ENRICHING THE CLASSIC TRADITION

CLASSIC FAVORITES

- BEOWULF
- THE CANTERBURY TALES by Geoffrey Chaucer
- SONNETS by William Shakespeare
- TO HIS COY MISTRESS by Andrew Marvell
- HOW SOON HATH TIME by John Milton
- THE DIARY OF SAMUEL PEPYS by Samuel Pepys
- A MODEST PROPOSAL by Jonathan Swift
- ELEGY WRITTEN IN A COUNTRY CHURCHYARD by Thomas Gray
- THE LAMB and THE TYGER by William Blake
- I WANDERED LONELY AS A CLOUD by William Wordsworth
- KUBLA KHAN by Samuel Taylor Coleridge
- TO A SKYLARK by Percy Bysshe Shelley
- ODE ON A GRECIAN URN by John Keats
- MY LAST DUCHESS by Robert Browning
- DOVER BEACH by Matthew Arnold
- THE DEMON LOVER by Elizabeth Bowen
- THE SECOND COMING by William Butler Yeats
- ARABY by James Joyce
- THE DISTANT PAST by William Trevor

MORE CLASSIC AUTHORS

Edmund Spenser
John Donne
Lord Byron
Charlotte Brontë
Virginia Woolf
D. H. Lawrence
Katherine Mansfield
T. S. Eliot
W. H. Auden
Doris Lessing
Seamus Heaney
Harold Pinter

LONGER PLAYS AND NOVELS

Macbeth
Hamlet
Pride and Prejudice
Jane Eyre
Tess of the d'Urbervilles
Pygmalion
1984
A Tale of Two Cities

CLASSIC TRADITIONS NEW PERSPECTIVES

World events and personal experiences all take on new dimensions when viewed through different lenses. The selections in this anthology were chosen to allow readers to see the world from a number of different perspectives.

Historical Connections

Many works in this book open a window on the past and offer fascinating insights into the eras and societies in which they were written.

THE PASTON LETTERS
by The Paston Family

THE DIARY OF SAMUEL PEPYS

THE DIARY AND LETTERS OF MADAME D'ARBLAY
by Fanny Burney

TESTAMENT OF YOUTH
by Vera Brittain

THE SPEECHES, MAY 19, 1940
by Winston Churchill

THE DISTANT PAST
by William Trevor

Women's Voices

Listen to the voices of these and other women throughout the ages:

Margery Kempe

Lady Mary Wortley Montagu

Mary Wollstonecraft

Elizabeth Barrett Browning

Charlotte Brontë

Virginia Woolf

Elizabeth Bowen

Margaret Atwood

Doris Lessing

Muriel Spark

Ruth Rendell

Contemporary Award Winners

Explore the world of contemporary literature in a rich mix of authors, including:

Nadine Gordimer

Stevie Smith

Seamus Heaney

Penelope Lively

Ted Hughes

Arthur C. Clarke

Chinua Achebe

Harold Pinter

World Perspective

Classic works of literature from around the world give you a fresh perspective on British literature. Here are some of the intriguing pairings we offer:

HEROIC TRADITIONS:
Beowulf
the **Iliad**

STORYTELLING TRADITIONS
Chaucer's **The Canterbury Tales**
Boccaccio's **The Decameron**

SONNET FORM:
Shakespeare
Petrarch

POETRY:
The ***nature poetry*** of William Blake
The ***Haiku poets*** of Japan

STUDENT FAVORITES

Our Student Board helped the authors and editors choose the selections in this anthology. Here are some of their favorites.

- In THE KING IS DEAD, LONG LIVE THE KING by Mary E. Coleridge, a dying king is given a chance to come back to life. Several Student Board members commented that they "couldn't put the story down."
- Algernon Blackwood's THE KIT-BAG is a spine-tingling tale of murder and terror in the night. One student reviewer said that this ghost story "had me on the edge of my seat."
- In the excerpt from TESTAMENT OF YOUTH, Vera Brittain relates some of the personal struggles and losses she suffered during World War I. One Student Board member noted that the excerpt "made me understand . . . how devastating war is."
- In the words of one Student Board reviewer, THE ROCKING-HORSE WINNER by D. H. Lawrence "really kept me guessing!" This story of obsession and strange forces at work is both fascinating and foreboding.
- "I really identified with the narrator," commented one Student Board member after reading AT THE PITT-RIVERS by Penelope Lively, a story about a teenage boy's observations and feelings.

"really kept me guessing"

"made me understand . . . how devastating war is"

"had me on the edge of my seat"

"couldn't put the story down"

"I really identified with the narrator"

YOUR CHOICE OF **PLAYS & NOVELS**

Choose from a wide array of **Literature Connections**, each with related readings. Listed below are some of the most popular choices to accompany this book.

CLASSIC

MACBETH by William Shakespeare
The classic drama about power, ambition, and murder

HAMLET by William Shakespeare
A tragedy of betrayal, revenge, and bitter choices

PRIDE AND PREJUDICE by Jane Austen
A witty satire on the pursuit of love

JANE EYRE by Charlotte Brontë
A young governess meets life and love with spirit and passion.

TESS OF THE D'URBERVILLES by Thomas Hardy
A story of innocence betrayed and the power of fate

PYGMALION by George Bernard Shaw
A classic play about transformation and love

THE CANTERBURY TALES by Geoffrey Chaucer
Your favorite tales from this master storyteller

A TALE OF TWO CITIES by Charles Dickens
An exciting story of love, intrigue, and sacrifice set during the French Revolution

CONTEMPORARY

THINGS FALL APART by Chinua Achebe
Tragic consequences result when two societies collide.

NERVOUS CONDITIONS by Tsitsi Dangarembga
A girl's coming of age in a world shaped by conflicting cultures

WHEN RAIN CLOUDS GATHER by Bessie Head
A South African refugee begins a new life in a village in Botswana.

1984 by George Orwell
Big Brother sees all in this bleak world of the future.

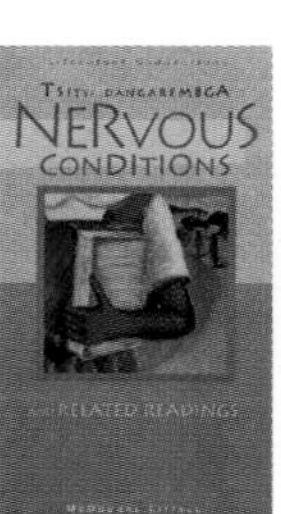

McDougal Littell

THE LANGUAGE OF LITERATURE

BRITISH LITERATURE

McDougal Littell

THE LANGUAGE OF LITERATURE

BRITISH LITERATURE

Arthur N. Applebee
Andrea B. Bermúdez
Sheridan Blau
Rebekah Caplan
Franchelle Dorn
Peter Elbow
Susan Hynds
Judith A. Langer
James Marshall

McDougal Littell
A HOUGHTON MIFFLIN COMPANY

Evanston, Illinois ▪ Boston ▪ Dallas

Acknowledgments

A. P. Watt Ltd.: "The Ant and the Grasshopper" by W. Somerset Maugham, from *The Collected Stories of W. Somerset Maugham.* Reprinted by permission of A. P. Watt Limited on behalf of the Royal Literary Fund.

Unit One

Dutton Signet: Excerpts from *Beowulf,* translated by Burton Raffel. Translation Copyright © 1963 by Burton Raffel, Afterword © 1963 by New American Library. "Fifth Day, Ninth Story" retitled "Federigo's Falcon," from *The Decameron* by Giovanni Boccaccio, translated by Mark Musa and Peter Bondanella, Translation copyright © 1982 by Mark Musa and Peter Bondanella. Introduction copyright © 1981, 1982 by Thomas Bergin.
From *Le Morte D'Arthur* by Sir Thomas Malory, translated by Keith Baines. Translation copyright © 1962 by Keith Baines, renewed © 1990 by Francesca Evans. Introduction © 1962 by Robert Graves, renewed © 1990 by Beryl Graves. Used by permission of Dutton Signet, a division of Penguin Books USA Inc.

Doubleday: Excerpts from *The Iliad* by Homer, translated by Robert Fitzgerald. Copyright © 1974 by Robert Fitzgerald. Used by permission of Doubleday, a division of Bantam Doubleday Dell Publishing Group, Inc.

Continued on page 1321

Cover Art

Background Photo: Big Ben and Houses of Parliament. Copyright © 1993 Romilly Lockyer/The Image Bank. **Queen Elizabeth:** Queen Elizabeth I of England when princess (about 1542–1547), unknown artist. The Granger Collection, New York. **Painting:** *Interior in Venice* (1898), John Singer Sargent. Royal Academy of Arts, London, Bridgeman/Art Resource, New York. **Silhouette:** UPI/ Bettmann. **Book:** Photo by Alan Shortall.

ISBN 0-395-73707-9

Printed in the United States of America.

2 3 4 5 6 7 8 9 – VJM – 01 00 99 98 97

Senior Consultants

The senior consultants guided the conceptual development for *The Language of Literature* series. They participated actively in shaping prototype materials for major components, and they reviewed completed prototypes and/or completed units to ensure consistency with current research and the philosophy of the series.

Arthur N. Applebee Professor of Education, State University of New York at Albany; Director, Center for the Learning and Teaching of Literature; Senior Fellow, Center for Writing and Literacy

Andrea B. Bermúdez Professor of Studies in Language and Culture; Director, Research Center for Language and Culture; Chair, Foundations and Professional Studies, University of Houston-Clear Lake

Sheridan Blau Senior Lecturer in English and Education and former Director of Composition, University of California at Santa Barbara; Director, South Coast Writing Project; Director, Literature Institute for Teachers; Vice President, National Council of Teachers of English

Rebekah Caplan Coordinator, English Language Arts K-12, Oakland Unified School District, Oakland, California; Teacher-Consultant, Bay Area Writing Project, University of California at Berkeley; served on the California State English Assessment Development Team for Language Arts

Franchelle Dorn Professor of Drama, Howard University, Washington, D.C.; Adjunct Professor, Graduate School of Opera, University of Maryland, College Park, Maryland; Co-founder of The Shakespeare Acting Conservatory, Washington, D.C.

Peter Elbow Professor of English, University of Massachusetts at Amherst; Fellow, Bard Center for Writing and Thinking

Susan Hynds Professor and Director of English Education, Syracuse University, Syracuse, New York

Judith A. Langer Professor of Education, State University of New York at Albany; Co-director, Center for the Learning and Teaching of Literature; Senior Fellow, Center for Writing and Literacy

James Marshall Professor of English and English Education, University of Iowa, Iowa City

Contributing Consultants

Tommy Boley Associate Professor of English, University of Texas at El Paso

Jeffrey N. Golub Assistant Professor of English Education, University of South Florida, Tampa

William L. McBride Reading and Curriculum Specialist; former middle and high school English instructor

Multicultural Advisory Board

The multicultural advisors reviewed literature selections for appropriate content and made suggestions for teaching lessons in a multicultural classroom.

Dr. Joyce M. Bell, Chairperson, English Department, Townview Magnet Center, Dallas, Texas

Dr. Eugenia W. Collier, author; lecturer; Chairperson, Department of English and Language Arts; teacher of Creative Writing and American Literature, Morgan State University, Maryland

Kathleen S. Fowler, President, Palm Beach County Council of Teachers of English, Boca Raton Middle School, Boca Raton, Florida

Noreen M. Rodriguez, Trainer for Hillsborough County School District's Staff Development Division, independent consultant, Gaither High School, Tampa, Florida

Michelle Dixon Thompson, Seabreeze High School, Daytona Beach, Florida

Teacher Review Panels

The following educators provided ongoing review during the development of the tables of contents, lesson design, and key components of the program.

FLORIDA

Judi Briant, English Department Chairperson, Armwood High School, Hillsborough County School District

Beth Johnson, Polk County English Supervisor, Polk County School District

Continued on page 1337

Manuscript Reviewers

The following educators reviewed prototype lessons and tables of contents during the development of *The Language of Literature* program.

Carol Alves, English Department Chairperson, Apopka High School, Apopka, Florida

Jacqueline Anderson, James A. Foshay Learning Center, Los Angeles, California

Kathleen M. Anderson-Knight, United Township High School, East Moline, Illinois

Anita Arnold, Thomas Jefferson High School, San Antonio, Texas

Cassandra L. Asberry, Justin F. Kimball High School, Dallas, Texas

Don Baker, English Department Chairperson, Peoria High School, Peoria, Illinois

Continued on page 1338

Student Board

The student board members read and evaluated selections to assess their appeal for twelfth-grade students.

Daniel Birdsall, Muhlenberg High School, Reading, Pennsylvania

Shane M. Cummins, Loudoun County High School, Leesburg, Virginia

Carrie Mitchell, Butler Traditional High School, Shively, Kentucky

Jennifer Schwab, MacArthur High School, San Antonio, Texas

Sarah Marie Slezak, Union High School, Grand Rapids, Michigan

Staci Talis Smith, Ramsay Alternative High School, Birmingham, Alabama

Eve E. Tanner, Justin F. Kimball High School, Dallas, Texas

CORE COMPONENTS

Student Anthology & Literature Connections

A rich mix of classic and contemporary literature

Longer works with related readings

FREE!
Choose from over
46 *Literature Connections* titles
when you adopt
The Language of Literature
from McDougal Littell
Call 800-323-5435 for details

Literature Connections

Each hardback volume contains

- **Novel or Play**
- **Related Readings**—poems, stories, plays, and articles that provide new perspectives on the longer works
- **Teacher's SourceBook** filled with background information and activities

Macbeth

by William Shakespeare

and Related Readings

Insomniac / POEM
Octavio Paz

Better Than Counting Sheep / POEM
Robert Penn Warren

Macbeth / LITERARY CRITICISM
Norrie Epstein

Like a Bad Dream / SHORT STORY
Heinrich Böll, translated by Leila Vennewitz

How Many Children Had Lady Macbeth? / PLAY
Don Nigro

Into Concrete Mixer Throw / POEM
Barbara Roe

Lady Macbeth's Trouble / PARODY
Maurice Baring

Yscolan / POEM
Myrddyn, translated by W.S. Merwin

Additional Literature Connections such as:

The Adventures of Huckleberry Finn*
Mark Twain

. . . And the Earth Did Not Devour Him*
Tomás Rivera

Animal Farm
George Orwell

The Crucible
Arthur Miller

Ethan Frome
Edith Wharton

Fallen Angels
Walter Dean Myers

The Friends
Rosa Guy

Hamlet
William Shakespeare

Jane Eyre*
Charlotte Brontë

Julius Caesar
William Shakespeare

Macbeth
William Shakespeare

A Midsummer Night's Dream
William Shakespeare

My Ántonia
Willa Cather

Nervous Conditions
Tsitsi Dangarembga

Picture Bride
Yoshiko Uchida

A Place Where the Sea Remembers
Sandra Benítez

Pygmalion
Bernard Shaw

A Raisin in the Sun
Lorraine Hansberry

The Scarlet Letter
Nathaniel Hawthorne

A Tale of Two Cities*
Charles Dickens

Things Fall Apart
Chinua Achebe

To Kill a Mockingbird, the Screenplay
Horton Foote

The Tragedy of Romeo and Juliet*
William Shakespeare

The Underdogs
Mariano Azuela

West with the Night
Beryl Markham

When Rain Clouds Gather
Bessie Head

*A Spanish version is also available.

UNIT ONE *The Anglo-Saxon and Medieval Periods* *449–1485* 10

Part 1 Tests of Courage 23

★ *Highlights*

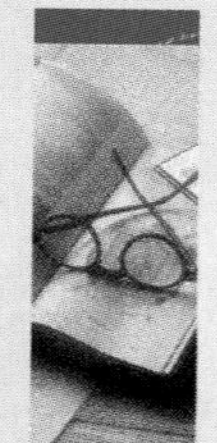

TEACHER RECOMMENDED
***from* Beowulf**

Burton Raffel's clear translation of this classic epic poem preserves the power of the original Anglo-Saxon verse, leading one member of our Teacher Board to comment that it "really bring the tale to life." (page 24)

CLASSIC FAVORITE
***from* The Canterbury Tales**

Geoffrey Chaucer is known for his wit, evocative detail, and shrewd insight. In *The Canterbury Tales* he vividly portrays 14th-century life by presenting 30 characters from various social classes. The description of the Pardoner is a fine example of his art. (page 87)

Part 2 Reflections of Everyday Life

WORLD PERSPECTIVE

Federigo's Falcon

Like Chaucer's *Canterbury Tales,* ***The Decameron,*** written by **Giovanni Boccaccio** offers a vivid picture of daily medieval life—in this case, in 14th-century Italy. The plot of this love story has some surprising and entertaining twists and turns. (page 109)

HISTORICAL CONNECTION

***from* The Paston Letters**

These letters reveal some of the ordinary and not-so-ordinary experiences of life in 15th-century England. Students and teachers alike will enjoy the glimpses into political intrigues, the parent-child struggles, and the plight of a pair of thwarted lovers. (page 118)

★ *Highlights*

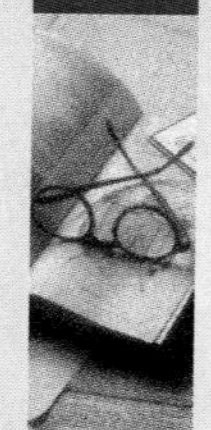

TEACHER RECOMMENDED

***from* Sir Gawain and the Green Knight**

This intriguing romance brings to life a magical world in the characters of King Arthur, the youthful Sir Gawain, and the awesome Green Knight. A Teacher Board member noted that John Gardner's brilliant translation "really engaged my students." (page 139)

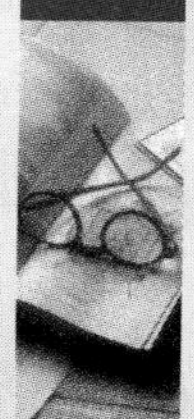

A WOMAN'S VOICE

***from* The Book of Margery Kempe**

This excerpt from the autobiography of **Margery Kempe,** one of the first women to write in English, speaks to her unusual perspectives and experiences. Her writing makes her forceful personality as strongly felt now as it was to her contemporaries. (page 184)

UNIT TWO *The English Renaissance* *1485–1660*

Part 1 Aspects of Love

REDISCOVERED CLASSIC

On Monsieur's Departure

This carefully constructed poem shows an unexpected side of **Elizabeth I.** Known for her strength, intelligence, and decisiveness, she is not often thought of in terms of the ambivalence and tenderness revealed here. (page 211)

CLASSIC FAVORITE

Sonnet 116

This well-known sonnet is perhaps one of the most famous love poems ever written. The emotions and thoughts expressed and the perfection of form are telling evidence of the genius of **William Shakespeare.** (page 228)

Literature Connections

RECOMMENDED FOR UNIT TWO

Macbeth
Hamlet
A Midsummer Night's Dream
Julius Caesar

Part 2 Facing Life's Limitations 252

★ Highlights

CLASSIC FAVORITE
A Valediction Forbidding Mourning

This lyric by **John Donne** includes one of the most striking images in English poetry—that of a draftsman's compass to represent two lovers. The power of this and other images in the poem has moved readers for generations. (page 267)

TEACHER RECOMMENDED
To His Coy Mistress

This monologue by **Andrew Marvell** is one of the best-known expressions of the philosophy of *carpe diem* in English literature. Numerous Teacher Board reviewers attested to the relevance of the poem's themes and the intensity of its passions. (page 281)

UNIT THREE

The Restoration and Enlightenment *1660–1798* 318

Part 1 Views of Society 328

HISTORICAL CONNECTION
***from* The Diary of Samuel Pepys**

These excerpts include Pepys's first-hand accounts of two great events in late 17th-century England—the coronation of Charles II and the Great Fire of London. Pepys also gives glimpses of life in Restoration England and of his life and personality. (page 329)

A WOMAN'S VOICE
Letter to Her Daughter

The strong personality and independent thinking of **Lady Mary Wortley Montagu** are evident in this letter discussing her granddaughter's future. Her views on education and marriage were unusual for her time and offer ideas still worth discussing. (page 356)

★ *Highlights*

REDISCOVERED CLASSIC
***from* An Academy for Women**

Before he wrote his famous novels, such a *Robinson Crusoe*, **Daniel Defoe** wrote proposals for social reform. His views on the education of women were radical in his day and are carefully argued in this fascinating excerpt from one of his essays. (page 379)

CLASSIC FAVORITE
A Modest Proposal

Few writers have been able to match the ability of **Jonathan Swift** to express social criticism through satire. The power of this essay to get the attention of the reader and to expose social and political ills is no less today than it was 250 years ago. (page 388)

Literature Connections

RECOMMENDED FOR UNIT THREE

A Tale of Two Cities

A Woman's Voice

***from* A Vindication of the Rights of Woman**

Mary Wollstonecraft was a rigorous thinker and a sophisticated writer. Her views on the rights of women, as expressed in this well-developed essay, reveal her thorough understanding of herself and society. (page 405)

World Perspective

***from* Memoirs of Madame Vigée-Lebrun**

The memoirs of **Élisabeth Vigée-Lebrun**, a painter in Paris during the French Revolution, depict French royalty and aristocracy and the terrors they faced. Like **James Boswell** and **Fanny Burney**, Vigée-Lebrun was a keen observer of human nature. (page 447)

UNIT FOUR *The Flowering of Romanticism* 1798–1832 472

Part 1 Seeking Truth 482

TEACHER RECOMMENDED
The Tyger
This famous poem by **William Blake** is characterized by powerful imagery and symbolism. One of our Teacher Board reviewers said, "I love to read this poem aloud to my students." (page 483)

WORLD PERSPECTIVE
Haiku
Like the English Romantic poets, Japan's great haiku poets often sought truth by observing the natural world. The haiku of **Matsuo Bashō** and **Kobayashi Issa** embody three qualities greatly valued in Japanese art: precision, economy, and delicacy. (page 491)

Literature Connections

RECOMMENDED FOR UNIT FOUR

Pride and Prejudice

CLASSIC FAVORITE

I Wandered Lonely As a Cloud

This reflective lyric by **William Wordsworth** is one of the simplest yet clearest expressions of the spirit of the romantic movement. Few fail to respond to the freshness of its description or to its appeal to the imagination. (page 496)

CLASSIC FAVORITE

Ode on a Grecian Urn

John Keats chose the traditional form of the ode to write about an ancient Greek urn. Keats's intense response to the beauty and mystery of the urn continues to stir the hearts and imaginations of readers. (page 552)

★ *Highlights*

A WOMAN'S VOICE
A Warning Against Passion

Charlotte Brontë, author of the classic novel *Jane Eyre,* reveals some personal views about love in this letter to a close friend. It also provides fascinating insight into Victorian attitudes in general. (page 597)

REDISCOVERED CLASSIC
Christmas Storms and Sunshine

This well-loved story by **Elizabeth Cleghorn Gaskell** resonates with her concern for the social relationships of everyday people. The characters—a young couple with a baby and an older childless couple—are drawn with realism, humor, and true feeling. (page 606)

Literature Connections

RECOMMENDED FOR UNIT FIVE

Jane Eyre
Tess of the d'Urbervilles

Part 2 New Directions 670

STUDENT FAVORITE
The King Is Dead, Long Live the King
In this ironic tale by **Mary E. Coleridge**, a king who has just died is given one more hour of life. One Student Board member thought that the feelings and behavior of the characters were "really true to life." (page 655)

TEACHER RECOMMENDED
The Importance of Being Earnest
In this classic farce, **Oscar Wilde** paints a satirical picture of the values and concerns of his day. "When my students read this aloud, they found it hilarious," said one Teacher Board member. (page 701)

UNIT SIX *Emerging Modernism* *1901–1950* 758

Part 1 Appearance Versus Reality 767

★*Highlights*

STUDENT FAVORITE
The Kit-Bag

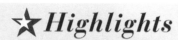

"This story had me on the edge of my seat," commented one of our Student Board reviewers. "I loved it!" **Algernon Blackwood** creates a tale of terror that is a chilling addition to the literary tradition of the ghost story. (page 768)

TEACHER RECOMMENDED
The Truth About George

The good-natured wit of **P. G. Wodehouse,** aptly named one of the greatest humorists of the 20th century, runs through this comic tale. "This one never fails with my students," noted a member of our Teacher Board. (page 793)

Part 2 Shocking Realities

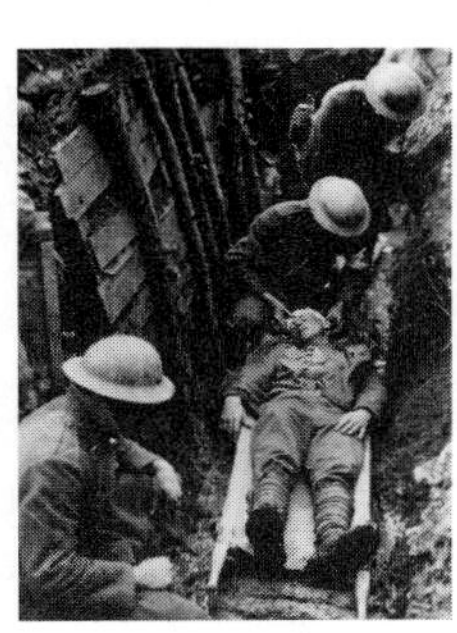

HISTORICAL CONNECTION
***from* Testament of Youth**

This excerpt provides a rare account of World War I from the perspective of a young woman. **Vera Brittain** served as a Red Cross nurse during the war, which "turned me from an ordinary patriotic young woman into a convinced pacifist." (page 850)

WORLD PERSPECTIVE
***from* Letters from Westerbork**

These excerpts from letters by **Etty Hillesum** provide insight into the suffering of Dutch Holocaust victims during World War II and give support to Churchill's description of the Nazi occupation as a "long night of barbarism." (page 871)

Literature Connections

RECOMMENDED FOR UNIT SIX

Pygmalion
1984

★ *Highlights*

CLASSIC FAVORITE
The Second Coming

Nobel Prize winner **William Butler Yeats** is considered by many to be the greatest poet of the 20th century, and this startling poem is among his best-known. (page 922)

STUDENT FAVORITE
At the Pitt-Rivers

Several Student Board members said that this story captured their feelings. No wonder a critic said of **Penelope Lively,** "She is particularly good at showing how one generation looks at, or ignores, the activities and preoccupations of another." (page 1011)

UNIT SEVEN *Contemporary Voices*
1950–Present 1002

Part 1 Moments of Insight 1010

A WOMAN'S VOICE
A Sunrise on the Veld

In this story, a shocking sight on an early-morning run leads a South African teenager to confront life head-on. As always, **Doris Lessing** reveals her remarkable ability to interpret the thoughts, feelings, and motivations of her characters. (page 1036)

TEACHER RECOMMENDED
Digging

Like much of the work of Nobel Prize winner **Seamus Heaney,** this poem contains images taken from rural life and reflects the poet's relationship with the past. The poem was a strong favorite with several of our Teacher Board reviewers. (page 1046)

Part 2 Culture and Conflict 1072

★ *Highlights*

HISTORICAL CONNECTION

The Distant Past

William Trevor, widely acclaimed as one of the greatest short story writers today, movingly explores the personal impact of the political divisions between Ireland and Britain. (page 1073)

NEW CLASSIC

Six Feet of the Country

Like much of the work of Nobel Prize winner **Nadine Gordimer,** this powerful story reflects the author's skill at showing how South Africa's system of apartheid could distort everyday relationships. (page 1099)

Literature Connections

RECOMMENDED FOR UNIT SEVEN

Things Fall Apart
Nervous Conditions
When Rain Clouds Gather

STUDENT FAVORITE
The First Year of My Life

In this biting satire by **Muriel Spark,** a very young narrator records her observations of world events as World War I draws to a close. One Student Board reviewer commented that the story "makes a serious point in an unusual and funny way." (page 1130)

A WOMAN'S VOICE
Paintbox Place

Best-selling author **Ruth Rendell** has received many awards for her mystery and detective fiction. In this story, in which an elderly woman is convinced she can solve a murder, Rendell takes a playful look at the detective in literature. (page 1149)

Electronic Library

The *Electronic Library* is a CD-ROM that contains additional fiction, nonfiction, poetry, and drama for each unit in *The Language of Literature*.

List of Titles, Grade 12 Electronic Library

Unit 1

Geoffrey Chaucer	*from* **The Canterbury Tales**
	The Prologue
	The Nun's Priest's Tale
Anonymous	**Everyman**

Unit 2

Sir Philip Sidney	**My True Love Hath My Heart**
George Herbert	**Virtue**
	Easter-Wings
Sir John Suckling	**The Constant Lover**
	Song
William Shakespeare	**Sonnet 30**
	Sonnet 73
	Sonnet 77
John Milton	**L'Allegro**
	Il Penseroso

Unit 3

John Dryden	**A Song for St. Cecilia's Day, 1687**
	Alexander's Feast
Jonathan Swift	**A Voyage to Lilliput,** *from* **Gulliver's Travels**
Robert Burns	**To a Mouse**
	A Red, Red Rose
	Afton Water

Unit 4

William Wordsworth	**She Was a Phantom of Delight**
	London, 1802
Samuel Taylor Coleridge	**The Rime of the Ancient Mariner**
Charles Lamb	**Dream-Children**
	A Dissertation upon Roast Pig

Note: A complete list of literature available for all grade levels accompanies each CD-ROM.

Lord Byron	*from* **Don Juan**
John Keats	**La Belle Dame sans Merci**
	Ode to a Nightingale
	On First Looking into Chapman's Homer
	Ode on Melancholy

Unit 5

Alfred, Lord Tennyson	**The Lady of Shalott**
	Song of the Lotos-Eaters
Dante Gabriel Rossetti	**The Blessed Damozel**
Christina Rossetti	**Goblin Market**
John Stuart Mill and Harriet Taylor Mill	**Early Essays on Marriage and Divorce**
Gerard Manley Hopkins	**God's Grandeur**
	The Windhover
	I Wake and Feel the Fell of Dark
Thomas Hardy	**The Darkling Thrush**
	The Convergence of the Twain
A. E. Housman	**Loveliest of Trees**
	With Rue My Heart Is Laden
	Terence, This Is Stupid Stuff

Unit 6

Virginia Woolf	**Professions for Women**
D. H. Lawrence	**The Horse Dealer's Daughter**
William Butler Yeats	**The Lake Isle of Innisfree**
	The Wild Swans at Coole
James Joyce	**The Boarding House**
Liam O'Flaherty	**Spring Sowing**
W. H. Auden	**The Shield of Achilles**
Katherine Mansfield	**Miss Brill**

Unit 7

V. S. Pritchett	**The Fly in the Ointment**
Margaret Drabble	**A Voyage to Cythera**

McDougal Littell
ELECTRONIC LIBRARY
A compendium of over 200 literary selections on CD ROM

Selections by Genre, Writing Workshops

Fiction

Nonfiction

Scripture

Drama

Poetry

Writing About Literature

Reading the World: Visual Literacy

Writing from Experience

LEARNING THE LANGUAGE OF

LITERATURE

What Stays with You?

When you see an elaborately detailed scene, like the one in this picture, certain objects catch your eye. Which ones are most noticeable? Before you answer that question, take the time to work through the activity below.

LOOK AGAIN

Get ready to notice what you notice. Find two or three other students to work with you.

1. Allow yourself 50 seconds to examine this photo. Then close your book and take two minutes to list as many items as you can recall.
2. Compare your results with those of the other members of your group.
3. Now look at the photo for 30 seconds. Close your book and again take two minutes to list as many objects as you can recall.
4. Compare your second list with your first. Which is longer?
5. Share your second list with your group. What do you notice about the group's lists this time around?
6. Put your lists away. With your book closed, try to visualize the picture in your mind. On a clean sheet of paper, list as many objects as you can remember. Which ones stayed with you? Why do you think you remembered them?

CONNECT TO LITERATURE

Literature, like this picture, presents a rich assortment of elements. When so much is being offered, it's only natural that different people benefit in different ways. You might remember details that no one else even noticed. What you remember says a lot about who you are. Turn the page to see how literature can give you souvenirs for a lifetime.

What Can Literature Offer You?

When you enter the world of literature, endless possibilities stretch before you. So, open your mind, extend your imagination, and get ready to gather many memories. Literature's offerings are yours to keep . . .

A NEW SENSE OF SELF

Reflecting on what you read sheds light on new aspects of yourself. Selections in this book begin with a **Previewing** page that provides you with background information and helps you tap into what you already know about a subject. For example, on page 211 you'll explore aspects of love and friendship before you read poems by Sir Thomas Wyatt and Elizabeth I. The **Responding** pages after a selection suggest activities you might use to further develop what you learned from the literature. For a sample, see page 215.

A PASSPORT TO IDEAS

In the world of literature, your travel options are limitless. With **literature selections** in this book as your vehicle, you will travel from bygone eras to modern culture, and you're certain to pick up keepsakes on the way. Take a look at Geoffrey Chaucer's *The Canterbury Tales* on page 88 and Doris Lessing's "A Sunrise on the Veld" on page 1037 for a preview of two very different destinations.

THE RIGHT WORDS

Experiencing other ways of life can make you wonder, "How am I ever going to describe all this?" The **Writing About Literature** workshops show you how to share your thoughts and questions with others. For example, the workshop on page 78 helps you interpret the values held by people and their communities. You'll also find opportunities to connect unit themes to real-world issues. For example, Unit Three explores society, change, and human nature, and the unit's **Writing from Experience** workshop, on page 462, invites you to write about a current condition, trend, or problem.

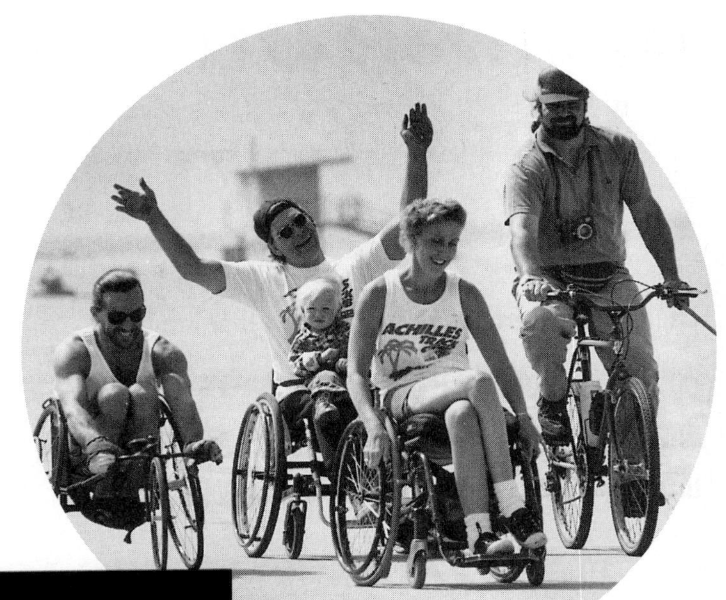

TOOLS FOR A LIFETIME

Literature can offer you insights and perspectives that encourage you to reevaluate the way you look at the world around you. In the **Reading the World** features, the strategies you use to uncover different layers of meaning in literature help you better understand everyday situations. See page 84 for an exercise in using details to make inferences about what you see.

How Do You Make It Your Own?

Literature has so much to offer you that knowing where to begin can be a real challenge. Several approaches will help you enter the world of literature and begin to stake your claim.

MULTIPLE PATHWAYS

How do you learn best? Would you rather work alone or with a friend? Do you prefer writing, talking, acting, or artwork? This book offers you a variety of learning options and allows you to choose the activities that best suit your strengths and interests. You'll be given opportunities to collaborate with classmates to share ideas, improve your writing, and make connections to other subject areas. Perhaps you will use technological tools such as the LaserLinks and the Writing Coach software program to further customize your learning.

PORTFOLIO

You may already know that many artists, photographers, designers, and writers keep samples of their work in a portfolio that they show to others. This year you will be collecting some of your work—writing samples, records of activities, artwork—in a portfolio. Probably you won't want to include all your work, just carefully chosen pieces. Discuss with your teacher portfolio options for this year. You will also find a variety of suggestions throughout this book.

Notebook

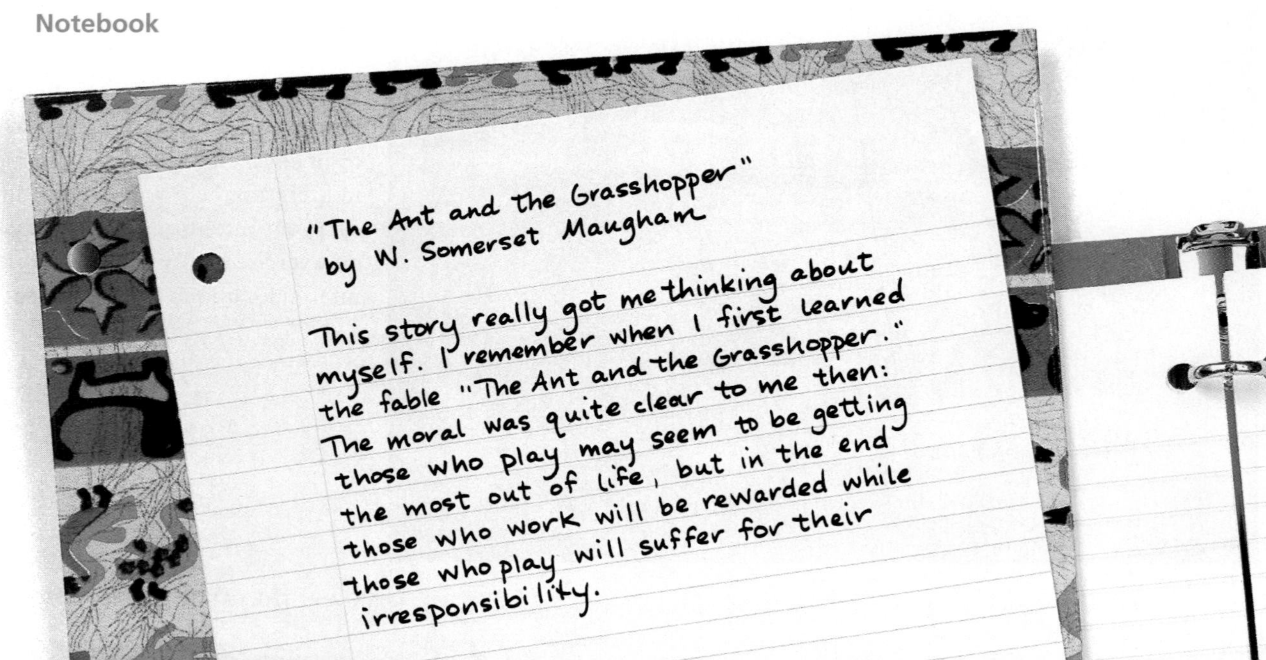

"The Ant and the Grasshopper"
by W. Somerset Maugham
This story really got me thinking about myself. I remember when I first learned the fable "The Ant and the Grasshopper." The moral was quite clear to me then: those who play may seem to be getting the most out of life, but in the end those who work will be rewarded while those who play will suffer for their irresponsibility.

Dreamily ch...
That once chased him.

The vet suggested inviting death.
But death saved me the decision
As gasping breath became shorter,
Then crashed into silence.

"It's only a dog," someone said.
He never felt the vacuum of loss,
Never dreamed of "only a dog"
And woke to the nightmare of nevermore.

Portfolio

NOTEBOOK

Select any type of notebook and dedicate it to your study of literature. Divide the notebook into three sections. Use the first section to jot down ideas, describe personal experiences, take notes, and express your thoughts before, while, and after you read a selection. Also include any charts, diagrams, and drawings that help you connect your reading to your life. The second section will be for your reading log, described below. Use the third section as a writer's notebook to record ideas and inspirations that you might want to write about later.

READING LOG

In your reading log you will record a special kind of response to literature—your direct comments as you read a selection. The reading strategies detailed at the right will help you think about what you are reading. In your reading log experiment with recording your own comments as you read. You will find specific opportunities to use your reading log throughout this book.

Reading Log

"The Ant and the Grasshopper"
by W. Somerset Maugham

The narrator says, "in an imperfect world industry is rewarded and giddiness punished." Why does he say "in an imperfect world"?

How can I admire the industrious ant when he cruelly leaves the grasshopper to suffer?

Strategies for Reading

Reading is not a passive activity. Quite the opposite—to get the most out of literature, you need to think as you read. The strategies below describe the kinds of thinking that active readers do. You can use these strategies, too.

QUESTION

Question what's happening while you read. Searching for reasons behind events and characters' feelings can help you feel closer to what you're reading. Note confusing words or statements, and keep them in mind. As you read on, you just might begin to understand them.

CONNECT

Connect personally with what you're reading. Think of similarities between the descriptions in the selection and what you have personally experienced, heard about, or read about.

PREDICT

Try to figure out what will happen next and how the selection might end. Then read on to see if you made good guesses.

CLARIFY

Stop occasionally to review what you understand, and expect to have your understanding change and develop as you read on. Also, watch for answers to questions you had earlier.

EVALUATE

Form opinions about what you read, both while you're reading and after you've finished. Try to visualize characters and develop your own ideas about events.

Now turn the page to see how two student readers put these strategies to work.

Alongside "The Ant and the Grasshopper" are comments made by two 12th-grade students, Christopher Domm and Marcy Ellis, while they were reading the story. Their comments provide a glimpse into the minds of readers actively engaged in the process of reading. You'll notice that Chris and Marcy quite naturally used the Strategies for Reading that were introduced on page 5. You'll also note that these readers responded differently to the story—no two readers think about or relate to a literary work in exactly the same way.

To benefit from this model of active reading, read the story first, jotting down your responses in your reading log. Then read Chris's and Marcy's comments and compare theirs with your own. The more you actively engage in reading and sharing ideas, the more you'll learn about yourself and others.

The Ant and the Grasshopper

W. SOMERSET MAUGHAM

The Brothers Bernheim-Jeune, Art Dealers and Publishers (early 20th century), Pierre Bonnard, Musée d'Orsay, Paris, France, Erich Lessing/Art Resource, New York.

When I was a very small boy I was made to learn by heart certain of the fables of La Fontaine, and the moral of each was carefully explained to me. Among those I learnt was *The Ant and The Grasshopper,* which is devised to bring home to the young the useful lesson that in an imperfect world industry is rewarded and giddiness punished. In this admirable fable (I apologize for telling something which everyone is politely, but inexactly, supposed to know) the ant spends a laborious summer gathering its winter store, while the grasshopper sits on a blade of grass singing to the sun. Winter comes and the ant is comfortably provided for, but the grasshopper has an empty larder: he goes to the ant and begs for a little food. Then the ant gives him her classic answer:

Chris: *I like this line right here—I think people can relate that to their own lives.*
EVALUATING

"What were you doing in the summer time?"

"Saving your presence, I sang, I sang all day, all night."

"You sang. Why, then go and dance."

I do not ascribe it to perversity on my part, but rather to the inconsequence of childhood, which is deficient in moral sense, that I could never quite reconcile myself to the lesson. My sympathies were with the grasshopper and for some time I never saw an ant without putting my foot on it. In this summary (and as I have discovered since, entirely human) fashion I sought to express my disapproval of prudence and common sense.

Marcy: *Wow! I always looked down on the grasshopper. It surprises me that the narrator looks down on the ant.*
CONNECTING/CLARIFYING

I could not help thinking of this fable when the other day I saw George Ramsay lunching by himself in a restaurant. I never saw anyone wear an expression of such deep gloom. He was staring into space. He looked as though the burden of the whole world sat on his shoulders. I was sorry for him: I suspected at once that his unfortunate brother had been causing trouble again. I went up to him and held out my hand.

"How are you?" I asked.

"I'm not in hilarious spirits," he answered.

"Is it Tom again?"

He sighed.

"Yes, it's Tom again."

"Why don't you chuck him? You've done everything in the world for him. You must know by now that he's quite hopeless."

Chris: *"Why don't you chuck him?" I don't really understand what he means.*
QUESTIONING

Marcy: *""Chuck him"? That's weird language!*
QUESTIONING/EVALUATING

I suppose every family has a black sheep. Tom had been a sore trial to his for twenty years. He had begun life decently enough: he went into business, married, and had two children. The Ramsays were perfectly respectable people and there was every reason to suppose that Tom Ramsay would have a useful and honorable career. But one day, without warning, he announced that he didn't like work and that he wasn't suited for marriage. He wanted to enjoy himself. He would listen to no expostulations. He left his wife and his office. He had a little money and he spent two happy years in the various capitals of Europe. Rumors of his doings reached his relations from time to time and they were

Marcy: *I'm seeing the parallel between the brother and the grasshopper. He'll probably be like him and fail.*
CLARIFYING/PREDICTING

Marcy: He reminds me of the father in As I Lay Dying. *The guy in* As I Lay Dying *thought that if he sweated, he would die. So he was always asking people to do things for him. Tom is always asking his friends for money and depending on his friends. They won't refuse him.*
CONNECTING

Marcy: This would be hard for me—to wash my hands of my family. I understand why he felt he had to, but I couldn't do it.
CONNECTING

Chris: Tom's taking advantage of his brother's friendship. It's probably going to come back to him further down the line.
PREDICTING

Chris: This reminds me of the brothers' relationship in A River Runs Through It. *The one brother is always out having fun . . . always taking advantage of the other brother.*
CONNECTING/EVALUATING

Marcy: Oh, they went out together! They were in cahoots. I would be mad, too.
CLARIFYING/CONNECTING

Marcy: 46—that's too old to be so irresponsible.
EVALUATING

profoundly shocked. He certainly had a very good time. They shook their heads and asked what would happen when his money was spent. They soon found out: he borrowed. He was charming and unscrupulous. I have never met anyone to whom it was more difficult to refuse a loan. He made a steady income from his friends and he made friends easily. But he always said that the money you spent on necessities was boring; the money that was amusing to spend was the money you spent on luxuries. For this he depended on his brother George. He did not waste his charm on him. George was a serious man and insensible to such enticements. George was respectable. Once or twice he fell to Tom's promises of amendment and gave him considerable sums in order that he might make a fresh start. On these Tom bought a motorcar and some very nice jewelry. But when circumstances forced George to realize that his brother would never settle down and he washed his hands of him, Tom, without a qualm, began to blackmail him. It was not very nice for a respectable lawyer to find his brother shaking cocktails behind the bar of his favorite restaurant or to see him waiting on the box seat of a taxi outside his club. Tom said that to serve in a bar or to drive a taxi was a perfectly decent occupation, but if George could oblige him with a couple of hundred pounds he didn't mind for the honor of the family giving it up. George paid.

Once Tom nearly went to prison. George was terribly upset. He went into the whole discreditable affair. Really Tom had gone too far. He had been wild, thoughtless, and selfish, but he had never before done anything dishonest, by which George meant illegal; and if he were prosecuted he would assuredly be convicted. But you cannot allow your only brother to go to jail. The man Tom had cheated, a man called Cronshaw, was vindictive. He was determined to take the matter into court; he said Tom was a scoundrel and should be punished. It cost George an infinite deal of trouble and five hundred pounds to settle the affair. I have never seen him in such a rage as when he heard that Tom and Cronshaw had gone off together to Monte Carlo the moment they cashed the check. They spent a happy month there.

For twenty years Tom raced and gambled, philandered with the prettiest girls, danced, ate in the most expensive restaurants, and dressed beautifully. He always looked as if he had just stepped out of a bandbox. Though he was forty-six you would never have taken him for more than thirty-five. He was a most amusing companion and though you knew he was perfectly worthless you could not but enjoy his society. He had high spirits, an unfailing gaiety, and incredible charm. I never grudged the contributions he regularly levied on me for the necessities of his existence. I never lent him fifty pounds without feeling that I was in his debt. Tom Ramsay knew everyone and everyone knew Tom Ramsay. You could not approve of him, but you could not help liking him.

Poor George, only a year older than his scapegrace brother, looked sixty. He had never taken more than a fortnight's holiday in the year for a quarter of a century. He was in his office every morning at nine-thirty and never left it till six. He was honest, industrious, and worthy. He had a good wife, to whom he had never been unfaithful even in thought, and four daughters to whom he was the best of fathers. He made a point of saving a third of his income and his plan was to retire at fifty-five to a little house in the country where he proposed to cultivate his garden and play golf. His life was blameless. He was glad that he was growing old because Tom was growing old too. He rubbed his hands and said:

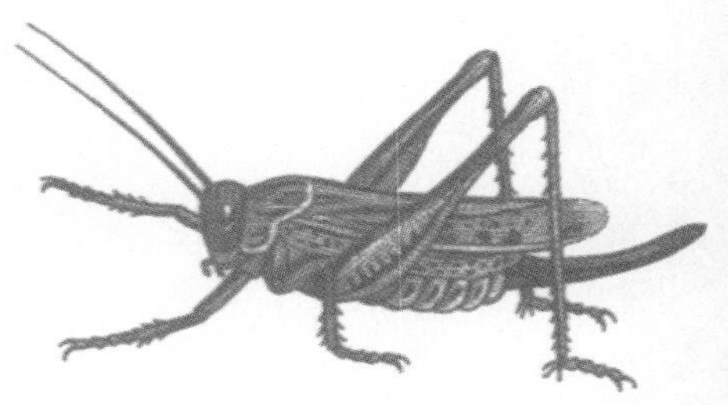

"It was all very well when Tom was young and good-looking, but he's only a year younger than I am. In four years he'll be fifty. He won't find life so easy then. I shall have thirty thousand pounds by the time I'm fifty. For twenty-five years I've said that Tom would end in the gutter. And we shall see how he likes that. We shall see if it really pays best to work or be idle."

Chris: *I think George is jealous of Tom's life.*
Evaluating

Poor George! I sympathized with him. I wondered now as I sat down beside him what infamous thing Tom had done. George was evidently very much upset.

"Do you know what's happened now?" he asked me.

I was prepared for the worst. I wondered if Tom had got into the hands of the police at last. George could hardly bring himself to speak.

"You're not going to deny that all my life I've been hardworking, decent, respectable, and straightforward. After a life of industry and thrift I can look forward to retiring on a small income in gilt-edged securities. I've always done my duty in that state of life in which it has pleased Providence to place me."

"True."

"And you can't deny that Tom has been an idle, worthless, dissolute, and dishonorable rogue. If there were any justice he'd be in the workhouse."

"True."

Chris: *I think this is funny right here. Tom's brother was so reserved and watched everything he did. Tom, on the other hand, took a chance in life. He didn't worry about the future; he just enjoyed life.*
Evaluating/Clarifying

George grew red in the face.

"A few weeks ago he became engaged to a woman old enough to be his mother. And now she's died and left him everything she had. Half a million pounds, a yacht, a house in London, and a house in the country."

Chris: *Usually the fable holds true to life, but this time it didn't.*
Clarifying

George Ramsay beat his clenched fist on the table.

"It's not fair, I tell you, it's not fair. Damn it, it's not fair."

I could not help it. I burst into a shout of laughter as I looked at George's wrathful face, I rolled in my chair, I very nearly fell on the floor. George never forgave me. But Tom often asks me to excellent dinners in his charming house in Mayfair, and if he occasionally borrows a trifle from me, that is merely from force of habit. It is never more than a sovereign.

Marcy: *It's not fair! I'd be upset. Of course George will still have his money—his retirement—but that's not much. Maybe Tom will share with George, but I don't think so. I doubt if he'll even pay back the money George gave him.*
Clarifying/Evaluating/Predicting

UNIT ONE

THE ANGLO-SAXON AND

The Bayeux tapestry (late 11th century–early 12th century). Musée de la Tapisserie, Bayeux, France, Giraudon/Art Resource New York.

449-1485

Medieval Periods

In reading great literature, I become a thousand men and yet remain myself.

C.S. Lewis
novelist and essayist

TIME LINE

The Anglo-Saxon & Medieval Periods 449–1485

407 ▲

Roman troops leave Britain

Hadrian's Wall, built by Romans (A.D. 122–128)

449

Traditional date of Anglo-Saxon invasion

597

Christian missionaries land in Kent; Christianity begins to spread among Anglo-Saxons

c. 750

Surviving version of *Beowulf* probably composed

793

First of many Viking raids ▶

871

Alfred the Great becomes king of Wessex (to 899)

c. 975

Anglo-Saxon verse collected in Exeter Book

1016

Canute, a Dane, becomes king of England (to 1035)

1066

Norman Conquest—William the Conqueror defeats Harold II at Hastings and becomes king of England

1166

Henry II institutes judge-and-jury system throughout England

c. 1170

Oxford University founded

1171

Henry II declares himself lord of Ireland, beginning centuries of English-Irish conflict

1215

King John signs Magna Carta

1282

England conquers Wales

Period *Pieces*

1295

Model Parliament assembled under Edward I

1337 ▲

Hundred Years' War with France begins (to 1453)

1347–1350

Black Death (bubonic plague) kills more than one-fourth of European population

c. 1375

Sir Gawain and the Green Knight composed

c. 1382

John Wycliffe has Bible translated into English

c. 1386 ▲

Chaucer begins *The Canterbury Tales*

Above: The Prioress

c. 1420

Earliest surviving Paston letter

1455

Beginning of Wars of the Roses (to 1485)

1485

William Caxton prints Sir Thomas Malory's *Le Morte d'Arthur* on England's first printing press

Roman sandals

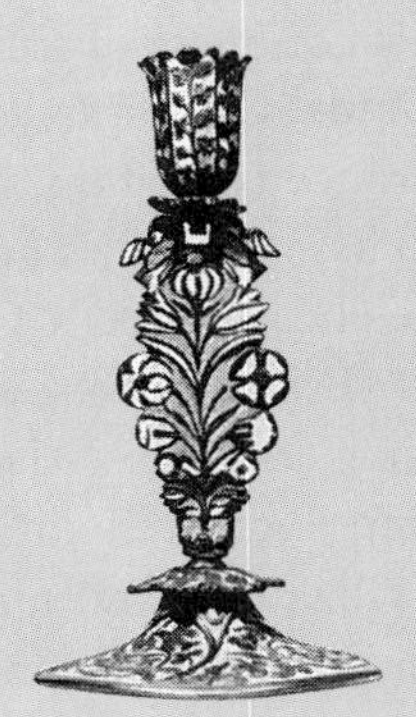

Medieval candlestick

Sundial for telling time

The Anglo-Saxon & Medieval Periods 449-1485

The British Isles, just off the west coast of continental Europe, enter recorded history in the writings of the Roman general Julius Caesar. In 55 B.C., fresh from his conquest of Celtic peoples known as Gauls, Caesar sailed from what is now France to Britain, largest of the British Isles, to assert Rome's authority over it. There he encountered a Celtic people called the Britons, from whom the island takes its name. Also living on Britain were Picts, remnants of a pre-Celtic civilization, and farther west, on Ireland (the next-largest British island) was another group of Celtic speakers, the Gaels.

The Britons had a thriving culture by most standards of the day. They were skilled in agriculture and metalwork, traded with their Celtic neighbors overseas, and had an oral tradition of literature and learning preserved by a priestly class known as druids. They were, however, no match for the Romans. About a century after Caesar's visit, Roman armies returned to Britain to make good his claim. Despite resistance, they rapidly conquered the Britons and drove the war-

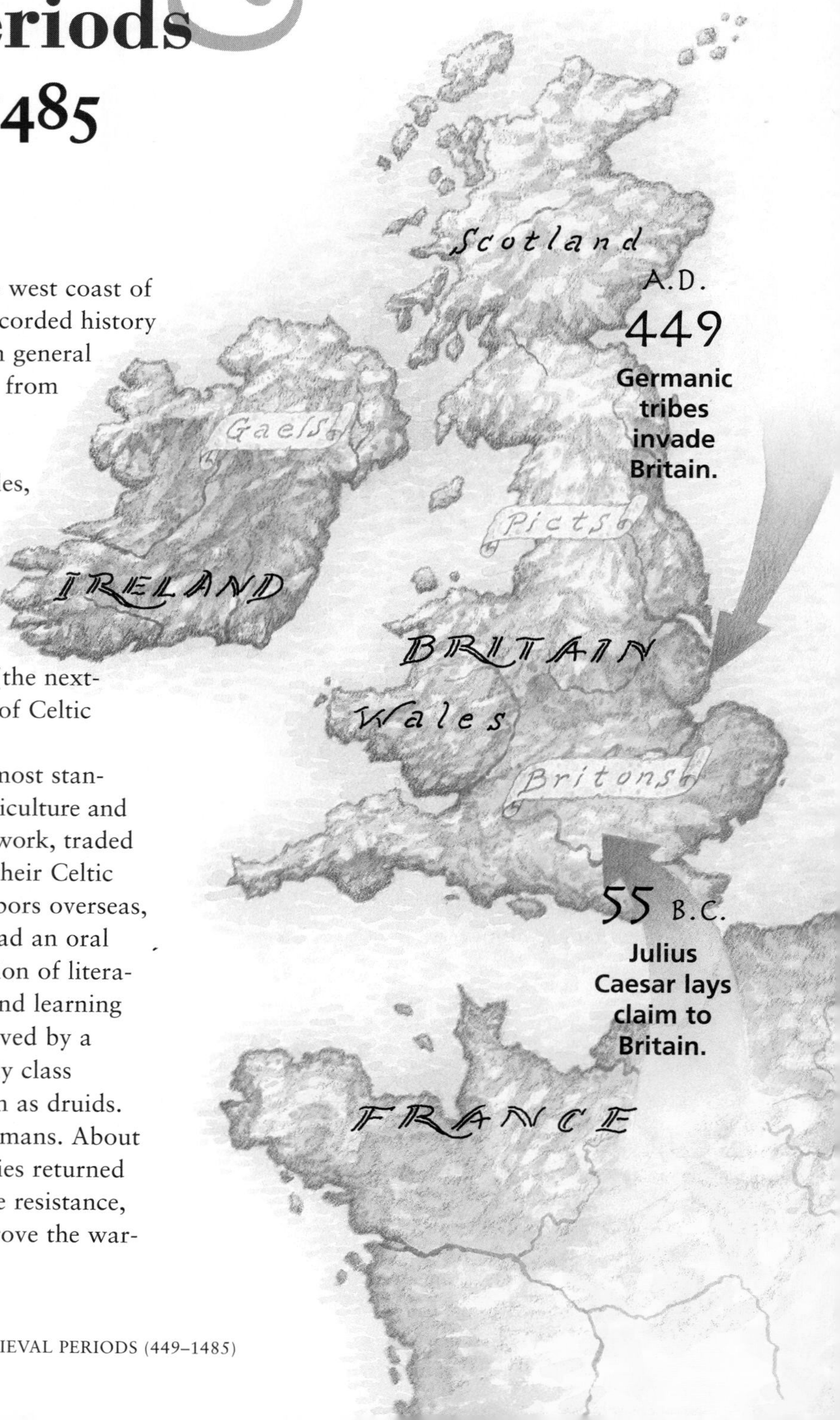

Detail of a Celtic container

A.D. 449
Germanic tribes invade Britain.

55 B.C.
Julius Caesar lays claim to Britain.

like Picts northward to what is now Scotland.

Britain became a province of the great Roman Empire, and the Romans introduced cities, fine stone roads, written scholarship, and eventually Christianity to the island. As they adapted to a more urban way of life, the "Romanized" Britons came to depend on the Roman military for protection; but early in the fifth century, with much of their empire being overrun by invaders, the Roman armies abandoned Britain to defend the city of Rome. It was not long before Britain too became the target of invasion.

Above: Celtic cross

The Anglo-Saxon Period
449-1066

In an invasion traditionally assigned to the year A.D. 449 but actually taking place over several decades, Angles, Saxons, and other Germanic peoples (such as Jutes and Frisians) left their northern European homelands and began settling on Britain's eastern and southern shores. The Britons—perhaps led by a Christian commander named Arthur—fought a series of legendary battles in an effort to stop the invasion. Eventually, however, they were driven to seek refuge in Cornwall and Wales on the western fringes of the island; in the northern area now called Scotland, where Gaels from Ireland were also settling; and in an area on the west coast of continental Europe that would come to be known as Britanny. In southern and central Britain, Celtic culture all but disappeared. The Germanic tribes eventually organized themselves into a confederation

Language

Just as Britain's fifth-century invaders eventually united into a nation called England, their closely related Germanic dialects evolved over time into a distinct language called English—today usually called Old English to distinguish it from later forms of the language. Old English was very different from the English we speak today. Harsher in sound, it was written phonetically, with no silent letters. Grammatically, it was more complex than modern English, with words changing form to indicate different functions, so that word order was more flexible than it is now. The most valuable characteristic of the language, however, was its ability to change and grow, adopting new words as the need arose.

Literature

Although the early Anglo-Saxons did have a writing system, called the runic alphabet, they used it mainly for inscriptions on coins, monuments, and the like. Their literature was composed and transmitted orally rather than in writing. In the mead halls of kings and nobles, where the Anglo-Saxons gathered to eat, drink, and socialize, oral poets called scops celebrated the deeds of heroic warriors in long **epic poems.** They also sang shorter, **lyric poems.** In some of these, deaths or other losses are mourned in the mood of bleak fatalism characteristic of early Anglo-Saxon times. Many of the lyrics composed after the advent of Christianity express religious faith or offer moral instruction. Others reflect a more playful nature: the brief Anglo-Saxon **riddles,** for example, describe familiar objects, like a ship or a bird, in ways that force the audience to guess their identity.

of seven kingdoms called the Heptarchy. In the southeast was Kent, kingdom of the Jutes. Further west were the Saxon kingdoms of Sussex, Essex, and Wessex. To the north were the kingdoms of the Angles—East Anglia, Mercia, and Northumbria. Perhaps because the Angles were dominant in the early history of the Heptarchy, the area of Germanic settlement became known as Angle-land, or England, and its people came to be called the English. Modern scholars, however, usually employ the term *Anglo-Saxon* to refer to the people and culture of this period of English history.

Like all cultures, that of the Anglo-Saxons changed over time. The early invaders were seafaring wanderers whose lives were bleak, violent, and short. With them, they brought their pagan religion—marked by a strong belief in *wyrd,* or fate—and their admiration for heroic warriors whose *wyrd* it was to prevail in battle. As they settled into their new land, however, the Anglo-Saxons became an agricultural people—less violent, more secure, more civilized. One of the most important civilizing forces was the Christianity they began accepting late in the sixth century.

The Growth of Christianity

Despite the collapse of Roman power there, Christianity had never completely died out in the British Isles. Early in the fifth century a Romanized Briton named Patrick had converted Ireland's Gaels to Christianity. When the Gaels began colonizing Scotland, they brought Christianity in their wake. From the isle of Iona off the Scottish coast, missionaries spread the faith among the Picts and Angles in the north. Later, in 597, a Roman missionary named Augustine arrived in the kingdom of Kent, where he established a monastery at Canterbury. From there, Christianity spread so rapidly that by 690 all of Britain was at least nominally Christian.

After the fall of the Roman Empire, monasteries became centers of intellectual, literary, artistic, and social activity. The Book of Kells is an illuminated gospel book begun in an Irish monastery in the late eighth century.

On Lindisfarne, a tiny island off the Northumbrian coast, monks produced the beautiful Bible manuscript known as the Lindisfarne Gospels.

The Danish Invasions

In the 790s, a new group of northern European invaders—the Danes, also known as the Vikings—began to devastate Northumbria's flourishing culture. Coming at first to loot monasteries, the Danes in time gained control of much of northern and eastern England. They were less successful in the south, where their advance was halted by a powerful king of Wessex, Alfred the Great. After inflicting defeats on the Danes in 878 and 886, Alfred forced them to agree to a truce and to accept Christianity.

Although Alfred's reign was a high point in Anglo-Saxon civilization, the tug-of-war with the Danes resumed after his death. In 1016 a Dane named Canute even managed to become king of all England; he proved a successful ruler and won the support of many Anglo-Saxon noblemen. Less successful was the deeply religious Edward the Confessor, who came to the throne in 1042. Edward, who had no children, had once sworn an oath making William, duke of Normandy, his heir—or so William claimed. Later, Edward was persuaded to name Harold, earl of Wessex, as his heir. When Edward died in 1066, the English witan (an advisory council of nobles and church officials) supported Harold's claim. Incensed, William led his Normans in what was to be the last successful invasion of the island of Britain: the Norman Conquest. Harold was killed at the Battle of Hastings, and on Christmas Day of 1066, a triumphant William—who would go down in history as William the Conqueror—was crowned king of England.

Ornamental pin commissioned by Alfred the Great

Literature

The spread of Christianity in Britain was accompanied by a spread of literacy and by the introduction of the Roman alphabet in place of the runic alphabet. Though poetry remained primarily an oral art, poems were now more likely to get written down. In this age before printing, however, the only books were manuscripts that scribes copied by hand. Thus, only a fraction of Anglo-Saxon poetry has survived, in manuscripts produced centuries after the poems were composed. The most famous survivor is the epic *Beowulf,* about a legendary hero of the northern European past. A manuscript known as the Exeter Book contains many of the surviving Anglo-Saxon lyrics, including "The Seafarer," "The Wife's Lament," and over 90 riddles.

Most Old English poems are anonymous. One of the few poets known

by name is a monk called Caedmon, described by the Venerable Bede in his famous eighth-century history of England. Like most scholars of his day, Bede wrote in Latin, the language of the church. It was not until the reign of Alfred the Great that writing in English began to be widespread. In 891, Alfred initiated the compiling of the *Anglo-Saxon Chronicle,* a historic record in poetry and prose that was added to, on and off, until early Norman times. He also encouraged English translations of portions of the Bible and other Latin works.

Inset above: Detail from an illuminated Bible

The Medieval Period
1066-1485

Like the Danes of Britain, the Normans (whose name means "north men") had originally been Viking raiders from northern Europe. However, after settling in the region that became known as Normandy, just northeast of Britanny on the coast of France, the Normans had adopted French ways. Now William introduced these practices to England, beginning the medieval (or middle) period in English history.

Probably the most significant of William's introductions was feudalism, a political and economic system in which the hierarchy of power was based on the premise that the king owned all the land in the kingdom. Keeping a fourth for himself and granting a fourth to the church, William parceled out the rest of England to loyal nobles—mostly Norman barons—who, in return, either paid him or supplied him with warriors called knights. The barons swore allegiance to the king, the knights to their barons, and so on down the social ladder. At the bottom of the ladder were the conquered Anglo-Saxons, many of whom were serfs—peasants bound to land they could not own. To protect Norman interests, barons were encouraged to build strong castles from which they could dominate the countryside and defend the realm from attack; at the same time, great cathedrals and abbeys were erected on the new church lands.

Because William's successors were less strong and organized than he, power struggles among the barons

Hoping to influence the church, Henry II appointed his friend Thomas à Becket archbishop of Canterbury. When the archbishop began favoring church interests over those of the crown, Henry's sharp criticisms prompted four loyal knights to murder Becket. Henry quickly proclaimed his innocence and reconciled with the church; Becket was declared a saint, his shrine at Canterbury becoming a popular destination for Christian pilgrims.

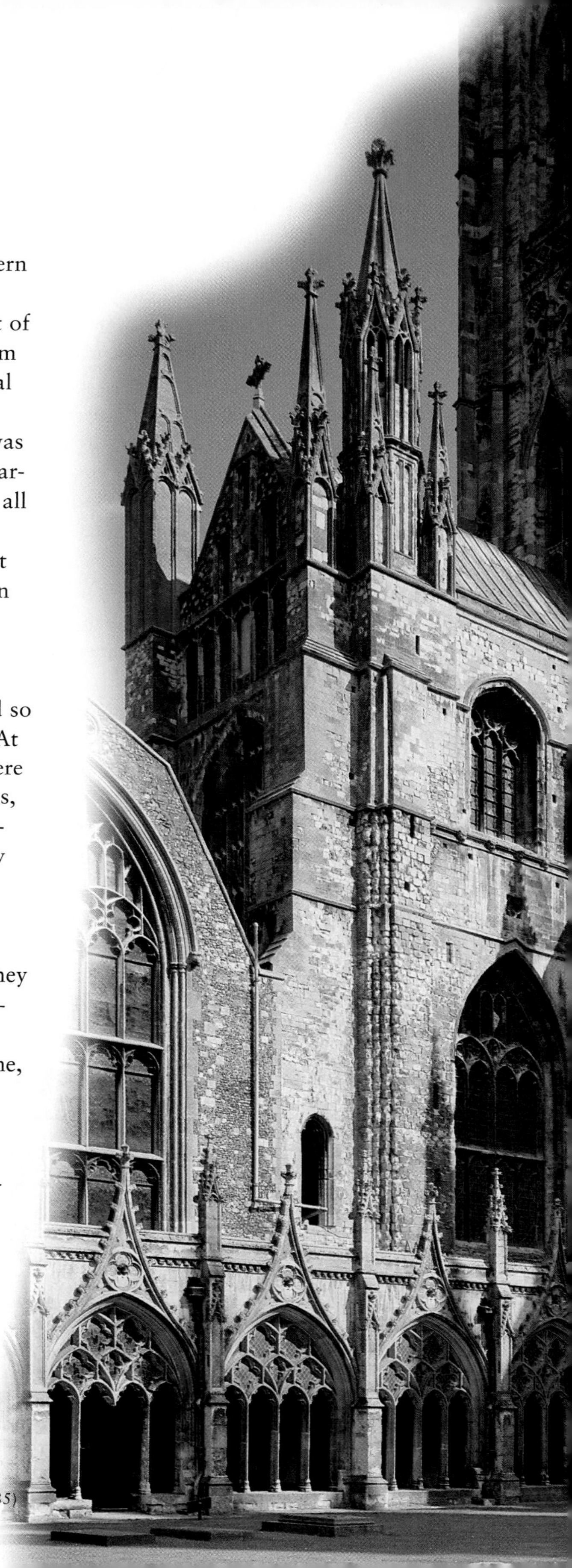

Canterbury Cathedral, begun in the 11th century, reflects the influence of Norman architecture.

were common in the decades after his death. When William's son Henry I died in 1135, the barons took sides in a violent struggle for power between Henry's daughter Matilda and his nephew Stephen. The near anarchy ended in 1154, when Matilda's son Henry Plantagenet took the throne as Henry II. One of medieval England's most memorable rulers, Henry reformed the judicial system, instituting royal courts throughout the country, establishing a system of juries, and initiating the formation of English common law out of a patchwork of centuries-old practices.

At least as colorful as Henry II was his wife, Eleanor of Aquitaine, a former French queen who had brought as her dowry vast landholdings in France. From French court circles she also brought the ideals of chivalry, a code of honor intended to govern knightly behavior. The code encouraged knights to honor and protect ladies and to go on holy quests—like the Crusades, the military expeditions in which European Christians attempted to wrest the holy city of Jerusalem from Moslem control.

Henry's son Richard I, called Richard the Lion-Hearted, spent much of his ten-year reign fighting in the Crusades and in France, where English possessions were threatened. During his absence, his treacherous brother John—the villain of many Robin Hood legends—plotted against him. When Richard died and John became king, he found that the royal

Jousting knights

Language

The Norman Conquest led to great changes in the English language. Despite their Viking origins, by 1066 the Normans spoke a dialect of Old French, which they brought to England with them. Norman French became the language of the English court, of government business, of the new nobility, and of the scholars, cooks, and craftspeople that the Norman barons brought with them to serve their more "refined" needs. The use of English became confined to the conquered, mostly peasant population. Ever adaptable, however, English soon incorporated thousands of words and many grammatical conventions from Norman French. These changes led to the development of Middle English, a form much closer than Old English to the language we speak today.

LITERATURE

As English became the language of a mostly illiterate peasantry, the common folk again relied on the oral tradition to tell their stories and express their feelings. Many of their compositions were folk ballads, brief narrative poems sung to musical accompaniment. The later Middle Ages saw the flowering of **mystery** and **miracle plays,** which dramatized episodes from the Bible and from saints' lives, and **morality plays,** which taught moral lessons. From these simple plays, intended to convey religious truths to an audience only partly literate, arose the great tradition of English drama.

Right: Flexible body armor called mail was made from iron links.

treasury had been bankrupted by overseas warfare. In 1215 he was forced to sign the Magna Carta ("Great Charter"), which limited royal authority by granting more power to the barons and thus was an early step on the road to democracy. During the reign of John's son Henry III, an advisory council of barons—now called a parliament—began to meet regularly. Under his successor, Edward I, the Model Parliament of 1295 established the inclusion of commoners (eventually to become the House of Commons) as well as barons (the "House of Lords") in the council.

The Decline of Feudalism

The growth of the commoners' power went hand in hand with the growth of medieval towns, a result of an increase in trade that was stimulated in part by the Crusades. In the towns, merchants and craftspeople formed organizations called guilds to control the flow and price of goods and to set up rules for advancing from apprentice to master craftsman. The

King Philip II of France *(above),* along with Richard the Lion-Hearted and Frederick I of Germany, was a leader of the forces attempting to recapture Jerusalem in the Third Crusade (1189–1192).

Right: Magna Carta, 1215

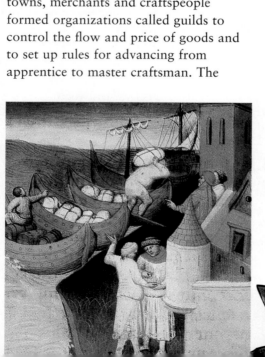

Wool, an important product in medieval commerce, was shipped from sheep farms to market towns, where merchants exchanged money for goods.

The spread of ideas was greatly assisted by a landmark innovation in 15th-century Europe—the printing press.

growth of towns meant the decline of feudalism, since wealth was no longer based exclusively on land ownership. On the other hand, the crowding of townspeople in conditions of poor sanitation ensured that diseases like plague could spread rapidly.

As towns were becoming centers of commerce, universities were becoming England's chief centers of learning. At Oxford University, 13th-century scholars like Roger Bacon advanced the study of science and mathematics. A century later, an Oxford scholar named John Wycliffe led an effort to end widespread church corruption. Though his followers, the Lollards, were suppressed, his ideas spread to John Huss in central Europe and through him influenced the later religious reformer Martin Luther.

The Hundred Years' War

Wycliffe's reform efforts took place during the Hundred Years' War, a long struggle between England and France that had begun in 1337 during the reign of Edward III. As the war continued on and off for more than a century, England also had to weather several domestic crises, including a great epidemic of plague known as the Black Death, which killed a third of England's popu-

Literature

Religious faith was a vital element of medieval English life and literature. One of the most distinctive products of the age is the long poem known as *Piers Plowman,* a dream vision that explores Christianity's spiritual mysteries. Religious devotion is also the key concern of *The Book of Margery Kempe,* an autobiography in which Kempe focuses on her spiritual growth. In contrast, far more worldly attitudes are expressed in the surviving correspondence of the Paston family. These remarkable letters, written from about 1420 to 1500 and discovered centuries later by one of the Pastons' descendants, provide fascinating glimpses of life in later medieval times.

Especially popular in the Middle Ages were **romances**—tales of chivalric knights, many of which feature King Arthur and the members of his court. For centuries the oral poets of the Britons in Wales had celebrated their legendary hero Arthur just as Anglo-Saxon scops had celebrated Beowulf. Then, about 1135, the monk Geoffrey of Monmouth produced a Latin "history" based on the old Welsh legends. Geoffrey's book caught the fancy of French, German, and English writers, who soon produced their own versions of the legends, updating them to reflect then-current notions of chivalry. In about 1375, an anonymous English poet produced *Sir Gawain and the Green Knight,* recounting the marvelous adventures of a knight of Arthur's court. A century later, in *Le Morte d'Arthur,* Sir Thomas Malory retold a number of the French Arthurian tales in Middle English.

Language

As warfare with France dragged on, English not only survived but triumphed. Among England's upper class it came to seem unpatriotic to use the language of the nation's number one enemy, especially since the Anglo-Norman variety of French was ridiculed by the "real" French speakers across the English Channel. By the end of the Hundred Years' War, English had once again become the first language of most of the English nobility.

LITERATURE

In the rebirth of English as a language of literature, no writer was more important than the 14th-century poet Geoffrey Chaucer, the towering figure of Middle English letters. Chaucer's masterpiece, *The Canterbury Tales,* is a collection of tales supposedly narrated by a group of pilgrims traveling from London to Canterbury to visit the shrine of Thomas à Becket. The pilgrims, who come from all walks of medieval life—the castle, the farm, the church, the town—are introduced in the famous "Prologue," where Chaucer weaves a vivid and charming tapestry of English life in the later Middle Ages.

lation; the Peasants' Revolt of 1381; and Richard II's forced abdication in 1399, which brought Henry IV to the English throne. The war itself had many famous episodes—like Henry V's great victory over the French at Agincourt and the French army's lifting of the siege of Orléans under the inspired leadership of the young peasant woman Joan of Arc. When the war finally ended in 1453, England had lost nearly all of its French possessions. It was also on the verge of a conflict in which two rival families claimed the throne—the house of York, whose symbol was a white rose, and the house of Lancaster, whose symbol was a red rose. The fighting, known as the Wars of the Roses, ended in 1485, when the Lancastrian Henry Tudor killed the Yorkist king Richard III at Bosworth Field and took the throne as Henry VII. This event is usually taken as marking the end of the Middle Ages in England.

In medieval art, the Black Death was often portrayed as a skeleton.

• *HISTORICAL LITERARY CONNECTION*

During the Hundred Years' War, the use of the longbow helped the English to inflict heavy casualties on the French, who were armed with the less efficient crossbow.

PART 1 *Tests of Courage*

The Anglo-Saxon and medieval periods were ones of turmoil and change—times when people's courage was frequently put to the test. Amid this turmoil, the tests of courage often took the form of physical challenges, such as confronting a dreaded foe or battling to survive on the high seas. Other tests of courage involved spiritual or emotional challenges, such as standing up for one's religious beliefs or enduring the absence of a loved one. As you read about tests of courage in this part of Unit One, try to place yourself in the distant past and imagine how you would respond to similar challenges.

PREVIEWING

EPIC POETRY

from Beowulf

The Beowulf Poet

Translated by Burton Raffel

PERSONAL CONNECTION

Beowulf is a long narrative poem about a legendary hero who battles evil. Like all heroes, Beowulf represents the values admired by his society. Think about the qualities of modern heroes and the enemies they battle. In your notebook, jot down ideas that come to mind about the qualities that make a hero.

HISTORICAL CONNECTION

After the fall of the Roman Empire, life in northern Europe was dominated by frequent bloody battles between Germanic tribes. Warriors were fiercely loyal to their leaders, and those who performed deeds of great strength or courage against their enemies were honored greatly. For entertainment, the warriors gathered in large wooden structures called mead halls, where they feasted, drank mead (an alcoholic beverage), and listened to tales of heroic achievements.

The heroic tales were presented in the form of long epic poems and shorter poetic narratives. Poet-singers called **scops** (shōps) recited the tales in a chanting voice, often accompanied by the music of a harp. *Beowulf,* the most famous of these heroic tales, is set in what is now Sweden and Denmark. Many scholars believe that *Beowulf* was composed in England during the eighth century but was not written down until 200 years later. It is regarded by many as the first major work in the history of English literature.

The surviving manuscript of *Beowulf* is written in Old English, the language of the Germanic inhabitants of Britain in the Anglo-Saxon period. Old English neither looks nor sounds like modern English and must be translated for most modern readers. The task of the translator goes beyond the literal deciphering of individual words and phrases; he or she must also make sure that the meaning of the original work is communicated to readers.

Old English

Đa com of more   under misthleoðum
grendel gongan–   godes yrre bær;
mynte se manscaða   manna cynnes
sumne besyrwan   in sele ðam hean.

As you read these excerpts from *Beowulf,* keep in mind that the words you are reading are those of the translator, Burton Raffel, but that the thoughts expressed are for the most part those of the original author.

Modern English

Out from the marsh, from the foot of misty
Hills and bogs, bearing God's hatred,
Grendel came, hoping to kill
Anyone he could trap on this trip to high Herot.

• *HISTORICAL CONNECTION*

READING CONNECTION

Reading Epic Poetry

An **epic** is a long narrative poem that deals with the adventures of a hero. Most epics possess some or all of the following characteristics:

1. The hero is a person of high social status and often of great historical or legendary importance.
2. The actions of the hero often determine the fate of a nation or group of people.
3. The hero performs exceedingly courageous, sometimes even superhuman, deeds that reflect the ideas and values of the era.
4. The plot is complicated by supernatural beings and events.
5. The setting is large in scale, involving more than one nation and often a long and dangerous journey through foreign lands.
6. Long, formal speeches are often delivered by the main character.
7. The poem treats universal ideas, such as good and evil, life and death.

As you read these excerpts from *Beowulf,* look for evidence of each of the seven epic characteristics. Record your findings in a chart like the one shown here. (If you have access to a computer word-processing program that allows you to create charts, you may want to use it to record your findings.)

Characteristics	Location of Evidence
1. Hero of high status	
2. Fateful actions	
3. Courageous deeds	
4. Supernatural complications	
5. Large-scale setting, long journey	
6. Formal speeches	
7. Universal ideas	

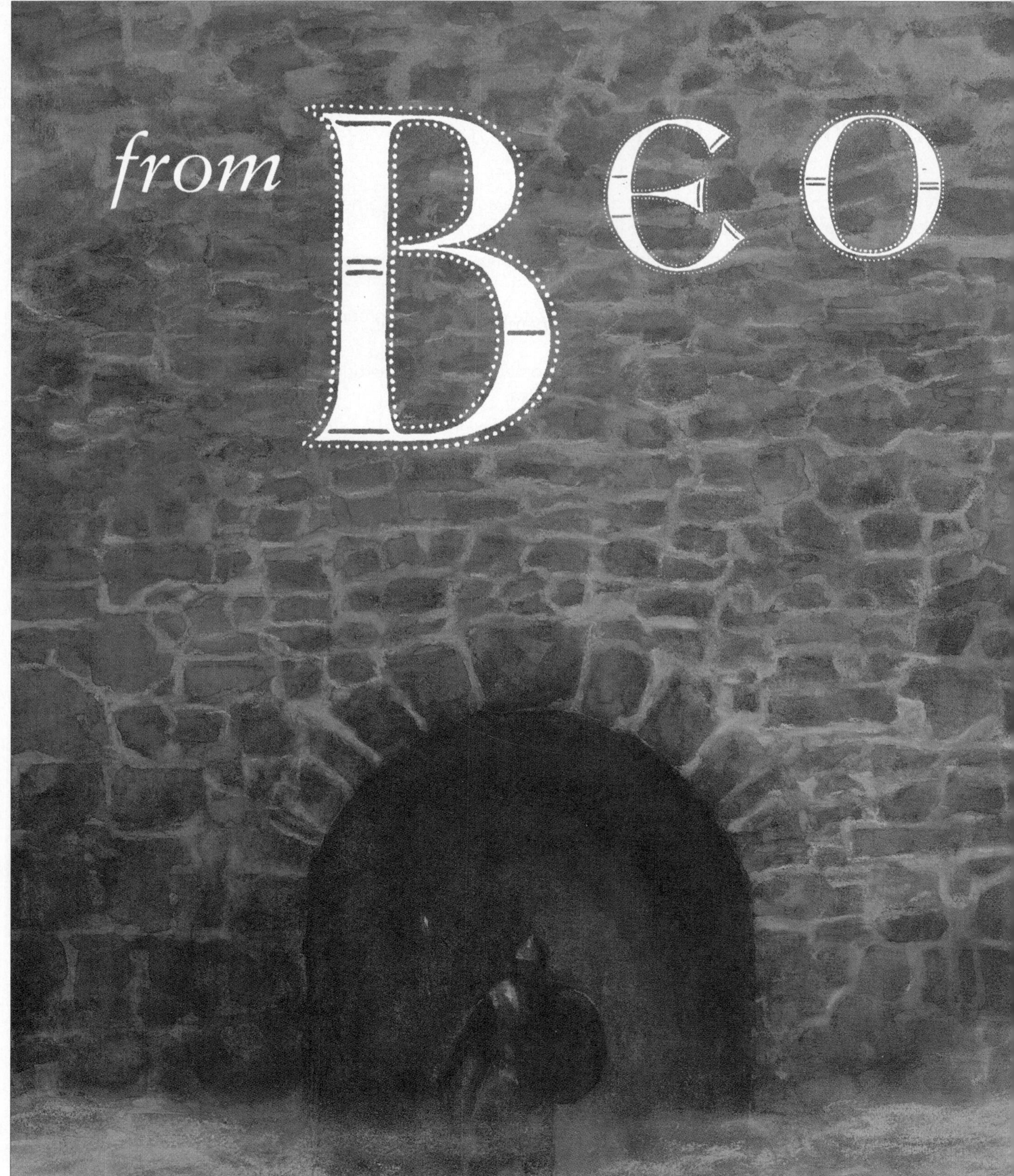
from
BEO

WULF

The tale of Beowulf tells about the heroes of two clans, the Danes and the Geats (gēts), who lived in Scandinavia. The introduction explains that Hrothgar (hrôth′gär), king of the Danes, built a wonderful mead hall that he called Herot (hâr′ət). In the passage you are about to read, Grendel, a fierce and powerful monster, invades the mead hall.

GRENDEL

A powerful monster, living down
In the darkness, growled in pain, impatient
As day after day the music rang
Loud in that hall, the harp's rejoicing
Call and the poet's clear songs, sung
Of the ancient beginnings of us all, recalling
The Almighty making the earth, shaping
These beautiful plains marked off by oceans,
Then proudly setting the sun and moon
To glow across the land and light it;
The corners of the earth were made lovely with trees
And leaves, made quick with life, with each
Of the nations who now move on its face. And then
As now warriors sang of their pleasure:
So Hrothgar's men lived happy in his hall
Till the monster stirred, that demon, that fiend,

Grendel, who haunted the moors, the wild
Marshes, and made his home in a hell
Not hell but earth. He was spawned in that slime,
Conceived by a pair of those monsters born
Of Cain, murderous creatures banished
By God, punished forever for the crime
Of Abel's death. The Almighty drove
Those demons out, and their exile was bitter,
Shut away from men; they split
Into a thousand forms of evil—spirits
And fiends, goblins, monsters, giants,
A brood forever opposing the Lord's
Will, and again and again defeated.
Then, when darkness had dropped, Grendel
Went up to Herot, wondering what the warriors
Would do in that hall when their drinking was done.
He found them sprawled in sleep, suspecting
Nothing, their dreams undisturbed. The monster's
Thoughts were as quick as his greed or his claws:
He slipped through the door and there in the silence
Snatched up thirty men, smashed them
Unknowing in their beds and ran out with their bodies,
The blood dripping behind him, back
To his lair, delighted with his night's slaughter.
At daybreak, with the sun's first light, they saw
How well he had worked, and in that gray morning
Broke their long feast with tears and laments
For the dead. Hrothgar, their lord, sat joyless
In Herot, a mighty prince mourning
The fate of his lost friends and companions,
Knowing by its tracks that some demon had torn
His followers apart. He wept, fearing
The beginning might not be the end. And that night
Grendel came again, so set
On murder that no crime could ever be enough,
No savage assault quench his lust
For evil. Then each warrior tried
To escape him, searched for rest in different
Beds, as far from Herot as they could find,
Seeing how Grendel hunted when they slept.
Distance was safety; the only survivors
Were those who fled him. Hate had triumphed.

GUIDE FOR READING

17 moors (mo͝orz): broad, open regions with patches of bog.

19 spawned: born.

21 Cain: the eldest son of Adam and Eve. According to the Bible (Genesis 4), he murdered his younger brother Abel.

19–29 Who were Grendel's earliest ancestors? How did he come to exist?

40 lair: the den of a wild animal.

49 What is meant by "The beginning might not be the end"?

58 In what way has hate triumphed?

WORDS TO KNOW

lament (lə-mĕnt′) *n.* an audible expression of grief; wail

So Grendel ruled, fought with the righteous,
One against many, and won; so Herot
Stood empty, and stayed deserted for years,
Twelve winters of grief for Hrothgar, king
Of the Danes, sorrow heaped at his door
By hell-forged hands. His misery leaped
The seas, was told and sung in all
Men's ears: how Grendel's hatred began,
How the monster relished his savage war
On the Danes, keeping the bloody feud
Alive, seeking no peace, offering
No truce, accepting no settlement, no price
In gold or land, and paying the living
For one crime only with another. No one
Waited for reparation from his plundering claws:
That shadow of death hunted in the darkness,
Stalked Hrothgar's warriors, old
And young, lying in waiting, hidden
In mist, invisibly following them from the edge
Of the marsh, always there, unseen.

64 What does the phrase "hell-forged hands" suggest about Grendel?

73 reparation: something done to make amends for loss or suffering. In Anglo-Saxon society, any person who killed another was expected to make a payment to the victim's family as a way of restoring peace.

BEOWULF

The story of Grendel's twelve years of terror has spread throughout the other clans. Beowulf, a young hero of the Geats, has received permission from his king, Higlac (hĭg′lăk), to sail with fourteen warriors to offer their help to the Danes. Arriving on the Danish shore, they are met by Hrothgar's men and escorted to Herot to greet the king.

"Hail, Hrothgar!
Higlac is my cousin and my king; the days
Of my youth have been filled with glory. Now Grendel's
Name has echoed in our land: sailors
Have brought us stories of Herot, the best
Of all mead-halls, deserted and useless when the moon
Hangs in skies the sun had lit,
Light and life fleeing together.
My people have said, the wisest, most knowing

Prow of ninth-century Oseberg ship

80 cousin: relative. Beowulf is Higlac's nephew as well as his subject.

WORDS TO KNOW
relish (rĕl′ĭsh) *v.* to enjoy keenly

And best of them, that my duty was to go to the Danes'
Great king. They have seen my strength for themselves,
Have watched me rise from the darkness of war,
Dripping with my enemies' blood. I drove
Five great giants into chains, chased
All of that race from the earth. I swam
In the blackness of night, hunting monsters
Out of the ocean, and killing them one
By one; death was my errand and the fate
They had earned. Now Grendel and I are called
Together, and I've come. Grant me, then,
Lord and protector of this noble place,
A single request! I have come so far,
Oh shelterer of warriors and your people's loved friend,
That this one favor you should not refuse me—
That I, alone and with the help of my men,
May purge all evil from this hall. I have heard,
Too, that the monster's scorn of men
Is so great that he needs no weapons and fears none.
Nor will I. My lord Higlac
Might think less of me if I let my sword
Go where my feet were afraid to, if I hid
Behind some broad linden shield: my hands
Alone shall fight for me, struggle for life
Against the monster. God must decide
Who will be given to death's cold grip."

110 linden shield: shield made from the wood of a linden tree.

110–112 Beowulf insists that he fight Grendel by himself, without weapons. Why is this so important to him?

THE BATTLE WITH GRENDEL

Out from the marsh, from the foot of misty
Hills and bogs, bearing God's hatred,
Grendel came, hoping to kill
Anyone he could trap on this trip to high Herot.
He moved quickly through the cloudy night,
Up from his swampland, sliding silently
Toward that gold-shining hall. He had visited Hrothgar's
Home before, knew the way—
But never, before nor after that night,
Found Herot defended so firmly, his reception
So harsh. He journeyed, forever joyless,

115 The reference to God shows the influence of Christianity. Whose side do you think God will be on?

WORDS TO KNOW

purge (pûrj) *v.* to cleanse or purify

Straight to the door, then snapped it open,
Tore its iron fasteners with a touch
And rushed angrily over the threshold.
He strode quickly across the inlaid
Floor, snarling and fierce: his eyes
Gleamed in the darkness, burned with a gruesome
Light. Then he stopped, seeing the hall
Crowded with sleeping warriors, stuffed
With rows of young soldiers resting together.
And his heart laughed, he relished the sight,
Intended to tear the life from those bodies
By morning; the monster's mind was hot
With the thought of food and the feasting his belly
Would soon know. But fate, that night, intended
Grendel to gnaw the broken bones
Of his last human supper. Human
Eyes were watching his evil steps,
Waiting to see his swift hard claws.
Grendel snatched at the first Geat
He came to, ripped him apart, cut
His body to bits with powerful jaws,
Drank the blood from his veins and bolted
Him down, hands and feet; death
And Grendel's great teeth came together,
Snapping life shut. Then he stepped to another
Still body, clutched at Beowulf with his claws,
Grasped at a strong-hearted wakeful sleeper
—And was instantly seized himself, claws
Bent back as Beowulf leaned up on one arm.
That shepherd of evil, guardian of crime,
Knew at once that nowhere on earth
Had he met a man whose hands were harder;
His mind was flooded with fear—but nothing
Could take his talons and himself from that tight
Hard grip. Grendel's one thought was to run
From Beowulf, flee back to his marsh and hide there:
This was a different Herot than the hall he had emptied.
But Higlac's follower remembered his final
Boast and, standing erect, stopped
The monster's flight, fastened those claws
In his fists till they cracked, clutched Grendel
Closer. The infamous killer fought

127 threshold: the strip of wood or stone at the bottom of a doorway.

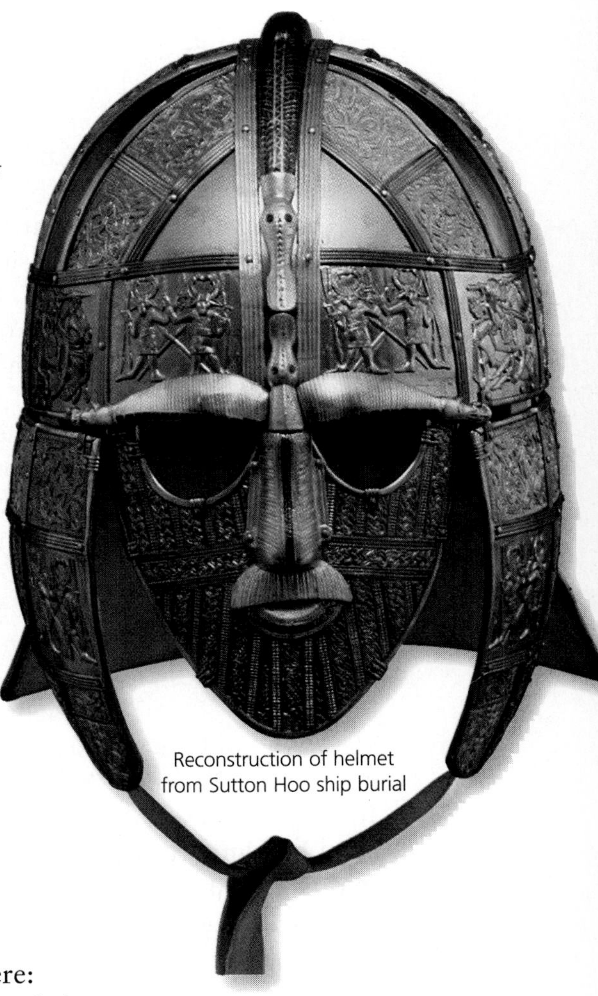

Reconstruction of helmet from Sutton Hoo ship burial

WORDS TO KNOW
talon (tăl′ən) *n.* a claw
infamous (ĭn′fə-məs) *adj.* having an unfavorable reputation; notorious

For his freedom, wanting no flesh but retreat,
Desiring nothing but escape; his claws
Had been caught, he was trapped. That trip to Herot
Was a miserable journey for the writhing monster!
The high hall rang, its roof boards swayed,
And Danes shook with terror. Down
The aisles the battle swept, angry
And wild. Herot trembled, wonderfully
Built to withstand the blows, the struggling
Great bodies beating at its beautiful walls;
Shaped and fastened with iron, inside
And out, artfully worked, the building
Stood firm. Its benches rattled, fell
To the floor, gold-covered boards grating
As Grendel and Beowulf battled across them.
Hrothgar's wise men had fashioned Herot
To stand forever; only fire,
They had planned, could shatter what such skill had put
Together, swallow in hot flames such splendor
Of ivory and iron and wood. Suddenly
The sounds changed, the Danes started
In new terror, cowering in their beds as the terrible
Screams of the Almighty's enemy sang
In the darkness, the horrible shrieks of pain
And defeat, the tears torn out of Grendel's
Taut throat, hell's captive caught in the arms
Of him who of all the men on earth
Was the strongest.
That mighty protector of men
Meant to hold the monster till its life
Leaped out, knowing the fiend was no use
To anyone in Denmark. All of Beowulf's
Band had jumped from their beds, ancestral
Swords raised and ready, determined
To protect their prince if they could. Their courage
Was great but all wasted: they could hack at Grendel
From every side, trying to open
A path for his evil soul, but their points
Could not hurt him, the sharpest and hardest iron
Could not scratch at his skin, for that sin-stained demon
Had bewitched all men's weapons, laid spells
That blunted every mortal man's blade.

159–170 Up to this point Grendel has killed his human victims easily. Why does he try to run away from Beowulf?

203–207 Why can no weapons hurt Grendel?

WORDS TO KNOW

writhing (rī′*th*ĭng) *adj.* twisting and turning in pain **writhe** *v.*

cowering (kou′ə-rĭng) *adj.* cringing in fear **cower** *v.*

taut (tôt) *adj.* pulled tight

And yet his time had come, his days
Were over, his death near; down
To hell he would go, swept groaning and helpless
To the waiting hands of still worse fiends.
Now he discovered—once the afflicter
Of men, tormentor of their days—what it meant
To feud with Almighty God: Grendel
Saw that his strength was deserting him, his claws
Bound fast, Higlac's brave follower tearing at
His hands. The monster's hatred rose higher,
But his power had gone. He twisted in pain,
And the bleeding sinews deep in his shoulder
Snapped, muscle and bone split
And broke. The battle was over, Beowulf
Had been granted new glory: Grendel escaped,
But wounded as he was could flee to his den,
His miserable hole at the bottom of the marsh,
Only to die, to wait for the end
Of all his days. And after that bloody
Combat the Danes laughed with delight.
He who had come to them from across the sea,
Bold and strong-minded, had driven affliction
Off, purged Herot clean. He was happy,
Now, with that night's fierce work; the Danes
Had been served as he'd boasted he'd serve them; Beowulf,
A prince of the Geats, had killed Grendel,
Ended the grief, the sorrow, the suffering
Forced on Hrothgar's helpless people
By a bloodthirsty fiend. No Dane doubted
The victory, for the proof, hanging high
From the rafters where Beowulf had hung it, was the monster's
Arm, claw and shoulder and all.
    And then, in the morning, crowds surrounded
Herot, warriors coming to that hall
From faraway lands, princes and leaders
Of men hurrying to behold the monster's
Great staggering tracks. They gaped with no sense
Of sorrow, felt no regret for his suffering,
Went tracing his bloody footprints, his beaten
And lonely flight, to the edge of the lake
Where he'd dragged his corpselike way, doomed
And already weary of his vanishing life.
The water was bloody, steaming and boiling
In horrible pounding waves, heat

219 sinews (sĭn′yo͞oz): the tendons that connect muscles to bones.

236–239 Why does Beowulf hang Grendel's arm from the rafters?

Sucked from his magic veins; but the swirling
Surf had covered his death, hidden
Deep in murky darkness his miserable
End, as hell opened to receive him.
Then old and young rejoiced, turned back
From that happy pilgrimage, mounted their hard-hooved
Horses, high-spirited stallions, and rode them
Slowly toward Herot again, retelling
Beowulf's bravery as they jogged along.
And over and over they swore that nowhere
On earth or under the spreading sky
Or between the seas, neither south nor north,
Was there a warrior worthier to rule over men.

During the night following Beowulf's defeat of Grendel, Grendel's mother, a monster who lives in the depths of a murky, cold lake, goes to Herot to seek revenge. She kills Hrothgar's closest friend and carries off Grendel's claw. When Beowulf is told of this attack, he immediately sets out to fight the monster. He descends for hours into the depths of the lake, where he engages in a horrendous battle with Grendel's mother. Using an enormous magic sword fashioned by giants, he finally defeats her, and peace is restored to the land of the Danes. Beowulf, laden with gifts given him by Hrothgar, returns to the land of his own people, the Geats, where he eventually becomes king and rules in peace and prosperity for 50 years.

In the land of the Geats, however, a dragon has been lying undisturbed in a tower for hundreds of years, keeping watch over a vast treasure. One day a thief enters the dragon's lair and steals a cup. The dragon is roused and begins terrorizing the land. Beowulf is an old man by now, but he takes on the challenge of fighting the dragon.

WORDS TO KNOW **pilgrimage** (pĭl'grə-mĭj) *n.* a journey to a sacred place or with a lofty purpose

BEOWULF'S LAST BATTLE

And Beowulf uttered his final boast:
"I've never known fear, as a youth I fought
In endless battles. I am old, now,
But I will fight again, seek fame still,
If the dragon hiding in his tower dares
To face me."
Then he said farewell to his followers,
Each in his turn, for the last time:
"I'd use no sword, no weapon, if this beast
Could be killed without it, crushed to death
Like Grendel, gripped in my hands and torn
Limb from limb. But his breath will be burning
Hot, poison will pour from his tongue.
I feel no shame, with shield and sword
And armor, against this monster: when he comes to me
I mean to stand, not run from his shooting
Flames, stand till fate decides
Which of us wins. My heart is firm,
My hands calm: I need no hot
Words. Wait for me close by, my friends.
We shall see, soon, who will survive
This bloody battle, stand when the fighting
Is done. No one else could do
What I mean to, here, no man but me
Could hope to defeat this monster. No one
Could try. And this dragon's treasure, his gold
And everything hidden in that tower, will be mine
Or war will sweep me to a bitter death!"
Then Beowulf rose, still brave, still strong,
And with his shield at his side, and a mail shirt on his breast,
Strode calmly, confidently, toward the tower, under
The rocky cliffs: no coward could have walked there!
And then he who'd endured dozens of desperate
Battles, who'd stood boldly while swords and shields
Clashed, the best of kings, saw
Huge stone arches and felt the heat
Of the dragon's breath, flooding down
Through the hidden entrance, too hot for anyone
To stand, a streaming current of fire
And smoke that blocked all passage. And the Geats'
Lord and leader, angry, lowered

293 mail: flexible armor made of metal links or overlapping metal scales.

His sword and roared out a battle cry,
A call so loud and clear that it reached through
The hoary rock, hung in the dragon's
Ear. The beast rose, angry,
Knowing a man had come—and then nothing
But war could have followed. Its breath came first,
A steaming cloud pouring from the stone,
Then the earth itself shook. Beowulf
Swung his shield into place, held it
In front of him, facing the entrance. The dragon
Coiled and uncoiled, its heart urging it
Into battle. Beowulf's ancient sword
Was waiting, unsheathed, his sharp and gleaming
Blade. The beast came closer; both of them
Were ready, each set on slaughter. The Geats'
Great prince stood firm, unmoving, prepared
Behind his high shield, waiting in his shining
Armor. The monster came quickly toward him,
Pouring out fire and smoke, hurrying
To its fate. Flames beat at the iron
Shield, and for a time it held, protected
Beowulf as he'd planned; then it began to melt,
And for the first time in his life that famous prince
Fought with fate against him, with glory
Denied him. He knew it, but he raised his sword
And struck at the dragon's scaly hide.
The ancient blade broke, bit into
The monster's skin, drew blood, but cracked
And failed him before it went deep enough, helped him
Less than he needed. The dragon leaped
With pain, thrashed and beat at him, spouting
Murderous flames, spreading them everywhere.
And the Geats' ring-giver did not boast of glorious
Victories in other wars: his weapon
Had failed him, deserted him, now when he needed it
Most, that excellent sword. Edgetho's
Famous son stared at death,
Unwilling to leave this world, to exchange it
For a dwelling in some distant place—a journey
Into darkness that all men must make, as death
Ends their few brief hours on earth.

Quickly, the dragon came at him, encouraged
As Beowulf fell back; its breath flared,
And he suffered, wrapped around in swirling

329–330 Why do you think Beowulf keeps fighting?

340–341 Edgetho's (ĕj′thōz′) . . . **son:** Beowulf.

Flames—a king, before, but now
A beaten warrior. None of his comrades
Came to him, helped him, his brave and noble
Followers; they ran for their lives, fled
Deep in a wood. And only one of them
Remained, stood there, miserable, remembering,
As a good man must, what kinship should mean.

Beowulf's remaining follower, Wiglaf, joins Beowulf, who attacks the dragon again singlehandedly; but the remnant of his sword shatters, and the monster wounds him in the neck. Wiglaf then strikes the dragon, and he and Beowulf together finally succeed in killing the beast. Their triumph is short-lived, however, because Beowulf's wound proves to be mortal.

THE DEATH OF BEOWULF

Beowulf spoke, in spite of the swollen,
Livid wound, knowing he'd unwound
His string of days on earth, seen
As much as God would grant him; all worldly
Pleasure was gone, as life would go,
Soon:
"I'd leave my armor to my son,
Now, if God had given me an heir,
A child born of my body, his life
Created from mine. I've worn this crown
For fifty winters: no neighboring people
Have tried to threaten the Geats, sent soldiers
Against us or talked of terror. My days
Have gone by as fate willed, waiting
For its word to be spoken, ruling as well
As I knew how, swearing no unholy oaths,
Seeking no lying wars. I can leave
This life happy; I can die, here,
Knowing the Lord of all life has never
Watched me wash my sword in blood
Born of my own family. Belovéd

Viking sword

WORDS TO KNOW

livid (lĭv'ĭd) *adj.* discolored; black-and-blue

Wiglaf, go, quickly, find
The dragon's treasure: we've taken its life,
But its gold is ours, too. Hurry,
Bring me ancient silver, precious
Jewels, shining armor and gems,
Before I die. Death will be softer,
Leaving life and this people I've ruled
So long, if I look at this last of all prizes."
        Then Wexstan's son went in, as quickly
As he could, did as the dying Beowulf
Asked, entered the inner darkness
Of the tower, went with his mail shirt and his sword.
Flushed with victory he groped his way,
A brave young warrior, and suddenly saw
Piles of gleaming gold, precious
Gems, scattered on the floor, cups
And bracelets, rusty old helmets, beautifully
Made but rotting with no hands to rub
And polish them. They lay where the dragon left them;
It had flown in the darkness, once, before fighting
Its final battle. (So gold can easily
Triumph, defeat the strongest of men,
No matter how deep it is hidden!) And he saw,
Hanging high above, a golden
Banner, woven by the best of weavers
And beautiful. And over everything he saw
A strange light, shining everywhere,
On walls and floor and treasure. Nothing
Moved, no other monsters appeared;

361–383 What values are reflected in Beowulf's speech?

384 Wexstan's son: Wiglaf.

Viking purse clip of gold, garnet, and glass, from Sutton Hoo ship burial

He took what he wanted, all the treasures
That pleased his eye, heavy plates
And golden cups and the glorious banner,
Loaded his arms with all they could hold.
Beowulf's dagger, his iron blade,
Had finished the fire-spitting terror
That once protected tower and treasures
Alike; the gray-bearded lord of the Geats
Had ended those flying, burning raids
Forever.
Then Wiglaf went back, anxious
To return while Beowulf was alive, to bring him
Treasure they'd won together. He ran,
Hoping his wounded king, weak
And dying, had not left the world too soon.
Then he brought their treasure to Beowulf, and found
His famous king bloody, gasping
For breath. But Wiglaf sprinkled water
Over his lord, until the words
Deep in his breast broke through and were heard.
Beholding the treasure he spoke, haltingly:
"For this, this gold, these jewels, I thank
Our Father in Heaven, Ruler of the Earth—
For all of this, that His grace has given me,
Allowed me to bring to my people while breath
Still came to my lips. I sold my life
For this treasure, and I sold it well. Take
What I leave, Wiglaf, lead my people,
Help them; my time is gone. Have
The brave Geats build me a tomb,
When the funeral flames have burned me, and build it
Here, at the water's edge, high
On this spit of land, so sailors can see
This tower, and remember my name, and call it
Beowulf's tower, and boats in the darkness
And mist, crossing the sea, will know it."
Then that brave king gave the golden
Necklace from around his throat to Wiglaf,
Gave him his gold-covered helmet, and his rings,
And his mail shirt, and ordered him to use them well:
"You're the last of all our far-flung family.
Fate has swept our race away,
Taken warriors in their strength and led them
To the death that was waiting. And now I follow them."

Viking cup, silver and gilt

The old man's mouth was silent, spoke
No more, had said as much as it could;
He would sleep in the fire, soon. His soul
Left his flesh, flew to glory. . . .

Then the warriors rose,
Walked slowly down from the cliff, stared
At those wonderful sights, stood weeping as they saw
Beowulf dead on the sand, their bold
Ring-giver resting in his last bed;
He'd reached the end of his days, their mighty
War-king, the great lord of the Geats,
Gone to a glorious death. . . .

Then the Geats built the tower, as Beowulf
Had asked, strong and tall, so sailors
Could find it from far and wide; working
For ten long days they made his monument,
Sealed his ashes in walls as straight
And high as wise and willing hands
Could raise them. And the riches he and Wiglaf
Had won from the dragon, rings, necklaces,
Ancient, hammered armor—all
The treasures they'd taken were left there, too,
Silver and jewels buried in the sandy
Ground, back in the earth, again
And forever hidden and useless to men.
And then twelve of the bravest Geats
Rode their horses around the tower,
Telling their sorrow, telling stories
Of their dead king and his greatness, his glory,
Praising him for heroic deeds, for a life
As noble as his name. So should all men
Raise up words for their lords, warm
With love, when their shield and protector leaves
His body behind, sends his soul
On high. And so Beowulf's followers
Rode, mourning their belovéd leader,
Crying that no better king had ever
Lived, no prince so mild, no man
So open to his people, so deserving of praise.

Pre-Viking helmet, A.D. 550–800

RESPONDING OPTIONS

FROM PERSONAL RESPONSE *TO* CRITICAL ANALYSIS

REFLECT 1. What impressions do you have of Beowulf after reading this poem? Record your impressions in your notebook.

RETHINK 2. The warriors who come to see evidence of Grendel's death swear that there is "nowhere . . . a warrior worthier [than Beowulf] to rule over men" (lines 261–264). Do you agree?

Consider
- Beowulf's ability to kill Grendel and the fire dragon
- the qualities needed for leadership in Beowulf's society
- the ideas about heroic qualities that you wrote for the Personal Connection on page 24

3. Why do you think Beowulf offers to help a clan other than his own in spite of the danger? Explain your answer.

4. What do you think causes Grendel to attack human beings?

Consider
- his relatives and ancestors
- his actions and attitudes
- the warriors' reaction to him

5. Beowulf is able to defeat evil in the form of both Grendel and the dragon, yet he ultimately loses his life in the process. From this fact, what conclusions can you draw about the struggle between good and evil?

RELATE 6. In today's society, we have our own kinds of monsters—enemies that threaten our safety or way of life. Who or what are today's monsters, and how do they threaten us? Who do you think the modern slayers of monsters are?

ANOTHER PATHWAY

Cooperative Learning

Review the chart that you made for the Reading Connection on page 25. Then compare your findings with those of several classmates. With these classmates, compile a group chart and pass out copies to be used as a reference for future writing assignments or tests.

QUICKWRITES

1. Imagine that you are one of Hrothgar's warriors. Write a **letter** to a comrade, describing Grendel, his nightly visits, and your fears.
2. Compose a **campaign speech** for Beowulf. Give reasons why you think he should be made king. Support your reasons with evidence from the poem.
3. Write a **news story** describing the conflict between Beowulf and either Grendel or the dragon. Include comments from imaginary witnesses to the event.
4. Develop an **outline** for an epic poem of your own. Tell about a hero who rescues society from one of the modern monsters you identified for question 6.

PORTFOLIO *Save your writing. You may want to use it later as a springboard to a piece for your portfolio.*

LITERARY CONCEPTS

Alliteration is a repetition of consonant sounds at the beginning of words, as in the phrase "slowly setting sun." Alliteration can be used to emphasize particular words, heighten a mood, or create a musical effect. In Old English poetry, alliteration played an especially important role. Read the following lines aloud. How does alliteration help develop the image of Grendel's movements?

> **He moved quickly through the cloudy night,**
> **Up from his swampland, sliding silently**
> **Toward that gold-shining hall. . . .**

Find other examples of alliteration in this selection and discuss how they contribute to the images in the poem.

ACROSS THE CURRICULUM

History Find out more about the Anglo-Saxons. Go beyond the information provided on pages 14–17 to investigate the lifestyles of different social classes—women and farmers as well as kings and warriors. Prepare a report on your findings.

ALTERNATIVE ACTIVITIES

1. With a small group of classmates, divide up the excerpts and practice an **oral reading** of *Beowulf.* Use your voices to convey excitement, suspense, sadness, and horror.
2. Illustrate the battle between Beowulf and Grendel or between Beowulf and the dragon in a **comic strip.** If you prefer, use a pad of paper and animate the battle by flipping pages so that the characters appear to move.
3. Find or create music to accompany the description of one of the battles. Prepare a **tape recording** that combines narration with the music.
4. Read excerpts from John Gardner's novel *Grendel,* a 20th-century version of the Beowulf story told from Grendel's point of view. Share your impressions of this modern telling.

THE WRITER'S STYLE

Burton Raffel's *Beowulf* is only one of many translations of the Old English epic. Here is a passage from Stanley B. Greenfield's translation:

> **So that lordly band lived joyfully,**
> **happily, until a hellish fiend**
> **inflicted painful crimes upon them:**
> **that gruesome demon was called Grendel;**
> **he haunted the waste borderland, held**
> **in fief the moors and fens and fastnesses.**

This is Burton Raffel's translation of the same passage:

> **So Hrothgar's men lived happily in his hall**
> **Till the monster stirred, that demon, that fiend,**
> **Grendel, who haunted the moors, the wild**
> **Marshes, and made his home in a hell**
> **Not hell but earth. . . .**

Compare the descriptions of Grendel in these two translations. Which do you think is more dramatic? Why?

WORDS TO KNOW

Review the Words to Know at the bottom of the selection pages. On your paper, write the vocabulary word that best completes each of the following sentences.

1. With each razor-sharp ______, Grendel tore his victim's flesh.
2. Grendel seemed to ______ his nightly visits to Herot.
3. Grendel's neck felt ______ in the strong grasp of Beowulf.
4. Grendel's evil acts made him ______ throughout the land.
5. Beowulf was not one of the warriors ______ in fear of the monster.
6. Grendel was left ______ in agony on the floor after the battle.
7. When Beowulf was finally able to ______ Herot of Grendel, the clan rejoiced.
8. Many people went on a ______ to see the lake where Grendel had sunk.
9. Beowulf's body was ______ after his battle with the dragon.
10. The Geats expressed their sorrow over Beowulf's death in a ______ of praise for their lost king.

THE BEOWULF POET

Nothing is known about the author of *Beowulf.* Certain references in the story suggest that it takes place in the sixth century; most scholars agree, however, that the poem itself was composed much later, probably in the eighth century.

The single surviving manuscript of *Beowulf* is believed to have been written by Anglo-Saxon monks around A.D. 1000. This manuscript, partially damaged by fire in 1731, is currently housed in the British Library in London.

Little information is available about the historical accuracy of the events described in *Beowulf.* Historical records show that a real Hygelac (the "Higlac" of this translation) fought another clan around A.D. 520. Whether Beowulf himself actually existed is uncertain. However, evidence from 20th-century archaeological digs—such as the well-preserved ship burial at Sutton Hoo in Suffolk, England—has shown that during this period people did live much as the poem describes.

LASERLINKS
• *STORYTELLER:* BEOWULF

PREVIEWING

EPIC POETRY

from the Iliad

Homer

Translated by Robert Fitzgerald

PERSONAL CONNECTION

If someone in your school insulted, threatened, or intentionally injured one of your close friends, how would you react? Would loyalty to your friend lead you to become involved in the conflict? What action, if any, would you take? Share your thoughts with a group of classmates.

HISTORICAL CONNECTION

The *Iliad* is an epic poem believed to be the work of a Greek poet named Homer in the eighth century B.C. The setting of the poem is the Trojan War, a conflict between Greeks and Trojans at the ancient city of Troy in Asia Minor. Although historians differ about the details, most believe that some type of conflict involving Greeks and Trojans did in fact occur around 1200 B.C.

According to Homer's poem, the Trojan War resulted when Paris, a prince of Troy, kidnapped Helen, the world's most beautiful woman, from her Greek home. This action naturally offended her husband, King Menelaus (mĕn′ə-lā′əs), who gathered an army of Greeks and set out to invade Troy and bring Helen home. Under the leadership of his brother Agamemnon (ăg′ə-mĕm′nŏn′), the Greeks laid siege to the walled city of Troy for ten years before finally achieving victory. The *Iliad* relates events that took place in the final year of that siege. The excerpts in the following selection illustrate the grim results of clashing loyalties.

READING CONNECTION

Classifying Characters The *Iliad* is a complex story involving many characters—both human and divine. Create a list of the following characters who play important roles in these excerpts: Achilles, Hector, Thetis, Zeus, Patroclus, Pallas Athena, Apollo, Hermes, and Priam. As you read this tale of clashing loyalties, use the notes that accompany the text to help you classify each character as a Greek, a Trojan, or a god. For each god, be sure to indicate whether the god is helping the Greeks or the Trojans.

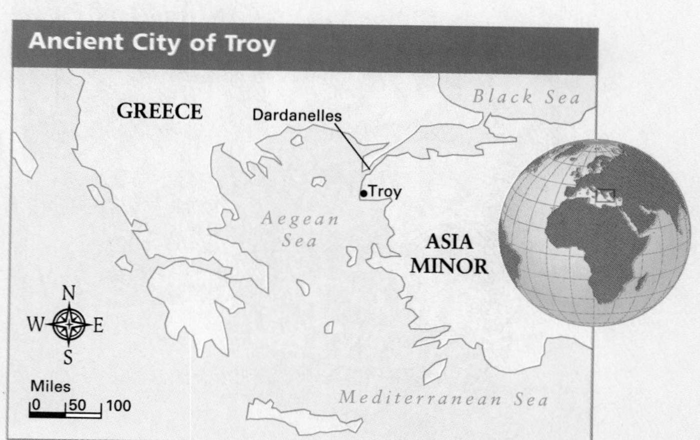

from **THE**

ILIAD

HOMER

Death of Hector, sixth-century B.C. Corinthian bowl painting

While the Greeks are laying siege to Troy, a quarrel breaks out between Agamemnon and his greatest warrior Achilles (ə-kĭl'ēz). As a result, the angry Achilles decides to remain in his tent and let the Greeks fight without him. With Achilles off the battlefield, the Trojans, under the leadership of Hector, are able to drive the Greeks back to the sea. During the battle, Hector kills Achilles' best friend, Patroclus (pə-trō'kləs). While grieving for his friend, Achilles is visited by his mother, Thetis (thē'tĭs), a goddess of the sea.

from Book 18

THE IMMORTAL SHIELD

Bending near
her groaning son, the gentle goddess wailed
and took his head between her hands in pity,
saying softly:

"Child, why are you weeping?
What great sorrow came to you? Speak out,

do not conceal it. Zeus
did all you asked: Achaean troops,
for want of you, were all forced back again
upon the ship sterns, taking heavy losses
none of them could wish."

The great runner
groaned and answered:

"Mother, yes, the master
of high Olympus brought it all about,
but how have I benefited? My greatest friend
is gone: Patroclus, comrade in arms, whom I
held dear above all others—dear as myself—
now gone, lost; Hector cut him down, despoiled him
of my own arms, massive and fine, a wonder
in all men's eyes. The gods gave them to Peleus
that day they put you in a mortal's bed—
how I wish the immortals of the sea
had been your only consorts! How I wish
Peleus had taken a mortal queen! Sorrow
immeasurable is in store for you as well,
when your own child is lost: never again
on his homecoming day will you embrace him!
I must reject this life, my heart tells me,
reject the world of men,
if Hector does not feel my battering spear
tear the life out of him, making him pay
in his own blood for the slaughter of Patroclus!"

Letting a tear fall, Thetis said:

"You'll be
swift to meet your end, child, as you say:
your doom comes close on the heels of Hector's own."

Achilles the great runner ground his teeth
and said:

"May it come quickly. As things were,
I could not help my friend in his extremity.
Far from his home he died; he needed me
to shield him or to parry the death stroke.
For me there's no return to my own country.

GUIDE FOR READING

6–7 Previously Achilles asked Thetis to persuade Zeus (zo͞os), ruler of the gods, to turn the tide of battle against the Greeks so that they would see how much they needed him.

7 Achaean (ə-kē′ən): Greek.

12 Olympus (ə-lĭm′pəs): the highest mountain in Greece, on whose peak the Greek gods and goddesses were thought to dwell.

16–17 Patroclus wore Achilles' armor to frighten the Trojans. "Despoiled him of my own arms" refers to Hector's taking the armor from Patroclus' corpse.

18 Peleus (pē′lē-əs): Achilles' human father.

38 parry: to turn aside the thrust of a sword.

Not the slightest gleam of hope did I
afford Patroclus or the other men
whom Hector overpowered. Here I sat,
my weight a useless burden to the earth,
and I am one who has no peer in war
among Achaean captains—
though in council
there are wiser. Ai! let strife and rancor
perish from the lives of gods and men,
with anger that envenoms even the wise
and is far sweeter than slow-dripping honey,
clouding the hearts of men like smoke: just so
the marshal of the army, Agamemnon,
moved me to anger. But we'll let that go,
though I'm still sore at heart; it is all past,
and I have quelled my passion as I must.

Now I must go to look for the destroyer
of my great friend. I shall confront the dark
drear spirit of death at any hour Zeus
and the other gods may wish to make an end.
Not even Heracles escaped that terror
though cherished by the Lord Zeus. Destiny
and Hera's bitter anger mastered him.
Likewise with me, if destiny like his
awaits me, I shall rest when I have fallen!
Now, though, may I win my perfect glory
and make some wife of Troy break down,
or some deep-breasted Dardan woman sob
and wipe tears from her soft cheeks. They'll know then
how long they had been spared the deaths of men,
while I abstained from war!
Do not attempt to keep me from the fight,
though you love me; you cannot make me listen."

46 rancor (răng'kər): bitter, long-lasting ill will.

48 envenoms (ĕn-vĕn'əmz): fills with poison.

59–61 Heracles (hĕr'ə-klēz'): the greatest legendary hero of ancient Greece, son of Zeus and a mortal woman named Alcmena (ălk-mē'nə). Zeus' wife, the goddess Hera (hîr'ə), hated and persecuted Heracles until his death.

62–63 How has Achilles' loyalty to Patroclus affected his attitude toward his own life?

66 Dardan (där'dn): Trojan.

Achilles seeks to avenge Patroclus by slaughtering Trojans. Apollo, a god who protects Troy, opens the gates of the city so that the Trojans can rush to safety inside the walls. Only Hector is left outside. Achilles chases him around the walls of Troy three times. Finally the goddess Pallas Athena (păl'əs ə-thē'nə), **disguised as Hector's brother Deiphobus** (dē-ĭf'ə-bəs), **appears to Hector and persuades him to fight Achilles.**

WORDS TO KNOW

quell (kwĕl) *v.* to quiet; suppress
abstain (ăb-stān') *v.* to hold oneself back deliberately

from Book 22

DESOLATION BEFORE TROY

And when at last the two men faced each other,
Hector was the first to speak. He said:

"I will no longer fear you as before,
son of Peleus, though I ran from you
round Priam's town three times and could not face you.
Now my soul would have me stand and fight,
whether I kill you or am killed. So come,
we'll summon gods here as our witnesses,
none higher, arbiters of a pact: I swear
that, terrible as you are,
I'll not insult your corpse should Zeus allow me
victory in the end, your life as prize.
Once I have your gear, I'll give your body
back to Achaeans. Grant me, too, this grace."

But swift Achilles frowned at him and said:

"Hector, I'll have no talk of pacts with you,
forever unforgiven as you are.
As between men and lions there are none,
no concord between wolves and sheep, but all
hold one another hateful through and through,
so there can be no courtesy between us,
no sworn truce, till one of us is down
and glutting with his blood the wargod Ares.
Summon up what skills you have. By god,
you'd better be a spearman and a fighter!
Now there is no way out. Pallas Athena
will have the upper hand of you. The weapon
belongs to me. You'll pay the reckoning
in full for all the pain my men have borne,
who met death by your spear."

He twirled and cast
his shaft with its long shadow. Splendid Hector,
keeping his eye upon the point, eluded it
by ducking at the instant of the cast,

76 Priam (prī'əm): the king of Troy.

80 arbiters (är'bĭ-tərz): judges; referees.

84–85 The Greeks and Trojans generally returned the bodies of the slain to their commanders or companions.

90 concord (kŏn'kôrd'): peace or harmony.

94 glutting with his blood the wargod Ares (âr'ēz): satisfying Ares, the god of war, by bleeding to death.

97–98 Pallas Athena, the goddess of wisdom, favors the Greeks.

WORDS TO KNOW

elude (ĭ-lo͞od') *v.* to avoid or escape

so shaft and bronze shank passed him overhead
and punched into the earth. But unperceived
by Hector, Pallas Athena plucked it out
and gave it back to Achilles. Hector said:

"A clean miss. Godlike as you are,
you have not yet known doom for me from Zeus.
You thought you had, by heaven. Then you turned
into a word-thrower, hoping to make me lose
my fighting heart and head in fear of you.
You cannot plant your spear between my shoulders
while I am running. If you have the gift,
just put it through my chest as I come forward.
Now it's for you to dodge my own. Would god
you'd give the whole shaft lodging in your body!
War for the Trojans would be eased
if you were blotted out, bane that you are."

With this he twirled his long spearshaft and cast it,
hitting his enemy mid-shield, but off
and away the spear rebounded. Furious
that he had lost it, made his throw for nothing,
Hector stood bemused. He had no other.
Then he gave a great shout to Deiphobus
to ask for a long spear. But there was no one
near him, not a soul. Now in his heart
the Trojan realized the truth and said:

"This is the end. The gods are calling deathward.
I had thought
a good soldier, Deiphobus, was with me.
He is inside the walls. Athena tricked me.
Death is near, and black, not at a distance,
not to be evaded. Long ago
this hour must have been to Zeus's liking
and to the liking of his archer son.
They have been well disposed before, but now
the appointed time's upon me. Still, I would not
die without delivering a stroke,
or die ingloriously, but in some action
memorable to men in days to come."

Achilles dragging the body of Hector around the walls of Troy (about 520 B.C.), attributed to the Antiope Group. Attic black figure hydria, courtesy of the Museum of Fine Arts, Boston, William Francis Warden Fund.

120 bane: a cause of distress, death, or ruin.

125 bemused (bĭ-myo͞ozd'): dazed; confused.

135–139 Zeus' "archer son" is Apollo, god of the sun, whose arrows may represent the sun's rays. Until now, Zeus and Apollo have assisted the Trojans.

WORDS TO KNOW

evade (ĭ-vād') *v.* to escape by cleverness or deception

With this he drew the whetted blade that hung
upon his left flank, ponderous and long,
collecting all his might the way an eagle
narrows himself to dive through shady cloud
and strike a lamb or cowering hare: so Hector
lanced ahead and swung his whetted blade.
Achilles with wild fury in his heart
pulled in upon his chest his beautiful shield—
his helmet with four burnished metal ridges
nodding above it, and the golden crest
Hephaestus locked there tossing in the wind.
Conspicuous as the evening star that comes,
amid the first in heaven, at fall of night,
and stands most lovely in the west, so shone
in sunlight the fine-pointed spear
Achilles poised in his right hand, with deadly
aim at Hector, at the skin where most
it lay exposed. But nearly all was covered
by the bronze gear he took from slain Patroclus,
showing only, where his collarbones
divided neck and shoulders, the bare throat
where the destruction of a life is quickest.
Here, then, as the Trojan charged, Achilles
drove his point straight through the tender neck,
but did not cut the windpipe, leaving Hector
able to speak and to respond. He fell
aside into the dust. And Prince Achilles
now exulted:

"Hector, had you thought
that you could kill Patroclus and be safe?
Nothing to dread from me; I was not there.
All childishness. Though distant then, Patroclus'
comrade in arms was greater far than he—
and it is I who had been left behind
that day beside the deepsea ships who now
have made your knees give way. The dogs and kites
will rip your body. His will lie in honor
when the Achaeans give him funeral."

Hector, barely whispering, replied:

153 Hephaestus (hĭ-fĕs′təs): the god of fire and blacksmith of the gods, who made Achilles' new armor.

160–161 Hector is wearing the armor of Achilles that he took from Patroclus' body.

177 kites: hawklike birds of prey.

178 "His [body]" refers to that of Patroclus.

WORDS TO KNOW

whetted (hwĕt′ĭd) *adj.* sharpened **whet** *v.*
ponderous (pŏn′dər-əs) *adj.* very heavy
exult (ĭg-zŭlt′) *v.* to feel great joy, especially in conquest or triumph

"I beg you by your soul and by your parents,
do not let the dogs feed on me
in your encampment by the ships. Accept
the bronze and gold my father will provide
as gifts, my father and her ladyship
my mother. Let them have my body back,
so that our men and women may accord me
decency of fire when I am dead."

Achilles the great runner scowled and said:

"Beg me no beggary by soul or parents,
whining dog! Would god my passion drove me
to slaughter you and eat you raw, you've caused
such agony to me! No man exists
who could defend you from the carrion pack—
not if they spread for me ten times your ransom,
twenty times, and promise more as well;
aye, not if Priam, son of Dardanus,
tells them to buy you for your weight in gold!
You'll have no bed of death, nor will you be
laid out and mourned by her who gave you birth.
Dogs and birds will have you, every scrap."

Then at the point of death Lord Hector said:

"I see you now for what you are. No chance
to win you over. Iron in your breast
your heart is. Think a bit, though: this may be
a thing the gods in anger hold against you
on that day when Paris and Apollo
destroy you at the Gates, great as you are."

Even as he spoke, the end came, and death hid him;
spirit from body fluttered to undergloom,
bewailing fate that made him leave his youth
and manhood in the world. And as he died
Achilles spoke again. He said:

"Die, make an end. I shall accept my own
whenever Zeus and the other gods desire."

At this he pulled his spearhead from the body,
laying it aside, and stripped

185–186 Hector's father is Priam, and his mother is Hecuba (hĕk'yə-bə).

188 Burning the bodies of the dead was customary. Truces were often arranged for this purpose.

194 carrion (kăr'ē-ən) **pack:** the wild animals that feed on dead flesh.

197 Dardanus (där'dn-əs): the founder of the line of Trojan kings. Here "son" means "descendant."

205–208 Although Achilles is still alive as the *Iliad* ends, other tales of the Trojan War tell how he is eventually killed by Hector's brother Paris, with the aid of Apollo.

Replica of Trojan Horse

the bloodstained shield and cuirass from his shoulders.
Other Achaeans hastened round to see
Hector's fine body and his comely face,
and no one came who did not stab the body.
Glancing at one another they would say:

"Now Hector has turned vulnerable, softer
than when he put the torches to the ships!"

And he who said this would inflict a wound.
When the great master of pursuit, Achilles,
had the body stripped, he stood among them,
saying swiftly:

"Friends, my lords and captains
of Argives, now that the gods at last have let me
bring to earth this man who wrought
havoc among us—more than all the rest—
come, we'll offer battle around the city,
to learn the intentions of the Trojans now.
Will they give up their strongpoint at this loss?
Can they fight on, though Hector's dead?

But wait:
why do I ponder, why take up these questions?
Down by the ships Patroclus' body lies
unwept, unburied. I shall not forget him
while I can keep my feet among the living.
If in the dead world they forget the dead,
I say there, too, I shall remember him,
my friend. Men of Achaea, lift a song!
Down to the ships we go, and take this body,
our glory. We have beaten Hector down,
to whom as to a god the Trojans prayed."

Indeed, he had in mind for Hector's body
outrage and shame. Behind both feet he pierced
the tendons, heel to ankle. Rawhide cords
he drew through both and lashed them to his chariot,
letting the man's head trail. Stepping aboard,
bearing the great trophy of the arms,
he shook the reins, and whipped the team ahead

218 cuirass (kwĭ-răs'): an armored breastplate.

224 Hector's torching of the ships occurred when the Trojans forced the Greeks (fighting without Achilles) back to the sea.

228–229 captains of Argives (är'jīvz'): Greek officers.

240 The "dead world" is the house of Hades, or the underworld, where the Greeks believed the shades of the dead to reside.

WORDS TO KNOW

vulnerable (vŭl'nər-ə-bəl) *adj.* open to attack; easily hurt
havoc (hăv'ək) *n.* widespread destruction

into a willing run. A dustcloud rose
above the furrowing body; the dark tresses
flowed behind, and the head so princely once
lay back in dust. Zeus gave him to his enemies
to be defiled in his own fatherland.
So his whole head was blackened. Looking down,
his mother tore her braids, threw off her veil,
and wailed, heartbroken to behold her son.
Piteously his father groaned, and round him
lamentation spread throughout the town,
most like the clamor to be heard if Ilion's
towers, top to bottom, seethed in flames.
They barely stayed the old man, mad with grief,
from passing through the gates. Then in the mire
he rolled, and begged them all, each man by name:

"Relent, friends. It is hard; but let me go
out of the city to the Achaean ships.
I'll make my plea to that demonic heart.
He may feel shame before his peers, or pity
my old age. His father, too, is old.
Peleus, who brought him up to be a scourge
to Trojans, cruel to all, but most to me,
so many of my sons in flower of youth
he cut away. And, though I grieve, I cannot
mourn them all as much as I do one,
for whom my grief will take me to the grave—
and that is Hector. Why could he not have died
where I might hold him? In our weeping, then,
his mother, now so destitute, and I
might have had surfeit and relief of tears."

263 Ilion (ĭl'ē-ən): another name for Troy.

268–270 Think about Priam's decision to approach Achilles. What does this reveal about his sense of honor and loyalty?

282 surfeit (sûr'fĭt): more than enough for satisfaction.

Achilles and his warriors return to their camp and carry out the burial rites for Patroclus. Three times, Achilles drags Hector's body behind his chariot around Patroclus' grave. Afterwards, the gods cleanse and restore the body, and Zeus asks Thetis to tell Achilles to return the body to the Trojans. Priam sets out for the Greek camp, accompanied only by an old servant, to ask Achilles to return the body. He is not aware that the god Hermes (hûr'mēz) **helps him by putting the sentries to sleep and opening the gates. Hermes leads Priam to Achilles' tent and then vanishes.**

WORDS TO KNOW

defile (dĭ-fīl') *v.* to make filthy; violate the honor of
clamor (klăm'ər) *n.* a loud, confused noise or outcry
scourge (skûrj) *n.* a source of great suffering or destruction
destitute (dĕs'tĭ-to͞ot') *adj.* lacking in resources; bereft

from Book 24

A GRACE GIVEN IN SORROW

Priam,
the great king of Troy, passed by the others,
knelt down, took in his arms Achilles' knees,
and kissed the hands of wrath that killed his sons.

When, taken with mad Folly in his own land,
a man does murder and in exile finds
refuge in some rich house, then all who see him
stand in awe.
So these men stood.
Achilles
gazed in wonder at the splendid king,
and his companions marveled too, all silent,
with glances to and fro. Now Priam prayed
to the man before him:

"Remember your own father,
Achilles, in your godlike youth: his years
like mine are many, and he stands upon
the fearful doorstep of old age. He, too,
is hard pressed, it may be, by those around him,
there being no one able to defend him
from bane of war and ruin. Ah, but he
may nonetheless hear news of you alive,
and so with glad heart hope through all his days
for sight of his dear son, come back from Troy,
while I have deathly fortune.

Noble sons
I fathered here, but scarce one man is left me.
Fifty I had when the Achaeans came,
nineteen out of a single belly, others
born of attendant women. Most are gone.
Raging Ares cut their knees from under them.
And he who stood alone among them all,
their champion, and Troy's, ten days ago
you killed him, fighting for his land, my prince,
Hector.

It is for him that I have come
among these ships, to beg him back from you,
and I bring ransom without stint.

316 stint: limitation.

Achilles,
be reverent toward the great gods! And take
pity on me, remember your own father.
Think me more pitiful by far, since I
have brought myself to do what no man else
has done before—to lift to my lips the hand
of one who killed my son."

Now in Achilles
the evocation of his father stirred
new longing, and an ache of grief. He lifted
the old man's hand and gently put him by.
Then both were overborne as they remembered:
the old king huddled at Achilles' feet
wept, and wept for Hector, killer of men,
while great Achilles wept for his own father
as for Patroclus once again; and sobbing
filled the room.

But when Achilles' heart
had known the luxury of tears, and pain
within his breast and bones had passed away,
he stood then, raised the old king up, in pity
for his grey head and greybeard cheek, and spoke
in a warm rush of words:

"Ah, sad and old!
Trouble and pain you've borne, and bear, aplenty.
Only a great will could have brought you here
among the Achaean ships, and here alone
before the eyes of one who stripped your sons,
your many sons, in battle. Iron must be
the heart within you. Come, then, and sit down.
We'll probe our wounds no more but let them rest,
though grief lies heavy on us. Tears heal nothing,
drying so stiff and cold. This is the way
the gods ordained the destiny of men,
to bear such burdens in our lives, while they
feel no affliction. At the door of Zeus
are those two urns of good and evil gifts
that he may choose for us; and one for whom
the lightning's joyous king dips in both urns
will have by turns bad luck and good. But one

326 overborne: overcome; overwhelmed.

Ajax and Achilles playing dice, Greek vase painting

336–348 Compare the impression of Achilles you got from lines 87–94 with the impression you get from these lines.

WORDS TO KNOW **evocation** (ĕv'ə-kā'shən) *n.* a bringing to mind

to whom he sends all evil—that man goes
contemptible by the will of Zeus; ravenous
hunger drives him over the wondrous earth,
unresting, without honor from gods or men.
Mixed fortune came to Peleus. Shining gifts
at the gods' hands he had from birth: felicity,
wealth overflowing, rule of the Myrmidons,
a bride immortal at his mortal side.
But then Zeus gave afflictions too—no family
of powerful sons grew up for him at home,
but one child, of all seasons and of none.
Can I stand by him in his age? Far from my country
I sit at Troy to grieve you and your children.
You, too, sir, in time past were fortunate,
we hear men say. From Macar's isle of Lesbos
northward, and south of Phrygia and the Straits,
no one had wealth like yours, or sons like yours.
Then gods out of the sky sent you this bitterness:
the years of siege, the battles and the losses.
Endure it, then. And do not mourn forever
for your dead son. There is no remedy.
You will not make him stand again. Rather
await some new misfortune to be suffered."

The old king in his majesty replied:

"Never give me a chair, my lord, while Hector
lies in your camp uncared for. Yield him to me
now. Allow me sight of him. Accept
the many gifts I bring. May they reward you,
and may you see your home again.
You spared my life at once and let me live."

Achilles, the great runner, frowned and eyed him
under his brows:

"Do not vex me, sir," he said.
"I have intended, in my own good time,
to yield up Hector to you. She who bore me,
the daughter of the Ancient of the sea,
has come with word to me from Zeus. I know
in your case, too—though you say nothing, Priam—
that some god guided you to the shipways here.

358 felicity (fĭ-lĭs'ĭ-tē): happiness; good fortune.

359 Myrmidons (mûr'mə-dŏnz'): a people of Thessaly in Greece, subjects of Achilles' father, Peleus.

363 "Of all seasons and of none" suggests that Achilles expects an early death for himself.

367–368 Lesbos (lĕz'bŏs) . . . **Phrygia** (frĭj'ē-ə) . . . **the Straits:** Lesbos is an island off the western coast of Asia Minor; Phrygia was an ancient kingdom in western Asia Minor; the Straits are the Dardanelles.

387 "The Ancient of the sea" is the sea god Nereus (nîr'ē-əs), father of Thetis.

No strong man in his best days could make entry
into this camp. How could he pass the guard,
or force our gateway?
Therefore, *let me be.*
Sting my sore heart again, and even here,
under my own roof, suppliant though you are,
I may not spare you, sir, but trample on
the express command of Zeus!"

When he heard this,
the old man feared him and obeyed with silence.
Now like a lion at one bound Achilles
left the room. Close at his back the officers
Automedon and Alcimus went out—
comrades in arms whom he esteemed the most
after the dead Patroclus. They unharnessed
mules and horses, led the old king's crier
to a low bench and sat him down.
Then from the polished wagon
they took the piled-up price of Hector's body.
One chiton and two capes they left aside
as dress and shrouding for the homeward journey.
Then, calling to the women slaves, Achilles
ordered the body bathed and rubbed with oil—
but lifted, too, and placed apart, where Priam
could not see his son—for seeing Hector
he might in his great pain give way to rage,
and fury then might rise up in Achilles
to slay the old king, flouting Zeus's word.
So after bathing and anointing Hector
they drew the shirt and beautiful shrouding over him.
Then with his own hands lifting him, Achilles
laid him upon a couch, and with his two
companions aiding, placed him in the wagon.
Now a bitter groan burst from Achilles,
who stood and prayed to his own dead friend:

"Patroclus,
do not be angry with me, if somehow
even in the world of Death you learn of this—
that I released Prince Hector to his father.
The gifts he gave were not unworthy. Aye,
and you shall have your share, this time as well."

395 suppliant (sŭp'lē-ənt): one who begs or pleads earnestly.

401 Automedon (ô-tŏm'ə-dn) . . . **Alcimus** (ăl'sə-məs).

408 chiton (kīt'n): a shirtlike garment; tunic.

WORDS TO KNOW

flouting (flout'ĭng) *adj.* disregarding in a contemptuous way; scorning **flout** *v.*

The Prince Achilles turned back to his quarters.
He took again the splendid chair that stood
against the farther wall, then looked at Priam
and made his declaration:

"As you wished, sir,
the body of your son is now set free.
He lies in state. At the first sight of Dawn
you shall take charge of him yourself and see him.
Now let us think of supper. We are told
that even Niobe in her extremity
took thought for bread—though all her brood had perished,
her six young girls and six tall sons. Apollo,
making his silver longbow whip and sing,
shot the lads down, and Artemis with raining
arrows killed the daughters—all this after
Niobe had compared herself with Leto,
the smooth-cheeked goddess.

She has borne two children,
Niobe said, How many have I borne!
But soon those two destroyed the twelve.

Besides,
nine days the dead lay stark, no one could bury them,
for Zeus had turned all folk of theirs to stone.
The gods made graves for them on the tenth day,
and then at last, being weak and spent with weeping,
Niobe thought of food. Among the rocks
of Sipylus' lonely mountainside, where nymphs
who race Achelous river go to rest,
she, too, long turned to stone, somewhere broods on
the gall immortal gods gave her to drink.

Like her we'll think of supper, noble sir.
Weep for your son again when you have borne him
back to Troy; there he'll be mourned indeed."

436–455 The mortal woman Niobe (nī'ə-bē) claimed that having so many children made her superior to the goddess Leto (lē'tō), who had only two. Leto's son and daughter, Apollo and Artemis (är'tə-mĭs), punished Niobe by killing all her children. After many days of grieving, Niobe asked the gods to relieve her by turning her to stone.

452 Sipylus (sĭp'ə-ləs): a mountain in west central Asia Minor.

453 Achelous (ăk'ə-lō'əs): a river near Mount Sipylus.

455 gall: bitterness; bile.

Priam and Achilles agree to an 11-day truce. During that time, the Trojans will mourn Hector's body before its burial.

RESPONDING OPTIONS

FROM PERSONAL RESPONSE *TO* CRITICAL ANALYSIS

REFLECT

1. What is your impression of Achilles? Jot down your thoughts in your notebook.

RETHINK

2. In your opinion, does Achilles' loyalty to his friend Patroclus justify the way he treats Hector? Explain your answer.
3. How would you describe the relationship between Achilles and Priam?

   Consider
   - Achilles' killing of Hector
   - the dialogue between the two men
   - why Achilles gives Hector's body to Priam
4. To what extent do Achilles and Hector correspond to your idea of a hero?

   Consider
   - the kind of warrior each man is
   - Achilles' loyalty to his friend
   - Hector's sense of loyalty
   - Hector's speech that begins "This is the end. . . ." (line 130, page 49)
   - Achilles' treatment of Hector's body
   - Achilles' response to Priam
5. Compare Achilles, Hector, and Priam. In your opinion, which character is the most courageous? Why?
6. How might your impression of Achilles be different if he refused to give Hector's body to Priam?

RELATE

7. Achilles and Hector fight one-on-one. Do you think leaders of rival nations, tribes, or groups should settle differences between themselves without involving their followers? Is it possible or practical to settle conflicts this way? Elaborate on your responses.

ANOTHER PATHWAY

Cooperative Learning

Look again at the list you created for the Reading Connection on page 44. Review the roles played by the gods and goddesses, and consider their importance to the advancement of the plot. Then, with four classmates, divide up the parts of Thetis, Zeus, Apollo, Athena, and Hermes. Role-play your character, explaining how you have directed or changed the course of events.

QUICKWRITES

1. As either a Greek or a Trojan general, write a **letter of commendation** for Achilles or Hector. Explain why you are awarding him your army's highest medal.
2. Think again about the relationship between Achilles and Priam. Then write a **character sketch** of Priam from Achilles' point of view.
3. Draft an **essay** explaining the messages about anger and revenge that are expressed in this selection.
4. Imagine events as they might have occurred without the gods and goddesses. Write an **outline** for a version of the poem in which the human characters determine their own fate.

PORTFOLIO *Save your writing. You may want to use it later as a springboard to a piece for your portfolio.*

LITERARY CONCEPTS

A **simile** is a figure of speech that makes a comparison between two things that are actually unlike yet have something in common. The comparison is expressed by means of the word *like* or *as.* "Silent as death" and "John went down like a stone" are examples of similes. **Epic similes** are long comparisons that often continue for a number of lines. (In a translation, the word *like* or *as* may not appear.) The epic simile in lines 145–148 of this selection compares Hector to an eagle. What does the simile suggest about Hector's character? Now analyze the simile in lines 154–158. How do the two similes contribute to the telling of the story?

ALTERNATIVE ACTIVITIES

1. With a classmate, give a **dramatic reading** of the encounter between Achilles and Priam. Use your voices and facial expressions to convey emotions such as sorrow, anger, desperation, compassion, and fear.
2. Create a **dance interpretation** of the battle between Hector and Achilles. Choose appropriate music to accompany it, and perform your dance for the class.
3. With a group of classmates, using large sheets of paper, sketch or paint a series of scenes from the *Iliad* and put them together to form a **mural** for your classroom.

LITERARY LINKS

Compare and contrast Achilles and Beowulf. Consider their actions and the reasons for those actions. Who do you think is more courageous? Who behaves more like a true epic hero?

ACROSS THE CURRICULUM

History Find out more about the real city of Troy. Where was it located? What have archaeologists discovered about the city? Present your findings to the class in an outline for a television documentary about Troy.

THE WRITER'S STYLE

In line 10, the reference to Achilles as "the great runner" is an example of an **epithet,** a brief phrase that refers to a characteristic of a particular person or thing. As this example shows, an epithet is often used in place of the name of the person or thing it describes. Identify to whom or what the following epithets refer: "the Trojan" (line 129), "Patroclus' comrade in arms" (lines 173–174), and "sad and old" (line 336). Then try to find other examples of epithets in this selection.

WORDS TO KNOW

Write the letter of the word that is not related in meaning to the other words in each set.

1. (a) face, (b) meet, (c) evade, (d) confront
2. (a) ponderous, (b) swift, (c) weighty, (d) hefty
3. (a) clamor, (b) peacefulness, (c) silence, (d) calmness
4. (a) dirty, (b) cleanse, (c) defile, (d) corrupt
5. (a) strong, (b) vulnerable, (c) weak, (d) defenseless
6. (a) dodge, (b) capture, (c) elude, (d) escape
7. (a) destruction, (b) disaster, (c) havoc, (d) protection
8. (a) whetted, (b) dull, (c) blunt, (d) rounded
9. (a) disobey, (b) flout, (c) punish, (d) disregard
10. (a) promise, (b) exult, (c) rejoice, (d) celebrate
11. (a) defender, (b) guardian, (c) protector, (d) scourge
12. (a) act, (b) abstain, (c) proceed, (d) perform
13. (a) remembrance, (b) calendar, (c) reminder, (d) evocation
14. (a) soothe, (b) quell, (c) scold, (d) hush
15. (a) destitute, (b) needy, (c) deprived, (d) injured

HOMER

Little is known about the Greek poet Homer. In fact, for centuries scholars have debated whether such a man ever really existed. Today, most agree that the author of two equally famous epics, the *Iliad* and the *Odyssey,* was indeed a man named Homer, who lived sometime between 800 and 600 B.C. Evidence of his life and authorship has been gathered indirectly from other writings of ancient Greece, from historical references, and from his poems. It seems likely that the mysterious poet was born either in western Asia Minor or on one of the nearby Aegean islands.

According to legend, Homer was blind; however, some scholars believe that this legend is not likely to be literally true. They point out that the typical ancient Greek portrayal of a sage or philosopher was of a blind man with exceptional inner vision. Ancient Greeks viewed the *Iliad* and the *Odyssey* as works that revealed all-important truths about human beings and their place in the universe. Often, Greek children were required to memorize portions of the epics and to model their behavior on the heroic code set forth by their author. With the possible exception of Shakespeare, no other poet in the Western world has been quoted more often than Homer.

Like *Beowulf,* Homer's poems probably had a long oral history before they were written down. It is believed that they were composed in verse partly because the meter made them easier to memorize. According to modern scholars, Homer was probably illiterate, living as he did at a time when writing was just being introduced among the Greeks. In his old age, the poet may have recited his epics for someone else to record.

LASERLINKS
• *ART GALLERY*

PREVIEWING

POETRY

from the Exeter Book

from The Seafarer   The Wife's Lament

PERSONAL CONNECTION

Think of situations in which people are forced to be separated from their families and friends for long periods of time. What problems might confront these people? What would your reaction to such a hardship be? Share your thoughts with your classmates. As you read the two poems that follow, compare your reflections on hardship with those experienced by the speakers.

HISTORICAL CONNECTION

Life in Anglo-Saxon society was filled with hardships, including separations from loved ones, outbreaks of disease, attacks by wild animals, and wars. Natural events such as storms were little understood and often terrifying. Even the dark, which could conceal unknown threats, was a source of fear. The people of the time therefore banded together in small communities or clans to protect one another from these common dangers.

A particular hardship presented itself to men who left behind their families and communities to travel the sea. They sailed the ocean for months in all kinds of weather, suffering many physical dangers and intense loneliness. The women and families they left behind also suffered, enduring months and even years of not knowing when the men they loved would return.

The Old English poems you are about to read reflect the intensity of Anglo-Saxon times and the human needs and loves of the people.

READING CONNECTION

Reading Old English Poetry When Old English poetry was first recorded, the scribes wrote it as prose, without breaks between lines. Modern editors, however, to show the poetry's rhythmic structure, print it in lines, with each line divided into two rhythmic units by a break called a **caesura** (sĭ-zho͝or'ə). The caesura signals a place where the scop probably paused momentarily, perhaps for breath, as he recited the poem. The translators of "The Seafarer" and "The Wife's Lament" have reproduced the caesuras in their translations. As you read each poem aloud, try pausing briefly at the caesuras.

from The Seafarer

A song I sing of my sea-adventure,
The strain of peril, the stress of toil,
Which oft I endured in anguish of spirit
Through weary hours of aching woe.
My bark was swept by the breaking seas;
Bitter the watch from the bow by night
As my ship drove on within sound of the rocks.
My feet were numb with the nipping cold,
Hunger sapped a sea-weary spirit,
And care weighed heavy upon my heart.
Little the landlubber, safe on shore,
Knows what I've suffered in icy seas
Wretched and worn by the winter storms,
Hung with icicles, stung by hail,
Lonely and friendless and far from home.
In my ears no sound but the roar of the sea,
The icy combers, the cry of the swan;
In place of the mead-hall and laughter of men

5 bark: boat or sailing ship.

11 landlubber: one who knows very little about traveling by sea.

17 combers (kō′mərz): waves breaking into foam as they approach a shore.

My only singing the sea-mew's call,
The scream of the gannet, the shriek of the gull;
Through the wail of the wild gale beating the bluffs
The piercing cry of the ice-coated petrel,
The storm-drenched eagle's echoing scream.
In all my wretchedness, weary and lone,
I had no comfort of comrade or kin.
Little indeed can he credit, whose town-life
Pleasantly passes in feasting and joy,
Sheltered from peril, what weary pain
Often I've suffered in foreign seas.
Night shades darkened with driving snow
From the freezing north, and the bonds of frost
Firm-locked the land, while falling hail,
Coldest of kernels, encrusted earth.
Yet still, even now, my spirit within me
Drives me seaward to sail the deep,
To ride the long swell of the salt sea-wave.
Never a day but my heart's desire
Would launch me forth on the long sea-path,
Fain of far harbors and foreign shores.
Yet lives no man so lordly of mood,
So eager in giving, so ardent in youth,
So bold in his deeds, or so dear to his lord,
Who is free from dread in his far sea-travel,
Or fear of God's purpose and plan for his fate.
The beat of the harp, and bestowal of treasure,
The love of woman, and worldly hope,
Nor other interest can hold his heart
Save only the sweep of the surging billows;
His heart is haunted by love of the sea.
Trees are budding and towns are fair,
Meadows kindle and all life quickens,
All things hasten the eager-hearted,
Who joyeth therein, to journey afar,
Turning seaward to distant shores.
The cuckoo stirs him with plaintive call,
The herald of summer, with mournful song,
Foretelling the sorrow that stabs the heart.
Who liveth in luxury, little he knows
What woe men endure in exile's doom.
Yet still, even now, my desire outreaches,
My spirit soars over tracts of sea,
O'er the home of the whale, and the world's expanse.

19–22 sea-mew . . . gannet . . . petrel: types of sea birds.

26 credit: believe.

39 fain of: longing for.

51 kindle: become bright; glow.

55 plaintive: sad; mournful.

Eager, desirous, the lone sprite returneth;
It cries in my ears and it urges my heart
To the path of the whale and the plunging sea.

Translated by Charles W. Kennedy

63 sprite: spirit.

The Whale. MS. Ashmole 1511, f. 86v, The Bodleian Library, Oxford, Great Britain.

FROM PERSONAL RESPONSE *TO* CRITICAL ANALYSIS

REFLECT 1. What images remain with you after reading this poem? Describe these images in your notebook, or sketch them.

RETHINK 2. How would you describe the seafarer's life?

Consider

- his experiences at sea
- his descriptions of life on land
- the thought he expresses when he says "His heart is haunted by love of the sea" (line 49)

3. Why do you think the seafarer tells about his hardships? Explain your opinion.

The Wife's Lament

Poverty carrying a sack of wheat to the mill reaches a dangerous bridge (about 1450–1475). From *Le mortifiement de vaine plaisance* of Rene I, duke of Anjou, M.705, f. 38v.

I make this song   about me full sadly
my own wayfaring.   I a woman tell
what griefs I had   since I grew up
new or old   never more than now.
Ever I know   the dark of my exile.

First my lord went out   away from his people
over the wave-tumult.   I grieved each dawn
wondered where my lord   my first on earth might be.
Then I went forth   a friendless exile
to seek service   in my sorrow's need.
My man's kinsmen   began to plot
by darkened thought   to divide us two
so we most widely   in the world's kingdom
lived wretchedly   and I suffered longing.

My lord commanded me   to move my dwelling here.
I had few loved ones   in this land
or faithful friends.   For this my heart grieves:
that I should find the man   well matched to me
hard of fortune   mournful of mind
hiding his mood   thinking of murder.

GUIDE FOR READING

2 wayfaring: journeying.

6 my lord: the speaker's husband.

7 wave-tumult: the sea. This is an example of a kenning—a compound epithet used in Old English poetry in place of the familiar name of an object. Here, the sea is pictured as a tumult, or chaos, of waves.

19 hard . . . mind: having a hard life and feeling sad.

Blithe was our bearing   often we vowed
that but death alone   would part us two
naught else.   But this is turned round
now . . .   as if it never were
our friendship.   I must far and near
bear the anger   of my beloved.
The man sent me out   to live in the woods
under an oak tree   in this den in the earth.
Ancient this earth hall.   I am all longing.

29 "Earth hall" refers to the speaker's living quarters. What kind of place do you think it is?

The valleys are dark   the hills high
the yard overgrown   bitter with briars
a joyless dwelling.   Full oft the lack of my lord
seizes me cruelly here.   Friends there are on earth
living beloved   lying in bed
while I at dawn   am walking alone
under the oak tree   through these earth halls.
There I may sit   the summerlong day
there I can weep   over my exile
my many hardships.   Hence I may not rest
from this care of heart   which belongs to me ever
nor all this longing   that has caught me in this life.

May that young man   be sad-minded always
hard his heart's thought   while he must wear
a blithe bearing   with care in the breast
a crowd of sorrows.   May on himself depend
all his world's joy.   Be he outlawed far
in a strange folk-land—   that my beloved sits
under a rocky cliff   rimed with frost
a lord dreary in spirit   drenched with water
in a ruined hall.   My lord endures
much care of mind.   He remembers too often
a happier dwelling.   Woe be to them
that for a loved one   must wait in longing.

42–50 In these lines, the speaker seems to wish for her husband the same sad, lonely life that he has forced her to endure.

Translated by Ann Stanford

RESPONDING OPTIONS

FROM PERSONAL RESPONSE *TO* CRITICAL ANALYSIS

REFLECT

1. What is your reaction to the wife's story in "The Wife's Lament"? Record your thoughts in your notebook.

RETHINK

2. Evaluate the kind of life the wife has led. Support your evaluation with details from the poem.
3. How would you describe the wife's opinion of her husband's behavior?
   Consider
   - the influence of her husband's kinsmen
   - the vow that the husband and wife made to each other
   - the wife's thoughts in lines 42–50
4. In your opinion, how might the husband respond to his wife's accusations?

RELATE

5. Compare and contrast the plights of the speakers of "The Seafarer" and "The Wife's Lament." Who do you think faces the most difficult hardships? Why?
6. In the modern world, many refugees leave their countries to escape dangers, not knowing when or if they will ever return to the homelands and people they love. How do you think the loneliness and other hardships they suffer compare with those endured in Anglo-Saxon times?

ANOTHER PATHWAY

Cooperative Learning

With a small group of classmates, stage a TV talk show and interview the speaker of each poem. Ask questions that will lead your guests to discuss their future hopes and plans as well as their past experiences.

QUICKWRITES

1. Imagine that you are the seafarer. Write a **diary entry** describing your experiences during a typical day at sea.
2. Write a **letter** to the speaker of "The Wife's Lament." Offer advice by explaining what you would do if confronted with similar hardships.
3. In a **paragraph,** describe a situation that has caused you to have conflicting responses similar to those of the seafarer.

PORTFOLIO *Save your writing. You may want to use it later as a springboard to a piece for your portfolio.*

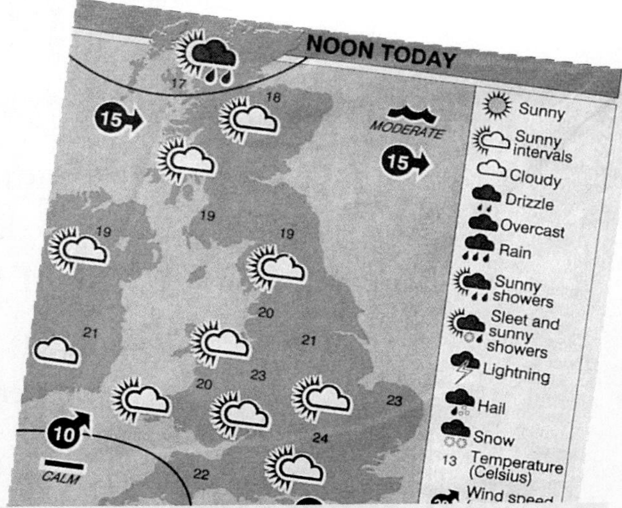

LITERARY CONCEPTS

Old English poetry has a strong **rhythm** that makes it easily chanted or sung. Each line has four stressed (´) syllables, two on either side of the caesura. The translators of "The Seafarer" and "The Wife's Lament" have reproduced this feature of Old English verse in their translations. Listen for the rhythm as you read aloud these lines from Charles W. Kennedy's version of "The Seafarer":

> In my eárs no soúnd but the róar of the séa,
> The ícy cómbers, the crý of the swán;

Emphasize the rhythm as you read another set of lines aloud with your classmates.

CONCEPT REVIEW: Alliteration Besides rhythm, the most important element of sound in Old English poetry is alliteration, the repetition of initial consonant sounds. Look for examples in both translations.

ALTERNATIVE ACTIVITIES

1. Research the weather patterns over the waters surrounding England. Draw a **map** showing the places where an Anglo-Saxon sailor may have encountered weather-related dangers and the types of dangers he may have faced.
2. Create an **illustration** for "The Wife's Lament." Using charcoal or watercolor, try to capture the mood of one of the scenes described by the speaker.

ACROSS THE CURRICULUM

History Investigate the discovery of the ship burial at Sutton Hoo in Suffolk, England. What kind of ship was buried there? What have the contents revealed about Anglo-Saxon culture?

THE AUTHORS

Nothing is known about the authors of "The Seafarer" and "The Wife's Lament." Both poems survive in the Exeter Book, a manuscript written around A.D. 975. Leofric, the first bishop of Exeter in England, had this collection of Anglo-Saxon poems in his personal library. After he donated it to the Exeter Cathedral library sometime between A.D. 1050 and 1072, the Exeter Book was neglected and abused for centuries, because few people were able to read the Old English language in which it was written. The original binding and an unknown number of pages were lost. Other pages were badly stained or scorched. Today the Exeter Book is handled with great care and treasured as one of the few surviving manuscripts from the Anglo-Saxon period.

PREVIEWING

NONFICTION

from A History of the English Church and People

The Venerable Bede

PERSONAL CONNECTION

Think about a time when you were challenged to make a major change in your life. Did you make the change? How did it affect the way you think or live? Share your experience with a group of classmates.

HISTORICAL CONNECTION

The Venerable Bede, regarded as the father of English history, lived and worked in a monastery in northern Britain during the late seventh and early eighth centuries. His most famous work, *A History of the English Church and People,* is a major source of information about life in Britain from the first successful Roman invasion, about A.D. 46, to A.D. 731. Bede was an unusually careful and thorough historian for his time. He sought out original documents and reliable eyewitness accounts on which to base his writing. Modern scholars consider his work to be an outstanding and largely trustworthy achievement.

Bede's *History* is filled with stories about the spread of Christianity among the English between A.D. 597 and 731. Christianity had been introduced into Britain during the Roman occupation, probably in the second century, and had flourished for a time. The Anglo-Saxon tribes who began invading around A.D. 450, however, were pagans and brought their religion with them. By the late sixth century, Christianity had been abandoned in many areas. In A.D. 597, missionaries from Rome began arriving in Britain to persuade the Anglo-Saxons to reject their pagan beliefs and accept the challenge of the Christian faith.

WRITING CONNECTION

In your notebook, write a brief description of a person you know or have heard of who, when faced with a difficult challenge in life, exhibited phenomenal courage and inner strength. What motivated this person to behave as he or she did? As you read this selection, discover what motivates two individuals of Anglo-Saxon times to face up to important challenges.

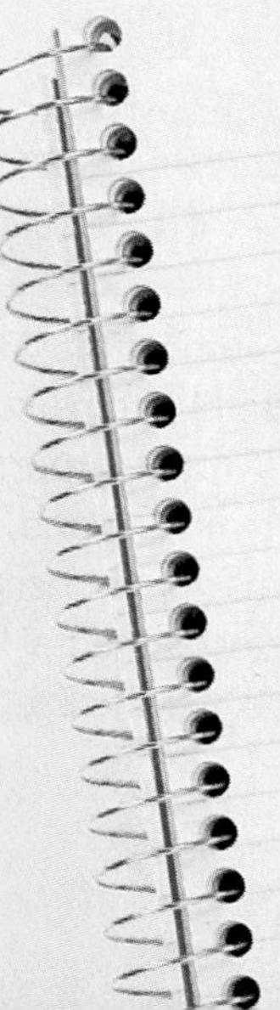

Brainstorm

-person who served in a war

-person who survived a natural disaster

-person who lost loved ones

-person who stood up for their rights

from **A History of the English Church and People**

The Venerable BEDE

King Edwin was a powerful ruler of Northumbria—a kingdom in northern Britain—during the early seventh century. Although a pagan, Edwin married a Christian, Ethelberga of Kent, and allowed her to practice her Christian faith. Ethelberga's chaplain, Paulinus, challenged her new husband to convert to Christianity.

Portrait of the scribe Eadwine

When Paulinus had spoken, the king answered that he was both willing and obliged to accept the Faith which he taught, but said that he must discuss the matter with his principal advisers and friends, so that if they were in agreement, they might all be cleansed together in Christ the Fount of Life. Paulinus agreed, and the king kept his promise. He summoned a council of the wise men, and asked each in turn his opinion of this new faith and new God being proclaimed.

Coifi, the High Priest, replied without hesitation: "Your Majesty, let us give careful consideration to this new teaching, for I frankly admit that, in my experience, the religion that we have hitherto professed seems valueless and powerless. None of your subjects has been more devoted to the service of the gods than myself, yet there are many to whom you show greater favor, who receive greater honors, and who are more successful in all their undertakings. Now, if the

WORDS TO KNOW **profess** (prə-fĕs') *v.* to claim belief in or allegiance to

gods had any power, they would surely have favored myself, who have been more zealous in their service. Therefore, if on examination these new teachings are found to be better and more effectual, let us not hesitate to accept them."

Another of the king's chief men signified his agreement with this prudent argument, and went on to say: "Your Majesty, when we compare the present life of man with that time of which we have no knowledge, it seems to me like the swift flight of a lone sparrow through the banqueting-hall where you sit in the winter months to dine with your thanes[1] and counselors. Inside there is a comforting fire to warm the room; outside, the wintry storms of snow and rain are raging. This sparrow flies swiftly in through one door of the hall, and out through another. While he is inside, he is safe from the winter storms; but after a few moments of comfort, he vanishes from sight into the darkness whence he came. Similarly, man appears on earth for a little while, but we know nothing of what went before this life, and what follows. Therefore if this new teaching can reveal any more certain knowledge, it seems only right that we should follow it." The other elders and counselors of the king, under God's guidance, gave the same advice.

Coifi then added that he wished to hear Paulinus' teaching about God in greater detail; and when, at the king's bidding, this had been given, the High Priest said: "I have long realized that there is nothing in what we worshiped, for the more diligently I sought after truth in our religion, the less I found. I now publicly confess that this teaching clearly reveals truths that will afford us the blessings of life, salvation, and eternal happiness. Therefore, Your Majesty, I submit that the temples and altars that we have dedicated to no advantage be immediately desecrated and burned." In short, the king granted blessed Paulinus full permission to preach, renounced idolatry, and professed his acceptance of the Faith of Christ. And when he asked the High Priest who should be the first to profane[2] the altars and shrines of the idols, together with the enclosures that surrounded them, Coifi replied: "I will do this myself, for now that the true God has granted me knowledge, who more suitably than I can set a public example, and destroy the idols that I worshiped in ignorance?" So he formally renounced his empty superstitions, and asked the king to give him arms and a stallion—for hitherto it had not been lawful for the High Priest to carry arms, or to ride anything but a mare—and, thus equipped, he set out to destroy the idols. Girded with a sword and with a spear in his hand, he mounted the king's stallion and rode up to the idols. When the crowd saw him, they thought he had gone mad, but without hesitation, as soon as he reached the temple, he cast a spear into it and profaned it. Then, full of joy at his knowledge of the worship of the true God, he told his companions to set fire to the temple and its enclosures and destroy them. The site where these idols once stood is still shown, not far east of York, beyond the river Derwent, and is known as Goodmanham. Here it was that the High Priest, inspired by the true God, desecrated and destroyed the altars that he had himself dedicated.

---

1. **thanes:** freemen attached to the household of an Anglo-Saxon lord, serving as his personal band of warriors.
2. **profane:** desecrate.

WORDS TO KNOW

zealous (zĕl'əs) *adj.* filled with enthusiasm; eager
effectual (ĭ-fĕk'cho͞o-əl) *adj.* able to produce a desired effect
prudent (pro͞od'nt) *adj.* showing wisdom or good judgment
desecrate (dĕs'ĭ-krāt') *v.* to violate the sacredness of
renounce (rĭ-nouns') *v.* to give up or reject

A page from the Venerable Bede's *History of the English Church and People*. The Granger Collection, New York.

Caedmon (kăd'mən) is the earliest English poet known to us by name. According to Bede, Caedmon composed many poems; however, only his first poem, a hymn to God the Creator, has survived. In the following account, Bede describes how Caedmon, who was an illiterate cowherd, became an accomplished poet.

Friars singing in choir, miniature from the Psalter of Henry VI (detail). Cotton Domitian A. XVII, f. 122v, by permission of The British Library.

In this monastery of Whitby there lived a brother[3] whom God's grace made remarkable. So skillful was he in composing religious and devotional songs, that he could quickly turn whatever passages of Scripture were explained to him into delightful and moving poetry in his own English tongue. These verses of his stirred the hearts of many folk to despise the world and aspire to heavenly things. Others after him tried to compose religious poems in English, but none could compare with him, for he received this gift of poetry as a gift from God and did not acquire it through any human teacher. For this reason he could never compose any frivolous or profane verses, but only such as had a religious theme fell fittingly from his devout lips. And although he followed a secular occupation until well advanced in years, he had never learned anything about poetry: indeed, whenever all those present at a feast took it in turns to sing and

3. **brother:** a man who lives in or works for a religious community but is not a priest or monk.

WORDS TO KNOW	
	aspire (ə-spīr') *v.* to strive to attain
	devout (dĭ-vout') *adj.* showing religious devotion and piety
	secular (sĕk'yə-lər) *adj.* unrelated to religion

entertain the company, he would get up from table and go home directly he saw the harp[4] approaching him.

On one such occasion he had left the house in which the entertainment was being held and went out to the stable, where it was his duty to look after the beasts that night. He lay down there at the appointed time and fell asleep, and in a dream he saw a man standing beside him who called him by name. "Caedmon," he said, "sing me a song." "I don't know how to sing," he replied. "It is because I cannot sing that I left the feast and came here." The man who addressed him then said: "But you shall sing to me." "What should I sing about?" he replied. "Sing about the Creation of all things," the other answered. And Caedmon immediately began to sing verses in praise of God the Creator that he had never heard before, and their theme ran thus: "Let us praise the Maker of the kingdom of heaven, the power and purpose of our Creator, and the acts of the Father of glory. Let us sing how the eternal God, the Author of all marvels, first created the heavens for the sons of men as a roof to cover them, and how their almighty Protector gave them the earth for their dwelling place." This is the general sense, but not the actual words that Caedmon sang in his dream; for however excellent the verses, it is impossible to translate them from one language into another[5] without losing much of their beauty and dignity. When Caedmon awoke, he remembered everything that he had sung in his dream, and soon added more verses in the same style to the glory of God.

Early in the morning he went to his superior the reeve,[6] and told him about this gift that he had received. The reeve took him before the abbess,[7] who ordered him to give an account of his dream and repeat the verses in the presence of many learned men, so that they might decide their quality and origin. All of them agreed that Caedmon's gift had been given him by our Lord, and when they had explained to him a passage of scriptural history or doctrine, they asked him to render it into verse if he could. He promised to do this, and returned next morning with excellent verses as they had ordered him. The abbess was delighted that God had given such grace to the man, and advised him to abandon secular life and adopt the monastic state. And when she had admitted him into the Community as a brother, she ordered him to be instructed in the events of sacred history.[8] So Caedmon stored up in his memory all that he learned, and like an animal chewing the cud, turned it into such melodious verse that his delightful renderings turned his instructors into his audience. He sang of the creation of the world, the origin of the human race, and the whole story of Genesis. He sang of Israel's departure from Egypt, their entry into the land of promise, and many other events of scriptural history. He sang of the Lord's Incarnation, Passion, Resurrection, and Ascension into heaven, the coming of the Holy Spirit, and the teaching of the Apostles. He also made many poems on the terrors of the Last Judgment, the horrible pains of Hell, and the joys of the kingdom of heaven. In addition to these, he composed several others on the blessings and judgments of God, by which he sought to turn his hearers from delight in wickedness, and to inspire them to love and do good. For Caedmon was a deeply religious man, who humbly submitted to regular discipline,[9] and firmly resisted all who tried to do evil, thus winning a happy death. ❖

---

4. **harp:** In Anglo-Saxon times, poetry was often recited to the accompaniment of a small harp.
5. **translate . . . another:** Caedmon's verses were composed in Old English, but Bede wrote in Latin.
6. **reeve:** the officer who oversaw the monastery's farms.
7. **abbess** (ăb′ĭs): a woman in charge of a convent or monastery. The abbess of Whitby at this time was named Hilda.
8. **sacred history:** the narratives in the Bible.
9. **regular discipline:** the rules of monastic life.

WORDS TO KNOW

render (rĕn′dər) *v.* to express in another language or form

RESPONDING OPTIONS

FROM PERSONAL RESPONSE *TO* CRITICAL ANALYSIS

REFLECT 1. What is your opinion of the way Bede describes historical events? Write down some of your thoughts in your notebook.

RETHINK 2. Why do you think the king seeks the advice of his counselors before responding to the challenge to accept Christianity?

3. In your opinion, does Coifi's destruction of the temples show great courage?

   Consider
   - Coifi's position as high priest of the pagan religion
   - his role as adviser to the king
   - the crowd's reaction at the temple

4. What do you think life would have been like for Caedmon if, after having his dream, he had chosen not to compose poetry?

RELATE 5. The decisions and actions of King Edwin and Coifi hastened the spread of Christianity throughout England in a relatively short time, producing a major shift in the entire society. Think of another time in history when a political decision or some significant event or development has had a great effect on a whole nation or culture. How did people respond to the challenges to their way of life?

ANOTHER PATHWAY

Imagine how the events in Bede's narratives would be described in a contemporary high school history book. Choose one of the excerpts and rewrite it from the point of view of a modern historian.

LITERARY CONCEPTS

Historical writing is a systematic account, often in narrative form, of the past of a nation or a group of people. Historical writing generally has the following characteristics: (1) it is concerned with real events, (2) the events are treated in chronological order, and (3) it is usually an objective retelling of facts rather than a personal interpretation. Think about Bede's writing. Do you think it displays all three of the aforementioned characteristics of historical writing?

Historical Writing
- concern with real events
- chronological order
- objective retelling of facts

QUICKWRITES

1. One of the king's advisers uses a simile, comparing human life to the flight of a sparrow. Write your own **simile** for life and explain your comparison.
2. Draft a short **essay** in which you compare and contrast the personal qualities of Coifi and Caedmon. Consider the temperament and behavior that each person displays when challenged to change his lifestyle.

PORTFOLIO *Save your writing. You may want to use it later as a springboard to a piece for your portfolio.*

ALTERNATIVE ACTIVITIES

Think about Caedmon's dream. Then create a **sketch** or **painting** of the man who appeared to Caedmon and inspired him to compose poetry.

LITERARY LINKS

Contrast the portrayals of life in Bede's *History* and in *Beowulf.* What aspects of Anglo-Saxon culture are emphasized in each work? What might account for the differences between the two portrayals?

ACROSS THE CURRICULUM

Geography Research travel between Rome and Britain during the time of Bede. Find a map showing Europe as it was in the seventh and eighth centuries. Trace the probable routes from Rome to Britain. What means of travel were used? How long would a trip from Rome to Britain have taken? What dangers would travelers have faced? Record your findings in an oral report.

CRITIC'S CORNER

In the introduction to his translation of Bede's *History,* Leo Sherley-Price writes, "Such is the interest of the subject matter and the vividness of Bede's characteristic style that the scenes and folk of long ago live again." Comment on whether the excerpts you have read support this view of Bede's writing.

WORDS TO KNOW

Decide whether the words in each of the following pairs are more nearly synonyms or antonyms. On your paper, write *S* for *Synonyms* or *A* for *Antonyms.*

1. zealous—enthusiastic
2. renounce—abandon
3. prudent—unwise
4. effectual—effective
5. devout—pious
6. desecrate—honor
7. aspire—desire
8. secular—religious
9. render—interpret
10. profess—deny

THE VENERABLE BEDE

673?–735

At the age of seven, Bede was taken by his parents to a monastery at Wearmouth, on the northeast coast of Britain, where he was left in the care of the abbot, Benedict Biscop (bĭsh'əp). It is not known why the boy's parents left him or whether he ever saw them again. When he was nine years old, Bede was moved a short distance to a new monastery at Jarrow, where he was to spend the rest of his life.

Bede seems to have been a naturally devout and studious child. He read widely in the monastery libraries, studied Latin and perhaps a little Greek, and participated fully in the religious life of the monastery. He was exposed to the art and learning of Europe through the paintings, books, and religious objects brought from Rome by Abbot Benedict. Bede became a deacon of the church at the age of 19, six years earlier than normal, and was ordained to the priesthood when he was 30.

Bede was a brilliant scholar and a gifted writer and teacher. He wrote about 40 books, including works on spelling, grammar, science, history, and religion. In addition, he popularized the dating of events from the birth of Christ, the system still in use today.

Bede's reputation as a scholar and a devout monk spread throughout Europe during his lifetime and in the centuries following. (The title "Venerable" was probably first applied to him during the century after his death.) Although Bede was influenced by the outlook of his time—as is evident in the miracle stories he included in his *History*—his carefulness and integrity are still respected and valued by scholars today, almost 1,300 years later.

LASERLINKS
• *AUTHOR BACKGROUND*

WRITING ABOUT
LITERATURE

EXAMINING VALUES

Reading literature that is set in a different time and place—like *Beowulf* and the *Iliad*—is like taking a trip to an unfamiliar country. One way to understand unfamiliar cultures and settings is to look closely at the people who populate these places and find out what's important to them. Then you can use the knowledge you've gained to infer the values of the cultures in which they live. The following pages will help you

- study how authors reveal the traits of characters
- write an interpretive essay analyzing the values of an unfamiliar culture
- use interpretive skills to understand modern communities

The Writer's Style: Characterization We can learn a lot about a person's background and beliefs by noting what the person says or does. Experienced writers know this and often use words and actions to reveal what a character is like.

Read the Literature

Notice what Beowulf's own words tell you about him.

Literature Model

Characterization Through Dialogue
On the basis of Beowulf's speech, what values do you think are important to him? What phrases support your answer?

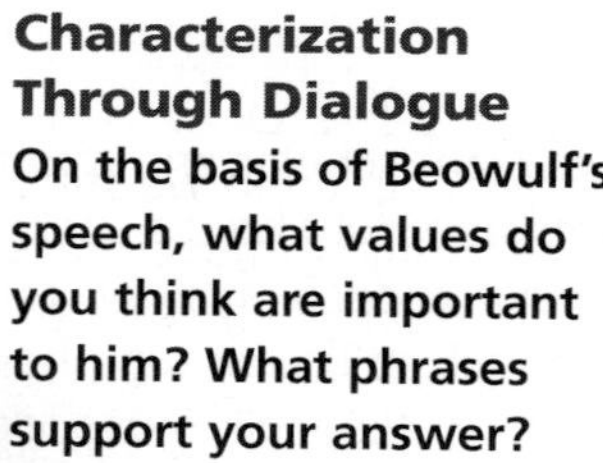

I have come so far,
Oh shelterer of warriors and your people's loved friend,
That this one favor you should not refuse me—
That I, alone and with the help of my men,
May purge all evil from this hall. I have heard,
Too, that the monster's scorn of men
Is so great that he needs no weapons and fears none.
Nor will I. My lord Higlac
Might think less of me if I let my sword
Go where my feet were afraid to, if I hid
Behind some broad linden shield: my hands
Alone shall fight for me, struggle for life
Against the monster.

from *Beowulf*
translated by Burton Raffel

Connect to Life

Journalists, like fiction writers, reveal the character of their subjects by showing what they say and what they do. Below, read about the actions of Johann Olav Koss, the Norwegian speed-skating champion who now helps others reach their goals.

Magazine Article

You see this as Koss—hero of the 1994 Winter Olympic Games, built like some Norse god, square-jawed, strapping, straight-nosed—walks to the start of the New York City Marathon on Nov. 6 with the 165 disabled runners of the Achilles Track Club. He helps a wheelchair-bound athlete over a curb, then unobtrusively clears the way for a one-legged runner on crutches.

E. M. Swift
from "Giving His All"
Sports Illustrated, December 19, 1994

Characterization Through Action
On the basis of his actions, what kind of person do you think Koss is? What values do you think he holds?

Try Your Hand: Using Characterization

1. **Round Out the Picture** Pick two people you know and jot down a distinctive character trait of each of them. Write a few sentences about each person, showing how he or she demonstrates that trait in his or her words and actions.
2. **Add a Twist to a QuickWrite** Find a QuickWrite in which you described a character and rewrite it, using another technique of characterization. For example, if you've described a character's actions, you may want to write a monologue for that person. It may reveal other aspects of the character.
3. **Create a Character** Write a paragraph in which the values of a real or fictional person are shown through both action and dialogue.

SkillBuilder

Using Dashes
When we talk, we often interrupt ourselves to explain something or to change our train of thought. When writing, you can use dashes to show these sorts of interruptions in sentences.

- Dashes are used to set off explanatory statements that interrupt the main idea of a sentence. The magazine-article excerpt on this page shows dashes used for that purpose.
- Dashes can also set off a summarizing statement from the rest of a sentence. The dash in the excerpt from *Beowulf* functions in this way.

APPLYING WHAT YOU'VE LEARNED
Use dashes to clarify the following sentences.

- Beowulf the warrior who could kill monsters with his bare hands would make an excellent hero in one of today's action-adventure movies.
- Although we still value physical strength and bravery, we no longer choose our leaders on the basis of those traits. Skill with people and words is more important.

GRAMMAR HANDBOOK

For more information on dashes, see page 1288 of the Grammar Handbook.

Interpretation

Stories entertain us, but they also communicate the values of the people who tell them. Learning to interpret these values can help you understand both fictional and real-life communities. Since heroes, real and fictitious, usually embody the values of the group to which they belong, one way to find out what is important to a community is to look at what its heroes say and do.

GUIDED ASSIGNMENT

Write an Interpretive Essay In interpretive essays, concrete examples are used to back up statements about what literature means. In this lesson, you'll interpret the values of the characters and community presented in one of the selections you just read.

1 Prewrite and Explore

Thinking about the values in your own world may help you to get started with this assignment. What do people strive for today? For what are they rewarded? How are resources divided? Discuss these thoughts with your classmates, then try asking similar questions about the selections.

Decision Point Since you will need specific examples to support the statements you make in your writing, you may want to consider which selections provide ample evidence of value systems. Then choose a selection to write about.

READ AND CONSIDER

Glance through the selection you have chosen, thinking about the values that are implied in it. You may want to ask yourself questions like the following:

- What motivates the characters?
- Who or what seems to get the most respect? Why?
- What qualities are mentioned often?

At this stage of the process, many writers put their thoughts on paper. Consider jotting down your first impressions in a list like the one shown at the left.

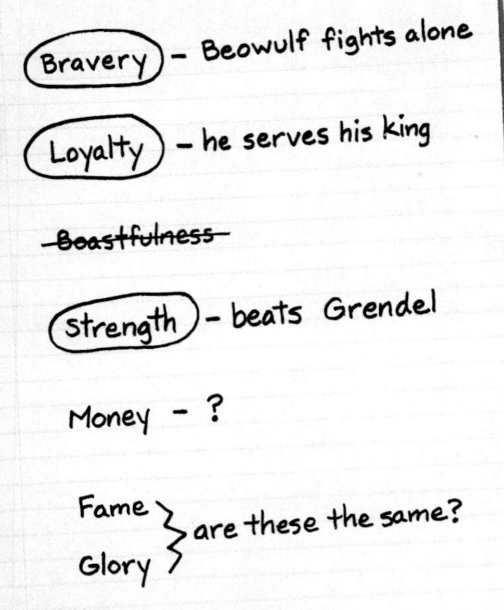

Bravery - Beowulf fights alone
Loyalty - he serves his king
~~Boastfulness~~
Strength - beats Grendel
Money - ?
Fame
Glory
are these the same?

❷ Collect the Evidence

Your list can help you decide what values were important to the group you're writing about. Keep track of the actions and dialogue that help you make this decision, because you'll need to cite them in your essay. You may want to record your information on note cards like the one below. Label each card with a value and a number, and write one supporting quote on it.

> 3
>
> Strength
>
> "I'd use no sword, no weapon, if this beast / Could be killed without it, crushed to death / Like Grendel, gripped in my hands and torn / Limb from limb."

❸ Draft and Share

You can use what you learned in step 2 to help you write a first draft. Look below to see how one student used information from note cards in a draft. You may also want to look at the SkillBuilder on organizing your essay.

Student's Draft

> Beowulf doesn't simply want to kill his enemies, he wants to show his strength by killing them with his bare hands. He says "I'd use no sword, no weapon, if this beast / Could be killed without it, crushed to death / Like Grendel, gripped in my hands and torn / Limb from limb."

After you've wrapped up your draft, consider asking another student to read your writing and give you feedback.

PEER RESPONSE

- What helped you understand why I thought these values were important?
- Which of my ideas do you agree with? Which do you disagree with?

SkillBuilder

WRITER'S CRAFT

Organizing Your Essay

Not only is an organized essay easier to read and follow; it's easier to write too. Consider using the following organizational structure when you write your interpretive essay.

Introduction The first paragraph should tell what your essay is about. You will probably want to include a thesis statement—one or two sentences that state the main idea of the essay.

Body The body of an essay presents the specific thinking and examples that back up your thesis statement. This information is usually organized into parts. For example, in an interpretive essay on values, you might write one body paragraph for each value mentioned.

Conclusion A conclusion should summarize or generalize about the information presented in the essay.

APPLYING WHAT YOU'VE LEARNED

After you've written your first draft, check to see whether your essay is organized effectively. If it's not, work on including the parts listed above in your revision.

4 Revise and Edit

Would a reader unfamiliar with your assignment understand what your essay is about? When you revise, make sure you state your topic clearly. Consider the Standards for Evaluation below and the Grammar in Context feature on the opposite page, which provides tips on how to strengthen your writing. After you've considered these resources, revise and edit your draft.

Student's Final Draft

In his first monologue, Beowulf boasts about how brave he is. He describes the bloody battles he has fought and claims he will confront Grendel with his bare hands. He says, "the monster's scorn of men / Is so great that he needs no weapons and fears none. / Nor will I." After he kills Grendel, Beowulf's bravery makes him famous. "Then old and young rejoiced . . . retelling / Beowulf's bravery as they jogged along."

How does the writer use concrete examples to demonstrate a point in the body of the essay?

In a time and place where monsters and dragons terrorized people, it is no surprise to find that society admired warrior traits. Beowulf's community respected loyalty, strength, and, most importantly, bravery. From the time he arrived on the shore of the Danes through fierce battles with three vicious monsters, Beowulf's actions and words proved his possession of these qualities. Even facing death, Beowulf showed loyalty, strength, and bravery. Because of this, he became not only a famous warrior and king but also a legendary hero.

After reading this conclusion, what information do you think the rest of the essay contained? How do you think it was organized?

Standards for Evaluation

An interpretive essay
- tells in the first paragraph what the essay is going to be about
- supports statements with details and examples from the selection
- concludes in a logical way

Grammar in Context

Active Voice of Verbs Your essay will be more memorable if you make your point clearly and strongly. Often, using verbs in the active voice instead of the passive voice can help you do this. The active voice is used when the subject of a sentence is the performer of the action. When the subject is the receiver of the action, the passive voice is used.

respected
Loyalty, strength, and most importantly, bravery ~~were respected by~~ Beowulf's community. From the time he arrived on the shore of the Danes through fierce battles with three vicious monsters, Beowulf's possession of these qualities ~~was proved by his~~ actions and words.
proved his

When the first sentence of the above excerpt is rewritten in the active voice, the auxiliary verb *were* is dropped and the subject is performing the action. This change gets rid of a wordy verb phrase and creates a more direct sentence.

Try Your Hand: Using Active Voice

On a separate sheet of paper, revise the following paragraph by changing verbs in the passive voice into active-voice verbs.

> Beowulf's superior bravery was obvious throughout the selection. Grendel was fought by him alone, while "the Danes started / In new terror, cowering in their beds." The dragon, too, was faced by Beowulf and no one else.

SkillBuilder

GRAMMAR FROM WRITING

Using *Having* with a Past Participle

When you want a sentence to show that one action was completed before another one, use *having* with the past participle in a participial phrase.

Incorrect: *Killing Grendel with his bare hands, Beowulf became famous in Denmark.*

Correct: *Having killed Grendel with his bare hands, Beowulf became famous in Denmark.*

APPLYING WHAT YOU'VE LEARNED

Combine each pair of sentences, using *having* and a past participle to show which action happened first.

1. The goddess noticed her son crying. She asked him what was the matter.
2. He lost his sword. Hector knew he would die.
3. Achilles killed Hector. He dragged the body through the camp.

GRAMMAR HANDBOOK

For more help with verb tenses and forms, see page 1277 of the Grammar Handbook.

R E A D I N G
THE WORLD

What's So Important?

The more you know about a group, the more likely you are to understand its people and appreciate their values. Watching what people say and do is one way to gather clues about a community's value system. Another way is to pay attention to what people own and how they live.

View Look closely at these scenes and record what you see. What objects are present? How are the people arranged? What is in the background?

Interpret What do the photos suggest about the way each group of people lives? What clues did you use to come up with your answer?

Discuss With a group, discuss what details you noticed. What do you think is important to the people in the photographs? What makes you think so? Now use the SkillBuilder to help with your inferences.

SkillBuilder

CRITICAL THINKING

Making Inferences

Whenever you come to a conclusion based on details you've seen, heard, or read, you're making an inference. You probably make a lot of inferences whenever you try to figure out what's important to a group of people. For example, as you approach the front door of relatives you've never met, you may notice a basketball net on their garage and a Seattle SuperSonics bumper sticker on their car. From these details you could infer that your relatives love basketball. Before you ring the doorbell, you might promise yourself not to mention that you hate all sports.

APPLYING WHAT YOU'VE LEARNED

Working with a small group, choose from a book or magazine a photo that shows a scene in a street, school, or home. Make a list of the details you notice in the picture, and then work with your group to make inferences about what might be important in the community shown. Make a chart to record the details you noticed and the inferences those details led you to make.

PART 2 *Reflections of Everyday Life*

What was life like for people in the Middle Ages? What made them laugh or cry? How did they carry out the business of living from day to day? In this part of Unit One, you will read selections that give insights into the nature of people's lives in the 14th and 15th centuries. The era will come alive for you as characters reveal their strengths and weaknesses, hopes and fears, joys and sorrows. Despite the hundreds of years that separate us from these interesting personalities, our similarities are quite astonishing.

PREVIEWING

POETRY

from The Canterbury Tales

from The Prologue *from* The Pardoner's Tale

Geoffrey Chaucer

Translated by Nevill Coghill

PERSONAL CONNECTION

A passage in the Bible states that "the love of money is the root of all evil." In your notebook write down your opinions about the influence of money. Try to answer these questions: How important is the accumulation of money to you? Have you ever met anyone who behaved dishonestly for money? What kind of desire for money, if any, would you characterize as normal or legitimate?

CULTURAL CONNECTION

In *The Canterbury Tales,* Chaucer vividly portrays 14th-century life by presenting 30 characters from various social classes. The characters include a virtuous knight, a love-struck squire, a lusty widow, a foul-mouthed miller, and a drunken cook. Pilgrims beginning a journey to the shrine of Thomas à Becket in Canterbury, England, the characters meet by chance at an inn and decide to travel together to the shrine and to tell stories to pass the time. The most entertaining storyteller is to be rewarded with a dinner.

One of the tales is that of the Pardoner—a clergyman with a license from the pope to grant indulgences (documents forgiving people for their sins). Indulgences were supposed to be granted only to people who had shown great charity; in practice, many pardoners simply sold their pardons to make money for the church or for themselves. To encourage business, unethical pardoners often threatened reluctant buyers with eternal damnation. Chaucer's Pardoner, whose desire for money outweighs his sense of honesty, is one of the least likable of the pilgrims.

READING CONNECTION

Analyzing Characterization There are a number of techniques that a writer can use to develop a character, including description of the character's physical appearance; presentation of the speech, thoughts, feelings, and actions of the character; and presentation of other characters' speech, thoughts, feelings, and actions. Create three word webs like the one shown here—one for the Summoner, one for the Pardoner, and one for the Host. Then, as you read, fill in the webs with words and phrases that describe the physical appearances and the personality traits of the characters.

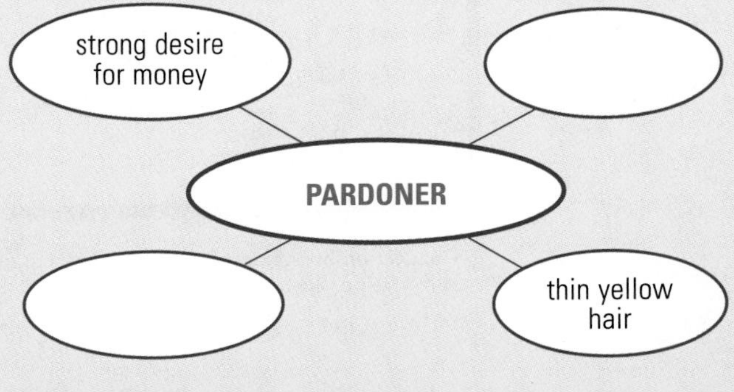

• *CULTURAL CONNECTION*

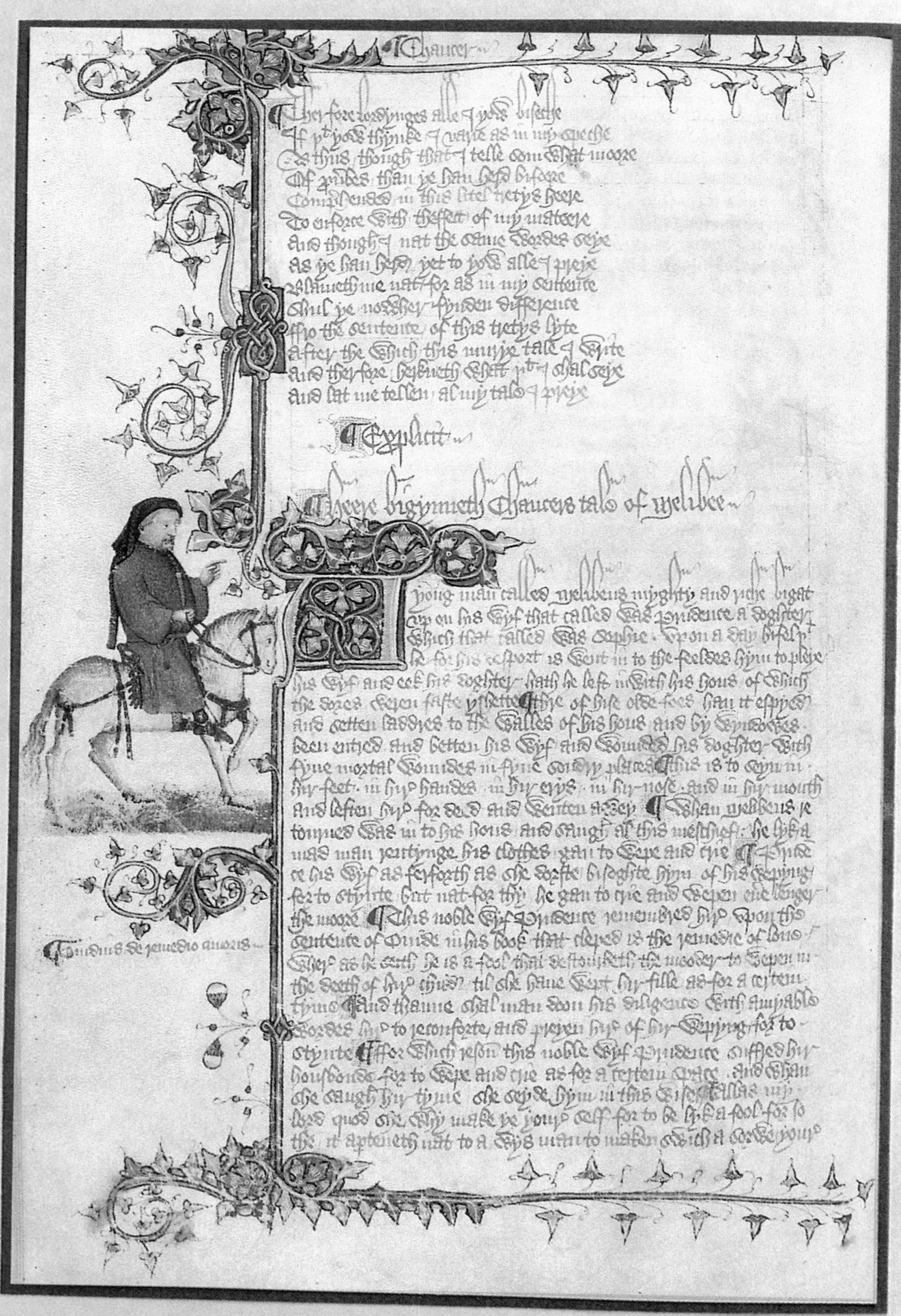

Chaucer on horseback. From the Ellesmere manuscript, EL 26 C 9, f. 153v, The Huntington Library, San Marino, California.

from The Prologue

When in April the sweet showers fall
And pierce the drought of March to the root, and all
The veins are bathed in liquor of such power
As brings about the engendering of the flower,
When also Zephyrus with his sweet breath
Exhales an air in every grove and heath
Upon the tender shoots, and the young sun
His half-course in the sign of the *Ram* has run,
And the small fowl are making melody
That sleep away the night with open eye
(So nature pricks them and their heart engages)
Then people long to go on pilgrimages
And palmers long to seek the stranger strands
Of far-off saints, hallowed in sundry lands,
And specially, from every shire's end
Of England, down to Canterbury they wend
To seek the holy blissful martyr, quick
To give his help to them when they were sick.

It happened in that season that one day
In Southwark, at *The Tabard,* as I lay
Ready to go on pilgrimage and start
For Canterbury, most devout at heart,
At night there came into that hostelry
Some nine and twenty in a company
Of sundry folk happening then to fall
In fellowship, and they were pilgrims all

GUIDE FOR READING

5 Zephyrus (zĕf'ər-əs): the Greek god of the west wind, an indicator of spring.

7–8 sun . . . run: The Ram, or Aries, is the first sign of the zodiac. In April, the sun passes through the last half of Aries and the first half of Taurus.

13 palmers: people journeying to religious shrines; pilgrims.

14 sundry (sŭn'drē): various.

16–17 down to Canterbury . . . martyr: The martyr is Thomas à Becket, archbishop of Canterbury, who was murdered in 1170; his tomb became a favorite destination of English pilgrims.

23 hostelry (hŏs'təl-rē): inn.

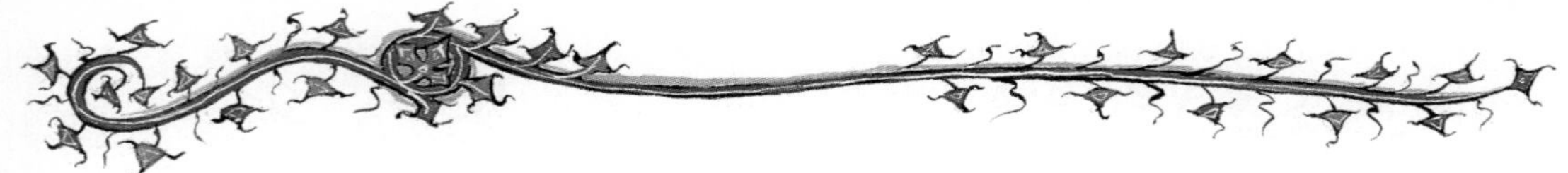

That towards Canterbury meant to ride.
The rooms and stables of the inn were wide;
They made us easy, all was of the best.
And, briefly, when the sun had gone to rest,
I'd spoken to them all upon the trip
And was soon one with them in fellowship,
Pledged to rise early and to take the way
To Canterbury, as you heard me say.

The speaker proceeds to describe the pilgrims, many of them in great detail. He concludes with portrayals of two men, the Summoner and the Pardoner, and with an account of how the Host of the Tabard Inn makes plans with the pilgrims to tell tales on the journey to and from Canterbury.

There was a *Summoner* with us at that Inn,
His face on fire, like a cherubin,
For he had carbuncles. His eyes were narrow,
He was as hot and lecherous as a sparrow.
Black scabby brows he had, and a thin beard.
Children were afraid when he appeared.
No quicksilver, lead ointment, tartar creams,
No brimstone, no boracic, so it seems,
Could make a salve that had the power to bite,
Clean up or cure his whelks of knobby white
Or purge the pimples sitting on his cheeks.
Garlic he loved, and onions too, and leeks,
And drinking strong red wine till all was hazy.
Then he would shout and jabber as if crazy,
And wouldn't speak a word except in Latin
When he was drunk, such tags as he was pat in;
He only had a few, say two or three,
That he had mugged up out of some decree;
No wonder, for he heard them every day.
And, as you know, a man can teach a jay
To call out "Walter" better than the Pope.
But had you tried to test his wits and grope
For more, you'd have found nothing in the bag.
Then "*Questio quid juris*" was his tag.
He was a noble varlet and a kind one,
You'd meet none better if you went to find one.
Why, he'd allow—just for a quart of wine—

35 Summoner: a person paid to summon sinners to church courts.

36 cherubin (chĕr'ə-bĭn'): a type of angel—in the Middle Ages frequently pictured as burning with heavenly fire.

37 carbuncles (kär'bŭng'kəlz): pimples and patches of inflamed skin, taken as a sign of drunkenness and lechery in the Middle Ages.

41–42 quicksilver . . . boracic: substances used as skin medicines during the medieval period.

44 whelks (hwĕlks): swellings.

50 tags: brief quotations.

54–55 a man can teach . . . better than the Pope: The Summoner is compared to a jay, a bird that can be taught to mimic human speech but which obviously has no understanding of what it says.

58 *Questio quid juris* (kwĕs'chō kwĭd jŏŏr'ĭs): Latin for "The question is, What is the law on this point?"

59 varlet: rascal; knave.

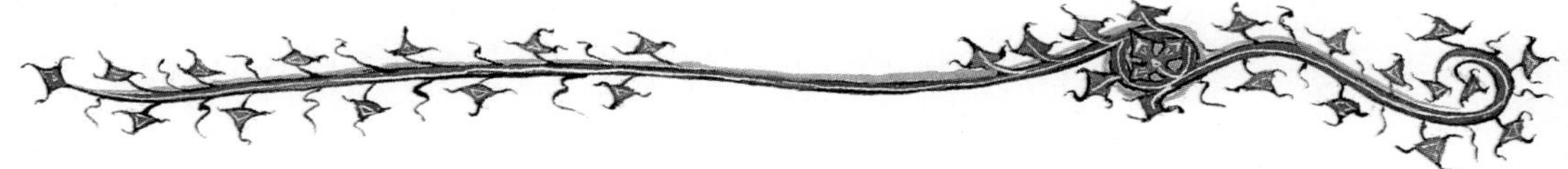

Any good lad to keep a concubine
A twelvemonth and dispense him altogether!
And he had finches of his own to feather:
And if he found some rascal with a maid
He would instruct him not to be afraid
In such a case of the Archdeacon's curse
(Unless the rascal's soul were in his purse)
For in his purse the punishment should be.
"Purse is the good Archdeacon's Hell," said he.
But well I know he lied in what he said;
A curse should put a guilty man in dread,
For curses kill, as shriving brings, salvation.
We should beware of excommunication.
Thus, as he pleased, the man could bring duress
On any young fellow in the diocese.
He knew their secrets, they did what he said.
He wore a garland set upon his head
Large as the holly-bush upon a stake
Outside an ale-house, and he had a cake,
A round one, which it was his joke to wield
As if it were intended for a shield.

He and a gentle *Pardoner* rode together,
A bird from Charing Cross of the same feather,
Just back from visiting the Court of Rome.
He loudly sang *"Come hither, love, come home!"*
The Summoner sang deep seconds to this song,
No trumpet ever sounded half so strong.
This Pardoner had hair as yellow as wax,
Hanging down smoothly like a hank of flax.
In driblets fell his locks behind his head
Down to his shoulders which they overspread;
Thinly they fell, like rat-tails, one by one.
He wore no hood upon his head, for fun;
The hood inside his wallet had been stowed,
He aimed at riding in the latest mode;
But for a little cap his head was bare
And he had bulging eye-balls, like a hare.
He'd sewed a holy relic on his cap;
His wallet lay before him on his lap,
Brimful of pardons come from Rome, all hot.

62 concubine (kŏng′kyə-bīn′): a woman who lives with a man as his spouse although not legally married to him.

69 The Summoner thinks that a sinner's punishment should be "in his purse." What do you think he means?

73 shriving: a priest's forgiving a sinner for his confessed sins.

74 excommunication: exclusion from participation in the rites of the church.

75 duress (dŏŏ-rĕs′): a condition of being forced, usually by threats, to do something.

76 diocese (dī′ə-sĭs): the district under a bishop's supervision.

84 Charing Cross: a section of London.

99 relic: an object revered for its association with a saint or holy person.

WORDS TO KNOW

wield (wēld) *v.* to handle skillfully
mode (mōd) *n.* a current fashion or style

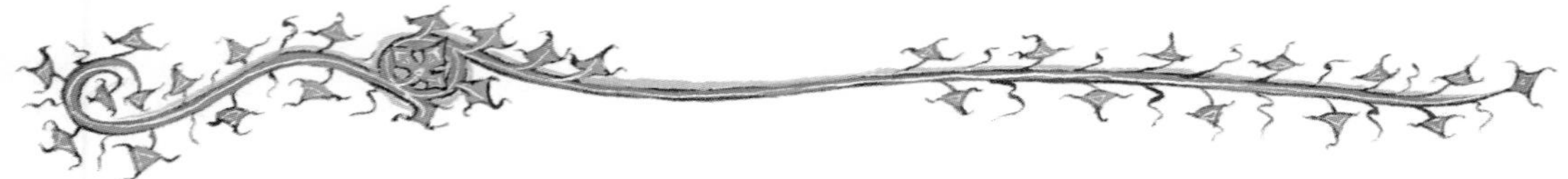

Pilgrims leaving Canterbury (about 1400). English manuscript illumination, The Granger Collection, New York.

He had the same small voice a goat has got.
His chin no beard had harbored, nor would harbor,
Smoother than ever chin was left by barber.
I judge he was a gelding, or a mare.
As to his trade, from Berwick down to Ware
There was no pardoner of equal grace,
For in his trunk he had a pillow-case
Which he asserted was Our Lady's veil.
He said he had a gobbet of the sail
Saint Peter had the time when he made bold
To walk the waves, till Jesu Christ took hold.
He had a cross of metal set with stones
And, in a glass, a rubble of pigs' bones.
And with these relics, any time he found
Some poor up-country parson to astound,

105 gelding (gĕl'dĭng): a castrated animal, especially a horse.

106 Berwick . . . Ware: Berwick is a village near the northern border of England; Ware, a village in the south of England, near London.

110 gobbet: piece or chunk.

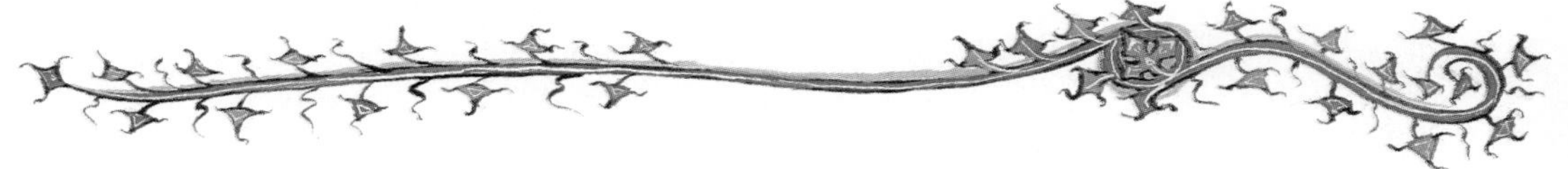

In one short day, in money down, he drew
More than the parson in a month or two,
And by his flatteries and prevarication
Made monkeys of the priest and congregation.
But still to do him justice first and last
In church he was a noble ecclesiast.
How well he read a lesson or told a story!
But best of all he sang an Offertory,
For well he knew that when that song was sung
He'd have to preach and tune his honey-tongue
And (well he could) win silver from the crowd.
That's why he sang so merrily and loud.

Now I have told you shortly, in a clause,
The rank, the array, the number and the cause
Of our assembly in this company
In Southwark, at that high-class hostelry
Known as *The Tabard,* close beside *The Bell.*
And now the time has come for me to tell
How we behaved that evening; I'll begin
After we had alighted at the Inn,
Then I'll report our journey, stage by stage,
All the remainder of our pilgrimage.
But first I beg of you, in courtesy,
Not to condemn me as unmannerly
If I speak plainly and with no concealings
And give account of all their words and dealings,
Using their very phrases as they fell.
For certainly, as you all know so well,
He who repeats a tale after a man
Is bound to say, as nearly as he can,
Each single word, if he remembers it,
However rudely spoken or unfit,
Or else the tale he tells will be untrue,
The things pretended and the phrases new.
He may not flinch although it were his brother,
He may as well say one word as another.
And Christ Himself spoke broad in Holy Writ,
Yet there is no scurrility in it,
And Plato says, for those with power to read,
"The word should be as cousin to the deed."
Further I beg you to forgive it me
If I neglect the order and degree

119 prevarication (prĭ-văr′ĭ-kā′shən): lying.

122 ecclesiast (ĭ-klē′zē-ăst′): clergyman.

124 Offertory: a chant preceding the ceremonial offering of bread and wine in the Roman Catholic Mass; afterwards, church members make monetary offerings to the church.

139–150 Chaucer, the narrator, apologizes in advance for using the exact words of his companions. Why would he make such an apology?

154 scurrility (skə-rĭl′ĭ-tē): vulgarity; coarseness.

And what is due to rank in what I've planned.
I'm short of wit as you will understand.

Our *Host* gave us great welcome; everyone
Was given a place and supper was begun.
He served the finest victuals you could think,
The wine was strong and we were glad to drink.
A very striking man our Host withal,
And fit to be a marshal in a hall.
His eyes were bright, his girth a little wide;
There is no finer burgess in Cheapside.
Bold in his speech, yet wise and full of tact,
There was no manly attribute he lacked,
What's more he was a merry-hearted man.
After our meal he jokingly began
To talk of sport, and, among other things
After we'd settled up our reckonings,
He said as follows: "Truly, gentlemen,
You're very welcome and I can't think when
—Upon my word I'm telling you no lie—
I've seen a gathering here that looked so spry,
No, not this year, as in this tavern now.
I'd think you up some fun if I knew how.
And, as it happens, a thought has just occurred
To please you, costing nothing, on my word.
You're off to Canterbury—well, God speed!
Blessed St. Thomas answer to your need!
And I don't doubt, before the journey's done
You mean to while the time in tales and fun.
Indeed, there's little pleasure for your bones
Riding along and all as dumb as stones.
So let me then propose for your enjoyment,
Just as I said, a suitable employment.
And if my notion suits and you agree
And promise to submit yourselves to me
Playing your parts exactly as I say
Tomorrow as you ride along the way,
Then by my father's soul (and he is dead)
If you don't like it you can have my head!
Hold up your hands, and not another word."

163 victuals (vĭt'lz): food.

166 marshal in a hall: an official in charge of the arrangements for a nobleman's banquet.

168 burgess (bûr'jĭs) **in Cheapside:** citizen in Cheapside, the main business district of London in Chaucer's day.

174 reckonings: bills.

188 dumb: silent.

Well, our opinion was not long deferred,
It seemed not worth a serious debate;
We all agreed to it at any rate
And bade him issue what commands he would.
"My lords," he said, "now listen for your good,
And please don't treat my notion with disdain.
This is the point. I'll make it short and plain.
Each one of you shall help to make things slip
By telling two stories on the outward trip
To Canterbury, that's what I intend,
And, on the homeward way to journey's end
Another two, tales from the days of old;
And then the man whose story is best told,
That is to say who gives the fullest measure
Of good morality and general pleasure,
He shall be given a supper, paid by all,
Here in this tavern, in this very hall,
When we come back again from Canterbury.
And in the hope to keep you bright and merry
I'll go along with you myself and ride
All at my own expense and serve as guide.
I'll be the judge, and those who won't obey
Shall pay for what we spend upon the way.
Now if you all agree to what you've heard
Tell me at once without another word,
And I will make arrangements early for it."

Of course we all agreed, in fact we swore it
Delightedly, and made entreaty too
That he should act as he proposed to do,
Become our Governor in short, and be
Judge of our tales and general referee,
And set the supper at a certain price.
We promised to be ruled by his advice
Come high, come low; unanimously thus
We set him up in judgment over us.
More wine was fetched, the business being done;
We drank it off and up went everyone
To bed without a moment of delay.

225 entreaty: an earnest request.

WORDS TO KNOW

defer (dĭ-fûr') *v.* to postpone
disdain (dĭs-dān') *n.* a show of contempt; scorn

Early next morning at the spring of day
Up rose our Host and roused us like a cock,
Gathering us together in a flock,
And off we rode at slightly faster pace
Than walking to St. Thomas' watering-place;
And there our Host drew up, began to ease
His horse, and said, "Now, listen if you please,
My lords! Remember what you promised me.
If evensong and matins will agree
Let's see who shall be first to tell a tale.
And as I hope to drink good wine and ale
I'll be your judge. The rebel who disobeys,
However much the journey costs, he pays.
Now draw for cut and then we can depart;
The man who draws the shortest cut shall start."

240 St. Thomas' watering-place: St. Thomas à Watering, a brook about two miles from London on the road to Canterbury.

244 evensong and matins (măt'nz): evening and morning prayer services; here used by the Host to mean "what you said last night and what you'll do this morning."

from The Pardoner's Prologue

"My lords," he said, "in churches where I preach
I cultivate a haughty kind of speech
And ring it out as roundly as a bell;
I've got it all by heart, the tale I tell.
I have a text, it always is the same
And always has been, since I learnt the game,
Old as the hills and fresher than the grass,
Radix malorum est cupiditas.

I preach, as you have heard me say before,
And tell a hundred lying mockeries more.
I take great pains, and stretching out my neck
To east and west I crane about and peck
Just like a pigeon sitting on a barn.
My hands and tongue together spin the yarn
And all my antics are a joy to see.
The curse of avarice and cupidity
Is all my sermon, for it frees the pelf.
Out come the pence, and specially for myself,
For my exclusive purpose is to win
And not at all to castigate their sin.

258 *Radix malorum est cupiditas* (rā'dĭks mă-lōr'əm ĕst kyo͞o-pĭd'ĭ-tăs'): Latin for "The love of money is the root of all evil"—a quotation from the Bible (1 Timothy 6:10).

260 mockeries: false tales.

266 cupidity (kyo͞o-pĭd'ĭ-tē): excessive desire for something, especially for money.

267 pelf: riches, especially those that are acquired dishonestly.

268 pence: pennies.

WORDS TO KNOW

avarice (ăv'ə-rĭs) *n.* an excessive desire for wealth; greed
castigate (kăs'tĭ-gāt') *v.* to criticize harshly

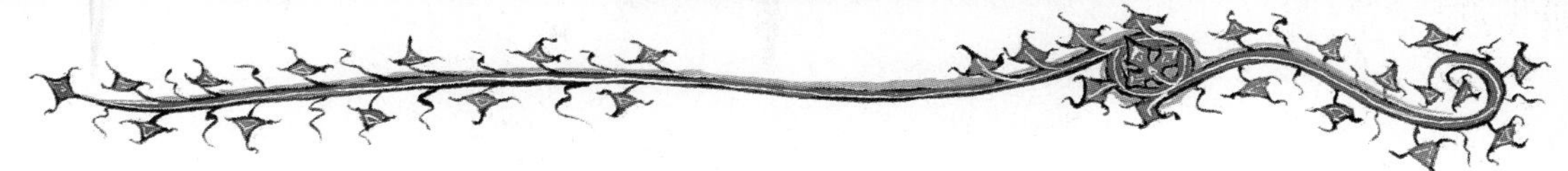

Once dead what matter how their souls may fare?
They can go blackberrying, for all I care!

269–272 What is the Pardoner's attitude toward those who listen to him preach?

And thus I preach against the very vice
I make my living out of—avarice.
And yet however guilty of that sin
Myself, with others I have power to win
Them from it, I can bring them to repent;
But that is not my principal intent.
Covetousness is both the root and stuff
Of all I preach. That ought to be enough.

"Well, then I give examples thick and fast
From bygone times, old stories from the past.
A yokel mind loves stories from of old,
Being the kind it can repeat and hold.
What! Do you think, as long as I can preach
And get their silver for the things I teach,
That I will live in poverty, from choice?
That's not the counsel of my inner voice!
No! Let me preach and beg from kirk to kirk
And never do an honest job of work,
No, nor make baskets, like St. Paul, to gain
A livelihood. I do not preach in vain.
There's no apostle I would counterfeit;
I mean to have money, wool and cheese and wheat
Though it were given me by the poorest lad
Or poorest village widow, though she had
A string of starving children, all agape.
No, let me drink the liquor of the grape
And keep a jolly wench in every town!

289 kirk: church.

"But listen, gentlemen; to bring things down
To a conclusion, would you like a tale?
Now as I've drunk a draught of corn-ripe ale,
By God it stands to reason I can strike
On some good story that you all will like.
For though I am a wholly vicious man
Don't think I can't tell moral tales. I can!
Here's one I often preach when out for winning. . . ."

WORDS TO KNOW
covetousness (kŭv′ĭ-təs-nĭs) *n.* an excessive desire for wealth or possessions

from The Pardoner's Tale

It's of three rioters I have to tell
Who, long before the morning service bell,
Were sitting in a tavern for a drink.
And as they sat, they heard the hand-bell clink
Before a coffin going to the grave;
One of them called the little tavern-knave
And said "Go and find out at once—look spry!—
Whose corpse is in that coffin passing by;
And see you get the name correctly too."
"Sir," said the boy, "no need, I promise you;
Two hours before you came here I was told.
He was a friend of yours in days of old,
And suddenly, last night, the man was slain,
Upon his bench, face up, dead drunk again.
There came a privy thief, they call him Death,
Who kills us all round here, and in a breath
He speared him through the heart, he never stirred.
And then Death went his way without a word.
He's killed a thousand in the present plague,
And, sir, it doesn't do to be too vague
If you should meet him; you had best be wary.
Be on your guard with such an adversary,
Be primed to meet him everywhere you go,
That's what my mother said. It's all I know."

The publican joined in with, "By St. Mary,
What the child says is right; you'd best be wary,

308 rioters: rowdy people; revelers.

311–312 hand-bell . . . grave: In Chaucer's time, a bell was carried beside the coffin in a funeral procession.

313 tavern-knave (nāv): a serving boy in an inn.

322 privy (prĭv′ē): hidden; secretive.

322–331 Death is personified as a thief in the night, who slays his victims and then flees. The plague, also known as the Black Death, killed at least a quarter of the population of Europe in the mid-14th century; in some areas, as much as two-thirds of the population may have perished.

332 publican: innkeeper; tavern owner.

WORDS TO KNOW

wary (wâr′ē) *adj.* cautious; on one's guard
adversary (ăd′vər-sĕr′ē) *n.* an enemy; opponent

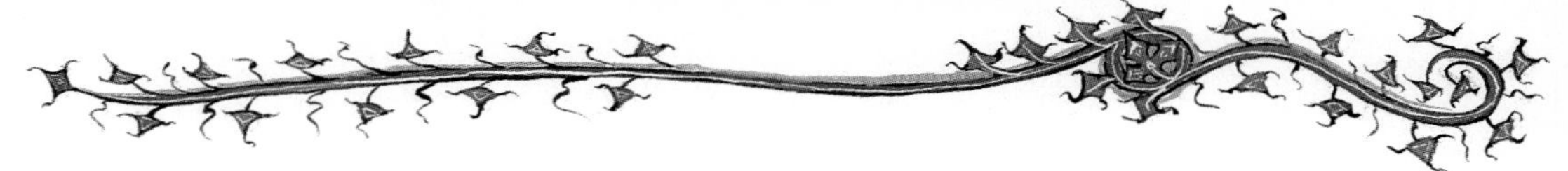

This very year he killed, in a large village
A mile away, man, woman, serf at tillage,
Page in the household, children—all there were.
Yes, I imagine that he lives round there.
It's well to be prepared in these alarms,
He might do you dishonor." "Huh, God's arms!"
The rioter said, "Is he so fierce to meet?
I'll search for him, by Jesus, street by street.
God's blessed bones! I'll register a vow!
Here, chaps! The three of us together now,
Hold up your hands, like me, and we'll be brothers
In this affair, and each defend the others,
And we will kill this traitor Death, I say!
Away with him as he has made away
With all our friends. God's dignity! Tonight!"

They made their bargain, swore with appetite,
These three, to live and die for one another
As brother-born might swear to his born brother.
And up they started in their drunken rage
And made towards this village which the page
And publican had spoken of before.
Many and grisly were the oaths they swore,
Tearing Christ's blessed body to a shred;
"If we can only catch him, Death is dead!"

349–357 How might the rioters' drinking be affecting their judgment and behavior?

When they had gone not fully half a mile,
Just as they were about to cross a stile,
They came upon a very poor old man
Who humbly greeted them and thus began,
"God look to you, my lords, and give you quiet!"
To which the proudest of these men of riot
Gave back the answer, "What, old fool? Give place!
Why are you all wrapped up except your face?
Why live so long? Isn't it time to die?"

359 stile: a stairway used to climb over a fence or wall.

The old, old fellow looked him in the eye
And said, "Because I never yet have found,
Though I have walked to India, searching round
Village and city on my pilgrimage,
One who would change his youth to have my age.

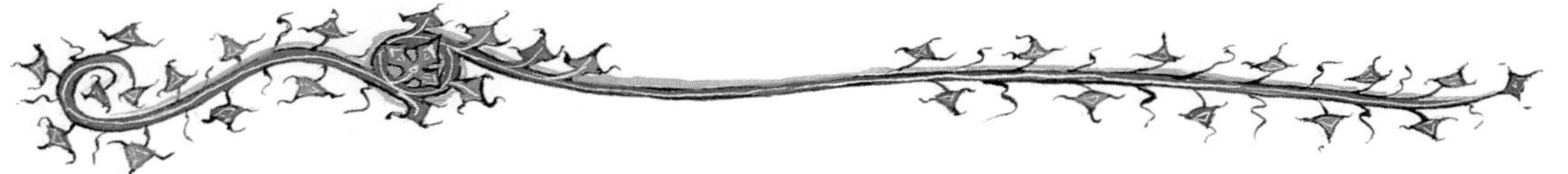

And so my age is mine and must be still
Upon me, for such time as God may will.

"Not even Death, alas, will take my life;
So, like a wretched prisoner at strife
Within himself, I walk alone and wait
About the earth, which is my mother's gate,
Knock-knocking with my staff from night to noon
And crying, 'Mother, open to me soon!
Look at me, mother, won't you let me in?
See how I wither, flesh and blood and skin!
Alas! When will these bones be laid to rest?
Mother, I would exchange—for that were best—
The wardrobe in my chamber, standing there
So long, for yours! Aye, for a shirt of hair
To wrap me in!' She has refused her grace,
Whence comes the pallor of my withered face.

"But it dishonored you when you began
To speak so roughly, sir, to an old man,
Unless he had injured you in word or deed.
It says in holy writ, as you may read,
'Thou shalt rise up before the hoary head
And honor it.' And therefore be it said
'Do no more harm to an old man than you,
Being now young, would have another do
When you are old'—if you should live till then.
And so may God be with you, gentlemen,
For I must go whither I have to go."

"By God," the gambler said, "you shan't do so,
You don't get off so easy, by St. John!
I heard you mention, just a moment gone,
A certain traitor Death who singles out
And kills the fine young fellows hereabout.
And you're his spy, by God! You wait a bit.
Say where he is or you shall pay for it,
By God and by the Holy Sacrament!
I say you've joined together by consent
To kill us younger folk, you thieving swine!"

379–386 The old man addresses the earth as his mother (compare the familiar expressions "Mother Earth" and "Mother Nature").

385 shirt of hair: a rough shirt made of animal hair, worn to punish oneself for one's sins.

392 hoary: gray or white with age.

404–408 What accusations against the old man does the young man make?

WORDS TO KNOW **pallor** (păl′ər) *n.* a lack of color; extreme paleness

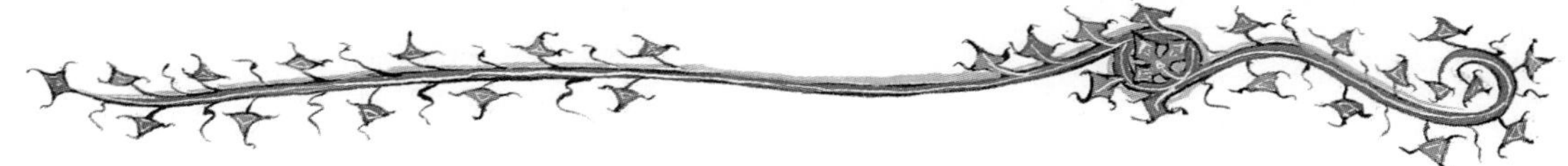

"Well, sirs," he said, "if it be your design
To find out Death, turn up this crooked way
Towards that grove, I left him there today
Under a tree, and there you'll find him waiting.
He isn't one to hide for all your prating.
You see that oak? He won't be far to find.
And God protect you that redeemed mankind,
Aye, and amend you!" Thus that ancient man.

At once the three young rioters began
To run, and reached the tree, and there they found
A pile of golden florins on the ground,
New-coined, eight bushels of them as they thought.
No longer was it Death those fellows sought,
For they were all so thrilled to see the sight,
The florins were so beautiful and bright,
That down they sat beside the precious pile.
The wickedest spoke first after a while.
"Brothers," he said, "you listen to what I say.
I'm pretty sharp although I joke away.
It's clear that Fortune has bestowed this treasure
To let us live in jollity and pleasure.
Light come, light go! We'll spend it as we ought.
God's precious dignity! Who would have thought
This morning was to be our lucky day?

419 florins: coins.

428 "Fortune" here means "fate." Do you think the young men will be blessed by Fortune?

"If one could only get the gold away,
Back to my house, or else to yours, perhaps—
For as you know, the gold is ours, chaps—
We'd all be at the top of fortune, hey?
But certainly it can't be done by day.
People would call us robbers—a strong gang,
So our own property would make us hang.
No, we must bring this treasure back by night
Some prudent way, and keep it out of sight.
And so as a solution I propose
We draw for lots and see the way it goes;
The one who draws the longest, lucky man,
Shall run to town as quickly as he can
To fetch us bread and wine—but keep things dark—
While two remain in hiding here to mark
Our heap of treasure. If there's no delay,

446 keep things dark: act in secret, without giving away what has happened.

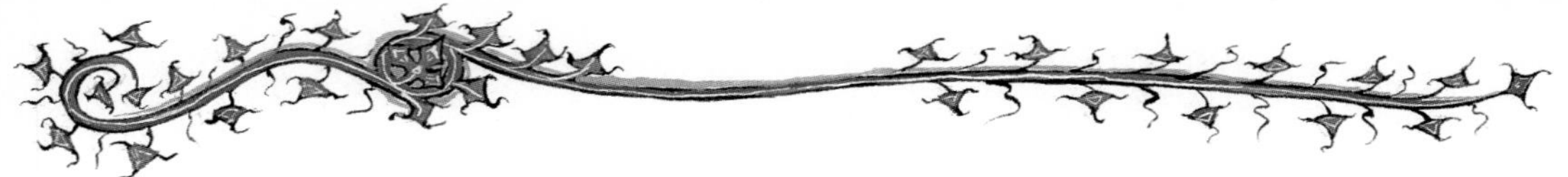

When night comes down we'll carry it away,
All three of us, wherever we have planned."

He gathered lots and hid them in his hand
Bidding them draw for where the luck should fall.
It fell upon the youngest of them all,
And off he ran at once towards the town.

As soon as he had gone the first sat down
And thus began a parley with the other:
"You know that you can trust me as a brother;
Now let me tell you where your profit lies;
You know our friend has gone to get supplies
And here's a lot of gold that is to be
Divided equally amongst us three.
Nevertheless, if I could shape things thus
So that we shared it out—the two of us—
Wouldn't you take it as a friendly act?"

"But how?" the other said. "He knows the fact
That all the gold was left with me and you;
What can we tell him? What are we to do?"

"Is it a bargain," said the first, "or no?
For I can tell you in a word or so
What's to be done to bring the thing about."
"Trust me," the other said, "you needn't doubt
My word. I won't betray you, I'll be true."

"Well," said his friend, "you see that we are two,
And two are twice as powerful as one.
Now look; when he comes back, get up in fun
To have a wrestle; then, as you attack,
I'll up and put my dagger through his back
While you and he are struggling, as in game;
Then draw your dagger too and do the same.
Then all this money will be ours to spend,
Divided equally of course, dear friend.
Then we can gratify our lusts and fill
The day with dicing at our own sweet will."

475–479 What does the young man's plan suggest about human nature and the desire for money?

483 dicing: gambling with dice.

WORDS TO KNOW

parley (păr′lē) *n.* a discussion or conference

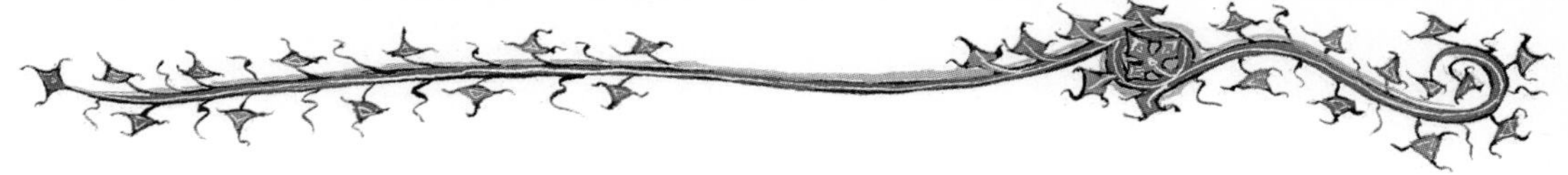

Thus these two miscreants agreed to slay
The third and youngest, as you heard me say.

The youngest, as he ran towards the town,
Kept turning over, rolling up and down
Within his heart the beauty of those bright
New florins, saying, "Lord, to think I might
Have all that treasure to myself alone!
Could there be anyone beneath the throne
Of God so happy as I then should be?"

And so the Fiend, our common enemy,
Was given power to put it in his thought
That there was always poison to be bought,
And that with poison he could kill his friends.
To men in such a state the Devil sends
Thoughts of this kind, and has a full permission
To lure them on to sorrow and perdition;
For this young man was utterly content
To kill them both and never to repent.

And on he ran, he had no thought to tarry,
Came to the town, found an apothecary
And said, "Sell me some poison if you will,
I have a lot of rats I want to kill
And there's a polecat too about my yard
That takes my chickens and it hits me hard;
But I'll get even, as is only right,
With vermin that destroy a man by night."

The chemist answered, "I've a preparation
Which you shall have, and by my soul's salvation
If any living creature eat or drink
A mouthful, ere he has the time to think,
Though he took less than makes a grain of wheat,
You'll see him fall down dying at your feet;
Yes, die he must, and in so short a while
You'd hardly have the time to walk a mile,
The poison is so strong, you understand."

484 miscreants (mĭs′krē-ənts): evildoers; villains.

493 Fiend: the Devil; Satan.

499 perdition: damnation; hell.

493–501 Why does the Devil have influence over the young man?

503 apothecary (ə-pŏth′ĭ-kĕr′ē): druggist.

The Pardoner, from the Ellesmere Manuscript

WORDS TO KNOW

vermin (vûr′mĭn) *n.* small animals that are destructive or carriers of disease

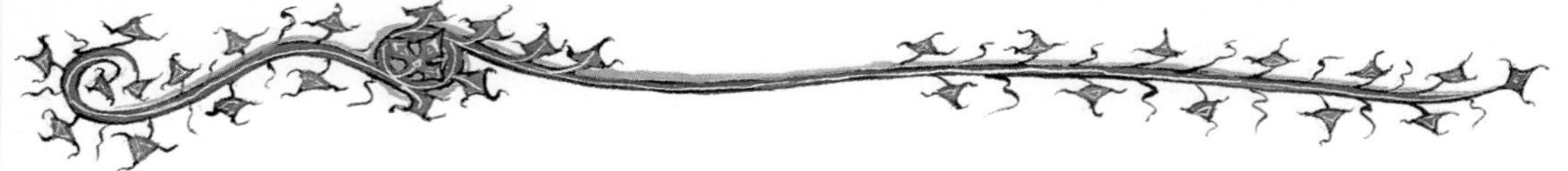

This cursed fellow grabbed into his hand
The box of poison and away he ran
Into a neighboring street, and found a man
Who lent him three large bottles. He withdrew
And deftly poured the poison into two.
He kept the third one clean, as well he might,
For his own drink, meaning to work all night
Stacking the gold and carrying it away.
And when this rioter, this devil's clay,
Had filled his bottles up with wine, all three,
Back to rejoin his comrades sauntered he.

Why make a sermon of it? Why waste breath?
Exactly in the way they'd planned his death
They fell on him and slew him, two to one.
Then said the first of them when this was done,
"Now for a drink. Sit down and let's be merry,
For later on there'll be the corpse to bury."
And, as it happened, reaching for a sup,
He took a bottle full of poison up
And drank; and his companion, nothing loth,
Drank from it also, and they perished both.

538 nothing loth: not at all unwilling.

There is, in Avicenna's long relation
Concerning poison and its operation,
Trust me, no ghastlier section to transcend
What these two wretches suffered at their end.
Thus these two murderers received their due,
So did the treacherous young poisoner too.

540 Avicenna's (ăv′ĭ-sĕn′əz) **long relation:** a medical text written by an 11th-century Islamic physician; it includes descriptions of various poisons and their effects.

544 Why does the Pardoner say that the young men "received their due"?

O cursed sin! O blackguardly excess!
O treacherous homicide! O wickedness!
O gluttony that lusted on and diced!

546 blackguardly: worthy of a scoundrel; villainous.

Dearly beloved, God forgive your sin
And keep you from the vice of avarice!
My holy pardon frees you all of this,
Provided that you make the right approaches,

549 The Pardoner is now addressing his fellow pilgrims.

WORDS TO KNOW

deftly (dĕft′lē) *adv.* in a quick, skillful manner
saunter (sôn′tər) *v.* to walk in a slow and leisurely manner; stroll
transcend (trăn-sĕnd′) *v.* to go beyond; surpass

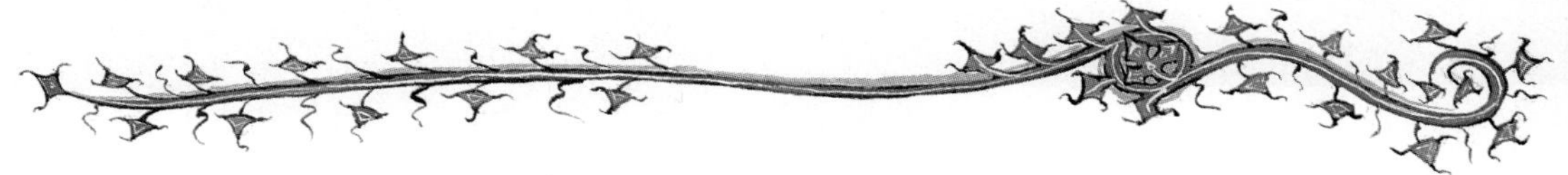

That is with sterling, rings, or silver brooches.
Bow down your heads under this holy bull!
Come on, you women, offer up your wool!
I'll write your name into my ledger; so!
Into the bliss of Heaven you shall go.
For I'll absolve you by my holy power,
You that make offering, clean as at the hour
When you were born. . . . That, sirs, is how I preach.
And Jesu Christ, soul's healer, aye, the leech
Of every soul, grant pardon and relieve you
Of sin, for that is best, I won't deceive you

One thing I should have mentioned in my tale,
Dear people. I've some relics in my bale
And pardons too, as full and fine, I hope,
As any in England, given me by the Pope.
If there be one among you that is willing
To have my absolution for a shilling
Devoutly given, come! and do not harden
Your hearts but kneel in humbleness for pardon;
Or else, receive my pardon as we go.
You can renew it every town or so
Always provided that you still renew
Each time, and in good money, what is due.
It is an honor to you to have found
A pardoner with his credentials sound
Who can absolve you as you ply the spur
In any accident that may occur.
For instance—we are all at Fortune's beck—
Your horse may throw you down and break your neck.
What a security it is to all
To have me here among you and at call
With pardon for the lowly and the great
When soul leaves body for the future state!
And I advise our Host here to begin,
The most enveloped of you all in sin.
Come forward, Host, you shall be the first to pay,
And kiss my holy relics right away.
Only a groat. Come on, unbuckle your purse!"

554 bull: an official document from the pope.

561 leech: physician.

569 absolution (ăb′sə-lo͞o′shən): forgiveness for sins; **shilling:** a coin worth twelve pence.

580–581 The Pardoner reminds the other pilgrims that death may come to them at any time. Why does he emphasize this point?

590 groat: a silver coin worth four pence.

RESPONDING OPTIONS

FROM PERSONAL RESPONSE *TO* CRITICAL ANALYSIS

REFLECT

1. Were you surprised by the ending of "The Pardoner's Tale"? Describe your response in your notebook.

RETHINK

2. Look again at the word webs you created for the Reading Connection on page 87. On the basis of the words and phrases you wrote down, how would you describe your opinions of the Summoner, the Host, and the Pardoner?
3. Why do you think the rioters in "The Pardoner's Tale" set out to kill Death?
   Consider
   - what they learn from the boy and the innkeeper
   - their view of themselves
   - other factors that may influence their judgment
4. Why do you think the character of the old man is included in "The Pardoner's Tale"?
   Consider
   - the story of his life
   - his views about Death
   - his directions for finding Death
5. Do you think the Pardoner's story will encourage the pilgrims to buy indulgences? Why or why not?
6. How would you describe the narrator's values?
   Consider
   - his choosing to characterize people like the Summoner and the Pardoner
   - his opinions of their actions
   - his description of himself as "short of wit" (line 160)

RELATE

7. Are there people in the world today who satisfy their desire for money by taking advantage of the guilt, fear, or ignorance of others? Explain your opinion.

ANOTHER PATHWAY

Write a summary of a contemporary version of "The Prologue." Update the setting, the characters, the destination, and the entertainment in accordance with modern careers and interests.

QUICKWRITES

1. Write a **news article** about the discovery of the rioters' bodies. Include interviews with the old man and with people at the tavern.
2. "The love of money is the root of all evil" is the lesson, or moral, of the tale that the Pardoner tells. Write your own **moral tale** that teaches the same lesson.
3. Write a Chaucerian **character sketch** of a friend or acquaintance, keeping in mind the techniques of characterization discussed in the Reading Connection on page 87.

PORTFOLIO *Save your writing. You may want to use it later as a springboard to a piece for your portfolio.*

LITERARY CONCEPTS

The **tone** of a literary work is the writer's expression of his or her attitude toward the work's subject. For example, the tone of a work might be described as serious, humorous, sarcastic, playful, bitter, or objective. The writer's choice of words and details helps establish the tone. In "The Prologue," Chaucer's restrained and detached tone accounts for much of the piece's humor. Instead of vehemently attacking the scoundrels of his age for their greed and hypocrisy, he speaks in an ironic, subdued voice that allows the reader to form his or her own conclusions. With a small group of classmates, go back through the excerpts from "The Prologue," "The Pardoner's Prologue," and "The Pardoner's Tale" and list key words and phrases that, in your opinion, help establish Chaucer's tone. Then choose a passage that your group thinks is especially effective in conveying humor.

CRITIC'S CORNER

One critic has described Chaucer as "a modern writer," one at home with every generation of readers. Do you agree with this observation? Support your answer with examples from the selection.

ACROSS THE CURRICULUM

History Write a brief research paper on the plague that spread through Europe in the mid-14th century. Include information about its origins and its effects on European life and culture. Be sure to document your sources.

ALTERNATIVE ACTIVITIES

1. Design a **poster** advertising the pilgrimage to Canterbury. You may use a computer to design your poster, or you could cut out words and pictures from magazines or even draw it by hand.
2. Imagine a live performance of "The Pardoner's Tale." Find or draw **costume sketches** to show how the characters might be dressed.
3. Chaucer's stories, written before the invention of the printing press, circulated in handmade manuscripts. Some of these manuscripts were embellished by artists, who added drawings and designs that explain or decorate the tales. Such manuscripts are said to be illuminated. Look at the page from an illuminated manuscript at the beginning of this selection. Then create your own **illuminated manuscript** of the first page of "The Prologue."

WORDS TO KNOW

Answer the following questions, and give reasons for your answers.

1. If the pilgrims were in a hurry, would they **saunter** to Canterbury?
2. Would a man accused of **avarice** be likely to count his money regularly?
3. Would guests at an inn be likely to order **vermin** and wine for dinner?
4. Might a good soldier be expected to **wield** a weapon?
5. If the Pardoner gave all his money to the church, would he be demonstrating **covetousness?**
6. Would you expect an **adversary** to disagree with you?
7. Could a **parley** lead to peace between warring countries?
8. If the rioters mistrusted one another, would you expect them to be **wary?**
9. Would the rosy-faced Summoner be said to exhibit **pallor?**
10. If the Host decided that the Pardoner's story was the best of all, would he have judged the story to **transcend** the others?
11. If the Host poured wine **deftly,** would you expect him to spill it?
12. Would a fashionable pilgrim dress according to the **mode?**
13. Is bad weather something that might **defer** a pilgrim's journey?
14. Would the greedy rioters look upon a pot of gold with **disdain?**
15. Would you be likely to **castigate** an author whose books you enjoy reading?

GEOFFREY CHAUCER

1343?–1400

The man who is often called the father of English poetry led a life almost as interesting as his writing. Geoffrey Chaucer was born into London's growing middle class. His father prepared him for a life of service to kings and nobles, and while still a teenager, Chaucer became an attendant to the king's daughter-in-law. It was probably during this time that he met his future wife, Philippa, who also served the royal family.

Although little is known about Chaucer's education, his writing indicates that he read and spoke French, Italian, and Latin, as well as his native Middle English. Through reading and travel, Chaucer learned about European literature and culture. In Italy in the 1370s, he became acquainted with the works of Dante, Petrarch, and Boccaccio, which were to influence his later poetry.

Chaucer held many jobs during his life. As a young man, he fought against France in an unsuccessful siege during the Hundred Years' War. Taken prisoner, he was later released when his ransom was paid, in part by the king. Back in England, he became a royal courtier, representing the king on important diplomatic missions to Flanders, France, Italy, and Spain. Chaucer also served as a controller of customs, a justice of the peace, a clerk of public works, and a member of Parliament. It is hard to imagine how this busy public servant found time to write.

Chaucer was a brilliant poet who knew how to laugh at human folly without viciousness. He even knew how to laugh at himself; his portrayal of himself as one of the Canterbury pilgrims is of a short, plump, slightly foolish man who commands no great respect. This plump and gentle poet gave the world some of the finest poetry and most memorable characters ever created in the English language.

LASERLINKS
• *AUTHOR BACKGROUND*

PREVIEWING

FICTION

from The Decameron
Federigo's Falcon

Giovanni Boccaccio (jō-vä′nē bō-kä′chē-ō′)

PERSONAL CONNECTION

In this story, Boccaccio tells about a man who makes great sacrifices for the woman he loves. Share examples of sacrifices for love that you have heard of or read about. What were the results of these sacrifices?

CULTURAL CONNECTION

Boccaccio lived in the 14th century, during the Italian Renaissance—a time of great achievements in art, music, and literature. Like Chaucer's *Canterbury Tales, The Decameron* is a collection of tales set within a frame story. The frame, or outer story, is about ten characters who flee to the country to escape a plague that is ravaging Florence, Italy. For ten days they amuse themselves by telling stories, each day selecting a person to serve as a "king" or "queen" who presides over the storytelling. Their 100 tales make up the bulk of *The Decameron.* As this selection begins, a lady named Filomena has just finished telling a story, and the queen of the day decides that it is time to tell her own story.

"Federigo's Falcon" is a tale of courtly love. In medieval times, marriages were arranged for reasons of wealth or position rather than love. As a result, couples sometimes looked outside marriage for romantic attachments. This practice was not considered scandalous as long as the love remained idealized. Federigo, a man of noble birth, is devoted to a married woman, Monna Giovanna (mō′nä jō′vä′nä), and will sacrifice anything to impress her and gain her love.

READING CONNECTION

Plotting Cause and Effect In a well-crafted story, a single event often starts a chain reaction: the event has an effect that becomes the cause of still another effect and so on. As you read this story about love and its sacrifices, try to keep track of the causes and effects by making a diagram like the one started here.

Federigo falls in love with Monna Giovanna.

↓

He spends all of his money to impress her.

↓

He is left with nothing but a small farm and his falcon.

↓

[ ]

LASERLINKS
• CULTURAL CONNECTION

GIOVANNI BOCCACCIO

Filomena had already finished speaking, and when the Queen saw there was no one left to speak except for Dioneo,[1] who was exempted because of his special privilege, she herself with a cheerful face said:

It is now my turn to tell a story and, dearest ladies, I shall do so most willingly with a tale similar in some respects to the preceding one, its purpose being not only to show you how much power your beauty has over the gentle heart, but also so that you yourselves may learn, whenever it is fitting, to be the donors of your favors instead of always leaving this act to the whim of Fortune,[2] who, as it happens, on most occasions bestows such favors with more abundance than discretion.

You should know, then, that Coppo di Borghese Domenichi,[3] who once lived in our city and perhaps still does, a man of great and respected authority in our times, one most illustrious and worthy of eternal fame both for his way of life and his ability much more than for the nobility of his blood, often took delight, when he was an old man, in discussing things from the past with his neighbors and with others. He knew how to do this well, for he was more logical and had a better memory and a more eloquent style of speaking than any other man. Among the many beautiful tales he told, there was one he would often tell about a young man who once lived in Florence named Federigo, the son of Messer Filippo Alberighi,[4] renowned above all other men in Tuscany for his prowess in arms and for his courtliness.

As often happens to most men of gentle breeding, he fell in love, with a noble lady named Monna Giovanna, in her day considered to be one of the most beautiful and most charming ladies that ever there was in Florence; and in order to win her love, he participated in jousts and tournaments, organized and gave banquets, spending his money without restraint; but she, no less virtuous than beautiful, cared little for these things he did on her behalf, nor did she care for the one who did them. Now, as Federigo was spending far beyond his means and getting nowhere, as can easily happen, he lost his wealth and was reduced to poverty, and was left with nothing to his name but his little farm (from whose revenues he lived very meagerly) and one falcon, which was among the finest of its kind in the world.

More in love than ever, but knowing that he would never be able to live the way he wished to in the city, he went to live at Campi, where his farm was. There he passed his time hawking whenever he could, imposing on no one, and enduring his poverty patiently. Now one day, during the time that Federigo was reduced to these extremes, it happened that the husband of Monna Giovanna fell ill, and realizing death was near, he made his last will: he was very rich, and he left everything to his son, who was just

---

1. **Dioneo** (dē′ô-nā′ō).
2. **Fortune:** a personification of the power that supposedly distributes good and bad luck to people.
3. **Coppo di Borghese Domenichi** (kôp′pō dē bōr-gā′zĕ dō-mĕ′nē-kē).
4. **Messer Filippo Alberighi** (mās′sĕr fē-lēp′pō äl′bĕ-rē′gē).

WORDS TO KNOW

discretion (dĭ-skrĕsh′ən) *n.* a sense of carefulness and restraint in one's actions or words

meagerly (mē′gər-lē) *adv.* poorly; scantily

La Pia de Tolommei (1868–1880), Dante Gabriel Rossetti. Oil on canvas, Spencer Museum of Art, University of Kansas.

growing up, and since he had also loved Monna Giovanna very much, he made her his heir should his son die without any legitimate children; and then he died.

Monna Giovanna was now a widow, and every summer, as our women usually do, she would go to the country with her son to one of their estates very close by to Federigo's farm. Now this young boy of hers happened to become more and more friendly with Federigo and he began to enjoy birds and dogs; and after seeing Federigo's falcon fly many times, it made him so happy that he very much wished it were his own, but he did not dare to ask for it, for he could see how precious it was to Federigo. During this time, it happened that the young boy took ill, and his mother was much grieved, for he was her only child and she loved him dearly; she would spend the entire day by his side, never ceasing to comfort him, asking him time and again if there was anything he wished, begging him to tell her what it might be, for if it was possible to obtain

WORDS TO KNOW

legitimate (lə-jĭt'ə-mĭt) *adj.* born of parents who are legally married to each other

She knew that Federigo had been in love with her for some time now.

it, she would certainly do everything in her power to get it. After the young boy had heard her make this offer many times, he said:

"Mother, if you can arrange for me to have Federigo's falcon, I think I would get well quickly."

When the lady heard this, she was taken aback for a moment, and then she began thinking what she could do about it. She knew that Federigo had been in love with her for some time now, but she had never deigned to give him a second look; so, she said to herself:

"How can I go to him, or even send someone, and ask for this falcon of his, which is, as I have heard tell, the finest that ever flew, and furthermore, his only means of support? And how can I be so insensitive as to wish to take away from this nobleman the only pleasure which is left to him?"

And involved in these thoughts, knowing that she was certain to have the bird if she asked for it, but not knowing what to say to her son, she stood there without answering him. Finally the love she bore her son persuaded her that she should make him happy, and no matter what the consequences might be, she would not send for the bird, but rather go herself to fetch it and bring it back to him; so she answered her son:

"My son, cheer up and think only of getting well, for I promise you that first thing tomorrow morning I shall go and fetch it for you."

The child was so happy that he showed some improvement that very day. The following morning, the lady, accompanied by another woman, as if they were out for a stroll, went to Federigo's modest little house and asked for him. Since the weather for the past few days had not been right for hawking, Federigo happened to be in his orchard attending to certain tasks, and when he heard that Monna Giovanna was asking for him at the door, he was so surprised and happy that he rushed there; as she saw him coming, she rose to greet him with womanly grace, and once Federigo had welcomed her most courteously, she said:

"How do you do, Federigo?" Then she continued, "I have come to make amends for the harm you have suffered on my account by loving me more than you should have, and in token of this, I intend to have a simple meal with you and this companion of mine this very day."

To this Federigo humbly replied: "Madonna,[5] I have no recollection of ever suffering any harm because of you; on the contrary: so much good have I received from you that if ever I was worth anything, it was because of your worth and the love I bore for you; and your generous visit is certainly so very dear to me that I would spend all over again all that I spent in the past, but you have come to a poor host."

And having said this, he humbly led her through the house and into his garden, and because he had no one there to keep her company, he said:

"My lady, since there is no one else, this good woman, who is the wife of the farmer here, will keep you company while I see to the table."

Though he was very poor, Federigo until now had never realized to what extent he had wasted his wealth; but this morning, the fact that he had nothing in the house with which he could honor the lady for the love of whom he had in the past entertained countless people, gave him cause to reflect: in great anguish, he cursed himself and his fortune, and like someone out of his senses he started running here and there throughout the house, but unable to find either money or anything he might be able to pawn, and since it

5. **Madonna:** Italian for "my lady," a polite form of address used in speaking to a married woman. "Monna" is a contraction of this term.

WORDS TO KNOW

deign (dān) *v.* to consider worthy of one's dignity; condescend

anguish (ăng′gwĭsh) *n.* agony

was getting late and he was still very much set on serving this noble lady some sort of meal, but unwilling to turn for help to even his own farmer (not to mention anyone else), he set his eyes upon his good falcon, which was sitting on its perch in a small room, and since he had nowhere else to turn, he took the bird, and finding it plump, he decided that it would be a worthy food for such a lady. So, without giving the matter a second thought, he wrung its neck and quickly gave it to his servant girl to pluck, prepare, and place on a spit to be roasted with care; and when he had set the table with the whitest of tablecloths (a few of which he still had left), he returned, with a cheerful face, to the lady in his garden and announced that the meal, such as he was able to prepare, was ready.

The lady and her companion rose and went to the table together with Federigo, who waited upon them with the greatest devotion, and they ate the good falcon without knowing what it was they were eating. Then, having left the table and spent some time in pleasant conversation, the lady thought it time now to say what she had come to say, and so she spoke these kind words to Federigo:

"Federigo, if you recall your former way of life and my virtue, which you perhaps mistook for harshness and cruelty, I have no doubt at all that you will be amazed by my presumption when you hear what my main reason for coming here is; but if you had children, through whom you might have experienced the power of parental love, I feel certain that you would, at least in part, forgive me. But, just as you have no child, I do have one, and I cannot escape the laws common to all mothers; the force of such laws compels me to follow them, against my own will and against good manners and duty, and to ask of you a gift which I know is most precious to you; and it is naturally so, since your extreme condition has left you no other delight,

Peregrine Falcon. Raja Serfogee of Tanjore Collection, by permission of The British Library.

no other pleasure, no other consolation; and this gift is your falcon, which my son is so taken by that if I do not bring it to him, I fear his sickness will grow so much worse that I may lose him. And therefore I beg you, not because of the love that you bear for me, which does not oblige you in the least, but because of your own nobleness, which you have shown to be greater than that of all others in practicing courtliness, that you be pleased to give it to me, so that I may say that I have saved the life of my son by means of this

WORDS TO KNOW

presumption (prĭ-zŭmp′shən) *n.* bold or outrageous behavior

compel (kəm-pĕl′) *v.* to urge irresistibly; constrain

oblige (ə-blīj′) *v.* to make it one's duty to act

gift, and because of it I have placed him in your debt forever."

When he heard what the lady requested and knew that he could not oblige her because he had given her the falcon to eat, Federigo began to weep in her presence, for he could not utter a word in reply. The lady at first thought his tears were caused more by the sorrow of having to part with the good falcon than by anything else, and she was on the verge of telling him she no longer wished it, but she held back and waited for Federigo's reply once he stopped weeping. And he said:

"My lady, ever since it pleased God for me to place my love in you, I have felt that Fortune has been hostile to me in many ways, and I have complained of her, but all this is nothing compared to what she has just done to me, and I shall never be at peace with her again, when I think how you have come here to my poor home, where, when it was rich, you never deigned to come, and how you requested but a small gift, and Fortune worked to make it impossible for me to give it to you; and why this is so I shall tell you in a few words. When I heard that you, out of your kindness, wished to dine with me, I considered it only fitting and proper, taking into account your excellence and your worthiness, that I should honor you, according to my possibilities, with a more precious food than that which I usually serve to other people. So I thought of the falcon for which you have just asked me and of its value and I judged it a food worthy of you, and this very day I had it roasted and served to you as best I could. But seeing now that you desired it another way, my sorrow in not being able to serve you is so great that never shall I be able to console myself again."

And after he had said this, he laid the feathers, the feet, and the beak of the bird before her as proof. When the lady heard and saw this, she first reproached him for having killed a falcon such as this to serve as a meal to a woman. But then to herself she commended the greatness of his spirit, which no poverty was able, or would be able, to diminish; then, having lost all hope of getting the falcon and thus, perhaps, of improving the health of her son, she thanked Federigo both for the honor paid to her and for his good intentions, and then left in grief to return to her son. To his mother's extreme sorrow, whether in disappointment in not having the falcon or because his illness inevitably led to it, the boy passed from this life only a few days later.

After the period of her mourning and her bitterness had passed, the lady was repeatedly urged by her brothers to remarry, since she was very rich and still young; and although she did not wish to do so, they became so insistent that remembering the worthiness of Federigo and his last act of generosity—that is, to have killed such a falcon to do her honor—she said to her brothers:

"I would prefer to remain a widow, if only that would be pleasing to you, but since you wish me to take a husband, you may be sure that I shall take no man other than Federigo degli Alberighi."

In answer to this, her brothers, making fun of her, replied:

"You foolish woman, what are you saying? How can you want him? He hasn't a penny to his name."

To this she replied: "My brothers, I am well aware of what you say, but I would much rather have a man who lacks money than money that lacks a man."

Her brothers, seeing that she was determined and knowing Federigo to be of noble birth, no matter how poor he was, accepted her wishes and gave her with all her riches in marriage to him; when he found himself the husband of such a great lady, whom he had loved so much and who was so wealthy besides, he managed his financial affairs with more prudence than in the past and lived with her happily the rest of his days. ❖

Translated by Mark Musa and Peter Bondanella

WORDS TO KNOW

reproach (rĭ-prōch') *v.* to express disapproval of or disappointment in

commend (kə-mĕnd') *v.* to express approval of; praise

RESPONDING OPTIONS

FROM PERSONAL RESPONSE *TO* CRITICAL ANALYSIS

REFLECT 1. What is your reaction to the events in this story? Respond in your notebook.

RETHINK 2. Do you think Federigo acts nobly or foolishly?

Consider
- what he sacrifices for love
- how his behavior affects other aspects of his life
- why he is drawn to Monna Giovanna

3. What is your opinion of Monna Giovanna?

Consider
- her response to Federigo's love for her
- her visit to Federigo's house
- her response when Federigo tells her of the bird's fate
- her reason for taking Federigo as her husband

4. What do you think is the most important message about human nature conveyed by this story? Explain your answer.

RELATE 5. In Boccaccio's time, women of Monna Giovanna's social class were expected to be married. Do women today feel the same pressure to marry? Are women and men under equal pressure to marry? Support your opinions with examples.

ANOTHER PATHWAY

If "Federigo's Falcon" were told from a contemporary perspective, how would the story be different? Rewrite the story from the point of view of either a man or a woman in today's society, then compare your story with a classmate's. Discuss how each differs from Boccaccio's story.

QUICKWRITES

1. Monna Giovanna says that she would "much rather have a man who lacks money than money that lacks a man." In a brief **paragraph,** give your interpretation and opinion of her statement.
2. Imagine Monna Giovanna's feelings when she discovers that she has dined on the falcon. Write a **diary entry** that she might compose to express her thoughts and feelings about the incident.
3. In a draft of an **essay,** compare and contrast your own views about love and marriage with those of either Federigo or Monna Giovanna. Include specific examples from the story and from your own observations.

PORTFOLIO *Save your writing. You may want to use it later as a springboard to a piece for your portfolio.*

LITERARY CONCEPTS

The **plot** of a literary work consists of all the actions and events in the work. A plot moves forward because of a **conflict**—a struggle between opposing forces. Most plots share four basic elements. In the **exposition,** the characters are introduced, the setting is established, and the major conflict is identified. In the **rising action,** suspense builds as the conflict intensifies and complications arise. The **climax,** or turning point, is the high point of the action, often occurring when a main character makes an important discovery or decision. Events that follow the climax, known as the **falling action,** show the results of the climax and tie up loose ends of the plot. Use the cause-and-effect diagram you made for the Reading Connection on page 109 to help you decide which events make up the exposition, the rising action, the climax, and the falling action of "Federigo's Falcon." Discuss your decisions with several of your classmates.

CRITIC'S CORNER

One critic has called "Federigo's Falcon" the "bare outline" of a story, suggesting that its effect on the reader might be different if the characters were developed more completely. Do you agree? Why or why not?

ALTERNATIVE ACTIVITIES

1. Think of the perfect wedding gift from Federigo to Monna Giovanna or from Monna Giovanna to Federigo. Then create the **gift** itself, or make a **model** or **illustration** of it. Keep in mind the giver's personality and financial status.
2. With a classmate, create a **pantomime** depicting Monna Giovanna's visit to Federigo's home. Make sure that your facial expressions and gestures reflect emotions appropriate to the actions.

ACROSS THE CURRICULUM

Science Find out more about falcons and falconry. How does a falcon go after its prey? How is a falcon trapped and trained for sport?

History Prepare an oral report on the traditions of courtly love during the Middle Ages and the Italian Renaissance. Include information on what men did to woo their ladies and how the ladies were expected to respond. You might even suggest other things Federigo might have done to win Monna Giovanna's love.

WORDS TO KNOW

EXERCISE A Classify the words in each of the following pairs as synonyms or antonyms.

1. legitimate—lawful
2. commend—blame
3. compel—force
4. reproach—compliment
5. discretion—recklessness
6. presumption—impudence
7. oblige—release
8. anguish—sorrow
9. meagerly—abundantly
10. deign—refuse

EXERCISE B Work with a small group of classmates to devise a game show, using the vocabulary words as either clues or answers. Think about popular game shows you have seen to help you decide on a format. From your group, pick a host, a helper, and judges, then play your game with the class.

GIOVANNI BOCCACCIO

1313–1375

Although Giovanni Boccaccio began writing poetry as a child, his early talent was not rewarded. Instead, his merchant father demanded that his son forget about writing and learn business. While still a teenager, he was sent from his home in Tuscany to Naples, where he was apprenticed to a banker. When he failed at banking, his father arranged for him to study religious law. Boccaccio was unsuccessful at law too, and after about 12 years in Naples, he returned home to seek other employment. None of his jobs were very satisfactory, however, and he often lived on the brink of poverty.

Fortunately, Boccaccio had continued to write in spite of his father's objections, and even during his unsuccessful venture in Naples, he produced an abundance of prose and poetry. It was also in Naples that he may have met his beloved "Fiammetta," a young lady who became the subject of much of his early writing and whose name he used for the narrator of "Federigo's Falcon" in *The Decameron*. The real identity of this woman has never been discovered.

Boccaccio complained that because his father "strove to bend" his talent, he was unable to become "a distinguished poet." Eventually, of course, he did achieve distinction as a great poet, storyteller, and scholar. Along with his friend Petrarch, an Italian poet whose writings you will encounter in Unit Two, Boccaccio helped to set new directions for Italian literature and for the study of the classical poets of ancient Rome. With the publication of *The Decameron,* he became an international celebrity. In addition to his contemporary Chaucer, many later poets writing in English—including Shakespeare, Dryden, Keats, Longfellow, and Tennyson—have been influenced by his work.

LASERLINKS
• *SCIENCE CONNECTION*

PREVIEWING

NONFICTION

from The Paston Letters

The Paston Family

PERSONAL CONNECTION

List the different methods you use to communicate with other people. Also list the kinds of information you exchange by each of the methods. Which method do you use most often? Might one form of communication be better than the others in a particular instance? Share your thoughts with classmates.

HISTORICAL CONNECTION

In England, the 15th century was a period of great unrest and lawlessness. Landowners often attacked their neighbors' estates and betrayed their political allies. The Wars of the Roses, a conflict between two royal families for control of the kingdom, ravaged England between 1455 and 1485. In addition, several outbreaks of the plague devastated many English families during the century.

A firsthand record of this turbulent era survives in the more than 1,000 surviving documents and letters of the Pastons, an English landowning family. During the early 1400s, William Paston, a lawyer, began accumulating property in Norfolk, a county of eastern England, both through purchases and through his acquisition of estates inherited by his wife, Agnes Berry. William's extensive landholdings and growing prosperity, however, made him a number of enemies. Some even challenged his claim to certain properties and brought grief to William's descendants for many years.

In their letters, the Pastons exchanged information about their legal disputes and other problems in considerable detail. Although writing letters had become an important means of communication by the 15th century, sending the letters was not easy. They had to be delivered by hand, often by a servant or even a total stranger. Weeks might pass before a letter reached its destination, and many never arrived. Consequently, the matters discussed in letters were seldom frivolous, usually being confined to important business or family news. Despite these limitations, the Pastons wrote hundreds of letters over the course of 90 years, leaving an invaluable source of information about the social and political conditions of the times.

READING CONNECTION

Using Graphic Devices

A graphic device can present information in a way that helps make a subject understandable. The graphic device on this page is a family tree. It shows the genealogy—that is, the relationships of birth and descent—of three generations of the Paston family. Before you read the letters, take some time to study these relationships. (The names in boldface type are those of the writers and recipients of the letters you will read.)

Notice that William Paston and Agnes Berry had five children. The oldest, John I, inherited much of the family property when his father died in 1444, and his marriage to Margaret Mautby led to the acquisition of even more property from his wife's family. Like his father, John I was a lawyer, possessed of skills that were much needed in his constant legal battles over claims to various properties. His many legal disputes required John I to stay in London for long periods of time, leaving Margaret to manage the Paston estates. Notice also that John and Margaret's large family included two sons named John. After the death of John I, his oldest son, John II, became responsible for much of the family business, even though Margaret was still living.

As you read the letters, refer often to the Paston family tree. Doing so may help you keep in mind that the people who communicated through these letters were real human beings who had many of the same needs, hopes, and fears that people have today.

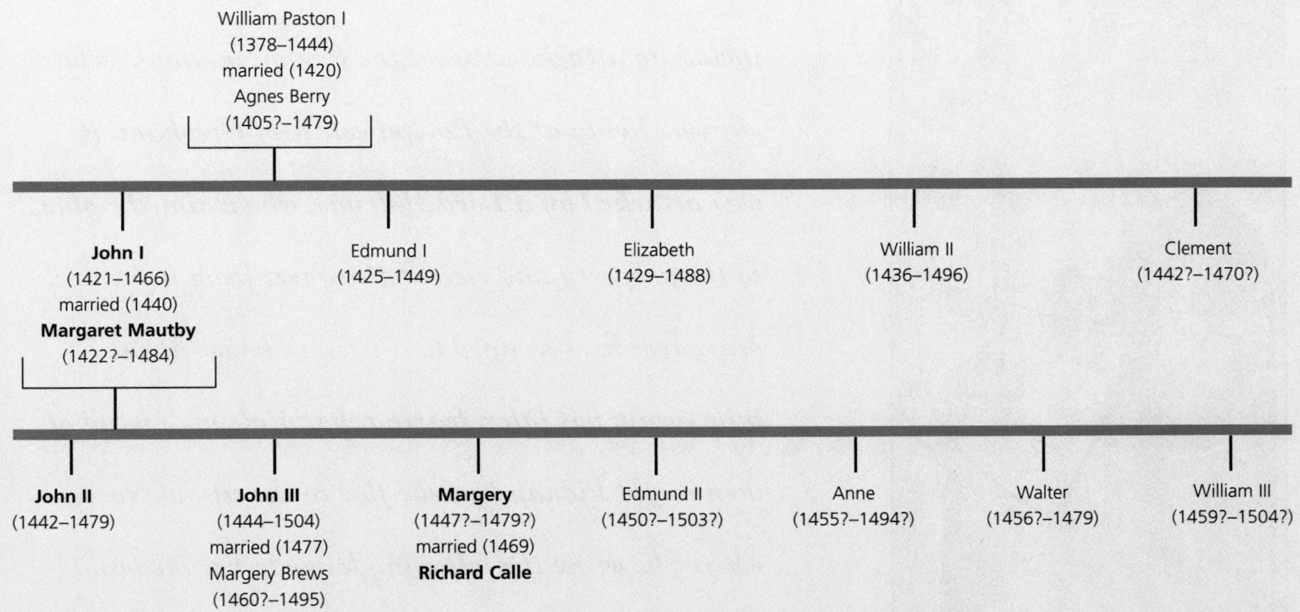

Women defending castle

from THE PASTON LETTERS

Margaret Paston, in the absence of her husband, John I, was able to deal equally well with small housekeeping problems and with family disasters, including attacks against the Paston manors. While she was living at the Paston estate of Gresham, it was attacked by a Lord Moleyns, who claimed rights to the property and ejected Margaret from her home. Margaret first escaped to a friend's house about a mile away; but later, fearing that Moleyns's band of men might kidnap her, she fled to the city of Norwich, where she wrote the following letter to her husband.

Margaret to John I

28 February 1449

Right worshipful husband, I commend myself to you, wishing with all my heart to hear that you are well, and begging that you will not be angry at my leaving the place where you left me. On my word, such news was brought to me by various people who are sympathetic to you and me that I did not dare stay there any longer. I will tell you who the people were when you come home. They let me know that various of Lord Moleyns' men said that if they could get their hands on me they would carry me off and keep me in the castle. They wanted you to get me out again, and said that it would not cause you much heart-ache. After I heard this news, I could not rest easy until I was here, and I did not dare go out of the place where I was until I was ready to ride away. Nobody in the place knew that I was leaving except the lady of the house, until an hour before I went. And I told her that I would come here to have clothes made for myself and the children, which I wanted made, and said I thought I would be here a fortnight[1] or three weeks. Please keep the reason for my departure a secret until I talk to you, for those who warned me do not on any account want it known.

I spoke to your mother as I came this way, and she offered to let me stay in this town, if you agree. She would very much like us to stay at her place, and will send me such things as she can spare so that I can set up house until you can get a place and things of your own to set up a household. Please let me know by the man who brings this what you would like me to do. I would be very unhappy to live so close to Gresham as I was until this matter is completely settled between you and Lord Moleyns.

Barow[2] told me that there was no better evidence in England than that Lord Moleyns has for [his title to] the manor of Gresham. I told him that I supposed the evidence was of the kind that William Hasard said yours was, and that the seals were not yet cold.[3] That, I said, was what I expected his lord's evidence to be like. I said I knew that your evidence was such that no one could have better evidence, and the seals on it were two hundred years older than he was. Then Barow said to me that if he came to London while you were there he would have a drink with you, to quell any anger there was between you. He said that he only acted as a servant, and as he was ordered to do. Purry[4] will tell you about the conversation between Barow and me when I came from Walsingham. I beg you with all my heart, for reverence of God, beware of Lord Moleyns and his men, however pleasantly they speak to you, and do not eat or drink with them; for they are so false that they cannot be trusted. And please take care when you eat or drink in any other men's company, for no one can be trusted.

I beg you with all my heart that you will be kind enough to send me word how you are, and how your affairs are going, by the man who brings this. I am very surprised that you do not send me more news than you have done. . . .

---

1. **fortnight:** two weeks.
2. **Barow:** one of Lord Moleyns's men.
3. **seals . . . cold:** A seal, often made by impressing a family emblem on hot wax, was placed on a document to show its authenticity. Margaret is suggesting that Lord Moleyns's documents are recent forgeries.
4. **Purry:** perhaps a servant or tenant of the Pastons.

In 1465, in still another property dispute, the Paston estate of Hellesdon was attacked by the duke of Suffolk, who had gained the support of several local officials. Although Margaret and John were not living at Hellesdon at the time, many of their servants and tenants suffered from the extensive damage. In the following two letters, Margaret tells her husband about the devastation.

Margaret to John I

17 October 1465

. . . On Tuesday morning John Botillere, also John Palmer, Darcy Arnald your cook and William Malthouse of Aylsham were seized at Hellesdon by the bailiff[5] of Eye, called Bottisforth, and taken to Costessey,[6] and they are being kept there still without any warrant or authority from a justice of the peace; and they say they will carry them off to Eye prison and as many others of your men and tenants as they can get who are friendly towards you or have supported you, and they threaten to kill or imprison them.

The duke came to Norwich at 10 o'clock on Tuesday with five hundred men and he sent for the mayor, aldermen and sheriffs, asking them in the king's name that they should enquire of the constables of every ward within the city which men had been on your side or had helped or supported your men at the time of any of these gatherings and if they could find any they should take them and arrest them and punish them; which the mayor did, and will do anything he can for him and his men. At this the mayor has arrested a man who was with me, called Robert Lovegold, a brazier,[7] and threatened him that he shall be hanged by the neck. So I would be glad if you could get a writ sent down for his release, if you think it can be done. He was only with me when Harlesdon[8] and others attacked me at Lammas.[9] He is very true and faithful to you, so I would like him to be helped. I have no one attending me who dares to be known, except Little John. William Naunton is here with me, but he dares not be known because he is much threatened. I am told that the old lady and the duke have been frequently set against us by what Harlesdon, the bailiff of Costessey, Andrews and Doget the bailiff's son and other false villains have told them, who want this affair pursued for their own pleasure; there are evil rumors about it in this part of the world and other places.

As for Sir John Heveningham, Sir John Wyndefeld and other respectable men, they have been made into their catspaws,[10] which will not do their reputation any good after this, I think. . . .

The lodge and remainder of your place was demolished on Tuesday and Wednesday, and the duke rode on Wednesday to Drayton and then to Costessey while the lodge at Hellesdon was being demolished. Last night at midnight Thomas Slyford, Green, Porter and John Bottisforth the bailiff of Eye and others got a cart and took away the featherbeds and all the stuff of ours that was left at the parson's and Thomas Water's house for safe-keeping. I will send you lists later, as accurately as I can, of the things we have lost. Please let me know what you want me to do, whether you want me to stay at Caister[11] or come to you in London.

I have no time to write any more. God have you in his keeping. Written at Norwich on St. Luke's eve.[12]

M.P.

---

5. **bailiff:** the manager of an estate.
6. **Costessey:** an estate owned by the duke of Suffolk.
7. **brazier** (brā′zhər): person who makes articles of brass.
8. **Harlesdon:** one of the duke of Suffolk's men.
9. **Lammas:** a religious feast that was celebrated on August 1.
10. **catspaws:** people who are deceived and used as tools by others.
11. **Caister:** one of the Paston estates.
12. **St. Luke's eve:** the eve of St. Luke's Day, a religious feast. Writers often dated letters in this way instead of using days and months.

Margaret to John I

27 October 1465

. . . I was at Hellesdon last Thursday and saw the place there, and indeed no one can imagine what a horrible mess it is unless they see it. Many people come out each day, both from Norwich and elsewhere, to look at it, and they talk of it as a great shame. The duke would have done better to lose £1000 than to have caused this to be done, and you have all the more goodwill from people because it has been done so foully. And they made your tenants at Hellesdon and Drayton, and others, help them to break down the walls of both the house and the lodge: God knows, it was against their will, but they did not dare do otherwise for fear. I have spoken with your tenants both at Hellesdon and Drayton, and encouraged them as best I can.

The duke's men ransacked the church, and carried off all the goods that were left there, both ours and the tenants, and left little behind; they stood on the high altar and ransacked the images, and took away everything they could find. They shut the parson out of the church until they had finished, and ransacked everyone's house in the town five or six times. The ringleaders in the thefts were the bailiff of Eye and the bailiff of Stradbroke, Thomas Slyford. And Slyford was the leader in robbing the church and, after the bailiff of Eye, it is he who has most of the proceeds of the robbery. As for the lead, brass, pewter, iron, doors, gates, and other household stuff, men from Costessey and Cawston have got it, and what they could not carry they hacked up in the most spiteful fashion. If possible, I would like some reputable men to be sent for from the king, to see how things are both there and at the lodge, before any snows come, so that they can report the truth, because otherwise it will not be so plain as it is now. For reverence of God, finish your business now, for the expense and trouble we have each day is horrible, and it will be like this until you have finished; and your men dare not go around collecting your rents, while we keep here every day more than twenty people to save ourselves and the place; for indeed, if the place had not been strongly defended, the duke would have come here. . . .

For the reverence of God, if any respectable and profitable method can be used to settle your business, do not neglect it, so that we can get out of these troubles and the great costs and expenses we have and may have in future. It is thought here that if my lord of Norfolk would act on your behalf, and got a commission to enquire into the riots and robberies committed on you and others in this part of the world, then the whole county will wait on him and do as you wish, for people love and respect him more than any other lord, except the king and my lord of Warwick. . . .

Please do let me know quickly how you are and how your affairs are going, and let me know how your sons are. I came home late last night, and will be here until I hear from you again. Wykes came home on Saturday, but he did not meet your sons.

God have you in his keeping and send us good news from you. Written in haste on the eve of St. Simon and St. Jude.

By yours, M.P.

During the fifteenth century, most marriages among the upper classes were arranged by families, usually to strengthen economic or political ties. The Paston family was greatly alarmed, therefore, when they learned that Margery, a daughter of Margaret and John I, had secretly become engaged to the Paston bailiff Richard Calle. Eventually, the two were married in spite of bitter opposition from Margery's family. In the following letter to Margery—the only piece of their correspondence to survive—Richard expresses his feelings about their predicament. The next letter is the response of Margery's mother, Margaret, to the situation, written to her son, John II.

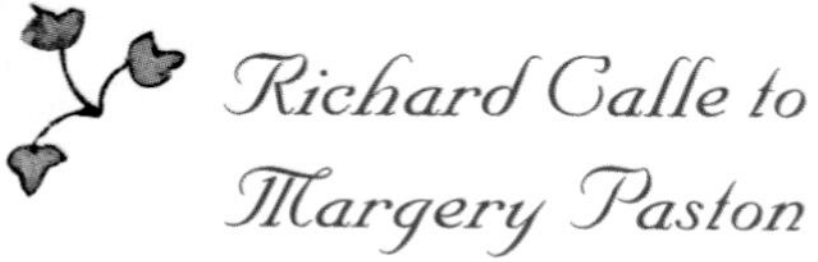

Richard Calle to Margery Paston

Spring-Summer 1469

My own lady and mistress, and indeed my true wife before God,[13] I commend myself to you with a very sad heart as a man who cannot be cheerful and will not be until things stand otherwise with us than they do now. This life that we lead now pleases neither God nor the world, considering the great bond of matrimony that is made between us, and also the great love that has been, and I trust still is, between us, and which for my part was never greater. So I pray that Almighty God will comfort us as soon as it pleases him, for we who ought by rights to be most together are most apart; it seems a thousand years since I last spoke to you. I would rather be with you than all the wealth in the world. Alas, also, good lady, those who keep us apart like this, scarcely realize what they are doing: those who hinder matrimony are cursed in church four times a year. It makes many men think that they can stretch a point of conscience in other matters as well as this one. But whatever happens, lady, bear it as you have done and be as cheerful as you can, for be sure, lady, that God in the long run will of his righteousness help his servants who mean to be true and want to live according to his laws.

I realize, lady, that you have had as much sorrow on my account as any gentlewoman has ever had in this world; I wish to God that all the sorrow you have had had fallen on me, so that you were freed of it; for indeed, lady, it kills me to hear that you are being treated otherwise than you should be. This is a painful life we lead; I cannot imagine that we live like this without God being displeased by it.

You will want to know that I sent you a letter from London by my lad, and he told me he could not speak to you, because so great a watch was kept on both you and him. He told me that John Thresher came to him in your name, and said that you had sent him to my lad for a letter or token which you thought I had sent you; but he did not trust him and would not deliver anything to him. After that he brought a ring, saying that you sent it to him, commanding him to deliver the letter or token to him, which I gather since then from my lad was not sent by you, but was a plot of my mistress [i.e., Margaret Paston] and James Gloys.[14] Alas, what do they intend? I suppose they think we are not engaged; and if this is the case I am very surprised, for they are not being sensible, remembering how plainly I told my mistress about everything at the beginning, and I think you have told her so too, if you have done as you should. And if you have denied it, as I have been told you have done, it was done neither with a good conscience nor to the pleasure of God, unless you did it for fear and to please those who were with you at the time. If this was the reason you did it, it was justified, considering how insistently you were

13. **my true wife before God:** In the 1400's, the spoken vow of a man and woman, even without a witness, was regarded as an official marriage.

14. **James Gloys:** the Paston family chaplain.

called on to deny it; and you were told many untrue stories about me, which, God knows, I was never guilty of.

My lad told me that your mother asked him if he had brought any letter to you, and she accused him falsely of many other things; among other things, she said to him in the end that I would not tell her about it at the beginning, but she expected that I would at the ending. As for that, God knows that she knew about it first from me and no one else. I do not know what my mistress means, for in truth there is no other gentlewoman alive who I respect more than her and whom I would be more sorry to displease, saving only yourself who by right I ought to cherish and love best, for I am bound to do so by God's law and will do so while I live, whatever may come of it. I expect that if you tell them the sober truth, they will not damn their souls for our sake. Even if I tell them the truth they will not believe me as much as they would you. And so, good lady, for reverence of God be plain with them and tell the truth, and if they will not agree, let it be between them, God and the devil; and as for the peril we should be in, I pray God it may lie on them and not on us. I am very sad and sorry when I think of their attitude. God guide them and send them rest and peace.

I am very surprised that they are as concerned about this affair as I gather that they are, in view of the fact that nothing can be done about it, and that I deserve better; from any point of view there should be no obstacles to it. Also their honor does not depend on your marriage, but in their own marriage [i.e., John II's]; I pray God send them a marriage which will be to their honor, to God's pleasure and to their heart's ease, for otherwise it would be a great pity.

Mistress, I am frightened of writing to you, for I understand that you have showed the letters that I have sent you before to others, but I beg you, let no one see this letter. As soon as you have read it, burn it, for I would not want anyone to see it. You have had nothing in writing from me for two years, and I will not send you any more: so I leave everything to your wisdom.

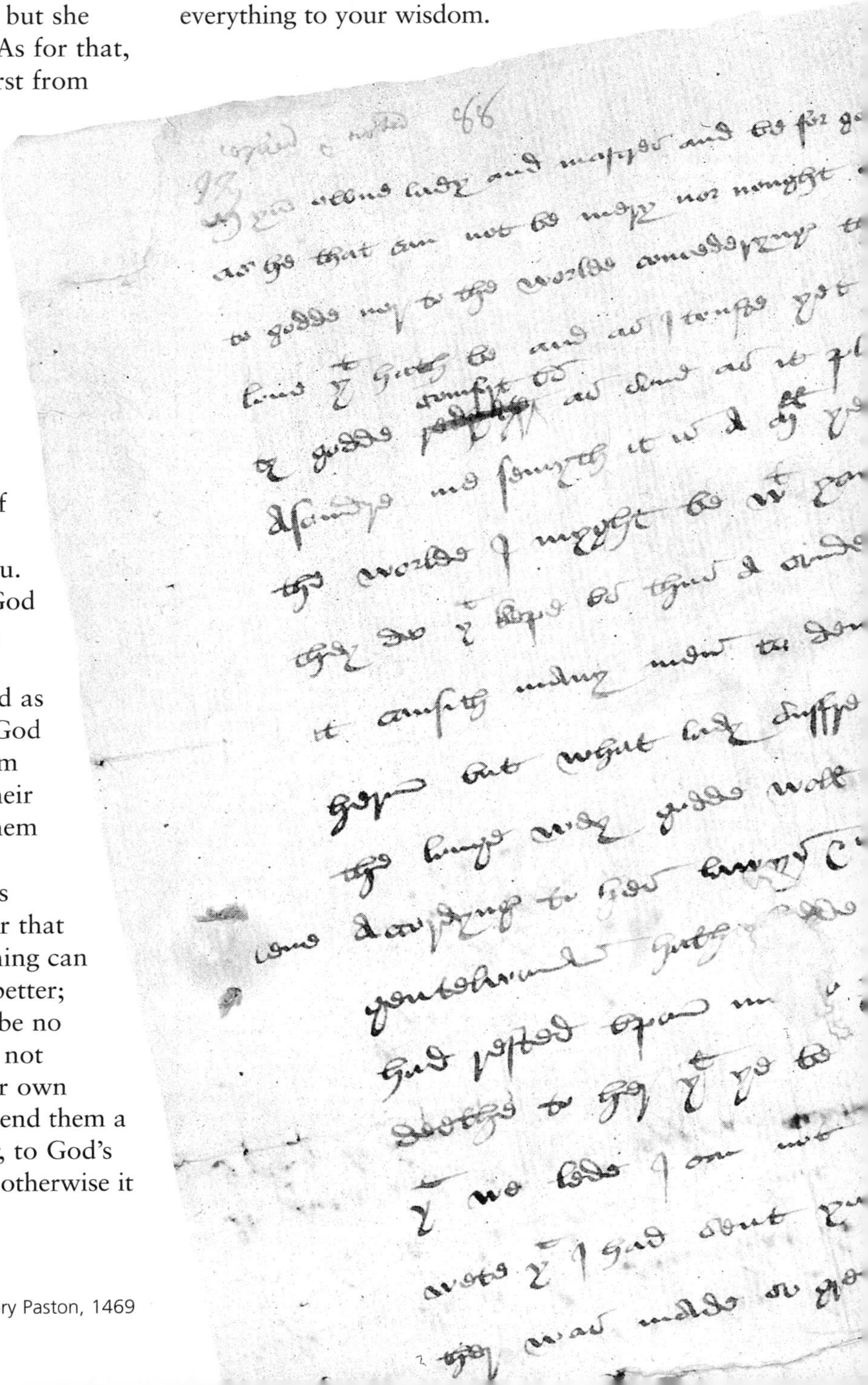

Letter from Richard Calle to Margery Paston, 1469

Almighty Jesu preserve, keep and give you your heart's desire, which I am sure will please God. This letter was written with as great difficulty as I ever wrote anything in my life, for I have been very ill, and am not yet really recovered, may God amend it.

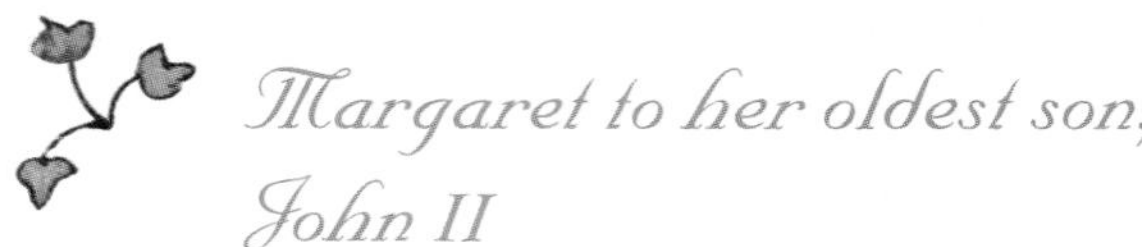

Margaret to her oldest son, John II

10 September 1469

. . . When I heard how she [Margery] had behaved, I ordered my servants that she was not to be allowed in my house. I had warned her, and she might have taken heed if she had been well-disposed. I sent messages to one or two others that they should not let her in if she came. She was brought back to my house to be let in, and James Gloys told those who brought her that I had ordered them all that she should not be allowed in. So my lord of Norwich has lodged her at Roger Best's, to stay there until the day in question; God knows it is much against his will and his wife's, but they dare not do otherwise. I am sorry that they are burdened with her, but I am better off with her there than somewhere else, because he and his wife are sober and well-disposed to us, and she will not be allowed to play the good-for-nothing there.

Please do not take all this too hard, because I know that it is a matter close to your heart, as it is to mine and other people's; but remember, as I do, that we have only lost a good-for-nothing in her, and take it less to heart: if she had been any good, whatever might have happened, things would not have been as they are, for even if he[15] were dead now, she would never be as close to me as she was. . . . You can be sure that she will regret her foolishness afterwards, and I pray to God that she does. Please, for my sake, be cheerful about all this. I trust that God will help us; may he do so in all our affairs. . . .

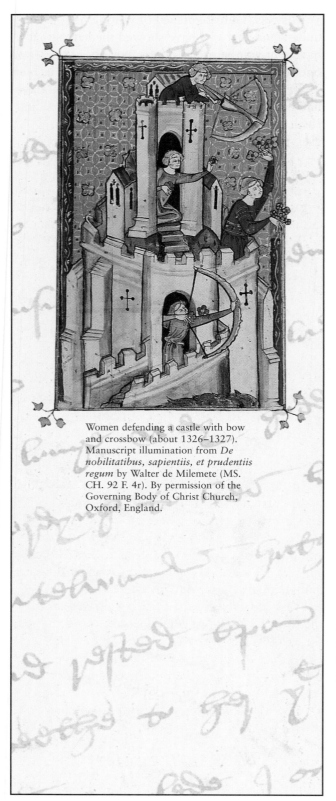

Women defending a castle with bow and crossbow (about 1326–1327). Manuscript illumination from *De nobilitatibus, sapientiis, et prudentiis regum* by Walter de Milemete (MS. CH. 92 F. 4r). By permission of the Governing Body of Christ Church, Oxford, England.

15. **he:** Richard Calle.

Although the Pastons were considered wealthy, they faced continual struggles. They even experienced occasional financial difficulties, particularly after the death of John I in 1466. John II, though frequently in London to deal with family legal matters, seems at times to have paid more attention to his own interests. The Pastons were also affected by the ravages of warfare and disease. The following three letters deal with some of their hardships.

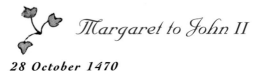

Margaret to John II

28 October 1470

. . . Unless you pay more attention to your expenses, you will bring great shame on yourself and your friends, and impoverish them so that none of us will be able to help each other, to the great encouragement of our enemies.

Those who claim to be your friends in this part of the world realize in what great danger and need you stand, both from various of your friends and from your enemies. It is rumored that I have parted with so much to you that I cannot help either you or any of my friends, which is no honor to us and causes people to esteem us less. At the moment it means that I must disperse my household and lodge somewhere, which I would be very loath to do if I were free to choose. It has caused a great deal of talk in this town and I would not have needed to do it if I had held back when I could. So for God's sake pay attention and be careful from now on, for I have handed over to you both my own property and your father's, and have held nothing back, either for myself or for his sake. . . .

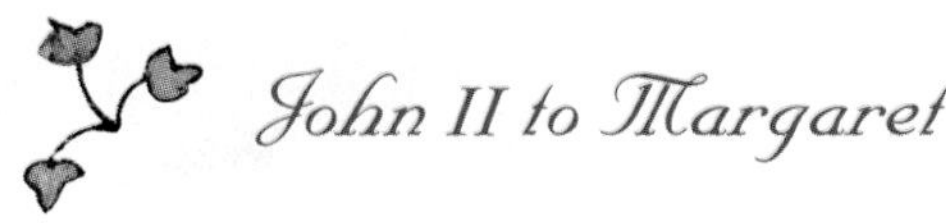

John II to Margaret

April 1471

Mother, I commend myself to you and let you know, blessed be God, my brother John is alive and well, and in no danger of dying. Nevertheless he is badly hurt by an arrow in his right arm below the elbow, and I have sent a surgeon to him, who has dressed the wound; and he tells me that he hopes he will be healed within a very short time. John Mylsent is dead. God have mercy on his soul; William Mylsent is alive and all his other servants seem to have escaped. . . .

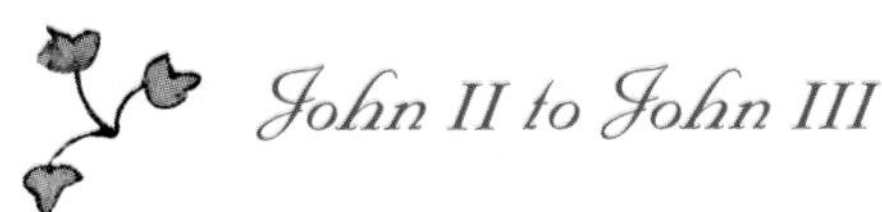

John II to John III

15 September 1471

. . . Please send me word if any of our friends or well-wishers are dead, for I fear that there is great mortality in Norwich and in other boroughs and towns in Norfolk: I assure you that it is the most widespread plague I ever knew of in England, for by my faith I cannot hear of pilgrims going through the country nor of any other man who rides or goes anywhere, that any town or borough in England is free from the sickness. May God put an end to it, when it please him. So, for God's sake, get my mother to take care of my younger brothers and see that they are not anywhere where the sickness is prevalent, and that they do not amuse themselves with other young people who go where the sickness is. If anyone has died of the sickness, or is infected with it, in Norwich, for God's sake let her send them to some friend of hers in the country; I would advise you to do the same. I would rather my mother moved her household into the country. . . . ❖

RESPONDING OPTIONS

FROM PERSONAL RESPONSE *TO* CRITICAL ANALYSIS

REFLECT 1. What do you think of the events described in the Paston family letters? Write down your thoughts in your notebook.

RETHINK 2. How would you describe Margaret Paston?
Consider
- the tone she communicates in her letters
- the nature of her responsibilities
- how she deals with problems
- her relationships with her husband and her children

3. On the basis of your reading of these letters, what qualities or values do you think were important to the Pastons? Give reasons for your answer.

4. What advice might you give Richard Calle and Margery Paston for dealing with their predicament?

RELATE 5. Margaret Paston was forced to take care of family business while her husband was away. How do you think a contemporary businesswoman would view Margaret's handling of these matters?

ANOTHER PATHWAY

Think about the limitations of communicating only through letters. If faster or easier methods of communication had been available to the Pastons, how might their lives have been different? With classmates, conduct a panel discussion in which you explore this question.

LITERARY CONCEPTS

Because of the turbulent times in which the Pastons lived, their letters present a number of **conflicts,** or struggles between opposing forces. In fiction, a conflict usually reaches a point of resolution; in a series of real letters, however, many of the conflicts described may necessarily remain unresolved.

With a group of classmates, go through the letters, creating a list of the various conflicts that are described by each writer. Decide whether each conflict is **external,** pitting a person against an outside force (such as another person, a physical obstacle, nature, or society), or **internal,** occurring within a person. Then choose one conflict and write an imaginative description of how it might have been resolved. If you like, include humor in your description. Share your group's work with the rest of the class.

QUICKWRITES

1. Imagine that you are Margery Paston. Write a **diary entry** in which you express your thoughts about your mother's reaction to your marriage plans.

2. In a **paragraph,** tell which of the persons mentioned in the Paston letters you would trust the most or the least. Explain your choice.

PORTFOLIO *Save your writing. You may want to use it later as a spring-board to a piece for your portfolio.*

ALTERNATIVE ACTIVITIES

1. On the map, locate the estate at Paston. Then use the mileage scale to estimate the distances between Paston and three other estates or towns mentioned in the letters you have read.
2. Research the fashions of 15th-century England. Then make an **illustration** showing clothing that would have been appropriate for a man or woman of the Paston family.
3. With several other students, give a short **dramatic presentation** of one of the letters.

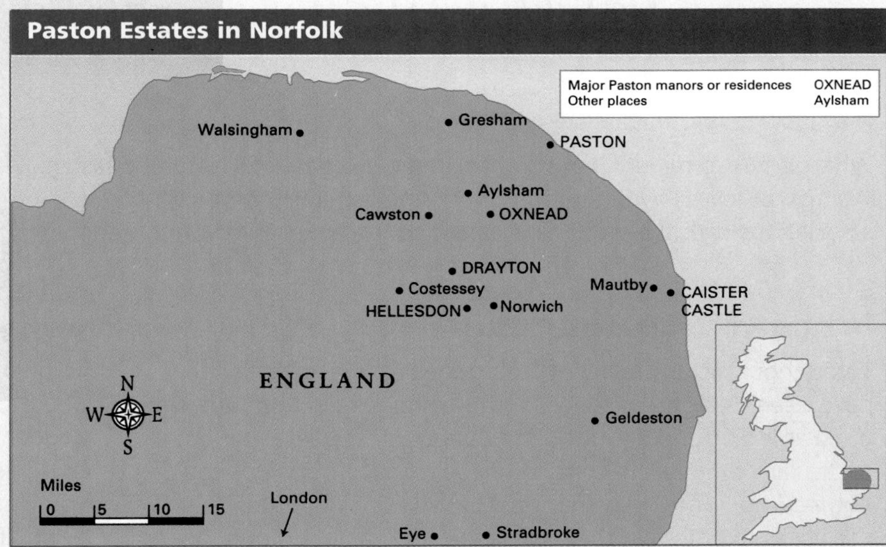

ACROSS THE CURRICULUM

Math Using dates from the Paston family tree on page 119, calculate the life span of each person shown in the diagram (for this activity, assume that all approximate dates are exact). What was the average life span of the men? of the women?

History *Cooperative Learning* With three classmates, investigate one of these topics related to the 15th century: the Wars of the Roses, courtship and marriage, education, religion, medicine and life expectancy, the role of women, art and music, or life on a medieval manor. Present your findings to the class.

CRITIC'S CORNER

Virginia Woolf wrote of the Paston letters that "in all this there is no writing for writing's sake; no use of the pen to convey pleasure or amusement." What does this observation suggest about the lives of the people who wrote these letters?

PREVIEWING

POETRY

Barbara Allan   Sir Patrick Spens

PERSONAL CONNECTION

What comes to mind when you hear the word *tragedy?* Natural disasters? Wars? Lost loves? With a group of classmates, brainstorm a variety of associations with the word, and record your responses in your notebook.

LITERARY CONNECTION

Throughout history, many of life's tragedies, real or fictional, have been depicted in song. Narrative songs called **ballads** were popular in England and Scotland during the medieval period, particularly among the common people, many of whom could not read nor write. Minstrels traveled about, singing these narratives to entertain their listeners with dramatic stories about ordinary people. The best of the early ballads were passed on orally from one generation to the next and sometimes from country to country. Stories often changed in the retelling, sometimes resulting in dozens of versions of the same ballad. Most composers of these popular, or folk, ballads remained anonymous, and the songs themselves were not written down before the 18th century.

The early popular ballads share certain characteristics common to oral traditions. The typical ballad focuses on a single incident, beginning in the middle of a crisis and proceeding directly to the resolution, with only the most sketchy background information, character development, and descriptive detail. Popular subjects of these early ballads include tragic love, domestic conflict, crime, war, and shipwreck.

In the ballads you are about to read, certain words of Scottish dialect appear—*rase* and *guid,* for example. Read each ballad through once, using the accompanying notes to help you decipher the dialect words. Then read the ballad again without referring to the notes. Allow the authentic sounds of the words to help you appreciate the texture and flavor of these old ballads.

WRITING CONNECTION

Think of an event you have heard or read about that you would call a tragedy—an accident resulting in death, for example, or a relationship ending in separation. In your notebook, write a description of this event. Then, as you read, compare your description with the ballads' accounts of two long-ago tragedies.

Minstrels often played the lute, a stringed instrument similar to the guitar, as accompaniment when singing ballads.

LASERLINKS
• LITERARY CONNECTION

Barbara Allan

It was in and about the Martinmas time,
When the green leaves were a-fallin';
That Sir John Graeme in the West Country
Fell in love with Barbara Allan.

He sent his man down through the town
To the place where she was dwellin':
"O haste and come to my master dear,
Gin ye be Barbara Allan."

O slowly, slowly rase she up,
To the place where he was lyin',
And when she drew the curtain by:
"Young man, I think you're dyin'."

"O it's I'm sick, and very, very sick,
And 'tis a' for Barbara Allan."
"O the better for me ye sal never be,
Though your heart's blood were a-spillin'.

"O dinna ye mind, young man," said she,
"When ye the cups were fillin',
That ye made the healths gae round and round,
And slighted Barbara Allan?"

He turned his face unto the wall,
And death with him was dealin':
"Adieu, adieu, my dear friends all,
And be kind to Barbara Allan."

And slowly, slowly, rase she up,
And slowly, slowly left him;
And sighing said she could not stay,
Since death of life had reft him.

She had not gane a mile but twa,
When she heard the dead-bell knellin',
And every jow that the dead-bell ga'ed
It cried, "Woe to Barbara Allan!"

"O mother, mother, make my bed,
O make it soft and narrow:
Since my love died for me today,
I'll die for him tomorrow."

1 Martinmas: November 11 (St. Martin's Day).

8 gin (gĭn): if.

9 rase (rāz): rose.

15 sal: shall.

17 dinna ye mind: don't you remember.

19 healths: toasts; **gae** (gā): go.

28 reft: deprived.

29 gane (gān): gone; **twa:** two.

30 dead-bell: a church bell rung to announce a person's death.

31 jow (jou): stroke; ga'ed: gave.

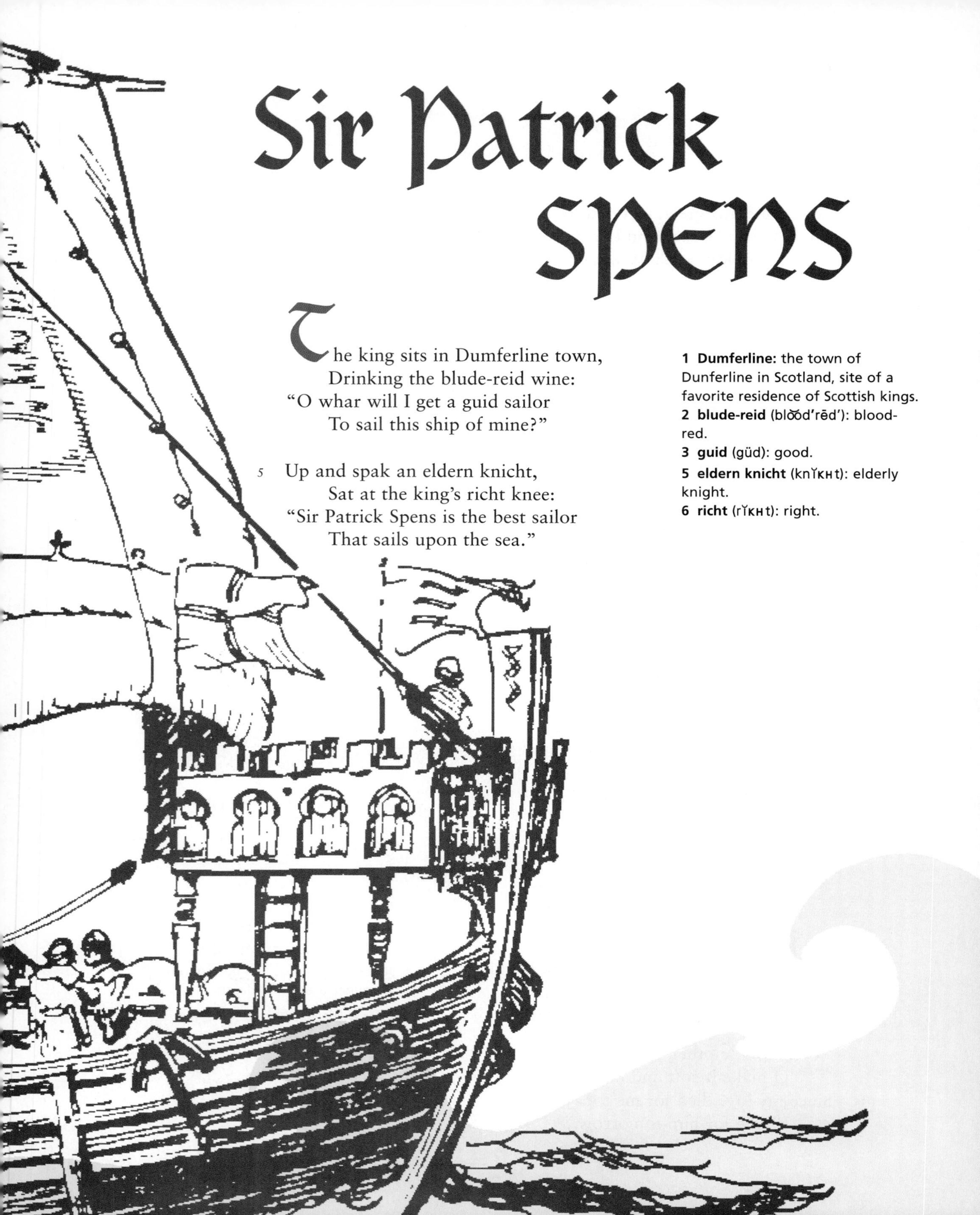

Sir Patrick Spens

The king sits in Dumferline town,
Drinking the blude-reid wine:
"O whar will I get a guid sailor
To sail this ship of mine?"

Up and spak an eldern knicht,
Sat at the king's richt knee:
"Sir Patrick Spens is the best sailor
That sails upon the sea."

1 Dumferline: the town of Dunferline in Scotland, site of a favorite residence of Scottish kings.

2 blude-reid (blo͝od′rēd′): blood-red.

3 guid (güd): good.

5 eldern knicht (knĭKHt): elderly knight.

6 richt (rĭKHt): right.

The king has written a braid letter
  And signed it wi' his hand,
And sent it to Sir Patrick Spens,
  Was walking on the sand.

The first line that Sir Patrick read,
  A loud lauch lauched he;
The next line that Sir Patrick read,
  The tear blinded his ee.

"O wha is this has done this deed,
  This ill deed done to me,
To send me out this time o' the year,
  To sail upon the sea?

"Make haste, make haste, my mirry men all,
  Our guid ship sails the morn."
"O say na sae, my master dear,
  For I fear a deadly storm.

"Late late yestre'en I saw the new moon
  Wi' the auld moon in her arm,
And I fear, I fear, my dear master,
  That we will come to harm."

O our Scots nobles were richt laith
  To weet their cork-heeled shoon,
But lang owre a' the play were played
  Their hats they swam aboon.

O lang, lang may their ladies sit,
  Wi' their fans into their hand,
Or e'er they see Sir Patrick Spens
  Come sailing to the land.

O lang, lang may the ladies stand,
  Wi' their gold kembs in their hair,
Waiting for their ain dear lords,
  For they'll see thame na mair.

Half o'er, half o'er to Aberdour
  It's fifty fadom deep,
And there lies guid Sir Patrick Spens,
  Wi' the Scots lords at his feet.

9 braid (brād): broad; emphatic.

14 lauch (loukh): laugh.

16 ee: eye.

17 wha: who.

23 na sae (nä sā): not so.

25 yestre'en (yĕ-strēn′): yesterday evening.
25–26 the new moon . . . arm: a thin crescent moon with the rest of the moon's disk faintly illuminated by light reflected from the earth.
26 auld (ould): old.
29 laith (lāth): loath; unwilling.
30 weet: wet; **shoon:** shoes.
31 lang owre a' (läng our ä): long before all.
32 aboon (ə-bo͞on′): above (them).

35 or e'er (ôr îr): before ever.

38 kembs: combs.

39 ain (ān): own.

40 na mair (nä mâr): no more.

41 half o'er: halfway over; **Aberdour:** a small town on the Scottish coast.
42 fadom (fä′dəm): fathoms.

RESPONDING OPTIONS

FROM PERSONAL RESPONSE *TO* CRITICAL ANALYSIS

REFLECT 1. How would you describe the moods created by the two ballads? Share your impressions with a classmate.

RETHINK 2. What is your opinion of the relationship between Barbara Allan and Sir John Graeme?

Consider
- his request to see her
- her reaction to the request
- the reason for his illness
- her claim that he has slighted her
- her statement "I'll die for him tomorrow" (line 36)

3. Why do you think Sir Patrick Spens chooses to sail the ship in spite of the risk?

Consider
- the elderly knight's opinion of him (lines 7–8)
- his reaction to the king's letter (lines 13–22)
- the warning from one of his men (lines 23–28)

RELATE 4. In your opinion, which of the ballads tells the more tragic story? Explain your opinion.

5. "Barbara Allan" and "Sir Patrick Spens" focus on two timeless tragic themes, an ill-fated love affair and a shipwreck. Reread the responses to the word *tragedy* that you recorded for the Personal Connection on page 130. What types of tragedies might you expect to find described in ballads written today?

ANOTHER PATHWAY

In most medieval ballads, the speaker has no personal involvement in the story. How might each of these two ballads be different if it were told from the point of view of someone affected by the events—the mother of Barbara Allan or a woman whose husband was lost at sea with Sir Patrick Spens? With a small group of classmates, explore the possibilities.

QUICKWRITES

1. Draft a **short story** in which you give a more detailed account of the relationship between Barbara Allan and Sir John Graeme. You might, for example, present events that may have occurred earlier in their relationship.
2. Create appropriate **epitaphs** for Barbara Allan and Sir Patrick Spens—brief statements, in prose or verse, that might be placed on their tombstones to memorialize their deaths.
3. Try to write your own **ballad** on a contemporary subject. Focus on events leading up to the climax of a dramatic or tragic situation. If you wish, use the event you described for the Writing Connection on page 130 as the basis of your ballad.

PORTFOLIO *Save your writing. You may want to use it later as a springboard to a piece for your portfolio.*

LITERARY CONCEPTS

Typically, a **ballad** consists of four-line stanzas, or **quatrains,** with the second and fourth lines of each stanza rhyming. Each stanza has a strong rhythmic pattern, usually with four stressed syllables in the first and third lines and three stressed syllables in the second and fourth lines. Most ballads also contain dialogue and repetitions of sounds, words, and phrases for emphasis. Notice the patterns of rhyme, rhythm, and repetition in the following stanza from "Barbara Allan." What effect do they create?

O slowly, slowly rase she up,
  To the place where he was lyin',
And when she drew the curtain by:
  "Young man, I think you're dyin'."

Select a stanza from "Sir Patrick Spens" and determine whether its patterns of rhyme and rhythm are the same as those in the stanza from "Barbara Allan." Share your findings with classmates.

ACROSS THE CURRICULUM

Music Research contemporary blues music and find examples of songs that combine characteristics of ballads with traditional tragic themes. Play recordings of these blues songs for your classmates.

Psychology Tragedy is still a common theme in contemporary forms of entertainment, such as plays, television dramas, soap operas, and documentaries. Discuss possible reasons for the popularity of tragic subjects throughout human history.

ALTERNATIVE ACTIVITIES

1. Imagine the exact circumstances of Sir Patrick Spens's death. Then create a **drawing** or **painting** of the incident.
2. Choreograph a **dance** that portrays the action of either "Barbara Allan" or "Sir Patrick Spens." Perform your dance for the class.

LITERARY LINKS

Both Sir Patrick Spens and the speaker of "The Seafarer" (pages 63–65) go off to sea despite anticipated danger. Compare and contrast their motives and attitudes.

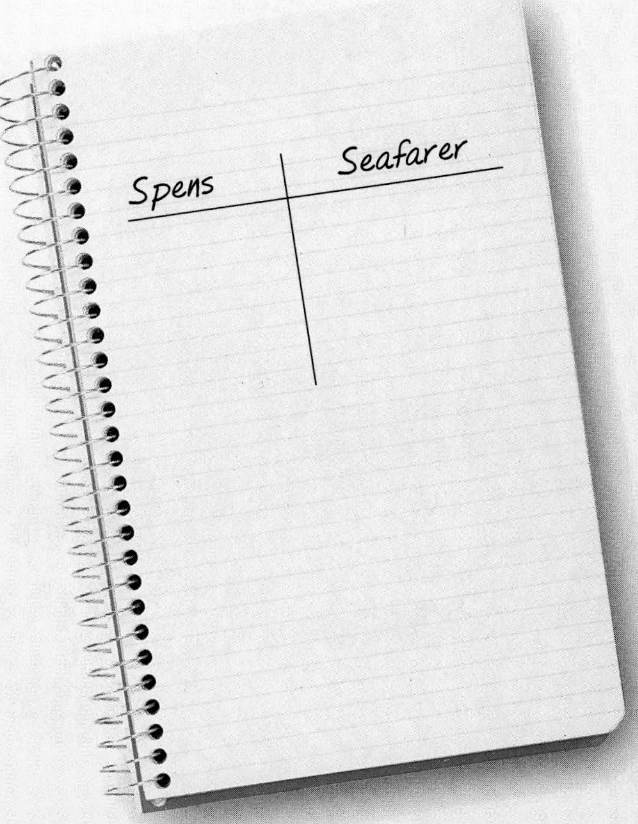

Get Up and Bar the Door

The anonymous poem "Get Up and Bar the Door" is another example of a Scottish ballad that has been handed down orally from generation to generation. Comparing it with the other ballads you have read, however, you may notice surprising differences in theme and tone.

It fell about the Martinmas time,
And a gay time it was then,
When our goodwife got puddings to make,
And she's boild them in the pan.

The wind sae cauld blew south and north,
And blew into the floor;
Quoth our goodman to our goodwife,
"Gae out and bar the door."

The Peasant Couple Dancing (1514), Albrecht Dürer. Engraving, The Metropolitan Museum of Art, New York, Fletcher Fund, 1919 (19.73.102).

"My hand is in my hussyfskap,
Goodman, as ye may see;
An it shoud nae be barrd this hundred year,
It's no be barrd for me."

They made a paction tween them twa,
They made it firm and sure,
That the first word whae'er shoud speak,
Shoud rise and bar the door.

Then by there came two gentlemen,
At twelve o'clock at night,
And they could neither see house nor hall,
Nor coal nor candle-light.

"Now whether is this a rich man's house,
Or whether is it a poor?"
But ne'er a word wad ane o' them speak,
For barring of the door.

And first they ate the white puddings,
And then they ate the black;
Tho muckle thought the goodwife to hersel,
Yet ne'er a word she spake.

Then said the one unto the other,
"Here, man, tak ye my knife;
Do ye tak aff the auld man's beard,
And I'll kiss the goodwife."

"But there's nae water in the house,
And what shall we do than?"
"What ails ye at the pudding-broo,
That boils into the pan?"

O up then started our goodman,
An angry man was he:
"Will ye kiss my wife before my een,
And scad me wi' pudding-bree?"

Then up and started our goodwife,
Gied three skips on the floor:
"Goodman, you've spoken the foremost word,
Get up and bar the door."

9 hussyfskap: household chores.

13 paction: agreement.

15 whae'er: whoever.

27 muckle: a great deal.

35–36 What . . . pan?: What's wrong with using the broth the puddings are boiling in?

40 scad: scald; **bree:** broth.

PART 3 *Attempts at Perfection*

Like the people of any age, those of the medieval period lived in an imperfect world. Nevertheless, they dreamed of what their lives could be. Some people looked to religion to teach them how to live virtuously. Others sought an idealized world in literature. Tales of chivalry, popular in this era, recount the adventures of heroic knights who live by a strict code of behavior. In this part of Unit One, you will read about characters who strive for—but don't quite attain—perfection. As you read, consider how your attitude toward them would be different if they were perfect.

PREVIEWING

ROMANCE

from Sir Gawain and the Green Knight

The Gawain Poet

Translated by John Gardner

PERSONAL CONNECTION

Suppose that you hear someone say, "The student-council president should be a person of honor." What qualities or ideals come to mind? Create a word web like the one shown, jotting down words or phrases that you think describe a person of honor.

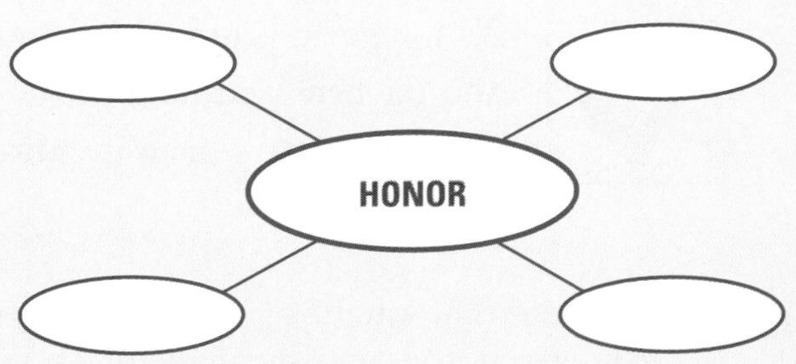

HISTORICAL CONNECTION

Medieval aristocrats relished tales of adventure, especially stories of brave and gallant knights. Although real knights were far from perfect, the knights of legend strove continually to obey a code of chivalry, a set of rules for gentlemanly and heroic behavior. Their code represented a combination of Christian and military ideals, including faith, modesty, loyalty, courtesy, bravery, and honor. The ideal knight respected and vigorously defended his church, his king, his country, and all victims of cruelty or injustice.

Especially popular during the medieval period were legends of King Arthur and his heroic knights of the Round Table. The popularity of these tales was due in part to the idealized world in which they were set. It was a world of castles, heroes, courtly love, and magical spells—a world quite unlike the real medieval England, with its plagues, political battles, and civil unrest. Although Launcelot was often presented as the greatest and most distinguished of Arthur's knights, in early tales that role was given to Arthur's nephew Gawain (gə-wān′), who was famous for his courage and especially for his unfailing chivalry.

READING CONNECTION

Reading a Narrative Poem Like all narrative poems, *Sir Gawain and the Green Knight* contains the same elements as a short story—setting, characters, and plot. As you read, keep track of the plot by writing brief notes about the actions of each character. Note the ways in which honor plays a role in the course of events.

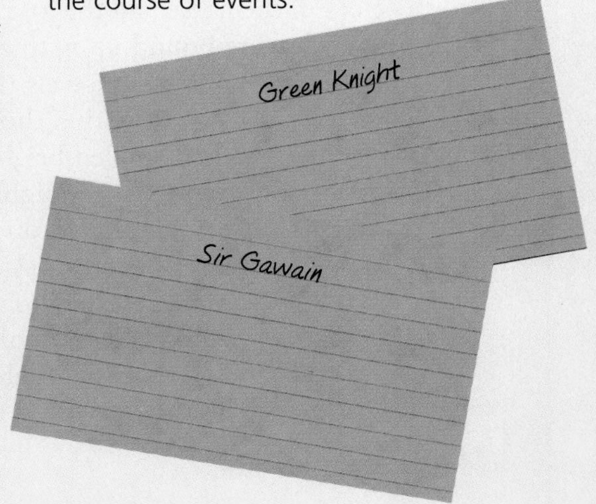

LASERLINKS
• *HISTORICAL CONNECTION*

from Sir Gawain and the

As the poem begins, Arthur and his knights are gathered to celebrate Christmas and the new year with feasting and revelry. In the midst of their festivities, an enormous man—who is entirely green—bounds through the door.

Splendid that knight errant stood in a splay of green,
And green, too, was the mane of his mighty destrier;
Fair fanning tresses enveloped the fighting man's shoulders,
And over his breast hung a beard as big as a bush;
The beard and the huge mane burgeoning forth from his head
Were clipped off clean in a straight line over his elbows,
And the upper half of each arm was hidden underneath
As if covered by a king's chaperon, closed round the neck.
The mane of the marvelous horse was much the same,
Well crisped and combed and carefully pranked with knots,
Threads of gold interwoven with the glorious green,
Now a thread of hair, now another thread of gold;
The tail of the horse and the forelock were tricked the same way,
And both were bound up with a band of brilliant green
Adorned with glittering jewels the length of the dock,
Then caught up tight with a thong in a criss-cross knot
Where many a bell tinkled brightly, all burnished gold.
So monstrous a mount, so mighty a man in the saddle
Was never once encountered on all this earth
till then;
His eyes, like lightning, flashed,
And it seemed to many a man,
That any man who clashed
With him would not long stand.

GUIDE FOR READING

1 knight errant (ĕr'ənt): a knight who wanders about, searching for adventure in order to prove his chivalry; **splay:** display.

2 destrier (dĕs'trē-ər): war horse.

5 burgeoning (bûr'jə-nĭng): growing.

8 chaperon (shăp'ə-rōn'): hood.

10 pranked with knots: decorated with bows.

13 forelock: the part of a horse's mane that falls forward between the ears.

15 dock: the fleshy part of an animal's tail.

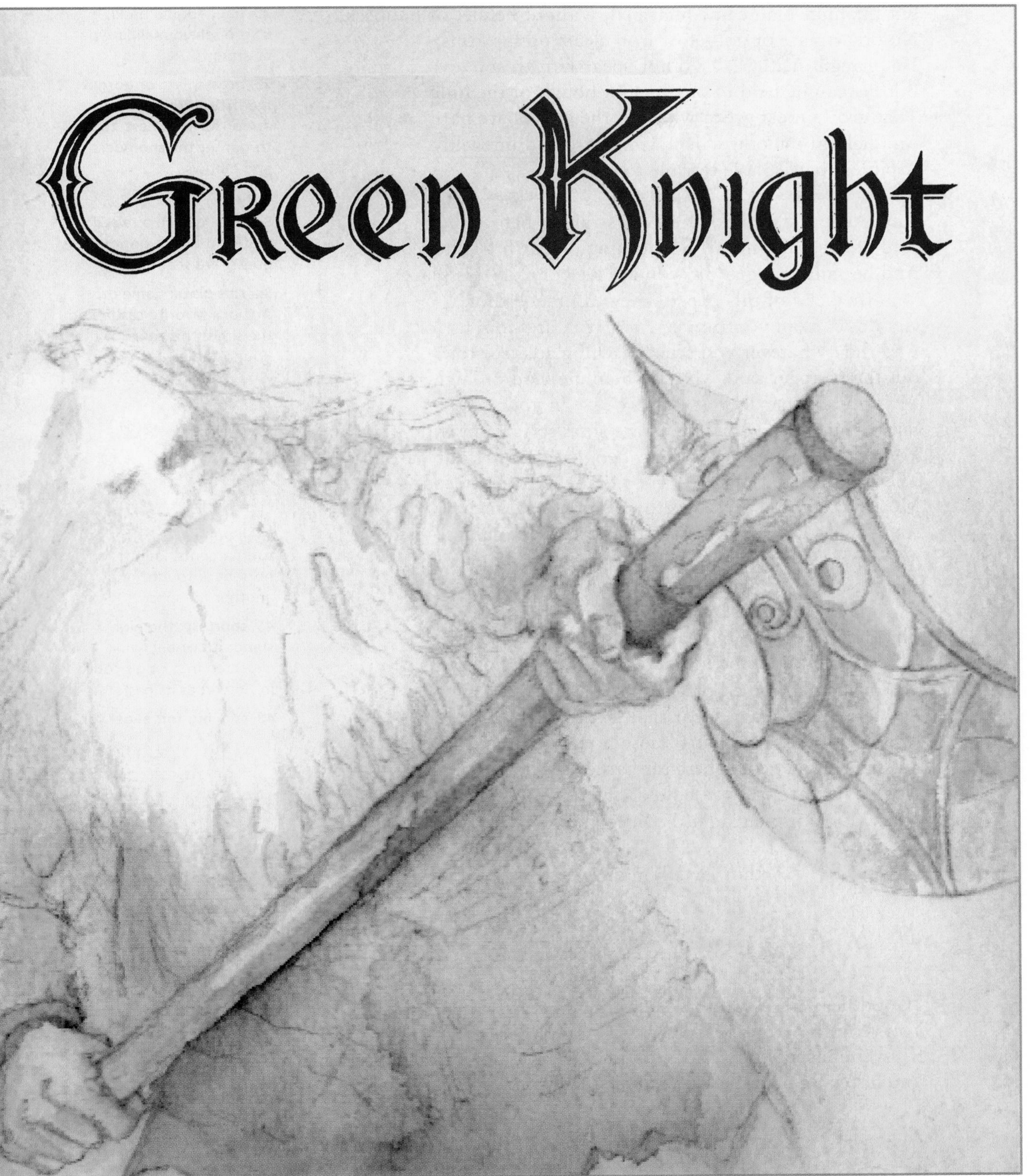
Green Knight

But the huge man came unarmed, without helmet or hauberk,
No breastplate or gorget or iron cleats on his arms;
He brought neither shield nor spearshaft to shove or to smite,
But instead he held in one hand a bough of the holly
That grows most green when all the groves are bare
And held in the other an ax, immense and unwieldy,
A pitiless battleblade terrible to tell of.

King Arthur stared down at the stranger before the high dais
And greeted him nobly, for nothing on earth frightened him.
And he said to him, "Sir, you are welcome in this place;
I am the head of this court. They call me Arthur.
Get down from your horse, I beg you, and join us for dinner,
And then whatever you seek we will gladly see to."
But the stranger said, "No, so help me God on high,
My errand is hardly to sit at my ease in your castle!
But friend, since your praises are sung so far and wide,
Your castle the best ever built, people say, and your barons
The stoutest men in steel armor that ever rode steeds,
Most mighty and most worthy of all mortal men
And tough devils to toy with in tournament games,
And since courtesy is in flower in this court, they say,
All these tales, in truth, have drawn me to you at this time.
You may be assured by this holly branch I bear
That I come to you in peace, not spoiling for battle.
If I'd wanted to come in finery, fixed up for fighting,
I have back at home both a helmet and a hauberk,
A shield and a sharp spear that shines like fire,
And other weapons that I know pretty well how to use.
But since I don't come here for battle, my clothes are mere cloth.
Now if you are truly as bold as the people all say,
You will grant me gladly the little game that I ask
as my right."
Arthur gave him answer
And said, "Sir noble knight,
If it's a duel you're after,
We'll furnish you your fight."

"Good heavens, I want no such thing! I assure you, Sire,
You've nothing but beardless babes about this bench!
If I were hasped in my armor and high on my horse,
You haven't a man that could match me, your might is so feeble.

25 hauberk (hô'bərk): a coat of chain mail (a type of armor).

26 breastplate or gorget (gôr'jĭt) **or iron cleats:** armor for the chest, the throat, or the shoulders and elbows.

32 dais (dā'ĭs): a raised platform where honored guests are seated.

34 this place: Camelot, Arthur's favorite castle and the site of his court of the Round Table.

44 In medieval tournaments, knights on horseback fought one another for sport.

45 courtesy: the high standards of behavior expected in a king's court; **in flower:** at its best.

48 spoiling for: eager for.

63 hasped: fastened.

61–64 What is the Green Knight's tone as he addresses King Arthur?

WORDS TO KNOW

unwieldy (ŭn-wēl'dē) *adj.* so large, heavy, or oddly shaped as to be difficult to hold or use

And so all I ask of this court is a Christmas game,
For the Yule is here, and New Year's, and here sit young men;
If any man holds himself, here in this house, so hardy,
So bold in his blood—and so brainless in his head—
That he dares to stoutly exchange one stroke for another,
I shall let him have as my present this lovely gisarme,
This ax, as heavy as he'll need, to handle as he likes,
And I will abide the first blow, bare-necked as I sit.
If anyone here has the daring to try what I've offered,
Leap to me lightly, lad; lift up this weapon;
I give you the thing forever—you may think it your own;
And I will stand still for your stroke, steady on the floor,
Provided you honor my right, when my inning comes,
to repay.
But let the respite be
A twelvemonth and a day;
Come now, my boys, let's see
What any here can say."

70 gisarme (gĭ-zärm′): a battle-ax with a long shaft and a two-edged head.

67–82 What challenge does the Green Knight offer?

If they were like stone before, they were stiller now,
Every last lord in the hall, both the high and the low;
The stranger on his destrier stirred in the saddle
And ferociously his red eyes rolled around;
He lowered his grisly eyebrows, glistening green,
And waved his beard and waited for someone to rise;
When no one answered, he coughed, as if embarrassed,
And drew himself up straight and spoke again:
"What! Can this be King Arthur's court?" said the stranger,
"Whose renown runs through many a realm, flung far and wide?
What has become of your chivalry and your conquest,
Your greatness-of-heart and your grimness and grand words?
Behold the radiance and renown of the mighty Round Table
Overwhelmed by a word out of one man's mouth!
You shiver and blanch before a blow's been shown!"
And with that he laughed so loud that the lord was distressed;
In chagrin, his blood shot up in his face and limbs
so fair;
More angry he was than the wind,
And likewise each man there;
And Arthur, bravest of men,
Decided now to draw near.

97 blanch: turn white.

99–101 Why is King Arthur so angry?

WORDS TO KNOW

respite (rĕs′pĭt) *n.* a period of rest or delay
renown (rĭ-noun′) *n.* fame
chagrin (shə-grĭn′) *n.* a feeling of embarrassment caused by humiliation or failure

And he said, "By heaven, sir, your request is strange;
But since you have come here for folly, you may as well find it.
I know no one here who's aghast of your great words.
Give me your gisarme, then, for the love of God,
And gladly I'll grant you the gift you have asked to be given."
Lightly the King leaped down and clutched it in his hand;
Then quickly that other lord alighted on his feet.
Arthur lay hold of the ax, he gripped it by the handle,
And he swung it up over him sternly, as if to strike.
The stranger stood before him, in stature higher
By a head or more than any man here in the house;
Sober and thoughtful he stood there and stroked his beard,
And with patience like a priest's he pulled down his collar,
No more unmanned or dismayed by Arthur's might
Than he'd be if some baron on the bench had brought him a glass
of wine.
Then Gawain, at Guinevere's side,
Made to the King a sign:
"I beseech you, Sire," he said,
"Let this game be mine.

"Now if you, my worthy lord," said Gawain to the King,
"Would command me to step from the dais and stand with you there,
That I might without bad manners move down from my place
(Though I couldn't, of course, if my liege lady disliked it)
I'd be deeply honored to advise you before all the court;
For I think it unseemly, if I understand the matter,
That challenges such as this churl has chosen to offer
Be met by Your Majesty—much as it may amuse you—
When so many bold-hearted barons sit about the bench:
No men under Heaven, I am sure, are more hardy in will
Or better in body on the fields where battles are fought;
I myself am the weakest, of course, and in wit the most feeble;
My life would be least missed, if we let out the truth.
Only as you are my uncle have I any honor,
For excepting your blood, I bear in my body slight virtue.
And since this affair that's befallen us here is so foolish,
And since I have asked for it first, let it fall to me.
If I've reasoned incorrectly, let all the court say,
without blame."
The nobles gather round
And all advise the same:
"Let the King step down
And give Sir Gawain the game!"

106 folly: dangerous and foolish activity.

118 unmanned: deprived of manly courage.

121 Guinevere: King Arthur's wife.

128 liege (lēj) **lady:** a lady to whom one owes loyalty and service; here used by Gawain to refer to Queen Guinevere.

131 churl: rude, uncouth person.

136–139 How does Gawain's description of himself reflect a knight's code of chivalry?

WORDS TO KNOW

aghast (ə-găst') *adj.* struck with terror or amazement; shocked

Arthur grants Gawain's request to take on the Green Knight's challenge. The Green Knight asks Gawain to identify himself, and the two agree on their pact. Gawain then prepares to strike his blow against the Green Knight.

On the ground, the Green Knight got himself into position,
His head bent forward a little, the bare flesh showing,
His long and lovely locks laid over his crown
So that any man there might note the naked neck.
Sir Gawain laid hold of the ax and he hefted it high,
His pivot foot thrown forward before him on the floor,
And then, swiftly, he slashed at the naked neck;
The sharp of the battleblade shattered asunder the bones
And sank through the shining fat and slit it in two,
And the bit of the bright steel buried itself in the ground.
The fair head fell from the neck to the floor of the hall
And the people all kicked it away as it came near their feet.
The blood splashed up from the body and glistened on the green,
But he never faltered or fell for all of that,
But swiftly he started forth upon stout shanks
And rushed to reach out, where the King's retainers stood,
Caught hold of the lovely head, and lifted it up,
And leaped to his steed and snatched up the reins of the bridle,
Stepped into stirrups of steel and, striding aloft,
He held his head by the hair, high, in his hand;
And the stranger sat there as steadily in his saddle
As a man entirely unharmed, although he was headless
on his steed.
He turned his trunk about,
That baleful body that bled,
And many were faint with fright
When all his say was said.

He held his head in his hand up high before him,
Addressing the face to the dearest of all on the dais;
And the eyelids lifted wide, and the eyes looked out,
And the mouth said just this much, as you may now hear:
"Look that you go, Sir Gawain, as good as your word,
And seek till you find me, as loyally, my friend,
As you've sworn in this hall to do, in the hearing of the knights.
Come to the Green Chapel, I charge you, and take
A stroke the same as you've given, for well you deserve
To be readily requited on New Year's morn.

162 shanks: legs.

163 retainers: servants or attendants.

172 baleful: threatening evil; sinister.

184 requited: paid back. For what does Gawain deserve to be requited? How do you expect this will be done?

WORDS TO KNOW
heft (hĕft) *v.* to lift up; hoist
pivot (pĭv′ət) *adj.* acting as a center around which something turns

Many men know me, the Knight of the Green Chapel;
Therefore if you seek to find me, you shall not fail.
Come or be counted a coward, as is fitting."
Then with a rough jerk he turned the reins
And haled away through the hall-door, his head in his hand,
And fire of the flint flew out from the hooves of the foal.
To what kingdom he was carried no man there knew,
No more than they knew what country it was he came from.
What then?
The King and Gawain there
Laugh at the thing and grin;
And yet, it was an affair
Most marvelous to men.

As the end of the year approaches, Gawain leaves on his quest to find the Green Chapel and fulfill his pledge. After riding through wild country and encountering many dangers, he comes upon a splendid castle. The lord of the castle welcomes Gawain and invites him to stay with him and his lady for a few days.

The lord proposes that he will go out to hunt each day while Gawain stays at the castle. At the end of the day, they will exchange what they have won. While the lord is out hunting, the lady attempts to seduce Gawain. Gawain resists her, however, and on the first two days accepts only kisses, which he gives to the lord at the end of each day in exchange for what the lord has gained in the hunt. On the third day Gawain continues to resist the lady, but she presses him to accept another gift.

She held toward him a ring of the yellowest gold
And, standing aloft on the band, a stone like a star
From which flew splendid beams like the light of the sun;
And mark you well, it was worth a rich king's ransom.
But right away he refused it, replying in haste,
"My lady gay, I can hardly take gifts at the moment;
Having nothing to give, I'd be wrong to take gifts in turn."
She implored him again, still more earnestly, but again
He refused it and swore on his knighthood that he could take nothing.
Grieved that he still would not take it, she told him then:
"If taking my ring would be wrong on account of its worth,
And being so much in my debt would be bothersome to you,
I'll give you merely this sash that's of slighter value."
She swiftly unfastened the sash that encircled her waist,
Tied around her fair tunic, inside her bright mantle;
It was made of green silk and was marked of gleaming gold

205 implored: begged.

212 tunic: a shirtlike garment worn by both men and women; **mantle:** a sleeveless cloak worn over the tunic.

Embroidered along the edges, ingeniously stitched.
This too she held out to the knight, and she earnestly begged him
To take it, trifling as it was, to remember her by.
But again he said no, there was nothing at all he could take,
Neither treasure nor token, until such time as the Lord
Had granted him some end to his adventure.
"And therefore, I pray you, do not be displeased,
But give up, for I cannot grant it, however fair
or right.
I know your worth and price,
And my debt's by no means slight;
I swear through fire and ice
To be your humble knight."

216 trifling: of little value.

"Do you lay aside this silk," said the lady then,
"Because it seems unworthy—as well it may?
Listen. Little as it is, it seems less in value,
But he who knew what charms are woven within it
Might place a better price on it, perchance.
For the man who goes to battle in this green lace,
As long as he keeps it looped around him,
No man under Heaven can hurt him, whoever may try,
For nothing on earth, however uncanny, can kill him."
The knight cast about in distress, and it came to his heart
This might be a treasure indeed when the time came to take
The blow he had bargained to suffer beside the Green Chapel.
If the gift meant remaining alive, it might well be worth it;
So he listened in silence and suffered the lady to speak,
And she pressed the sash upon him and begged him to take it,
And Gawain did, and she gave him the gift with great pleasure
And begged him, for her sake, to say not a word,
And to keep it hidden from her lord. And he said he would,
That except for themselves, this business would never be known
to a man.
He thanked her earnestly,
And boldly his heart now ran;
And now a third time she
Leaned down and kissed her man.

242 Why do you think Gawain finally accepts the green sash?

When the lord returns at the end of the third day, Gawain gives him a kiss but does not reveal the gift of the sash.

WORDS TO KNOW

ingeniously (ĭn-jēn′yəs-lē) *adv.* in a way marked by skill and imagination; cleverly
uncanny (ŭn-kăn′ē) *adj.* frighteningly unnatural or supernatural; mysterious

On New Year's Day Gawain must go to meet the Green Knight. Wearing the green sash, he sets out before dawn. Gawain arrives at a wild, rugged place, where he sees no chapel but hears the sound of a blade being sharpened. Gawain calls out, and the Green Knight appears with a huge ax. The Green Knight greets Gawain, who, with pounding heart, bows his head to take his blow.

Quickly then the man in the green made ready,
Grabbed up his keen-ground ax to strike Sir Gawain;
With all the might in his body he bore it aloft
And sharply brought it down as if to slay him;
Had he made it fall with the force he first intended
He would have stretched out the strongest man on earth.
But Sir Gawain cast a side glance at the ax
As it glided down to give him his Kingdom Come,
And his shoulders jerked away from the iron a little,
And the Green Knight caught the handle, holding it back,
And mocked the prince with many a proud reproof:
"*You* can't be Gawain," he said, "who's thought so good,
A man who's never been daunted on hill or dale!
For look how you flinch for fear before anything's felt!
I never heard tell that Sir Gawain was ever a coward!
I never moved a muscle when *you* came down;
In Arthur's hall I never so much as winced.
My head fell off at my feet, yet I never flickered;
But you! You tremble at heart before you're touched!
I'm bound to be called a better man than you, then,
my lord."
Said Gawain, "I shied once:
No more. You have my word.
But if my head falls to the stones
It cannot be restored.

"But be brisk, man, by your faith, and come to the point!
Deal out my doom if you can, and do it at once,
For I'll stand for one good stroke, and I'll start no more
Until your ax has hit—and that I swear."
"Here goes, then," said the other, and heaves it aloft
And stands there waiting, scowling like a madman;
He swings down sharp, then suddenly stops again,
Holds back the ax with his hand before it can hurt,
And Gawain stands there stirring not even a nerve;

258 his Kingdom Come: his death and entry into the afterlife; a reference to the sentence "Thy kingdom come" in the Lord's Prayer.

274–275 The Green Knight has proclaimed himself a better man than Gawain. How does Gawain dispute that idea in these lines?

WORDS TO KNOW

reproof (rĭ-pro͞of′) *n.* an expression of disapproval; criticism
daunt (dônt) *v.* to destroy the courage of; dismay
flinch (flĭnch) *v.* to pull back from something unpleasant or surprising
wince (wĭns) *v.* to spring back involuntarily, as in pain

He stood there still as a stone or the stock of a tree
That's wedged in rocky ground by a hundred roots.
O, merrily then he spoke, the man in green:
"Good! You've got your heart back! Now I can hit you.
May all that glory the good King Arthur gave you
Prove efficacious now—if it ever can—
And save your neck." In rage Sir Gawain shouted,
"*Hit* me, hero! I'm right up to here with your threats!
Is it *you* that's the cringing coward after all?"
"Whoo!" said the man in green, "he's wrathful, too!
No pauses, then; I'll pay up my pledge at once,
I vow!"
He takes his stride to strike
And lifts his lip and brow;
It's not a thing Gawain can like,
For nothing can save him now!

He raises that ax up lightly and flashes it down,
And that blinding bit bites in at the knight's bare neck—
But hard as he hammered it down, it hurt him no more
Than to nick the nape of his neck, so it split the skin;
The sharp blade slit to the flesh through the shiny hide,
And red blood shot to his shoulders and spattered the ground.
And when Gawain saw his blood where it blinked in the snow
He sprang from the man with a leap to the length of a spear;
He snatched up his helmet swiftly and slapped it on,
Shifted his shield into place with a jerk of his shoulders,
And snapped his sword out faster than sight; said boldly—
And, mortal born of his mother that he was,
There was never on earth a man so happy by half—
"No more strokes, my friend; you've had your swing!
I've stood one swipe of your ax without resistance;
If you offer me any more, I'll repay you at once
With all the force and fire I've got—as you
will see.
I take one stroke, that's all,
For that was the compact we
Arranged in Arthur's hall;
But now, no more for me!"

The Green Knight remained where he stood, relaxing on his ax—
Settled the shaft on the rocks and leaned on the sharp end—
And studied the young man standing there, shoulders hunched,

314–322 At this moment, how do you think Gawain would explain the fact that he has received only a slight cut from the Green Knight's ax?

WORDS TO KNOW

efficacious (ĕf'ĭ-kā'shəs) *adj.* effective

And considered that staunch and doughty stance he took,
Undaunted yet, and in his heart he liked it;
And then he said merrily, with a mighty voice—
With a roar like rushing wind he reproved the knight—
"Here, don't be such an ogre on your ground!
Nobody here has behaved with bad manners toward you
Or done a thing except as the contract said.
I owed you a stroke, and I've struck; consider yourself
Well paid. And now I release you from all further duties.
If I'd cared to hustle, it may be, perchance, that I might
Have hit somewhat harder, and then you might well be cross!
The first time I lifted my ax it was lighthearted sport,
I merely feinted and made no mark, as was right,
For you kept our pact of the first night with honor
And abided by your word and held yourself true to me,
Giving me all you owed as a good man should.
I feinted a second time, friend, for the morning
You kissed my pretty wife twice and returned me the kisses;
And so for the first two days, mere feints, nothing more
severe.
A man who's true to his word,
There's nothing he needs to fear;
You failed me, though, on the third
Exchange, so I've tapped you here.

"That sash you wear by your scabbard belongs to me;
My own wife gave it to you, as I ought to know.
I know, too, of your kisses and all your words
And my wife's advances, for I myself arranged them.
It was I who sent her to test you. I'm convinced
You're the finest man that ever walked this earth.
As a pearl is of greater price than dry white peas,
So Gawain indeed stands out above all other knights.
But you lacked a little, sir; you were less than loyal;
But since it was not for the sash itself or for lust
But because you loved your life, I blame you less."
Sir Gawain stood in a study a long, long while,
So miserable with disgrace that he wept within,
And all the blood of his chest went up to his face
And he shrank away in shame from the man's gentle words.
The first words Gawain could find to say were these:
"Cursed be cowardice and covetousness both,
Villainy and vice that destroy all virtue!"
He caught at the knots of the girdle and loosened them
And fiercely flung the sash at the Green Knight.

326 staunch: firm; **doughty** (dou′tē): brave.

338 feinted (fān′tĭd): pretended to attack.

337–343 What does the Green Knight reveal about himself?

350 scabbard (skăb′ərd): a sheath for a dagger or sword.

354 What was the Green Knight's test?

368 girdle: sash.

"There, there's my fault! The foul fiend vex it!
Foolish cowardice taught me, from fear of your stroke,
To bargain, covetous, and abandon my kind,
The selflessness and loyalty suitable in knights;
Here I stand, faulty and false, much as I've feared them,
Both of them, untruth and treachery; may they see sorrow
and care!
I can't deny my guilt;
My works shine none too fair!
Give me your good will
And henceforth I'll beware."

At that, the Green Knight laughed, saying graciously,
"Whatever harm I've had, I hold it amended
Since now you're confessed so clean, acknowledging sins
And bearing the plain penance of my point;
I consider you polished as white and as perfectly clean
As if you had never fallen since first you were born.
And I give you, sir, this gold-embroidered girdle,
For the cloth is as green as my gown. Sir Gawain, think
On this when you go forth among great princes;
Remember our struggle here; recall to your mind
This rich token. Remember the Green Chapel.
And now, come on, let's both go back to my castle
And finish the New Year's revels with feasting and joy,
not strife,
I beg you," said the lord,
And said, "As for my wife,
She'll be your friend, no more
A threat against your life."

"No, sir," said the knight, and seized his helmet
And quickly removed it, thanking the Green Knight,
"I've reveled too well already; but fortune be with you;
May He who gives all honors honor you well."

And so they embraced and kissed and commended each other
To the Prince of Paradise, and parted then
in the cold;
Sir Gawain turned again
To Camelot and his lord;
And as for the man in green,
He went wherever he would.

370 vex: harass; torment.

371–372 What does Gawain mean when he says, "Foolish cowardice taught me . . . to bargain . . . and abandon my kind"?

384 penance: punishment accepted by a person to show sorrow for wrongdoing; **point:** blade.

382–386 The Green Knight is saying that Gawain has paid for his fault by admitting it and offering his head to the ax.

387–388 Why do you think the Green Knight gives Gawain the sash?

WORDS TO KNOW
amended (ə-mĕn′dĭd) *adj.* corrected **amend** *v.*

RESPONDING OPTIONS

FROM PERSONAL RESPONSE *TO* CRITICAL ANALYSIS

REFLECT

1. What is your reaction to this romance? In your notebook, elaborate on your thoughts.

RETHINK

2. Why do you think Gawain requests to take up the Green Knight's challenge?
   Consider
   - the Green Knight's behavior
   - the response of the other knights
   - the code of chivalry
3. In your opinion, how well does Gawain fulfill the Green Knight's challenge? Use details from the poem to support your opinion.
4. What might have happened if Gawain had refused to accept the sash? Explain your answer.
5. Think about the way in which the Green Knight tests Gawain's virtues at the castle. Do you think the test is fair? Why or why not?
6. Look again at the word web you created for the Personal Connection on page 139. Compare and contrast your own concept of honor with that of Gawain.
   Consider
   - his attitude toward King Arthur
   - his response to the lady in the castle
   - his reaction when he is told that he has failed the Green Knight's test

RELATE

7. King Arthur and his knights were judged by their conduct, specifically by how well they followed the code of chivalry. Do you think today's leaders are judged by a specific code of conduct? If so, what is it?

ANOTHER PATHWAY

Gawain uses the words *cowardice, covetousness, villainy, untruth,* and *treachery* to describe his own behavior. With a small group of classmates, act as a mock jury and determine whether Gawain is guilty of any or all of these offenses.

QUICKWRITES

1. Imagine that you are King Arthur presiding over the Round Table. Write the **speech** that you would make upon Gawain's safe return to Camelot.
2. Prepare a **list of questions** that you would ask the Green Knight in an interview for your school paper.
3. Suppose that Gawain failed to meet the Green Knight in 12 months and a day. In prose, write a new **story ending** to show what you think might happen.
4. You have read that *Sir Gawain and the Green Knight* is a medieval romance. In a short **essay,** explain why you think the romance remains a popular narrative form.

PORTFOLIO *Save your writing. You may want to use it later as a springboard to a piece for your portfolio.*

LITERARY CONCEPTS

The **romance** has been a popular narrative form since the Middle Ages. Generally, the term *romance* refers to any imaginative adventure concerned with noble heroes, gallant love, a chivalric code of honor, and daring deeds. Romances usually have faraway settings, depict events unlike those of ordinary life, and idealize their heroes as well as the eras in which the heroes lived. Medieval romances are often lighthearted in tone and involve fantasy. What characteristics of romance can you find in this excerpt from *Sir Gawain and the Green Knight?* Cite specific examples from the story.

THE WRITER'S STYLE

In translating *Sir Gawain and the Green Knight,* John Gardner attempted to preserve the alliterative style of the original Middle English poem. How do you think the alliteration affects the description in lines 1–8? in lines 152–157?

CRITIC'S CORNER

J.R.R. Tolkien, who also translated *Sir Gawain and the Green Knight,* said that Gawain's being less than perfect makes him more human and believable. Do you agree with this opinion? Support your answer with evidence from the poem.

ACROSS THE CURRICULUM

History Find out more about the armor and weaponry used in medieval England. How did real-life warriors typically prepare for battle? What were their weapons? If you have access to a CD-ROM encyclopedia or an on-line encyclopedia, you might use a computer to start your research.

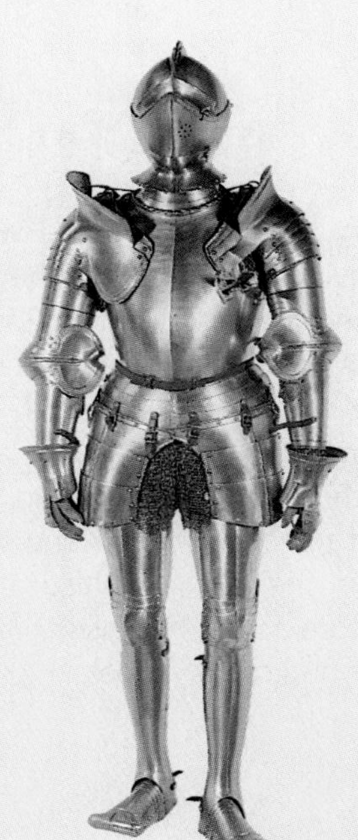

ALTERNATIVE ACTIVITIES

1. Investigate the techniques used to create special effects in movies. Then draw a **diagram** that illustrates the technique you would use to film the beheading of the Green Knight.
2. Devise a **computer game** based on the Green Knight's challenge. Make one or more drawings to illustrate the way the game would be played.
3. With a small group of classmates, prepare a **dramatic interpretation** of a scene from the poem. After deciding on roles, lines, and actions, rehearse your performance before presenting it to the class.

LITERARY LINKS

Compare and contrast Gawain and Beowulf. In your opinion, who is the more honorable character?

WORDS TO KNOW

EXERCISE A Write the letter of the pair of terms that express the relationship closest to that of the capitalized pair.

1. RENOWN : FAME :: (a) greed : cowardice, (b) courtesy : politeness, (c) friendship : conflict, (d) honor : reward
2. DAUNT : ENCOURAGE :: (a) notify : warn, (b) neglect : leave, (c) frighten : injure, (d) rejoice : mourn
3. WEIGHT LIFTER : HEFT :: (a) pianist : piano, (b) artist : draw, (c) actor : applaud, (d) gardener : tool
4. ERROR : AMENDED :: (a) accident : avoided, (b) storm : predicted, (c) crack : repaired, (d) sack : crumpled
5. PAINFUL : WINCE :: (a) proud : succeed, (b) satisfied : eat, (c) funny : laugh, (d) noisy : listen
6. RESPITE : WEEKEND :: (a) exercise : jogging, (b) failure : victory, (c) problem : food, (d) fortune : lucky
7. AGHAST : SHOCKED :: (a) angry : jealous, (b) surprised : shy, (c) terrified : unhappy, (d) cautious : careful
8. GHOST : UNCANNY :: (a) comedian : serious, (b) scholar : intelligent, (c) volunteer : numerous, (d) detective : mysterious
9. EFFICACIOUS : USELESS :: (a) loyal : unfaithful, (b) honest : wise, (c) important : significant, (d) desirable : good
10. FLINCH : UNSHAKABLE :: (a) perspire : cold, (b) gamble : daring, (c) smile : friendly, (d) brag : intelligent
11. MANAGEABLE : UNWIELDY :: (a) wide : deep, (b) lost : crumpled, (c) closed : unopened, (d) light : heavy
12. INGENIOUSLY : CLEVERLY :: (a) slowly : speedily, (b) joyfully : nicely, (c) carelessly : recklessly, (d) brilliantly : carefully
13. PIVOT : TURNING :: (a) vehicle : moving, (b) axis : rotating, (c) crosswalk : stopping, (d) trampoline : bouncing
14. CHAGRIN : UNPLEASANT :: (a) regret : amused, (b) bliss : joyful, (c) impatience : calm, (d) horror : curious
15. REPROOF : APPROVE :: (a) hatred : oppose, (b) assistance : encourage, (c) recognition : ignore, (d) permission : allow

EXERCISE B Find an object (or a picture of an object) that can be described with one of the adjectives among the vocabulary words.

The Gawain Poet

The identity of the author of *Sir Gawain and the Green Knight* is unknown. The only surviving early manuscript of the poem, produced by an anonymous copyist around 1400, contains three other poems—*Pearl, Purity,* and *Patience*—that are believed to be the work of the same man. (Since *Pearl* is the most technically brilliant of the four poems, their author is also known as the Pearl Poet.) The Gawain Poet's descriptions and language suggest that he wrote in the second half of the 14th century and was therefore a contemporary of Chaucer. His dialect, however, indicates that he was not a Londoner like Chaucer but lived somewhere in the northwestern part of England.

The Gawain Poet's works reveal that he was widely read in French and Latin and had some knowledge of law and theology. Although he was familiar with many details of medieval aristocratic life, his descriptions and metaphors also show a love of the countryside and rural life. Because of his rich imagination, sophisticated technique, and wide knowledge, he is considered one of the greatest of medieval English poets.

PREVIEWING

ROMANCE

from Le Morte d'Arthur

Sir Thomas Malory

Retold by Keith Baines

PERSONAL CONNECTION

Have you ever done or said something that you later regretted? If so, why did you regret it? Given a second chance, how would you have behaved differently? Share your thoughts with your classmates.

HISTORICAL CONNECTION

The legend of King Arthur is one of the most popular and enduring legends in Western culture. Some historians believe that the fictional Arthur was modeled on a real fifth- or sixth-century Celtic military leader whose cavalry defended Britain against the invading Anglo-Saxons. However, the historical Arthur was undoubtedly very different from the king of later legend, who ruled an idealized world of romance, chivalry, and magic.

Since the sixth century, there have been many variations of the stories celebrating King Arthur. Most English-speaking readers have been introduced to the Arthurian legends through Thomas Malory's *Le Morte d'Arthur* or one of its many adaptations. Malory's work consists of a number of interwoven tales that chronicle the rise and fall of the Arthurian world. These tales are based on earlier English and French stories about Arthur's court and are populated by such famous characters as Merlin the magician, Queen Gwynevere (also spelled *Guinevere*), and a host of knights, including Sir Launcelot, Sir Gawain—whom you encountered in the previous selection—Sir Tristram, and Sir Galahad. Although the title *Le Morte d'Arthur* ("The Death of Arthur") perhaps applies best to the last section of Malory's work, it is by this title that the entire work has come to be known.

WRITING CONNECTION

The excerpt you are about to read depicts the death of King Arthur. Reflect on the images that come to mind when you think of King Arthur and his world. In your notebook, try to predict the type of end that Arthur will meet. Keep your prediction in mind as you read this legendary tale of characters whose regrets cannot prevent a fateful conclusion.

Richard Harris as King Arthur in the 1967 film *Camelot*. Photofest.

KING ARTHUR'S FAVORITE KNIGHT, **SIR LAUNCELOT**, HAS FALLEN **IN LOVE** WITH THE KING'S WIFE, **GWYNEVERE**. THE SECRET LOVE **AFFAIR** IS EXPOSED BY SIR MODRED, ARTHUR'S SON BY **ANOTHER** WOMAN, AND GWYNEVERE IS **SENTENCED** TO **BURN** AT THE STAKE. WHILE RESCUING THE **IMPRISONED** GWYNEVERE, LAUNCELOT SLAYS TWO **KNIGHTS** WHO, UNKNOWN TO HIM AT THE TIME, ARE THE BROTHERS OF **SIR GAWAIN**, A FAVORITE NEPHEW OF ARTHUR'S. AFTER A **RECONCILIATION**, LAUNCELOT RETURNS **GWYNEVERE** TO ARTHUR TO BE REINSTATED AS **QUEEN**. AT THE URGING OF SIR GAWAIN, WHO STILL WANTS **REVENGE** ON LAUNCELOT, THE KING BANISHES LAUNCELOT TO **FRANCE**, WHERE THE FOLLOWING EXCERPT **BEGINS**.

Detail of Arthur from the Nine Heroes Tapestries (about 1385), probably Nicolas Bataille. The Metropolitan Museum of Art, New York, The Cloisters Collection, Munsey Fund, 1932 (32.130.3a).

SIR THOMAS MALORY

from LE MORTE D'ARTHUR

The Siege of Benwick

When Sir Launcelot had established dominion over France, he garrisoned the towns and settled with his army in the fortified city of Benwick, where his father King Ban had held court.

King Arthur, after appointing Sir Modred ruler in his absence, and instructing Queen Gwynevere to obey him, sailed to France with an army of sixty thousand men, and, on the advice of Sir Gawain, started laying waste[1] all before him.

News of the invasion reached Sir Launcelot, and his counselors advised him. Sir Bors spoke first:

"My lord Sir Launcelot, is it wise to allow King Arthur to lay your lands waste when sooner or later he will oblige you to offer him battle?"

Sir Lyonel spoke next: "My lord, I would recommend that we remain within the walls of our city until the invaders are weakened by cold and hunger, and then let us sally forth[2] and destroy them."

Next, King Bagdemagus: "Sir Launcelot, I understand that it is out of courtesy that you permit the king to ravage your lands, but where will this courtesy end? If you remain within the city, soon everything will be destroyed."

Then Sir Galyhud: "Sir, you command knights of royal blood; you cannot expect them to remain meekly within the city walls. I pray you, let us encounter the enemy on the open field, and they will soon repent of their expedition."

And to this the seven knights of West Britain all muttered their assent. Then Sir Launcelot spoke:

"My lords, I am reluctant to shed Christian blood in a war against my own liege;[3] and yet I do know that these lands have already suffered depredation in the wars between King Claudas and my father and uncle, King Ban and King Bors. Therefore I will next send a messenger to King Arthur and sue[4] for peace, for peace is always preferable to war."

1. **laying waste:** destroying.
2. **sally forth:** rush out suddenly in an attack.
3. **liege** (lēj): a lord or ruler to whom one owes loyalty and service.
4. **sue:** appeal; beg.

WORDS TO KNOW

ravage (răv'ĭj) *v.* to cause great damage to; devastate
depredation (dĕp'rĭ-dā'shən) *n.* destruction caused by robbery or looting

Accordingly a young noblewoman accompanied by a dwarf was sent to King Arthur. They were received by the gentle knight Sir Lucas the Butler.

"My lady, you bring a message from Sir Launcelot?" he asked.

"My lord, I do. It is for the king."

"Alas! King Arthur would readily be reconciled to Sir Launcelot, but Sir Gawain forbids it; and it is a shame, because Sir Launcelot is certainly the greatest knight living."

The young noblewoman was brought before the king, and when he had heard Sir Launcelot's entreaties for peace he wept, and would readily have accepted them had not Sir Gawain spoken up:

"My liege, if we retreat now we will become a laughingstock, in this land and in our own. Surely our honor demands that we pursue this war to its proper conclusion."

"Sir Gawain, I will do as you advise, although reluctantly, for Sir Launcelot's terms are generous and he is still dear to me. I beg you make a reply to him on my behalf."

Sir Gawain addressed the young noblewoman:

"Tell Sir Launcelot that we will not bandy words with him, and it is too late now to sue for peace. Further that I, Sir Gawain, shall not cease to strive against him until one of us is killed."

The young noblewoman was escorted back to Sir Launcelot, and when she had delivered Sir Gawain's message they both wept. Then Sir Bors spoke:

"My lord, we beseech you, do not look so dismayed! You have many trustworthy knights behind you; lead us onto the field and we will put an end to this quarrel."

"My lords, I do not doubt you, but I pray you, be ruled by me: I will not lead you against our liege until we ourselves are endangered; only then can we honorably sally forth and defeat him."

Sir Launcelot's nobles submitted; but the next day it was seen that King Arthur had laid siege to the city of Benwick. Then Sir Gawain rode before the city walls and shouted a challenge:

"My lord Sir Launcelot: have you no knight who will dare to ride forth and break spears with me? It is I, Sir Gawain."

Sir Bors accepted the challenge. He rode out of the castle gate, they encountered, and he was wounded and flung from his horse. His comrades helped him back to the castle, and then Sir Lyonel offered to joust. He too was overthrown and helped back to the castle.

Thereafter, every day for six months Sir Gawain rode before the city and overthrew whoever accepted his challenge. Meanwhile, as a result of skirmishes, numbers on both sides were beginning to dwindle. Then one day Sir Gawain challenged Sir Launcelot:

"My lord Sir Launcelot: traitor to the king and to me, come forth if you dare and meet your mortal foe, instead of lurking like a coward in your castle!"

Sir Launcelot heard the challenge, and one of his kinsmen spoke to him:

"My lord, you must accept the challenge, or be shamed forever."

"Alas, that I should have to fight Sir Gawain!" said Sir Launcelot. "But now I am obliged to."

Sir Launcelot gave orders for his most powerful courser[5] to be harnessed, and when he had armed, rode to the tower and addressed King Arthur:

"My lord King Arthur, it is with a heavy heart that I set forth to do battle with one of your own blood; but now it is incumbent upon my honor to do so. For six months I have suffered your majesty to lay my lands waste and to besiege me in my own city. My courtesy is repaid with insults, so deadly and shameful that now I must by force of arms seek redress."

"Have done, Sir Launcelot, and let us to battle!" shouted Sir Gawain.

---

5. **courser:** a horse trained for battle.

WORDS TO KNOW

entreaty (ĕn-trē′tē) *n.* an earnest request; plea
dwindle (dwĭn′dl) *v.* to become steadily less
incumbent (ĭn-kŭm′bənt) *adj.* required as a duty or obligation
redress (rĭ-drĕs′) *n.* repayment for a wrong or injury

Sir Launcelot rode from the city at the head of his entire army. King Arthur was astonished at his strength and realized that Sir Launcelot had not been boasting when he claimed to have acted with forbearance. "Alas, that I should ever have come to war with him!" he said to himself.

It was agreed that the two combatants should fight to the death, with interference from none. Sir Launcelot and Sir Gawain then drew apart and galloped furiously together, and so great was their strength that their horses crashed to the ground and both riders were overthrown.

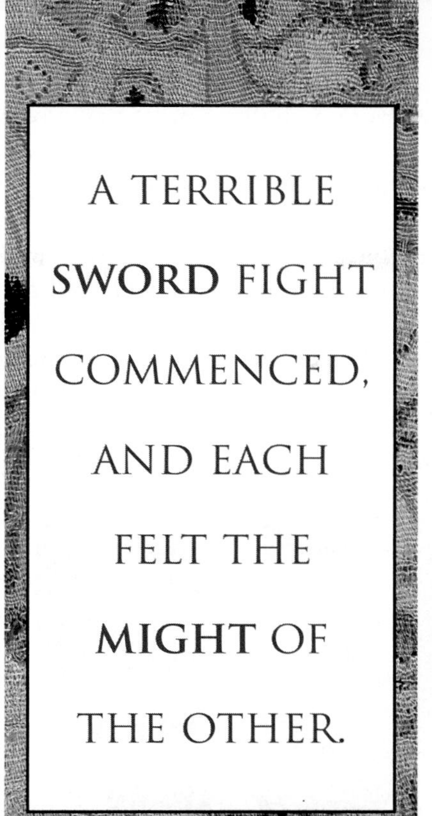
A TERRIBLE
SWORD FIGHT
COMMENCED,
AND EACH
FELT THE
MIGHT OF
THE OTHER.

A terrible sword fight commenced, and each felt the might of the other as fresh wounds were inflicted with every blow. For three hours they fought with scarcely a pause, and the blood seeped out from their armor and trickled to the ground. Sir Launcelot found to his dismay that Sir Gawain, instead of weakening, seemed to increase in strength as they proceeded, and he began to fear that he was battling not with a knight but with a fiend incarnate.[6] He decided to fight defensively and to conserve his strength.

It was a secret known only to King Arthur and to Sir Gawain himself that his strength increased for three hours in the morning, reaching its zenith[7] at noon, and waning again. This was due to an enchantment that had been cast over him by a hermit[8] when he was still a youth. Often in the past, as now, he had taken advantage of this.

Thus when the hour of noon had passed, Sir Launcelot felt Sir Gawain's strength return to normal, and knew that he could defeat him.

"Sir Gawain, I have endured many hard blows from you these last three hours, but now beware, for I see that you have weakened, and it is I who am the stronger."

Thereupon Sir Launcelot redoubled his blows, and with one, catching Sir Gawain sidelong on the helmet, sent him reeling to the ground. Then he courteously stood back.

"Sir Launcelot, I still defy you!" said Sir Gawain from the ground. "Why do you not kill me now? for I warn you that if ever I recover I shall challenge you again."

"Sir Gawain, by the grace of God I shall endure you again," Sir Launcelot replied, and then turned to the king:

"My liege, your expedition can find no honorable conclusion at these walls, so I pray you withdraw and spare your noble knights. Remember me with kindness and be guided, as ever, by the love of God."

"Alas!" said the king, "Sir Launcelot scruples[9] to fight against me or those of my blood, and once more I am beholden to him."

Sir Launcelot withdrew to the city and Sir Gawain was taken to his pavilion, where his wounds were dressed. King Arthur was doubly grieved, by his quarrel with Sir Launcelot and by the seriousness of Sir Gawain's wounds.

For three weeks, while Sir Gawain was recovering, the siege was relaxed and both sides skirmished only halfheartedly. But once recovered,

6. **fiend incarnate:** devil in human form.
7. **zenith:** highest point; peak.
8. **hermit:** a person living in solitude for religious reasons.
9. **scruples:** hesitates for reasons of principle.

WORDS TO KNOW

forbearance (fôr-bâr′əns) *n.* self-control; patient restraint
reeling (rē′lĭng) *adj.* falling back **reel** *v.*

Sir Gawain rode up to the castle walls and challenged Sir Launcelot again:

"Sir Launcelot, traitor! Come forth, it is Sir Gawain who challenges you."

"Sir Gawain, why these insults? I have the measure of your strength and you can do me but little harm."

"Come forth, traitor, and this time I shall make good my revenge!" Sir Gawain shouted.

"Sir Gawain, I have once spared your life; should you not beware of meddling with me again?"

Sir Launcelot armed and rode out to meet him. They jousted and Sir Gawain broke his spear and was flung from his horse. He leaped up immediately, and putting his shield before him, called on Sir Launcelot to fight on foot.

"The issue[10] of a mare has failed me; but I am the issue of a king and a queen and I shall not fail!" he exclaimed.

As before, Sir Launcelot felt Sir Gawain's strength increase until noon, during which period he defended himself, and then weaken again.

"Sir Gawain, you are a proved knight, and with the increase of your strength until noon you must have overcome many of your opponents, but now your strength has gone, and once more you are at my mercy."

Sir Launcelot struck out lustily and by chance reopened the wound he had made before. Sir Gawain fell to the ground in a faint, but when he came to he said weakly:

"Sir Launcelot, I still defy you. Make an end of me, or I shall fight you again!"

"Sir Gawain, while you stand on your two feet I will not gainsay[11] you; but I will never strike a knight who has fallen. God defend me from such dishonor!"

Sir Launcelot walked away and Sir Gawain continued to call after him: "Traitor! Until one of us is dead I shall never give in!"

For a month Sir Gawain lay recovering from his wounds, and the siege remained; but then, as Sir Gawain was preparing to fight Sir Launcelot once more, King Arthur received news which caused him to strike camp and lead his army on a forced march to the coast, and thence to embark for Britain.

---

10. **issue:** offspring.

11. **gainsay:** deny.

The Day of Destiny

During the absence of King Arthur from Britain, Sir Modred, already vested with sovereign powers,[12] had decided to usurp the throne. Accordingly, he had false letters written—announcing the death of King Arthur in battle—and delivered to himself. Then, calling a parliament, he ordered the letters to be read and persuaded the nobility to elect him king. The coronation took place at Canterbury and was celebrated with a fifteen-day feast.

Sir Modred then settled in Camelot and made overtures to Queen Gwynevere to marry him. The queen seemingly acquiesced, but as soon as she had won his confidence, begged leave to make a journey to London in order to prepare her trousseau.[13] Sir Modred consented, and the queen rode straight to the Tower which, with the aid of her loyal nobles, she manned and provisioned for her defense.

Sir Modred, outraged, at once marched against her, and laid siege to the Tower, but despite his large army, siege engines, and guns, was unable to effect a breach. He then tried to entice the queen from the Tower, first by guile and then by threats, but she would listen to neither. Finally the Archbishop of Canterbury came forward to protest:

"Sir Modred, do you not fear God's displeasure? First you have falsely made yourself king; now you, who were begotten by King Arthur on his aunt, try to marry your father's wife! If you do not revoke your evil deeds I shall curse you with bell, book, and candle."[14]

"Fie on you! Do your worst!" Sir Modred replied.

"Sir Modred, I warn you take heed! or the wrath of the Lord will descend upon you."

"Away, false priest, or I shall behead you!"

The Archbishop withdrew, and after excommunicating Sir Modred, abandoned his office and fled to Glastonbury. There he took up his abode as a simple hermit, and by fasting and prayer sought divine intercession[15] in the troubled affairs of his country.

Sir Modred tried to assassinate the Archbishop, but was too late. He continued to assail the queen with entreaties and threats, both of which failed, and then the news reached him that King Arthur was returning with his army from France in order to seek revenge.

Sir Modred now appealed to the barony to support him, and it has to be told that they came forward in large numbers to do so. Why? it will be asked. Was not King Arthur, the noblest sovereign Christendom had seen, now leading his armies in a righteous cause? The answer lies in the people of Britain, who, then as now, were fickle. Those who so readily transferred their allegiance to Sir Modred did so with the excuse that whereas King Arthur's reign had led them into war and strife, Sir Modred promised them peace and festivity.

Hence it was with an army of a hundred thousand that Sir Modred marched to Dover to battle against his own father, and to withhold from him his rightful crown.

As King Arthur with his fleet drew into the harbor, Sir Modred and his army launched forth

---

12. **vested with sovereign powers:** given the authority of a king.
13. **trousseau** (tro͞o′sō): clothes and linens that a bride brings to her marriage.
14. **I shall curse you with bell, book, and candle:** The archbishop is threatening to excommunicate Modred—that is, to deny him participation in the rites of the church. In the medieval ritual of excommunication, a bell was rung, a book was shut, and a candle was extinguished.
15. **divine intercession:** assistance from God.

WORDS TO KNOW

usurp (yo͞o-sûrp′) *v.* to seize unlawfully by force
acquiesce (ăk′wē-ĕs′) *v.* to agree or give in without protest
guile (gīl) *n.* clever trickery; deceit
assail (ə-sāl′) *v.* to attack, either with blows or with words

in every available craft, and a bloody battle ensued in the ships and on the beach. If King Arthur's army were the smaller, their courage was the higher, confident as they were of the righteousness of their cause. Without stint[16] they battled through the burning ships, the screaming wounded, and the corpses floating on the bloodstained waters. Once ashore they put Sir Modred's entire army to flight.

The battle over, King Arthur began a search for his casualties, and on peering into one of the ships found Sir Gawain, mortally wounded. Sir Gawain fainted when King Arthur lifted him in his arms; and when he came to, the king spoke:

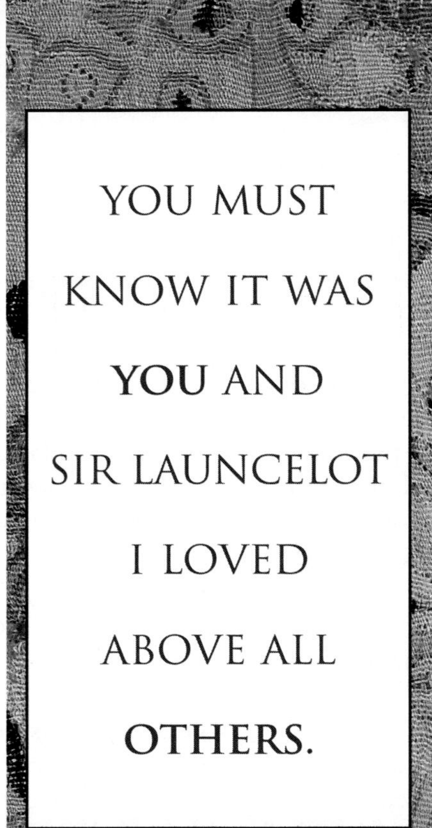
YOU MUST KNOW IT WAS YOU AND SIR LAUNCELOT I LOVED ABOVE ALL OTHERS.

"Alas! dear nephew, that you lie here thus, mortally wounded! What joy is now left to me on this earth? You must know it was you and Sir Launcelot I loved above all others, and it seems that I have lost you both."

"My good uncle, it was my pride and my stubbornness that brought all this about, for had I not urged you to war with Sir Launcelot your subjects would not now be in revolt. Alas, that Sir Launcelot is not here, for he would soon drive them out! And it is at Sir Launcelot's hands that I suffer my own death: the wound which he dealt me has reopened. I would not wish it otherwise, because is he not the greatest and gentlest of knights?

"I know that by noon I shall be dead, and I repent bitterly that I may not be reconciled to Sir Launcelot; therefore I pray you, good uncle, give me pen, paper, and ink so that I may write to him."

A priest was summoned and Sir Gawain confessed; then a clerk brought ink, pen, and paper, and Sir Gawain wrote to Sir Launcelot as follows:

"Sir Launcelot, flower of the knighthood: I, Sir Gawain, son of King Lot of Orkney and of King Arthur's sister, send you my greetings!

"I am about to die; the cause of my death is the wound I received from you outside the city of Benwick; and I would make it known that my death was of my own seeking, that I was moved by the spirit of revenge and spite to provoke you to battle.

"Therefore, Sir Launcelot, I beseech you to visit my tomb and offer what prayers you will on my behalf; and for myself, I am content to die at the hands of the noblest knight living.

"One more request: that you hasten with your armies across the sea and give succor to our noble king. Sir Modred, his bastard son, has usurped the throne and now holds against him with an army of a hundred thousand. He would have won the queen, too, but she fled to the Tower of London and there charged her loyal supporters with her defense.

"Today is the tenth of May, and at noon I shall give up the ghost; this letter is written partly with my blood. This morning we fought our way ashore, against the armies of Sir Modred, and that is how my wound came to be reopened. We won the day, but my lord King Arthur needs you, and I too, that on my tomb you may bestow your blessing."

---

16. **stint:** holding back.

WORDS TO KNOW

ensue (ĕn-so͞o') *v.* to occur as a result; follow
succor (sŭk'ər) *n.* aid in a time of need; relief

Sir Gawain fainted when he had finished, and the king wept. When he came to he was given extreme unction,[17] and died, as he had anticipated, at the hour of noon. The king buried him in the chapel at Dover Castle, and there many came to see him, and all noticed the wound on his head which he had received from Sir Launcelot.

Then the news reached Arthur that Sir Modred offered him battle on the field at Baron Down. Arthur hastened there with his army, they fought, and Sir Modred fled once more, this time to Canterbury.

When King Arthur had begun the search for his wounded and dead, many volunteers from all parts of the country came to fight under his flag, convinced now of the rightness of his cause. Arthur marched westward, and Sir Modred once more offered him battle. It was assigned for the Monday following Trinity Sunday, on Salisbury Down.

Sir Modred levied fresh troops from East Anglia and the places about London, and fresh volunteers came forward to help Arthur. Then, on the night of Trinity Sunday, Arthur was vouchsafed[18] a strange dream:

He was appareled in gold cloth and seated in a chair which stood on a pivoted scaffold. Below him, many fathoms deep, was a dark well, and in the water swam serpents, dragons, and wild beasts. Suddenly the scaffold tilted and Arthur was flung into the water, where all the creatures struggled toward him and began tearing him limb from limb.

Arthur cried out in his sleep and his squires hastened to waken him. Later, as he lay between waking and sleeping, he thought he saw Sir Gawain, and with him a host of beautiful noblewomen. Arthur spoke:

"My sister's son! I thought you had died; but now I see you live, and I thank the lord Jesu! I pray you, tell me, who are these ladies?"

"My lord, these are the ladies I championed[19] in righteous quarrels when I was on earth. Our lord God has vouchsafed that we visit you and plead with you not to give battle to Sir Modred tomorrow, for if you do, not only will you yourself be killed, but all your noble followers too. We beg you to be warned, and to make a treaty with Sir Modred, calling a truce for a month, and granting him whatever terms he may demand. In a month Sir Launcelot will be here, and he will defeat Sir Modred."

Thereupon Sir Gawain and the ladies vanished, and King Arthur once more summoned his squires and his counselors and told them his vision. Sir Lucas and Sir Bedivere were commissioned to make a treaty with Sir Modred. They were to be accompanied by two bishops and to grant, within reason, whatever terms he demanded.

The ambassadors found Sir Modred in command of an army of a hundred thousand and unwilling to listen to overtures of peace. However, the ambassadors eventually prevailed on him, and in return for the truce granted him suzerainty[20] of Cornwall and Kent, and succession to the British throne when King Arthur died. The treaty was to be signed by King Arthur and Sir Modred the next day. They were to meet between the two armies, and each was to be accompanied by no more than fourteen knights.

Both King Arthur and Sir Modred suspected the other of treachery, and gave orders for their armies to attack at the sight of a naked sword. When they met at the appointed place the treaty was signed and both drank a glass of wine.

---

17. **extreme unction:** a ritual in which a priest anoints and prays for a dying person.
18. **vouchsafed:** granted.
19. **championed:** defended or fought for.
20. **suzerainty** (so͞o′zər-ən-tē): the position of feudal lord.

Then, by chance, one of the soldiers was bitten in the foot by an adder[21] which had lain concealed in the brush. The soldier unthinkingly drew his sword to kill it, and at once, as the sword flashed in the light, the alarums[22] were given, trumpets sounded, and both armies galloped into the attack.

"Alas for this fateful day!" exclaimed King Arthur, as both he and Sir Modred hastily mounted and galloped back to their armies. There followed one of those rare and heartless battles in which both armies fought until they were destroyed. King Arthur, with his customary valor, led squadron after squadron of cavalry into the attack, and Sir Modred encountered him unflinchingly. As the number of dead and wounded mounted on both sides, the active combatants continued dauntless until nightfall, when four men alone survived.

King Arthur wept with dismay to see his beloved followers fallen; then, struggling toward him, unhorsed and badly wounded, he saw Sir Lucas the Butler and his brother, Sir Bedivere.

"Alas!" said the king, "that the day should come when I see all my noble knights destroyed! I would prefer that I myself had fallen. But what has become of the traitor Sir Modred, whose evil ambition was responsible for this carnage?"

Looking about him King Arthur then noticed Sir Modred leaning with his sword on a heap of the dead.

"Sir Lucas, I pray you give me my spear, for I have seen Sir Modred."

"Sire, I entreat you, remember your vision—how Sir Gawain appeared with a heaven-sent message to dissuade you from fighting Sir Modred. Allow this fateful day to pass; it is ours, for we three hold the field, while the enemy is broken."

"My lords, I care nothing for my life now! And while Sir Modred is at large I must kill him: there may not be another chance."

"God speed you, then!" said Sir Bedivere.

When Sir Modred saw King Arthur advance with his spear, he rushed to meet him with drawn sword. Arthur caught Sir Modred below the shield and drove his spear through his body; Sir Modred, knowing that the wound was mortal, thrust himself up to the handle of the spear, and then, brandishing his sword in both hands, struck Arthur on the side of the helmet, cutting through it and into the skull beneath; then he crashed to the ground, gruesome and dead.

King Arthur fainted many times as Sir Lucas and Sir Bedivere struggled with him to a small chapel nearby, where they managed to ease his wounds a little. When Arthur came to, he thought he heard cries coming from the battlefield.

"Sir Lucas, I pray you, find out who cries on the battlefield," he said.

Wounded as he was, Sir Lucas hobbled painfully to the field, and there in the moonlight saw the camp followers stealing gold and jewels from the dead, and murdering the wounded. He returned to the king and reported to him what he had seen, and then added:

"My lord, it surely would be better to move you to the nearest town?"

"My wounds forbid it. But alas for the good Sir Launcelot! How sadly I have missed him today! And now I must die—as Sir Gawain warned me I would—repenting our quarrel with my last breath."

Sir Lucas and Sir Bedivere made one further attempt to lift the king. He fainted as they did so. Then Sir Lucas fainted as part of his intestines broke through a wound in the stomach. When the king came to, he saw Sir Lucas lying dead with foam at his mouth.

"Sweet Jesu, give him succor!" he said. "This noble knight has died trying to save my life—alas that this was so!"

Sir Bedivere wept for his brother.

---

21. **adder:** a poisonous snake.

22. **alarums:** calls to arms.

WORDS TO KNOW

dissuade (dĭ-swād') *v.* to divert from a course of action by persuasion

"Sir Bedivere, weep no more," said King Arthur, "for you can save neither your brother nor me; and I would ask you to take my sword Excalibur to the shore of the lake and throw it in the water. Then return to me and tell me what you have seen."

"My lord, as you command, it shall be done."

Sir Bedivere took the sword, but when he came to the water's edge, it appeared so beautiful that he could not bring himself to throw it in, so instead he hid it by a tree, and then returned to the king.

"Sir Bedivere, what did you see?"

"My lord, I saw nothing but the wind upon the waves."

"Then you did not obey me; I pray you, go swiftly again, and this time fulfill my command."

Sir Bedivere went and returned again, but this time too he had failed to fulfill the king's command.

"Sir Bedivere, what did you see?"

"My lord, nothing but the lapping of the waves."

"Sir Bedivere, twice you have betrayed me! And for the sake only of my sword: it is unworthy of you! Now I pray you, do as I command, for I have not long to live."

This time Sir Bedivere wrapped the girdle around the sheath and hurled it as far as he could into the water. A hand appeared from below the surface, took the sword, waved it thrice, and disappeared again. Sir Bedivere returned to the king and told him what he had seen.

"Sir Bedivere, I pray you now help me hence, or I fear it will be too late."

Sir Bedivere carried the king to the water's edge, and there found a barge in which sat many beautiful ladies with their queen. All were wearing black hoods, and when they saw the king, they raised their voices in a piteous lament.

"I pray you, set me in the barge," said the king.

Sir Bedivere did so, and one of the ladies laid the king's head in her lap; then the queen spoke to him:

"My dear brother, you have stayed too long: I fear that the wound on your head is already cold."

Thereupon they rowed away from the land and Sir Bedivere wept to see them go.

"My lord King Arthur, you have deserted me! I am alone now, and among enemies."

"Sir Bedivere, take what comfort you may, for my time is passed, and now I must be taken to Avalon[23] for my wound to be healed. If you hear of me no more, I beg you pray for my soul."

The barge slowly crossed the water and out of sight while the ladies wept. Sir Bedivere walked alone into the forest and there remained for the night.

In the morning he saw beyond the trees of a copse[24] a small hermitage. He entered and found a hermit kneeling down by a fresh tomb. The hermit was weeping as he prayed, and then Sir Bedivere recognized him as the Archbishop of Canterbury, who had been banished by Sir Modred.

"Father, I pray you, tell me, whose tomb is this?"

"My son, I do not know. At midnight the body was brought here by a company of ladies. We buried it, they lit a hundred candles for the service, and rewarded me with a thousand bezants."[25]

"Father, King Arthur lies buried in this tomb."

Sir Bedivere fainted when he had spoken, and when he came to he begged the Archbishop to allow him to remain at the hermitage and end his days in fasting and prayer.

"Father, I wish only to be near to my true liege."

"My son, you are welcome; and do I not recognize you as Sir Bedivere the Bold, brother to Sir Lucas the Butler?"

---

23. **Avalon:** an island paradise of Celtic legend, where heroes are taken after death.

24. **copse** (kŏps): a grove of small trees.

25. **bezants** (bĕz′ənts): gold coins.

Thus the Archbishop and Sir Bedivere remained at the hermitage, wearing the habits of hermits and devoting themselves to the tomb with fasting and prayers of contrition.[26]

Such was the death of King Arthur as written down by Sir Bedivere. By some it is told that there were three queens on the barge: Queen Morgan le Fay, the Queen of North Galys, and the Queen of the Waste Lands; and others include the name of Nyneve, the Lady of the Lake who had served King Arthur well in the past, and had married the good knight Sir Pelleas.

In many parts of Britain it is believed that King Arthur did not die and that he will return to us and win fresh glory and the Holy Cross of our Lord Jesu Christ; but for myself I do not believe this, and would leave him buried peacefully in his tomb at Glastonbury, where the Archbishop of Canterbury and Sir Bedivere humbled themselves, and with prayers and fasting honored his memory. And inscribed on his tomb, men say, is this legend:

HIC IACET **ARTHURUS,**
REX **QUONDAM** REXQUE FUTURUS.[27]

---

26. **contrition** (kən-trĭsh′ən): sincere regret for wrongdoing.

27. ***Hic iacet Arthurus, rex quondam rexque futurus*** (hĭk yä′kĕt är-to͞o′ro͝os rāks kwôn′däm rāk′skwĕ fo͝o-to͞o′ro͝os) *Latin:* Here lies Arthur, the once and future king.

INSIGHT

from PREFACE TO FIRST EDITION OF *LE MORTE D'ARTHUR*

1485

William Caxton

I have, after the simple cunning that God hath sent to me, under the favor and correction of all noble lords and gentlemen, enprised to enprint a book of the noble histories of the said King Arthur and of certain of his knights, after a copy unto me delivered, which copy Sir Thomas Malory did take out of certain books of French and reduced it into English.

And I, according to my copy, have done set it in enprint to the intent that noble men may see and learn the noble acts of chivalry, the gentle and virtuous deeds that some knights used in tho[se] days, by which they came to honor, and how they that were vicious were punished and oft put to shame and rebuke; humbly beseeching all noble lords and ladies with all other estates, of what estate or degree they been of, that shall see and read in this said book and work, that they take the good and honest acts in their remembrance, and to follow the same; wherein they shall find many joyous and pleasant histories and noble and renowned acts of humanity, gentleness, and chivalries. For herein may be seen noble chivalry, courtesy, humanity, friendliness, hardiness, love, friendship, cowardice, murder, hate, virtue and sin. Do after the good and leave the evil, and it shall bring you to good fame.

RESPONDING OPTIONS

FROM PERSONAL RESPONSE *TO* CRITICAL ANALYSIS

REFLECT 1. What thoughts were in your mind as you finished reading this selection? Share them with the class.

RETHINK 2. In your opinion, which character in the selection is most admirable, and which is least admirable?

Consider

- the ways in which Launcelot shows loyalty and disloyalty to the king
- Gawain's pursuit of vengeance against Launcelot
- Arthur's willingness to forget his loyalty to Launcelot and follow Gawain's advice
- Modred's seizure of the throne and the support he gets from the people
- Gwynevere's involvement with Launcelot and her actions against Modred
- the regrets expressed by Arthur, Launcelot, and Gawain

3. How much choice do you think Arthur has in determining his own fate?

Consider

- the importance of chivalry to his followers
- the consequences of his long stay in France
- the warnings he receives in his dreams

4. If Arthur, Launcelot, and Gawain were given a second chance to resolve their conflicts, what do you think they might do differently?

RELATE 5. Would you say that the forces that end Arthur's reign are the same forces that bring down governments in the real world? Support your answer with examples from local, national, or world history.

6. Review the Insight selection on page 166. Which of the characteristics named in William Caxton's preface—noble chivalry, courtesy, humanity, friendliness, hardiness, love, friendship, cowardice, murder, hate, virtue, and sin—would you say are represented in this excerpt?

ANOTHER PATHWAY

Cooperative Learning

Imagine that *Le Morte d'Arthur* did not end with this excerpt. With a partner, draft an outline of an additional tale that Malory might have chosen to write. Compare your story ideas with those of other students.

QUICKWRITES

1. Assume the identity of any major character in this selection—Arthur, Launcelot, Gawain, Modred, or Gwynevere. Retell any portion of the selection as an **internal monologue** in the character's voice.
2. Write a **television news report** in which you announce details of the conflict between Arthur and Modred and describe the events leading up to their deaths.
3. As Launcelot, write a **eulogy** for Arthur.
4. Think of current film actors whom you believe to be suited to play the characters in this selection. Write a **proposal** to a motion-picture studio, explaining your choices.

PORTFOLIO *Save your writing. You may want to use it later as a springboard to a piece for your portfolio.*

LITERARY CONCEPTS

Characterization is the way in which writers guide readers' impressions of characters. There are four basic methods of developing a character: (1) description of the character's physical appearance; (2) presentation of the character's speech, thoughts, feelings, and actions; (3) presentation of other characters' speech, thoughts, feelings, and actions; and (4) direct comments about the character's nature. With a group of classmates, look back through this selection, identifying passages that help create readers' impressions of Arthur, Launcelot, Gawain, Modred, and Gwynevere. Record the method of characterization used in each passage, and jot down a word or phrase to describe the qualities of character that are revealed in the passage.

CONCEPT REVIEW: Romance The tales in *Le Morte d'Arthur* are romances—imaginative adventure stories about noble heroes and daring deeds. What characteristics of romance can you find in this excerpt?

ACROSS THE CURRICULUM

Art History Investigate the different styles that have been used over the centuries to illustrate the legends of the Round Table. Share your findings with classmates.

Illustration of a knight (1917), N. C. Wyeth. Oil on canvas, 40″ × 32″, private collection. From *The Boy's King Arthur,* edited by Sidney Lanier, with permission of Charles Scribner's Sons, New York.

CRITIC'S CORNER

In describing Malory's characterizations, one critic has said that Launcelot always seems noble in spite of his faults. Do you agree with this opinion? Cite evidence from the selection to support your answer.

LITERARY LINKS

Compare and contrast the characterization of Gawain in this excerpt from *Le Morte d'Arthur* with the characterization of him in the excerpt from *Sir Gawain and the Green Knight.*

ALTERNATIVE ACTIVITIES

1. Imagine that you are producing a play based on this selection. Choose a scene and design a miniature **set** for it, depicting the scenery, the props, and the characters.
2. With several classmates, create a **newspaper** based on the events in the selection. Include standard newspaper features, such as news articles, editorials, obituaries, a fashion section, comics, want ads, and political cartoons.

WORDS TO KNOW

Review the Words to Know at the bottom of the selection pages and list them on your paper. Then choose the word that could be substituted for the italicized word or phrase in each sentence below.

1. The king's followers began to *attack* his honor.
2. Everyone marveled at the *patience* with which he reacted to the attacks.
3. The king's enemies tried to *unlawfully take over* the throne.
4. The king hoped to *discourage* them from doing harm.
5. The enemies ignored the king's *plea* for peace.
6. They used *trickery* and threats to turn people against the king.
7. The king had to *agree without protest* to a declaration of war.
8. He felt that it was *laid as a duty* on him to fight for his honor.
9. His army sought *repayment* for crimes against the king.
10. The king knew that after he issued his challenge, a full-scale war would *follow.*
11. His advisers warned that the war would *greatly damage* the land.
12. The number of healthy soldiers began to *decline.*
13. Wounded soldiers were seen *falling back* all over the battlefield.
14. Other kingdoms were asked to give *assistance* to the weakened army.
15. The plundering soldiers caused *damage* and sorrow throughout the land.

Sir Thomas Malory

1405?–1471

A son of prosperous parents, the Thomas Malory who many scholars think to be the author of *Le Morte d'Arthur* led a surprisingly unsettled life that ended in prison. A native of Warwickshire, England, he fought in the Hundred Years' War, was knighted around 1442, and was elected to Parliament in 1445. Malory then became embroiled in the violent political conflicts that preceded the outbreak of the Wars of the Roses. A staunch supporter of the house of Lancaster and its claim to the throne, Malory was imprisoned repeatedly by the Yorkist government on a variety of charges, including robbery, cattle rustling, bribery, and attempted murder. He pleaded innocent to all the charges, and his guilt was never proven. It is possible that his outspoken opposition to the ruling family provoked enemies to accuse him falsely in some instances.

Malory seems to have written *Le Morte d'Arthur* while he served a series of prison terms that began in 1451. He finished the book about two years before his death in 1471. William Caxton, who introduced the art of printing to England, published the first edition of Malory's work in 1485, giving the book the title by which it is known today. *Le Morte d'Arthur* remains the most complete English version of the Arthurian legends and has been the source of many later adaptations of the tales.

LASERLINKS
• *AUTHOR BACKGROUND*

PREVIEWING

EPIC

from the Ramayana (rä-mä'yə-nə)

Valmiki (väl-mē'kē)

Translated and adapted by R. K. Narayan

PERSONAL CONNECTION

Think of someone who is a hero to a large segment of the population. He or she might be a sports figure, a spiritual or political leader, a military figure, or some other individual admired by many. What actions or qualities make that person heroic? As you read this selection, consider whether similar heroic qualities are displayed by the hero in the epic battle depicted.

LITERARY/CULTURAL CONNECTION

The great Indian epic *Ramayana* was composed in verse by the poet Valmiki, probably between 300 and 200 B.C. Over the centuries, it has been translated and adapted by many authors, including the 20th-century writer R. K. Narayan. The *Ramayana* pervades the culture of India. According to Narayan, "Everyone of whatever age, outlook, education, or station in life knows the essential part of the epic and adores the main figures in it." For Hindu men in particular, the hero of the *Ramayana* serves as a model of devotion and duty.

Like epics of other cultures, the *Ramayana* celebrates the achievements of both human heroes and divine beings. It is the story of Rama (rä'mə), a royal prince who is the seventh incarnation, or embodiment, of the god Vishnu (vĭsh'no͞o). The epic describes Rama's life, love, battles, and hardships. At the point of the story where this excerpt begins, Rama's wife Sita (sē'tä) has been kidnapped by Ravana (rä'və-nə), the 10-headed, 20-armed demon-king of the island of Lanka (ləng'kä). Hanuman (hə'no͝o-män), a flying monkey in Rama's army, has located Sita and helped build a bridge to Lanka so that all of Rama's forces can cross over and rescue her. Meanwhile, Ravana prepares to defend his land.

READING CONNECTION

Keeping Track of Characters In this selection, the hero Rama and his followers engage in a major battle with the demon-king Ravana and his allies. To keep track of the characters on each side of the conflict, make a chart like the one below. As you read, group the participants according to their loyalty to Rama or to Ravana.

Rama	Ravana
Sugreeva	sorcerer

LASERLINKS
• LITERARY/CULTURAL CONNECTION

from the RAMAYANA

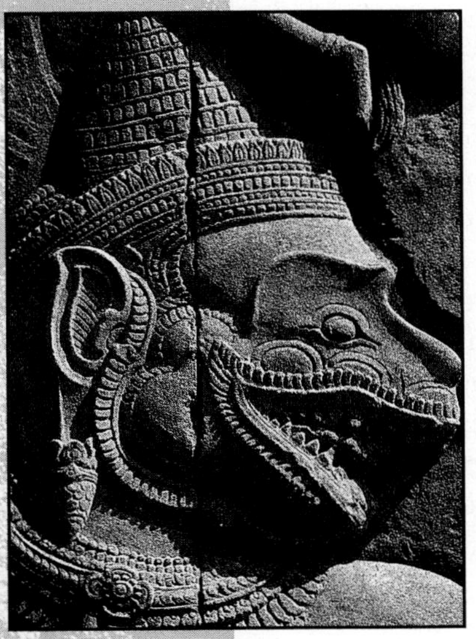

Sculpture of Hanuman

THE SIEGE OF LANKA

Ravana deployed the pick of his divisions to guard the approaches to the capital and appointed his trusted generals and kinsmen in special charge of key places. Gradually, however, his world began to shrink. As the fight developed he lost his associates one by one. No one who went out returned.

He tried some devious measures in desperation. He sent spies in the garb of Rama's monkey army across to deflect and corrupt some of Rama's staunchest supporters, such as Sugreeva,[1] on whom rested the entire burden of this war. He employed sorcerers to disturb the mind of Sita, hoping that if she yielded, Rama would ultimately lose heart. He ordered a sorcerer to create a decapitated head resembling Rama's and placed it before Sita as evidence of Rama's defeat. Sita, although shaken at first, very soon recovered her composure and remained unaffected by the spectacle.

---

1. **Sugreeva** (so͝o-grē′və).

At length a messenger from Rama arrived, saying, "Rama bids me warn you that your doom is at hand. Even now it is not too late for you to restore Sita and beg Rama's forgiveness. You have troubled the world too long. You are not fit to continue as King. At our camp, your brother, Vibishana,[2] has already been crowned the King of this land, and the world knows all people will be happy under him."

Ravana ordered the messenger to be killed instantly. But it was more easily said than done, the messenger being Angada,[3] the son of mighty Vali.[4] When two rakshasas[5] came to seize him, he tucked one of them under each arm, rose into the sky, and flung the rakshasas down. In addition, he kicked and broke off the tower of Ravana's palace, and left. Ravana viewed the broken tower with dismay.

Rama awaited the return of Angada, and, on hearing his report, decided that there was no further cause to hope for a change of heart in Ravana and immediately ordered the assault on Lanka.

As the fury of the battle grew, both sides lost sight of the distinction between night and day. The air was filled with the cries of fighters, their challenges, cheers, and imprecations; buildings and trees were torn up and, as one of his spies reported to Ravana, the monkeys were like a sea overrunning Lanka. The end did not seem to be in sight.

At one stage of the battle, Rama and Lakshmana[6] were attacked by Indrajit,[7] and the serpent darts employed by him made them swoon on the battlefield. Indrajit went back to his father to proclaim that it was all over with Rama and Lakshmana and soon, without a leader, the monkeys would be annihilated.

Ravana rejoiced to hear it and cried, "Did not I say so? All you fools believed that I should surrender." He added, "Go and tell Sita that Rama and his brother are no more. Take her high up in Pushpak Vimana,[8] my chariot, and show her their bodies on the battlefield." His words were obeyed instantly. Sita, happy to have a chance to glimpse a long-lost face, accepted the chance, went high up, and saw her husband lying dead in the field below. She broke down. "How I wish I had been left alone and not brought up to see this spectacle. Ah, me . . . Help me to put an end to my life."

Trijata,[9] one of Ravana's women, whispered to her, "Don't lose heart, they are not dead," and she explained why they were in a faint.

In due course, the effect of the serpent darts was neutralized when Garuda,[10] the mighty eagle, the born enemy of all serpents, appeared on the scene; the venomous darts enveloping Rama and Lakshmana scattered at the approach of Garuda and the brothers were on their feet again.

From his palace retreat Ravana was surprised to hear again the cheers of the enemy hordes outside the ramparts; the siege was on again. Ravana still had about him his commander-in-chief, his son Indrajit, and five or six others on whom he felt he could rely at the last instance. He sent them one by one. He felt shattered when news came of the death of his commander-in-chief.

"No time to sit back. I will myself go and destroy this Rama and his horde of monkeys," he said and got into his chariot and entered the field.

At this encounter Lakshmana fell down in a faint, and Hanuman hoisted Rama on his shoulders and charged in the direction of Ravana.

---

2. **Vibishana** (vĭ-bē′shə-nə).
3. **Angada** (əng′gə-də).
4. **Vali** (və′lē): king of the monkeys.
5. **rakshasas** (räk′shə-səz): demons.
6. **Lakshmana** (lək′shmə-nə).
7. **Indrajit** (ĭn′drə-jēt): Ravana's son.
8. **Pushpak Vimana** (po͝osh′pək vĭ-mä′nə).
9. **Trijata** (trĭ′jə-tä).
10. **Garuda** (gə-ro͞o′də).

WORDS TO KNOW

imprecation (ĭm′prĭ-kā′shən) *n.* a curse
rampart (răm′pärt′) *n.* an embankment or wall for defense against attack

The main combatants were face to face for the first time. At the end of this engagement Ravana was sorely wounded, his crown was shattered, and his chariot was broken. Helplessly, barehanded, he stood before Rama, and Rama said, "You may go now and come back tomorrow with fresh weapons." For the first time in his existence of many thousand years, Ravana faced the humiliation of accepting a concession, and he returned crestfallen to his palace.

He ordered that his brother Kumbakarna,[11] famous for his deep sleep, should be awakened. He could depend upon him, and only on him now. It was a mighty task to wake up Kumbakarna. A small army had to be engaged. They sounded trumpets and drums at his ears and were ready with enormous quantities of food and drink for him, for when Kumbakarna awoke from sleep, his hunger was phenomenal and he made a meal of whomever he could grab at his bedside. They cudgelled, belaboured, pushed, pulled, and shook him, with the help of elephants; at last he opened his eyes and swept his arms about and crushed quite a number among those who had stirred him up. When he had eaten and drunk, he was approached by Ravana's chief minister and told, "My lord, the battle is going badly for us."

"Which battle?" he asked, not yet fully awake.

And they had to refresh his memory. "Your brother has fought and has been worsted; our enemies are breaking in, our fort walls are crumbling. . . ."

Kumbakarna was roused. "Why did not anyone tell me all this before? Well, it is not too late; I will deal with that Rama. His end is come." Thus saying, he strode into Ravana's chamber and said, "Don't worry about anything any more. I will take care of everything."

Ravana spoke with anxiety and defeat in his voice. Kumbakarna, who had never seen him in this state, said, "You have gone on without heeding anyone's words and brought yourself to this pass. You should have fought Rama and acquired Sita. You were led away by mere lust and never cared for anyone's words. . . . Hm . . . This is no time to speak of dead events. I will not forsake you as others have done. I'll bring Rama's head on a platter."

Kumbakarna's entry into the battle created havoc. He destroyed and swallowed hundreds and thousands of the monkey warriors and came very near finishing off the great Sugreeva himself. Rama himself had to take a hand at destroying this demon; he sent the sharpest of his arrows, which cut Kumbakarna limb from limb; but he fought fiercely with only inches of his body remaining intact. Finally Rama severed his head with an arrow. That was the end of Kumbakarna.

When he heard of it, Ravana lamented, "My right hand is cut off."

One of his sons reminded him, "Why should you despair? You have Brahma's[12] gift of invincibility. You should not grieve." Indrajit told him, "What have you to fear when I am alive?"

Indrajit had the power to remain invisible and fight, and accounted for much destruction in the invader's camp. He also created a figure resembling Sita, carried her in his chariot, took her before Rama's army and killed her within their sight.

This completely demoralized the monkeys, who suspended their fight, crying, "Why should we fight when our goddess Sita is thus gone?" They were in a rout until Vibishana came to their rescue and rallied them again.

Indrajit fell by Lakshmana's hand in the end. When he heard of his son's death, Ravana shed bitter tears and swore, "This is the time to kill that woman Sita, the cause of all this misery."

11. **Kumbakarna** (ko͝om′bə-kər′nə).

12. **Brahma's** (brä′məz): given by Brahma—in the Hindu religion, the creator of the universe and one of a trinity of gods that make up the Supreme God.

WORDS TO KNOW **invincibility** (ĭn-vĭn′sə-bĭl′ĭ-tē) *n.* a state of being unbeatable

A few encouraged this idea, but one of his councillors advised, "Don't defeat your own purpose and integrity by killing a woman. Let your anger scorch Rama and his brother. Gather all your armies and go and vanquish Rama and Lakshmana, you know you can, and then take Sita. Put on your blessed armour and go forth."

RAMA AND RAVANA IN BATTLE

Every moment, news came to Ravana of fresh disasters in his camp. One by one, most of his commanders were lost. No one who went forth with battle cries was heard of again. Cries and shouts and the wailings of the widows of warriors came over the chants and songs of triumph that his courtiers arranged to keep up at a loud pitch in his assembly hall. Ravana became restless and abruptly left the hall and went up on a tower, from which he could obtain a full view of the city. He surveyed the scene below but could not stand it. One who had spent a lifetime in destruction, now found the gory spectacle intolerable. Groans and wailings reached his ears with deadly clarity; and he noticed how the monkey hordes revelled in their bloody handiwork. This was too much for him. He felt a terrific rage rising within him, mixed with some admiration for Rama's valour. He told himself, "The time has come for me to act by myself again."

He hurried down the steps of the tower, returned to his chamber, and prepared himself for the battle. He had a ritual bath and performed special prayers to gain the benediction of Shiva; donned his battle dress, matchless armour, armlets, and crowns. He had on a protective armour for every inch of his body. He girt his sword-belt and attached to his body his accoutrements for protection and decoration.

When he emerged from his chamber, his heroic appearance was breathtaking. He summoned his chariot, which could be drawn by horses or move on its own if the horses were hurt or killed. People stood aside when he came out of the palace and entered his chariot. "This is my resolve," he said to himself: "Either that woman Sita, or my wife Mandodari,[13] will soon have cause to cry and roll in the dust in grief. Surely, before this day is done, one of them will be a widow."

The gods in heaven noticed Ravana's determined move and felt that Rama would need all the support they could muster. They requested Indra to send down his special chariot for Rama's use. When the chariot appeared at his camp, Rama was deeply impressed with the magnitude and brilliance of the vehicle. "How has this come to be here?" he asked.

"Sir," the charioteer answered, "my name is Matali.[14] I have the honour of being the charioteer of Indra. Brahma, the four-faced god and the creator of the Universe, and Shiva, whose power has emboldened Ravana now to challenge you, have commanded me to bring it here for your use. It can fly swifter than air over all obstacles, over any mountain, sea, or sky, and will help you to emerge victorious in this battle."

Rama reflected aloud, "It may be that the rakshasas have created this illusion for me. It may be a trap. I don't know how to view it." Whereupon Matali spoke convincingly to dispel the doubt in Rama's mind. Rama, still hesitant, though partially convinced, looked at Hanuman and Lakshmana and asked, "What do you think of it?" Both answered, "We feel no doubt that this chariot is Indra's; it is not an illusory creation."

Rama fastened his sword, slung two quivers full of rare arrows over his shoulders, and climbed into the chariot.

The beat of war drums, the challenging cries of soldiers, the trumpets, and the rolling chariots speeding along to confront each other, created a deafening mixture of noise. While Ravana had

13. **Mandodari** (mən-dō′də-rē).

14. **Matali** (mä′tə-lē).

instructed his charioteer to speed ahead, Rama very gently ordered his chariot-driver, "Ravana is in a rage; let him perform all the antics he desires and exhaust himself. Until then be calm; we don't have to hurry forward. Move slowly and calmly, and you must strictly follow my instructions; I will tell you when to drive faster."

Ravana's assistant and one of his staunchest supporters, Mahodara[15]—the giant among giants in his physical appearance—begged Ravana, "Let me not be a mere spectator when you confront Rama. Let me have the honour of grappling with him. Permit me to attack Rama."

"Rama is my sole concern," Ravana replied. "If you wish to engage yourself in a fight, you may fight his brother Lakshmana."

Noticing Mahodara's purpose, Rama steered his chariot across his path in order to prevent Mahodara from reaching Lakshmana. Whereupon Mahodara ordered his chariot-driver, "Now dash straight ahead, directly into Rama's chariot."

The charioteer, more practical-minded, advised him, "I would not go near Rama. Let us keep away." But Mahodara, obstinate and intoxicated with war fever, made straight for Rama. He wanted to have the honour of a direct encounter with Rama himself in spite of Ravana's advice; and for this honour he paid a heavy price, as it was a moment's work for Rama to destroy him, and leave him lifeless and shapeless on the field. Noticing this, Ravana's anger mounted further. He commanded his driver, "You will not slacken now. Go." Many ominous signs were seen now—his bow-strings suddenly snapped; the mountains shook; thunders rumbled in the skies; tears flowed from the horses' eyes; elephants with decorated foreheads moved along dejectedly. Ravana, noticing them, hesitated only for a second, saying, "I don't care. This mere mortal Rama is of no account, and these omens do not concern me at all." Meanwhile, Rama paused for a moment to consider his next step; and suddenly turned towards the armies supporting Ravana, which stretched away to the horizon, and destroyed them. He felt that this might be one way of saving Ravana. With his armies gone, it was possible that Ravana might have a change of heart. But it had only the effect of spurring Ravana on; he plunged forward and kept coming nearer Rama and his own doom.

Rama's army cleared and made way for Ravana's chariot, unable to stand the force of his approach. Ravana blew his conch[16] and its shrill challenge reverberated through space. Following it another conch, called "Panchajanya,"[17] which belonged to Mahavishnu[18] (Rama's original form before his present incarnation), sounded of its own accord in answer to the challenge, agitating the universe with its vibrations. And then Matali picked up another conch, which was Indra's, and blew it. This was the signal indicating the commencement of the actual battle. Presently Ravana sent a shower of arrows on Rama; and Rama's followers, unable to bear the sight of his body being studded with arrows, averted their heads. Then the chariot horses of Ravana and Rama glared at each other in hostility, and the flags topping the chariots—Ravana's ensign of the Veena[19] and Rama's with the whole universe on it—clashed, and one heard the stringing and twanging of bow-strings on both sides, overpowering in volume all other sound. Then followed a shower of arrows from Rama's own bow. Ravana stood gazing at the chariot sent by Indra and swore, "These gods, instead of supporting me, have gone to the support of this

---

15. **Mahodara** (mə-hō′də-rä).
16. **conch** (kŏngk): a large spiral seashell, used as a trumpet.
17. **Panchajanya** (pän′chə-jən′yə).
18. **Mahavishnu** (mə-hä′vĭsh′no͞o): the Supreme God in Hinduism, who divides himself into the trinity of Brahma, Vishnu, and Shiva.
19. **Veena** (vē′nə): a stringed musical instrument.

WORDS TO KNOW **incarnation** (ĭn′kär-nā′shən) *n.* a bodily form taken on by a spirit

petty human being. I will teach them a lesson. He is not fit to be killed with my arrows but I shall seize him and his chariot together and fling them into high heaven and dash them to destruction." Despite his oath, he still strung his bow and sent a shower of arrows at Rama, raining in thousands, but they were all invariably shattered and neutralized by the arrows from Rama's bow, which met arrow for arrow. Ultimately Ravana, instead of using one bow, used ten with his twenty arms, multiplying his attack tenfold; but Rama stood unhurt.

Ravana suddenly realized that he should change his tactics and ordered his charioteer to fly the chariot up in the skies. From there he attacked and destroyed a great many of the monkey army supporting Rama. Rama ordered Matali, "Go up in the air. Our young soldiers are being attacked from the sky. Follow Ravana, and don't slacken."

There followed an aerial pursuit at dizzying speed across the dome of the sky and rim of the earth. Ravana's arrows came down like rain; he was bent upon destroying everything in the world. But Rama's arrows diverted, broke, or neutralized Ravana's. Terror-stricken, the gods watched this pursuit. Presently Ravana's arrows struck Rama's horses and pierced the heart of Matali himself. The charioteer fell. Rama paused for a while in grief, undecided as to his next step. Then he recovered and resumed his offensive. At that moment the divine eagle Garuda was seen perched on Rama's flagpost, and the gods who were watching felt that this could be an auspicious sign.

After circling the globe several times, the duelling chariots returned, and the fight continued over Lanka. It was impossible to be very clear about the location of the battleground as the fight occurred here, there, and everywhere. Rama's arrows pierced Ravana's armour and made him wince. Ravana was so insensible to pain and impervious to attack that for him to wince was a good sign, and the gods hoped that this was a turn for the better. But at this moment, Ravana suddenly changed his tactics. Instead of merely shooting his arrows, which were powerful in themselves, he also invoked several supernatural forces to create strange effects: He was an adept in the use of various asthras[20] which could be made dynamic with special incantations. At this point, the fight became one of attack with supernatural powers, and parrying of such an attack with other supernatural powers.

Ravana realized that the mere aiming of shafts with ten or twenty of his arms would be of no avail because the mortal whom he had so contemptuously thought of destroying with a slight effort was proving formidable, and his arrows were beginning to pierce and cause pain. Among the asthras sent by Ravana was one called "Danda," a special gift from Shiva, capable of pursuing and pulverizing its target. When it came flaming along, the gods were struck with fear. But Rama's arrow neutralized it.

Now Ravana said to himself, "These are all petty weapons. I should really get down to proper business." And he invoked the one called "Maya"—a weapon which created illusions and confused the enemy.

With proper incantations and worship, he sent off this weapon and it created an illusion of reviving all the armies and its leaders—Kumbakarna and Indrajit and the others—and bringing them back to the battlefield. Presently Rama found all those who, he thought, were no

20. **asthras** (əs'thrəz): arrows or other weapons powered by supernatural forces.

WORDS TO KNOW

impervious (ĭm-pûr'vē-əs) *adj.* incapable of being penetrated; unaffected

incantation (ĭn'kăn-tā'shən) *n.* a chant intended to bring forth supernatural powers; magic spell

parrying (păr'ē-ĭng) *n.* warding off or turning aside **parry** *v.*

formidable (fôr'mĭ-də-bəl) *adj.* hard to handle or overcome

more, coming on with battle cries and surrounding him. Every man in the enemy's army was again up in arms. They seemed to fall on Rama with victorious cries. This was very confusing and Rama asked Matali, whom he had by now revived, "What is happening now? How are all these coming back? They were dead." Matali explained, "In your original identity you are the creator of illusions in this universe. Please know that Ravana has created phantoms to confuse you. If you make up your mind, you can dispel them immediately." Matali's explanation was a great help. Rama at once invoked a weapon called "Gnana"[21]—which means "wisdom" or "perception." This was a very rare weapon, and he sent it forth. And all the terrifying armies who seemed to have come on in such a great mass suddenly evaporated into thin air.

Ravana then shot an asthra called "Thama," whose nature was to create total darkness in all the worlds. The arrows came with heads exposing frightening eyes and fangs, and fiery tongues. End to end the earth was enveloped in total darkness and the whole of creation was paralysed. This asthra also created a deluge of rain on one side, a rain of stones on the other, a hail-storm showering down intermittently, and a tornado sweeping the earth. Ravana was sure that this would arrest Rama's enterprise. But Rama was able to meet it with what was named "Shivasthra."[22] He understood the nature of the phenomenon and the cause of it and chose the appropriate asthra for counteracting it.

Ravana now shot off what he considered his deadliest weapon—a trident[23] endowed with extraordinary destructive power, once gifted to Ravana by the gods. When it started on its journey there was real panic all round. It came on flaming toward Rama, its speed or course unaffected by the arrows he flung at it.

When Rama noticed his arrows falling down

Rama and Lakshmana fight the demoness Taraka (1587–1598, India, Mughal, school of Akbar), Mushfiq. Leaf from a manuscript, opaque colors and gold on paper, 27.5 cm x 15.2 cm, courtesy of the Freer Gallery of Art, Smithsonian Institution, Washington, D.C. (07.217 35v).

21. **Gnana** (gnä′nə).

22. **Shivasthra** (shĭ-vəs′thrə).

23. **trident** (trīd′nt): a spear with three prongs.

ineffectively while the trident sailed towards him, for a moment he lost heart. When it came quite near, he uttered a certain mantra[24] from the depth of his being and while he was breathing out that incantation, an esoteric syllable in perfect timing, the trident collapsed. Ravana, who had been so certain of vanquishing Rama with his trident, was astonished to see it fall down within an inch of him, and for a minute wondered if his adversary might not after all be a divine being although he looked like a mortal. Ravana thought to himself, "This is, perhaps, the highest God. Who could he be? Not Shiva, for Shiva is my supporter; he could not be Brahma, who is four faced; could not be Vishnu, because of my immunity from the weapons of the whole trinity. Perhaps this man is the primordial being, the cause behind the whole universe. But whoever he may be, I will not stop my fight until I defeat and crush him or at least take him prisoner."

With this resolve, Ravana next sent a weapon which issued forth monstrous serpents vomiting fire and venom, with enormous fangs and red eyes. They came darting in from all directions.

Rama now selected an asthra called "Garuda" (which meant "eagle"). Very soon thousands of eagles were aloft, and they picked off the serpents with their claws and beaks and destroyed them. Seeing this also fail, Ravana's anger was roused to a mad pitch and he blindly emptied a quiverful of arrows in Rama's direction. Rama's arrows met them half way and turned them round so that they went back and their sharp points embedded themselves in Ravana's own chest.

Ravana was weakening in spirit. He realized that he was at the end of his resources. All his learning and equipment in weaponry were of no avail and he had practically come to the end of his special gifts of destruction. While he was going down thus, Rama's own spirit was soaring up. The combatants were now near enough to grapple with each other and Rama realized that this was the best moment to cut off Ravana's heads. He sent a crescent-shaped arrow which sliced off one of Ravana's heads and flung it far into the sea, and this process continued; but every time a head was cut off, Ravana had the benediction of having another one grown in its place. Rama's crescent-shaped weapon was continuously busy as Ravana's heads kept cropping up. Rama lopped off his arms but they grew again and every lopped-off arm hit Matali and the chariot and tried to cause destruction by itself, and the tongue in a new head wagged, uttered challenges, and cursed Rama. On the cast-off heads of Ravana devils and minor demons, who had all along been in terror of Ravana and had obeyed and pleased him, executed a dance of death and feasted on the flesh.

Ravana was now desperate. Rama's arrows embedded themselves in a hundred places on his body and weakened him. Presently he collapsed in a faint on the floor of his chariot. Noticing his state, his charioteer pulled back and drew the chariot aside. Matali whispered to Rama, "This is the time to finish off that demon. He is in a faint. Go on. Go on."

But Rama put away his bow and said, "It is not fair warfare to attack a man who is in a faint. I will wait. Let him recover," and waited.

When Ravana revived, he was angry with his charioteer for withdrawing, and took out his sword, crying, "You have disgraced me. Those who look on will think I have retreated." But his charioteer explained how Rama suspended the fight and forebore to attack when he was in a faint. Somehow, Ravana appreciated his explanation and patted his back and resumed his attacks. Having exhausted his special weapons, in desperation Ravana began to throw on Rama

---

24. **mantra** (măn′trə): a word, sound, or phrase used as a prayer or spell.

WORDS TO KNOW

esoteric (ĕs′ə-tĕr′ĭk) *adj.* understood only by a chosen few
primordial (prī-môr′dē-əl) *adj.* first existing; original

all sorts of things such as staves, cast-iron balls, heavy rocks, and oddments he could lay hands on. None of them touched Rama, but glanced off and fell ineffectually. Rama went on shooting his arrows. There seemed to be no end of this struggle in sight.

Now Rama had to pause to consider what final measure he should take to bring this campaign to an end. After much thought, he decided to use "Brahmasthra,"[25] a weapon specially designed by the Creator Brahma on a former occasion, when he had to provide one for Shiva to destroy Tripura,[26] the old monster who assumed the forms of flying mountains and settled down on habitations and cities, seeking to destroy the world. The Brahmasthra was a special gift to be used only when all other means had failed. Now Rama, with prayers and worship, invoked its fullest power and sent it in Ravana's direction, aiming at his heart rather than his head; Ravana being vulnerable at heart. While he had prayed for indestructibility of his several heads and arms, he had forgotten to strengthen his heart, where the Brahmasthra entered and ended his career.

Rama watched him fall headlong from his chariot face down onto the earth, and that was the end of the great campaign. Now one noticed Ravana's face aglow with a new quality. Rama's arrows had burnt off the layers of dross,[27] the anger, conceit, cruelty, lust, and egotism which had encrusted his real self, and now his personality came through in its pristine form—of one who was devout and capable of tremendous attainments. His constant meditation on Rama, although as an adversary, now seemed to bear fruit, as his face shone with serenity and peace. Rama noticed it from his chariot above and commanded Matali, "Set me down on the ground." When the chariot descended and came to rest on its wheels, Rama got down and commanded Matali, "I am grateful for your services to me. You may now take the chariot back to Indra."

Surrounded by his brother Lakshmana and Hanuman and all his other war chiefs, Rama approached Ravana's body, and stood gazing on it. He noted his crowns and jewellery scattered piecemeal on the ground. The decorations and the extraordinary workmanship of the armour on his chest were blood-covered. Rama sighed as if to say, "What might he not have achieved but for the evil stirring within him!"

At this moment, as they readjusted Ravana's blood-stained body, Rama noticed to his great shock a scar on Ravana's back and said with a smile, "Perhaps this is not an episode of glory for me as I seem to have killed an enemy who was turning his back and retreating. Perhaps I was wrong in shooting the Brahmasthra into him." He looked so concerned at this supposed lapse on his part that Vibishana, Ravana's brother, came forward to explain. "What you have achieved is unique. I say so although it meant the death of my brother."

"But I have attacked a man who had turned his back," Rama said. "See that scar."

Vibishana explained, "It is an old scar. In ancient days, when he paraded his strength around the globe, once he tried to attack the divine elephants that guard the four directions. When he tried to catch them, he was gored in the back by one of the tuskers and that is the scar you see now; it is not a fresh one though fresh blood is flowing on it."

Rama accepted the explanation. "Honour him and cherish his memory so that his spirit may go to heaven, where he has his place. And now I will leave you to attend to his funeral arrangements, befitting his grandeur." ❖

---

25. **Brahmasthra** (brə-məs′thrə).

26. **Tripura** (trĭ-po͞o′rə).

27. **dross:** waste matter; impurities.

RESPONDING OPTIONS

FROM PERSONAL RESPONSE *TO* CRITICAL ANALYSIS

REFLECT **1.** What is your reaction to the battle between Rama and Ravana? Record your response in your notebook.

RETHINK **2.** Ravana, with his 10 heads and 20 arms, would seem to have an advantage over Rama. Why do you think Rama is able to defeat him?

3. How would you describe Rama's heroic code of conduct?

Consider
- the offer he sends to Ravana by messenger
- the two chances he gives Ravana to recover
- his strategy and behavior in battle
- what he tells Ravana's brother after Ravana has been killed

4. Do you think that Ravana is heroic?

Consider
- the heroic qualities you identified for the Personal Connection on page 170
- the tricks Ravana uses in his combat with Rama
- the differences and similarities between Ravana and Rama
- the description of Ravana as he falls to earth from his chariot

RELATE **5.** In India, Rama has been celebrated as a hero for centuries. Compare Rama's heroic qualities with those displayed by heroes of your own country.

LITERARY CONCEPTS

Epics often journey into the realm of the supernatural. **Supernatural elements** include any beings, powers, or events that are unexplainable by the known forces or laws of nature. List the supernatural elements in this excerpt from the *Ramayana.* How important are they to the story? Why do you think supernatural elements are found in the literatures of nearly all cultures?

ANOTHER PATHWAY

Cooperative Learning

With a small group of classmates, analyze the battle strategies employed by Rama and Ravana. Begin by listing the various strategies each character uses against his adversary. Then decide what each strategy reveals about the character who makes use of it.

QUICKWRITES

1. Suppose you were asked to direct a film version of the *Ramayana.* In a **memo** to the film's producer, share your thoughts on the appeal of such a movie to contemporary audiences.

2. Ravana has many supernatural powers that he uses to trick his enemy. If you could choose to have any three supernatural powers for a day, which three would you choose? In a **paragraph,** describe the three supernatural powers and explain why you would choose them.

PORTFOLIO *Save your writing. You may want to use it later as a spring-board to a piece for your portfolio.*

THE WRITER'S STYLE

The *Ramayana* was originally composed in verse, and there have been many verse translations of it. Compare the following verse description of Kumbakarna's death with the corresponding passage in R. K. Narayan's prose translation (page 173). Which version do you think is more effective?

> Deadly arrows keen and flaming from the
> hero's weapon broke,
> Kumbha-karna faint and bleeding felt his
> death at every stroke,
>
> Last, an arrow pierced his armor, from his
> shoulders smote his head,
> Kumbha-karna, lifeless, headless, rolled
> upon the gory bed,
>
> Hurled unto the heaving ocean
> Kumbha-karna's body fell,
> And as shaken by a tempest, mighty was
> the ocean's swell!
>
> *Translated by Romesh C. Dutt*

ART CONNECTION

Examine the image of the monkey-god on page 171. How does it compare with your mental image of Hanuman, the flying monkey in Rama's army?

LITERARY LINKS

Compare the conflict between Rama and Ravana with that between Achilles and Hector in the *Iliad*. In what ways are Rama and Achilles alike? How do they differ? In your opinion, which character is more heroic?

WORDS TO KNOW

Review the Words to Know at the bottom of the selection pages. Then write the word that best fits in each blank.

Zing, the hero of the Zoori nation, was an ___1___ of Erg, the god of energy. According to legend, Zing was a ___2___ being, the first and greatest of the Zoori man-gods. He fought bravely from behind a ___3___ when attacked by Zud, the six-fisted demon. The nasty Zud, with his superior weapons, was a ___4___ opponent. Because of his many fists and scaly skin, Zud seemed ___5___ to harm. Zing recited an ___6___, seeking aid from his divine protectors. His words were ___7___ and meant only for heavenly ears. An army of sacred zebras arrived to help Zing ___8___ the many swords and spears of his foe. Zing and his army proved their ___9___, easily overpowering Zud and his evil followers. Zud shouted a hateful ___10___, shook his six fists, and retired from the battlefield.

VALMIKI

According to current versions of the *Ramayana,* the story of Rama was told to the wise man Valmiki by the divine sage Narada. Although little is known about the poet, some scholars believe that Valmiki was indeed a man of genius. They regard him as the "first poet" of India and the inventor of the *sloka,* the poetic meter used in the *Ramayana* and popular in later Indian poetry.

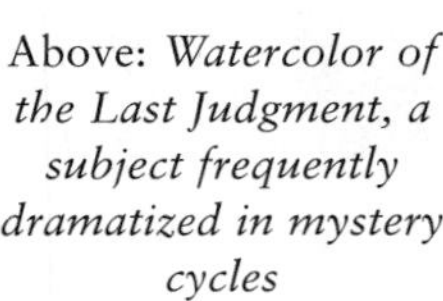

Above: *Watercolor of the Last Judgment, a subject frequently dramatized in mystery cycles*

Above right: *Miniature from a manuscript of* Li Romans d'Alixandre *(about 1340), showing people wearing animal masks, perhaps for an entertainment at court*

Mystery, Miracle, & Morality *Plays*

During the early Middle Ages, in order to make church teachings accessible to the common people, clergymen began to dramatize stories from the Bible and episodes from the lives of saints. The clerics themselves played the roles in the dramas, bringing sacred history to life as part of church services. These dramatized stories soon became a popular part of church life.

Staging diagram for The Castle of Perseverance, *one of the earliest surviving English morality plays*

As time passed, these plays developed into more elaborate productions, known as **mystery plays** (the biblical dramas) and **miracle plays** (the dramas of saints' lives), that were unsuitable for performance inside a church. The job of presenting the mystery plays was taken over by trade and craft guilds, or unions. Each guild took responsibility for one or two plays, building a pageant wagon and making costumes, props, and scenery. On a feast day, the guilds would load their props and scenery onto their wagons, form a procession, and take turns performing the plays at prearranged sites. Together, the plays formed what is called a mystery cycle, covering the whole history of the world, from the creation of Adam and Eve to the Last Judgment.

The mystery cycles were fabulous events. They often ran from sunrise to sunset, sometimes for three or more days, and included music, dance, comedy skits, and special effects to create the illusion of rain, lightning, and flying. These spectacular productions whetted the English appetite for drama. By the 1400s, professional acting troupes were traveling the countryside, performing plays of their own—called **morality plays**—that dealt with the moral struggles of everyday people.

Morality plays dramatized the inner conflicts of characters such as Everyman, an average man who is summoned by Death. Everyman tries to soften his fate by appealing to friends with names like Kindred and Fellowship, but in the face of Death they desert him. He can bring only Good Deeds along with him to the grave.

The message, of course, was crystal clear, but the play *Everyman* was more than a sermon or fable. To a large extent, morality plays such as this represented a step away from the religious drama and toward a popular English secular drama. By the 1500s, morality plays were a regular part of street pageants and began to adopt elements of court entertainments, such as mummers plays (pantomimes), tournaments, and masquerades.

As morality plays grew more varied and sophisticated, their popularity increased. The English people became a nation of theatergoers, and a wide range of dramatic entertainments became part of England's cultural life. In this way, the morality plays—like the mystery and miracle plays before them—set the stage for Elizabethan drama and the genius of playwrights like William Shakespeare.

Above:
Woodcut illustrating John Skot's edition of Everyman *(about 1503)*

Left:
In a mystery cycle, a trade or craft guild might produce a play related to its members' occupation. A shipbuilders' guild, for example, might produce a play about Noah's ark.

PREVIEWING

NONFICTION

from The Book of Margery Kempe

Margery Kempe

PERSONAL CONNECTION

Think of a time when you experienced a great deal of stress or anxiety—perhaps a time when you were facing a serious illness or a major change in your life. How did you handle the experience? Did you do anything special to help yourself cope?

HISTORICAL/BIOGRAPHICAL CONNECTION

During the Middle Ages, religion influenced all aspects of life, and the clergy was a powerful force in both spiritual and political matters. Like the rest of medieval society, the religious hierarchy was controlled by men. A woman who wished to pursue a spiritual calling was expected to join a convent or to live as a recluse. Margery Kempe did neither. Although a wife and mother, she was determined to devote her life to Christ and, at the age of 40, became a religious visionary, traveling and preaching extensively in England, Europe, and the Holy Land. In the 1430s, Kempe dictated to two different scribes the story of her spiritual life, *The Book of Margery Kempe,* which was not published in its entirety until 1936. It is the earliest surviving autobiography in the English language.

Margery Kempe was born about 1373 in Lynn—a town in the county of Norfolk, England—where her father served five terms as mayor. Although born to a prominent family, Kempe, like most women of her time, received little education. Around the age of 20, she married John Kempe, a tax collector, with whom she had 14 children. The text of Kempe's autobiography begins with the birth of her first child and describes a deeply troubling experience that would affect the course of her life.

READING CONNECTION

Reading an Autobiography Typically, writers of autobiographies—accounts of the writers' own lives—recount their experiences in the first person, using the pronouns *I* and *me.* Margery Kempe, however, tells her story in the third person, referring to herself as "this creature" and using the pronouns *she* and *her.* As you read about Kempe's experience, think of some reasons why she might have chosen to use the third-person, rather than the first-person, point of view.

Detail of *The Harvesters* (1565), Pieter Brueghel the Elder. Panel, 46½" × 63¼", The Metropolitan Museum of Art, The Rogers Fund, 1919.

from The Book of Margery Kempe

Chapter One Illness and Recovery

Woman tending fire and reading, from an illuminated manuscript

When this creature was twenty years of age, or somewhat more, she was married to a worshipful burgess[1] [of Lynn] and was with child within a short time, as nature would have it. And after she had conceived, she was troubled with severe attacks of sickness until the

1. **burgess** (bûr′jĭs): a citizen of an English town.

child was born. And then, what with the labor-pains she had in childbirth and the sickness that had gone before, she despaired of her life, believing she might not live. Then she sent for her confessor,[2] for she had a thing on her conscience which she had never revealed before that time in all her life. For she was continually hindered by her enemy—the devil—always saying to her while she was in good health that she didn't need to confess but to do penance by herself alone, and all should be forgiven, for God is merciful enough. And therefore this creature often did great penance in fasting on bread and water, and performed other acts of charity with devout prayers, but she would not reveal that one thing in confession.

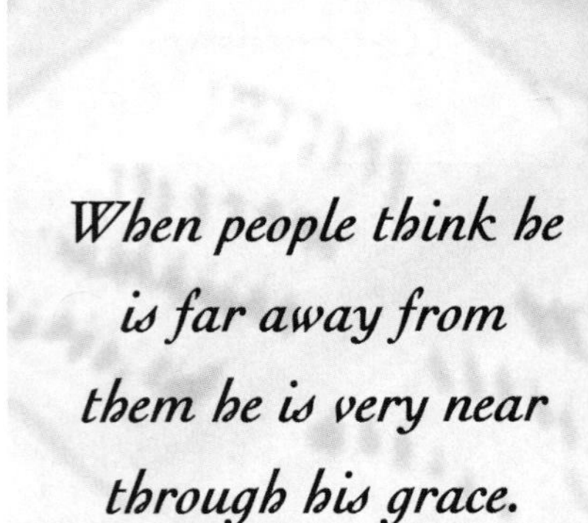
When people think he
is far away from
them he is very near
through his grace.

And when she was at any time sick or troubled, the devil said in her mind that she should be damned, for she was not shriven[3] of that fault. Therefore, after her child was born, and not believing she would live, she sent for her confessor, as said before, fully wishing to be shriven of her whole lifetime, as near as she could. And when she came to the point of saying that thing which she had so long concealed, her confessor was a little too hasty and began sharply to reprove her before she had fully said what she meant, and so she would say no more in spite of anything he might do. And soon after, because of the dread she had of damnation on the one hand, and his sharp reproving of her on the other, this creature went out of her mind and was amazingly disturbed and tormented with spirits for half a year, eight weeks and odd days.

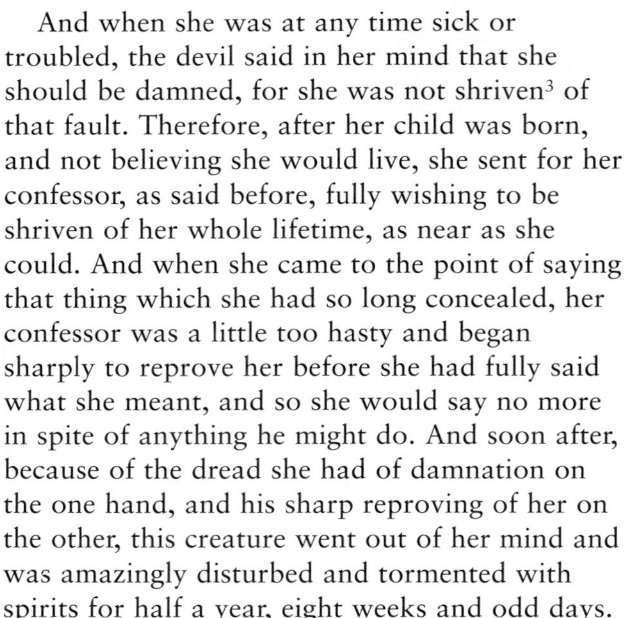

And in this time she saw, as she thought, devils opening their mouths all alight with burning flames of fire, as if they would have swallowed her in, sometimes pawing at her, sometimes threatening her, sometimes pulling her and hauling her about both night and day during the said time. And also the devils called out to her with great threats, and bade her that she should forsake her Christian faith and belief, and deny her God, his mother, and all the saints in heaven, her good works and all good virtues, her father, her mother, and all her friends. And so she did. She slandered her husband, her friends, and her own self. She spoke many sharp and reproving words; she recognized no virtue nor goodness; she desired all wickedness; just as the spirits tempted her to say and do, so she said and did. She would

2. **confessor:** spiritual adviser; the priest to whom Margery confessed her sins.

3. **shriven:** absolved; forgiven.

have killed herself many a time as they stirred her to, and would have been damned with them in hell, and in witness of this she bit her own hand so violently that the mark could be seen for the rest of her life. And also she pitilessly tore the skin on her body near her heart with her nails, for she had no other implement, and she would have done something worse, except that she was tied up and forcibly restrained both day and night so that she could not do as she wanted.

And when she had long been troubled by these and many other temptations, so that people thought she should never have escaped from them alive, then one time as she lay by herself and her keepers were not with her, our merciful Lord Christ Jesus—ever to be trusted, worshiped be his name, never forsaking his servant in time of need—appeared to his creature who had forsaken him, in the likeness of a man, the most seemly, most beauteous, and most amiable that ever might be seen with man's eye, clad in a mantle of purple silk, sitting upon her bedside, looking upon her with so blessed a countenance that she was strengthened in all her spirits, and he said to her these words: "Daughter, why have you forsaken me, and I never forsook you?"

And as soon as he had said these words, she saw truly how the air opened as bright as any lightning, and he ascended up into the air, not hastily and quickly, but beautifully and gradually, so that she could clearly behold him in the air until it closed up again.

And presently the creature grew as calm in her wits and her reason as she ever was before, and asked her husband, as soon as he came to her, if she could have the keys of the buttery[4] to get her food and drink as she had done before. Her maids and her keepers advised him that he should not deliver up any keys to her, for they said she would only give away such goods as there were, because she did not know what she was saying, as they believed.

Nevertheless, her husband, who always had tenderness and compassion for her, ordered that they should give her the keys. And she took food and drink as her bodily strength would allow her, and she once again recognized her friends and her household, and everybody else who came to her in order to see how our Lord Jesus Christ had worked his grace in her—blessed may he be, who is ever near in tribulation.[5] When people think he is far away from them he is very near through his grace. Afterwards this creature performed all her responsibilities wisely and soberly enough, except that she did not truly know our Lord's power to draw us to him.[6] ❖

4. **buttery:** pantry.
5. **tribulation:** suffering or distress.
6. **did not . . . power:** did not feel the full attraction of God's grace. Kempe is saying that her total devotion to the Lord did not come until later.

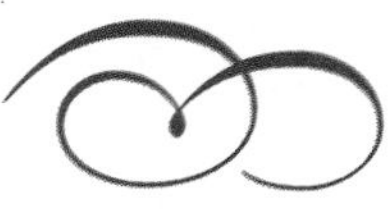

RESPONDING OPTIONS

FROM PERSONAL RESPONSE *TO* CRITICAL ANALYSIS

REFLECT

1. How did Margery Kempe's description of her illness affect you? Share your thoughts with the class.

RETHINK

2. On the basis of your reading, how would you describe Margery Kempe?

Consider
- her reasons for talking to a confessor
- the way she handles stress and anxiety
- her response to the spiritual vision

3. Do you think Kempe's account of her illness and recovery is believable? Why or why not?

4. What does Kempe's experience tell you about her society's attitude toward mental illness?

RELATE

5. Think about modern views of mental illness. Do you think the mentally ill are better able to cope today? Is our society more understanding of those who suffer from mental illness? Explain your opinion.

ANOTHER PATHWAY

Assume the role of Margery Kempe's husband, and describe her experience from his point of view. What additional information do you think his account might contain?

QUICKWRITES

1. As Kempe's confessor, write a **letter** to John Kempe, giving your opinion or explanation of the illness and visions his wife has experienced.
2. Write a **script** for a dialogue in which Kempe and her husband discuss her recovery after more than eight months of mental disturbances.
3. Think about a time when you recovered from an illness. Make a **list** of the things that gave you the most pleasure after you got well. For example, you may have enjoyed tasting your dinner, playing sports outside, or seeing friends.

PORTFOLIO *Save your writing. You may want to use it later as a springboard to a piece for your portfolio.*

LITERARY CONCEPTS

An **autobiography** is a writer's account of his or her own life. Autobiographies often convey profound insights as writers recount past events from the perspective of greater understanding and distance. List various reasons why someone might be inspired to write an autobiography, and then decide which of those reasons, or what other reasons, might have prompted Kempe to record her life story. Share your ideas with the class.

ALTERNATIVE ACTIVITIES

1. ***Cooperative Learning*** Create an **autobiographical account** of one incident in your life, using Kempe's method of dictating to scribes. Form a group with two of your classmates, and describe the incident in private, first to one and then to the other. Have each write down an account of the incident; then meet with them and compare the two versions. Discuss how Kempe's story may have been altered as it was dictated and recorded in writing.
2. Make a **drawing** or **painting** of one of the visions Kempe experienced during her illness.
3. Design and create a **book jacket** for Kempe's autobiography. Use images from the selection.

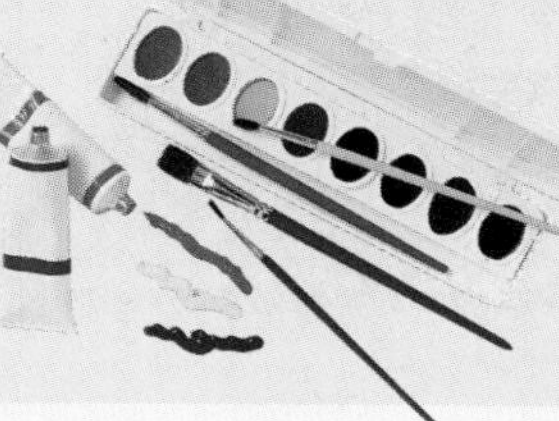

ACROSS THE CURRICULUM

Science Investigate the nature of medical care during the 14th and 15th centuries. Present your findings in an oral report to the class.

CRITIC'S CORNER

A critic has said that Margery Kempe exhibits contradictory qualities, appearing to be both humble and forceful, both devout and arrogant. Try to find evidence of these contradictory qualities in the selection.

MARGERY KEMPE

1373?–1439?

At around the age of 40, after bearing 14 children, Margery Kempe decided to become a "bride of Christ"—to live in chastity and preach her visions to the world. As a vocal, outgoing speaker she was quite an oddity at a time when most women remained at home as wives and mothers. Although many men and women she met considered her a model of human compassion and devotion, many others disapproved of her lifestyle.

Once Kempe had made her commitment to God, she began a series of religious pilgrimages to Jerusalem, Spain, Italy, and Germany. It was in Jerusalem that she received her "gift" of weeping. She would fall into violent fits of crying at unpredictable times throughout the rest of her life, often during church service. Both the clergy and the common people found her hysterical crying at best annoying, at worst heretical. As a result, Kempe encountered a good deal of persecution and ridicule, although she maintained that her tears were a special gift from God, a physical token of her special worth in his eyes. She was also censured by many for dressing all in white, which at the time was a symbol of both chastity and piety.

Her autobiography, *The Book of Margery Kempe,* is important for several reasons. The work serves as a sort of time capsule, preserving for the reader the social customs, speech, and attitudes of the day. It also reveals the singular character of Kempe herself, a strong woman of faith who lived by her convictions despite intense social criticism and opposition. Finally, as an autobiography it is unique in its purpose: Kempe felt her story to be worth the telling not as a record of her life, which she probably thought too unimportant to merit a written account, but as a testament to God's power and his wonderful dealings with "this creature" Margery Kempe.

WRITING FROM EXPERIENCE

WRITING TO REFLECT

In Unit One you've encountered people who have had their courage tested. You've probably faced challenges in your own life at times—perhaps not monsters or fierce warriors, but tests as important to you as their own were to Beowulf, Achilles, and other legendary heroes.

GUIDED ASSIGNMENT

Write a Reflective Essay In a reflective essay you think about the meaning of an experience, incident, or event. You look for a lesson about life that the experience taught you. This type of essay, written in the first person, allows you to share your personal reaction to an experience.

Newspaper Story

Attempt to Integrate Central High Fails

LITTLE ROCK, ARK., Sept. 4, 1957

A hostile mob prevented Elizabeth Eckford from entering Little Rock's all-white Central High School today. Eckford was one of nine black students who tried to end racial segregation in the school.

1 Look for Ideas

Be Open to Life's Lessons Have you ever had an experience or read an article that contained an important lesson or nugget of wisdom? The activities below may help you recall experiences that can serve as springboards to some truth about life:

- Think about your own experiences. What was the worst thing that ever happened to you? the best thing? the most frightening thing? Do you recall the first time you did something? What event will you remember forever?
- Talk with friends or acquaintances about experiences that had particular meaning for them. (You can start with the questions above.)
- Think about things you've read, heard, or seen on TV. For example, what lessons can be found in the news stories on these pages?

Quotation from TV Documentary

"We do not want to be called heroes. We are people first and our disabilities, well, they are just a fact of life."

Itzhak Perlman, violinist and childhood polio victim, from "Bodies in Motion"

Examine the photos that accompany the two news stories. List the ways in which these photos extend your understanding of the stories.

Newspaper Feature Story

How Muggsy Overcame Long Odds

The subject of the interview was Tyrone Bogues Sr., known universally as Muggsy, who is 30 years old and stands 5 feet 3 inches tall. He is the speedy, stocky, starting point guard for the Hornets, the team's most valuable player last year and the shortest player in the history of the National Basketball Association.

The interviewer was his son, Tyrone Jr., age 3, who comes about up to his father's hip and is the shortest person in the Bogues household.

"Daddy," said Ty Jr., holding up a microphone, "Alonzo Mourning is this big"—Ty Jr. held his hand over his head—"and you are this big." He dropped his hand to his knee. "Alonzo Mourning can dunk the basketball and you can't. Why's that?"

"Why's that?" asked the startled father. "What kind of interview is this? What show am I on, anyway? I'm leaving."

All this drew a laugh from everyone but the interviewer, who still waited, microphone in hand, for the answer.

And Muggsy gave it. "Two is two," he said.

"What?" Ty Jr. asked.

"It doesn't matter how you do something," Muggsy said. "The only thing that matters is what you do. And a basket counts for 2 points any way it goes in."

What challenges did Muggsy face when he was my age?

And there in the few moments of this interview, the life of Muggsy Bogues passed before him. Every day of his life, he has said, he has to prove himself over again. Every day of his life, he has to demonstrate that someone his size can accomplish the improbable. And every day of his life, he confronts and ultimately confounds his critics, whether they are in the press, on the basketball court, or, even, in his den.

Do I agree that it doesn't matter how you do something?

Ira Berkow
from the *New York Times*, February 26, 1995

2 Record Your Ideas

As you collect experiences to write about, think about their meanings. What significance, what lessons about life, do the experiences hold? Do they suggest ideas about courage, attempts at perfection, or other important themes, ideas, or truths? Freewrite for several minutes to get your first thoughts on paper. If a printed source inspired you, you can attach self-stick notes to your source, as shown above.

PREWRITING

Exploring Experiences

The Selection Process You've begun thinking about experiences and may already have some ideas about what lessons they can teach. Now you're ready to begin seriously investigating your thoughts. The following steps will help you focus on an experience and explore the ways in which it conveys a lesson about life.

1 Look for Meaning

After considering ideas from your own life and other sources, think about how an experience can inspire a reflective essay. Begin by listing some of the experiences you've been considering, and think about the meanings you can find in each one. A planning chart like the one at the right can help you begin sorting out your ideas. Don't stop after your first thought. Dig deeper and see what other lessons you can learn from an experience.

Student's Planning Chart

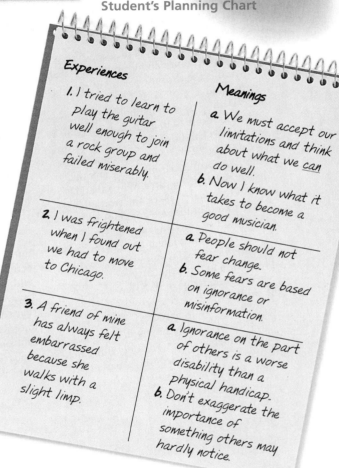

Experiences	Meanings
1. I tried to learn to play the guitar well enough to join a rock group and failed miserably.	a. We must accept our limitations and think about what we can do well. b. Now I know what it takes to become a good musician.
2. I was frightened when I found out we had to move to Chicago.	a. People should not fear change. b. Some fears are based on ignorance or misinformation.
3. A friend of mine has always felt embarrassed because she walks with a slight limp.	a. Ignorance on the part of others is a worse disability than a physical handicap. b. Don't exaggerate the importance of something others may hardly notice.

2 Capture the Main Idea

Find a Thesis Look at your planning chart or list of ideas and find the experience you think is the most promising. In one or two sentences, try to capture the broader meaning or lesson the experience suggests. This broader meaning will be your thesis, the main point of your essay. For example, any of the meanings recorded in the planning chart at the right could be developed as the thesis of a reflective essay.

Find Further Support Look for other examples that will further support your thesis. These examples can come from your own experiences or from the experiences of other people you've talked to or interviewed. Your reading is another potential source of examples. Newspaper and magazine stories, biographies, and even fiction may contain experiences that will support or help you focus on your thesis.

3 Talk About It

Talk your ideas over with others. Do they agree or disagree with your thesis? They may be able to offer new insights or further examples to support your thesis.

4 Take Stock

Think about what you've accomplished so far. You might ask yourself the following questions.

- Have I thoroughly explored the basic theme of my essay—the truth I mean to get out of the experience I am describing? Have I also considered secondary meanings?
- Which details of the experience can best help me bring out that truth?
- Which other examples will help me?

SkillBuilder

CRITICAL THINKING

Generalizing

Generalizing involves using something specific as the basis for a statement of a general principle. For example, the experience of failing to become a good rock guitarist, backed up by one or two similar experiences, could lead you to the generalization that people must learn to live with their limitations—in other words, we must learn to accept what life hands us.

APPLYING WHAT YOU'VE LEARNED

Form a generalization based on each of the following instances:

1. Muggsy Bogues decides to become a basketball player in spite of his small stature and becomes a star in the NBA.
2. Thomas Edison experiments with hundreds of substances before discovering the right filament material for the first practical electric light bulb.

THINK & PLAN

Reflecting on Your Ideas

1. Have you found sufficient support for your thesis? If not, where can you look for more?
2. How can you weave into your essay the information necessary to support your thesis?
3. How can you convey the impact your experience had on you?

DRAFTING

Getting Your Ideas Down

A Framework for Thinking In many reflective essays, the writer starts with one experience, uses it as a springboard to establish a thesis, and then expands upon the thesis with additional examples. Your narrative of the main experience may take up a major part of your essay, or it may be related very briefly, with most of the essay being expository reflection on the theme.

1 Write a Rough Draft

You might begin by retelling the incident that led to your discovery, then telling what you learned from it. Afterward, you can elaborate on what you've written and generalize to form your thesis. Finally, you can expand your idea with additional examples. The Writing Coach can help you with this stage.

Student's Rough Draft

Conquering Crime

My Rough Draft	My Comments My Rough Draft
Three years ago I found out my family would be moving to Chicago. The news meant that I'd have to leave behind all my friends and the life I knew in the small Iowa town I'd been brought up in. I'd be going to a place I'd never seen. The whole idea of moving scared me, and I was pretty miserable until I got to know something about Chicago and gradually lost my fear.	Might be good to start with some reflections on the basic idea of fear of change, then relate my experience (with more detail to bring it alive), then get in some additional examples before arriving at a final conclusion.
Thinking about that experience now—and how it turned out—I know that my fears were largely a fear of change. Everything at home seemed safe and familiar, everything in Chicago frightening and unfamiliar. Some fear of change may be natural; at any rate, it's pretty common. However, if we let the fear affect us as much as mine did, it can be damaging.	
A lot of people have this fear of change. I remember my dad, usually so confident, being scared when he had to learn to use a computer at work. A much more serious example would be the feelings of many people in the South when the Supreme Court said they had to integrate their schools. I can recall a picture of an African American girl walking through a jeering crowd, their faces distorted with hatred.	What other examples can I add? Who were those people in England during the Industrial Revolution who went around smashing machines? Additional comments: The ideas are good, but this isn't yet an essay. It has some good raw material, however.

❷ Analyze Your Rough Draft

After finishing your rough draft, analyze what you've done. Ask yourself questions such as the following:

- Have I made the importance of the experience and the lesson I learned from it clear?
- Have I included all necessary details? too many details?
- Does any part need to be expanded?
- What parts of my draft do I particularly like? dislike?

Read the notes the writer of the draft on the left made in the analysis stage. Would similar notes help you analyze your draft?

❸ Rework and Share

You can use the guidelines below as you turn your rough draft into a more polished first draft.

- Create a strong opening. Try to capture your readers' attention in your first paragraph.
- Choose a method of organization that suits your purpose. The narrative section may require a chronological order, but you could use other methods to explore the idea. You might decide to reflect on the thesis or the truth you discovered before you start your narrative.
- The two strongest positions in an essay are its beginning and its end. You might use one or both of these positions to bring out the truth you mean to explore.

PEER RESPONSE

A peer reviewer can help you identify the strengths and weaknesses of your draft. Ask a peer reviewer questions such as the following:

- What lesson did my essay convey to you?
- Which examples best illustrate my point?
- What did you find least effective in my essay?

SkillBuilder

WRITER'S CRAFT

Writing an Introduction

You can begin a reflective essay in a number of ways. Here are some openings used for this type of expository writing.

- Start with a statement of your main idea or thesis.
- Tell an anecdote that relates to your thesis.
- Pose a question that you intend to answer or explore.
- Use a quotation that relates to your theme or thesis.

In addition, since your essay may include a narrative section, you may choose to start at some dramatic moment in the incident.

WRITING HANDBOOK

For more information on writing introductions, see pages 1220–1221 of the Writing Handbook.

APPLYING WHAT YOU'VE LEARNED

Draft an opening paragraph for your reflective essay, using one of the techniques described above.

RETHINK & EVALUATE

Preparing to Revise

1. What additional examples can you use to strengthen your thesis?
2. How can you encourage your readers to think about the meaning of the experience you are describing?

Finishing Your Essay

A Last Look This is the stage at which you revise and edit your work. You might want to let your essay sit overnight or longer so that you can give it a fresh look before you begin revising it into a final draft. The information on these pages offers some suggestions about revising and editing.

1 Revise and Edit

Look at your draft with a critical eye. Try to see it as an outsider rather than as the writer. The following tips can help you as you prepare to revise your essay:

- Make sure there is a clear relationship between the experience you describe and the truth you draw out of it.
- Be sure you have chosen the best examples to illustrate your thesis.
- Review peer comments with an open mind. You may decide to ignore them, act on only some of them, or accept everything.
- Use the Standards for Evaluation and the Editing Checklist in the SkillBuilder on the next page as you revise, edit, and proofread your essay.

How does this opening compare with the one in the student's rough draft?

Student's Revised Essay

Our lives are filled with fears we must conquer. We may not have our courage tested by monsters and dragons, but we all have our inner demons. Some people fear heights or closed places or become frightened by peer pressures. Seniors may be uneasy about what lies ahead after graduation. My fear was a fear of change, and I faced a big test when I was fourteen.

I learned something important as a result of this experience. Moving to Chicago brought big changes to my life and my lifestyle, but I faced the changes, adapted to them, and eventually became grateful for them. Although anxiety about change is natural, even useful at times, being terrified by it, I realized, is foolish.

The machinery-smashing workers of the 1800s and some southerners at the time of the civil rights movement let their fears drive them to violence. People who are frightened today by computers or genetic engineering need to realize that these developments can allow them to do things they never dreamed of once they get past their fear of change. Change is here to stay. It's the one thing we can always count on. To fear what's going to happen anyway is senseless.

How does the writer's use of comparison and contrast help support the conclusion?

Find out what video equipment is available and if you can get help in using it.

2 Share Your Work

The way you publish your final version depends on your intended audience and your goal. Below are some additional publishing possibilities for sharing a reflective essay.

PUBLISHING IDEAS

- Present your essay as a dramatic monologue before a live audience or recorded on videotape.
- Save your essay as part of a collection of personal writing you might be able to draw on sometime in the future.
- Submit your essay to your school newspaper or magazine.
- Send it to friends or to a general audience on the Internet.

Standards for Evaluation

A reflective essay
- is written from the first-person point of view
- includes an introduction that attracts readers' attention
- relates an experience from the writer's—or some other person's—life
- uses the experience as a basis for a general observation about life
- allows readers to think about the significance of the experience in the light of their own lives

SkillBuilder

GRAMMAR FROM WRITING

Using Quotation Marks

In relating an incident, you may include dialogue. In passages of dialogue, be sure you use quotation marks correctly, especially with other marks of punctuation.

GRAMMAR HANDBOOK

For more information on using quotation marks, see pages 1292–1293 of the Grammar Handbook.

Editing Checklist Use the following revision and editing tips as you revise your draft:

- Did you use quotation marks and other punctuation correctly?
- Did you use verb tenses correctly to distinguish between present and past events?
- Did you proofread your draft carefully?

REFLECT & ASSESS

Evaluate the Experience

1. What did you learn about yourself as you worked on your reflective essay? What did you learn about life?
2. What new skills did you use in writing your essay? What writing skills do you think you need to develop further?

PORTFOLIO Add your essay to your portfolio along with a note telling what you learned in writing it.

Reflect & Assess

UNIT ONE: THE ANGLO-SAXON AND MEDIEVAL PERIODS

How has reading the selections in this unit added to your understanding of the Anglo-Saxon and medieval periods? What new insights did you gain into life during these times, and how does it compare with life as you know it? Explore these questions by completing one or more options in each of the following sections.

REFLECTING ON THE UNIT

OPTION 1 **Comparing Challenges** Many of the people you have encountered in this unit—both real and fictitious—endure physical, spiritual, and emotional challenges. Select an individual from each of the three parts of the unit, and then write a few paragraphs comparing the ways in which the three people confront their challenges. Explain which person's methods of coping with adversity might be most useful in today's society.

OPTION 2 **Resetting the Scene** With a small group of classmates, discuss which selections in this unit stand out in your mind as being most representative of life in medieval times. Then choose a scene from one of these selections and perform it as a short skit for the rest of the class. If possible, use costumes and background music to help you convey the feeling of the period.

OPTION 3 **Role-Playing** With four or five classmates, hold a "meeting of the minds" in which you role-play several heroic individuals from this unit who sit down to reflect on their lives and times. You may wish to have them praise, criticize, or question one another's actions as they are depicted in the selections.

REFLECT & ASSESS *Self-Assessment: Make a list of the impressions you had about people of the Anglo-Saxon and medieval periods before you read the selections in Unit One. Then note whether your reading has confirmed these preconceptions or proved them wrong.*

REVIEWING LITERARY CONCEPTS

OPTION 1 **Assessing Conflict** The individuals portrayed in this unit become involved in a variety of conflicts, both external and internal. In a chart similar to the one shown, list at least six characters or historical figures from the unit. Describe the main conflict that each faces, and note whether that conflict is external or internal. Are most of the conflicts external, or are most internal? On the basis of your findings, what kinds of problems would you say the people of these times were concerned with?

Character	Main Conflict	Type of Conflict
Beowulf	He must battle with Grendel and the fire dragon.	External

OPTION 2 **Understanding Characterization** Many selections in this unit feature both heroes and villains. Which heroes and villains were the most memorable? List them, and then note the techniques that the writers used to guide your impressions of these characters. With a partner, discuss what could be done to make some of the heroes less appealing and some of the villains more sympathetic.

REFLECT & ASSESS *Self-Assessment: On a sheet of paper, copy the following list of literary terms introduced in this unit. Put a question mark next to each term that you do not fully understand. Consult the Handbook of Literary Terms (page 1192) to clarify the meanings of the terms you've marked with question marks.*

alliteration
simile
epic simile
rhythm
historical writing
tone
plot
conflict
ballad form
romance
characterization
supernatural elements
autobiography

PORTFOLIO BUILDING

- **QuickWrites** Many of the QuickWrites assignments in this unit asked you to assume the identities of characters and people depicted in the selections. From your responses, choose two that you think are particularly successful at conveying the individuals' personalities. In a cover note, explain what you think makes each piece of writing so effective. Then add the pieces and the cover notes to your portfolio.
- **Writing About Literature** Earlier in this unit, you wrote an essay in which you interpreted the values of characters and their community. Reread the essay now. If you could ask the characters four questions, what would they be? How do you think the characters would answer them?
- **Writing from Experience** By now you've written an essay on what you learned from your own or someone else's experience. Reread the essay now. Write a moral that sums up the lesson you learned from that experience. Attach it to your essay if you choose to add the essay to your portfolio.
- **Personal Choice** Reflect on all the activities and writing assignments you have worked on in this unit, including any you might have done independently. Which project would you like to expand into a larger piece? Write a note that explains your plans, and add it to your portfolio.

REFLECT & ASSESS *Self-Assessment: At this point, you are probably just beginning your portfolio for the school year. Review the pieces you have chosen to include so far. What generalizations can you make about your writing strengths and interests?*

SETTING GOALS

As you worked through the reading and writing activities in the unit, you probably became aware of areas in which your work could use some improvement. After thinking over the work you did for this unit, create a list of skills or concepts that you would like to work on in the next unit.

UNIT TWO

No man is an island,
entire of itself;
every man is a piece of the
continent,
a part of the main.

John Donne
poet

1485–1660

The ENGLISH Renaissance

Detail of the altarpiece of the *Virgin of the Navigators* (16th century), unknown artist. Seville, Spain, Reales Alcázares.

TIME LINE

The English Renaissance

1485–1660

1485

Henry Tudor defeats Richard III and takes throne as Henry VII

1492

Columbus lands in New World

1509

Reign of Henry VIII begins

1516

Thomas More publishes *Utopia*

1517

German cleric Martin Luther criticizes Roman Catholic Church, initiating Protestant Reformation

1534

At insistence of Henry VIII, Parliament passes Act of Supremacy, completing break with Roman Catholic Church

1543

Theory of Polish astronomer Nicolaus Copernicus, that earth and other planets revolve around sun, published

1547

Reign of Edward VI begins

1553

Reign of Mary I begins

1558

Reign of Elizabeth I begins

1576

England's first permanent public theater built near London

1588

English navy defeats Spanish Armada

c. 1595

William Shakespeare completes *Romeo and Juliet*

Period *Pieces*

1603

James VI of Scotland becomes king of England as James I

1607

English establish Jamestown colony in Virginia

1609

Irish uprisings quelled; most land in northern Ireland redistributed to English and Scottish Protestants

1611

King James Bible completed

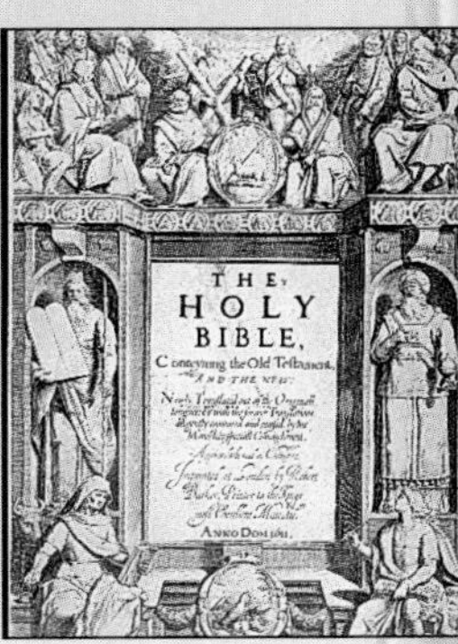
THE HOLY BIBLE,

1620

Pilgrims establish Plymouth colony in Massachusetts

1625

Reign of Charles I begins

1633

John Donne's *Poems* published posthumously

1642

English civil war begins

1649

Charles I beheaded

1660

Monarchy restored with accession of Charles II

Early microscope

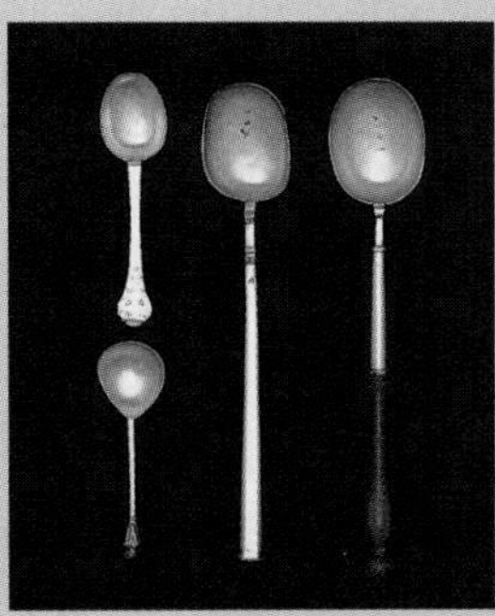

Household items

Engraved floral clock from mid-17th century

INTRODUCTION

The English Renaissance 1485–1660

Above: Henry VIII
Right: Self-portrait of Leonardo da Vinci, artistic and scientific genius of the Italian Renaissance

At certain points in history, factors converge to cause dramatic shifts in human values and perceptions. One such shift, beginning in 14th-century Italy, launched the period of European history known as the Renaissance ("rebirth"). During the Renaissance, the medieval world view, focused on religion and the afterlife, was replaced by a more modern view, stressing human life here on earth. Renaissance Europeans delighted in the arts and literature, in the beauty of nature, in human impulses, and in a new sense of mastery over the world. They reinterpreted Europe's pre-Christian past, using the arts and philosophies of ancient Greece and Rome as models for their own achievements. Surging with creative energy, they expanded the scientific, geographical, and philosophical boundaries of the medieval world, often questioning timeworn truths and challenging authority. A new emphasis was placed on the individual and on the development of human potential. The ideal "Renaissance man" was a many-faceted person who cultivated his innate talents to the fullest.

In England, political instability delayed the advent of Renaissance ideas, but they began to penetrate English society after 1485, when the Wars of the Roses ended and Henry Tudor took the throne as Henry VII. A shrewd if colorless monarch, Henry exercised strong authority at home and negotiated favorable commercial treaties abroad. He built up the nation's merchant fleet and financed expeditions that established English claims in the New World. He also engineered a clever political alliance by arranging for his eldest son, Arthur, to marry Catherine of Aragon, daughter of King Ferdinand and Queen Isabella of Spain, England's greatest New World rival. When Arthur died unexpectedly, the pope granted a special dispensation allowing Arthur's younger brother Henry, the new heir to the throne, to marry Catherine. The marriage would have startling consequences.

Stained-glass panels depicting Henry VIII and Catherine of Aragon

The Reign of Henry VIII

Henry VIII succeeded his father in 1509. A true Renaissance prince, Henry was a skilled athlete, poet, and musician, well educated in French, Italian, and Latin. During his reign, the Protestant Reformation was sweeping northern Europe, propelled by discontent with church abuses and a growing nationalism that resented the influence of Rome. While many in England sympathized with Protestant reforms, Henry at first remained loyal to Rome. However, after 18 years of marriage he had only one child, Mary, and he became obsessed with producing a male heir. Insisting that the papal dispensation had been a mistake, he requested that his marriage be annulled so that he could wed Catherine's court attendant Anne Boleyn. When the pope refused to comply, Henry broke with Rome and in 1534 declared himself head of the Church of England, or Anglican Church.

Top: Armor made for a slim and youthful Henry VIII
Bottom: Anne Boleyn

Language

During the 1400s, the pronunciation of most English long vowels changed, in what is referred to as the Great Vowel Shift. In addition, the final *e* in words like *take* was no longer pronounced. By 1500, Middle English had evolved into an early form of the modern English spoken today. In spite of the changes in pronunciation, however, early printers continued to use Middle English spellings—retaining, for example, the *k* and *e* in *knife,* even though the letters were no longer pronounced. This practice resulted in many of the inconsistent spellings for which modern English is known.

Printing helped stabilize the language, so that the differences between Renaissance English and our own are comparatively minor. Nevertheless, there are some differences. In the Renaissance, *thou, thee, thy,* and *thine* were used for familiar address, while *you, your,* and *yours* were reserved for more formal and impersonal situations. Renaissance speakers and writers also distinguished between "this tree" (near), "that tree" (farther), and "yon tree" (even farther). They used the verb ending *-est* or *-st* with the second-person singular subject *thou* ("thou leadest," "thou canst") and *-eth* or *-th* with third-person singular subjects ("she looketh," "he doth"). They also used fewer helping verbs, especially in questions ("Saw you the bird?").

The English vocabulary grew as new ideas and discoveries demanded new words. The Renaissance interest in the classics gave rise to new formations from Greek and Latin roots. Trade brought English speakers into contact with languages such as Spanish, Portuguese, Italian, Dutch, and Arabic—as well as various African, Indian, and American languages—and English borrowed words from all of them. The Renaissance spirit also encouraged writers to coin new words. Shakespeare is credited with some 2000 coinages, many involving the use of nouns as verbs and verbs as nouns.

Growing English nationalism and the spread of Protestant ideas brought popular support for Henry's action; those who openly opposed it frequently paid with their lives.

Ironically, Anne Boleyn produced only a daughter, Elizabeth, and eventually Anne was executed on a charge of adultery. A third marriage finally gave Henry his long-sought son, the frail and sickly Edward VI, who in 1547, at the age of ten, succeeded his father. During his six-year reign, the Church of England became more truly Protestant, clarifying its beliefs and establishing its rituals in a landmark publication, the Book of Common Prayer. When Edward died, however, his half-sister Mary took the throne and tried to reintroduce Roman Catholicism. The move was unpopular, as was her marriage to her cousin Philip II of Spain, and her persecution of Protestants earned her the nickname Bloody Mary. On her death in 1558, most welcomed the succession of her half-sister Elizabeth.

Top to bottom: Edward, Prince of Wales, son of Henry VIII and Jane Seymour; Mary, daughter of Henry VIII and Catherine of Aragon; Elizabeth I, daughter of Henry VIII and Anne Boleyn

The Elizabethan Era

Elizabeth I, the unwanted daughter of Henry VIII and Anne Boleyn, proved to be one of the ablest monarchs in English history. During her long reign, the English Renaissance reached its full flower, and England enjoyed a time of unprecedented prosperity and international prestige. A practical and disciplined ruler, Elizabeth loved pomp and ceremony but was nevertheless frugal and intent on balancing the national budget. She was also a consummate politician, exercising absolute authority while remaining sensitive to public opinion and respectful of Parliament. In religious matters she steered a middle course. Reestablishing the independent Church of England, she made it a buffer between Roman Catholics and radical Protestants, now often called Puritans because they sought to "purify" the church of all remaining Roman Catholic practices.

In foreign policy, Elizabeth was a shrewd strategist who kept England out of costly wars and ended the unpopular Spanish alliance. Though she never married, for 20 years she used the possibility of her marriage to utmost advantage, feigning interest in one European prince after another. Convinced by advisers that the path to national prosperity lay in New World riches, she encouraged overseas ventures, including Sir Francis Drake's circumnavigation of the globe and Sir Walter Raleigh's attempt to establish a colony in Virginia. In secret, she funded pirate raids against the ships of Spain, while publicly denouncing such "unlawful acts" of plunder.

The quarrel with Catholic Spain intensified in 1587, when Elizabeth reluctantly executed her cousin Mary Stuart, the Roman Catholic queen of Scotland, for conspiracy. Catholics, who questioned the legitimacy of Elizabeth's parents' marriage, had believed Mary to be the rightful heir to the English throne and had participated in a number of foreign-backed plots against Elizabeth. A year after Mary's execution, Spain's Philip II sent a great armada, or fleet of warships, to challenge the English navy. Aided by a violent storm, the smaller, more maneuverable English ships defeated the Spanish Armada, making Elizabeth the undisputed leader of a great military power.

The Rise of the Stuarts

With Elizabeth's death in 1603, the powerful Tudor dynasty came to an end, and the rule of England fell into the hands of the weaker house of Stuart. Elizabeth was succeeded by her cousin James VI of Scotland, son of Mary Stuart, who ascended

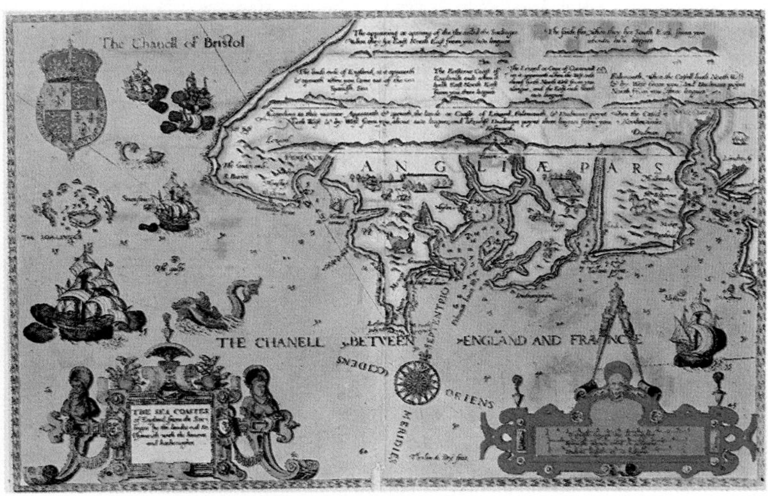

Map published in 1588, depicting the approach of the Spanish Armada

Literature

Although the zenith of English Renaissance literature was not reached until Elizabeth's reign, a number of earlier writers paved the way. Among them were Sir Thomas Wyatt and Henry Howard, earl of Surrey, court poets of Henry VIII's reign who introduced into England the Italian verse form called the **sonnet**. During Elizabethan times, the sonnet became the most popular form of love lyric. Sonnets were often published in sequences, such as Edmund Spenser's *Amoretti,* addressed to his future wife. William Shakespeare's magnificent sonnets do not form a clear sequence, but several address a mysterious figure known as the Dark Lady, who some scholars think may have been the poet Amelia Lanier.

Shakespeare left an even clearer mark on drama, which came of age in the Renaissance. Although most plays of medieval times had treated religious themes, Renaissance drama was concerned with the complexities of human life here on earth. Plays were often staged at court, in the homes of wealthy nobles, and in inn yards, where spectators could sit on the ground in front of the stage or in balconies overlooking it. A similar plan was used in England's first theaters, like the famous Globe Theater in London. Most of the plays were written mainly or entirely in verse. Among the era's finest playwrights other than Shakespeare were Christopher Marlowe and Ben Jonson. Jonson was influential in shaping English drama on the basis of classical models, distinguishing clearly between **tragedies,** which end with their heroes' downfall, and **comedies,** which end happily.

the throne of England as James I. Separated from his mother in childhood, James was happy to support the Church of England, but both Roman Catholic and Protestant extremists expected otherwise—Catholics because he was Mary Stuart's son, Puritans because he was king of Presbyterian Scotland. Problems with Roman Catholics arose early in his reign, when a group including Guy Fawkes conspired to kill him and blow up Parliament in the unsuccessful Gunpowder Plot of 1605. Later, James had greater difficulties with the Puritans, and these problems only worsened when his son Charles I took the throne in 1625.

James and Charles lacked the political savvy and frugality of Elizabeth, and both aroused opposition by their belief in the divine right of kings, considering themselves God's representatives in all civil and religious matters. Their contempt for Parliament and their shocking extravagance met with much hostility in the House of Commons, now dominated by Puritans. Even more offensive to the Puritans was the kings' preference for "High-Church" rituals in the Anglican Church—rituals that seemed to smack of Roman Catholicism.

In 1629, with the situation deteriorating, Charles I dismissed Parliament, refusing to summon it again for 11 years. During this time he took strong measures against his political opponents through the royal Courts of the Star Chamber, which operated without trial by jury. The result of these oppressive measures was a deepening of religious, political, and economic unrest. Thousands of English citizens—especially Puritans—emigrated to North America, making the Stuart years England's first period of major colonial expansion. Then, in 1637, Charles's attempt to introduce Anglican prayers and practices in Scotland's Presbyterian churches led to open rebellion there. In need of funds to suppress the Scots, Charles was forced to reconvene Parliament. In a session known as the Long Parliament, many of his powers were stripped. He responded with a show of military force, and England was soon plunged into civil war.

Top: James I
Bottom: Charles I, depicted as a knight on horseback

The Pilgrims begin their voyage to the New World after living in the Netherlands for 12 years.

Oliver Cromwell in his military finery

The Defeat of the Monarchy

The English civil war pitted the Royalists, or supporters of the monarchy—mainly Roman Catholics, Anglicans, and members of the nobility—against the supporters of Parliament, consisting principally of Puritans, smaller landowners, and middle-class town dwellers. Under the skilled leadership of General Oliver Cromwell, the devout, disciplined Puritan army soundly defeated the Royalists in 1645, and the king surrendered a year later. Cromwell's army, now in control of Parliament, ordered stiff retaliatory measures against the Royalists. In 1649, the king himself was executed.

The members of Parliament had difficulty in deciding on an alternative to monarchy. At first they established a commonwealth with Cromwell as head; later they made him "lord protector" for life. Under the Puritan-dominated government, England's theaters were closed and most forms of recreation suspended; Sunday became a day of prayer, when even walking for pleasure was forbidden. A reluctant but able politician, Cromwell curbed quarrels among members of the military, religious leaders, and discontented government officials. When Cromwell died in 1658, his son inherited his title. Richard Cromwell, however, showed little of his father's ability to control the country's political wrangling and increasingly unruly public. Puritan government had proved no less autocratic than the Stuart reign, and in 1660 a new Parliament invited Charles II, son of Charles I, to return from exile and assume the throne. His reign ushered in a new chapter in English history, known as the Restoration.

LASERLINKS
• *HISTORICAL LITERARY CONNECTION*

Literature

Like Shakespeare, Marlowe and Jonson were fine lyric poets. Marlowe's "The Passionate Shepherd to His Love" is a famous example of **pastoral verse,** which praises the simple joys of rural life. Jonson's lyrics influenced many of the younger poets of the age, such as Robert Herrick and Richard Lovelace. Jonson's contemporary John Donne broke with poetic conventions, employing unusual imagery and elaborate metaphors to produce what came to be called **metaphysical poetry.** His blend of passion and intellect was especially influential among younger religious poets, such as George Herbert.

The English Renaissance was also a high point in the history of epic poetry. Edmund Spenser dedicated his action-packed romantic epic *The Faerie Queene* to Elizabeth I. Some decades later, the Puritan poet John Milton penned the lofty epic *Paradise Lost,* retelling the story of the fall of Adam and Eve in the Garden of Eden. The Bible, Milton's main source of inspiration, had been made accessible to all English people in 1611, with the publication of the magnificent King James Bible—the culmination of years of effort by many translators, most notably the Protestant reformer William Tyndale. Although this translation rivals Shakespeare's plays in its use of memorable poetic language, most sections are in fact prose. Among the era's other influential prose works are the essays of Sir Francis Bacon, who pioneered the essay form in English, and the sermons and meditations of John Donne.

PART 1 *Aspects of Love*

The Renaissance was a time of rapid change in the arts, literature, and learning. New ideas were embraced, and old ones—including the concept of love—were examined from different perspectives. In sonnets and other forms of verse, English poets of the period explored the many aspects of love: unrequited love, constant love, timeless love, and love that is subject to change. As you read the poems in this part of Unit Two, compare your own ideas about love with those expressed in these works.

PREVIEWING

POETRY

My Lute, Awake!

Sir Thomas Wyatt

On Monsieur's Departure

Elizabeth I

PERSONAL CONNECTION

Suppose that you loved or liked someone who did not return your love or your friendship. How would you react? In your notebook, write a short paragraph describing the effect that such a rejection might have on you.

LITERARY CONNECTION

Sir Thomas Wyatt, a diplomat in the service of King Henry VIII, traveled widely and was responsible for introducing various forms of Italian lyric poetry to England. Although this achievement was of great importance to the development of English poetry, many of Wyatt's best poems are in the style of the native English dance song, or ballet (băl'ət). The ballet was a lively and forceful kind of verse written to be sung to the accompaniment of the lute, a stringed instrument popular in the 16th century.

The writer of "On Monsieur's Departure," Elizabeth I, was a daughter of Henry VIII and queen of England during the flowering of the English Renaissance. Elizabeth was unusually well educated for a woman of her time and wrote several poems, all of which seem to be based on events in her life.

One of the popular themes of love poetry in the 16th century was unrequited love—love that is ignored or rejected. In the tradition of earlier European poems of courtly love, such poetry portrayed the rejected lover as desolate and anguished, totally in the power of the beloved. These poems by Wyatt and Elizabeth I are both concerned with the theme of unrequited love. The individuality of each poem lies in the way the poet works subtle variations on the traditional situations and responses.

READING CONNECTION

Clarifying Meaning in Older Works of Literature Poetry and other literature of the Renaissance can be challenging to modern readers. If you find the syntax or the order of the words hard to follow, try rephrasing the lines until the sense becomes clear. In addition, refer to any notes that explain difficult words or phrases. If an unfamiliar word is not annotated, or if a familiar word seems to be used in an unconventional way, consult a dictionary. Finally, reread each selection as many times as necessary—aloud as well as silently—concentrating on the main ideas and the way they fit together.

My Lute, Awake!

Sir Thomas Wyatt

My lute, awake! Perform the last
Labor that thou and I shall waste,
And end that I have now begun;
For when this song is sung and past,
My lute, be still, for I have done.

As to be heard where ear is none,
As lead to grave in marble stone,
My song may pierce her heart as soon.
Should we then sigh or sing or moan?
No, no, my lute, for I have done.

The rocks do not so cruelly
Repulse the waves continually
As she my suit and affection.
So that I am past remedy,
Whereby my lute and I have done.

Proud of the spoil that thou hast got
Of simple hearts, thorough love's shot;
By whom, unkind, thou hast them won,
Think not he hath his bow forgot,
Although my lute and I have done.

6–8 as to be heard . . . as soon: My song's having an effect on her emotions is as unlikely as sound being heard without an ear or soft lead carving hard marble.

13 suit: wooing; courtship.

17 thorough love's shot: through the arrow of Cupid, the god of love.

Vengeance shall fall on thy disdain
That makest but game on earnest pain.
Think not alone under the sun
Unquit to cause thy lovers plain,
Although my lute and I have done.

23–24 think not . . . plain: Do not think that you alone under the sun will escape unrevenged for causing your lovers to lament.

Perchance thee lie withered and old
The winter nights that are so cold,
Plaining in vain unto the moon.
Thy wishes then dare not be told.
Care then who list, for I have done.

30 list: likes; wishes.

And then may chance thee to repent
The time that thou hast lost and spent
To cause thy lovers sigh and swoon.
Then shalt thou know beauty but lent,
And wish and want as I have done.

Now cease, my lute. This is the last
Labor that thou and I shall waste,
And ended is that we begun.
Now is this song both sung and past;
My lute, be still, for I have done.

FROM PERSONAL RESPONSE *TO* CRITICAL ANALYSIS

REFLECT

1. In your notebook, jot down words or phrases that describe your impression of this poem.

RETHINK

2. How would you describe the speaker's attitude toward the woman who is the subject of the poem?
3. If the speaker's wishes came true, what do you think would happen to the woman? Explain your answer.
4. Do you think the speaker is sincere when he says "I have done"? Why or why not?

ELIZABETH I

On Monsieur's Departure

Young Elizabeth

I grieve and dare not show my discontent,
I love and yet am forced to seem to hate,
I do, yet dare not say I ever meant,
I seem stark mute but inwardly do prate.
I am and not, I freeze and yet am burned,
Since from myself another self I turned.

My care is like my shadow in the sun,
Follows me flying, flies when I pursue it,
Stands and lies by me, doth what I have done.
His too familiar care doth make me rue it.
No means I find to rid him from my breast,
Till by the end of things it be suppressed.

Some gentler passion slide into my mind,
For I am soft and made of melting snow;
Or be more cruel, love, and so be kind.
Let me or float or sink, be high or low.
Or let me live with some more sweet content,
Or die and so forget what love ere meant.

4 prate: chatter.

6 another self: The man referred to in this poem is thought by some to be a French duke who had been involved in negotiations for marriage to Elizabeth; by others, to be the earl of Essex, a favorite courtier of Elizabeth's who was executed for treason in 1601.
7 care: sorrow.
9 doth . . . done: does all that I do.
10 his too familiar care . . . it: His too easy and superficial sorrow makes me regret my own feelings of sorrow.

RESPONDING OPTIONS

FROM PERSONAL RESPONSE *TO* CRITICAL ANALYSIS

REFLECT 1. Do you feel sympathy for the speaker of "On Monsieur's Departure"? Why or why not?

RETHINK 2. What conflicts does the speaker seem to be experiencing?

Consider
- the contrasts she presents in lines 1–5
- what she says in line 6
- the references to her care and "his too familiar care"

3. Do you think the speaker is responsible for the situation she finds herself in? Why or why not?

4. How would you explain the speaker's wish in the last stanza?

5. How does knowing that this poem was written by Queen Elizabeth I affect your interpretation of it?

RELATE 6. Compare the portrayals of unrequited love in "My Lute, Awake!" and "On Monsieur's Departure."

Consider
- the attitudes and actions of the man and the woman in each poem
- the tone of each poem
- the traditional portrayal of unrequited love in courtly-love poetry

ANOTHER PATHWAY

Cooperative Learning

With a group of three or four classmates, write a plot outline for a contemporary soap opera based on one of the poems. Create a story that includes events leading up to and following the situation described in the poem. Develop one of the scenes in detail and act it out for the class.

QUICKWRITES

1. Imagine that you are Elizabeth I and have just read "My Lute, Awake!" Write a **letter** to a friend, expressing your reaction to Wyatt's poem.
2. Imagine that you are a newspaper advice columnist. Write an **advice column** suggesting ways of coping with the dilemma described by the speaker of one of these poems.
3. Write a **poem** about unrequited love, either real or imaginary. If you like, you can write your poem in the form of a ballad or as lyrics for a country-and-western song.

PORTFOLIO *Save your writing. You may want to use it later as a springboard to a piece for your portfolio.*

LITERARY CONCEPTS

A **rhyme scheme** is the pattern of end rhyme in a poem. The rhyme scheme is charted by assigning a letter of the alphabet, beginning with *a,* to each line. Lines that rhyme are given the same letter—in "My Lute, Awake!," for example, the rhyme scheme of each stanza is *aabab.* (The rhyme may not always be exact. In the first stanza of "My Lute, Awake!" the word *waste* is meant to rhyme with *last* and *past.*) Using the letters *a, b,* and *c,* chart the rhyme scheme of the stanzas of "On Monsieur's Departure."

ALTERNATIVE ACTIVITIES

1. Listen to some recordings of Renaissance music, both vocal and instrumental. Select a group of pieces that you think reflect the mood of either "My Lute, Awake!" or "On Monsieur's Departure." Then make a **tape recording** of the pieces and play it for the class. Explain your choices, and ask for feedback from your classmates.
2. Create a **montage** that expresses your conception of unrequited love. Use drawings, photographs, fabric, images from magazines and greeting cards, and any other materials that convey your impressions and ideas.

ACROSS THE CURRICULUM

Music Research the types of musical instruments used during the Renaissance. Try to find pictures of the instruments, information about the materials used in making them, and descriptions of how they were played. If possible, arrange for musicians who own replicas of Renaissance instruments to play the instruments for your class.

SIR THOMAS WYATT

1503–1542

As a courtier and diplomat for Henry VIII, Sir Thomas Wyatt was alternately in and out of favor with the whimsical king. Henry ordered Wyatt imprisoned twice, once for quarreling with a duke and once for treason, both times threatening him with execution. Each time, however, Wyatt was pardoned and accepted back into the king's service.

A skilled musician and amateur poet, Wyatt wrote lyrics in his leisure time to amuse himself and other courtiers. As was usual during the Renaissance, his poems were circulated privately, and only a few were published during his lifetime. Critical opinion of Wyatt's poems varies—some think their rhythm too irregular and rough, while others consider them fresh and vigorous. Most critics agree, however, that his most inventive work is to be found in the songs he wrote for lute accompaniment and that his introduction of the Italian sonnet form into English was a significant contribution to English literature.

OTHER WORKS "Whoso List to Hunt," "Blame Not My Lute," "My Galley Charged with Forgetfulness"

ELIZABETH I

1533–1603

Elizabeth I, daughter of King Henry VIII and Anne Boleyn, had an unsettling and probably lonely childhood. Her father, hoping for a male heir, was disappointed at Elizabeth's birth and two years later ordered her mother executed, supposedly for treason. Despite his bitterness at not having a son, Henry provided Elizabeth with the rigorous education normally given only to boys. She learned Latin, Greek, French, Italian, history, and theology, and her literary output includes speeches, translations, and a small collection of poems focusing on events in her personal life.

Elizabeth ascended the throne in 1558 and ruled for 45 years. Her reign was a glorious period in English history, a time of great prosperity, artistic achievement, and international prestige. Although she considered a number of marriage proposals, Elizabeth rejected all of them, ignoring the advisers who hoped she would marry and provide an heir to the throne.

OTHER WORKS "The Doubt of Future Foes," "Speech to the Troops at Tilbury"

- *AUTHOR BACKGROUND*
- *MUSIC CONNECTION*

PREVIEWING

POETRY

Sonnet 30 Sonnet 75

Edmund Spenser

PERSONAL CONNECTION

Romantic love can generate a variety of intense feelings and conflicting emotions. Recall a character in a book or a movie—or perhaps someone you know—who has seemed to respond to romantic love in an unusually intense way. With a group of classmates, briefly discuss the emotions and reactions of that individual, explaining why you think the individual reacted as he or she did.

LITERARY CONNECTION

During the 16th century, the sonnet became one of the most popular poetic forms in England. Originally developed in Italy in the 13th century, the sonnet was used to convey deep and intense amorous feelings, often expressing an idealized love reminiscent of the courtly love of the Middle Ages. In many Renaissance sonnets, the speaker—typically a man—tells of his intense love and of the anxiety and distress he feels as his beloved remains aloof and unreachable.

"Sonnet 30" and "Sonnet 75" by Edmund Spenser are part of a collection of sonnets he called *Amoretti,* which can be translated roughly as "intimate little tokens of love." Published in 1595, the sonnets in *Amoretti* are arranged in a narrative sequence that simulates the ritual and emotions of a courtship. Many of them were written during Spenser's courtship of his second wife, Elizabeth Boyle, and the details and emotions they present are thought to be in part autobiographical.

WRITING CONNECTION

If you were going to write a poem expressing intense feelings of love, what images would you include? In your notebook, jot down words and phrases that come to mind. (You might find it helpful to look at the examples shown here.) Then, as you read Spenser's sonnets, compare the images he uses with your own.

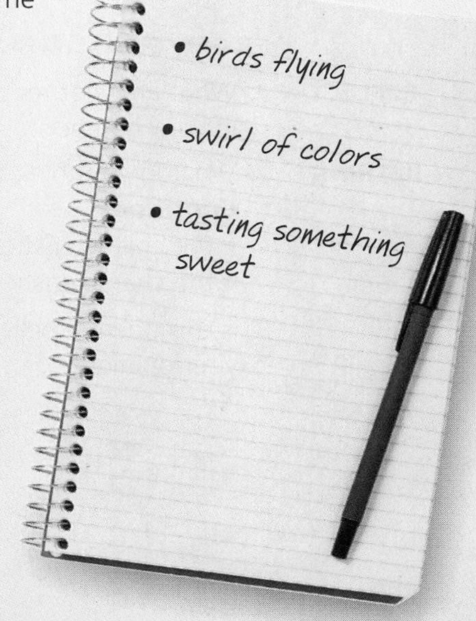

• birds flying
• swirl of colors
• tasting something sweet

SONNET 30

Edmund Spenser

My love is like to ice, and I to fire;
How comes it then that this her cold so great
Is not dissolved through my so hot desire,
But harder grows the more I her entreat?
Or how comes it that my exceeding heat
Is not delayed by her heart-frozen cold:
But that I burn much more in boiling sweat,
And feel my flames augmented manifold?
What more miraculous thing may be told
That fire which all things melts, should harden ice:
And ice which is congealed with senseless cold,
Should kindle fire by wonderful device.
Such is the pow'r of love in gentle mind,
That it can alter all the course of kind.

4 entreat: plead with.

8 augmented manifold: greatly increased.

11 congealed: solidified.

14 kind: nature.

FROM PERSONAL RESPONSE *TO* CRITICAL ANALYSIS

REFLECT **1.** What are your reactions to the speaker's feelings about love? Jot down your responses in your notebook.

RETHINK **2.** Why do you think Spenser chose to use the images of fire and ice?

Consider

- the characteristics usually associated with fire and ice
- the characteristics of fire and ice in this sonnet

3. Is this poem a believable description of a love relationship? Explain your opinion.

SONNET 75

Edmund Spenser

One day I wrote her name upon the strand,
But came the waves and washéd it away:
Again I wrote it with a second hand,
But came the tide, and made my pains his prey.
"Vain man," said she, "that dost in vain assay,
A mortal thing so to immortalize.
For I myself shall like to this decay,
And eke my name be wipéd out likewise."
"Not so," quod I, "let baser things devise
To die in dust, but you shall live by fame:
My verse your virtues rare shall eternize,
And in the heavens write your glorious name,
Where whenas death shall all the world subdue,
Our love shall live, and later life renew."

1 **strand:** beach.

5 **assay:** try.

8 **eke:** also.

9 **quod:** said.

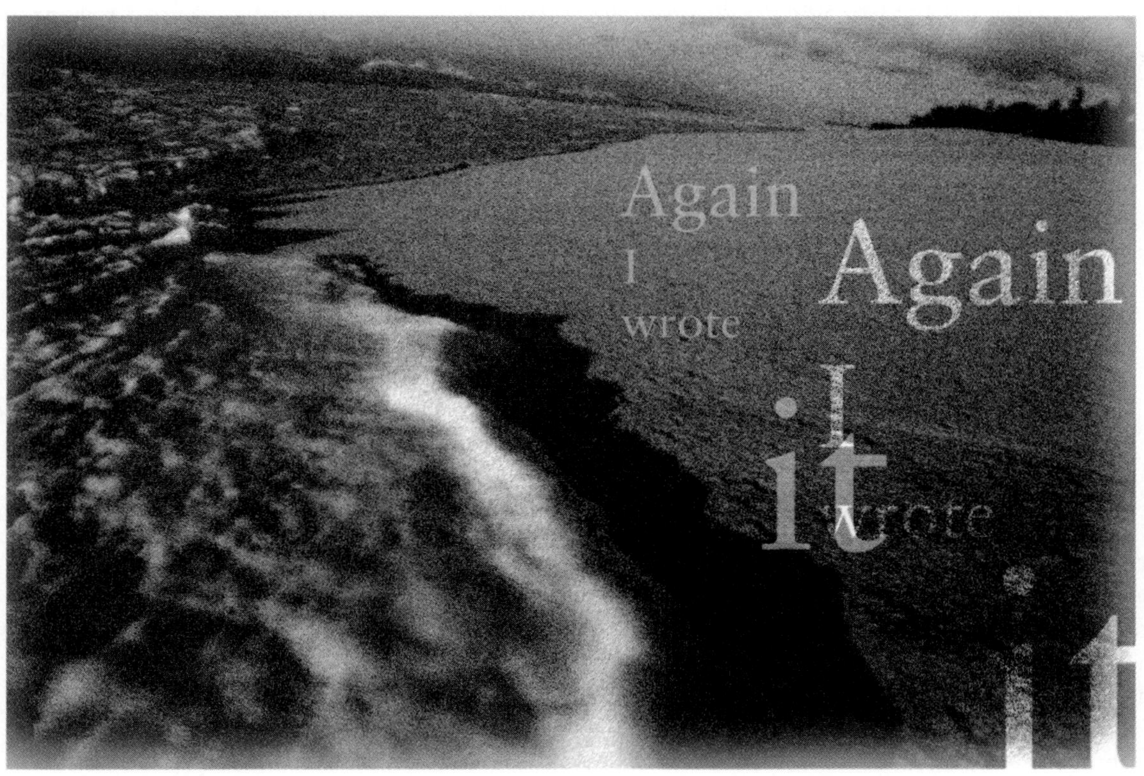

RESPONDING OPTIONS

FROM PERSONAL RESPONSE *TO* CRITICAL ANALYSIS

REFLECT

1. What images remain in your mind after your reading of "Sonnet 75"? Record your thoughts in your notebook.

RETHINK

2. Why do you think the speaker wants to immortalize his love? Explain your thinking.
3. Reread lines 13 and 14. Do you agree with the speaker that love can overcome death?

   Consider
   - the woman's statement that she and her name will be "wiped out"
   - the speaker's assertion in line 11
   - your own observations about love

RELATE

4. Compare the attitude of the woman toward the speaker in "Sonnet 30" with that in "Sonnet 75." In what ways are the attitudes alike? In what ways are they different?
5. Which of the two sonnets do you think conveys more intense feelings of love? Support your opinion with details from the poems.

ANOTHER PATHWAY

Spenser's sonnets are identified only by numbers. Create a title for each of the two poems, choosing words or phrases that reflect the thoughts and intense feelings of each speaker. With your classmates, hold a contest and vote on the best titles.

LITERARY LINKS

Compare Spenser's "Sonnet 30" with Elizabeth I's "On Monsieur's Departure," paying particular attention to similarities and differences in the poets' uses of opposites in their descriptions of love relationships.

THE WRITER'S STYLE

Reread "Sonnet 75" aloud. Notice the repetition of consonant sounds at the beginnings of words (alliteration) and the repetition of vowel sounds (assonance). What effect do you think these repetitions of sounds create?

QUICKWRITES

1. In "Sonnet 30," Spenser compares his feelings to fire. Write a **paragraph** in which you make your own comparison between love and some aspect of nature. Explain the reasons for your comparison.
2. In "Sonnet 75," the speaker suggests that he can immortalize his love in verse. Make a **list** of other ways in which people try to immortalize themselves.
3. Using the images you jotted down for the Writing Connection on page 217, create your own **sonnet** on the subject of love. You might use a traditional, serious approach or try experimenting with humor.

PORTFOLIO *Save your writing. You may want to use it later as a springboard to a piece for your portfolio.*

LITERARY CONCEPTS

A **sonnet** is a 14-line poem with a fixed pattern of rhythm and rhyme. Many English sonnets consist of three 4-line units, called **quatrains,** followed by a **couplet** (two rhymed lines). The three quatrains express three different but related thoughts, with the couplet providing the conclusion.

Notice the progression of the speaker's thoughts about the intensity of love in each of Spenser's sonnets. Work with classmates to break each sonnet down into its three quatrains and couplet and to summarize the meaning expressed in each of the parts. For each poem, create a chart like the one shown.

Poem/Line Numbers	Meaning Expressed
1. Sonnet 30, lines 1-4	
2.	

ALTERNATIVE ACTIVITIES

1. Using watercolors or acrylic paints, create a **painting** that conveys your impression of the opposing attitudes presented in "Sonnet 30." Experiment with colors and the use of abstract forms in addition to realistic images in creating your desired effect.
2. Conduct an **opinion poll** in which you ask ten or more participants to complete the sentence "Love is like . . ." Record their responses on tape or in your notebook. Share any unusual responses with the class.

EDMUND SPENSER

1552?–1599

Born to a relatively poor London family, Edmund Spenser was able to work his way through Cambridge University as a "poor scholar." He read extensively, becoming acquainted with Latin, Greek, French, and Italian literature. His earliest publication was of translations of several French poems, written when he was 16 years old. While at Cambridge, Spenser established literary friendships and showed that he had ambitious plans for a poetic career.

After receiving his master of arts degree in 1576, Spenser served as secretary to several influential men, including the earl of Leicester. His employment in Leicester's household was important, for it was there that he met and developed a friendship with Sir Philip Sidney and other court writers who were promoting the new English poetry of the Elizabethan Age. In his own poetry, Spenser often experimented with verse forms and used archaic language for its rustic and musical effect. He was respected and imitated by his contemporaries, as he has been by many later poets.

One year after publishing his first major work, *The Shepheardes Calender,* which he dedicated to Sidney, Spenser moved to Ireland, where he held various minor government jobs and continued his writing. It was there that he wrote one of the greatest poetic romances in English literature, *The Faerie Queene.* Spenser spent most of his remaining life in Ireland, but after his home near Dublin was destroyed during a civil war, he returned to England, where he died a few years later almost impoverished despite his many years of service to nobility. In honor of his great literary achievements, Spenser was buried near Geoffrey Chaucer—one of his favorite poets—in what is now called the Poets' Corner of Westminster Abbey.

OTHER WORKS "Sonnet 26," "Sonnet 67," "Sonnet 71," and "Sonnet 72"

LASERLINKS
• *AUTHOR BACKGROUND*

PREVIEWING

POETRY

The Passionate Shepherd to His Love
Christopher Marlowe

The Nymph's Reply to the Shepherd
Sir Walter Raleigh

PERSONAL CONNECTION

Close your eyes and think of a place you have visited. What images make up your mental picture of the place? Create a word web similar to the one shown, identifying the place in the center oval and surrounding it with words and phrases that describe the images you associate with the place. Which of your images do you consider realistic? Which would you describe as romantic or idealized?

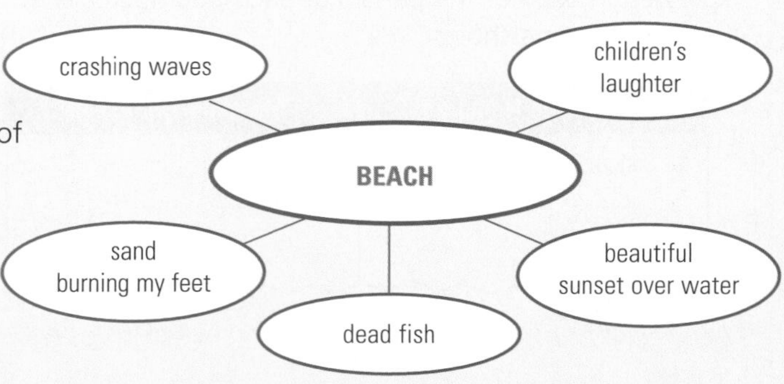

CULTURAL/BIOGRAPHICAL CONNECTION

The Renaissance was a period of creativity and new ideas, a time in which knowledge and skills were cultivated in a broad range of fields, from music, art, and literature to science and athletics. According to writers of the time, the ideal "Renaissance man" should develop himself in every possible way. The terms *Renaissance man* and *Renaissance woman* are still used today to describe people who pursue a broad spectrum of interests. Perhaps you know someone who fits this description.

Included in the ranks of the true Renaissance men were two kindred spirits, Christopher Marlowe and Sir Walter Raleigh. During his short life, Marlowe studied religion, became a talented and recognized poet and playwright, conducted secret government business, and engaged in philosophical discussions with his friend Raleigh. As a statesman, writer, soldier, scientist, adventurer, and explorer, Raleigh lived a life of action as well as contemplation.

Marlowe was an extraordinary poet and dramatist. His poem "The Passionate Shepherd to His Love" became so famous that other poets wrote responses to it. The most notable of these is "The Nymph's Reply to the Shepherd," written by Raleigh. Together, the two poems enact a debate about the realities of love.

WRITING CONNECTION

Think about the different ways love is depicted in books, music, and movies. Do these depictions usually reflect a realistic view of love, or are they based on a romantic or idealized notion of love? In your notebook, record some of your observations. Then explain whether you think your own attitude toward love is realistic or idealistic. As you read these two poems, decide which speaker's attitude is closer to your own.

LASERLINKS
• *CULTURAL/BIOGRAPHICAL CONNECTION*

Christopher Marlowe

The Passionate Shepherd *to* His Love

The Hireling Shepherd (1851), William Holman Hunt. Manchester (U.K.) City Art Gallery/A.K.G., Berlin/Superstock.

Come live with me and be my love,
And we will all the pleasures prove
That valleys, groves, hills, and fields,
Woods, or steepy mountain yields.

And we will sit upon the rocks,
Seeing the shepherds feed their flocks,
By shallow rivers to whose falls
Melodious birds sing madrigals.

2 prove: experience.

8 madrigals: songs of a type popular during the Renaissance.

And I will make thee beds of roses
And a thousand fragrant posies,
A cap of flowers, and a kirtle
Embroidered all with leaves of myrtle;

A gown made of the finest wool
Which from our pretty lambs we pull;
Fair lined slippers for the cold,
With buckles of the purest gold;

A belt of straw and ivy buds,
With coral clasps and amber studs:
And if these pleasures may thee move,
Come live with me, and be my love.

The shepherds' swains shall dance and sing
For thy delight each May morning:
If these delights thy mind may move,
Then live with me and be my love.

11 kirtle: skirt.

21 swains: youths.

FROM PERSONAL RESPONSE *TO* CRITICAL ANALYSIS

REFLECT **1.** What is your opinion of the gifts that the shepherd offers to his beloved?

RETHINK **2.** How serious or realistic do you think the shepherd's offer is?

Consider
- the way he describes the setting
- the gifts he promises

3. Why do you think Marlowe chose the setting described in the poem?

Sir Walter Raleigh

The Nymph's Reply to the Shepherd

If all the world and love were young,
And truth in every shepherd's tongue,
These pretty pleasures might me move
To live with thee and be thy love.

Time drives the flocks from field to fold
When rivers rage and rocks grow cold,
And Philomel becometh dumb;
The rest complains of cares to come.

The flowers do fade, and wanton fields
To wayward winter reckoning yields;
A honey tongue, a heart of gall,
Is fancy's spring, but sorrow's fall.

Thy gowns, thy shoes, thy beds of roses,
Thy cap, thy kirtle, and thy posies
Soon break, soon wither, soon forgotten—
In folly ripe, in reason rotten.

Thy belt of straw and ivy buds,
Thy coral clasps and amber studs,
All these in me no means can move
To come to thee and be thy love.

But could youth last and love still breed,
Had joys no date nor age no need,
Then these delights my mind might move
To live with thee and be thy love.

5 fold: a pen for animals, especially sheep.

7 Philomel: the nightingale; **dumb:** silent.

9 wanton: producing abundant crops; luxuriant.

22 date: ending.

RESPONDING OPTIONS

FROM PERSONAL RESPONSE *TO* CRITICAL ANALYSIS

REFLECT 1. Were you surprised by the nymph's response in "The Nymph's Reply to the Shepherd"? Share your thoughts with a classmate.

RETHINK 2. How would you describe the nymph's attitude toward life?

Consider

- the connection she makes between youth and love
- her descriptions of the effects of time

3. Do you agree with the nymph's reasons for not accepting the shepherd's offer? Why or why not?

4. On the basis of the first and last stanzas, what do you think might convince the nymph to accept the shepherd's offer?

RELATE 5. What message is conveyed when "The Passionate Shepherd to His Love" and "The Nymph's Reply to the Shepherd" are read together?

ANOTHER PATHWAY

Divide the class into two groups, the Nymphs and the Shepherds. Using the poems for support, plan and stage a debate on the question, What is the better attitude toward love—idealistic or realistic? Be sure to use specific descriptions and ideas from the poems to defend your position.

LITERARY CONCEPTS

A **pastoral** is a poem presenting shepherds in rural settings, usually in an idealized manner. The style of pastorals may seem unnatural, since the supposedly simple, rustic characters tend to use very formal, courtly language; however, Renaissance poets were drawn to this form not as a means of accurately portraying rustic life but as a means of conveying their own emotions and ideas in an artistic way.

Marlowe's "The Passionate Shepherd to His Love" is a perfect example of a pastoral. Find at least four pastoral descriptions in Marlowe's poem that are directly challenged in "The Nymph's Reply to the Shepherd." Create a chart to share your examples with the class.

QUICKWRITES

1. Write a **parody,** or humorous imitation, of "The Passionate Shepherd to His Love." In place of the shepherd, substitute a person with a different job (for example, an accountant, a truck driver, a plumber, or a chef) and select an appropriate setting.
2. Imagine that you are the shepherd. Write a **diary entry** expressing your thoughts and feelings after hearing the nymph's reply.
3. Write a **magazine article** in which you compare realistic and idealistic attitudes toward love in modern society. You may use examples from popular culture, such as movies and music, or cite examples from the lives of people you know.

PORTFOLIO *Save your writing. You may want to use it later as a spring-board to a piece for your portfolio.*

LITERARY LINKS

Who do you think would be more likely to share the shepherd's attitude toward love—the speaker of Wyatt's "My Lute, Awake!" or the speaker of Spenser's "Sonnet 75"? Explain your opinion.

ALTERNATIVE ACTIVITIES

1. With a partner, act out a **telephone conversation** in which the shepherd attempts to persuade the nymph to accept his offer.
2. Using either an abstract or a realistic style, create a single **drawing** or **painting** that depicts the contrasting scenes described in the two poems.

THE WRITER'S STYLE

Reread the poems, paying attention to the rhythm and rhymes. What effect is created by the strong rhythmic pattern and the rhyming couplets used in each poem?

CHRISTOPHER MARLOWE

1564–1593

Christopher Marlowe is best remembered for writing plays in which his use of what Ben Jonson dubbed his "mighty line," or blank verse, transformed the British theater. The son of a shoemaker, Marlowe attended Cambridge University on a scholarship but was almost denied his master's degree because he was suspected of conspiring against the queen. A letter from the queen's Privy Council excused the young man, hinting that he was active in Elizabeth's secret service.

Marlowe wrote his first successful play, *Tamburlaine the Great,* at the age of 23. He lived only six more years but wrote five plays during that time, including *The Jew of Malta* and *Dr. Faustus,* works that would profoundly influence the development of Elizabethan drama. Like his friend Sir Walter Raleigh, Marlowe was a freethinker who was suspected of treasonous and antichurch sentiment. In 1593, at the age of 29, Marlowe was murdered in a tavern, allegedly during an argument over the bill.

SIR WALTER RALEIGH

1552?–1618

Sir Walter Raleigh was a man of action and intellect. He attended Oxford University, studied law, and was widely read in chemistry, mathematics, and medicine. He also wrote history and poetry. By helping to quell an Irish rebellion in 1580, he won the affection of Queen Elizabeth. As the queen's favorite, Raleigh was granted land, made a vice-admiral, knighted, and appointed governor of Jersey, an island in the English Channel.

Raleigh fell out of favor with the jealous queen in 1592, when she found out that he had seduced and married one of her ladies in waiting. After this, his life became even more adventurous; among his activities were the establishment of the short-lived Roanoke colony in North America and the leading of an expedition to South America in search of gold. His unorthodox ideas and violent temper made him many enemies, including Elizabeth's successor, King James I. In 1603, he was charged with treason and imprisoned for 13 years. Afterward, Raleigh led another expedition to South America but fell into disfavor once again when his soldiers burned a local settlement. On his return to London, he was imprisoned and executed.

LASERLINKS
• *LITERARY CONNECTION*

PREVIEWING

POETRY

Sonnet 29 Sonnet 116 Sonnet 130

William Shakespeare

PERSONAL CONNECTION

Think about two people you know who have a strong love relationship that has lasted for many years. Consider the qualities of each of the persons involved in the relationship. Do you think those qualities help explain the strength of the relationship? Share your thoughts with classmates.

BIOGRAPHICAL/LITERARY CONNECTION

William Shakespeare, best known for his plays, also wrote nondramatic poetry, including a series of 154 sonnets. In the 1590s many English poets wrote sonnet sequences, groups of sonnets with an overall narrative structure, usually addressed to an idealized but unattainable woman. Typical themes included the woman's great beauty, her coldness and disdain, the suffering of the poet-lover, and the immortality of poetry.

Shakespeare almost certainly wrote his sonnets—which were not published until 1609—during the 1590s too, but they differ in some ways from the sonnets written by other poets. First, they are addressed to at least three different people: a young man, whom the poet urges to marry and have children; a "dark lady," who is unlike the ideal beautiful woman of the time; and a rival poet. Second, the themes of Shakespeare's sonnets are more complex and less predictable than those of other poets' sonnets. Shakespeare writes, for example, of time, change, and death as well as of love and beauty. Third, Shakespeare developed the sonnet form to its highest artistic level; today, the English sonnet is often referred to as the Shakespearean sonnet.

There has been much speculation about the relationship of Shakespeare's sonnets to his private life. Scholars have suggested various identities for the three people addressed, but no clear evidence on which to base conclusions has emerged. The most that can be said is that many of the sonnets seem to spring from strong love relationships.

WRITING CONNECTION

Think about the kinds of problems that might stand in the way of developing a strong love relationship. What circumstances might test such a relationship? How do you think the passage of time might affect it? What could destroy it? List some of your thoughts in your notebook. Keep your ideas in mind as you read these three sonnets by a master of poetic expression.

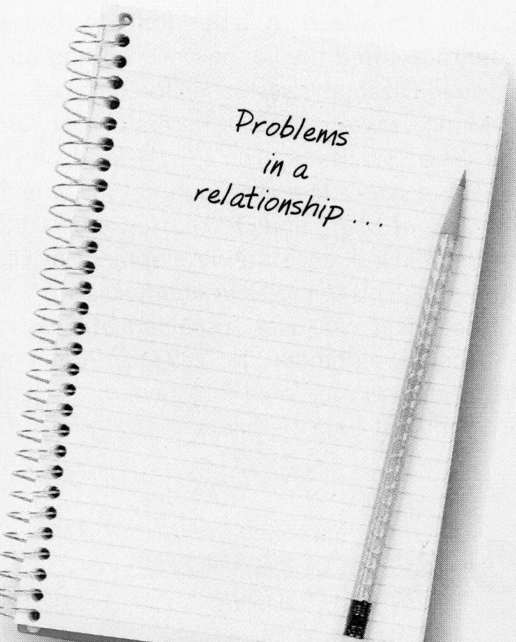

SONNET 29

WILLIAM SHAKESPEARE

When in disgrace with Fortune and men's eyes
I all alone beweep my outcast state,
And trouble deaf heaven with my bootless cries,
And look upon myself and curse my fate,
Wishing me like to one more rich in hope,
Featur'd like him, like him with friends possess'd,
Desiring this man's art, and that man's scope,
With what I most enjoy contented least;
Yet in these thoughts myself almost despising,
Haply I think on thee, and then my state
(Like to the lark at break of day arising
From sullen earth) sings hymns at heaven's gate,
For thy sweet love rememb'red such wealth brings,
That then I scorn to change my state with kings.

2 state: condition.

3 bootless: futile; useless.

6 featur'd like him: with his features—that is, handsome.

7 scope: intelligence.

11 lark: the English skylark, noted for its beautiful singing while soaring in flight.

FROM PERSONAL RESPONSE *TO* CRITICAL ANALYSIS

REFLECT 1. Can you identify in any way with the speaker of this poem? Share your thoughts with classmates.

RETHINK 2. What do you think are the speaker's strongest feelings in this sonnet? Explain your answer.

SONNET 116

WILLIAM SHAKESPEARE

Let me not to the marriage of true minds
Admit impediments; love is not love
Which alters when it alteration finds,
Or bends with the remover to remove.
O no, it is an ever-fixéd mark
That looks on tempests and is never shaken;
It is the star to every wand'ring bark,
Whose worth's unknown, although his height be taken.
Love's not Time's fool, though rosy lips and cheeks
Within his bending sickle's compass come,
Love alters not with his brief hours and weeks,
But bears it out even to the edge of doom.
    If this be error and upon me proved,
    I never writ, nor no man ever loved.

2 impediments: obstacles. The traditional marriage service reads in part, "If any of you know cause or just impediment why these persons should not be joined together . . ."
5 mark: seamark—a landmark that can be seen from the sea and used as a guide in navigation.
7 bark: sailing ship.
8 whose . . . height be taken: a reference to the star, whose value is measureless even though its altitude is measured by navigators.
10 within . . . compass: within the range of his curving sickle.
12 bears it out: endures; **doom:** Doomsday; Judgment Day.

Anne of Gonzaga, Nathaniel Hatch. Victoria & Albert Museum, London/Art Resource, New York.

FROM PERSONAL RESPONSE *TO* CRITICAL ANALYSIS

REFLECT

1. What is your response to the description of love in this poem?
2. What kind of person might the speaker be?
   Consider
   - the likely age of such a person
   - the experiences that such a person might have had

RETHINK

3. Do you think the speaker's concept of love is realistic? Why or why not?

SONNET 130

WILLIAM SHAKESPEARE

Catherine Howard, John Hoskins. Victoria & Albert Museum, London/Art Resource, New York.

My mistress' eyes are nothing like the sun;
Coral is far more red than her lips' red;
If snow be white, why then her breasts are dun;
If hairs be wires, black wires grow on her head.
I have seen roses damask'd, red and white,
But no such roses see I in her cheeks,
And in some perfumes is there more delight
Than in the breath that from my mistress reeks.
I love to hear her speak, yet well I know
That music hath a far more pleasing sound;
I grant I never saw a goddess go,
My mistress when she walks treads on the ground.
    And yet, by heaven, I think my love as rare
    As any she belied with false compare.

3 dun: tan.

5 damask'd: with mingled colors.

8 reeks: is exhaled (used here without the word's present reference to offensive odors).

11 go: walk.

14 as . . . compare: as any woman misrepresented by exaggerated comparisons.

RESPONDING OPTIONS

FROM PERSONAL RESPONSE *TO* CRITICAL ANALYSIS

REFLECT 1. Were you surprised by the description in "Sonnet 130"? Share your reactions with your classmates, then record them in your notebook.

RETHINK 2. What do you think is the speaker's attitude toward the woman he loves?

Consider
- his descriptions of her physical characteristics
- his description of her voice
- his conclusion in the couplet

3. What do you think might have been Shakespeare's purpose in writing this sonnet?

RELATE 4. In your opinion, which of the three sonnets expresses the strongest commitment to a love relationship? Explain your answer.

5. Renaissance sonnets often focus on the great beauty of the beloved. How important is physical beauty or attractiveness in today's society?

ANOTHER PATHWAY

Cooperative Learning

Create a Venn diagram like the one shown. In the appropriate spaces, write down ideas and emotions that appear in one sonnet (spaces where a circle does not overlap with others), in two of the sonnets (spaces where two circles overlap), and in all three sonnets (the space common to all three).

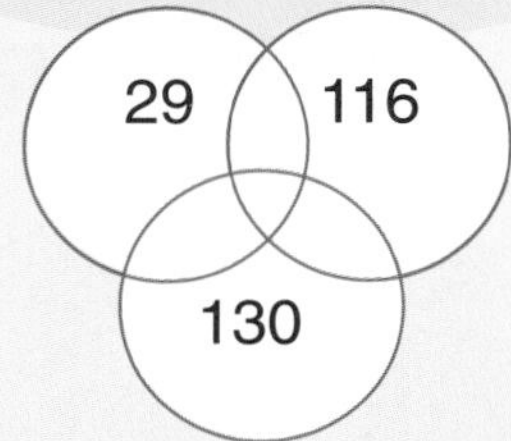

LITERARY CONCEPTS

Language that conveys meanings beyond the literal meanings of the words is called **figurative language. Similes** and **metaphors** are types of figurative language that consist of comparisons between things that are basically unlike but have something in common. In a simile the word *like* or *as* is used; in a metaphor it is not. Identify one simile or metaphor in each sonnet, and explain the comparison and its effect.

CONCEPT REVIEW: Rhyme Scheme Like Spenser, Shakespeare uses the structure of three quatrains and a couplet in his sonnets. However, he uses the rhyme scheme *abab cdcd efef gg* instead of the Spenserian pattern *(abab bcbc cdcd ee).* Reread Shakespeare's three sonnets and discuss with your classmates how the rhyme scheme contributes to the meaning and appeal of each poem.

QUICKWRITES

1. Write a **poem** describing someone you love or greatly admire. Use at least one simile or metaphor.
2. As the speaker of "Sonnet 116," write a **character sketch** of the ideal partner in a strong love relationship. Make sure to identify various qualities the person would need to possess.
3. Imagine that you are the woman described in "Sonnet 130." In a **letter** to the speaker, give your opinion of his description.

PORTFOLIO *Save your writing. You may want to use it later as a springboard to a piece for your portfolio.*

ALTERNATIVE ACTIVITIES

1. With a partner, stage a **television talk show** in which the host interviews William Shakespeare about the meaning of love.
2. Prepare a **scrapbook** of items—such as photos, drawings, poems, and sayings—that express your conception of a strong love relationship.
3. With a small group of classmates, investigate some of Shakespeare's other sonnets. Have each group member prepare a **reading** of his or her favorite sonnet. Discuss the feelings and ideas expressed in each poem, and compare it with one or more of the three sonnets you have read in this lesson.
4. Reread each of the three sonnets, and choose your favorite. Think of films, novels, short stories, works of art, and musical compositions that in some way reflect the mood of the poem or the ideas and images in it. Prepare a **list of resources** that could be used by other readers to explore different treatments of the subject of the poem.

LITERARY LINKS

The speaker of "Sonnet 130," like the speaker of Spenser's "Sonnet 75," uses the word *rare* to describe his beloved. Compare the thoughts and emotions of the two speakers. Whom would you more likely enjoy meeting? Why?

ART CONNECTION

Look again at the two small portraits of women on pages 230–231. Why do you think they were chosen to illustrate "Sonnet 116" and "Sonnet 130"?

ACROSS THE CURRICULUM

Art Find some books with portraits of women painted in England during the Renaissance. Look at several of the portraits and think about whether they seem idealized or realistic. How does the portrayal of women in painting of the period compare with the portrayal of women in Renaissance poetry?

Psychology For most people, love is one of the most important aspects of life. Investigate some of the definitions and analyses of love in the writings of contemporary psychologists. Share what you find with the class, and discuss any relationships you can see between Shakespeare's views of love and the psychologists'.

CRITIC'S CORNER

One critic has called Shakespeare's sonnets "explorations of the human spirit." Discuss ways in which this interpretation does or does not apply to the three sonnets you have read. Use details from the poems to support your conclusions.

William Shakespeare

1564–1616

William Shakespeare, considered by many to be the greatest writer of the Western world, was the son of a merchant of Stratford-upon-Avon, England. Although never educated at a university, he attended the Stratford Grammar School, where he would have studied the standard curriculum of the day: Latin grammar, composition, and literature. Many have speculated about Shakespeare's youth and early adulthood, but only a few facts are known. In 1582, at the age of 18, he married Anne Hathaway, with whom he was to have two daughters and a son. Probably during the 1580s, he moved to London, where he began a career as an actor and playwright for the Lord Chamberlain's Men (later known as the King's Men), London's leading theater company.

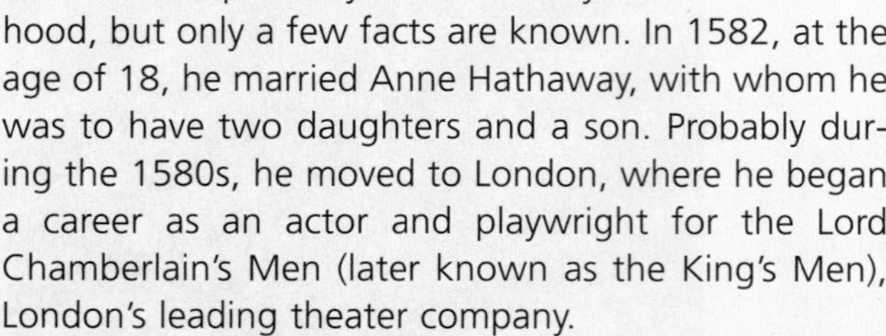

Shakespeare quickly became one of London's most prominent and successful playwrights. His plays appealed to everyone, from refined aristocrats to rowdy and uneducated peasants. No other playwright of the period could match his range. Shakespeare's imaginative world is populated with tragic kings, feisty adolescents, prudish servants, witty tavern keepers, lovesick aristocrats, treasonous advisers, and a host of other interesting characters from all segments of society. He understood human psychology, and he shaped and interpreted his material without moralizing or imposing judgments. His audiences responded strongly to his memorable and recognizably human characters.

Shakespeare was also clever and imaginative in his use of language, playing on ambiguities, connotations, and double meanings and creating vivid images and figures of speech. He used the rhythm of blank verse to produce powerful effects, and he made bold experiments with spoken English, seen in his juxtaposition of formal diction with slang and prose with poetry. Shakespeare drew upon an enormous vocabulary that has been estimated at more than 25,000 words, over four times the number used in the King James Bible.

During his lifetime, Shakespeare composed 154 sonnets, 2 narrative poems, and more than 35 plays, including comedies (*As You Like It* and *The Taming of the Shrew,* for example), tragedies (including *Romeo and Juliet, Macbeth, Hamlet,* and *King Lear*), and histories (such as *Julius Caesar, Richard II,* and *Henry IV, Parts 1 and 2*). His success made him a wealthy and important citizen. He was one of the seven shareholders who financed the construction of the Globe Theater in 1599, and his plays were performed before Queen Elizabeth I and King James I. Shakespeare was a welcome visitor in the homes of some of the finest families in London, a respected figure in the literary establishment, a loyal friend to fellow actors, and apparently a shrewd investor who was able to live in comfortable retirement after he left the theater in 1613. Ben Jonson, a rival poet and playwright, predicted that Shakespeare would be "not of an age, but for all time." His prediction has come true. Even today, Shakespeare's plays are performed more frequently, and in more countries, than the works of any other playwright.

OTHER WORKS "Sonnet 18," "Sonnet 30," "Sonnet 73," "Sonnet 97," "Sonnet 138," *Romeo and Juliet, Othello, Macbeth, Twelfth Night, A Midsummer Night's Dream, As You Like It, The Taming of the Shrew*

LASERLINKS
- *AUTHOR BACKGROUND*
- *CONTEMPORARY CONNECTION*

PREVIEWING

POETRY

Sonnet 169 Sonnet 292

Francesco Petrarch (frän-chäs'kō pē'trärk')

PERSONAL CONNECTION

Love can sometimes be painful, especially the loss of love. You may know or have read about someone who has experienced such a loss. Think about how that person reacted to the loss of love. Did the reaction seem reasonable to you? Share your thoughts with your classmates. Then, as you read these two sonnets, notice the way in which the speakers express their reactions to the loss of love.

LITERARY CONNECTION

Although sonnets had been written in Italy for nearly a hundred years before Petrarch wrote his, it was he who established the sonnet as a major poetic form. He perfected the sonnet style that 200 years later was adapted and used by Wyatt, Spenser, Shakespeare, and other English poets.

Petrarch's sonnets, the output of a lifetime of work, show his longing for a woman named Laura, with whom he reportedly fell passionately in love on Good Friday, April 6, 1327, after seeing her in church. Even though Laura did not return his love, she was the inspiration for over 300 of Petrarch's poems. Like many of Petrarch's contemporaries, Laura died in the plague that devastated much of Europe in the mid-14th century. "Sonnet 292" was written after her death.

READING CONNECTION

Summarizing the Main Ideas of a Sonnet Create a chart like the one shown. As you read each of Petrarch's sonnets, jot down phrases that summarize the main idea of each stanza.

	Sonnet 169	Sonnet 292
Lines 1–4		
Lines 5–8		
Lines 9–11		
Lines 12–14		

FRANCESCO PETRARCH

SONNET 169

Rapt in the one fond thought that makes me stray
from other men and walk this world alone,
sometimes I have escaped myself and flown
to seek the very one that I should flee;

so fair and fell I see her passing by
that the soul trembles to take flight again,
so many arméd sighs are in her train,
this lovely foe to Love himself and me!

And yet, upon that high and clouded brow
I seem to see a ray of pity shine,
shedding some light across the grieving heart:

so I call back my soul, and when I vow
at last to tell her of my hidden pain,
I have so much to say I dare not start.

Translated by Anthony Mortimer

1 rapt: deeply absorbed.

5 fell: cruel.

7 train: a group of people following in attendance.

FROM PERSONAL RESPONSE *TO* CRITICAL ANALYSIS

REFLECT **1.** What are your thoughts about the feelings the speaker expresses in this poem? Record your impressions in your notebook.

RETHINK **2.** How would you describe the relationship between the speaker and his beloved?

Consider

- the conflict the speaker expresses in lines 3–4
- his description of how his soul "trembles to take flight again" (line 6)
- his use of contradictory phrases in describing the beloved, such as "fair and fell" (line 5) and "lovely foe" (line 8)
- the needs he suggests in lines 12–14

Portrait of a Man and Woman at a Casement (about 1440–1445), Fra Filippo Lippi. Tempera on wood, 25¼″ × 16½″, The Metropolitan Museum of Art, New York, gift of Henry G. Marquand, 1889, Marquand Collection (89.15.19).

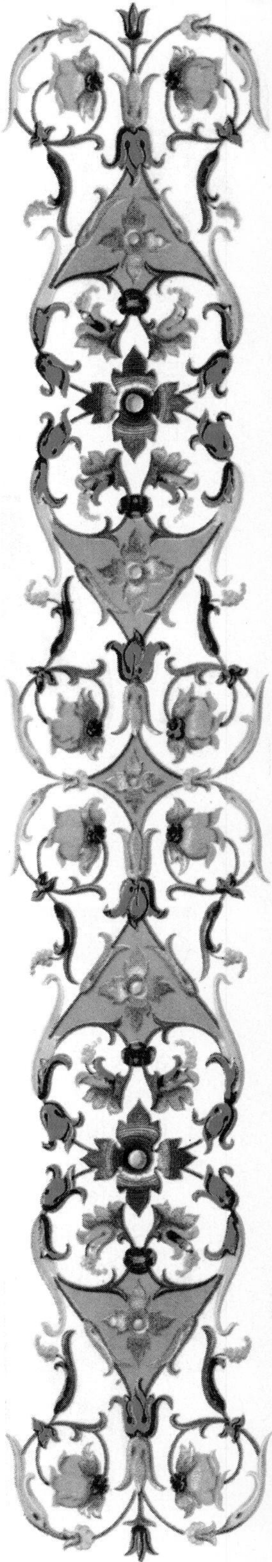

SONNET 292

The eyes I spoke of once in words that burn,
the arms and hands and feet and lovely face
that took me from myself for such a space
of time and marked me out from other men;

the waving hair of unmixed gold that shone,
the smile that flashed with the angelic rays
that used to make this earth a paradise,
are now a little dust, all feeling gone;

and yet I live, grief and disdain to me,
left where the light I cherished never shows,
in fragile bark on the tempestuous sea.

Here let my loving song come to a close,
the vein of my accustomed art is dry,
and this, my lyre, turned at last to tears.

Translated by Anthony Mortimer

11 bark: sailing ship; **tempestuous:** stormy.

14 lyre (līr): a stringed musical instrument of the harp family, used in ancient Greece.

RESPONDING OPTIONS

FROM PERSONAL RESPONSE TO CRITICAL ANALYSIS

REFLECT 1. Find a recording of music that conveys the overall mood of "Sonnet 292," and play it for the rest of the class.

RETHINK 2. How would you describe the speaker's feelings over the loss of love?
Consider
- his description of his beloved's physical attributes
- his attitude toward his own life (lines 9–11)
- what he means by "the vein of my accustomed art is dry" (line 13)

3. How does the speaker's reaction to the loss of love compare with the reactions you discussed for the Personal Connection on page 235?

RELATE 4. Compare the attitudes of the speakers at the end of the two sonnets. In your opinion, which speaker faces a more difficult situation? Explain your answer.

ANOTHER PATHWAY

Using as a starting point the chart you made for the Reading Connection on page 235, write a prose description of what happens in each poem. Include Petrarch's vivid images as you expand his thoughts into longer passages of narrative.

LITERARY CONCEPTS

The **Italian sonnet** written by Petrarch is different in form from the English sonnet. The 14 lines of the Italian sonnet are divided into two parts: an **octave** (the first 8 lines) and a **sestet** (the last 6 lines). Generally, the octave tells a story, introduces a situation, or raises a question. In the sestet, the speaker comments on the story, situation, or question.

Refer to the sonnets by Spenser in this part of Unit Two, then compare the style of these Italian sonnets with that of Spenser's English sonnets. Which form do you think gives the writer more liberties? Which form seems to you to fit more situations or themes? Discuss your conclusions with your classmates.

Italian Sonnet
- Octave (first 8 lines)
- Sestet (last 6 lines)

QUICKWRITES

1. Create a **title** for each of Petrarch's two sonnets.
2. Write an **outline** for a series of soap-opera episodes based on the sonnets. Describe the speaker and the woman he loves. Add details to explain the speaker's "hidden pain" and grief.
3. Write an **inscription** for a monument that the speaker of "Sonnet 292" might erect in honor of the woman he loved.

PORTFOLIO *Save your writing. You may want to use it later as a springboard to a piece for your portfolio.*

ALTERNATIVE ACTIVITIES

1. Choreograph a **dance interpretation** of one of the sonnets. Create different movements to express the speaker's thoughts and emotions. Perform your dance for the class.
2. Create a **design** for the monument described in QuickWrites. Let your imagination be inspired by the images and mood of the sonnet.

CRITIC'S CORNER

Edgar Quinet, a 19th-century French critic, said that "Petrarch's originality consists in having realized, for the first time, that every moment of our existence contains in itself the substance of a poem." Read Petrarch's sonnets again. Do you agree that everyday incidents can in themselves be poetic?

THE WRITER'S STYLE

Compare the use of language and imagery in the two sonnets. Find examples of descriptive words, phrases, or images in "Sonnet 169" that are repeated in "Sonnet 292."

LITERARY LINKS

Review the various sonnets you have read in this part of Unit Two. Which sonnet did you find the most rewarding to read? Give reasons for your choice.

FRANCESCO PETRARCH

1304–1374

Although born in Italy, Petrarch moved with his family to France, where his father had accepted a job. It was in France that Petrarch, on his father's insistence, began his study of law, later returning to Italy to continue his education. After his father's death in 1326, however, Petrarch abandoned law, a subject for which he had little inclination, to study Greek and Latin literature and to write poetry.

In the spirit of the Renaissance, Petrarch had varied interests, ranging from the scholarly and literary to a love of and fascination with nature. In 1336, together with his brother, he climbed Mt. Ventoux in the Alps; the climb was quite unusual in an age that showed little interest in nature. He also had a deep interest in religious studies, which led him to join the clergy. The church positions he held provided him not only with a modest means of income but also with much free time to devote to literature. He studied, wrote, and traveled extensively and was highly regarded as a literary and cultural leader of his time.

In 1340, Petrarch received invitations from both Paris and Rome to become poet laureate. He chose Rome, and in 1341 received the honor of being its first poet laureate since ancient times. Most of the 366 poems in the *Canzoniere* ("Book of Songs"), Petrarch's poetic masterpiece, are written about his love for Laura, who also appears in his *Trionfi* ("Triumphs"). Petrarch never lost his love of writing. He spent the last years of his life composing and revising his literary works, and he died in his study, at work at his desk.

LASERLINKS
• *AUTHOR BACKGROUND*

Fear No More the Heat o' the Sun

William Shakespeare

Songs appear in many of Shakespeare's plays. Although the songs serve specific purposes, such as heightening the mood of particular scenes, they can be enjoyed on their own. They are superb lyrics, full of wit and charm, sometimes humorous and sometimes poignant. The following song is from the play *Cymbeline,* written by Shakespeare during the last years of his life. Two young princes recite the song (it is one of the few songs not actually sung) over the supposedly dead body of their sister, Imogen.

Fear no more the heat o' the sun,
Nor the furious winter's rages,
Thou thy worldly task hast done,
Home art gone, and ta'en thy wages.
Golden lads and girls all must,
As chimney-sweepers, come to dust.

Fear no more the frown o' the great,
Thou art past the tyrant's stroke;
Care no more to clothe and eat,
To thee the reed is as the oak.
The scepter, learning, physic, must
All follow this and come to dust.

Fear no more the lightning-flash.
Nor the all-dreaded thunder-stone.
Fear not slander, censure rash.
Thou hast finish'd joy and moan.
All lovers young, all lovers must
Consign to thee and come to dust.

No exorciser harm thee.
Nor no witchcraft charm thee.
Ghost unlaid forbear thee.
Nothing ill come near thee.
Quiet consummation have,
And renownéd be thy grave.

10 reed: a type of grass with a hollow stalk, frequently used as a symbol of frailness.
11 the scepter, learning, physic: kingship, scholarship, and medical science.

14 thunder-stone: The sound of thunder was thought to be caused by falling stones.

18 consign to thee: submit to the same conditions as you.

19 exorciser: one who calls up spirits.

21 unlaid: not properly buried and therefore still walking the earth; **forbear:** leave alone.
23 consummation: death.

Milestones in British Literature

William Shakespeare

The PLAYS *of* SHAKESPEARE

Right:
Sir John Falstaff, the most famous comic character created by Shakespeare.

What do the Japanese art film *Ran,* the Jane Smiley novel *A Thousand Acres,* and the 1950s musical *West Side Story* have in common? They're all based on plays by William Shakespeare. During his lifetime, Shakespeare wrote at least 37 tragedies, comedies, histories, and romances. These plays have inspired countless novels, plays, poems, films, and essays, not to mention works of art, music, and dance. They have been performed in parks, parodied by other playwrights, and quoted in *Star Trek* movies.

What generates the near-fanatical devotion Shakespeare inspires? Perhaps it is his fine ear for the English language. Some of the most familiar quotations in English are from Shakespeare's plays: "O Romeo, Romeo, wherefore art thou Romeo?" is from *Romeo and Juliet,* "Friends, Romans, countrymen, lend me your ears" is from *Julius Caesar,* and "To be or not to be . . ." is from *Hamlet.* Shakespeare also coined many popular phrases, such as *fair play, foregone conclusion,* and *catch cold.* He even invented words, including *assassination, bump,* and *lonely.*

Above:
The Globe Theater, home of Shakespeare's theatrical company. Common folk could view plays from the floor of the Globe for the price of a single penny.

❦

Left:
Laurence Olivier, the great 20th-century actor, as Hamlet.

❦

Left:
The romantic comedy A Midsummer Night's Dream *juxtaposes the lives of humans with the mysterious and merry world of fairies. Shown is one of Arthur Rackham's famous illustrations of* A Midsummer Night's Dream, *1908.*

Noting Shakespeare's natural skill with language, the British writer George Orwell called him a "word musician." Yet language alone cannot explain Shakespeare's appeal. The stories themselves are compelling, and they unfold with an understanding of human emotion and an appreciation of dramatic effect rarely equaled in theater. Shakespeare valued dramatic effect so much that it got him in trouble with Elizabethan critics. They were shocked and dismayed by this "Upstart Crow" who repeatedly ignored the unities of time and place. Critics also complained when he combined elements of tragedy and comedy, especially in romances like *The Tempest.*

Obviously, sticking to convention was not Shakespeare's primary concern. He knew the "rules" of dramatic writing and routinely wrote plays having the classical five-act structure: *The Comedy of Errors* and *The Merry Wives of Windsor* are models of classical correctness. However, when a story called for a dream sequence, a new location, or a word that had not been invented, he had no trouble breaking the rules.

Shakespeare's disregard for the unities of time and place was matched only by his insistence on unity of purpose. He focused with laserlike precision on his goal of reflecting the speech, actions, and values of his time. The comedies mirrored Elizabethan manners. The tragedies offered glimpses of souls in torment. In attempting to reflect his time, however, Shakespeare succeeded in doing much more; he proved to be—as Ben Jonson, a rival poet and playwright, wrote—"not of an age, but for all time."

WRITING ABOUT
LITERATURE

USING YOUR IMAGINATION

What movies or songs do you know that have the same theme of unrequited love as Spenser's Sonnet 30 or Wyatt's "My Lute, Awake!"? Recognizing that the same theme can occur in different time periods and different media will help you understand literature and inspire your own writing. In the following pages you will

- study how writers use figurative language
- write a creative response inspired by a poem from Unit Two
- examine the effects of different media on the same subject

The Writer's Style: Figurative Language Writers use figurative language, or figures of speech, to make associations that go beyond the literal meanings of the words and create vivid descriptions and explain abstract ideas.

Read the Literature

Similes and metaphors are two figures of speech. Both compare unlike things. In the excerpts below, notice how similes use *like* or *as* to signal a comparison.

Literature Models

Abstract Ideas
To what does the speaker compare himself and the woman he loves? How is the comparison used in each line of the excerpt?

My love is like to ice, and I to fire;
How comes it then that this her cold so great
Is not dissolved through my so hot desire,
But harder grows the more I her entreat?

Edmund Spenser
from Sonnet 30

Vivid Descriptions
What image does this simile form for you? What does this tell you about the actions of the beloved?

The rocks do not so cruelly
Repulse the waves continually
As she my suit and affection.
So that I am past remedy,
Whereby my lute and I have done.

Sir Thomas Wyatt
from "My Lute, Awake!"

Connect to Life

Metaphors don't use the words *like* or *as*, but they imply comparisons nevertheless. Since these figures of speech can help us see or understand something in a new way, writers use them in everything from poetry to magazine articles.

Magazine Article

When the mood came on him, Ernest Hemingway fancied himself in a boxing ring with Tolstoy. For Hemingway, novel-writing was a competitive sport, so naturally he felt obliged to go a few rounds with Count Leo.

Peter S. Prescott
from "Tinker, Tailor, Soldier, Spy"
Newsweek, September 30, 1991

Direct Comparisons
What is novel-writing being compared to in this excerpt?

Try Your Hand: Using Figurative Language

1. Make Comparisons Use a simile or metaphor to describe the following items in a new, surprising way. For example, you might describe a nose as a quivering pink mouse.
   - a pet dog
   - a driveway
   - a shopping cart
2. Express Your Ideas Find a portfolio piece in which you write about your reactions to a poem. Where appropriate, add similes or metaphors to express your ideas more clearly.
3. Write a Poem Have you ever seen or experienced anything you've found difficult to explain to others? Write a poem or paragraph that uses similes and metaphors to describe a unique experience.

SkillBuilder

WRITER'S CRAFT

Avoiding Clichés

Clichés are similes, metaphors, and other expressions that are so overused they have lost their ability to describe.

She looked pretty as a picture in that dress.

When writing, replace clichés with precise expressions. Visualizing your subject or free associating about it may help you come up with fresh comparisons.

The billowing sleeves and wide skirt of her magenta dress made her look like some kind of exotic butterfly.

APPLYING WHAT YOU'VE LEARNED

Rewrite each sentence, replacing the cliché with a more vivid expression.

1. His singing voice was clear as a bell.
2. When I shook her hand, it was cold as ice.
3. Roberto had puppy dog eyes and coal black hair.

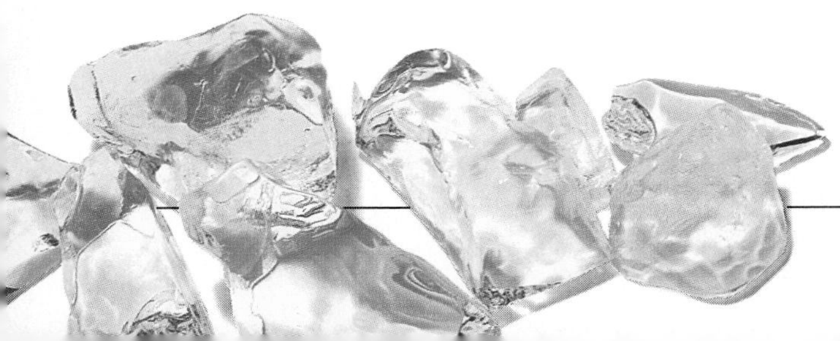

Creative Response

"Morphing" is not just a special effect seen on film. It occurs with literature all the time. Books turn into movies, poems turn into songs, and short stories become plays. Changing the form of a story is sometimes the best way to continue to enjoy or explore it.

GUIDED ASSIGNMENT

Transform a Poem On the next few pages, you'll transform one or more of the poems in Unit Two into another kind of writing. For example, you may want to write a skit about what would happen if the shepherd and his nymph got married or a rap song expressing the sentiments of Spenser's Sonnet 75.

1 Prewrite and Explore

Choose a poem from the ones you just read that has a situation or character you can relate to. Ask yourself questions like the following:

- What is the situation in the poem?
- What are the people like?
- Does the poem reflect feelings people have today?

USE YOUR IMAGINATION

Think about how the information in the poem could be used in different ways. What happens if the speaker's beloved talks back? What if the situation in the poem were taking place today? Don't worry if your ideas seem outrageous; just jot them down as they come to you. You may want to use the SkillBuilder on generating information to help you create details about the characters and situations in the poem you have chosen.

THINK ABOUT FORM

In order to get started, you need to know what it is you'll be writing. The information in the chart below may help you weigh the benefits and limitations of different kinds of writing.

short story	needs a beginning, middle, and end and includes a conflict that is worked through to a resolution
song	doesn't need a plot, just a sentiment, but there's not much opportunity to develop characters
skit	lets you work with characters, but the whole story needs to be told through dialogue

Decision Point Decide what kind of writing will allow you to explore the most interesting aspect of your selection.

② Plan the Change

Transformation always means change, but how much you alter the poem you've chosen depends on the ideas you want to explore and the kind of writing you want to create. Making a chart like the one below may help you figure out what to do in order to transform a poem into another writing form.

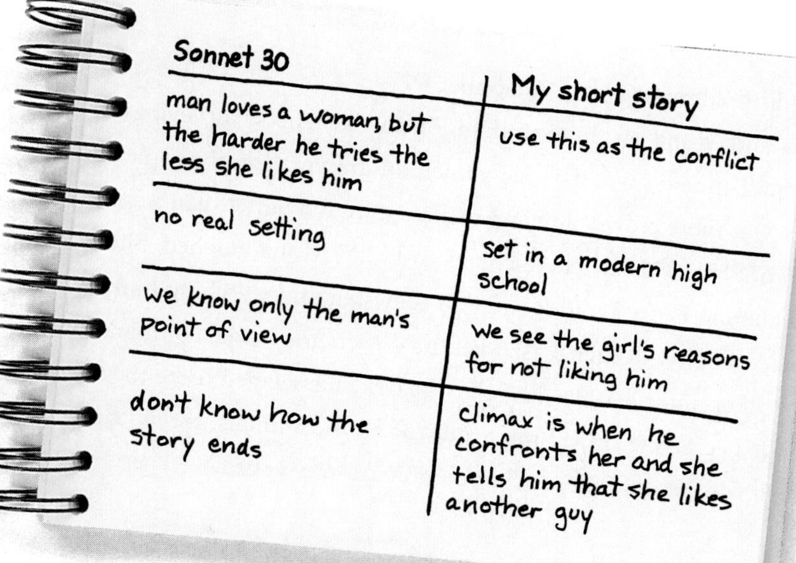

Sonnet 30
My short story
man loves a woman, but the harder he tries the less she likes him
use this as the conflict
no real setting
set in a modern high school
we know only the man's point of view
we see the girl's reasons for not liking him
don't know how the story ends
climax is when he confronts her and she tells him that she likes another guy

③ Draft and Share

The changes you came up with in step 2 can help you turn your ideas into a draft. You may want to refer to the chart on the opposite page to make sure that your piece has all the characteristics of its form. Consider asking another student to read your draft and give you feedback.

 PEER RESPONSE

- What specific images can you recall?
- What part of the draft confused you, if any?
- How can you tell what poem I was transforming?

SkillBuilder

 CRITICAL THINKING

Generating Information About a Character

The more you know about your subject, the more likely you are to be able to write well about it. One way to learn about the characters or situations in your writing is to ask yourself questions about them.

- Start by asking *who, what, where, when,* and *why* questions about the characters or story you want to write about. For example, *What does the main character want?*
- Consider asking category questions such as *What is my subject similar to?*
- You may also want to ask *what if* questions. For example, *What if the characters changed their roles?*

APPLYING WHAT YOU'VE LEARNED

Conduct an imaginary interview with a character you're planning to write about. Write down several different kinds of questions and then record the answers.

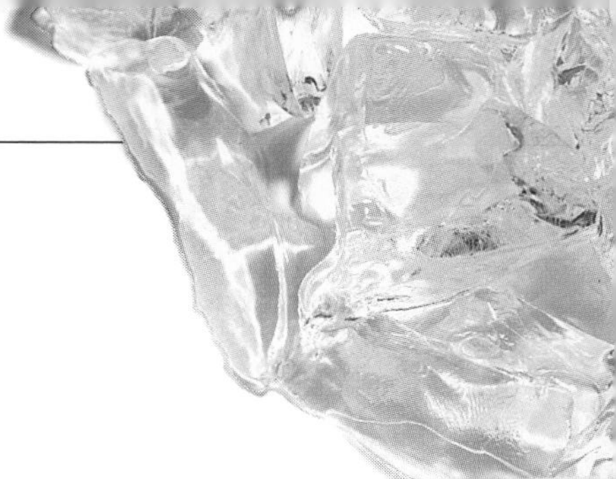

4 Revise and Edit

The revise stage is the time to work on creating vivid, clear sentences. Remember that similes and metaphors can help you do that, and look to the Standards for Evaluation for other writing tips. When you have finished revising, decide how to share your final draft with the class.

What specific actions show how Lecia feels about Robert? What is similar about this story and Sonnet 30? What is different?

Hot Blood versus Cold

(inspired by Edmund Spenser's Sonnet 30)

Lecia and Mona sat thigh to thigh on the bleachers, surveying the milling half-time crowd. The big game had drawn a lot of people and the gym was more crowded than a rock concert and hotter than a sauna.

"Oh no," said Lecia, "here comes Robert." Mona laughed. She'd been watching Lecia avoid Robert all semester, and watching him try harder to get close to her. Last week he'd even gotten the combination to her locker and filled it with teddy bears. This seemed to be the final straw for Lecia. She ripped the heads off all the animals, threw them in the trash can, and got her locker combination changed.

Robert stared over at Lecia. She had moved down two rows to sit by Ramon Denito, the guy who looked like he was slipping on banana peels every time he ran down the gym floor, and she was smiling into his down-turned face.

"That girl is one cold-blooded snake," he said to Jon.

"Well, hey, forget about her. I hear Joanna likes you, anyway."

"No way. Lecia's the best thing in this school. I already bought her a Christmas present."

How does the writer use metaphor to create a sensory experience and a vivid image?

Standards for Evaluation

A creative transformation
- demonstrates an understanding of the original form
- effectively translates characteristics of one form to those of another
- uses language creatively and effectively

Grammar in Context

Degrees of Comparison When the talk turns to love, you'll probably want to use comparative and superlative phrases. After all, how else can you say that somebody is the most fabulous person you've ever met? Remember that regular adjectives and adverbs form the comparative and superlative degrees in one of two ways.

- One-syllable modifiers and a few two-syllable ones form the comparative and superlative by adding *-er* and *-est.*
- Most modifiers with two syllables and all modifiers with three or more syllables use *more* and *most* to form comparative and superlative degrees.

> The big game had drawn a lot of people and the gym was crowdeder than a rock concert and ~~more~~ hot than a sauna.
>
> "Oh no," said Lecia, "here comes Robert." Mona laughed. She'd been watching Lecia avoid Robert all semester and watching him try ~~more~~ hard to get close to her.

In the example above, incorrect use of the degrees of adjectives and adverbs makes the writing sound choppy and awkward. When in doubt about how to form the comparative or superlative degree of a modifier, look the modifier up in the dictionary under its positive form. For more information about comparison, see page 1273 of the Grammar Handbook.

Try Your Hand: Using Comparatives and Superlatives

Rewrite the following sentences, using the correct comparative or superlative degree of adjectives and adverbs.

- He is the annoyingest person I've ever met.
- As he came closer to her, his smile became more wide.
- Lecia became more angry the more Robert talked.

SkillBuilder

GRAMMAR FROM WRITING

Avoiding Double Comparisons

When you form the comparative or superlative degree of an adjective or adverb you either add *-er* or *-est* or you place the word *more* or *most* before the modifier. Using both *more* or *most* and *-er* or *-est* results in a double comparison, and is incorrect.

Incorrect: *But the more harder I try to get her to like me, the less she does.*

Correct: *But the harder I try to get her to like me, the less she does.*

APPLYING WHAT YOU'VE LEARNED
On a separate piece of paper, rewrite the following sentences.

1. "On Monsieur's Departure" is the most saddest thing I have ever read.
2. Love, which should make you more happier than anything else, is making the narrator miserable.
3. She seems to think the most best thing that could happen would be for her to forget love.

Now examine your draft to make sure you haven't used any double comparisons.

GRAMMAR HANDBOOK

For more help with modifiers, see pages 1272–1276 of the Grammar Handbook.

Self-Portrait in Red Jacket by Mary Mabbutt, May 1987

READING THE WORLD

Changing Media

Just as you might get a great idea for a project while you're watching a TV commercial, a painter might find inspiration in a news story. But whenever ideas from one medium are translated into another, changes take place. For one thing, the artist's personal vision often enters into the mix. Recognizing similarities and differences between similar subjects portrayed in different media can help you appreciate the strengths and limitations of each form.

View What do you see when you look at the self-portrait on the opposite page? What are the proportions of the figure? What do the colors and forms make you think of?

Interpret What similarities and differences do you see between the photograph of the artist and the portrait?

Discuss With a group, discuss the different kinds of information you receive from the photograph and from the painting. Refer to the SkillBuilder at the right for help in comparing and contrasting the two images.

Mary Mabbutt

SkillBuilder

CRITICAL THINKING

Comparing and Contrasting
Noticing the similarities and differences between two portrayals of the same subject can help you understand your reactions to each one. There are a variety of ways to compare and contrast, and each method provides different results.

- Compare and contrast your initial reaction to a subject with a later reaction.
- Compare all the similarities between two subjects, and then contrast all the differences.
- Break the subjects down into categories or aspects and then compare and contrast them feature by feature.

APPLYING WHAT YOU'VE LEARNED
With a partner, decide how you would use comparing and contrasting to explore the different effects the items in each pair below might have on you. Explain your reasoning.

- A current event and the TV movie made about it
- *Romeo and Juliet* and a modern-day story of star-crossed love
- A documentary and a fictionalized movie about the same subject

PART 2 *Facing Life's Limitations*

Many people of the Renaissance sought answers to questions about life's limitations. Some found comfort in the lessons of the Bible. Others read works such as those in this part of Unit Two in which writers reflected on love, death, and the role of men and women. You may find that the questions posed are still relevant today.

PREVIEWING

SCRIPTURE

from the King James Bible
from Ecclesiastes, Chapter 3
Psalm 23
Parable of the Prodigal Son

PERSONAL CONNECTION

Think about events that have occurred in your life. Do any of these events stand out in your mind as being particularly important? Create a time line, charting significant events and phases. If appropriate, include times when you made major changes in your attitude and times when you learned valuable lessons about life.

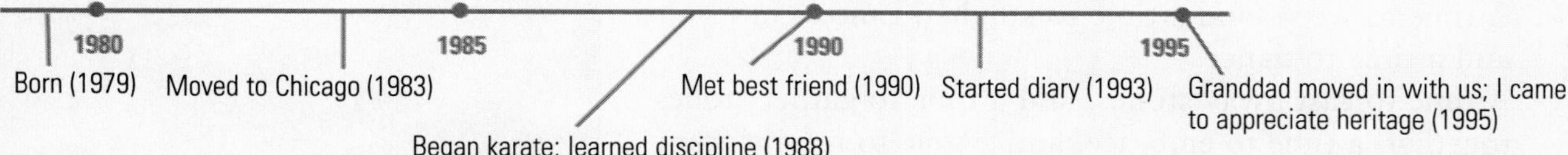

HISTORICAL/CULTURAL CONNECTION

When James I, the successor of Elizabeth I, became king of England in 1603, Puritan leaders petitioned him to support a new translation of the Bible. Although he bore no great love for the Puritans, he agreed that English worshipers needed a translation better than the ones in popular use. In 1604, the king appointed 54 distinguished scholars and clergymen to create a new translation—one that would be more accurate than previous English versions and more beautiful in its use of language. The result—the King James Bible—was the main Protestant Bible in English for over 300 years. Even today, although many other translations are available, it remains the most important and influential of all versions.

The following passages from the King James Bible illustrate different types of scriptural writing, each designed to impart spiritual lessons about life. The selection from Ecclesiastes is an example of what is called wisdom literature—literature intended to help human beings find the meaning of life. The second selection is a psalm, or song of praise. The last is a parable, a brief story that is meant to teach a moral or religious lesson.

WRITING CONNECTION

As you read these biblical selections, record in your notebook any lines or sentences that you find especially meaningful. Briefly state why they appeal to you, and describe any lessons about life that can be learned from them.

from the King James Bible

from Ecclesiastes, Chapter 3

1 To every thing there is a season, and a time to every purpose under the heaven:
2 A time to be born, and a time to die; a time to plant, and a time to pluck up that which is planted;
3 A time to kill, and a time to heal; a time to break down, and a time to build up;
4 A time to weep, and a time to laugh; a time to mourn, and a time to dance;
5 A time to cast away stones, and a time to gather stones together; a time to embrace, and a time to refrain from embracing;
6 A time to get,[1] and a time to lose; a time to keep, and a time to cast away;
7 A time to rend,[2] and a time to sew; a time to keep silence, and a time to speak;
8 A time to love, and a time to hate; a time of war, and a time of peace.

1. **get:** gain; win.
2. **rend:** tear or rip.

Month of July from *Très riches heures du duc de Berry* (about 1415), Limbourg brothers. Musée Condé, Chantilly, France. Giraudon/Art Resource, New York.

FROM PERSONAL RESPONSE *TO* CRITICAL ANALYSIS

REFLECT **1.** Share with your classmates one of the lines from Ecclesiastes that you recorded in your notebook. Discuss its appeal.

RETHINK **2.** Do you agree with the message conveyed in this excerpt?

Consider

- the meaning of the statement "To every thing there is a season" (line 1)
- the contrasting examples given throughout the excerpt

RELATE **3.** Which lines do you think have special relevance to contemporary life?

Psalm 23

A Psalm of David

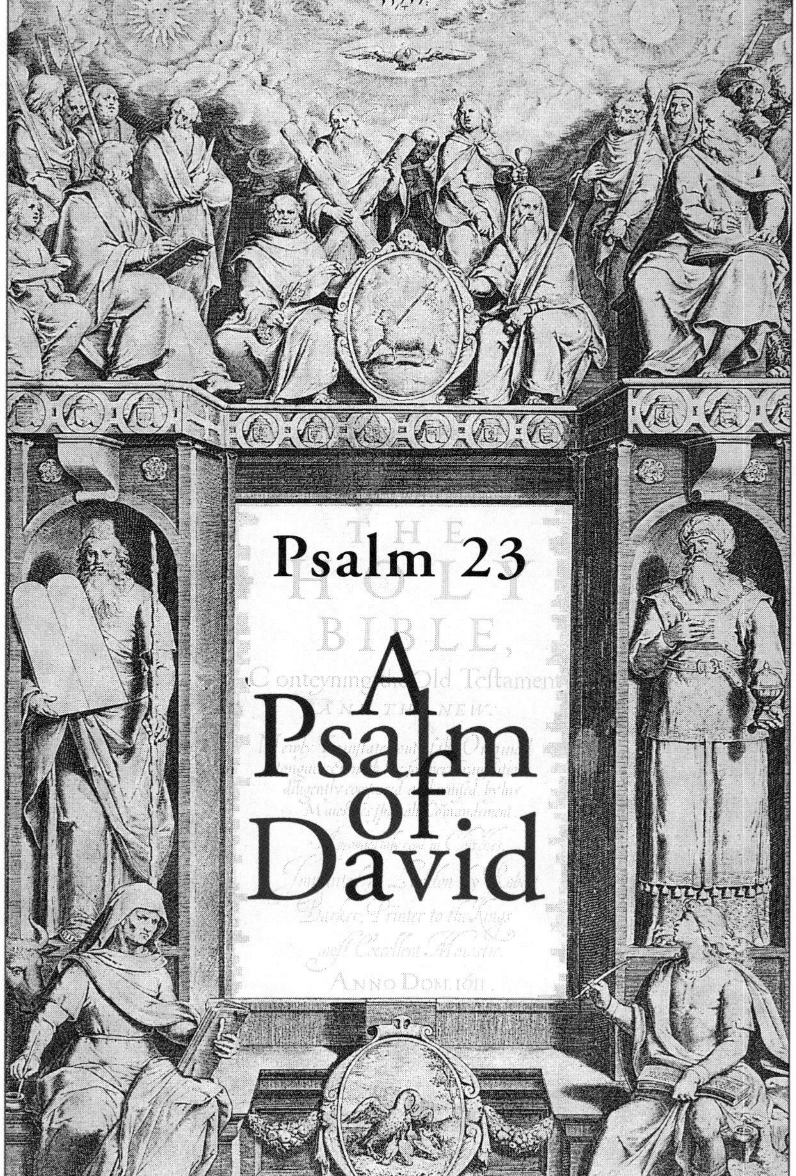

Title page of the first edition of the King James Bible, London, 1611. The Granger Collection, New York.

1 The Lord is my shepherd; I shall not want.[1]

2 He maketh me to lie down in green pastures: he leadeth me beside the still waters.

3 He restoreth my soul: he leadeth me in the paths of righteousness for his name's sake.

4 Yea, though I walk through the valley of the shadow of death, I will fear no evil: for thou art with me; thy rod and thy staff they comfort me.

5 Thou preparest a table before me in the presence of mine enemies: thou anointest my head with oil; my cup runneth over.[2]

6 Surely goodness and mercy shall follow me all the days of my life: and I will dwell in the house of the Lord for ever.

---

1. **want:** be in need.
2. **Thou preparest . . . runneth over:** In this verse, the Lord is presented as a generous host who offers his guest food, oil for grooming, and an overflowing cup of wine. In ancient times, olive oil was used as a cleansing agent and was quite expensive.

FROM PERSONAL RESPONSE *TO* CRITICAL ANALYSIS

REFLECT **1.** What images are you left with after reading this psalm? Describe them in your notebook.

RETHINK **2.** In your opinion, how might this psalm affect someone trying to cope with life's difficulties or limitations?

3. Psalm 23 is part of a group of psalms often called "songs of trust." Why do you think it is included in this group?

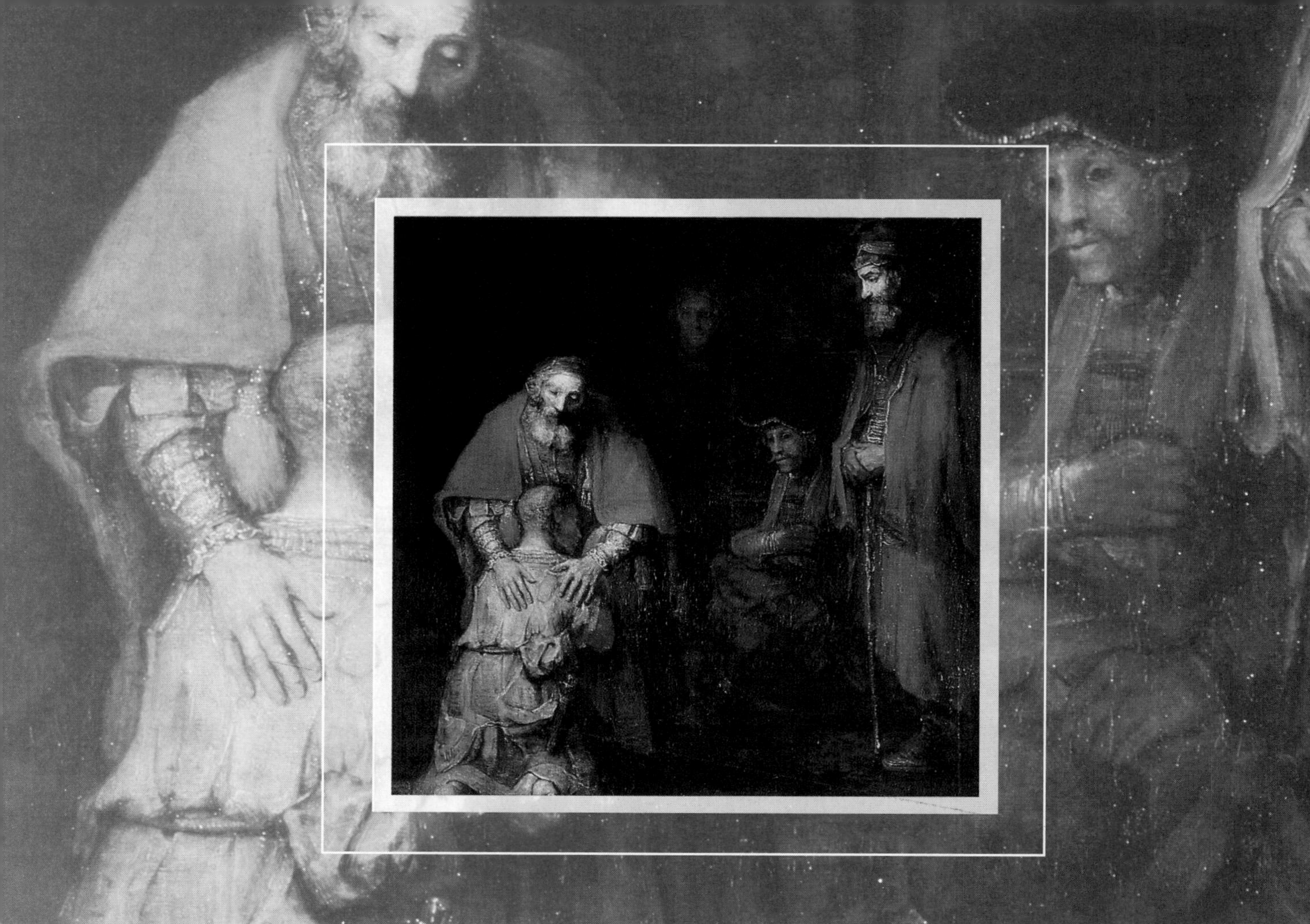

Return of the Prodigal Son (1667–1668), Rembrandt van Rijn. The Hermitage Museum, St. Petersburg, Russia. Bridgeman Art Library, London/Superstock.

from Luke, Chapter 15

Parable of the Prodigal Son

11 And he said, A certain man had two sons:
12 And the younger of them said to his father, Father, give me the
portion of goods that falleth to me. And he divided unto them
his living.
13 And not many days after the younger son gathered all together,
and took his journey into a far country, and there wasted his
substance with riotous living.
14 And when he had spent all, there arose a mighty famine in that
land; and he began to be in want.

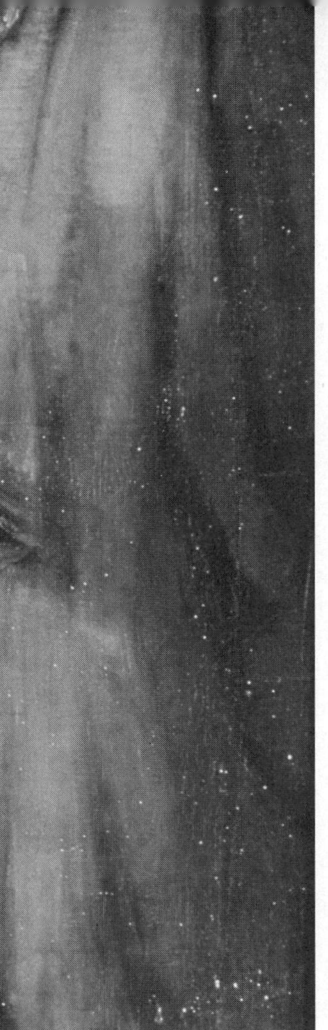

15 And he went and joined himself to a citizen of that country;
and he[1] sent him into his fields to feed swine.
16 And he would fain[2] have filled his belly with the husks that the
swine did eat: and no man gave unto him.
17 And when he came to himself, he said, How many hired servants
of my father's have bread enough and to spare, and I perish
with hunger!
18 I will arise and go to my father, and will say unto him, Father, I
have sinned against heaven, and before thee,
19 And am no more worthy to be called thy son: make me as one of
thy hired servants.
20 And he arose, and came to his father. But when he was yet a great
way off, his father saw him, and had compassion, and ran, and fell
on his neck, and kissed him.
21 And the son said unto him, Father, I have sinned against heaven,
and in thy sight, and am no more worthy to be called thy son.
22 But the father said to his servants, Bring forth the best robe, and
put it on him; and put a ring on his hand, and shoes on his feet:
23 And bring hither the fatted calf, and kill it; and let us eat, and
be merry:
24 For this my son was dead, and is alive again; he was lost, and is
found. And they began to be merry.
25 Now his elder son was in the field: and as he came and drew nigh
to the house, he heard musick and dancing.
26 And he called one of the servants, and asked what these things meant.
27 And he said unto him, Thy brother is come; and thy father hath
killed the fatted calf, because he hath received him safe and sound.
28 And he was angry, and would not go in: therefore came his father
out, and intreated[3] him.
29 And he answering said to his father, Lo, these many years do I serve
thee, neither transgressed[4] I at any time thy commandment: and yet
thou never gavest me a kid,[5] that I might make merry with my friends:
30 But as soon as this thy son was come, which hath devoured thy living
with harlots, thou hast killed for him the fatted calf.
31 And he said unto him, Son, thou art ever with me, and all that I have
is thine.
32 It was meet[6] that we should make merry, and be glad: for this thy
brother was dead, and is alive again; and was lost, and is found.

---

1. **he:** the citizen.
2. **fain:** gladly.
3. **intreated:** entreated; urged.
4. **transgressed:** violated; broke.
5. **kid:** young goat.
6. **meet:** fitting; proper.

RESPONDING OPTIONS

FROM PERSONAL RESPONSE *TO* CRITICAL ANALYSIS

REFLECT 1. How did you respond to the three characters in the parable of the prodigal son? Jot down your responses in your notebook.

RETHINK 2. If you were in the father's place, would you react to the younger son's return as he does?

Consider

- the father's reaction to the words spoken by the younger son upon his return
- the father's explanation to his older son
- your own feelings about forgiveness

3. In your opinion, what is the message or lesson of this parable?

RELATE 4. Think about the different spiritual lessons presented in the passage from Ecclesiastes, Psalm 23, and the parable of the prodigal son. Do you think it is difficult to put these lessons into practice today? Give reasons for your opinion.

5. How might readers of different ages—for example, a teenager and an elderly person—differ in their reactions to the selection from Ecclesiastes, to Psalm 23, or to the parable?

ANOTHER PATHWAY

The philosopher George Santayana once said that "there is no cure for birth and death save to enjoy the interval." How does his reflection on life compare with the spiritual lessons taught in these three selections? Draft an essay to answer this question, using specific lines or sentences from the three selections to support your opinion.

THE WRITER'S STYLE

Note that the King James Bible contains verb forms ending in *-eth* and *-est.* Look up these endings in a dictionary. How far back do they go in the history of the language? Which ending is used for the second person, and which for the third person? In most dictionaries, terms such as *colloquial, slang, poetic,* and *archaic* are used to describe certain words. Which term is applied to these endings?

QUICKWRITES

1. Decide what might happen next in the parable of the prodigal son. Write a **continuation** of the story.
2. Think of a simple lesson about life that you would like to teach others. Then write a modern **parable,** in either a serious or a humorous style, to convey the lesson.
3. Pretend that you work for your local newspaper. Write an **editorial** relating the message of one of these selections to contemporary life. Describe how a community or world situation might be improved if people took the message to heart.

PORTFOLIO *Save your writing. You may want to use it later as a springboard to a piece for your portfolio.*

LITERARY CONCEPTS

Used in both poetry and prose, **repetition** is a technique in which a word or group of words is repeated throughout a selection. Repetition of words and phrases often helps to reinforce meaning and to create an appealing rhythm. Find examples of repetition in the excerpt from Ecclesiastes and in the parable of the prodigal son. In which selection do you think repetition plays a more important role?

LITERARY LINKS

Look again at the excerpt from *The Book of Margery Kempe* (page 185). Which of the three selections from the Bible do you think would offer the greatest comfort to Kempe?

ART CONNECTION

One critic has stated that Rembrandt's *Return of the Prodigal Son* (page 256) represents the artist's idea of Christian forgiveness and mercy. Look closely at the painting. In addition to the subject matter, what qualities of the painting do you think express the idea of mercy or forgiveness?

ACROSS THE CURRICULUM

Art Find a painting that you think illustrates Psalm 23. Bring a copy of the painting to class and explain to others why you made your choice.

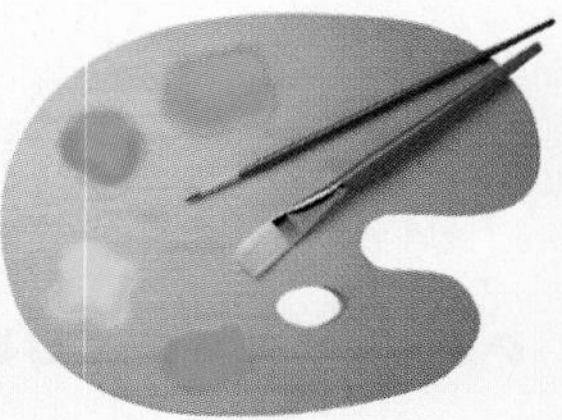

Music Find and share with classmates the Byrds' 1966 recording of the song "Turn, Turn, Turn." Compare the lyrics of the song with the passage from Ecclesiastes that you have read. Then discuss the significance of the song's title.

ALTERNATIVE ACTIVITIES

1. Design a 12-month **calendar** that contains your favorite lines from the selections. Choose one line for each month, then find appropriate art to accompany the texts or use a computer to make your own illustrations.
2. Imagine that you are the older son in the parable of the prodigal son. Rehearse and perform a **dramatic soliloquy**—a speech revealing your innermost thoughts about events in your life.
3. Create a **collage** of images that reflect your understanding of the excerpt from Ecclesiastes. You may choose to use fine art, photographs, illustrations, or a combination of the three.

LASERLINKS
- *ART GALLERY*

PREVIEWING

NONFICTION

from Essays

Sir Francis Bacon

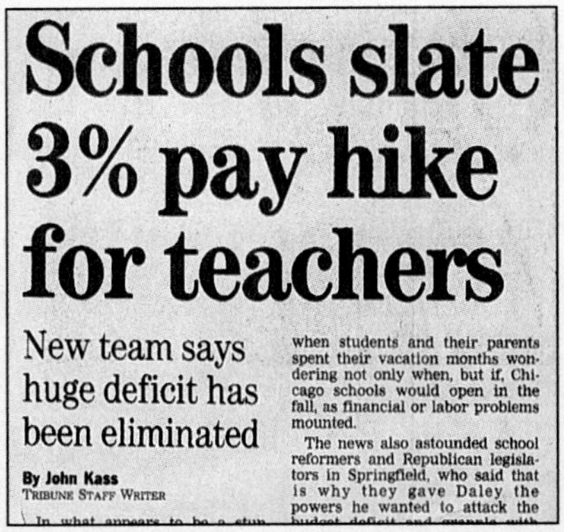

Schools slate 3% pay hike for teachers

New team says huge deficit has been eliminated

By John Kass
TRIBUNE STAFF WRITER

when students and their parents spent their vacation months wondering not only when, but if, Chicago schools would open in the fall, as financial or labor problems mounted.

The news also astounded school reformers and Republican legislators in Springfield, who said that is why they gave Daley the powers he wanted to attack the

PERSONAL CONNECTION

Most people have strong opinions about certain topics or issues. In your notebook, jot down some thoughts about an issue that concerns you—perhaps something that affects you personally, such as a school policy or a community problem, or a more universal issue, such as crime, censorship, the protection of the environment, or individual rights. Then get together with a group of classmates and share your opinion.

LITERARY CONNECTION

Sir Francis Bacon is often called the father of the English essay. In 1597, he published ten essays, the first examples of that literary form to gain popularity in England. Bacon actually borrowed the title and concept for his *Essays* from the French author Michel de Montaigne, who had published a similar work, titled *Essais,* in 1580. In contrast with Montaigne's writing—which is light and personal, revealing glimpses of the author's own life and personality—Bacon's essays are more philosophical, offering opinions on the nature of human behavior and motivation and generalizing about what humans do and ought to do. In writing his essays, Bacon had a single purpose in mind—to give instruction and advice to young men who were ambitious to succeed. His first collection included "Of Studies," one of the essays presented on the following pages. His final collection was published in 1625, a year before his death, and included 58 essays on subjects ranging from love, friendship, and beauty to superstition, death, and revenge.

READING CONNECTION

Identifying Opinion When you are reading nonfiction, it is important to evaluate opinions as you encounter them. Make two charts like the one shown, one for each of Bacon's essays. As you read each essay, look for statements of opinion with which you generally agree or definitely disagree. Write these statements under the appropriate headings in your charts.

"Of Studies"	
Agree	Disagree

Of Studies

Sir Francis Bacon

wise men use them

Crafty men contemn studies

Abeunt studia in mores

natural abilities are like natural plants

Detail of *Still Life with Old Books* (17th century), unknown French artist. Courtesy of the Musée de Brou, Bourg-en-Bresse, France.

Reading maketh a full man

Some books are to be tasted

simple men admire them

Studies serve for delight, for ornament, and for ability. Their chief use for delight is in privateness and retiring; for ornament, is in discourse;[1] and for ability, is in the judgment and disposition of business. For expert men can execute, and perhaps judge of particulars, one by one; but the general counsels, and the plots and marshaling of affairs, come best from those that are learned. To spend too much time in studies is sloth; to use them too much for ornament is affectation;[2] to make judgment wholly by their rules is the humor[3] of a scholar. They perfect

1. **discourse:** conversation.
2. **affectation:** something done just for show or to give a false impression.
3. **humor:** whim; temperament.

nature, and are perfected by experience; for natural abilities are like natural plants, that need pruning by study; and studies themselves do give forth directions too much at large, except they be bounded in by experience. Crafty men contemn[4] studies, simple men admire them, and wise men use them, for they teach not their own use; but that is a wisdom without them, and above them, won by observation. Read not to contradict and confute,[5] nor to believe and take for granted, nor to find talk and discourse, but to weigh and consider. Some books are to be tasted, others to be swallowed, and some few to be chewed and digested; that is, some books are to be read only in parts; others to be read, but not curiously;[6] and some few to be read wholly, and with diligence and attention. Some books also may be read by deputy and extracts made of them by others, but that would be only in the less important arguments and the meaner sort of books; else[7] distilled[8] books are like common distilled waters,[9] flashy[10] things. Reading maketh a full man, conference[11] a ready man, and writing an exact man. And therefore, if a man write little, he had need have a great memory; if he confer little, he had need have a present wit;[12] and if he read little, he had need have much cunning, to seem to know that he doth not. Histories make men wise; poets, witty; the mathematics, subtle; natural philosophy, deep; moral, grave; logic and rhetoric, able to contend. *Abeunt studia in mores.*[13] Nay, there is no stond[14] or impediment in the wit but may be wrought out by fit studies, like as diseases of the body may have appropriate exercises. Bowling is good for the stone and reins,[15] shooting for the lungs and breast, gentle walking for the stomach, riding for the head, and the like. So if a man's wit be wandering, let him study the mathematics; for in demonstrations, if his wit be called away never so little, he must begin again. If his wit be not apt to distinguish or find differences, let him study the schoolmen,[16] for they are *cumini sectores.*[17] If he be not apt to beat over[18] matters and to call up one thing to prove and illustrate another, let him study the lawyer's cases. So every defect of the mind may have a special receipt.[19] ❖

---

4. **contemn:** view with contempt, hate.
5. **confute:** prove wrong.
6. **curiously:** carefully or thoroughly.
7. **else:** in other respects.
8. **distilled:** having only the important elements extracted or taken out.
9. **common distilled waters:** herbal home remedies.
10. **flashy:** tasteless; dull.
11. **conference:** conversation.
12. **present wit:** active intelligence.
13. ***Abeunt studia in mores*** (ä′bĕ-o͝ont sto͞o′dē-ä ĭn mō′rāz) *Latin:* Studies show themselves in manners.
14. **stond:** stoppage.
15. **the stone and reins:** kidney stones and other kidney disorders.
16. **schoolmen:** medieval scholastic philosophers.
17. ***cumini sectores*** (ko͞o′mĭ-nē sĕk-tō′rāz) *Latin:* cutters of herbs—that is, people who make extremely fine distinctions; hairsplitters.
18. **beat over:** reason through.
19. **receipt:** remedy; prescription.

FROM PERSONAL RESPONSE *TO* CRITICAL ANALYSIS

REFLECT

1. What was your first reaction to Bacon's views on studies? Jot down your thoughts in your notebook.

RETHINK

2. Do you think that different kinds of studies can have different effects on you? Give reasons for your opinion.
3. Have Bacon's opinions changed your attitude toward studies or toward the reading of books? Explain your answer.

Of Marriage and Single Life

Sir Francis Bacon

Vetulam suam praetulit immortalitati

single men . . . are more cruel and hard-hearted

single life is liberty

It is often seen that BAD husbands have very *good* wives

Unmarried men are best friends . . . but not always best subjects

wife and children are a kind of discipline of humanity

. . . those that have children should have greatest care of future times

He that hath wife and children hath given hostages to fortune; for they are impediments to great enterprises, either of virtue or mischief. Certainly the best works, and of greatest merit for the public, have proceeded from the unmarried or childless men, which both in affection and means have married and endowed the public. Yet it were great reason that those that have children should have greatest care of future times, unto which they know they must transmit their dearest pledges. Some there are who, though they lead a single life, yet their thoughts do end with themselves, and account future times impertinences.[1] Nay, there are some other that account wife and children but as bills of charges. Nay more, there are some foolish rich covetous men that take a pride in having no children, because they may be thought so much the richer. For perhaps they have heard some talk, "Such an one is a great rich man," and another except to it, "Yea, but he hath a great charge of children"; as if it were an abatement[2] to his riches. But the most ordinary cause of a single life is liberty, especially in certain self-pleasing and humorous[3] minds, which are so sensible of every restraint, as they will go near to think their girdles and garters to be bonds and shackles. Unmarried men are best friends, best masters, best servants, but not always best subjects, for they are light to run away, and almost all fugitives are of that condition. A single life doth well with churchmen, for charity will hardly water the ground where it must first fill a pool. It is indifferent for judges and magistrates, for if they be facile[4] and corrupt, you shall have a servant five times worse than a wife. For soldiers, I find the generals commonly in their hortatives[5] put men in mind of their wives and children; and I think the despising of marriage amongst the Turks maketh the vulgar[6] soldier more base. Certainly wife and children are a kind of discipline of humanity; and single men, though they be many times more charitable, because their means are less exhaust,[7] yet, on the other side, they are more cruel and hard-hearted (good to make severe inquisitors), because their tenderness is not so oft called upon. Grave natures, led by custom, and therefore constant, are commonly loving husbands, as was said of Ulysses, *Vetulam suam praetulit immortalitati.*[8] Chaste women are often proud and froward,[9] as presuming upon the merit of their chastity. It is one of the best bonds, both of chastity and obedience, in the wife if she think her husband wise, which she will never do if she find him jealous. Wives are young men's mistresses, companions for middle age, and old men's nurses, so as a man may have a quarrel[10] to marry when he will. But yet he was reputed one of the wise men that made answer to the question when a man should marry: "A young man not yet, an elder man not at all." It is often seen that bad husbands have very good wives; whether it be that it raiseth the price of their husbands' kindness when it comes, or that the wives take a pride in their patience. But this never fails, if the bad husbands were of their own choosing, against their friends' consent; for then they will be sure to make good their own folly. ❖

A single life doth well with churchmen

Wives are young men's mistresses, . . . and old men's nurses

1. **impertinences** (ĭm-pûr′tn-ən-səz): irrelevant concerns; things not worthy of attention.
2. **abatement** (ə-bāt′mənt): a reduction.
3. **humorous:** whimsical.
4. **facile** (făs′əl): easily influenced or persuaded.
5. **hortatives** (hôr′tə-tĭvz): speeches to encourage troops before battle.
6. **vulgar:** common; ordinary.
7. **exhaust:** depleted; drained.
8. ***Vetulam suam praetulit immortalitati*** (vĕ′to͝o-läm so͞o′äm prī′to͝o-lĭt ĭm-môr-tä′lĭ-tä′tē) *Latin:* He preferred his aged wife to immortality.
9. **froward** (frō′wərd): stubborn.
10. **quarrel:** reason; excuse.

RESPONDING OPTIONS

FROM PERSONAL RESPONSE *TO* CRITICAL ANALYSIS

REFLECT

1. Did any of the statements in "Of Marriage and Single Life" startle you? Share your thoughts with your classmates.

RETHINK

2. Which do you think Bacon respects more, the married life or the single life? Support your answer with details from the essay.

3. How would you describe Bacon's views of men and of women?

Consider

- the assumptions he makes about men and about women
- the different roles he assigns to men and women
- his opinion of the relationship between men and women

4. Think about the aspects of marriage that Bacon describes in his essay. In your opinion, why has he failed to mention love?

RELATE

5. Today there is a great deal of discussion about what makes a good marriage. Do you think any of Bacon's views are relevant to contemporary ideas about marriage? Provide supporting details for your conclusions.

ANOTHER PATHWAY

Cooperative Learning

Recall that one of Bacon's main purposes in writing his essays was to give advice to young men who wanted to succeed in life. As a class, divide into two groups. With your group, make a list of guidelines from each essay that could be included in a book of "rules for success." Share your list with the class.

LITERARY CONCEPTS

An **essay** is a brief work of nonfiction that offers an opinion on a subject. The purpose of an essay may be to express ideas and feelings, to inform, to entertain, or to persuade. The main point of an essay is often presented in the opening sentences and then supported by a series of examples, facts, or reasons. Bacon's essays are persuasive, designed to convince the reader to accept certain ideas. Do you think Bacon's statements are well supported with examples, facts, and reasons? Try to find supporting material for three of the opinions you included in the charts you made for the Reading Connection on page 260.

QUICKWRITES

1. Select one of Bacon's statements with which you disagree. In a **letter** to the author, give reasons why you do not share his opinion.

2. Draft a **persuasive essay** about the issue you selected for the Personal Connection on page 260. State your opinion regarding the issue, and give reasons for it.

3. Create a **list of questions** for an opinion poll on study or on marriage. Include some questions that reflect Bacon's ideas.

PORTFOLIO *Save your writing. You may want to use it later as a springboard to a piece for your portfolio.*

ALTERNATIVE ACTIVITIES

1. Put together a **collection of images**—either paintings or photographs—that could be used to illustrate some of the ideas and impressions in "Of Studies" or in "Of Marriage and Single Life." Show your collection to the class and ask them what passage they think each image is related to. Discuss the reasons for your choices.
2. With a partner, conduct the **opinion poll** described in the third activity under "QuickWrites." Question both students and adults, and videotape their responses if possible. Show your video to the class.
3. Review Bacon's division of books into three categories. Then, with a small group of classmates, identify five books that belong to each category. Compile the work of all the groups in your class, and make a **chart** of books to be read for different purposes.

THE WRITER'S STYLE

Bacon often uses identical grammatical structures to express related ideas. This technique, called **parallelism,** is illustrated in the statement "Crafty men contemn studies, simple men admire them, and wise men use them." Find other examples of parallelism in the two essays.

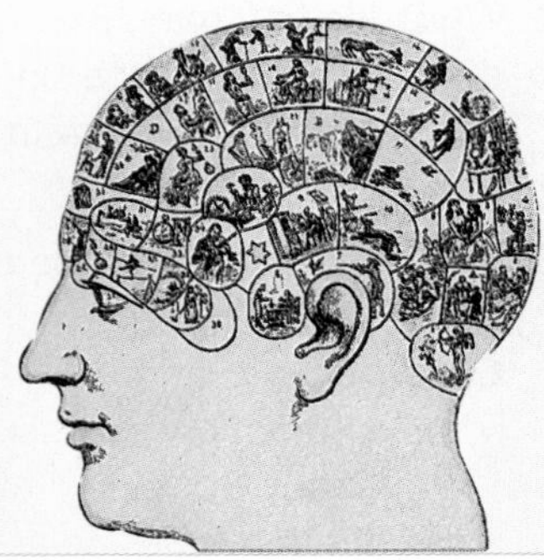

ACROSS THE CURRICULUM

Biology In Bacon's opinion, a variety of studies is needed to stimulate the different functions of the brain. Investigate current research on the brain and its functions. Report on two or three of the functions, listing activities that can strengthen each of them.

SIR FRANCIS BACON

1561–1626

Like Marlowe and Raleigh, Francis Bacon was a Renaissance man. His interests extended from law and public service to philosophy and science. Although he entered Cambridge University at the age of 12, he stayed there just two years. He began his legal studies only when faced with financial difficulties, but he became an ambitious public servant and rose steadily in royal service, acting as legal counsel both to Elizabeth I and to James I. Bacon was eventually knighted and in 1618 was appointed to the highest judicial position in England. Three years later, his career ended in scandal when he was charged with—and admitted—accepting bribes.

Banished from public service, Bacon directed his full attention to other interests. He was a prolific writer and produced, in addition to his famous essays, many philosophical and scientific treatises. Unfortunately, his avid interest in scientific discovery led ultimately to his death. Curious about the preservative effects of refrigeration, Bacon killed a hen and carefully stuffed it with snow. Chilled by the experiment, he developed bronchitis, from which he died on April 9, 1626.

OTHER WORKS "Of Truth," "Of Great Place"

PREVIEWING

POETRY/NONFICTION

A Valediction: Forbidding Mourning
Holy Sonnet 10
from Meditation 17

John Donne

PERSONAL CONNECTION

Many writers struggle with life's difficult questions and try to come to terms with their own doubts and fears by writing about them. Think about how you strive to find answers to your most challenging questions about life. How do you express your thoughts and concerns? Record your reflections in your notebook.

BIOGRAPHICAL/LITERARY CONNECTION

As a young man, John Donne wrote passionate love poems and sought the admiration of numerous women. Later in life, Donne made a notable change. He married, fathered 12 children, entered the ministry, and authored over 160 sermons. "Jack" Donne, the spirited young romantic, became Dr. John Donne, a highly respected preacher and the dean of St. Paul's Cathedral in London.

Donne was an intellectual who contemplated life's most perplexing questions, particularly those involving death—a common literary theme of the time. During the Renaissance, the threat of death could never be disregarded. Medical knowledge was limited, and effective medicines were rare. It was not unusual for people to die well before the age of 50. Many women died during childbirth, children died from illnesses that are easily treated today, and epidemics killed thousands of people at a time. Donne's own wife died at the age of 33, shortly after giving birth to their 12th child. Two of his children were stillborn, and others died at the ages of 3, 7, and 19.

The selections on the following pages reflect Donne's keen awareness of the briefness and fragility of existence and show how he coped with life's limitations. "A Valediction: Forbidding Mourning" is one of several poetic valedictions (farewells) that Donne composed. Written prior to the poet's departure for France in 1611, the poem was intended to console his wife, who was distressed over her husband's impending long absence. "Holy Sonnet 10," part of a collection of 26 poems, reflects Donne's concerns about spiritual matters, particularly death and salvation. Donne wrote "Meditation 17" in 1623 while recovering from a serious illness. He was inspired in part by hearing the ringing of church bells to announce a person's death.

LASERLINKS
• *BIOGRAPHICAL CONNECTION*

READING CONNECTION

Understanding Metaphysical Poetry

The term ***metaphysical poetry*** is used to describe a style of poetry cultivated by a group of 17th-century poets, of whom Donne was the first. The metaphysical poets rejected the conventions of Elizabethan love poetry, with its sweet, musical quality and themes of courtly love. Instead, they approached subjects such as religion, death, and even love by analyzing them logically and philosophically. The metaphysical poets were intellectuals who, like the ideal Renaissance man, were well-read in a broad spectrum of subjects. Donne himself studied philosophy, theology, science, law, and medicine, and his writing reflects the scope of his reading as well as images from everyday life.

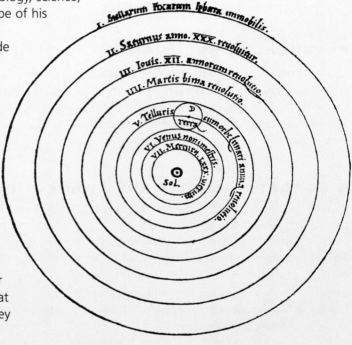

The characteristics of metaphysical poetry include more than just an intellectual approach to subject matter. Instead of the lyrical style of most Elizabethan poetry, the metaphysical poets used a more colloquial, or conversational, style. In spite of the simplicity of the words, the ideas may seem obscure or confusing at first, for metaphysical poets loved to play with language. Donne's writing is filled with surprising twists: unexpected images and comparisons and an occasional **paradox**—a statement that seems to contradict itself but, in fact, reveals some element of truth.

Make a chart like the one shown below. Then, as you read these selections, record any unusual or unexpected images, comparisons, or paradoxes that you find. Think about how such devices help convey Donne's attitude toward life's limitations.

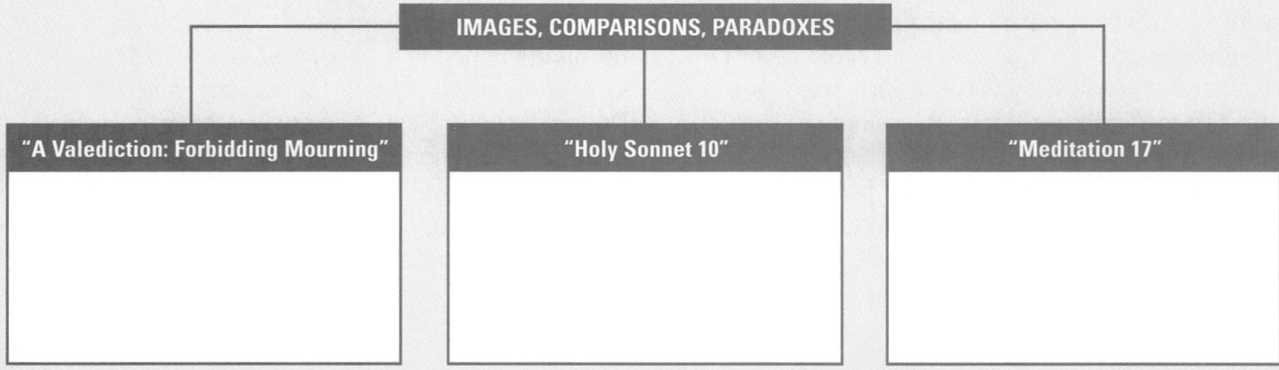

A Valediction: Forbidding Mourning

John Donne

As virtuous men pass mildly away,
    And whisper to their souls to go,
Whilst some of their sad friends do say
    The breath goes now, and some say, No;

So let us melt, and make no noise,
    No tear-floods, nor sigh-tempests move,
'Twere profanation of our joys
    To tell the laity our love.

Moving of th' earth brings harms and fears,
    Men reckon what it did and meant;
But trepidation of the spheres,
    Though greater far, is innocent.

5 melt: part; dissolve our togetherness.
7 profanation (prŏf′ə-nā′shən): an act of contempt for what is sacred or respected.
8 laity (lā′ĭ-tē): persons without understanding of the "religion" of love.
9 moving of th' earth: an earthquake.
11 trepidation of the spheres: apparently irregular movements of heavenly bodies.
12 innocent: harmless.

Dull sublunary lovers' love
    (Whose soul is sense) cannot admit
Absence, because it doth remove
    Those things which elemented it.

But we by a love so much refined
    That our selves know not what it is,
Inter-assuréd of the mind,
    Care less, eyes, lips, and hands to miss.

Our two souls therefore, which are one,
    Though I must go, endure not yet
A breach, but an expansion,
    Like gold to airy thinness beat.

If they be two, they are two so
    As stiff twin compasses are two;
Thy soul, the fixed foot, makes no show
    To move, but doth, if th' other do.

And though it in the center sit,
    Yet when the other far doth roam,
It leans and hearkens after it,
    And grows erect, as that comes home.

Such wilt thou be to me, who must
    Like th' other foot, obliquely run;
Thy firmness makes my circle just,
    And makes me end where I begun.

13 sublunary (sŭb'lo͞o-nĕr'ē) **lovers' love:** the love of earthly lovers, which, like all things beneath the moon, is subject to change and death.
14 soul: essence; **sense:** sensuality.
16 elemented: composed.

19 inter-assuréd of the mind: confident of each other's love.

22 endure not yet: do not, nevertheless, suffer.

26 twin compasses: the two legs of a compass used for drawing circles.

32 as that comes home: when the moving foot returns to the center as the compass is closed.

34 obliquely (ō-blēk'lē): not in a straight line.
35 firmness: constancy; **just:** perfect.

FROM PERSONAL RESPONSE *TO* CRITICAL ANALYSIS

REFLECT 1. What image in this poem made the greatest impression on you? Why did it impress you? Jot down your thoughts in your notebook.

RETHINK 2. How do you think the speaker would define true love?

Consider
- his description of "sublunary lovers' love" (lines 13–16)
- the comparison in lines 25–36
- the title of the poem

RELATE 3. In your opinion, is the message of this poem still relevant? Explain your answer.

Detail of Nativity of Christ. Stained glass, Abbey Ste. Foy, Conques, France. Giraudon/Art Resource, New York.

Holy Sonnet 10

John Donne

Death, be not proud, though some have callèd thee
Mighty and dreadful, for thou art not so;
For those whom thou think'st thou dost overthrow
Die not, poor Death, nor yet canst thou kill me.
From rest and sleep, which but thy pictures be,
Much pleasure; then from thee much more must flow,
And soonest our best men with thee do go,
Rest of their bones, and soul's delivery.
Thou art slave to fate, chance, kings, and desperate men,
And dost with poison, war, and sickness dwell,
And poppy or charms can make us sleep as well
And better than thy stroke; why swell'st thou then?
One short sleep past, we wake eternally
And death shall be no more; Death, thou shalt die.

5–6 From rest . . . flow: Since we derive pleasure from rest and sleep, which are only likenesses of death, we should derive much more from death itself.
8 soul's delivery: the freeing of the soul from the body.

11 poppy: opium, a narcotic drug made from the juice of the poppy plant.
12 swell'st: swell with pride.

FROM PERSONAL RESPONSE *TO* CRITICAL ANALYSIS

REFLECT **1.** What are your thoughts about the speaker's attitude toward death? Share your response with your classmates.

RETHINK **2.** Why do you think the speaker addresses death as a person?

3. How do you interpret the speaker's statement "Death, thou shalt die"? Explain your response.

from

Meditation 17

John Donne

Perchance he for whom this bell tolls may be so ill as that he knows not it tolls for him; and perchance I may think myself so much better than I am, as that they who are about me and see my state may have caused it to toll for me, and I know not that. The church is catholic,[1] universal, so are all her actions; all that she does belongs to all. When she baptizes a child, that action concerns me; for that child is thereby connected to that body which is my head too, and ingrafted into that body whereof I am a member.[2] And when she buries a man, that action concerns me: all mankind is of one author and is one volume; when one man dies, one chapter is not torn out of the book, but translated into a better language; and every chapter must be so translated. God employs several translators; some pieces are translated by age, some by sickness, some by war, some by justice; but God's hand is in every translation, and his hand shall bind up all our scattered leaves again for that library where every book shall lie open to one another. As therefore the bell that rings to a sermon calls not upon the preacher only, but upon the congregation to come, so this bell calls us all; but how much more me, who am brought so near the door by this sickness. . . . Who casts not up his eye to the sun when it rises? but who takes off his eye from a comet when that breaks out? Who bends not his ear to any bell which upon any occasion rings? but who can remove it from that bell which is passing a piece of himself out of this world? No man is an island, entire of itself; every man is a piece of the continent, a part of the main.[3] If a clod be washed away by the sea, Europe is the less, as well as if a promontory[4] were, as well as if a manor of thy friend's or of thine own were. Any man's death diminishes me because I am involved in mankind, and therefore never send to know for whom the bell tolls; it tolls for thee. ❖

Nunc lento sonitu dicunt, morieris.

Now this bell tolling softly for another, says to me, Thou must die.

---

1. **is catholic:** embraces all humankind.
2. **body which is my head . . . member:** Donne likens the church to the head, which controls every part of the body, and to the body itself, because it is made up of interconnected parts (the individuals who compose it).
3. **main:** mainland.
4. **promontory** (prŏm′ən-tôr′ē): a ridge of land jutting out into a body of water.

RESPONDING OPTIONS

FROM PERSONAL RESPONSE *TO* CRITICAL ANALYSIS

REFLECT 1. Which part of the excerpt from Donne's "Meditation 17" did you find most thought-provoking? Discuss your choice with your classmates.

RETHINK 2. Explain in your own words what you think Donne is saying in the last three sentences.

Consider
- the statement "No man is an island"
- Donne's reference to the bell that "tolls for thee"

3. In your opinion, how might the thoughts recorded in this meditation help someone to cope with life's limitations?

4. Donne says that when a person dies, the person's "chapter is not torn out of the book, but translated into a better language." What do you think he means by this statement?

RELATE 5. In their writings, Donne and many of his contemporaries tried to unravel the mysteries of death. Do you think the level of interest in death is as great in today's society? Why or why not?

ANOTHER PATHWAY

Cooperative Learning

As a class, divide into three discussion groups, one for each selection. Work with your group to draft a letter in which you respond to the speaker's ideas. Include passages from the selection to support your reply. Share your group's letter with the rest of the class.

LITERARY CONCEPTS

Donne's writing contains several types of figurative language, including **extended metaphors.** Like any metaphor, an extended metaphor is a comparison between two essentially unlike things that does not contain the word *like* or *as.* A metaphor becomes extended when the two things are compared at length and in a number of ways—perhaps throughout a stanza, a paragraph, or even an entire work.

Refer to the chart you made for the Reading Connection on page 268. Are any of the comparisons you noted metaphors? If so, highlight them. Then decide which of those metaphors might be considered extended metaphors. Compare your findings with those of your classmates.

QUICKWRITES

1. In a draft of an **essay,** compare Donne's views of death in "Holy Sonnet 10" and in "Meditation 17."
2. Create your own **extended metaphor** to depict either love or death. You may choose to write your metaphor in the form of a paragraph or a short poem.
3. Write a **short story** titled "No Man Is an Island." In the story, present an incident, true or imaginary, that reflects your interpretation of the title.
4. Using the title "A Valediction," write a **poem** of your own in which you describe your thoughts about going away and leaving someone you love behind.

PORTFOLIO Save your writing. You may want to use it later as a spring-board to a piece for your portfolio.

ALTERNATIVE ACTIVITIES

1. Using appropriate colors, shapes, and images, create an abstract or representational **painting** or **collage** that reflects the mood conveyed by one of the Donne selections.
2. Listen to recordings of contemporary songs or Renaissance songs to find some metaphors for love. Write down the lyrics and prepare a **recitation** along with a partner.

CRITIC'S CORNER

The scholar C. S. Lewis commented that much of Donne's writing deals with rather grim themes. On the basis of your understanding of these three selections, do you agree or disagree with Lewis? Give evidence to support your answer.

LITERARY LINKS

Compare Donne's depiction of love in "A Valediction: Forbidding Mourning" with Shakespeare's depiction of love in "Sonnet 116." Do the two speakers appear to agree or to disagree? Explain your opinion.

JOHN DONNE

1572–1631

John Donne was born into a Roman Catholic family at a time when the Protestant majority had no tolerance for religious ideas different from their own. Although he attended Oxford University for several years, he was not eligible for a degree because of his religious beliefs. In 1593, his only brother died while imprisoned for sheltering a Jesuit priest.

At the age of 25, Donne became the personal secretary of Sir Thomas Egerton, a distinguished official of the royal court. A few years later, he married Egerton's niece, Ann More, secretly and without seeking permission. When the marriage was discovered, Donne lost his job. He was left nearly penniless and battled poverty for many years thereafter. Eventually, King James I recruited the struggling poet to the cause of Protestantism, and Donne became an Anglican priest in 1615. Within six years, he was named dean of St. Paul's Cathedral, a position he held until his death. Donne was hailed as a dynamic preacher who incorporated wit and poetic language into his sermons.

Donne, whose writing is filled with paradoxes, was something of a paradox himself—a poet turned preacher, a sensualist and a scholar, a doubter and a believer. He was both dramatic and introspective, worldly and spiritual. Steeped in medieval learning, he was at the same time open to the fresh currents of 17th-century science and discovery. It is said that Donne "married passion to reason," and his example has influenced writers from his own time to the 20th century.

OTHER WORKS "The Canonization," "The Flea," "Holy Sonnet 7"

PREVIEWING

POETRY

On My First Son   Still to Be Neat

Ben Jonson

PERSONAL CONNECTION

Most of us make various assumptions as we go through life. For example, we might assume that certain events will happen as we have planned or that people will behave as we expect. Do you tend to make assumptions about yourself and others? Have you ever been surprised when something did not happen the way you assumed it would? In your notebook, jot down thoughts about assumptions you have made about yourself or others.

BIOGRAPHICAL CONNECTION

Ben Jonson was a literary giant who knew most of London's important writers, including Francis Bacon, John Donne, and William Shakespeare. Like Shakespeare, Jonson has been remembered chiefly as a great playwright—in fact, his influence on English drama may have been equal to that of his more celebrated contemporary. However, Jonson also wrote some of the finest poetry in the English language.

The selections on the following pages show two of Jonson's varied poetic styles. Each poem deals with a speaker's assumptions about life and people. "On My First Son" is the poet's response to the death of his son, Benjamin. Like John Donne and others in his society, Jonson was forced on more than one occasion to experience the anguish of an untimely death. Both of his children died at very young ages, his son at the age of seven, a victim of the plague, and his daughter, Mary, in infancy. The second poem, "Still to Be Neat," is a song from one of Jonson's major plays, the comedy *Epicene;* or, *The Silent Woman.* In it, the speaker shares his assumptions about a "neat" woman.

Portrait said to be of Ben Jonson and William Shakespeare playing chess (1603), Karel van Mander. Courtesy of Frank de Heyman, Brooklyn, New York.

READING CONNECTION

Understanding the Speaker in Poetry
The speaker in a poem is often thought to be the writer, but in many cases this assumption is not valid. Though a writer may speak with his or her own voice in a poem, the speaker is often a voice or character made up by the writer. Two poems by the same writer may therefore have very different speakers. As you read these poems by Ben Jonson, note the differences in the speakers. In which poem is Jonson obviously the speaker? What can you infer about the other speaker?

On My First Son

Ben Jonson

Farewell, thou child of my right hand, and joy;
My sin was too much hope of thee, loved boy:
Seven years thou wert lent to me, and I thee pay,
Exacted by thy fate, on the just day.
O could I lose all father now! for why
Will man lament the state he should envy,
To have so soon 'scaped world's and flesh's rage,
And, if no other misery, yet age?
Rest in soft peace, and asked, say, "Here doth lie
Ben Jonson his best piece of poetry."
For whose sake henceforth all his vows be such
As what he loves may never like too much.

1 child of my right hand: The Hebrew name *Benjamin* means "son of the right hand."

4 just: required.

5 lose all father: lose the feeling of being a father.

Detail of *The Graham Children* (1742), William Hogarth. Oil on canvas. The Granger Collection, New York.

FROM PERSONAL RESPONSE *TO* CRITICAL ANALYSIS

REFLECT

1. What is your attitude toward the speaker after reading the poem? Jot your reaction in your notebook.

RETHINK

2. In your opinion, what are some of the emotions and issues the speaker is grappling with as a result of his son's death?

Consider

- the "sin" he describes in line 2
- the comparison he makes in lines 3–4
- his resolve in lines 11–12

3. The English poet Alfred, Lord Tennyson, once wrote, "'Tis better to have loved and lost / Than never to have loved at all." How do you think Jonson would have responded to Tennyson's statement?

Portrait of Frances Howard, Countess of Essex and Somerset, Isaac Oliver. Victoria & Albert Museum, London/Art Resource, New York.

Still to Be Neat

BEN JONSON

Still to be neat, still to be dressed,
As you were going to a feast;
Still to be powdered, still perfumed;
Lady, it is to be presumed,
Though art's hid causes are not found,
All is not sweet, all is not sound.

Give me a look, give me a face
That makes simplicity a grace;
Robes loosely flowing, hair as free;
Such sweet neglect more taketh me
Than all th'adulteries of art.
They strike mine eyes, but not my heart.

1 still: always.

11 adulteries: impurities; debasements.

RESPONDING OPTIONS

FROM PERSONAL RESPONSE *TO* CRITICAL ANALYSIS

REFLECT 1. Do you agree with the ideas expressed by the speaker of "Still to Be Neat"? Write your opinion in your notebook.

RETHINK 2. What do you think the speaker assumes about the "powdered" and "perfumed" woman?

Consider

- his reference to "art's hid causes" (line 5)
- what he means by "All is not sweet, all is not sound" (line 6)
- his use of the word "adulteries" to describe the ways in which a woman tries to improve her appearance (line 11)

3. On the basis of your reading of the poem and your work for the Reading Connection on page 276, what is your opinion of the speaker of "Still to Be Neat"?

RELATE 4. Do you think "Still to Be Neat" could have been written about a contemporary woman? Explain your opinion, keeping in mind the values of today's society.

5. Compare the tones, or attitudes, of the speakers of Jonson's two poems. How does the poet communicate tone in each poem?

ANOTHER PATHWAY

If you have read more than one work by a particular writer, you have probably noticed that the works share certain qualities. At the same time, most writers strive to make each of their works unique. Think about "On My First Son" and "Still to Be Neat." Create a Venn diagram that expresses their similarities and differences.

LITERARY CONCEPTS

An **epitaph** is an inscription placed on a tomb or monument to honor the memory of the person buried there. The term *epitaph* has also been used more loosely to describe any verse commemorating someone who has died. Although a few humorous epitaphs have been composed, most are serious in tone. "On My First Son" is sometimes called an epitaph. Which lines do you think are especially deserving of this label?

CONCEPT REVIEW: Repetition Find examples of repetition in "Still to Be Neat." Discuss why Jonson might have chosen to repeat certain words. How does the repetition affect your reading of the poem?

QUICKWRITES

1. Write a **sympathy note** to Ben Jonson, offering him advice or comfort on the occasion of the death of his son. You may refer to his poem "On My First Son" in your note and try to help him with some of the issues he raises.
2. Think of a quality or trait that you particularly dislike in a person. Using that trait as your subject, write a **parody,** or imitation, of the first stanza of "Still to Be Neat."

PORTFOLIO *Save your writing. You may want to use it later as a springboard to a piece for your portfolio.*

ALTERNATIVE ACTIVITIES

1. Create a **sketch** of a tombstone or monument that Jonson might have erected in memory of his son.
2. Put together a **pictorial essay** depicting the contrast between natural beauty and the "adulteries of art."
3. The next writer you will study in this unit is Robert Herrick. Herrick was a great admirer of Jonson's work. He wrote a poem called "Delight in Disorder" in response to Jonson's "Still to Be Neat." Find a copy of his poem and give an **oral reading** of it for your classmates. Then discuss with the class the similarities and differences between the two poems.

LITERARY LINKS

Reread lines 5–8 of "On My First Son." Then compare Jonson's attitude toward death with that of John Donne in "Holy Sonnet 10."

BEN JONSON

1572–1637

In spite of a quarrelsome nature, Ben Jonson was a leader in the literary world and was greatly admired by a group of young poets—including Robert Herrick and Sir John Suckling—who proudly called themselves the sons of Ben. Although well-educated as a child, Jonson never attended a university. He worked a short time as a bricklayer and then joined the British army. While aiding the Dutch in their war against Spain, Jonson killed the enemy's best soldier in single combat. Returning to England, he pursued a career in the theater, faring poorly as an actor but gaining extensive popularity as a playwright.

A man of great bulk, with what he described as a "mountain belly" and a "rocky face," Jonson lived life with gusto. Unfortunately, his volcanic temperament led to occasional scrapes with the law. Once, he barely escaped hanging after killing a fellow actor in a duel. Because a knowledge of Latin was largely confined to clergymen in Renaissance England, Jonson eluded death by reading a "neck verse"—a passage from the Latin Bible—so that he could be tried by a church court rather than a more harsh criminal court. He was, however, branded on the thumb as a convicted felon. He was also twice imprisoned when he offended authorities with his plays.

Satire, which was just emerging as a popular dramatic form, was well suited to Jonson's combative nature and scathing wit. He gained fame for his satiric comedies, two of which, *Volpone* and *The Alchemist,* are still staged in theaters today. Many of his plays were performed at the Globe Theater, and Shakespeare himself acted in Jonson's first comedy, *Every Man in His Humor.* In 1616, Jonson published a volume of his plays and poems under the title *Works.* At that time, only more intellectual subjects, such as history and theology, were considered important enough to be presented as "works." The volume therefore became quite controversial, as Jonson undoubtedly had hoped. In his later years, Jonson wrote elaborate entertainments for the royal court and was rewarded with a sizable pension. His tombstone in Westminster Abbey bears the epitaph "O rare Ben Jonson."

OTHER WORKS "Song, to Celia," "To the Memory of My Beloved, the Author Master William Shakespeare," "Epitaph on Elizabeth, L. H."

PREVIEWING

POETRY

To the Virgins, to Make Much of Time
Robert Herrick

To His Coy Mistress
Andrew Marvell

To Lucasta, Going to the Wars
Richard Lovelace

PERSONAL CONNECTION

The Latin expression *carpe diem* (kär'pĕ dē'ĕm)—"seize the day"—comes from a poem in which the Roman poet Horace advocates enjoying life fully because death is inevitable. This philosophy of life has been embraced by various individuals over the centuries and is still popular with some people today. With a group of classmates, discuss your opinion of this approach to life.

Flower Still Life (1614), Ambrosius Bosschaert the Elder. Collection of the J. Paul Getty Museum, Malibu, California (83.PC.386).

HISTORICAL/LITERARY CONNECTION

The Stuart king Charles I—successor to James I—believed that he had a divine right to rule, independent of Parliament. Tension grew between Charles and members of the legislative body, and in 1629 the king suspended Parliament. Thirteen years later, in 1642, England erupted in a civil war between those who supported the monarchy, who were called Cavaliers, and those who supported Parliament, known as Roundheads. The Cavaliers included a group of poets whose musical, lighthearted verse was popular among members of the royal court. The Cavalier poets focused on themes of love, war, honor, and courtly behavior and frequently advocated the philosophy of *carpe diem,* or living for the moment.

Prominent among the Cavalier poets were Robert Herrick and Richard Lovelace. Another 17th-century poet, Andrew Marvell, although not a Cavalier in political sympathies, is often grouped with the Cavaliers because of his poetic style. His combination of the intellectual depth and wit of the metaphysical poets with the lighthearted and melodious style of the Cavaliers makes him difficult to categorize.

WRITING CONNECTION

In your notebook, write a description of a person you know or have heard of who, in your opinion, lives according to the philosophy of *carpe diem.* Include examples of the person's behavior. Then, as you read these three poems, compare the person's attitude with the attitudes expressed by the poems' speakers.

LASERLINKS
• *HISTORICAL CONNECTION*

To the Virgins, to Make Much of Time

Robert Herrick

Gather ye rosebuds while ye may,
    Old time is still a-flying;
And this same flower that smiles today
    Tomorrow will be dying.

The glorious lamp of heaven, the sun,
    The higher he's a-getting,
The sooner will his race be run,
    And nearer he's to setting.

That age is best which is the first,
    When youth and blood are warmer;
But being spent, the worse, and worst
    Times still succeed the former.

Then be not coy, but use your time,
    And, while ye may, go marry;
For, having lost but once your prime,
    You may forever tarry.

GUIDE FOR READING

9–12 How does the speaker appear to feel about old age? Do you agree with his opinion?

13 coy: hesitant; modest.

15–16 How do these lines reflect the philosophy of *carpe diem?*
16 tarry: wait.

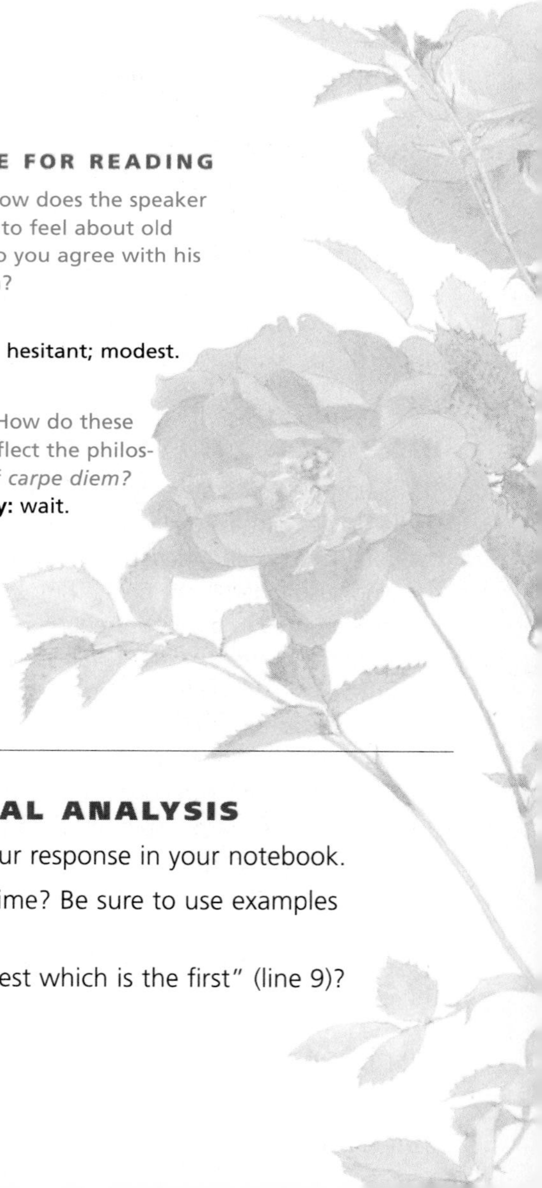

FROM PERSONAL RESPONSE *TO* CRITICAL ANALYSIS

REFLECT **1.** What was your overall reaction to this poem? Record your response in your notebook.

RETHINK **2.** How would you describe the speaker's thoughts about time? Be sure to use examples from the poem to help explain your opinion.

3. Do you agree with the speaker's idea that "that age is best which is the first" (line 9)? Why or why not?

The Proposal (1872), Adolphe-William Bouguereau. Oil on canvas, 64⅜″ × 44″, The Metropolitan Museum of Art, New York, gift of Mrs. Elliot L. Kamen in memory of her father, Bernard R. Armour, 1960 (60.122).

To His Coy Mistress

Andrew Marvell

Had we but world enough, and time,
This coyness, lady, were no crime.
We would sit down, and think which way
To walk, and pass our long love's day.
Thou by the Indian Ganges' side
Shouldst rubies find; I by the tide
Of Humber would complain. I would
Love you ten years before the flood,
And you should, if you please, refuse

GUIDE FOR READING

5 Ganges (găn′jēz′): a great river of northern India.

7 Humber: a river of northern England, flowing through Marvell's hometown; **complain:** sing melancholy love songs.

5–7 Why do you think the speaker chooses to place his lover at the Ganges and himself at the Humber? What is his argument and his objective?

8 flood: the biblical Flood.

Till the conversion of the Jews.
My vegetable love should grow
Vaster than empires and more slow;
An hundred years should go to praise
Thine eyes, and on thy forehead gaze;
Two hundred to adore each breast,
But thirty thousand to the rest;
An age at least to every part,
And the last age should show your heart.
For, lady, you deserve this state,
Nor would I love at lower rate.
    But at my back I always hear
Time's wingéd chariot hurrying near;
And yonder all before us lie
Deserts of vast eternity.
Thy beauty shall no more be found,
Nor, in thy marble vault, shall sound
My echoing song; then worms shall try
That long-preserved virginity,
And your quaint honor turn to dust,
And into ashes all my lust:
The grave's a fine and private place,
But none, I think, do there embrace.
    Now therefore, while the youthful hue
Sits on thy skin like morning dew,
And while thy willing soul transpires
At every pore with instant fires,
Now let us sport us while we may,
And now, like amorous birds of prey,
Rather at once our time devour
Than languish in his slow-chapped power.
Let us roll all our strength and all
Our sweetness up into one ball,
And tear our pleasures with rough strife
Thorough the iron gates of life:
Thus, though we cannot make our sun
Stand still, yet we will make him run.

10 till . . . Jews: In Marvell's day, Christians believed that all Jews would convert to Christianity just before the Last Judgment and the end of the world.

11 vegetable love: a love that grows like a plant (an oak tree, for example)—slowly but with the power to become very large.

19 state: dignity.

20 How would you describe the speaker's tone up to this point?

32 Has the speaker's tone changed?

35 transpires: breathes.

37–40 Consider the title of this part of Unit Two, "Facing Life's Limitations." How is the speaker trying to deal with life's limitations?

40 slow-chapped: slow-jawed.

44 thorough: through.

FROM PERSONAL RESPONSE *TO* CRITICAL ANALYSIS

REFLECT

1. In your notebook, make a sketch based on your image of this poem's speaker.

RETHINK

2. Do you think the speaker's argument about time is convincing? Explain your opinion, using support from the poem.

3. In your opinion, is the speaker sincere in his description of the way he would go about loving his mistress if he had more time?

To Lucasta,
GOING TO THE WARS

Tell me not, Sweet, I am unkind
That from the nunnery
Of thy chaste breast and quiet mind,
To war and arms I fly.

True, a new mistress now I chase,
The first foe in the field;
And with a stronger faith embrace
A sword, a horse, a shield.

Yet this inconstancy is such
As you too shall adore;
I could not love thee, Dear, so much,
Loved I not honor more.

RICHARD LOVELACE

GUIDE FOR READING

4 Think about the speaker's use of the word *arms.* Why is it especially appropriate for the speaker to talk about flying to arms?

7 What is the "stronger faith" the speaker mentions in this line?

Sir Philip Sidney (about 1576), unknown artist. The Granger Collection, New York.

RESPONDING OPTIONS

FROM PERSONAL RESPONSE *TO* CRITICAL ANALYSIS

REFLECT 1. In your notebook, jot down words or phrases that convey your impression of the speaker of "To Lucasta, Going to the Wars." Share them with a partner.

RETHINK 2. Which do you think the speaker prefers, love or war?

Consider
- his description of Lucasta
- what he means by "stronger faith" in line 7
- his thoughts about honor

3. Why do you think the speaker uses words like *mistress, embrace, inconstancy,* and *adore* in referring to his duty?

4. If you were the speaker's beloved, how might you react to lines 11–12?

RELATE 5. Think about the ways in which women are described in "To the Virgins, to Make Much of Time," "To His Coy Mistress," and "To Lucasta, Going to the Wars." Do you think the speakers share the same attitude toward women? Explain your opinion.

6. Think about the philosophy of *carpe diem* as it is expressed in these poems. How might this philosophy be a way of facing life's limitations?

ANOTHER PATHWAY

With three or four classmates, plan and act out a talk-show interview with the speakers of these three poems. Prepare questions and responses that reveal the speakers' views on the concepts of *carpe diem* and honor and on their attitudes toward women. You may also want to consider their probable reactions to contemporary events.

LITERARY CONCEPTS

Hyperbole is figurative language that greatly exaggerates facts or ideas for emphasis or for humorous effect. "Standing by the garage was a dog the size of a bus" is an example of hyperbole. What examples of hyperbole, or extreme exaggeration, can you find in "To His Coy Mistress"? How do they help the speaker develop his argument?

QUICKWRITES

1. Draft a short **comparison-contrast essay** in which you compare the poems "To His Coy Mistress" and "To the Virgins, to Make Much of Time," concentrating on their speakers, themes, and styles.
2. Write a **speech** in which you use your own examples of hyperbole to convince your listeners to "seize the day."
3. Write a **letter** from Lucasta to her lover after he's left for the war. Be sure to mention how you feel about his choice to leave you and go fight in a war.

PORTFOLIO *Save your writing. You may want to use it later as a springboard to a piece for your portfolio.*

ALTERNATIVE ACTIVITIES

1. Arrange images and words to create a classroom **banner** on the *carpe diem* theme.
2. Prepare a **booklet** of quotations about the fleeting nature of time. Be sure to include Marvell's reference to "time's wingéd chariot."
3. Draw single-panel **cartoons** depicting some of the ideas and objects that are personified in the poems—for example, "old time . . . still a-flying."

ART CONNECTION

Look again at Adolphe-William Bouguereau's painting *The Proposal* on page 283. In your opinion, does this painting capture the mood of Marvell's poem "To His Coy Mistress"? Give reasons for your answer.

LITERARY LINKS

In your opinion, what would each of the speakers of these poems think of the kind of love described in Donne's "A Valediction: Forbidding Mourning"?

ACROSS THE CURRICULUM

History Find out more about life during the reign of Charles I—including court life, the lifestyle of the Cavalier poets, and the events that led up to the civil war.

ROBERT HERRICK

1591–1674

As a young man, Robert Herrick tried his hand at goldsmithing, the family trade, before going off to Cambridge University. There he received two degrees and, a few years later, was ordained a priest. An ardent admirer of Ben Jonson, Herrick was one of the "sons of Ben" and an active member of London society. He loved the city and was disappointed when assigned to a rural church in Devonshire. Because of his loyalty to the king, he was deprived of this post for 15 years under the Parliamentary government but was reassigned to Devonshire when the monarchy was restored.

While in London in 1648, Herrick published his only book, *Hesperides,* which contained over 1,400 poems on both worldly and religious themes. Unfortunately, because of the civil war, society was not very interested in Herrick's light, playful verse, and his work was not much appreciated until the 19th century. After returning to the country, Herrick settled down to his life as a country priest, spending his days in enjoyment of nature and the quiet life and writing no more poetry. Herrick's poetry is greatly appreciated today, and he has been called "the greatest song-writer ever born of English race."

OTHER WORKS "Corinna's Going A-Maying," "Delight in Disorder," "The Argument of His Book"

Andrew Marvell

1621–1678

During his lifetime, Andrew Marvell was known for his political activities rather than his poetry. After receiving a degree from Cambridge University, he traveled abroad for several years before returning to England in 1650 to tutor the daughter of the Parliamentary general Lord Fairfax. It was while living at the Fairfax estate that he wrote most of his nonsatirical poetry. Three years later, Marvell became tutor to Oliver Cromwell's ward, William Dutton.

Marvell wrote a number of poems about Cromwell, including "An Horatian Ode upon Cromwell's Return from Ireland," perhaps the greatest political poem in English. In 1657 he became an assistant to John Milton, the Latin secretary for the Parliamentary government, and in 1659 was himself elected to membership in Parliament, an office he held until his death. After the Restoration, he seems to have been influential in securing Milton's deliverance from prison and from possible execution. During this time he also wrote many political satires attacking the king's policies. Marvell's poetry was not published until after his death, and his true talent as a poet was not fully recognized until the 20th century.

OTHER WORKS "The Mower's Song," "The Garden," "On a Drop of Dew"

Richard Lovelace

1618–1657

A courtier, soldier, poet, lover, and connoisseur of the arts said to have been one of the most handsome men in England, Richard Lovelace had all of the qualities of the perfect Cavalier. He was born into a wealthy military family and was educated at Oxford. On a visit to the university, the king and queen admired him so much that they granted him a master's degree on the spot. Naturally, he fought for the monarchy during the civil war.

Lovelace was imprisoned twice, once for petitioning Parliament in the king's favor and again for his involvement in an uprising against the legislative body. It was while he was imprisoned that he wrote his best and most famous poems, "To Althea, from Prison" and "To Lucasta, Going to the Wars." In 1646, he was badly wounded while fighting the Spanish in France.

Lovelace depleted most of his fortune trying to help the king and spent the last years of his life dependent on the charity of friends. During his lifetime, Lovelace's poems were popular and even set to music, but after his death they were forgotten for over 100 years.

OTHER WORKS "To Amarantha, That She Would Dishevel Her Hair," "To Lucasta, Going Beyond the Seas," "To Althea, from Prison"

PREVIEWING

POETRY

from the Rubáiyát (roo͞′bē-yät′)

Omar Khayyám (ō′mär kī-yäm′)

Translated by Edward FitzGerald

PERSONAL CONNECTION

You may have heard expressions such as "Life is a bowl of cherries" or "Life's a beach." In your notebook, complete the sentence "Life is a(n) . . ." with an original comparison that expresses your view of life. Briefly explain why you think the comparison is valid. Then, as you read these poems, be aware of the ways in which their speaker uses comparisons to express a philosophy of life.

CULTURAL CONNECTION

The *Rubáiyát* is probably the work of Persian literature best known in the West. It has been translated into almost every major language of the world. The word *rubáiyát* is the plural form of *ruba'i,* the name of a Persian poetic form. A ruba'i is a quatrain, or four-line poem, in which the first, second, and fourth lines rhyme.

In its entirety, the *Rubáiyát* contains more than 400 of these quatrains. Each quatrain conveys a single thought about a subject such as beauty, love, death, or the fleeting nature of time. The theme of *carpe diem*—"seize the day"—is dominant in the *Rubáiyát,* just as it is in the poems of the English Cavalier poets. Although at one time all 400 poems were attributed to the 12th-century Persian poet Omar Khayyám, scholars now believe that he perhaps wrote no more than 250.

In 1859, the British writer Edward FitzGerald translated 75 of the poems into English. FitzGerald tried to remain true to Omar's expression of his philosophy of life by respecting the poems' form and individual themes, but he did modify the images somewhat to fit the tastes of his Victorian audience. Because the original quatrains were rather disconnected, FitzGerald rearranged them into a more unified and continuous sequence.

READING CONNECTION

Linking Imagery and Tone Frequently, a writer relies on imagery to convey his or her tone, or attitude toward a subject. The writer's tone, in turn, usually reflects his or her philosophy of life. As you read these poems, decide how you would describe the speaker's tone in each of them. Look for imagery, or descriptive language, that helps establish the tone. Then record your thoughts in a chart like the one shown.

Poem	Tone	Imagery
1	forceful	Field of Night, Shaft of Light
7		
12		

FROM THE

Rubáiyát

Omar Khayyám

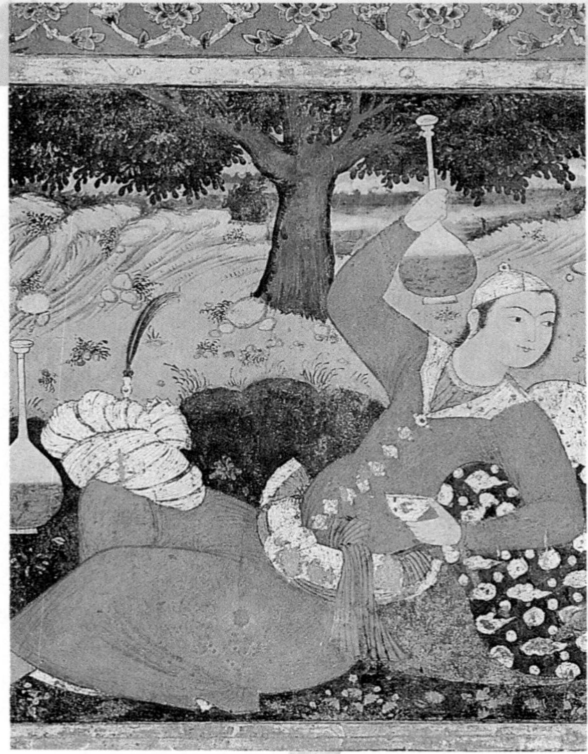

Joy of Wine fresco. Chehel Sotün Palace, Isfahan, Iran. Photo by Roloff Beny, courtesy of the National Archives of Canada (PA-1986-009).

1

Wake! For the Sun, who scatter'd into flight
The Stars before him from the Field of Night,
    Drives Night along with them from Heav'n, and strikes
The Sultán's Turret with a Shaft of Light.

4 Sultán's Turret: a tower in the palace of a Moslem ruler.

7

Come, fill the Cup, and in the fire of Spring
Your Winter-garment of Repentance fling:
    The Bird of Time has but a little way
To flutter—and the Bird is on the Wing.

12

A Book of Verses underneath the Bough,
A Jug of Wine, a Loaf of Bread—and Thou
Beside me singing in the Wilderness—
Oh, Wilderness were Paradise enow!

12 enow: enough.

63

Oh, threats of Hell and Hopes of Paradise!
One thing at least is certain—*This* Life flies;
One thing is certain and the rest is Lies;
The Flower that once has blown for ever dies.

64

Strange, is it not? that of the myriads who
Before us pass'd the door of Darkness through,
Not one returns to tell us of the Road,
Which to discover we must travel too.

17 myriads (mĭr'ē-ədz): countless numbers (of people).

68

We are no other than a moving row
Of Magic Shadow-shapes that come and go
Round with the Sun-illumined Lantern held
In Midnight by the Master of the Show;

69

But helpless Pieces of the Game He plays
Upon this Checker-board of Nights and Days;
Hither and thither moves, and checks, and slays,
And one by one back in the Closet lays.

27 hither and thither: here and there.

96

Yet Ah, that Spring should vanish with the Rose!
That Youth's sweet-scented manuscript should close!
The Nightingale that in the branches sang,
Ah, whence, and whither flown again, who knows!

99

Ah, Love! could you and I with Him conspire
To grasp this sorry Scheme of Things entire,
Would not we shatter it to bits—and then
Re-mold it nearer to the Heart's Desire!

RESPONDING OPTIONS

FROM PERSONAL RESPONSE *TO* CRITICAL ANALYSIS

REFLECT

1. In your notebook, freewrite about the thoughts you had after reading these poems.

RETHINK

2. How would you describe the philosophy of life expressed by the speaker?

Consider

- what he compares time to in poem 7
- the actions he advocates in poems 1, 7, and 12
- his view of death in poems 63 and 64
- what he compares human beings to in poems 68 and 69

3. How do you think the speaker views the relationship between human beings and God?

4. Which idea expressed in the poems seems to come closest to your own philosophy of life? Explain your response.

RELATE

5. The speaker suggests that happiness can be achieved very simply, with "a Book of Verses . . . a Jug of Wine, a Loaf of Bread—and Thou." Do you think most people can be satisfied with such simple pleasures? Give reasons for your opinion.

LITERARY LINKS

Which of these poems from the *Rubáiyát* seem most closely related to the ideas expressed in Robert Herrick's "To the Virgins, to Make Much of Time" (page 282)? What theme do they share with Herrick's poem?

CRITIC'S CORNER

One critic, Gordon S. Haight, stated that the *Rubáiyát* "will always attract some readers by its dark philosophy." What do you think Haight meant by "dark philosophy"? Explain your interpretation.

ANOTHER PATHWAY

Cooperative Learning

Reread the poems from the *Rubáiyát,* looking for examples of ways in which metaphors can help convey insights about life. Create an original one- or two-line simile or metaphor that expresses one of the ideas in the poems. Then, as a class, compile a "mini-*Rubáiyát.*"

metaphor	simile
is	like or as

QUICKWRITES

1. In a **paragraph,** identify the person whom you think the speaker is addressing in these poems. Give reasons for your opinion.
2. Select one poem with which you strongly agree or disagree. Write a **letter** to Omar Khayyám, explaining your thoughts about his ideas.
3. Write a **list** of questions about life and death that you think the speaker of these poems would like to have answered.

PORTFOLIO *Save your writing. You may want to use it later as a springboard to a piece for your portfolio.*

LITERARY CONCEPTS

The **theme** of a literary work is a message or insight about life or human nature that the writer wishes to communicate to the reader. For example, "The love of money is the root of all evil" is a theme of Chaucer's "Pardoner's Tale" (page 98). Although some works are written purely for entertainment, most serious works make at least one point about life or the human condition. Sometimes a theme is quite subtle, and often different readers will discover different themes in the same work. What themes can you find in these poems from the *Rubáiyát?*

CONCEPT REVIEW: Metaphor As you may recall, a metaphor is a comparison that does not contain the word *like* or *as.* Sometimes the comparison is stated directly, as in "Life is a broken-winged bird"; sometimes it is implied, as in "the Bird of Time." In poetry, metaphors often help convey themes. For example, in poem 7, time is compared to a bird that has already completed part of a short journey. This comparison reflects the theme that time is limited and passes quickly. What other metaphors can you find in these poems, and what themes do they help express?

ALTERNATIVE ACTIVITIES

1. Read other poems from the *Rubáiyát* and choose two to share with classmates. In a brief **oral report,** tell how you think each poem reflects the speaker's philosophy of life.
2. Create a **mural** depicting images or ideas presented in some or all of the poems.

ACROSS THE CURRICULUM

History Investigate the culture of 12th-century Persia—the culture in which Omar Khayyám wrote his poems. Find information on the topic of religion, education, or government, and report your findings to the class.

OMAR KHAYYÁM

1050?–1123?

Omar Khayyám lived in Persia, the region now occupied by the nation of Iran. During his lifetime, he was more famous for his work as a scientist than for his poetry. The name *Khayyám* means "tentmaker"; thus, the author of the *Rubáiyát* is sometimes called Omar the Tentmaker. It is possible that Omar briefly engaged in this line of work before going on to more scholarly pursuits; however, it is more likely that his father was the tentmaker.

In any case, Omar was an exceptionally brilliant man who mastered the subjects of mathematics, astronomy, philosophy, history, medicine, and law. He was the author of important works on astronomy, geometry, and algebra as well as poetry. Because of his scientific genius, Omar was asked to make the astronomical calculations that were needed to reform the calendar in use at the time. He was later asked to help in the design and building of an observatory in the city of Isfahan. Despite his many scientific contributions, however, Omar's worldwide reputation is based mainly on his poetry.

PREVIEWING

POETRY

How Soon Hath Time
When I Consider How My Light Is Spent

John Milton

PERSONAL CONNECTION

Think about someone you know or have read about—such as a musician or an athlete—who has suffered disappointment in trying to reach a desired goal or realize a dream. In your notebook, record your impressions of how that person reacted to disappointment and how he or she carried on afterward.

BIOGRAPHICAL CONNECTION

John Milton studied continually, even as a child. Because of his scholarly and literary gifts, he was encouraged to enter the ministry. He chose instead to dedicate his life to writing but maintained a deep concern with religious issues, particularly God's relationship to human beings. He was also a strong advocate of the Puritans, a strict religious group who supported the Parliamentarians in their war against the monarchy during the 1640s.

The poems on the following pages were written more than 20 years apart, at two critical junctures in Milton's life. In the first poem, written on the occasion of his 23rd birthday, he reflects upon his disappointment at the meagerness of his creative output. The second poem reveals the disappointment with which the poet viewed his loss of sight at the age of 43. It is believed that the strain of continual reading in poor lighting contributed to this untimely affliction.

READING CONNECTION

Clarifying Meaning The literature of Milton's time can be challenging to modern readers. If the word order seems odd, try rephrasing the sentences until they sound more natural to you. As you read these poems, refer to the notes that explain some of the words and phrases. If an unfamiliar word is not explained, or if a familiar word is used in an unconventional way, consult a dictionary. Finally, reread each poem as many times as necessary, concentrating on how the ideas fit together.

HOW SOON HATH TIME

JOHN MILTON

How soon hath Time, the subtle thief of youth,
Stoln on his wing my three and twentieth year!
My hasting days fly on with full career,
But my late spring no bud or blossom show'th.
Perhaps my semblance might deceive the truth,
That I to manhood am arrived so near,
And inward ripeness doth much less appear,
That some more timely-happy spirits endu'th.
Yet be it less or more, or soon or slow,
It shall be still in strictest measure even
To that same lot, however mean or high,
Toward which Time leads me, and the will of Heaven;
All is, if I have grace to use it so,
As ever in my great Taskmaster's eye.

3 **career:** speed.

5 **semblance:** outward appearance.

8 **more timely-happy spirits:** people who have accomplished more at an early age; **endu'th:** endows.

10 **still:** always; **even:** adequate.

11 **lot:** fate.

14 **ever:** eternally.

FROM PERSONAL RESPONSE *TO* CRITICAL ANALYSIS

REFLECT **1.** Do the ideas in this poem seem optimistic or pessimistic to you? In your notebook, write a brief explanation of your opinion.

RETHINK **2.** Do you think Milton, at age 23, would have described himself as a youth or as a man?

Consider

- his statement that "no bud or blossom show'th"
- his reference to his appearance in line 5
- the "inward ripeness" he mentions in line 7

3. What conclusions does the speaker seem to reach by the end of the poem?

Illustration (about 1856),
Birket Foster.

When I Consider How My Light Is Spent

John Milton

When I consider how my light is spent
Ere half my days, in this dark world and wide,
And that one talent which is death to hide,
Lodged with me useless, though my soul more bent
To serve therewith my Maker, and present
My true account, lest he returning chide;
"Doth God exact day-labor, light denied?"
I fondly ask; but Patience to prevent
That murmur, soon replies, "God doth not need
Either man's work or his own gifts; who best
Bear his mild yoke, they serve him best. His state
Is kingly. Thousands at his bidding speed
And post o'er land and ocean without rest:
They also serve who only stand and wait."

3 talent: a reference to the biblical parable of the talents (Matthew 25:14–30), in which a servant who has hidden his one talent (a sum of money) in the earth is reprimanded for not putting it to good use.

8 fondly: foolishly.

12 thousands: here, thousands of angels.

RESPONDING OPTIONS

FROM PERSONAL RESPONSE *TO* CRITICAL ANALYSIS

REFLECT 1. What are your thoughts about the last line of "When I Consider How My Light Is Spent"? Share them with your classmates.

RETHINK 2. What do you think troubles Milton most about his loss of sight? Find lines in the poem that support your response.

3. Do you think Milton will be able to follow the advice of Patience? Why or why not?

RELATE 4. Compare and contrast Milton's attitudes in "How Soon Hath Time" and "When I Consider How My Light Is Spent." Pay particular attention to his feelings about his talent and about his relationship with God.

5. On the basis of your reading of both poems, would you say that Milton's reactions to life's disappointments are praiseworthy? Why or why not?

ANOTHER PATHWAY

Cooperative Learning

Working with a group, prepare two charts—one for each poem—in which you list the thoughts and feelings expressed in the poems. Share your findings with the other groups, highlighting or circling the entries that your charts have in common.

Thoughts and Feelings Expressed	Words or Lines in Poem
1.	
2.	
3.	
4.	

LITERARY CONCEPTS

An **allusion** is a reference to a historical or fictional person, place, or event with which the reader is assumed to be familiar. Writers use allusions to make their works more meaningful. In what way do you think Milton's allusion to the biblical parable of the talents gives additional meaning to the poem "When I Consider How My Light Is Spent"? Explain and support your answer.

CONCEPT REVIEW: Sonnet Both of these poems are Italian sonnets. For each sonnet, explain the relationship between the content of the octave (the first eight lines) and the content of the sestet (the last six lines).

QUICKWRITES

1. Refer to the impressions you recorded for the Personal Connection on page 294. In a short **essay,** compare Milton's reactions to disappointment with those of the person you wrote about.
2. In a **paragraph,** summarize the religious theme, or message, of one of these poems.
3. Write a **biographical entry** about yourself that might appear in a book called *Who's Who in (name of your town).* Describe your achievements as they might be when you are 23.

PORTFOLIO *Save your writing. You may want to use it later as a springboard to a piece for your portfolio.*

ALTERNATIVE ACTIVITIES

1. Using pastels and ink, create an **illustration** depicting the ideas conveyed in one of the two poems. Experiment with bold as well as subtle colors to achieve the effect you want.
2. Investigate and prepare an **oral report** on the achievements of another well-known figure who has learned to cope with blindness. Share your findings with the class.

CRITIC'S CORNER

The poet Samuel Taylor Coleridge once remarked upon the "calmness" and "self-possession," or self-confidence, that Milton displays in his poetry. What evidence of those personal traits can you find in these two poems?

LITERARY LINKS

Compare and contrast Milton's reactions to the swiftness of time with the reactions of the speaker in Robert Herrick's "To the Virgins, to Make Much of Time."

ACROSS THE CURRICULUM

Science In 1638, while traveling in Italy, Milton met Galileo, the famous astronomer and physicist. Research the life and times of this scientist, who is viewed as the founder of modern experimental science.

Science Investigate the various causes of blindness. How has the treatment of eye disorders changed since Milton's time?

The Blind Milton Dictating to His Daughters (1878), Mihály von Munkácsy. Oil on canvas, The Granger Collection, New York.

ART CONNECTION

Look again at the two depictions of the phases of the moon on page 295. Why do you think these images were chosen to illustrate the poem "How Soon Hath Time"?

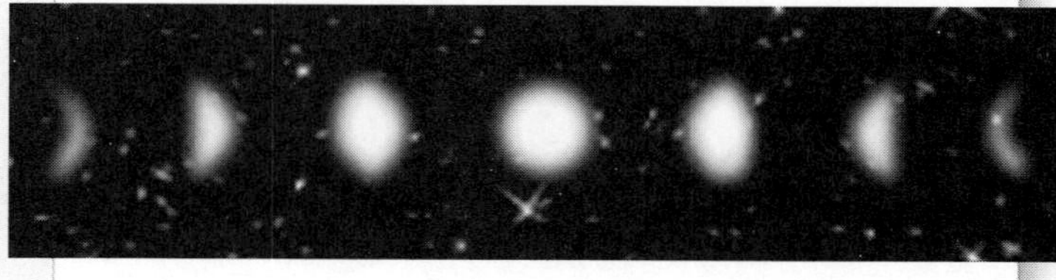

JOHN MILTON

1608–1674

While still a teenager, John Milton decided that he would become an important poet. That he achieved his goal is undoubted: he became one of the greatest writers in English history. In addition, he is considered one of the leading interpreters of Puritan thought.

As a young man, Milton had the best of educations and spent extended periods of time in independent study and travel. Although he earned two degrees from Cambridge University, he was not particularly popular at that institution. He often criticized the curriculum and on one occasion was suspended briefly for arguing with a tutor.

Milton had adversaries in the political arena as well. When civil war erupted in 1642, he devoted his energies to writing political pamphlets in support of the Puritan Roundheads. After the Parliamentary forces defeated the forces of King Charles I, he accepted the position of Latin secretary to Oliver Cromwell, leader of the Commonwealth—the new Parliamentary government. When the monarchy was restored in 1660, Milton was arrested for his earlier political activities, but he avoided execution and imprisonment, perhaps because of his blindness.

In his later years, Milton began serious work on his epic masterpiece *Paradise Lost;* its sequel, *Paradise Regained;* and the dramatic poem *Samson Agonistes.* He had conceived the idea for an epic poem when he was 19 but did not begin composing it until he was in his 50s and totally blind. In writing *Paradise Lost,* Milton composed over 10,000 lines of verse in his head, dictating 20 or 30 lines at a time to friends, relatives, and paid assistants.

OTHER WORKS "L'Allegro," "Il Penseroso"

LASERLINKS
• *AUTHOR BACKGROUND*

MILESTONES IN BRITISH LITERATURE

John Milton

PARADISE LOST

How did the world come to be created? Where do we human beings fit in? Why is there suffering, pain, and death? These fundamental questions engaged John Milton throughout his life. In 1658, at the age of 50, the blind poet undertook to compose a poem he had had in mind since he was 19, one that would "justify the ways of God to man." Using the biblical account in Genesis as his basic source, he constructed long, flowing sentences in rhythmic blank verse, which he then dictated 20 or 30 lines at a time to paid assistants, friends, and relatives. Within seven years, he had finished his ambitious masterpiece, *Paradise Lost,* considered by many to be the finest epic poem in the English language.

Right:
The Expulsion from Paradise *by Italian painter Masaccio (1401–1428).*

Below:
Like most educated men of his time, Milton knew that the earth revolves around the sun. Many people, however, still envisioned the earth as the center of the universe, so Milton presented the cosmos in a way that his readers could imagine.

In *Paradise Lost,* Milton describes a civil war that takes place in heaven when God appoints his Son to the seat of honor, a position coveted by Satan. After Satan and his band of rebel angels are defeated and cast into Hell, Satan vows to corrupt God's latest creation—humanity. This he accomplishes through the temptation of the first woman, Eve, in the Garden of Eden.

When Eve and her mate, Adam, realize that they have disobeyed God, they are overcome with grief and despair. Yet they experience God's

Left:
Satan in His Original Glory: "Thou Wast Perfect Till Iniquity Was Found in Thee" *by William Blake (about 1805)*

Below:
First page of the manuscript of Paradise Lost

mercy as well as his wrath: by the end of the epic, Adam and Eve have some hope for the future. Their banishment from the Garden of Eden has been softened by the promise of a Messiah. Milton's *Paradise Regained*, completed two years after *Paradise Lost,* presents the fulfillment of that promise.

In *Paradise Lost,* Milton probes the relationships between free will and destiny and between freedom and responsibility. Praised for its mastery of poetic style, the work has served as an inspiration to generations of writers, including Joseph Addison, Samuel Johnson, William Blake, and Percy Bysshe Shelley.

Left:
In Paradise Lost, *the cosmos is suspended by a golden chain from Heaven's floor. Far below is Hell—but the devils have built a causeway to reach our world.*

ON YOUR OWN

Female Orations

MARGARET CAVENDISH, DUCHESS OF NEWCASTLE

Margaret Cavendish lived at a time when female writers were few and tended to concentrate on such subjects as family, religion, romance, and the responsibilities of keeping a household. Modesty was highly valued as a feminine virtue, so most women writers of the time never published their work. Cavendish was keenly aware of the limitations placed on women in her society, yet she published her unorthodox writings despite them. She became the subject of considerable criticism and scorn for publishing her thoughts on subjects that were considered off-limits to female interpretation. In Female Orations, *she records an imaginary debate between women with differing points of view on the role of women in society.*

Young Woman Standing at a Virginal (about 1670), Jan Vermeer. The Granger Collection, New York.

I

Ladies, gentlewomen, and other inferior women, but not less worthy: I have been industrious to assemble you together, and wish I were so fortunate as to persuade you to make frequent assemblies, associations, and combinations amongst our sex, that we may unite in prudent counsels, to make ourselves as free, happy, and famous as men; whereas now we live and die as if we were produced from beasts, rather than from men; for men are happy, and we women are miserable; they possess all the ease, rest, pleasure, wealth, power, and fame; whereas women are restless with labor, easeless with pain, melancholy for want of pleasures, helpless for want of power, and die in oblivion, for want of fame. Nevertheless, men are so unconscionable and cruel against us that they endeavor to bar us of all sorts of liberty, and will not suffer us freely to associate amongst our own sex; but would fain[1] bury us in their houses or beds, as in a grave. The truth is, we live like bats or owls, labor like beasts, and die like worms.

II

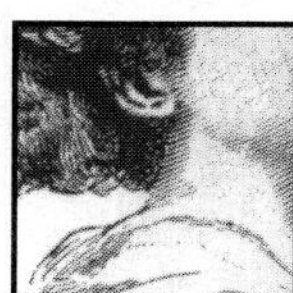

Ladies, gentlewomen, and other inferior women: The lady that spoke to you hath spoken wisely and eloquently, in expressing our unhappiness; but she hath not declared a remedy, or showed us a way to come out of our miseries; but, if she could or would be our guide, to lead us out of the labyrinth men have put us into, we should not only praise and admire her, but adore and worship her as our goddess: but alas! men, that are not only our tyrants but our devils, keep us in the hell of subjection, from whence I cannot perceive any redemption or getting out; we may complain and bewail our condition, yet that will not free us; we may murmur and rail against men, yet they regard not what we say. In short, our words to men are as empty sounds; our sighs, as puffs of winds; and our tears, as fruitless showers; and our power is so inconsiderable, that men laugh at our weakness.

III

Ladies, gentlewomen, and other inferior women: The former orations were exclamations against men, repining[2] at their condition and mourning for our own; but we have no reason to speak against men, who are our admirers and lovers; they are our protectors, defenders, and maintainers; they admire our beauties, and love our persons; they protect us from injuries, defend us from dangers, are industrious for our subsistence, and provide for our children; they swim great voyages by sea, travel long journeys by land, to get us rarities and curiosities; they dig to the center of the earth for gold for us; they dive to the bottom of the sea for jewels for us: they build to the skies houses for us: they hunt, fowl, fish, plant, and reap for food for us. All which, we could not do ourselves; and yet we complain of men, as if they were our enemies, whenas[3] we could not possibly live without them, which shows we are as ungrateful as inconstant. But we have more reason to murmur against Nature, than against men, who hath made men more ingenious, witty,[4] and wise than women; more strong, industrious, and laborious than women; for women are witless and strengthless, and unprofitable creatures, did they not bear children. Wherefore, let us love men, praise men, and pray for men; for without men, we should be the most miserable creatures that Nature hath made or could make.

---

1. **fain:** gladly.
2. **repining:** complaining.
3. **whenas:** when in fact.
4. **witty:** intelligent.

IV

Noble ladies, gentlewomen, and other inferior women: The former oratoress says we are witless and strengthless; if so, it is that we neglect the one and make no use of the other, for strength is increased by exercise, and wit is lost for want of conversation. But to show men we are not so weak and foolish as the former oratoress doth express us to be, let us hawk, hunt, race, and do the like exercises that men have; and let us converse in camps,[5] courts, and cities; in schools, colleges, and courts of judicature; in taverns, brothels, and gaming houses; all of which will make our strength and wit known, both to men and to our own selves, for we are as ignorant of ourselves as men are of us. And how should we know ourselves, when we never made a trial of ourselves? Or how should men know us, when they never put us to the proof? Wherefore my advice is, we should imitate men; so will our bodies and minds appear more masculine, and our power will increase by our actions.

V

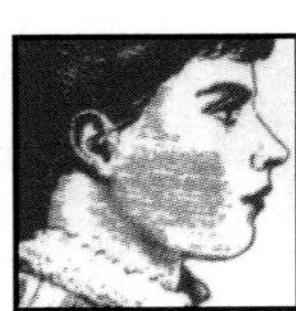

Noble, honorable, and virtuous women: The former oration was to persuade us to change the custom of our sex, which is a strange and unwise persuasion, since we cannot change the nature of our sex, nor make ourselves men; and to have female bodies, and yet to act masculine parts, will be very preposterous and unnatural. In truth, we shall make ourselves like the defects of Nature, and be hermaphroditical,[6] neither perfect women, nor perfect men, but corrupt and imperfect creatures. Wherefore let me persuade you, since we cannot alter the nature of our persons, not to alter the course of our lives; but to rule so our lives and behaviors that we be acceptable and pleasing to God and men; which is, to be modest, chaste, temperate, humble, patient, and pious; also, be housewifely, cleanly, and of few words. All which will gain us praise from men and blessing from Heaven; love in this world and glory in the next.

VI

Worthy women: The former oratoress's oration endeavored to persuade us that it would not only be a reproach and disgrace, but unnatural, for women in their actions and behavior to imitate men: we may as well say it will be a reproach, disgrace, and unnatural to imitate the gods, which imitation we are commanded both by the gods and their ministers; and shall we neglect the imitation of men, which is more easy and natural than the imitation of the gods? For how can terrestrial[7] creatures imitate celestial deities?[8] Yet one terrestrial may imitate another, although in different sorts of creatures. Wherefore, since all terrestrial imitations ought to ascend to the better and not to descend to the worse, women ought to imitate men, as being a degree in nature more perfect than they themselves; and all masculine women ought to be as much praised as effeminate men to be dispraised; for the one advances to perfection, the other sinks to imperfection; that so, by our industry, we may come, at last, to equal men, both in perfection and power.

---

5. **camps:** military encampments.
6. **hermaphroditical** (hər-măf′rə-dĭt′ĭ-kəl): having both male and female characteristics in one body.
7. **terrestrial:** earthly.
8. **celestial deities:** heavenly gods.

VII

Noble ladies, honorable gentlewomen, and worthy female-commoners: The former oratoress's speech was to persuade us out of ourselves and to be that which Nature never intended us to be, to wit, masculine. But why should we desire to be masculine, since our own sex and condition is far the better? For if men have more courage, they have more danger; and if men have more strength, they have more labor than women have; if men are more eloquent in speech, women are more harmonious in voice; if men be more active, women are more graceful; if men have more liberty, women have more safety; for we never fight duels nor battles; nor do we go long travels or dangerous voyages; we labor not in building nor digging in mines, quarries, or pits, for metal, stone, or coals; neither do we waste or shorten our lives with university or scholastical studies, questions, and disputes; we burn not our faces with smiths' forges or chemists'[9] furnaces; and hundreds of other actions which men are employed in; for they would not only fade the fresh beauty, spoil the lovely features, and decay the youth of women, causing them to appear old, when they are young; but would break their small limbs, and destroy their tender lives. Wherefore women have no reason to complain against Nature or the god of Nature, for although the gifts are not the same as they have given to men, yet those gifts they have given to women are much better; for we women are much more favored by Nature than men, in giving us such beauties, features, shapes, graceful demeanor, and such insinuating and enticing attractives, that men are forced to admire us, love us, and be desirous of us; insomuch that rather than not have and enjoy us, they will deliver to our disposals their power, persons, and lives, enslaving themselves to our will and pleasures; also, we are their saints, whom they adore and worship; and what can we desire more than to be men's tyrants, destinies, and goddesses? ❖

9. **chemists':** alchemists'.

Margaret Cavendish

1623?–1674

Born Margaret Lucas, Margaret Cavendish was two years old when her father died. Her mother, who assumed control of the family's extensive estate, was regarded as a shrewd and ambitious businessperson and, as a result, was not well liked by her neighbors. The Lucas family further alienated their neighbors by allying themselves with the monarchy during the conflicts between the king and Parliament. Margaret became an attendant to the queen, whom she accompanied to Paris in 1645. There she met and married William Cavendish, the duke of Newcastle.

As an English nobleman and supporter of the monarchy, the duke had voluntarily fled to France during England's civil war. As the new duchess of Newcastle, Margaret Cavendish was forced to live in exile as well, and in poverty, until the monarchy was restored. It was during her exile that the childless Cavendish began writing with the intent of publishing her work.

After the Restoration, Cavendish and her husband returned to England, where she began to pursue a literary career in earnest. Cavendish wrote about science, mathematics, and philosophy—subjects considered beyond the capacities of women in the 17th century—and produced numerous works of poetry, prose, and drama. Her bold writings and strange manner earned her the nickname "Mad Madge of Newcastle." Her husband, however, supported her throughout and at her death in 1674 wrote, in the inscription he composed for her tombstone, ". . . This Dutches was a wise, wittie and learned Lady, which her many Bookes do well testifie. . . ."

from Eve's Apology in Defense of Women

Amelia Lanier

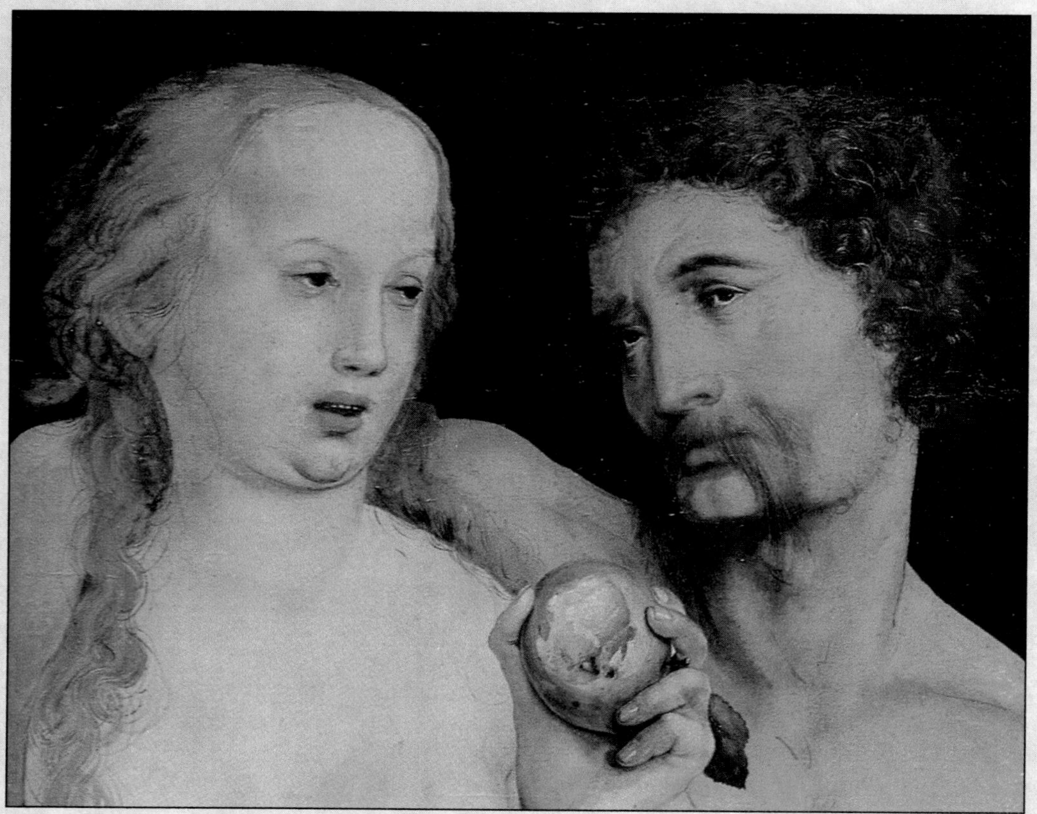

Adam Tempted by Eve (1517), Hans Holbein the Younger. Öffentliche Kunstsammlung Basel, Switzerland (313).

In the biblical Book of Genesis, Eve is tempted by a serpent to eat the fruit of the forbidden tree of knowledge, and she, in turn, offers it to Adam. As a result of their disobedience, God expels them from the Garden of Eden, taking away the gift of human immortality. These stanzas are from Amelia Lanier's defense of Eve, in which the poet (1570?–1640?) adopts a position that was quite radical in its time.

But surely Adam cannot be excused;
Her fault though great, yet he was most to blame.
What weakness offered, strength might have refused;
Being lord of all, the greater was his shame;
Although the serpent's craft had her abused,
God's holy word ought all his actions frame;
    For he was lord and king of all the earth,
    Before poor Eve had either life or breath,

Who being framed by God's eternal hand
The perfectest man that ever breathed on earth,
And from God's mouth received that strait command,
The breach whereof he knew was present death;
Yea, having power to rule both sea and land,
Yet with one apple won to lose that breath
    Which God had breathéd in his beauteous face,
    Bringing us all in danger and disgrace;

And then to lay the fault on patience's back,
That we (poor women) must endure it all;
We know right well he did discretion lack,
Being not persuaded thereunto at all.
If Eve did err, it was for knowledge sake;
The fruit being fair persuaded him to fall.
    No subtle serpent's falsehood did betray him;
    If he would eat it, who had power to stay him?

Not Eve, whose fault was only too much love,
Which made her give this present to her dear,
That what she tasted he likewise might prove,
Whereby his knowledge might become more clear;
He never sought her weakness to reprove
With those sharp words which he of God did hear;
    Yet men will boast of knowledge, which he took
    From Eve's fair hand, as from a learned book.

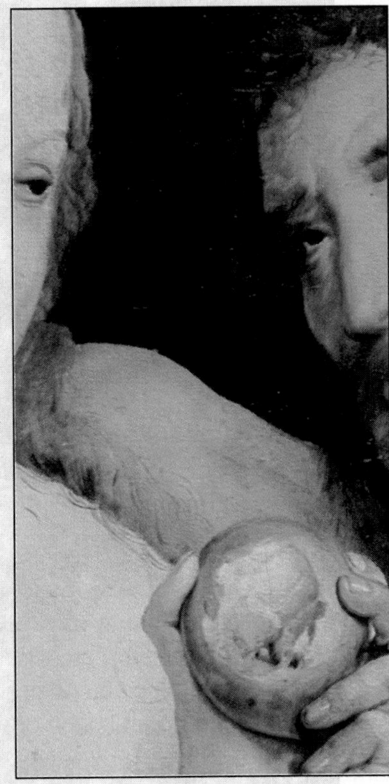

WRITING FROM EXPERIENCE

WRITING TO EXPRESS

English Renaissance poets didn't consider themselves professional poets. Shakespeare was an actor and a playwright, John Donne and Robert Herrick were clergymen, others held positions in government, and Elizabeth I, of course, was the Queen of England. But they all used poetry to express feelings about love and about facing life's limitations. Poetry is a powerful medium for expressing feelings and ideas.

GUIDED ASSIGNMENT

Write a Poem Write a poem that expresses some of your own feelings about love, life's limitations, or some other deeply felt feeling or idea.

Student's Scrapbook

Prose—words in their best order; poetry—the best words in their best order.

Samuel Taylor Coleridge

A conversation I overheard:
"You look like you lost your best friend."
"I did, sort of. My dog died last night."

I was really crushed when my dog died. That's an emotion I could write about.

1 Be Open to Inspiration

Be aware of the subjects and situations around you that are waiting to be made into poems. Do the items shown on these pages give you any ideas for a poem? Sometimes an idea can occur to you without your even thinking about it. If that fails to happen, however, you can use a variety of sources for inspiration. List at least two ideas for a poem drawn from each of the following sources.

Searching Your Memory Can you recall an event, a person, a place, an image that left you with some powerful feeling—happiness, sadness, exaltation, rage, fear, hilarity, frustration?

Using Your Senses Look around you. Observe carefully what you see at school, at home—wherever you are. Use your other senses as well. Something you hear, smell, taste, or feel might bring up an image or an idea you can explore.

Using Your Reading Think about the things you have read or are reading—stories, articles, poems, advertising copy—just about any reading matter might give you an idea for a poem.

Talking About It Talk with others about ideas for poems. Your own poem will most likely spring from something personal, but talking may remind you of something or help focus your ideas.

2 Play with Ideas

Once you've decided on an image or idea you want to explore, write down any related words or phrases that occur to you. Some of these words or phrases may provide you with a useful start when you're ready to begin drafting your poem.

DIRE STRAITS
LOVE

Love over Gold

You walk out on the high wire
you're a dancer on thin ice
you pay no heed to the danger
and less to advice
your footsteps are forbidden
but with knowledge of your sin
you throw your love to all the strangers
and caution to the wind

And you go dancing through doorways
just to see what you will find
leaving nothing to interfere
with the crazy balance of your mind
and when you finally reappear
at the place where you came in
you've thrown your love to all the strangers
and caution to the wind

It takes love over gold
and mind over matter
to do what you do that you must
when the things that you hold
can fall and be shattered
or run through your fingers like dust

Mark Knopfler
from the album *Love over Gold* by Dire Straits

I could write a song, or I could just write a poem and think about setting it to music later.

Song Lyrics

Words That Inspire

EQUALITY

A word can inspire a poem. Certain words, especially abstract ones, can arouse strong feelings or powerful memories.

PREWRITING

Working with Your Ideas

Words That Evoke Images Crafting a poem is similar to working on a painting, a sculpture, or a piece of music. Like those art forms, a poem comes into being—is discovered—gradually as its maker shapes it and reshapes it until it "feels right." The poet's raw materials, however, are not shapes, colors, or musical tones, but words that express images and feelings.

1 Use Your Imagination

Close your eyes. Picture the scene or event that inspired you. Try to mentally relive that scene or event so that you can recall the feelings it evoked. If you think it may help, try drawing a picture of what you recall.

2 Start Writing

As you think about the thing that inspired you, jot down everything that occurs to you. Put down scraps of ideas, descriptions, images, and words or phrases that appeal to you. Don't worry about the order of your ideas or about writing too much. You won't use everything you write, but at this stage you're exploring. After a while, you may find a line or two, or maybe just a phrase, that you particularly like. Use that as a new start and continue exploring.

Notes for poem

People saying "it's only a dog" when Sam died. What do they know?

Sam was like the brother I never had

Always cheerful, ready to play

The way he warmed my bed on cold nights

The fun we had together

His tail sending signals of happiness

Playing the hunting dog—stalking birds (until the day an enormous crow sent him scurrying)

Cold, wet nose against my cheek

The way he died, drifting into sleep without complaining

My feelings when he died:

- relief (no more suffering, no need for me to make a decision about "putting him to sleep")
- sadness
- an empty feeling in my stomach

3 Start Pulling It Together

As you look over your notes, you may want to try some of the following suggestions. They can help you start pulling together the ideas that will grow into your poem.

- Look over your notes and underline or highlight words, phrases, ideas, descriptions, or images that stand out. Cross out the ideas that are clearly not going to be of use.
- Look for ideas that are particularly important or effective in capturing the feelings you want your poem to express.
- Look for connections in your recorded thoughts. Do any patterns emerge that will help you shape your poem?
- Look for something—a word or phrase, a central image, perhaps a title or a first line—that can help you begin drafting your poem.

4 Think About Shape and Form

The poem you write can be structured with a regular pattern of line length, rhythm, and rhymes, or free verse, in which line length and rhythm can vary and rhymes can be irregular or not used at all. You can find examples of many types of poems in this book. Looking at them will help you see the many options available to you.

When you begin drafting your own poem, you may want to experiment with different shapes and forms. Keep trying until you find the one that best fits what you are trying to express.

SkillBuilder

CRITICAL THINKING

Formulating Analogies
Shakespeare uses an analogy, a figure of speech in which a comparison is made, in these lines from *King Lear.*

As flies to wanton boys, are we
to the gods;
They kill us for their sport.

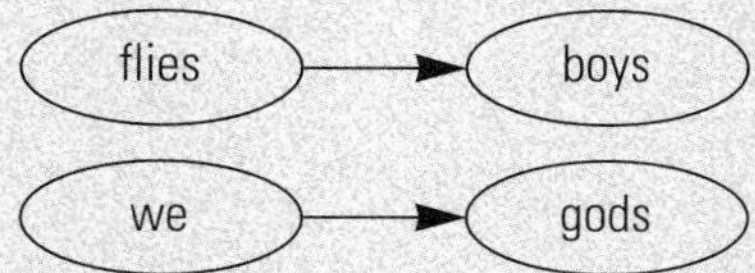

Like metaphors and similes, analogies can create vivid—often startling—images in a poem or other writing. Reading or hearing Shakespeare's lines, you can picture nasty little boys killing flies for fun. This helps us feel the despair of the character in *King Lear* who speaks the lines.

APPLYING WHAT YOU'VE LEARNED
Complete the following analogies as imaginatively as you can.

1. Light is to darkness as . . .
2. Gymnasts are to sport as . . .
3. Chocolate is to me as . . .

THINK & PLAN

Weighing Your Options

1. Will your work be a conventional poem, the lyrics for a song, or a rap? Will it rhyme?
2. What images have you thought of? Are they appropriate?
3. How will you begin your poem?

Drafting Your Poem

Poet at Work Poetry demands almost continuous revision. Your final version of a poem may look nothing like your first draft, but you need that first draft to get you started on the long series of revisions.

1 Draft Your Poem

Once you decide on a topic and have a general idea of what you are trying to convey, plunge right into your rough draft. In fact, you may want to try several different drafts using different styles or forms. Never mind if you can tell as you write that you won't be happy with the result. You can change anything—or everything—when you revise. For now, just concentrate on getting a complete poem on paper.

Student's Rough Draft

Sam was my playmate, companion, and friend,
Brother I never had, faithful to the end,
Bed warmer,
Never-tiring jokester,
Tennis shoe terminator—
But that was then.

Opening lines too maudlin, corny, I let the rhymes dictate my word choices. Forget rhyme?

As ~~creeping~~ furtive age crawled closer
Wet-nosed kisses dried up,
Flying paws were grounded.
His tail a less frequent~~ly waving~~ semaphore
Sending messages of happiness and mischief.
But never complaining.

These 3 lines are pretty good. Expand here?

Then the night he didn't get into my bed,
The morning he was slow to get out of his,
A slower gait, a sadder look,
Clouded eyes and legs that shook.
Soon an almost imperceptible whine.
Followed by a heavy breath,
And then silence.

Can I give the poem a meaning beyond the death of a dog? How?

2 Analyze Your Rough Draft

After you've completed your draft, read it critically. Note your general reactions alongside the draft, as the writer of the poem at the left did. Mark the parts you like—the words, phrases, images, or lines you think you'd like to keep. If specific changes occur to you, make them on the draft.

3 Revise and Share

As you revise, think about how some of the poetic devices and characteristics of poetry can be used in your work.

Mood What mood are you trying to create? Do you want your poem to be light and humorous, solemn and serious, angry, melancholy, or tender? What words, what images will suit your intended mood?

Figures of Speech Figures of speech create images that will make your descriptions and ideas come alive. Think about how you can use metaphors, similes, personification, or analogies in your writing. (See the SkillBuilder sections on page 311 and this page for more on analogies and personification.)

Sound Devices Consider what your words sound like and how they work together. You can use devices such as repetition (*a happy, happy, happy time*), alliteration (repeating initial sounds in a series of words: *a torturous and terrible time*), and onomatopoeia (words that imitate sounds: *buzzing*).

Remember that the devices you use should suit your subject and support the ideas and feelings you want to convey. Also remember as you revise that it's sometimes a good idea to put a poem aside for a while. A little distance and a fresh start can give you a whole new outlook.

PEER RESPONSE

Show your draft to a peer reviewer and ask questions like these.

- How did my poem affect you? What mood or feeling did you get from it?
- What title would you give to my draft? Why?
- What words, phrases, lines, or images impressed you? Did any of them seem out of place?

SkillBuilder

WRITER'S CRAFT

Using Personification
Sir Thomas Wyatt uses personification when he begins his poem with the words "My lute, awake!" Wyatt speaks of his lute as though it were a sleeping person. **Personification** is a figure of speech in which something inanimate, abstract, or nonhuman is given human characteristics.

Whenever you read of shadows "creeping along the floor," animals "conversing seriously," or spring "strewing her flowers," personification is at work. Like other figures of speech, personification is used in prose as well as in poetry.

APPLYING WHAT YOU'VE LEARNED
Turn back to Marlowe's "The Passionate Shepherd to His Love" (page 223) and Raleigh's "The Nymph's Reply to the Shepherd" (page 225). See how many uses of personification you can find in each poem and list them.

RETHINK & EVALUATE

Preparing to Revise

1. What additions or deletions do you want to make?
2. How effectively have you used poetic devices to create the mood you are trying to convey?
3. Where can you strengthen your poem with more-vivid images or better word choices?

Finishing Your Poem

A Last Look You may think, after several revisions, that your poem is finished, but is it? Once again, it might be a good idea to let it rest for a while. Come back to your poem after not thinking about it for a day or two, and you may find more ways to bring it closer to the perfection poetry demands.

1 Revise and Edit

Go over your poem carefully. Read it aloud a few times, listening to its rhythms and the sounds of its words. As you start your final draft, you can use the following questions as well as the Standards for Evaluation and Editing Checklist on the next page.

- Is each word the right word in the right place?
- Should line lengths be more varied or more regular, longer or shorter?
- Does the rhythm seem natural? Is it appropriate to the subject or the mood you mean to create?
- Did you state something that could be better stated with an image—through simile, metaphor, analogy, or personification?
- Are your rhymes good rhymes?
- Would added uses of such sound devices as repetition, alliteration, and onomatopoeia help?

Student's Final Draft

Why do you think the writer used this title for the poem?

Only a Dog

"It's only a dog," someone said.
Childhood playmate,
Bed warmer (though Mom said no),
Tennis-shoe terminator,
Untiring jokester,
Cohort in mischief,
Unwaveringly loyal friend,
Brother I never had.

As furtive age crawled closer
Wet-nosed kisses dried up,
Flying paws were grounded,
Breath became wheeze,
Tail a less frequent semaphore
Signaling happiness.
Every sign of healthy vigor
Seemed suddenly gone.

No longer waiting
For silent signals of safety
To creep into my bed,
He kept to his,
Tossing with memories of better days.
Legs jerked with nocturnal vigor,
Dreamily chasing the stubborn crow
That once chased him.

The vet suggested inviting death.
But death saved me the decision
As gasping breath became shorter,
Then crashed into silence.

"It's only a dog," someone said.
He never felt the vacuum of loss,
Never dreamed of "only a dog"
And woke to the nightmare of nevermore.

How does this version of the poem differ from the rough draft? What changes seem especially effective?

② Share Your Work

The printed page has never been the only outlet for poets. The poets of Ancient Greece sang their odes in public and recited their epics with a musical background. Many Renaissance poems were written as songs; others were later turned into songs. Today, the options for sharing your work are even more numerous.

PUBLISHING IDEAS

- Start a class or school poetry magazine in which all students can share their poems.
- Organize a school or class poetry festival at which students can read their poems aloud.
- Find a poetry forum for young writers on the Internet and send your poem to it.
- Working alone or collaborating with a musician friend, write music to accompany your poem. You can set the poem as a song or provide background music for it.
- A local or neighborhood newspaper may publish submissions by budding poets. A local coffee house or public-access TV station may provide time for young writers to read their poems to audiences. Investigate the possibilities.

Standards for Evaluation

A poem
- focuses on a single event or experience
- creates a mood appropriate to its subject
- uses precise and effective language, with no unnecessary words
- uses appropriate, fresh images that support its meaning
- uses sounds to support its meaning and effect

SkillBuilder

GRAMMAR FROM WRITING

Using Capitalization and Punctuation in Poetry
Until you build your confidence as a poet, it might be best to follow the standard conventions for capitalizing and punctuating poetry. The rules are very simple, as the Editing Checklist below shows.

 GRAMMAR HANDBOOK

For additional information on using capitalization and punctuation, see page 1281 of the Grammar Handbook.

Editing Checklist Use the following revision and editing tips as you revise your poem.

- Did you capitalize the first word of each line and all proper nouns in your poem?
- Did you use commas, periods, and other punctuation just as you would in prose?

REFLECT & ASSESS

Evaluate the Experience

1. How would you evaluate your success with poetry?
2. What skills that you used in writing your poem will be useful in your prose writing?

PORTFOLIO Write an introduction to your poem telling about the experience of writing it. Add it and your poem to your portfolio.

Reflect & Assess

UNIT TWO: THE ENGLISH RENAISSANCE

From reading this unit, what have you learned about the interests and problems of people who lived during the English Renaissance? What connections have you discovered between life then and your life now? Explore these questions by completing one or more options in each of the following sections.

REFLECTING ON THE UNIT

OPTION 1 **Drafting an Essay** Many of the works in this unit deal with various aspects of the theme of love. Which of these works did you find the most meaningful for life today? Explore this question in a brief essay, drawing connections between the works and experiences you have had, heard about, or witnessed.

OPTION 2 **Focusing on Important Issues** After reading the selections in this unit, you should be able to identify some of the main issues with which English Renaissance writers were concerned. Develop a list of generalizations about concerns that can be inferred from the selections. To illustrate each generalization, quote a sentence or a line of poetry from the unit. Then, working with your classmates, combine the quotations with appropriate images to create a collage that conveys the spirit of the English Renaissance.

OPTION 3 **Interpreting a Quotation** Recall the quotation from John Donne at the beginning of this unit: "No man is an island, entire of itself; every man is a piece of the continent, a part of the main." Choose your two favorite writers in this unit (other than Donne himself). In your notebook, create a diary entry for each of them in which you explore what the writer's reaction to the quotation might be. Then jot down your thoughts about what the quotation means to you.

Self-Assessment: To explore how your understanding of the English Renaissance has developed over the course of the unit, jot down words and phrases that come to mind when you think of this historical period. Then circle at least three words and phrases that you think describe the English Renaissance most accurately. Get together with a partner and compare what the two of you have noted. Feel free to make changes in your own list on the basis of your partner's ideas.

REVIEWING LITERARY CONCEPTS

OPTION 1 **Identifying Figurative Language** Most of the poetry you have read in this unit contains figurative language, including metaphor, simile, personification, and hyperbole. In a chart like the one shown, name at least two poems that contain figurative language in each part of the unit. Quote an example of figurative language from each poem, and note what type of figurative language it is. When you have completed the chart, identify the example of figurative language you find the most interesting or appealing, as well as your reasons for finding it so.

Poems	Example of Figurative Language	Type of Figurative Language
"My Lute, Awake!"	"Perform the last / Labor that thou and I shall waste" (ll. 1–2)	Personification

OPTION 2 **Understanding Theme** You have learned that the theme of a literary work is a message or insight about life or human nature that the writer communicates to readers. Review the selections in this unit and determine the main theme of each. Because different readers may discover different themes in the same work, be sure to discuss your opinions with your classmates.

REFLECT & ASSESS *Self-Assessment: Did you understand figurative language and theme well enough to complete one of the options above? On a sheet of paper, copy the following list of literary terms introduced in this unit. Rank the terms to show your understanding of their meanings, from 1 (the term that you feel you understand most fully) to 15 (the term you understand the least). Your ranking should help you decide which concepts you need to review.*

rhyme scheme	*essay*
sonnet	*extended metaphor*
pastoral	*personification*
figurative language	*epitaph*
metaphor	*hyperbole*
simile	*theme*
Italian sonnet	*allusion*
repetition	

PORTFOLIO BUILDING

- **QuickWrites** Several of the QuickWrites assignments in this unit asked you to analyze attitudes and ideas presented in the selections. Choose two pieces of writing that you think represent your best attempts at analyzing the literature in this unit. Write a cover note supporting your choices, then add the note and the two pieces to your portfolio.
- **Writing About Literature** Earlier in this unit, you transformed a poem into another kind of writing. Reread your writing now and compare it with the poem on which it is based. If you had to nominate one of the two works for a creative prize, which would you select? What reasons would you give for your nomination?
- **Writing from Experience** In some ways a poem is never finished; it may require repeated reevaluation and revision until its writer is satisfied with it. Reread the poem you wrote for the Writing from Experience feature. Which images and words capture your ideas the best? If you were to revise your poem now, which words and images would you change? Attach your answers to these questions to your poem if you choose to add it to your portfolio.
- **Personal Choice** Reflect on all the activities and writing that you have worked on for this unit, including work that you have done on your own. Also look over the evaluations and responses that you have received from your peers. Which of the activities or writing assignments proved the most rewarding? Write a note that explains your choice, and add it to your portfolio.

REFLECT & ASSESS *Self-Assessment: Now that you have a handful of writing pieces in your portfolio, look them over and decide which are examples of your strongest work. Are there any pieces that you consider weak and may wish to replace as the year goes on?*

SETTING GOALS

As you worked through the reading and writing activities in this unit, you probably became more aware of your interests and abilities. Are there any skills on which you feel you still need improvement? Are there any particular writers or genres that you would like to investigate further? Create a list of these skills and interests.

UNIT THREE

Spring Gardens, Ranelagh, Thomas Rowlandson.
Victoria & Albert Museum, London/Superstock.

The Restoration and Enlightenment

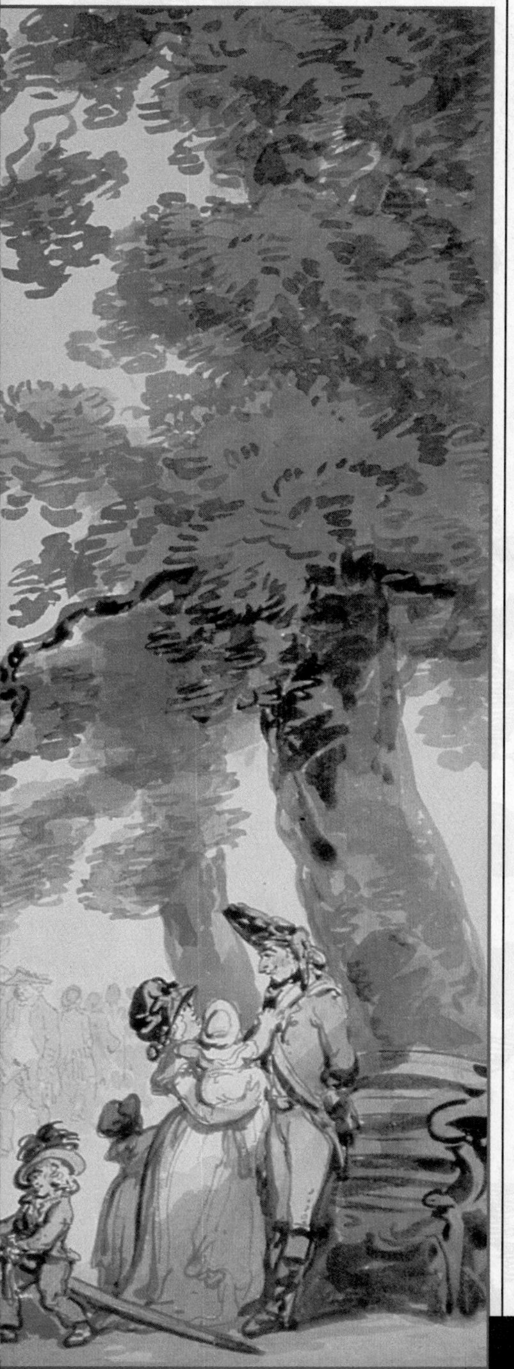

1660–1798

Let observation with extensive view,
Survey mankind, from China to Peru;
Remark each anxious toil, each eager strife
And watch the busy scenes of crowded life.

SAMUEL JOHNSON
critic and scholar

TIME LINE

The Restoration & Enlightenment 1660-1798

1660

Restoration of monarchy with accession of Charles II; Samuel Pepys begins his diary

1666

Great Fire of London

1668

John Dryden appointed first official poet laureate

1678

Puritan author John Bunyan publishes *The Pilgrim's Progress*

1685

Reign of James II begins

1689

Parliament passes English Bill of Rights

1702

Reign of Anne, England's last Stuart monarch, begins

1707

Act of Union officially unites England and Scotland as Great Britain

1709

Richard Steele begins periodical *The Tatler*

1714

Reign of George I, first Hanoverian monarch, begins

1721

Robert Walpole, first political leader to be called prime minister, takes office

1727

Reign of George II begins

1740

Publication of Samuel Richardson's *Pamela,* generally considered first modern English novel

1753

British Museum founded in London

1760

Reign of George III begins

1763

Britain defeats France in Seven Years' (French and Indian) War, acquiring French Canada

Coin commemorating capture of Quebec, 1759

1768

Royal Academy of Arts founded, with portrait painter Joshua Reynolds as first president; publication of *Encyclopaedia Britannica* begins in Scotland

1776–1783

American Revolution—Britain loses 13 colonies

1784

Religious reformer John Wesley, founder of Methodism, officially splits with Church of England

1788

First British settlement in Australia

1793

Louis XVI executed; beginning of war between Britain and revolutionary France; France swept by Reign of Terror

Period *Pieces*

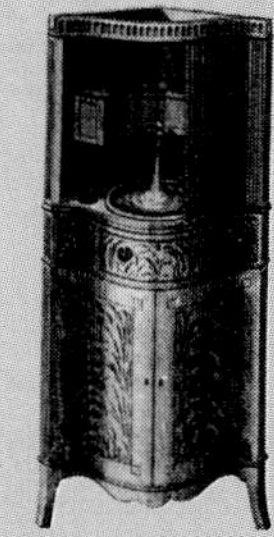

Personal cleanliness began to assume more importance. Pictured is a drawing of an 18th-century washstand.

Day-bed, *c.* 1695

Painted watch dial from latter half of the 18th century

The Restoration & Enlightenment 1660-1798

Charles II wearing finery inspired by the French fashions he saw during his exile

The palace and grounds of Versailles, residence of the French king Louis XIV

After the restoration of the monarchy in 1660, England turned its back on the grim era of Puritan rule and entered a lively period in which the glittering Stuart court set the tone for upper-class social and political life. Charles II had spent much of his long exile in France, absorbing the glamour, elegance, and intrigue of the court of Louis XIV, and after his return to England he and his courtiers tried to emulate the French court's sophistication and splendor. Lords and ladies dressed in rich silks and lace-trimmed finery, wearing elaborate wigs and sparkling jewels. They performed intricate, stately dances at elegant balls and flocked to London's newly reopened theaters. Like Louis XIV, Charles was a patron of the arts and sciences, appointing England's first official poet laureate and chartering the scientific organization known as the Royal Society. Clever and cynical, the king was also extremely self-indulgent, and his excesses both shocked and titillated the English public.

With the Restoration came a return to Anglicanism as England's state religion and a realization that future monarchs would have to share their authority with Parliament, whose influence had increased substantially. An astute

Left: Hand bells were rung to warn of approaching carts filled with victims of the Great Plague of 1665.

Below: Sir Christopher Wren designed the new St. Paul's Cathedral (completed 1710) to replace one that had been destroyed by the Great Fire of London in 1666.

politician, Charles at first won widespread support in Parliament, weathering a series of disasters that included the Great Plague of 1665 and the Great Fire of London a year later. Soon, however, old political rivalries resurfaced, creating two factions that became the nation's chief political parties: the Tories and the Whigs. The Tory party—supporters of royal authority—consisted mainly of landowning aristocrats and conservative Anglicans, who had little tolerance for Protestant dissenters and no desire for war with France. The Whigs, who wanted to limit royal authority, included several powerful nobles as well as wealthy merchants and financiers. Suspicious of the king's Catholic advisers and his pro-French sympathies, the Whigs favored leniency toward Protestant dissenters and sought to curb French expansion in Europe and North America, which they saw as a threat to England's commercial interests.

William and Mary

Political conflict increased when Charles, who had no legitimate children, was succeeded in 1685 by his Catholic brother, James. A blundering, tactless statesman, James II was determined to restore Roman Catholicism as England's state religion, thereby losing the support even of many Tories. As a result, the Whigs in Parliament met with little opposition when they began negotiating to replace James with his Protestant daughter Mary and her husband, the Dutch nobleman William of Orange. In 1688, James was forced to abdicate, and William and Mary took the English throne peacefully in what would become known as the Glorious (or Bloodless)

William and Mary, who ruled England jointly after the Glorious Revolution

Language

During the Enlightenment, emphasis on reason and logic led to efforts to stabilize and systematize the English language. In 1693 the influential writer John Dryden complained, "We have yet no prosodia, not so much as a tolerable dictionary or grammar, so that our language is in a manner barbarous," and over the next decades scholars worked to remedy the situation. One such scholar was Samuel Johnson, whose *Dictionary of the English Language* was published in 1755. Although Johnson recognized that language is always changing, he also recognized the importance of a standard for pronunciation, usage, and spelling. Seven years later Robert Lowth published *A Short Introduction to English Grammar,* in which he attempted to establish a system of rules for judging correctness in matters under dispute. Since early grammarians like Lowth based their ideas on Latin, however, their rules often proved inappropriate for English. For example, they considered the infinitive form of an English verb to consist of two words ("to stun"); but because Latin infinitives are single words, they deemed it incorrect to "split" an English infinitive with an adverb ("to completely stun"), thus creating a puzzling "rule" that has bedeviled generations of schoolchildren.

Despite the Enlightenment scholars' search for uniformity and stability, overseas colonization was bringing variety and growth to English. New environments demanded new vocabulary, often borrowed from the native languages of the regions (like *raccoon* and *chipmunk* from Native American tongues and *kangaroo* from the language of Australian Aborigines). In addition, the great distance of the colonies from the homeland and the slow methods of communication allowed differences between the colonists' English and that spoken in Britain to grow.

Revolution—a triumph of Parliamentary rule over the divine right of kings. The next year, Parliament passed the English Bill of Rights, which put specific limits on royal authority. The remaining supporters of James II—and later those who supported the royal claims of his Catholic son, James Edward Stuart—were known as Jacobites (from *Jacobus,* the Latin form of *James*).

As a Dutchman and a Protestant, King William (who ruled alone after Mary died) was a natural enemy of Catholic France and its expansionist threats to Holland. From the first year of his reign, with Whig support, he took every opportunity to oppose the ambitions of Louis XIV with English military power, beginning a series of wars with France that some historians consider a "Second Hundred Years' War." A year before William's death, Parliament passed the Act of Settlement, which permanently barred Catholics from the throne. In 1702, therefore, the crown passed to Mary's Protestant sister, Anne, a somewhat stodgy but undemanding ruler who faithfully tended to her royal duties. During her reign, Scotland officially united with England to form Great Britain, and war with France continued—although Anne, unlike William, sided with the Tories who opposed it. A peace treaty arranged by her Tory ministers, or advisers, in 1713 procured what was to be only a brief lull in British-French antagonisms.

German-born George I was the first Hanoverian ruler of England.

Portrait of George III with his wife Charlotte and the first 6 of their 15 children

The House of Hanover

Outliving all 16 of her children, Anne was the last monarch of the house of Stuart. With her death in 1714, the crown passed to a distant cousin of hers—the ruler of Hanover in Germany—who as George I became the first ruler of Britain's house of Hanover. The new king spoke no English and was viewed with contempt by many Tories, some of whom supported James Edward

Stuart's bid for the throne in the unsuccessful Jacobite rebellion of 1715. The Whigs, on the other hand, favored the Hanoverian succession and won the new king's loyalty. Because of the language barrier, George I relied heavily on his Whig ministers; and Robert Walpole, the head of the Whig party, emerged as the king's "prime minister" (the first official to be so called)—a position he continued to hold under George II, who succeeded his father in 1727. Toward the end of George II's reign, another able prime minister, William Pitt (the Elder), arose on the political scene. Pitt led the nation to victory over France in the Seven Years' War (called the French and Indian War in America), which resulted in Britain's acquisition of French Canada.

The Seven Years' War was still being fought when George III, grandson of George II, succeeded to the throne in 1760. The first British-born monarch of the house of Hanover, George III sought a more active role in governing the country, but his highhanded ways soon antagonized many. Scornful of the Whigs, George had trouble working with nearly everyone, partly because he suffered from a mental illness that grew worse over the years. During the first few decades of his 60-year reign, he led Britain into a series of political blunders that ultimately resulted in the loss of the American colonies.

In 1770, British soldiers attacked American colonists in the Boston Massacre, one of the events leading to the American Revolution.

Literature

The literary style that prevailed from the Restoration nearly to the end of the 18th century is called **neoclassicism** ("new classicism"). Neoclassical writers modeled their works on those of ancient Greece and Rome—especially those of Rome—emulating the supposed restraint, rationality, and dignity of classical writing. Neoclassicists stressed balance, order, logic, sophisticated wit, and emotional restraint, focusing on society and the human intellect and avoiding personal feelings. The neoclassical era in English literature is often divided into three periods: the Restoration (1660–1700), the Augustan Age (1700–1750), and the Age of Johnson (1750–1784).

During the Restoration, drama flourished in England's newly reopened theaters. Influenced by the French "comedy of manners," witty **Restoration comedies** portrayed and often satirized the artificial, sophisticated society centered in the Stuart court. Equally popular were **heroic dramas,** tragedies or tragicomedies featuring idealized heroes, dastardly villains, exciting action, and spectacular staging. Although many of the comedies were in prose, the heroic dramas were usually written in **heroic couplets** (iambic pentameter lines rhyming in pairs), the dominant verse form of the neoclassical period.

Both the Restoration comedies and the heroic dramas appealed primarily to the elite. Attracting a much wider audience was *The Pilgrim's Progress* (1678), a prose allegory by the Puritan John Bunyan, in which he extolled the virtues of faith, hope, and charity and condemned the shallow inhabitants of a worldly place called Vanity Fair. Another great Restoration prose work was the personal diary of Samuel Pepys, not published until 1825.

THE AGE OF REASON

Despite recurring warfare with France and the disaster of the American Revolution, the 18th century was a time of relative stability in Britain. The thought of the time was heavily influenced by the Enlightenment, a philosophical movement inspired by the works of such late-17th-century figures as John Locke, the political philosopher who had provided a logical justification for the Glorious Revolution, and Sir Isaac Newton, the scientist who had provided rational explanations of gravity and motion. Order, balance, logic, and reason were the paramount ideals of the day—so much so that the 18th century is often called the Age of Reason. The methods of scientific inquiry were applied to everything from farming to politics. Religion, the source of so much bloodshed a century earlier, became a far less emotional issue, although John Wesley did lead an evangelical revival that gave rise not only to the new Methodist groups but also to a revivalist movement within the Church of England.

Sir Isaac Newton is considered the father of modern science.

Women at a salon, about 1780

Many British citizens lived well during the 18th century, and a few lived sumptuously. Wealthy aristocrats built lavish country estates filled with furnishings of exquisite craftsmanship and surrounded by beautifully tended lawns and gardens. When Parliament was in session, members relocated to their London townhouses on the spacious new streets and squares that had been laid out after the Great Fire. Writers, artists, politicians, and other educated members of society gathered daily in London's coffeehouses to exchange ideas, conduct business, and gossip. Educated women sometimes held salons, or private gatherings, where they too could participate in the nation's intellectual life.

By producing larger animals, breeding experiments led to an improved diet, with more meat for more people.

Advances and Changes

The spirit of the Enlightenment led to many improvements in living conditions. Early in the century, Lady Mary Wortley Montagu, the wife of a British ambassador, brought back from Turkey the idea of inoculation to prevent smallpox, and by the end of the 1700s, Edward Jenner had developed an effective smallpox vaccination. Dramatic advances in agriculture helped improve Britain's food supply as wealthy landowners developed more productive methods of cultivating and harvesting crops. Breeding experiments resulted in larger animals: by the end of the century, the average weight of sheep and cattle had more than doubled. Unfortunately, putting these improvements into practice drove thousands of peasant farmers off the land. Increasingly, the open fields that had formerly been available to villagers for livestock grazing were being enclosed into large, separate tracts, held by the prosperous landowners who could then make use of the agricultural innovations. Although this enclosure of the land improved farming efficiency and output, it destroyed the traditional way of life of the English village.

Many of the villagers forced off the land sought jobs at the factories that had begun to dot the landscape. Britain, with its wealth of inventions, ample coal and iron, and ready colonial markets, was becoming a pioneer in the use of machines and steam power to manufacture goods that had formerly been made by hand. This Industrial Revolution changed the very fabric of British life. Sleepy towns in the north and west, near the sources of coal, iron, and water power, were transformed into grimy manufacturing centers in which workers—many of them women and children—labored long hours for low pay. By the end of the century, Britain had produced not only a solid commercial and industrial base but also a growing mass of restless, impoverished workers. The stability that had marked 18th-century life was beginning to crumble.

LASERLINKS

• *HISTORICAL LITERARY CONNECTION*

Literature

Neoclassicism reached its zenith in the Augustan Age—so named because its writers likened their society to that of Rome in the prosperous, stable reign of the emperor Augustus, when the finest Roman literature was produced. An alternative name for the period is the Age of Pope, because Alexander Pope dominated the literary world of the day with his epigrammatic and satiric verses. **Satire** also characterized the poetry and prose of Jonathan Swift and the essays of Joseph Addison and Richard Steele, which appeared in the early English magazines *The Tatler* and *The Spectator.*

The 18th century also saw the birth of **novels** as we know them. Early examples of these works of fiction include Daniel Defoe's episodic tale of adventure *Robinson Crusoe,* the sentimental stories of Samuel Richardson, and the comic works of Tobias Smollett and Henry Fielding.

The name "Age of Johnson" is a tribute to Samuel Johnson, Britain's most influential man of letters in the second half of the 18th century. Johnson was at the center of a circle that included his biographer James Boswell, the historian Edward Gibbon, the novelist and diarist Fanny Burney, and the comic dramatist Richard Brinsley Sheridan. Though Johnson and most of his associates affirmed neoclassical ideals, during this time poetry entered a transitional stage in which poets began writing simpler, freer lyrics on subjects close to the human heart. The reflective poetry of Oliver Goldsmith and Thomas Gray and the lyrical songs of Scotland's Robert Burns anticipate the first stirrings of romanticism at the very end of the century.

PART 1 *Views of Society*

In the second half of the 17th century, English writers sought to make sense of their world by observing human society and reflecting on both its positive and its negative attributes. In this part of Unit Three, some of the writers of the time offer their views on the restored monarchy, human nature, the proper behavior of children, and the role of women in society. As you read the selections, decide what these observations reveal about English society of this era.

PREVIEWING

NONFICTION

from The Diary of Samuel Pepys

Samuel Pepys (pēps)

PERSONAL CONNECTION

Many people exaggerate when relating stories about themselves. Think of people you know who exaggerate their own qualities and experiences. Which do they tend to exaggerate most—their good qualities or their bad ones? Do you know any people who always describe their experiences honestly, giving a balanced, candid portrayal of themselves and their activities?

HISTORICAL CONNECTION

Few descriptions of daily life in any period of history are as vivid as those found in *The Diary of Samuel Pepys*—a rare firsthand account of events that occurred over 300 years ago, long before the advent of telecommunications and eyewitness news reports. Begun in 1660, the historic year of the Restoration, the diary not only records the drama of public events but provides a candid portrayal of the social and domestic life of a middle-class Londoner. Although Samuel Pepys wrote his diary in shorthand to ensure the privacy of his thoughts, he was undoubtedly aware of its immense value to future generations, since he eventually bequeathed his library, including the diary, to Cambridge University.

Pepys had an intimate view of some of the most dramatic events of his time. As personal secretary to a British admiral, he was aboard the ship on which King Charles II returned to England after a long exile in France. As a prosperous Londoner, Pepys was able to enjoy the entertainments and luxuries that again became a feature of English social life after the overthrow of the Puritan Commonwealth. He also witnessed the Great Fire of London in 1666, which destroyed more than 13,000 homes, at least 80 churches, and most of London's government buildings.

WRITING CONNECTION

Reflect upon an incident that you have witnessed or experienced in the recent past, preferably one involving other people. Then write a brief diary entry describing the incident and the behavior of the people involved. Give a candid portrayal of what you observed and of what your own actions and emotions were at the time.

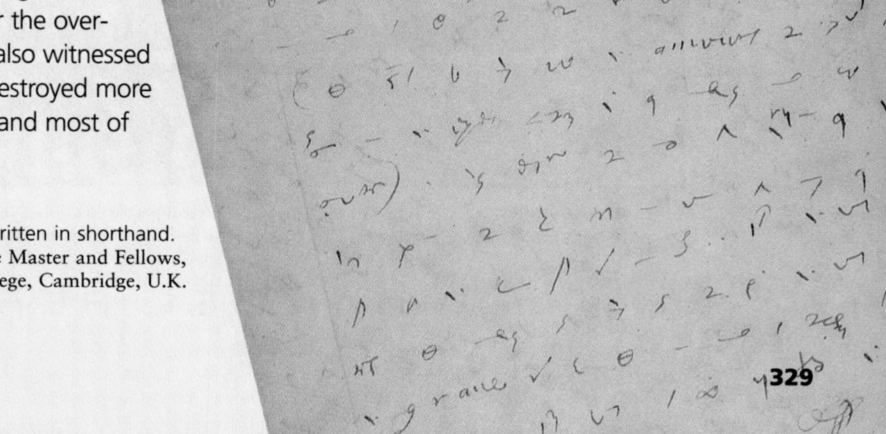

Pepys's diary, written in shorthand. Courtesy of The Master and Fellows, Magdalene College, Cambridge, U.K.

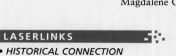

LASERLINKS
• *HISTORICAL CONNECTION*

from

THE DIARY OF Samuel Pepys

Samuel Pepys (1666), John Hayls. Oil on canvas. The Granger Collection, New York. *Frame:* The last page of Pepys's diary. Courtesy of The Master and Fellows, Magdalene College, Cambridge, U.K.

SAMUEL PEPYS

The Restoration of Charles II

1660

March 16. . . . To Westminster Hall, where I heard how the Parliament had this day dissolved themselves[1] and did pass very cheerfully through the Hall and the Speaker without his mace.[2] The whole Hall was joyful thereat, as well as themselves; and now they begin to talk loud of the King. . . .

May 22. . . . News brought that the two dukes are coming on board, which, by and by they did in a Dutch boat, the Duke of York in yellow trimming, the Duke of Gloucester in gray and red. My Lord[3] went in a boat to meet them, the captain, myself, and others standing at the entering port. . . .

May 23. . . . All the afternoon the King walking here and there, up and down (quite contrary to what I thought him to have been), very active and stirring. Upon the quarter-deck he fell in discourse of his escape from Worcester.[4] Where it made me ready to weep to hear the stories that he told of his difficulties that he had passed through. As his traveling four days and three nights on foot, every step up to his knees in dirt, with nothing but a green coat and a pair of country breeches on and a pair of country shoes, that made him so sore all over his feet that he could scarce stir. Yet he was forced to run away from a miller and other company that took them for rogues. His sitting at table at one place, where the master of the house, that had not seen him in eight years, did know him but kept it private; when at the same table there was one that had been of his own regiment at Worcester, could not know him but made him drink the King's health and said that the King was at least four fingers higher than he. Another place, he was by some servants of the house made to drink, that they might know him not to be a Roundhead,[5] which they swore he was. In another place, at his inn, the master of the house, as the King was standing with his hands upon the back of a chair by the fire-side, he kneeled down and kissed his hand privately, saying that he would not ask him who he was, but bid God bless him whither that he was going. . . .

The Coronation of the King

1661

April 23. . . . About 4 in the morning I rose. . . . And got to the Abbey,[6] . . . where with a great deal of patience I sat from past 4 till 11 before the King came in. And a pleasure it was to see the Abbey raised in the middle, all covered with red and a throne (that is a chair) and footstool on the top of it. And all the officers of all kinds, so much as the very fiddlers, in red vests. At last comes in the dean and prebends of Westminster with the bishops (many of them in cloth-of-gold copes[7]); and after them the nobility all in their parliament-robes, which was a most magnificent sight. Then

1. **Parliament . . . themselves:** This Parliament abolished the government established by Oliver Cromwell and restored the monarchy under Charles II, who had been living in exile in France.
2. **mace:** a staff used as a symbol of authority.
3. **my Lord:** Sir Edward Montagu, Pepys's employer, who was in command of the fleet that brought Charles II back to England.
4. **his escape from Worcester** (wo͝os′tər): Charles II, at the head of a Scottish army, had been defeated by Cromwell's troops at the Battle of Worcester in 1651. He had gone into hiding, journeyed secretively to the coast, and escaped to France.
5. **Roundhead:** a supporter of Cromwell's Puritan government.
6. **Abbey:** Westminster Abbey, the London church where monarchs are crowned.
7. **copes:** long robes worn by church officials while performing services or rites.

the duke and the King with a scepter (carried by my Lord of Sandwich) and sword and mond[8] before him, and the crown too.

The King in his robes, bare-headed, which was very fine. And after all had placed themselves—there was a sermon and the service. And then in the choir at the high altar he passed all the ceremonies of the coronation—which, to my very great grief, I and most in the Abbey could not see. The crown being put upon his head, a great shout begun. And he came forth to the throne and there passed more ceremonies: as, taking the oath and having things read to him by the bishop, and his lords (who put on their caps as soon as the King put on his crown) and bishops came and kneeled before him. And three times the king-at-arms[9] went to the three open places on the scaffold and proclaimed that if any one could show any reason why Ch. Stuart[10] should not be King of England, that now he should come and speak. And a general pardon also was read by the Lord Chancellor; and medals flung up and down by my Lord Cornwallis—of silver; but I could not come by any.

But so great a noise, that I could make but little of the music; and indeed, it was lost to everybody. . . . I went out a little while before the King had done all his ceremonies and went round the Abbey to Westminster Hall, all the way within rails, and 10,000 people, with the ground covered with blue cloth—and scaffolds all the way. Into the hall I got—where it was very fine with hangings and scaffolds, one upon another, full of brave ladies. And my wife in one little one on the right hand. Here I stayed walking up and down; and at last, upon one of the side-stalls, I stood and saw the King come in with all the persons (but the soldiers) that were yesterday in the cavalcade; and a most pleasant sight it was to see them in their several robes. And the King came in with his crown on and his scepter in his hand—under a canopy borne up by six silver staves, carried by barons of the Cinque Ports[11]—and little bells at every end.

And after a long time he got up to the farther end, and all set themselves down at their several tables—and that was also a rare sight. And the King's first course carried up by the Knights of the Bath. And many fine ceremonies there was of the heralds leading up people before him and bowing; and my Lord of Albemarle going to the kitchen and ate a bit of the first dish that was to go to the Kings's table. . . .

The Great London Fire

1666

September 2. (Lord's day) Some of our maids sitting up late last night to get things ready against our feast today, Jane called us up, about 3 in the morning, to tell us of a great fire they saw in the city. So I rose, and slipped on my nightgown and went to her window, and thought it to be on the back side of Mark Lane at the furthest; but being unused to such fires as followed, I thought it far enough off, and so went to bed again and to sleep. About 7 rose again to dress myself, and there looked out at the window and saw the fire not so much as it was, and further off. So to my closet to set things to rights after yesterday's cleaning. By and by Jane comes and tells me that she hears that above 300 houses have been burned down tonight by the fire we saw, and that it was now burning down all Fish Street by London Bridge. So I made myself ready presently, and walked to the Tower[12] and there got up upon one of the high places, Sir J. Robinson's little son

8. **mond:** a sphere with a cross on top, used as a symbol of royal power and justice.
9. **king-at-arms:** one of the chief heralds assigned to make official proclamations.
10. **Ch. Stuart:** Charles Stuart. (Charles II was one of the Stuart line of English monarchs.)
11. **Cinque** (sĭngk) **Ports:** a group of seaports of southeastern England that formed a defensive association.
12. **Tower:** the Tower of London, a group of buildings built as a fortress and later used as a royal residence and a prison for political offenders.

The Great Fire of London (1666), Dutch school. The Granger Collection, New York.

going up with me; and there I did see the houses at that end of the bridge all on fire, and an infinite great fire on this and the other side the end of the bridge—which, among other people, did trouble me for poor little Michell and our Sarah on the bridge.[13] So down, with my heart full of trouble, to the Lieutenant of the Tower, who tells me that it begun this morning in the King's baker's house in Pudding Lane, and that it hath burned down St. Magnus Church and most part of Fish Street already. So I down to the water-side and there got a boat and through bridge, and there saw a lamentable fire. Poor Michell's house, as far as the Old Swan, already burned that way and the fire running further, that in a very little time it got as far as the steelyard while I was there. Everybody endeavoring to remove their goods, and flinging into the river or bringing them into lighters that lay off. Poor people staying in their houses as long as till the very fire touched them, and then running into boats or clambering from one pair of stair by the water-side to another. And among other things, the poor pigeons I perceive were loath to leave their houses, but hovered about the windows and balconies till they were some of them burned, their wings, and fell down.

. . . At last met my Lord Mayor in Canning Street, like a man spent, with a handkerchief about his neck. To the King's message, he cried like a fainting woman, "Lord, what can I do? I am spent. People will not obey me. I have been pull[ing] down houses. But the fire overtakes us faster than we can do it." That he needed no more soldiers; and that for himself, he must go and refresh himself, having been up all night. So he left me, and I him, and walked home—seeing people all almost distracted and no manner of means used to quench the fire. The houses too, so very thick thereabouts, and full of matter for burning, as pitch and tar, in Thames Street—and warehouses of oil and wines and brandy and other things. . . .

13. **on the bridge:** in one of the houses on Old London Bridge. (London was so crowded that this bridge bore an entire superstructure of houses and shops.)

Having seen as much as I could now, I away to Whitehall[14] by appointment, and there walked to St. James's Park, and there met my wife and Creed and Wood and his wife and walked to my boat, and there upon the water again, and to the fire up and down, it still increasing and the wind great. So near the fire as we could for smoke; and all over the Thames,[15] with one's face in the wind you were almost burned with a shower of firedrops—this is very true—so as houses were burned by these drops and flakes of fire, three or four, nay five or six houses, one from another. When we could endure no more upon the water, we to a little alehouse on the bankside over against the Three Cranes, and there stayed till it was dark almost and saw the fire grow; and as it grew darker, appeared more and more, and in corners and upon steeples and between churches and houses, as far as we could see up the hill of the city, in a most horrid malicious bloody flame, not like the fine flame of an ordinary fire. Barbary and her husband away before us. We stayed till, it being darkish, we saw the fire as only one entire arch of fire from this to the other side the bridge, and in a bow up the hill, for an arch of above a mile long. It made me weep to see it. The churches, houses, and all on fire and flaming at once, and a horrid noise the flames made, and the cracking of houses at their ruin. So home with a sad heart, and there find everybody discoursing and lamenting the fire. . . .

September 3. About 4 o'clock in the morning, my Lady Batten sent me a cart to carry away all my money and plate and best things to Sir W. Rider's at Bethnal Green; which I did, riding myself in my nightgown in the cart; and Lord, to see how the streets and the highways are crowded with people, running and riding and getting of carts at any rate to fetch away thing[s]. . . .

September 8. . . . I met with many people undone, and more that have extraordinary great losses. People speaking their thoughts variously about the beginning of the fire and the rebuilding of the city. . . .

September 20. . . . In the afternoon out by coach, my wife with me (which we have not done several weeks now), through all the ruins to show her them, which frets her much—and is a sad sight indeed. . . .

September 25. . . . So home to bed—and all night still mightily troubled in my sleep with fire and houses pulling down.

Domestic Affairs

1663

January 13. So my poor wife rose by 5 o'clock in the morning, before day, and went to market and bought fowl and many other things for dinner—with which I was highly pleased. And the chine of beef was down also before 6 o'clock, and my own jack,[16] of which I was doubtful, doth carry it very well. Things being put in order and the cook come, I went to the office, where we sat till noon; and then broke up and I home—whither by and by comes Dr. Clerke and his lady—his sister and a she-cousin, and Mr. Pierce and his wife, which was all my guest[s].

I had for them, after oysters—at first course, a hash of rabbits and lamb, and a rare chine of beef—next, a great dish of roasted fowl, cost me about 30*s*, and a tart; and then fruit and cheese. My dinner was noble and enough. I had my house mighty clean and neat, my room below with a good fire in it—my dining-room above, and my chamber being made a withdrawing-chamber, and my wife's a good fire also. I find my new table very proper, and will hold nine or ten people well, but eight with great room. After dinner, the women to cards in my wife's chamber and the doctor [and] Mr. Pierce in mine, because the dining-room smokes unless I keep a good charcoal fire, which I was not then provided with. . . .

---

14. **Whitehall:** a wide road in London, the location of many government offices.

15. **Thames** (tĕmz): the principal river flowing through London.

16. **jack:** a device for roasting meat.

October 21. This evening after I came home, I begun to enter my wife in arithmetic, in order to her studying of the globes,[17] and she takes it very well—and I hope with great pleasure I shall bring her to understand many fine things.

1667

January 7. . . . To the duke's house and saw *Macbeth;* which though I saw it lately, yet appears a most excellent play in all respects, but especially in divertisement,[18] though it be a deep tragedy; which is a strange perfection in a tragedy, it being most proper here and suitable. . . .

May 26. (Lord's day) . . . After dinner, I by water alone to Westminster . . . toward the parish church. . . . I did entertain myself with my perspective glass[19] up and down the church, by which I had the great pleasure of seeing and gazing a great many very fine women; and what with that and sleeping, I passed away the time till sermon was done. . . .

May 27. . . . Stopped at the Bear Garden[20] stairs, there to see a prize fought; but the house so full, there was no getting in there; so forced to [go] through an alehouse into the pit where the bears are baited, and upon a stool did see them fight, which they did very furiously, a butcher and a waterman. The former had the better all along, till by and by the latter dropped his sword out of his hand, and the butcher, whether not seeing his sword dropped or I know not, but did give him a cut over the wrist, so as he was disabled to fight any longer. But Lord, to see how in a minute the whole stage was full of watermen to revenge the foul play, and the butchers to defend their fellow, though most blamed him; and there they all fell to it, to knocking down and cutting many of each side. It was pleasant to see, but that I stood in the pit and feared that in the tumult I might get some hurt. At last the rabble broke up, and so I away. . . .

1669

January 12. . . . This evening I observed my wife mighty dull; and I myself was not mighty fond, because of some hard words she did give me at noon, out of a jealousy at my being abroad this morning; when, God knows, it was upon the business of the office unexpectedly; but I to bed, not thinking but she would come after me; but waking by and by out of a slumber, which I usually fall into presently after my coming into the bed, I found she did not prepare to come to bed, but got fresh candles and more wood for her fire, it being mighty cold too. At this being troubled, I after a while prayed her to come to bed, all my people being gone to bed; so after an hour or two, she silent, and I now and then praying her to come to bed, she fell out into a fury, that I was a rogue and false to her. . . . At last, about 1 o'clock, she came to my side of the bed and drew my curtain open, and with the tongs, red hot at the ends, made as if she did design to pinch me with them; at which in dismay I rose up, and with a few words she laid them down and did by little and little, very sillily, let all the discourse fall; and about 2, but with much seeming difficulty, came to bed and there lay well all night. . . .

---

17. **the globes:** geography (the terrestrial globe) and astronomy (the celestial globe).
18. **divertisement** (dĭ-vûr′tĭs-mənt): diversion; amusement.
19. **perspective glass:** small telescope.
20. **Bear Garden:** an establishment in which bears were chained to a post and tormented by dogs as a form of entertainment. It was also the site of scheduled fights between men.

RESPONDING OPTIONS

FROM PERSONAL RESPONSE TO CRITICAL ANALYSIS

REFLECT

1. What are your impressions of Pepys? Record them in your notebook.

RETHINK

2. What do you think might have been Pepys's purpose in keeping his diary?

   Consider
   - the variety of events he describes
   - what types of people he chooses to describe
   - whether his observations are primarily objective or subjective

3. Does Pepys seem to you to give a candid portrayal of himself, or do you think he exaggerates his best qualities? Support your answer with details from the selection.

RELATE

4. Suppose that Pepys were living today and had witnessed a recent memorable event—for example, an inauguration, a meeting of world leaders, or a natural disaster, such as a hurricane, an earthquake, or a flood. What aspects of the event would he most likely highlight in his diary?

ANOTHER PATHWAY

Cooperative Learning

Working in small groups, make a list of the personality traits that you think Samuel Pepys possessed. Cite evidence from the selection to support the traits you identify. Then get together with the other groups. Develop a class character sketch of Pepys, and use it to decide what actor should play the part of Pepys in a movie about his life.

LITERARY CONCEPTS

A **diary** is a writer's personal day-to-day account of his or her experiences and impressions. Most diaries are private and not intended to be shared. Some, however, have been published because they are well written and provide useful perspectives on historical events or on the everyday life of particular eras. What unique insights into a public event might be found in a diary but not in a more formal account of the event?

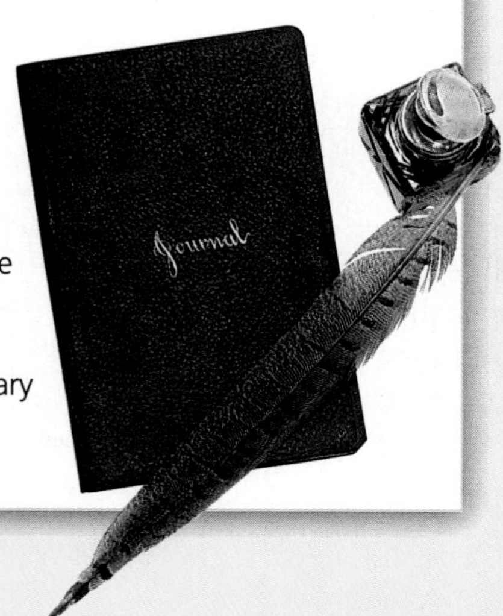

QUICKWRITES

1. Imagine Mrs. Pepys's reactions to the events of January 13, 1663, or January 12, 1669. Then compose a **diary entry** that she might have written on one of those days.
2. Write a **newspaper article** about either the coronation of Charles II or the Great Fire of London. Use facts from Pepys's diary, but present your account in the detached and objective style characteristic of a news report.

***PORTFOLIO** Save your writing. You may want to use it later as a springboard to a piece for your portfolio.*

ALTERNATIVE ACTIVITIES

1. With a partner, perform an **improvisation** of the conversation and events Pepys describes in the diary entry of January 12, 1669.
2. Design a **set** for a movie depiction of the Great Fire of London. Be sure to include specific details from Pepys's description.
3. Prepare a **time capsule** from Pepys's era. Construct or illustrate objects that reflect the events and culture of his time. Try to think of the kinds of things that Pepys would be likely to include.

CRITIC'S CORNER

The author Virginia Woolf once said that the "chief delight" of Pepys's diary might be its revelation of "those very weaknesses and idiosyncrasies which in our own case we would die rather than reveal." What do you think Woolf meant? What effect do Pepys's "weaknesses" have on you as you read the diary?

ACROSS THE CURRICULUM

History Investigate the events that led to the downfall of the Puritan Commonwealth and the restoration of the English monarchy under Charles II. What was the mood of the people? How was the Parliamentary government overthrown?

SAMUEL PEPYS

1633–1703

The son of a tailor, Samuel Pepys received a scholarship to Cambridge University, where he earned both a bachelor's and a master's degree. Pepys had an insatiable curiosity and strove to learn all that he could about every subject. His interests ranged from music and theater to science, history, and mathematics. It was undoubtedly this fascination with life that inspired him, at the age of 26, to begin keeping the diary in which he would eventually set down more than 1.2 million words. After faithfully making entries for nine years, he was forced to abandon his diary because of poor eyesight.

Shortly after starting the diary, Pepys became a clerk in the Royal Navy office, where he decided to prove his own worth by becoming a naval expert. His hard work and honesty, as well as his saving of the navy office during the Great Fire of London, led eventually to his appointment as secretary of the admiralty. In that capacity, he doubled the number of battleships and restored the previously weakened Royal Navy as a major sea power.

During his years of public service, Pepys enjoyed an active social life amid a circle of friends that included such notables as Sir Isaac Newton and John Dryden. However, Pepys also made enemies in his rise to power. In 1678, some of his adversaries tried unsuccessfully to ruin his reputation. They first tried to implicate Pepys in the murder of a London official, then falsely accused him of treason. Although Pepys was imprisoned briefly, the intervention of King Charles II kept him from further punishment, and in 1683 he returned once again to public service.

Pepys lived in retirement for the last 14 years of his life. He spent his time amassing a large personal library, collecting material for a history of the navy—which he unfortunately never completed—and corresponding with various artists and scholars. He died at the home of his friend and former servant, William Hewer.

PREVIEWING

POETRY

from An Essay on Man
Epigrams, *from* An Essay on Criticism

Alexander Pope

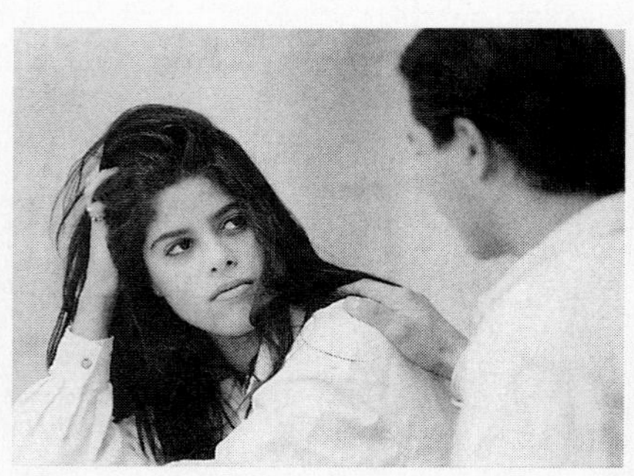

PERSONAL CONNECTION

Recall some recent social events in which you have participated—parties or dances, perhaps, or more informal get-togethers with friends. Jot down words that describe your attitude or behavior in each situation. Were you friendly or sympathetic on one occasion and hostile or insensitive on another? Did you act wisely one time and foolishly another? If so, how do you account for the contradictions in your behavior?

LITERARY CONNECTION

In England, the literary movement of neoclassicism began about 1660 and persisted throughout much of the 18th century. Neoclassical writers modeled their works on the literature of ancient Greece and Rome, which they believed contained universal truths and rules of form important in writing. Neoclassicists emphasized reason, common sense, good taste, simplicity, emotional restraint, order, and balance. In response to the contradictions and weaknesses of society, many writers concentrated on the exposure of human frailties; some gave moral instruction.

Two concepts important to neoclassicists were nature and wit. *Nature* generally referred to the universal principles of truth underlying the structure of the world. Nature was viewed as a source of order and harmony both in society and in individual behavior. The word *wit* had a number of meanings, ranging from "intellect" to "imagination" to "cleverness."

Alexander Pope was a neoclassical writer in both thought and style; the two verse essays *An Essay on Man* and *An Essay on Criticism* reflect many of the neoclassical ideals. In *An Essay on Criticism,* which Pope began writing when he was just 17, he made use of the **epigram,** a literary form that had originated in ancient Greece. The epigram developed from simple inscriptions on monuments into a literary genre—a short poem or saying characterized by conciseness, balance, clarity, and wit.

READING CONNECTION

Analyzing an Author's Ideas In his verse essays, Pope expresses opinions about the contradictions in human nature and experience. As you read these excerpts, analyze the author's ideas, using diagrams like the one shown here to record the contradictions that Pope presents in each poem.

An Essay on Man

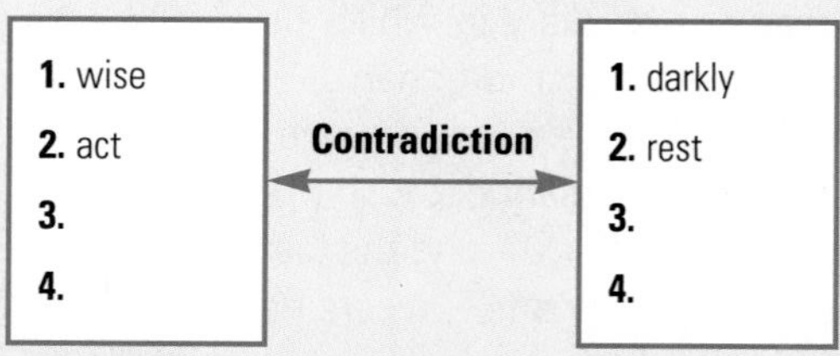

FROM AN ESSAY ON MAN

ALEXANDER POPE

Know then thyself, presume not God to scan;
The proper study of mankind is man.
Placed on this isthmus of a middle state,
A being darkly wise, and rudely great:
With too much knowledge for the Skeptic side,
With too much weakness for the Stoic's pride,
He hangs between; in doubt to act, or rest;
In doubt to deem himself a god, or beast;
In doubt his mind or body to prefer;
Born but to die, and reasoning but to err;
Alike in ignorance, his reason such,
Whether he thinks too little, or too much:
Chaos of thought and passion, all confused;
Still by himself abused, or disabused;
Created half to rise, and half to fall;
Great lord of all things, yet a prey to all;
Sole judge of truth, in endless error hurled:
The glory, jest, and riddle of the world!

3 **isthmus** (ĭs'məs): a narrow strip of land connecting larger bodies of land.
4 **rudely:** in a rough or clumsy way.
5 **Skeptic side:** the Greek philosophy of skepticism, whose adherents held that sure knowledge is unattainable.
6 **Stoic's** (stō'ĭks) **pride:** the haughty behavior of an adherent of the Greek philosophy of Stoicism, which taught that human beings should be indifferent to all pleasure and pain.
8 **deem:** judge; consider.

FROM PERSONAL RESPONSE *TO* CRITICAL ANALYSIS

REFLECT **1.** What is your reaction to Pope's style and manner of writing? Take a few moments to record your impressions in your notebook.

RETHINK **2.** Why do you think Pope says that human beings are continually "in doubt" (lines 7–9)? Use evidence from the poem to support your ideas.

3. Referring to the diagram you developed for the Reading Connection on page 338, summarize the understanding of human nature that you think Pope expresses in this poem.

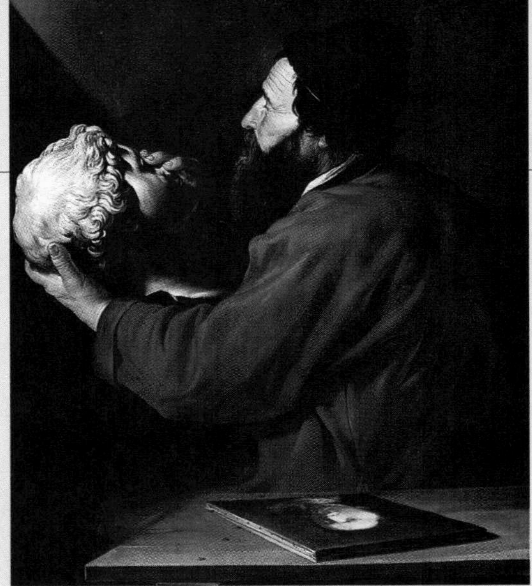

EPIGRAMS

from AN ESSAY ON CRITICISM

ALEXANDER POPE

The Sense of Touch (about 1615–1616), Jusepe de Ribera. Oil on canvas, 45⅝″ × 34¾″, The Norton Simon Foundation, Pasadena, California.

First follow Nature, and your judgment frame
By her just standard, which is still the same:
Unerring Nature, still divinely bright,
One clear, unchanged, and universal light,
Life, force, and beauty, must to all impart,
At once the source, and end, and test of art.

■

Of all the causes which conspire to blind
Man's erring judgment, and misguide the mind,
What the weak head with strongest bias rules,
Is pride, the never-failing vice of fools.

■

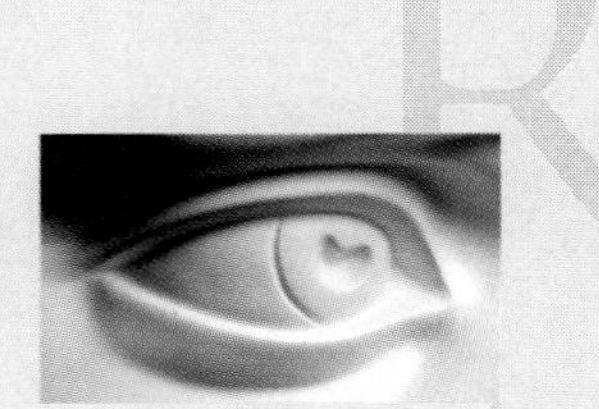

Pride, where wit fails, steps in to our defense,
And fills up all the mighty void of sense.
If once right reason drives that cloud away,
Truth breaks upon us with resistless day.
Trust not yourself; but your defects to know,
Make use of every friend—and every foe.

A little learning is a dangerous thing;
Drink deep, or taste not the Pierian spring:
There shallow draughts intoxicate the brain,
And drinking largely sobers us again.

■

12 void: emptiness; vacuum.

18 Pierian (pī-îr′ē-ən) **spring:** a spring sacred to the Muses and therefore considered a source of inspiration. (In Greek mythology, the Muses—nine daughters of Zeus and Memory—were the goddesses of all artistic and intellectual pursuits.)

19 draughts (dräfts): gulps or swallows.

In wit, as Nature, what affects our hearts
Is not th' exactness of peculiar parts;
'Tis not a lip, or eye, we beauty call,
But the joint force and full result of all.

22 **peculiar:** individual.

■

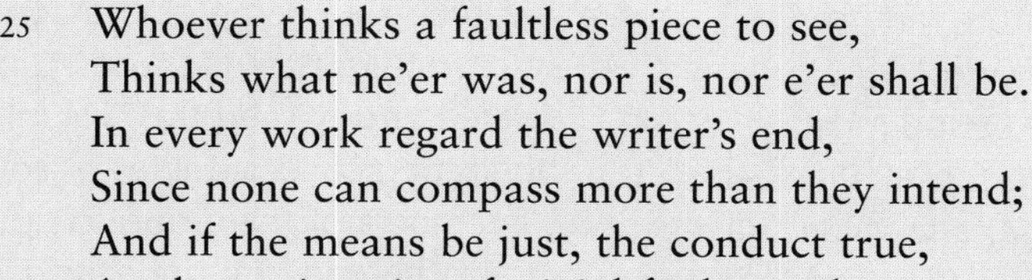

Whoever thinks a faultless piece to see,
Thinks what ne'er was, nor is, nor e'er shall be.
In every work regard the writer's end,
Since none can compass more than they intend;
And if the means be just, the conduct true,
Applause, in spite of trivial faults, is due.

27 **end:** goal or intention.

28 **compass:** accomplish.

■

True wit is Nature to advantage dressed,
What oft was thought, but ne'er so well expressed;
Something, whose truth convinced at sight we find,
That gives us back the image of our mind.

■

True ease in writing comes from art, not chance,
As those move easiest who have learned to dance.
'Tis not enough no harshness gives offense,
The sound must seem an echo to the sense.

■

Avoid extremes; and shun the fault of such,
Who still are pleased too little or too much.

■

Regard not then if wit be old or new,
But blame the false, and value still the true.

■

Good nature and good sense must ever join;
To err is human, to forgive, divine.

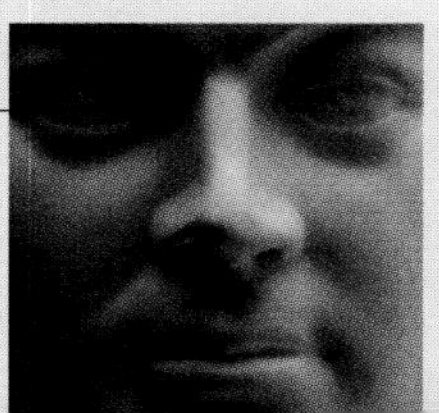

RESPONDING OPTIONS

FROM PERSONAL RESPONSE *TO* CRITICAL ANALYSIS

REFLECT 1. Write down two of your favorite epigrams from *An Essay on Criticism,* and share them with another student.

RETHINK 2. What seem to be some of Pope's main concerns in these epigrams?

Consider
- his references to nature, art, and wit
- what he says about pride
- his statements "the sound must seem an echo to the sense" (line 38) and "blame the false, and value still the true" (line 42)

3. What ideas does Pope convey through contradictory statements in these epigrams?

Consider
- his advice to "make use of every friend—and every foe" (line 16)
- his statement that "those move easiest who have learned to dance" (line 36)

RELATE 4. Compare the views of human nature and experience that Pope expresses in the excerpts from *An Essay on Man* and *An Essay on Criticism.*

ANOTHER PATHWAY

Cooperative Learning

Organize a game of charades based on your interpretations of these selections. With the class divided into two groups, volunteers in each group should try acting out lines or couplets for the other members of the group to guess. If any of the charades are not solved, they should be acted out again for the whole class.

LITERARY CONCEPTS

A **heroic couplet** consists of two rhyming lines written in **iambic pentameter**—a metrical pattern of five feet (units), each of which is made up of two syllables, the first unstressed and the second stressed. Pope's masterful use of the heroic couplet made it a popular verse form during the neoclassical period. The following lines from *An Essay on Criticism* are one of many possible examples from his work:

Ăvoíd ĕxtrémes; ănd shún thĕ fáult ŏf súch,
Whŏ stíll ăre pleásed tŏo líttlĕ ór tŏo múch.

Heroic couplets are especially well suited to writing epigrams. Choose one of the epigrams you wrote down for question 1 and note Pope's use of the heroic couplet in it. Read the epigram aloud and mark the unstressed and stressed syllables. Is the pattern of stresses strictly iambic, or are there some variations?

QUICKWRITES

1. Using ideas presented in the two selections, write a set of **maxims**—sayings that express guidelines for behavior—that could be titled "Pope's Rules for Life."
2. Convey your own message about human nature in an **epigram** consisting of one or more heroic couplets.
3. In an **autobiographical account,** describe a personal experience that illustrates one of the ideas expressed in these selections.

PORTFOLIO *Save your writing. You may want to use it later as a springboard to a piece for your portfolio.*

ALTERNATIVE ACTIVITIES

1. Create a **political cartoon** based on an idea expressed in either *An Essay on Man* or *An Essay on Criticism.*
2. Make a **list** of TV or movie characters who exhibit some of the contradictory qualities suggested in the excerpt from *An Essay on Man.*

ART CONNECTION

Look again at the reproduction of the painting *The Sense of Touch* on page 340, in which a man is shown holding a piece of sculpture. Notice that the man's eyes are shut and that a portrait is lying on the table. What do you think the artist is trying to convey? In what ways might the painting reflect some of the concerns Pope expresses in the epigrams?

LITERARY LINKS

How might the descriptions of events in *The Diary of Samuel Pepys* (page 330) be used to illustrate Pope's idea that a human being is "great lord of all things, yet a prey to all"?

ACROSS THE CURRICULUM

History/Philosophy In the history of Western thought, the 18th century is often referred to as the Age of Reason or the Enlightenment. Most of the philosophers of the time considered reason to be the only road to truth and were therefore particularly interested in the methods and laws of science and mathematics. Investigate some of the ideas of the Age of Reason, and share your findings with the class. Pay particular attention to ideas that you see reflected in Pope's work.

ALEXANDER POPE

1688–1744

From childhood, Alexander Pope was plagued by ill health. As a result of tuberculosis of the spine, he suffered constant physical pain and grew to a height of only four feet six inches. Although he was therefore severely limited in his physical activities, it is likely that these limitations may have contributed to his early devotion to reading and writing and to his ultimate success as a writer.

Pope was raised as a Roman Catholic during a period in England's history when only Protestants could obtain a university education or hold public office. For this reason, he was largely self-taught. He was an exceptional child, however, and his genius as a poet was recognized at an early age. Pope maintained that he began writing verse before the age of 12. By the time he was 17, his poems were being read and admired by many of England's best literary critics. Unlike most of his predecessors in the literary world, Pope was able to prosper with writing as his sole career. His prosperity was achieved primarily through his translations of Homer's *Iliad* and *Odyssey,* products of an enormous amount of work for which he was handsomely rewarded.

Pope's friends included the distinguished writers Richard Steele, Joseph Addison, Jonathan Swift, and John Gay. Along with Swift and Gay, he was a member of the Scriblerus Club, a group devoted to the writing of satires. Because of his sharp tongue, Pope was often the object of criticism by less talented writers, with several of whom he engaged in lifelong feuds.

OTHER WORKS *The Rape of the Lock,* "Epistle to Miss Blount"

LASERLINKS
• *HISTORICAL CONNECTION*

PREVIEWING

FABLE

The Acorn and the Pumpkin
The Value of Knowledge

Jean de La Fontaine (zhän′ də lə fôn-tān′)

PERSONAL CONNECTION

What stories have you read that teach a lesson or convey a meaningful message about life? Think about the sorts of messages these stories convey and how the stories instruct readers. Share your recollections with your classmates.

HISTORICAL CONNECTION

In France, the neoclassical movement began around 1600, roughly 60 years before the advent of English neoclassicism. Jean de La Fontaine and other 17th-century French writers, like their later English counterparts, placed great emphasis on reason, intellect, order, and simplicity in thought and actions. Many focused on the flaws in human nature, pointing out society's weaknesses and giving moral instruction.

Like the English writers of the late 1600s, La Fontaine was inspired by his reading of ancient authors; he borrowed ideas for many of his fables from the tales traditionally ascribed to Aesop, a Greek slave who lived around 600 B.C. In his masterful verse retellings of Aesop's fables, La Fontaine employed a natural, relaxed style that made the tales more appealing to readers, often using humor to reveal human shortcomings and to convey meaningful messages about life. The two poems you are about to read are from his *Fables,* a collection of over 200 moral tales that have entertained readers for centuries.

WRITING CONNECTION

Proverbs and sayings such as "Haste makes waste" and "A penny saved is a penny earned" have traditionally been passed down from generation to generation. In your notebook, create a chart like the one shown, recording some other familiar sayings that come to mind. Then put a check by those that you think offer the most meaningful messages about life.

✓	Familiar Sayings
	1.
	2.
	3.
	4.
	5.

The Acorn and the Pumpkin

Jean de La Fontaine

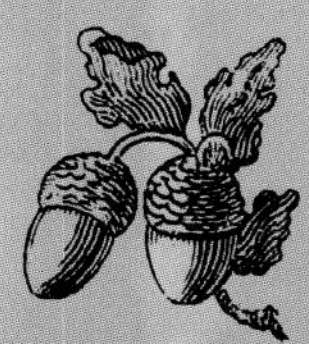

The Lord knows best what He's about.
No need to search for proof throughout
The universe. Look at the pumpkin.
It gives us all the proof we need. To wit:
The story of a village bumpkin—
Garo by name—who found one, gazed at it,
And wondered how so huge a fruit could be
Hung from so slight a stem: "It doesn't fit!
God's done it wrong! If He'd asked me,
He'd hang them from those oaks. Big fruit, big tree.
Too bad someone so smart and strong—
At least that's what the vicar's always saying
With all his preaching and his praying—
Didn't have me to help His work along!
I'd hang the acorn from this vine instead . . .
No bigger than my nail . . . It's like I said:
God's got things backwards. It's all wrong . . .
Well, after all that weighty thought I'd best
Take me a nap. We thinkers need our rest."
No sooner said than done. Beneath an oak
Our Garo laid his head in sweet repose.
Next moment, though, he painfully awoke:
An acorn, falling, hit him on the nose.
Rubbing his face, feeling his bruises,
He finds it still entangled in his beard.
"A bloody nose from this?" he muses.
"I must say, things aren't quite what they appeared.
My goodness, if this little nut
Had been a pumpkin or a squash, then what?
God knows His business after all, no question!
It's time I changed my tune!" With that suggestion,
Garo goes home, singing the praise
Of God and of His wondrous ways.

Translated by Norman R. Shapiro

4 to wit: that is to say (used to introduce an explanation or example).

26 muses: thinks to himself; ponders.

FROM PERSONAL RESPONSE *TO* CRITICAL ANALYSIS

REFLECT **1.** How did you react to the story of Garo? Record your impressions in your notebook.

RETHINK **2.** What is your opinion of the logic that Garo uses? Explain your response.

3. What message do you think the speaker is trying to convey? Support your opinion.

THE VALUE OF KNOWLEDGE

Jean de La Fontaine

Betwixt two burghers there arose
A row. One, quick of wit, was poor;
The other, rich, but much the boor.
The latter, twitting, clucks and crows:
Surely his bookish rival owes
The likes of him respect, and should—
If he, indeed, had any sense—
Pay homage to his opulence.
("Sense"? Hardly! Rather say "foolhardihood"!
For why revere mere wealth without
Real worth? It's meaningless.) "So, brother,"
Brashly the lout would taunt and flout
The other;
"Doubtless you think yourself my better; but
How often do you have your friends to dinner?
What good are books? Will reading fill their gut?
The wretches just grow poorer, thinner;
Up in their garrets, garbed all year the same;
No servants but their shadows! Fie! For shame!
The body politic has little use
For those who never buy. Wealth and excess—
Luxury, in a word—produce
The greatest deal of human happiness.
Our pleasures set the wheel a-turning:
Earning and spending; spending, earning.

1 burghers: citizens of a town.

3 boor (bo͝or): a rude, ill-mannered person.

4 twitting: mocking; ridiculing.

8 opulence: wealth.

10 revere: regard with great respect; honor.

12 flout: show contempt for; scorn.

18 garrets: rooms on the top floor of buildings; attics.

19 fie: an interjection used to express disapproval or distaste.

20 body politic: the people of a nation or state.

Each of us, Heaven knows, must play his part:
Spinners and seamsters, fancy beaus and belles
Who buy the finery the merchant sells;
And even you, who with your useless art,
Toady to patrons ever quick to pay."
Our bookman doesn't deign respond:
There's much too much that he might say.
But still, revenge is his, and far beyond
Mere satire's meager means. For war breaks out,
And Mars wreaks havoc round about.
Homeless, our vagabonds must beg their bread.
Scorned everywhere, the boor meets glare and glower;
Welcomed, the wit is plied with board and bed.

So ends their quarrel. Fools take heed: knowledge is power!

Translated by Norman R. Shapiro

27 beaus (bōz) **and belles** (bĕlz): fashionable men and women.

30 toady: act in a subservient way, using flattery to get what one wants.

31 Our bookman . . . respond: Our scholar thinks it beneath his dignity to reply.

35 Mars wreaks (rēks) **havoc:** war causes great destruction. (In Roman mythology, Mars was the god of war.)

38 plied: continually supplied.

Engraving by Gustave Doré.

RESPONDING OPTIONS

FROM PERSONAL RESPONSE *TO* CRITICAL ANALYSIS

REFLECT **1.** Were you satisfied with the way "The Value of Knowledge" ended? Share your thoughts with the class.

RETHINK **2.** Why do you think the wit is welcomed and the boor rejected at the end of the poem?
Consider
- the description of the boor
- the conditions after the outbreak of war
- what the speaker means by the statement that "knowledge is power"

3. Do you agree with any of the rich burgher's opinions? Explain your response.

4. What messages about human nature do you think the poem expresses?

RELATE **5.** According to the rich burgher, "Wealth and excess— / Luxury in a word—produce / The greatest deal of human happiness." Do you think most people would agree with him? Why or why not? What do you consider the greatest source of happiness?

6. In your opinion, which poem—"The Acorn and the Pumpkin" or "The Value of Knowledge"—proves its point more effectively? Support your opinion.

ANOTHER PATHWAY

Cooperative Learning

Work in a group to convert one of the poems into a storybook for young children. Keep the same message, but use only words that an elementary reader will be able to understand. Include illustrations, and design a cover. If you use a computer, experiment with larger fonts and spacing to make the pages appropriate for young readers.

LITERARY CONCEPTS

A **fable** is a brief tale, in either prose or verse, told to illustrate a moral or teach a lesson. Often, the moral of a fable appears in a distinct and memorable statement near the tale's beginning or end. Which statements in "The Acorn and the Pumpkin" and "The Value of Knowledge" do you think express the morals of the fables? Support your responses with evidence from the poems.

QUICKWRITES

1. As the poor burgher, write an **interior monologue** in which you respond to some of the rich burgher's taunts or criticisms about your position in life.
2. Rewrite the **ending** of "The Value of Knowledge." Change the actions and events depicted in lines 33–38, but keep the same conclusion: "Knowledge is power."
3. Compose an original **fable** to illustrate one of the sayings you recalled for the Writing Connection on page 344. Include the saying as the moral of your fable.

PORTFOLIO *Save your writing. You may want to use it later as a springboard to a piece for your portfolio.*

ALTERNATIVE ACTIVITIES

1. With several of your classmates, present a **debate** on the pros and cons of the lifestyles of the two characters in "The Value of Knowledge." Include visual aids, such as charts or diagrams, to help you illustrate your points. Ask the class to vote on which side presents the most logical and effective argument.
2. Create a **comic strip** based on the story of Garo in "The Acorn and the Pumpkin."
3. With a partner, perform a **dramatic reading** of one of the poems. Use appropriate gestures, movements, and props to enhance your presentation.

LITERARY LINKS

Compare La Fontaine's poetic fables with the epigrams from Pope's *An Essay on Criticism* (page 340). How do fables and epigrams differ in style? in tone? Can you think of any situations in which one of these forms of moral instruction might be preferable to the other? Explain your thoughts.

ACROSS THE CURRICULUM

Economics Investigate the life of a 17th-century French writer, artist, or musician. How did his or her economic situation compare with that of the wit in "The Value of Knowledge"? Would any of the boor's comments have been applicable to him or her?

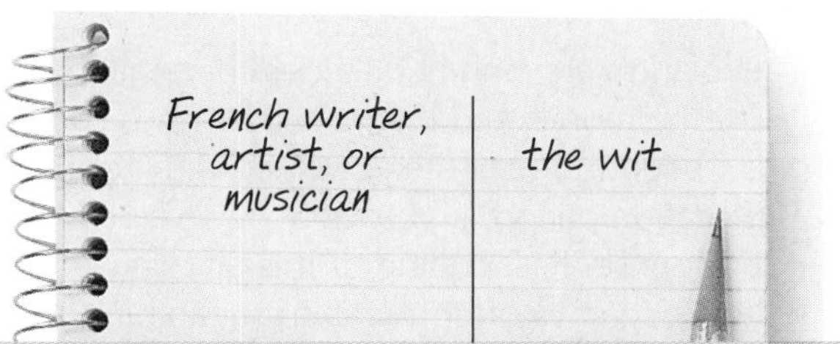

JEAN DE LA FONTAINE

1621–1695

As a young man, Jean de La Fontaine was rather restless, with no apparent goals in life and little inclination to work. Born into a middle-class family in the Champagne region of France, La Fontaine began studying for the priesthood at the age of 19 but after a very short time switched to the study of law. His father, an inspector of waterways and forests, arranged for his son to take over his position, one that La Fontaine was to occupy—with little interest or attention—for almost 20 years.

Although he read a great deal of poetry, especially the works of classical authors, La Fontaine did not begin writing original poems until he was in his mid-30s. In 1656, he moved to Paris, where for several years the financial support of a succession of wealthy patrons enabled him to devote his time to writing. He also frequented Parisian literary circles, becoming acquainted with such important French writers as Molière and Racine.

La Fontaine produced great quantities of prose and poetry, but his lasting fame depends chiefly on his *Fables*. These poetic tales are an important part of French culture and are enjoyed by people of all ages, from small schoolchildren to world-renowned scholars.

OTHER WORKS "The Crow and the Fox," "The Stag Who Saw Himself in the Water," "The Hen Who Laid Golden Eggs"

PREVIEWING

NONFICTION

from The Spectator

Joseph Addison

PERSONAL CONNECTION

Most major newspapers publish daily or weekly feature columns by noted journalists. Many of these columns are extremely popular. Think of some columnists whose articles you have read. What kinds of topics do they usually discuss? Are they concerned with everyday life, or do they focus on other issues? Discuss why these columnists enjoy such a wide readership.

CULTURAL/LITERARY CONNECTION

In the late 1600s, England's growing middle class became increasingly concerned with the morals and manners of English society. Popular thought had begun to react negatively to the moral excesses of the Restoration period, and society now valued moderation and good sense. Responding to this popular sentiment, certain writers began to offer moral instruction in their work, displaying a casual, good-natured approach to society's ills. Middle-class Londoners eagerly read the many new periodicals of the day and gathered in coffeehouses to share their thoughts on social, political, and philosophical issues.

Although hundreds of these periodicals were published before the 18th century, none enjoyed the popularity of those written by Joseph Addison and his friend Richard Steele in the early 1700s. Together, Addison and Steele created a form of writing that has remained popular for nearly three centuries—a predecessor of the articles in modern newsmagazines. In 1709, Steele began issuing *The Tatler* three times a week, and Addison was a frequent contributor to the periodical. Shortly after the demise of *The Tatler,* Addison and Steele jointly launched *The Spectator,* a periodical dealing with issues of everyday life. It was distributed six days a week for nearly two years.

Addison, who wrote most of the articles in *The Spectator,* frequently satirized the morals and manners of his day with refined and gentle humor. He and Steele were the first journalists to write deliberately for women as well as men and to publish letters from both male and female readers.

WRITING CONNECTION

If you were a newspaper columnist, what aspects of everyday life would you choose to write about? Think about topics that you find amusing, disturbing, or intriguing; then choose seven that you might like to discuss in a daily column. List the topics in your notebook, and as you read the following excerpts, compare them with those chosen by Joseph Addison.

Teresa Wiltz
Off the cuff

Ads get attention, all right, for stupidity, offensiveness

He gave in.

Mind you, kiddie porn was not the phrase that leapt to mind when I first viewed Calvin

breathing Bruce Weber).

There's the below-the-wais shot of a young man clad in a Gianni Versace jock strap with a football sandwiched between his thighs. The

from The SPECTATOR

JOSEPH ADDISON

PLAN *and* PURPOSE

It is with much satisfaction that I hear this great city inquiring day by day after these my papers, and receiving my morning lectures with a becoming seriousness and attention. My publisher tells me that there are already three thousand of them distributed every day. . . . Since I have raised to myself so great an audience, I shall spare no pains to make their instruction agreeable, and their diversion useful. For which reasons I shall endeavor to enliven morality with wit, and to temper wit with morality, that my readers may, if possible, both ways find their account in the speculation of the day. . . . The mind that lies fallow[1] but a single day, sprouts up in follies that are only to be killed by a constant and assiduous culture. It was said of Socrates, that he brought philosophy down from heaven to inhabit among men; and I shall be ambitious to have it said of me, that I have brought philosophy out of closets and libraries, schools and colleges, to dwell in clubs and assemblies, at tea tables and in coffeehouses.

I would therefore in a very particular manner recommend these my speculations to all well-regulated families, that set apart an hour in every morning for tea and bread and butter; and would earnestly advise them for their good to order this paper to be punctually served up and to be looked upon as a part of the tea equipage. . . .[2]

---

1. **lies fallow:** is uncultivated, like a field in which no crops have been sown.
2. **equipage:** equipment.

WORDS TO KNOW	
	temper (tĕm′pər) *v.* to make less intense; moderate
	speculation (spĕk′yə-lā′shən) *n.* a consideration of a subject
	assiduous (ə-sĭj′o͞o-əs) *adj.* steadily and carefully attentive

COUNTRY MANNERS

The first and most obvious reflections which arise in a man who changes the city for the country are upon the different manners of the people whom he meets with in those two different scenes of life. By manners I do not mean morals, but behavior and good breeding, as they show themselves in the town and in the country. . . .

Patience in a Punt (1792), Henry William Bunbury. Watercolor, 8″ × 12⅜″, The Paul Mellon Collection, Upperville, Virginia.

Rural politeness is very troublesome to a man of my temper, who generally takes the chair that is next me and walks first or last, in the front or in the rear, as chance directs. I have known my friend Sir Roger's dinner almost cold before the company could adjust the ceremonial and be prevailed upon to sit down. . . . Honest Will Wimble, who I should have thought had been altogether uninfected with ceremony, gives me abundance of trouble in this particular. Though he has been fishing all the morning, he will not help himself at dinner till I am served. When we are going out of the hall, he runs behind me; and last night, as we were walking in the fields, stopped short at a stile[3] till I came up to it, and upon my making signs to him to get over, told me, with a serious smile, that sure I believed they had no manners in the country. . . .

On COURTSHIP *and* MARRIAGE

Before marriage we cannot be too inquisitive and discerning in the faults of the person beloved, nor after it too dim-sighted and superficial. However perfect and accomplished the person appears to you at a distance, you will find many blemishes and imperfections in her humor,[4] upon a more intimate acquaintance, which you never discovered or perhaps suspected. Here therefore discretion and good nature are to show their strength; the first will hinder your thoughts from dwelling on what is disagreeable, the other will raise in you all the tenderness of compassion and humanity, and by degrees soften those very imperfections into beauties. . . .

---

3. **stile:** a set of steps for climbing over a fence.
4. **humor:** disposition; temperament.

WORDS TO KNOW

superficial (so͞o′pər-fĭsh′əl) *adj.* showing little attention to detail; shallow

LUGUBRIOUS PEOPLE

There are many persons, who, by a natural uncheerfulness of heart, mistaken notions of piety, or weakness of understanding, love to indulge this uncomfortable way of life, and give up themselves a prey to grief and melancholy. Superstitious fears, and groundless scruples, cut them off from the pleasures of conversation, and all those social entertainments which are not only innocent but laudable; as if mirth was made for reprobates, and cheerfulness of heart denied those who are the only persons that have a proper title to it.

Sombrius is one of these sons of sorrow. He thinks himself obliged in duty to be sad and disconsolate. He looks on a sudden fit of laughter, as a breach of his baptismal vow. An innocent jest startles him like blasphemy. Tell him of one who is advanced to a title of honor, he lifts up his hands and eyes; describe a public ceremony, he shakes his head. . . . All the little ornaments of life are pomps and vanities. Mirth is wanton,[5] and wit profane. He is scandalized at youth for being lively, and at childhood for being playful. He sits at a Christening, or a marriage feast, as at a funeral; sighs at the conclusion of a merry story; and grows devout when the rest of the company grow pleasant. . . .

ADVANTAGES *of* MARRIAGE

There is another accidental advantage in marriage, which has likewise fallen to my share; I mean having a multitude of children. These I cannot but regard as very great blessings. When I see my little troop before me, I rejoice in the additions which I have made to my species, to my country, and to my religion, in having produced such a number of reasonable creatures, citizens, and Christians. I am pleased to see myself thus perpetuated, and as there is no production comparable to that of a human creature, I am more proud of having been the occasion of ten such glorious productions, than if I had built a hundred pyramids at my own expense, or published as many volumes of the finest wit and learning. . . . ❖

5. **wanton:** immoral or impure.

WORDS TO KNOW

lugubrious (lo͝o-go͞o'brē-əs) *adj.* dismal or gloomy to an exaggerated degree
indulge (ĭn-dŭlj') *v.* to yield to; devote oneself to
scruple (skro͞o'pəl) *n.* an uneasiness about the rightness of an action
laudable (lô'də-bəl) *adj.* praiseworthy
reprobate (rĕp'rə-bāt') *n.* an immoral person; one without principles
disconsolate (dĭs-kŏn'sə-lĭt) *adj.* unable to be comforted; cheerless and gloomy

RESPONDING OPTIONS

FROM PERSONAL RESPONSE TO CRITICAL ANALYSIS

REFLECT 1. What is your overall impression of these excerpts from *The Spectator?* Write your thoughts in your notebook.

RETHINK 2. On the basis of these excerpts, how would you describe Addison?

Consider
- his goals, as stated under "Plan and Purpose"
- the kinds of topics he addresses
- his tone, or attitude toward the topics

3. What messages about everyday life do you think Addison hoped to convey to his readers?

Consider
- the lifestyles and manners he praises
- the types of behavior he criticizes

4. Considering the popularity of Addison's writing when it first appeared, what can you conclude about his audience? Give evidence to support your conclusions.

RELATE 5. Do you think any of the opinions expressed in the excerpts could be applied to contemporary life? Explain your answer and, if appropriate, support it with examples.

ANOTHER PATHWAY

Cooperative Learning

Plan and publish a class newspaper or newsmagazine in the style of *The Spectator.* Use some of the topics you listed for the Writing Connection on page 350, and add others that you think will appeal to readers your own age. Use a desktop-publishing program if one is available on a computer in your school.

LITERARY CONCEPTS

Through their periodicals, Addison and Steele increased the popularity of the informal essay. An **informal essay** presents an opinion on a subject, but not in a completely serious or formal tone. Characteristics of this type of essay include humor, a personal or confidential approach, a loose and sometimes rambling style, and often a surprising or unconventional topic. With a partner, look for these characteristics in the excerpts from *The Spectator.* Why do you think the informal essay was particularly suited to Addison's purpose?

QUICKWRITES

1. Write copy for a **handbill** or **advertisement** that would inspire 18th-century readers to subscribe to *The Spectator.*
2. In a **letter to the editor,** state your approval or disapproval of the ideas expressed in one of the excerpts. Give reasons for your opinions.
3. Write a **character sketch** of someone you know who exhibits qualities either praised or criticized by Addison.

PORTFOLIO *Save your writing. You may want to use it later as a springboard to a piece for your portfolio.*

ALTERNATIVE ACTIVITIES

Prepare a classroom **exhibit** of recent newspaper columns. Organize them according to topic, and identify those that most closely resemble the excerpts from *The Spectator* in subject or tone.

ACROSS THE CURRICULUM

Journalism Research the history of newspapers and periodicals prior to 1700. What were some of the earliest forms of journalistic publications, and what subjects did they deal with?

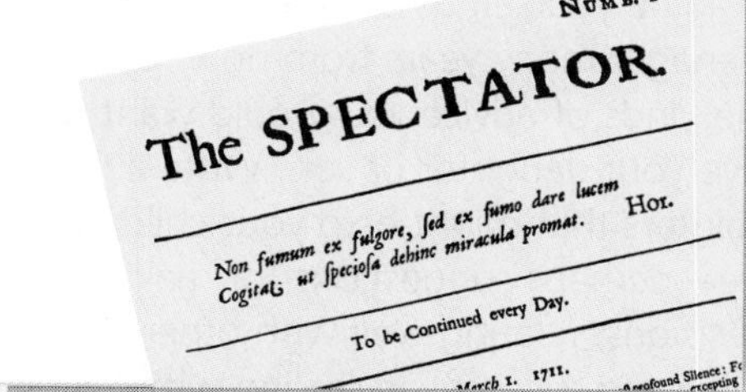

NUMB. 1

The SPECTATOR.

Non fumum ex fulgore, sed ex fumo dare lucem
Cogitat, ut speciosa dehinc miracula promat. HOR.

To be Continued every Day.

March 1. 1711.

LITERARY LINKS

Compare the excerpts from Addison's essays with Sir Francis Bacon's essay "Of Marriage and Single Life" (page 263). What similarities and differences in subject matter and tone do you see?

WORDS TO KNOW

EXERCISE A Write the letter of the word that is a synonym of the boldfaced word.

1. **temper:** (a) modify, (b) gratify, (c) explain
2. **assiduous:** (a) critical, (b) diligent, (c) flexible
3. **disconsolate:** (a) forlorn, (b) argumentative, (c) separated
4. **lugubrious:** (a) huge, (b) difficult, (c) mournful
5. **indulge:** (a) praise, (b) submit, (c) ruin

EXERCISE B For each phrase in the first column, write the letter of the rhyming phrase in the second column that has a similar meaning.

1. shame the villain	a. quadruple your **scruples**
2. distinct and admirable	b. humiliate the **reprobate**
3. a shallow administrator	c. a **speculation** on inflation
4. greatly increase your ethics	d. audible and **laudable**
5. a pondering about the economy	e. a **superficial** official

JOSEPH ADDISON

1672–1719

Joseph Addison's name is inseparably linked with that of his friend Richard Steele because of their collaboration on *The Tatler* and *The Spectator.* Addison and Steele's long friendship began when they were teenagers at the same London school. Both attended Oxford University and later became strong supporters of the liberal political party known as the Whigs.

At Oxford, Addison received a master's degree and distinguished himself as a master of Latin verse. He later served as a member of the British and Irish parliaments and held several important government posts, including that of secretary of state.

In his statement of the plan and purpose of *The Spectator,* Addison remarked that it was his ambition to bring "philosophy out of closets and libraries, schools and colleges, to dwell in clubs and assemblies, at tea tables and in coffeehouses." He was successful in his endeavor, partly because the light, humorous style of his writing made its moral content acceptable to 18th-century readers. By praising marriage, honesty, and simplicity while ridiculing hypocrisy and pride, Addison and Steele sought to improve the morals and manners of their audience; and by writing about the events and scenes of everyday life, they have given future generations a good idea of how people lived in their time.

PREVIEWING

NONFICTION

from Letters to His Son
Philip Stanhope, Lord Chesterfield

Letter to Her Daughter
Lady Mary Wortley Montagu

PERSONAL CONNECTION

Most parents feel that they have a responsibility to advise their children and attempt to do so in various ways. Think about your own response to advice from parents or older family members. What is the most important or helpful advice that a parent can give a child?

LITERARY CONNECTION

The popularity of letter writing during the 1700s resulted in collections of correspondence that have become an important part of English literary tradition. Among the most notable are the letters written by Philip Stanhope, Lord Chesterfield, to his son and godson and those written by Lady Mary Wortley Montagu to her husband, sister, and daughter. Because these letters were personal and meant to be read only by their recipients, they offer unique perspectives on 18th-century society.

Chesterfield wrote letters nearly every day for more than 30 years, most of them dealing with matters of etiquette and social awareness. An able statesman, he was known as a man of wit and elegance. The published correspondence of Montagu, who traveled widely and was a leading figure in society, consists of almost 900 letters. In them she reveals her views on society both in England and abroad, focusing particularly on the lives and education of women. Also the author of poems and essays, Montagu was encouraged in her pursuits by her friend Mary Astell, who argued for a woman's right to a challenging and balanced education. In their correspondence to their children, both Chesterfield and Montagu impart extensive parental advice as well as their personal views on the characteristics and imperfections of society.

WRITING CONNECTION

Imagine yourself as the parent of a teenager many years from now. Consider the kinds of advice you would want to give your daughter or son. Write a list of pointers that might help your child in life—perhaps suggestions for making decisions, relating well with other people, achieving success, or dealing with problems. Then, as you read these letters, compare your advice with that offered by Chesterfield and Montagu.

George Morland (about 1785–1810), Thomas Rowlandson. British Museum, London, Bridgeman/Art Resource.

from Letters *to His* Son

PHILIP STANHOPE,
LORD CHESTERFIELD

SPA, JULY 25, 1741

Dear Boy,

I have often told you in my former letters (and it is most certainly true) that the strictest and most scrupulous honor and virtue can alone make you esteemed and valued by mankind; that parts and learning can alone make you admired and celebrated by them; but that the possession of lesser talents was most absolutely necessary towards making you liked, beloved, and sought after in private life. Of these lesser talents, good-breeding is the principal and most necessary one, not only as it is very important in itself; but as it adds great luster to the more solid advantages both of the heart and the mind.

I have often touched upon good-breeding to you before; so that this letter shall be upon the next necessary qualification to it, which is a genteel, easy manner and carriage, wholly free from those odd tricks, ill habits, and awkwardnesses, which even very many worthy and sensible people have in their behavior. However trifling a genteel manner may sound, it is of very great consequence towards pleasing in private life, especially the women; which, one time or other, you will think worth pleasing; and I have known many a man, from his awkwardness, give people such a dislike of him at first, that all his merit could not get the better of it afterwards. Whereas a genteel manner prepossesses people in your favor, bends them towards you, and makes them wish to like you.

WORDS TO KNOW

scrupulous (skrōō'pyə-ləs) *adj.* showing great strictness and care, especially in matters of right and wrong

prepossess (prē'pə-zĕs') *v.* to influence beforehand; prejudice

Awkwardness can proceed but from two causes; either from not having kept good company, or from not having attended to it. As for your keeping good company, I will take care of that; do you take care to observe their ways and manners, and to form your own upon them. Attention is absolutely necessary for this, as indeed it is for everything else; and a man without attention is not fit to live in the world. When an awkward fellow first comes into a room, it is highly probable that his sword gets between his legs, and throws him down, or makes him stumble at least; when he has recovered this accident, he goes and places himself in the very place of the whole room where he should not; there he soon lets his hat fall down; and, taking it up again, throws down his cane; in recovering his cane, his hat falls a second time; so that he is a quarter of an hour before he is in order again. If he drinks tea or coffee, he certainly scalds his mouth, and lets either the cup or the saucer fall, and spills the tea or coffee in his breeches. At dinner, his awkwardness distinguishes itself particularly, as he has more to do: there he holds his knife, fork, and spoon differently from other people; eats with his knife to the great danger of his mouth, picks his teeth with his fork, and puts his spoon, which has been in his throat twenty times, into the dishes again. If he is to carve, he can never hit the joint; but, in his vain efforts to cut through the bone, scatters the sauce in everybody's face. He generally daubs himself with soup and grease, though his napkin is commonly stuck through a button-hole, and tickles his chin. When he drinks, he infallibly coughs in his glass, and besprinkles the company. Besides all this, he has strange tricks and gestures; such as snuffing up his nose, making faces, putting his fingers in his nose, or blowing it and looking afterwards in his handkerchief, so as to make the company sick. His hands are troublesome to him, when he has not something in them, and he does not know where to put them; but they are in perpetual motion between his bosom and his breeches: he does not wear his clothes, and in short does nothing, like other people. All this, I own, is not in any degree criminal; but it is highly disagreeable and ridiculous in company, and ought most carefully to be avoided by whoever desires to please.

AWKWARDNESS CAN PROCEED BUT FROM TWO CAUSES; EITHER FROM NOT HAVING KEPT GOOD COMPANY, OR FROM NOT HAVING ATTENDED TO IT.

From this account of what you should not do, you may easily judge what you should do; and a due attention to the manners of people of fashion, and who have seen the world, will make it habitual and familiar to you.

There is, likewise, an awkwardness of expression and words, most carefully to be avoided; such as false English, bad pronunciation, old sayings, and common proverbs; which are so many proofs of having kept bad and low company. For example: if, instead of saying that tastes are different, and that every man has his own peculiar one, you should let off a proverb, and say, That what is one man's meat is another man's poison; or else, Every one as they like, as the good man said when he kissed his cow; everybody would be persuaded that you had never kept company with anybody above footmen and housemaids.

Attention will do all this; and without attention nothing is to be done: want of attention, which is really want of thought, is either folly or madness. You should not only have attention to everything, but a quickness of attention, so as to observe, at once, all the people in the room; their motions, their looks, and their words; and yet without staring at them, and seeming to be an observer. This quick and unobserved observation is of infinite advantage in life, and is to be acquired with care; and, on the contrary, what is called absence, which is a thoughtlessness, and want of attention about what is doing, makes a man so like either a fool or a madman, that, for my part, I see no real difference. A fool never had thought; a madman has lost it; and an absent man is, for the time, without it.

Adieu! Direct your next to me, *chez Monsieur Chabert, Banquier, à Paris;*[1] and take care that I find the improvements I expect at my return.

London, September 5, 1748

Dear Boy,

. . . As women are a considerable, or at least a pretty numerous part, of company; and as their suffrages[2] go a great way towards establishing a man's character in the fashionable part of the world (which is of great importance to the fortune and figure he proposes to make in it), it is necessary to please them. I will therefore, upon this subject, let you into certain *arcana,*[3] that will be very useful for you to know, but which you must, with the utmost care, conceal, and never seem to know.

Women, then, are only children of a larger growth; they have an entertaining tattle and sometimes wit; but for solid, reasoning good-sense, I never in my life knew one that had it, or who reasoned or acted consequentially[4] for four-and-twenty hours together. Some little passion or humor always breaks in upon their best resolutions. Their beauty neglected or controverted, their age increased, or their supposed understandings depreciated, instantly kindles their little passions, and overturns any system of consequential conduct, that in their most reasonable moments they might have been capable of forming. A man of sense only trifles with them, plays with them, humors and flatters them, as he does with a sprightly, forward child; but he neither consults them about, nor trusts them with, serious matters; though he often makes them believe that he does both; which is the thing in the world that they are proud of; for they love mightily to be dabbling in business (which by the way, they always spoil); and being justly distrustful, that men in general look upon them in a trifling light, they almost adore that man, who talks more seriously to them, and who seems to consult and trust them; I say, who seems, for weak men really do, but wise ones only seem to do it. No flattery is either too high or too low for them. They will greedily swallow the highest, and gratefully accept of the lowest; and you may safely flatter any woman, from her understanding down to the exquisite taste of her fan.

Women who are either indisputably beautiful, or indisputably ugly, are best flattered upon the score of their understandings; but those who are in a state of mediocrity, are best flattered upon their beauty, or at least their graces; for every woman who is not absolutely ugly, thinks herself handsome; but, not hearing often that she is so, is the more grateful and the more obliged to the few who tell her so; whereas a decided and conscious beauty looks upon every tribute paid to her beauty, only as her due; but wants to shine, and to be considered on the side of her understanding; and a woman who is ugly enough to know that she is so, knows that she has nothing left for it but her understanding, which is consequently (and probably in more senses than one) her weak side.

But these are secrets which you must keep inviolably, if you would not, like Orpheus, be torn

1. ***chez*** (shā) **. . . *à Paris*** (ä pä-rē′) *French:* at the house of . . . in Paris. (Chesterfield is giving the address where he can be reached.)
2. **suffrages** (sŭf′rĭ-jĭz): signs of approval.
3. ***arcana*** (är-kā′nə) *Latin:* secrets; mysteries.
4. **consequentially:** in a logically consistent manner.

WORDS TO KNOW

controverted (kŏn′trə-vûr′tĭd) *adj.* disputed; denied **controvert** *v.*
inviolably (ĭn-vī′ə-lə-blē) *adv.* with absolute security

to pieces by the whole sex;[5] on the contrary, a man who thinks of living in the great world, must be gallant, polite, and attentive to please the women. They have, from the weakness of men, more or less influence in all Courts; they absolutely stamp every man's character in the *beau monde*,[6] and make it either current, or cry it down, and stop it in payments. It is, therefore, absolutely necessary to manage, please, and flatter them; and never to discover the least marks of contempt, which is what they never forgive; but in this they are not singular, for it is the same with men; who will much sooner forgive an injustice than an insult. Every man is not ambitious, or covetous, or passionate; but every man has pride enough in his composition to feel and resent the least slight and contempt. Remember, therefore, most carefully to conceal your contempt, however just, wherever you would not make an implacable enemy. Men are much more unwilling to have their weaknesses and their imperfections known, than their crimes; and, if you hint to a man that you think him silly, ignorant, or even ill-bred or awkward, he will hate you more, and longer, than if you tell him plainly that you think him a rogue. Never yield to that temptation, which to most young men is very strong, of exposing other people's weaknesses and infirmities, for the sake either of diverting the company, or of showing your own superiority. You may get the laugh on your side by it, for the present; but you will make enemies by it for ever; and even those who laugh with you then will, upon reflection, fear, and consequently hate you; besides that, it is ill-natured, and a good heart desires rather to conceal than expose other people's weaknesses or misfortunes. If you have wit, use it to please, and not to hurt: you may shine like the sun in the temperate zones, without scorching. Here it is wished for: under the line[7] it is dreaded.

These are some of the hints which my long experience in the great world enables me to give you; and which, if you attend to them, may prove useful to you in your journey through it. I wish it may be a prosperous one; at least, I am sure that it must be your own fault if it is not.

Make my compliments to Mr. Harte, who, I am very sorry to hear, is not well. I hope by this time he is recovered. ❖

Adieu!

5. **like Orpheus** (ôr′fē-əs) **. . . sex:** a reference to a Greek myth in which the musician Orpheus is torn limb from limb by maenads—women frenzied under the influence of the god Dionysus.

6. ***beau monde*** (bō môɴd) *French:* the fashionable world; high society.

7. **line:** equator.

FROM PERSONAL RESPONSE *TO* CRITICAL ANALYSIS

REFLECT **1.** What is your reaction to Chesterfield after reading his letters? Record your opinions in your notebook.

RETHINK **2.** What attitudes and behavior seem to be most important to Chesterfield?

Consider
- the kind of advice he offers and the examples he gives
- what he hopes to accomplish
- his views of men and women

3. How would you describe Chesterfield's relationship with his son? Support your ideas with evidence from the letters.

WORDS TO KNOW

implacable (ĭm-plăk′ə-bəl) *adj.* impossible to appease; unforgiving
diverting (dĭ-vûr′tĭng) *n.* entertaining; amusing **divert** *v.*

Letter to Her Daughter

Lady Mary Wortley Montagu

January 28, 1753

Dear Child,

You have given me a great deal of satisfaction by your account of your eldest daughter. I am particularly pleased to hear she is a good arithmetician; it is the best proof of understanding. The knowledge of numbers is one of the chief distinctions between us and brutes. If there is anything in blood you may reasonably expect your children should be endowed with an uncommon share of good sense. Mr. Wortley's family and mine have both produced some of the greatest men that have been born in England. I mean Admiral Sandwich, and my great-grandfather who was distinguished by the name of Wise William. I have heard Lord Bute's father mentioned as an extraordinary genius (though he had not many opportunities of showing it), and his uncle the present Duke of Argyle has one of the best heads I ever knew.

Lady Mary Wortley Montagu (about 1725), Jonathan Richardson. Private collection, courtesy of the Earl of Harrowby.

I will therefore speak to you as supposing Lady Mary not only capable but desirous of learning. In that case, by all means let her be indulged in it. You will tell me, I did not make it a part of your education. Your prospect was very different from hers, as you had no defect either in mind or person to hinder, and much in your circumstances to attract, the highest offers. It seemed your business to learn how to live in the world, as it is hers to know how to be easy out of it. It is the common error of builders and parents to follow some plan they think beautiful (and perhaps is so) without considering that nothing is beautiful that is misplaced. Hence we see so many edifices raised that the raisers can never inhabit, being too large for their fortunes. Vistas are laid open over barren heaths, and apartments contrived for a coolness very agreeable in Italy but killing in the north of Britain. Thus every woman endeavors to breed her daughter a fine lady, qualifying her for a station in which she will never appear, and at the same time incapacitating her for that retirement to which she is destined. Learning (if she has a real taste for it) will not only make her contented but happy in it. No entertainment is so cheap as reading, nor any pleasure so lasting. She will not want new fashions nor regret the loss of expensive diversions or variety of company if she can be amused with an author in her closet. To render this amusement extensive, she should be permitted to learn the languages. I have heard it lamented that boys lose so many years in mere learning of words. This is no objection to a girl, whose time is not so precious. She cannot advance herself in any profession, and has therefore more hours to spare; and as you say her memory is good she will be very agreeably employed this way.

There are two cautions to be given on this subject: first, not to think herself learned when she can read Latin or even Greek. Languages are more properly to be called vehicles of learning than learning itself, as may be observed in many schoolmasters, who though perhaps critics in grammar are the most ignorant fellows upon earth. True knowledge consists in knowing things, not words. I would wish her no further a linguist than to enable her to read books in their originals, that are often corrupted and always injured by translations. Two hours application every morning will bring this about much sooner

WORDS TO KNOW

edifice (ĕd′ə-fĭs) *n.* a building, especially a large and impressive one
contrive (kən-trīv′) *v.* to plan cleverly; devise

than you can imagine, and she will have leisure enough beside to run over the English poetry, which is a more important part of a woman's education than it is generally supposed. Many a young damsel has been ruined by a fine copy of verses, which she would have laughed at if she had known it had been stolen from Mr. Waller.[1] I remember when I was a girl I saved one of my companions from destruction, who communicated to me an epistle[2] she was quite charmed with. As she had a natural good taste she observed the lines were not so smooth as Prior's or Pope's,[3] but had more thought and spirit than any of theirs. She was wonderfully delighted with such a demonstration of her lover's sense and passion, and not a little pleased with her own charms, that had force enough to inspire such elegancies. In the midst of this triumph I showed her they were taken from Randolph's *Poems,* and the unfortunate transcriber was dismissed with the scorn he deserved. To say truth, the poor plagiary[4] was very unlucky to fall into my hands; that author, being no longer in fashion, would have escaped anyone of less universal reading than myself. You should encourage your daughter to talk over with you what she reads, and as you are very capable of distinguishing, take care she does not mistake pert folly for wit and humor, or rhyme for poetry, which are the common errors of young people, and have a train of ill consequences.

Christie's Images.

The second caution to be given her (and which is most absolutely necessary) is to conceal whatever learning she attains, with as much solicitude as she would hide crookedness or lameness. The parade of it can only serve to draw on her the envy, and consequently the most inveterate hatred of all he and she fools, which will certainly be at least three parts in four of all her acquaintance. The use of knowledge in our sex (beside the amusement of solitude) is to moderate the passions and learn to be contented with a small expense, which are the certain effects of a studious life and, it may be, preferable even to that fame which men have engrossed to themselves and will not suffer us to share. You will tell me I have not observed this rule myself, but you are mistaken; it is only inevitable accident that has given me any reputation that way. I have always carefully avoided it, and ever thought it a misfortune.

The explanation of this paragraph would occasion a long digression, which I will not trouble you with, it being my present design only to say what I think useful for the instruction of my granddaughter, which I have much at heart. If she has the same inclination (I should say passion) for learning that I was born with, history, geography, and philosophy will furnish her with materials to pass away cheerfully a longer life than is allotted to mortals. I believe there are few heads capable of making Sir Isaac Newton's calculations, but the result of them is not difficult to be understood by a moderate capacity. Do not fear this should make her affect the character of Lady———, or Lady————, or Mrs.———. Those women are ridiculous not because they have learning but because they have

1. **Mr. Waller:** the English poet Edmund Waller.
2. **epistle:** letter.
3. **as Prior's or Pope's:** as those of Matthew Prior or Alexander Pope, both English poets.
4. **plagiary:** plagiarist—one who copies someone else's writing and presents it as his or her own.

WORDS TO KNOW

inveterate (ĭn-vĕt′ər-ĭt) *adj.* firmly established and deep-rooted

it not. One thinks herself a complete historian after reading Echard's *Roman History,*[5] another a profound philosopher having got by heart some of Pope's unintelligible essays, and a third an able divine[6] on the strength of Whitefield's sermons.[7] Thus you hear them screaming politics and controversy. It is a saying of Thucydides:[8] Ignorance is bold, and knowledge reserved. Indeed it is impossible to be far advanced in it without being more humbled by a conviction of human ignorance than elated by learning.

At the same time I recommend books I neither exclude work nor drawing. I think it as scandalous for a woman not to know how to use a needle, as for a man not to know how to use a sword. I was once extreme fond of my pencil, and it was a great mortification to me when my father turned off my master,[9] having made a considerable progress for the short time I learned. My over-eagerness in the pursuit of it had brought a weakness on my eyes that made it necessary to leave it off, and all the advantage I got was the improvement of my hand. I see by hers that practice will make her a ready writer. She may attain it by serving you for a secretary when your health or affairs make it troublesome to you to write yourself, and custom will make it an agreeable amusement to her. She cannot have too many for that station in life which will probably be her fate. The ultimate end of your education was to make you a good wife (and I have the comfort to hear that you are one); hers ought to be, to make her happy in a virgin state. I will not say it is happier, but it is undoubtedly safer than any marriage. In a lottery where there is (at the lowest computation) ten thousand blanks to a prize it is the most prudent choice not to venture.

I have always been so thoroughly persuaded of this truth that notwithstanding the flattering views I had for you (as I never intended you a sacrifice to my vanity) I thought I owed you the justice to lay before you all the hazards attending matrimony. You may recollect I did so in the strongest manner. Perhaps you may have more success in the instructing your daughter. She has so much company at home she will not need seeking it abroad, and will more readily take the notions you think fit to give her. As you were alone in my family, it would have been thought a great cruelty to suffer you no companions of your own age, especially having so many near relations, and I do not wonder their opinions influenced yours. I was not sorry to see you not determined on a single life, knowing it was not your father's intention, and contented myself with endeavoring to make your home so easy that you might not be in haste to leave it.

I am afraid you will think this a very long and insignificant letter. I hope the kindness of the design will excuse it, being willing to give you every proof in my power that I am your most affectionate mother,

M. Wortley

---

5. **Echard's *Roman History:*** a book by Lawrence Echard, an English historian.
6. **able divine:** knowledgeable religious scholar.
7. **Whitefield's sermons:** the printed sermons of George Whitefield, a famous English preacher.
8. **Thucydides** (thōō-sĭd′ĭ-dēz′): an ancient Greek historian.
9. **turned off my master:** discharged my art instructor.

WORDS TO KNOW **mortification** (môr′tə-fĭ-kā′shən) *n.* extreme embarrassment; humiliation

from Some Reflections upon Marriage

MARY ASTELL

According to the rate that young women are educated, according to the way their time is spent, they are destined to folly and impertinence, to say no worse, and, which is yet more inhuman, they are blamed for that ill conduct they are not suffered to avoid, and reproached for those faults they are in a manner forced into; so that if Heaven has bestowed any sense on them, no other use is made of it, than to leave them without excuse. So much, and no more, of the world is shown them, than serves to weaken and corrupt their minds, to give them wrong notions, and busy them in mean pursuits; to disturb, not to regulate their passions; to make them timorous and dependent, and, in a word, fit for nothing else but to act a farce for the diversion of their governors.

RESPONDING OPTIONS

FROM PERSONAL RESPONSE *TO* CRITICAL ANALYSIS

REFLECT

1. Does Montagu strike you as an appealing person? Jot down some of your impressions in your notebook.

RETHINK

2. What is your opinion of Montagu's views on education and marriage for women? Explain your reaction.
3. What factors do you think might have influenced Montagu to give this kind of advice about the raising of her granddaughter?
4. How do you think Montagu's granddaughter might have felt about her grandmother's advice?

RELATE

5. With a partner, role-play a conversation in which Montagu and Chesterfield discuss the role of women in society.
6. Reread the Insight excerpt from Mary Astell's *Some Reflections upon Marriage.* In what ways might the letters of Chesterfield and Montagu be used to support Astell's claims about the treatment of women? Be specific in your answer.

ANOTHER PATHWAY

With a partner, draw some conclusions about 18th-century England, based on the information and views presented in these three letters. Carefully read each letter again, looking for evidence about the attitudes, lifestyles, and manners of the day. Then analyze the evidence and decide what it tells you about 18th-century society. Discuss your findings with the class.

LITERARY LINKS

Compare the letters of Montagu and Chesterfield with those written in the 15th century by Margaret Paston (page 121). Consider the purpose, subject matter, and tone of the letters. How are they similar? How do they differ?

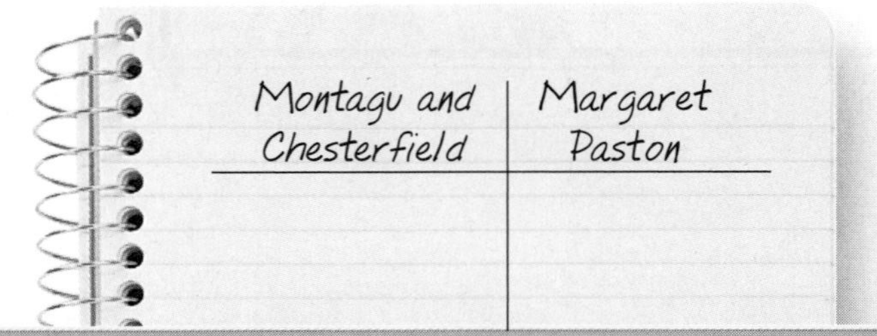

QUICKWRITES

1. Work with a partner to write an exchange of **letters** in which Chesterfield's son and Montagu's daughter discuss their feelings about the parental advice they have received.
2. Reread the three letters and choose a statement that intrigues you or that is controversial. Draft a brief **essay** in which you analyze the statement and explain why you do or do not agree with it.
3. Use the information in the letters to write a **character sketch** of Chesterfield's son or Montagu's granddaughter. Your approach may be serious or humorous.

PORTFOLIO *Save your writing. You may want to use it later as a springboard to a piece for your portfolio.*

WORDS TO KNOW

Review the Words to Know at the bottom of the selection pages. Then, on your paper, write the vocabulary words that are suggested by the phrases in items 1–5 and by the groups of idioms in items 6–10.

1. how secrets should be kept and deep friendships preserved
2. what you do when you make a friend expect a blind date to be terrific
3. what the White House and Buckingham Palace are examples of
4. the kind of behavior that is so habitual that it can never be changed
5. what inventors, architects, and schemers do
6. nearly die of shame, blow one's cool, be red as a beet, feel like two cents
7. dotting all the *i's,* being as good as one's word, taking pains, following through
8. no way, on the contrary, have a bone to pick, in a pig's eye
9. just for laughs, stop and smell the roses, take a break, live a little
10. carry a grudge, heart of stone, hard as nails, not give an inch

Philip Stanhope, Lord Chesterfield

1694–1773

Philip Stanhope was raised and educated by his grandmother and largely ignored by his aristocratic father. He studied briefly at Cambridge University, then left the university to travel abroad, where he eagerly observed and imitated French manners and culture. At an early age, he was elected to Parliament and appointed to a position at court, and in 1728 he was made ambassador to Holland. He became a capable statesman and diplomat, eventually serving as secretary of state.

Chesterfield was a friend of Pope, Swift, and Voltaire, and as a patron of the arts he gave financial assistance to many struggling writers. Although he contributed numerous essays to periodicals, he is remembered chiefly for his letters to his son and godson. Although the attitudes he displays in his letters have frequently been criticized, the polish and wit of his writing continue to be admired by readers.

Lady Mary Wortley Montagu

1689–1762

Lady Mary Wortley Montagu, a gifted poet and essayist, was acquainted with many literary figures, including Pope, Addison, and Steele. Her first published work was an essay contributed to *The Spectator.*

A daughter of London aristocrats, Montagu educated herself in her father's library. In 1712, to escape an arranged marriage, she eloped with Edward Wortley Montagu. When Edward was appointed ambassador to Turkey, Lady Mary accompanied him to Constantinople, where she wrote more than 50 letters describing Turkish culture. After her return to England in 1718, she courageously promoted the Turkish practice of inoculating against smallpox, a disease that had killed her brother and marred her own appearance.

Lady Mary and her husband grew apart, and in 1739 she left him and England, beginning what was to be nearly 23 years of living and traveling in Italy and France. Her Turkish letters were published in 1763, but a full edition of her letters was not available until 1967.

MILESTONES IN BRITISH LITERATURE

Daniel Defoe

Robinson Crusoe

If you were marooned on a remote and wild island, how would you respond to the challenges of nature? What would you eat? Where would you sleep? Would you go mad from isolation—or use the experience as a chance to grow? These are some of the issues confronted by the hero of Daniel Defoe's masterful adventure story *Robinson Crusoe.*

The plot of *Robinson Crusoe* is based on the true story of Alexander Selkirk, a sailor who had been stranded for 52 months on an uninhabited island near Chile. Defoe capitalized on public interest in Selkirk by producing a memoir of a fictional castaway—Robinson Crusoe—using the first-person narrative, exact details, and precise chronology that would be found in the journal of a seasoned seafarer. The resulting story was so popular that unscrupulous publishers scrambled to produce and sell their own editions. Even today, the book is available in many editions, some lavishly illustrated, and the story of Robinson Crusoe is used as a basis for comic books, feature films, and science fiction adventures.

In his 28 years on the island, Crusoe learns how to make tools, plant seeds, and domesticate animals. Slowly, he turns the untamed land into a secure and productive homestead.

In addition to chronicling the adventures of a castaway, Defoe explored the social and moral values of his time. For example, he portrays Crusoe as a willful son whose disregard for the wishes of his parents leads him into danger, slavery, and shipwreck. He also shows how the experience of life alone on the island leads Crusoe to appreciate the moral and social values back home. Only when Crusoe begins to apply these values, along with his native talents, does he begin to prosper. He teaches himself carpentry, pottery, agriculture, and animal husbandry. He learns the geography of his island. He rescues from cannibals a man whom he names Friday and who becomes his devoted servant. Finally, he saves the captain of a passing ship from mutineers. Leaving the mutineers on the island, Crusoe and the captain sail with Friday to England, where Crusoe assumes a place in English society.

At one time or another, almost everyone has wondered what it would be like to have to survive in a wilderness. In *Robinson Crusoe,* Defoe presents a man who not only survives but thrives—who transforms the wilderness into an expression of humanity. The result is a story that appeals to everyone who yearns for adventure.

Left:
Despite ominous mishaps, including a severe storm, Robinson Crusoe is determined to make his fortune at sea.

Center:
Crusoe, the disheveled castaway

Right:
For 26 of his years on the island, Crusoe's only companions are a dog, some cats, a goat, and his parrot, which he teaches to say "Poor Robin Crusoe! Where are you?"

WRITING ABOUT LITERATURE

TAKE MY ADVICE

Like those who came before them, people in 18th-century England loved to comment on human behavior. Modern Americans also like to give each other advice. Now you will give some advice of your own. How will you help people see your point? This lesson will allow you to

- learn how writers use tone to show attitude
- write an advice essay about a real-world issue
- evaluate the sources of conflicting advice

Writer's Style: Using Tone A writer uses tone to communicate a certain attitude to a particular audience. The range of tones is as great as the range of human emotions. Tones such as anger, humor, admiration, and seriousness can all be conveyed through language.

Read the Literature

In a letter of advice to his son, this father describes the behavior of an awkward man. How does his language convey his attitude about this subject?

Choice of Tone
What tone has this writer chosen? What does this tone communicate? Which words and phrases set the tone?

Literature Model

At dinner, his awkwardness distinguishes itself particularly, as he has more to do: there he holds his knife, fork, and spoon differently from other people; eats with his knife to the great danger of his mouth, picks his teeth with his fork, and puts his spoon, which has been in his throat twenty times, into the dishes again. If he is to carve, he can never hit the joint; but, in his vain efforts to cut through the bone, scatters the sauce in everybody's face. He generally daubs himself with soup and grease, though his napkin is commonly stuck through a buttonhole, and tickles his chin. When he drinks, he infallibly coughs in his glass, and besprinkles the company.

Philip Stanhope, Lord Chesterfield
from *Letters to His Son*

Connect to Life

People haven't stopped giving advice over the years. Today, you can find an advice column in almost any newspaper you open. The tone of these columns varies, depending on what kind of advice is being given. The model below shows a response to a mother whose 20-year-old son refuses to get a job and move out.

Advice Columnist

Dear Had It: In Schenectady your son is an adult at eighteen, and he has no more right to live on your property than a stranger. You can give him the official thirty-days' notice to move out of your house, and if he refuses, the court will advise him that he has ten days to move, after which they will "help" him.

Abigail Van Buren
from *The Best of Dear Abby*

Use of Tone
What tone does the writer use in this column? What message does this tone convey?

Try Your Hand: Using Tone

1. **Change the Tone** Write your own advice to "Had It" but try using a humorous or insincere tone.
2. **Pretend It Matters** Give advice to one of your classmates about how to walk down the hallway, but do it in the most formal, stiff, stilted tone you can. Pretend it is a matter of national security. How will you begin the note?
3. **Try Two Approaches** Make two posters for the door of your locker or room, telling people to stay out. In one poster, use a humorous tone. For the other, use a serious or angry tone. Which do you think would be more effective?

SkillBuilder

WRITER'S CRAFT

Using Hyperbole

Whenever you exaggerate to make a point or create a humorous tone, you are using **hyperbole.** Read the following excerpt from *Letters to His Son* by Lord Chesterfield.

Women, then, are only children of a larger growth; they have an entertaining tattle and sometimes wit; but for solid, reasoning good-sense, I never in my life knew one that had it, or who reasoned or acted consequentially for four-and-twenty hours together.

The writer is exaggerating when he says that he has never known a woman who had acted reasonably for 24 hours. However, by saying so, he emphasizes his opinion of the women he knows.

APPLYING WHAT YOU'VE LEARNED
Use hyperbole to add humor or emphasis to the following sentences. For example, you could rewrite the sentence *I have a better idea* to read *I have an idea that could save the planet from destruction*.

- That lunch was bad.
- Your proposal sounds difficult.
- I liked her performance.

WRITING ABOUT LITERATURE

Creative Response

When you see people in a situation you've already experienced, you're probably tempted to give them suggestions on how to handle it. But how do you convince them that the advice you have to give is the advice they should follow? Giving suggestions to someone else may help you appreciate the choices writers in Unit Three made when they wrote to advise.

GUIDED ASSIGNMENT

Write an Advice Essay Advice essays can be serious, or they can be very humorous. The next few pages will guide you through the writing of an advice essay.

1 Prewrite and Explore

Advice is a personal recommendation based on a blend of knowledge and experience. To give believable advice, make sure you know something about your subject.

WHAT'S THE PROBLEM?

Look around you. Who looks like they could use a little advice? What problems are these people dealing with? Talk to your friends and classmates. Find out what people your age are confused about. You might want to use a chart like the one below to identify problems.

WHAT DO YOU KNOW?

You know who needs advice, but what are you qualified to give advice about? Think about what you know. Also consider the things you've experienced. Are you always able to find a job? Do you get along well with your friends? On your chart, circle or highlight topics you feel qualified to comment on.

Decision Point Which topic will you give advice about?

Student's Prewriting Chart

2 Write a Rough Draft

Now that you have a topic, how will you present your advice? Will you write a letter, a satire, an advice column, or an essay? What tone will you use? Will it be humorous, sarcastic, professional, or familiar? Look through all the selections in Unit Three for inspiration before you write a rough draft.

Student's Rough Draft

Keep it light so I don't sound like a know-it-all!

Remember that adults have different ideas about what looks good than teenagers do. We forget this because most of us spend time with people our own age. When you're looking for a job, you are probably going to be interviewed and hired by an adult. One time I was applying for a job with a girl who was dressed as if she were going to a party. I saw her résumé, and she had a lot more experience than I did. Still, I got the job because I had dressed conservatively.

I should give more examples from my experience.

3 Draft and Share

As you turn your rough draft into a more focused piece of writing, remember to state your subject and your qualifications for giving advice in the introductory paragraph. When your draft is completed, consider asking a classmate to read it and give you feedback.

PEER RESPONSE

- How did I convince you that I am qualified to give advice on this subject? If I didn't convince you, what was missing?
- How did the tone of my writing affect the way you responded to my advice?
- If you were giving advice on this topic, what would you include that I didn't?

SkillBuilder

WRITER'S CRAFT

Identifying Your Audience

Knowing who will read what you write—your audience—will help you tailor your writing to meet your readers' needs. The type of audience determines what information you provide and also influences your word choice, language, and tone. Sometimes the audience will be predetermined. For example, when you write a letter to a relative or friend, you know who is going to read it. At other times you can choose who your audience will be or decide whether you even want to share your work with others—you may write an essay for young kids, for example, or you may want to write about your feelings in a confidential diary.

APPLYING WHAT YOU'VE LEARNED

As you work on your advice essay, try to meet your readers' needs by asking questions like the following:

- What do my readers already know about the topic?
- How big a stake do the readers have in this topic?
- Will readers agree or disagree with my advice?
- What approach will make my essay most effective?
- What tone should I use to make the advice acceptable to the reader?

4 Revise and Edit

As you revise, make sure your tone is consistent throughout your draft. Also consider the Standards for Evaluation below and the Grammar in Context feature on the opposite page. When you're finished, read some of your classmates' pieces and reflect on the variety of tones and formats used to give advice. Consider which advice you would be most likely to follow, and why.

Student's Final Draft

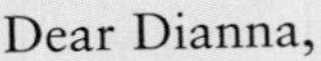

Dear Dianna,

Aunt Josefina told me you're looking for a job. Girl, I remember how tough that was for me at first. I applied for fifteen jobs before I finally got this good one at the video store. I'll tell you what I learned about job hunting—appearance counts.

You're probably thinking you know how important appearance is, right? You've got a closet full of clothes, and you wake up an hour early every morning to do your hair. But something we forget when we're in high school is that adults have a different idea of what looks good than we do. It took me a while to catch on to this myself.

What qualifies this student to give advice on making a good appearance?

Second of all, you have to know whom you're dealing with. In other words, don't show up for a job interview dressed as if you're going to a party. When I applied for the job in the video store, I wore a button-down shirt and tan pants. I didn't think I would get the job because a girl with experience was also applying. She was wearing a red Lycra dress and rhinestone earrings. Also, she kept blowing huge bubbles with her gum. Finally a bubble popped and stuck to her chin, right below her bright red lips. That girl had work experience, but she did not have a good appearance, and it was little old me who got the job.

Who is this writer's audience? How does the writer suit her tone to this reader?

Standards for Evaluation

An advice essay

- provides the qualifications of the writer
- states the subject
- has a consistent tone throughout
- gives reasons to follow the advice being given

Grammar in Context

Complex Sentences When revising and editing your advice essay, you can show the relationships between ideas by using complex sentences. A complex sentence contains one independent clause, which can stand alone as a sentence, and one or more subordinate clauses, which cannot stand alone.

> When I applied for the job in the video store, I wore a button-down shirt and tan pants. I didn't think I would get the job because a girl with experience was also applying.

In the example above, the short, simple sentences are combined into complex sentences that further explain the relationships between the ideas.

In a complex sentence, a subordinate clause functions as a noun or a modifier. As a modifier, it modifies a word in the independent clause. If the subordinate clause functions as a noun in a complex sentence, it can be the subject, object, or complement in the independent clause.

Try Your Hand: Using Complex Sentences

Revise the following paragraph by making some of the simple sentences into complex sentences, using conjunctions such as *because, when, after, before, until, unless,* or *if.*

> You shouldn't risk making a bad impression on a potential employer. First impressions make a big impact. Check out what the other employees are wearing before you apply. You'll be prepared for the interview.

Check your advice essay to see if using complex sentences can help show the relationships between ideas.

SkillBuilder

GRAMMAR FROM WRITING

Using Subordinating Conjunctions

Using the correct subordinating conjunction to introduce a subordinate clause will help clarify the relationship between ideas. Subordinating conjunctions express relationships of time, manner, cause, reason, comparison, condition, and purpose.

Some Subordinating Conjunctions	
Time	after, as, before, since, until, when, whenever, while
Manner	as, as if
Place	where, wherever
Cause or Reason	because, since
Comparison	as, as much as, than, whereas
Condition	although, as long as, even though, if, though, unless
Purpose	in order that, that

APPLYING WHAT YOU'VE LEARNED
Use a subordinating conjunction to combine the sentences in each pair.

1. I lost my purse. I left it on my seat.
2. Rodney lost the race. He tried very hard.
3. I swim. My eyes get red.

GRAMMAR HANDBOOK

For more information on subordinating conjunctions, see page 1287 of the Grammar Handbook.

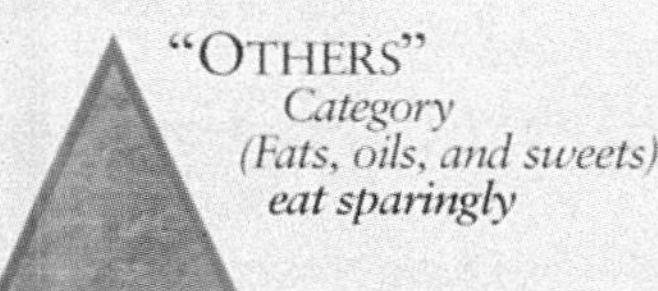
FOOD GUIDE PYRAMID
"OTHERS"
Category
(Fats, oils, and sweets)
eat sparingly

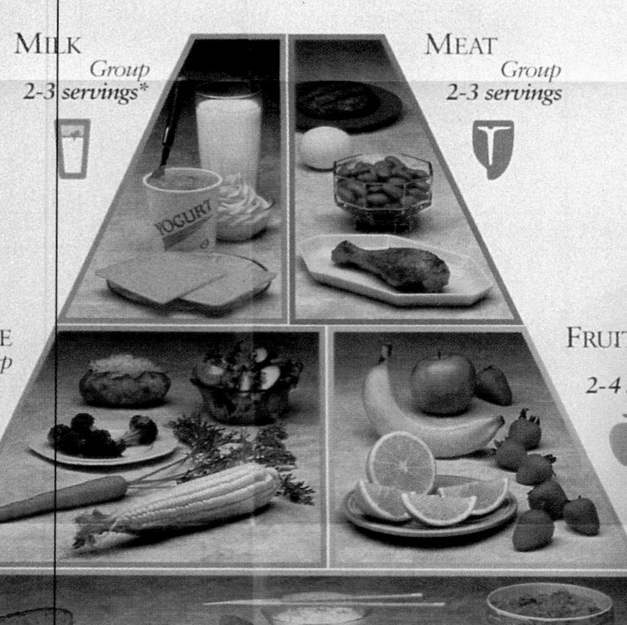
MILK
Group
2-3 servings*
MEAT
Group
2-3 servings
FRUIT
Group
2-4 servings
YOGURT
Need more information on serving sizes or the variety of foods in each food group? Ask for a copy of Dairy Council's GUIDE to GOOD EATING.

THE NEW 4
FOOD GROUPS
VEGGIES
GRAINS
FRUITS
LEGUMES
LIVE LONGER. LIVE BETTER.
GO VEGETARIAN.
PHYSICIANS COMMITTEE FOR RESPONSIBLE MEDICINE

R E A D I N G
THE WORLD

CONFLICTING ADVICE

"Drink your milk." "Eat two to three servings of meat a day." "Cut down on fatty foods." You're bombarded with advice every day. How can you figure out what to believe?

View Look closely at this scene. What advice is the poster from the National Dairy Council providing? What advice is the Physicians Committee for Responsible Medicine giving on its T-shirt?

Interpret How do the two advisory messages contradict each other? What choices is this person making? Which advice would you follow?

Discuss How do you think the sources of the advice at the left affect the messages being given? What kinds of conflicting dietary advice do you hear? How do you decide what to believe? You may want to refer to the SkillBuilder on evaluating sources as you discuss these issues.

SkillBuilder

CRITICAL THINKING

Evaluating Sources

As you sift through the huge amount of advice directed at you, it's a good idea to consider where it came from. A group with a vested interest in a subject may provide biased information about it. Other sources may be more objective. How do you know whom to believe? Ask yourself the following questions when evaluating a source:

- Who is publishing, writing, or saying this? If I followed this advice, how would it affect the source?
- Where did the source get this information? What have they studied or experienced? What makes them experts on this subject?
- What kind of medium presents the information? Is it a popular magazine? a TV show? a scientific journal?
- When was this information published? Has new information come out since then?

APPLYING WHAT YOU'VE LEARNED
With a partner, flip through a newspaper or magazine. Circle any pieces of advice you find. They could be in the form of advice columns, editorials, movie reviews, or articles. For each piece of advice, evaluate the source by using the criteria above. Make a decision on whether the source is credible or questionable.

PART 2 *Arguments for Change*

Social and economic conditions improved for many people during the Enlightenment. However, the wealth and privilege enjoyed by the middle and upper classes contrasted strikingly with the poverty suffered by the rest of the people. Many writers fought against the injustices they perceived by arguing in favor of social reforms. Some, including several of the essayists in this part of Unit Three, supported equal opportunities for women. Others penned stinging satires attacking the treatment of the poor. As you read the selections, think about what changes you would promote in today's society.

PREVIEWING

NONFICTION

from An Academy for Women

Daniel Defoe

PERSONAL CONNECTION

In the 17th and early 18th centuries, the only females who received an education were those whose families could afford private lessons, and even they were taught only a few subjects and were barred from attending universities. On the basis of your understanding of history and social customs, why do you think females were prevented from receiving the same education as males? Record your thoughts in your notebook.

HISTORICAL/CULTURAL CONNECTION

Although the education of females in 17th-century England was not entirely neglected, the only schooling available to them was private tutoring, which was usually shared with siblings or cousins. Such tutoring was an option only for the upper classes, and then only if the father or husband allowed it. Despite their limited education, a few women began to express themselves publicly in books, pamphlets, and essays during the 1600s. Some called for more rights for women, including the right to an education. In most circles, however, such ideas were ignored or ridiculed.

Following the Restoration, England experienced a period of growth in social awareness as well as in industry and commerce. More and more individuals looked for practical ways to correct what they perceived as society's flaws. One of those individuals was Daniel Defoe. Best known today as a novelist, Defoe was also involved in both commerce and social reform. One of his first publications, written in 1697, was *An Essay on Projects,* a series of proposals advocating, among other things, the establishment of banks, insurance companies, and credit unions—and, in "An Academy for Women," the education of females.

READING CONNECTION

Following a Formal Argument In a formal argument, a writer makes a proposal and then presents facts, reasons, or examples to support it. The proposal is generally a call to action and usually appears near the beginning of the argument. Make a chart like the one shown, and as you read this selection on the education of females, use it to record Defoe's main proposal and supporting details.

Proposal	Supporting Details
	1. 2. 3. 4.

Using Your Reading Log The reading strategies introduced on page 5 are based on the kinds of connections active readers make when they read. To help you practice some of those strategies, questions have been inserted at certain points in this excerpt from "An Academy for Women." Record your response to each of the questions in your reading log. Also record other thoughts and feelings that come to you as you read.

• *CULTURAL CONNECTION*

FROM An Academy *for* WOMEN

Daniel Defoe

I have often thought of it as one of the most barbarous customs in the world, considering us as a civilized and a Christian country, that we deny the advantages of learning to women. We reproach the sex every day with folly and impertinence, while I am confident, had they the advantages of education equal to us, they would be guilty of less than ourselves.

One would wonder, indeed, how it should happen that women are conversible[1] at all, since they are only beholden to natural parts for all their knowledge. Their youth is spent to teach them to stitch and sew or make baubles. They are taught to read indeed, and perhaps to write their names or so, and that is the height of a woman's education. And I would but ask any who slight the sex for their understanding, what is a man (a gentleman, I mean) good for that is taught no more? . . .

The soul is placed in the body like a rough diamond, and must be polished, or the luster of it will never appear: and it is manifest that as the rational soul distinguishes us from brutes, so education carries on the distinction and makes some less brutish than others. This is too evident to need any demonstration. But why then should women be denied the benefit of instruction? If knowledge and understanding had been useless additions to the sex, God Almighty would never have given them capacities, for He made nothing needless. Besides, I would ask such what they can see in ignorance that they should think it a necessary ornament to a woman? or how much worse is a wise woman than a fool? or what has the woman done to forfeit the privilege of being taught? Does she plague us with her pride and impertinence? Why did we not let her learn, that she might have had more wit? Shall we upbraid women with folly,[2] when it is only the error of this inhuman custom that hindered them being made wiser?

The capacities of women are supposed to be greater and their senses quicker than those of the men; and what they might be capable of being bred to is plain from some instances of female wit, which this age is not without; which upbraids us with injustice, and looks as if we denied women the advantages of education for fear they should vie with the men in their improvements.

To remove this objection, and that women might have at least a needful opportunity of

1. **conversible:** able to carry on a conversation.
2. **upbraid women with folly:** scold women for foolishness.

WORDS TO KNOW

manifest (măn′ə-fĕst′) *adj.* obvious; clear
vie (vī) *v.* to compete

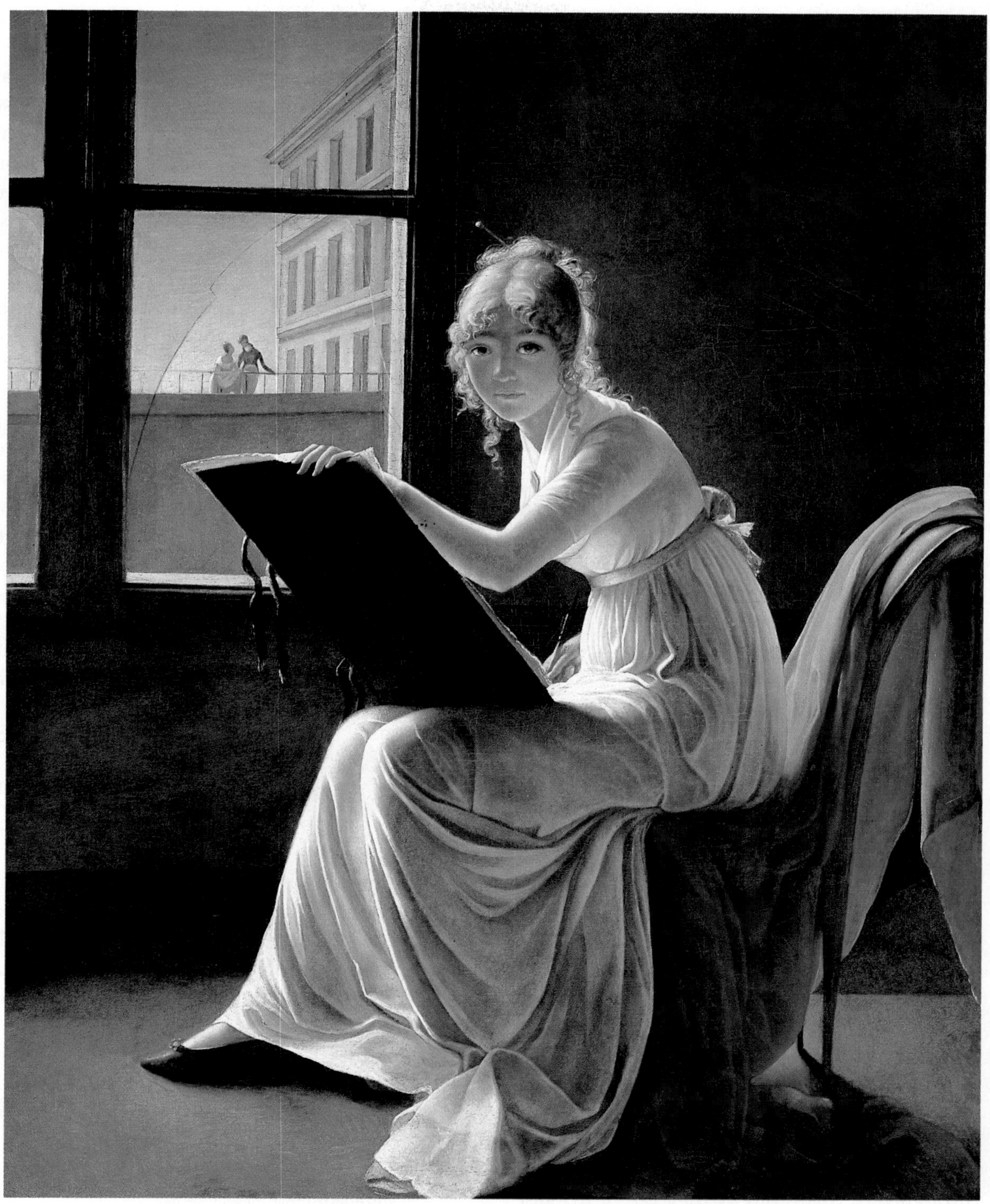

Portrait of a Young Woman, called Mademoiselle Charlotte du Val d'Ognes (about 1800), unknown French artist. Oil on canvas, 63½″ × 50⅝″, The Metropolitan Museum of Art, bequest of Isaac D. Fletcher, 1917. Mr. and Mrs. Isaac D. Fletcher Collection (17.120.204). Copyright © 1989 The Metropolitan Museum of Art.

education in all sorts of useful learning, I propose the draft of an academy for that purpose. . . .

The academy I propose should differ but little from public schools, wherein such ladies as were willing to study should have all the advantages of learning suitable to their genius. . . .

The persons who enter should be taught all sorts of breeding suitable to both their genius and their quality, and in particular music and dancing, which it would be cruelty to bar the sex of, because they are their darlings; but besides this, they should be taught languages, as particularly French and Italian; and I would venture the injury of giving a woman more tongues than one.

The great distinguishing difference which is seen in the world between men and women is in their EDUCATION.

They should, as a particular study, be taught all the graces of speech and all the necessary air of conversation, which our common education is so defective in that I need not expose it. They should be brought to read books, and especially history, and so to read as to make them understand the world, and be able to know and judge of things when they hear of them.

EVALUATE

What is your opinion of the areas of study that Defoe proposes?

To such whose genius would lead them to it I would deny no sort of learning; but the chief thing in general is to cultivate the understandings of the sex, that they may be capable of all sorts of conversation; that their parts and judgments being improved, they may be as profitable in their conversation as they are pleasant.

Women, in my observation, have little or no difference in them, but as they are or are not distinguished by education. Tempers indeed may in some degree influence them, but the main distinguishing part is their breeding.

The whole sex are generally quick and sharp. I believe I may be allowed to say generally so, for you rarely see them lumpish and heavy when they are children, as boys will often be. If a woman be well-bred, and taught the proper management of her natural wit, she proves generally very sensible and retentive; and without partiality, a woman of sense and manners is the finest and most delicate part of God's creation; the glory of her Maker, and the great instance of His singular regard to man, His darling creature, to whom He gave the best gift either God could bestow or man receive. And it is the sordidest[3] piece of folly and ingratitude in the world to withhold from the sex the due luster which the advantages of education gives to the natural beauty of their minds.

A woman well-bred and well taught, furnished with the additional accomplishments of knowledge and behavior, is a creature without comparison; her society is the emblem of sublimer[4] enjoyments; her person is angelic and her conversation heavenly; she is all softness and sweetness, peace, love, wit, and delight. She is every way suitable to the sublimest wish, and the man that has such a one to his portion has nothing to do but to rejoice in her and be thankful.

On the other hand, suppose her to be the very same woman, and rob her of the benefit of education, and it follows thus:

3. **sordidest:** most meanly selfish.

4. **sublimer:** more noble or exalted.

WORDS TO KNOW

retentive (rĭ-tĕn'tĭv) *adj.* able to retain knowledge or information easily

If her temper be good, want of education makes her soft and easy.

Her wit, for want of teaching, makes her impertinent and talkative.

Her knowledge, for want of judgment and experience, makes her fanciful and whimsical.

If her temper be bad, want of breeding makes her worse, and she grows haughty, insolent, and loud.

If she be passionate, want of manners makes her termagant[5] and a scold, which is much at one with lunatic.

If she be proud, want of discretion (which still is breeding) makes her conceited, fantastic, and ridiculous.

And from these she degenerates to be turbulent, clamorous, noisy, nasty, and the devil.

Methinks mankind for their own sakes, since, say what we will of the women, we all think fit one time or other to be concerned with them, should take some care to breed them up to be suitable and serviceable, if they expected no such thing as delight from them. Bless us! what care do we take to breed up a good horse and to break him well, and what a value do we put upon him when it is done, and all because he should be fit for our use; and why not a woman? Since all her ornaments and beauty without suitable behavior is a cheat in nature, like the false tradesman who puts the best of his goods uppermost that the buyer may think the rest are of the same goodness. . . .

QUESTION

What point is Defoe making in his simile of the false tradesman?

But to come closer to the business, the great distinguishing difference which is seen in the world between men and women is in their education, and this is manifested by comparing it with the difference between one man or woman and another.

And herein it is that I take upon me to make such a bold assertion that all the world are mistaken in their practice about women; for I cannot think that God Almighty ever made them so delicate, so glorious creatures, and furnished them with such charms, so agreeable and so delightful to mankind, with souls capable of the same accomplishments with men, and all to be only stewards of our houses, *cooks and slaves.*

. . . I remember a passage which I heard from a very fine woman; she had wit and capacity enough, an extraordinary shape and face, and a great fortune, but had been cloistered up all her time, and for fear of being stolen, had not had the liberty of being taught the common necessary knowledge of women's affairs; and when she came to converse in the world, her natural wit made her so sensible of the want of education, that she gave this short reflection on herself: "I am ashamed to talk with my very maids," says she, "for I don't know when they do right or wrong. I had more need to go to school than be married."

I need not enlarge on the loss the defect of education is to the sex, nor argue the benefit of the contrary practice; it is a thing will be more easily granted than remedied. This chapter is but an essay at the thing, and I refer the practice to those happy days, if ever they shall be, when men shall be wise enough to mend it. ❖

5. **termagant** (tûr'mə-gənt): a quarrelsome woman.

WORDS TO KNOW

degenerate (dĭ-jĕn'ə-rāt') *v.* to sink to a lower condition; deteriorate
cloister (kloi'stər) *v.* to confine or seclude, as in a convent

RESPONDING OPTIONS

FROM PERSONAL RESPONSE *TO* CRITICAL ANALYSIS

REFLECT **1.** What thoughts came to mind when you finished reading this essay? Share your thoughts with the class.

RETHINK **2.** Refer to the chart you created for the Reading Connection on page 379. In your opinion, does Defoe present a convincing argument? Why or why not?

3. How would you describe Defoe's attitude toward women?

Consider
- the qualities he attributes to women
- the areas of study he proposes for them
- his description of an uneducated woman
- the possible motives behind his proposal

RELATE **4.** How might a contemporary feminist or defender of women's rights respond to Defoe's essay?

5. Do you think that any issues related to the education or training of women are still controversial? Explain your opinion.

ANOTHER PATHWAY

Defoe's proposal in "An Academy for Women" challenged the traditional thinking of his day. With a partner, read through the selection again. Look for two types of statements: ones that portray Defoe as a man ahead of his time and ones that reflect the typical thinking of the late 1600s. Share your ideas in a discussion with the whole class.

LITERARY CONCEPTS

In a **persuasive essay,** a writer attempts to convince readers to adopt a particular opinion or to perform a certain action. Most persuasive essays present a series of facts, reasons, or examples in support of an opinion or proposal. Effective persuasion appeals to both the intelligence and the emotions of its intended audience. Of the supporting details in Defoe's essay, which kinds do you think appeal to readers' intelligence? Which appeal to their emotions?

LITERARY LINKS

Compare Defoe's opinions on the education of women with those expressed by Lady Mary Wortley Montagu in her letter to her daughter (page 361). What opinions do Defoe and Montagu seem to share? On what issues might they disagree?

QUICKWRITES

1. Imagine that you are an educated 17th-century male. Write a **letter to the editor** conveying your response to Defoe's proposal.
2. Write **dialogue** for an imaginary interview between Defoe and a contemporary female television or radio talk-show host.
3. Defoe claims that "the great distinguishing difference . . . between men and women is in their education" (page 383). Draft a **short essay** in which you explain whether you think his argument supports this idea.

PORTFOLIO *Save your writing. You may want to use it later as a springboard to a piece for your portfolio.*

ART CONNECTION

Look closely at the portrait of Mademoiselle Charlotte du Val d'Ognes on page 381. In your opinion, what specific elements of the painting reflect ideas presented in this selection?

ACROSS THE CURRICULUM

History Investigate the education of women in England after 1700. What types of formal education were offered to females? What subjects were taught? When were women's colleges founded in the major universities?

WORDS TO KNOW

For each group of words below, write the letter of the word that is an antonym of the boldfaced word.

1. **degenerate:** (a) produce, (b) improve, (c) accelerate
2. **retentive:** (a) forgetful, (b) selfish, (c) graceful
3. **vie:** (a) startle, (b) cooperate, (c) lose
4. **cloister:** (a) free, (b) organize, (c) praise
5. **manifest:** (a) hurtful, (b) questionable, (c) timid

DANIEL DEFOE

1660–1731

"No man has tasted differing fortunes more, / And thirteen times I have been rich and poor." In this self-description, Daniel Defoe summarized the many ups and downs of his career. Fascinated with the world of trade, Defoe became a merchant, dealing at different times in an assortment of products, from bricks to insurance. Although he amassed great wealth in many of his ventures, occasional bad investments led him to bankruptcy.

As a devout Presbyterian and a critic of the Church of England, Defoe was barred from attending a university and went instead to an academy for religious dissenters. His interest in politics stemmed largely from his desire to "purify" the Church of England. At various times in his career, he was allied with both the Tories and the Whigs, and he was later accused of acting as a double agent, performing secret intelligence work for both parties.

Defoe wrote many political pamphlets, one of which led to his imprisonment. His punishment included time in the pillory, a wooden device with holes for the prisoner's head and hands. Prisoners in the pillory were usually pelted with rotten fruit and vegetables by onlookers, but Defoe's views were so popular that the public drank to his health and threw flowers instead. One of his political poems, *The True-Born Englishman,* reportedly sold more copies than any poem published in England before that time.

Today Defoe is most recognized for his novels, which he did not begin writing until he was in his late 50s. His most famous novel, *Robinson Crusoe,* was the first book other than the Bible to be widely read by members of all levels of English society.

OTHER WORKS *Moll Flanders, Roxana, Colonel Jack*

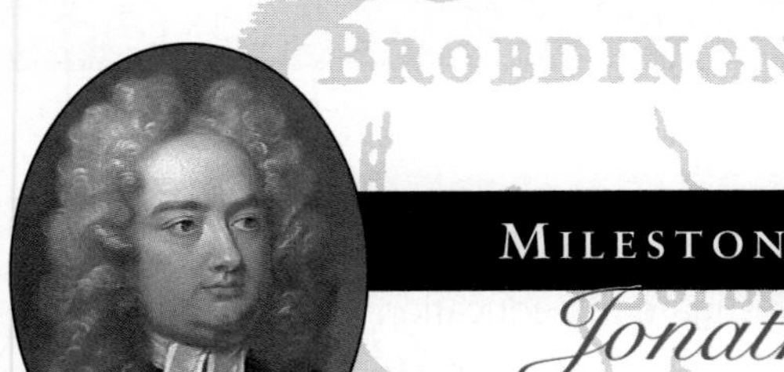

MILESTONES IN BRITISH LITERATURE

Jonathan Swift

Gulliver's TRAVELS

After looking at the title, introductions, and convincing maps, many readers concluded that Gulliver's Travels *was a true account of an English sailor.*

Below:
Gulliver and two of the Houyhnhnms (hwĭn′əmz), *horses that are rational and sophisticated beings*

Consider for a moment the startling notion that life exists elsewhere in the universe. Imagine a place, as yet undiscovered, whose 6-inch people regard you as a monster. Think about a land of 72-foot giants who can hold you like a pet in the palm of one hand. Or dream up a world where horses are intelligent creatures and humanoids are brutish beasts. Those are the kinds of worlds Jonathan Swift imagined when he wrote his fantasy masterpiece *Travels into Several Remote Nations of the World, in Four Parts, by Lemuel Gulliver, First a Surgeon, and Then a Captain of Several Ships. Gulliver's Travels* tells what happens when an ordinary sailor gets shipwrecked in extraordinary places—and learns to see life at home in new ways.

By the time Swift published *Gulliver's Travels* in 1726, he was already well-known for his clever wit and biting satire; yet *Gulliver's Travels* added a new dimension to his reputation. The book contained such delightful fantasy and uproarious humor that it became an immediate success. It inspired letters from readers eager to meet Mr. Gulliver, sequels by writers hoping to cash in on the work's popularity, and a humorous poem by Alexander Pope, telling of Mrs. Gulliver's troubles with her husband. Later, at the end of the 18th century, a Glasgow painter produced a children's version of Gulliver's first two adventures, and Swift's fantastic characters moved into the mainstream of British culture.

More than 250 years after it first appeared, *Gulliver's Travels* is still an amazing popular success. Children love it for its fantastic adventures, while adults delight in its wit and social commentary. The story has been performed on stage, adapted in animated films, and illustrated in comic books. It has set a standard for political satire and provided a groundwork for contemporary works of fantasy and science fiction. Swift's Gulliver may have peacefully retired to the English county of Nottinghamshire, but the influence of his adventures reaches far into the future.

Think about a land where a 72-foot giant can hold you like a pet in the palm of one hand.

Above:
The Yahoos, who resemble human beings, are nothing more than greedy, filthy beasts.

PREVIEWING

NONFICTION

A Modest Proposal

Jonathan Swift

PERSONAL CONNECTION

Think of writers and entertainers who use humor to call attention to the faults of society or government. Do you think that their humor can lead to reforms? In your notebook, write down your thoughts about humor and its potential for bringing about changes in society.

HISTORICAL/BIOGRAPHICAL CONNECTION

Although of English ancestry, Jonathan Swift began and ended his life in Ireland. English influence in Ireland, which began during the Middle Ages, had grown so strong by 1700 that the English Parliament completely dominated Irish politics and religion. Ireland's own parliament was virtually powerless, and most of the laws it passed were dictated by the English government. Although the vast majority of Irish citizens were Roman Catholics, the English allowed only Anglicans (members of the Protestant Church of England) to serve in the Irish parliament. The anti-Catholic legislation passed by these Anglicans—such as laws prohibiting Catholics from purchasing or inheriting land—created tremendous discord between Protestants and Catholics in Ireland, a conflict that has lasted to this day.

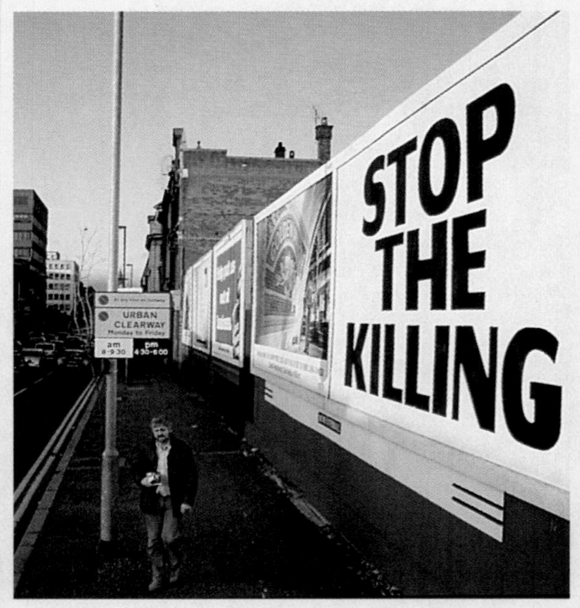

During the late 1600s, Ireland's economy suffered greatly from England's domination. Absentee landlords charged exceedingly high rents, driving many workers off the land. Moreover, an English law passed in 1699 placed strict limitations on Ireland's trade, which caused workers to lose their jobs. The country soon faced widespread poverty.

Because of Swift's English ancestry and Anglican faith, he had a natural love of England, where he lived for most of his youth. In fact, he was reluctant to return to Ireland when he was appointed to a church post there. Nevertheless, he became a strong defender of Irish rights. Considered the most distinguished satirist to have written in the English language, Swift used humor to confront and expose the political, social, economic, and religious injustices that were tearing at the heart of the Irish people.

READING CONNECTION

Reading Satire

The 18th century has been called "the golden age of satire." Literary giants such as Swift, Defoe, Dryden, Pope, Addison, and Fielding showed their mastery of satire in various literary forms, including poetry, novels, essays, and drama. An understanding of the purpose and characteristics of satire may help you fully appreciate "A Modest Proposal."

Satire is a literary technique that mixes criticism with humor. The satirist uses laughter as a weapon, usually to encourage some type of social reform. In addition to literary figures, the list of well-known satirists includes news commentators, newspaper columnists, screenwriters, songwriters, and comedians. Occasionally the object of a satire is an individual person, but more often it is a group of people, an institution, a whole country, or—as in the case of Swift's *Gulliver's Travels*—all of humanity.

There are two main types of satire, named for the Roman satirists Horace and Juvenal, which differ chiefly in tone. **Horatian satire** is playfully amusing and seeks to correct vice or foolishness with gentle laughter and sympathetic understanding. **Juvenalian satire** provokes a darker kind of laughter. It is bitter and criticizes corruption or incompetence with scorn and outrage. Whether Horatian or Juvenalian, effective satire always contains an element of humor and never descends to abusive language or sarcastic insults. Swift once stated that he advocated the kind of satire that "gives the least offense; which, instead of lashing, laughs men out of their follies and vices; and . . . gives Horace the preference to Juvenal."

Literary satirists often use **irony**—a contrast between expectation and reality—to convey their messages. Often, a satirist will distance himself or herself from a subject by creating a fictional speaker—usually a calm, and often a naive, observer—who can address the topic without revealing the true emotions of the writer. As you read "A Modest Proposal," look for the different characteristics of satire that Swift uses to help deliver his message. Decide whether his satire is of the Horatian type—the type he advocated as least offensive.

Satire

- *humor playful or bitter*
- *criticism of a large group or institution*
- *irony*
- *naive narrator*

Using Your Reading Log Use your reading log to record your responses to the questions inserted in this selection. Also jot down other thoughts and feelings that come to you as you read.

A Modest Proposal

FOR PREVENTING THE CHILDREN OF POOR PEOPLE IN IRELAND FROM BEING A BURDEN TO THEIR PARENTS OR COUNTRY, AND FOR MAKING THEM BENEFICIAL TO THE PUBLIC

Jonathan Swift

Industry and Idleness: The Idle 'Prentice Executed at Tyburn (1747), William Hogarth. Steel engraving. The Granger Collection, New York.

It is a melancholy object to those who walk through this great town[1] or travel in the country, when they see the streets, the roads, and cabin doors, crowded with beggars of the female sex, followed by three, four, or six children, all in rags and importuning every passenger for an alms. These mothers, instead of being able to work for their honest livelihood, are forced to employ all their time in strolling to beg sustenance for their helpless infants, who, as they grow up, either turn thieves for want of work, or leave their dear native country

1. **this great town:** Dublin.

to fight for the Pretender[2] in Spain, or sell themselves to the Barbadoes.[3]

I think it is agreed by all parties that this prodigious number of children in the arms, or on the backs, or at the heels of their mothers, and frequently of their fathers, is in the present deplorable state of the kingdom a very great additional grievance; and therefore whoever could find out a fair, cheap, and easy method of making these children sound, useful members of the commonwealth would deserve so well of the public as to have his statue set up for a preserver of the nation.

But my intention is very far from being confined to provide only for the children of professed beggars; it is of a much greater extent, and shall take in the whole number of infants at a certain age who are born of parents in effect as little able to support them as those who demand our charity in the streets.

As to my own part, having turned my thoughts for many years upon this important subject, and maturely weighed the several schemes of other projectors, I have always found them grossly mistaken in their computation. It is true, a child just dropped from its dam[4] may be supported by her milk for a solar year, with little other nourishment; at most not above the value of two shillings, which the mother may certainly get, or the value in scraps, by her lawful occupation of begging; and it is exactly at one year old that I propose to provide for them in such a manner as instead of being a charge upon their parents or the parish, or wanting food and raiment for the rest of their lives, they shall on the contrary contribute to the feeding, and partly to the clothing, of many thousands.

There is likewise another great advantage in my scheme, that it will prevent those voluntary abortions, and that horrid practice of women murdering their bastard children, alas, too frequent among us, sacrificing the poor innocent babes, I doubt, more to avoid the expense than the shame, which would move tears and pity in the most savage and inhuman breast.

The number of souls in this kingdom being usually reckoned one million and a half, of these I calculate there may be about two hundred thousand couple whose wives are breeders; from which number I subtract thirty thousand couples who are able to maintain their own children, although I apprehend there cannot be so many under the present distresses of the kingdom; but this being granted, there will remain an hundred and seventy thousand breeders. I again subtract fifty thousand for those women who miscarry, or whose children die by accident or disease within the year. There only remain an hundred and twenty thousand children of poor parents annually born. The question therefore is, how this number shall be reared and provided for, which, as I have already said, under the present situation of affairs, is utterly impossible by all the methods hitherto proposed. For we can neither employ them in handicraft or agriculture; we neither build houses (I mean in the country) nor cultivate land. They can very seldom pick up

EVALUATE

What tone is conveyed by the speaker's mathematical calculations?

2. **Pretender:** James Edward Stuart—the "pretender," or claimant, to the English throne, from which his father, James II, had been deposed in 1688. Because he was Roman Catholic, the common people of Ireland were loyal to him.

3. **sell . . . the Barbadoes** (bär-bā′dōz): To escape extreme poverty, some of the Irish migrated to the West Indies, obtaining money for their passage by agreeing to work in servitude on plantations there for a set time.

4. **dam:** female parent (used almost exclusively of farm animals).

WORDS TO KNOW

prodigious (prə-dĭj′əs) *adj.* enormous
deplorable (dĭ-plôr′ə-bəl) *adj.* miserable; woeful

a livelihood by stealing till they arrive at six years old, except where they are of towardly parts;[5] although I confess they learn the rudiments much earlier, during which time they can however be looked upon only as probationers, as I have been informed by a principal gentleman in the county of Cavan, who protested to me that he never knew above one or two instances under the age of six, even in a part of the kingdom so renowned for the quickest proficiency in that art.

I am assured by our merchants that a boy or girl before twelve years old is no salable commodity; and even when they come to this age they will not yield above three pounds, or three pounds and half a crown at most on the Exchange; which cannot turn to account either to the parents or the kingdom, the charge of nutriment and rags having been at least four times that value.

I shall now therefore humbly propose my own thoughts, which I hope will not be liable to the least objection.

I have been assured by a very knowing American of my acquaintance in London, that a young healthy child well nursed is at a year old a most delicious, nourishing, and wholesome food, whether stewed, roasted, baked, or boiled; and I make no doubt that it will equally serve in a fricassee or a ragout.[6]

I do therefore humbly offer it to public consideration that of the hundred and twenty thousand children, already computed, twenty thousand may be reserved for breed, whereof only one fourth part to be males, which is more than we allow to sheep, black cattle, or swine; and my reason is that these children are seldom the fruits of marriage, a circumstance not much regarded by our savages, therefore one male will be sufficient to serve four females. That the remaining hundred thousand may at a year old be offered in sale to the persons of quality and fortune through the kingdom, always advising the mother to let them suck plentifully in the last month, so as to render them plump and fat for a good table. A child will make two dishes at an entertainment for friends; and when the family dines alone, the fore or hind quarter will make a reasonable dish, and seasoned with a little pepper or salt will be very good boiled on the fourth day, especially in winter.

I have reckoned upon a medium that a child just born will weigh twelve pounds, and in a solar year if tolerably nursed increaseth to twenty-eight pounds.

I grant this food will be somewhat dear, and therefore very proper for landlords, who, as they have already devoured most of the parents, seem to have the best title to the children.

QUESTION

What does the speaker mean by "landlords, who . . . have already devoured most of the parents"?

Infant's flesh will be in season throughout the year, but more plentiful in March, and a little before and after. For we are told by a grave author, an eminent French physician,[7] that fish being a prolific[8] diet, there are more children born in Roman Catholic countries about nine months after Lent than at any other season; therefore, reckoning a year after Lent, the markets will be more glutted than usual, because the number of popish[9] infants is at least three to one in this kingdom; and therefore it will have one other collateral advantage, by lessening the number of Papists[10] among us.

I have already computed the charge of nursing a beggar's child (in which list I reckon all

5. **are of towardly parts:** have a promising talent.
6. **fricassee** (frĭk′ə-sē′) **. . . ragout** (ră-gōō′): types of meat stews.
7. **grave . . . physician:** François Rabelais (1494?–1553), a French satirist.
8. **prolific:** promoting fertility.
9. **popish** (pō′pĭsh): Roman Catholic.
10. **Papists** (pā′pĭsts): Roman Catholics.

WORDS TO KNOW

rudiment (rōō′də-mənt) *n.* a basic principle or skill
proficiency (prə-fĭsh′ən-sē) *n.* competence; expertise

cottagers, laborers, and four fifths of the farmers), to be about two shillings per annum, rags included; and I believe no gentleman would repine to give ten shillings for the carcass of a good fat child, which, as I have said, will make four dishes of excellent nutritive meat, when he hath only some particular friend or his own family to dine with him. Thus the squire will learn to be a good landlord, and grow popular among the tenants; the mother will have eight shillings net profit, and be fit for work till she produces another child.

Those who are more thrifty (as I must confess the times require) may flay the carcass; the skin of which artificially dressed will make admirable gloves for ladies, and summer boots for fine gentlemen.

As to our city of Dublin, shambles[11] may be appointed for this purpose in the most convenient parts of it, and butchers we may be assured will not be wanting; although I rather recommend buying the children alive, and dressing them hot from the knife as we do roasting pigs.

A very worthy person, a true lover of his country, and whose virtues I highly esteem, was lately pleased in discoursing on this matter to offer a refinement upon my scheme. He said that many gentlemen of this kingdom, having of late destroyed their deer, he conceived that the want of venison might be well supplied by the bodies of young lads and maidens, not exceeding fourteen years of age nor under twelve, so great a number of both sexes in every county being now ready to starve for want of work and service; and these to be disposed of by their parents, if alive, or otherwise by their nearest relations. But with due deference to so excellent a friend and so deserving a patriot, I cannot be altogether in his sentiments; for as to the males, my American acquaintance assured me from frequent experience that their flesh was generally tough and lean, like that of our schoolboys, by continual exercise, and their taste disagreeable; and to fatten them would not answer the charge. Then as to the females, it would, I think with humble submission, be a loss to the public, because they soon would become breeders themselves; and besides, it is not improbable that some scrupulous people might be apt to censure such a practice (although indeed very unjustly) as a little bordering upon cruelty; which, I confess, hath always been with me the strongest objection against any project, how well soever intended.

But in order to justify my friend, he confessed that this expedient was put into his head by the famous Psalmanazar,[12] a native of the island Formosa, who came from thence to London above twenty years ago, and in conversation told my friend that in his country when any young person happened to be put to death, the executioner sold the carcass to persons of quality as a prime dainty; and that in his time the body of a plump girl of fifteen, who was crucified for an attempt to poison the emperor, was sold to his Imperial Majesty's prime minister of state, and other great mandarins of the court, in joints from the gibbet,[13] at four hundred crowns. Neither indeed can I deny that if the same use were made of several plump young girls in this town, who without one single groat[14] to their fortunes cannot stir abroad without a chair, and appear at the playhouse and assemblies in foreign fineries which they never will pay for, the kingdom would not be the worse.

Some persons of a desponding spirit are in great concern about that vast number of poor people

11. **shambles:** slaughterhouses.

12. **Psalmanazar** (săl′mə-năz′ər): a French impostor in London, who called himself George Psalmanazar and pretended to be from Formosa (now Taiwan)—where, he said, cannibalism was practiced.

13. **gibbet** (jĭb′ĭt): gallows.

14. **groat:** an old British coin worth four pennies.

WORDS TO KNOW

deference (dĕf′ər-əns) *n.* courteous regard or respect
expedient (ĭk-spē′dē-ənt) *n.* a means to an end

who are aged, diseased, or maimed, and I have been desired to employ my thoughts what course may be taken to ease the nation of so grievous an encumbrance. But I am not in the least pain upon that matter, because it is very well known that they are every day dying and rotting by cold and famine, and filth and vermin, as fast as can be reasonably expected. And as to the younger laborers, they are now in almost as hopeful a condition. They cannot get work, and consequently pine away for want of nourishment to a degree that if at any time they are accidentally hired to common labor, they have not strength to perform it; and thus the country and themselves are happily delivered from the evils to come.

I have too long digressed, and therefore shall return to my subject. I think the advantages by the proposal which I have made are obvious and many, as well as of the highest importance.

For first, as I have already observed, it would greatly lessen the number of Papists, with whom we are yearly overrun, being the principal breeders of the nation as well as our most dangerous enemies; and who stay at home on purpose to deliver the kingdom to the Pretender, hoping to take their advantage by the absence of so many good Protestants, who have chosen rather to leave their country than stay at home and pay tithes against their conscience to an Episcopal curate.[15]

Secondly, the poorer tenants will have something valuable of their own, which by law may be made liable to distress,[16] and help to pay their landlord's rent, their corn and cattle being already seized and money a thing unknown.

Thirdly, whereas the maintenance of an hundred thousand children, from two years old and upwards, cannot be computed at less than ten shillings a piece per annum, the nation's stock will be thereby increased fifty thousand pounds per annum, besides the profit of a new dish introduced to the tables of all gentlemen of fortune in the kingdom who have any refinement in taste. And the money will circulate among ourselves, the goods being entirely of our own growth and manufacture.

Fourthly, the constant breeders, besides the gain of eight shillings sterling per annum by the sale of their children, will be rid of the charge of maintaining them after the first year.

Fifthly, this food would likewise bring great custom to taverns, where the vintners will certainly be so prudent as to procure the best receipts for dressing it to perfection, and consequently have their houses frequented by all the fine gentlemen, who justly value themselves upon their knowledge in good eating; and a skillful cook, who

15. **Protestants . . . curate:** Swift is referring to Anglo-Irish landowners who lived—and spent the income from their property—in England.

16. **distress:** seizure for the payment of debts.

WORDS TO KNOW

encumbrance (ĕn-kŭm'brəns) *n.* a burden

understands how to oblige his guests, will contrive to make it as expensive as they please.

Sixthly, this would be a great inducement to marriage, which all wise nations have either encouraged by rewards or enforced by laws and penalties. It would increase the care and tenderness of mothers toward their children, when they were sure of a settlement for life to the poor babes, provided in some sort by the public, to their annual profit instead of expense. We should see an honest emulation among the married women, which of them could bring the fattest child to the market. Men would become as fond of their wives during the time of their pregnancy as they are now of their mares in foal, their cows in calf, or sows when they are ready to farrow; nor offer to beat or kick them (as is too frequent a practice) for fear of a miscarriage.

EVALUATE

What effect is the speaker trying to create by listing the advantages of the proposal?

Many other advantages might be enumerated. For instance, the addition of some thousand carcasses in our exportation of barreled beef, the propagation of swine's flesh, and improvement in the art of making good bacon, so much wanted among us by the great destruction of pigs, too frequent at our tables, which are no way comparable in taste or magnificence to a well-grown, fat, yearling child, which roasted whole will make a considerable figure at a lord mayor's feast or any other public entertainment. But this and many others I omit, being studious of brevity.

Supposing that one thousand families in this city would be constant customers for infants' flesh, besides others who might have it at merry meetings, particularly weddings and christenings, I compute that Dublin would take off annually about twenty thousand carcasses, and the rest of the kingdom (where probably they will be sold somewhat cheaper) the remaining eighty thousand.

I can think of no one objection that will possibly be raised against this proposal, unless it should be urged that the number of people will be thereby much lessened in the kingdom. This I freely own, and it was indeed one principal design in offering it to the world. I desire the reader will observe, that I calculate my remedy for this one individual kingdom of Ireland and for no other that ever was, is, or I think ever can be upon earth. Therefore let no man talk to me of other expedients: of taxing our absentees at five shillings a pound: of using neither clothes nor household furniture except what is of our own growth and manufacture: of utterly rejecting the materials and instruments that promote foreign luxury: of curing the expensiveness of pride, vanity, idleness, and gaming in our women: of introducing a vein of parsimony,[17] prudence, and temperance: of learning to love our country, in the want of which we differ even from Laplanders and the inhabitants of Topinamboo:[18] of quitting our animosities and factions, nor acting any longer like the Jews, who were murdering one another at the very moment their city was taken:[19] of being a little cautious not to sell our country and conscience for nothing: of teaching landlords to have at least one degree of

17. **parsimony** (pär'sə-mō'nē): frugality; thrift.
18. **Topinamboo** (tŏp'ĭ-năm'bo͞o): an area in Brazil.
19. **Jews . . . taken:** In A.D. 70, during a Jewish revolt against Roman rule, the inhabitants of Jerusalem, by fighting among themselves, made it easier for the future Roman emperor Titus to capture the city.

WORDS TO KNOW

emulation (ĕm'yə-lā'shən) *n.* an effort to equal or outdo another person; rivalry

animosity (ăn'ə-mŏs'ĭ-tē) *n.* hostility; hatred

mercy toward their tenants: lastly, of putting a spirit of honesty, industry, and skill into our shopkeepers; who, if a resolution could now be taken to buy only our native goods, would immediately unite to cheat and exact upon us in the price, the measure, and the goodness, nor could ever yet be brought to make one fair proposal of just dealing, though often and earnestly invited to it.

QUESTION

What might be the speaker's source for the "other expedients" he lists?

Therefore I repeat, let no man talk to me of these and the like expedients,[20] till he hath at least some glimpse of hope that there will ever be some hearty and sincere attempt to put them in practice.

But as to myself, having been wearied out for many years with offering vain, idle, visionary thoughts, and at length utterly despairing of success, I fortunately fell upon this proposal, which, as it is wholly new, so it hath something solid and real, of no expense and little trouble, full in our own power, and whereby we can incur no danger in disobliging England. For this kind of commodity will not bear exportation, the flesh being of too tender a consistence to admit a long continuance in salt, although perhaps I could name a country which would be glad to eat up our whole nation without it.

After all, I am not so violently bent upon my own opinion as to reject any offer proposed by wise men, which shall be found equally innocent, cheap, easy, and effectual. But before something of that kind shall be advanced in contradiction to my scheme, and offering a better, I desire the author or authors will be pleased maturely to consider two points. First, as things now stand, how they will be able to find food and raiment for an hundred thousand useless mouths and backs. And secondly, there being a round million of creatures in human figure throughout this kingdom, whose sole subsistence put into a common stock would leave them in debt two millions of pounds sterling, adding those who are beggars by profession to the bulk of farmers, cottagers, and laborers, with their wives and children who are beggars in effect; I desire those politicians who dislike my overture, and may perhaps be so bold to attempt an answer, that they will first ask the parents of these mortals whether they would not at this day think it a great happiness to have been sold for food at a year old in the manner I prescribe, and thereby have avoided such a perpetual scene of misfortunes as they have since gone through by the oppression of landlords, the impossibility of paying rent without money or trade, the want of common sustenance, with neither house nor clothes to cover them from the inclemencies of the weather, and the most inevitable prospect of entailing the like or greater miseries upon their breed forever.

I profess, in the sincerity of my heart, that I have not the least personal interest in endeavoring to promote this necessary work, having no other motive than the public good of my country, by advancing our trade, providing for infants, relieving the poor, and giving some pleasure to the rich. I have no children by which I can propose to get a single penny; the youngest being nine years old, and my wife past childbearing. ❖

20. **let no man . . . expedients:** Swift had, in his writings, suggested the "other expedients" without success.

WORDS TO KNOW

perpetual (pər-pĕch′o͞o-əl) *adj.* everlasting; continual

RESPONDING OPTIONS

FROM PERSONAL RESPONSE *TO* CRITICAL ANALYSIS

REFLECT 1. What was your first reaction to the speaker's proposal? Jot down your thoughts in your notebook.

RETHINK 2. How would you describe the speaker? Use details to support your answer.

3. What response do you think Swift hoped to get from readers of "A Modest Proposal"?

4. In your opinion, why did Swift have the speaker list "other expedients" to Ireland's problem?

Consider
- the types of proposals the speaker mentions
- the contrast between those proposals and the "modest proposal"
- Swift's overall purpose for writing the essay

RELATE 5. Poverty and starvation in 18th-century Ireland inspired Swift to write "A Modest Proposal." What are some of the social and political issues that might inspire satirists today?

ANOTHER PATHWAY

Cooperative Learning

Pretend it is the year 1729. Organize a "town meeting" to discuss "A Modest Proposal." Begin by writing a list of questions and comments that various citizens—Roman Catholics, Protestants, mothers, fathers, children, government officials—might have. Then select a moderator, and conduct your meeting.

LITERARY CONCEPTS

An important element in satirical writing is **irony,** or contrast between expectation and reality. Irony is often subtle and easily overlooked or misinterpreted. One type of irony that is typical of satirical prose is **verbal irony.** Verbal irony occurs when what is said is not what is meant—as when words of praise actually convey criticism or words of criticism are used to praise. This incongruity often has the effect of surprising the reader. What irony do you find in the title "A Modest Proposal"? In what other ways is irony used in the selection?

CRITIC'S CORNER

Some critics, including Samuel Johnson, have suggested that Swift was a misanthrope—a hater of humanity. On the basis of your understanding of "A Modest Proposal," would you agree or disagree with this evaluation? Explain your reasons.

QUICKWRITES

1. Imagine that you are the editor of an 18th-century periodical. To help you decide whether to print Swift's essay, write a **memo** in which you list the pros and cons of publishing it.
2. Write a draft of a **satiric essay** of your own, titled "A Modest Proposal." Offer a humorous or outrageous proposal for reforming a current social or political problem.
3. Write a **biographical sketch** of Jonathan Swift, basing your description of him on what you know about his motivations for writing "A Modest Proposal."

PORTFOLIO *Save your writing. You may want to use it later as a springboard to a piece for your portfolio.*

ALTERNATIVE ACTIVITIES

Draw a **political cartoon** that might have appeared in newspapers in response to the original publication of Swift's essay.

ACROSS THE CURRICULUM

History Investigate the history of religious strife in Ireland. What changes occurred in the relationship between Protestants and Catholics after the 18th century? How did those changes affect the political climate in Ireland?

ART CONNECTION

Look again at the Hogarth illustration on pages 390–391, and think about the "proposal" you have just read. Why do you think this illustration was chosen to accompany Swift's "A Modest Proposal"?

THE WRITER'S STYLE

In this essay, Swift often uses words and phrases that might shock or offend his readers—for example, "I am assured by our merchants that a boy or girl before twelve years old is no salable commodity; and even when they come to this age they will not yield above three pounds." Find other similar examples. Why do you think Swift chose to use this type of language?

WORDS TO KNOW

Decide whether the words in each of the following pairs are synonyms or antonyms. On your paper, write *S* for *Synonyms* or *A* for *Antonyms.*

1. animosity—admiration
2. prodigious—small
3. perpetual—temporary
4. deference—esteem
5. expedient—device
6. proficiency—incompetence
7. deplorable—wretched
8. emulation—cooperation
9. encumbrance—asset
10. rudiment—basis

JONATHAN SWIFT

1667–1745

Although not a particularly good student, Jonathan Swift did earn a degree from Trinity College in Dublin. His father had died before he was born, and, though poor, Swift was given a superior education by wealthy relatives. In 1689, during a time of religious turmoil, he moved to England, where he lived at the elegant estate of a retired diplomat. There he met some of London's most important writers and politicians.

After Swift was ordained a priest of the Church of England in 1695, he began to return to Ireland intermittently to work in various church posts. His literary reputation was established in 1704 with the publication of *A Tale of a Tub,* a satire on religious and cultural topics. During the next decade, he wrote many political articles and pamphlets—first for the Whigs but later, having grown dissatisfied with Whig policies, for the Tories. In 1713, as a reward for his service to the Tories, Swift was appointed dean of St. Patrick's Cathedral in Dublin, where he spent the remainder of his life. There, he directed his energies to creating many of the great works upon which his fame rests. Swift's Latin epitaph, which he wrote himself, ends in lines that can be translated, "Go, traveler, and imitate if you can a man who was an undaunted champion of liberty."

OTHER WORKS *Gulliver's Travels, The Battle of the Books, The Journal to Stella*

PREVIEWING

NONFICTION

from The Crisis

Thomas Paine

PERSONAL CONNECTION

Think about the types of injustices, or unfair conditions, that have existed in the world at various points in history—such as slavery, political repression, racial discrimination, and unjust imprisonment. How have the victims of some of these injustices responded to their situations? In your opinion, what responses have been the most effective? Share your thoughts with classmates.

HISTORICAL CONNECTION

During the 18th century, political unrest and a passion for liberty began to emerge both in Britain and in its American colonies. In Britain, the working classes revolted against the economic injustice they were experiencing. In America, the colonists protested unfair regulations and taxes imposed on them by Parliament. The British government reacted to the colonists' protests by imposing even tighter restrictions and by sending more British troops to the colonies.

When Thomas Paine arrived in America in 1774, the colonists were on the brink of war. Although a loyal British citizen, Paine sympathized with the plight of common people everywhere. In early 1776, he anonymously published a pamphlet called *Common Sense,* in which he urged Americans to seek independence. This pamphlet was extremely popular and undoubtedly influenced the drafting of the Declaration of Independence.

After the outbreak of the American Revolution, Paine joined the patriots as a general's aide. In the early days of the war, he found himself retreating with George Washington's troops, who had been driven out of New York by a larger British force. Casualties and desertions had severely diminished the colonial troops, and Washington's army was on the verge of disintegration. Observing the desperation of the soldiers, Paine wrote another powerful essay, the first in a series later to be titled *The Crisis.* After reading Paine's essay, Washington ordered it read aloud to the disheartened troops camped at Valley Forge.

WRITING CONNECTION

Unjust Situation	Possible Response

In your notebook, mark off two columns. In the first column, list three or four current national or international situations in which people are confronting injustices. In the second column, describe the way you would respond if you were a victim of the injustices. Then, as you read this selection, note the way in which Thomas Paine responded to unjust conditions in colonial America.

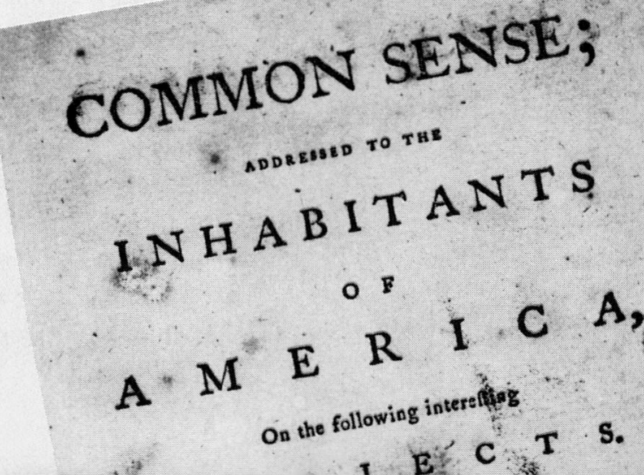

LASERLINKS
• HISTORICAL CONNECTION

from

THE CRISIS, NUMBER 1

THOMAS PAINE

These are the times that try men's souls. The summer soldier and the sunshine patriot will in this crisis, shrink from the service of his country; but he that stands it NOW, deserves the love and thanks of man and woman. Tyranny, like hell, is not easily conquered; yet we have this consolation with us, that the harder the conflict, the more glorious the triumph. What we obtain too cheap, we esteem too lightly; 'tis dearness[1] only that gives everything its value. Heaven knows how to put a proper price upon its goods; and it would be strange indeed, if so celestial an article as FREEDOM should not be highly rated. Britain, with an army to enforce her tyranny, has declared that she has a right (not only to TAX) but "to BIND us in ALL CASES WHATSOEVER," and if being bound in that manner, is not slavery, then is there not such a thing as slavery upon earth. Even the expression is impious,[2] for so unlimited a power can belong only to God. . . .

I have as little superstition in me as any man living, but my secret opinion has ever been, and still is, that God Almighty will not give up a people to military destruction, or leave them unsupportedly to perish, who have so earnestly and so repeatedly sought to avoid the calamities of war, by every decent method which wisdom could invent. Neither have I so much of the

1. **dearness:** high cost; expensiveness.
2. **impious** (ĭm′pē-əs): lacking in religious devotion and respect.

infidel[3] in me, as to suppose that he has relinquished the government of the world, and given us up to the care of devils; and as I do not, I cannot see on what grounds the king of Britain can look up to heaven for help against us: a common murderer, a highwayman, or a house-breaker, has as good a pretense as he. . . .

I once felt all that kind of anger, which a man ought to feel, against the mean[4] principles that are held by the Tories:[5] a noted one, who kept a tavern at Amboy, was standing at his door, with as pretty a child in his hand, about eight or nine years old, as I ever saw, and after speaking his mind as freely as he thought was prudent, finished with this unfatherly expression, *"Well! give me peace in my day."* Not a man lives on the continent but fully believes that a separation must some time or other finally take place, and a generous parent should have said, *"If there must be trouble let it be in my day, that my child may have peace";* and this single reflection, well applied, is sufficient to awaken every man to duty. Not a place upon earth might be so happy as America. Her situation is remote from all the wrangling world, and she has nothing to do but to trade with them. A man can distinguish himself between temper and principle, and I am as confident, as I am that God governs the world, that America will never be happy till she gets clear of foreign dominion. Wars, without ceasing, will break out till that period arrives, and the continent must in the end be conqueror; for though the flame of liberty may sometimes cease to shine, the coal can never expire. . . .

The heart that feels not now, is dead: the blood of his children will curse his cowardice, who shrinks back at a time when a little might have saved the whole, and made *them* happy. (I love the man that can smile at trouble; that can gather strength from distress, and grow brave by reflection.) 'Tis the business of little minds to shrink; but he whose heart is firm, and whose conscience approves his conduct, will pursue his principles unto death. My own line of reasoning is to myself as straight and clear as a ray of light. Not all the treasures of the world, so far as I believe, could have induced[6] me to support an offensive war, for I think it murder; but if a thief breaks into my house, burns and destroys my property, and kills or threatens to kill me, or those that are in it, and *to "bind me in all cases whatsoever,"* to his absolute will, am I to suffer it? What signifies it to me, whether he who does it is a king or a common man; my countryman, or not my countryman; whether it be done by an individual villain or an army of them? If we reason to the root of things we shall find no difference; neither can any just cause be assigned why we should punish in the one case and pardon in the other. ❖

3. **infidel** (ĭn′fĭ-dəl): a person who does not hold accepted religious beliefs.
4. **mean:** small-minded; selfish.
5. **Tories:** colonists loyal to Britain.
6. **induced:** persuaded.

RESPONDING OPTIONS

FROM PERSONAL RESPONSE *TO* CRITICAL ANALYSIS

REFLECT

1. What words or phrases remain in your mind after your reading of this excerpt from *The Crisis?* Jot down a few of them in your notebook.

RETHINK

2. What three or four statements in this excerpt do you think express Paine's basic principles or beliefs about life?
3. In your opinion, what qualities or attitudes anger Paine?

   Consider
   - what he means by "summer soldier" and "sunshine patriot"
   - his anecdote about the Tory
   - his praise of "the man that can smile at trouble . . . gather strength from distress, and grow brave by reflection"
4. How would you describe Paine's view of war? Support your ideas with details from his essay.
5. What effects do you think Paine's essay might have had on the people who read it or heard it read?

RELATE

6. Paine states that America "is remote from all the wrangling world, and she has nothing to do but to trade with them." Has this view, in your opinion, been borne out by the later relationships between the United States and other nations? Support your answer with examples.

ANOTHER PATHWAY

With a partner, analyze the language Paine uses in *The Crisis* to sway his readers. Make a list of words or phrases that you think are designed to appeal to certain emotions, and then describe those emotions. Share and discuss your list with the rest of the class.

LITERARY CONCEPTS

Parallelism is the use of similar grammatical constructions to express ideas that are related or equal in importance. The parallel elements may be words, phrases, sentences, or paragraphs. For example, the first paragraph of this excerpt contains the parallelisms "the harder the conflict, the more glorious the triumph" and "what we obtain too cheap, we esteem too lightly." What other examples of parallelism can you find in Paine's essay? What effect does his use of parallelism have on the reader?

QUICKWRITES

1. Create copy for a **handbill** to recruit volunteer soldiers for the American Revolution. Reflect ideas expressed in *The Crisis.*
2. How might Thomas Paine react to the injustices you identified for the Writing Connection on page 400? Write notes for a **speech** in which he urges people to remedy one of the injustices.
3. Write your own **definition** of *summer soldier* or *sunshine patriot.* Give examples from contemporary society.

PORTFOLIO *Save your writing. You may want to use it later as a springboard to a piece for your portfolio.*

ALTERNATIVE ACTIVITIES

1. Design and create several **political buttons,** using thought-provoking sentences or phrases from Paine's essay.
2. Practice and perform an **oral reading** of this selection. Pretend that you are speaking to Washington's troops at Valley Forge.
3. Create a **collage** of photographs and illustrations that reflect Paine's statement "'Tis the business of little minds to shrink; but he whose heart is firm, and whose conscience approves his conduct, will pursue his principles unto death."

CRITIC'S CORNER

One critic has written that "the single most important clue to Paine's writings is that they are *dynamic.*" Do you think the excerpt you have read supports this conclusion? Explain your answer.

ACROSS THE CURRICULUM

History Research the attitudes of the British people toward the American colonists in the years leading up to the American Revolution. What attitudes were most widespread? Did all British citizens have basically the same views? Summarize your findings for the class.

THOMAS PAINE

1737–1809

Thomas Paine understood the struggles of the working class. At the age of 13 he began working for his father as a corset maker in Thetford, England. Disliking this job, he attempted a number of other kinds of work over a period of years, including seafaring, teaching, and tax collecting. He was not very successful in any of these occupations, but by the time he was in his 30s, he had become interested in political issues and had begun writing political pamphlets. While in London in 1774, he met Benjamin Franklin, who encouraged Paine to look for opportunities in America.

Paine arrived in Philadelphia in November 1774 and found work as a magazine editor. He quickly became committed to the American cause and supported it throughout the Revolution, both as a writer and as an aide to military and political leaders. Although Paine's patriotic pamphlets were extremely popular, he was virtually penniless by the end of the war, partly because he had donated substantial amounts of money to help provide supplies for soldiers. In return for his services during the war, the state of New York gave him a farm, where he spent his time working on various inventions, including an improved iron bridge. In 1787, on a trip to Europe to promote his bridge, he became embroiled in the French Revolution and was inspired to write a defense of the revolutionaries, called *Rights of Man.* Ironically, the French revolutionaries later arrested Paine for arguing that the French king should be banished rather than executed.

While imprisoned in France, Paine began writing *The Age of Reason,* in which he acknowledged God but opposed organized religion. On his return to America in 1802, he discovered that his contributions to the American cause had largely been forgotten. Widely criticized for his unorthodox religious views, Paine had few friends in his later years. For more than a century after his death, he was regarded as someone who had done more harm than good. In recent years, however, his achievements have been honored by a new generation of historians, and a number of monuments have been erected in his memory.

OTHER WORKS *Common Sense, Rights of Man*

PREVIEWING

NONFICTION

from A Vindication of the Rights of Woman

Mary Wollstonecraft

PERSONAL CONNECTION

Women's rights have been debated for centuries. From your knowledge of history, what has caused this debate? Do you think that women's rights are still a controversial issue in our society? Why or why not? Share your thoughts with your classmates.

BIOGRAPHICAL CONNECTION

Although a number of 18th-century British writers discussed the role of women in society, none became as celebrated for their feminist views as Mary Wollstonecraft. Early in her life, Wollstonecraft learned the value of independence and became openly critical of a society that treated females as inferior creatures who were socially, financially, and legally dependent on men. Her concern for humanity was not limited to compassion for downtrodden women, though. Like her friend Thomas Paine, she advocated the equality and independence of all human beings. Even before Paine wrote his more famous *Rights of Man,* Wollstonecraft had written a defense of the French Revolution entitled *A Vindication of the Rights of Men.* Published in 1790, it was controversial not only for its radical ideas but for being a woman's venture into political writing. In 1792, Wollstonecraft continued the controversy with her publication of *A Vindication of the Rights of Woman,* in which she called for an end to the prevailing injustices against females. Although her opinions on women's rights may seem conservative by modern standards, they were radical in 18th-century Britain, where most women accepted their inferior status or at least refrained from expressing their discontent.

An 18th-century London literary circle

WRITING CONNECTION

Brainstorm a list of words and phrases that you think describe the typical 18th-century British woman. Make sure that your list addresses such topics as education, rights as a citizen, marriage and customs, and social behavior. Then, as you read this selection, compare your image of the typical woman in 18th-century Britain with Wollstonecraft's depiction.

Using Your Reading Log Use your reading log to record your responses to the questions inserted in this selection. Also jot down other thoughts and feelings that come to you as you read.

FROM

A VINDICATION OF THE RIGHTS OF WOMAN

MARY WOLLSTONECRAFT

FROM THE INTRODUCTION

After considering the historic page, and viewing the living world with anxious solicitude, the most melancholy emotions of sorrowful indignation have depressed my spirits, and I have sighed when obliged to confess, that either nature has made a great difference between man and man, or that the civilization which has hitherto taken place in the world has been very partial. I have turned over various books written on the subject of education, and patiently observed the conduct of parents and the management of schools; but what has been the result?—a profound conviction that the neglected education of my fellow-creatures is the grand source of the misery I deplore; and that women, in particular, are rendered weak and wretched by a variety of concurring causes, originating from one hasty conclusion. The conduct and manners of women, in fact, evidently prove that their minds are not in a healthy state; for, like the flowers which are planted in too rich

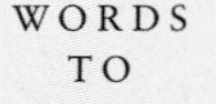

WORDS TO KNOW

solicitude (sə-lĭs'ĭ-to͞od') *n.* care or concern
concurring (kən-kûr'ĭng) *adj.* occurring at the same time; acting together
concur *v.*

a soil, strength and usefulness are sacrificed to beauty; and the flaunting leaves, after having pleased a fastidious eye, fade, disregarded on the stalk, long before the season when they ought to have arrived at maturity. One cause of this barren blooming I attribute to a false system of education, gathered from the books written on this subject by men who, considering females rather as women than human creatures, have been more anxious to make them alluring mistresses than affectionate wives and rational mothers; and the understanding of the sex has been so bubbled by this specious homage, that the civilized women of the present century, with a few exceptions, are only anxious to inspire love, when they ought to cherish a nobler ambition, and by their abilities and virtues exact respect.

In a treatise,[1] therefore, on female rights and manners, the works which have been particularly written for their improvement must not be overlooked; especially when it is asserted, in direct terms, that the minds of women are enfeebled by false refinement; that the books of instruction, written by men of genius, have had the same tendency as more frivolous productions; and that . . . they are treated as a kind of subordinate beings, and not as a part of the human species, when improvable reason is allowed to be the dignified distinction which raises men above the brute creation, and puts a natural scepter in a feeble hand.

Yet, because I am a woman, I would not lead my readers to suppose that I mean violently to agitate the contested question respecting the quality or inferiority of the sex; but as the subject lies in my way, and I cannot pass it over without subjecting the main tendency of my reasoning to misconstruction, I shall stop a moment to deliver, in a few words, my opinion. In the government of the physical world it is observable that the female in point of strength is, in general, inferior to the male. This is the law of nature; and it does not appear to be suspended or abrogated[2] in favor of woman. A degree of physical superiority cannot, therefore, be denied—and it is a noble prerogative! But not content with this natural pre-eminence, men endeavor to sink us still lower merely to render us alluring objects for a moment; and women, intoxicated by the adoration which men, under the influence of their senses, pay them, do not seek to obtain a durable interest in their hearts, or to become the friends of the fellow creatures who find amusement in their society.

QUESTION

Why does Wollstonecraft blame both men and women for society's attitude toward women?

I am aware of an obvious inference: from every quarter have I heard exclamations against masculine women; but where are they to be found? If by this appellation men mean to inveigh against their ardor[3] in hunting, shooting, and gaming, I shall most cordially join in the cry; but if it be against the imitation of manly virtues, or, more properly speaking, the attainment of those talents and virtues, the exercise of which ennobles the human character, and which raise females in the scale of animal being, when they are comprehensively termed mankind; all those who view them with a philosophic eye must, I should think, wish with me, that they may every day grow more and more masculine. . . .

My own sex, I hope, will excuse me, if I treat them like rational creatures, instead of flattering their *fascinating* graces, and viewing them

1. **treatise** (trē′tĭs): a formal, detailed article or book on a particular subject.
2. **abrogated** (ăb′rə-gā′tĭd): canceled; repealed.
3. **if by . . . ardor:** if by this word (that is, *masculine*) men mean to condemn some women's enthusiasm.

WORDS TO KNOW

specious (spē′shəs) *adj.* attractive in a deceptive or insincere way
subordinate (sə-bôr′dn-ĭt) *adj.* less important; lower in rank

as if they were in a state of perpetual childhood, unable to stand alone. I earnestly wish to point out in what true dignity and human happiness consists—I wish to persuade women to endeavor to acquire strength, both of mind and body, and to convince them that the soft phrases, susceptibility of heart, delicacy of sentiment, and refinement of taste, are almost synonymous with epithets[4] of weakness, and that those beings who are only the objects of pity and that kind of love, which has been termed its sister, will soon become objects of contempt. . . .

The education of women has, of late, been more attended to than formerly; yet they are still reckoned a frivolous sex, and ridiculed or pitied by the writers who endeavor by satire or instruction to improve them. It is acknowledged that they spend many of the first years of their lives in acquiring a smattering of accomplishments; meanwhile strength of body and mind are sacrificed to libertine[5] notions of beauty, to the desire of establishing themselves—the only way women can rise in the world—by marriage. And this desire making mere animals of them, when they marry they act as such children may be expected to act: they dress; they paint, and nickname God's creatures. Surely these weak beings are only fit for a seraglio![6] Can they be expected to govern a family with judgment, or take care of the poor babes whom they bring into the world?

If then it can be fairly deduced from the present conduct of the sex, from the prevalent fondness for pleasure which takes place of ambition and those nobler passions that open and enlarge the soul; that the instruction which women have hitherto received has only tended, with the constitution of civil society, to render them insignificant objects of desire—mere propagators of fools!—if it can be proved that in aiming to accomplish them, without cultivating their understandings, they are taken out of their sphere of duties, and made ridiculous and useless when the short-lived bloom of beauty is over, I presume that *rational* men will excuse me for endeavoring to persuade them to become more masculine and respectable.

Indeed the word masculine is only a bugbear:[7] there is little reason to fear that women will acquire too much courage or fortitude; for their apparent inferiority with respect to bodily strength, must render them, in some degree, dependent on men in the various relations of life; but why should it be increased by prejudices that give a sex to virtue, and confound simple truths with sensual reveries?[8]

FROM CHAPTER 2

Youth is the season for love in both sexes; but in those days of thoughtless enjoyment provision should be made for the more important years of life, when reflection takes place of sensation. But Rousseau, and most of the male writers who have followed his steps, have warmly inculcated[9] that the whole tendency of female education ought to be directed to one point: to render them pleasing.

Let me reason with the supporters of this opinion who have any knowledge of human nature, do they imagine that marriage can eradicate the habitude of life? The woman who

4. **epithets:** descriptive terms.
5. **libertine** (lĭb′ər-tēn′): indecent or unseemly.
6. **seraglio** (sə-răl′yō): harem.
7. **bugbear:** an object of exaggerated fear.
8. **confound . . . reveries:** confuse simple truths with sexual daydreams.
9. **inculcated** (ĭn-kŭl′kā′tĭd): taught.

has only been taught to please will soon find that her charms are oblique sunbeams, and that they cannot have much effect on her husband's heart when they are seen every day, when the summer is passed and gone. Will she then have sufficient native energy to look into herself for comfort, and cultivate her dormant faculties? or, is it not more rational to expect that she will try to please other men; and, in the emotions raised by the expectation of new conquests, endeavor to forget the mortification her love or pride has received? When the husband ceases to be a lover—and the time will inevitably come, her desire of pleasing will then grow languid, or become a spring of bitterness; and love, perhaps, the most evanescent[10] of all passions, gives place to jealousy or vanity.

I now speak of women who are restrained by principle or prejudice; such women, though they would shrink from an intrigue with real abhorrence, yet, nevertheless, wish to be convinced by the homage of gallantry that they are cruelly neglected by their husbands; or, days and weeks are spent in dreaming of the happiness enjoyed by congenial souls till their health is undermined and their spirits broken by discontent. How then can the great art of pleasing be such a necessary study? it is only useful to a mistress; the chaste wife, and serious mother, should only consider her power to please as the polish of her virtues, and the affection of her husband as one of the comforts that render her talk less difficult and her life happier. But, whether she be loved or neglected, her first wish should be to make herself respectable, and not to rely for all her happiness on a being subject to like infirmities with herself.

QUESTION

How does Wollstonecraft suggest that a woman "make herself respectable"?

The worthy Dr. Gregory fell into a similar error. I respect his heart; but entirely disapprove of his celebrated Legacy to his Daughters. . . .

He actually recommends dissimulation,[11] and advises an innocent girl to give the lie to her feelings, and not dance with spirit, when gaiety of heart would make her feet eloquent without making her gestures immodest. In the name of truth and common sense, why should not one woman acknowledge that she can take more exercise than another? or, in other words, that she has a sound constitution; and why, to damp innocent vivacity, is she darkly to be told that men will draw conclusions which she little thinks of? Let the libertine draw what inference he pleases; but, I hope, that no sensible mother will restrain the natural frankness of youth by instilling such indecent cautions. Out of the abundance of the heart the mouth speaketh; and a wiser than Solomon hath said, that the heart should be made clean, and not trivial ceremonies observed, which it is not very difficult to fulfil with scrupulous exactness when vice reigns in the heart.

Women ought to endeavor to purify their heart; but can they do so when their uncultivated understandings make them entirely dependent on their senses for employment and amusement, when no noble pursuit sets them above the little vanities of the day, or enables them to curb the wild emotions that agitate a reed over which every passing breeze has power? To gain the affections of a virtuous man, is affectation necessary? Nature has given woman a weaker frame than man; but, to ensure her husband's affections, must a wife, who by the exercise of

10. **evanescent** (ĕv′ə-nĕs′ənt): quickly vanishing; fleeting.

11. **dissimulation:** a concealing of one's true feelings; pretense.

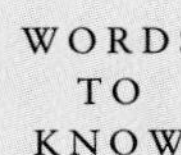

WORDS TO KNOW

languid (lăng′gwĭd) *adj.* sluggish; weak
vivacity (vĭ-văs′ĭ-tē) *n.* liveliness
affectation (ăf′ĕk-tā′shən) *n.* unnatural behavior; conduct intended to give a false impression

her mind and body whilst she was discharging the duties of a daughter, wife, and mother, has allowed her constitution to retain its natural strength, and her nerves a healthy tone, is she, I say, to condescend to use art and feign a sickly delicacy in order to secure her husband's affection? Weakness may excite tenderness, and gratify the arrogant pride of man; but the lordly caresses of a protector will not gratify a noble mind that pants for, and deserves to be respected. Fondness is a poor substitute for friendship! . . .

Besides, the woman who strengthens her body and exercises her mind will, by managing her family and practicing various virtues, become the friend, and not the humble dependent of her husband; and if she, by possessing such substantial qualities, merit his regard, she will not find it necessary to conceal her affection, nor to pretend to an unnatural coldness of constitution to excite her husband's passions. . . .

EVALUATE

What type of marriage is Wollstonecraft condemning?

If all the faculties of woman's mind are only to be cultivated as they respect her dependence on man; if, when a husband be obtained, she have arrived at her goal, and meanly proud rests satisfied with such a paltry crown, let her grovel contentedly, scarcely raised by her employments above the animal kingdom; but, if, struggling for the prize of her high calling, she look beyond the present scene, let her cultivate her understanding without stopping to consider what character the husband may have whom she is destined to marry. Let her only determine, without being too anxious about present happiness, to acquire the qualities that ennoble a rational being, and a rough inelegant husband may shock her taste without destroying her peace of mind. She will not model her soul to suit the frailties of her companion, but to bear with them: his character may be a trial, but not an impediment to virtue. . . .

These may be termed Utopian dreams. Thanks to that Being who impressed them on my soul, and gave me sufficient strength of mind to dare to exert my own reason, till, becoming dependent only on him for the support of my virtue, I view, with indignation, the mistaken notions that enslave my sex.

I love man as my fellow; but his scepter, real, or usurped, extends not to me, unless the reason of an individual demands my homage; and even then the submission is to reason, and not to man. In fact, the conduct of an accountable being must be regulated by the operations of its own reason; or on what foundation rests the throne of God?

It appears to me necessary to dwell on these obvious truths, because females have been insulated, as it were; and, while they have been stripped of the virtues that should clothe humanity, they have been decked with artificial graces that enable them to exercise a short-lived tyranny. Love, in their bosoms, taking place of every nobler passion, their sole ambition is to be fair, to raise emotion instead of inspiring respect; and this ignoble desire, like the servility in absolute monarchies, destroys all strength of character. Liberty is the mother of virtue, and if women be, by their very constitution, slaves, and not allowed to breathe the sharp invigorating air of freedom, they must ever languish like exotics,[12] and be reckoned beautiful flaws in nature.

12. **languish like exotics:** wilt like plants grown away from their natural environment.

WORDS TO KNOW

feign (fān) *v.* to give a false appearance of; simulate or counterfeit
grovel (grŏv′əl) *v.* to behave with exaggerated submission or humility
ignoble (ĭg-nō′bəl) *adj.* not noble; degrading; contemptible

RESPONDING OPTIONS

FROM PERSONAL RESPONSE *TO* CRITICAL ANALYSIS

REFLECT 1. Would you like to hear Wollstonecraft speak on women's rights? Explain why or why not in your notebook.

RETHINK 2. Draw two circles. In one circle, list words that you think express Wollstonecraft's concept of weakness. In the other, list words that you think express her concept of strength.

3. In your opinion, what "manly virtues" does Wollstonecraft want women to imitate?

4. How do you think Wollstonecraft would describe a good marriage?

   Consider
   - the kinds of female behavior she criticizes
   - her complaints about the attitude of men toward women
   - the qualities she would like women to acquire
   - her reasons for encouraging women to strengthen their minds

5. Do you think Wollstonecraft believes in the complete equality of men and women?

RELATE 6. Look back at the list you created for the Writing Connection on page 405. On the basis of what you've learned from the selection, how accurate was your image of women and their rights in 18th-century Britain?

7. In your opinion, what social issues would concern Wollstonecraft today? Would she still feel a need to defend women's rights?

ANOTHER PATHWAY

Create a bar graph like the one shown. At the bottom, list negative attitudes toward women that Wollstonecraft observed in the 18th century. Then draw bars to indicate the degrees to which you think those attitudes have changed.

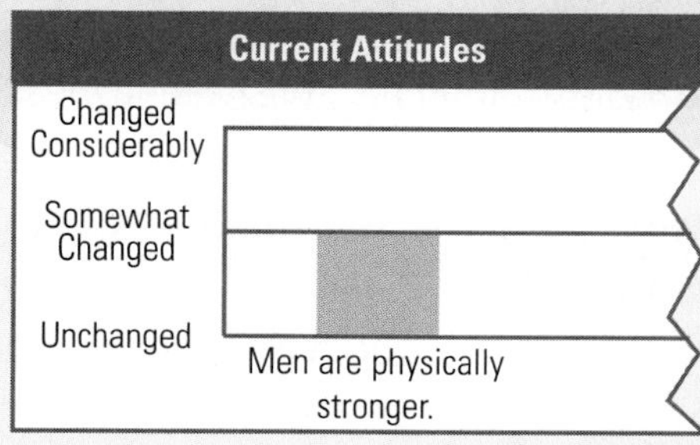

LITERARY CONCEPTS

Argumentation is speech or writing intended to convince an audience that a proposal should be adopted or rejected. Most argumentation begins with a statement of an idea or opinion, which is then supported with logical evidence. Another technique of argumentation is the anticipation and rebuttal of opposing views. What idea or opinion forms the basis of Wollstonecraft's argument? How does she anticipate and respond to opposing views? Cite specific examples.

QUICKWRITES

1. Create a **conversation** in which Wollstonecraft discusses women's rights with one of her female contemporaries.
2. Draft an **opinion paper** on the importance of cultivating one's mind. Use any of Wollstonecraft's reasons with which you concur, but also add some of your own.

PORTFOLIO *Save your writing. You may want to use it later as a springboard to a piece for your portfolio.*

LITERARY LINKS

Compare Wollstonecraft's views with those expressed by Defoe in "An Academy for Women" (page 380). How are their attitudes toward women alike? How are they different?

ALTERNATIVE ACTIVITIES

With a small group of classmates, conduct a **press conference** in which reporters question Wollstonecraft about her views on women.

WORDS TO KNOW

Use your knowledge of the boldfaced words to answer the following questions.

1. Are people who **feign** friendship being loyal, being rude, or being phony?
2. Is a person who displays **vivacity** showing conceit, showing pep, or showing wealth?
3. Is a **specious** statement a truth, a mistake, or a lie?
4. Which is a sign of **solicitude**—a salute, a yawn, or a pat on the shoulder?
5. Would a person who feels **subordinate** speak forcefully, moderately, or timidly?
6. Would a person who's feeling **languid** be most likely to want to sit on the beach, to climb a mountain, or to dig at an archaeological site?
7. Are people who **grovel** while asking for something most likely to ask on their knees, with their noses in the air, or while shaking their fists?
8. Is an **ignoble** man most likely to be described as a prince of a fellow, a giant in his field, or a real rat?
9. If you felt that someone was displaying **affectation,** would you say that the person was cracking the whip, was putting on airs, or was looking on the bright side?
10. If you can't take Beginning Art and Advanced Drama because they are **concurring** classes, is your problem due to a scheduling conflict, a lack of training, or a lack of space?

MARY WOLLSTONECRAFT

1759–1797

Mary Wollstonecraft's unusual and difficult childhood taught her to question conventional attitudes about women. Her family moved frequently as her father pursued a series of unsuccessful farming ventures, in which he used up the family's money, including the money promised to his daughters by their grandfather. Fearing her father's alcoholism and violence, Wollstonecraft would sometimes sleep on the floor outside her mother's room to protect her mother from him. In this impoverished, chaotic household, Wollstonecraft received only six or seven years of formal education and was mostly self-taught.

At age 19, Wollstonecraft left home to take a job as companion to a rich widow. When she was 22, she opened a private school near London, and although the project was short-lived, it introduced her to important friends who encouraged her to write. Wollstonecraft had taught herself French and German, and in 1787 she was hired as a translator for a new monthly journal. She often participated in discussions with the journal's publisher, Joseph Johnson, and his circle of intellectual friends, including Thomas Paine, the poet William Blake, and the philosopher William Godwin.

Wollstonecraft later developed a close friendship with Godwin and, at the age of 37, married him. Their happy but brief relationship ended unexpectedly when Wollstonecraft died less than a year later from inept medical care following childbirth. The couple's daughter—the future Mary Wollstonecraft Shelley—was to become famous in her own right as the author of *Frankenstein* and the wife of the poet Percy Bysshe Shelley.

PART 3 *Revelations About Human Nature*

In this part of Unit Three, the people of the 18th century come to life in biographical sketches, essays, letters, and poems that offer interesting perspectives on the human condition. The writers of the selections reveal their thoughts on everything from bad habits and other everyday concerns to such universal topics as war, aging, and death. Some even take a humorous look at themselves and the people around them. As you read these writings, you may find yourself confronted with aspects of your own nature.

PREVIEWING

NONFICTION

from The Rambler On Spring *from* The Idler On Idleness

Samuel Johnson

PERSONAL CONNECTION

"It's human nature" is an expression often used to justify the behavior of an individual or a group. In your notebook, describe an experience that gave you valuable insights into human nature. What did the experience tell you about the way people sometimes think or act?

BIOGRAPHICAL CONNECTION

Among students of English literature, the years 1750–1784 are often called the Age of Johnson—a tribute to the influence of Samuel Johnson, the literary leader of his day. Although known today chiefly for his *Dictionary of the English Language,* Johnson was also a talented poet, essayist, and critic. His knowledge and opinions were greatly respected by his contemporaries, many of whom asked him to write prefaces and dedications for, and reviews of, their own literary works. Perhaps even more famous than Johnson's literary achievements, however, was his witty conversation. He met regularly with a circle of friends, whom he often entertained with his profound wisdom and outrageous opinions.

Much of Johnson's own writing was prompted by financial problems. Even while compiling his dictionary, he relied on journalistic writing to help pay his bills. Two of his journalistic essays, one from *The Rambler* and one from *The Idler,* appear on the following pages. Johnson launched *The Rambler,* a twice-weekly periodical, in 1750. Each issue consisted of a single essay, often laced with moral instruction. In 1758, he began writing *The Idler,* a weekly feature that appeared for two years in a London newspaper. His keen insights into human nature revealed a recognition of his own shortcomings as well. *The Idler* featured an assortment of fictional characters with self-descriptive names, such as Mr. Sober, Bob Sturdy, and Tom Tempest. Many scholars consider Mr. Sober to be Johnson's caricature of himself.

READING CONNECTION

Determining Meanings of Lengthy Sentences Many of the sentences in Johnson's essays are quite lengthy. His insights into human nature, though perceptive, are often embedded in a series of related thoughts. You might want to approach these selections by reading each sentence slowly, looking for the main idea. Then read the sentence again, concentrating on phrases or clauses that add meaning to the main point.

> It is lucky for a man, in whom this temper prevails, when he turns his hopes upon things wholly out of his own power; since he forbears then to precipitate his affairs, for the sake of the great event that is to complete his felicity, and waits for the blissful hour, with less neglect of the measures necessary to be taken in the mean time.

Samuel Johnson

ON Spring

TUESDAY, *April* 3, 1750

ET NUNC OMNIS AGER, NUNC OMNIS PARTURIT ARBOS,
NUNC FRONDENT SILVAE, NUNC FORMOSISSIMUS ANNUS.

VIRGIL, *Eclogues*[1] 3.56–57

Now ev'ry field, now ev'ry tree is green;
Now genial nature's fairest face is seen.[2]

Elphinston

Every man is sufficiently discontented with some circumstances of his present state, to suffer his imagination to range more or less in quest of future happiness, and to fix upon some point of time, in which, by the removal of the inconvenience which now perplexes him, or acquisition of the advantage which he at present wants, he shall find the condition of his life very much improved.

When this time, which is too often expected with great impatience, at last arrives, it generally comes without the blessing for which it was desired; but we solace ourselves with some new prospect, and press forward again with equal eagerness.

It is lucky for a man, in whom this temper prevails, when he turns his hopes upon things wholly out of his own power; since he forbears then to precipitate his affairs,[3] for the sake of the great event that is to complete his felicity,[4] and waits for the blissful hour, with less neglect of the measures necessary to be taken in the mean time.

I have long known a person of this temper, who indulged his dream of happiness with less hurt to himself than such chimerical[5] wishes commonly produce, and adjusted his scheme with such address, that his hopes were in full bloom three parts of the year, and in the other part never

1. *Eclogues* (ĕk'lôgz'): a book of pastoral poems by the Roman poet Virgil.
2. **Now ev'ry . . . is seen:** a free translation of Virgil's lines.
3. **forbears . . . affairs:** refrains from acting rashly or impetuously.
4. **felicity:** happiness.
5. **chimerical** (kī-mĕr'ĭ-kəl): unrealistic and fantastic; fanciful.

WORDS TO KNOW

suffer (sŭf'ər) *v.* to allow; permit
solace (sŏl'ĭs) *v.* to console; comfort

wholly blasted.[6] Many, perhaps, would be desirous of learning by what means he procured to himself such a cheap and lasting satisfaction. It was gained by a constant practice of referring the removal of all his uneasiness to the coming of the next spring; if his health was impaired, the spring would restore it; if what he wanted was at a high price, it would fall in value in the spring.

The spring, indeed, did often come without any of these effects, but he was always certain that the next would be more propitious; nor was ever convinced that the present spring would fail him before the middle of summer; for he always talked of the spring as coming till it was past, and when it was once past, everyone agreed with him that it was coming.

By long converse with this man, I am, perhaps, brought to feel immoderate pleasure in the contemplation of this delightful season; but I have the satisfaction of finding many, whom it can be no shame to resemble, infected with the same enthusiasm; for there is, I believe, scarce any poet of eminence, who has not left some testimony of his fondness for the flowers, the zephyrs,[7] and the warblers of the spring. Nor has the most luxuriant imagination been able to describe the serenity and happiness of the golden age, otherwise than by giving a perpetual spring, as the highest reward of uncorrupted innocence.

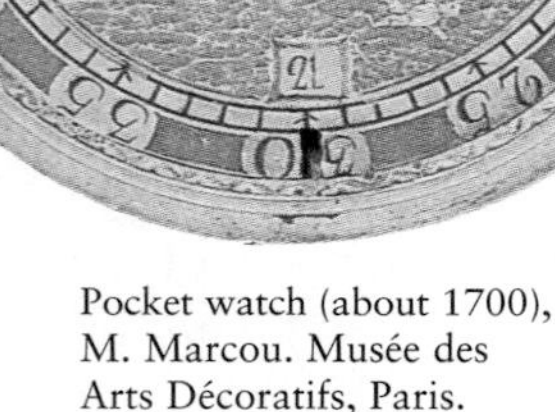

Pocket watch (about 1700), M. Marcou. Musée des Arts Décoratifs, Paris.

There is, indeed, something inexpressibly pleasing, in the annual renovation of the world, and the new display of the treasures of nature. The cold and darkness of winter, with the naked deformity of every object on which we turn our eyes, make us rejoice at the succeeding season, as well for what we have escaped, as for what we may enjoy; and every budding flower, which a warm situation brings early to our view, is considered by us as a messenger to notify the approach of more joyous days.

The spring affords to a mind, so free from the disturbance of cares or passions as to be vacant to calm amusements, almost every thing that our present state makes us capable of enjoying. The variegated verdure[8] of the fields and woods, the succession of grateful odors, the voice of pleasure pouring out its notes on every side, with the gladness apparently conceived by every animal, from the growth of his food, and the clemency of the weather, throw over the whole earth an air of gaiety, significantly expressed by the smile of nature.

Yet there are men to whom these scenes are able to give no delight, and who hurry away from all the varieties of rural beauty, to lose their hours, and divert their thoughts by cards, or assemblies, a tavern dinner, or the prattle of the day.

It may be laid down as a position which will seldom deceive, that when a man cannot bear his own company there is something wrong. He must fly from himself, either because he feels a

6. **blasted:** shriveled; withered.

7. **zephyrs** (zĕf′ərz): gentle breezes.

8. **variegated verdure** (vâr′ē-ĭ-gā′tĭd vûr′jər): greenery of many hues.

WORDS TO KNOW

procure (prō-kyŏŏr′) *v.* to obtain; acquire

propitious (prə-pĭsh′əs) *adj.* favorable; advantageous

clemency (klĕm′ən-sē) *n.* mildness

Sandleford Priory (1744), Edward Haytley. Oil on canvas, The Leger Galleries Ltd., London.

tediousness in life from the equipoise[9] of an empty mind, which, having no tendency to one motion more than another but as it is impelled by some external power, must always have recourse to foreign objects; or he must be afraid of the intrusion of some unpleasing ideas, and, perhaps, is struggling to escape from the remembrance of a loss, the fear of a calamity, or some other thought of greater horror.

Those whom sorrow incapacitates to enjoy the pleasures of contemplation, may properly apply to such diversions, provided they are innocent, as lay strong hold on the attention; and those, whom fear of any future affliction chains down to misery, must endeavor to obviate the danger.

My considerations shall, on this occasion, be turned on such as are burthensome[10] to themselves merely because they want subjects for reflection, and to whom the volume of nature is thrown open, without affording them pleasure or instruction, because they never learned to read the characters.

A French author has advanced this seeming paradox, that *very few men know how to take a walk;* and, indeed, it is true, that few know how to take a walk with a prospect of any other pleasure, than the same company would have afforded them at home.

There are animals that borrow their color from the neighboring body, and, consequently, vary their hue as they happen to change their place. In like manner it ought to be the endeavor of every man to derive his reflections from the objects about him; for it is to no purpose that he alters his position, if his attention continues fixed to the same point. The mind should be kept open to the access of every new idea, and so far disengaged from the predominance of particular thoughts, as easily to accommodate itself to occasional entertainment.

A man that has formed his habit of turning every new object to his entertainment, finds in the productions of nature an inexhaustible stock of materials upon which he can employ himself, without any temptations to envy or malevolence; faults, perhaps, seldom totally avoided by those, whose judgment is much exercised upon the works of art. He has always a certain prospect of discovering new reasons for adoring the sovereign

9. **equipoise:** state of balance; lack of direction.
10. **burthensome:** an obsolete spelling of *burdensome.*

WORDS TO KNOW

obviate (ŏb′vē-āt′) *v.* to prevent; avert
paradox (păr′ə-dŏks′) *n.* a statement that appears to be self-contradictory or contrary to common sense but may nevertheless be true
malevolence (mə-lĕv′ə-ləns) *n.* wickedness; ill will

author of the universe, and probable hopes of making some discovery of benefit to others, or of profit to himself. There is no doubt but many vegetables and animals have qualities that might be of great use, to the knowledge of which there is not required much force of penetration, or fatigue of study, but only frequent experiments, and close attention. What is said by the chemists of their darling mercury,[11] is, perhaps, true of everybody through the whole creation, that if a thousand lives should be spent upon it, all its properties would not be found out.

Mankind must necessarily be diversified by various tastes, since life affords and requires such multiplicity of employments, and a nation of naturalists is neither to be hoped, or desired; but it is surely not improper to point out a fresh amusement to those who languish in health, and repine[12] in plenty, for want of some source of diversion that may be less easily exhausted, and to inform the multitudes of both sexes, who are burthened with every new day, that there are many shows which they have not seen.

He that enlarges his curiosity after the works of nature, demonstrably multiplies the inlets to happiness; and, therefore, the younger part of my readers, to whom I dedicate this vernal[13] speculation, must excuse me for calling upon them, to make use at once of the spring of the year, and the spring of life; to acquire, while their minds may be yet impressed with new images, a love of innocent pleasures, and an ardor for useful knowledge; and to remember, that a blighted spring makes a barren year, and that the vernal flowers, however beautiful and gay, are only intended by nature as preparatives to autumnal fruits. ❖

11. **chemists . . . mercury:** The properties (characteristics) of mercury and its compounds made the silvery liquid metal fascinating to early chemists.

12. **repine:** feel dissatisfied; complain.

13. **vernal:** having to do with spring.

FROM PERSONAL RESPONSE *TO* CRITICAL ANALYSIS

REFLECT 1. What is your overall impression of this essay? Write your reaction in your notebook.

RETHINK 2. How would you describe Johnson's attitude toward spring?

3. Why do you think Johnson, in the last paragraph, dedicates his essay to "the younger part of my readers"?

Consider
- his recommended approach to life
- the types of behavior he condemns
- the hope he expresses for those in "the spring of life"

WORDS TO KNOW

languish (lăng'gwĭsh) *v.* to be weak or depressed

Mr. and Mrs. Andrews (late 1700s), Thomas Gainsborough. National Gallery, London. Bridgeman/Art Resource.

On Idleness

SAMUEL JOHNSON

Saturday, November 18, 1758

Many moralists have remarked, that Pride has of all human vices the widest dominion, appears in the greatest multiplicity of forms, and lies hid under the greatest variety of disguises; of disguises, which, like the moon's veil of brightness, *are both* its luster and its shade, *and betray it to others, though they hide it from ourselves.*

It is not my intention to degrade Pride from this pre-eminence of mischief, yet I know not whether Idleness may not maintain a very doubtful and obstinate competition.

There are some that profess Idleness in its full dignity, who call themselves the Idle, as Busiris in the play[1] "calls himself the Proud"; who boast that they do nothing, and thank their stars that they have nothing to do; who sleep every night till they can sleep no longer, and rise only that exercise may enable them to sleep again; who prolong the reign of darkness by double curtains, and never see the sun but to "tell him how they hate his beams"; whose whole labor is to vary the postures of indulgence, and whose day differs from their night but as a couch or chair differs from a bed.

These are the true and open votaries[2] of Idleness, for whom she weaves the garlands of poppies, and into whose cup she pours the waters of oblivion;[3] who exist in a state of unruffled stupidity, forgetting and forgotten; who have long ceased to live, and at whose death the survivors can only say, that they have ceased to breathe.

But Idleness predominates in many lives where it is not suspected; for being a vice which terminates in itself, it may be enjoyed without injury to others; and is therefore not watched like Fraud, which endangers property, or like Pride, which naturally seeks its gratifications in another's inferiority. Idleness is a silent and peaceful quality, that neither raises envy by ostentation, nor hatred by opposition; and therefore nobody is busy to censure or detect it.

As Pride sometimes is hid under humility, Idleness is often covered by turbulence and hurry. He that neglects his known duty and real employment, naturally endeavors to crowd his mind with something that may bar out the remembrance of his own folly, and does any thing but what he ought to do with eager diligence, that he may keep himself in his own favor.

Some are always in a state of preparation, occupied in previous measures, forming plans, accumulating materials, and providing for the main affair. These are certainly under the secret power of Idleness. Nothing is to be expected from the workman whose tools are forever to be sought. I was once told by a great master, that no man ever excelled in painting, who was eminently curious about pencils and colors.

IDLENESS IS A SILENT AND PEACEFUL QUALITY, THAT NEITHER RAISES ENVY BY OSTENTATION, NOR HATRED BY OPPOSITION.

1. **Busiris** (byōō-sī′rĭs) **in the play:** a reference to the play *Busiris, King of Egypt* by the English poet Edward Young. A figure in Greek mythology, Busiris put to death all strangers who entered his kingdom and was himself killed by Hercules.
2. **votaries:** worshipers; devotees.
3. **waters of oblivion:** in Greek mythology, the waters of the river Lethe, which produce forgetfulness

WORDS TO KNOW

ostentation (ŏs′tĕn-tā′shən) *n.* a showy display, especially of wealth or knowledge; boastful showiness

There are others to whom Idleness dictates another expedient, by which life may be passed unprofitably away without the tediousness of many vacant hours. The art is, to fill the day with petty business, to have always something in hand which may raise curiosity, but not solicitude, and keep the mind in a state of action, but not of labor.

This art has for many years been practiced by my old friend Sober, with wonderful success. Sober is a man of strong desires and quick imagination, so exactly balanced by the love of ease, that they can seldom stimulate him to any difficult undertaking; they have, however, so much power, that they will not suffer him to lie quite at rest, and though they do not make him sufficiently useful to others, they make him at least weary of himself.

Mr. Sober's chief pleasure is conversation; there is no end of his talk or his attention; to speak or to hear is equally pleasing; for he still fancies that he is teaching or learning something, and is free for the time from his own reproaches.

But there is one time at night when he must go home, that his friends may sleep; and another time in the morning, when all the world agrees to shut out interruption. These are the moments of which poor Sober trembles at the thought. But the misery of these tiresome intervals, he has many means of alleviating. He has persuaded himself that the manual arts are undeservedly overlooked; he has observed in many trades the effects of close thought, and just ratiocination.[4] From speculation he proceeded to practice, and supplied himself with the tools of a carpenter, with which he mended his coalbox very successfully, and which he still continues to employ, as he finds occasion.

He has attempted at other times the crafts of the shoemaker, tinman, plumber, and potter; in all these arts he has failed, and resolves to qualify himself for them by better information. But his daily amusement is chemistry. He has a small furnace, which he employs in distillation,[5] and which has long been the solace of his life. He draws oils and waters, and essences and spirits, which he knows to be of no use; sits and counts the drops as they come from his retort,[6] and forgets that, whilst a drop is falling, a moment flies away.

Poor Sober! I have often teased him with reproof, and he has often promised reformation; for no man is so much open to conviction as the Idler, but there is none on whom it operates so little. What will be the effect of this paper I know not; perhaps he will read it and laugh, and light the fire in his furnace; but my hope is that he will quit his trifles, and betake himself to rational and useful diligence. ❖

---

4. **ratiocination** (răsh′ē-ŏs′ə-nā′shən): systematic and logical thought.

5. **distillation:** the separation of parts of a liquid mixture by condensing and collecting the vapors produced when it is heated.

6. **retort:** a vessel used for distilling liquids.

from

A Dictionary of the English Language

Samuel Johnson

ADU'LT. A person above the age of infancy, or grown to some degree of strength; sometimes full grown: a word used chiefly by medicinal writers.

TO A'MBLE. To move easily, without hard shocks, or shaking.

APE. A kind of monkey remarkable for imitating what he sees.

BA'SKET. A vessel made of twigs, rushes, or splinters, or some other slender body interwoven.

CORN. The seeds which grow in ears, not in pods; such as are made into bread.

CRU'EL. Pleased with hurting others; inhuman; hardhearted; without pity; without compassion; savage; barbarous; unrelenting.

DULL. Not exhilarating; not delightful; as, *to make dictionaries is* dull *work.*

FISH. An animal that inhabits the water.

TO HISS. To utter a noise like that of a serpent and some other animals. It is remarkable, that this word cannot be pronounced without making the noise which it signifies.

LOUSE. A small animal, of which different species live on the bodies of men, beasts, and perhaps of all living creatures.

MI'SER. A wretched person; one overwhelmed with calamity.

MOULD. A kind of concretion on the top or outside of things kept, motionless and damp; now discovered by microscopes to be perfect plants.

MOUSE. The smallest of all beasts; a little animal haunting houses and corn fields, destroyed by cats.

NO'VEL. A small tale, generally of love.

POP. A small smart quick sound. It is formed from the sound.

RE'CIPE. A medical prescription.

RI'VER. A land current of water bigger than a brook.

TO SLU'BBER. To do any thing lazily, imperfectly, or with idle hurry.

SUN. The luminary that makes the day.

TE'MPEST. The utmost violence of the wind; the names by which the wind is called according to the gradual increase of its force seems to be, a breeze; a gale; a gust; a storm; a tempest.

WA'RREN. A kind of park for rabbits.

RESPONDING OPTIONS

FROM PERSONAL RESPONSE *TO* CRITICAL ANALYSIS

REFLECT 1. Discuss your reactions to Johnson's essay "On Idleness" with a classmate.

RETHINK 2. Do you think Johnson views idleness as a serious character flaw?

Consider
- the tone of the essay
- his examples of idleness
- his expectations regarding Sober's reformation

3. What insights about himself do you think Johnson reveals through the character of Mr. Sober?

4. According to Johnson, idleness is "a vice which terminates in itself" and therefore can be indulged in "without injury to others." Do you agree? Explain your opinion.

RELATE 5. Would you say that Johnson's tone is the same in "On Spring" and "On Idleness"? Support your answer.

6. Look again at the Insight selection on page 422. Compare some of the entries in Johnson's dictionary with entries for the same words in a modern dictionary. What similarities and differences do you notice?

ANOTHER PATHWAY

Cooperative Learning

Work with a group to create a proposal for a book modernizing Johnson's ideas. It should be addressed to a prospective publisher and should include an introduction, in which you state your purpose, and an outline of your modernization. Be sure to make Johnson's main points accessible to modern readers.

LITERARY CONCEPTS

An **aphorism** is a brief statement that expresses a general observation about life in a clever or forceful way. Unlike proverbs, which stem from oral folk tradition, aphorisms can be assigned to specific authors. Because they are generalizations, aphorisms are meaningful even when taken out of their original contexts. "A blighted spring makes a barren year," in the last sentence of "On Spring," is an example of a statement that could be called an aphorism. What other aphorisms can you find in these essays?

Aphorism
A brief statement that expresses a general observation about life in a clever or forceful way.

QUICKWRITES

1. Write an **anecdote** about a friend, a family member, or an acquaintance who exhibits one or more of the traits Johnson describes in these essays.
2. Imagine that you are Mr. Sober. Write a **letter** to Johnson, defending your behavior.
3. In a **paragraph,** explain why you agree or disagree with Johnson's claim, in "On Spring," that "every man is sufficiently discontented with some circumstances of his present state" to look forward to a time when he will find "the condition of his life very much improved."

PORTFOLIO Save your writing. You may want to use it later as a springboard to a piece for your portfolio.

ALTERNATIVE ACTIVITIES

1. In a humorous **monologue,** attempt to defend idleness as preferable to diligence.
2. Create a visual **caricature** portraying one of the personality types described by Johnson in these essays.

LITERARY LINKS

Compare these essays of Johnson's with the excerpts from Joseph Addison's *Spectator* essays (page 350). Which of Johnson's essays is more similar in tone to Addison's writing? Support your answer with details from the essays.

WORDS TO KNOW

EXERCISE A For each word in the first column, write the letter of the best antonym in the second column.

1. procure	a. thrive
2. languish	b. forbid
3. obviate	c. lose
4. malevolence	d. permit
5. suffer	e. kindness

EXERCISE B Review the Words to Know at the bottom of the selection pages. Then write the word, not used in Exercise A, described by each sentence below.

1. "It was the best of times, it was the worst of times" is an example of this.
2. "Red sky in the morning, sailor take warning; red sky at night, sailor's delight" means that a red sunset is a sign of this kind of weather on the next day.
3. "Peacock, look at your legs!" is a reminder that this can be foolish.
4. "When in disgrace with Fortune and men's eyes / I all alone beweep my outcast state" shows that the speaker of the sonnet needs someone to do this to him.
5. "Power can do by gentleness what violence fails to accomplish" indicates that this can be an effective quality.

SAMUEL JOHNSON

1709–1784

Born in Lichfield, England, Samuel Johnson was the son of a prominent but impoverished bookseller. During infancy, he contracted scrofula, a tubercular infection that left him with a disfigured face and impaired vision and hearing. He attended public schools until he was 17 and read widely in his father's shop, but Johnson's family could not afford to give him the higher education he craved. Although a small inheritance of his mother's allowed him to enroll in Oxford University in 1728, he was forced to leave after only 13 months when the money ran out.

For many years, Johnson earned a meager income by teaching and by translating books. Then, at the age of 27, determined to make a name for himself, he walked to London to seek a career in writing. Within a year he had published his first significant poem and had begun to gain recognition as a literary talent.

Johnson's literary achievements during the next 30 years—particularly his dictionary, an edition of Shakespeare's works, and a series of critical biographies of English poets in which he proves himself a forerunner of modern literary critics—earned him fame, as well as honorary doctorates from Oxford University and Trinity College in Dublin. Nevertheless, he was still on the brink of poverty in 1756, when he was briefly imprisoned for his many debts. In 1762, Johnson's financial woes finally ended when the king awarded him an annual pension.

OTHER WORKS *Lives of the Poets,* "Preface" in *A Dictionary of the English Language*

PREVIEWING

NONFICTION

from The Life of Samuel Johnson

James Boswell

PERSONAL CONNECTION

People have always been curious about the lives of famous people. Think of a current celebrity who interests you. What kinds of things would you like to know about this person? Where would you go to find such information? In your notebook, jot down some possible sources and the kinds of information you might find in them.

BIOGRAPHICAL CONNECTION

Samuel Johnson was one of the most extraordinary scholars and personalities of his time. Despite years of struggle and hardship, he pursued his literary and intellectual interests and eventually became respected as a poet, essayist, journalist, and critic. He also devoted ten years of his life to compiling a massive dictionary. Though Johnson was a leading figure of his day, his opinions were controversial and often inspired heated reactions.

James Boswell, 31 years younger than Johnson, was a university-trained lawyer from a wealthy Scottish family. He had a lifelong fascination with London and the variety of experiences to be found there. He also had a great desire to meet the famous Samuel Johnson. In 1763, when Boswell was only 22, he was unexpectedly introduced to Johnson in the back room of a bookseller's shop in London. Although Johnson was at first annoyed by Boswell's questions and impertinences, he quickly warmed to the young man.

During the next 21 years, Boswell chronicled in great detail his conversations, experiences, and travels with Johnson. After Johnson's death in 1784, Boswell spent 7 years writing the great man's biography. Unlike earlier biographies, which emphasized the positive aspects of their subjects' lives and were often excessively flattering, Boswell's presents a full and accurate portrait that includes both the good and the bad, giving the reader a vivid sense of Johnson as a real person.

James Boswell

READING CONNECTION

Reading Biography Think about what you might expect to find in a biography of a famous writer and intellectual of the 18th century. In the first column of a chart like the one shown, list the kinds of details and topics that you think might be included. Then, as you read these excerpts from Boswell's biography of Johnson, look for details and topics that are similar to and different from what you expected. Note these in the second and third columns of the chart. You may want to use your computer to create your chart.

What I Expect	Similar to Expectations	Unexpected

FROM THE LIFE OF

On Eating (1763)

At supper this night he talked of good eating with uncommon satisfaction. "Some people (said he,) have a foolish way of not minding, or pretending not to mind, what they eat. For my part, I mind my belly very studiously, and very carefully; for I look upon it, that he who does not mind his belly will hardly mind anything else."

He now appeared to me *Jean Bull philosophe,*[1] and he was, for the moment, not only serious but vehement. Yet I have heard him, upon other occasions, talk with great contempt of people who were anxious to gratify their palates; and the 206th number of his *Rambler* is a masterly essay against gulosity.[2] His practice, indeed, I must acknowledge, may be considered as casting the balance of his different opinions upon this subject; for I never knew any man who relished good eating more than he did. When at table, he was totally absorbed in the business of the moment; his looks seemed riveted to his plate; nor would he, unless when in very high company, say one word, or even pay the least attention to what was said by others, till he had satisfied his appetite, which was so fierce, and indulged with such intenseness, that while in the act of eating, the veins of his forehead swelled, and generally a strong perspiration was visible. To those whose sensations were delicate, this could not but be disgusting; and it was doubtless not very suitable to the character of a philosopher, who should be distinguished by self-command. But it must be owned, that Johnson, though he could be rigidly *abstemious,*[3] was not a *temperate* man either in eating or drinking. He could refrain, but he could not use moderately. He told me, that he had fasted two days without inconvenience, and that he had never been hungry but once. They who beheld with wonder how much he ate upon all occasions when his dinner was to his taste, could not easily conceive what he must have meant by hunger; and not only was he remarkable for the extraordinary quantity which he ate, but he was, or affected to be, a man of very nice discernment in the science of cookery. He used to descant[4] critically on the dishes which had been at table where he had dined or supped, and to recollect very minutely what he had liked. . . .

When invited to dine, even with an intimate friend, he was not pleased if something better than a plain dinner was not prepared for him. I have heard him say on such an occasion, "This was a good dinner enough, to be sure; but it was not a dinner to *ask* a man to." On the other hand, he was wont to express, with great glee, his satisfaction when he had been entertained quite to his mind.

1. ***Jean Bull philosophe*** (zhäɴ′ bo͞ol′ fē-lô-zôf′) *French:* John Bull philosopher. (John Bull is a figure representing the typical Englishman—honest, hearty, and gruff.)
2. **gulosity** (gyo͞o-lŏs′ĭ-tē): excessive appetite; gluttony.
3. **abstemious** (ăb-stē′mē-əs): self-denying; abstinent.
4. **descant** (dĕs′kănt′): speak at length.

WORDS TO KNOW

vehement (vē′ə-mənt) *adj.* forceful in expression or feeling; intense
temperate (tĕm′pər-ĭt) *adj.* moderate; restrained
discernment (dĭ-sûrn′mənt) *n.* good judgment

Samuel Johnson

James Boswell

Oliver Goldsmith, James Boswell, and Dr. Samuel Johnson at the Mitre Tavern, London (19th century), unknown artist. Colored engraving, The Granger Collection, New York.

On Equality of the Sexes (1778)

Mrs. Knowles affected to complain that men had much more liberty allowed them than women.

JOHNSON. "Why, Madam, women have all the liberty they should wish to have. We have all the labor and the danger, and the women all the advantage. We go to sea, we build houses, we do everything, in short, to pay our court to the women."

MRS. KNOWLES. "The Doctor reasons very wittily, but not convincingly. Now, take the instance of building; the mason's wife, if she is ever seen in liquor, is ruined; the mason may get himself drunk as often as he pleases, with little loss of character; nay, may let his wife and children starve."

JOHNSON. "Madam, you must consider, if the mason does get himself drunk, and let his wife and children starve, the parish will oblige him to find security for their maintenance. We have different modes of restraining evil. Stocks for the men, a ducking-stool for women, and a pound for beasts. If we require more perfection from women than from ourselves, it is doing them honor. And women have not the same temptations that we have: they may always live in virtuous company;

Johnson and Boswell (late 1700s), engraving by unknown artist.

men must mix in the world indiscriminately. If a woman has no inclination to do what is wrong being secured from it is no restraint to her. I am at liberty to walk into the Thames; but if I were to try it, my friends would restrain me in Bedlam,[5] and I should be obliged to them."

MRS. KNOWLES. "Still, Doctor, I cannot help thinking it a hardship that more indulgence is allowed to men than to women. It gives a superiority to men, to which I do not see how they are entitled."

JOHNSON. "It is plain, Madam, one or other must have the superiority. As Shakespeare says, 'If two men ride on a horse, one must ride behind.'"

DILLY. "I suppose, Sir, Mrs. Knowles would have them to ride in panniers,[6] one on each side."

JOHNSON. "Then, Sir, the horse would throw them both."

MRS. KNOWLES. "Well, I hope that in another world the sexes will be equal."

BOSWELL. "That is being too ambitious, Madam. *We* might as well desire to be equal with the angels. *We* shall all, I hope, be happy in a future state, but we must not expect to be all happy in the same degree. It is enough if we be happy according to our several capacities. A worthy carman[7] will get to heaven as well as Sir Isaac Newton.[8] Yet, though equally good, they will not have the same degrees of happiness."

JOHNSON. "Probably not."

On the Fear of Death (1769)

I mentioned to him that I had seen the execution of several convicts at Tyburn,[9] two days before, and that none of them seemed to be under any concern.

JOHNSON. "Most of them, Sir, have never thought at all."

BOSWELL. "But is not the fear of death natural to man?"

JOHNSON. "So much so, Sir, that the whole of life is but keeping away the thoughts of it."

He then, in a low and earnest tone, talked of his meditating upon the awful hour of his own dissolution,[10] and in what manner he should conduct himself upon that occasion: "I know not (said he,) whether I should wish to have a friend by me, or have it all between God and myself." . . .

When we were alone, I introduced the subject of death, and endeavored to maintain that the fear of it might be got over. I told him that David Hume[11] said to me, he was no more uneasy to think he should *not be* after this life, than that he *had not been* before he began to exist.

JOHNSON. "Sir, if he really thinks so, his perceptions are disturbed; he is mad: if he does not think so, he lies. He may tell you, he holds his finger in the flame of a candle, without feeling pain; would you believe him? When he dies, he at least gives up all he has."

BOSWELL. "Foote,[12] Sir, told me, that when he was very ill he was not afraid to die."

JOHNSON. "It is not true, Sir. Hold a pistol to Foote's breast, or to Hume's breast, and threaten to kill them, and you'll see how they behave."

BOSWELL. "But may we not fortify our minds for the approach of death?"

Here I am sensible[13] I was in the wrong, to bring before his view what he ever looked upon with horror; for although when in a celestial frame, in his "Vanity of Human Wishes," he has supposed death to be "kind Nature's signal for retreat," from this state of being to "a happier seat," his thoughts upon this awful change were in general full of dismal apprehensions. His mind

5. **Bedlam:** a London institution for the mentally ill.
6. **panniers** (păn′yərz): a pair of baskets hung across the back of a pack animal.
7. **carman:** carriage driver.
8. **Sir Isaac Newton:** a famous English mathematician.
9. **Tyburn:** the former site of public hangings in London.
10. **awful . . . dissolution:** awe-inspiring hour of his own death.
11. **David Hume:** a Scottish philosopher and historian.
12. **Foote:** Samuel Foote, an actor and dramatist.
13. **sensible:** aware.

resembled the vast amphitheater, the Colosseum at Rome. In the center stood his judgment, which, like a mighty gladiator, combated those apprehensions that, like the wild beasts of the *Arena,* were all around in cells, ready to be let out upon him. After a conflict, he drove them back into their dens; but not killing them, they were still assailing him. To my question, whether we might not fortify our minds for the approach of death, he answered, in a passion, "No, Sir, let it alone. It matters not how a man dies, but how he lives. The act of dying is not of importance, it lasts so short a time." He added, (with an earnest look,) "A man knows it must be so, and submits. It will do him no good to whine."

I attempted to continue the conversation. He was so provoked, that he said, "Give us no more of this"; and was thrown into such a state of agitation, that he expressed himself in a way that alarmed and distressed me; showed an impatience that I should leave him, and when I was going away, called to me sternly, "Don't let us meet to-morrow."

On Johnson's Physical Courage (1775)

. . . No man was ever more remarkable for personal courage. He had, indeed, an awful dread of death, or rather, "of something after death"; and what rational man, who seriously thinks of quitting all that he has ever known, and going into a new and unknown state of being, can be without that dread? But his fear was from reflection; his courage natural. His fear, in that one instance, was the result of philosophical and religious consideration. He feared death, but he feared nothing else, not even what might occasion death. Many instances of his resolution may be mentioned. One day, at Mr. Beauclerk's house in the country, when two large dogs were fighting, he went up to them, and beat them till they separated; and at another time, when told of the danger there was that a gun might burst if charged with many balls, he put in six or seven, and fired it off against a wall. Mr. Langton told me, that when they were swimming together near Oxford, he cautioned Dr. Johnson against a pool, which was reckoned particularly dangerous; upon which Johnson directly swam into it. He told me himself that one night he was attacked in the street by four men, to whom he would not yield, but kept them all at bay, till the watch came up, and carried both him and them to the roundhouse.[14] In the playhouse at Lichfield, as Mr. Garrick informed me, Johnson having for a moment quitted a chair which was placed for him between the side-scenes, a gentleman took possession of it, and when Johnson on his return civilly demanded his seat, rudely refused to give it up; upon which Johnson laid hold of it, and tossed him and the chair into the pit. Foote, who so successfully revived the old comedy, by exhibiting living characters, had resolved to imitate Johnson on the stage, expecting great profits from his ridicule of so celebrated a man. Johnson being informed of his intention, and being at dinner at Mr. Thomas Davies's the bookseller, from whom I had the story, he asked Mr. Davies "what was the common price of an oak stick"; and being answered sixpence, "Why then, Sir, (said he,) give me leave to send your servant to purchase me a shilling one. I'll have a double quantity; for I am told Foote means to *take me off,* as he calls it, and I am determined the fellow shall not do it with impunity." Davies took care to acquaint Foote of this, which effectually checked the wantonness of the mimic. Mr. Macpherson's menaces[15] made Johnson provide himself with the same implement of defense; and had he been attacked, I have no doubt that, old as he was, he would have made his corporal prowess be felt as much as his intellectual. ❖

14. **roundhouse:** jail.

15. **Mr. Macpherson's menaces:** the threats of James Macpherson, a Scottish poet whose "translations" of alleged third-century poems had been exposed as frauds by Johnson.

WORDS TO KNOW

impunity (ĭm-pyo͞o′nĭ-tē) *n.* freedom from punishment or penalty
corporal (kôr′pər-əl) *adj.* bodily; physical

RESPONDING OPTIONS

FROM PERSONAL RESPONSE *TO* CRITICAL ANALYSIS

REFLECT 1. Which of these excerpts did you find most interesting? Jot down the reasons for your choice in your notebook.

RETHINK 2. Why do you think Boswell decided to include a discussion of Johnson's eating habits?

3. Do you think that Johnson's opinions are fair and based on adequate evidence? Support your conclusion with details from the selection.

4. How do you account for Johnson's willingness to risk his life despite his great fear of death?

Consider
- Johnson's response to a challenge
- his forcefulness in expressing himself
- Boswell's statement that Johnson's "fear was from reflection; his courage natural"

5. What do you think might account for Johnson's becoming such a well-known figure in his time?

RELATE 6. The four subjects treated in these excerpts—eating, the equality of men and women, death, and courage—are still important issues. Choose one of the four subjects and compare the aspects of it that concerned Johnson with the aspects that are most commonly discussed today.

ANOTHER PATHWAY

Cooperative Learning

Work with a partner to compile a list of Samuel Johnson's actions and a list of his statements. What can you infer about Johnson's character from his actions and words? Are there contradictions or surprises in what he does and says? Does he seem likable? Share your conclusions with your classmates.

LITERARY CONCEPTS

A **biography** is an account of a person's life written by another person. In a good biography, the presentation of the subject's life is comprehensive, unified, and accurate, and the information is interpreted to provide the reader with a full picture of the subject's personality. Look back at the chart you made for the Reading Connection on page 425. What kinds of details, conversations, and incidents does Boswell include in these excerpts? Do you think Boswell gives a balanced portrayal of Johnson?

QUICKWRITES

1. Create a **list** of questions you would like to ask Samuel Johnson if you were to interview him.
2. Write a **character sketch** of Johnson that could help a casting director choose an actor to play the part of him in a play. In your description, include details of physical appearance, personality, and voice.
3. Think about the famous person you identified for the Personal Connection on page 425. Write a brief **proposal** outlining your ideas for a biography of the person.

PORTFOLIO *Save your writing. You may want to use it later as a springboard to a piece for your portfolio.*

ALTERNATIVE ACTIVITIES

1. With a partner, role-play a **conversation** in which Johnson and a nutrition expert discuss their ideas about good eating.
2. Work with one or more classmates to present in **pantomime** one of the scenes portrayed in these excerpts. Use gestures and facial expressions to convey your impression of the characters' personalities.

WORDS TO KNOW

Review the Words to Know at the bottom of the selection pages. Then write the word that best completes each sentence.

1. When Johnson was attacked physically or verbally, he was likely to respond in a ______ manner.
2. Surely Johnson's threatening to take a stick to an actor who made fun of him was not the reaction of a ______ man.
3. Johnson frequently used biting sarcasm to attack people who offended him, but at times his attack would be more ______.
4. People quickly found that they could not be rude to Johnson with ______.
5. Clearly, a person with a reasonable amount of ______ would have hesitated to insult or offend Johnson unnecessarily.

THE WRITER'S STYLE

In his biography of Samuel Johnson, Boswell recounts many humorous moments and conversations. Look for two or three examples of humor in the excerpts you have read. What part does humor seem to play in Boswell's portrayal of Johnson's personality?

JAMES BOSWELL

1740–1795

Born in Edinburgh, Scotland, James Boswell was the oldest son of Lord Auchinleck, a wealthy landowner and prominent judge. Under his father's prodding, young Boswell reluctantly took up the study of law, and he did eventually practice law, marry, raise a family, and manage the Auchinleck estate; but his real passion was London—its zest, elegance, and wit. Because he was charming and had a gift for friendship, he became well-known and widely liked in the city.

His most famous friendship, of course, was with Samuel Johnson, though the two men could not have been more different. Whereas Johnson was learned, deeply religious, and revered for the logic, seriousness, and elegance of his writings, Boswell was gregarious, insatiably curious, and frivolous. Beneath Boswell's apparent superficiality, however, lay a great ability to listen to other people and to record their words and behavior in astonishing detail.

Boswell began keeping a diary at about the age of 16. It was thought for many years that his personal papers had been destroyed, but during the 1920s and 1930s, in a series of events that read like a detective story, 8,000 pages of Boswell's journal came to light—many at a castle in Ireland. The diary reveals the extent of Boswell's genius. With a prodigious memory for detail, he described events, recorded impressions, and reconstructed entire conversations with unparalleled immediacy and vividness. Ironically, Boswell died thinking himself a failure, never to know that he would be acclaimed as both the world's greatest biographer and a brilliant diarist.

OTHER WORKS *The Journal of a Tour to the Hebrides, with Samuel Johnson, LL.D.; Boswell's London Journal: 1762–1763*

PREVIEWING

POETRY

Elegy Written in a Country Churchyard

Thomas Gray

PERSONAL CONNECTION

Think about times when you have traveled past or visited a cemetery. What thoughts and feelings did you have? Did you feel sad? Did you wonder about the lives of the people buried there? With a group of classmates, explore your reactions by completing a word web similar to the one shown.

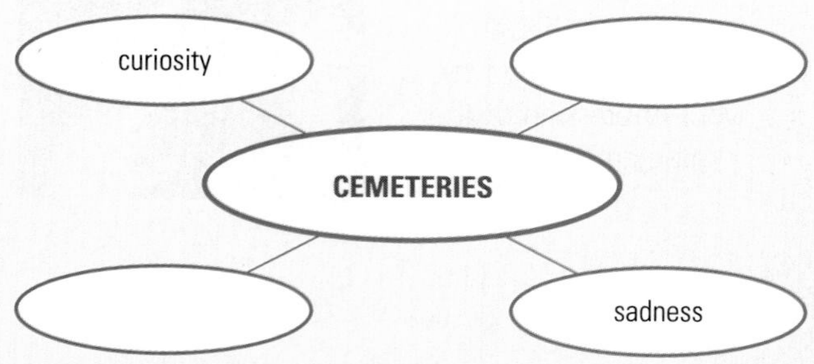

BIOGRAPHICAL/LITERARY CONNECTION

Thomas Gray is one the transitional poets sometimes called preromantic. These poets typically employed the elaborate, stately diction of the neoclassicists but used it to treat different subjects and explore new outlooks. Whereas many neoclassical writers focused on city life, for example, Gray often found his subject matter in the country and in nature. Neoclassicists emphasized simplicity and emotional restraint, but Gray dared to describe intense personal feelings. The topics explored by neoclassical writers tended to be universal, embracing the whole of humanity; Gray, however, brazenly talked about himself. Such bold departures were scorned by Samuel Johnson and other advocates of the rule-bound restraint characteristic of much 18th-century writing.

Gray began "Elegy Written in a Country Churchyard" after his close friend Richard West died at the age of 26. The melancholy and depression Gray suffered as a result of this loss inspired some portions of the elegy, which he spent eight years writing and revising. Although the sense of loss it expresses may be personal, the poem nevertheless clearly has relevance to the lives of all people. This universal appeal has made it one of the most-quoted poems in English literature.

READING CONNECTION

Forming Impressions from Description
As you read this poem, let Gray's descriptions guide you in forming an impression of the lives of the people he presents.

Elegy Written in a Country Churchyard

Thomas Gray

The curfew tolls the knell of parting day,
The lowing herd wind slowly o'er the lea,
The plowman homeward plods his weary way,
And leaves the world to darkness and to me.

Now fades the glimmering landscape on the sight,
And all the air a solemn stillness holds,
Save where the beetle wheels his droning flight,
And drowsy tinklings lull the distant folds;

Save that from yonder ivy-mantled tower
The moping owl does to the moon complain
Of such, as wandering near her secret bower,
Molest her ancient solitary reign.

GUIDE FOR READING

2 lea (lē): meadow.

Beneath those rugged elms, that yew tree's shade,
    Where heaves the turf in many a moldering heap,
Each in his narrow cell forever laid,
    The rude forefathers of the hamlet sleep.

The breezy call of incense-breathing Morn,
    The swallow twittering from the straw-built shed,
The cock's shrill clarion, or the echoing horn,
    No more shall rouse them from their lowly bed.

For them no more the blazing hearth shall burn,
    Or busy housewife ply her evening care;
No children run to lisp their sire's return,
    Or climb his knees the envied kiss to share.

Oft did the harvest to their sickle yield,
    Their furrow oft the stubborn glebe has broke;
How jocund did they drive their team afield!
    How bowed the woods beneath their sturdy stroke!

Let not Ambition mock their useful toil,
    Their homely joys, and destiny obscure;
Nor Grandeur hear with a disdainful smile
    The short and simple annals of the poor.

The boast of heraldry, the pomp of power,
    And all that beauty, all that wealth e'er gave,
Awaits alike the inevitable hour.
    The paths of glory lead but to the grave.

Nor you, ye proud, impute to these the fault,
    If Memory o'er their tomb no trophies raise,
Where through the long-drawn aisle and fretted vault
    The pealing anthem swells the note of praise.

Can storied urn or animated bust
    Back to its mansion call the fleeting breath?
Can Honor's voice provoke the silent dust,
    Or Flattery soothe the dull cold ear of Death?

16 rude: unsophisticated; rustic. Where is the speaker?

26 glebe: soil; earth.

27 jocund (jŏk'ənd): merry.

32 annals: descriptive records; history. What is the speaker's attitude toward the dead?

33 heraldry: noble birth.

35 What is meant by "the inevitable hour"?

37 impute . . . fault: assign the blame to them.

38 trophies: sculptures depicting the achievements of the deceased.

39 fretted vault: space enclosed under a decorated arched ceiling.

41 storied . . . bust: an urn for the ashes of the deceased, decorated with scenes from the person's life, or a lifelike portrait sculpture.

43 provoke: call forth.

Perhaps in this neglected spot is laid
    Some heart once pregnant with celestial fire;
Hands that the rod of empire might have swayed,
    Or waked to ecstasy the living lyre.

But Knowledge to their eyes her ample page
    Rich with the spoils of time did ne'er unroll;
Chill Penury repressed their noble rage,
    And froze the genial current of the soul.

Full many a gem of purest ray serene,
    The dark unfathomed caves of ocean bear:
Full many a flower is born to blush unseen,
    And waste its sweetness on the desert air.

Some village Hampden, that with dauntless breast
    The little tyrant of his fields withstood;
Some mute inglorious Milton here may rest,
    Some Cromwell guiltless of his country's blood.

The applause of listening senates to command,
    The threats of pain and ruin to despise,
To scatter plenty o'er a smiling land,
    And read their history in a nation's eyes,

Their lot forbade: nor circumscribed alone
    Their growing virtues, but their crimes confined;
Forbade to wade through slaughter to a throne,
    And shut the gates of mercy on mankind,

The struggling pangs of conscious truth to hide,
    To quench the blushes of ingenuous shame,
Or heap the shrine of Luxury and Pride
    With incense kindled at the Muse's flame.

Far from the madding crowd's ignoble strife,
    Their sober wishes never learned to stray;
Along the cool sequestered vale of life
    They kept the noiseless tenor of their way.

48 lyre: a small harplike musical instrument used in ancient Greece to accompany the singing of poetry and therefore frequently used as a symbol of the poetic art.

51–52 penury (pĕn'yə-rē): extreme poverty; **genial current:** warm, life-giving power. Why has poverty held back their "noble rage" and "genial current"?

57 Hampden: John Hampden, a 17th-century English politician who opposed the "tyrant" Charles I over unjust taxation.

60 Cromwell: Oliver Cromwell, leader of the Parliamentary forces in the English Civil War and head of the English government from 1653 to 1658.

65 circumscribed: limited; confined.

69 conscious truth: conscience.

72 incense . . . flame: poetic praise.

73 madding: wildly excited; disorderly.

75 sequestered: isolated; secluded.

76 tenor: unwavering course.

Yet even these bones from insult to protect
Some frail memorial still erected nigh,
With uncouth rhymes and shapeless sculpture decked,
Implores the passing tribute of a sigh.

Their name, their years, spelt by the unlettered Muse,
The place of fame and elegy supply:
And many a holy text around she strews,
That teach the rustic moralist to die.

For who to dumb Forgetfulness a prey,
This pleasing anxious being e'er resigned,
Left the warm precincts of the cheerful day,
Nor cast one longing lingering look behind?

On some fond breast the parting soul relies,
Some pious drops the closing eye requires;
Even from the tomb the voice of Nature cries,
Even in our ashes live their wonted fires.

For thee, who mindful of the unhonored dead
Dost in these lines their artless tale relate;
If chance, by lonely contemplation led,
Some kindred spirit shall inquire thy fate,

Haply some hoary-headed swain may say,
"Oft have we seen him at the peep of dawn
Brushing with hasty steps the dews away
To meet the sun upon the upland lawn.

"There at the foot of yonder nodding beech
That wreathes its old fantastic roots so high,
His listless length at noontide would he stretch,
And pore upon the brook that babbles by.

"Hard by yon wood, now smiling as in scorn,
Muttering his wayward fancies he would rove,
Now drooping, woeful wan, like one forlorn,
Or crazed with care, or crossed in hopeless love.

81 unlettered Muse: the "inspiration" of the uneducated stonecutters who carved the inscriptions on the tombstones.

85–88 For who . . . behind?: For who has ever accepted that he will be forgotten, leaving the warmth of earthly life without any regret?

90 drops: tears.

92 wonted (wôn'tĭd): accustomed.

93 thee: that is, Gray himself.

97 hoary-headed swain: white-haired peasant.

104 pore: to gaze intently.

"One morn I missed him on the customed hill,
   Along the heath and near his favorite tree;
Another came; nor yet beside the rill,
   Nor up the lawn, nor at the wood was he;

"The next with dirges due in sad array
   Slow through the churchway path we saw him borne.
Approach and read (for thou canst read) the lay,
   Graved on the stone beneath yon aged thorn."

111 rill: brook.

113 dirges: funeral hymns.

115 lay: poem.

116 thorn: hawthorn.

The Epitaph

Here rests his head upon the lap of Earth
   A youth to fortune and to Fame unknown.
Fair Science frowned not on his humble birth,
   And Melancholy marked him for her own.

Large was his bounty, and his soul sincere,
   Heaven did a recompense as largely send:
He gave to Misery all he had, a tear,
   He gained from Heaven ('twas all he wished) a friend.

No farther seek his merits to disclose,
   Or draw his frailties from their dread abode
(There they alike in trembling hope repose),
   The bosom of his Father and his God.

117–128 What do you learn about Gray from this epitaph?

RESPONDING OPTIONS

FROM PERSONAL RESPONSE *TO* CRITICAL ANALYSIS

REFLECT 1. Decide on a color that, in your opinion, represents the mood of this poem. Explain your choice to your classmates.

RETHINK 2. What ideas about the lives of people are conveyed by the poem?

Consider
- the reference to "the inevitable hour" in line 35
- the speculations about the "forefathers of the hamlet" throughout the poem
- the roles of Knowledge and Penury in lines 49–52
- the sentiments expressed in lines 57–72

3. Review the word web you created for the Personal Connection on page 432. How does your reaction to cemeteries compare with Gray's?

4. How would you describe Gray's attitude toward death?

Consider
- your answer to question 2
- Gray's description of what someone might say about his own death (lines 98–116)
- his inclusion of his own epitaph

5. Consider how different readers might react to this poem. For example, how might the reaction of a 20-year-old reader differ from that of a 70-year-old reader?

RELATE 6. In your opinion, does this poem have relevance to the lives of people today? Why or why not?

ANOTHER PATHWAY

Cooperative Learning

Review the descriptive details that Gray uses to help the reader form an impression of the lives of the people he presents. Then work with a small group to create a list of facts about these people. Next to each fact, cite the line or lines of the poem that convey the information. Compare your lists with those of other groups.

LITERARY CONCEPTS

Personification is a type of figurative language in which human qualities are attributed to an object, animal, or idea. In line 117 of Gray's elegy, for example, Earth is personified as a motherly figure upon whose lap the dead may rest their head. With a partner, find some other examples of personification in the poem.

QUICKWRITES

1. In a **paragraph,** explain what you think is meant by "Full many a flower is born to blush unseen, / And waste its sweetness on the desert air" (lines 55–56).
2. Give the poem a new **title** that conveys either the poem's mood or an aspect of its subject.
3. Write your own **epitaph,** describing yourself and indicating the qualities for which you hope to be remembered.

PORTFOLIO *Save your writing. You may want to use it later as a springboard to a piece for your portfolio.*

ALTERNATIVE ACTIVITIES

1. Draw a charcoal or pencil **sketch** to illustrate one of the examples of personification in the poem. Experiment with shading and texture to create an appropriate background for your image.
2. Create a recording of **background music** to accompany an oral reading of the poem. For the recording, select an instrumental work or a song (or excerpts from several pieces) that you think complements the poem's mood. Play your recording as you read the poem aloud for your classmates.

THE WRITER'S STYLE

The typical word order in an English sentence is subject-verb-object. In this poem, Gray frequently uses **inversions,** or rearrangements of this typical order. For example, in the clause "all the air a solemn stillness holds" (line 6), the order is object-subject-verb. Inversion is often used in poetry to emphasize words or ideas. Find at least three other examples of inversion in the poem. How would each passage read if the words were arranged in the usual order?

LITERARY LINKS

Compare the speakers of "Elegy Written in a Country Churchyard" and Shakespeare's "Fear No More the Heat o' the Sun" (page 240). Do you notice any similarities or differences in their attitudes toward death? Discuss your observations with your classmates, and compare your ideas with theirs.

ACROSS THE CURRICULUM

History Investigate Gray's allusions, in lines 57–60, to events of the reign of Charles I. What circumstances caused the king to be viewed as a "tyrant." How was he challenged?

THOMAS GRAY

1716–1771

The only one of his parents' 12 children to survive past infancy, Thomas Gray was rather delicate and frail as a child. Although his mother adored and sheltered her son, his ill-tempered, abusive father frequently vented his rage on the family. Gray was able to escape his uneasy, frightening home life, however, when at the age of eight he entered boarding school at Eton College. A studious, sensitive boy, he disliked boisterous games and sports and chose friends who shared his scholarly interests. Among these were Horace Walpole—the son of Britain's most prominent Whig leader—and Richard West, a fellow poet.

At about the age of 18, Gray entered Cambridge University. There he embarked upon the study of law, but after several years he abandoned his studies to accompany his friend Walpole on a tour of Europe. The trip ended in a bitter quarrel, which severed their friendship for many years.

In 1742, the year of Richard West's early death, Gray returned to Cambridge. There he continued his studies, obtained his degree, and wrote a number of carefully crafted poems. In 1757, the government was ready to offer him the position of poet laureate; however, not wanting to write poems on request and always hesitant to publish his poetry, he declined. Gray remained at Cambridge, rarely leaving its grounds, for the rest of his life. He died at the age of 55 and was buried beside his mother in the rural churchyard at Stoke Poges in Buckinghamshire, the setting of his famous elegy.

OTHER WORKS "Ode on a Distant Prospect of Eton College," "Ode on the Spring"

PREVIEWING

NONFICTION

from The Diary and Letters of Madame d'Arblay

Fanny Burney

PERSONAL CONNECTION

Think about your initial conversation with a person you met recently. Did the conversation leave you with a distinct impression of the person? In your opinion, what personality traits can be revealed in a brief conversation? Share your thoughts with your classmates.

CULTURAL/BIOGRAPHICAL CONNECTION

Conversation was a fashionable activity in London throughout the 18th century, but after 1750 the preferred setting for conversation changed from coffeehouses to private homes. Parties intended chiefly as occasions for conversation were often hosted by women, particularly the members of a literary group known as the bluestockings. Members of both sexes were invited, and the guests usually included one or more distinguished writers, artists, or musicians. The scope of the entertainment might extend beyond conversation to literary readings, dramatic performances, and occasionally even dancing or card playing.

One of London's most prominent social hostesses was Hester Thrale, whose prestigious guests included the renowned author Samuel Johnson, the playwright Richard Brinsley Sheridan, the painter Joshua Reynolds, the actor David Garrick, the philosopher Edmund Burke, and a young writer named Fanny Burney. At the age of 26, Burney had anonymously published her first novel, *Evelina.* An instant success, *Evelina* had won the approval of even the most critical readers, including Johnson. When Burney was eventually identified as the book's author, she became the darling of literary circles and a sought-after guest at social gatherings.

Although Burney (known after her marriage as Madame d'Arblay) achieved immediate fame through her novels, readers today are more familiar with her diary, which she began when she was 15 and wrote in regularly for 70 years. A number of the entries are copies of letters to relatives and close friends. Like the letter you are about to read, many were addressed to Burney's sister and best friend, Susan Burney Phillips.

WRITING CONNECTION

In this selection, Fanny Burney presents a vivid record of the conversation at a party. Try to recall a conversation that you recently took part in or overheard. Use a script format like the one shown to record as accurately as possible the exact words spoken by each participant. Then, as you read Burney's letter to her sister, compare her recollection of conversation with your own.

FROM

The Diary and Letters of MADAME D'ARBLAY

FANNY BURNEY

Letter to Mrs. Phillips, Her Sister

I thank you most heartily for your two sweet letters, my ever dearest Susy, and equally for the kindness they contain and the kindness they accept. And, as I have a frank[1] and a subject, I will leave my *bothers,* and write you and my dear brother Molesworth a little account of a *rout*[2] I have just been at, at the house of Mr. Paradise.

You will wonder, perhaps, in this time of hurry, why I went thither; but when I tell you Pacchierotti[3] was there, you will not think it surprising.

There was a crowd of company; Charlotte and I went together; my father came afterwards. Mrs. Paradise received us very graciously, and led me immediately up to Miss Thrale, who was sitting by the Pac.[4] The Miss Kirwans, you may be sure, were not far off, and so I did pretty well. There was nobody else I knew but Dr. Solander, Mr. Coxe, the traveler, Sir Sampson and Lady Gideon (Streatham acquaintances), Mr. Sastres, and Count Zenobia, a noble Venetian, whom I have often met lately at Mrs. Thrale's.

We were very late, for we had waited cruelly for the coach, and Pac. had sung a song out of *Artaxerxes,*[5] composed for a tenor, which we lost, to my infinite regret. Afterwards he sang "Dolce speme," set by Bertoni, less elegantly than by Sacchini, but more expressively for the words. He sang it delightfully. It was but the second time I have heard him in a room since his return to England.

---

1. **frank:** an envelope marked by an official so that it can be mailed without postage.
2. **rout:** party.
3. **Pacchierotti** (päk′yĕ-rôt′tē): a well-known operatic singer of the time.
4. **Pac.:** an abbreviation of *Pacchierotti.*
5. ***Artaxerxes*** (är′tə-zûrk′sēz′): an opera by the 18th-century British composer Thomas Arne.

The Porten Family, Gawen Hamilton. Museum of Fine Arts, Springfield, Massachusetts, James Philip Gray Collection.

After this he went into another room, to try if it would be cooler; and Mrs. Paradise, leaning over the Kirwans and Charlotte, who hardly got a seat all night for the crowd, said she begged to speak to me. I squeezed my great person out, and she then said,

"Miss Burney, Lady Say and Sele[6] desires the honor of being introduced to you."

Her ladyship stood by her side. She seems pretty near fifty—at least turned forty; her head was full of feathers, flowers, jewels, and geegaws, and as high as Lady Archer's; her dress was trimmed with beads, silver, persian sashes, and all sort of fine fancies; her face is thin and fiery, and her whole manner spoke a lady all alive.

"Miss Burney," cried she, with great quickness, and a look all curiosity, "I am very happy to see you; I have longed to see you a great while; I have read your performance, and I am quite delighted with it. I think it's the most elegant novel I ever read in my life. Such a style! I am quite surprised at it. I can't think where you got so much invention!"

You may believe this was a reception not to make me very loquacious. I did not know which way to turn my head.

"I must introduce you," continued her ladyship, "to my sister; she'll be quite delighted to see you. She has written a novel herself; so you are sister authoresses. A most elegant thing it is, I assure you; almost as pretty as yours, only not quite so elegant. She has written two novels, only one is not so pretty as the other. But I shall insist upon your seeing them. One is in letters, like yours, only yours is prettiest; it's called the *Mausoleum of Julia!*"

What unfeeling things, thought I, are *my* sisters! I'm sure I never heard them go about thus praising *me!*

6. **Lady Say and Sele:** the title of the wife of Baron Say and Sele.

WORDS TO KNOW **loquacious** (lō-kwā′shəs) *adj.* very talkative

Mrs. Paradise then again came forward, and taking my hand, led me up to her ladyship's sister, Lady Hawke, saying aloud, and with a courteous smirk, "Miss Burney, ma'am, authoress of *Evelina.*"

"Yes," cried my friend, Lady Say and Sele, who followed me close, "it's the authoress of *Evelina;* so you are sister authoresses!"

Lady Hawke arose and curtsied. She is much younger than her sister, and rather pretty; extremely languishing, delicate, and pathetic; apparently accustomed to be reckoned the genius of her family, and well contented to be looked upon as a creature dropped from the clouds.

I was then seated between their ladyships, and Lady S. and S., drawing as near to me as possible, said,

"Well, and so you wrote this pretty book!—and pray did your papa know of it?"

"No, ma'am; not till some months after the publication."

"So I've heard; it's surprising! I can't think how you invented it!—there's a vast deal of invention in it! And you've got so much humor, too! Now my sister has no humor—hers is all sentiment. You can't think how I was entertained with that old grandmother and her son!"

I suppose she meant Tom Branghton for the son.

"How much pleasure you must have had in writing it; had not you?"

"Y—e—s, ma'am."

"So has my sister; she's never without a pen in her hand; she can't help writing for her life. When Lord Hawke is traveling about with her, she keeps writing all the way."

"Yes," said Lady Hawke; "I really can't help writing. One has great pleasure in writing the things; has not one, Miss Burney?"

"Y—e—s, ma'am."

"But your novel," cried Lady Say and Sele, "is in such a style!—so elegant! I am vastly glad you made it end happily. I hate a novel that don't end happy."

"Yes," said Lady Hawke, with a languid smile, "I was vastly glad when she married Lord Orville. I was sadly afraid it would not have been."

"My sister intends," said Lady Say and Sele, "to print her *Mausoleum,* just for her own friends and acquaintances."

"Yes," said Lady Hawke, "I have never printed yet."

"I saw Lady Hawke's name," quoth I to my first friend, "ascribed to the play of *Variety.*"

"Did you indeed?" cried Lady Say, in an ecstasy. "Sister! do you know Miss Burney saw your name in the newspapers, about the play!"

"Did she?" said Lady Hawke, smiling complacently. "But I really did not write it; I never wrote a play in my life."

"Well," cried Lady Say, "but do repeat that sweet part that I am so fond of—you know what I mean; Miss Burney *must* hear it,—out of your novel, you know!"

Lady H.—No I can't; I have forgot it.

Lady S.—Oh no! I am sure you have not; I insist upon it.

Lady H.—But I know you can repeat it yourself; you have so fine a memory; I am sure you can repeat it.

Lady S.—Oh, but I should not do it justice! that's all,—I should not do it justice!

Lady Hawke then bent forward, and repeated—"'If, when he made the declaration of his love, the sensibility that beamed in his eyes was felt in his heart, what pleasing sensations and soft alarms might not that tender avowal awaken!'"

"And from what, ma'am," cried I, astonished, and imagining I had mistaken them, "is this taken?"

"From my sister's novel!" answered the delighted Lady Say and Sele, expecting my raptures to be equal to her own; "it's in the *Mausoleum,*—did not you know that? Well, I can't think how you can write these sweet novels! And it's all just like that part. Lord Hawke himself says it's all poetry. For my part, I'm sure I never could write so. I suppose, Miss

WORDS TO KNOW

ascribed (ə-skrībd') *adj.* assigned; referred to as a source **ascribe** *v.*
complacently (kəm-plā'sənt-lē) *adv.* in a contented, self-satisfied way; smugly

Burney, you are producing another,—a'n't you?"

"No, ma'am."

"Oh, I daresay you are. I daresay you are writing one at this very minute!"

Mrs. Paradise now came up to me again, followed by a square man, middle-aged, and humdrum, who, I found, was Lord Say and Sele, afterwards from the Kirwans; for though they introduced him to me, I was so confounded by their vehemence and their manners, that I did not hear his name.

"Miss Burney," said Mrs. P., presenting me to him, "authoress of *Evelina.*"

"Yes," cried Lady Say and Sele, starting up, "'tis the authoress of *Evelina!*"

"Of what?" cried he.

"Of *Evelina.* You'd never think it,—she looks so young, to have so much invention, and such an elegant style! Well, I could write a play, I think, but I'm sure I could never write a novel."

"Oh yes, you could, if you would try," said Lady Hawke.

"Oh no, I could not," answered she; "I could not get a style—that's the thing—I could not tell how to get a style! and a novel's nothing without a style, you know!"

"Why no," said Lady Hawke; "that's true. But then you write such charming letters, you know!"

"Letters!" repeated Lady S. and S., simpering; "do you think so? Do you know I wrote a long letter to Mrs. Ray just before I came here, this very afternoon,—quite a long letter! I did, I assure you!"

Here Mrs. Paradise came forward with another gentleman, younger, slimmer, and smarter, and saying to me, "Sir Gregory Page Turner," said to him, "Miss Burney, authoress of *Evelina.*"

At which Lady Say and Sele, in fresh transport, again arose, and rapturously again repeated—"Yes, she's authoress of *Evelina!* Have you read it?"

"No; is it to be had?"

"Oh dear, yes! it's been printed these two years! You'd never think it! But it's the most elegant novel I ever read in my life. Writ in such a style!"

"Certainly," said he, very civilly; "I have every inducement to get it. Pray where is it to be had? everywhere, I suppose?"

"Oh, nowhere, I hope!" cried I, wishing at that moment it had been never in human ken.[7]

My *square* friend, Lord Say and Sele, then putting his head forward, said, very solemnly, "I'll purchase it!"

His lady then mentioned to me a hundred novels that I had never heard of, asking my opinion of them, and whether I knew the authors; Lady Hawke only occasionally and languidly joining in the discourse: and then Lady S. and S., suddenly arising, begged me not to move, for she should be back again in a minute, and flew to the next room.

I took, however, the first opportunity of Lady Hawke's casting down her eyes, and reclining her delicate head, to make away from this terrible set; and, just as I was got by the piano-forte,[8] where I hoped Pacchierotti would soon present himself, Mrs. Paradise again came to me, and said,

"Miss Burney, Lady Say and Sele wishes vastly to cultivate your acquaintance, and begs to know if she may have the honor of your company to an assembly at her house next Friday?—and I will do myself the pleasure to call for you, if you will give me leave."

"Her ladyship does me much honor, but I am unfortunately engaged," was my answer, with as much promptness as I could command. ❖

---

7. **ken:** range of vision; sight.

8. **piano-forte** (pē-ăn′ō-fôr′tā): piano.

WORDS TO KNOW

transport (trăns′pôrt′) *n.* a state of being carried away by emotion; a state of bliss

inducement (ĭn-dōōs′mənt) *n.* a motive for action; incentive

RESPONDING OPTIONS

FROM PERSONAL RESPONSE *TO* CRITICAL ANALYSIS

REFLECT 1. In your notebook, jot down your impression of Burney's experience at the party.

RETHINK 2. In your opinion, what different aspects of human nature are illuminated by the conversation Burney recounts?

Consider

- the reasons for Burney's popularity
- the conduct of Mrs. Paradise
- the sentiments expressed by Lady Say and Sele
- the attitude of Lady Hawke

3. How would you describe Burney's attitude toward her experience?

Consider

- the tone she adopts in recounting the conversation
- her depiction of people's responses to her fame as an author
- her desire to hear the opera singer

RELATE 4. Have you ever met or observed a person who behaved like Lady Say and Sele? What do you think motivated the person's behavior?

5. Look again at the conversation you recorded for the Writing Connection on page 440. How is it similar to the conversation recorded in Burney's letter? How is it different?

ANOTHER PATHWAY

Cooperative Learning

With three or four classmates, prepare to act out the scene described by Burney. As you rehearse, decide on mannerisms and voice patterns for each character. Then present your drama to the class. After each group has performed, discuss the various portrayals of Burney and her acquaintances.

LITERARY CONCEPTS

Written conversation between two or more people, in either fiction or nonfiction, is called **dialogue.** Writers use dialogue to bring characters to life and to give readers insights into the characters' qualities, personality traits, and reactions to other people. Do you think Burney's account of the party would have been as effective without dialogue? Use examples to explain your opinion.

QUICKWRITES

1. Write a **gossip column** that Lady Say and Sele might have written for the society page of a local paper after her meeting with Fanny Burney.
2. Create a **script** for the scene Burney describes. Be sure to include any stage directions and director's notes that you think are needed to flesh out the scene.
3. Use the conversation you recorded for the Writing Connection as the basis for a **diary entry** written, like Burney's, as a letter to a friend or sibling.

PORTFOLIO *Save your writing. You may want to use it later as a springboard to a piece for your portfolio.*

ALTERNATIVE ACTIVITIES

1. Draw a humorous **caricature** of Lady Say and Sele, based on the information revealed in this selection. Try to capture her personality as well as her appearance.
2. Create a **photo essay** called "Conversations." Include pictures that show a variety of facial expressions and gestures.

ACROSS THE CURRICULUM

History Research the origin of the term *bluestocking.* What role did the bluestockings play in the history of English literature? Did they change society's attitudes toward women?

LITERARY LINKS

Compare the ways in which Fanny Burney and Samuel Pepys describe social gatherings. How do they differ in the types of details they record? What do the differences reveal about the writers? Justify your answers with examples from the selections in this book.

WORDS TO KNOW

EXERCISE A Review the Words to Know at the bottom of the selection pages. Then write the word suggested by each of the following sets of idioms.

1. on cloud nine, walking on air
2. rattle on, run off at the mouth
3. point the finger, give credit where it's due
4. dangle a carrot in front of, light a fire under
5. without batting an eye, not give a hoot

EXERCISE B Look for images that illustrate the meanings of at least three vocabulary words.

FANNY BURNEY

1752–1840

Largely self-taught, Fanny Burney was an avid reader who, by the time she was ten, had begun writing stories, poems, and plays. As a girl, she stood timidly in the background at her father's parties, listening closely to the guests; her remarkable memory allowed her to recall conversations word for word. Even after becoming a successful novelist, she remained modest around her ardent admirers.

Burney's novels influenced a number of later female novelists, particularly Jane Austen. *Evelina* was a forerunner of the "novel of manners," a genre in which the customs and conventions of social life occupy a prominent place. None of Burney's other novels had the success of *Evelina,* although Austen was to find both the title and the theme for her *Pride and Prejudice* in Burney's second novel, *Cecilia.*

In 1786, Burney's life took a new direction when she reluctantly accepted a position at the court of King George III. It was an unpleasant experience that allowed her little time to write, and she left the court after five years. At age 41, she married Alexandre d'Arblay, a French general who had fled to England during the French Revolution. Although d'Arblay was poor, the proceeds from Burney's third novel, *Camilla,* enabled them to live comfortably. In 1802, a visit to France became a ten-year exile for the d'Arblays and their son when the country suddenly became engaged in war with England. During her later years, back in London, Burney published her father's memoirs. Her own diary was not published until long after her death.

PREVIEWING

NONFICTION

from Memoirs of Madame Vigée-Lebrun

Élisabeth Vigée-Lebrun (vē-zhā′ lə-brœN′)

PERSONAL CONNECTION

Imagine a society divided between a few extremely rich aristocrats and many desperately poor people. If you lived among the rich, how might you feel about the poor? How might they feel about you? Write down some of your thoughts in your notebook.

HISTORICAL CONNECTION

In these excerpts from her memoirs, Élisabeth Vigée-Lebrun—a gifted artist who painted portraits of the French nobility—recalls events of her own life amidst the turmoil of the French Revolution, which began in 1789. Like James Boswell and Fanny Burney, Vigée-Lebrun was a keen observer of human nature and offers a unique perspective on some of the famous as well as the ordinary people of her time.

Before the Revolution, France was ruled by a king, who had almost unlimited authority, and by the privileged nobility and clergy. These groups obtained most of the money they needed to maintain their rich lifestyles by taxing peasant farmers and other poor workers. In 1789, the French government's finances were in a shambles; the country's support of the American Revolution had raised French debt to unprecedented levels. Peasants and farmers were angry because their requests for a voice in government had been denied. Facing food shortages and other economic hardships, they revolted and stormed the Bastille, a Paris fortress-prison that was a hated symbol of royal authority and oppression. Workers throughout the countryside pillaged and burned the elegant chateaus of the nobility.

A long period of struggle and increasing violence ensued, during which King Louis XVI and his wife, Marie Antoinette, were imprisoned and later executed—the king in January 1793 and the queen in October. The most horrific months of the Revolution, known as the Reign of Terror, came in late 1793 and 1794, when thousands of citizens were imprisoned and executed.

READING CONNECTION

Interpreting Details Élisabeth Vigée-Lebrun includes many descriptive details in her writing. As you read her memoirs, use a chart like the one shown to note words and phrases she uses to describe the people, both rich and poor, whom she encounters.

Rich People	Poor People

Queen Marie Antoinette on the Way to the Scaffold (about 1793), Jacques Louis David. Pen drawing, 15 cm × 10 cm, E. de Rothschild Collection, Musée du Louvre, Paris.

• *HISTORICAL CONNECTION*

from

MEMOIRS OF MADAME VIGÉE-LEBRUN

It was in the year 1779 that I painted the Queen for the first time; *she was then in the heyday of her youth and beauty. Marie Antoinette was tall and admirably built, being somewhat stout, but not excessively so. Her arms were superb, her hands small and perfectly formed, and her feet charming. She had the best walk of any woman in France, carrying her head erect with a dignity that stamped her queen* in the midst of her whole court, her majestic mien, however, not in the least diminishing the sweetness and amiability of her face. To anyone who has not seen the Queen it is difficult to get an idea of all the graces and all the nobility combined in her person. Her features were not regular; she had inherited that long and narrow oval peculiar to the Austrian nation. Her eyes were not large; in color they were almost blue, and they were at the same time merry and kind. Her nose was slender and pretty, and her mouth not too large, though her lips were rather thick. But the most remarkable thing about her face was the splendor of her complexion. I never have seen one so brilliant, and brilliant is the word, for her skin was so transparent that it bore no umber[1] in the painting. Neither could I render the real effect of it as I wished. I had no colors to paint such freshness, such delicate tints, which were hers alone, and which I had never seen in any other woman.

At the first sitting the imposing air of the Queen at first frightened me greatly, but Her Majesty spoke to me so graciously that my fear was soon dissipated. It was on that occasion that I began the picture representing her with a large basket, wearing a satin dress, and holding a rose in her hand. This portrait was destined for her brother, Emperor Joseph II, and the Queen ordered two copies besides—one for the Empress of Russia, the other for her own apartments at Versailles or Fontainebleau.[2]

I painted various pictures of the Queen at different times. In one I did her to the knees, in a pale orange-red dress, standing before a table on which she was arranging some flowers in a vase. It may be well imagined that I preferred to paint her in a plain gown and especially without a wide hoopskirt. She usually gave these portraits to her friends or to foreign diplomatic envoys. One of them shows her with a straw hat on, and a white muslin dress, whose sleeves are turned up, though quite neatly. When this work was exhibited at the Salon,[3] malignant folk did not fail to make the remark that the Queen had been painted in her chemise,[4] for we were then in 1786, and calumny[5] was already busy concerning her. Yet in spite of all this the portraits were very successful.

Toward the end of the exhibition a little piece was given at the Vaudeville Theater, bearing the title, I think, "The Assembling of the Arts." Brongniart,[6] the architect, and his wife, whom the author had taken into his confidence, had taken a box on the first tier, and called for me on the day of the first performance. As I had no suspicion of the surprise in store for me, judge of my emotion when Painting appeared on the scene and I saw the actress representing that art copy me in the act of painting a portrait of the Queen. The same moment everybody in the parterre[7] and the boxes turned toward me and applauded to bring the roof down. I can hardly believe that anyone was ever more moved and more grateful than I was that evening.

I was so fortunate as to be on very pleasant terms with the Queen. When she heard that I had something of a voice we rarely had a sitting without singing some duets by Grétry[8] together, for she was exceedingly fond of music, although she did not sing very true. As for her conversation, it would be difficult for me to convey all its charm, all its affability. I do not think that Queen Marie Antoinette ever missed an opportunity of saying something pleasant to those who had the honor of being presented to her, and the

1. **umber:** a brown pigment.
2. **Versailles** (vĕr-sī′) . . . **Fontainebleau** (fôN-tĕn-blō′): sites of royal palaces.
3. **Salon:** an annual French art exhibition.
4. **chemise** (shə-mēz′): a woman's loose-fitting undergarment.
5. **calumny** (kăl′əm-nē): the making of false statements intended to injure a person's reputation; slander.
6. **Brongniart** (brôN-nyär′).
7. **parterre** (pär-târ′): the seating area nearest the stage on the main floor of a theater.
8. **Grétry** (grā-trē′): an 18th-century French composer of operas.

WORDS TO KNOW

mien (mēn) *n.* the manner in which one carries and conducts oneself; demeanor
amiability (ā′mē-ə-bĭl′ĭ-tē) *n.* good nature; friendliness

kindness she always bestowed upon me has ever been one of my sweetest memories.

One day I happened to miss the appointment she had given me for a sitting; I had suddenly become unwell. The next day I hastened to Versailles to offer my excuses. The Queen was not expecting me; she had had her horses harnessed to go out driving, and her carriage was the first thing I saw on entering the palace yard. I nevertheless went upstairs to speak with the chamberlains on duty. One of them, M. Campan, received me with a stiff and haughty manner, and bellowed at me in his stentorian voice, "It was yesterday, madame, that Her Majesty expected you, and I am very sure she is going out driving, and I am very sure she will give you no sitting today!" Upon my reply that I had simply come to take Her Majesty's orders for another day, he went to the Queen, who at once had me conducted to her room. She was finishing her toilet,[9] and was holding a book in her hand, hearing her daughter repeat a lesson. My heart was beating violently, for I knew that I was in the wrong. But the Queen looked up at me and said most amiably, "I was waiting for you all the morning yesterday; what happened to you?"

"I am sorry to say, Your Majesty," I replied, "I was so ill that I was unable to comply with Your Majesty's commands. I am here to receive more now, and then I will immediately retire."

"No, no! Do not go!" exclaimed the Queen. "I do not want you to have made your journey for nothing!" She revoked the order for her carriage and gave me a sitting. I remember that, in my confusion and my eagerness to make a fitting response to her kind words, I opened my paint-box so excitedly that I spilled my brushes on the floor. I stooped down to pick them up. "Never mind, never mind," said the Queen, and, for aught I could say, she insisted on gathering them all up herself.

When the Queen went for the last time to Fontainebleau, where the court, according to custom, was to appear in full gala, I repaired there to enjoy that spectacle. I saw the Queen in her grandest dress; she was covered with diamonds, and as the brilliant sunshine fell upon her she seemed to me nothing short of dazzling. Her head, erect on her beautiful Greek neck, lent her as she walked such an imposing, such a majestic air, that one seemed to see a goddess in the midst of her nymphs. During the first sitting I had with Her Majesty after this occasion I took the liberty of mentioning the impression she had made upon me, and of saying to the Queen how the carriage of her head added to the nobility of her bearing. She answered in a jesting tone, "If I were not Queen they would say I looked insolent, would they not?"

The Queen neglected nothing to impart to her children the courteous and gracious manners which endeared her so to all her surroundings. I once saw her make her six-year-old daughter dine with a little peasant girl and attend to her wants. The Queen saw to it that the little visitor was served first, saying to her daughter, "You must do the honors."

The last sitting I had with Her Majesty was given me at Trianon, where I did her hair for the large picture in which she appeared with her children. After doing the Queen's hair, as well as separate studies of the Dauphin,[10] Madame Royale, and the Duke de Normandie, I busied myself with my picture, to which I attached great importance, and I had it ready for the Salon of 1788. The frame, which had been taken there alone, was enough to

9. **toilet:** the process of dressing or grooming oneself.

10. **Dauphin** (dō-făɴ′): the eldest son of the king of France.

evoke a thousand malicious remarks. "That's how the money goes," they said, and a number of other things which seemed to me the bitterest comments. At last I sent my picture, but I could not muster up the courage to follow it and find out what its fate was to be, so afraid was I that it would be badly received by the public. In fact, I became quite ill with fright. I shut myself in my room, and there I was, praying to the Lord for the success of my "Royal Family," when my brother and a host of friends burst in to tell me that my picture had met with universal acclaim. After the Salon, the King, having had the picture transferred to Versailles, M. d'Angevilliers,[11] then minister of the fine arts and director of royal residences, presented me to His Majesty. Louis XVI vouchsafed[12] to talk to me at some length and to tell me that he was very much pleased. Then he added, still looking at my work, "I know nothing about painting, but you make me like it."

Marie Antoinette and Her Children (about 1785), Élisabeth Vigée-Lebrun. Chateau Versailles, France. Giraudon/Art Resource, New York.

The picture was placed in one of the rooms at Versailles, and the Queen passed it going to mass and returning. After the death of the Dauphin, which occurred early in the year 1789, the sight of this picture reminded her so keenly of the cruel loss she had suffered that she could not go through the room without shedding tears. She then ordered M. d'Angevilliers to have the picture taken away, but with her usual consideration she informed me of the fact as well, apprising me of her motive for the removal. It is really to the Queen's sensitiveness that I owed the preservation of my picture, for the fishwives[13] who soon afterward came to Versailles for Their Majesties would certainly have destroyed it, as they did the Queen's bed, which was ruthlessly torn apart.

I never had the felicity of setting eyes on Marie Antoinette after the last court ball at Versailles. The ball was given in the theater, and the box where I was seated was so situated that I could hear what the Queen said. I observed that she was

---

11. **d'Angevilliers** (dänzh-vēl-yā').
12. **vouchsafed** (vouch-sāft'): granted in a gracious manner; condescended.
13. **fishwives:** women who sell fish (a derogatory reference to the common women who supported the French Revolution).

very excited, asking the young men of the court to dance with her, such as M. Lameth, whose family had been overwhelmed with kindness by the Queen, and others, who all refused, so that many of the dances had to be given up. The conduct of these gentlemen seemed to me exceedingly improper; somehow their refusal likened a sort of revolt—the prelude to revolts of a more serious kind. The Revolution was drawing near; it was, in fact, to burst out before long. . . .

It was in 1786 that I went for the first time to Louveciennes,[14] where I had promised to paint Mme. Du Barry. She might then have been about forty-five years old. She was tall without being too much so; she had a certain roundness, her throat being rather pronounced but very beautiful; her face was still attractive, her features were regular and graceful; her hair was ashy, and curly like a child's. But her complexion was beginning to fade. She received me with much courtesy, and seemed to me very well behaved, but I found her more spontaneous in mind than in manner: her glance was that of a coquette,[15] for her long eyes were never quite open, and her pronunciation had something childish which no longer suited her age.

She lodged me in a part of the building where I was greatly put out by the continual noise. Under my room was a gallery, sadly neglected, in which busts, vases, columns, the rarest marbles, and a quantity of other valuable articles were displayed without system or order. These remains of luxury contrasted with the simplicity adopted by the mistress of the house, with her dress and her mode of life. Summer and winter Mme. Du Barry wore only a dressing-robe of cotton cambric or white muslin, and every day, whatever the weather might be, she walked in her park, or outside of it, without ever incurring disastrous consequences, so sturdy had her health become through her life in the country. She had maintained no relations with the numerous court that surrounded her so long. In the evening we were usually alone at the fireside, Mme. Du Barry and I. She sometimes talked to me about Louis XV and his court. She showed herself a worthy person by her actions as well as her words, and did a great deal of good at Louveciennes, where she helped all the poor. Every day after dinner we took coffee in the pavilion which was so famous for its rich and tasteful decorations. The first time Mme. Du Barry showed it to me she said: "It is here that Louis XV did me the honor of coming to dinner. There was a gallery above for musicians and singers who performed during the meal."

When Mme. Du Barry went to England, before the Terror, to ger back her stolen diamonds, which, in fact, she recovered there, the English received her very well. They did all they could to prevent her from returning to France. But it was not long before she succumbed to the fate in store for everybody who had some possessions. She was informed against and betrayed by a little Negro called Zamore, who is mentioned in all the memoirs of the period as having been overwhelmed with kindness by her and Louis XV. Being arrested and thrown into prison, Mme. Du Barry was tried and condemned to death by the Revolutionary tribunal at the end of 1793. She was the only woman, among all who perished in those dreadful days, unable to face the scaffold with firmness; she screamed, she sued for pardon to the hideous mob surrounding her, and that mob became moved to such a degree that the executioner hastened to finish his task. This has always confirmed my belief that if the victims of that

14. **Louveciennes** (lo͞ov-syĕn′): an estate given to Madame Du Barry by Louis XV.

15. **coquette** (kō-kĕt′): a woman who tries to get men to notice and admire her; a flirt.

period of execrable memory had not had the noble pride of dying with fortitude the Terror would have ceased long before it did.

I made three portraits of Mme. Du Barry. In the first I painted her at half length, in a dressing-gown and straw hat. In the second she is dressed in white satin; she holds a wreath in one hand, and one of her arms is leaning on a pedestal. The third portrait I made of Mme. Du Barry is in my own possession. I began it about the middle of September, 1789. From Louveciennes we could hear shooting in the distance, and I remember the poor woman saying, "If Louis XV were alive I am sure this would not be happening." I had done the head, and outlined the body and arms, when I was obliged to make an expedition to Paris. I hoped to be able to return to Louveciennes to finish my work, but heard that Berthier and Foulon[16] had been murdered. I was now frightened beyond measure, and thenceforth thought of nothing but leaving France. The fearful year 1789 was well advanced, and all decent people were already seized with terror. I remember perfectly that one evening when I had gathered some friends about me for a concert, most of the arrivals came into the room with looks of consternation; they had been walking at Longchamps that morning, and the populace assembled at the Étoile gate had cursed at those who passed in carriages in a dreadful manner. Some of the wretches had clambered on the carriage steps, shouting, "Next year you will be behind your carriages and we shall be inside!" and a thousand other insults.

As for myself, I had little need to learn fresh details in order to foresee what horrors impended. I knew beyond doubt that my house in the Rue Gros Chenet, where I had settled but three months since, had been singled out by the criminals. They threw sulphur into our cellars through the airholes. If I happened to be at my window, vulgar ruffians would shake their fists at me. Numberless sinister rumors reached me from every side; in fact, I now lived in a state of continual anxiety and sadness. My health became sensibly affected, and two of my best friends, the architect Brongniart and his wife, when they came to see me, found me so thin and so changed that they besought me to come and spend a few days with them, which invitation I thankfully accepted. Brongniart had his lodgings at the Invalides, whither I was conducted by a physician attached to the Palais Royal, whose servants wore the Orléans livery,[17] the only one then held in any respect. There I was given everything of the best. As I was unable to eat, I was nourished on excellent Burgundy wine and soup, and Mme. Brongniart was in constant attendance upon me. All this solicitude ought to have quieted me, especially as my friends took a less black view of things than I did. Nevertheless, they did not succeed in banishing my evil forebodings. "What is the use of living; what is the use of taking care of oneself?" I would often ask my good friends, for the fears that the future held over me made life distasteful to me. But I must acknowledge that even with the furthest stretch of my imagination I guessed only at a fraction of the crimes that were to be committed. . . .

16. **Berthier** (bĕr-tyā′): a French aristocrat; **Foulon** (fo͞o-lôɴ′): a government minister of war and finance who increased his own wealth at the expense of the poor.

17. **livery:** the uniform of a servant.

WORDS TO KNOW

execrable (ĕk′sĭ-krə-bəl) *adj.* detestable; hateful

fortitude (fôr′tĭ-to͞od′) *n.* the strength to bear misfortune or pain calmly and patiently; firm courage

consternation (kŏn′stər-nā′shən) *n.* a sudden fear or amazement that makes one feel helpless; dismay

Self-Portrait (late 1700s), Élisabeth Vigée-Lebrun. Oil on canvas, Uffizi, Florence, Italy. Scala/Art Resource, New York.

I had made up my mind to leave France. For some years I had cherished the desire to go to Rome. The large number of portraits I had engaged to paint had, however, hindered me from putting my plan into execution. But I could now paint no longer; my broken spirit, bruised with so many horrors, shut itself entirely to my art. Besides, dreadful slanders were pouring upon my friends, my acquaintances and myself, although, Heaven knows, I had never hurt a living soul. I thought like the man who said, "I am accused of having stolen the towers of Notre Dame; they are still in their usual place, but I am going away, as I am evidently to blame." I left several portraits I had begun, among them Mlle. Contat's. At the same time I refused to paint Mlle. de Laborde (afterward Duchess de Noailles),[18] brought to me by her father. She was scarcely sixteen, and very charming, but it was no longer a question of success or money—it was only a question of saving one's head. I had my carriage loaded, and my passport ready, so that I might leave next day with my daughter and her governess, when a crowd of national guardsmen burst into my room with their muskets. Most of them were drunk and shabby, and had terrible faces. A few of them came up to me and told me in the coarsest language that I must not go, but that I must remain. I answered that since everybody had been called upon to enjoy his liberty, I intended to make use of mine. They would barely listen to me, and kept on repeating, "You will not go, citizeness; you will not go!" Finally they went away. I was plunged into a state of cruel anxiety when I saw two of them return. But they did not frighten me, although they belonged to the gang, so quickly did I recognize that they wished me no harm. "Madame," said one of them, "we are your neighbors, and we have come to advise you to leave, and as soon as possible. You cannot live here; you are changed so much that we feel sorry for you. But do not go in your carriage: go in the stage-coach; it is much safer." I thanked them with all my heart, and followed their good advice. I had three places reserved, as I still wanted to take my daughter, who was then five or six years old, but was unable to secure them until a fortnight later, because all who exiled themselves chose the stage-coach, like myself. At last came the long-expected day.

It was the 5th of October, and the King and Queen were conducted from Versailles to Paris surrounded by pikes. The events of that day filled me with uneasiness as to the fate of Their Majesties and that of all decent people, so that I was dragged to the stage-coach at midnight in a dreadful state of mind. I was very much afraid of the Faubourg Saint Antoine, which I was obliged to traverse to reach the Barrière du Trône.[19] My brother and my husband escorted me as far as this gate without leaving the door of the coach for a moment; but the suburb that I was so frightened of was perfectly quiet. All its inhabitants, the workmen and the rest, had been to Versailles after the royal family, and fatigue kept them all in bed.

Opposite me in the coach was a very filthy man, who stunk like the plague, and told me quite simply that he had stolen watches and

18. **Noailles** (nô-ī′).

19. **Faubourg Saint Antoine** (fō-bo͞or′ săɴ äɴ-twän′) . . . **Barrière de Trône** (bä-ryĕr′ də trōn′).

other things. Luckily he saw nothing about me to tempt him, for I was only taking a small amount of clothing and eighty louis for my journey. I had left my principal effects and my jewels in Paris, and the fruit of my labors was in the hands of my husband, who spent it all. I lived abroad solely on the proceeds of my painting.

Not satisfied with relating his fine exploits to us, the thief talked incessantly of stringing up such and such people on lamp-posts, naming a number of my own acquaintances. My daughter thought this man very wicked. He frightened her, and this gave me the courage to say, "I beg you, sir, not to talk of killing before this child." That silenced him, and he ended by playing at battle with my daughter. On the bench I occupied there also sat a mad Jacobin[20] from Grenoble, about fifty years old, with an ugly, bilious[21] complexion, who each time we stopped at an inn for dinner or supper made violent speeches of the most fearful kind. At all of the towns a crowd of people stopped the coach to learn the news from Paris. Our Jacobin would then exclaim: "Everything is going well, children! We have the baker and his wife safe in Paris. A constitution will be drawn up, they will be forced to accept it, and then it will be all over." There were plenty of ninnies and flatheads who believed this man as if he had been an oracle. All this made my journey a very melancholy one. I had no further fears for myself, but I feared greatly for everybody else—for my mother, for my brother, and for my friends. I also had the gravest apprehensions concerning Their Majesties, for all along the route, nearly as far as Lyons, men on horseback rode up to the coach to tell us that the King and Queen had been killed and that Paris was on fire. My poor little girl got all a-tremble; she thought she saw her father dead and our house burned down, and no sooner had I succeeded in reassuring her than another horseman appeared and told us the same stories.

I cannot describe the emotions I felt in passing over the Beauvoisin[22] Bridge. Then only did I breathe freely. I had left France behind, that France which nevertheless was the land of my birth, and which I reproached myself with quitting with so much satisfaction. The sight of the mountains, however, distracted me from all my sad thoughts. I had never seen high mountains before; those of the Savoy[23] seemed to touch the sky, and seemed to mingle with it in a thick vapor. My first sensation was that of fear, but I unconsciously accustomed myself to the spectacle, and ended by admiring it. A certain part of the road completely entranced me; I seemed to see the "Gallery of the Titans,"[24] and I have always called it so since. Wishing to enjoy all these beauties as fully as possible, I got down from the coach, but after walking some way I was seized with a great fright, for there were explosions being made with gunpowder, which had the effect of a thousand cannon shots, and the din echoing from rock to rock was truly infernal.

I went up Mount Cenis, as other strangers were doing, when a postilion[25] approached me, saying, "The lady ought to take a mule; to climb up on foot is too fatiguing." I answered that I was a work-woman and quite accustomed to walking. "Oh! no!" was the laughing reply. "The lady is no work-woman; we know who she is!" "Well, who am I, then?" I asked him. "You are Mme. Lebrun, who paints so well, and we are all very glad to see you safe from those bad people." I never guessed how the man could have learned my name, but it proved to me how many secret agents the Jacobins must have had. Happily I had no occasion to fear them any longer. ❖

M^{de} LeBrun

20. **Jacobin:** radical revolutionary.

21. **bilious** (bĭl′yəs): sickly yellow.

22. **Beauvoisin** (bō-vwä-zăɴ′).

23. **the Savoy:** the mountainous region along the border between France and Italy.

24. **Titans:** a group of giants in Greek mythology.

25. **postilion:** a person who helps guide a coach by riding on one of the lead horses.

RESPONDING OPTIONS

FROM PERSONAL RESPONSE *TO* CRITICAL ANALYSIS

REFLECT 1. As you read, how did you feel about the situation Vigée-Lebrun found herself in? Jot down your reactions in your notebook and share some of them with your classmates.

RETHINK 2. Explain Vigée-Lebrun's feelings about the French Revolution, as revealed in her comments about the rich and the poor.

Consider
- the encounters she has with aristocrats and with revolutionaries
- the terms that she uses to refer to the aristocracy and the revolutionaries
- her acceptance by the French aristocracy

3. What impression of Marie Antoinette's character do you think Vigée-Lebrun wished to convey? Why might she have wanted to convey that impression? Use details from the selection to support your opinions.

4. Do you find Vigée-Lebrun a sympathetic person? Why or why not?

RELATE 5. Problems between the rich and the poor continue to exist in modern life. Think about how the rich and the poor view one another in contemporary American society. What do you think would be the best ways of resolving misunderstandings and conflicts between the two groups?

ANOTHER PATHWAY

Cooperative Learning

Interview five classmates about whether, on the basis of this memoir, they would condemn or defend Marie Antoinette and Madame Du Barry. Develop a questionnaire for use during the interview. Be sure to ask those you interview to support their opinions. Summarize your survey and share it with classmates.

LITERARY CONCEPTS

Description is writing that helps a reader to picture scenes, events, and characters. It helps the reader understand exactly what someone or something is like. An effective description is often like a good painting: it provides visual details of color, size, and shape that give the reader a clear impression of the person, place, object, or event being described. Look back at the words and phrases you noted in your chart for the Reading Connection on page 447, and decide what descriptive passage in the selection you think is the most effective. Explain your choice.

QUICKWRITES

1. Write a **description** of Madame Vigée-Lebrun from the viewpoint of the "mad Jacobin from Grenoble," her fellow passenger in the stagecoach leaving France.
2. Keeping in mind Vigée-Lebrun's use of detailed description to portray the events and people she writes about in her memoirs, write a brief **memoir** of an incident in your own life, perhaps one connected with a significant historical or community event. Try to make the people, places, and actions seem alive and vital, so that a person two centuries from now would find them interesting to read about.

PORTFOLIO Save your writing. You may want to use it later as a springboard to a piece for your portfolio.

ALTERNATIVE ACTIVITIES

1. Imagine that you are a French peasant woman living in Vigée-Lebrun's time. In a **dramatic monologue,** express your feelings about your situation and your attitude toward the aristocracy.
2. Role-play the **conversation** that Madame Du Barry and Vigée-Lebrun might have had during their last portrait session in 1789. Use details from the excerpt to help you create realistic characterizations.
3. Prepare a **time line** that reflects both historical and personal events that Vigée-Lebrun describes in this excerpt. Add illustrations or other visual images to represent the various occurrences.

LITERARY LINKS

Compare this excerpt from Vigée-Lebrun's memoir with the excerpt of Samuel Pepys's diary on page 330. How would you characterize the tone of each of these works of nonfiction? Which did you find more interesting?

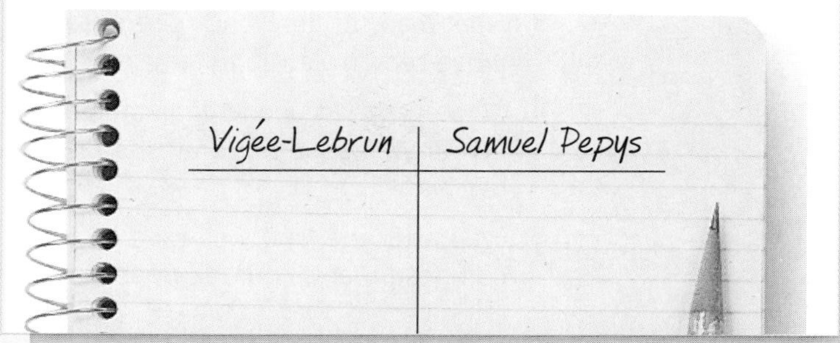

ART CONNECTION

Look again at the painting *Marie Antoinette and Her Children* on page 451. What descriptive details of Marie Antoinette given in the selection are reflected in the painting?

ACROSS THE CURRICULUM

History Recall that Vigée-Lebrun tells of a time when Marie Antoinette made her six-year-old daughter dine with a little peasant girl and attend to her wants. Research life and culture at the time of the French Revolution. For example, what would it have been like to be a peasant girl before and after the uprising? Hold a panel discussion in which you share what you have learned about life during this turbulent time.

WORDS TO KNOW

Review the Words to Know at the bottom of the selection pages. Then write the word that best completes each sentence.

1. It was reported that Marie Antoinette, when told that the poor had no bread, responded, "Let them eat cake," and such a response was thought to be truly _____.
2. That story fit the common perception of the queen as haughty and uncaring; Madame Vigée-Lebrun, on the other hand, praises her for her _____.
3. What many of the French people saw as an air of arrogance, Vigée-Lebrun viewed as a majestic _____.
4. Whatever the queen's character, her awareness that her power was gone and that she faced death must have filled her with _____.
5. Even after the king was executed, however, she showed composure and courage in prison—surely a sign of _____.

Élisabeth Vigée-Lebrun

1755–1842

As a child, Élisabeth Vigée-Lebrun drew miniature portraits in the margins of her schoolbooks and even on the dormitory walls of the convent school she attended in Paris. She received some instruction from her father, a minor painter, and from artist friends, but she was mainly self-taught. When she was 13, her father died, and Vigée-Lebrun began supporting her mother and younger brother by painting portraits.

The young artist quickly gained a following, and her reputation as a portrait painter of the nobility was established by the time she was 19. When she was 20, she married a picture dealer, Jean Lebrun. Though his gambling losses drained much of her sizable income, he was a valuable critic of her work and made many great paintings available to her for study. At the age of 24, she was invited to do her first portrait of Marie Antoinette. The many portraits of the queen that followed are among the artist's most famous works.

Because she painted and mingled with the aristocracy, Vigée-Lebrun felt especially threatened by the events leading up to the French Revolution. After she fled Paris in 1789, she traveled and lived in various parts of Europe and England and was sought as a painter wherever she went. She returned to France in 1810 and published her memoirs in the 1830s.

During her long and illustrious career, Vigée-Lebrun created more than 800 paintings, including more than 600 portraits. Although her portraits of women were usually flattering—undoubtedly one reason for her popularity—her talent and the stature of her work are undisputed. Upon her death in 1842, Vigée-Lebrun was buried near her country home at Louveciennes. In accordance with her wishes, a paint palette and brushes were carved on her tombstone.

LASERLINKS
• *ART GALLERY*

Thirty-Eight

CHARLOTTE SMITH

Charlotte Smith was a well-known poet and novelist of the late 18th century. This poem is apparently addressed to Eliza Hayley, Smith's neighbor and the wife of another popular 18th-century poet, William Hayley. Smith, who was a year older than Eliza Hayley, probably wrote the poem in honor of her neighbor's 38th birthday.

In early youth's unclouded scene,
The brilliant morning of eighteen,
With health and sprightly joy elate
    We gazed on life's enchanting spring,
    Nor thought how quickly time would bring
The mournful period—Thirty-eight.

Then the starch maid or matron sage,
Already of that sober age,
We viewed with mingled scorn and hate,
    In whose sharp words or sharper face
    With thoughtless mirth we loved to trace
The sad effects of—Thirty-eight.

Till saddening, sickening at the view,
We learned to dread what time might do;
And then preferred a prayer to fate
    To end our days ere that arrived,
    When (power and pleasure long survived)
We met neglect and—Thirty-eight.

7 sage: wise.

Detail of *Lady Sophia Charlotte Sheffield* (late 1700s), Thomas Gainsborough. Courtesy of Waddesdon Manor.

But time, in spite of wishes, flies,
And fate our simple prayer denies,
And bids us death's own hour await:
    The auburn locks are mixed with grey,
    The transient roses fade away,
But reason comes at—Thirty-eight.

Her voice the anguish contradicts
That dying vanity inflicts;
Her hand new pleasures can create.
    For us she opens to the view
    Prospects less bright—but far more true,
And bids us smile at—Thirty-eight.

No more shall scandal's breath destroy
The social converse we enjoy
With bard or critic tête à tête;
    O'er youth's bright blooms her blights shall pour,
    But spare the improving friendly hour
That science gives to—Thirty-eight.

Stripped of their gaudy hues by truth,
We view the glitt'ring toys of youth,
And blush to think how poor the bait
    For which to public scenes we ran
    And scorned of sober sense the plan
Which gives content at—Thirty-eight.

23 transient: not lasting long; temporary.

33 with bard . . . tête à tête (tāt'ə-tāt'): with a poet or a critic, in privacy.

Though time's inexorable sway
Has torn the myrtle bands away,
For other wreaths 'tis not too late;
    The amaranth's purple glow survives,
    And still Minerva's olive lives
On the calm brow of—Thirty-eight.

With eye more steady we engage
To contemplate approaching age,
And life more justly estimate.
    With firmer souls and stronger powers,
    With reason, faith, and friendship ours,
    We'll not regret the stealing hours
That lead from Thirty—even to Forty-eight.

44 myrtle bands: wreaths made of the foliage of the myrtle, the sacred plant of Venus, the Roman goddess of love.

46 amaranth's purple glow: the purplish foliage of the amaranth, a plant used to symbolize immortality.

47 Minerva's olive: The olive tree was the sacred plant of Minerva, the Roman goddess of wisdom.

Charlotte Smith

1749–1806

Charlotte Smith grew up in London and on her father's country estate, surrounded by elegant comforts and receiving the best education available to girls living in 18th-century England. She became quite accomplished in dancing and acting and was an avid reader. Her life changed drastically, however, when just before her 16th birthday she entered into an arranged marriage with the son of a prosperous merchant. She quickly realized that the marriage was a mistake; her husband did not share her intellectual pursuits and was an incorrigible spendthrift.

In 1783, Smith's husband was sent to debtor's prison, and she, as the dutiful wife, joined him there, leaving their children in the care of her brother. Realizing that she needed to find an independent means of relieving the family's debt and providing for her children, Smith turned her considerable talent to writing. In 1784, while still residing in debtor's prison, she published *Elegiac Sonnets and Other Essays.* The work was an immediate success.

In 1787, Smith legally separated from her husband and began raising and educating her children on her own. Aware that prose was more profitable than poetry, Smith produced ten novels in the decade between 1788 and 1798. One of her best works, *The Old Manor House,* was published in 1793. Smith nevertheless maintained her commitment to writing poetry and continually expanded her editions of poems. By 1800, *Elegiac Sonnets and Other Essays* had been reprinted eight times.

Smith's writing remained popular for a number of years. Nearly 30 years after her death, her contribution to English poetry was recognized by William Wordsworth, one of the leading poets of the romantic movement. By the later years of the 19th century, however, her works—like those of many of the female writers of her time—had been almost forgotten. Today her writing is more widely read, and she is regarded by many literary critics as one of the forerunners of romanticism in poetry.

WRITING FROM EXPERIENCE

WRITING TO EXPLAIN

Some of the writers you studied in this unit wrote about social conditions or problems in their society. Using facts from different sources, they formed conclusions. You've probably done this yourself. This technique of putting together pieces of information is important in research, problem solving, and decision making.

GUIDED ASSIGNMENT

Write an Informative Essay Write an informative essay about some current condition, trend, or problem in society. Use the evidence you find to help you understand the situation and explore its impact on society.

1 Make Connections

Look at the clippings on these pages. Think about the issue or issues underlying each one. What causes or effects might be associated with each situation?

2 Look for a Topic

Think about the world around you. Have you noticed or been touched by some recent trend or social problem? Look for ideas you can explore further, and make a list of possible topics. Here are some sources you can explore for ideas:

- the literature selections
- the clippings on these pages
- articles in recent newspapers and newsmagazines
- the results of recent opinion polls or surveys

Why do people feel this way? Are kids getting more violent?

News Article

Treat Kid Crooks Like Adults

According to a recently released Roper poll, most Americans think that juveniles who commit violent crimes should be treated the same as adults. A majority of 68 percent said that juveniles should be given the same treatment adults get. Only 13 percent of the 1,516 people polled opted for more lenient treatment.

Graph

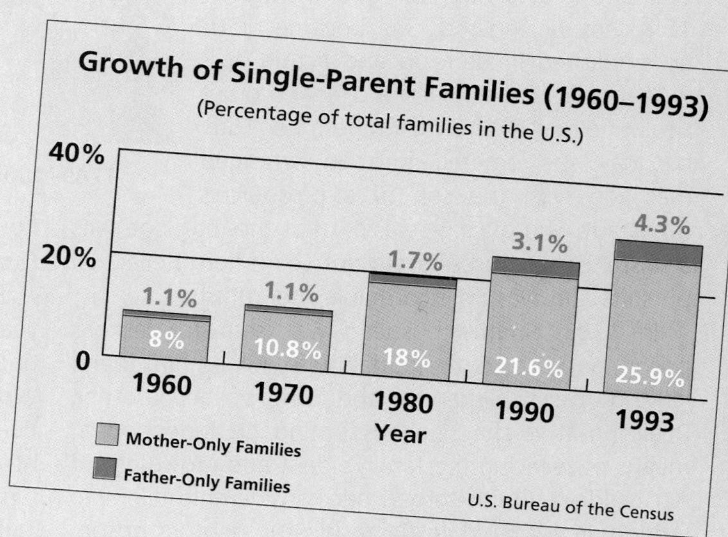

Husband Wishes His Work Didn't Rate Comments

Because I married a wonderful woman in a demanding medical residency, I have—without benefit of training—been put in charge of running our household.

It's logical. My schedule is more flexible than my wife's. But now, as I do the marketing, cleaning, and cooking and errand-running, I find that people marvel at my dexterity. And I marvel at how differently I am treated from women while doing these traditionally female things.

Take marketing, for example. I tend to do it during mid-afternoons when the stores are less crowded. Not surprisingly, my only company is a couple of stressed-out moms squeezing tomatoes in the produce aisle. But being the only male shopper in the place seems to have conferred on me a special status, because more often than not, if I am waiting in a checkout line, another one will be opened for me. I have made a conscious study of this phenomenon, and it does not happen with nearly the same frequency for women.

The implicit message, it seems to me, is that my time is more valuable than theirs.

If I manage to shave a few dollars off my tab with coupons, the cashier congratulates me. Yet I have seen some women so deftly use cents-off coupons that the market practically has to pay them for shopping there, all without a compliment from anyone.

So what do I have to complain about, anyway? Consider all the pluses of being a man in a woman's world: As a male, I can claim ignorance about a host of things, from selecting fresh fruit to ordering meat, all without reproach. Society does not expect expertise from me in these areas.

Michael Africk
from *Chicago Tribune*

How could I find out if the number of men doing shopping and other such tasks is increasing?

Feature Article

What other lifestyle changes occur if both husband and wife have jobs?

3 What's the Question?

Before researching a topic, you need to find an approach to it. You can start by finding a question you want to answer. The question about lifestyle changes in the stick-on note at the right is an example. Look over your list of topics and freewrite questions that arise from each one. Then examine your questions. Do they help you make sense of the topics? Do they help you decide which topic to choose for your essay?

What trends do you see in the graph at the left? What do you think might have caused these trends? How could you investigate the topic further?

Exploring Your Topic

Focusing Your Ideas Social trends rarely have simple explanations. If you want to understand such trends, you need to examine many possibilities and pull together information from a variety of sources. This bringing together of varied pieces of information in order to come to a conclusion is called synthesizing.

1 Lay the Groundwork

After you've chosen your topic, take a few minutes to freewrite on what you already know about it. Then try to form a hypothesis to guide your further research. For example, suppose your topic is the growing number of single-parent families. You might hypothesize that the percentage of such families will continue to grow. You could then guide your research to find whether your hypothesis is likely to be correct.

Gather Information Here are some sources you can use to gather information:

- Explore your personal observations and recollections.
- Talk with peers and get their insights.
- Interview experts on the topic.
- Conduct surveys or polls.
- Use print or electronic resources to do further reading about your topic.

Consider Your Goals What do you hope to achieve in your essay? Do you want to inform your readers about your topic or prove a point? Do you want to recommend some kind of action? Decide what your goals are. They will help determine the kinds of information you'll look for.

For information on using electronic resources, see pages 1244–1245 of the Multimedia Handbook.

2 Evaluate Your Sources

Consider the usefulness and the meaning of the information you gather. Ask yourself questions like the following as you examine your sources:

- Is this material relevant to my essay?
- Is the information recent enough?
- Is the writer an expert on the topic? If the source is written by a nonexpert, have specialists been interviewed and quoted?
- Can I confirm these facts by looking at another source?
- Do sources contradict each other?
- Is the writer biased? If so, how?
- Do I agree or disagree with the writer's opinions? Why?

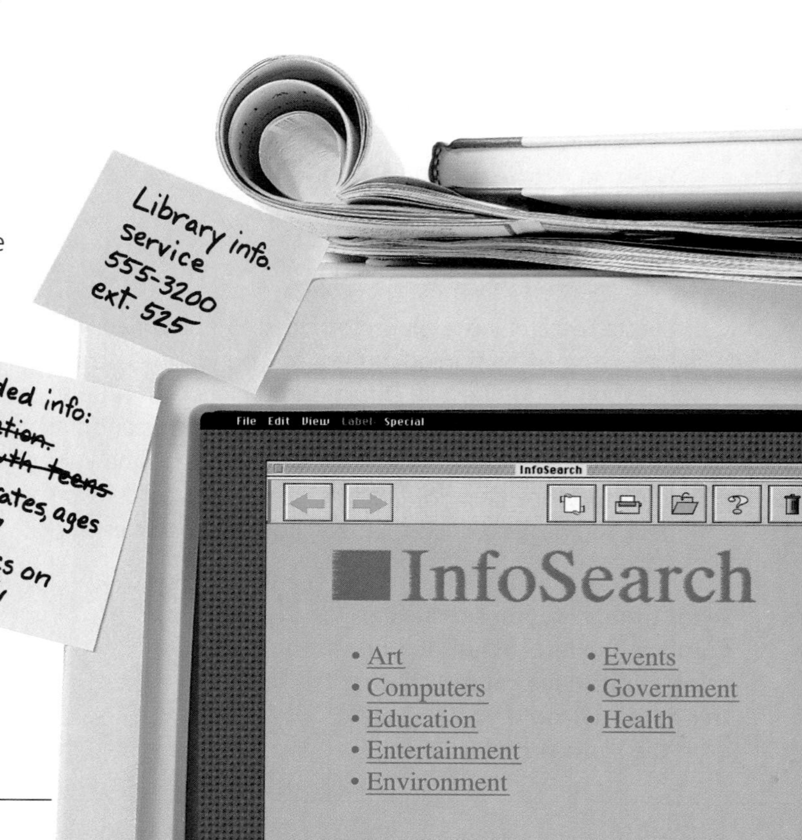

3 Look for Connections

Analyze the information you've gathered. Look for trends, relationships, or patterns, and think about what they mean. Examine any relationships you find. What conclusions can you draw? For example, one student investigating the topic of juvenile crime found that over the past 25 years both juvenile crime and the number of children living in poverty rose significantly. She wondered whether there was a relationship between the two.

4 State a Tentative Conclusion

Use logic, inference, past experience, and the results of your research to draw a conclusion. The student working on juvenile crime, for example, eventually found several likely causes for the increase. She formed the tentative conclusion that increased juvenile crime was not the result of a single cause but of several causes working together. For more help on drawing conclusions, see the SkillBuilder on this page.

Think about all you've learned about your topic. Can you find a central truth, condition, meaning, or problem that the information points to? Form a generalization out of this understanding, and make it your tentative conclusion. Keep in mind that a tentative conclusion can be changed as you continue to learn and think about your topic.

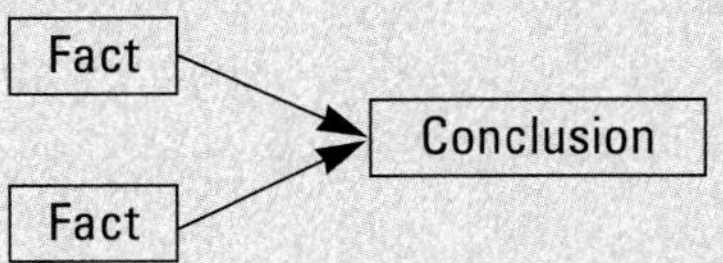

Drawing Conclusions
A conclusion brings a collection of facts together.

Fact → Conclusion
Fact → Conclusion

Any collection of facts can lead to a number of different conclusions, but whatever your conclusion is, each fact you use must support it.

APPLYING WHAT YOU'VE LEARNED

1. What two different conclusions can you draw from the following statistics?

People Committed to Prison for Drug Offenses, 1960 and 1989	
1960	3,148
1989	87,859

2. What additional facts would help support your conclusions?

THINK & PLAN

Prewriting Checkup

1. Do all of your facts support your tentative conclusion? If not, how can you revise your conclusion?
2. Have you been able to resolve any inconsistencies or differences of opinion that have turned up in your research?

DRAFTING

Discover Through Writing

Getting Started After collecting your information, start pulling ideas together. What connections, patterns, or trends do you find? Start stating your findings. Some writers begin by organizing their material into an outline. Others just start writing. You can experiment with either approach or both. The Writing Coach example below uses a discovery draft, in which the writing helps the writer discover an approach to the topic.

1 Try a Discovery Draft

Your discovery draft may begin as a group of facts and a tentative conclusion. Don't worry about organization at this point; you'll take care of that when you begin revising. Even your tentative conclusion may change as you think about what your facts show. Just start writing to see what you can discover about your topic.

Student's Discovery Draft

Juvenile Crime

My Discovery Draft	My Comments My Discovery Draft
Juvenile violent crime is increasing. In the period 1986–1991, the rate of homicides by adults 25 years and older fell; the rate among teens aged 14–17 rose 124%. Rates for other crimes by juveniles are also rising. Why?	Need an opening that will really grab readers.
Some possible causes: **Demographic changes:** A new generation of baby boomers is reaching adolescence, the years when they're most likely to become involved in crimes. **Poverty:** More than 1 in 5 American children live below the poverty line. Numbers are growing. **Breakdown of family:** Growing numbers of divorces, both parents working, one-parent families, teenage pregnancies, runaways. All put a strain on family connections.	I'll need some statistics to support this. Other causes will also need support from statistics or authorities.
Gangs: Many kids lack good role models. Join gangs to get a feeling of belonging (or are pressured to join). Gang members are more likely to become involved in crime. **Violence in the media:** Violent movies and TV get kids so used to seeing violence they're no longer repelled by it. **Guns and drugs:** Both too easily available to young people. War on Drugs was a flop. Tentative conclusion: Simple, one-cause explanations won't wash. Not one cause but many.	Are any of these various causes connected? If so, how? Additional comments: Have I missed any other explanations? Is every explanation valid? Are the causes equally significant, or are some of them more powerful than others?

2 Organize Your Essay

After analyzing your discovery draft, think about how you will organize your essay. One way is to start with the facts and end with the conclusion you've drawn. Another way is to start with your conclusion and then supply the facts that support it. The chart below shows a third method of organization. Start with a question or situation—for example, the question you hoped to answer when you chose your topic. Then continue with the facts and a conclusion.

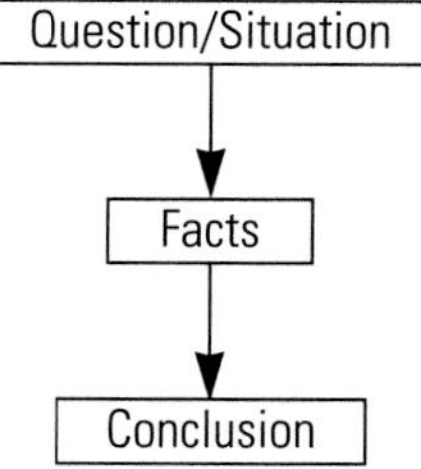

This method can allow you to use some narrative writing in your essay. You can share with your readers how you went about exploring your topic. See the SkillBuilder at the right for more about using other writing modes in your essay.

3 Rework and Share

After reworking your essay, share your draft with a peer reader. Asking questions like the following will help you evaluate your conclusion and the facts used to support it.

PEER RESPONSE

- How would you restate my conclusion?
- Do my facts support my conclusion?
- Have I left out facts that might strengthen my conclusion?
- Do you agree or disagree with my conclusion? Why?

SkillBuilder

WRITER'S CRAFT

Using a Variety of Modes

A synthesis may be mainly an expository essay, but that doesn't mean it must be exclusively so. Think about how you could use any of the following alternatives.

- Use description to help your readers picture your topic.
- Use a narrative to relate an anecdote or example that ties to your topic.
- If your conclusion leads to a recommended course of action, use persuasion.
- Use any combination of the above methods as they suit your purpose.

APPLYING WHAT YOU'VE LEARNED

Using ideas from your draft, write a sentence or two illustrating the use of description, narration, or persuasion in a synthesis.

RETHINK & EVALUATE

Preparing to Revise

1. How will you organize your essay? Why?
2. Is your tentative conclusion still appropriate? If not, how can you modify it?
3. Have you included enough facts to back up your conclusion?

Polishing Your Essay

Finalizing Your Draft Now's the time to think about getting your essay ready for publication. As you begin your last revisions, remember that your essay should include enough facts to support any conclusion you come to. If you haven't already done so, you also should think about the form in which you will publish your essay. See Share Your Work on the next page for some possibilities.

1 Revise and Edit

These questions can help you revise your essay.

- Will your introduction attract a reader's attention?
- Does your organization help your ideas flow naturally from one to the next?
- Do you need to clarify anything with more details, definitions, or background information?
- Is your style appropriate to your audience?
- Have you tried using any elements of descriptive, narrative, or persuasive writing to help get across your ideas?

Be sure to check your work against the Standards for Evaluation, and use the Editing Checklist in the SkillBuilder as you prepare your essay for publication.

Student's Final Draft

Two boys, aged fourteen and sixteen, are arrested and charged with burglary and vandalism.

A three-year-old girl sitting on her porch is killed in a drive-by shooting. Police arrest four gang members. The youngest is a fourteen-year-old girl.

Sound familiar? Such reports are becoming commonplace. Juvenile crime—particularly violent crime—is increasing. Why? What's responsible for this alarming trend?

How does this conclusion compare with the writer's earlier tentative conclusion?

Many people blame the media for violent behavior. Others blame the problem on gangs, guns, drugs, the breakdown of the family, or poverty. As I've tried to show, changes such as rising birth rates combined with gangs, drugs, guns, increasing poverty, the breakdown of the family, and violence in the media all play a part in creating and maintaining the problem. These causes are tangled, but all work toward the same effect. Proposed actions that address a single cause—such as censorship of the media, tougher penalties for offenders, or more prisons—are not likely to solve this complex problem. Only when people admit that there are no simple solutions can they begin the hard work of trying to decrease juvenile crime.

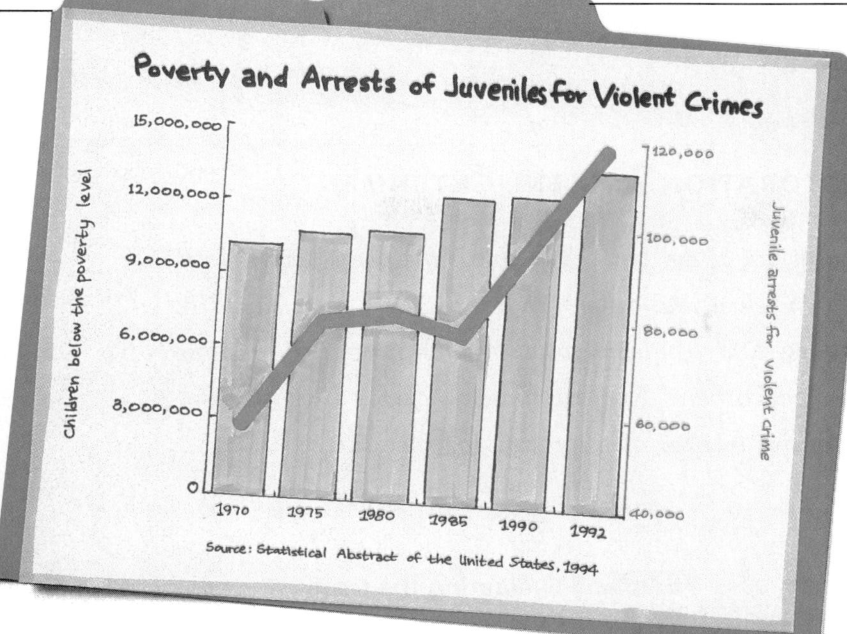

The writer of the essay about juvenile crime made this graph to accompany the essay.

2 Share Your Work

Think about how you could make your essay available to a wider audience. Will you do a written essay, an oral report, an article for the school newspaper, some kind of cooperative presentation (such as a panel discussion with a few classmates), or some other publishing option? Think about how your publishing option will affect the kinds of alterations you will need to make on your final draft.

Standards for Evaluation

An informative essay
- includes an appealing and appropriate introduction, a body, and a conclusion based on sufficient and pertinent evidence
- explains all evidence and qualifies or limits its observations as necessary
- draws on reliable sources
- avoids unsupported generalizations
- uses language and details appropriate to the audience
- may include elements of descriptive, narrative, and persuasive writing as well as exposition

SkillBuilder

GRAMMAR FROM WRITING

Using Active Voice
As you edit your writing, remember that the active voice is more effective than the passive voice.

Passive voice: A rising rate of juvenile crime has been noted.
Active voice: People have noted a rising rate of juvenile crime.

GRAMMAR HANDBOOK

See page 1299 of the Grammar Handbook for more information on active and passive voice.

Editing Checklist Use the following editing tips as you revise your draft:

- Have you used punctuation correctly?
- Do your subjects and verbs agree grammatically?
- Are there shorter sentences that could be combined for greater effectiveness?
- Have you used active rather than passive voice?

REFLECT & ASSESS

Evaluate the Experience

1. Do you believe that you came to the right conclusion?
2. What would you change if you were to write your essay again?

PORTFOLIO Write the answers to the above questions in a note that accompanies your essay in your portfolio.

REFLECT & ASSESS

UNIT THREE: THE RESTORATION AND ENLIGHTENMENT

As you read the selections in this unit, what did you learn about the ways people in the 17th and 18th centuries viewed themselves and others? What did they see clearly? In what areas did they have blind spots? Did you learn anything about yourself and the ways people today view themselves and others? Explore these questions by completing one or more of the options in each of the following sections.

REFLECTING ON THE UNIT

OPTION 1 **Gaining Insights** Some of the writers represented in this unit portrayed life as it was in the late 17th century and the 18th century, whereas others portrayed life as they thought it should be. Choose two of the writers—one to represent each perspective. What does the work of each reveal about how people see themselves and others? Which had the greatest impact on your understanding of human nature and society? Explain your choices in one or two paragraphs.

OPTION 2 **Examining Form and Content** The selections in this unit include essays, poetry, a diary, letters, biography, and autobiography. Which kind of writing did you enjoy reading the most? Which do you think gives the clearest, most objective view of human nature? Make a chart in which you list the literary forms and identify at least one example of each among the selections in this unit. Then jot down one strength and one weakness of each form.

OPTION 3 **Evaluating the Issues** The selections in this unit reveal a variety of human weaknesses and problems. How clearly did the people of the time understand their own faults and those of others? Which of their concerns seem trivial? Which seem significant? Are any of their concerns important to people today? Get together with some of your classmates to discuss your conclusions.

REFLECT & ASSESS *Self-Assessment: To explore what you have learned about human nature from this unit, create a three-column chart. In the first column, list four insights you have gained into how people view themselves and others; in the second, identify the source of each insight; in the third, rank the insights according to how important each is to you.*

REVIEWING LITERARY CONCEPTS

OPTION 1 **Analyzing Essays** Several of the prose selections in this unit are informal or persuasive essays. Make a chart like the one shown, listing the selections that are essays and identifying each as informal or persuasive. Briefly explain the purpose of each essay and evaluate how effectively the purpose is carried out.

Selection	Type of Essay	Purpose	Effectiveness
from *The Spectator*	informal	entertainment, mild criticism of human weaknesses	enjoyable humor, accurate perceptions of human nature

OPTION 2 **Recognizing Irony and Satire** Writers often use irony and satire to reveal human defects and weaknesses. Think about the selections that you read from this unit that use these techniques. Which examples are most effective? Why? Compare your choices with those of your classmates and discuss any differences in your opinions.

REFLECT & ASSESS *Self-Assessment: On a piece of paper, copy the following list of literary terms introduced in this unit. Put checks next to those you understand well and question marks next to those that are still unclear to you. Then find a partner and exchange lists. Take turns defining the terms that one of you understands well but the other is having difficulty with. Work together to define any terms whose meanings you are both unsure of.*

diary	*parallelism*
heroic couplet	*argumentation*
iambic pentameter	*aphorism*
fable	*biography*
informal essay	*personification*
persuasive essay	*dialogue*
satire	*description*
irony	

PORTFOLIO BUILDING

- **QuickWrites** Many of the QuickWrites assignments in this unit asked you to observe and comment on aspects of human behavior. Look over your work for these assignments and pick two pieces that you think contain your most perceptive ideas. Write a brief cover note in which you explain why these pieces show particularly clear insights, and add them, along with the note, to your portfolio.
- **Writing About Literature** In this unit you wrote an advice essay based on your knowledge and experience. For the moment, imagine that you are the person receiving your advice. What is your initial reaction? What is your opinion of the writer's qualifications? Is the tone of the essay effective, or does it make you distrust the advice? Would you follow the advice? On the basis of your answers to these questions, decide what changes you might make to your essay so that readers would be more likely to heed your advice.
- **Writing from Experience** Reread the informative essay you wrote about a societal trend or problem, paying special attention to the examples you used to support your conclusion. Which example do you think is the most powerful, and why? Since completing your essay, what additional examples have you found that either support or challenge your conclusion? Jot down responses to these questions, and attach your notes to your essay if you choose.
- **Personal Choice** Think back on all the activities, projects, and writing you have worked on in the course of this unit—either for assignments or on your own—that have involved some kind of imaginative response. Which of them was the most creative experience for you? Write a note explaining your choice, and add the note to your portfolio.

REFLECT & ASSESS *Self-Assessment: You are now beginning to build up a variety of writing pieces in your portfolio. Look through them. Do you find a stronger sense of confidence in your more recent writing? What is your favorite piece so far?*

SETTING GOALS

As you reviewed your work for this section, you probably noticed some aspects of your writing that are not as strong as others. Identify the weak areas that need continued attention and the skills that need practice. Keep these in mind as you work through the next unit.

UNIT FOUR

To see the world in a grain of sand
And heaven in a wild flower,
Hold infinity in the palm of your hand
And eternity in an hour.

William Blake
POET AND ARTIST

The Lake, Petworth: Sunset, Fighting Bucks (about 1828), Joseph Mallord William Turner. Clore Collection, Tate Gallery, London/Art Resource, New York.

1798-1832

The Flowering of Romanticism

1798-1832

TIME LINE

The Flowering of Romanticism

1798-1832

1798

William Wordsworth and Samuel Taylor Coleridge's *Lyrical Ballads* published

1800

Dorothy Wordsworth begins keeping "Grasmere Journal" in Lake District

1800

Act of Union passed, creating United Kingdom of Great Britain and Ireland

1805

Admiral Horatio Nelson dies as British fleet defeats French navy in Battle of Trafalgar

1805

Landscape painter J. M. W. Turner, precursor of artistic movement known as impressionism, paints *The Shipwreck*

The Shipwreck (1805), Joseph Mallord William Turner. Clore Collection, Tate Gallery, London/ Art Resource, New York.

1806

Deaths of William Pitt the Younger and Charles James Fox

1811

George III declared permanently insane; his eldest son George, Prince of Wales, is named regent

1812

Lord Byron wins fame with first two sections of *Childe Harold's Pilgrimage*

1812

Napoleon escalates invasions across Europe

1812

Britain fights United States in War of 1812

1813

Jane Austen publishes *Pride and Prejudice*

1814

Sir Walter Scott publishes first historical novel, *Waverley*

1815

Napoleon returns from exile and is defeated in Battle of Waterloo

1818

First crossing of Atlantic Ocean by steamship

1818

Mary Shelley's *Frankenstein* published anonymously

1819

"Peterloo Massacre"—11 killed in St. Peter's Fields, Manchester, when cavalry charges social reformers

1819

Percy Bysshe Shelley writes "Ode to the West Wind"; John Keats writes "Ode on a Grecian Urn" and "To Autumn"

1820

Regency ends with death of George III and crowning of Prince of Wales as George IV

1829

First water-purification plant built in London

1829

Catholic Emancipation Act passed; Irish Catholic politician Daniel O'Connell takes seat in House of Commons

1830

George IV dies; reign of his brother, William IV, begins

1830

Liverpool-to-Manchester railway opens

1832

First Reform Bill extends voting rights

Period *Pieces*

Combination night lamp and tea warmer

Iron in which heated brick was inserted

Twelve-month equation clock

INTRODUCTION

The Flowering of Romanticism 1798-1832

Great change swept the Western world at the end of the 18th century. A successful revolution in America and an ongoing one in France shattered the political stability of the day. In Britain, revolutions in industry and agriculture rocked the social and economic structure of the nation. Reflecting and responding to these dramatic changes was a movement that came to be called romanticism, which dominated Western intellectual and artistic life in the early 19th century.

Romanticism was an outgrowth of 18th-century neoclassicism as well as a reaction against it. The spiritual father of the movement was the French Enlightenment thinker Jean Jacques Rousseau. Rousseau's argument that human society is based on a contract between the government and the governed echoed earlier ideas of England's John Locke and helped inspire the French Revolution. Rousseau attributed evil not to human nature but to society, insisting that in the natural state a human being was essentially good and happy—a "noble savage." This idealization of nature and human beings became basic tenets of romantic thinking. Also basic was an emphasis on the individual, the personal, and the emotional—

Top: *Portrait of Jean Jacques Rousseau* (1753), Maurice Quentin de La Tour. Musée d'Art et d'Histoire, Geneva, Switzerland, Giraudon/Art Resource, New York.
Bottom: *Taking of the Bastille on July 14, 1789* (about 1789–1800), unknown French artist. Giraudon/Art Resource, New York.

in sharp contrast to the emphasis on society, science, and reason that had been at the root of neoclassical thought.

Literary romanticism was pioneered in Germany by Johann Wolfgang von Goethe and in Britain by William Wordsworth and Samuel Taylor Coleridge. However, unlike the artistic ideals of neoclassicism, those of romanticism did not reflect the mainstream views of British society. During its peak period from 1798 to 1832, while the political instability and violence emanating from continental Europe prompted a conservative reaction throughout most levels of British society, romanticism flowered mainly as a movement of protest—a powerful expression of a desire for personal freedom and radical reform.

WILLIAM PITT THE YOUNGER

In the 1780s, before the conservative reaction set in, the need for reform was apparent not only to members of Britain's more liberal Whig party but also to the new Tory prime minister, William Pitt the Younger (son of the prime minister who led Britain through the Seven Years' War). The nation's growing cities were beset with a host of problems, including crime and poor sanitation. Child labor and other factory abuses were not being addressed, the emerging industrial centers in the north and west had no representation in Parliament, and archaic laws denied rights to many religious groups, including the Catholic majority in Ireland. Britain had lost its American colonies, primarily because of incompetent management, and the rest of its overseas empire faced a number of difficulties, ranging from corruption in India to the evils of the slave trade.

Although Pitt came to power as a reformer, his reform plans were pushed aside when the French Revolution erupted in 1789. Initial British sympathy for the revolution soon died down when France's revolutionary moderates fell from power. The Whig politician

Language

The democratic attitudes of romanticism helped broaden the concept of "acceptable" English and narrow the gap between the language of scholars and aristocrats and that of the common people. In their efforts to create literature based on natural speech, romantic writers sometimes employed regional dialects, colloquialisms, and even slang—to the dismay of more conservative critics. Romantic writers who were interested in capturing the flavor of the legendary past sometimes even used archaic language (*quoth* instead of *said,* for example).

In the aftermath of the American Revolution, British and American English grew further apart. A major figure in the development of American English was Connecticut-born Noah Webster, who patriotically set about proving that the new nation's language was as good as its mother tongue. His *American Spelling Book* went through over 300 editions from 1788 to 1829, and his 1828 *American Dictionary of the English Language* became a national institution. It was in part through Webster's influence that Americans dropped the *k* at the end of words like *publick* and *traffick;* eliminated the *u* in words such as *colour, flavour,* and *splendour* (but not, for some reason, in *glamour*); and changed the British *re* to *er* in words like *centre.*

William Pitt Addressing the House of Commons in 1793, Karl Anton Hickel. Oil on canvas, The Granger Collection, New York.

Edmund Burke, who had supported the American Revolution, was among the first to attack the excesses of the increasingly radical government of France. Burke's attacks created a rift within the Whig party, leaving the party's leader, Charles James Fox, with little support. As the violence of the French radicals increased, so did the British reaction, especially when France began exporting revolution beyond its borders. In 1793, after French troops invaded Holland, Britain entered upon a war with France that would ultimately last for over 25 years. Pitt was forced to succumb to fearful voices equating all reform efforts with revolution and arguing for domestic repression to keep Britain from falling victim to the violence and anarchy seen in France.

Near the end of the century, rebellious Irishmen, encouraged by the promise of French assistance, rose up against their British masters. Though this rebellion was quelled after poor weather prevented a major French landing, the threat of a French invasion of Britain by way of Ireland remained. To combat the threat, Pitt offered to sponsor various reforms, including the granting of voting rights to Roman Catholics, if the Irish Parliament would agree to dissolve itself and join politically with the British Parliament. The passage of the Act of Union in 1800 formalized this arrangement, creating the United Kingdom of Great Britain and Ireland, but George III—still on the throne despite his periodic bouts of madness—refused to allow voting rights for Catholics. Pitt was forced to resign, just when his nation needed him most—when the brilliant Corsican general Napoleon Bonaparte had emerged as the dominant force on the French political scene.

Above: *Napoleon Bonaparte Crossing the Alps* (about 1801), Jacques Louis David. Chateau de Malmaison, Rueil-Malmaison, France, Giraudon/Art Resource, New York.

Created as a symbol of the union of Great Britain and Ireland, this flag—known as the Union Jack—has served as the national flag of the United Kingdom since 1801. It consists of elements taken from earlier flags of England (red cross on white), Scotland (diagonal white cross on blue), and Ireland (diagonal red cross on white).

The Rise and Fall of Napoleon

In late 1799, when Napoleon had taken control of France's revolutionary government, his charisma and acceptance of democratic principles had won him the admiration of reform-minded intellectuals throughout Europe. Soon, however, his hunger for power became clear. In 1804 he crowned himself emperor of France, and over the next several years his military and political maneuvers allowed him to establish control over most of continental Europe. Called back to power in 1804, Pitt tried to prepare Britain for a seemingly inevitable French invasion. Fortunately, in 1805 the British fleet under Horatio Nelson succeeded in destroying the French navy in the Battle of Trafalgar off the coast of Spain, ending the threat of invasion. The victory was bittersweet, however, for Nelson himself was killed in the battle, and within months Pitt was also gone, dying of overwork at the age of 46.

His plans of invasion thwarted, Napoleon tried to break Britain economically by closing the ports of continental Europe to British trade. Tightening his grip on the Iberian Peninsula (Spain and Portugal), Napoleon deposed the Spanish king and placed his brother Joseph on the throne. In the "Peninsular War" that followed, British troops—commanded first by Sir John Moore (killed in action in 1809) and then by Sir Arthur Wellesley—gradually liberated the Iberian Peninsula from French control.

In 1811, with the Peninsular War in full swing, George III was declared insane and his eldest son and heir—George, Prince of Wales—became Britain's regent, or acting ruler. A spendthrift with loose personal morals, Prince George had been a gambling buddy of the now-deceased Whig leader Charles James Fox and (unlike George III) had always favored the Whigs. Now, however, he abandoned them and sided with the Tories, once again quashing hopes of domestic reform. Anyone who criticized the regent too openly became subject to arrest and imprisonment.

In 1812, Napoleon made the mistake of invading Russia, a nation with which he had enjoyed an uneasy peace. Though his army got as far as Moscow, the brutal Russian winter forced it into a retreat during which starvation, the freezing weather, and Cossack raids managed to kill off most of the French troops. Meanwhile, Wellesley's British forces were closing in on France from the south. At the Battle of Leipzig in 1813, the nations allied against Napoleon dealt him what seemed a death blow.

LITERATURE

Although the beginning of Britain's romantic period is traditionally assigned to the year 1798, aspects of romanticism are evident in earlier British literature. Writing in the dialect of Lowland Scotland, Robert Burns, who died in 1796, produced heartfelt lyrics about love, nature, and the Scottish past, many of which were meant to be sung to familiar tunes. William Blake, who began publishing in the 1780s, expressed his rebellious spirit and his mystical view of the nature of good and evil in such works as *The French Revolution, The Marriage of Heaven and Hell,* and the contrasting poems of *Songs of Innocence* and *Songs of Experience.*

Nevertheless, the real flowering of romanticism came with the 1798 publication of William Wordsworth and Samuel Taylor Coleridge's landmark collection *Lyrical Ballads.* The two men, who had first met in 1795, were united by their shared desire to explore new modes of literary expression. Wordsworth, who had visited France when the revolution began, was deeply committed to the common people and sought to express individual human experiences in a natural language. Coleridge, in poems like "Kubla Khan," focused on more exotic experiences, letting his imagination wander in realms of mystery and the supernatural. Both poets rejected the world of science and industry, feeling that insight into human experience flows most freely from communion with nature. With Wordsworth's sister, Dorothy—whose diaries reveal much about the two poets' personalities—they spent a good deal of their time in the rural Lake District of northwestern England, so that they and their friend Robert Southey are sometimes referred to as the Lake Poets.

Above: Early 19th-century improvements in public hygiene included the construction of sewers.

When the allied forces entered Paris a year later, Napoleon was captured and exiled to the island of Elba; but while allied ministers met to decide Europe's fate at the Congress of Vienna, Napoleon escaped and returned to the French throne for the so-called Hundred Days. He was finally defeated at the Battle of Waterloo in Belgium in 1815 and exiled to the more remote island of St. Helena. Wellesley (recently ennobled as the duke of Wellington), who commanded the British troops that bore the brunt of the battle, was the hero of the hour, and "to meet one's Waterloo" became synonymous with "to suffer a decisive defeat."

In August 1819, workers met in St. Peter's Fields, Manchester, to peacefully demonstrate their discontent with Britain's economic and labor policies and to call for reform. The local militia, ordered to arrest the protest's leader, instead launched an attack that resulted in 11 deaths and hundreds of injuries. The incident, likened to the Battle of Waterloo, became known as the Peterloo Massacre.

The Aftermath of the War

The end of the war with France did not mean an immediate end to reactionary British domestic policies, for the fear of revolution still remained strong. To Britain's growing mass of restless laborers were added thousands of discharged veterans returning to a nation in which jobs were scarce, wages low, and poverty widespread. Large landowners successfully pressured the Tory government to continue the Corn Laws, which barred cheap foreign grain from British markets and so kept the price of food high. Industry, in contrast, operated under the economic philosophy of laissez-faire capitalism, which held that government should not interfere in private enterprise. Thus, workers remained at the mercy of factory owners. They were even forbidden from banding together in labor unions that might pressure owners into improving work conditions and wages.

The Regency ended in 1820, when George III died and the Prince of Wales officially took the throne as George IV. Over the next several years, the Tories gradually began to institute some of the reforms that the nation so sorely needed. Sir Robert Peel revamped Britain's harsh criminal code and organized the nation's first professional civilian police force. The duke of Wellington, now serving as prime minister, pushed the Catholic Emancipation Act through Parliament in 1829, just in time to allow the newly elected Irish Catholic political leader Daniel O'Connell to take his seat in the House of Commons. Wellington's more conservative fellow Tories opposed the bill, however, and like Pitt before him, he was forced to resign over the issue. Thus, the passage of the Reform Bill of 1832, which more fairly distributed seats in Parliament and extended the vote to middle-class men, would be a Whig effort, not a Tory one. This landmark bill marks the end of the romantic period and the start of the mainstream reform efforts that characterized the dawning Victorian era.

Above: Although certain reforms were made in the education of females, mid-century educational policies were still extremely limiting.

Literature

Wordsworth and Coleridge belonged to the so-called first generation of romantic writers. The leading poets of the second generation, which rose to prominence during the Regency, were Lord Byron, Percy Bysshe Shelley, and John Keats. Byron, in both his poetry and his personal life, helped popularize the brooding, self-absorbed romantic figure now sometimes known as the Byronic hero. Both he and his friend Shelley, a brilliant lyric poet, were members of the upper class whose radical politics and personal affairs eventually made them figures of scandal, leading to their self-imposed exile from Britain. The equally brilliant John Keats, a less-well-born acquaintance of Shelley's, also left Britain, seeking a cure for his tuberculosis in the warmer climate of Italy. All three poets died young while living abroad.

Though best known for poetry, the romantic period also was a time when many memorable works of prose were produced. The romantic emphasis on personal experience is evident in the fine personal essays of Charles Lamb, William Hazlitt, and Thomas De Quincey, many of which first appeared in literary journals. Sir Walter Scott, the most popular novelist of the day, pioneered the historical novel in his best-selling *Waverley* (1814), set in his native Scotland. Also popular were gothic novels of mystery and horror, such as *Frankenstein* (1818) by Mary Wollstonecraft Shelley, the wife of Percy Bysshe Shelley and the daughter of Mary Wollstonecraft (see page 412). Jane Austen, on the other hand, remained in many ways a neoclassical writer, penning ironic novels of manners such as *Pride and Prejudice* (1813) and *Emma* (1815). Nevertheless, Austen's introduction of more dialogue into fiction helped pave the way for the realistic novels of the Victorian era.

LASERLINKS
• *HISTORICAL LITERARY CONNECTION*

PART 1 *Seeking Truth*

The poets of the romantic period turned their attention from the common experience of society in order to focus on the experiences of the individual, believing that emotion was more important than reason as a way of understanding life. Many rejected the formal style of the neoclassicists and instead employed more lyrical poetic forms to express themselves. Romantic poets looked in particular to the natural world as a source of truth and inspiration, as you will see in this part of Unit Four.

PREVIEWING

POETRY

Selected Poems

William Blake

PERSONAL CONNECTION

Have you ever wondered what inspired an author to write a particular story or poem? Briefly describe to the class one of your favorite novels, short stories, or poems. Then share your thoughts and speculations about the source of the author's inspiration.

BIOGRAPHICAL/LITERARY CONNECTION

William Blake was an artist, a poet, and a visionary. His work was so incompatible with the taste of his day that his contemporaries could not appreciate his accomplishments. Some believed him to be inspired but irrational; others thought him to be mad. Throughout his life, Blake saw visions—from angels sitting in a tree to messages from his dead brother—which he attributed not to a supernatural source but to the interaction of his imagination with the world and with infinity, or God. This interaction was the inspiration for both his poetry and his art. His work reflects highly original interpretations of human experience and of the relationship between the human and the divine.

In 1789, using his own method of producing books with hand-colored illustrations, Blake published his first major work, *Songs of Innocence*, a group of poems modeled on the street ballads and rhymes sung by London's children. In 1794, he added to these poems a group of contrasting poems called *Songs of Experience*. Many of the poems in *Songs of Innocence* have matching poems in *Songs of Experience*—for example, "The Lamb" is paired with "The Tyger." In the subtitle for this combined edition of the two collections, Blake indicated that his purpose in putting them together was to show "the two contrary states of the human soul."

The Tyger (1794), William Blake. Color relief etching, The Granger Collection, New York.

WRITING CONNECTION

Focus on one natural object—perhaps a tree, an animal, or a star. With that object as your inspiration, generate ideas for a poem and for a story. Jot down some of your ideas in a diagram like the one shown.

IDEAS

POEM

Source of Inspiration

STORY

from **Songs of**

SONGS

William Blake

The Lamb

Little Lamb, who made thee?
Dost thou know who made thee?
Gave thee life & bid thee feed,
By the stream & o'er the mead;[1]
Gave thee clothing of delight,
Softest clothing wooly bright;
Gave thee such a tender voice,
Making all the vales[2] rejoice!
Little Lamb who made thee?
Dost thou know who made thee?

Little Lamb I'll tell thee,
Little Lamb I'll tell thee!
He is calléd by thy name,
For he calls himself a Lamb:[3]
He is meek & he is mild,
He became a little child:
I a child & thou a lamb,
We are calléd by his name.
Little Lamb God bless thee.
Little Lamb God bless thee.

1. **mead:** meadow.
2. **vales:** valleys.
3. In the New Testament, Jesus is sometimes referred to as the Lamb of God.

Innocence

The Little Boy Lost

"Father, father, where are you going?
O do not walk so fast.
Speak father, speak to your little boy,
Or else I shall be lost."

The night was dark, no father was there;
The child was wet with dew;
The mire[1] was deep, & the child did weep,
And away the vapor[2] flew.

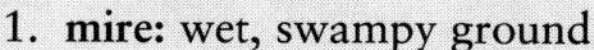

1. **mire:** wet, swampy ground.
2. **vapor:** mist; fog.

Detail of title page of *Songs of Innocence* (1789), William Blake. The Granger Collection, New York.

The Little Boy Found

The little boy lost in the lonely fen,[1]
Led by the wand'ring light,
Began to cry, but God ever nigh,
Appear'd like his father in white.

He kissed the child & by the hand led
And to his mother brought,
Who in sorrow pale, thro' the lonely dale,
Her little boy weeping sought.

1. **fen:** swamp; marsh.

FROM PERSONAL RESPONSE *TO* CRITICAL ANALYSIS

REFLECT **1.** What thoughts went through your mind as you were reading these poems? Describe your reactions in your notebook.

RETHINK **2.** What ideas about life do you think the speakers of these poems express?
Consider
- the speaker's thoughts about the lamb's creation
- what happens to the lost boy

3. Do you think the title *Songs of Innocence* is appropriate for these poems? Explain your answer.

from **Songs of**

SONGS

William Blake

The TYGER

Tyger! Tyger! burning bright
In the forests of the night,
What immortal hand or eye
Could frame thy fearful symmetry?

In what distant deeps or skies
Burnt the fire of thine eyes?
On what wings dare he aspire?
What the hand dare seize the fire?

And what shoulder, & what art,
Could twist the sinews of thy heart?
And when thy heart began to beat,
What dread hand? & what dread feet?

What the hammer? what the chain?
In what furnace was thy brain?
What the anvil? what dread grasp
Dare its deadly terrors clasp?

When the stars threw down their spears
And water'd heaven with their tears,
Did he smile his work to see?
Did he who made the Lamb make thee?

Tyger! Tyger! burning bright
In the forests of the night,
What immortal hand or eye
Dare frame thy fearful symmetry?

4 symmetry: balance of form.

7 he: the tiger's creator; **aspire:** soar; ascend; aim for something great.

10 sinews (sĭn′yo͞oz): tendons.

The *Fly*

Little Fly,
Thy summer's play
My thoughtless hand
Has brush'd away.

Am not I
A fly like thee?
Or art not thou
A man like me?

For I dance
And drink & sing,
Till some blind hand
Shall brush my wing.

If thought is life
And strength & breath,
And the want
Of thought is death,

Then am I
A happy fly
If I live
Or if I die.

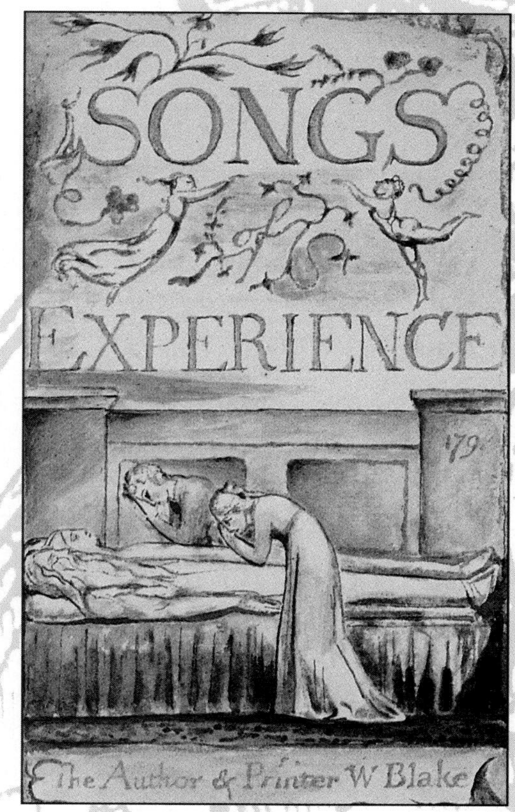

Title page of *Songs of Experience* (1794), William Blake. The Granger Collection, New York.

from Songs *of* Experience

William Blake

The Sick Rose

O Rose, thou art sick.
The invisible worm
That flies in the night
In the howling storm

Has found out thy bed
Of crimson joy,
And his dark secret love
Does thy life destroy.

RESPONDING OPTIONS

FROM PERSONAL RESPONSE *TO* CRITICAL ANALYSIS

REFLECT **1.** Jot down some of the images that came to mind as you read "The Tyger," "The Fly," and "The Sick Rose."

RETHINK **2.** What view of experience do you think is reflected in these poems?

Consider
- the questions the speaker asks about the tiger
- the reasons the speaker compares himself to a fly
- the image of the worm in the rose

3. What seems to be the attitude of the speaker in each of these poems?

RELATE **4.** What understanding of innocence and experience do you find reflected in these poems from *Songs of Innocence* and *Songs of Experience*?

5. Compare the attitudes of the speakers in *Songs of Innocence* with those of the speakers in *Songs of Experience*. Consider similarities as well as differences.

6. What do you think might have been the sources of Blake's inspiration for these poems? Consider feelings and thoughts as well as aspects of the external world.

ANOTHER PATHWAY

Cooperative Learning

Work with a small group of classmates to list some of the issues about life and death that Blake raises in these six poems. Prepare a set of questions that your group could use to lead a discussion of the main themes in *Songs of Innocence* and *Songs of Experience*. Then choose one of your questions to discuss with the rest of the class.

LITERARY CONCEPTS

A **symbol** is a person, place, object, or activity that stands for something beyond itself. Literary symbols take on meaning within the context of the works in which they occur. Sometimes a literary symbol has more than one possible meaning. For example, the rose in Blake's poem might symbolize goodness, innocence, or all of humanity. In a chart like the one shown, identify the qualities of the lamb and the tiger and tell what you think each animal symbolizes. Then identify any other objects in the six Blake poems that you think might be considered symbols.

Object	Qualities	Symbol of . . .
Lamb		
Tiger		

QUICKWRITES

1. Think back to Blake's statement (quoted in the Biographical/Literary Connection on page 483) that he paired *Songs of Innocence* with *Songs of Experience* to show "the two contrary states of the human soul." Write a **critique** of the two groups of poems, in which you evaluate how well they fulfill that purpose.
2. Use one of the ideas you generated for the Writing Connection on page 483 to write a **poem** or a **story.**

PORTFOLIO *Save your writing. You may want to use it later as a springboard to a piece for your portfolio.*

ALTERNATIVE ACTIVITIES

1. Create a **montage**—a composite picture made up of a variety of photos or parts of photos—to illustrate Blake's concept of innocence. Then create a similar montage to illustrate his concept of experience.
2. Choreograph and perform for the class a **dance interpretation** expressing the contrast between "The Lamb" and "The Tyger." Perform your dance to a taped reading of the poems.

ART CONNECTION

Look at the two illustrations of Blake's on pages 485 and 487. How do the scenes depicted reflect the themes of innocence and experience?

CRITIC'S CORNER

One critic has commented that for Blake "even the most casual acts of perception are acts of imaginative sculpture." Explain the ways in which the poems you have read do or do not, in your opinion, support this idea.

LITERARY LINKS

Compare the views of life expressed in these poems from *Songs of Innocence* and *Songs of Experience* with the views of life presented in the excerpts from the King James Bible in Unit Two. What similarities and differences do you see?

WILLIAM BLAKE

1757–1827

William Blake's life was at once extraordinary and uneventful. Although his imaginative life was rich and astonishingly creative, his everyday life was lived in obscurity and near poverty. The son of a London clothing merchant, Blake showed an early flair for drawing and began attending art school when he was only 10. He spoke of having visions from the time he was a young child, and he was already writing poetry by the age of 12. When he was 14 he entered a seven-year apprenticeship to an engraver, after which he studied engraving at the Royal Academy of Arts.

When Blake was 24, he married Catherine Boucher, a poor and illiterate young woman. Blake taught her to read, and she later helped him in his engraving and printing work. In 1784, Blake opened his own print shop, where he developed an engraving technique that he called "illuminated printing." The method involved printing both text and illustration on a page at the same time, then coloring the illustration by hand. *Songs of Innocence* was one of the first works he printed in this manner. Because the process was time-consuming, Blake produced only a few copies of each of his books, undoubtedly one of the reasons that his works were not widely known during his lifetime.

Blake's later works were on a grand scale, marked by prophetic and mythic visions, richly illustrated, and difficult to understand. These complex works were almost totally ignored by readers in his own day. During his 60s, Blake stopped writing poetry and devoted all his time to pictorial art. He finally gained the recognition of a small group of artists who admired his work, and it was during this period that he created some of his best designs, including illustrations for Dante's *Divine Comedy* and designs for the book of Job. Blake died three months before his 70th birthday, confident of the value of his work but still relatively unknown, his stunning originality as a poet and artist not to be recognized until well into the 20th century.

OTHER WORKS "Introduction" and "The Chimney Sweeper" in *Songs of Innocence*, "Introduction" and "The Chimney Sweeper" in *Songs of Experience*

PREVIEWING

POETRY

Haiku

Matsuo Bashō (mät-so͝o'ō bä'shō)

Kobayashi Issa (kō-bä-yä'shē ēs'sä)

PERSONAL CONNECTION

Shakespeare wrote that "brevity is the soul of wit." What do you think he meant? Do you think important ideas or impressions can be imparted in just a few words? Share your thoughts or examples with your classmates.

LITERARY CONNECTION

Haiku (hī'ko͞o) is a form of Japanese poetry that embodies three qualities greatly valued in Japanese art: precision, economy, and delicacy. Like the English romantic poets, Japanese haiku poets found nature to be an important source of inspiration. The rules of haiku are strict—in only 17 syllables, arranged in 3 lines of 5, 7, and 5 syllables, the poet must create a clear picture of a single aspect of nature that evokes a strong emotional response in the reader. The brevity of haiku can be misleading; their powerful effect comes as much from what is suggested as from what is directly said.

Matsuo Bashō was a 17th-century teacher of haiku. Idolized in his own lifetime, he is still regarded as the greatest of all Japanese haiku poets. Kobayashi Issa, who composed nearly 20,000 haiku, achieved fame a century later. Although Bashō and Issa followed the strict requirements of the haiku form, the exact number and pattern of syllables in their poems cannot usually be reproduced in English versions, as you may notice when you read these translations.

WRITING CONNECTION

Close your eyes and picture yourself in a favorite natural setting—perhaps a beach, a park, the woods, or the mountains. Let your imagination focus on one fragment of that setting, such as a single bird or a lone cloud. In just one brief sentence, try to capture the image, action, or mood of that scene.

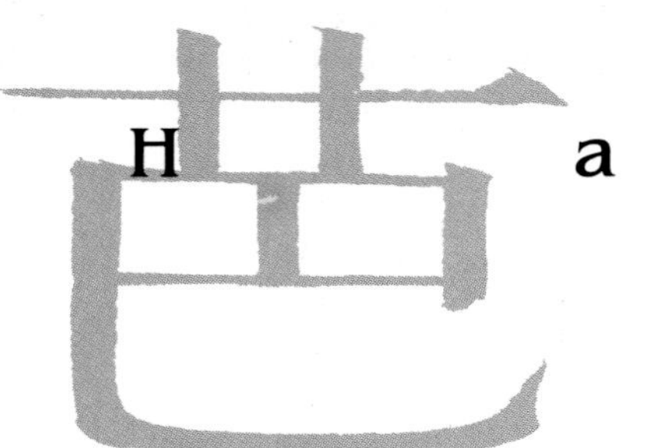

Haiku

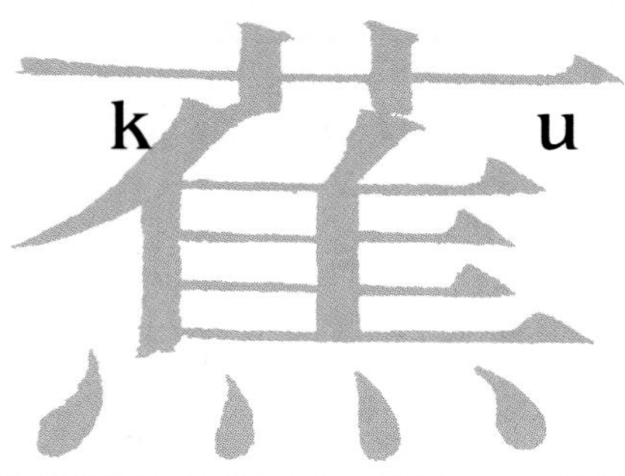

Autumn—
even the birds
and clouds look old.

Bashō

Wintry day,
on my horse
a frozen shadow.

Bashō

Skylark
sings all day,
and day not long enough.

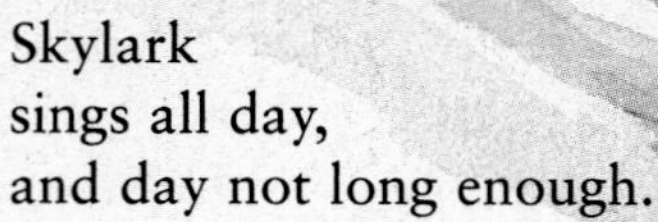

Bashō

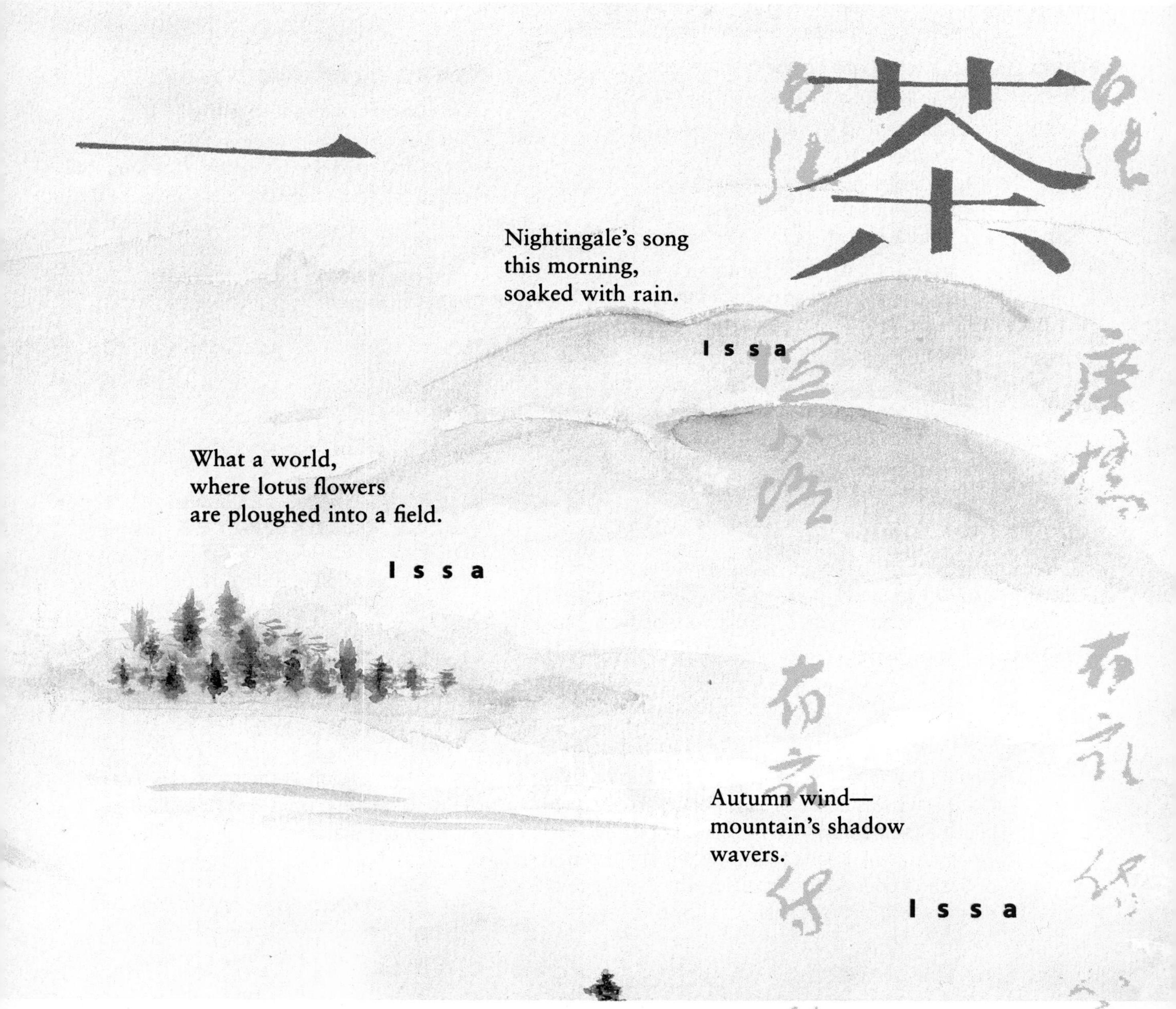

一茶

Nightingale's song
this morning,
soaked with rain.

Issa

What a world,
where lotus flowers
are ploughed into a field.

Issa

Autumn wind—
mountain's shadow
wavers.

Issa

Translated by Lucien Stryk and Takashi Ikemoto

RESPONDING OPTIONS

FROM PERSONAL RESPONSE *TO* CRITICAL ANALYSIS

REFLECT 1. Which of these haiku did you enjoy the most? In your notebook, jot down reasons for your choice.

RETHINK 2. What emotions do the haiku evoke in you?

3. What impressions of nature do the two poets seem to share?

   Consider
   - their descriptions of seasons
   - the words they use to describe the natural world

4. If the two haiku about autumn were about spring instead, what images might be used?

RELATE 5. On the basis of your reading of these poems, do you think haiku have relevance for all cultures and times, or are they more relevant to a specific culture or era? Support your answer with evidence from the poems.

ANOTHER PATHWAY

Cooperative Learning

With two classmates, explore the ideas suggested by the haiku in this lesson. One student in your group might identify the main idea of each haiku, another might suggest emotions that the words and images bring to mind, and the third might analyze the form of the haiku. Present your findings to the class.

LITERARY LINKS

Compare the haiku of Bashō and Issa with the poems of William Blake. Do you think Blake and the Japanese poets viewed nature in the same way? Explain your opinion.

CRITIC'S CORNER

Donald Keene, a scholar of Japanese literature, wrote that Bashō was able "to capture at once the eternal and the momentary" in his haiku. Briefly explain what you think Keene meant by this characterization of Bashō's poems. Then explain why you agree or disagree with the comment.

QUICKWRITES

1. Write an original **haiku** that conveys your reaction to one aspect of nature. You might use the sentence you wrote for the Writing Connection on page 491 as a springboard for your haiku.
2. The architect Ludwig Mies Van Der Rohe summed up his theory of modern design in the sentence "Less is more." In a **paragraph,** explain how this statement might be applied to the haiku form.

PORTFOLIO Save your writing. You may want to use it later as a springboard to a piece for your portfolio.

ALTERNATIVE ACTIVITIES

1. Using watercolors, pen and ink, or both media, create an **illustration** for one of the haiku.
2. Read other haiku by Japanese poets. Then create a **booklet** of your favorite haiku. You might want to use a computer graphics program to design borders for your pages.

ACROSS THE CURRICULUM

History Investigate some of the principles of Zen Buddhism. What aspects of Zen do you think might have influenced haiku poets like Bashō and Issa? Discuss your findings with your classmates.

Art Explore the Japanese arts of woodblock printing, calligraphy, painting, and pottery. What do these arts have in common with haiku? Create a bulletin-board display to illustrate the connections.

MATSUO BASHŌ

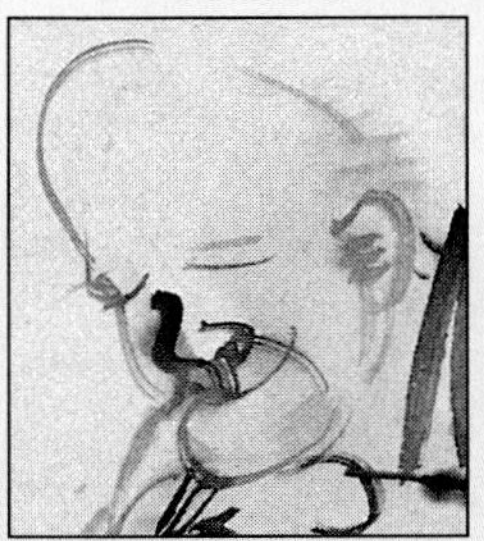

1644–1694

Bashō was born to a family of modest means. Early in life, he became friends with the son of a noble family, whose royal connections allowed Bashō to study with a prominent teacher of haiku. After his friend died at an early age, Bashō pursued a career as a professional haiku poet in Edo (now Tokyo).

Around 1677, Bashō started his own school of haiku and by 1680 was the most famous Japanese poet of his day. Neither writing nor teaching provided much income, though, and he lived modestly throughout his life. In 1684, he began the first of many journeys through Japan—journeys that provided inspiration for much of his poetry. Teaching wherever he traveled, he had more than 2,000 students by the time of his death.

One day, according to legend, a student announced that he had thought of a poem: "Pluck off the wings of a bright red dragonfly and there a pepper pod will be." Bashō informed him that he would never be a poet. A poet, according to Bashō, would have said: "Add but the wings to a bright red pepper pod and there a dragonfly will be." Whether or not the story is true, it reflects a compassion for living things that, along with his superb technical skills as a poet, has made Bashō a major figure in world literature.

KOBAYASHI ISSA

1763–1828

Although born into a fairly prosperous family, Kobayashi Issa was forced to leave home at the age of 14 because of difficulties with his stepmother. He moved to Edo, where he studied under Chikua, a prominent haiku poet. When Chikua died in 1790, Issa took over as head of his school, where he continued to display his talent as a master of the haiku form. Issa is known for simple, personal poetry that often touches upon two subjects: his love for insects and small animals and his poverty. Like Bashō, Issa traveled to many parts of Japan and was honored by leading poets of the day.

Issa dealt with adversity all his life. In spite of his talent, he lived most of his life in poverty, occasionally being forced to rely on friends for shelter. In 1813, a small inheritance from his family may have given Issa, then in his 50s, the means to marry for the first time. His first four children died in infancy, and his wife eventually died in childbirth. Issa's second marriage ended unhappily, and his only healthy child, the offspring of a third marriage, was born after the poet's death.

LASERLINKS
- *CULTURAL CONNECTION*
- *ART GALLERY*

PREVIEWING

POETRY

Selected Poems

William Wordsworth

PERSONAL CONNECTION

Think about the ways in which you react to different aspects of nature, such as a rainy day, the first signs of spring, or waves crashing against rocks. Do you think nature can affect the way a person thinks, feels, or acts? Share your thoughts with the class.

BIOGRAPHICAL/LITERARY CONNECTION

In his poetry, William Wordsworth urged his readers to look to nature for an understanding of life, and in so doing, he became a major force behind the romantic movement. Romantic writers emphasized the importance of the individual, valued imagination and the emotions more than reason and abstract ideas, and looked to nature as a source of truth and inspiration.

Grasmere, William Havell (1782–1857). Private collection.

For a time, Wordsworth and his friend Samuel Taylor Coleridge discussed poetry almost daily and collaborated on a number of poems. In 1798 they jointly published a collection of their poetry, titled *Lyrical Ballads,* that included Coleridge's "The Rime of the Ancient Mariner" and Wordsworth's "Lines Composed a Few Miles Above Tintern Abbey." Praised as a literary breath of spring, the volume sold out within two years.

In 1800 Wordsworth published a new edition of *Lyrical Ballads*, adding a second volume of his own poems. He also added a preface containing ideas that seemed radical to many of his contemporaries. In it, he rejected the formal style and diction of neoclassical poetry, maintaining that poetry should be written in simple, spontaneous language—the language of all mankind rather than of a literary elite—and should deal with everyday events, common people, and the passions of the human heart.

Much of Wordsworth's poetry was inspired by his reaction to nature during his frequent walks with his sister, Dorothy, in the green, mountainous splendor of the Lake District in northwestern England. In her journals, Dorothy recorded her own observations about the sights they encountered. (The Insight selection on page 508 is an excerpt from one of these journals.) It was not unusual for Wordsworth to read and borrow from his sister's descriptions, particularly when reflecting upon a scene that they had observed months, or even years, before.

READING CONNECTION

Form and Meaning in Poetry

Although the romantic poets experimented with a variety of verse forms, both traditional and innovative, they held it as a basic premise that the form of a poem must be compatible with its content and meaning. The term *form* refers to all the principles of arrangement in a poem—the ways in which the words and images are organized and patterned to produce a pleasing whole. Elements of form—such as the sound devices of rhythm, rhyme, alliteration, consonance, and assonance—work together with other poetic elements to shape a poem, convey meaning, and create a total experience for the reader.

The following lines from William Blake's "The Lamb" (page 484) provide an example of how various literary elements can combine to create meaning:

> **Little Lamb, who made thee?**
> **Dost thou know who made thee?**
> **Gave thee life & bid thee feed,**
> **By the stream & o'er the mead;**
> **Gave thee clothing of delight,**
> **Softest clothing wooly bright;**

First, notice how the speaker uses figurative language—in this case, personification—in addressing the lamb. Then notice how sound devices—rhythm, rhyme, and repetition—create a lyrical, carefree quality that echoes the innocence and youth described in the poem. The shortness of the lines also contributes to this childlike effect. Finally, note the imagery that the poet uses in the last two lines to describe the lamb's appearance. Clearly, in these lines of Blake's poem, form and meaning are inseparable parts of a whole.

As you read each of these poems by Wordsworth, think about the elements of form that help convey the speaker's response to nature. Read each poem aloud, concentrating on the elements of sound. Then, in your notebook, chart your evaluation of the relationship between the poem's form and its meaning. Rank each poem using a scale of 1 to 5, with 1 indicating that you think the form does not reinforce the meaning and 5 indicating that, in your opinion, the form plays a significant role in conveying meaning.

Rank	Poem
	"Lines Composed a Few Miles Above Tintern Abbey"
	"Composed upon Westminster Bridge"
	"The World Is Too Much with Us"
	"It Is a Beauteous Evening"
	"I Wandered Lonely As a Cloud"

LASERLINKS
• *VISUAL VOCABULARY*

Lines Composed a Few Miles Above Tintern Abbey

Five years have passed; five summers, with the length
Of five long winters! and again I hear
These waters, rolling from their mountain-springs
With a soft inland murmur. Once again
Do I behold these steep and lofty cliffs,
That on a wild secluded scene impress
Thoughts of more deep seclusion; and connect
The landscape with the quiet of the sky.
The day is come when I again repose
Here, under this dark sycamore, and view
These plots of cottage ground, these orchard tufts,
Which at this season, with their unripe fruits,
Are clad in one green hue, and lose themselves
'Mid groves and copses. Once again I see
These hedgerows, hardly hedgerows, little lines
Of sportive wood run wild; these pastoral farms,
Green to the very door; and wreaths of smoke
Sent up, in silence, from among the trees!
With some uncertain notice, as might seem
Of vagrant dwellers in the houseless woods,
Or of some Hermit's cave, where by his fire
The Hermit sits alone.

These beauteous forms,
Through a long absence, have not been to me
As is a landscape to a blind man's eye;
But oft, in lonely rooms, and 'mid the din
Of towns and cities, I have owed to them,

GUIDE FOR READING

9 repose: lie at rest.

14 copses (kŏp′sĭz): thickets of small trees.

16 pastoral (păs′tər-əl): rural and serene.

20 vagrant: wandering.

The Seine at Giverny, Morning Mists (1897), Claude Monet. North Carolina Museum of Art, Raleigh, purchased with funds from the Sarah Graham Kenan Foundation and the North Carolina Art Society (Robert F. Phifer Bequest).

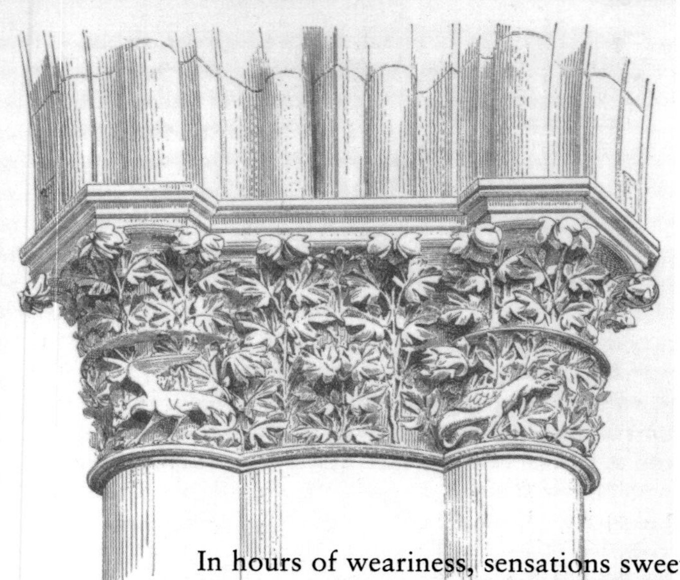

In hours of weariness, sensations sweet,
Felt in the blood, and felt along the heart;
And passing even into my purer mind,
With tranquil restoration—feelings too
Of unremembered pleasure; such, perhaps,
As have no slight or trivial influence
On that best portion of a good man's life,
His little, nameless, unremembered, acts
Of kindness and of love. Nor less, I trust,
To them I may have owed another gift,
Of aspect more sublime; that blessed mood,
In which the burthen of the mystery,
In which the heavy and the weary weight
Of all this unintelligible world,
Is lightened—that serene and blessed mood,
In which the affections gently lead us on—
Until, the breath of this corporeal frame
And even the motion of our human blood
Almost suspended, we are laid asleep
In body, and become a living soul;
While with an eye made quiet by the power
Of harmony, and the deep power of joy,
We see into the life of things.

If this
Be but a vain belief, yet, oh! how oft—
In darkness and amid the many shapes
Of joyless daylight; when the fretful stir
Unprofitable, and the fever of the world,
Have hung upon the beatings of my heart—
How oft, in spirit, have I turned to thee,
O sylvan Wye! thou wanderer through the woods,
How often has my spirit turned to thee!

38 burthen: burden.

43 corporeal (kôr-pôr'ē-əl): bodily.

56 sylvan: located in a wood or forest; **Wye:** a river in Wales and England.

22–57 What effect do you think the memory of the "beauteous forms" has on the speaker?

And now, with gleams of half-extinguished thought
With many recognitions dim and faint,
And somewhat of a sad perplexity,
The picture of the mind revives again;
While here I stand, not only with the sense
Of present pleasure, but with pleasing thoughts
That in this moment there is life and food
For future years. And so I dare to hope,
Though changed, no doubt, from what I was when first
I came among these hills; when like a roe
I bounded o'er the mountains, by the sides
Of the deep rivers, and the lonely streams,
Wherever nature led—more like a man
Flying from something that he dreads than one
Who sought the thing he loved. For nature then
(The coarser pleasures of my boyish days,
And their glad animal movements all gone by)
To me was all in all.—I cannot paint
What then I was. The sounding cataract
Haunted me like a passion; the tall rock,
The mountain, and the deep and gloomy wood,
Their colors and their forms, were then to me
An appetite; a feeling and a love,
That had no need of a remoter charm,
By thought supplied, nor any interest
Unborrowed from the eye.—That time is past,
And all its aching joys are now no more,
And all its dizzy raptures. Not for this
Faint I, nor mourn nor murmur; other gifts
Have followed; for such loss, I would believe,
Abundant recompense. For I have learned
To look on nature, not as in the hour
Of thoughtless youth; but hearing oftentimes
The still, sad music of humanity,
Nor harsh nor grating, though of ample power
To chasten and subdue. And I have felt
A presence that disturbs me with the joy
Of elevated thoughts; a sense sublime
Of something far more deeply interfused,
Whose dwelling is the light of setting suns,
And the round ocean and the living air,
And the blue sky, and in the mind of man:

64–65 What does the speaker suggest by saying "there is life and food / For future years"?

67 roe: deer.

67–83 Notice how the speaker formerly responded to nature.

76 cataract: waterfall.

88 recompense: compensation. Here the speaker begins to describe what he has received in place of the "aching joys" and "dizzy raptures" of youth.

93 chasten (chā'sən): scold; make modest.

A motion and a spirit, that impels
All thinking things, all objects of all thought,
And rolls through all things. Therefore am I still
A lover of the meadows and the woods,
And mountains; and of all that we behold
From this green earth; of all the mighty world
Of eye, and ear—both what they half create,
And what perceive; well pleased to recognize
In nature and the language of the sense
The anchor of my purest thoughts, the nurse,
The guide, the guardian of my heart, and soul
Of all my moral being.

Nor perchance,
If I were not thus taught, should I the more
Suffer my genial spirits to decay:
For thou art with me here upon the banks
Of this fair river; thou my dearest Friend,
My dear, dear Friend; and in thy voice I catch
The language of my former heart, and read
My former pleasures in the shooting lights
Of thy wild eyes. Oh! yet a little while
May I behold in thee what I was once,
My dear, dear Sister! and this prayer I make,
Knowing that Nature never did betray
The heart that loved her; 'tis her privilege,
Through all the years of this our life, to lead
From joy to joy: for she can so inform
The mind that is within us, so impress
With quietness and beauty, and so feed
With lofty thoughts, that neither evil tongues,
Rash judgments, nor the sneers of selfish men,
Nor greetings where no kindness is, nor all
The dreary intercourse of daily life,
Shall e'er prevail against us, or disturb
Our cheerful faith, that all which we behold
Is full of blessings. Therefore let the moon
Shine on thee in thy solitary walk;
And let the misty mountain winds be free
To blow against thee: and, in after years,
When these wild ecstasies shall be matured
Into a sober pleasure; when thy mind
Shall be a mansion for all lovely forms,
Thy memory be as a dwelling place
For all sweet sounds and harmonies; oh! then,

115 thou my dearest Friend: Wordsworth's sister, Dorothy.

119–120 The speaker sees in his sister's response to nature a mirror of his own youthful response.

121 Note the "prayer" the speaker has made. What does he hope for his sister?

If solitude, or fear, or pain, or grief
Should be thy portion, with what healing thoughts
Of tender joy wilt thou remember me,
And these my exhortations! Nor, perchance—
If I should be where I no more can hear
Thy voice, nor catch from thy wild eyes these gleams
Of past existence—wilt thou then forget
That on the banks of this delightful stream
We stood together; and that I, so long
A worshiper of Nature, hither came
Unwearied in that service; rather say
With warmer love—oh! with far deeper zeal
Of holier love. Nor wilt thou then forget,
That after many wanderings, many years
Of absence, these steep woods and lofty cliffs,
And this green pastoral landscape, were to me
More dear, both for themselves and for thy sake!

146 exhortations: words of encouraging advice.

FROM PERSONAL RESPONSE *TO* CRITICAL ANALYSIS

REFLECT **1.** In your notebook, sketch a memorable scene depicted in the poem. If you like, share it with classmates.

RETHINK **2.** What effect does nature seem to have on the speaker? Use details from the poem to support your answer.

3. Do you think the speaker regrets his loss of youth?

Consider

- the way he reacted to nature as a youth (lines 67–83)
- his reference to "other gifts" (line 86)
- his reaction to his sister's presence

William Wordsworth

Composed upon Westminster Bridge,

September 3, 1802

The Thames Below Westminster (1871), Claude Monet. National Gallery, London, Bridgeman/Art Resource, New York.

Earth has not anything to show more fair:
Dull would he be of soul who could pass by
A sight so touching in its majesty;
This City now doth, like a garment, wear
The beauty of the morning; silent, bare,
Ships, towers, domes, theaters, and temples lie
Open unto the fields, and to the sky;
All bright and glittering in the smokeless air.
Never did sun more beautifully steep
In his first splendor, valley, rock, or hill;
Ne'er saw I, never felt, a calm so deep!
The river glideth at his own sweet will:
Dear God! the very houses seem asleep;
And all that mighty heart is lying still!

GUIDE FOR READING

4 this City: London.

9 steep: soak; saturate.

12 the river: the Thames (tĕmz)—the principal river in London.

13 houses: Westminster Bridge is next to the Houses of Parliament; this word may therefore have a double meaning.

14 What do you think "that mighty heart" might be?

William Wordsworth

The World Is Too Much with Us

The world is too much with us; late and soon,
Getting and spending, we lay waste our powers;
Little we see in Nature that is ours;
We have given our hearts away, a sordid boon!
This Sea that bares her bosom to the moon,
The winds that will be howling at all hours,
And are up-gathered now like sleeping flowers,
For this, for everything, we are out of tune;
It moves us not.—Great God! I'd rather be
A Pagan suckled in a creed outworn;
So might I, standing on this pleasant lea,
Have glimpses that would make me less forlorn;
Have sight of Proteus rising from the sea;
Or hear old Triton blow his wreathéd horn.

GUIDE FOR READING

2–3 What does the speaker say alienates us from nature?

4 sordid boon: selfish or ignoble gift.

10 a Pagan: a non-Christian (in this case, a worshiper of the gods of ancient Greece). In the following lines, note what the speaker thinks a pagan could do that he cannot.

11 lea: meadow.

13–14 Proteus (prō′tē-əs) . . . **Triton** (trīt′n): sea gods of Greek mythology. Why do you think the speaker considers it an advantage to be able to see Proteus or hear Triton?

FROM PERSONAL RESPONSE *TO* CRITICAL ANALYSIS

REFLECT **1.** In your notebook, jot down a few words that describe your reaction to "Composed upon Westminster Bridge, September 3, 1802" and "The World Is Too Much with Us."

RETHINK **2.** With which of these two poems' speakers do you identify more strongly? Explain your response.

3. In "Composed upon Westminster Bridge, September 3, 1802," Wordsworth embraces the city of London in all its glory. In "The World Is Too Much with Us," he seems to find more value in the natural world. How do you explain this apparent contradiction in the two poems?

William Wordsworth 

Mortlake Terrace (1827), Joseph Mallord William Turner. Oil on canvas, 36¼" × 48⅛", National Gallery of Art, Washington, D.C., Andrew W. Mellon Collection. Photo by Richard Carafelli.

It Is a Beauteous Evening

It is a beauteous evening, calm and free,
The holy time is quiet as a Nun
Breathless with adoration; the broad sun
Is sinking down in its tranquility;
The gentleness of heaven broods o'er the Sea:
Listen! the mighty Being is awake,
And doth with his eternal motion make
A sound like thunder—everlastingly.
Dear Child! dear Girl! that walkest with me here,
If thou appear untouched by solemn thought,
Thy nature is not therefore less divine:
Thou liest in Abraham's bosom all the year,
And worship'st at the Temple's inner shrine,
God being with thee when we know it not.

GUIDE FOR READING

5 broods: hovers protectively.

9 dear Child: Wordsworth's daughter Caroline.

10–14 Why does the speaker say that the child's less thoughtful response to the evening does not imply a less divine nature?

12 in Abraham's bosom: in the presence of God.

William Wordsworth

I WANDERED LONELY *As* A CLOUD

I wandered lonely as a cloud
That floats on high o'er vales and hills,
When all at once I saw a crowd,
A host, of golden daffodils;
Beside the lake, beneath the trees,
Fluttering and dancing in the breeze.

Continuous as the stars that shine
And twinkle on the milky way,
They stretched in never-ending line
Along the margin of a bay:
Ten thousand saw I at a glance,
Tossing their heads in sprightly dance.

The waves beside them danced; but they
Outdid the sparkling waves in glee;
A poet could not but be gay,
In such a jocund company;
I gazed—and gazed—but little thought
What wealth the show to me had brought:

For oft, when on my couch I lie
In vacant or in pensive mood,
They flash upon that inward eye
Which is the bliss of solitude;
And then my heart with pleasure fills,
And dances with the daffodils.

GUIDE FOR READING

16 jocund (jŏk'ənd): merry.

20 pensive: dreamily thoughtful.

21 What do you think the speaker is referring to when he speaks of "that inward eye"?

INSIGHT

Dorothy Wordsworth

from the GRASMERE JOURNALS

Apr. 15. It was a threatening misty morning—but mild. We [Dorothy and William] set off after dinner from Eusemere. Mrs. Clarkson went a short way with us but turned back. The wind was furious and we thought we must have returned. We first rested in the large Boat-house, then under a furze Bush opposite Mr. Clarkson's. Saw the plough going in the field. The wind seized our breath the Lake was rough. There was a Boat by itself floating in the middle of the Bay below Water Millock. We rested again in the Water Millock Lane. The hawthorns are black and green, the birches here and there greenish but there is yet more of purple to be seen on the Twigs. We got over into a field to avoid some cows—people working, a few primroses by the roadside, wood-sorrel flower, the anemone, scentless violets, strawberries, and that starry yellow flower which Mrs. C. calls pile wort. When we were in the woods beyond Gowbarrow park we saw a few daffodils close to the water side. We fancied that the lake had floated the seeds ashore and that the little colony had so sprung up. But as we went along there were more and yet more and at last under the boughs of the trees, we saw that there was a long belt of them along the shore, about the breadth of a country turnpike road. I never saw daffodils so beautiful they grew among the mossy stones about and about them, some rested their heads upon these stones as on a pillow for weariness and the rest tossed and reeled and danced and seemed as if they verily laughed at the wind that blew upon them over the lake, they looked so gay ever glancing ever changing. This wind blew directly over the lake to them. There was here and there a little knot and a few stragglers a few yards higher up but they were so few as not to disturb the simplicity and unity and life of that one busy highway. We rested again and again. The Bays were stormy, and we heard the waves at different distances and in the middle of the water like the sea.

Silhouette of Dorothy Wordsworth, unknown artist. The Wordsworth Trust.

RESPONDING OPTIONS

FROM PERSONAL RESPONSE *TO* CRITICAL ANALYSIS

REFLECT **1.** Record in your notebook some of the images that remain in your mind after reading "It Is a Beauteous Evening" and "I Wandered Lonely As a Cloud."

RETHINK **2.** How would you describe the speakers of these two poems?

Consider

- each speaker's reaction to nature
- what the speaker tells his daughter in lines 10–14 of "It Is a Beauteous Evening"
- the reference to "that inward eye" in "I Wandered Lonely As a Cloud" (line 21)

RELATE **3.** Review each of the five Wordsworth poems. Then reread the evaluations you made for the Reading Connection on page 497 and revise any rankings about which you've changed your mind. According to your chart, in which of the poems does form play the most important role in conveying meaning?

4. Compare Wordsworth's reflections upon nature in "I Wandered Lonely As a Cloud" with his sister's description of the same scene in the Insight on page 508.

ANOTHER PATHWAY

Cooperative Learning

Wordsworth, like most romantic poets, viewed nature as a source of truth. With a small group of classmates, look for evidence of this attitude in each of the five poems. In addition to the speaker's physical and emotional reactions, consider what he appears to sense or "see" in nature. Share the group's ideas with the entire class.

LITERARY CONCEPTS

Imagery consists of words and phrases that re-create sensory experiences for a reader. Though many images are visual, some appeal to the sense of smell, hearing, taste, or touch or to several of the senses. For example, in "Lines Composed a Few Miles Above Tintern Abbey," the description of "waters, rolling . . . / With a soft inland murmur" appeals to two senses—sight and hearing. Look for other examples of imagery in these poems of Wordsworth's. In a chart like the one shown, list two or three examples from each poem and identify the senses they appeal to. Afterward, share your findings with the class and discuss the role of imagery in creating the mood of each poem.

Imagery	Poem/Line(s)	Sense Appealed To
"waters, rolling . . . / With a soft inland murmur."	"Lines Composed a Few Miles . . . ," lines 3–4	sight, hearing

QUICKWRITES

1. Compose a **journal entry** that Dorothy Wordsworth might have written after visiting Tintern Abbey.
2. Recall a place that you have visited both as a child and as a teenager. Describe the place in two **paragraphs** — one written from your perspective as a child and the other written from your perspective as a teenager.
3. In a short **poem,** written in either rhymed or unrhymed verse, describe your own recollections of a natural setting that left a strong impression on your "inward eye."

PORTFOLIO *Save your writing. You may want to use it later as a spring-board to a piece for your portfolio.*

ALTERNATIVE ACTIVITIES

1. With several classmates, plan and create a **mural** depicting the setting described in "Lines Composed a Few Miles Above Tintern Abbey."
2. With a partner, conduct a **debate** on the merits of experiencing nature in the city versus the merits of a more rustic setting. Use lines from the poems to support your opinions when possible.

CRITIC'S CORNER

Samuel Taylor Coleridge praised Wordsworth for capturing "the perfect truth of nature in his images and descriptions." Do you agree with this assessment of Wordsworth's writing? Cite examples from the poems to support your answer.

LITERARY LINKS

Compare Wordsworth's treatment of innocence and experience with that of William Blake. How do the two poets differ in their attitudes toward experience and loss of youth?

ACROSS THE CURRICULUM

Geography Investigate the English settings that inspired Wordsworth, particularly the Lake District and the Wye Valley. Then present your findings in a booklet titled *A Travel Guide to Wordsworth Country.* Include maps, information about current landmarks that date back to Wordsworth's time, and descriptions of the climate and terrain. If you have access to a computer, use it to arrange the text and create graphics.

WILLIAM WORDSWORTH

1770–1850

As a child, William Wordsworth spent his free time walking through the English countryside near Esthwaite Lake, taking in the sights and sounds of nature and getting to know the local farmers and shepherds. Orphaned at the age of 13, he was placed in the care of his uncles, who educated him at the best schools, including Cambridge University. Wordsworth had already developed a deep appreciation for nature and its power to comfort; by contrast, he found university life stifling and artificial.

In the summer of 1790, while on break from Cambridge, Wordsworth and a friend hiked through France and the Alps. A year later, after completing his studies, he returned to France, where his sympathy for the plight of common people made him a supporter of the French Revolution. He also met and fell in love with a young French woman, Annette Vallon, who bore him a daughter. However, financial circumstances and the outbreak of war between England and France prevented their marriage, and Wordsworth was forced to return to England. The next several years were extremely unhappy for the young poet, who suffered greatly from guilt as well as conflicting loyalties to England and France.

In 1795, Wordsworth and his beloved sister, Dorothy, settled for a time in the southwestern county of Dorset, where they began their long friendship with the poet Samuel Taylor Coleridge. In 1802, Wordsworth married Mary Hutchinson, whom he had known since childhood.

Although Wordsworth continued writing throughout his long life, his most celebrated poems were written before 1807. Wordsworth's poetic genius was officially recognized when he was appointed poet laureate in 1843, an honor he held until his death seven years later at the age of 80.

OTHER WORKS "My Heart Leaps Up," "The Tables Turned," "Ode: Intimations of Immortality," "The Solitary Reaper"

LASERLINKS
- *ART GALLERY*

PREVIEWING

POETRY

Kubla Khan

Samuel Taylor Coleridge

PERSONAL CONNECTION

Have you ever had a dream so vivid that you wanted to write it down or tell someone about it? Were you able to capture the mood of your dream when you retold it? Discuss your experiences with your classmates.

BIOGRAPHICAL/LITERARY CONNECTION

Samuel Taylor Coleridge was an influential poet, critic, and philosopher who, like his good friend William Wordsworth, was a leading figure in the English romantic movement. Like other poets of this era, Coleridge responded to nature with intense emotion. In poems such as "Kubla Khan," he wrote enthusiastically not only about the beauty and serenity of nature but also about its savagery and wildness.

The circumstances surrounding the composition of "Kubla Khan" are almost as well-known as the poem itself. According to Coleridge, he had been reading about the building of a summer palace for Kublai Khan, the great 13th-century Mongol ruler, when he fell asleep in his chair as a result of a painkilling drug he had taken. In his sleep, Coleridge later reported, the images of the poem "rose up before him as *things*, . . . without any sensation or consciousness of effort." When he awoke, he began writing the poem down, but at line 54 he was interrupted by someone who needed to see him on business. When he returned to the poem, he was unable to remember the rest of his dream. He therefore called the lines he had written a "fragment" and "a vision in a dream."

READING CONNECTION

Reading Poetry Aloud Most poetry is meant to be heard, and the dreamlike "Kubla Khan" is no exception. After you have read the poem silently, try reading it aloud. As you do, listen for **alliteration** (the repetition of initial consonant sounds) and for **onomatopoeia** (the use of words, like *buzz* and *murmur,* whose sounds echo their meanings). Consider how these and other sound devices enhance the effect of the poem.

Kublai Khan, Chinese silk album leaf by unknown artist, Yuan Dynasty. The Granger Collection, New York.

LASERLINKS
• *LITERARY CONNECTION*

Samuel Taylor Coleridge

Kubla

In Xanadu did Kubla Khan
A stately pleasure dome decree:
Where Alph, the sacred river, ran
Through caverns measureless to man
Down to a sunless sea.
So twice five miles of fertile ground
With walls and towers were girdled round:
And there were gardens bright with sinuous rills,
Where blossomed many an incense-bearing tree;
And here were forests ancient as the hills,
Enfolding sunny spots of greenery.

But oh! that deep romantic chasm which slanted
Down the green hill athwart a cedarn cover!
A savage place! as holy and enchanted
As e'er beneath a waning moon was haunted
By woman wailing for her demon lover!
And from this chasm, with ceaseless turmoil seething,
As if this earth in fast thick pants were breathing,
A mighty fountain momently was forced:
Amid whose swift half-intermitted burst
Huge fragments vaulted like rebounding hail,
Or chaffy grain beneath the thresher's flail:
And 'mid these dancing rocks at once and ever
It flung up momently the sacred river.
Five miles meandering with a mazy motion
Through wood and dale the sacred river ran,
Then reached the caverns measureless to man,
And sank in tumult to a lifeless ocean:
And 'mid this tumult Kubla heard from far
Ancestral voices prophesying war!
The shadow of the dome of pleasure
Floated midway on the waves;
Where was heard the mingled measure
From the fountain and the caves.
It was a miracle of rare device,
A sunny pleasure dome with caves of ice!

A damsel with a dulcimer
In a vision once I saw:

GUIDE FOR READING

1 Xanadu (zăn′ə-do͞o′): Shangdu, one of Kublai Khan's residences in what is now northern China.

8 sinuous rills: winding streams.

13 athwart a cedarn cover: across a grove of cedar trees.

19 momently: at every moment.

20 intermitted: interrupted.

30 What does this line suggest about Kubla's destiny?

35 device: design.

37 dulcimer: a stringed musical instrument played with small hammers.

Khan

It was an Abyssinian maid,
And on her dulcimer she played,
Singing of Mount Abora.
Could I revive within me
Her symphony and song,
To such a deep delight 'twould win me,
That with music loud and long,
I would build that dome in air,
That sunny dome! those caves of ice!
And all who heard should see them there,
And all should cry, Beware! Beware!
His flashing eyes, his floating hair!
Weave a circle round him thrice,
And close your eyes with holy dread,
For he on honeydew hath fed,
And drunk the milk of Paradise.

39 Abyssinian: from Abyssinia, now called Ethiopia.

41 Mount Abora: a legendary earthly paradise like Kubla Khan's.

46 What would the speaker do if he were able? What do you think the Abyssinian maid symbolizes?

48 Note in the following lines what effect the speaker's song and appearance will have on others.

53 honeydew: an ideally sweet or luscious substance.

54 What kind of experience would it be to drink "the milk of Paradise"?

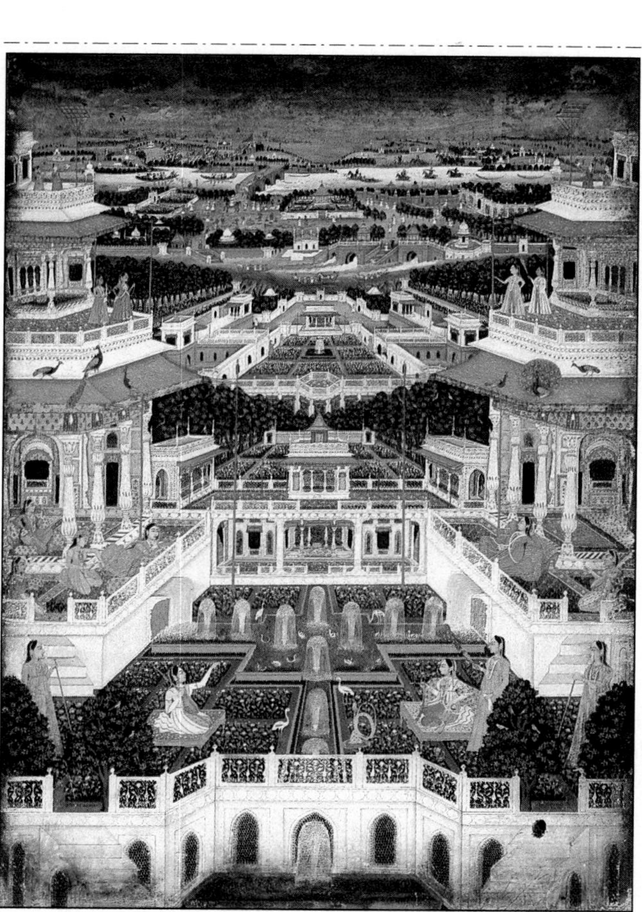

In a Harem Garden (about 1765), attributed to Faiz Allah of Faizabad, Mughal empire. Opaque watercolor on paper. The David Collection, Copenhagen, Denmark.

RESPONDING OPTIONS

FROM PERSONAL RESPONSE *TO* CRITICAL ANALYSIS

REFLECT **1.** In your notebook, make a quick sketch showing your impression of the pleasure dome. Compare your vision with your classmates' interpretations.

RETHINK **2.** How would you describe the world of Kubla Khan?

Consider
- the description of Xanadu (lines 6–11)
- the description of the chasm (lines 12–16)
- the description of the sacred river (lines 17–28)

3. Which lines and images in the poem seem most dreamlike to you?

4. Which do you think contributes more to the beauty of Kubla Khan's pleasure dome—human effort or nature?

5. Reread lines 37–54. Why would those who heard the speaker's music cry, "Beware! Beware!"?

RELATE **6.** The world represented in "Kubla Khan" is strange and exotic, even magical. Think about modern movies, books, and television shows that feature magical or unusual situations. Do you think people today are still fascinated by the exotic?

LITERARY CONCEPTS

Comprehending the **structure** of a poem—the sequence of thoughts and images that work together to convey its meaning—can help a reader to understand the poem better. "Kubla Khan" can be divided into three parts, which might be called the thesis, the antithesis, and the synthesis. The first part presents a vision of a paradise, the second provides a sinister and turbulent contrast, and the third introduces another vision and pulls together the first two sections, showing that the speaker who can build such a dome "in air" can also inspire a "holy dread." Where do you think the divisions between these three parts are in the poem? How does this structure help create the poem's meaning?

ANOTHER PATHWAY

This poem contains a curious blend of images of lush natural beauty and images of sinister, dark mystery. With a partner, create a chart like the one shown, listing images of beauty and more sinister or savage images. Discuss how these contrasting images affected you as you read the poem. Why do you think the poet used such contradictory images?

Beautiful Images	Sinister Images
sunny spots of greenery	a sunless sea

QUICKWRITES

1. Coleridge called "Kubla Khan" a fragment. Write an **outline** for a possible continuation of the poem, using the fragment as a springboard for the actions that might later take place.
2. Write the text for a **travel brochure** inviting vacationers to visit Xanadu. Include sketches of illustrations that you would use, providing a caption for each.
3. For five days, keep a **journal** in which you record what you remember about your dreams. Describe your dreams as vividly as possible.

PORTFOLIO *Save your writing. You may want to use it later as a springboard to a piece for your portfolio.*

ALTERNATIVE ACTIVITIES

1. Alone or with a small group of classmates, create a **dance** based on a section of "Kubla Khan," using the poem's imagery for your inspiration. Through your movements, try to capture some of the poem's mystery, power, and dreamlike quality.
2. Create a **collage** of the poem's strong images. Try to capture the mood of the poem in your collage.

CRITIC'S CORNER

Algernon Charles Swinburne, a noted 19th-century English poet and critic, wrote, "In reading it ["Kubla Khan"] we seem rapt into that paradise . . . where music and color and perfume were one, where you could hear the hues and see the harmonies of heaven." Do you agree? Reread the poem to help you decide.

ACROSS THE CURRICULUM

Science To ease Coleridge's severe pain from physical ailments, doctors prescribed laudanum—a solution of opium in alcohol. Coleridge eventually developed an addiction to the drug, with which he struggled for the rest of his life. Research the use of laudanum and some of the other medical practices of the late 18th and early 19th centuries. Present your findings in an oral report.

SAMUEL TAYLOR COLERIDGE

1772–1834

As a schoolboy, Coleridge was precocious, reading for amusement the most difficult passages of the ancient Roman poet Virgil. Although already a devoted scholar when he entered Cambridge University, Coleridge did not care for college life and at one point left to enlist in a cavalry unit called the Light Dragoons. When his escapade was discovered by his brothers, he was promptly returned to school; but he left Cambridge in 1794 without having received a degree.

That year, Coleridge met the author Robert Southey, and together they dreamed about establishing an ideal community in the United States on the banks of the Susquehanna River. Their community was to be a pantisocracy, a society ruled equally by all its members. Southey backed out of the project, however, and their dream was never realized.

In 1795 Coleridge had the extraordinary good fortune to meet William Wordsworth. They became close friends, traveling and writing together and often helping each other with their poetry. *Lyrical Ballads,* the joint collection they published in 1798, included Coleridge's famous poem "The Rime of the Ancient Mariner."

Most of Coleridge's best poetry was written early in his career. Later he turned to philosophy and literary criticism, becoming the most influential literary critic of the romantic movement. In his later years, Coleridge moved in with a Dr. Gillman at Highgate, north of London. The doctor helped him control an addiction to opium, and Coleridge seemed more at peace with himself. His rooms became a center of conversation for an admiring crowd that dubbed him the Sage of Highgate.

OTHER WORKS "The Rime of the Ancient Mariner," "Christabel," "Dejection: An Ode"

Milestones in British Literature

Jane Austen

PRIDE & PREJUDICE

Imagine that you are living in England around the turn of the 19th century, standing on the threshold of adulthood. You are a woman, so your only career option is marriage. The match you make will reflect your values and desires—and determine the manner in which you spend the rest of your life.

This is the world of *Pride and Prejudice,* Jane Austen's insightful and clever examination of English manners and morals. The novel centers on the roundabout courtship of a proud young man, Fitzwilliam Darcy, and a spirited but judgmental young woman, Elizabeth Bennet, who fall in dislike at first sight. Elizabeth's and Darcy's friends and families provide a cast of characters whose traits Jane Austen depicts with irony and humor. For example, the silly schemes with which Elizabeth's mother—who has no real understanding of good manners, good breeding, or good sense—tries to ensure that her daughters will marry well cause Elizabeth no end of painful embarrassment. Elizabeth's good-natured

The Cloakroom, Clifton Assembly Rooms, *Rolinda Sharples (1794–1838). City of Bristol Museum and Art Gallery, Bristol, Great Britain.*

Painting of Jane Austen by her sister, 1804. Robert Harding Picture Library.

but ineffectual father contributes to the near ruin of the family by neglecting to rein in his wife and younger daughters. Elizabeth's best friend astonishes her when she agrees to marry a pompous suitor of Elizabeth's not for love, or even riches, but for security.

In the course of the novel, Austen exposes the ever-changing nature of public opinion, ridicules the assumed superiority of the upper class, and shows how prejudice can lead to premature and even dangerous conclusions. She gently but firmly chides two young lovers who are so mild and polite in expressing their feelings that they almost lose each other, and she celebrates the independent spirit that leads two unlikely lovers to forge a bond of enduring joy.

Soon after *Pride and Prejudice* was published, critics began comparing Jane Austen to Shakespeare. They admired her command of language, her use of comic fools, and her dramatic presentation of characters in action. In addition, they noticed a kinship between the hard-won affection of Elizabeth and Darcy and the reluctant love of Beatrice and Benedick in Shakespeare's *Much Ado About Nothing.*

Unlike Shakespeare's lovers, however, Austen's characters are not tricked into love. Instead, they hammer out their own romance, allowing for shared values and mutual respect. Their integrity, independence, and well-deserved love has made *Pride and Prejudice* a perennial favorite among novels as well as a classic celebration of joyous love between independent equals.

A Darcy-like character wearing gentleman's clothing typical of the day

WRITING ABOUT
LITERATURE

FINDING MEANING

What did Wordsworth's walk by the daffodils mean to him? What attitude does Shelley seem to have toward Ozymandias? When you read a poem, its message may not be clear to you at first. You may need to reread the poem two or three times, look up words in the dictionary, and let images form in your mind. These habits can help you find poems that speak to you. In the following pages you will

- learn how writers use denotation and connotation
- interpret a poem by studying your own response to it
- uncover meaning in the world around you

Writer's Style: Denotation and Connotation One way writers create meaning is by choosing their words carefully. When they select a word, they think of both its denotation, or literal meaning, and its connotation, the attitudes and feelings associated with it.

Read the Literature

Read the excerpts below to see how the connotations of words can affect the mood of a poem, as well as its meaning.

Literature Models

Negative Connotations
How would the effect change if Shelley had used the word *smile* instead of *sneer*? What other words with negative connotations can you find?

. . . Near them, on the sand,
Half sunk, a shattered visage lies, whose frown,
And wrinkled lip, and sneer of cold command,
Tell that its sculptor well those passions read

Percy Bysshe Shelley,
from "Ozymandias"

Positive Connotations
What mood do these lines suggest to you? Which words help to convey this mood?

The beauty of the morning; silent, bare,
Ships, towers, domes, theaters, and temples lie
Open unto the fields, and to the sky;
All bright and glittering in the smokeless air.

William Wordsworth,
from "Composed upon Westminster Bridge,
September 3, 1802"

Connect to Life

When people want to make something sound good, they use words that have positive connotations. Advertisers do this when they're writing ads to convince you to buy something, and you probably use connotation when you try to convince a friend that the movie you've suggested will prove to be the ideal choice.

Magazine Article

Let's say you're trying to peddle some fake flowers. Do you call yourself a fake-flower peddler? Of course not; you're a *floral marketer*, artificial-flower division.

Now you look at your product—sometimes quite beautiful, petals made of silk or whatever—and you ask yourself, "Why *artificial*?" That's a word that turns buyers off. You brood about that, and come up with a fresh-as-a-daisy answer: you'll create a market for *permanent flowers*.

William Safire,
from "On Language," *The New York Times Magazine*, January 16, 1994

Word Choice
What do you think of when you hear the word *fake*? Why might a salesperson want to call a product *permanent* rather than *artificial*?

Try Your Hand: Using Connotation

1. **Write Sentence Pairs** Use words with similar denotations and different connotations to write an insult and a compliment that mean basically the same thing. For example: "I am determined. He is stubborn." Create three sentence pairs.
2. **Change the Meaning** Use connotation to write two different descriptions of the same kind of food.
3. **Make It Convincing** Write a paragraph, an advertisement, or a speech in which you use connotation to make an undesirable proposition sound great.

SkillBuilder

Using Sensory Details

At its best, reading can make you feel like you're visiting another place. Sensory details—words that appeal to the sense of sight, smell, taste, touch, or hearing—help writers provide readers with just such experiences. They also help make writing clearer and more engaging. Notice which senses this excerpt from Coleridge's "Kubla Khan" appeals to.

And there were gardens bright with sinuous rills, / Where blossomed many an incense-bearing tree, / And here were forests ancient as the hills, / Enfolding sunny spots of greenery.

When you're writing, decide which senses are important to the experience you're describing. Also, consider the connotations of the words you use in sensory descriptions. For example, the word *moist* creates a different sensory experience than the word *clammy*.

APPLYING WHAT YOU'VE LEARNED
Use sensory details to write brief descriptions of the following experiences:

- walking at night
- being alone in your home
- waiting to get a test back

For more information on descriptive writing, see pages 1226–1227 of the Writing Handbook.

WRITING ABOUT LITERATURE

Personal Response

You've probably encountered things in life—books, movies, real-world situations—that you don't immediately understand. When you look again, you may notice details that help you become aware of what's going on. A third look may uncover even more clues. Over time, you may be able to interpret what was once a mystery to you.

GUIDED ASSIGNMENT

Write a Process Response On the next few pages you'll read a poem several times, note how your responses to it change, and describe in an essay how your ideas developed.

Student's Notes

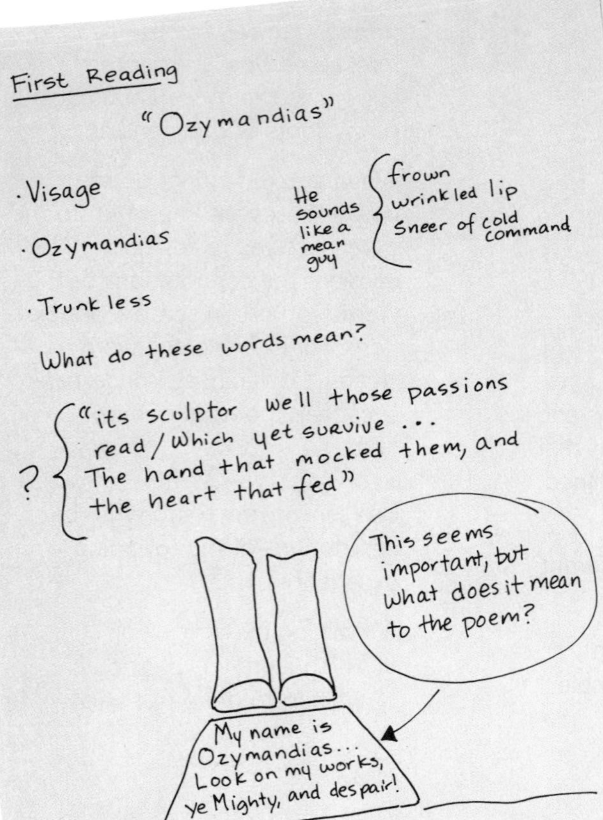

First Reading
"Ozymandias"
· Visage
· Ozymandias
· Trunk less
He sounds like a mean guy
frown
wrinkled lip
Sneer of cold command
What do these words mean?
"its sculptor well those passions read / Which yet survive . . . The hand that mocked them, and the heart that fed"
?
This seems important, but what does it mean to the poem?
My name is Ozymandias... Look on my works, ye Mighty, and despair!

1 Prewrite and Explore

Choose a poem from Unit Four that intrigues you. As you read the poem, document your responses to it, including the words or phrases that triggered your reactions. You may want to record questions and impressions in your notebook, or you may want to use some other method, such as a chart, to keep track of your thinking. Ask yourself the following questions as you read.

- Which phrases or images are especially beautiful or strange?
- What don't I understand?
- Which words carry strong positive or negative connotations?
- What do I think is going on?
- What was the poet trying to say?

REREAD

When you read the poem again, try to answer some of the questions raised in the first reading. You will probably want to pay attention to repetition in the poem and to look up unfamiliar words in the dictionary. Continue to document your responses, noting any new questions that have arisen.

2 Interpret

What conclusions have you come to after rereading? Formulate your interpretation of the poem, reading it one more time if you need to. The model below shows how one student used previous responses to figure out what a poem means.

Student's Notes

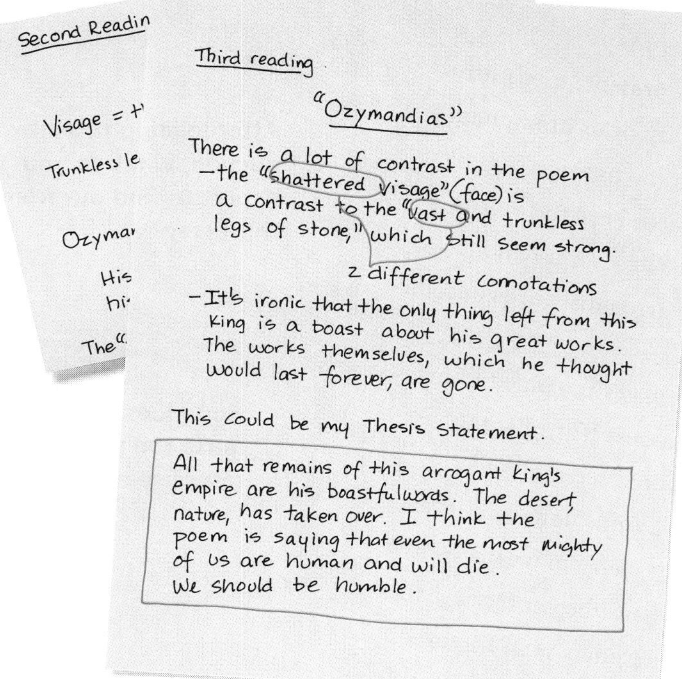
Second Readin

Visage = t

Trunkless le

Ozymar

His
hi

The "

Third reading

"Ozymandias"

There is a lot of contrast in the poem
—the "shattered visage" (face) is a contrast to the "vast and trunkless legs of stone," which still seem strong.
2 different connotations

—It's ironic that the only thing left from this king is a boast about his great works. The works themselves, which he thought would last forever, are gone.

This could be my Thesis statement.

All that remains of this arrogant king's empire are his boastful words. The desert, nature, has taken over. I think the poem is saying that even the most mighty of us are human and will die. We should be humble.

3 Draft and Share

In a draft, discuss your interpretation and the process you used to arrive at it. Remember to do the following things:

- State your main idea in the first paragraph.
- Refer back to your notes to help you describe each stage of your response.
- Support your statements with examples from the poem.
- Refer to the Skillbuilder on Writing a Conclusion for tips on closing your essay.

- How did my response change with each reading?
- Why do you agree or disagree with my impressions?
- Where do I need to provide more support for my ideas?

SkillBuilder

WRITER'S CRAFT

Writing a Conclusion
The conclusion of a piece of writing should follow the logic of what has come before and should leave the reader feeling satisfied that the issues brought up have been discussed. Some suggestions on how to conclude your writing are listed below.

Restate Your Thesis If in the body of your essay you have presented examples to back up your main idea, a reader may benefit from reading the thesis statement again.

Generalize About the Information You Have Given
If you have presented quite a bit of detailed information in your body paragraphs, you may want to end by drawing conclusions and making generalizations about the information.

Ask a Question If you'd like your reader to use the information you've presented to think about a certain topic, you may want to conclude by asking a question.

APPLYING WHAT YOU'VE LEARNED
Use one of the above suggestions to conclude your essay in a satisfying way.

WRITING HANDBOOK

For more information on writing conclusions, see pages 1228–1229 of the Writing Handbook.

4 Revise and Edit

Consider sharing your final version with other students who wrote about the same poem you did. Discuss where your interpretations differ and reflect on the reasons for the differences. The Standards for Evaluation below and the Grammar in Context feature on the opposite page can also give you tips on what to look for as you revise.

Student's Final Draft

The Sands of Time

"Ozymandias" by Percy Bysshe Shelley presents a beautiful and sad reminder that even the most mighty of us are human and that we all become insignificant with the passage of time. Once I understood the poem, I could almost hear the words dying out in the desert wind, but it took me several readings to fully see the contrast between the king's arrogant words and the humble end they have come to.

After reading this introduction, what do you expect to find out from this essay?

When I first read the poem, several images remained in my mind. I could picture the "vast and trunkless legs of stone" standing in the desert on a pedestal. I could see the huge expanse of "boundless and bare" desert with "lone and level sands" stretching far away. These images left me with a feeling of vastness and loneliness. Although when I began reading the poem I didn't know who or what Ozymandias was, I figured out he was an ancient king. I also figured out he was probably a cruel and arrogant person because of the words used to describe him: *frown, wrinkled lip,* and *sneer of cold command.*

How does this student make the process of response clear?

Standards for Evaluation

A process response essay
- introduces its subject and presents the reader's reaction in the introduction
- shows changes in the responses over several readings
- supports responses with examples from the poem
- concludes in a way that follows the logic of the rest of the essay

Grammar in Context

Dangling Modifiers A dangling modifier is one that doesn't seem to be related to any word in the sentence. When you use a modifier to describe your response to a poem, make sure your sentence names who or what is being modified. Otherwise, you will end up with a dangling modifier, which can distort meaning or produce unintentional humor. What is the dangling modifier in the sentence below?

> On the third reading, the sentence structure of "Ozymandias" reinforces its meaning.

Dangling modifiers often appear at the beginning of a sentence. You can correct a dangling modifier by rewriting the sentence to tell whom or what the modifier refers to. Try to place the modifying word, phrase, or clause as close as possible to the word it modifies.

> On the third reading, I realized that the sentence structure of "Ozymandias" reinforces the poem's meaning.

For more information about correcting dangling modifiers, see page 1274 of the Grammar Handbook.

Try Your Hand: Correcting Dangling Modifiers

Read the following paragraph. On a separate piece of paper, rewrite those sentences that contain dangling modifiers.

> Buried in the sand, the artist who carved the sneer and frown must have had reason to be afraid of the king. However, time has made this tyrant safe. Reading the poem, the image of his "vast and trunkless legs" shows both how powerful he was and how meaningless this power became over time. Although Ozymandias sounds like an arrogant and cruel king, somehow I felt sorry for him the more I read this poem. I felt a little sorry for all humans.

SkillBuilder

GRAMMAR FROM WRITING

Avoiding Misplaced Modifiers

Sometimes a modifier and the word it modifies are placed so far apart that the intended meaning is unclear. This situation results in a misplaced modifier, and the effects are occasionally humorous.

I learned that Samuel Coleridge was the last of ten children from my teacher.

In the above example, the phrase *from my teacher* appears to modify *children*, but it was meant to modify *learned*. To avoid misplaced modifiers, put the modifier as close as possible to the word it modifies.

I learned from my teacher that Samuel Coleridge was the last of ten children.

APPLYING WHAT YOU'VE LEARNED
Correct the misplaced modifiers by putting them closer to the word they modify.

- Mary Wollstonecraft Godwin married the 24-year-old Percy Bysshe Shelley at the age of 19.
- The friendships in movies she and Shelley had with other romantic writers have been discussed.

GRAMMAR HANDBOOK

For more information on misplaced modifiers, see page 1274 of the Grammar Handbook.

GUNN WALL
HARDWARE
Dutch Boy
Paints
HARDWARE
UEN CAFE
國
華
699 JACKSON
JACKSON

R E A D I N G
THE WORLD

LOOKING CLOSELY

Whether you're reading a poem or walking around an unfamiliar neighborhood, there's almost always more to art and life than first meets the eye. Just as you did in your process response, you can usually figure out what you're looking at or where you are by asking yourself questions, looking again, and thinking things through.

View Look quickly at the scene shown on these pages. Then jot down your first responses. What did you see? What details did you notice?

Interpret Where do you think this scene takes place? What do you think is going on? Who do you think lives nearby?

Discuss Look more closely at the scene. What details are you noticing for the first time? In a group, discuss how your first impression may have changed and why. Refer to the SkillBuilder at the right for help with analyzing details.

SkillBuilder

CRITICAL THINKING

Analyzing Details

Analyzing is a way of thinking that involves taking something apart, examining the parts, and using what you've learned about them to explain the whole subject or idea.

When you're analyzing a picture or a scene, the parts you want to examine are the details. You may get an overall impression when you first view an image, but until you look closely at a particular component, you won't know if that general impression is correct.

Questions like the following may help you identify important details in an image:

- What kinds of objects are present? What do you know about those objects?
- What is in the background?
- What kinds of people can be seen? Are they young? old? alone? in groups? What are they doing?
- What is there to read? What does it say?

APPLYING WHAT YOU'VE LEARNED
With a partner, find a scene in a book or magazine. What's your first impression of it? Analyze the scene, making a list of details you notice and discussing each one. When you can use what you learned from the details to explain the scene, present your analysis to another set of partners.

PART 2 # *Embracing the Imagination*

Romantic poets passionately embraced the concept of creative self-expression, giving free rein to their imaginations in an effort to convey their personal visions of love and life. In this part of Unit Four, you will read poems in which writers imagine what it would be like to embody the ocean's majesty, to soar and sing like a bird, and to defy the ravages of time. As you read these poems, consider what images your own imagination might conjure up as a means of creative self-expression.

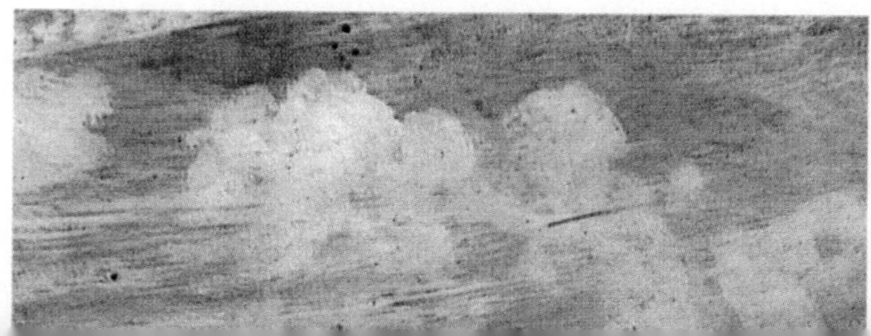

PREVIEWING

POETRY

Selected Poems

George Gordon, Lord Byron

PERSONAL CONNECTION

Think of someone in your family, school, or community who conveys strong emotions when speaking. Does the person usually express the emotions in ordinary conversation, or does he or she do so in speeches, sermons, or other public presentations? Do you think the ability to express powerful emotions is an advantage or a disadvantage? Write your thoughts in your notebook.

BIOGRAPHICAL/LITERARY CONNECTION

During the romantic period, no English poet achieved greater popularity than George Gordon, Lord Byron. Because the heroes he created in many of his works were rebellious, moody figures of great passion and strong will, Byron was extolled during most of the 19th century as the ideal example of the romantic spirit. He attracted admirers throughout Europe, and his influence was felt not only in the poetry of his many imitators but in art and music as well.

Even though Byron became a symbol of romanticism, his poetry was rooted in 18th-century forms, as is evident in the first two poems that you will read. He avoided, and actually scorned, the experimental poetry of his contemporaries; but he was nevertheless decidedly romantic in his emphasis on freedom and the individual and in his expression of powerful emotions. In the words of one of his university instructors, Byron was "a young gentleman of tumultuous passions."

Byron's immense popularity originated with the publication of the first two sections of his poetic travelogue *Childe Harold's Pilgrimage* in 1812. The young poet acquired the material for this work and several other poems during an adventurous two-year excursion through Portugal, Spain, Malta, Greece, and Asia Minor. For 19th-century readers, part of the appeal of *Childe Harold's Pilgrimage* was the excitement of reading about countries or scenery they had never seen.

READING CONNECTION

Understanding Apostrophe The romantic poets frequently used **apostrophe,** a literary device associated with the expression of powerful emotions. Apostrophe is a figure of speech in which an object, an abstract quality, or an absent or imaginary person is addressed directly, as if present and able to understand. The excerpt from *Childe Harold's Pilgrimage* on the following pages contains an apostrophe to the ocean. As you read it, consider the effect the poet creates by the use of apostrophe rather than simple description of the ocean.

Lord Byron (1813), Thomas Phillips. Oil on canvas, The Granger Collection, New York.

SHE WALKS IN BEAUTY

GEORGE GORDON, LORD BYRON

Comus, Disguised as a Rustic, Addresses the Lady in the Wood (1801-1802), William Blake. Henry E. Huntington Library and Art Gallery, San Marino, California.

She walks in beauty, like the night
Of cloudless climes and starry skies;
And all that's best of dark and bright
Meet in her aspect and her eyes:
Thus mellowed to that tender light
Which heaven to gaudy day denies.

One shade the more, one ray the less,
Had half impaired the nameless grace
Which waves in every raven tress,
Or softly lightens o'er her face;
Where thoughts serenely sweet express
How pure, how dear their dwelling place.

And on that cheek, and o'er that brow,
So soft, so calm, yet eloquent,
The smiles that win, the tints that glow,
But tell of days in goodness spent,
A mind at peace with all below,
A heart whose love is innocent!

2 climes: regions; climates.

4 aspect: appearance.

9 tress: lock of hair.

When We Two Parted

When we two parted
In silence and tears,
Half broken-hearted
To sever for years,
Pale grew thy cheek and cold,
Colder thy kiss;
Truly that hour foretold
Sorrow to this.

The dew of the morning
Sunk chill on my brow—
It felt like the warning
Of what I feel now.
Thy vows are all broken,
And light is thy fame;
I hear thy name spoken,
And share in its shame.

They name thee before me,
A knell to mine ear;
A shudder comes o'er me—
Why wert thou so dear?
They know not I knew thee,
Who knew thee too well—
Long, long shall I rue thee,
Too deeply to tell.

In secret we met—
In silence I grieve,
That thy heart could forget,
Thy spirit deceive.
If I should meet thee
After long years,
How should I greet thee?—
With silence and tears.

18 knell: the ringing of a bell to announce a death.

23 rue: remember with feelings of sorrow; regret.

SILENCE AND TEARS.

FROM PERSONAL RESPONSE *TO* CRITICAL ANALYSIS

REFLECT **1.** Did you identify with the situation in one of these poems more than the other? Write your thoughts in your notebook.

RETHINK **2.** What kinds of relationships does the poet seem to be presenting in the two poems? Support your answer with details from the poems.

3. How would you describe the different emotions expressed by the speakers of these poems?

from Childe Harold's

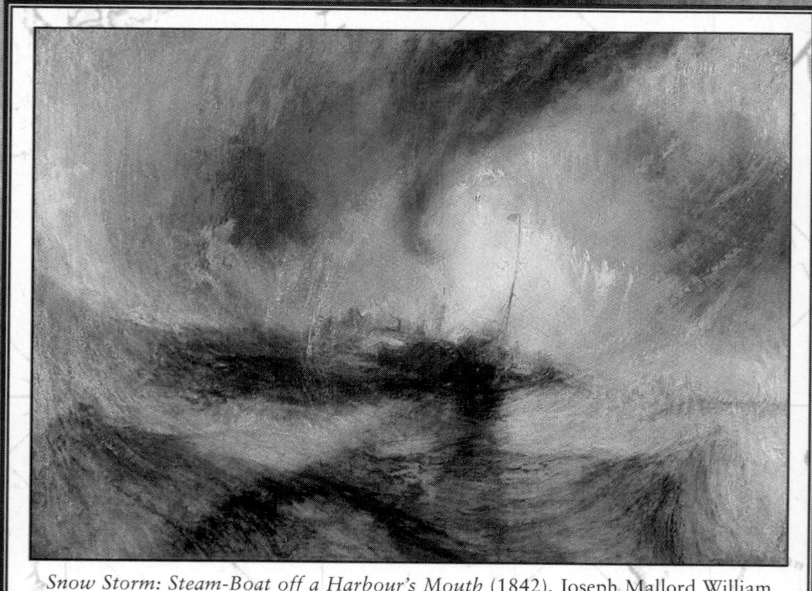

Snow Storm: Steam-Boat off a Harbour's Mouth (1842), Joseph Mallord William Turner. Clore Collection, Tate Gallery, London/Art Resource, New York.

Pilgrimage

George Gordon, Lord Byron

Apostrophe to the Ocean

There is a pleasure in the pathless woods,
There is a rapture on the lonely shore,
There is society where none intrudes,
By the deep Sea, and music in its roar:
I love not Man the less, but Nature more,
From these our interviews, in which I steal
From all I may be or have been before,
To mingle with the Universe, and feel
What I can ne'er express, yet can not all conceal.

Roll on, thou deep and dark blue Ocean, roll!
Ten thousand fleets sweep over thee in vain;
Man marks the earth with ruin, his control
Stops with the shore; upon the watery plain
The wrecks are all thy deed, nor doth remain
A shadow of man's ravage, save his own,
When, for a moment, like a drop of rain,
He sinks into thy depths with bubbling groan,
Without a grave, unknell'd, uncoffin'd, and unknown.

15 ravage: destruction.

18 unknell'd: with no announcement of his death.

His steps are not upon thy paths, thy fields
Are not a spoil for him,—thou dost arise
And shake him from thee; the vile strength he wields
For earth's destruction thou dost all despise,
Spurning him from thy bosom to the skies,
And send'st him, shivering in thy playful spray
And howling, to his Gods, where haply lies
His petty hope in some near port or bay,
And dashest him again to earth:—there let him lay.

25 haply: perhaps.

The armaments which thunderstrike the walls
Of rock-built cities, bidding nations quake
And monarchs tremble in their capitals,
The oak leviathans, whose huge ribs make
Their clay creator the vain title take
Of lord of thee and arbiter of war,—
These are thy toys, and, as the snowy flake,
They melt into thy yeast of waves, which mar
Alike the Armada's pride or spoils of Trafalgar.

Thy shores are empires, changed in all save thee—
Assyria, Greece, Rome, Carthage, what are they?
Thy waters wash'd them power while they were free,
And many a tyrant since; their shores obey
The stranger, slave, or savage; their decay
Has dried up realms to deserts:—not so thou,
Unchangeable save to thy wild waves' play;
Time writes no wrinkle on thine azure brow;
Such as creation's dawn beheld, thou rollest now.

Thou glorious mirror, where the Almighty's form
Glasses itself in tempests; in all time,
Calm or convulsed—in breeze, or gale, or storm,
Icing the pole, or in the torrid clime
Dark-heaving;—boundless, endless, and sublime—
The image of Eternity—the throne
Of the Invisible; even from out thy slime
The monsters of the deep are made; each zone
Obeys thee; thou goest forth, dread, fathomless, alone.

And I have loved thee, Ocean! and my joy
Of youthful sports was on thy breast to be
Borne, like thy bubbles, onward. From a boy
I wanton'd with thy breakers—they to me
Were a delight; and if the freshening sea
Made them a terror—'t was a pleasing fear,
For I was as it were a child of thee,
And trusted to thy billows far and near,
And laid my hand upon thy mane—as I do here.

31 oak leviathans: large ships.

32 their clay creator: humankind.

33 arbiter: a person with the power of judging or ruling.

35 yeast: turbulent froth.

36 Armada's . . . Trafalgar (trə-făl′gər): The mighty Spanish Armada was defeated by the British fleet in 1588; Trafalgar is a Spanish cape, the site of a great British naval victory over the French and Spanish in 1805.

38 Assyria . . . Carthage: four powerful ancient civilizations.

44 azure (ăzh′ər): sky blue.

47 glasses itself: is reflected.

49 torrid clime: the intensely hot regions near the equator.

53 zone: one of the five climatic regions of the earth.

54 fathomless: too deep to be measured; also, beyond comprehension.

58 wanton'd: frolicked playfully; **breakers:** large waves.

RESPONDING OPTIONS

FROM PERSONAL RESPONSE *TO* CRITICAL ANALYSIS

REFLECT 1. In your notebook, describe your reaction to Byron's use of apostrophe in this excerpt from *Childe Harold's Pilgrimage*.

RETHINK 2. What aspects of the ocean do you think the speaker admires most?

3. What different emotions does the ocean seem to inspire in the speaker?
   Consider
   - his description of the ocean's relationship to humanity
   - what he means when he calls the ocean "the throne / Of the Invisible" (lines 51–52)
   - his remembrance of his youth

4. How would you describe the ocean's relationship to other aspects of nature mentioned in the excerpt?

RELATE 5. According to the speaker, "Man marks the earth with ruin, his control / Stops with the shore." Do you think this statement is true? Give examples to support your answer.

6. Which of the three poems—"She Walks in Beauty," "When We Two Parted," or the excerpt from *Childe Harold's Pilgrimage*—do you think conveys the strongest emotions? Give reasons for your opinion.

ANOTHER PATHWAY

Work with a partner to create a chart like the one shown for each of the three poems, listing the emotions, thoughts, and wishes expressed by the poem's speaker. After you complete the three charts, discuss what seem to be the main characteristics of the speakers and the similarities and differences between them.

"She Walks in Beauty"		
Emotions	**Thoughts**	**Wishes**

LITERARY CONCEPTS

In *Childe Harold's Pilgrimage*, Byron used a verse form called the **Spenserian stanza.** Named for Edmund Spenser, who invented it for his romance *The Faerie Queene,* the Spenserian stanza consists of nine iambic lines rhyming in the pattern *ababbcbcc*. Each of the first eight lines contains five stressed syllables, and the ninth line contains six—as is shown in the last two lines of the first stanza:

˘ ˊ ˘ ˊ ˘ ˊ ˘ ˊ ˘ ˊ
To mingle with the Universe, and feel

˘ ˊ ˘ ˊ ˘ ˊ ˘ ˊ ˘ ˊ ˘ ˊ
What I can never express, yet can not all conceal.

Why do you think Byron chose to use the Spenserian stanza for *Childe Harold's Pilgrimage*? Support your ideas with examples from the poem.

QUICKWRITES

1. Write a **character sketch** conveying your impression of the woman described in "She Walks in Beauty."
2. Write **dialogue** for an imaginary conversation between the speaker of "When We Two Parted" and the person he addresses.
3. As the speaker of *Childe Harold's Pilgrimage*, write an **opinion column** for a weekly newsmagazine, expressing your views on the foibles of society.

PORTFOLIO *Save your writing. You may want to use it later as a springboard to a piece for your portfolio.*

ALTERNATIVE ACTIVITIES

1. Create **border designs** for an illuminated manuscript of "She Walks in Beauty."
2. With a partner, plan and conduct an imaginary **interview** with Lord Byron. Include questions, based on your reading of the excerpt from *Childe Harold's Pilgrimage*, about his attitudes toward society.

ART CONNECTION

Look again at the Turner seascape on page 530. What aspects of the excerpt from *Childe Harold's Pilgrimage* do you see reflected in the painting?

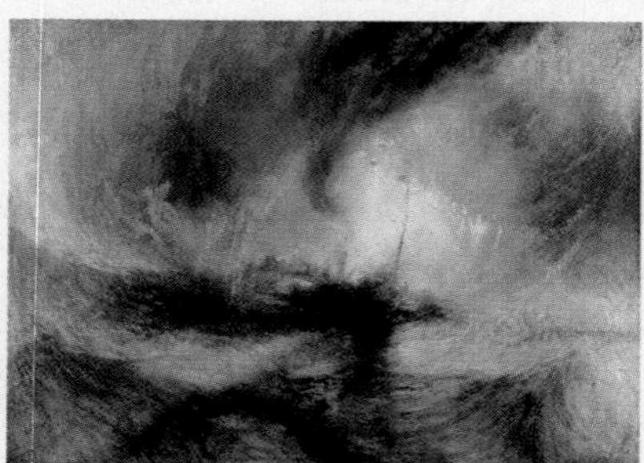

LITERARY LINKS

Like Wordsworth, Byron refers to his childhood as well as his present life in his poetry. Compare the views of childhood and adulthood presented in "Lines Composed a Few Miles Above Tintern Abbey" (page 498) and the excerpt from *Childe Harold's Pilgrimage*. What similarities and differences do you find?

THE WRITER'S STYLE

"She Walks in Beauty" was written to be set to music. What elements of the poem do you think give it a musical quality? Compare your ideas with those of your classmates.

ACROSS THE CURRICULUM

History Research the Battle of Trafalgar. Who was involved in the battle? What were its causes? What long-range effects did it have? Report your findings to the class.

GEORGE GORDON, LORD BYRON

1788–1824

Lord Byron is one of the most handsome and daring figures in literary history. Born into a family of hot-tempered soldiers, seamen, and fighters, he lived a dramatic life. He had a fierce determination to test himself physically—a response, in part, to his having been born with a clubfoot that gave him a slight limp throughout his life. At school, Byron enthusiastically engaged in vigorous sports, including swimming, boxing, riding, and fencing. Later, while traveling in Europe, he frequently sought out dangerous ventures that frightened his companions.

At the age of 10, Byron inherited an ancestral estate from his great-uncle—and with it the title of sixth Baron Byron. He was only in his 20s when the first parts of *Childe Harold's Pilgrimage* were published and, as he put it, "I awoke one morning and found myself famous." Unfortunately, he had a reckless and dissipated lifestyle that often left him in debt and suffering from extreme melancholy. He entered into many romantic alliances throughout his life, but his one marriage lasted only a year. The rumors arising from its failure caused a decline in Byron's popularity in England, and in 1816 he left the country for good, living first in Switzerland and then for several years in Italy, where he began work on what was to be his masterpiece, *Don Juan*. In 1823, impelled by his love of the Greek people, he embarked on a mission to help them in their war for independence from Turkish rule. While training soldiers, he contracted a fever and died shortly thereafter, just after his 36th birthday. Byron is still regarded as a national hero in Greece, not for his poetry but for his dedication to the country's revolution.

OTHER WORKS "So We'll Go No More A-Roving," "On This Day I Complete My Thirty-Sixth Year"

PREVIEWING

POETRY

Selected Poems

Percy Bysshe Shelley

PERSONAL CONNECTION

What aspirations do people your age tend to have? Survey ten students in your class to find out some of their hopes and dreams for the future. Compare their responses. Are their aspirations practical and realistic? lofty and idealistic? Discuss your findings with your classmates.

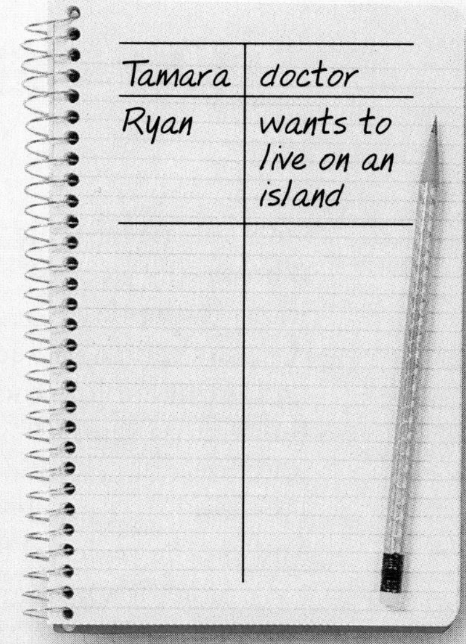

BIOGRAPHICAL/LITERARY CONNECTION

Percy Bysshe Shelley was an idealist and a nonconformist who passionately opposed all injustice and dreamed of changing the world through love, imagination, and poetry. Now ranked among the greatest of the English romantic poets, Shelley was rebuked by his contemporaries for his radical views and was unable to publish some of his best poetry.

As a young man, Shelley fiercely opposed the oppression and poverty he saw in places like Ireland and Wales. When his efforts at reform met with resistance and failure, however, he turned to poetry as a means of expressing and fulfilling his aspirations. He wrote with the conviction that through the imagination of the poet and the power of love, humanity could perceive and transcend the evils of society. In his essay *A Defense of Poetry,* Shelley declared that "poets are the unacknowledged legislators of the world."

Shelley was a skillful craftsman who explored a wide array of poetic forms and rhythmic patterns in his work. "Ozymandias" is a sonnet in which he experiments with rhyme and rhythm. "Ode to the West Wind" and "To a Skylark" are examples of the **ode**—an exalted, complex lyric that develops a dignified theme, such as the celebration of an element of nature.

WRITING CONNECTION

What are some of your own aspirations for the future? What obstacles or limits, if any, might you encounter in your attempts to fulfill your dreams? Jot down some of your thoughts in your notebook. Then, as you read these poems, note the ways in which they give expression to human aspirations.

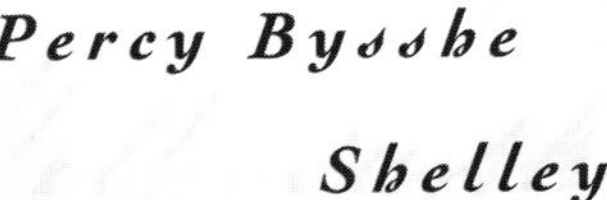

Percy Bysshe Shelley

Ozymandias

I met a traveler from an antique land
Who said: Two vast and trunkless legs of stone
Stand in the desert . . . Near them, on the sand,
Half sunk, a shattered visage lies, whose frown,
And wrinkled lip, and sneer of cold command,
Tell that its sculptor well those passions read
Which yet survive, stamped on these lifeless things,
The hand that mocked them, and the heart that fed:
And on the pedestal these words appear:
"My name is Ozymandias, king of kings:
Look on my works, ye Mighty, and despair!"
Nothing beside remains. Round the decay
Of that colossal wreck, boundless and bare
The lone and level sands stretch far away.

GUIDE FOR READING

2 trunkless legs: legs separated from the rest of the body.

4 visage (vĭz′ĭj): face.

6 those passions: that is, Ozymandias' passions.

8 This line may be paraphrased as "The sculptor's hand, which mocked the passions of the king, and the king's heart, which fed those passions."

10 Ozymandias (ŏz′ĭ-măn′dyəs): the Greek form of "Usermare," a title of the Egyptian pharaoh Rameses II, who reigned from 1304 to 1237 B.C.

11 What is ironic about the boast inscribed on the pedestal?

FROM PERSONAL RESPONSE *TO* CRITICAL ANALYSIS

REFLECT

1. Does this poem remind you of anything you have seen in your own experiences? Jot down your thoughts in your notebook.

RETHINK

2. How would you describe Ozymandias? Use details from the poem to support your answer.
3. What message about life do you think is conveyed in this poem?
   Consider
   - the words Ozymandias had carved on the pedestal
   - the aspirations Ozymandias seems to have had
   - what has happened to the statue

Ode to the West Wind

Percy Bysshe Shelley

Detail of *Cloud Study* (about 1821), John Constable, R.A. Oil on canvas, Victoria and Albert Museum, London/Art Resource, New York.

I

O wild West Wind, thou breath of Autumn's being,
Thou, from whose unseen presence the leaves dead
Are driven, like ghosts from an enchanter fleeing,

Yellow, and black, and pale, and hectic red,
Pestilence-stricken multitudes: O thou,
Who chariotest to their dark wintry bed

The wingéd seeds, where they lie cold and low,
Each like a corpse within its grave, until
Thine azure sister of the Spring shall blow

Her clarion o'er the dreaming earth, and fill
(Driving sweet buds like flocks to feed in air)
With living hues and odors plain and hill:

Wild Spirit, which art moving everywhere;
Destroyer and preserver; hear, oh, hear!

4 hectic: feverish.

9 sister . . . Spring: the reviving south wind of spring.

10 clarion: a trumpet with a clear, ringing tone.

II

Thou on whose stream, mid the steep sky's commotion,
Loose clouds like earth's decaying leaves are shed,
Shook from the tangled bough of Heaven and Ocean,

Angels of rain and lightning: there are spread
On the blue surface of thine aëry surge,
Like the bright hair uplifted from the head

Of some fierce Maenad, even from the dim verge
Of the horizon to the zenith's height,
The locks of the approaching storm. Thou dirge

Of the dying year, to which this closing night
Will be the dome of a vast sepulcher,
Vaulted with all thy congregated might

Of vapors, from whose solid atmosphere
Black rain, and fire, and hail will burst: oh, hear!

III

Thou who didst waken from his summer dreams
The blue Mediterranean, where he lay,
Lulled by the coil of his crystálline streams,

Beside a pumice isle in Baiae's bay,
And saw in sleep old palaces and towers
Quivering within the wave's intenser day,

All overgrown with azure moss and flowers
So sweet, the sense faints picturing them! Thou
For whose path the Atlantic's level powers

Cleave themselves into chasms, while far below
The sea-blooms and the oozy woods which wear
The sapless foliage of the ocean, know

Thy voice, and suddenly grow gray with fear,
And tremble and despoil themselves: oh, hear!

IV

If I were a dead leaf thou mightest bear;
If I were a swift cloud to fly with thee;
A wave to pant beneath thy power, and share

18 angels: messengers.

19 aëry: airy.

20–23 The speaker is saying that the clouds lie in streaks, looking like the streaming hair of a maenad (mē′năd′)—a wildly dancing female worshiper of Dionysus, the Greek god of wine.

23 dirge: funeral song.

25 sepulcher (sĕp′əl-kər): tomb.

31 crystálline (krĭs-tăl′ĭn) **streams:** the different-colored transparent currents of the Mediterranean Sea.

32 pumice (pŭm′ĭs): a light volcanic rock; **Baiae's** (bī′ēz′) **bay:** the Bay of Naples, site of the ancient Roman resort of Baiae.

37 level powers: surface.

The impulse of thy strength, only less free
Than thou, O uncontrollable! If even
I were as in my boyhood, and could be

The comrade of thy wanderings over Heaven,
As then, when to outstrip thy skyey speed
Scarce seemed a vision; I would ne'er have striven

As thus with thee in prayer in my sore need.
Oh, lift me as a wave, a leaf, a cloud!
I fall upon the thorns of life! I bleed!

A heavy weight of hours has chained and bowed
One too like thee: tameless, and swift, and proud.

V

Make me thy lyre, even as the forest is:
What if my leaves are falling like its own!
The tumult of thy mighty harmonies

Will take from both a deep, autumnal tone,
Sweet though in sadness. Be thou, Spirit fierce,
My spirit! Be thou me, impetuous one!

Drive my dead thoughts over the universe
Like withered leaves to quicken a new birth!
And, by the incantation of this verse,

Scatter, as from an unextinguished hearth
Ashes and sparks, my words among mankind!
Be through my lips to unawakened earth

The trumpet of a prophecy! O Wind,
If Winter comes, can Spring be far behind?

50 thy skyey (skī'ē) **speed:** the swiftness of clouds moving quickly across the sky.

51 vision: here, something impossible to achieve.

57 lyre: here, a reference to the Aeolian harp, an instrument whose strings make musical sounds when the wind blows over them.

62 impetuous (ĭm-pĕch'o͞o-əs): violently forceful; impulsive.

65 incantation: recitation, as of a magic spell.

FROM PERSONAL RESPONSE *TO* CRITICAL ANALYSIS

REFLECT

1. In your notebook, sketch one of the pictures that remain in your mind after reading "Ode to the West Wind."

RETHINK

2. How would you describe the speaker's feelings about the wind? Explain your answer.
3. What aspirations does the speaker appear to have?

   Consider
   - what he means by "the thorns of life" in line 54
   - his request in lines 63–67

To a Skylark

PERCY BYSSHE SHELLEY

Hail to thee, blithe Spirit!
Bird thou never wert,
That from Heaven, or near it,
Pourest thy full heart
In profuse strains of unpremeditated art.

Higher still and higher
From the earth thou springest
Like a cloud of fire;
The blue deep thou wingest,
And singing still dost soar, and soaring ever singest.

In the golden lightning
Of the sunken sun,
O'er which clouds are bright'ning,
Thou dost float and run;
Like an unbodied joy whose race is just begun.

The pale purple even
Melts around thy flight;
Like a star of Heaven,
In the broad daylight
Thou art unseen, but yet I hear thy shrill delight,

Keen as are the arrows
Of that silver sphere,
Whose intense lamp narrows
In the white dawn clear
Until we hardly see—we feel that it is there.

5 unpremeditated (ŭn'prĭ-mĕd'ĭ-tā'tĭd): natural; not planned out ahead of time.

16 even: evening.

22 silver sphere: the planet Venus, often called the morning star because it is visible in the east just before daybreak.

All the earth and air
With thy voice is loud,
As, when night is bare,
From one lonely cloud
The moon rains out her beams, and Heaven is overflowed.

What thou are we know not;
What is most like thee?
From rainbow clouds there flow not
Drops so bright to see
As from thy presence showers a rain of melody.

Like a Poet hidden
In the light of thought,
Singing hymns unbidden,
Till the world is wrought
To sympathy with hopes and fears it heeded not:

Like a high-born maiden
In a palace tower
Soothing her love-laden
Soul in secret hour
With music sweet as love, which overflows her bower:

45 bower: private room; boudoir.

Like a glowworm golden
In a dell of dew,
Scattering unbeholden
Its aërial hue
Among the flowers and grass, which screen it from the view!

Like a rose embowered
In its own green leaves,
By warm winds deflowered,
Till the scent it gives
Makes faint with too much sweet those heavy-wingéd thieves:

53 deflowered: fully opened.

55 thieves: the warm winds.

Sound of vernal showers
On the twinkling grass,
Rain-awakened flowers,
All that ever was
Joyous, and clear, and fresh, thy music doth surpass:

56 vernal: spring.

Teach us, Sprite or Bird,
What sweet thoughts are thine:
I have never heard
Praise of love or wine
That panted forth a flood of rapture so divine.

Detail of *Cloud Study* (1821), John Constable, R.A. Oil on paper laid on board, 9¾″ × 11⅞″, Yale Center for British Art, Paul Mellon Collection (B1981.25.155).

Chorus Hymeneal,
Or triumphal chant,
Matched with thine would be all
But an empty vaunt,
A thing wherein we feel there is some hidden want.

What objects are the fountains
Of thy happy strain?
What fields, or waves, or mountains?
What shapes of sky or plain?
What love of thine own kind? what ignorance of pain?

With thy clear keen joyance
Languor cannot be:
Shadow of annoyance
Never came near thee:
Thou lovest—but ne'er knew love's sad satiety.

Waking or asleep,
Thou of death must deem
Things more true and deep
Than we mortals dream,
Or how could thy notes flow in such a crystal stream?

66 chorus Hymeneal (hī′mə-nē′əl): a wedding song.

69 vaunt: boast.

71 fountains: sources.

77 languor (lăng′gər): lack of energy; listlessness.

80 satiety (sə-tī′ĭ-tē): the weariness or disgust caused by having a desire fulfilled to excess.

82 deem: know.

We look before and after,
And pine for what is not:
Our sincerest laughter
With some pain is fraught;
Our sweetest songs are those that tell of saddest thought.

Yet if we could scorn
Hate, and pride, and fear;
If we were things born
Not to shed a tear,
I know not how thy joy we ever should come near.

91 if: even if.

Better than all measures
Of delightful sound,
Better than all treasures
That in books are found,
Thy skill to poet were, thou scorner of the ground!

Teach me half the gladness
That thy brain must know,
Such harmonious madness
From my lips would flow
The world should listen then—as I am listening now.

INSIGHT

from A Defense of Poetry

PERCY BYSSHE SHELLEY

Poetry turns all things to loveliness; it exalts the beauty of that which is most beautiful, and it adds beauty to that which is most deformed; it marries exultation and horror, grief and pleasure, eternity and change; it subdues to union under its light yoke all irreconcilable things. It transmutes all that it touches, and every form moving within the radiance of its presence is changed by wondrous sympathy to an incarnation of the spirit which it breathes; its secret alchemy turns to potable[1] gold the poisonous waters which flow from death through life; it strips the veil of familiarity from the world, and lays bare the naked and sleeping beauty which is the spirit of its forms.

1. **potable** (pō′tə-bəl): drinkable.

RESPONDING OPTIONS

FROM PERSONAL RESPONSE *TO* CRITICAL ANALYSIS

REFLECT

1. In your notebook, list some words and phrases that convey your impressions of "To a Skylark."

RETHINK

2. How would you describe the attitude of the speaker toward the skylark?
3. How do you think the speaker might like to change his own life?
   Consider
   - the qualities he seems to admire most in the bird
   - what he means by "Such harmonious madness / From my lips would flow" (lines 103–104)

RELATE

4. Compare "Ozymandias," "Ode to the West Wind," and "To a Skylark." In your opinion, which poem best conveys the power of nature?
5. On the basis of the three poems you have read, do you think Shelley's poetry achieves the effects he describes in the Insight on page 543?

ANOTHER PATHWAY

Cooperative Learning

In each of the three poems, the speaker comments on the obstacles that prevent people from fulfilling their aspirations. In small groups, decide what ideas each poem conveys about the limits of human aspiration. Look for inferences as well as direct statements. Write down your thoughts and discuss them with the class.

LITERARY CONCEPTS

Meter is a regular repetition of a rhythmic unit in a line of poetry. Each unit, or **foot,** consists of a combination of stressed and unstressed syllables. The following line from the sonnet "Ozymandias" is written in **iambic pentameter**—a meter in which the line is made up of five feet called iambs, each consisting of an unstressed syllable followed by a stressed syllable:

˘ ´ ˘ ´ ˘ ´ ˘ ´ ˘ ´
The lone and level sands stretch far away.

Poets use different meters, as well as variations within a regular metrical pattern—adding an extra syllable or reversing the stressed and unstressed syllables in a foot—to create the effects they want and to reinforce meaning. Choose another line from "Ozymandias" and two lines each from "Ode to the West Wind" and "To a Skylark." Mark the stressed and unstressed syllables, and then compare the meters and variations. Discuss the effects Shelley creates with different rhythmic patterns.

QUICKWRITES

1. Think back to the personal aspirations you noted for the Writing Connection on page 535. Choose an element of nature—such as a tree, a lake, or a season—that might symbolize one of your personal aspirations. Write a **free-verse poem** in which you describe the element of nature and express what it symbolizes for you.
2. Create a **travel brochure** advertising the desert landmark described in "Ozymandias."

PORTFOLIO Save your writing. You may want to use it later as a springboard to a piece for your portfolio.

ALTERNATIVE ACTIVITIES

1. Design and create a clay **statue** of Ozymandias, based on your impression of the king as he is portrayed in Shelley's poem.
2. Draw or paint a **mural** illustrating the effects of the west wind on the land, the sky, and the sea.
3. In the role of either the speaker of "Ode to the West Wind" or the speaker of "To a Skylark," deliver a **soliloquy** expressing your aspirations and frustrations as a poet.

LITERARY LINKS

Compare Shelley's "To a Skylark" with Matsuo Bashō's haiku about a skylark (page 492). Are there any similarities in the poems' messages? Which poem do you think is more effective? Give reasons for your answer.

ACROSS THE CURRICULUM

History Investigate the reign of Rameses II, the Ozymandias of Shelley's poem. What type of leader was he? Are the descriptions of him in historical accounts compatible with the depiction in Shelley's poem?

Head of Ramses. Photo Copyright © A Bolesta/H. Armstrong Roberts.

PERCY BYSSHE SHELLEY

1792–1822

Percy Bysshe Shelley led a driven and tumultuous life that ended tragically and prematurely. Born into an aristocratic and wealthy family, he was sent away to boarding school at the age of ten. There, he endured bullying and teasing from the other boys, painful experiences that fueled his hatred of injustice. As an adolescent, Shelley embraced many radical views, including atheism, and rejected most of the institutions of society. When he was expelled from Oxford University during his first year for circulating an essay defending atheism, his family was scandalized; he and his father remained alienated for the rest of Shelley's life.

In 1811, a few months after leaving Oxford, Shelley eloped to Scotland with Harriet Westbrook, who was only 16. Their relationship was not a strong one, and in 1814, despite the fact that Harriet was expecting their second child, Shelley abandoned her for Mary Wollstonecraft Godwin, the daughter of the philosopher William Godwin and the feminist author Mary Wollstonecraft.

Shelley's radical ideas and personal behavior drew criticism from his family and friends, and he began to view himself as an outcast. In 1818, following the death of Harriet, Shelley finally married Mary Godwin, and they moved permanently to Italy. In 1819, despite his despair at the deaths of his two infant children within a period of nine months, he produced much of his greatest poetry, including "Ode to the West Wind" and his masterpiece, the verse drama *Prometheus Unbound.*

The years 1820–1822 were ones of relative stability, during which Shelley wrote many fine lyrics, including "To a Skylark" and "Adonais," an elegy in memory of John Keats. In the last stanza of this poem, he speaks of his spirit as a ship "borne darkly, fearfully, afar." On July 8, 1822, Shelley and a friend were drowned when their boat capsized in a sudden storm. Shelley's ashes were buried in Rome, near the graves of John Keats and Shelley's son William.

OTHER WORKS "Hymn to Intellectual Beauty," "The Cloud," "To Night," "Love's Philosophy," "Adonais"

LASERLINKS
• *CULTURAL CONNECTION*

PREVIEWING

POETRY

The Lotus-Blossom Cowers

Heinrich Heine (hīn′rĭk hī′nə)

PERSONAL CONNECTION

If a radio disc jockey offered to play your favorite love song, which song would you choose? What kind of relationship does the song describe? Share your thoughts with your classmates.

LITERARY/BIOGRAPHICAL CONNECTION

The romantic movement influenced the literature of almost every country in Europe. In Germany, the romantic period extended from approximately 1790 to 1830. In literature, it was characterized by an interest in folksongs, fables, and medieval romances and by an outpouring of poetry dealing with the themes of love, melancholy, and the beauty of nature.

The early poetry of Heinrich Heine exemplifies the style of the period. In 1827, Heine published *The Book of Songs,* a large collection of lyric poems that includes "The Lotus-Blossom Cowers." Containing love songs, ballads, and sonnets—many of which were later set to music—this volume was responsible for Heine's international reputation as a respected and influential poet.

Eventually, Heine turned from composing love poems to writing poetry and essays about political and social issues. Like the English romantic poet Percy Bysshe Shelley, Heine was an outspoken and often bitter critic of social injustice who was rejected in his homeland for expressing radical and unpopular opinions. Unlike Shelley, however, Heine was not a romantic in spirit. He was skeptical of the power of the imagination and did not believe that romantic idealism was the answer to society's ills. Although his earlier love poems are definitely romantic in style, his later writing places him in the "post-romantic" period of German literature.

WRITING CONNECTION

Jot down several ideas for a contemporary love song. Using the idea you like best, try to write the lyrics for at least one verse of an original love song. As an alternative, you might compose new lyrics for the song you identified for the Personal Connection. Then, as you read "The Lotus-Blossom Cowers," notice the similarities and differences between your lyrics and Heine's poem.

The Lotus-Blossom Cowers

Heinrich Heine

The lotus-blossom cowers
    Under the sun's bright beams;
Her forehead drooping for hours,
    She waits for the night among dreams.

The Moon, he is her lover,
    He wakes her with his gaze;
To him alone she uncovers
    The fair flower of her face.

She glows and grows more radiant,
    And gazes mutely above;
Breathing and weeping and trembling
    With love—and the pain of love.

RESPONDING OPTIONS

FROM PERSONAL RESPONSE *TO* CRITICAL ANALYSIS

REFLECT 1. Did you find anything surprising in this poem? Jot down your response in your notebook.

RETHINK 2. What qualities of the lotus-blossom stand out in your mind?

3. How would you describe the speaker's attitude toward love?
   Consider
   - the way the lotus-blossom responds to the moon
   - what the speaker means by "the pain of love" (line 12)

4. Why do you think Heine chose a lotus-blossom as the subject of this poem?

RELATE 5. Do you think pain is an integral part of every love relationship? Why or why not?

ANOTHER PATHWAY

Each time you reread a poem, you may discover images or ideas you missed in previous readings. Read the poem three times. After each reading, note images and your reactions to specific lines. After the final reading, compare your impressions. How did they change? Did you discover any images or ideas that you hadn't noticed in your first reading?

LITERARY CONCEPTS

Mood is the feeling or atmosphere that a writer creates for the reader. One element that contributes to the mood of a poem is **imagery**—the words and phrases that re-create sensory experiences for the reader. In the center of a word web, describe the mood of Heine's poem. Then, in the surrounding circles, list words or images that contribute to the mood. If you think the poem has more than one mood, complete a word web for each mood you identify.

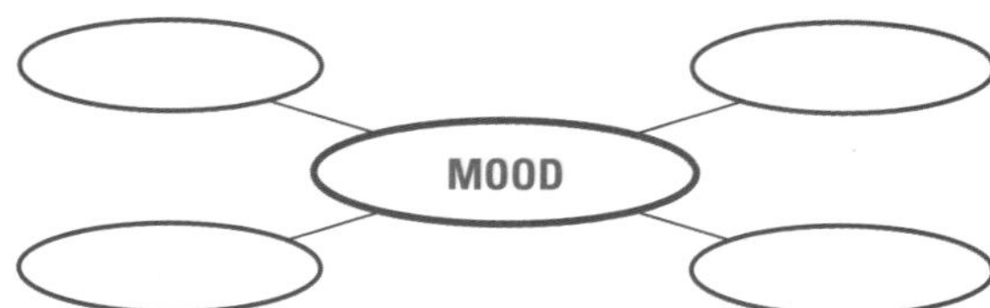

CONCEPT REVIEW: Personification Heine makes use of personification when he gives human qualities to a flower. Working with a partner, rewrite "The Lotus-Blossom Cowers," eliminating all instances of personification. How does the absence of personification change the poem?

QUICKWRITES

1. Compose a **haiku** based on an idea or image in Heine's poem.
2. Imagining yourself to be the speaker of "The Lotus-Blossom Cowers," write your **definition** of love.
3. Write a descriptive **paragraph** in which you give human qualities to some aspect of nature—for example, a flower, a tree, an animal, the sun, or a storm.

PORTFOLIO *Save your writing. You may want to use it later as a springboard to a piece for your portfolio.*

ALTERNATIVE ACTIVITIES

1. Using images from the poem, design a **postage stamp** celebrating love.
2. Look for a **musical recording** that in your opinion conveys the mood and emotions of the poem. Play the recording for your class.

LITERARY LINKS

Compare the imagery in "The Lotus-Blossom Cowers" with that in Lord Byron's "She Walks in Beauty" (page 528). What similarities can you find? In your opinion, which poet paints a more vivid or striking picture? Give reasons for your answer.

THE WRITER'S STYLE

Heine wrote his poems in German, his native language, but they have been translated into English many times. What difficulties would you expect a writer to encounter in translating a poem from one language to another? What aspects of a poem might be changed in the process of translation?

ACROSS THE CURRICULUM

Science ***Cooperative Learning*** As a group, research the habitat and characteristics of the lotus, or water lily. What type of growing conditions does it require? What are its primary characteristics? What unique qualities of the plant might have inspired Heinrich Heine to write "The Lotus-Blossom Cowers"? Discuss your findings with the class.

HEINRICH HEINE

1797–1856

Born in Düsseldorf, Germany (then Prussia), to Jewish parents, Heinrich Heine was greatly influenced by an uncle who tried unsuccessfully to push his nephew into business. When he was 17, Heine began to halfheartedly pursue a series of apprenticeships, but he succeeded at none. His uncle finally agreed to provide him with a university education, and although the young man was more interested in writing poetry, he eventually received a degree in law. Intent on finding a job, Heine reluctantly converted to Protestantism because government positions were not open to Jews at the time; but his conversion was in vain, for he was never offered any of the jobs he desired.

During his university days, Heine became concerned about political and social injustice. Throughout his life, he searched for a solution to such injustice, exploring ideas ranging from various forms of socialism to the communism espoused by his acquaintance Karl Marx. None of these options totally satisfied Heine, however, for he always worried that any radical changes in social order might destroy the literature, art, and music that he so dearly loved.

In 1831, Heine moved to Paris, which at the time was a haven for freethinkers. He was heartily welcomed into French social and literary circles, where he found many admirers of his work. In his essays, he began speaking out against the governments of both France and Germany, but these works were poorly received in his homeland. Many Germans considered him unpatriotic, and the government attempted to ban all of his works. This hostility toward Heine lasted for a long time. Many years after his death, efforts to erect memorials to the poet in Germany were met with violent protests that in some cities erupted into riots.

In 1848, Heine entered a long period of declining health. A serious illness left him partially paralyzed, and for eight years the poet was confined to his bed—or as he termed it, his "mattress grave." Although often in tremendous pain, he continued to write until his death, producing some of his best poetry during the last years of his life.

OTHER WORKS *The Book of Songs, Poems of Heinrich Heine*

MILESTONES IN BRITISH LITERATURE

Mary Wollstonecraft Shelley

Frankenstein

What if you discovered the secret of creation? Suddenly, you would know how to generate life. You could invent a new kind of being, eliminate aging, perhaps conquer death! You might give life to a new species, which would credit you forever as its creator. Would you be willing to dedicate your energy and intellect, forsake your friends, and give up your youth for the sake of such an experiment?

And what if—after all your sacrifice and sweat—your work didn't turn out quite as planned? What if your creation turned out to be ugly, frightful, or grotesque? Would you find it in your heart to embrace your creation—or would you flee from it in terror? These are some of the issues Mary Wollstonecraft Shelley raised when she wrote her classic horror novel *Frankenstein; or, The Modern Prometheus.*

The daughter of the authors William Godwin and Mary Wollstonecraft and the second wife of the poet Percy Bysshe Shelley, Mary Shelley was keenly aware of the close relationship between life and danger, even death. Her mother had died while giving birth to her. Her own first child, born prematurely, died after two weeks. When Lord Byron first proposed that she write a ghost story, Mary Shelley was only 18 years old, pregnant with her second child, and haunted by suicides in both her husband's family and her own. It is little to be wondered at that she responded by writing a novel of creation gone awry.

Published in 1818, *Frankenstein* received strong, albeit mixed, reviews. One magazine, for example, declared the story "excellent," whereas another called it a "tissue of horrible and disgusting absurdity." Most everyone, however, was struck by the terrifying and pathetic monster created by the scientist Victor Frankenstein. Beginning life as an affectionate creature, the monster became evil only after he was cruelly rejected by Frankenstein and other human beings. Throughout the years, his creator has been compared to Prometheus, Percy Bysshe Shelley, the biblical Adam, and the spirit of science itself.

Today, in our scientific age, Mary Shelley's novel is best known as a tale of scientific horror. Whether on paper or on film, the monster still finds significance and meaning in people's imaginations and hearts.

Top:
Frontispiece from an 1831 edition of Mary Wollstonecraft Shelley's Frankenstein
Middle:
Charles Ogle as Frankenstein's monster in the first movie version, 1910. British Film Institute.
Bottom:
Boris Karloff as the monster, 1931. Photofest.

PREVIEWING

POETRY

Selected Poems

John Keats

PERSONAL CONNECTION

Using a chart like the one shown, list at least ten things—objects, people, qualities, experiences, ideas, or places—that have special significance for you. Which of these do you think of as permanent, and which ones seem transient, or temporary? Share your charts with your classmates.

Objects	People	Qualities	Experiences	Ideas	Places

BIOGRAPHICAL CONNECTION

Although John Keats died of tuberculosis at a tragically young age, he was one of the most gifted English romantic poets. Keats began writing poetry at age 18, and by the time of his death at age 25 he had written poems that would establish him as a major poet. In 1819 alone—a year of extreme emotional distress—Keats composed a series of masterpieces, including a narrative poem, numerous sonnets, and five odes. Three of those poems appear on the following pages.

Although his work reflects the powerful emotions typically found in romantic poetry, Keats did not share the social and political concerns of many of his contemporaries. He was not influenced by the revolutionary ideals of the time and did not, like Percy Bysshe Shelley or Heinrich Heine, search for solutions to society's ills. Keats was more concerned with the qualities of beauty and with the private emotions of the individual, such as the joys or pains of love and the anxieties inspired by an uncertain future.

John Keats (1821), Joseph Severn. Oil on canvas, The Granger Collection, New York.

READING CONNECTION

Understanding the Ode In many of his best poems, Keats reveals his mastery of the ode. Popular among romantic poets, the ode is an elaborate lyric poem, written in language that is dignified and exalted as well as enthusiastic. Odes usually address serious subjects, such as the transience of life, and appeal to both the imagination and the intellect. They are sometimes reflective and may express intense emotions. As you read "Ode on a Grecian Urn" and "To Autumn," look for characteristics that identify them as odes.

ODE ON A GRECIAN URN

Courtesy of the Keats-Shelley Memorial House, Rome.

John Keats

Thou still unravish'd bride of quietness,
Thou foster-child of silence and slow time,
Sylvan historian, who canst thus express
A flowery tale more sweetly than our rhyme:
What leaf-fring'd legend haunts about thy shape
Of deities or mortals, or of both,
In Tempe or the dales of Arcady?
What men or gods are these? What maidens loath?
What mad pursuit? What struggle to escape?
What pipes and timbrels? What wild ecstasy?

Heard melodies are sweet, but those unheard
Are sweeter; therefore, ye soft pipes, play on;
Not to the sensual ear, but, more endear'd,
Pipe to the spirit ditties of no tone:
Fair youth, beneath the trees, thou canst not leave
Thy song, nor ever can those trees be bare;
Bold lover, never, never canst thou kiss,
Though winning near the goal—yet, do not grieve;
She cannot fade, though thou hast not thy bliss,
For ever wilt thou love, and she be fair!

GUIDE FOR READING

1 Do you think *still* means "as yet" or "motionless" here?

3 sylvan: pertaining to trees or woods.

5 haunts about: surrounds.

7 Tempe (tĕm′pē′) . . . **Arcady** (är′kə-dē): two places in Greece that are traditional settings in literary works dealing with idealized rustic life. Tempe is a beautiful valley; Arcady (Arcadia) is a mountainous region.

8 loath: unwilling; reluctant.

10 timbrels: tambourines.

11–12 Why might unheard melodies be sweeter than heard ones?

Ah, happy, happy boughs! that cannot shed
Your leaves, nor ever bid the spring adieu;
And, happy melodist, unweariéd,
For ever piping songs for ever new;
More happy love! more happy, happy love!
For ever warm and still to be enjoyed,
For ever panting, and for ever young;
All breathing human passion far above,
That leaves a heart high-sorrowful and cloy'd,
A burning forehead, and a parching tongue.

29 cloy'd: having had too much of something; oversatisfied.

Who are these coming to the sacrifice?
To what green altar, O mysterious priest,
Lead'st thou that heifer lowing at the skies,
And all her silken flanks with garlands drest?
What little town by river or sea shore,
Or mountain-built with peaceful citadel,
Is emptied of this folk, this pious morn?
And, little town, thy streets for evermore
Will silent be; and not a soul to tell
Why thou art desolate, can e'er return.

38–40 Why do you think the speaker says that the little town will be forever silent and desolate?

O Attic shape! Fair attitude! with brede
Of marble men and maidens overwrought,
With forest branches and the trodden weed;
Thou, silent form, dost tease us out of thought
As doth eternity: Cold Pastoral!
When old age shall this generation waste,
Thou shalt remain, in midst of other woe
Than ours, a friend to man, to whom thou say'st,
"Beauty is truth, truth beauty,"—that is all
Ye know on earth, and all ye need to know.

41 Attic: pure and classical, in the Athenian style; **brede:** interwoven design.

45 pastoral (păs'tər-əl): an artistic work that portrays rural life in an idealized way. Why do you suppose the speaker calls it "cold"?

FROM PERSONAL RESPONSE *TO* CRITICAL ANALYSIS

REFLECT

1. How did you react to the language of this poem? Briefly describe your reactions in your notebook.

RETHINK

2. What does the speaker seem to admire most about the urn?

3. What role do you think the speaker's imagination plays in his thoughts?
Consider
- his reference to unheard melodies
- what has inspired his questions about the "little town"

4. What messages about life do you think the poem conveys?

To AUTUMN

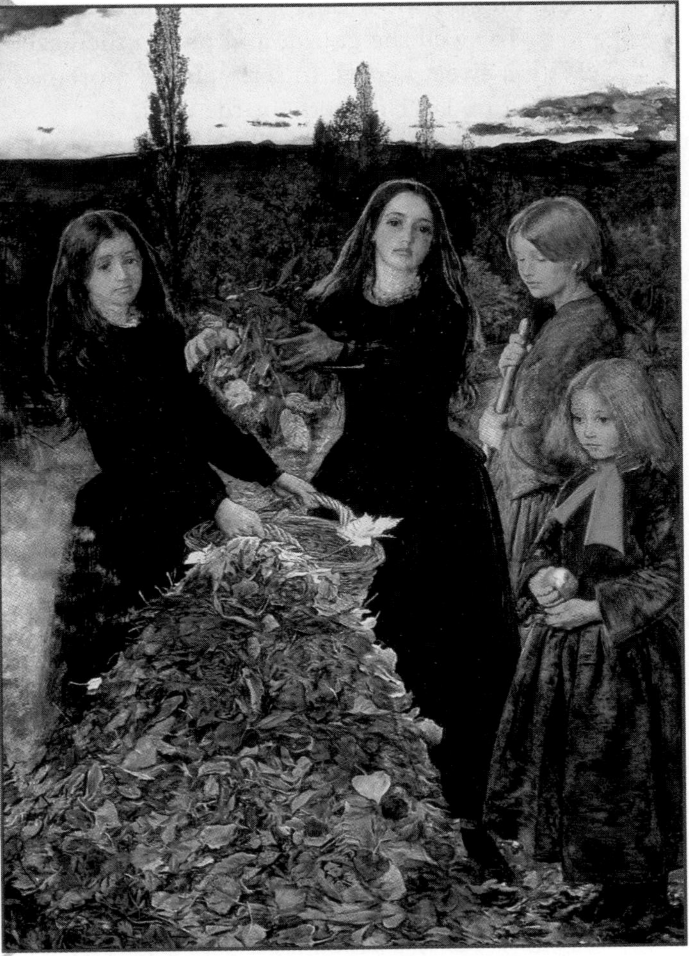

Autumn Leaves, Sir John Everett Millais (1829–1896). Copyright © Manchester (Great Britain) City Art Galleries.

John Keats

GUIDE FOR READING

1 Note the bounty of the harvest the speaker describes in this line and those that follow.

Season of mists and mellow fruitfulness,
  Close bosom-friend of the maturing sun;
Conspiring with him how to load and bless
  With fruit the vines that round the thatch-eaves run;
To bend with apples the mossed cottage-trees,

And fill all fruit with ripeness to the core;
To swell the gourd, and plump the hazel shells
With a sweet kernel; to set budding more,
And still more, later flowers for the bees,
Until they think warm days will never cease,
For Summer has o'er-brimmed their clammy cells.

Who hath not seen thee oft amid thy store?
Sometimes whoever seeks abroad may find
Thee sitting careless on a granary floor,
Thy hair soft-lifted by the winnowing wind;
Or on a half-reaped furrow sound asleep,
Drowsed with the fume of poppies, while thy hook
Spares the next swath and all its twinéd flowers:
And sometimes like a gleaner thou dost keep
Steady thy laden head across a brook;
Or by a cider-press, with patient look,
Thou watchest the last oozings hours by hours.

Where are the songs of Spring? Aye, where are they?
Think not of them, thou hast thy music too—
While barred clouds bloom the soft-dying day,
And touch the stubble-plains with rosy hue;
Then in a wailful choir the small gnats mourn
Among the river sallows, borne aloft
Or sinking as the light wind lives or dies;
And full-grown lambs loud bleat from hilly bourn;
Hedge crickets sing; and now with treble soft
The redbreast whistles from a garden croft;
And gathering swallows twitter in the skies.

12 Whom does the speaker seem to be addressing?

15 winnowing (wĭn'ō-ĭng): separating chaff from grain by blowing the chaff away.

17 hook: scythe (a tool with a long curved blade used for mowing and reaping).

18 swath: a row of grain to be cut.

28 sallows: willow trees.

30 bourn: region.

32 croft: a small enclosed field.

FROM PERSONAL RESPONSE *TO* CRITICAL ANALYSIS

REFLECT 1. What parts of Keats's description of autumn appeal most to you? List them in your notebook.

RETHINK 2. Why do you think Keats addresses autumn as though it were a person?

3. How would you describe the mood of this poem?

Far Left: John Keats (1819), Charles Armitage Brown. Pencil drawing, The Granger Collection, New York.

Left: Deathbed portrait of Keats, unknown artist. Reproduced by permission of the London Borough of Camden from the collections at Keats House, Hampstead, Great Britain.

When I Have Fears That I May Cease to Be

John Keats

GUIDE FOR READING

1 Note, in the lines that follow, the reasons for the speaker's fear.

3 charactry: handwriting.

4 garners: storage bins.

9 Why is the "fair creature" described as "of an hour"?

When I have fears that I may cease to be
  Before my pen has glean'd my teeming brain,
Before high piled books, in charactry,
  Hold like rich garners the full ripen'd grain;
When I behold, upon the night's starr'd face,
  Huge cloudy symbols of a high romance,
And think that I may never live to trace
  Their shadows, with the magic hand of chance;
And when I feel, fair creature of an hour,
  That I shall never look upon thee more,
Never have relish in the fairy power
  Of unreflecting love;—then on the shore
Of the wide world I stand alone, and think
Till love and fame to nothingness do sink.

RESPONDING OPTIONS

FROM PERSONAL RESPONSE *TO* CRITICAL ANALYSIS

REFLECT 1. In your notebook, describe your reaction to the speaker of "When I Have Fears That I May Cease to Be."

RETHINK 2. What specific concerns does the speaker appear to have?

Consider
- his mention of his pen and books
- what he is afraid he'll "never live to trace" (lines 6–8)
- the "fair creature" (line 9)

3. What conclusion does the speaker draw in the last lines of the poem?

4. Given what you know of Keats's illness, do you think his concerns about the transience of life are justified? Support your opinion.

RELATE 5. Compare "Ode on a Grecian Urn," "To Autumn," and "When I Have Fears That I May Cease to Be." Do you think any of the poems convey similar messages about life?

ANOTHER PATHWAY

Cooperative Learning

Get together with four classmates, with each member of the group choosing one of the five senses (sight, smell, hearing, touch, and taste). Then look through these three poems for examples of imagery that appeal to the sense each of you has chosen. Share your findings with your group, and then discuss them with the class.

LITERARY CONCEPTS

Poets often use the sound devices of assonance and consonance. **Assonance** is the repetition of a vowel sound within words—for example, the repetition of the long *e* sound in the following line:

> When I have f<u>ea</u>rs that I may c<u>ea</u>se to b<u>e</u>

Consonance is the repetition of consonant sounds within and at the ends of words, like that of the *st* and *z* sounds in this line:

> Thou watche<u>st</u> the la<u>st</u> oo<u>z</u>ing<u>s</u> hour<u>s</u> by hour<u>s</u>.

Find other examples of assonance and consonance in the three poems. Then explain why you think Keats uses these sound devices in his poetry.

CONCEPT REVIEW: Alliteration Keats also uses alliteration, or the repetition of consonant sounds at the beginning of words. Find examples of alliteration in each poem.

QUICKWRITES

1. Rewrite one **stanza** from "To Autumn," using images that portray another season of the year.
2. Draft an **essay** in which you explain your interpretation of the statement "Beauty is truth, truth beauty."
3. Make a **list** of contemporary subjects that you think would be appropriate topics for an ode.

PORTFOLIO *Save your writing. You may want to use it later as a springboard to a piece for your portfolio.*

CRITIC'S CORNER

The famous American writer Edgar Allan Poe praised the work of Keats, saying, "Beauty is always his aim." Cite examples of lines from the three poems that help support this claim.

ALTERNATIVE ACTIVITIES

1. With a partner, design and create a **collage** that captures the mood of "To Autumn." You might want to use a variety of forms and materials, including drawings, photographs, leaf rubbings, dried leaves and grasses, nuts, seeds, and so on.
2. In a dramatic **oral reading** of one of the poems, try to convey the intense emotions that might have inspired the poet.

LITERARY LINKS

Compare Keats's "When I Have Fears That I May Cease to Be" with John Milton's "How Soon Hath Time" (page 295). Do the two poems' speakers share the same attitude toward time? Explain your answer.

ACROSS THE CURRICULUM

Art Investigate the art of ancient Greece. Try to locate illustrations of the kinds of vases and sculptures that inspired Keats's "Ode on a Grecian Urn." What kinds of designs typically adorn these early works of art?

American School of Classical Studies at Athens, Angora Excavations.

JOHN KEATS

1795–1821

John Keats's life was brief but intense. As a young child, he was indifferent to his studies and high-spirited. When he was about 13, however, he developed a passion for reading and within a short time read every book in his school library. He was strongly encouraged by a teacher, Charles Cowden Clarke, who remained a friend and literary influence in his life.

Keats's father had died when Keats was 8, and his mother died when he was 14. He was then taken out of school by his guardian and apprenticed to a surgeon. When he was 18 he began writing poetry, which became the driving force of his life. Although he qualified to practice surgery, by 1817 he had abandoned medicine for the less certain career of poet. He was not immediately successful. In fact, an early narrative poem, *Endymion*, was savagely attacked by London critics. Although Keats was painfully disappointed, fortunately he did not allow the reviews to deter him from continuing his work.

Beginning in 1818, Keats had to confront a series of physical and emotional crises. During the summer he developed the early symptoms of tuberculosis, the same disease that had killed his mother. His brother Tom was also suffering from tuberculosis and died in the autumn of 1818. After his brother's death, Keats moved to a friend's house and fell passionately in love with an 18-year-old neighbor, Fanny Brawne. Although he became engaged to Fanny, he was prevented by poverty and poor health from marrying her, a situation that added greatly to his distress. Amazingly, in the midst of this great emotional turmoil, Keats produced his greatest works, which were received with more favorable critical recognition than *Endymion* had been.

In the fall of 1820, as his illness progressed, Keats followed the advice of friends and moved to Italy in search of a milder climate. He died less than six months later and was buried in Rome under an epitaph he had composed for himself: "Here lies one whose name was writ in water."

OTHER WORKS "Ode to a Nightingale," "Solitude," "On First Looking into Chapman's Homer," "La Belle Dame Sans Merci," "To One Who Has Been Long in City Pent"

LASERLINKS
• *ART GALLERY*

Bright STAR, Would I

John Keats

Keats wrote this sonnet in 1819, two years before he succumbed to tuberculosis. The "bright star" is the North Star, which had inspired the poet during a walking tour of England's Lake District in 1818.

Bright STAR, would I were steadfast as thou art—
Not in lone splendor hung aloft the night
And watching, with eternal lids apart,
Like nature's patient, sleepless Eremite,
The moving waters at their priestlike task
Of pure ablution round earth's human shores,
Or gazing on the new soft fallen mask
Of snow upon the mountains and the moors—
No—yet still steadfast, still unchangeable,
Pillowed upon my fair love's ripening breast,
To feel forever its soft fall and swell,
Awake forever in a sweet unrest,
Still, still to hear her tender-taken breath,
And so live ever—or else swoon to death.

4 Eremite (âr′ə-mīt′): hermit.

6 ablution (ə-blo͞o′shən): a ritual washing of the body.

Were Steadfast As Thou Art

The Starry Night (1889), Vincent van Gogh. Oil on canvas, 29″ × 36¼″, The Museum of Modern Art, New York, acquired through the Lillie P. Bliss Bequest. Photo Copyright © 1995 The Museum of Modern Art, New York.

WRITING FROM EXPERIENCE

WRITING TO EXPLAIN

Most of the the writers you have studied in Unit Four, "The Flowering of Romanticism," were seekers of truth. They looked for answers to such questions as What is beauty? What is art? What can we (or should we) learn from nature? Analysis is one method of looking into such big questions—and more-limited, everyday questions as well. Is space exploration still worthwhile? Have voters lost interest in government? Why is one short story better than another? Is this CD really a classic? Analysis can help answer such questions.

GUIDED ASSIGNMENT

Write an Analysis Analysis involves taking something apart in order to examine and explain it. Write an essay using analysis to explore a subject and to discover your own truth.

Quotation from Science Article

The Future of
Genetic Engineering

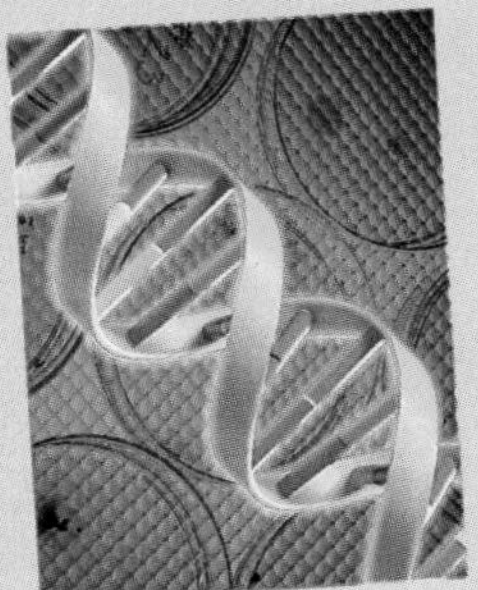

The ability to manipulate genes—in animals and plants, as well as humans—could eventually change everything: what we eat, what we wear, how we live, how we die and how we see ourselves in relation to our fate.

from "The Genetic Revolution," *Time*

This is frightening. Has anyone thought about the consequences of these changes?

1 Look for Ideas

What will you analyze? A good choice might be a topic you don't fully understand, a problem you uncovered, or an issue that troubles you. The following are some ways in which you can discover ideas.

- Get together with a group of classmates and brainstorm. Talk about such fields as music, art, literature, sports, science, technology, and politics.
- Interview people who have interesting jobs, hobbies, or expertise in areas you'd like to learn more about.
- Think about recent books you have read, movies you have seen, music you have heard, or other activities that can lead you to a topic worth analyzing.
- Consider the items shown on these two pages.

What topics suitable for analysis do these activities suggest? Make a list of the topics as they occur to you.

2 Formulate Questions

Analysis can begin with one or more questions you want answered. The self-stick notes on the items on these pages are examples of questions you might ask about a particular topic. Can you see a common idea within these items or find an important issue raised by one or more of them? After you've made a generalization about the items, turn it into a question you would like to answer.

Select a few topics from those you listed in your exploration and think about the questions they raise. Write down one or two questions for each topic.

A New Divide Between Haves and Have-Nots?

If there was any lingering doubt that the computer has become ensconced as a member of the American family, it was dispelled at the turn of the year by some startling statistics. For the first time ever, consumers in 1994 bought $8 billion worth of PCs—just a smidgen away from the $8.3 billion they spent on TVs. The sales record in terms of dollars is bound to fall to the computer soon, though the TV's cheaper price guarantees its dominion in numbers for a while yet.

In the nation's poorer areas, however—places like Washington's Anacostia neighborhood, the hollows of Appalachia or Miami's Liberty City—families with IBM Activas, NEC CD-ROM drives, modems, Internet connections and all the other paraphernalia so beloved by computer users are few and far between. Therein lies one of the most troubling aspects of the emerging information age. In an era in which success is increasingly identified with the ability to use computers and gain access to cyberspace, will the new technology only widen the gap between rich and poor, educated and uneducated, blacks, whites, and Hispanics? As Commerce Secretary Ronald Brown puts it, "How do you create an environment so that once we've built this information infrastructure, you do not create a society of haves and have-nots?"

from *Time*

Won't computers, like television, eventually be available for everyone?

Will this new division come about? Can we keep it from happening?

Technology Article

LASERLINKS
• *WRITING SPRINGBOARD*

WRITING COACH

Book

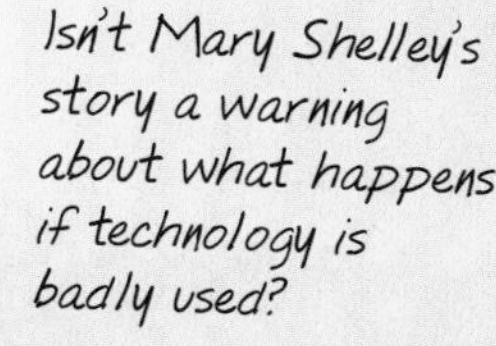

Isn't Mary Shelley's story a warning about what happens if technology is badly used?

FRANKENSTEIN

OR THE MODERN PROMETHEUS BY MARY WOLLSTONECRAFT SHELLEY

PREWRITING

Working with Your Ideas

First Steps By now you should have several promising topics and questions that can serve as pathways into your analysis. These two pages will help you focus on ways of making discoveries about your topic. They'll get you ready to write an analysis that will help both you and your readers understand your topic.

1 Choose, Explore, and Focus

Choose Look over the topics you listed and wrote questions about earlier. Spend a few minutes freewriting on each idea to see where it takes you. If necessary, do further questioning and brainstorming in order to find the topic you want to write an essay on.

Student's Notes

How is my life influenced by technology?

Describe—Meals prepared in microwaves; home entertainment from direct satellite transmission, cable, tapes, videodiscs, CDs

Compare—When my parents were my age, only the government and big businesses had computers; no one had cellular phones or CDs.

Associate—Personal computers and VCRs are so much a part of my life that I don't even think of them as a "new technology."

Analyze—Breakdown of technological influences: at school, at work, at home, at play, while traveling

Apply—Technological changes already affect, to some extent, nearly every aspect of my life.

Argue for or against—We can't stop change, so we need to adapt to it and benefit from it but keep it from ruling our lives or changing them for the worse.

Determine Purpose Think about the purpose of your analysis. Is it only to inform your readers, or do you want to convince them of an opinion? It's also possible that your purpose will be more personal. You may want to understand your topic better in order to make a decision or a judgment.

Explore Start exploring your chosen topic by jotting down what you know about it. To consider various approaches, try making notes about the topic under different headings, as shown in the student example at the left. This student began with the question "How is my life influenced by technology?" and then examined different aspects of the question. This technique, called cubing, looks at a topic in six different ways.

Focus Think about the question or problem you want to analyze. Look at your freewriting and your notes. Try to find one aspect of the topic that you want to focus your analysis on.

2 Break Your Subject into Parts

Analysis involves breaking a topic apart and examining each part to see how it fits into the whole. Most topics can be broken apart in more than one way. Here are some ways in which the topic of technological influence can be broken down.

By use: at home, at school, at work
By industry: health care, communications
By fields: engineering, genetics, chemistry
By qualities: benefits, problems

3 Gather Information

Make a list of questions you want your essay to answer and then look for answers in the most appropriate source for each question. You can gather information from books, magazines, reference works, interviews, and any other sources appropriate to your topic. Refer to the Multimedia Handbook if you need help in locating or using CD-ROM or on-line sources.

4 Write a Thesis Statement

After gathering all the information you need, write a thesis statement. Look over your research notes and decide what main idea you want to stress in your essay. Try to sum up that main idea in a single sentence. You may decide to revise this thesis sentence later, but it will help you focus on your topic as you start writing.

Research Materials

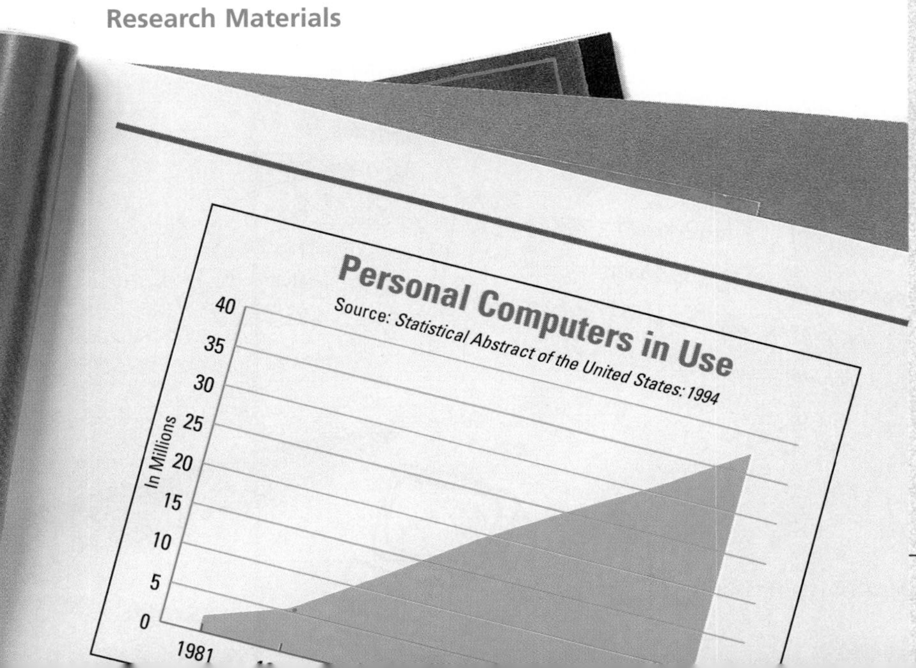

SkillBuilder

CRITICAL THINKING

Classifying Information

Classifying is a useful technique for analyzing a topic. When you classify, you organize information into groups that share similar qualities or functions. If you were analyzing technology, for example, you might start classifying it as follows. Keep in mind that there can be more than one way to classify items within a topic.

Technology

Electronics	Chemistry
Cable TV	Pharmaceuticals
Lasers	Synthetics
Computers	Textiles

APPLYING WHAT YOU'VE LEARNED

Pick a topic (either the one you've decided to write about or a different one). Use classification to group the parts of your topic into categories. Keep in mind that there may be more than one way to classify its parts.

THINK & PLAN

Reflecting on Your Topic

1. How will you break down your topic for analysis?
2. Have you learned all you need to know about your topic? Where can you get more information if you need it?
3. What is the purpose of your analysis?

DRAFTING

Discover Through Writing

Just Start After collecting data on a complex topic, you still may be uncertain of what all your information means. Or you may have no idea how to put it all together in an essay. The best thing to do is just start writing. As you write, you'll probably discover your essay gradually taking shape.

1 Begin a Rough Draft

Your rough draft is a means of exploring your topic, determining its limits, and deciding what conclusion your evidence leads to. It may also help you determine the format for your final version. Will it be a typed essay, a pamphlet, a speech, or something else?

Student's Rough Draft

Technology: Blessing or Curse?

Mary Shelley's horror story Frankenstein is a particularly meaningful story for the world today. Just about every part of our lives today is touched by technology. What are the consequences of these innovations, many of them unknown a generation ago?

I shouldn't take it for granted that everyone knows Shelley's book. I'll need to tell more about Frankenstein. The opening needs to be snappier anyway.

There are thousands of ways in which we are influenced by technology. Let's consider the impact on our lives of some major technological changes in the area of electronics, including computers (including the Net) and such other communications media as cellular phones, direct satellite TV, and home entertainment centers.

This category is still too broad. I've tried to cover too much and only scratched the surface of each item. Focus on computers only.

The electronic category contains the most familiar examples of how technology influences our lives. We can hardly escape them. Computers are used at home, at school, and at our workplaces. Almost anyplace we go—stores, supermarkets, restaurants, hotels, banks, ticket offices for trains, buses, airlines, and so on—we will find ourselves facing a computer terminal.

Computers keep track of our school and employment records, our medical problems, our spending and debts, the things we buy or sell, the places we go to and the places we've been to—in fact, just about everything between, and including, our birth and our death.

These two paragraphs are pretty good. Just need to fix first sentence for the narrower topic.

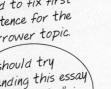

I should try sending this essay to "Your Turn" in the News.

2 Organize Your Draft

Below are some techniques you can use to develop and organize your ideas within your analysis.

Describe Examine the characteristics of each part of the thing your are analyzing.

Define Define key parts, characteristics, or terms, particularly if your topic is a technical one.

Compare/Contrast Show how your subject or its parts are similar to or different from others.

Classify/Categorize Organize the subject of your analysis into categories according to qualities or functions.

Sequence/Order Show how things function in a specific sequence or order (especially important when you analyze a process).

The following is a simple organizational model you can try.

1. Get your readers' attention with a good introduction.
2. Identify your topic and your purpose.
3. Describe the parts of your topic.
4. Examine each part and tell how it's related to the other parts and to the whole.
5. Come to a conclusion that gives your analysis a meaning.

3 Rework and Share Your Draft

Ask yourself these questions as you rework your draft.

- Did I clearly introduce my topic and my purpose?
- Could I further use any of the organizing tips listed above?
- Have I covered everything that's needed? Can any of the information I've included be eliminated?
- Have I achieved my purpose?

PEER RESPONSE

A peer reviewer can help you evaluate your draft. Ask her or him questions like these.

- What do you think is the main point of my essay?
- How can I make my analysis clearer?
- What things should I further define or describe?
- How can I make my ideas flow more naturally?

SkillBuilder

WRITER'S CRAFT

Comparing and Contrasting

Comparison is a way of analyzing a subject. To make a comparison, think about how one thing is similar to and different from another thing. A Venn diagram can help you.

Printing Press	Both	Internet
• developed in 15th century • needs paper	resulted in increased availability of information	• developed in late 20th century • needs computers

WRITING HANDBOOK

For more information on comparing and contrasting, see page 1233 of the Writing Handbook

APPLYING WHAT YOU'VE LEARNED

Think of two things or ideas that you could compare and contrast. Use a Venn diagram if you wish.

RETHINK & EVALUATE

Preparing to Revise

1. What conclusion have you come to about your topic?
2. What evidence will you need to support that conclusion?
3. How can you get your readers' attention in your introduction?
4. How will you organize your revised draft?

Polishing Your Analysis

Final Thoughts Before you start polishing your analysis, take a few minutes to think about it. Have you worked through the information enough to answer your own questions and come to a satisfying conclusion? How will you explain your topic and your purpose to your audience? Try to have a complete picture of your analysis in your head before you start revising your draft.

Student's Published Article

page 14

YOUR TURN

Computers: Blessing or Curse?

(continued from page 12)

Computers also have widened our community. Using the Internet, we not only can play a computer game with a friend next door but can communicate almost instantly with someone halfway around the world or get information from hundreds of libraries, museums, data banks, and other sources.

On the other hand, others can get to us just as easily. The Internet may become the junk-mail carrier of tomorrow, drowning us in unwanted advertising copy.

The possibility of information theft is far more dangerous. Information about almost every aspect of our lives ends up in data banks. Without effective safeguards—and so far, they don't exist—government agencies, private businesses, computer criminals, or just curious hackers can get at this information without our permission or our knowledge.

Victor Frankenstein, the obsessed doctor in Mary Shelley's novel *Frankenstein,* created a new type of human being that turned out to be a monster who brought tragedy to the doctor and those he loved. Frankenstein wanted to use technology to conquer death. His mistake was that he failed to take responsibility for or think about the consequences of what he achieved.

Mary Shelley's horror story can be read as a warning against blind acceptance of new technologies. Will computers end up enriching our lives or controlling them? Will new technologies bring about new dangers? Who is thinking about the responsibility for advances in technology that could become tomorrow's monsters?

1 Revise and Edit

Use the following tips to make sure your revision meets the Standards for Evaluation listed on the next page.

- Will your opening attract your readers' attention as well as introduce your topic?
- Are the parts of your topic clearly defined and adequately presented? Have you shown how the parts relate to one another?
- Did your peer comments suggest a need to add or change anything to make your analysis clearer?
- Have you drawn a logical conclusion that gives your analysis a purpose?

INTERNET
COMPUTER SECURITY
Import files from only reliable, virus-free sources.
Use a password that only you know and that nobody else can guess.
Use virus-protection software.

Visual Aids for an Oral Presentation

2 Share Your Work

In addition to, or instead of, presenting a written essay, think about sharing your ideas in one of the following formats or in some other suitable format. In the example shown above, the student used charts to supplement an oral analysis.

PUBLISHING IDEAS

- Give your report orally, using photos, charts, graphs, artwork, or a video to supplement it.
- Present your ideas as your opening statement in a panel discussion on your topic.
- Submit your analysis to a newspaper or to a magazine that specializes in your topic.

Standards for Evaluation

An effective analysis

- includes an interesting and informative introduction
- identifies the parts that make up the topic
- uses appropriate strategies to examine and explain each part
- presents its information in a logical order
- includes an effective and well-developed introduction, body, and conclusion

SkillBuilder

GRAMMAR FROM WRITING

Using Comparisons
If you make comparisons in your analysis, be sure you use the correct forms of comparative adjectives and adverbs. Be careful with irregular comparative forms.

Positive	Comparative	Superlative
good	better	best
bad	worse	worst

Use a dictionary for help if you are unsure of which form to use.

GRAMMAR HANDBOOK

For more information on comparisons, see page 1273 of the Grammar Handbook.

Editing Checklist Use these revision and editing tips.

- Have you used the correct forms of comparatives?
- Did you check the spelling of any proper nouns or terms that are new to you?
- Did you proofread carefully?

REFLECT & ASSESS

Evaluate the Experience

1. What have you learned about your topic?
2. How will writing an analysis help you resolve questions in the future?

PORTFOLIO Consider the above questions in an introduction to your essay. Add it and your essay to your portfolio.

REFLECT & ASSESS

UNIT 4: THE FLOWERING OF ROMANTICISM

What new understanding of the romantic poets have you gained by reading and discussing the poetry in this unit? In your opinion, how do the romantics' views of nature and love compare with the views held by people today? Explore these questions by completing one or more options in each of the following sections.

REFLECTING ON THE UNIT

OPTION 1 **Analyzing Similarities** Recall the quotation from William Blake at the beginning of this unit:

To see the world in a grain of sand
And heaven in a wild flower,
Hold infinity in the palm of your hand
And eternity in an hour.

Working with a small group of classmates, discuss what you think this quotation means. Then, with your group, create a graph like the one shown, indicating how similar the messages of five of the poems in the unit are to the message of Blake's lines.

	Slightly Similar → → → Very Similar
"The World Is Too Much with Us"	

OPTION 2 **Comparing Times** Many of the romantic poets were inspired to write about their observations of, and powerful responses to, the natural world. From each part of the unit, select one poem in which the observations and responses are, in your opinion, especially pertinent to issues in today's world. In a paragraph or two, explain how the two poems affected you and how the messages or truths they convey relate to contemporary issues.

OPTION 3 **Defining Romanticism** How would you define the term *romanticism?* With a group of classmates, create a list of words and phrases that you associate with the romantic movement. Highlight the words and phrases that you think are particularly relevant to the era. Then compare your list with those of other groups.

REFLECT & ASSESS

Self-Assessment: Review your understanding of the poems in this unit by creating a two-column chart. In the first column, list your five favorites among the poems, in order of your preference. In the second, summarize each poem's message and tell why you like the poem.

REVIEWING LITERARY CONCEPTS

OPTION 1 **Examining Imagery, Symbol, and Mood** The poets represented in this unit all share a purpose: to express themselves through their poetry. Although some of the poems focus on feelings and others on ideas, all of them depend to some degree on imagery—and many depend on symbols—to convey moods and to present the poets' attitudes toward their subjects. Select six or more of the poems in this unit. Decide what mood each evokes, and identify at least two images or symbols that help sustain the mood. Share your conclusions with a partner.

OPTION 2 **Appreciating Sound and Meter** Think again about some of the elements—such as rhythm, rhyme, alliteration, consonance, and assonance—that work together to create a total experience for readers of poetry. In what passages of the poems in this unit do you think sound and meter are employed in particularly interesting ways? Identify ten noteworthy examples in various poems; then, with a small group, create a list of the five most effective uses of sound and meter.

REFLECT & ASSESS

Self-Assessment: The following literary terms were discussed in Unit Four. Copy the list in your notebook, circling any terms that you do not completely understand. Use the Handbook of Literary Terms (page 1192) to check the definitions of the circled terms.

symbol	*Spenserian stanza*
form	*ode*
imagery	*meter*
alliteration	*foot*
onomatopoeia	*mood*
structure	*assonance*
apostrophe	*consonance*

PORTFOLIO BUILDING

- **QuickWrites** Many of the QuickWrites assignments in this unit asked you to recall your own experiences with nature or your impressions of nature—a particular place, an element of nature, a season. Select two pieces of your writing that you think successfully recreate your impressions or experiences. Write a cover note explaining your choices. Then add the note and the two pieces to your portfolio.
- **Writing About Literature** Earlier in this unit, you wrote an essay about your changing understanding of a poem. Reread your essay and the poem now. Imagine that the poet is having lunch with you in your school's cafeteria. If you could ask him three questions about the poem, what would you ask? Write your questions and attach them to the essay.
- **Writing from Experience** In this unit, you were asked to analyze a subject in order to develop your own understanding. Reread your essay now. What is the most compelling piece of evidence that supports your recommendation? Jot down your ideas and attach them to your essay.
- **Personal Choice** Think about the writing assignments and other activities—including independent and group projects—that you completed for this unit. Which activity or writing assignment did you enjoy most? Write a note explaining your choice and giving your evaluation of the project's success. Include the note in your portfolio.

REFLECT & ASSESS

Self-Assessment: Look over the writing that you have chosen for your portfolio so far. Create a list in which you rank the pieces according to how pleased you are with the results. On the list, note any particular writing strengths you have discovered, along with any skills you want to work on in subsequent units. Date your list and add it to your portfolio.

SETTING GOALS

As you worked through the reading and writing activities in this unit, you very likely developed a deeper understanding of the nature of poetry. Are there any poets you studied in this unit whose work you would like to read more of? Do you have any ideas for poetry of your own? Do you still feel that you are reluctant to read poetry? Develop a list of goals for enhancing your own knowledge and appreciation of poetry.

UNIT FIVE

THE VICTORIANS

1832-1901

Our deeds determine us, as much as we determine our deeds.

George Eliot
novelist

The Stone Pickers (1887), George Clausen, Oil on canvas, 42″ x 31″, Tyne and Wear Museums, Newcastle upon Tyne, England.

CLAUSEN

TIME LINE

The Victorians
1832-1901

1833

Slavery is abolished in British Empire

1837

William IV dies and is succeeded by his niece Victoria; Charles Dickens publishes first magazine installment of *Oliver Twist*

1840

Queen Victoria weds Prince Albert; Britain annexes New Zealand and agrees to unite Lower Canada and Upper Canada as single colony

1847

Charlotte Brontë publishes *Jane Eyre;* her sister Emily publishes *Wuthering Heights*

1848

University of London grants admission to women students

1850

Alfred, Lord Tennyson, publishes *In Memoriam* and is appointed poet laureate upon death of Wordsworth; Elizabeth Barrett Browning publishes *Sonnets from the Portuguese*

1854

Crimean War—in which Britain, Turkey, France, and Austria fight Russia—begins

1859

Charles Darwin publishes *On the Origin of Species*

1860

Florence Nightingale founds school for nurses

1861

Prince Albert dies; George Eliot publishes novel *Silas Marner*

1865

Transatlantic telegraph cable is completed; Joseph Lister, building on work of French scientist Louis Pasteur, introduces modern antiseptic surgery; Lewis Carroll publishes *Alice's Adventures in Wonderland*

1870

National Education Act authorizes local governments to establish public schools; Married Women's Property Act gives women economic rights

1875

Public Health Act expands sanitary laws; new sewer system is installed in London

1876

Disraeli secures title "Empress of India" for Victoria; collective bargaining by trade unions is legalized

1877

Britain annexes Transvaal in South Africa

1879

Irish nationalist Charles Stewart Parnell organizes Land League and pressures for Irish home rule

1883

Robert Louis Stevenson publishes adventure novel *Treasure Island*

1887

Sir Arthur Conan Doyle publishes *A Study in Scarlet*, first work featuring Sherlock Holmes

1891

Thomas Hardy publishes *Tess of the D'Urbervilles*

1895

First production of Oscar Wilde's *The Importance of Being Earnest;* H. G. Wells publishes landmark science fiction novel *The Time Machine*

1901

Queen Victoria dies

Period *Pieces*

The Benz Viktoria, 1893

Mangle, used to squeeze water from laundry

Big Ben, tower clock installed in Houses of Parliament, 1859

INTRODUCTION

The Victorians 1832-1901

Britain's Victorian era was a time of overseas expansion and domestic reform. During this period of growth and change, the numbers of the middle class swelled, the lives of the working class improved, and the nation was set on the road to democracy. Its advances included the laying of a transatlantic telegraph cable and the advent of the automobile, electric lighting, and antiseptic medicine. Nevertheless, for many people today the term *Victorian* implies only stuffy complacency, hypocrisy, and prudishness. These characteristics did exist, but they by no means sum up the era.

Victoria was only 18 when she began her reign in 1837. Mindful of the scandalous conduct of her royal uncles, George IV and William IV, the queen placed great emphasis on moral behavior and was scrupulous in the performance of her royal duties. Ably tutored by the Whig prime minister Lord Melbourne, the young queen accepted—as her predecessors had not—the idea of a constitutional monarchy in which the monarch gave advice rather than orders. In 1840 Melbourne helped arrange the marriage of Victoria and her German cousin Prince Albert of Saxe-Coburg-Gotha, to whom she became deeply devoted. After Albert died in 1861, Victoria mourned him for the rest of her life, retiring even further from the daily affairs of government. Fortunately, during Victoria's 64-year reign (the longest in British history) she and the nation would be served by a number of talented prime ministers—including, in addition to Melbourne, Sir Robert Peel in the early Victorian years, Lord Palmerston in the mid-Victorian era, and the rival politicians Benjamin Disraeli and William E.

Top: Portrait of Queen Victoria, painted in the year of her marriage
Above: The Great Exhibition of 1851, held in London's Crystal Palace, celebrated industry and technology.
Left: An Indian floral pattern of the sort that had a major influence on Victorian design
Right: Removal of Irish tenants during the potato famine

Gladstone in later Victorian times. These leaders helped guide Britain through a remarkable period of social, economic, and political change.

An Era of Reform

Under Lord Melbourne and the Whigs, who held power throughout much of the 1830s, many long-sought reforms were passed, including the abolition of slavery in the British Empire and the first restrictions on child labor in factories. Nevertheless, the Whigs' goal was not democracy but an enlightened government by an educated upper class. Their best-known achievement, the Reform Bill of 1832, expanded voting rights only to men with a certain amount of property. When members of the working-class movement called Chartism demanded universal male suffrage, the demand went unheeded.

After the 1841 election brought Sir Robert Peel and the Tories to power, gradual reform continued, with new laws addressing safety in the mines and factories. Peel, however, faced agitation from both Chartists and the Anti–Corn Law League, which sought to repeal the laws protecting British farmers from foreign competition. The league's cause was advanced by the devastating rains of 1845, which ruined England's wheat crop and allowed disease to wipe out Ireland's harvest of potatoes, the staple

Language

In Victorian times, as education spread and people entering the middle class attempted to speak "proper" English, the English language became more homogeneous. Increased literacy also stabilized English, since the written language tends to change more slowly than the spoken. The period also saw the beginning of an effort to compile a definitive record of the histories, uses, and meanings of English words, resulting in the massive *Oxford English Dictionary,* the first volume of which was published in 1884. This landmark work, not completed until 1928 and revised several times since, traces each word's changes in meaning from its first recorded use to the present.

Victorian advances in the natural and social sciences spurred the coinage of new words, such as *telephone, photography, psychiatrist,* and *feminist*. As the new fields of study developed their own jargons, their specialized and technical vocabulary began to infiltrate everyday speech. Euphemisms—mild, indirect, or vague terms substituted for ones considered harsh or offensive—also grew more popular as Victorian propriety made certain words taboo. A chicken breast became "white meat"; its legs, "drumsticks." Even words that today seem rather benign—such as *belly, buck,* and *stallion*—were prudishly avoided.

Although "proper" circles frowned on slang, it was widely used among the lower classes as a means of conversing safely in the presence of outsiders, including the police. The Cockneys of London's East End developed an elaborate system of rhyming slang in early Victorian times—using, for example, *loaf* to mean "head" because *loaf* is the first word in the expression *loaf of bread,* which rhymes with *head.* The expression "use your loaf" is still common in the East End today.

food of the Irish poor. With famine stalking Ireland, Peel agreed that foreign grain could ease conditions and introduced a bill to abolish the Corn Laws. The bill passed too late to help most of the Irish, but it did mark the beginning of free trade in Britain.

International Affairs

The free-trade issue divided the Tories and led some of them to join the Whigs to form a new political party, the Liberal party. During this realignment, the dominant political figure was the independent Lord Palmerston, a moderate Whig who served as foreign minister for much of the 1830s and 1840s. In that capacity he had successfully overseen the expansion of Britain's empire—including, in 1840, the annexation of New Zealand and the beginning of a war with China that led to the British acquisition of Hong Kong two years later. Palmerston's clever diplomacy, backed up by the British fleet, had also kept France out of Egypt and Russia out of Turkey. Then, in 1854, with Turkey again threatened and Palmerston out of office, Britain joined the fight against Russia in the Crimean War. By the next year, after a series of British military blunders and defeats, the public was clamoring for change. At this point Palmerston became prime minister, and it was he who received credit for ending the war with the 1856 treaty ensuring Turkish sovereignty. Two years later, following a mutiny by native troops in British India, Palmerston's government attempted to end corruption there by removing control of the colony from the hands of the East India Company. This change had mixed results but was generally applauded in Britain.

Top: Disraeli and Gladstone
Above: Florence Nightingale caring for wounded soldiers
Left: Portrait of Nightingale
Below: The advent of the railroad revolutionized the transportation of both people and goods.

Prosperity and Advances

Though Palmerston showed little interest in domestic reform, free trade and the expansion of empire helped make the mid-Victorian period a prosperous time in Britain, both for aristocrats and for the growing middle class. Despite the repeal of the Corn Laws, the introduction of the McCormick reaper from America prevented an agricultural decline. Textile exports were booming, and industry in general benefited from Henry Bessemer's new steel-making process. Steamships and railways revolutionized the transportation of goods and people, making travel quicker, cheaper, and far more comfortable than ever before. Communications improved with the advent of the telegraph. Growing literacy and improvements in printing spurred the publication of books, magazines, and newspapers. Advances in medicine included the introduction of antiseptic surgery by Joseph Lister and the founding of the first modern nursing school by Florence Nightingale, who had become famous as a volunteer nurse in the Crimean War.

Nightingale's volunteer spirit was echoed in the foundation of the YMCA, the Salvation Army, and a host of new charitable organizations. In mid-Victorian Britain—a society at once deeply religious and highly materialistic—most people viewed charity as a Christian duty and shared an optimistic faith in humanity's ability to achieve happiness through economic and material progress. John Stuart Mill, the most influential economist of the period, argued for gradual, steady social reform and for the abandonment of the strict laissez-faire (government-noninterference) policies of earlier British liberals. Many of Mill's ideas were put into practice after Palmerston's death, when Gladstone and Disraeli rose on the political scene.

Gladstone and Disraeli

As head of the new Liberal party, Gladstone wore the mantle of reform, but Disraeli also realized the importance of political and social reforms in attracting working-class support for his revitalized Tory party. Gladstone won passage of bills for land reform in Ireland and for the establishment of public schools and secret balloting in elections. Disraeli won passage of the landmark Second Reform Bill of 1867, which extended the vote to working-class males, as well

Literature

Though no longer the radical movement it once was, **romanticism** continued to influence Victorian writing; but a new movement, called **realism,** increasingly began to take hold. Realism sought to capture everyday life as it really was lived. Instead of turning away from science and industry as romanticism had done, realism focused on the effects of the Industrial Revolution, often bringing social problems to public attention. Many early Victorian novels blend romanticism and realism. Charles Dickens, the era's most popular storyteller, produced entertaining novels with farfetched plots that nevertheless exposed real social problems—such as the plight of orphans in *Oliver Twist* (1837–1839) and *Nicholas Nickleby* (1838–1839). In *Wuthering Heights* (1847), Emily Brontë, one of a growing number of women writers, set a melodramatic plot with a Byronic hero against a realistic Yorkshire landscape; in *Jane Eyre* (1847), her sister Charlotte blended gothic elements with realistic social details. Realism is an even stronger element in the novels of William Makepeace Thackeray and Anthony Trollope.

Later in the century, new ideas in the natural and social sciences prompted the style known as **psychological realism,** which focused not on external realities but on the inner realities of the mind, and **naturalism,** an offshoot of realism that viewed nature and society as forces indifferent to human suffering. One of the pioneering psychological realists was the novelist George Meredith. The beginnings of naturalism are evident in the novels of George Eliot (Mary Ann Evans), but even more strongly naturalistic is the pessimistic fiction of Thomas Hardy, set in the author's native Wessex.

as bills that improved housing and sanitation, legalized trade unions, and reformed factory conditions. Where the two rivals differed most was in their personal styles and their attitudes toward British imperialism. A staid, morally righteous figure, Gladstone was a "Little Englander" who believed that Britain should take care of its own problems rather than involve itself in costly expansion abroad. The more flamboyant Disraeli linked prosperity to colonial expansion and patriotically equated imperialism with Britain's destiny. In 1875 he secretly negotiated the British government's purchase of a large interest in the newly completed Suez Canal in Egypt, which cut thousands of miles off the sea trip to India. A year later, he maneuvered Parliament into conferring the title "Empress of India" on Victoria. He also acquired the Mediterranean island of Cyprus and annexed the Transvaal, a South African republic that had been established by the Boers, settlers of mostly Dutch descent. Disraeli's policies enjoyed the support of the queen, who could not conceal her dislike for the self-righteous Gladstone.

Fascinated by the heroic exploits of their explorers, missionaries, and empire builders in Africa and Asia, most British citizens also supported Disraeli's imperialism, although by the time of his death in 1881, that support was waning. Disraeli's effort to prevent a Russian domination of Afghanistan, which threatened British India, resulted in two years of costly warfare there. Similarly, his annexation of the Transvaal led to conflicts with the native Zulu and with the Boers, who regained control of the Transvaal in 1881. Events such as these introduced the nation to the downside of imperialism, much as Gladstone had warned.

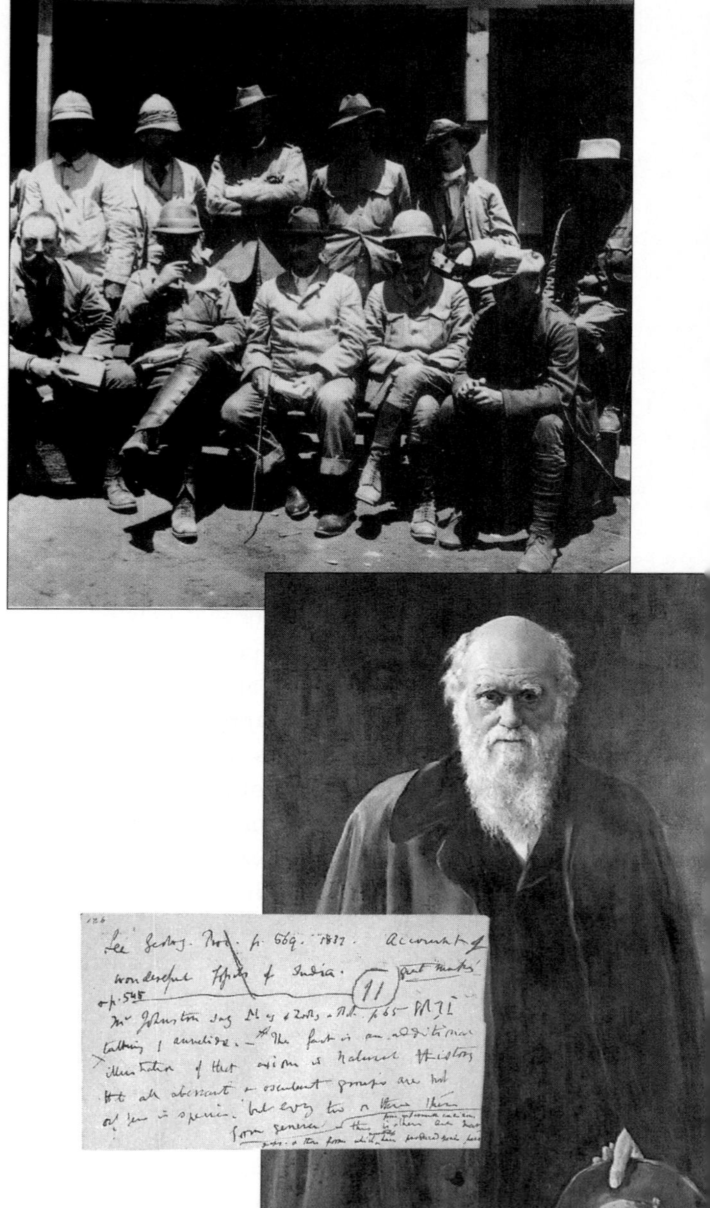

Top: Boer War soldiers
Above: Charles Darwin; *inset:* detail from Darwin's notebooks
Right: Portrait of an older Queen Victoria
Far right: Victorian bicycle

New Directions

During the last decades of the Victorian era, the confident optimism of earlier times was tinged with an undercurrent of anxiety. To be sure, most people patriotically celebrated Victoria's Golden Jubilee, marking 50 years of her rule, in 1887 and her Diamond Jubilee a decade later. Nevertheless, the complacency of mid-Victorian times was beginning to shatter as new ideas took hold. The writings of the scientist Charles Darwin created a rift between liberal Christians, whose interpretation of the Bible allowed the acceptance of Darwin's theory of evolution, and fundamentalist Christians, whose interpretation did not. Applying Darwin's ideas to human society, the philosopher Herbert Spencer coined the phrase "survival of the fittest," which conservatives—called social Darwinists—used to justify a return to government noninterference, saying that nature should be allowed to weed out the "unfit." This thinking brought the social Darwinists into conflict with the increasingly socialist labor movement, which supported industrial reform through government control and ownership. The socialism of the labor movement also frayed its ties to moderate Liberals just as the Liberal party was falling into disarray over the issue of Irish home rule. Then, in 1899, British colonial expansion in Africa resulted in the Boer War, which galvanized public patriotism and further weakened the anti-imperialist Liberal party. A new party formed in 1900—the Labor party— would become a dominant political force in the new century, and the Boer War would be a prelude to the far more devastating warfare of the modern age.

LASERLINKS

• *HISTORICAL LITERARY CONNECTION*

Literature

Extremely popular in Victorian times, novels often were serialized in magazines aimed at the growing middle class. Toward the 19th century's end the short story also grew popular, in hands such as those of Rudyard Kipling, who championed British imperialism in rousing tales drawn from his experiences in India, and Sir Arthur Conan Doyle, creator of the master detective Sherlock Holmes. The Victorian emphasis on family life also spurred a boom in children's literature, including Lewis Carroll's *Alice's Adventures in Wonderland* (1865) and *Through the Looking Glass* (1872).

Poetry also thrived during Victorian times. Alfred, Lord Tennyson, who became poet laureate in 1850, wrote musical public verse like "The Charge of the Light Brigade," as well as more personal poetry such as that of *In Memoriam* (1850). Elizabeth Barrett Browning produced a bestseller with *Sonnets from the Portuguese* (1850), a volume of love poems to her husband Robert, who himself pioneered the verse form called the dramatic monologue. Poets of the Pre-Raphaelite movement, such as Dante Gabriel Rossetti and his sister Christina, repudiated Victorian excess and sought to return to the clarity of medieval Italian works. The more pessimistic mood of late Victorian times is evident in the verse of Thomas Hardy and A. E. Housman. Gerard Manley Hopkins is noted for his modern experiments in poetic rhythm.

The Victorian era was not an age of great drama, although Oscar Wilde wrote some fine comedies in the 1890s. The era's most enduringly popular stage creations are the comic operas of W. S. Gilbert and Arthur Sullivan, which ridicule social pretense with a vitality that is still admired today.

PART 1 *Personal Relationships*

During the Victorian era, the Industrial Revolution brought increased productivity and economic growth to much of England. However, it also brought poverty, overcrowding, and appalling work conditions to the many people who had flocked to the cities from rural areas, hoping for a better life. As the world became a confusing and often brutal place, personal relationships—love, marriage, friendship—became especially important to the Victorians. Of course, as the writers in this part of Unit Five suggest, not all such relationships provide comfort. Some, twisted by jealousy, turn dark—even criminal. In these selections, you may encounter experiences and questions that continue to concern people.

PREVIEWING

POETRY

from In Memoriam

Alfred, Lord Tennyson

PERSONAL CONNECTION

Think about people you have known or read about who have experienced the death of a close friend or loved one. How did they express their loss and feelings of grief? What helped them cope? Share your thoughts with your classmates.

BIOGRAPHICAL CONNECTION

Alfred, Lord Tennyson, was a true spokesperson for middle-class Victorians. His poetry reflected many of the prevailing attitudes of the day, especially the moral and religious concerns of individuals living in a universe redefined by scientific discoveries. Nevertheless, his output was diverse, ranging from optimistic verse written to please the public to wistful, melancholic poems expressing his own thoughts and feelings.

In 1833, Tennyson was overwhelmed with grief by the sudden death of his best friend, Arthur Henry Hallam, who had recently become engaged to Tennyson's sister and was just 22 years old. In response to this loss, Tennyson began writing *In Memoriam,* an elegy mourning the death of a man of great talent cut off before he is able to fulfill the promise of his youth. Written over a period of 17 years, the poem consists of 132 sections, 3 of which are included in the selection presented here.

Arthur Henry Hallam (about 1830), unknown artist. Engraving after a contemporary drawing by Mrs. Weld, The Granger Collection, New York.

WRITING CONNECTION

Imagine that you have been asked to give a speech entitled "In Memoriam" to honor the memory of a friend or family member who has died. How would you address your own grief, and the grief of others, over the loss of this loved one? List in your notebook a few of the general topics that you would cover in your speech. Then, as you read these excerpts from Tennyson's poem, compare your topics with those that he touches upon.

FROM

In Memoriam

ALFRED, LORD TENNYSON

27

I envy not in any moods
The captive void of noble rage,
The linnet born within the cage,
That never knew the summer woods;

I envy not the beast that takes
His license in the field of time,
Unfettered by the sense of crime,
To whom a conscience never wakes;

Nor, what may count itself as blest,
The heart that never plighted troth
But stagnates in the weeds of sloth;
Nor any want-begotten rest.

I hold it true, whate'er befall;
I feel it, when I sorrow most;
'Tis better to have loved and lost
Than never to have loved at all.

2 void of: lacking in.

3 linnet: a kind of small songbird.

6 license: freedom of action; liberty.

7 unfettered: unrestricted.

9–12 nor, what . . . rest: nor do I envy the supposed peace of mind that arises from remaining sunk in inaction, never pledging one's love, or from any deficiency.

May Day (1960), Andrew Wyeth. Watercolor. Copyright © 1995 Andrew Wyeth.

54

O, yet we trust that somehow good
Will be the final goal of ill,
To pangs of nature, sins of will,
Defects of doubt, and taints of blood;

That nothing walks with aimless feet;
That not one life shall be destroyed,
Or cast as rubbish to the void,
When God hath made the pile complete;

That not a worm is cloven in vain;
That not a moth with vain desire
Is shriveled in a fruitless fire,
Or but subserves another's gain.

Behold, we know not anything;
I can but trust that good shall fall
At last—far off—at last, to all,
And every winter change to spring.

So runs my dream; but what am I?
An infant crying in the night;
An infant crying for the light,
And with no language but a cry.

130

Thy voice is on the rolling air;
I hear thee where the waters run;
Thou standest in the rising sun,
And in the setting thou art fair.

What are thou then? I cannot guess;
But though I seem in star and flower
To feel thee some diffusive power,
I do not therefore love thee less.

My love involves the love before;
My love is vaster passion now;
Though mixed with God and Nature thou,
I seem to love thee more and more.

Far off thou art, but ever nigh;
I have thee still, and I rejoice;
I prosper, circled with thy voice;
I shall not lose thee though I die.

19 pangs of nature: physical pain.

20 taints of blood: inherited faults.

23 void: empty space.

25 cloven: split.

28 subserves: promotes or assists.

Portrait of Lord Tennyson (about 1856–1859), George Frederick Watts. Oil on wood panel, 61 cm × 50.4 cm, National Gallery of Victoria, Melbourne, Australia, purchased 1888.

43 diffusive: scattered about.

49 nigh: nearby.

RESPONDING OPTIONS

FROM PERSONAL RESPONSE *TO* CRITICAL ANALYSIS

REFLECT **1.** With your classmates, discuss your thoughts after reading these sections of *In Memoriam*.

RETHINK **2.** What different reactions to grief and loss does the speaker seem to experience?

Consider

- the last stanza of section 27
- his expression of trust in section 54, especially in lines 30–33
- his thoughts leading up to the statement "I have thee still, and I rejoice" in line 50

3. What do you think brings the speaker consolation?

Consider

- what he states he hears and feels in lines 37–44
- his thoughts about love in lines 45–48
- his statement "I shall not lose thee . . ." in line 52

4. Many Victorians were optimistic about the future. Do you think the speaker is? Support your opinion with evidence from the excerpts.

RELATE **5.** Share with the class your opinion of the speaker's comment that it is "better to have loved and lost / Than never to have loved at all."

ANOTHER PATHWAY

With a partner, examine how the speaker struggles, in each section of *In Memoriam*, to cope with his grief and the loss of his friend. In a chart like the one shown, summarize the speaker's thoughts and compare his tones in the three sections. Share your ideas with the class.

	Section 27	Section 54	Section 130
Speaker's thoughts			
Speaker's tone			

LITERARY CONCEPTS

Tennyson's *In Memoriam* is one of the most famous elegies in English literature. An **elegy** is an extended meditative poem in which the speaker reflects upon death—often in tribute to a person who has died recently—or an equally serious subject. Most elegies are written in formal, dignified language and are serious in tone. Thomas Gray's "Elegy Written in a Country Churchyard" (page 432) is another well-known example of this genre. List the purposes you think Tennyson had for writing his elegy. Give evidence to support your ideas.

QUICKWRITES

1. Write individual **titles** for these three sections of *In Memoriam*. Make sure that each reflects the principal theme of the section to which it applies.
2. Compose an **epitaph** for Arthur Hallam, based on Tennyson's reaction to his friend's death.
3. Using the list you made for the Writing Connection on page 583 as a starting point, write a short **speech** in which you eulogize someone who has died.

PORTFOLIO *Save your writing. You may want to use it later as a springboard to a piece for your portfolio.*

ALTERNATIVE ACTIVITIES

1. Create a three-part **collage** to convey the speaker's moods or attitudes in the three excerpts. Use background colors, photographs, found objects, and perhaps drawings of your own to compose your visual statement.
2. ***Cooperative Learning*** With several classmates, stage a **mixed-media performance** that evokes the feelings of grief and loss expressed in this selection. Use a combination of oral reading of the excerpts, modern dance, and appropriate music and images.

LITERARY LINKS

Compare these excerpts from *In Memoriam* with Ben Jonson's "On My First Son" (page 276). What differences do you see in the two speakers' ways of coping with their grief? Share your thoughts with the class.

ACROSS THE CURRICULUM

Psychology Research current theories of grief and loss. What are the normal stages of the grieving process? What are the most helpful things people can do to confront and resolve their grief? Share your findings in a brief oral report to the class.

ALFRED, LORD TENNYSON

1809–1892

The fourth son in a family of 12 children, Alfred Tennyson grew up in Somersby, England, where his father was a clergyman. Even as a child, Tennyson displayed an interest in poetry. He began learning to write poems at age eight by imitating the styles of Milton, Byron, and others. While a teenager, he collaborated with his brother on a collection of poems, which they published in 1826.

Although Tennyson's father tutored his children to prepare them for a university education, family life at Somersby was problematical. The Reverend Dr. Tennyson's dissatisfaction with his profession led to periods of drunkenness that caused his family distress. Tensions in the family were increased by the opium addiction of one child and the severe mental illness of another.

In 1827, Tennyson entered Cambridge University, where he won a poetry contest in his first year. His achievements caught the attention of a group of gifted undergraduates who called themselves the Apostles. Under the leadership of Arthur Henry Hallam, the Apostles urged Tennyson to pursue a career as a poet. Unfortunately, lack of funds forced the promising young poet to leave the university in 1831 and return home without taking a degree.

In the following years, Tennyson endured many difficulties, including the calamity of Hallam's death, financial problems, and an engagement complicated by the disapproval of his future wife's father. Throughout this time, however, he persisted with his writing, and in 1850 *In Memoriam* was published to impressive reviews. Tennyson had at last received literary recognition, and later that year he was invited by Queen Victoria to succeed Wordsworth as poet laureate.

Tennyson lived a long life, during which he became a living legend—one of the most beloved figures of the Victorian era. He was a colorful character of large stature who delighted audiences with his thunderous voice. In 1884, at the government's urging, he accepted the rank of baron and, along with it, the title *Lord.*

OTHER WORKS "The Charge of the Light Brigade," "The Lady of Shalott," "Ulysses," "Crossing the Bar," *Idylls of the King*

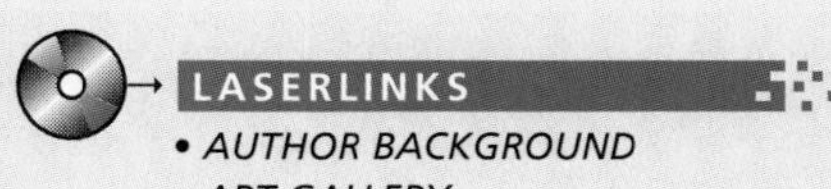

- *AUTHOR BACKGROUND*
- *ART GALLERY*

MILESTONES IN BRITISH LITERATURE

Charles Dickens

THE NOVELS OF CHARLES DICKENS

"It was the best of times, it was the worst of times": so begins Charles Dickens's novel *A Tale of Two Cities,* set at the time of the French Revolution. In many respects, this description can also be applied to Dickens's own era. Depending on one's perspective, Victorian Britain was the bright new dawning of the Industrial Revolution, or it was a filthy, brutal, and dehumanizing period best gotten over with. Dickens was able to see and comment upon both views of 19th-century life. With humor and intensity, his work shed light on London's criminals, businessmen, and working poor.

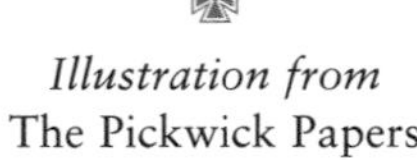

Illustration from The Pickwick Papers

Born in Portsmouth but raised in London from the age of two, Dickens used events from his own life as starting points for many of his novels. His early career as a newspaper reporter sharpened his eye for detail and his ear for dialogue, giving him an uncanny ability to make his stories spring to life.

Dickens's first literary success was *The Posthumous Papers of the Pickwick Club*—usually known as *The Pickwick Papers*—in which he chronicled the humorous misadventures of eccentric characters in London and the countryside. The novel was an immediate

W. C. Fields and Freddie Bartholomew in the 1935 film version of David Copperfield

success, catapulting Dickens into sudden and lasting fame. After this lighthearted bestseller, Dickens wrote 14 other novels, as well as numerous short stories and works of nonfiction.

Although Dickens's early novels, including *Oliver Twist* and *Nicholas Nickleby,* address such serious topics as crime, greed, and the mistreatment of children, they are also filled with lighter, humorous moments. His later novels, such as *Bleak House* and *A Tale of Two Cities,* present a grimmer, harsher world, and are etched with irony and satire. In the midst of this later phase of his literary output, however, Dickens also created two celebrated tales of youth and discovery—*David Copperfield,* a largely autobiographical work, and *Great Expectations,* considered by many to be his finest work.

Although Dickens died at the age of 58, his popularity did not. To this day, his works are enjoyed both in their original form and in adaptations as films and plays. An eight-hour stage production of *Nicholas Nickleby* recently enjoyed widespread popularity, and *A Christmas Carol* has become a delightful part of the Christmas tradition in countries around the world. Dickens's novels are an indispensable part of our literary landscape—and our modern social conscience as well.

Upper left:
Dickens's study
Lower left:
Earliest known photograph of Dickens, 1852. Photofest.

PREVIEWING

POETRY

My Last Duchess   Porphyria's Lover

Robert Browning

PERSONAL CONNECTION

Consider the potential consequences of jealousy in a love relationship. Do you think jealousy is normal in such a relationship? Are there different degrees of this emotion? Share your thoughts with classmates.

LITERARY CONNECTION

Although Robert Browning is best known as one of the greatest of Victorian poets, he actually devoted many years to writing plays. The techniques he learned as a playwright undoubtedly led to his mastery of the **dramatic monologue**—a type of poem in which a fictional speaker addresses a silent listener about a critical experience in his or her life. "My Last Duchess" and "Porphyria's (pôr-fîr'yəz) Lover" are among Browning's best dramatic monologues.

"My Last Duchess" takes place in 16th-century Italy and reflects the esteem for art that characterized the Italian Renaissance. Loosely based on actual events in the life of Alfonso II, duke of Ferrara, the poem presents a single episode in the duke's negotiations to marry the daughter of a powerful count. As the poem begins, the duke is showing a portrait of his former wife to the count's agent. The painting of the duchess "looking as if she were alive" is typical of Renaissance portraits, in which painters endeavored to portray their sitters as accurately and realistically as possible.

"Porphyria's Lover" first appeared with another dramatic monologue under the title *Madhouse Cells,* a title that reveals the poet's fascination with abnormal states of mind. Though Browning was a respectable, well-balanced person, the fictional speakers in his poems—ranging from corrupt bishops to insanely jealous lovers—often display abnormal behavior.

READING CONNECTION

Making Inferences An inference is a logical guess or conclusion based on evidence. You often need to make inferences to figure out what is unstated yet implied in a literary work. You might, for example, use clues provided by a writer to infer, simply from the way a character acts, that the character is jealous of another character. As you read each of these poems, jot down, in a chart like the one shown, any inferences you make about the speaker, the woman he describes, the setting, or past events.

Inferences		
	"My Last Duchess"	"Porphyria's Lover"
Speaker		
Woman		
Setting		
Past events		

My Last Duchess

Robert Browning

Vespertina Quies (1893), Sir Edward Burne-Jones. Oil on canvas 120.6 cm × 62.2 cm, bequeathed by Miss Maud Beddington, 1940, Tate Gallery, London/Art Resource, New York.

That's my last Duchess painted on the wall,
Looking as if she were alive. I call
That piece a wonder, now: Frà Pandolf's hands
Worked busily a day, and there she stands.
Will't please you sit and look at her? I said
"Frà Pandolf" by design, for never read
Strangers like you that pictured countenance,
The depth and passion of its earnest glance,
But to myself they turned (since none puts by
The curtain I have drawn for you, but I)
And seemed as they would ask me, if they durst,
How such a glance came there; so, not the first
Are you to turn and ask thus. Sir, 'twas not
Her husband's presence only, called that spot
Of joy into the Duchess' cheek: perhaps
Frà Pandolf chanced to say "Her mantle laps
Over my lady's wrist too much," or "Paint
Must never hope to reproduce the faint
Half-flush that dies along her throat": such stuff
Was courtesy, she thought, and cause enough
For calling up that spot of joy. She had
A heart—how shall I say?—too soon made glad,
Too easily impressed; she liked whate'er
She looked on, and her looks went everywhere.

GUIDE FOR READING

1 What can you infer from the duke's use of the word *last?*

3 Frà Pandolf's: of Brother Pandolf, a fictitious friar-painter.

7 countenance: face.

9–10 What might it mean that no one save the duke draws the curtain?

11 durst: dared. (Note the hint that the strangers feel some sense of fear about questioning the duke.)

16 mantle: cloak.

21–24 How do you think the duke feels about the duchess's tendency to be easily pleased?

Sir, 'twas all one! My favor at her breast,
The dropping of the daylight in the West,
The bough of cherries some officious fool
Broke in the orchard for her, the white mule
She rode with round the terrace—all and each
Would draw from her alike the approving speech,
Or blush, at least. She thanked men—good! but thanked
Somehow—I know not how—as if she ranked
My gift of a nine-hundred-years-old name
With anybody's gift. Who'd stoop to blame
This sort of trifling? Even had you skill
In speech—(which I have not)—to make your will
Quite clear to such an one, and say, "Just this
Or that in you disgusts me; here you miss,
Or there exceed the mark"—and if she let
Herself be lessoned so, nor plainly set
Her wits to yours, forsooth, and made excuse
—E'en then would be some stooping; and I choose
Never to stoop. Oh sir, she smiled, no doubt,
Whene'er I passed her; but who passed without
Much the same smile? This grew; I gave commands;
Then all smiles stopped together. There she stands
As if alive. Will't please you rise? We'll meet
The company below, then. I repeat,
The Count your master's known munificence
Is ample warrant that no just pretense
Of mine for dowry will be disallowed;
Though his fair daughter's self, as I avowed
At starting, is my object. Nay, we'll go
Together down, sir. Notice Neptune, though,
Taming a sea horse, thought a rarity,
Which Claus of Innsbruck cast in bronze for me!

27 officious: offering unwanted services; meddling.

35 trifling: actions of little importance.

41 forsooth: in truth; indeed.

46 What do you think happened to make the smiles stop?

49 munificence (myo͞o-nĭf'ĭ-səns): generosity.

50 just pretense: legitimate claim.

51 dowry (dou'rē): a financial settlement given to a groom by the bride's father.

53–54 The count's agent has gestured for the duke, because of his higher social status, to descend first. The duke responds that they will go down together. In your opinion, is the duke's graciousness in ignoring social differences genuine?

54 Neptune: in Roman mythology, the god of the sea.

55 What comparison can you draw between the duke and duchess's relationship and Neptune's taming the sea horse?

56 Claus of Innsbruck: a fictitious Austrian sculptor. What can you infer from the last two words of the poem?

FROM PERSONAL RESPONSE *TO* CRITICAL ANALYSIS

REFLECT 1. In your notebook, explain your reaction to this poem.

RETHINK 2. How would you describe the speaker's attitude toward his former wife?

Consider

- where he keeps his wife's picture
- his reaction to the courtesy Frà Pandolf shows her
- how he feels about her response to his "gift of a nine-hundred-years-old name" (lines 32–34)
- why he chooses "never to stoop" (lines 42–43)

3. Think about what might have happened to the duchess. Why do you suppose the poet never tells us exactly what happened to her?

PORPHYRIA'S LOVER

ROBERT BROWNING

The Model (1939), Georges Braque. Oil on canvas, 100 cm × 100 cm, private collection, New York. Copyright © 1995 Artists Rights Society (ARS), New York/ADAGP, Paris.

The rain set early in tonight,
    The sullen wind was soon awake,
It tore the elm-tops down for spite,
    And did its worst to vex the lake:
    I listened with heart fit to break.
When glided in Porphyria; straight
    She shut the cold out and the storm,
And kneeled and made the cheerless grate
    Blaze up, and all the cottage warm;
    Which done, she rose, and from her form
Withdrew the dripping cloak and shawl,
    And laid her soiled gloves by, untied
Her hat and let the damp hair fall,
    And, last, she sat down by my side
    And called me. When no voice replied,

GUIDE FOR READING

4 vex: to disturb; trouble the surface of.

6 straight: immediately.

6–9 What do you think Porphyria's first actions reveal about her?

8 grate: fireplace.

15 Although the speaker has heard Porphyria, he does not reply. Why do you think he remains silent?

She put my arm about her waist,
And made her smooth white shoulder bare,
And all her yellow hair displaced,
And, stooping, made my cheek lie there,
And spread, o'er all, her yellow hair,
Murmuring how she loved me—she
Too weak, for all her heart's endeavor,
To set its struggling passion free
From pride, and vainer ties dissever,
And give herself to me forever.
But passion sometimes would prevail,
Nor could tonight's gay feast restrain
A sudden thought of one so pale
For love of her, and all in vain:
So, she was come through wind and rain.
Be sure I looked up at her eyes
Happy and proud; at last I knew
Porphyria worshiped me: surprise
Made my heart swell, and still it grew
While I debated what to do.
That moment she was mine, mine, fair,
Perfectly pure and good: I found
A thing to do, and all her hair
In one long yellow string I wound
Three times her little throat around,
And strangled her. No pain felt she;
I am quite sure she felt no pain.
As a shut bud that holds a bee,
I warily oped her lids: again
Laughed the blue eyes without a stain.
And I untightened next the tress
About her neck; her cheek once more
Blushed bright beneath my burning kiss:
I propped her head up as before,
Only, this time my shoulder bore
Her head, which droops upon it still:
The smiling rosy little head,
So glad it has its utmost will,
That all it scorned at once is fled,
And I, its love, am gained instead!
Porphyria's love: she guessed not how
Her darling one wish would be heard.
And thus we sit together now,
And all night long we have not stirred,
And yet God has not said a word!

22–25 What is Porphyria unable to do? What might the "vainer ties" be?

27–30 Porphyria has left a party in order to be with the speaker.

35 Note that the speaker feels that he must make a decision.

44 In your opinion, why does the speaker open Porphyria's eyes "warily" (cautiously)?

52–55 The speaker here claims that he knows Porphyria's mind.

56–57 What is the speaker claiming?

RESPONDING OPTIONS

FROM PERSONAL RESPONSE *TO* CRITICAL ANALYSIS

REFLECT 1. Were you surprised by the events presented in "Porphyria's Lover"? Why or why not? Record your thoughts in your notebook.

RETHINK 2. Why do you think the speaker kills Porphyria?
Consider
- what the speaker expects in a love relationship
- his opinion of Porphyria's activities
- what he hopes to achieve by his action

3. Do you think the speaker feels guilty about what he has done?
Consider
- the tone in which he speaks
- his reason for strangling Porphyria
- his attempt to make her look as she did before the murder (lines 44–49)
- his comment about God's response to the deed (line 60)

4. Using pantomime, try to portray the changing moods of the speaker throughout the poem.

RELATE 5. Compare the love relationships in "My Last Duchess" and "Porphyria's Lover," drawing on the inferences you noted for the Reading Connection on page 590. How are the relationships alike? How are they different?

ANOTHER PATHWAY

The speaker of a dramatic monologue often reveals to the reader characteristics or feelings of which the speaker is unaware. For each of these poems, make a Venn diagram to compare your own opinion of the speaker with his apparent view of himself. Then share and discuss your diagrams with the class.

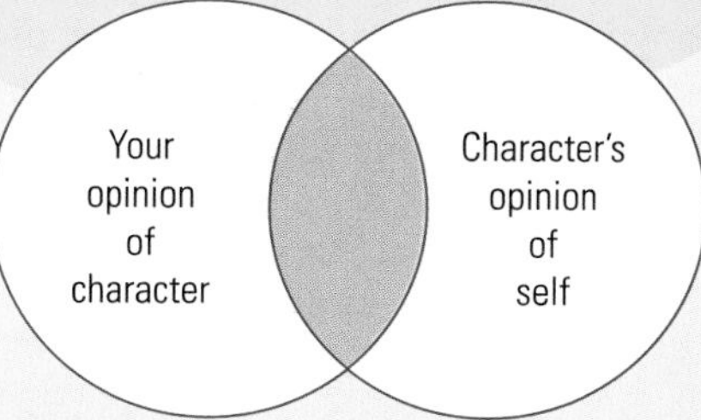

LITERARY CONCEPTS

In a **dramatic monologue,** the speaker describes a crucial experience to one or more listeners who remain silent, allowing the speaker to proceed without interruption or argument. The effect on the reader is that of hearing just one side of a conversation. This technique allows the poet to focus on the feelings, personality, and motivations of the speaker—in a sense, taking the reader inside the speaker's mind. How might Browning's choice of the dramatic-monologue form have determined the kinds of situations he presented in his poems? In your opinion, what types of characters make the best speakers of dramatic monologues?

QUICKWRITES

1. Imagine that you are the silent listener in "My Last Duchess" and write a **list** of questions you would like to ask the speaker.
2. Write a **synopsis** of a television mystery in which the incident described in "Porphyria's Lover" is either the first or the last scene.

PORTFOLIO *Save your writing. You may want to use it later as a springboard to a piece for your portfolio.*

ALTERNATIVE ACTIVITIES

1. ***Cooperative Learning*** With a group of classmates, conduct a **trial** of Porphyria's lover on the charge of murder. Students acting as lawyers should question the defendant, and after deliberating, a jury should deliver their verdict.
2. In a pencil or oil **portrait,** try to convey some of the characteristics of one of the poem's speakers. Your portrait may be realistic or abstract.

LITERARY LINKS

Contrast the speakers of "My Last Duchess" and "Porphyria's Lover" with the speaker of Lord Byron's "She Walks in Beauty" (page 528). How do the speakers differ in their attitudes toward women?

CRITIC'S CORNER

The 19th-century novelist George Eliot stated that Browning "sets our thoughts at work rather than our emotions." What do you think she meant, and do you agree with her? Cite evidence from these two poems to support your answer.

ACROSS THE CURRICULUM

Psychology Research theories on jealousy, looking for answers to these questions: What causes some people to be more jealous than others? What is the relationship between jealousy and self-esteem? Can feelings of jealousy be avoided or overcome? Report your findings to the class.

ROBERT BROWNING

1812–1889

Born and raised near London, Robert Browning lived with his parents until he married at the age of 34. Although he attended the University of London for a brief period, his real education took place at home, where he was tutored in literature, history, and music, as well as boxing and horsemanship. Browning's parents agreed to financially support their son in his attempt to make a living writing poetry, and at the age of 21 he published his first poem, "Pauline," which was savagely criticized for displaying too much emotion. The criticism embarrassed the young poet, who vowed to keep his writing totally objective, free from personal feelings, in the future. It was at this time that he began to write plays and dramatic monologues. His plays were not well received, and for many years critics claimed that his poetry was too difficult to read.

In 1845, Browning met the poet Elizabeth Barrett, six years his senior, and began a famous romance that has been memorialized in both film and literature. The couple eloped in 1846 and moved to Italy. Although Browning wrote very little during his marriage, he lived happily for the next 15 years. After his wife's death in 1861, he returned to London with his young son and concentrated for the next few years on the writing of *The Ring and the Book,* a series of dramatic monologues based on the records of a 17th-century Roman murder trial. The publication of *The Ring and the Book* made Browning famous and finally obtained for his poetry the recognition it deserved.

OTHER WORKS "Count Gismond," "The Bishop Orders His Tomb at St. Praxed's Church," "Home Thoughts, from Abroad," "Prospice," "The Pied Piper of Hamelin"

LASERLINKS
- *FILM CONNECTION*
- *ART GALLERY*

PREVIEWING

POETRY/NONFICTION

Sonnet 43
Elizabeth Barrett Browning

A Warning Against Passion
Charlotte Brontë

PERSONAL CONNECTION

The two selections you are about to read express very different attitudes toward romantic relationships. How would you describe your approach to romance? Try judging yourself on the four scales shown. For each pair of opposite qualities, decide at approximately which point of the scale you think your romantic personality falls.

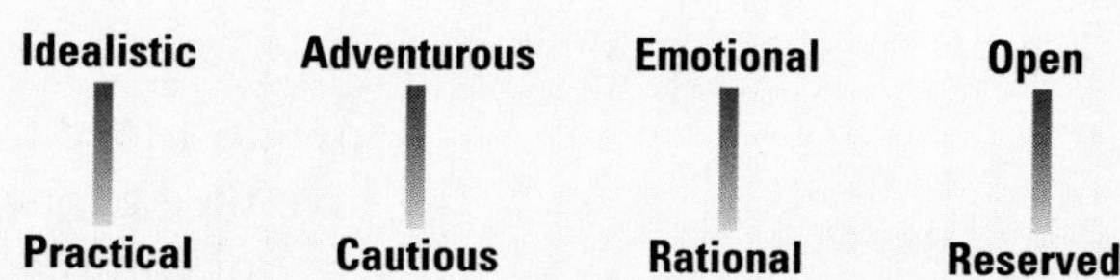

BIOGRAPHICAL CONNECTION

Elizabeth Barrett and Robert Browning were one of Victorian England's most famous couples. When they met, Elizabeth, an invalid, was a well-known poet, but Robert—six years her junior—was still struggling to gain recognition. Elizabeth's over-protective father strongly opposed Robert's attentions; the couple, however, married without his knowledge and moved to Italy, where Elizabeth's health improved and her career flourished. During their courtship, Elizabeth had secretly written a group of sonnets, including "Sonnet 43," about her romance with Robert, but she did not show them to him until after they were married. She titled them *Sonnets from the Portuguese* and published them as translations of another poet's work to hide her identity as the author.

Charlotte Brontë, the author of the famous romantic novel *Jane Eyre,* reveals some of her attitudes toward love in a personal letter to her close friend Ellen Nussey. Ellen, or Nell, had asked Brontë for advice in handling the attentions of a Mr. Vincent, whom she was thinking of marrying, even though she did not know him well and was not strongly attracted to him. Brontë offers her friend several perspectives on the situation.

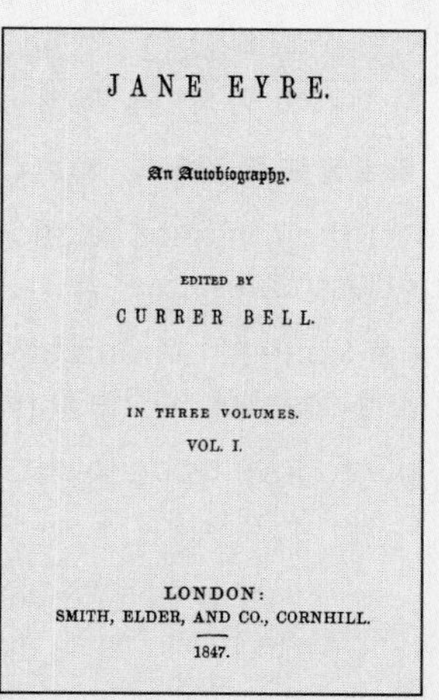
JANE EYRE.

An Autobiography.

EDITED BY

CURRER BELL.

IN THREE VOLUMES.

VOL. I.

LONDON:
SMITH, ELDER, AND CO., CORNHILL.
1847.

READING CONNECTION

Relating Form and Meaning Writers choose different forms—such as poems, essays, and stories—to convey different ideas, attitudes, and feelings. In these selections, Barrett Browning conveys her thoughts about love in a poem, and Brontë conveys her thoughts about love in a letter. As you read, note what qualities of love each writer emphasizes and how the form she has chosen helps to highlight those qualities.

SONNET 43

Elizabeth Barrett Browning

How do I love thee? Let me count the ways.
I love thee to the depth and breadth and height
My soul can reach, when feeling out of sight
For the ends of Being and ideal Grace.
I love thee to the level of everyday's
Most quiet need, by sun and candlelight.
I love thee freely, as men strive for Right;
I love thee purely, as they turn from Praise.
I love thee with the passion put to use
In my old griefs, and with my childhood's faith.
I love thee with a love I seemed to lose
With my lost saints,—I love thee with the breath,
Smiles, tears, of all my life!—and, if God choose,
I shall but love thee better after death.

FROM PERSONAL RESPONSE *TO* CRITICAL ANALYSIS

REFLECT **1.** What is your impression of the romantic relationship described in this sonnet? Share your thoughts with your classmates.

RETHINK **2.** Look again at the Personal Connection on page 597. On each of the scales shown, where would you place the speaker of the sonnet?

3. Do you think it is desirable to love or be loved in this way? Explain your answer.

Warning Against Passion

Charlotte Brontë

November 20th, 1840.

My dearest Nell,—That last letter of thine treated of matters so high and important I cannot delay answering it for a day—

Now, Nell, I am about to write thee a discourse and a piece of advice which thou must take as if it came from thy grandmother—but in the first place—before I begin with thee, I have a word to whisper in the ear of Mr. Vincent and I wish it could reach him.

In the name of St. Chrysostom, St. Simon and St. Jude,[1] why does not that amiable young gentleman come forward like a man and say all that he has to say to yourself personally—instead of trifling with kinsmen and kinswomen? "Mr. Vincent," I say—"walk or ride over to Brookroyd . . . and say, 'Miss Ellen, I want to speak to you.' Miss Ellen will of course civilly answer, 'I'm at your service, Mr. Vincent' and then when the room is cleared of all but *yourself* and *herself* just take a chair near her, insist upon her laying down that silly . . . basketwork, and listening to *you.* Then begin in a clear, distinct, deferential, but determined voice—'Miss Ellen, I have a question to put to you, a very important question—will you take me as your husband, for better for worse? I am not a rich man, but I have sufficient to support us—I am not a great man, but I love you honestly and truly—Miss Ellen, if you knew the world better you would see that this is an offer not to be despised—a kind attached heart, and a moderate competency.'[2] Do this, Mr. Vincent, and you may succeed—go on writing sentimental and love-sick letters to Henry[3] and I would not give sixpence for your suit."[4]

So much for Mr. Vincent—now, Nell, your turn comes to swallow the black bolus[5]—called a friend's advice. . . . Is the man a fool? is he a knave,[6] a humbug, a hypocrite, a ninny, a noodle? If he is any or all of these things, of course there is no sense in trifling with him—cut him short at once—Blast his hopes with lightning rapidity and keenness.

Is he something better than this? has he at least common sense—a good disposition, a manageable temper? Then, Nell, consider the matter. You feel a disgust towards him *now,* an utter repugnance—very likely—but be so good as to remember you don't know him—you have only had three or four days' acquaintance with him—longer and closer intimacy might reconcile you to a wonderful extent. And now I'll tell you a word of truth at which you may be offended or not as you like—From what I know of your character—and I think I know it pretty well—I should say you will never *love before* marriage—After that ceremony is over, and after you have had some months to settle down, and to get accustomed to the creature you have taken for your worse half—you will probably make a most affectionate and happy wife—even if the individual should not prove all you could wish—you will be indulgent towards his little follies and foibles—and will not feel much annoyance at them. This will especially be the case if he should have sense sufficient to allow you to guide him in important matters. Such being the case, Nell, I hope you will not have the romantic folly to wait for the awakening of what the French call "Une grande *passion*"—My good girl, "une grande passion" is "*une* grande *folie.*"[7] . . .

I hope you will not have the romantic folly to wait for the awakening of what the French call "Une grande *passion*" —My good girl, "une grande passion" is "*une* grande *folie.*"

1. **St. Chrysostom** (krĭs′əs-təm), **St. Simon, and St. Jude:** saints known for their honesty, sincerity, and courage.
2. **competency:** income or means sufficient to meet one's needs.
3. **Henry:** Ellen Nussey's brother.
4. **suit:** courtship.
5. **black bolus:** a round, bitter medicinal preparation, larger than an ordinary pill.
6. **knave:** an unprincipled, crafty fellow.
7. **"Une grande *passion*"** (ün gräɴd′ pä-syôɴ′) . . . **"*une* grande *folie*"** (ün gräɴd′ fô-lē′) *French:* a great passion . . . a great foolishness.

WORDS TO KNOW

discourse (dĭs′kôrs′) *n.* a discussion of a subject in speech or writing
deferential (dĕf′ə-rĕn′shəl) *adj.* showing courteous respect
repugnance (rĭ-pŭg′nəns) *n.* an extreme dislike or distaste
foible (foi′bəl) *n.* a minor weakness or character flaw

Mediocrity[8] in all things is wisdom—mediocrity in the sensations is superlative wisdom. When you are as old as I am, Nell— (I am sixty at least being your grandmother) you will find that the majority of those worldly precepts—whose seeming coldness shocks and repels us in youth—are founded in wisdom. Did you not once say to me in all childlike simplicity, "I thought, Charlotte—no young ladies should fall in love, till the offer was actually made." . . . The maxim is just . . . I will even extend and confirm it—no young lady should fall in love till the offer has been made, accepted—the marriage ceremony performed and the first half year of wedded life has passed away—a woman may then begin to love, but with great precaution—very coolly—very moderately—very rationally—if she ever loves so much that a harsh word or a cold look from her husband cuts her to the heart—she is a fool—if she ever loves so much that her husband's will is her law—and that she has got into a habit of watching his looks in order that she may anticipate his wishes she will soon be a neglected fool.

Couple in a Garden (about 1840), H. Robinson. Engraving after a Daniel Maclise illustration for a Thomas Moore poem, Mary Evans Picture Library, London.

Did I not once tell you of an instance of a relative of mine who cared for a young lady till he began to suspect that she cared more for him and then instantly conceived a sort of contempt for her?[9] . . .

I have two studies—*you* are my study for the success, the credit, and the respectability of a quiet, tranquil character. Mary is my study—for the contempt, the remorse—the misconstruction which follow the development of feelings in themselves noble, warm—generous—devoted and profound—but which being too freely revealed—too frankly bestowed—are not estimated at their real value. . . . I never hope to see in this world a character more truly noble—she would *die* willingly for one she loved—her intellect and her attainments are of the very highest standard, yet I doubt whether Mary will ever marry. . . . ❖

8. **mediocrity** (mē′dē-ŏk′rĭ-tē): a state of being midway between two extremes. (The word is used here without any negative connotation.)

9. **relative of mine . . . contempt for her:** a reference to a failed romance between another friend, Mary Taylor, and Brontë's brother, Branwell.

WORDS TO KNOW

precept (prē′sĕpt′) *n.* a rule or principle of conduct

RESPONDING OPTIONS

FROM PERSONAL RESPONSE *TO* CRITICAL ANALYSIS

REFLECT 1. What is your opinion of Brontë's advice in "A Warning Against Passion"? Jot down your thoughts in your notebook.

RETHINK 2. How would you summarize the main points of Brontë's advice about love and marriage?

Consider
- her proposed advice to Mr. Vincent
- her view of falling in love
- her view of possible relationships between husbands and wives

3. How would you describe Brontë's views of men and women?

RELATE 4. Issues relating to love and marriage continue to be of great concern to people. Do you think Brontë's advice has relevance today? Explain your answer.

5. What do you think Brontë and Barrett Browning would say about each other's attitude toward romantic relationships?

ANOTHER PATHWAY

Cooperative Learning

How do you think Barrett Browning and Brontë would define love? Work with a small group of classmates to make a cluster diagram, like the one shown, for each selection. Record the aspects of love that you think would be important elements in each writer's definition of the emotion.

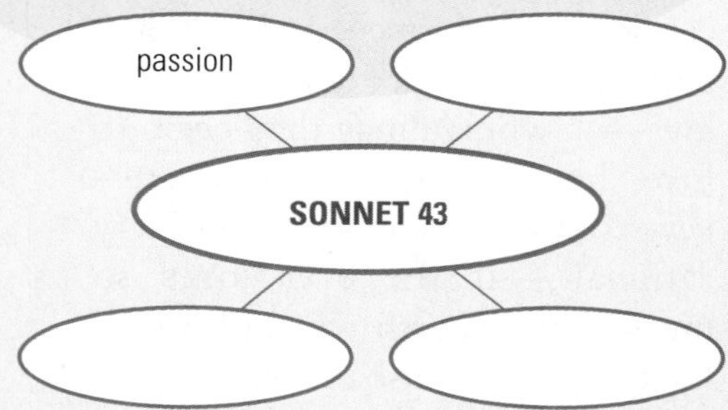

LITERARY CONCEPTS

An **author's purpose** may be to entertain, to inform, to express opinions, or to persuade. Although a writer can fulfill more than one of these purposes in a work, one is usually the most important. What seems to be the main purpose of "Sonnet 43"? of "A Warning Against Passion"? Do they share any purposes? Explain your answer.

LITERARY LINKS

Reread Spenser's "Sonnet 30" (page 218) and Shakespeare's "Sonnet 116" (page 230). Compare these two sonnets with Barrett Browning's "Sonnet 43." Which of the three poems expresses the emotion of love most convincingly for you?

QUICKWRITES

1. Write a **letter** in which Ellen Nussey responds to Brontë's advice.
2. Write a **parody,** or humorous imitation, of "Sonnet 43," describing a less-than-ideal relationship. A good opening might be "How can I stand thee? . . ."

PORTFOLIO Save your writing. You may want to use it later as a springboard to a piece for your portfolio.

ALTERNATIVE ACTIVITIES

1. With a partner, stage an imaginary **conversation** between Ellen Nussey and Mr. Vincent after Nussey has read the letter from Brontë.
2. Conduct a **survey** of some of your classmates to determine what they think are the most important elements of a successful marriage. Ask them to comment on the perspectives in Barrett Browning's poem and Brontë's letter.

WORDS TO KNOW

Review the Words to Know at the bottom of the selection pages. Then choose the word that is most closely related to each of the following sets.

1. lecture, speech, persuasive essay
2. bowing to a queen, giving someone else first choice of a seat
3. walking out of a movie, boycotting a product
4. "Waste not, want not," "Act in haste, repent at leisure."
5. being late all the time, forgetting to return borrowed items

ELIZABETH BARRETT BROWNING

1806–1861

Elizabeth Barrett was the oldest of 11 children in a prosperous family. A precocious child, she read constantly and had her first poem published by the time she was 14. She became ill when she was about 15, and from that time until she eloped with Robert Browning in 1846, she lived the life of an invalid. Her mother died in 1828, and the drowning of her favorite brother in 1840 plunged her into depression. Throughout her illness and grief, however, she continued to write, eventually becoming one of England's most popular poets.

During the 15 years of her marriage, Barrett Browning was intensely happy. She gave birth to a son, wrote a wide variety of poems, and ardently supported such causes as the abolition of slavery, the reform of child labor practices, and women's rights. The Brownings' home in Florence, Italy, became a gathering place for people prominent in politics and the arts. Barrett Browning's most ambitious poem, the verse novel *Aurora Leigh,* was the first work by an Englishwoman in which the main character is herself a writer.

OTHER WORKS "Sonnet 22," *The Cry of the Children*

CHARLOTTE BRONTË

1816–1855

Charlotte Brontë developed her literary gift in the face of tragedy. One of six children, she lived with her family in the remote Yorkshire village of Haworth, where her father was a clergyman. After the death of her mother when she was 5 and of her two oldest sisters when she was 9, she and her sisters Emily and Anne and her brother, Branwell, became inseparable companions. They wrote constantly.

After periods of schooling and work as a teacher away from home, Charlotte returned to Haworth in her late 20s to try to open a school for girls with her sisters. The scheme failed, however, and in 1846 they turned to publishing some of their writing. Their first efforts received little attention, but when Charlotte's novel *Jane Eyre* appeared in 1847, it was an immediate success.

Sadly, Charlotte's triumph was soon eclipsed by further tragedy. During the next two years, Branwell, Emily, and Anne all died, leaving Charlotte heartbroken and lonely. Nevertheless, she wrote two more novels and corresponded regularly with her friends. In 1854 she married her father's assistant, but within a year she was dead as a result of pregnancy complications.

OTHER WORKS *Shirley, Villette*

• *AUTHOR BACKGROUND*

MILESTONES IN BRITISH LITERATURE

Charlotte and Emily Brontë

The Brontë Novels

"*Wuthering Heights* was hewn in a wild workshop, with simple tools, out of homely materials," wrote Charlotte Brontë in an introduction to her sister Emily's novel. The same could be said of Charlotte's masterpiece *Jane Eyre,* for although these novels were published in 1847, when Charlotte was 31 and Emily 29, the imaginations that inspired them were developed at an early age and evident in the childhood games they played in their father's parsonage on the Yorkshire moors. Using wooden soldiers and a toy village, the six Brontë children created a world called the Great Glass Town Confederacy, consisting of tiny kingdoms inhabited by characters based on their favorite heroes. All of them, but especially Charlotte and Emily, wrote everything down—composing stories, essays, and songs about

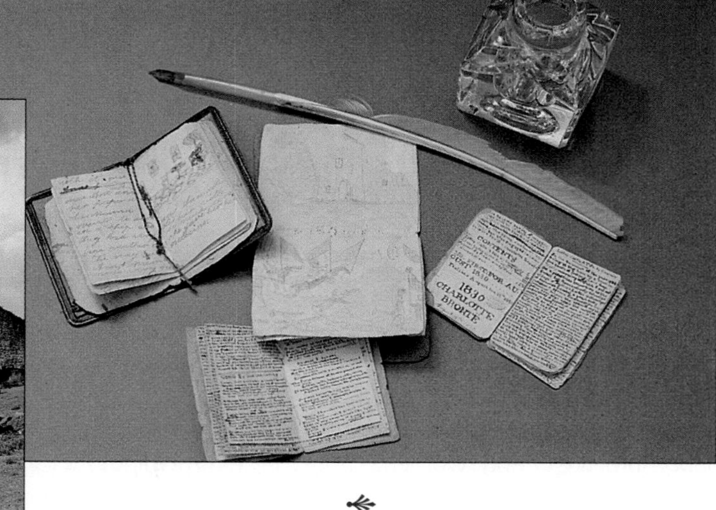

Left:
Photograph of the Yorkshire moor where the Brontë children grew up
Above:
The Brontë children wrote their tiny books by hand on folded sheets of paper measuring about 2 inches by 1½ inches. The covers were made of paper from sugar bags or wrapping paper from local shops.

their kingdoms and binding the writings into tiny books. As the children grew, the Glass Town games fell off, but the Brontë girls continued to write, their works springing from the worlds they continued to create within.

As a young adult, Charlotte discovered a stack of Emily's poems. Elated at their high quality, she convinced Emily and Anne, another sister, to combine their poems with hers in a single volume. The three sisters, adopting the pseudonyms "Currer Bell," "Ellis Bell," and "Acton Bell," published their book in 1846. Although only two copies were sold, the young Brontës were not deterred from continuing to write.

It was with their novels that the sisters would achieve their greatest success, even though when Emily's *Wuthering Heights* was published, it was largely ignored. Nevertheless, this fierce, brooding story—set on the moors—of the star-crossed love between Heathcliff and Catherine eventually came to be considered one of the most original novels of all time. Charlotte's *Jane Eyre* became an immediate critical and popular success as readers fell in love with her noble and passionately independent heroine.

Soon afterward, when Anne published *The Tenant of Wildfell Hall,* rumors circulated that Acton, Currer, and Ellis Bell were all the same man; so the sisters revealed their true identities, and their public literary life began. The triumph was muted, however, by their brother Branwell's sudden death, followed closely by the deaths of Emily and Anne. By the time Charlotte was 33, she was the sole survivor of the six Brontë children. Still, she continued to write.

The Brontës' novels, most notably Charlotte's *Jane Eyre* and Emily's *Wuthering Heights,* have remained popular works of literature for nearly 150 years. Through them, readers can experience the imaginations of two women who, despite the male domination of the Victorian literary world, were able to make their voices heard.

Top:
Painting by Thomas Davidson, depicting the scene from Jane Eyre *in which Jane meets Rochester*
Bottom:
Watercolor by Emily of her pet hawk, 1841. All of the Brontë children drew and painted.

PREVIEWING

FICTION

Christmas Storms and Sunshine

Elizabeth Cleghorn Gaskell

PERSONAL CONNECTION

Have you ever given someone you didn't know very well the "cold shoulder"? Think about what might have prompted you to act this way. Were your actions based on sound reasoning, or were they based on a mere first impression of the person or on what someone else had said? Get together with a few other students and share your experiences.

HISTORICAL CONNECTION

The early Victorian era was a time of political reform, as the old aristocracy reluctantly gave way to a more democratic system. The First Reform Bill, passed in 1832, gave voting rights to the middle class and, as a result, made the upper class less powerful. The Tories, a political party that had controlled the government for almost 50 years, represented the interests of wealthy landowners and opposed the democratic reforms. The Tories were conservative, and they scorned their opponents, the "Radical" Whigs, for supporting reforms that gradually allowed the middle class to become a major force in England's economy.

Many Victorian writers focused on topics that appealed to the growing number of readers in the newly powerful middle class, writing about the social and personal relationships of ordinary people. The popular Victorian novelist Elizabeth Cleghorn Gaskell, a member of the growing middle class, lived in Manchester, one of England's most industrial cities. Her writing deals with the manners and morals of upper- and middle-class Victorian society as well as the living and working conditions of the lower class, and her stories are often set in industrial cities much like Manchester. The story you are about to read involves the first impressions of two families who live in the same house.

WRITING CONNECTION

In your notebook, make a list like the one shown, recording the qualities or details that you use to formulate your first impressions of people. Place a check by any qualities or details that might change once you learn more about each individual. As you read the selection, you may decide to add other qualities to your list.

First Impressions

Possibly Change	Qualities/Details
	1. facial features
✓	2. friendly
	3.

Christmas Storms and Sunshine

ELIZABETH CLEGHORN GASKELL

In the town of—(no matter where) there circulated two local newspapers (no matter when). Now the *Flying Post* was long-established and respectable—alias bigoted and Tory; the *Examiner* was spirited and intelligent—alias newfangled and democratic. Every week these newspapers contained articles abusing each other, as cross and peppery as articles could be, and evidently the production of irritated minds, although they seemed to have one stereotyped commencement[1]—"Though the article appearing in our

1. **stereotyped commencement:** a beginning that was repeatedly used without variation.

last week's *Post* (or *Examiner*) is below contempt, yet we have been induced," &c. &c.; and every Saturday the Radical shopkeepers shook hands together, and agreed that the *Post* was done for by the slashing, clever *Examiner*; while the more dignified Tories began by regretting that Johnson should think that low paper, only read by a few of the vulgar, worth wasting his wit upon; however, the *Examiner* was at its last gasp.

It was not, though. It lived and flourished; at least it paid its way, as one of the heroes of my story could tell. He was chief compositor, or whatever title may be given to the headman of the mechanical part of a newspaper. He hardly confined himself to that department. Once or twice, unknown to the editor, when the manuscript had fallen short, he had filled up the vacant space by compositions of his own; announcements of a forthcoming crop of green peas in December; a grey thrush having been seen, or a white hare, or such interesting phenomena; invented for the occasion, I must confess; but what of that? His wife always knew when to expect a little specimen of her husband's literary talent by a peculiar cough, which served as prelude; and, judging from this encouraging sign, and the high-pitched and emphatic voice in which he read them, she was inclined to think, that an "Ode to an Early Rosebud," in the corner devoted to original poetry, and a letter in the correspondence department, signed "Pro Bono Publico,"[2] were her husband's writing, and to hold up her head accordingly.

I never could find out what it was that occasioned the Hodgsons to lodge in the same house as the Jenkinses. Jenkins held the same office in the Tory Paper as Hodgson did in the *Examiner*, and, as I said before, I leave you to give it a name. But Jenkins had a proper sense of his position, and a proper reverence for all in authority, from the king down to the editor and sub-editor. He would as soon have thought of borrowing the king's crown for a nightcap, or the king's scepter for a walking-stick as he would have thought of filling up any spare corner with any production of his own; and I think it would have even added to his contempt of Hodgson (if that were possible), had he known of the "productions of his brain," as the latter fondly alluded to the paragraphs he inserted, when speaking to his wife.

Jenkins had his wife too. Wives were wanting[3] to finish the completeness of the quarrel which existed one memorable Christmas week, some dozen years ago, between the two neighbors, the two compositors. And with wives, it was a very pretty, a very complete quarrel. To make the opposing parties

2. **"Pro Bono Publico"** (prō bō′nō pŭb′lĭ-kō′): a Latin phrase meaning "for the public good."

3. **wanting:** required; needed.

WORDS TO KNOW
allude (ə-lo͞od′) *v.* to make an indirect reference

still more equal, still more well-matched, if the Hodgsons had a baby ("such a baby!—a poor, puny little thing"), Mrs. Jenkins had a cat ("such a cat! a great, nasty, miowling tom-cat, that was always stealing the milk put by for little Angel's supper"). And now, having matched Greek with Greek, I must proceed to the tug of war.[4] It was the day before Christmas; such a cold east wind! such an inky sky! such a blue-black look in people's faces, as they were driven out more than usual, to complete their purchases for the next day's festival.

Before leaving home that morning, Jenkins had given some money to his wife to buy the next day's dinner.

"My dear, I wish for turkey and sausages. It may be a weakness, but I own I am partial to sausages. My deceased mother was. Such tastes are hereditary. As to the sweets—whether plum-pudding or mince-pies—I leave such considerations to you; I only beg you not to mind expense. Christmas comes but once a year."

And again he called out from the bottom of the first flight of stairs, just close to the Hodgsons' door ("such ostentatiousness," as Mrs. Hodgson observed), "You will not forget the sausages, my dear!"

"I should have liked to have had something above common, Mary," said Hodgson, as they too made their plans for the next day; "but I think roast beef must do for us. You see, love, we've a family."

"Only one, Jem! I don't want more than roast beef, though, I'm sure. Before I went to service,[5] mother and me would have thought roast beef a very fine dinner."

"Well, let's settle it, then, roast beef and a plum-pudding; and now, good-bye. Mind and take care of little Tom. I thought he was a bit hoarse this morning."

And off he went to his work.

Now, it was a good while since Mrs. Jenkins and Mrs. Hodgson had spoken to each other, although they were quite as much in possession of the knowledge of events and opinions as though they did. Mary knew that Mrs. Jenkins despised her for not having a real lace cap, which Mrs. Jenkins had; and for having been a servant, which Mrs. Jenkins had not; and the little occasional pinchings which the Hodgsons were obliged to resort to, to make both ends meet, would have been very patiently endured by Mary, if she had not winced under Mrs. Jenkins's knowledge of such economy. But she had her revenge. She had a child, and Mrs. Jenkins had none. To have had a child, even such a puny baby as little Tom, Mrs. Jenkins would have worn commonest caps, and cleaned grates, and drudged her fingers to the bone. The great unspoken disappointment of her life soured her temper, and turned her thoughts inward, and made her morbid and selfish.

"Hang that cat! he's been stealing again! he's gnawed the cold mutton in his nasty mouth till it's not fit to set before a Christian; and I've nothing else for Jem's dinner. But I'll give it him now I've caught him, that I will!"

So saying, Mary Hodgson caught up her husband's Sunday cane, and despite pussy's cries and scratches, she gave him such a beating as she hoped might cure him of his thievish propensities; when, lo! and behold, Mrs. Jenkins stood at the door with a face of bitter wrath.

"Aren't you ashamed of yourself, ma'am, to abuse a poor dumb animal, ma'am, as knows no better than to take food when he sees it, ma'am?

4. **having matched . . . tug of war:** a reference to the proverb "When Greek meets Greek, then comes the tug of war," meaning that when evenly matched opponents fight, the battle will be fierce.

5. **went to service:** took employment as a servant.

WORDS TO KNOW

propensity (prə-pĕn′sĭ-tē) *n.* an inclination or tendency

He only follows the nature which God has given, ma'am; and it's a pity your nature, ma'am, which I've heard is of the stingy saving species, does not make you shut your cupboard door a little closer. There is such a thing as law for brute animals. I'll ask Mr. Jenkins, but I don't think them Radicals has done away with that law yet, for all their Reform Bill, ma'am. My poor precious love of a Tommy, is he hurt? and is his leg broke for taking a mouthful of scraps, as most people would give away to a beggar—if he'd take 'em!" wound up Mrs. Jenkins, casting a contemptuous look on the remnant of a scrag end of mutton.

Mary felt very angry and very guilty. For she really pitied the poor limping animal as he crept up to his mistress, and there lay down to bemoan himself; she wished she had not beaten him so hard, for it certainly was her own careless way of never shutting the cupboard-door that had tempted him to his fault. But the sneer at her little bit of mutton turned her penitence to fresh wrath, and she shut the door in Mrs. Jenkins's face, as she stood caressing her cat in the lobby, with such a bang, that it wakened little Tom, and he began to cry.

Everything was to go wrong with Mary today. Now baby was awake, who was to take her husband's dinner to the office? She took the child in her arms and tried to hush him off to sleep again, and as she sung she cried, she could hardly tell why,—a sort of reaction from her violent angry feelings. She wished she had never beaten the poor cat; she wondered if his leg was really broken. What would her mother say if she knew how cross and cruel her little Mary was getting? If she should live to beat her child in one of her angry fits?

It was of no use lullabying while she sobbed so; it must be given up, and she must just carry her baby in her arms, and take him with her to the office, for it was long past dinner-time. So she pared the mutton carefully, although by so doing she reduced the meat to an infinitesimal quantity, and taking the baked potatoes out of the oven, she popped them piping hot into her basket, with the etceteras of plate, butter, salt, and knife and fork.

It was, indeed, a bitter wind. She bent against it as she ran, and the flakes of snow were sharp and cutting as ice. Baby cried all the way, though she cuddled him up in her shawl. Then her husband had made his appetite up for a potato pie, and (literary man as he was) his body got so much the better of his mind, that he looked rather black at the cold mutton. Mary had no appetite for her own dinner when she arrived at home again. So, after she had tried to feed baby, and he had fretfully refused to take his bread and milk, she laid him down as usual on his quilt, surrounded by playthings, while she sided away, and chopped suet for the next day's pudding. Early in the afternoon a parcel came, done up first in brown paper, then in such a white, grass-bleached, sweet-smelling towel, and a note from her dear, dear mother; in which quaint writing she endeavored to tell her daughter that she was not forgotten at Christmas time; but that, learning that Farmer Burton was killing his pig, she had made interest for some of his famous pork, out of which she had manufactured some sausages, and flavored them just as Mary used to like when she lived at home.

"Dear, dear mother!" said Mary to herself. "There never was any one like her for remembering other folk. What rare sausages she used to make! Home things have a smack with 'em no bought things can ever have. Set them up with their sausages! I've a notion if Mrs. Jenkins had

ever tasted mother's she'd have no fancy for them townmade things Fanny took in just now."

And so she went on thinking about home, till the smiles and the dimples came out again at the remembrance of that pretty cottage, which would look green even now in the depth of winter, with its pyracanthus,[6] and its holly-bushes, and the great Portugal laurel that was her mother's pride. And the back path through the orchard to Farmer Burton's, how well she remembered it! The bushels of unripe apples she had picked up there and distributed among his pigs, till he had scolded her for giving them so much green trash!

She was interrupted—her baby (I call him a baby, because his father and mother did, and because he was so little of his age, but I rather think he was eighteen months old,) had fallen asleep some time before among his playthings; an uneasy, restless sleep; but of which Mary had been thankful, as his morning's nap had been too short, and as she was so busy. But now he began to make such a strange crowing noise, just like a chair drawn heavily and gratingly along a kitchen floor! His eyes were open, but expressive of nothing but pain.

"Mother's darling!" said Mary, in terror, lifting him up. "Baby, try not to make that noise. Hush, hush, darling; what hurts him?" But the noise came worse and worse.

"Fanny! Fanny!" Mary called in mortal fright, for her baby was almost black with his gasping breath, and she had no one to ask for aid or sympathy but her landlady's daughter, a little girl of twelve or thirteen, who attended to the house in her mother's absence, as daily cook in gentlemen's families. Fanny was more especially considered the attendant of the upstairs lodgers (who paid for the use of the kitchen, "for Jenkins could not abide the smell of meat cooking"), but just now she was fortunately sitting at her afternoon's work of darning stockings, and hearing Mrs. Hodgson's cry of terror, she ran to her sitting-room, and understood the case at a glance.

"He's got the croup![7] O Mrs. Hodgson, he'll die as sure as fate. Little brother had it, and he died in no time. The doctor said he could do nothing for him—it had gone too far. He said if we'd put him in a warm bath at first, it might have saved him; but, bless you! he was never half so bad as your baby." Unconsciously there mingled in her statement some of a child's love of producing an effect; but the increasing danger was clear enough.

"Oh, my baby! my baby! Oh, love, love! don't look so ill! I cannot bear it. And my fire so low!

6. **pyracanthus** (pī′rə-kăn′thəs): a thorny evergreen shrub.

7. **croup** (kro͞op): a respiratory disease in children, marked by difficulty in breathing and a sharp cough.

WORDS TO KNOW

mortal (môr′tl) *adj.* intense or severe

Newgate (late 1800s), Frank Holl. Royal Holloway and Bedford Collection, New College, Egham, Surrey, Great Britain. Bridgeman/Art Resource, New York.

There, I was thinking of home, and picking currants, and never minding the fire. O Fanny! what is the fire like in the kitchen? Speak."

"Mother told me to screw it up, and throw some slack[8] on as soon as Mrs. Jenkins had done with it, and so I did. It's very low and black. But, oh, Mrs. Hodgson! let me run for the doctor—I cannot abear to hear him, it's so like little brother."

Through her streaming tears Mary motioned her to go; and trembling, sinking, sick at heart, she laid her boy in his cradle, and ran to fill her kettle.

Mrs. Jenkins, having cooked her husband's snug little dinner, to which he came home; having told him her story of pussy's beating, at which he was justly and dignifiedly (?) indignant, saying it was all of a piece with that abusive *Examiner;* having received the sausages, and turkey, and mince pies, which her husband had ordered; and cleaned up the room, and prepared everything for tea, and coaxed and duly bemoaned her cat (who had pretty nearly forgotten his beating, but very much enjoyed the petting); having done all these and many other things, Mrs. Jenkins sat down to get up the real lace cap. Every thread was pulled out separately, and carefully stretched: when—what was that? Outside, in the street, a chorus of piping children's voices sang the old carol she had heard a hundred times in the days of her youth—

"As Joseph was a walking he heard an angel sing,

'This night shall be born our heavenly King.

He neither shall be born in housen nor in hall,

Nor in the place of Paradise, but in an ox's stall.

He neither shall be clothed in purple nor in pall,

But all in fair linen, as were babies all:

He neither shall be rocked in silver nor in gold,

But in a wooden cradle that rocks on the mould,' " &c.

She got up and went to the window. There, below, stood the group of black little figures, relieved[9] against the snow, which now enveloped everything. "For old sake's sake," as she phrased it, she counted out a halfpenny apiece for the singers, out of the copper bag, and threw them down below.

The room had become chilly while she had been counting out and throwing down her money, so she stirred her already glowing fire, and sat down right before it—but not to stretch her lace; like Mary Hodgson, she began to think over long past days, on softening remembrances of the dead and gone, on words long forgotten, on holy stories heard at her mother's knee.

"I cannot think what's come over me tonight," said she, half aloud, recovering herself by the sound of her own voice from her train of thought—"My head goes wandering on them old times. I'm sure more texts have come into my head with thinking on my mother within this last half-hour, than I've thought on for years and years. I hope I'm not going to die. Folks says, thinking too much on the dead betokens we're going to join 'em; I should be loth[10] to go just yet—such a fine turkey as we've got for dinner tomorrow too!"

Knock, knock, knock, at the door, as fast as knuckles could go. And then, as if the comer could not wait, the door was opened, and Mary Hodgson stood there as white as death.

"Mrs. Jenkins!—oh, your kettle is boiling, thank God! Let me have the water for my baby, for the love of God! He's got croup, and is dying!"

Mrs. Jenkins turned on her chair with a wooden, inflexible look on her face, that (between ourselves) her husband knew and dreaded for all his pompous dignity.

8. **slack:** fragments of coal.
9. **relieved:** set off by contrast.
10. **loth** (lōth): unwilling; reluctant.

WORDS TO KNOW **pompous** (pŏm′pəs) *adj.* characterized by excessive pride or exaggerated dignity

"I'm sorry I can't oblige you, ma'am; my kettle is wanted for my husband's tea. Don't be afeared, Tommy, Mrs. Hodgson won't venture to intrude herself where she's not desired. You'd better send for the doctor, ma'am, instead of wasting your time in wringing your hands, ma'am—my kettle is engaged."

Mary clasped her hands together with passionate force, but spoke no word of entreaty to that wooden face—that sharp, determined voice; but, as she turned away, she prayed for strength to bear the coming trial, and strength to forgive Mrs. Jenkins.

Mrs. Jenkins watched her go away meekly, as one who has no hope, and then she turned upon herself as sharply as she ever did on any one else.

"What a brute I am, Lord forgive me! What's my husband's tea to a baby's life? In croup, too, where time is everything. You crabbed old vixen, you!—any one may know you never had a child!"

She was downstairs (kettle in hand) before she had finished her self-upbraiding;[11] and when in Mrs. Hodgson's room, she rejected all thanks (Mary had not the voice for many words), saying, stiffly, "I do it for the poor baby's sake, ma'am, hoping he may live to have mercy to poor dumb beasts, if he does forget to lock his cupboards."

But she did everything, and more than Mary, with her young inexperience, could have thought of. She prepared the warm bath, and tried it with her husband's own thermometer (Mr. Jenkins was as punctual as clockwork in noting down the temperature of every day). She let his mother place her baby in the tub, still preserving the same rigid, affronted aspect, and then she went upstairs without a word. Mary longed to ask her to stay, but dared not; though, when she left the room, the tears chased each other down her cheeks faster than ever. Poor young mother! how she counted the minutes till the doctor should come. But, before he came, down again stalked Mrs. Jenkins, with something in her hand.

"I've seen many of these croup-fits, which, I take it, you've not, ma'am. Mustard plasters[12] is very sovereign,[13] put on the throat; I've been up and made one, ma'am, and, by your leave, I'll put it on the poor little fellow."

Mary could not speak, but she signed her grateful assent.

It began to smart while they still kept silence; and he looked up to his mother as if seeking courage from her looks to bear the stinging pain; but she was softly crying to see him suffer, and her want of courage reacted upon him, and he began to sob aloud. Instantly Mrs. Jenkins's apron was up, hiding her face: "Peep-bo, baby," said she, as merrily as she could. His little face brightened, and his mother having once got the cue, the two women kept the little fellow amused, until his plaster had taken effect.

"He's better—oh, Mrs. Jenkins, look at his eyes! how different! And he breathes quite softly"—

As Mary spoke thus, the doctor entered. He examined his patient. Baby was really better.

"It has been a sharp attack, but the remedies you have applied have been worth all the Pharmacopoeia[14] an hour later.—I shall send a powder," &c. &c.

Mrs. Jenkins stayed to hear this opinion; and (her heart wonderfully more easy) was going to leave the room, when Mary seized her hand and kissed it; she could not speak her gratitude.

Mrs. Jenkins looked affronted and awkward, and as if she must go upstairs and wash her hand directly.

But, in spite of these sour looks, she came softly down an hour or so afterwards to see how baby was.

---

11. **self-upbraiding:** self-scolding.
12. **mustard plaster:** a paste made of powdered mustard, water, and vinegar that causes localized irritation when applied to the skin and is intended to relieve inflamed tissues.
13. **sovereign** (sŏv′ər-ĭn): effective.
14. **Pharmacopoeia** (fär′mə-kə-pē′ə): all the medicinal drugs listed in the standard reference work on the subject.

WORDS TO KNOW **affronted** (ə-frŭn′tĭd) *adj.* offended **affront** *v.*

The little gentleman slept well after the fright he had given his friends; and on Christmas morning, when Mary awoke and looked at the sweet little pale face lying on her arm, she could hardly realize the danger he had been in.

When she came down (later than usual), she found the household in a commotion. What do you think had happened? Why, pussy had been traitor to his best friend, and eaten up some of Mr. Jenkins's own especial sausages; and gnawed and tumbled the rest so, that they were not fit to be eaten! There were no bounds to that cat's appetite! he would have eaten his own father if he had been tender enough. And now Mrs. Jenkins stormed and cried—"Hang the cat!"

Christmas Day, too! and all the shops shut! "What was turkey without sausages?" gruffly asked Mr. Jenkins.

"O Jem!" whispered Mary, "hearken what a piece of work he's making about sausages—I should like to take Mrs. Jenkins up some of mother's; they're twice as good as bought sausages."

"I see no objection, my dear. Sausages do not involve intimacies, else his politics are what I can no ways respect."

"But, oh, Jem, if you had seen her last night about baby! I'm sure she may scold me forever, and I'll not answer. I'd even make her cat welcome to the sausages." The tears gathered to Mary's eyes as she kissed her boy.

"Better take 'em upstairs, my dear, and give them to the cat's mistress." And Jem chuckled at his saying.

Mary put them on a plate, but still she loitered.

"What must I say, Jem? I never know."

"Say—I hope you'll accept of these sausages, as my mother—no, that's not grammar;—say what comes uppermost, Mary, it will be sure to be right."

So Mary carried them upstairs and knocked at the door; and when told to "come in," she looked very red, but went up to Mrs. Jenkins, saying, "Please take these. Mother made them." And was away before an answer could be given.

Just as Hodgson was ready to go to church, Mrs. Jenkins came downstairs, and called Fanny. In a minute, the latter entered the Hodgsons' room, and delivered Mr. and Mrs. Jenkins's compliments, and they would be particular glad if Mr. and Mrs. Hodgson would eat their dinner with them.

"And carry baby upstairs in a shawl, be sure," added Mrs. Jenkins's voice in the passage, close to the door, whither she had followed her messenger. There was no discussing the matter, with the certainty of every word being overheard.

Mary looked anxiously at her husband. She remembered his saying he did not approve of Mr. Jenkins's politics.

"Do you think it would do for baby?" asked he.

"Oh, yes," answered she eagerly; "I would wrap him up so warm."

"And I've got our room up to sixty-five already, for all it's so frosty," added the voice outside.

Now, how do you think they settled the matter? The very best way in the world. Mr. and Mrs. Jenkins came down into the Hodgsons' room and dined there. Turkey at the top, roast beef at the bottom, sausages at one side, potatoes at the other. Second course, plum pudding at the top, and mince pies at the bottom.

And after dinner, Mrs. Jenkins would have baby on her knee, and he seemed quite to take to her; she declared he was admiring the real lace on her cap, but Mary thought (though she did not say so) that he was pleased by her kind looks and coaxing words. Then he was wrapped up and carried carefully upstairs to tea, in Mrs. Jenkins's room. And after tea, Mrs. Jenkins, and Mary, and her husband, found out each other's mutual liking for music, and sat singing old glees and catches,[15] till I don't know what o'clock, without one word of politics or newspapers.

Before they parted, Mary had coaxed pussy on to her knee; for Mrs. Jenkins would not part with baby, who was sleeping on her lap.

"When you're busy bring him to me. Do, now, it will be a real favor. I know you must have a deal to do, with another coming; let him come up to me. I'll take the greatest of cares of him; pretty darling, how sweet he looks when he's asleep!"

When the couples were once more alone, the husbands unburdened their minds to their wives.

Mr. Jenkins said to his— "Do you know, Burgess tried to make me believe Hodgson was such a fool as to put paragraphs into the *Examiner* now and then; but I see he knows his place, and has got too much sense to do any such thing."

Hodgson said— "Mary, love, I almost fancy from Jenkins's way of speaking (so much civiler than I expected), he guesses I wrote that 'Pro Bono' and the 'Rosebud,'—at any rate, I've no objection to your naming it, if the subject should come uppermost; I should like him to know I'm a literary man."

Well! I've ended my tale; I hope you don't think it too long; but, before I go, just let me say one thing.

If any of you have any quarrels, or misunderstandings, or coolnesses, or cold shoulders, or shynesses, or tiffs, or miffs, or huffs, with anyone else, just make friends before Christmas,—you will be so much merrier if you do.

I ask it of you for the sake of that old angelic song, heard so many years ago by the shepherds, keeping watch by night, on Bethlehem Heights. ❖

15. **glees and catches:** types of unaccompanied part songs for several voices.

RESPONDING OPTIONS

FROM PERSONAL RESPONSE *TO* CRITICAL ANALYSIS

REFLECT **1.** Which character in the story is most appealing to you? In your notebook, jot down reasons for your choice. Share your thoughts with your classmates.

RETHINK **2.** How would you describe the characters' first impressions of one another?

Consider
- Mr. Hodgson's and Mr. Jenkins's jobs
- the makeup of each family
- the personal opinions and feelings each character reveals
- the social attitudes or class consciousness each character exhibits

3. Do you find the events in the latter part of the story believable? Support your response with details from the story.

4. How might the outcome of the story be different if it didn't take place at Christmas? Give reasons for your answer.

RELATE **5.** Mr. Jenkins and Mr. Hodgson have opposing political views. Do you think strong political differences always create difficulties in a personal relationship? Support your answer with examples or reasons.

ANOTHER PATHWAY

Cooperative Learning

With a small group of classmates, identify and describe the different emotions experienced by Mrs. Hodgson and Mrs. Jenkins as the story progresses. Try to determine the cause of each emotion from actions in the story. Record your observations about each character in a chart like the one shown. Share your ideas with the class.

Mrs. Hodgson	
Emotion	**Cause**
annoyance	Cat eats cold mutton.

LITERARY CONCEPTS

Many stories are told from the **third-person point of view**—that is, by a narrator who is outside the action of the story. Occasionally, a story is told from an omniscient, or all-knowing, third-person point of view. In stories told from an **omniscient point of view,** the narrator sees into the minds of more than one character. What evidence of an omniscient point of view can you find in "Christmas Storms and Sunshine"? How do you think this narrative method affects the story?

QUICKWRITES

1. Pretend that you are Mary Hodgson. In a **letter** to your mother, describe the experience you have just had with the Jenkinses.

2. Imagine that you are Mr. Hodgson and write a short **editorial** for the *Examiner.* Deliver a message to readers, based on what you have learned over the Christmas holiday.

3. Suppose that the Jenkinses discover that Mr. Hodgson really does put his own compositions into the *Examiner.* Write the **dialogue** that might occur between Mr. and Mrs. Jenkins after this revelation.

PORTFOLIO *Save your writing. You may want to use it later as a springboard to a piece for your portfolio.*

ALTERNATIVE ACTIVITIES

1. With a partner or group, plan a **dramatic interpretation** of one or more scenes from the story. Determine how to portray each character and what lines and actions you will use. Then rehearse your presentation, and give your final performance for the entire class.
2. Create a drawing or model of the **set design** you would use for a dramatized version of "Christmas Storms and Sunshine."
3. With a partner, improvise a **conversation** in which Mary Hodgson tells her son, who is now a teenager, about the incidents described in this story.

CRITIC'S CORNER

A student reviewer, Dan Birdsall, thought that "the irony of the ending was cool—it seems like the two families would end up enemies again after a while." Do you agree that the new friendship of the Hodgsons and the Jenkinses is unlikely to last? With your classmates, discuss your thoughts on this possibility. Support your ideas with evidence from the selection.

ACROSS THE CURRICULUM

History Look up information on life in English industrial cities—such as Manchester—during the early 19th century. What kind of housing was available? What were the popular social activities? How did life differ for various social classes?

Journalism Find out what the leading newspapers were in 19th-century England. What were their names, their prices, their political leanings? How were they received by the people of their time?

THE WRITER'S STYLE

In her writing, Gaskell often includes parenthetical remarks (information separated from the rest of the story by parentheses), as in the clause ". . . I think it would have even added to his contempt of Hodgson (if that were possible) . . ." Look for other examples of this technique in the story. What kinds of information does Gaskell usually convey in parentheses? What effect does this technique have on your reading?

ART CONNECTION

What thoughts come to mind when you look at the woman in *Newgate* on page 612? How do these thoughts relate to your impression of Mrs. Hodgson in "Christmas Storms and Sunshine"? Discuss your ideas with your classmates.

WORDS TO KNOW

Review the Words to Know at the bottom of the selection pages. Then write the word that best completes each of the following sentences.

1. Since it is always easier to see things from one's own point of view, Mrs. Hodgson and Mrs. Jenkins have a _____ to blame each other for any quarrel they have.
2. Mrs. Jenkins might be shocked to discover that what she thinks is simple self-respect and good breeding could be seen by Mrs. Hodgson as _____ haughtiness.
3. Mrs. Hodgson might be surprised to find out that while Mrs. Jenkins is behaving coldly and showing _____ indignation, she is really quite worried about the Hodgson baby.
4. After all, the Hodgson baby is in serious, even _____, danger, and Mrs. Jenkins has humanity's normal protective impulses toward helpless babies.
5. A bitter memory makes Mrs. Jenkins _____ to an earlier quarrel by saying, "I do it for the poor baby's sake, ma'am, hoping he may live to have mercy to poor dumb beasts, if he does forget to lock his cupboards."

ELIZABETH CLEGHORN GASKELL

1810–1865

Elizabeth Cleghorn, only 13 months old when her mother died, was taken from her London home to be raised by her mother's sister in a rural village. In this calm, country setting she learned to appreciate and carefully observe all the details of the natural world. At the age of 12, she was sent to boarding school, where she developed a love of reading and a sympathetic nature. Occasionally she saw her father, who had remained in London and remarried, and from his intensive tutoring she gained a proficiency in languages. These early experiences combined to give her not only the sensitivity which would later manifest itself in a deep concern for the less fortunate but also the desire and skill to write about their lives.

In 1831, while visiting relatives in Manchester, she met William Gaskell, a Unitarian minister, and the following year they married. As a minister's wife, she devoted much time to helping those in need. She was also kept busy raising and educating four daughters. Her first serious efforts at writing, however, did not occur until she was in her thirties and recovering from the death in 1845 of her infant son.

Gaskell drew upon her firsthand experiences with the poor in writing her first novel, *Mary Barton,* which was extremely successful and won her the approval of such literary figures as Charles Dickens and Charlotte Brontë. On Dickens's urging, Gaskell contributed stories to his new periodical, *Household Words,* in which two of her novels, *Cranford* and *North and South,* would be published in weekly installments. Gaskell and Brontë admired each other's work and eventually became close friends. Shortly after her dear friend's untimely death, and at the request of Brontë's father, Gaskell wrote her first and only biography, *The Life of Charlotte Brontë.* Gaskell herself died quite suddenly at the age of 55, while having tea and conversing with her family at the country home where she planned one day to retire with her husband.

Gaskell sympathized deeply with her poor fellow citizens and was committed to raising the social awareness of her readers. Since some Victorians did not consider it proper to discuss or write about social problems, Gaskell created controversy in her time by honestly depicting the appallingly squalid housing of the poor and vividly portraying working-class life.

OTHER WORKS "My Lady Ludlow," "Cousin Phillis," "Half a Life-Time Ago"

George Eliot

The Novels of GEORGE ELIOT

Who is George Eliot? This question tantalized the literary world and tormented townspeople throughout 1858, the year John Blackwood published Eliot's two-volume *Scenes of Clerical Life.* Critics admired the work; literary figures discussed it; Warwickshire residents were shocked to recognize themselves in print. Then, in 1859, when Blackwood published a novel by Eliot, *Adam Bede,* the rumors fairly flew. Celebrities clamored to know the author, whom critics declared one of the "masters of the art." Townspeople searched for and found a local man to promote as Eliot unmasked.

Meanwhile, the true author, Mary Ann Evans, and her partner George Lewes were doing all they could to keep people off the track. When Blackwood guessed Eliot's identity, she begged him to keep the secret, and he agreed. Evans wanted her work to be judged on its merits, not on the basis of its author's gender. However, the similarities between her characters and real-life people and places made continued anonymity nearly impossible. Within two years, the secret was out.

Top:
"My new story," wrote Eliot in 1857, "will be a country story—full of the breath of the cows and the scent of hay." Adam Bede *richly celebrates the vanishing world of the rural community, as depicted by John Constable in his painting* The Hay Wain. The Hay Wain, *(1821) John Constable. National Gallery, London/Bridgeman Art Library, London/Superstock.*

Above:
Scene from the production of Middlemarch *broadcast by PBS in 1994*

Left:
Manuscript page of "Legend of St. Ogg"

Armed with knowledge of Eliot's gender, critics reexamined her work and found it deeply immoral. One critic even accused George Eliot of destroying "all comfortable notions of right and wrong, true and false." These complaints distressed Eliot, but she had this consolation: although Mary Ann Evans's reviews were terrible, George Eliot's had been good. It's little wonder, therefore, that she retained her pen name.

The complaining critics seem to have been unable to see that Eliot's novels actually have a strong moral tone. In *The Mill on the Floss,* for example, a sister rejected by her judgmental brother nevertheless saves his life at the cost of her own. In *Silas Marner,* an alienated miser adopts a foundling and gains for himself both love and redemption. In *Middlemarch,* one of the greatest novels of the 19th century, a woman who must choose between security and love gives up everything—and finds that she is glad she did. These heroes, torn by conflicting desires, struggle mightily to do what's right, and whether or not they succeed, good always wins in the end.

Now that Eliot's gender is not an issue, critics and readers alike enjoy the power and suspense of her novels. She has become respected and admired for the unfailing idealism and tough realism she showed both in her novels and in her life.

PREVIEWING

FICTION

The Miracle of Purun Bhagat

Rudyard Kipling

PERSONAL CONNECTION

Do you know or have you read about someone who decided to change his or her life in a major way? Perhaps the person took a new job, moved, or married. What kinds of things did this person value most before and after the change in his or her lifestyle? Share your thoughts with your classmates.

HISTORICAL/CULTURAL CONNECTION

England's first settlements in India were trading posts established during the 1600s. Taking advantage of a weak Indian government, British agents were in control of India by 1774. Although Indian soldiers revolted against foreign rule in 1857, British forces successfully quelled the rebellion. Shortly thereafter, Queen Victoria appointed a viceroy to head India's government and to carry out the wishes of Parliament. Most Indian princes agreed to abide by British law, and government posts were given to a few Indians who supported the British presence. During the late 19th century, the British changed many of India's laws and constructed both railroad and telegraph systems to improve what they viewed as a primitive, or backward, civilization.

A number of British citizens moved to India during its years as a British colony. Among them were the parents of the writer Rudyard Kipling, who was born in India in 1865. Even as a child, Kipling was fascinated by Indian culture and values; later, he would vividly depict Indian life in his stories.

Most Indians are Hindus, and for them Hinduism is not only a religion but a way of life. Hindus are divided into castes, or social classes, and according to Hindu laws, a person can never leave the caste into which he or she is born. Each person's lifestyle—including eating habits, employment, and choice of friends and a marriage partner—is determined by his or her caste.

WRITING CONNECTION

Look back on your life and think about how your interests and values have changed over the years. In your notebook, create a "ladder" like the one shown, jotting down between the rungs things that you have valued, and that you predict you will value, at various stages of your life. As you read you may think of additional ideas for your ladder chart.

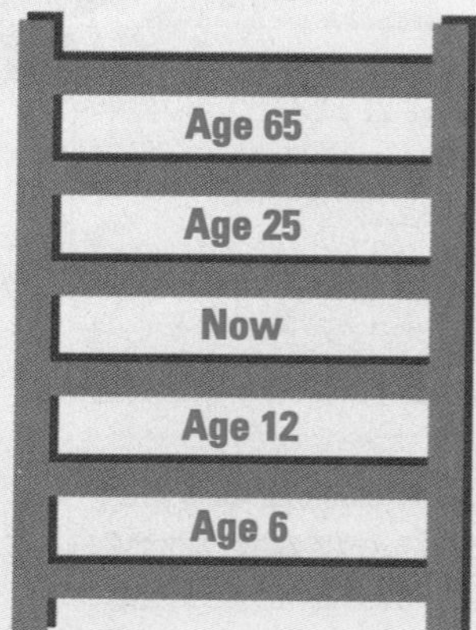

Using Your Reading Log Use your reading log to record your responses to the questions inserted at various points in the selection. Also jot down other thoughts and feelings that come to you as you read.

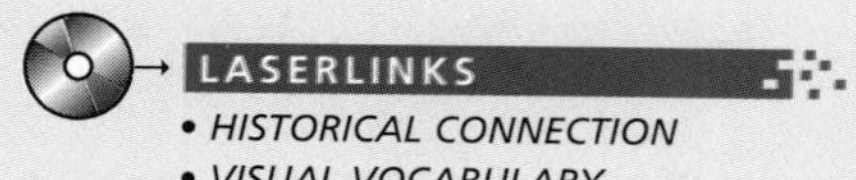

- *HISTORICAL CONNECTION*
- *VISUAL VOCABULARY*

The Miracle of Purun Bhagat

Rudyard Kipling

There was once a man in India who was Prime Minister of one of the semi-independent native States in the north-western part of the country.

La coupe de mystère [The chalice of mystery] (1890), Odilon Redon. Oil on paper mounted on linen, 22½″ × 14″, collection of the Walker Art Center, Minneapolis, Minnesota, gift of Alexander M. Bing, 1953 (53.53).

He was a Brahmin,[1] so high-caste that caste ceased to have any particular meaning for him; and his father had been an important official in the gay-colored tag-rag and bob-tail[2] of an old-fashioned Hindu Court. But as Purun Dass grew up he realized that the ancient order of things was changing, and that if any one wished to get on he must stand well with the English, and imitate all the English believed to be good. At the same time a native official must keep his own master's favor. This was a difficult game, but the quiet, close-mouthed young Brahmin, helped by a good English education at a Bombay University, played it coolly, and rose, step by step, to be Prime Minister of the kingdom. That is to say, he held more real power than his master, the Maharajah.[3]

When the old king—who was suspicious of the English, their railways and telegraphs—died, Purun Dass stood high with his young successor, who had been tutored by an Englishman; and between them, though he always took care that his master should have the credit, they established schools for little girls, made roads, and started State dispensaries[4] and shows of agricultural implements, and published a yearly blue-book on the "Moral and Material Progress of the State," and the Foreign Office and the Government of India were delighted. Very few native States take up English progress without reservations, for they will not believe, as Purun Dass showed he did, that what is good for the Englishman must be twice as good for the Asiatic. The Prime Minister became the honored friend of Viceroys[5] and Governors, and Lieutenant-Governors, and medical missionaries, and common missionaries, and hard-riding English officers who came to shoot in the State preserves, as well as of whole hosts of tourists who travelled up and down India in the cold weather, showing how things ought to be managed. In his spare time he would endow scholarships for the study of medicine and manufactures on strictly English lines, and write letters to the *Pioneer,* the greatest Indian daily paper, explaining his master's aims and objects.

At last he went to England on a visit, and had to pay enormous sums to the priests when he came back; for even so high-caste a Brahmin as Purun Dass lost caste by crossing the black sea. In London he met and talked with every one worth knowing—men whose names go all over the world—and saw a great deal more than he said. He was given honorary degrees by learned universities, and he made speeches and talked of Hindu social reform to English ladies in evening dress, till all London cried, "This is the most fascinating man we have ever met at dinner since cloths were first laid!"

When he returned to India there was a blaze of glory, for the Viceroy himself made a special visit to confer upon the Maharajah the Grand Cross of the Star of India—all diamonds and ribbons and enamel; and at the same ceremony, while the cannon boomed, Purun Dass was made a Knight Commander of the Order of the Indian Empire; so that his name stood Sir Purun Dass, K.C.I.E.

That evening at dinner in the big Viceregal[6] tent he stood up with the badge and the collar of the Order on his breast, and replying to the toast of his master's health, made a speech that few Englishmen could have surpassed.

Next month, when the city had returned to its sun-baked quiet, he did a thing no Englishman would have dreamed of doing, for, so far as the world's affairs went, he died. The jeweled order of his knighthood returned to the Indian Government, and a new Prime Minister was appointed to the charge of affairs, and a great game of General Post[7] began in all the subordinate

1. **Brahmin:** a member of the highest Hindu caste.
2. **tag-rag and bob-tail:** a phrase meaning "a diverse and disorderly assemblage of people."
3. **Maharajah** (mä′hə-rä′jə): an Indian king or prince.
4. **dispensaries:** medical clinics.
5. **Viceroys** (vīs′roiz′): officials ruling as representatives of the sovereign.
6. **Viceregal** (vīs-rē′gəl): belonging to the viceroy.
7. **General Post:** a game in which, at a summons, all players change places.

appointments. The priests knew what had happened and the people guessed; but India is the one place in the world where a man can do as he pleases and nobody asks why; and the fact that Dewan Sir Purun Dass, K.C.I.E., had resigned position, palace, and power, and taken up the begging-bowl and ochre-colored dress of a Sunnyasi[8] or holy man, was considered nothing extraordinary. He had been, as the Old Law recommends, twenty years a youth, twenty years a fighter—though he had never carried a weapon in his life—and twenty years head of a household. He had used his wealth and his power for what he knew both to be worth; he had taken honor when it came his way; he had seen men and cities far and near, and men and cities had stood up and honored him. Now he would let these things go, as a man drops the cloak he needs no longer.

Behind him, as he walked through the city gates, an antelope skin and brass-handled crutch under his arm, and a begging-bowl of polished brown *coco-de-mer*[9] in his hand, barefoot, alone, with eyes cast on the ground—behind him they were firing salutes from the bastions[10] in honor of his happy successor. Purun Dass nodded. All that life was ended; and he bore it no more ill-will or good-will than a man bears to a colorless dream of the night. He was a Sunnyasi—a houseless, wandering mendicant,[11] depending on his neighbors for his daily bread; and so long as there is a morsel to divide in India neither priest nor beggar starves. He had never in his life tasted meat, and very seldom eaten even fish. A five-pound note would have covered his personal expenses for food through any one of the many years in which he had been absolute master of millions of money. Even when he was being lionized[12] in London he had held before him his dream of peace and quiet—the long, white, dusty Indian road, printed all over with bare feet, the incessant, slow-moving traffic, and the sharp-smelling wood-smoke curling up under the fig-trees in the twilight, where the wayfarers sat at their evening meal.

When the time came to make that dream true the Prime Minister took the proper steps, and in three days you might more easily have found a bubble in the trough of the long Atlantic seas than Purun Dass among the roving, gathering, separating millions of India.

NOW HE WOULD LET THESE THINGS GO, AS A MAN DROPS THE CLOAK HE NEEDS NO LONGER.

8. **Sunnyasi** (sŭn-yä′sē).
9. ***coco-de-mer*** (kō′kō-də-mâr′): the shell of a huge nut, resembling two joined coconut shells.
10. **bastions:** projecting parts of a fortification.
11. **mendicant** (mĕn′dĭ-kənt): beggar.
12. **lionized:** treated as a celebrity.

CLARIFY

What evidence suggests that Purun Dass has changed his life willingly?

At night his antelope skin was spread where the darkness overtook him—sometimes in a Sunnyasi monastery by the roadside; sometimes by a mud pillar shrine of Kala Pir, where the Jogis, who are another misty division of holy men, would receive him as they do those who know what castes and divisions are worth; sometimes on the outskirts of a little Hindu village, where the children would steal up with the food their parents had prepared; and sometimes on the pitch of the bare grazing-grounds where the flame of his stick fire waked the drowsy camels. It was all one to Purun Dass—or Purun Bhagat,[13] as he called himself now. Earth, people, and food were all one. But, unconsciously, his feet drew him northward and eastward; from the south to Rohtak; from Rohtak to Kurnool; from Kurnool to ruined Samanah, and then up-stream along the dried bed of the Gugger river that fills only when the rain falls in the hills, till, one day, he saw the far line of the great Himalayas.

Then Purun Bhagat smiled, for he remembered that his mother was of Rajput Brahmin birth, from Kulu way—a Hill-woman, always homesick for the snows—and that the least touch of Hill blood draws a man in the end back to where he belongs.

"Yonder," said Purun Bhagat, breasting the lower slopes of the Sewaliks, where the cacti stand up like seven-branched candlesticks, "yonder I shall sit down and get knowledge"; and the cool wind of the Himalayas whistled about his ears as he trod the road that led to Simla.

The last time he had come that way it had been in state, with a clattering cavalry escort, to visit the gentlest and most affable of Viceroys; and the two had talked for an hour together about mutual friends in London, and what the Indian common folk really thought of things. This time Purun Bhagat paid no calls, but leaned on the rail of the Mall,[14] watching the glorious view of the Plains spread out forty miles below, till a native Mohammedan policeman told him he was obstructing traffic; and Purun Bhagat salaamed[15] reverently to the Law, because he knew the value of it, and was seeking for a Law of his own. Then he moved on, and slept that night in an empty hut at Chota Simla, which looks like the very last end of the earth, but it was only the beginning of his journey. He followed the Himalaya-Thibet[16] road, the little ten-foot track that is blasted out of solid rock, or strutted out on timbers over gulfs a thousand feet deep; that dips into warm, wet, shut-in valleys, and climbs across bare, grassy hill-shoulders where the sun strikes like a burning-glass; or turns through dripping, dark forests where the tree-ferns dress the trunks from head to heel, and the pheasant calls to his mate. And he met Thibetan herdsmen with their dogs and flocks of sheep, each sheep with a little bag of borax on his back,[17] and wandering wood-cutters, and cloaked and blanketed Lamas[18] from Thibet, coming into India on pilgrimage, and envoys[19] of little solitary Hill-states, posting furiously on ring-streaked and piebald ponies, or the cavalcade[20] of a Rajah paying a visit, or else for a long, clear day he would see nothing more than a black bear grunting and rooting down below in the valley. When he first started, the roar of the

CLARIFY

What kind of "Law" might Purun Bhagat be seeking?

13. **Bhagat** (bəg′ət): The Hindi word *bhagat* means "a devout person or saint."

14. **Mall:** a major roadway in Simla.

15. **salaamed** (sə-lämd′): bowed deeply, with the right palm pressed to the forehead, to show respect.

16. **Thibet:** a variant form of *Tibet.*

17. **borax on his back:** Tibet was the first important source of borax, a mineral with many industrial uses. In Tibet, sheep are often used as beasts of burden.

18. **Lamas:** Buddhist monks.

19. **envoys** (ĕn′voiz′): government representatives or agents.

20. **cavalcade:** a procession of riders on horseback or in horse-drawn carriages.

world he had left still rang in his ears, as the roar of a tunnel rings a little after the train has passed through; but when he had put the Mutteeanee Pass behind him that was all done, and Purun Bhagat was alone with himself, walking, wondering, and thinking, his eyes on the ground, and his thoughts with the clouds.

One evening he crossed the highest pass he had met till then—it had been a two days' climb—and came out on a line of snow-peaks that belted all the horizon—mountains from fifteen to twenty thousand feet high, looking almost near enough to hit with a stone, though they were fifty or sixty miles away. The pass was crowned with dense, dark forest—deodar, walnut, wild cherry, wild olive, and wild pear but mostly deodar, which is the Himalayan cedar; and under the shadow of the deodars stood a deserted shrine to Kali—who is Durga, who is Sitala, who is sometimes worshipped against the smallpox.[21]

Purun Dass swept the stone floor clean, smiled at the grinning statue, made himself a little mud fireplace at the back of the shrine, spread his antelope skin on a bed of fresh pine needles, tucked his *bairagi*—his brass-handled crutch—under his armpit, and sat down to rest.

Immediately below him the hillside fell away, clean and cleared for fifteen hundred feet, to where a little village of stone-walled houses, with roofs of beaten earth, clung to the steep tilt. All round it tiny terraced fields lay out like aprons of patchwork on the knees of the mountain, and cows no bigger than beetles grazed between the smooth stone circles of the threshing-floors. Looking across the valley the eye was deceived by the size of things, and could not at first realize that what seemed to be low scrub, on the opposite mountain-flank, was in truth a forest of hundred-foot pines. Purun Bhagat saw an eagle swoop across the enormous hollow, but the great bird dwindled to a dot ere it was half-way over. A few bands of scattered clouds strung up and down the valley, catching on a shoulder of the hills, or rising up and dying out when they were level with the head of the pass. And "Here shall I find peace," said Purun Bhagat.

Now, a Hill-man makes nothing of a few hundred feet up or down, and as soon as the villagers saw the smoke in the deserted shrine, the village priest climbed up the terraced hillside to welcome the stranger.

When he met Purun Bhagat's eyes—the eyes of a man used to control thousands—he bowed to the earth, took the begging-bowl without a word, and returned to the village, saying, "We have at last a holy man. Never have I seen such a man. He is of the plains—but pale colored—a Brahmin of the Brahmins." Then all the housewives of the village said, "Think you he will stay with us?" and each did her best to cook the most savory meal for the Bhagat. Hill-food is very simple, but with buckwheat and Indian corn, and rice and red pepper, and little fish out of the stream in the little valley, and honey from the flue-like hives built in the stone walls, and dried apricots, and turmeric,[22] and wild ginger, and bannocks[23] of flour, a devout woman can make good things; and it was a full bowl that the priest carried to the Bhagat. Was he going to stay? asked the priest. Would he need a *chela*—a disciple—to beg for him? Had he a blanket against the cold weather? Was the food good?

Purun Bhagat ate, and thanked the giver. It was in his mind to stay. That was sufficient, said the priest. Let the begging-bowl be placed outside the shrine, in the hollow made by those two twisted roots, and daily should the Bhagat be fed; for the village felt honored that such a man—he looked timidly into the Bhagat's face—should tarry among them.

That day saw the end of Purun Bhagat's

21. **Kali . . . smallpox:** In Hinduism, the supreme goddess Devi takes many forms; one of these is Kali, goddess of destruction, who is also identified with the goddesses Durga (another deity of destruction) and Sitala (the deity of smallpox).

22. **turmeric** (tûr′mər-ĭk): a spice made from the roots of the turmeric plant.

23. **bannocks:** flat loaves of unleavened bread.

wanderings. He had come to the place appointed for him—the silence and the space. After this, time stopped, and he, sitting at the mouth of the shrine, could not tell whether he were alive or dead; a man with control of his limbs, or a part of the hills, and the clouds, and the shifting rain, and sunlight. He would repeat a Name softly to himself a hundred hundred times, till, at each repetition, he seemed to move more and more out his body, sweeping up to the doors of some tremendous discovery; but, just as the door was opening, his body would drag him back, and, with grief, he felt he was locked up again in the flesh and bones of Purun Bhagat.

Every morning the filled begging-bowl was laid silently in the crotch of the roots outside the shrine. Sometimes the priest brought it; sometimes a Ladakhi[24] trader, lodging in the village, and anxious to get merit, trudged up the path; but, more often, it was the woman who had cooked the meal overnight; and she would murmur, hardly above her breath: "Speak for me before the gods, Bhagat. Speak for such an one, the wife of so-and-so!" Now and then some bold child would be allowed the honor, and Purun Bhagat would hear him drop the bowl and run as fast as his little legs could carry him, but the Bhagat never came down to the village. It was laid out like a map at his feet. He could see the evening gatherings held on the circle of the threshing-floors, because that was the only level ground; could see the wonderful unnamed green of the young rice, the indigo blues of the Indian corn; the dock-like patches of buckwheat, and, in its season, the red bloom of the amaranth, whose tiny seeds, being neither grain nor pulse,[25] make a food that can be lawfully eaten by Hindus in time of fasts.

When the year turned, the roofs of the huts were all little squares of purest gold, for it was on the roofs that they laid out their cobs of the corn to dry. Hiving and harvest, rice-sowing and husking, passed before his eyes, all embroidered down there on the many-sided fields, and he thought of them all, and wondered what they all led to at the long last.

Even in populated India a man cannot a day sit still before the wild things run over him as though he were a rock; and in that wilderness very soon the wild things, who knew Kali's Shrine well, came back to look at the intruder. The *langurs,* the big gray-whiskered monkeys of the Himalayas, were, naturally, the first, for they are alive with curiosity; and when they had upset the begging-bowl, and rolled it round the floor, and tried their teeth on the brass-handled crutch, and made faces at the antelope skin, they decided that the human being who sat so still was harmless. At evening, they would leap down from the pines, and beg with their hands for things to eat, and then swing off in graceful curves. They liked the warmth of the fire, too, and huddled round it till Purun Bhagat had to push them aside to throw on more fuel; and in the morning, as often as not, he would find a furry ape sharing his blanket. All day long, one or other of the tribe would sit by his side, staring out at the snows, crooning and looking unspeakably wise and sorrowful.

After the monkeys came the *barasingh,* that big deer which is like our red deer, but stronger. He wished to rub off the velvet of his horns against the cold stones of Kali's statue, and stamped his feet when he saw the man at the shrine. But Purun Bhagat never moved, and, little by little, the royal stag edged up and nuzzled his shoulder. Purun Bhagat slid one cool hand along the hot antlers, and the touch soothed the fretted beast, who bowed his head, and Purun Bhagat very softly rubbed and ravelled off the velvet. Afterwards, the *barasingh* brought his doe and fawn—gentle things that mumbled on the holy man's blanket—or would come alone at night, his eyes green in the fire-flicker, to take his share of fresh walnuts. At last, the musk-deer, the

---

24. **Ladakhi** (lə-dä′kē): from Ladakh, a region in the upper Indus River valley—at the time, part of northwestern India.

25. **pulse:** the edible seeds of certain pod-bearing plants, such as peas and beans.

shyest and almost the smallest of the deerlets, came, too, her big, rabbity ears erect; even brindled, silent *mushick-nabha* must needs find out what the light in the shrine meant, and drop her moose-like nose into Purun Bhagat's lap, coming and going with the shadows of the fire. Purun Bhagat called them all "my brothers," and his low call of *"Bhai! Bhai!"* would draw them from the forest at noon if they were within earshot. The Himalayan black bear, moody and suspicious—Sona, who has the V-shaped white mark under his chin—passed that way more than once; and since the Bhagat showed no fear, Sona showed no anger, but watched him, and came closer, and begged a share of the caresses, and a dole of bread or wild berries. Often, in the still dawns, when the Bhagat would climb to the very crest of the notched pass to watch the red day walking along the peaks of the snows, he would find Sona shuffling and grunting at his heels, thrusting a curious forepaw under fallen trunks, and bringing it away with a *whoof* of impatience; or his early steps would wake Sona where he lay curled up, and the great brute, rising erect, would think to fight, till he heard the Bhagat's voice and knew his best friend.

Nearly all hermits and holy men who live apart from the big cities have the reputation of being able to work miracles with the wild things, but all the miracle lies in keeping still, in never making a hasty movement, and, for a long time, at least, in never looking directly at a visitor. The villagers saw the outlines of the *barasingh* stalking like a shadow through the dark forest behind the shrine; saw the *minaul,* the Himalayan pheasant, blazing in her best colors before Kali's statue; and the *langurs* on their haunches, inside, playing with the walnut shells. Some of the children, too, had heard Sona singing to himself, bear-fashion, behind the fallen rocks, and the Bhagat's reputation as miracle-worker stood firm.

Yet nothing was further from his mind than miracles. He believed that all things were one big Miracle, and when a man knows that much he knows something to go upon. He knew for a certainty that there was nothing great and nothing little in this world; and day and night he strove to think out his way into the heart of things, back to the place whence his soul had come.

So thinking, his untrimmed hair fell down about his shoulders, the stone slab at the side of the antelope-skin was dented into a little hole by the foot of his brass-handled crutch, and the place between the tree-trunks, where the begging-bowl rested day after day, sunk and wore into a hollow almost as smooth as the brown shell itself; and each beast knew his exact place at the fire. The fields changed their colors with the seasons; the threshing-floors filled and emptied, and filled again and again; and again and again, when winter came, the *langurs* frisked among the branches feathered with light snow, till the mother-monkeys brought their sad-eyed little babies up from the warmer valleys with the spring. There were few changes in the village. The priest was older, and many of the little children who used to come with the begging-dish sent their own children now; and when you asked of the villagers how long their holy man had lived in Kali's Shrine at the head of the pass, they answered, "Always."

EVALUATE

How would you describe the relationship between the villagers and Purun Bhagat?

Then came such summer rains as had not been known in the Hills for many seasons. Through three good months the valley was wrapped in cloud and soaking mist—steady, unrelenting downfall, breaking off into thunder-shower after thunder-shower. Kali's Shrine stood above the clouds, for the most part, and there was a whole month in which the Bhagat never caught a glimpse of his village. It was packed away under a white floor of cloud that swayed and shifted and rolled on itself and bulged upward, but never broke from its piers—the streaming flanks of the valley.

All that time he heard nothing but the sound of a million little waters, overhead from the trees, and underfoot along the ground, soaking through the pine-needles, dripping from the tongues of draggled fern, and spouting in newly-torn muddy channels down the slopes. Then the sun came out, and drew forth the good incense of the deodars and the rhododendrons, and that far-off, clean smell the Hill People call "the smell of the snows." The hot sunshine lasted for a week, and then the rains gathered together for their last downpour, and the water fell in sheets that flayed off the skin of the ground and leaped back in mud. Purun Bhagat heaped his fire high that night, for he was sure his brothers would need warmth; but never a beast came to the shrine, though he called and called till he dropped asleep, wondering what had happened in the woods.

It was in the black heart of the night, the rain drumming like a thousand drums, that he was roused by a plucking at his blanket, and, stretching out, felt the little hand of a *langur*. "It is better here than in the trees," he said sleepily, loosening a fold of blanket; "take it and be warm." The monkey caught his hand and pulled hard. "Is it food, then?" said Purun Bhagat. "Wait awhile, and I will prepare some." As he kneeled to throw fuel on the fire the *langur* ran to the door of the shrine, crooned, and ran back again, plucking at the man's knee.

"What is it? What is thy trouble, Brother?" said Purun Bhagat, for the *langur's* eyes were full of things that he could not tell. "Unless one of thy caste be in a trap—and none set traps here—I will not go into that weather. Look, Brother, even the *barasingh* comes for shelter."

PREDICT

The animals are behaving strangely. What might be happening?

The deer's antlers clashed as he strode into the shrine, clashed against the grinning statue of Kali. He lowered them in Purun Bhagat's direction and stamped uneasily, hissing through his half-shut nostrils.

"Hai! Hai! Hai!" said the Bhagat, snapping his fingers. "Is *this* payment for a night's lodging?" But the deer pushed him towards the door, and as he did so Purun Bhagat heard the sound of something opening with a sigh, and saw two slabs of the floor draw away from each other, while the sticky earth below smacked its lips.

"Now I see," said Purun Bhagat. "No blame to my brothers that they did not sit by the fire to-night. The mountain is falling. And yet—why should I go?" His eye fell on the empty begging-bowl, and his face changed. "They have given me good food daily since—since I came, and, if I am not swift, tomorrow there will not be one mouth in the valley. Indeed, I must go and warn them below. Back there, Brother! Let me get to the fire."

The *barasingh* backed unwillingly as Purun Bhagat drove a torch deep into the flame, twirling it till it was well lit. "Ah! ye came to warn me," he said, rising. "Better than that we shall do, better than that. Out, now, and lend me thy neck, Brother, for I have but two feet."

He clutched the bristling withers[26] of the *barasingh* with his right hand, held the torch away with his left, and stepped out of the shrine into the desperate night. There was no breath of wind, but the rain nearly drowned the torch as the great deer hurried down the slope, sliding on his haunches. As soon as they were clear of the forest more of the Bhagat's brothers joined them. He heard, though he could not see, the *langurs* pressing about him, and behind them the *uhh! uhh!* of Sona. The rain matted his long white hair into ropes; the water splashed beneath his bare feet, and his yellow robe clung to his frail old body, but he stepped down steadily, leaning against the *barasingh*. He was no longer a holy man, but Sir Purun Dass, K.C.I.E., Prime Minister of no small State, a man accustomed to command, going out to save life. Down the steep plashy path they poured all together, the Bhagat and his brothers, down and down till the deer clicked and stumbled on the wall of a threshing-floor, and snorted because he smelt Man. Now they were at the head of the one crooked village

26. **withers:** the high part of the deer's back, between the shoulder blades.

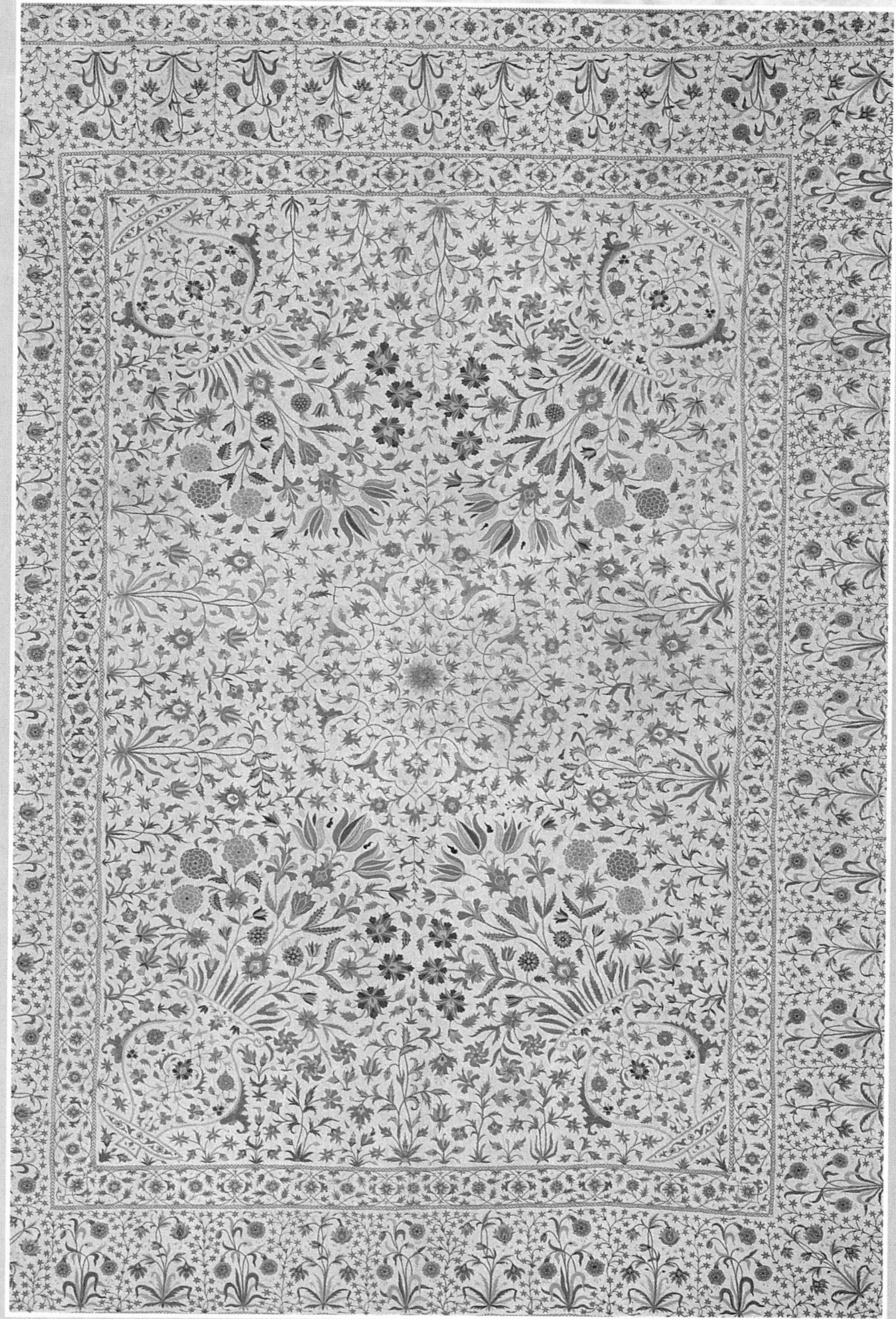

Mughal floorspread (about 1700). Cotton embroidered with silk, 269 cm × 203 cm, Victoria and Albert Museum, London/Art Resource, New York.

street, and the Bhagat beat with his crutch at the barred windows of the blacksmith's house as his torch blazed up in the shelter of the eaves. "Up and out!" cried Purun Bhagat; and he did not know his own voice, for it was years since he had spoken aloud to a man. "The hill falls! The hill is falling! Up and out, oh, you within!"

"It is our Bhagat," said the blacksmith's wife. "He stands among his beasts. Gather the little ones and give the call."

It ran from house to house, while the beasts, cramped in the narrow way, surged and huddled round the Bhagat, and Sona puffed impatiently.

The people hurried into the street—they were no more than seventy souls all told—and in the glare of their torches they saw their Bhagat holding back the terrified *barasingh,* while the monkeys plucked piteously at his skirts, and Sona sat on his haunches and roared.

"Across the valley and up the next hill!" shouted Purun Bhagat. "Leave none behind! We follow!"

Then the people ran as only Hill-folk can run, for they knew that in a landslip you must climb for the highest ground across the valley. They fled, splashing through the little river at the bottom, and panted up the terraced fields on the far side, while the Bhagat and his brethren followed. Up and up the opposite mountain they climbed, calling to each other by name—the roll-call of the village—and at their heels toiled the big *barasingh,* weighted by the failing strength of Purun Bhagat. At last the deer stopped in the shadow of a deep pine-wood, five hundred feet up the hillside. His instinct, that had warned him of the coming slide, told him he would be safe here.

HIS INSTINCT, THAT HAD WARNED HIM OF THE COMING SLIDE, TOLD HIM HE WOULD BE SAFE HERE.

Purun Bhagat dropped fainting by his side, for the chill of the rain and that fierce climb was killing him; but first he called to the scattered torches ahead, "Stay and count your numbers;" then, whispering to the deer as he saw the lights gather in a cluster: "Stay with me, Brother. Stay—till—I—go!"

There was a sigh in the air that grew to a mutter, and a mutter that grew to a roar, and a roar that passed all sense of hearing, and the hillside on which the villagers stood was hit in the darkness, and rocked to the blow. Then a note as steady, deep, and true as the deep C of the organ drowned everything for perhaps five minutes, while the very roots of the pines quivered to it. It died away, and the sound of the rain falling on miles of hard ground and grass changed to the muffled drums of water on soft earth. That told its own tale.

Never a villager—not even the priest—was bold enough to speak to the Bhagat who had saved their lives. They crouched under the pines and waited till the day. When it came they looked across the valley, and saw that what had been forest, and terraced field, and track-threaded grazing-ground was one raw, red, fan-shaped smear, with a few trees flung head-down on the scarp.[27] That red ran high up the hill of their refuge, damming back the little river, which had begun to spread into a brick-colored lake. Of the village, of the road to the shrine, of the shrine itself, and the forest behind, there was no trace. For one mile in width and two thousand feet in sheer depth the mountain-side had come away bodily, planed clean from head to heel.

And the villagers, one by one, crept through the wood to pray before their Bhagat. They saw the *barasingh* standing over him, who fled when they came near, and they heard the *langurs* wailing in the branches, and Sona moaning up the hill; but their Bhagat was dead, sitting cross-legged, his back against a tree, his crutch under his armpit, and his face turned to the north-east.

The priest said: "Behold a miracle after a miracle, for in this very attitude must all Sunnyasis be buried! Therefore, where he now is we will build the temple to our holy man."

They built the temple before a year was ended, a little stone and earth shrine, and they called the hill the Bhagat's Hill, and they worship there with lights and flowers and offerings to this day. But they do not know that the saint of their worship is the late Sir Purun Dass, K.C.I.E., D.C.L.,[28] Ph.D., etc., once Prime Minister of the progressive and enlightened state of Mohiniwala, and honorary or corresponding member of more learned and scientific societies than will ever do any good in this world or the next. ❖

27. **scarp:** escarpment—a steep slope or cliff separating two level areas of different elevations.

28. **K.C.I.E., D.C.L.:** abbreviations of the titles *Knight Commander of the Indian Empire* and *Doctor of Civil Law.*

RESPONDING OPTIONS

FROM PERSONAL RESPONSE TO CRITICAL ANALYSIS

REFLECT 1. What is your impression of Purun and his actions? Take a moment to jot down your thoughts in your notebook.

RETHINK 2. Do you admire Purun more in his role as Purun Dass or in his role as Purun Bhagat? Explain your answer.

3. Why do you think Purun changes his life so drastically?

   Consider
   - his cultural heritage
   - his values as a young man
   - his accomplishments as prime minister
   - the values he expresses as he begins his new life

4. What, in your opinion, is the miracle of Purun Bhagat? Share your ideas with your classmates.

5. How believable do you find this story?

   Consider
   - the change Purun undergoes
   - the villagers' reaction to him
   - the animals' behavior
   - Purun's saving of the villagers

RELATE 6. Early in the story, Purun Dass seems to believe that "what is good for the Englishman must be twice as good for the Asiatic." How do you think most people would respond to that type of thinking today?

ANOTHER PATHWAY

Cooperative Learning

With a small group of classmates, list the things that seem to matter most to Purun Dass. Then list the values, interests, and goals that seem most important to Purun Bhagat. Which set of values do you find more worthwhile? Discuss your list and share your opinions with the class.

LITERARY CONCEPTS

The **setting** of a story is the time and place of the action. Setting often plays an important role in a story's events. How important do you think the setting of "The Miracle of Purun Bhagat" is? Discuss with your classmates how the events of the story might have been different if Purun Bhagat had become a Sunnyasi but remained in the city.

QUICKWRITES

1. Using details from the story, write an **obituary** of Purun Bhagat for an Indian newspaper.
2. Imagine that you are a villager on the mountainside and that you have just learned about Purun Bhagat's former life as Purun Dass. In a **diary entry,** record your reaction to this news.
3. Use the diagram you made for the Writing Connection on page 622 as a starting point for a **paragraph** in which you explain what you value most in life.

PORTFOLIO *Save your writing. You may want to use it later as a springboard to a piece for your portfolio.*

ALTERNATIVE ACTIVITIES

1. With a partner, present a **dramatic dialogue** in which Purun Dass, the government official, and Purun Bhagat, the holy man, discuss the pros and cons of their lifestyles.
2. Select a favorite descriptive passage from the story and depict it visually in a **watercolor painting.** Add penciling later to accentuate details if you wish.

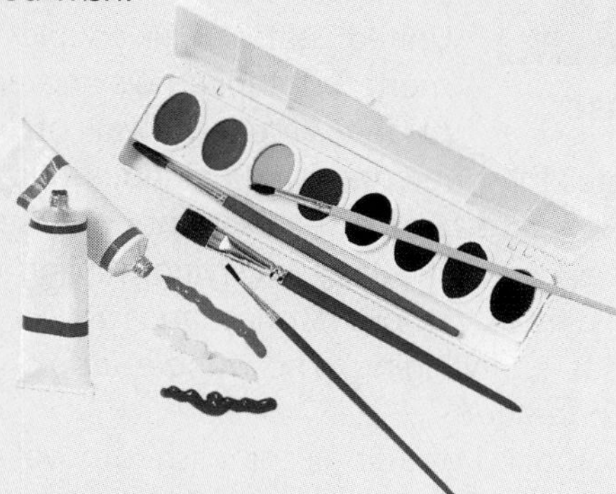

3. Create a design or model of a **statue** that honors Purun by reflecting both phases of his life.

LITERARY LINKS

The heroic code of Rama, as depicted in the *Ramayana* (page 170), is revered by all Hindus and serves as a model of devotion and duty for Hindu men. Do you think that Purun lives his whole life in accordance with that code? Give reasons for your answer.

CRITIC'S CORNER

The student reviewer Shane Cummins found it interesting that Purun dies "sitting 'Indian-style' against the tree." What parts of the story did you find memorable? Share and discuss them with the class.

ACROSS THE CURRICULUM

History Find out more about India's caste system and its effects on the lifestyle of the Indian people. What constitutes a caste? What kinds of rules govern each caste? Has the caste system changed at all since the 19th century? Share your findings with your classmates.

Geography Select several of the villages, cities, and regions named in the story, and find out about the present-day terrain, climate, vegetation, and living conditions in those places. Compile your findings in an illustrated booklet to share with the class. If you have access to a computer, use it to help design the booklet's cover and arrange the text.

THE WRITER'S STYLE

By including many vivid details, Kipling creates for the reader a strong visual image of the different scenes, actions, and events in "The Miracle of Purun Bhagat." What three scenes in the story stand out most vividly in your mind? Recall specific details used in the presentation of these scenes, and give your opinion of why Kipling might have made certain scenes more striking or distinctive than others.

Rudyard Kipling

1865–1936

Although born in Bombay, Joseph Rudyard Kipling spent many of his childhood years in England, unhappily separated from his family. His English parents had moved to India shortly after their marriage, when his father was assigned to a teaching position at an art school. At that time, it was customary for British residents in India to send their children back to Britain for schooling. When Kipling was 6 years old, therefore, his parents took him and his younger sister to Southsea, England, and placed them in a foster home for the next five years. Kipling felt abandoned and later described his stay in Southsea as a period of extreme unhappiness and anxiety. At the age of 12, Kipling was sent to the United Services College, an inexpensive boarding school in Devon, England. Although Kipling later recalled the bullying and unruliness of the students, his school experiences were generally pleasant enough, and his assignment as editor of the school magazine eventually led him to a career in journalism.

In 1882, at the age of 16, Kipling returned to India, where he worked as a newspaper reporter for the next seven years. Many of his early stories were published in a series of paperback books that were sold in train stations. International travelers soon spread word of his work beyond the boundaries of India, and when he returned to England in 1889, his reputation as a great writer had preceded him. He very quickly became one of England's favorite writers.

In 1892, Kipling married an American, Carrie Balestier, and moved with her to the United States. The couple settled in Vermont, but Kipling was never able to adjust to the American way of life. Four years later they were back in England, where Kipling would live the rest of his life. Even though his stay in America was not particularly satisfying, Kipling wrote many of his most famous stories and novels in the United States, including *The Jungle Books* and *Captains Courageous*.

Kipling was an accomplished novelist and poet, as well as the author of over 300 short stories. He is perhaps best known today for his children's stories, particularly the widely read *Just So Stories.* Many of his works—including his most famous novel, *Kim*—reveal his lifelong fascination with the people and animals of India. In 1907, he became the first English writer to be awarded the Nobel Prize for literature.

OTHER WORKS "The Man Who Would Be King," "The Strange Ride of Morrowbie Jukes," "The Maltese Cat," "The King's Ankus," "The Return of Imray"

LASERLINKS
• *GEOGRAPHICAL CONNECTION*

PREVIEWING

FICTION

What Men Live By

Leo Tolstoy

PERSONAL CONNECTION

Think about a time when you or someone you know encountered a stranger in need. How did you or the other person react to the stranger? Write about the experience in your notebook, and then share your writing.

CULTURAL/BIOGRAPHICAL CONNECTION

During the 19th century, the peasants of Russia were poor and struggling. Russia was still a Christian nation then, and it was ruled by an emperor called the czar. Although the peasants were freed from a form of slavery called serfdom during the 1800s, their standard of living remained far lower than that of the wealthy landowners.

Even though Leo Tolstoy was himself an aristocrat and a wealthy landowner, he became a leader in the fight to change society and educate the peasant class. Like the British authors Elizabeth Gaskell and Charles Dickens, Tolstoy often used his writing to call attention to social and moral issues—especially the plight of the poor. Toward the end of his writing career, he began writing down and adapting the folk tales through which peasants conveyed messages about the meaning of life. He believed that these messages revealed truths that could improve the quality of life for all. In "What Men Live By," you will read about a 19th-century Russian peasant and his encounter with a stranger in need.

Leo Tolstoy

READING CONNECTION

Understanding the Title of a Work The title of a literary work often contains important clues to the content, tone, and theme of the work. What can you predict about this story on the basis of the title "What Men Live By"? As you read Tolstoy's tale about a stranger in need, think about the title and its possible meaning.

Using Your Reading Log Use your reading log to record your responses to questions inserted in this selection. Also jot down other thoughts and feelings that come to you as you read.

LASERLINKS
• *CULTURAL CONNECTION*

What Men Live By

LEO TOLSTOY

I

A shoemaker named Simon, who had neither house nor land of his own, lived with his wife and children in a peasant's hut and earned his living by his work. Work was cheap but bread was dear, and what he earned he spent for food. The man and his wife had but one sheep-skin coat between them for winter wear, and even that was worn to tatters, and this was the second year he had been wanting to buy sheep-skins for a new coat. Before winter Simon saved up a little money: a three-ruble note[1] lay hidden in his wife's box, and five rubles and twenty kopeks[2] were owed him by customers in the village.

---

1. **three-ruble** (ro͞o′bəl) **note:** a piece of paper money. The ruble is the main monetary unit of Russia.
2. **kopeks:** one-hundredths of a ruble.

So one morning he prepared to go to the village to buy the sheep-skins. He put on over his shirt his wife's wadded nankeen[3] jacket, and over that he put his own cloth coat. He took the three-ruble note in his pocket, cut himself a stick to serve as a staff, and started off after breakfast. "I'll collect the five rubles that are due to me," thought he, "add the three I have got, and that will be enough to buy sheep-skins for the winter coat."

He came to the village and called at a peasant's hut, but the man was not at home. The peasant's wife promised that the money should be paid next week, but she would not pay it herself. Then Simon called on another peasant, but this one swore he had no money, and would only pay twenty kopeks which he owed for a pair of boots Simon had mended. Simon then tried to buy the sheep-skins on credit, but the dealer would not trust him.

"Bring your money," said he, "then you may have your pick of the skins. We know what debt-collecting is like."

So all the business the shoemaker did was to get the twenty kopeks for boots he had mended and to take a pair of felt boots a peasant gave him to sole with leather.

Simon felt downhearted. He spent the twenty kopeks on vodka and started homewards without having bought any skins. In the morning he had felt the frost; but now, after drinking the vodka, he felt warm even without a sheep-skin coat. He trudged along, striking his stick on the frozen earth with one hand, swinging the felt boots with the other, and talking to himself.

"I'm quite warm," said he, "though I have no sheep-skin coat. I've had a drop and it runs through my veins. I need no sheep-skins. I go along and don't worry about anything. That's the sort of man I am! What do I care? I can live without sheep-skins. I don't need them. My wife will fret, to be sure. And, true enough, it *is* a shame; one works all day long and then does not get paid. Stop a bit! If you don't bring that money along, sure enough I'll skin you, blessed if I don't. How's that? He pays twenty kopeks at a time! What can I do with twenty kopeks? Drink it—that's all one can do! Hard up, he says he is! So he may be—but what about me? You have house, and cattle, and everything; I've only what I stand up in! You have corn of your own growing, I have to buy every grain. Do what I will, I must spend three rubles every week for bread alone. I come home and find the bread all used up and I have to work out another ruble and a half. So just you pay up what you owe, and no nonsense about it!"

By this time he had nearly reached the shrine at the bend of the road. Looking up, he saw something whitish behind the shrine. The daylight was fading, and the shoemaker peered at the thing without being able to make out what it was. "There was no white stone here before. Can it be an ox? It's not like an ox. It has a head like a man, but it's too white; and what could a man be doing there?"

He came closer, so that it was clearly visible. To his surprise it really was a man, alive or dead, sitting naked, leaning motionless against the shrine. Terror seized the shoemaker, and he thought, "Some one has killed him, stripped him, and left him here. If I meddle I shall surely get into trouble."

So the shoemaker went on. He passed in front of the shrine so that he could not see the man. When he had gone some way he looked back, and saw that the man was no longer leaning against the shrine but was moving as if looking towards him. The shoemaker felt more frightened than before, and thought, "Shall I go back to him or shall I go on? If I go near him something dreadful may happen. Who knows who the fellow is? He has not come here for any good. If I go near him he may jump up and throttle me, and there will be no getting away. Or if not, he'd still be a burden on one's hands. What could I do with a naked man? I couldn't give him my last clothes. Heaven only help me to get away!"

So the shoemaker hurried on, leaving the shrine

3. **nankeen:** a sturdy, cotton cloth.

behind him—when suddenly his conscience smote[4] him and he stopped in the road.

"What are you doing, Simon?" said he to himself. "The man may be dying of want, and you slip past afraid. Have you grown so rich as to be afraid of robbers? Ah, Simon, shame on you!"

So he turned back and went up to the man.

II

Simon approached the stranger, looked at him and saw that he was a young man, fit, with no bruises on his body, but evidently freezing and frightened, and he sat there leaning back without looking up at Simon, as if too faint to lift his eyes. Simon went close to him and then the man seemed to wake up. Turning his head, he opened his eyes and looked into Simon's face. That one look was enough to make Simon fond of the man. He threw the felt boots on the ground, undid his sash, laid it on the boots, and took off his cloth coat.

"It's not a time for talking," said he. "Come, put this coat on at once!" And Simon took the man by the elbows and helped him to rise. As he stood there, Simon saw that his body was clean and in good condition, his hands and feet shapely, and his face good and kind. He threw his coat over the man's shoulders, but the latter could not find the sleeves. Simon guided his arms into them, and drawing the coat on well, wrapped it closely about him, tying the sash round the man's waist.

Simon even took off his cap to put it on the man's head, but then his own head felt cold and he thought: "I'm quite bald, while he has long curly hair." So he put his cap on his own head again. "It will be better to give him something for his feet," thought he; and he made the man sit down and helped him to put on the felt boots, saying, "There, friend, now move about and warm yourself. Other matters can be settled later on. Can you walk?"

The man stood up and looked kindly at Simon but could not say a word.

"Why don't you speak?" said Simon. "It's too cold to stay here, we must be getting home. There now, take my stick, and if you're feeling weak lean on that. Now step out!"

The man started walking and moved easily, not lagging behind.

As they went along, Simon asked him, "And where do you belong to?"

"I'm not from these parts."

"I thought as much. I know the folks hereabouts. But how did you come to be there by the shrine?"

"I cannot tell."

"Has some one been ill-treating you?"

"No one has ill-treated me. God has punished me."

"Of course God rules all. Still, you'll have to find food and shelter somewhere. Where do you want to go to?"

"It is all the same to me."

Simon was amazed. The man did not look like a rogue, and he spoke gently, but yet he gave no account of himself. Still Simon thought, "Who knows what may have happened?" And he said to the stranger: "Well then, come home with me and at least warm yourself awhile."

So Simon walked towards his home, and the stranger kept up with him, walking at his side. The wind had risen and Simon felt it cold under his shirt. He was getting over his tipsiness by now and began to feel the frost. He went along sniffling and wrapping his wife's coat round him, and he thought to himself: "There now—talk about sheep-skins! I went out for sheep-skins and come home without even a coat to my back, and what is more, I'm bringing a naked man along with me. Matrëna won't be pleased!" And when he thought of his wife he felt sad, but when he looked at the stranger and remembered how he had looked up at him at the shrine, his heart was glad.

PREDICT

How do you think Simon's wife will react to the stranger?

4. **smote:** dealt a blow to; sharply affected.

Nightfall at Hradčany (1909–1913), Jakub Schikaneder. Oil on canvas, 33.7″ × 41.9″, National Gallery, Prague, Czech Republic.

III

Simon's wife had everything ready early that day. She had cut wood, brought water, fed the children, eaten her own meal, and now she sat thinking. She wondered when she ought to make bread: now or tomorrow? There was still a large piece left.

"If Simon has had some dinner in town," thought she, "and does not eat much for supper, the bread will last out another day."

She weighed the piece of bread in her hand again and again and thought: "I won't make any more today. We have only enough flour left to bake one batch. We can manage to make this last out till Friday."

So Matrëna put away the bread and sat down at the table to patch her husband's shirt. While she worked she thought how her husband was buying skins for a winter coat.

"If only the dealer does not cheat him. My good man is much too simple; he cheats nobody, but any child can take him in. Eight rubles is a lot of money—he should get a good coat at that price. Not tanned skins, but still a proper winter coat. How difficult it was last winter to get on without a winter coat. I could neither get down to the river nor go out anywhere. When he went out he put on all we had, and there was nothing left for me. He did not start very early today, but still it's time he was back. I only hope he has not gone on the spree!"

Hardly had Matrëna thought this than steps were heard on the threshold and some one entered. Matrëna stuck her needle into her work and went out into the passage. There she saw two men: Simon, and with him a man without a hat and wearing felt boots.

Matrëna noticed at once that her husband smelt of spirits. "There now, he has been drinking," thought she. And when she saw that he was coatless, had only her jacket on, brought no parcel, stood there silent, and seemed ashamed, her heart was ready to break with disappointment. "He has drunk the money," thought she, "and has been on the spree with some good-for-nothing fellow whom he has brought home with him."

Matrëna let them pass into the hut, followed them in, and saw that the stranger was a young, slight man, wearing her husband's coat. There was no shirt to be seen under it, and he had no hat. Having entered, he stood neither moving nor raising his eyes, and Matrëna thought: "He must be a bad man—he's afraid."

Matrëna frowned, and stood beside the stove looking to see what they would do.

Simon took off his cap and sat down on the bench as if things were all right.

"Come, Matrëna; if supper is ready, let us have some."

Matrëna muttered something to herself and did not move but stayed where she was, by the stove. She looked first at the one and then at the other of them and only shook her head. Simon saw that his wife was annoyed, but tried to pass it off. Pretending not to notice anything, he took the stranger by the arm.

"Sit down, friend," said he, "and let us have some supper."

The stranger sat down on the bench.

"Haven't you cooked anything for us?" said Simon.

Matrëna's anger boiled over. "I've cooked, but not for you. It seems to me you have drunk your wits away. You went to buy a sheep-skin coat but come home without so much as the coat you had on and bring a naked vagabond home with you. I have no supper for drunkards like you."

"That's enough, Matrëna. Don't wag your tongue without reason! You had better ask what sort of man—"

"And you tell me what you've done with the money?"

Simon found the pocket of the jacket, drew out the three-ruble note, and unfolded it.

"Here is the money. Trifonov did not pay, but promises to pay soon."

Matrëna got still more angry; he had bought no sheep-skins but had put his only coat on some naked fellow and had even brought him to their house.

She snatched up the note from the table, took it to put away in safety, and said: "I have no supper for you. We can't feed all the naked drunkards in the world."

"There now, Matrëna, hold your tongue a bit. First hear what a man has to say—!"

"Much wisdom I shall hear from a drunken fool. I was right in not wanting to marry you—a drunkard. The linen my mother gave me you drank; and now you've been to buy a coat—and have drunk it too!"

Simon tried to explain to his wife that he had only spent twenty kopeks; tried to tell how he had found the man—but Matrëna would not let him get a word in. She talked nineteen to the dozen[5] and dragged in things that had happened ten years before.

Matrëna talked and talked, and at last she flew at Simon and seized him by the sleeve.

"Give me my jacket. It is the only one I have, and you must needs take it from me and wear it yourself. Give it here, you mangy dog, and may the devil take you."

Simon began to pull off the jacket, and turned a sleeve of it inside out; Matrëna seized the jacket and it burst its seams. She snatched it up, threw it over her head, and went to the door. She meant to go out, but stopped undecided—she wanted to work off her anger, but she also wanted to learn what sort of a man the stranger was.

IV

Matrëna stopped and said: "If he were a good man he would not be naked. Why, he hasn't even a shirt on him. If he were all right, you would say where you came across the fellow."

"That's just what I am trying to tell you," said

---

5. **talked nineteen to the dozen:** chattered on excessively.

Simon. "As I came to the shrine I saw him sitting all naked and frozen. It isn't quite the weather to sit about naked! God sent me to him or he would have perished. What was I to do? How do we know what may have happened to him? So I took him, clothed him, and brought him along. Don't be so angry, Matrëna. It is a sin. Remember, we must all die one day."

Angry words rose to Matrëna's lips, but she looked at the stranger and was silent. He sat on the edge of the bench, motionless, his hands folded on his knees, his head drooping on his breast, his eyes closed, and his brows knit as if in pain. Matrëna was silent, and Simon said: "Matrëna, have you no love of God?"

Matrëna heard these words, and as she looked at the stranger, suddenly her heart softened towards him. She came back from the door, and going to the stove she got out the supper. Setting a cup on the table, she poured out some kvas.[6] Then she brought out the last piece of bread and set out a knife and spoons.

"Eat, if you want to," said she.

Simon drew the stranger to the table.

"Take your place, young man," said he.

Simon cut the bread, crumbled it into the broth, and they began to eat. Matrëna sat at the corner of the table, resting her head on her hand and looking at the stranger.

And Matrëna was touched with pity for the stranger and began to feel fond of him. And at once the stranger's face lit up; his brows were no longer bent, he raised his eyes and smiled at Matrëna.

When they had finished supper, the woman cleared away the things and began questioning the stranger. "Where are you from?" said she.

"I am not from these parts."

"But how did you come to be on the road?"

"I may not tell."

"Did some one rob you?"

"God punished me."

"And you were lying there naked?"

"Yes, naked and freezing. Simon saw me and had pity on me. He took off his coat, put it on me, and brought me here. And you have fed me, given me drink, and shown pity on me. God will reward you!"

Matrëna rose, took from the window Simon's old shirt she had been patching, and gave it to the stranger. She also brought out a pair of trousers for him.

"There," said she, "I see you have no shirt. Put this on, and lie down where you please, in the loft or on the stove."[7]

QUESTION

Why do you think Matrëna's attitude toward the stranger has changed?

The stranger took off the coat, put on the shirt, and lay down in the loft. Matrëna put out the candle, took the coat, and climbed to where her husband lay on the stove.

Matrëna drew the skirts of the coat over her and lay down but could not sleep; she could not get the stranger out of her mind.

When she remembered that he had eaten their last piece of bread and that there was none for tomorrow and thought of the shirt and trousers she had given away, she felt grieved; but when she remembered how he had smiled, her heart was glad.

Long did Matrëna lie awake, and she noticed that Simon also was awake—he drew the coat towards him.

"Simon!"

"Well?"

"You have had the last of the bread and I have not put any to rise. I don't know what we shall do tomorrow. Perhaps I can borrow some of neighbor Martha."

"If we're alive we shall find something to eat."

The woman lay still awhile, and then said, "He seems a good man, but why does he not tell us who he is?"

---

6. **kvas** (kväs): a Russian drink, similar to beer, made from fermented grains.

7. **on the stove:** The large stoves and ovens in Russian peasant homes often had tops large enough to sleep on for extra warmth.

"I suppose he has his reasons."

"Simon!"

"Well?"

"We give; but why does nobody give us anything?"

Simon did not know what to say; so he only said, "Let us stop talking" and turned over and went to sleep.

V

In the morning Simon awoke. The children were still asleep; his wife had gone to the neighbor's to borrow some bread. The stranger alone was sitting on the bench, dressed in the old shirt and trousers, and looking upwards. His face was brighter than it had been the day before.

Simon said to him, "Well, friend; the belly wants bread and the naked body clothes. One has to work for a living. What work do you know?"

"I do not know any."

This surprised Simon, but he said, "Men who want to learn can learn anything."

"Men work and I will work also."

"What is your name?"

"Michael."

"Well, Michael, if you don't wish to talk about yourself, that is your own affair; but you'll have to earn a living for yourself. If you will work as I tell you, I will give you food and shelter."

"May God reward you! I will learn. Show me what to do."

Simon took yarn, put it round his thumb and began to twist it.

Grain Harvest (1908), Natalia Sergeevna Goncharova. Oil on canvas, 96 cm × 103 cm, The State Russian Museum, St. Petersburg, Russia.

"It is easy enough—see!"

Michael watched him, put some yarn round his own thumb in the same way, caught the knack, and twisted the yarn also.

Then Simon showed him how to wax the thread. This also Michael mastered. Next Simon showed him how to twist the bristle in, and how to sew, and this, too, Michael learned at once.

Whatever Simon showed him he understood at once, and after three days he worked as if he had sewn boots all his life. He worked without stopping and ate little. When work was over he sat silently, looking upwards. He hardly went into the street, spoke only when necessary, and neither joked nor laughed. They never saw him smile, except that first evening when Matrëna gave him supper.

VI

Day by day and week by week the year went round. Michael lived and worked with Simon. His fame spread till people said that no one sewed boots so neatly and strongly as Simon's workman, Michael; from all the district round people came to Simon for their boots, and he began to be well off.

One winter day, as Simon and Michael sat working, a carriage on sledge-runners, with three horses and with bells, drove up to the hut. They looked out of the window; the carriage stopped at their door; a fine servant jumped down from the box and opened the door. A gentleman in a fur coat got out and walked up to Simon's hut. Up jumped Matrëna and opened the door wide. The gentleman stooped to enter the hut, and when he drew himself up again his head nearly reached the ceiling and he seemed quite to fill his end of the room.

Simon rose, bowed, and looked at the gentleman with astonishment. He had never seen any one like him. Simon himself was lean, Michael was thin, and Matrëna was dry as a bone, but this man was like some one from another world: red-faced, burly, with a neck like a bull's, and looking altogether as if he were cast in iron.

The gentleman puffed, threw off his fur coat, sat down on the bench, and said, "Which of you is the master bootmaker?"

"I am, your Excellency," said Simon, coming forward.

Then the gentleman shouted to his lad, "Hey, Fédka, bring the leather!"

The servant ran in, bringing a parcel. The gentleman took the parcel and put it on the table.

"Untie it," said he. The lad untied it.

The gentleman pointed to the leather.

"Look here, shoemaker," said he, "do you see this leather?"

"Yes, your honor."

"But do you know what sort of leather it is?"

Simon felt the leather and said, "It is good leather."

"Good, indeed! Why, you fool, you never saw such leather before in your life. It's German and cost twenty rubles."

Simon was frightened and said, "Where should I ever see leather like that?"

"Just so! Now, can you make it into boots for me?"

"Yes, your Excellency, I can."

Then the gentleman shouted at him: "You *can,* can you? Well, remember whom you are to make them for, and what the leather is. You must make me boots that will wear for a year, neither losing shape nor coming unsewn. If you can do it, take the leather and cut it up; but if you can't, say so. I warn you now, if your boots come unsewn or lose shape within a year I will have you put in prison. If they don't burst or lose shape for a year, I will pay you ten rubles for your work."

Simon was frightened and did not know what to say. He glanced at Michael and nudging him with his elbow, whispered: "Shall I take the work?"

Michael nodded his head as if to say, "Yes, take it."

Simon did as Michael advised and undertook

to make boots that would not lose shape or split for a whole year.

Calling his servant, the gentleman told him to pull the boot off his left leg, which he stretched out.

"Take my measure!" said he.

Simon stitched a paper measure seventeen inches long, smoothed it out, knelt down, wiped his hands well on his apron so as not to soil the gentleman's sock, and began to measure. He measured the sole, and round the instep, and began to measure the calf of the leg, but the paper was too short. The calf of the leg was as thick as a beam.

"Mind you don't make it too tight in the leg."

Simon stitched on another strip of paper. The gentleman twitched his toes about in his sock looking round at those in the hut, and as he did so he noticed Michael.

"Whom have you there?" asked he.

"That is my workman. He will sew the boots."

"Mind," said the gentleman to Michael, "remember to make them so that they will last me a year."

Simon also looked at Michael and saw that Michael was not looking at the gentleman, but was gazing into the corner behind the gentleman, as if he saw some one there. Michael looked and looked, and suddenly he smiled, and his face became brighter.

"What are you grinning at, you fool?" thundered the gentleman. "You had better look to it that the boots are ready in time."

"They shall be ready in good time," said Michael.

"Mind it is so," said the gentleman, and he put on his boots and his fur coat, wrapped the latter round him, and went to the door. But he forgot to stoop, and struck his head against the lintel.[8]

He swore and rubbed his head. Then he took his seat in the carriage and drove away.

When he had gone, Simon said: "There's a figure of a man for you! You could not kill him with a mallet. He almost knocked out the lintel, but little harm it did him."

And Matrëna said: "Living as he does, how should he not have grown strong? Death itself can't touch such a rock as that."

VII

Then Simon said to Michael: "Well, we have taken the work, but we must see we don't get into trouble over it. The leather is dear, and the gentleman hot-tempered. We must make no mistakes. Come, your eye is truer and your hands have become nimbler than mine, so you take this measure and cut out the boots. I will finish off the sewing of the vamps."[9]

Michael did as he was told. He took the leather, spread it out on the table, folded it in two, took a knife and began to cut out.

Matrëna came and watched him cutting and was surprised to see how he was doing it. Matrëna was accustomed to seeing boots made, and she looked and saw that Michael was not cutting the leather for boots, but was cutting it round.

She wished to say something, but she thought to herself: "Perhaps I do not understand how gentlemen's boots should be made. I suppose Michael knows more about it—and I won't interfere."

When Michael had cut up the leather he took a thread and began to sew not with two ends, as boots are sewn, but with a single end, as for soft slippers.

Again Matrëna wondered, but again she did not interfere. Michael sewed on steadily till noon. Then Simon rose for dinner, looked around, and saw that Michael had made slippers out of the gentleman's leather.

"Ah!" groaned Simon, and he thought, "How is it that Michael, who has been with me a whole year and never made a mistake before, should do

8. **lintel:** the horizontal beam at the top of a door frame.

9. **vamps:** the upper parts of shoes or boots, covering the instep or the instep and the toes.

such a dreadful thing? The gentleman ordered high boots, welted,[10] with whole fronts, and Michael has made soft slippers with single soles and has wasted the leather. What am I to say to the gentleman? I can never replace leather such as this."

And he said to Michael, "What are you doing, friend? You have ruined me! You know the gentleman ordered high boots, but see what you have made!"

Hardly had he begun to rebuke Michael, when "rat-tat" went the iron ring hung at the door. Some one was knocking. They looked out of the window; a man had come on horseback and was fastening his horse. They opened the door, and the servant who had been with the gentleman came in.

"Good day," said he.

"Good day," replied Simon. "What can we do for you?"

"My mistress has sent me about the boots."

"What about the boots?"

"Why, my master no longer needs them. He is dead."

"Is it possible?"

"He did not live to get home after leaving you but died in the carriage. When we reached home and the servants came to help him alight, he rolled over like a sack. He was dead already, and so stiff that he could hardly be got out of the carriage. My mistress sent me here, saying: 'Tell the bootmaker that the gentleman who ordered boots of him and left the leather for them no longer needs the boots, but that he must quickly make soft slippers for the corpse. Wait till they are ready and bring them back with you.' That is why I have come."

Michael gathered up the remnants of the leather; rolled them up, took the soft slippers he had made, slapped them together, wiped them down with his apron, and handed them and the roll of leather to the servant, who took them and said: "Good-bye, masters, and good day to you!"

QUESTION

How do you think Michael knew that he should make slippers?

VIII

Another year passed, and another, and Michael was now living his sixth year with Simon. He lived as before. He went nowhere, only spoke when necessary, and had only smiled twice in all those years—one when Matrëna gave him food, and a second time when the gentleman was in their hut. Simon was more than pleased with his workman. He never now asked him where he came from and only feared lest Michael should go away.

They were all at home one day. Matrëna was putting iron pots in the oven; the children were running along the benches and looking out of the window; Simon was sewing at one window and Michael was fastening on a heel at the other.

One of the boys ran along the bench to Michael, leant on his shoulder, and looked out of the window.

"Look, Uncle Michael! There is a lady with little girls! She seems to be coming here. And one of the girls is lame."

When the boy said that, Michael dropped his work, turned to the window, and looked out into the street.

Simon was surprised. Michael never used to look out into the street, but now he pressed against the window, staring at something. Simon also looked out and saw that a well-dressed woman was really coming to his hut, leading by the hand two little girls in fur coats and woolen shawls. The girls could hardly be told one from the other, except that one of them was crippled in her left leg and walked with a limp.

The woman stepped into the porch and entered the passage. Feeling about for the entrance she found the latch, which she lifted, and opened the door. She let the two girls go in first, and followed them into the hut.

"Good day, good folk!"

10. **welted:** with a leather strip stitched between the sole and the upper.

"Pray come in," said Simon. "What can we do for you?"

The woman sat down by the table. The two little girls pressed close to her knees, afraid of the people in the hut.

"I want leather shoes made for these two little girls, for spring."

"We can do that. We never have made such small shoes, but we can make them; either welted or turnover shoes, linen lined. My man, Michael, is a master at the work."

Simon glanced at Michael and saw that he had left his work and was sitting with his eyes fixed on the little girls. Simon was surprised. It was true the girls were pretty, with black eyes, plump, and rosy-cheeked, and they wore nice kerchiefs and fur coats, but still Simon could not understand why Michael should look at them like that—just as if he had known them before. He was puzzled but went on talking with the woman and arranging the price. Having fixed it, he prepared the measure. The woman lifted the lame girl on to her lap and said: "Take two measures from this little girl. Make one shoe for the lame foot and three for the sound one. They both have the same-sized feet. They are twins."

Simon took the measure and, speaking of the lame girl, said: "How did it happen to her? She is such a pretty girl. Was she born so?"

"No, her mother crushed her leg."

Then Matrëna joined in. She wondered who this woman was and whose the children were, so she said: "Are not you their mother, then?"

"No, my good woman; I am neither their mother nor any relation to them. They were quite strangers to me, but I adopted them."

"They are not your children and yet you are so fond of them?"

"How can I help being fond of them? I fed them both at my own breasts. I had a child of my own, but God took him. I was not so fond of him as I now am of these."

"Then whose children are they?"

IX

The woman, having begun talking, told them the whole story.

"It is about six years since their parents died, both in one week: their father was buried on the Tuesday, and their mother died on the Friday. These orphans were born three days after their father's death, and their mother did not live another day. My husband and I were then living as peasants in the village. We were neighbors of theirs, our yard being next to theirs. Their father was a lonely man, a wood-cutter in the forest. When felling trees one day they let one fall on him. It fell across his body and crushed his bowels out. They hardly got him home before his soul went to God; and that same week his wife gave birth to twins—these little girls. She was poor and alone; she had no one, young or old, with her. Alone she gave them birth, and alone she met her death.

"The next morning I went to see her, but when I entered the hut, she, poor thing, was already stark and cold. In dying she had rolled on to this child and crushed her leg. The village folk came to the hut, washed the body, laid her out, made a coffin, and buried her. They were good folk. The babies were left alone. What was to be done with them? I was the only woman there who had a baby at the time. I was nursing my first-born—eight weeks old. So I took them for a time. The peasants came together, and thought and thought what to do with them; and at last they said to me: 'For the present, Mary, you had better keep the girls, and later on we will arrange what to do for them.' So I nursed the sound one at my breast, but at first I did not feed this crippled one. I did not suppose she would live. But then I thought to myself, why should the poor innocent suffer? I pitied her and began to feed her. And so I fed my own boy and these two—the three of them—at my own breast. I was young and strong and had good food, and God gave me so much milk that at times it even overflowed. I used sometimes to feed two at a time, while the third was waiting. When one had had enough I nursed

Photo by Kari Haavisto.

the third. And God so ordered it that these grew up, while my own was buried before he was two years old. And I had no more children, though we prospered. Now my husband is working for the corn merchant at the mill. The pay is good and we are well off. But I have no children of my own, and how lonely I should be without these little girls! How can I help loving them! They are the joy of my life!"

CLARIFY

How were the twins able to survive after their mother's death?

She pressed the lame little girl to her with one hand, while with the other she wiped the tears from her cheeks.

And Matrëna sighed, and said: "The proverb is true that says, 'One may live without father or mother, but one cannot live without God.' "

So they talked together, when suddenly the whole hut was lighted up as though by summer lightning from the corner where Michael sat. They all looked towards him and saw him sitting, his hands folded on his knees, gazing upwards and smiling.

The woman went away with the girls. Michael rose from the bench, put down his work, and took off his apron. Then, bowing low to Simon and his wife, he said: "Farewell, masters. God has forgiven me. I ask your forgiveness, too, for anything done amiss."

And they saw that a light shone from Michael. And Simon rose, bowed down to Michael, and said: "I see, Michael, that you are no common man, and I can neither keep you nor question you. Only tell me this: how is it that when I found you and brought you home, you were gloomy, and when my wife gave you food you smiled at her and became brighter? Then when the gentleman came to order the boots, you smiled again and became brighter still? And now, when this woman brought the little girls, you smiled a third time and have become as bright as day? Tell me, Michael, why does your face shine so, and why did you smile those three times?"

And Michael answered: "Light shines from me because I have been punished, but now God has pardoned me. And I smiled three times, because God sent me to learn three truths, and I have learnt them. One I learnt when your wife pitied me, and that is why I smiled the first time. The second I learnt when the rich man ordered the boots, and then I smiled again. And now, when I saw those little girls, I learnt the third and last, and I smiled the third time."

And Simon said, "Tell me, Michael, what did God punish you for? and what were the three truths? that I, too, may know them."

And Michael answered: "God punished me for disobeying him. I was an angel in heaven and disobeyed God. God sent me to fetch a woman's soul. I flew to earth and saw a sick woman lying alone who had just given birth to twin girls. They moved feebly at their mother's side but she could not lift them to her breast. When she saw me, she understood that God had sent me for her soul, and she wept and said: 'Angel of God! My husband has just been buried, killed by a falling tree. I have neither sister, nor aunt, nor mother: no one to care for my orphans. Do not take my soul! Let me nurse my babes, feed them, and set them on their feet before I die. Children cannot live without father or mother.' And I hearkened to her. I placed one child at her breast and gave the other into her arms, and returned to the Lord in heaven. I flew to the Lord, and said: 'I could not take the soul of the mother. Her husband was killed by a tree; the woman has twins and prays that her soul may not be taken. She says: "Let me nurse and feed my children, and set them on their feet. Children cannot live without father or mother." I have not taken her soul.' And God said: 'Go—take the mother's soul, and learn three truths: Learn *What dwells in man, What is not given to man,* and *What men live by*. When thou hast learnt these things, thou shalt return to heaven.' So I flew again to earth and took the mother's soul. The babes dropped from her breasts. Her body rolled over on the bed and crushed one babe, twisting its leg. I rose above the village, wishing to take her soul to God, but a wind seized me and my wings drooped and dropped off. Her soul rose alone to God, while I fell to earth by the roadside."

CLARIFY

For what was Michael punished?

XI

And Simon and Matrëna understood who it was that had lived with them and whom they had clothed and fed. And they wept with awe and with joy. And the angel said: "I was alone in the field, naked. I had never known human needs, cold and hunger, till I became a man. I was famished, frozen, and did not know what to do. I saw, near the field I was in, a shrine built for God, and I went to it hoping to find shelter. But the shrine was locked and I could not enter. So I sat down behind the shrine to shelter myself at least from the wind. Evening drew on, I was hungry, frozen, and in pain. Suddenly I heard a man coming along the road. He carried a pair of boots and was talking to himself. For the first time since I became a man I saw the mortal face of a man, and his face seemed terrible to me and I turned from it. And I heard the man talking to himself of how to cover his body from the cold in winter, and how to feed wife and children. And I thought: 'I am perishing of cold and hunger and here is a man thinking only of how to clothe himself and his wife, and how to get bread for themselves. He cannot help me.' When the man saw me he frowned and became still more terrible and passed me by on the other side. I despaired; but suddenly I heard him coming back. I looked up and did not recognize the same man: before, I had seen death in his face; but now he was alive and I recognized in him the presence of God. He came up to me, clothed me, took me with him, and brought me to his home. I entered the house; a woman came to meet us and began to speak. The woman was still more terrible than the man had been; the spirit of death came from her mouth; I could not breathe for the stench[11] of death that spread around her. She wished to drive me out into the cold, and I knew that if she did so she would die. Suddenly her husband spoke to her of God, and the woman changed at once. And when she brought me food and looked at me, I glanced at her and saw that death no longer dwelt in her; she had become alive, and in her too I saw God.

"Then I remembered the first lesson God had set me: *'Learn what dwells in man.'* And I understood that in man dwells Love! I was glad that God had already begun to show me what He had promised, and I smiled for the first time.

11. **stench:** foul smell.

But I had not yet learnt all. I did not yet know *What is not given to man,* and *What men live by.*

"I lived with you and a year passed. A man came to order boots that should wear for a year without losing shape or cracking. I looked at him, and suddenly, behind his shoulder, I saw my comrade—the angel of death. None but me saw that angel; but I knew him, and knew that before the sun set he would take the rich man's soul. And I thought to myself, 'The man is making preparation for a year and does not know that he will die before evening.' And I remembered God's second saying, *'Learn what is not given to man.'*

"What dwells in man I already knew. Now I learnt what is not given him. It is not given to man to know his own needs. And I smiled for the second time. I was glad to have seen my comrade angel—glad also that God had revealed to me the second saying.

"But I still did not know all. I did not know *What men live by.* And I lived on, waiting till God should reveal to me the last lesson. In the sixth year came the girl-twins with the woman; and I recognized the girls and heard how they had been kept alive. Having heard the story, I thought, 'Their mother besought[12] me for the children's sake, and I believed her when she said that children cannot live without father or mother; but a stranger has nursed them and has brought them up.' And when the woman showed her love for the children that were not her own and wept over them, I saw in her the living God, and understood *What men live by.* And I knew that God had revealed to me the last lesson and had forgiven my sin. And then I smiled for the third time."

XII

And the angel's body was bared, and he was clothed in light so that eye could not look on him; and his voice grew louder, as though it came not from him but from heaven above. And the angel said: "I have learnt that all men live not by care for themselves, but by love.

"It was not given to the mother to know what her children needed for their life. Nor was it given to the rich man to know what he himself needed. Nor is it given to any man to know whether, when evening comes, he will need boots for his body or slippers for his corpse.

"I remained alive when I was a man, not by care of myself but because love was present in a passer-by and because he and his wife pitied and loved me. The orphans remained alive not because of their mother's care, but because there was love in the heart of a woman, a stranger to them, who pitied and loved them. And all men live not by the thought they spend on their own welfare, but because love exists in man.

"I knew before that God gave life to men and desires that they should live; now I understood more than that.

"I understood that God does not wish men to live apart, and therefore he does not reveal to them what each one needs for himself; but he wishes them to live united, and therefore reveals to each of them what is necessary for all.

"I have now understood that though it seems to men that they live by care for themselves, in truth it is love alone by which they live. He who has love, is in God, and God is in him, for God is love."

And the angel sang praise to God, so that the hut trembled at his voice. The roof opened, and a column of fire rose from earth to heaven. Simon and his wife and children fell to the ground. Wings appeared upon the angel's shoulders and he rose into the heavens.

And when Simon came to himself the hut stood as before, and there was no one in it but his own family. ❖

Translated by Louise and Aylmer Maude

12. **besought** (bĭ-sôt′): begged.

RESPONDING OPTIONS

FROM PERSONAL RESPONSE *TO* CRITICAL ANALYSIS

REFLECT 1. What is your reaction to Michael's explanation of what men live by? Write down your thoughts in your notebook.

RETHINK 2. Compare the reaction to a needy stranger you wrote about for the Personal Connection on page 637 with Simon's reaction when he encounters Michael. Do you think most people would be likely to react as Simon does? Why or why not?

3. Do you think Simon and Matrëna are basically similar or basically different? Explain your answer.

Consider
- their initial reactions to Michael and the changes in their attitudes
- how each of them copes with poverty
- the role of God in each of their lives

4. Do you think Michael has deserved to be punished by God? Give reasons for your opinion.

5. Think again about the three lessons that Michael learns about life. Do you think any one of the lessons is more important than the others?

Consider
- why Matrëna's behavior changes from bitter and selfish to kind and generous
- why Michael knows that he should make slippers for the rich man
- why the twins were able to survive without their natural mother

RELATE 6. Summarize in one sentence what you think the theme of the story is. Do you think the theme is valid as a principle for living today? Explain your opinion.

7. What do you think would happen if Michael appeared in your neighborhood as a stranger in need of food, clothing, and shelter? Do you think it would be possible for him to learn the same lessons? Give reasons for your answers.

ANOTHER PATHWAY

This story can be divided into four main parts (sections I–V, sections VI–VII, sections VIII–IX, and sections X–XII). Summarize the plot of the story by creating an appropriate subtitle for each of the four parts. With your classmates, discuss everyone's subtitles and pick the most appropriate for each section.

QUICKWRITES

1. Write an **episode** that occurs in the lives of Simon and Matrëna after Michael has left them. Imitate the style of the story, and try to show how Michael has affected the couple's life.

2. Write your own three **maxims** for living that might help people lead more meaningful and rewarding lives. Feel free to include ideas that are very different from those in the story.

PORTFOLIO Save your writing. You may want to use it later as a springboard to a piece for your portfolio.

LITERARY CONCEPTS

A **folk tale** is a story that is handed down, usually by word of mouth, from generation to generation. Folk tales reflect the unique characteristics of the regions they come from, showing how the inhabitants live and what their values are. Many involve supernatural events, and most suggest morals. Often, things happen in threes in folk tales. What characters and events in this story characterize it as a folk tale?

ART CONNECTION

Look again at the painting *Nightfall at Hradčany* on page 641. In your opinion, how closely does this painting reflect the mood of the story?

LITERARY LINKS

Consider Michael's comment that "men live not by care for themselves, but by love." How does this message relate to the theme of Elizabeth Gaskell's story "Christmas Storms and Sunshine" (page 606)?

ALTERNATIVE ACTIVITIES

1. Design a **storyboard,** or series of sketches, for one part of the story. Each sketch should show the setting and the actions of the characters. Display your storyboard in class.
2. Near the end of the story, Michael says, "I have learnt that all men live not by care for themselves, but by love." With your classmates, collect and create a **display** of newspaper columns that could serve to illustrate Michael's comment by showing that people still help one another.
3. Design a **monument** to be placed at the spot where the angel first appeared to Simon. Try to visually convey the lesson that Michael learned during his time with Simon.

CRITIC'S CORNER

Virginia Woolf had this to say about Tolstoy's writing: "He notices the blue or red of a child's frock; the way a horse shifts its tail; the sound of a cough; the action of a man trying to put his hands into pockets that have been sewn up. And what his infallible eye reports of a cough or a trick of the hands his infallible brain refers to something hidden in the character so that we know his people, not only by the way they love and their views on politics and the immortality of the soul, but also by the way they sneeze and choke." Find at least three passages in "What Men Live By" that support this comment about Tolstoy's descriptive style.

ACROSS THE CURRICULUM

Economics Find out about the differences between the economic conditions of Russian aristocrats and peasants in the 19th century. What were the causes of the huge economic gap between the rich and the poor? Report your findings to the class.

Leo Tolstoy

1828–1910

Although Leo Tolstoy was orphaned as a young child, his early years were rather uneventful. He was raised by relatives and lived most of his life in Yasnaya Polyana, about 100 miles south of Moscow. At the age of 16, he entered a university, but he returned home after a few years to educate himself. In 1852, determined to change his rather aimless lifestyle, he joined the army and began to spend much of his free time writing. When his stories based on his experiences during the Crimean War were well received, his literary career was launched.

In the late 1850s, Tolstoy returned to his family estate and, unhappy with the education available to the peasants there, developed his own school, eliminating all grades, punishments, and rewards. In 1862 he married, and for the next 15 years he devoted his time to his wife, his 13 children, and the writing of his two greatest works, *War and Peace* and *Anna Karenina*. It took him 7 years to complete *War and Peace,* now regarded as one of the greatest novels in world literature.

In spite of his relative success in life, Tolstoy began to suffer a spiritual and emotional crisis during his middle years. He found comfort in Christian principles and decided that he must shed his worldly possessions, give away his wealth, and live the honest, simple life of a Russian peasant. His resolve was not shared by his family, however, and bitter quarrels ensued. To appease them, Tolstoy signed his entire estate over to his wife, thereafter devoting his time to writing essays and stories dealing with religious, social, and moral issues. He dressed in the clothes of a peasant, gave up drinking and smoking, and became a vegetarian. He simplified his life as much as possible but remained unsatisfied. Finally, at the age of 82, accompanied by his youngest daughter and a doctor, Tolstoy left home to search for a simpler existence. He died of pneumonia in a train station a few days later.

OTHER WORKS "How Much Land Does a Man Need?" "Three Questions," "Two Old Men," "Alyosha Gorshok"

THE KING IS DEAD, LONG LIVE THE KING

Mary E. Coleridge

A moderately successful writer during the late 19th century, Mary E. Coleridge is probably better known as the great-grandniece of the romantic poet Samuel Taylor Coleridge. In several of her works—including this story—she, like her more famous relation, touches upon themes of fantasy and the supernatural. This similarity once inspired a critic to call her "the tail of the comet S. T. C."

It was not very quiet in the room where the king lay dying. People were coming and going, rustling in and out with hushed footsteps, whispering eagerly to each other; and where a great many people are all busy making as little noise as possible, the result is apt to be a kind of bustle, that weakened nerves can scarcely endure.

But what did that matter? The doctors said he could hear nothing now. He gave no sign that he could. Surely the sobs of his beautiful young wife, as she knelt by the bedside, must else have moved him.

For days the light had been carefully shaded. Now, in the hurry, confusion, and distress, no one remembered to draw the curtains close, so that the dim eyes might not be dazzled. But what did that matter? The doctors said he could see nothing now.

For days no one but his attendants had been allowed to come near him. Now the room was free for all who chose to enter. What did it matter? The doctors said he knew no one.

So he lay for a long time, one hand flung out upon the counterpane,[1] as if in search of something. The queen took it softly in hers, but there was no answering pressure. At length the eyes and mouth closed, and the heart ceased to beat.

"How beautiful he looks," they whispered one to another.

When the king came to himself it was all very still—wonderfully and delightfully still, as he thought, wonderfully and delightfully dark. It was a strange, unspeakable relief to him—he lay as if in heaven. The room was full of the scent of flowers, and the cool night air came pleasantly through an open window. A row of wax tapers burned with soft radiance at the foot of the bed on which he was lying, covered with a velvet pall, only his head and face exposed. Four or five men were keeping guard around him, but they had fallen fast asleep.

So deep was the feeling of content which he experienced that he was loth[2] to stir. Not till the great clock of the palace struck eleven, did he so much as move. Then he sat up with a light laugh.

He remembered how, when his mind was failing him, and he had rallied all his powers in one last passionate appeal against the injustice which was taking him away from the world just when the world most needed him, he had heard a voice saying, "I will give thee yet one hour after death. If, in that time, thou canst find three that desire thy life, live!"

This was his hour, his hour that he had snatched away from death. How much of it had he lost already? He had been a good king; he had worked night and day for his subjects: he had nothing to fear, and he knew that it was very pleasant to live, how pleasant he had never known before, for, to do him justice, he was not selfish; it was his unfinished work that he grieved about when the decree went forth against him. Yet, as he passed out of the room where the watchers sat heavily sleeping, things were changed to him somehow. The burning sense of injustice was gone. Now that he came to think of it, he had done very little. True that it was his utmost, but there were many better men in the world, and the world was large, very large it seemed to him now. Everything had grown larger. He loved his country and his home as well as ever, but in the night it had seemed as if they must perish with him, and now he knew that they were still unchanged.

---

1. **counterpane:** bedspread.
2. **loth** (lōth): unwilling.

> "I WILL GIVE THEE YET ONE HOUR AFTER DEATH. IF, IN THAT TIME, THOU CANST FIND THREE THAT DESIRE THY LIFE, LIVE!"

Outside the door he paused a moment, hesitating whither to go first. Not to the queen. The very thought of her grief unnerved him. He would not see her till he could once more clasp her in his arms, and bid her weep tears of joy only because he was come again. After all, he had but an hour to wait. Before the castle clock struck twelve, he would be back again in life, remembering these things only as a dream. He sighed a little to think of it.

"All that to do over again some day," he said, as he recalled his last moments.

Almost he turned again to the couch he had so lately left.

"But I have never yet done anything through fear," said the king.

And he smiled as he thought of the terms of the compact. His city lay before him in the moonlight.

"I could find three thousand as easily as three," he said. "Are they not all my friends?"

As he passed out of the gate, he saw a child sitting on the steps, crying bitterly.

"What is the matter, little one?" said the sentinel on guard, stopping a moment.

"Father and mother have gone to the castle, because the king's dead," sobbed the child, "and they've never come back again; and I'm so tired and so hungry! And I've had no supper, and my doll's broken. Oh! I do wish the king were alive again!"

And she burst into a fresh storm of weeping. It amused the king not a little.

"So this is the first of my subjects that wants me back!" he said.

He had no child of his own. He would have liked to try and comfort the little maiden, but there were other calls upon him just then. He was on his way to the house of his great friend, the man whom he loved more than all others. A kind of malicious delight possessed him, as he pictured to himself the deep dejection he should find him in.

"Poor Amyas!" he said. "I know what I should be feeling in his place. I am glad he was not taken. I could not have borne his loss."

As he entered the courtyard of his friend's house, lights were being carried to and fro, horses were being saddled, an air of bustle and excitement pervaded the place. Look where he might, he could not see the face he knew so well. He entered at the open door. His friend was not in the hall. Room after room he vainly traversed—they were all empty. A sudden horror took him. Surely Amyas was not dead of grief?

He came at length to a small private apartment, in which they had spent many a happy, busy hour together; but his friend was not here either, though, to judge by appearances, he could only just have left it. Books and papers were tumbled all about in strange confusion, and bits of broken glass strewed the floor.

A little picture was lying on the ground. The king picked it up, and recognized a miniature of himself, the frame of which had been broken in the fall. He let it drop again, as if it had burnt him. The fire was blazing brightly, and the fragments of a half-destroyed letter lay, unconsumed as yet, in the fender.[3] It was in his own writing. He snatched it up, and saw it was the last he had written, containing the details of an elaborate scheme which he had much at heart. He had only just thrown it back into the flames when two people entered the room, talking together, one a lady, the other a man, booted and spurred as though he came from a long distance.

"Where is Amyas?" he asked.

"Gone to proffer[4] his services to the new king, of course," said the lady. "We are, as you may think, in great anxiety. He has none of the ridiculous notions of his predecessor,[5] who, indeed, hated him cordially. The very favor Amyas has hitherto enjoyed will stand in his way at the new court. I only hope he may be in time to make his peace. He can, with trust, say that he utterly disapproved of the foolish reforms which his late master was bent on making. Of course, he was fond of him in a way; but we must think of ourselves, you know. People in our position have no time for sentiment. He started almost immediately after the king's death. I am sending his retinue[6] after him."

"Quite right," said the gentleman, whom the king now knew as one of his ambassadors. "I shall follow him at once. Between you and me, it is no bad thing for the country. That poor boy had no notion of statesmanship. He forced me to conclude a peace which would have been disastrous to all our best interests. Happily, we shall have war directly now. Promotions in the army would have been at a standstill if he had had his way."

The king did not stay to hear more.

"I will go to my people," he said. "They at least have no interest to make peace with my successor. He will but take from them what I gave."

He heard the clock strike the first quarter as he went. He was, indeed, a very remarkable king, for he knew his way to the poorest part of his dominions. He had been there before, often and often, unknown to any one; and the misery which he had there beheld had stirred and steeled him to attempt what had never before been attempted.

No one about the palace knew where he had caught the malignant fever which carried him off. He had a shrewd suspicion himself, and he went straight to that quarter.

"Fevers won't hurt me now," he said laughing. The houses were as wretched, the people looked as sickly and squalid[7] as ever. They were standing about in knots in the streets, late though it was, talking together about him. His name was in every mouth. The details of his illness, and the probable day of his funeral, seemed to interest them more than anything else.

Five or six men were sitting drinking round a table in a disreputable-looking public-house,[8] and he stopped to overhear their conversation.

"And a good riddance, too!" said one of them, whom he knew well. "What's the use of a king as never spends a farthing more than he can help? It gives no impetus[9] to trade, it don't. The new fellow's a very different sort. We shall have fine doings soon."

---

3. **fender:** a short metal screen in front of a fireplace.
4. **proffer** (prŏf′ər): to offer for acceptance.
5. **predecessor:** the former holder of an office or position.
6. **retinue** (rĕt′n-o͞o′): a group of attendants; entourage.
7. **squalid** (skwŏl′ĭd): dirty and wretched from poverty or lack of care.
8. **public-house:** tavern.
9. **impetus** (ĭm′pĭ-təs): incentive; stimulus.

Romance (about 1924), Maxfield Parrish. Cover lining for *The Knave of Hearts* by Louise Saunders, oil on panel, courtesy of New York Graphic Society Ltd. Photo by Allen Photography.

"Ay!" struck in another, "a meddlesome, priggish[10] sort of chap, he was, always aworritting us about clean houses, and such like. What right's *he* got to interfere, I'd like to know?"

"Down with all kings! says I," put in a third: "but if we're to have 'em, let 'em behave as sich. I like a young fellow as isn't afraid of his missus, and knows port wine from sherry."

"Wanted to abolish capital punishment, he did!" cried a fourth. "Thought he'd get more work out of the poor fellows in prison, I suppose? Depend on it, there's some reason like that at the bottom of it. We ain't so very perticular about the lives of our subjects for nothing, we ain't"; an expression of opinion in which all the rest heartily concurred. The clock struck again as the king turned away; he felt as if a storm of abuse from some one he had always hated would be a precious balm[11] just then. He entered the state prison, and made for the condemned cell. Capital punishment was not abolished yet, and in this particular instance he had certainly felt glad of it.

The cell was tenanted only by a little haggard[12] looking man, who was writing busily on his knee. The king had only seen him once before, and he looked at him curiously.

Presently, the jailer entered, and with him the

10. **priggish:** irritatingly concerned with proper behavior.

11. **balm:** something that soothes, heals, or comforts.

12. **haggard:** worn and exhausted in appearance.

first councillor, a man whom his late master had greatly loved and esteemed. The convict looked up quickly.

"It was not to be till to-morrow," he said. Then, as if afraid he had betrayed some cowardice, "but I am ready at any moment. May I ask you to give this paper to my wife?"

"The king is dead," said the first councillor gravely. "You are reprieved. His present majesty has other views. You will, in all probability, be set at large to-morrow."

"Dead?" said the man with a stunned look.

"Dead!" said the first councillor, with the impressiveness of a whole board.

The man stood up, passing his hand across his brow.

"Sir," he said earnestly, "I respected him. For all he was a king, he treated me like a gentleman. He, too, had a young wife. Poor fellow, I wish he were alive again!"

There were tears in the man's eyes as he spoke.

he third quarter struck as the king left the prison. He felt unutterably humiliated. The pity of his foe was harder to bear than the scorn of his friends. He would rather have died a thousand deaths than owe his life to such a man. And yet, because he was himself noble, he could not but rejoice to find nobility in another. He said to himself sternly that it was not worth what he had gone through. He reviewed his position in no very self-complacent[13] mood. The affection he had so confidently relied upon was but a dream. The people he was fain[14] to work for were not ripe for their own improvement. A foolish little child, a generous enemy, these were his only friends. After all, was it worth while to live? Had he not better go back quietly and submit, making no further effort? He had learnt his lesson; he could "lie down in peace, and sleep, and take his rest." The eternal powers had justified themselves. What matter though every man had proved a liar? The bitterness had passed away, and he seemed to see clearly.

Thick clouds had gathered over the moon, and the cold struck through him. All at once a sense of loneliness that cannot be described rushed over him, and his heart sank. Was there really no one who cared—no one? He would have given anything at that moment for a look, a single word of real sympathy. He longed with sick longing for the assurance of love.

There were yet a few moments left. How had he borne to wait so long? This, at least, he was sure of, and this was all the world to him. He began to find comfort and consolation in the thought; he forgave—indeed he almost forgot—the rest. Yet he had fallen very low, for, as he stood at the door of his wife's room, he hesitated whether to go in. What if this, too, were an illusion? Had he not best go back before he knew?

"But I have never yet done anything through fear," said the king.

His wife was sitting by the fire alone, her face hidden, her long hair falling round her like a veil. At the first sight of her, a pang of self-reproach shot through him. How could he ever have doubted?

She was wearing a ring that he had given her—a ring she wore always, and the light sparkled and flashed from the jewel. Except for this, there was nothing bright in the room.

He ardently desired to comfort her. He wondered why all her ladies had left her. Surely one might have stayed with her on this first night of her bereavement?[15] She seemed to be lost in thought. If she would only speak, or call his name! But she was quite silent.

A slight noise made the king start. A secret door in the wall opened, the existence of which he had thought was known only to himself and his queen, and a man stood before her.

---

13. **self-complacent:** self-satisfied; smug.

14. **fain:** ready and willing.

15. **bereavement:** the loss of a loved one to death.

She put her finger to her lips, as though to counsel silence, and then threw herself into his arms.

"You have come," she said— "Oh, I am so glad! I had to hold his hand when he was dying. I was frightened sitting here by myself. I thought his ghost would come back, but he will never come back any more. We may be happy always now," and drawing the ring from her finger, she kissed it, weeping, and gave it to him.

When midnight struck, the watchers wakened with a start, to find the king lying stark and stiff, as before, but a great change had come over his countenance.[16]

"We must not let the queen see him again," they said. ❖

16. **countenance:** face.

Mary E. Coleridge

1861–1907

Although she never achieved the fame of her ancestor, Mary Coleridge was a talented writer in a variety of literary forms, including novels, short stories, poetry, and essays. Born in London, Coleridge received an excellent education at home and, according to one of her friends, could read Hebrew, French, Italian, and German by the time she was 19 years old. Her father was a well-read lawyer who often entertained noted authors, including the poets Tennyson and Browning. Coleridge herself studied both literature and philosophy, eventually obtaining a job as an instructor of English literature in a working-women's college, a position she held for the last 12 years of her life. She never married and lived with her parents until her death at age 46.

Coleridge did not publish her first major work until she was in her 30s. Although her first novel, *The Seven Sleepers of Ephesus,* was not generally well received, it was praised by Robert Louis Stevenson, and several of her subsequent novels became quite popular. In addition, she regularly contributed stories and essays to various journals, including *The Cornhill Magazine* and *The Times Literary Supplement.* As a poet, she was reluctant to publish, or even talk about, her own work. At the urging of a family friend—the poet Robert Bridges—she eventually allowed two small collections of her poems to be published under the pseudonym Anodos. The rest were not made public until after her death. Bridges said of her poems, "They are both beautiful and original, and often exhibit imagination of a very rare kind, conveyed by the identical expression of true feeling and artistic insight."

WRITING ABOUT
LITERATURE

CRITICAL EYE

A movie that makes you furious may cause someone else to stand up and cheer. People's opinions about art are strongly affected by whether or not they agree with the ideas a particular work expresses. In order to understand your own opinion, you need to identify ideas and examine their presentation. In the following pages, you will

- study how writers use elaboration to support their ideas
- write a critical essay expressing your opinion
- make a judgment about the way ideas are expressed

Writer's Style: Elaboration Elaboration is the process of developing a writing idea by adding specific supporting details.

Read the Literature

Writers consider their purpose, audience, and form when deciding how to elaborate on their ideas. What methods of elaboration have the writers of the following excerpts chosen?

Literature Models

Elaboration Through Incidents and Detail
What is the general idea stated in this excerpt? Which details help you see, smell, taste, feel, or hear the events being described?

Even in populated India a man cannot a day sit still before the wild things run over him as though he were a rock; and in that wilderness very soon the wild things, who knew Kali's Shrine well, came back to look at the intruder. The *langurs,* the big gray-whiskered monkeys of the Himalayas, were, naturally, the first, for they are alive with curiosity; and when they had upset the begging-bowl, and rolled it round the floor, and tried their teeth on the brass-handled crutch, and made faces at the antelope skin, they decided that the human being who sat so still was harmless.

Rudyard Kipling, from "The Miracle of Purun Bhagat"

Elaboration Through Example
What is the example? What idea does it elaborate on?

Simon then tried to buy the sheep-skins on credit, but the dealer would not trust him.

"Bring your money," said he, "then you may have your pick of the skins."

Leo Tolstoy, from "What Men Live By"

Connect to Life

In addition to supporting their ideas and providing details, nonfiction writers may use elaboration to verify the truth of their claims. One way they do this is by using visual aids like the graph below to highlight facts and statistics.

Magazine Graph

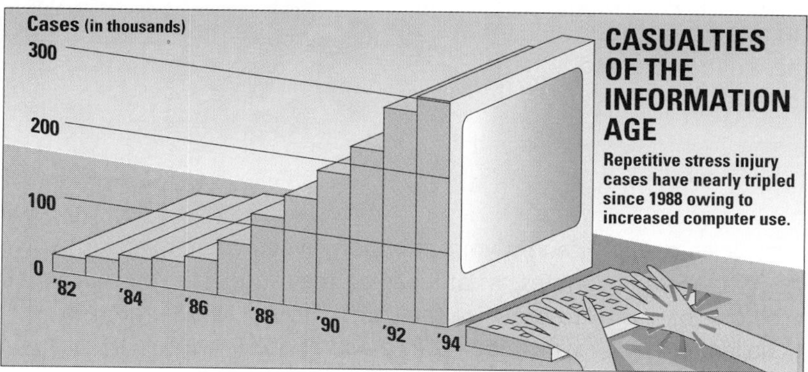

Elaboration Through Facts and Statistics

Repetitive stress injuries cause severe wrist pain. How is the claim being made by this graph supported with details?

Try Your Hand: Using Elaboration

1. **Elaborate on Ideas** For each of the following, write a sentence that elaborates on the idea presented.
   - Flying in an airplane is safer than driving in a car.
   - We always want what we don't have.
   - Mickey was a disruptive student.
2. **Find Examples of Elaboration** Look through a newspaper or magazine article and make a list of the quotations, statistics, and other details that develop the main idea.
3. **Elaborate on Your Opinion** When was the last time you said, "I love it when . . ." or "I hate that . . ."? Write a paragraph in which you elaborate on your opinion.

SkillBuilder

Using Compound Verbs

When two or more verbs or verb phrases are joined by a conjunction and share the same subject, they form a compound verb. Compound verbs can help you elaborate by allowing you to include extra information in a single sentence

The Englishman Rudyard Kipling began his life, started his career, and achieved early fame in colonial India.

Compound verbs can also allow you to combine two sentences into one.

Purun Dass received an English education.

He grew up to champion Western ways.

Purun Dass received an English education and grew up to champion Western ways.

APPLYING WHAT YOU'VE LEARNED

Using the verbs below, and supplying your own if you wish to, write three sentences with compound verbs. One of the sentences should include a compound verb made up of more than two verbs.

stretched	antagonized
ran	apologized
rotated	realized
leapt	squandered
limped	achieved

Criticism

Whether you agree or disagree with the ideas in the selections you just read, you'll probably have the urge to share your opinion with somebody else. Learning to be critical, or to evaluate whether something is worth the effort it takes to read, can help you articulate your thoughts to other people.

GUIDED ASSIGNMENT

Evaluate Ideas The next few pages will help you write a critical essay on the ideas presented in a selection. You will identify the ideas, evaluate how well the writer presented them, and then evaluate the ideas themselves.

1 Prewrite and Explore

Fiction often deals with important issues, such as morality, faith, love, and human nature. Was there a Unit Five selection that helped you see one of these ideas in a new way? Were you challenged or disturbed by anything one of the writers said?

Decision Point Choose a selection that had statements, opinions, or ideas worth exploring further.

IDENTIFY THE IDEAS

Look through the selection, listing points you think the writer was trying to make. If these points are hard to identify, use your notebook or note cards to record the phrases and incidents that caught your attention. When you reread your notes, what ideas do they suggest? You may want to organize the cards into stacks according to which idea they elaborate on.

Student's Prewriting Notes

"The Miracle of Purun Bhagat" 1

It "was considered nothing extraordinary" when Purun Dass resigned his position, took up a begging-bowl, and became a holy man.

"The Miracle of Purun Bhagat" 2

"He had used his wealth and his power for what he knew both to be worth. ... Now he would let these things go, as a man drops the cloak he needs no longer."

One idea is that people in India can decide to give up material things and lead a spiritual life.

EXPLORE THE PRESENTATION

Once you have identified some key ideas, think about how the writer communicated each point in the selection. Consider questions like the following:

- Are the ideas clearly stated, or are they implied?
- Are opposing ideas discussed? Why do you think that is?
- Does one character represent the ideas?

Remember to keep track of the specific examples that help you answer these questions, so you can elaborate on the points you make in your critical essay.

❷ Freewrite About Your Opinion

How did you react to the ideas presented in the selection? Freewrite about your opinions. As you're writing, you may want to ask yourself questions like the following:

- Do the ideas have both positive aspects and negative ones? What are they?
- How did the way the author presented the ideas affect the way I reacted to them?
- What kind of place would the world be if everyone followed these ideas?

Student's Freewriting

I like the idea that in India anybody can drop out of society and become a holy man. This seems like a more balanced approach to life than we have here, where you are expected to work hard all your life to buy as many things as you can. It seems that in this story, it is acceptable to give up material wealth.

I should tell how the change in Purun's life helped me question my own values.

❸ Draft and Share

When you write your draft, include the information you uncovered in the prewriting stage as well as the opinions you discussed in your freewriting. Be sure to tell how the presentation of the ideas affected your reaction to them and to elaborate on your thoughts. After you've completed a first draft, ask another student to read it and give you feedback.

- What is my opinion of the ideas I am discussing?
- What helped you understand why I reacted to the ideas the way I did?
- What do you agree with or disagree with? Why?

SkillBuilder

WRITER'S CRAFT

Achieving Unity Within Paragraphs

A paragraph is unified when all its sentences support one main idea, which is often expressed in a topic sentence. However, you don't need a topic sentence to create unity. You can also relate all the sentences to an implied main idea.

The longer I spent in India, the less material possessions meant to me. I gave away a lot of my belongings and started spending hours just sitting quietly under a tree or alongside a river. There are temples everywhere in India, small ones nestled in alleys and huge ones atop mountains, and I was drawn to them all.

All the sentences in the above paragraph support the idea that the narrator became more spiritual in India.

APPLYING WHAT YOU'VE LEARNED

In order to achieve unity in your paragraphs, reread your writing and delete any sentences that don't support the main idea. If a paragraph seems to deal with two ideas, consider creating two paragraphs from it.

4 Revise and Edit

When you revise, make sure that your essay tells readers whether or not the selection you chose is worth reading. Remember that you don't need to agree with the ideas presented in a piece in order to respect or enjoy it. When you're finished writing, reread your paper and try to think of real-life examples of the ideas you discussed.

Student's Final Draft

From Politician to Pauper

Rudyard Kipling's "The Miracle of Purun Bhagat" tells the story of a British-influenced Indian politician, Purun Dass. This man decides to change his name to Purun Bhagat, disappear from society, and become a poor holy man. This transformation allows us to compare "civilized" Western ways with those ways that bring about a spiritual life. Through the main character, Kipling shows that fame and material wealth are not the only situations to value in life.

What ideas will be discussed in the body of the essay? What is the writer's opinion of those ideas?

How does the student elaborate on the ideas presented in Kipling's story?

Purun Dass resigns his position, gives up his worldly goods, and becomes a penniless holy man. Kipling writes, "Now he would let these things go, as a man drops the cloak he needs no longer." As the story progresses, Purun's life takes on new meaning as he finds inner peace, living a "rich" life though money has no part in it.

Standards for Evaluation

A critical essay
- identifies the ideas in the selection
- states an opinion about the ideas
- evaluates how well the writer presented those ideas
- supports all reasons with specific examples

Grammar in Context

Adjective Clauses An adjective clause is a subordinate clause that modifies a noun or pronoun. The clause usually follows the noun or pronoun it modifies, and begins with a word such as *who*, *whose*, *that*, *when*, or *where*. Because an adjective clause answers the question *Which one?* or *What kind?* it can be used to provide details of elaboration.

The punctuation of an adjective clause depends on whether it is essential or nonessential. An essential adjective clause is necessary to the meaning of a sentence and is not set off with commas.

> The change, that Purun Bhagat made in his life, was as drastic as it was sudden.

A nonessential adjective clause adds additional information to a sentence and is not necessary to its meaning. One or two commas should be used to set off a nonessential clause from the rest of the sentence.

> Kipling, who himself lived in India, skillfully encourages us to compare the Western ways of Purun Dass with the spiritual ways of Purun Bhagat.

Try Your Hand: Using Adjective Clauses

Combine each pair of sentences by turning the second sentence into an adjective clause.

- Purun Bhagat settled in the mountains.
  His mother's family came from the mountains.
- The village priest represented the community.
  He welcomed Purun Bhagat to the village.
- The rains pounded down for three months.
  The downpour caused damage to the village.
- The animals issued the warning.
  The animals were Purun Bhagat's friends.

SkillBuilder

GRAMMAR FROM WRITING

Using Relative Pronouns
Many adjective clauses are introduced by relative pronouns such as *who*, *whom*, *whose*, *that*, and *which*. These words relate the clauses to the nouns or pronouns they modify.

India, which is cut off from the rest of Asia by mountains, is the second most populous country in the world.

India is the antecedent of *which*.

A relative pronoun may serve as the subject of a clause, as in the example above, or it may serve as the direct object in a clause. It may also serve as the object of a preposition or as a modifier within the clause.

India, with which England had a troubled relationship, gained its independence in 1947.

APPLYING WHAT YOU'VE LEARNED
Use relative pronouns to introduce adjective clauses into the following sentences.

- In the United States, there is no tradition of wandering holy men.
- Most Americans do not think of it as an honor to feed beggars.
- There is less traditional life in this country than in India.

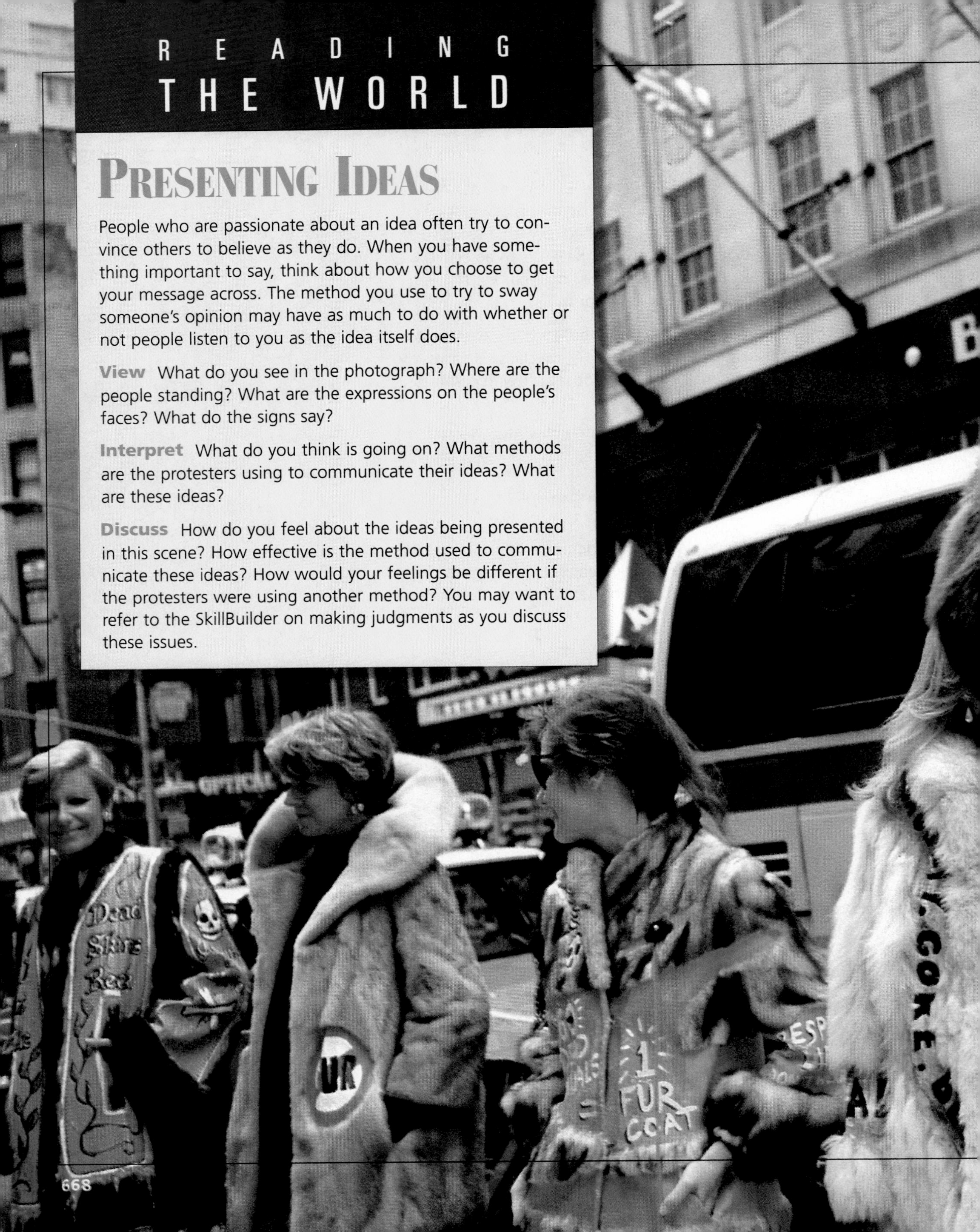

READING

THE WORLD

PRESENTING IDEAS

People who are passionate about an idea often try to convince others to believe as they do. When you have something important to say, think about how you choose to get your message across. The method you use to try to sway someone's opinion may have as much to do with whether or not people listen to you as the idea itself does.

View What do you see in the photograph? Where are the people standing? What are the expressions on the people's faces? What do the signs say?

Interpret What do you think is going on? What methods are the protesters using to communicate their ideas? What are these ideas?

Discuss How do you feel about the ideas being presented in this scene? How effective is the method used to communicate these ideas? How would your feelings be different if the protesters were using another method? You may want to refer to the SkillBuilder on making judgments as you discuss these issues.

SkillBuilder

CRITICAL THINKING

Making Judgments

The method used to communicate an idea will probably affect your first response to it. Depending on what you already know, feel, and believe, some methods may have a positive effect on how you view the idea and other methods may have a negative effect. In order to make a judgment about the idea itself, it is useful to be able to separate the method of communication from the message. In order to do that, state the idea being expressed in one or two sentences. Then ask questions like the following.

- Is this method of communication appealing to my heart, head, or wallet?
- Which emotions is this method appealing to? How?
- What facts and statistics is this method presenting? What facts and statistics are being ignored?
- Does the method imply ideas other than the one being discussed? Does it imply certain values, for example? Or does it imply attitudes about certain groups of people?

APPLYING WHAT YOU'VE LEARNED
Find an ad, a picture, or an article that communicates an idea. Write down your first response to the idea. Then write down the answers to the questions above. Discuss whether your response to the idea changed or remained the same.

PART 2 # *New Directions*

Industrial growth, social upheaval, and a new interest in science changed the direction of Victorian life. A prosperous middle class emerged even as the problems of the poor increased, and scientific theories challenged traditional religious beliefs. Some poets, reflecting on the loss of old certainties, wrote thoughtful poems about humankind's isolation and the fleeting nature of youth, beauty, and fame. Other writers, however, took a more lighthearted view—satirizing, for example, the upper class's adherence to a rigid code of manners. As you read the selections in this part of Unit Five, compare the fears and foibles of Victorian society with those of today's world.

PREVIEWING

POETRY

Dover Beach
To Marguerite—Continued
Matthew Arnold

PERSONAL CONNECTION

What comes to mind when you hear the word *isolation?* Think about situations that might cause a person to experience feelings of isolation. Do you think such feelings occur only when a person is physically separated from other people? Share your thoughts with your classmates.

HISTORICAL/BIOGRAPHICAL CONNECTION

In Great Britain, the Victorian era was a time of rapid change in social, economic, and religious life. The growth of industrialization and commercialism created both increasing prosperity and social unrest. The development of new scientific theories challenged traditional beliefs and eroded old assumptions about the nature of the world. Matthew Arnold, who was a social and literary critic as well as a poet, was concerned throughout his life with the questions and struggles of his time. As a critic, he was also disturbed by what he perceived as the complacency of much of society toward the emerging changes and toward the importance of beauty and culture.

In his poetry Arnold deals with the loneliness of humankind in an indifferent universe, bereft of old certainties. Although Arnold thought that religion was an essential part of culture, his poems nonetheless reflect his personal sense of isolation, doubt, and at times even despair. In his poem "Stanzas from the Grande Chartreuse," he speaks of himself as "Wandering between two worlds, one dead, / The other powerless to be born." "Dover Beach," possibly written just after the poet's visit to Dover, England, on his honeymoon in 1851, is probably the most famous of his poems. "To Marguerite—Continued" is one of a series of poems believed to have been written to a woman he met in the 1840s.

WRITING CONNECTION

Suppose that you are preparing to write a poem or story in which you want to convey a particular feeling or mood, such as a sense of isolation. In your notebook create a cluster diagram like the one shown in which you identify various settings or situations that might help create such a feeling. As you read Arnold's poems, notice the setting and details that help create the mood of each poem.

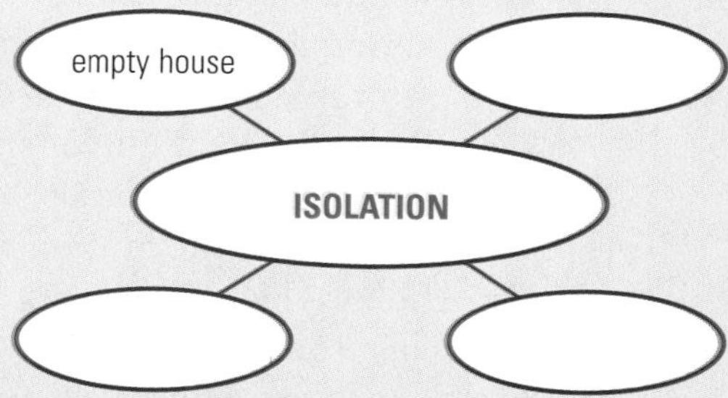

LASERLINKS
• *GEOGRAPHICAL CONNECTION*

Dover Beach

Matthew Arnold

The sea is calm tonight.
The tide is full, the moon lies fair
Upon the straits—on the French coast the light
Gleams and is gone; the cliffs of England stand,
Glimmering and vast, out in the tranquil bay.
Come to the window, sweet is the night air!
Only, from the long line of spray
Where the sea meets the moon-blanched land,
Listen! you hear the grating roar
Of pebbles which the waves draw back, and fling,
At their return, up the high strand,
Begin, and cease, and then again begin,
With tremulous cadence slow, and bring
The eternal note of sadness in.

3 straits: the Strait of Dover, a narrow channel separating England and France, at the northern end of the English Channel.

8 moon-blanched: shining palely in the moonlight.

13 tremulous cadence: trembling rhythm.

Sophocles long ago
Heard it on the Aegean, and it brought
Into his mind the turbid ebb and flow
Of human misery; we
Find also in the sound a thought,
Hearing it by this distant northern sea.

The Sea of Faith
Was once, too, at the full, and round earth's shore
Lay like the folds of a bright girdle furled.
But now I only hear
Its melancholy, long, withdrawing roar,
Retreating, to the breath
Of the night wind, down the vast edges drear
And naked shingles of the world.

Ah, love, let us be true
To one another! for the world, which seems
To lie before us like a land of dreams,
So various, so beautiful, so new,
Hath really neither joy, nor love, nor light,
Nor certitude, nor peace, nor help for pain;
And we are here as on a darkling plain
Swept with confused alarms of struggle and flight,
Where ignorant armies clash by night.

15 Sophocles (sŏf′ə-klēz′): an ancient Greek writer of tragic plays.

16 Aegean (ĭ-jē′ən): the Aegean Sea—part of the Mediterranean Sea, between Greece and Turkey.

17 turbid: in a state of turmoil; muddled.

21 Sea of Faith: traditional religious beliefs about God and the world, long viewed as true and unshakable.

23 girdle: a belt or sash worn around the waist.

27 drear: dreary.

28 shingles: pebbly beaches.

FROM PERSONAL RESPONSE *TO* CRITICAL ANALYSIS

REFLECT **1.** What images stand out in your mind after reading the poem? Describe them in your notebook.

RETHINK **2.** How would you describe the speaker's view of the world?

Consider

- his responses to what he sees and hears at the beach
- what he says about the Sea of Faith
- the images in lines 35–37

3. Why do you think the poem is addressed to the speaker's loved one?

To Marguerite —Continued

Matthew Arnold

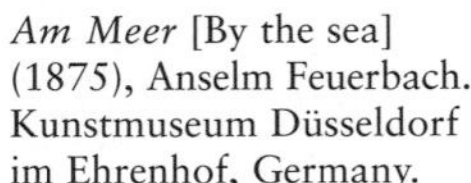

Am Meer [By the sea] (1875), Anselm Feuerbach. Kunstmuseum Düsseldorf im Ehrenhof, Germany.

Yes! in the sea of life enisled,
With echoing straits between us thrown,
Dotting the shoreless watery wild,
We mortal millions live *alone*.
The islands feel the enclasping flow,
And then their endless bounds they know.

But when the moon their hollows lights,
And they are swept by balms of spring,
And in their glens, on starry nights,
The nightingales divinely sing;
And lovely notes, from shore to shore,
Across the sounds and channels pour—

Oh! then a longing like despair
Is to their farthest caverns sent;
For surely once, they feel, we were
Parts of a single continent!
Now round us spreads the watery plain—
Oh might our marges meet again!

Who ordered that their longing's fire
Should be, as soon as kindled, cooled?
Who renders vain their deep desire?—
A God, a God their severance ruled!
And bade betwixt their shores to be
The unplumbed, salt, estranging sea.

1 enisled (ĕn-īld′): separated, like islands.

6 bounds: limits or boundaries.

8 balms: soothing scents and airs.

9 glens: valleys.

12 sounds: long, wide bodies of water, larger than channels.

18 marges: margins.

22 severance: separation.

24 unplumbed: unmeasured; **estranging** (ĭ-strān′jĭng): alienating.

RESPONDING OPTIONS

FROM PERSONAL RESPONSE *TO* CRITICAL ANALYSIS

REFLECT 1. In your notebook, jot down words and phrases that describe your reaction to the speaker of "To Marguerite—Continued." Share your thoughts with classmates.

RETHINK 2. How would you describe the mood of the poem?

3. What seems to be the theme or message of this poem?
   Consider
   - the reference to living alone in line 4
   - the imagery of islands
   - the statement that "a God their severance ruled" (line 22)

4. How do you think the speaker would describe his relationship with Marguerite?

5. Role-play the speaker of "To Marguerite—Continued," giving a dramatic explanation of how you view your relationship to the rest of the world.

RELATE 6. Compare the imagery in the two poems. Discuss possible reasons for the images Arnold chose to convey his ideas.

ANOTHER PATHWAY

Cooperative Learning

With the class divided into two groups, each focusing on one of Arnold's poems, discuss your responses to the speaker's thoughts about life. Then, with your group, compose a letter to the speaker in which you express your ideas. Share and discuss your letter with the rest of the class.

LITERARY CONCEPTS

Poets often use a controlling image to convey their thoughts or feelings. A **controlling image** is a single image or comparison that extends throughout a literary work and shapes its meaning. Often, the controlling image is an **extended metaphor,** a comparison of two unlike things at some length and in several ways. Reread "To Marguerite—Continued" and identify the extended metaphor that acts as the controlling image. Note what objects and ideas are being compared. Do you think there is a controlling image in "Dover Beach"? Explain your answer.

CONCEPT REVIEW: Allusion "Dover Beach" contains an allusion, or reference, to a well-known literary figure. What is the allusion? What is its function in the poem?

QUICKWRITES

1. Write **lecture notes** in which you either support or refute the idea, stated in "To Marguerite—Continued," that "we mortal millions live *alone.*"

2. Imagine that you are the "love" addressed in line 29 of "Dover Beach." Write a **diary entry** expressing your reaction to what the speaker has said.

3. In an original **simile** or **metaphor,** try to express the concept of being isolated from the world. You might consider using one of the settings or situations you listed for the Writing Connection on page 671.

PORTFOLIO *Save your writing. You may want to use it later as a springboard to a piece for your portfolio.*

ALTERNATIVE ACTIVITIES

1. Create a **drawing** or **painting** to illustrate one of the images in either "Dover Beach" or "To Marguerite—Continued."
2. Make a **set design** for a dance based on one of the poems. Include brief notes describing the mood you hope to create.
3. Create a **montage** of pictures and words to convey emotions or sentiments expressed in one of the poems. You might want to "design" your words on a computer, using a variety of type fonts.

LITERARY LINKS

Compare the attitudes toward life expressed in "Dover Beach" and "To Marguerite—Continued" with the attitude expressed by Tennyson in the excerpt from "In Memoriam" (page 583). In your opinion, which of the three poems reflects the most positive attitude toward the future?

ACROSS THE CURRICULUM

Music Locate and play a recording of the musical composition "Dover Beach" by Samuel Barber, which was based on Arnold's poem. Do you think the music effectively conveys the feelings and ideas expressed in the poem? Explain your answer.

CRITIC'S CORNER

In an essay on "Dover Beach," the American poet and novelist James Dickey speaks of the "subtlety, force, and conviction" of the poem. Look for evidence in the poem to support or refute his comments.

MATTHEW ARNOLD

1822–1888

Matthew Arnold grew up under the scholarly influence of his father, a well-known clergyman and renowned headmaster of the distinguished Rugby School. Unlike his father, however, the younger Arnold was high-spirited and mischievous. At Oxford University, he spent more time socializing than studying and, as a result, barely passed his exams. He did, however, win a prestigious award for one of his poems.

In 1847, Arnold became the private secretary to an English lord. With the help of his employer, he later acquired a job as inspector of schools, a post he held for 35 years. The position required Arnold to travel constantly and gave him the opportunity to observe English culture and society closely. Arnold wrote during his spare time and published his first poems anonymously. His growing reputation as a poet led to his appointment in 1857 as professor of poetry at Oxford, a part-time post that he retained for 10 years.

After 1867, Arnold devoted most of his efforts to writing critical essays on poetry and on problems in English society. He attacked the provincialism of his time and argued for a broader intellectual life and a greater awareness and appreciation of the arts. Arnold also wrote extensively on the religious controversies of his time. Although he felt strongly that religion was a necessary part of what he called culture, he thought that traditional religious views and institutions needed examination. Finally, Arnold made significant efforts to improve English education by visiting schools in Europe and writing forceful reports on his ideas for reform. He died suddenly at the age of 66 and was buried next to the three sons who had preceded him in death.

OTHER WORKS "Isolation: To Marguerite," "The Buried Life," "Lines Written in Kensington Gardens," "A Summer Night"

LASERLINKS
• *FILM CONNECTION*

PREVIEWING

POETRY

Pied Beauty
Spring and Fall: To a Young Child

Gerard Manley Hopkins

PERSONAL CONNECTION

Think about a time when you closely examined a single leaf or flower. What unique details do you remember observing? Do you think it is possible to convey the unique qualities of a natural object in a poem or a painting? Share your thoughts with your classmates.

LITERARY/BIOGRAPHICAL CONNECTION

Gerard Manley Hopkins was an innovator whose poetry was not published or understood until decades after his death. Hopkins developed a revolutionary style, one unlike that of his contemporaries or of any poet before him. He experimented with language and form, inventing new words, using inverted word order, and developing nontraditional rhythmic patterns, which he called **sprung rhythm.** Hopkins is now regarded as a major poet of the Victorian era, whose work became a pivotal influence in the development of modern poetry.

Hopkins responded with intensity to the natural world. He invented a word, *inscape,* to describe the qualities of nature he tried to convey in his poems. Generally, inscape seems to be an inner landscape of meaning, derived from the unique qualities of natural objects, that one can experience through close observation. For almost eight years, Hopkins recorded his impressions of the natural world in a journal, which he illustrated with detailed drawings of flowers and trees. Descriptions from his journal often appeared later in his poetry. Hopkins was an aspiring painter and talented musician as well as a poet, and his talent in both art and music is reflected in his poems.

READING CONNECTION

Recognizing Coined Words Hopkins frequently coined, or invented, words to capture his impressions of nature's uniqueness or special qualities. Usually, his new words contain familiar word parts. In some cases, the coined word is actually a compound made by joining two familiar words in an unfamiliar arrangement. As you read the following poems, make a list of the coined words that you discover. Also jot down the image or feeling that you think each word conveys. The annotations will help you with the meaning of some words.

LASERLINKS
• *PERSONAL CONNECTION*

Pied Beauty

GERARD MANLEY HOPKINS

Glory be to God for dappled things—
For skies of couple-color as a brinded cow;
For rose-moles all in stipple upon trout that swim;
Fresh-firecoal chestnut-falls; finches' wings;
Landscape plotted and pieced—fold, fallow, and plough;
And áll trádes, their gear and tackle and trim.

All things counter, original, spare, strange;
Whatever is fickle, freckled (who knows how?)
With swift, slow; sweet, sour; adazzle, dim;
He fathers-forth whose beauty is past change:
Praise him.

1 dappled: spotted or splashed with color.

2 brinded: brindled—streaked or spotted with a darker color.

3 rose-moles . . . stipple: spots of pink in flecks or speckles.

4 fresh-firecoal chestnut-falls: fallen chestnuts that are the color of glowing coals.

5 fold: a pen for animals; **fallow:** land left unseeded.

6 trim: equipment.

7 counter: opposing.

10 fathers-forth: creates.

FROM PERSONAL RESPONSE *TO* CRITICAL ANALYSIS

REFLECT 1. In your notebook, draw or describe one image that remains in your mind from your reading of "Pied Beauty."

RETHINK 2. Why do you think the speaker is so fascinated by "dappled things"?

Consider
- the details the speaker describes
- the question in parentheses in line 8
- the references to God in lines 1, 10, and 11

3. Why do you think Hopkins includes "all trades" with the details from nature?

4. Think back to the discussion you had for the Personal Connection on page 677. How successful do you think Hopkins is in conveying unique qualities in nature? Support your answer with evidence from the poem.

Spring (late 1800s), Frederick Walker. Victoria and Albert Museum, London/Art Resource, New York.

SPRING and FALL:

To a Young Child

GERARD MANLEY HOPKINS

Márgarét, are you griéving
Over Goldengrove unleaving?
Leáves, líke the things of man, you
With your fresh thoughts care for, can you?
Áh! ás the heart grows older
It will come to such sights colder
By and by, nor spare a sigh
Though worlds of wanwood leafmeal lie;
And yet you *will* weep and know why.
Now no matter, child, the name:
Sórrow's springs áre the same.
Nor mouth had, no nor mind, expressed
Whát heart heard of, ghost guessed:
It ís the blight man was born for,
It is Margaret you mourn for.

1 Hopkins often included stress marks in his poems to indicate the rhythms he intended.

2 unleaving: losing its leaves.

3–4 Leaves . . . can you?: Do you in your innocence grieve about falling leaves as though they were equal to human loss?

8 wanwood: faded woodland; **leafmeal:** dry, ground-up leaves.

12 nor: neither.

13 ghost: spirit; soul.

14 blight: a condition that stops growth and brings withering and death.

INSIGHT

from

Journal

GERARD MANLEY HOPKINS

September 17, 1868—Fine.—Chestnuts as bright as coals or spots of vermilion.[1]

July 8, 1871—After much rain, some thunder, and no summer as yet, the river swollen and golden and, where charged with air, like ropes and hills of melting candy, there was this day a thunderstorm on a greater scale—huge rocky clouds lit with livid[2] light, hail and rain that flooded the garden, and thunder ringing and echoing round like brass. . . .

June 16, 1873— . . . I saw [a pigeon] up on the eaves of the roof: as it moved its head a crush of satin green came and went, a wet or soft flaming of the light. . . .

August 9, 1873— . . . From the cliffs I saw the sea paved with wind—clothed and purpled all over with ribbons of wind. . . .

October 17, 1873— . . . At the end of the month hard frosts.

Wonderful downpour of leaf: when the morning sun began to melt the frost they fell at one touch and in a few minutes a whole tree was flung of them; they lay masking and papering the ground at the foot. . . .

August 8, 1874— . . . All the west country seems to me to have soft maroon or rosy cocoa-dust-colored handkerchiefs or ploughfields, sometimes delicately combed with rows of green, their hedges bending in flowing outlines and now misted a little by the beginning of twilight run down into it upon the shoulders of the hills; in the bottom crooked rows of rich tall elms. . . .

1. **vermilion:** bright red.
2. **livid:** ashen or pale.

RESPONDING OPTIONS

FROM PERSONAL RESPONSE *TO* CRITICAL ANALYSIS

REFLECT 1. What impressions of Margaret do you have after reading "Spring and Fall: To a Young Child"? Share your reactions with your classmates.

RETHINK 2. How would you describe the speaker's relationship to Margaret?

Consider
- the speaker's two questions
- the prediction in lines 5–8
- the statements in lines 9 and 11

3. How does the speaker seem to interpret Margaret's grieving?

RELATE 4. Compare the speakers of "Pied Beauty" and "Spring and Fall: To a Young Child." What similarities and differences do you find in their attitudes toward nature?

5. What connections do you see between the descriptions of nature in Hopkins's journal entries (see the Insight selection on page 680) and the images of nature in his poetry?

ANOTHER PATHWAY

Cooperative Learning

With a group of classmates, discuss the meanings of the titles "Pied Beauty" and "Spring and Fall: To a Young Child." Evaluate the effectiveness of each title and discuss your ideas with the class.

LITERARY CONCEPTS

In order to approximate the rhythms of natural speech in his poetry, Hopkins ignored traditional patterns of rhythm, instead using what he called sprung rhythm. The lines of a poem written in **sprung rhythm** have fixed numbers of stressed syllables but varying numbers of unstressed syllables. As in the example below, a line may contain several consecutive stressed syllables, or a stressed syllable may be followed by one, two, or even three unstressed syllables.

Lándscăpe plóttĕd ănd piécĕd—fóld, fállŏw, ănd plóugh;
Ănd áll trádes, théir géar ănd táckle ănd trím.

Read "Pied Beauty" and "Spring and Fall: To a Young Child" aloud. In which lines do you think Hopkins comes closest to reproducing the rhythms of natural speech?

CONCEPT REVIEW: Alliteration Notice the many examples of alliteration, or repetition of initial consonant sounds, in both poems. Why do you think Hopkins used alliteration so extensively?

QUICKWRITES

1. Create a **dictionary** of your own coined words to describe various unique qualities in nature. Include a brief definition of each word.
2. Write a short **poem** in which you express your enthusiasm for a unique quality or pattern in nature.
3. Write an **entry** for a nature journal, recording your close observations and impressions of one aspect of the natural world.

PORTFOLIO *Save your writing. You may want to use it later as a springboard to a piece for your portfolio.*

ALTERNATIVE ACTIVITIES

1. Work with a partner to create a watercolor **mural** depicting some of the images in these two poems. Display your finished mural in the classroom.
2. ***Cooperative Learning*** With a group of classmates, compile a class **nature journal** that includes the poems and journal entries you wrote for the QuickWrite activities. Add other poems and descriptive passages that you find, and include illustrations, photographs, and natural objects, such as pressed flowers or leaves.

CRITIC'S CORNER

One critic has observed that for Hopkins "words are a means of possessing nature." Think about what this statement might mean. Look for words in the two poems that might be a "means of possessing nature."

LITERARY LINKS

Compare "Pied Beauty" and "Spring and Fall: To a Young Child" with Wordsworth's "Lines Composed a Few Miles Above Tintern Abbey" (page 498), Shelley's "To a Skylark" (page 540), and Keats's "To Autumn" (page 555). Identify any attitudes toward nature that you think Hopkins shares with the three romantic poets.

GERARD MANLEY HOPKINS

1844–1889

Gerard Manley Hopkins grew up in a family of writers and artists and showed early promise as both a poet and painter. He won a prize for his poetry while still a teenager and continued to write while attending Balliol College at Oxford University, where he was a brilliant student. It was also at Oxford that the deeply religious young man began struggling with his Protestant faith and, in 1866, joined the Roman Catholic Church. This action alienated him from his parents, who could never understand their son's decision. The rift grew even wider when Hopkins joined the Jesuit order and was eventually ordained a priest.

Hopkins preached and taught for many years at a number of parishes in England and Scotland. In 1884, he was assigned to teach Greek literature at University College in Dublin, where he would spend his last years. Hopkins did not enjoy his assignment in Ireland, however, because he was overworked and in declining health. At age 44, he died of typhoid fever.

As a young man, Hopkins experienced a continuing conflict between his desire to write poetry and his religious commitment. He burned most of his early poems when he entered the Jesuit order, and he did not write poetry again for seven years, although he did continue to write in his journal. In 1874, Hopkins went to a Jesuit college in rural Wales to study theology. He was deeply happy during his three years there, and with encouragement from his superiors, he eventually returned to writing poetry. When he tried to get his first major poem published, however, it was rejected, and after that he showed his work to only a few friends. A collection of Hopkins's poetry was published in 1918, but it was not until 1930, when a second edition appeared, that his work finally received full recognition.

OTHER WORKS "God's Grandeur," "Hurrahing in Harvest," "Binsey Poplars"

PREVIEWING

POETRY

The Man He Killed
Ah, Are You Digging on My Grave?
Thomas Hardy

PERSONAL CONNECTION

Think about someone you know whose life has unexpectedly changed, or consider a time when your life took a completely unexpected turn. What happened? How did you or the person you know react to the change? Share your thoughts with classmates.

LITERARY/BIOGRAPHICAL CONNECTION

Thomas Hardy is one of the most widely recognized authors of the Victorian era. As a novelist, he focused on the bitter and often disastrous ironies of life. Most of his contemporaries thought he was overly pessimistic, but Hardy once denied the charge, calling himself a "meliorist"—someone who thinks humanity has the ability to make the world better. Although known primarily as a novelist, Hardy was also a gifted poet. After devoting the first 25 years of his literary career to writing fiction, including 14 novels, he turned his attention almost completely to writing poetry. Hardy's life spanned 88 years, and although his novels were composed during the Victorian era, most of his poetry was actually written in the 20th century.

Hardy's style of poetry is unlike that of most of his contemporaries. In fact, his departure from the typical language and form of Victorian poetry led some of his contemporaries to complain that his poems seemed more like prose than poetry. Characteristics of the novel that might be observed in some of his poems include the use of dialogue; a relaxed narrative style; simple, unadorned language; and the framework of a plot, often with interaction between characters, dramatic moments, and unexpected twists.

Tess of the d'Urbervilles
by Thomas Hardy
With an Introduction by Robert B. He
Signet Classic
Thomas Hardy
Jude The Obscure

WRITING CONNECTION

Good stories often have unexpected, and sometimes startling, twists in their plots. What books or movies with such unexpected twists do you know about? In your notebook, list the books or movies, and briefly explain the unusual turn of events that takes place in each. Then, as you read these poems, note the unexpected twists in them.

THE MAN HE KILLED

Thomas Hardy

"Had he and I but met
By some old ancient inn,
We should have sat us down to wet
Right many a nipperkin!

"But ranged as infantry,
And staring face to face,
I shot at him as he at me,
And killed him in his place.

4 nipperkin: a container holding about half a pint of beer or ale.

"I shot him dead because—
Because he was my foe,
Just so: my foe of course he was;
That's clear enough; although

"He thought he'd 'list, perhaps,
Off-hand like—just as I—
Was out of work—had sold his traps—
No other reason why.

"Yes; quaint and curious war is!
You shoot a fellow down
You'd treat if met where any bar is,
Or help to half-a-crown."

13 'list: enlist.

15 traps: personal belongings.

20 half-a-crown: an old British coin.

FROM PERSONAL RESPONSE *TO* CRITICAL ANALYSIS

REFLECT 1. Does the speaker of this poem react to killing an enemy in a way that you would expect? In your notebook, jot down reasons for your answer.

RETHINK 2. Do you think the speaker is satisfied with the reason he provides for killing his enemy?
Consider
- his repetition of the word *because* (lines 9–10)
- his repetition of his reason for shooting the man (lines 10–11)
- the emphasis on the word *although* (line 12)

RELATE 3. Does the theme or message of this poem have relevance in today's world?

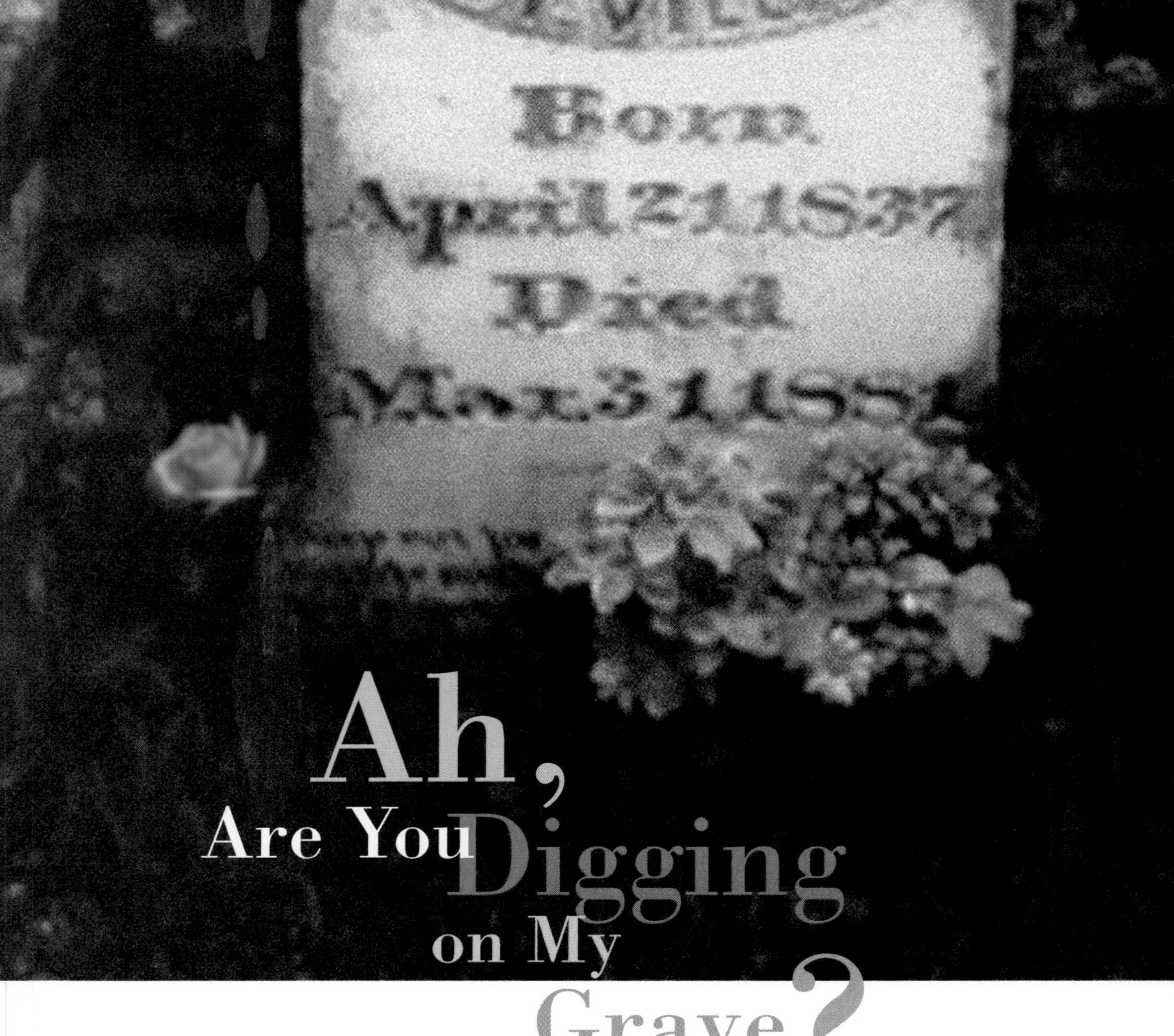

Ah, Are You Digging on My Grave?

Thomas Hardy

"Ah, are you digging on my grave,
    My loved one?—planting rue?"
—"No: yesterday he went to wed
One of the brightest wealth has bred.
'It cannot hurt her now,' he said,
    'That I should not be true.' "

2 rue: an herb that, because its name is identical to the word *rue* (meaning "sorrow" or "regret"), is often used as a symbol of repentance.

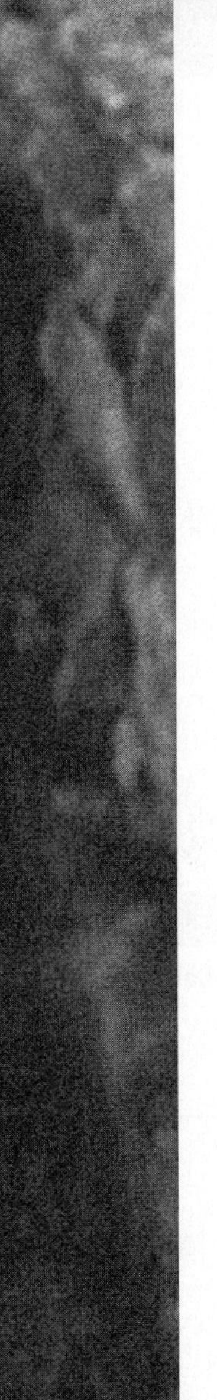

"Then who is digging on my grave?
My nearest dearest kin?"
—"Ah, no: they sit and think, 'What use!
What good will planting flowers produce?
No tendance of her mound can loose
Her spirit from Death's gin.'"

11 tendance: attendance; watchful care.

12 gin: a snare or trap.

"But someone digs upon my grave?
My enemy?—prodding sly?"
—"Nay: when she heard you had passed the Gate
That shuts on all flesh soon or late,
She thought you no more worth her hate,
And cares not where you lie."

"Then, who is digging on my grave?
Say—since I have not guessed!"
—"O it is I, my mistress dear,
Your little dog, who still lives near,
And much I hope my movements here
Have not disturbed your rest?"

"Ah yes! *You* dig upon my grave . . .
Why flashed it not on me
That one true heart was left behind!
What feeling do we ever find
To equal among human kind
A dog's fidelity!"

30 fidelity: faithfulness.

"Mistress, I dug upon your grave
To bury a bone, in case
I should be hungry near this spot
When passing on my daily trot.
I am sorry, but I quite forgot
It was your resting place."

RESPONDING OPTIONS

FROM PERSONAL RESPONSE *TO* CRITICAL ANALYSIS

REFLECT

1. In your notebook, describe your reaction to the unexpected twist in "Ah, Are You Digging on My Grave?" Share your thoughts with classmates.

RETHINK

2. What reactions to her death does the first speaker seem to expect?
3. Why do you think the poet conceals the identity of the second speaker until the fourth stanza?
4. What do you think the poet might be implying in this poem?

RELATE

5. Are "The Man He Killed" and "Ah, Are You Digging on My Grave" similar in tone? Give reasons to support your answer.
6. Look back at the description of Hardy's poems in the Literary/Biographical Connection on page 683. What characteristics of the novel can you find in these poems?

ANOTHER PATHWAY

Cooperative Learning

With a small group of classmates, decide what each poem reveals about its main speaker. Look not only for what is stated directly but also for what can be inferred, or guessed, on the basis of clues in the poems. Present your impressions in a chart like the one shown, and discuss your ideas with the class.

The Speaker in [title of poem]			
Personality	Lifestyle	Past Activities	Conflicts

LITERARY CONCEPTS

Satire is a literary technique in which ideas or customs are ridiculed for the purpose of improving society. The tone of satire may be gently witty, mildly abrasive, or bitterly ironic. For example, in "Ah, Are You Digging on My Grave?" Hardy reacts against the romantic notions of some Victorians by satirizing typically sentimental ideas about love, loyalty, and death. With a partner, list phrases or lines from the poem "The Man He Killed" that reveal a satirical tone.

QUICKWRITES

1. Write a **summary** of a short story based on the situation described in "The Man He Killed." Include events before and after the time of the poem.
2. Write the **epitaph** that the first speaker in "Ah, Are You Digging on My Grave?" might have wished were on her gravestone.
3. Write a **review** of one of the books or movies that you listed for the Writing Connection on page 683. In your review, compare the unexpected twist in the book or movie with the twist in one of Hardy's poems.

PORTFOLIO *Save your writing. You may want to use it later as a springboard to a piece for your portfolio.*

ALTERNATIVE ACTIVITIES

1. Draw a **war poster** that the speaker of "The Man He Killed" might have designed.
2. With a partner, practice and present a **dramatic reading** of "Ah, Are You Digging on My Grave?" in which you try to convey the attitude of each speaker. Be sure to pay attention to the punctuation as an indicator of shifts between speakers.
3. ***Cooperative Learning*** Work with a small group of classmates to present an **interview** with the survivors in "Ah, Are You Digging on My Grave?" Allow each survivor to describe his or her relationship with the speaker.

CRITIC'S CORNER

Lytton Strachey, a well-known biographer and a contemporary of Thomas Hardy, described one of Hardy's poems as depicting a scene that might easily be "the turning point in a realistic psychological novel." Do you think Strachey's description fits either or both of the poems you have read? Give reasons to support your answer.

THE WRITER'S STYLE

In his poetry, Hardy sometimes uses an English **dialect**—a variety of language spoken in a specific region. A dialect can include distinctive words and phrases, grammatical constructions, and pronunciations. Look for examples of dialect in these poems. Why do you think Hardy used dialect in his writing?

THOMAS HARDY

1840–1928

The son of a builder, Thomas Hardy was reared and educated in southwestern England, a setting he later used in his novels. Apprenticed to a local architect at the age of 15, he left six years later for London, where he studied and worked as an architect for many years. During his stay in London, he began to write both poetry and fiction, and his first published novel appeared anonymously in 1871. Although the response to it was lukewarm, Hardy continued to write, finally achieving success with *Far from the Madding Crowd,* published in 1874. The popularity of that novel inspired him to give up architecture and devote his life to writing.

As a novelist, Hardy produced a series of mostly successful works, including *The Return of the Native,* considered one of the best novels in English literature. In 1891, however, his novel *Tess of the D'Urbervilles* was harshly criticized for its sympathetic treatment of what many readers viewed as immoral behavior. His next novel, *Jude the Obscure,* also met with hostility and was censored by one of England's most prominent bookstores. Disgusted by these reactions, Hardy abandoned the novel form altogether and turned to writing poetry.

As a poet, Hardy created ironic anecdotes in verse, often using the rhythm of the ballad to emphasize the timelessness of his themes. His poetry has none of the self-pity so common in Victorian verse; his tone is stern and unflinching, his poetry straightforward and authentic—attributes still admired by critics and readers.

OTHER WORKS "The Darkling Thrush," "Channel Firing," "The Going," "Neutral Tones," "The Duel"

PREVIEWING

POETRY

When I Was One-and-Twenty
To an Athlete Dying Young

A. E. Housman

PERSONAL CONNECTION

Think of conversations you have heard in which older adults, perhaps some of your family members, talked about their youth. What aspects of their younger days did they recall? Share your thoughts with the class.

LITERARY/BIOGRAPHICAL CONNECTION

A. E. Housman composed most of his poems in his early 20s. Although not a prolific poet, he was nevertheless an influential literary figure, admired by many other poets, who emulated his concisely crafted short lyrics, and by the public, who appreciated his universal themes and grace of style.

The two poems in this lesson are from Housman's first collection of poetry, *A Shropshire Lad.* In the 63 poems of that book, Housman disguised any autobiographical points by creating an imaginary speaker—a young farmer named Terence Hearsay. Like most of Housman's poems, these focus on youth.

WRITING CONNECTION

In your notebook, write one or two paragraphs explaining the characteristics that you associate with youthfulness. Also explain at what point you think a person's youth ends and his or her adulthood begins. As you read the two poems, pay particular attention to the ideas that the poems convey about youth and aging.

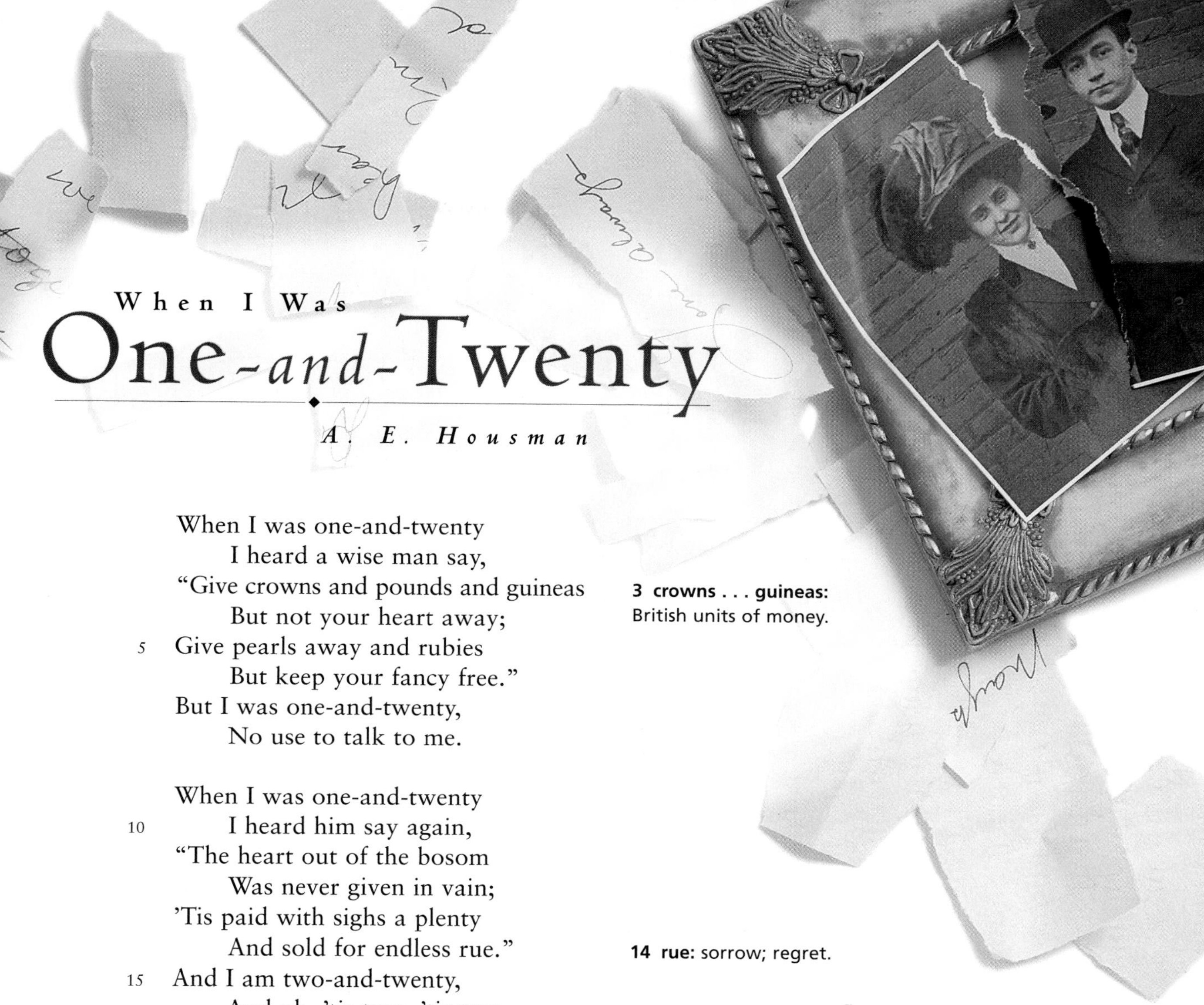

When I Was One-and-Twenty

A. E. Housman

When I was one-and-twenty
I heard a wise man say,
"Give crowns and pounds and guineas
But not your heart away;
Give pearls away and rubies
But keep your fancy free."
But I was one-and-twenty,
No use to talk to me.

When I was one-and-twenty
I heard him say again,
"The heart out of the bosom
Was never given in vain;
'Tis paid with sighs a plenty
And sold for endless rue."
And I am two-and-twenty,
And oh, 'tis true, 'tis true.

3 crowns . . . guineas: British units of money.

14 rue: sorrow; regret.

FROM PERSONAL RESPONSE *TO* CRITICAL ANALYSIS

REFLECT 1. What is your reaction to the words of the wise man? Jot down some of your thoughts in your notebook.

RETHINK 2. What do you think could account for the change in the speaker's attitude? Give reasons for your answer.

3. What message do you think the speaker is trying to convey?

TO AN ATHLETE DYING YOUNG

A. E. HOUSMAN

The time you won your town the race
We chaired you through the market-place;
Man and boy stood cheering by,
And home we brought you shoulder-high.

Today, the road all runners come,
Shoulder-high we bring you home,
And set you at your threshold down,
Townsman of a stiller town.

Smart lad, to slip betimes away
From fields where glory does not stay
And early though the laurel grows
It withers quicker than the rose.

Eyes the shady night has shut
Cannot see the record cut,
And silence sounds no worse than cheers
After earth has stopped the ears:

2 chaired: carried publicly on a chair or seat, in triumph.

9 betimes: early.

11 laurel: Wreaths made of leaves of the laurel tree were worn by victorious athletes in ancient times as a token of honor and glory.

14 cut: broken.

Now you will not swell the rout
Of lads that wore their honors out,
Runners whom renown outran
And the name died before the man.

So set, before its echoes fade,
The fleet foot on the sill of shade,
And hold to the low lintel up
The still-defended challenge-cup.

And round that early-laurelled head
Will flock to gaze the strengthless dead,
And find unwithered on its curls
The garland briefer than a girl's.

17 rout (rout): crowd.

22 sill: threshold.

23 lintel: the beam across the top of a door frame.

28 garland: a wreath or woven chain of leaves or flowers.

RESPONDING OPTIONS

FROM PERSONAL RESPONSE *TO* CRITICAL ANALYSIS

REFLECT 1. What are your thoughts after reading "To an Athlete Dying Young"? Share them with your classmates.

RETHINK 2. How would you describe the speaker's response to the young man's death?

Consider
- his reference to the athlete as a "smart lad" (line 9)
- what the eyes and ears will not see or hear (lines 13–16)
- his reference to a name's dying "before the man" (line 20)
- the images he presents in the last two stanzas

3. Do you agree with the speaker's ideas about fame? Why or why not?

RELATE 4. Think about how people today typically respond to the untimely death of a famous athlete. Do you think this poem would comfort them? Explain your response.

5. Compare and contrast the portrayals of youth in "When I Was One-and-Twenty" and "To an Athlete Dying Young." Cite lines from each poem to support your ideas.

ANOTHER PATHWAY

Cooperative Learning

Working with a small group, list the advantages and disadvantages each speaker might attribute to youth and adulthood. Then have the members of your group add to the list their own personal ideas about the advantages and disadvantages of youth and adulthood. Share your group's results with the class.

LITERARY CONCEPTS

Although **rhythm** and **rhyme** usually work together to enhance the meaning of a poem, the effect is more noticeable in some poems than others. On a sheet of paper, copy the first stanza of each of these poems. Read each stanza aloud, then mark the meter of each. How do the meters of the poems differ? In which poem do you think the rhythm and rhyme are more obvious? In the poem you selected, what effect do you think the rhythm and rhyme create?

QUICKWRITES

1. Reflecting on "When I Was One-and-Twenty," write a **personal anecdote** in which you describe a time when you did not heed the warning of another person, only to learn later that the warning was justified.
2. Using examples from contemporary life, draft a short **opinion paper** in which you either support or oppose the thoughts about fame and glory expressed in "To an Athlete Dying Young."
3. Echoing the ideas of romanticism, Housman maintained that poetry cannot be explained or analyzed because it is an experience not of intellect but of emotion. Draft an **essay** explaining whether you agree or disagree with Housman's theory.

PORTFOLIO *Save your writing. You may want to use it later as a springboard to a piece for your portfolio.*

ALTERNATIVE ACTIVITIES

1. Practice and present a **rebuttal** of the views expressed in "When I Was One-and-Twenty."
2. Use pencil or charcoal to create a **drawing** illustrating an image or idea in one of Housman's poems.
3. Create a clay or wire **sculpture** that reflects your impression of the runner described in "To an Athlete Dying Young."

LITERARY LINKS

Housman said that Shakespeare's "Fear No More the Heat o' the Sun" (page 240) had a particular influence on him. Compare "To an Athlete Dying Young" with this poem of Shakespeare's. What similarities can you find? Explain your answer, citing support from both poems.

CRITIC'S CORNER

In 1936, the American poet Conrad Aiken commented that the thoughts expressed in Housman's poetry have an "adolescent note," or "boyishness." Would you use the word *adolescent* or *mature* to describe the thoughts expressed in "To an Athlete Dying Young" and "When I Was One-and-Twenty"? Give reasons to support your answer.

ACROSS THE CURRICULUM

Music Some of Housman's poems have been set to music by composers such as Ralph Vaughan Williams, George Butterworth, John Ireland, and Arnold Bax. Which poems did they use? How did they happen to write music for these poems? If possible, locate recordings of some of the compositions and play them for the class.

A. E. Housman

1859–1936

Alfred Edward Housman spent more years working on scholarly Latin translations than writing poetry. His interest in classical studies began in grammar school, where he studied Greek and Latin and developed a skill of creating remarkably clear translations. Although he displayed intellectual prowess early in life, periods of emotional distress plagued his youth and may have contributed to the melancholy later reflected in his poetry. His mother's death when he was just 12 years old upset him greatly. While a student at Oxford University, he faced further personal anxieties that left him in a state of emotional turmoil and caused him to fail his final exams. After leaving the university without a degree, Housman worked in London as a clerk in the patent office for 10 years.

During his years as a clerk, Housman continued to study Latin on his own, wrote articles for journals, and eventually earned recognition as a brilliant scholar and critic of Latin texts. In 1892, he was made professor of Latin at University College in London, where he taught until 1911. He then became a professor at Cambridge University, teaching there until shortly before his death. In his later years, Housman turned down various awards and honors, including the government's coveted Order of Merit and an appointment as England's poet laureate.

OTHER WORKS "Bredon Hill," "Is My Team Ploughing?" "Loveliest of Trees," "On Moonlit Heath and Lonesome Bank"

PREVIEWING

POETRY

1996

Rabindranath Tagore

PERSONAL CONNECTION

Science fiction writers often write about life in future centuries. Think about the science fiction stories and movies being produced today. What kind of life do their writers seem to anticipate 100 or more years from now? Share your thoughts with classmates.

HISTORICAL/BIOGRAPHICAL CONNECTION

During the 19th century, British colonial rule brought dramatic changes to India's educational system as well as its government. Parliament insisted that Indian schools offer instruction not only in the English language but also in English literature. Although this directive displeased many Indians, the people living in the eastern province of Bengal were generally receptive to learning about the culture of their English rulers.

Born in India in 1861, the Bengali poet Rabindranath Tagore was influenced by the works of both English and Bengali authors. Although the Tagore family welcomed the opportunity to study Western culture, they also promoted Bengali arts and traditions. They read widely in English literature, but when writing their own poems, plays, and stories, they wrote in Bengali. It was not until Rabindranath Tagore was in his 50s that he began translating his poems into English, reluctantly honoring a promise he had made to an English admirer. In 1913, shortly after his translations reached the Western world, Tagore was awarded the Nobel Prize in literature, becoming the first Asian to receive that honor.

Tagore looked for the best in every culture and advocated for his own country a balance between the traditions of East and West. He worried about the tensions between cultures and wondered how they would affect the future of the world. It may have been this contemplation of the future that inspired Tagore to write in 1896 the poem you are about to read, called "1996."

WRITING CONNECTION

Suppose that you were to write a letter to be placed in a time capsule and opened 100 years from now. What message would you want to convey to people in the future? What questions might you ask them about their world? In your notebook, write a draft of your letter. As you read Tagore's poem, compare his message to future readers with your own.

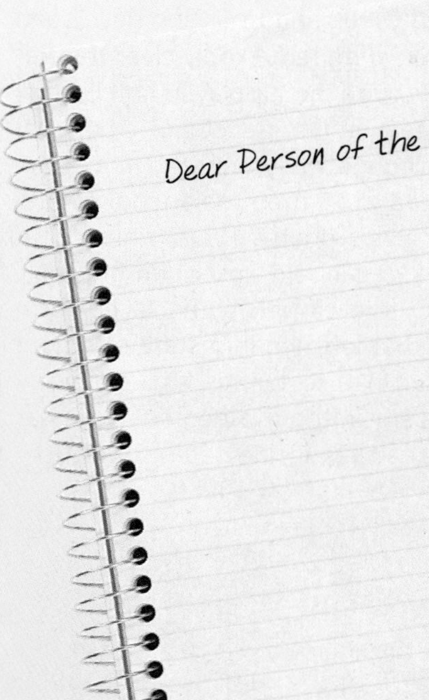

1996

Rabindranath Tagore

Who are you reading curiously this poem of mine
a hundred years from now?
Shall I be able to send to you
—steeped in the love of my heart—
the faintest touch of this spring morning's joy,
the scent of a flower,
a bird-song's note,
a spark of today's blaze of color
a hundred years from now?

Yet, for once, open your window on the south
and from your balcony

Rabindranath Tagore, 1896

gaze at the far horizon.
Then, sinking deep in fancy
think of the ecstasies of joy
that came floating down
from some far heaven of bliss
to touch the heart of the world
a hundred years ago;
think of the young spring day
wild, impetuous and free;
and of the south wind
—fragrant with the pollen of flowers—
rushing on restless wings to paint the earth
with the radiant hues of youth
a hundred years before your day.

And think, how his heart aflame,
his whole being rapt in song,
a poet was awake that day
to unfold like flowers
his myriad thoughts
with what wealth of love!—
one morning a hundred years ago.

A hundred years from now
who is the new poet singing his songs to you?
Across the years I send him
the joyous greeting of this spring.
May my song echo for a while,
on your spring day,
in the beating of your heart,
in the murmur of bees,
in the rustling of leaves,—
a hundred years from today.

February, 1896

20 impetuous (ĭm-pĕch'o͞o-əs): impulsive.

27 rapt: deeply absorbed.

30 myriad (mĭr'ē-əd): countless.

RESPONDING OPTIONS

FROM PERSONAL RESPONSE *TO* CRITICAL ANALYSIS

REFLECT **1.** What impressions of Rabindranath Tagore do you have after reading this poem? Jot down your thoughts in your notebook.

RETHINK **2.** How do you think Tagore would explain the purpose of his poem?

Consider

- what he hopes to "send" to the reader (line 3)
- why he wants the reader to "gaze at the far horizon" (line 12)
- his desire "to unfold like flowers / his myriad thoughts" (lines 29–30)

3. Why do you think Tagore chose images of spring and nature to relay his message to future readers?

4. Do you think Tagore expects the world to change much in 100 years? Use evidence from the poem to support your answer.

5. Look back at your draft of a letter for the Writing Connection on page 696. Do you notice any similarities between your message and the message conveyed by Tagore? Discuss what these similarities, as well as any differences, might indicate.

RELATE **6.** Think about the message that Tagore sends to his future readers. Do you think a contemporary poet might send a similar message to future readers? Why or why not?

ANOTHER PATHWAY

Plan what you would say in a poem called "2096." In a chart like the one shown here, compare Tagore's "1996" with the poem you would compose. How would your poem differ from Tagore's in theme and tone? Share your ideas with classmates.

	Theme	Tone
Tagore's "1996"		
My "2096"		

LITERARY LINKS

In "1996," Tagore seems to express a belief that appreciation of nature will endure throughout time. Compare Tagore's views with Wordsworth's impressions of the effects of time on public appreciation of nature in "Lines Composed a Few Miles Above Tintern Abbey" (page 498).

QUICKWRITES

1. Jot down some **images** that come to mind when you think of a spring day. Then place a check beside those that you think would most appeal to Rabindranath Tagore.
2. Write a short **autobiographical sketch** that answers Tagore's question "Who are you reading curiously this poem of mine . . . ?"
3. Write **dialogue** for a conversation in which Tagore and a present-day author discuss the role of the poet.

***PORTFOLIO** Save your writing. You may want to use it later as a springboard to a piece for your portfolio.*

LITERARY CONCEPTS

The **title** of a literary work introduces readers to the piece and usually reveals something about its subject or theme. Although some poems are merely identified by their first line, most literary works have been carefully and deliberately titled. Some titles are straightforward, stating exactly what the reader can expect to discover in the work. Others merely tickle the imagination, perhaps hinting at the subject and forcing the reader to search for deeper meaning. Before you began reading this poem, what thoughts or predictions did you have about its theme or message, based on the title "1996"?

CRITIC'S CORNER

In awarding Rabindranath Tagore the 1913 Nobel Prize in literature, Harald Hjärne, chairman of the Nobel committee, praised Tagore's poetry for its "rhythmically balanced style." What evidence of rhythmic balance can you find in "1996"?

THE WRITER'S STYLE

In "1996," Tagore addresses the reader directly. What is your reaction to this technique? What effect do you think the poet is trying to achieve?

ALTERNATIVE ACTIVITIES

1. Prepare an **anthology** of contemporary poetry as an answer to Tagore's question ". . . who is the new poet . . . ?"
2. ***Cooperative Learning*** With classmates, prepare a **triptych**—an artwork in three panels—to illustrate your impressions of the world in Tagore's time, the world today, and the world as it might appear 100 years from now.

Rabindranath Tagore

1861–1941

Born into one of the most intellectual and talented Indian families of the time, Rabindranath Tagore wrote his first poem at the age of 8. By the time he was 15, he had published one poem and was reading his work aloud at public gatherings. In spite of his thirst for learning, Tagore disliked his childhood school experiences and rebelled against his rigidly institutionalized education. At the age of 17, he traveled to London, enrolled at University College, and, following his family's wishes, began to study law. Two years later, however, he gave up his studies and returned to India to devote his life to literary pursuits.

Although born in the city of Calcutta, Tagore seemed to prefer life in the rural areas of Bengal. He had a fascination with nature that was strengthened during a boyhood trip to northern India and the Himalayas. In later years, he managed his family's estates and composed numerous literary works in rural Bengal, where he eventually founded his own school. In an effort to blend the best of Indian and Western traditions, he introduced many new educational techniques, including coeducation and the elimination of all caste, or class, distinctions. After World War I, he expanded his local school into an international university.

By the time of his death at the age of 80, Tagore had composed numerous short stories, novels, and plays, as well as 60 volumes of poetry. He was also a gifted painter and musician and had set many of his poems to music. Reflected in some of his best poetry is the intense sadness he experienced after the deaths of his wife, a daughter, and a son within a five-year period. Much of his writing was also inspired by a deep concern for India's poor and by a desire for social and political reforms. Besides being a leader in the arts, Tagore was one of India's leading activists for independence. His death came six years before his country gained its freedom from British rule.

OTHER WORKS *Gitanjali (Song Offerings), The Crescent Moon,* "The Cabuliwallah," "The Babus of Nayanjore"

PREVIEWING

DRAMA

The Importance of Being Earnest

Oscar Wilde

PERSONAL CONNECTION

Think about different comedies—plays, movies, or situation comedies on TV—that you have watched during the past year. Were all of the performances similar in style and subject matter, or were some more ridiculous or absurd than others? Make a list of the various elements that make a comedy absurd. Then share your thoughts with classmates.

LITERARY/CULTURAL CONNECTION

Victorian writers produced very little in the way of noteworthy drama until the end of the 19th century. The masterpiece of that period was undoubtedly Oscar Wilde's *The Importance of Being Earnest*. Although this play is similar in some ways to the Restoration comedies of the late 17th century, its comic style, especially the witty dialogue and emphasis on absurd situations, was new to Victorian theatergoers.

Wilde's plays offered audiences a fresh contrast to the somber tone of Victorian dramas and to the emphasis on proper manners and rigid morals for which Victorian society is often remembered. The original subtitle of *The Importance of Being Earnest* was "A Trivial Comedy for Serious People." Typically, fashionable society in the 19th century placed great importance on family background, rank, financial status, appropriate dress, social observances, and adherence to a code of manners and morals. In his comedies, Wilde takes a satirical look at the values and concerns of many of his contemporaries, especially the segment of society that he once called "the beautiful people."

Wilde's plays were performed in both London and New York between 1892 and 1895. *The Importance of Being Earnest* was the last of a series of comedies that he wrote during his brief career as a dramatist. It was first performed in London in February 1895 and was instantly popular. One of the actors in the original production declared that in over 50 years of acting he had never before experienced such admiration from an audience. A favorite of theater directors for most of the 20th century, the play is famous for its witty lines and absurd comic situations in which paradox is used to undermine convention.

Scene from 1953 movie.
Photofest.

• *READING CONNECTION*

READING CONNECTION

Visualizing Drama in Performance

Every drama is a story that was meant to be staged—to be brought to life before an audience. In order to fully appreciate a play, you should try to visualize a performance of it as you read. Much of the entertainment in reading a play comes from being able to visualize the setting and action and to imagine the way the characters speak their lines. If you use a little imagination, your reading experience can be almost as satisfying as watching a live performance. Using your imagination is especially important in reading a comedy, because so much of the experience depends upon the audience's reaction to the humor. *The Importance of Being Earnest*, because of its witty dialogue and absurd comic situations, especially profits from being visualized by the reader.

When reading a drama for the first time, imagine that you are a theater director planning a stage performance of the play. Pretend that it is your job to decide how the play will be staged, what kinds of actors will be used, and how each actor will portray his or her character. As you read, pay attention to the stage directions—the notes in the script that describe settings, sound effects, and characters' movements, expressions, and tones of voice. Picture the scenery, the props, and the costumes needed for each scene. Then decide how each character should be portrayed—what special traits or qualities an actor would need to emphasize. Also think about appropriate tones of voice, facial expressions, gestures, and movements for the actors.

Many dramas contain scenes in which the dialogue and situations cannot be fully understood without reference to visual effects. For example, an actor's costume, expressions, gestures, or handling of a prop might convey a meaning that is not evident in the dialogue alone. As the director, you would need to carefully stage these scenes so that they affect the audience in the way the playwright intended. As you read *The Importance of Being Earnest*, try to visualize a live performance of the play. In a chart like the one shown, jot down examples of visual effects that you think might be important for a complete understanding of the dialogue, the characters, and the absurd or ridiculous situations in particular scenes.

The Importance of Being Earnest

Visual Effect	Examples
Costumes	Clothing of upper class
Expressions	
Gestures	
Handling of props	

The Importance of Being Earnest

Oscar Wilde

Cast of Characters

John Worthing, Justice of the Peace
Algernon Moncrieff
Rev. Canon Chasuble
Merriman, a butler
Lane, a manservant
Lady Bracknell
Hon. Gwendolen Fairfax
Cecily Cardew
Miss Prism, a governess

The Scenes of the Play

Act I ALGERNON MONCRIEFF'S FLAT IN HALF-MOON STREET, W.
Act II THE GARDEN AT THE MANOR HOUSE, WOOLTON.
Act III DRAWING-ROOM AT THE MANOR HOUSE, WOOLTON.

Time: THE PRESENT

First Act

Scene:

Morning-room in Algernon's flat in Half-Moon Street. The room is luxuriously and artistically furnished. The sound of a piano is heard in the adjoining room.

(Lane *is arranging afternoon tea on the table, and after the music has ceased,* Algernon *enters.*)

Algernon. Did you hear what I was playing, Lane?

Lane. I didn't think it polite to listen, sir.

Algernon. I'm sorry for that, for your sake. I don't play accurately—any one can play accurately—but I play with wonderful expression. As far as the piano is concerned, sentiment is my forte. I keep science for Life.

Lane. Yes, sir.

Algernon. And, speaking of the science of Life, have you got the cucumber sandwiches cut for Lady Bracknell?

Lane. Yes, sir. (*hands them on a salver*[1])

1. **salver:** serving tray.

WORDS TO KNOW

forte (fôrt) *n.* something at which a person excels

Algernon (*inspects them, takes two, and sits down on the sofa*). Oh! . . . by the way, Lane, I see from your book that on Thursday night, when Lord Shoreman and Mr. Worthing were dining with me, eight bottles of champagne are entered as having been consumed.

Lane. Yes, sir; eight bottles and a pint.

Algernon. Why is it that at a bachelor's establishment the servants invariably drink the champagne? I ask merely for information.

Lane. I attribute it to the superior quality of the wine, sir. I have often observed that in married households the champagne is rarely of a first-rate brand.

Algernon. Good heavens! Is marriage so demoralizing[2] as that?

Lane. I believe it *is* a very pleasant state, sir. I have had very little experience of it myself up to the present. I have only been married once. That was in consequence of a misunderstanding between myself and a young person.

Algernon (*languidly*). I don't know that I am much interested in your family life, Lane.

Lane. No, sir; it is not a very interesting subject. I never think of it myself.

Algernon. Very natural, I am sure. That will do, Lane, thank you.

Lane. Thank you, sir.

(Lane *goes out.*)

Algernon. Lane's views on marriage seem somewhat lax. Really, if the lower orders don't set us a good example, what on earth is the use of them? They seem, as a class, to have absolutely no sense of moral responsibility.

(*Enter* Lane.)

Lane. Mr. Ernest Worthing.

(*Enter* Jack.)

(Lane *goes out.*)

Algernon. How are you, my dear Ernest? What brings you up to town?

Jack. Oh, pleasure, pleasure! What else should bring one anywhere? Eating as usual, I see, Algy!

Algernon (*stiffly*). I believe it is customary in good society to take some slight refreshment at five o'clock. Where have you been since last Thursday?

Jack (*sitting down on the sofa*). In the country.

Algernon. What on earth do you do there?

Jack (*pulling off his gloves*). When one is in town one amuses oneself. When one is in the country one amuses other people. It is excessively boring.

Algernon. And who are the people you amuse?

Jack (*airily*). Oh, neighbors, neighbors.

Algernon. Got nice neighbors in your part of Shropshire?

Jack. Perfectly horrid! Never speak to one of them.

Algernon. How immensely you must amuse them! (*goes over and takes sandwich*) By the way, Shropshire is your county, is it not?

Jack. Eh? Shropshire? Yes, of course. Hello! Why all these cups? Why cucumber sandwiches? Why such reckless extravagance in one so young? Who is coming to tea?

Algernon. Oh! merely Aunt Augusta and Gwendolen.

Jack. How perfectly delightful!

Algernon. Yes, that is all very well; but I am afraid Aunt Augusta won't quite approve of your being here.

Jack. May I ask why?

Algernon. My dear fellow, the way you flirt with Gwendolen is perfectly disgraceful. It is almost as bad as the way Gwendolen flirts with you.

Jack. I am in love with Gwendolen. I have come up to town expressly to propose to her.

Algernon. I thought you had come up for pleasure? . . . I call that business.

Jack. How utterly unromantic you are!

---

2. **demoralizing:** This word has three meanings: (1) "disheartening," (2) "wild, confusing, and disorderly," and (3) "morally corrupting." Algernon may have any or all of the meanings in mind.

Algernon. I really don't see anything romantic in proposing. It is very romantic to be in love. But there is nothing romantic about a definite proposal. Why, one may be accepted. One usually is, I believe. Then the excitement is all over. The very essence of romance is uncertainty. If ever I get married, I'll certainly try to forget the fact.

Jack. I have no doubt about that, dear Algy. The Divorce Court was specially invented for people whose memories are so curiously constituted.

Algernon. Oh! there is no use speculating on that subject. Divorces are made in Heaven—(Jack *puts out his hand to take a sandwich.* Algernon *at once interferes.*) Please don't touch the cucumber sandwiches. They are ordered specially for Aunt Augusta. (*takes one and eats it*)

Jack. Well, you have been eating them all the time.

Algernon. That is quite a different matter. She is my aunt. (*takes plate from below*) Have some bread and butter. The bread and butter is for Gwendolen. Gwendolen is devoted to bread and butter.

Jack (*advancing to table and helping himself*). And very good bread and butter it is too.

Algernon. Well, my dear fellow, you need not eat as if you were going to eat it all. You behave as if you were married to her already. You are not married to her already, and I don't think you ever will be.

Jack. Why on earth do you say that?

Algernon. Well, in the first place girls never marry the men they flirt with. Girls don't think it right.

Jack. Oh, that is nonsense!

Algernon. It isn't. It is a great truth. It accounts for the extraordinary number of bachelors that one sees all over the place. In the second place, I don't give my consent.

Jack. Your consent!

Algernon. My dear fellow, Gwendolen is my first cousin. And before I allow you to marry her, you will have to clear up the whole question of Cecily. (*rings bell*)

Jack. Cecily! What on earth do you mean? What do you mean, Algy, by Cecily! I don't know any one of the name of Cecily.

(*Enter* Lane.)

Algernon. Bring me that cigarette case Mr. Worthing left in the smoking-room the last time he dined here.

Lane. Yes, sir.

(Lane *goes out.*)

Jack. Do you mean to say you have had my cigarette case all this time? I wish to goodness you had let me know. I have been writing frantic letters to Scotland Yard about it. I was very nearly offering a large reward.

Algernon. Well, I wish you would offer one. I happen to be more than usually hard up.

Jack. There is no good offering a large reward now that the thing is found.

(*Enter* Lane *with the cigarette case on a salver.* Algernon *takes it at once.* Lane *goes out.*)

Algernon. I think that is rather mean of you, Ernest, I must say. (*opens case and examines it*) However, it makes no matter, for, now that I look at the inscription inside, I find that the thing isn't yours after all.

Jack. Of course it's mine. (*moving to him*) You have seen me with it a hundred times, and you have no right whatsoever to read what is written inside. It is a very ungentlemanly thing to read a private cigarette case.

Algernon. Oh! it is absurd to have a hard and fast rule about what one should read and what one shouldn't. More than half of modern culture depends on what one shouldn't read.

Jack. I am quite aware of the fact, and I don't propose to discuss modern culture. It isn't the sort of thing one should talk of in private. I simply want my cigarette case back.

Algernon. Yes; but this isn't your cigarette case. This cigarette case is a present from some one of the name of Cecily, and you said you didn't know any one of that name.

Jack. Well, if you want to know, Cecily happens to be my aunt.

Algernon. Your aunt!

Jack. Yes. Charming old lady she is, too. Lives at Tunbridge Wells. Just give it back to me, Algy.

Algernon (*retreating to back of sofa*). But why does she call herself little Cecily if she is your aunt and lives at Tunbridge Wells? (*reading*) "From little Cecily with her fondest love."

Jack (*moving to sofa and kneeling upon it*). My dear fellow, what on earth is there in that? Some aunts are tall, some aunts are not tall. That is a matter that surely an aunt may be allowed to decide for herself. You seem to think that every aunt should be exactly like your aunt! That is absurd! For Heaven's sake give me back my cigarette case. (*follows* Algernon *round the room*)

Algernon. Yes. But why does your aunt call you her uncle? "From little Cecily, with her fondest love to her dear Uncle Jack." There is no objection, I admit, to an aunt being a small aunt, but why an aunt, no matter what her size may be, should call her own nephew her uncle, I can't quite make out. Besides, your name isn't Jack at all; it is Ernest.

Jack. It isn't Ernest; it's Jack.

Algernon. You have always told me it was Ernest. I have introduced you to everyone as Ernest. You answer to the name of Ernest. You look as if your name was Ernest. You are the most earnest-looking person I ever saw in my life. It is perfectly absurd your saying that your name isn't Ernest. It's on your cards. Here is one of them. (*taking it from case*) "Mr. Ernest Worthing, B. 4, The Albany." I'll keep this as a proof that your name is Ernest if ever you attempt to deny it to me, or to Gwendolen, or to any one else. (*puts the card in his pocket*)

Jack. Well, my name is Ernest in town and Jack in the country, and the cigarette case was given to me in the country.

Algernon. Yes, but that does not account for the fact that your small Aunt Cecily, who lives at Tunbridge Wells, calls you her dear uncle. Come, old boy, you had much better have the thing out at once.

Jack. My dear Algy, you talk exactly as if you were a dentist. It is very vulgar to talk like a dentist when one isn't a dentist. It produces a false impression.

Algernon. Well, that is exactly what dentists always do. Now, go on! Tell me the whole thing. I may mention that I have always suspected you of being a confirmed and secret Bunburyist; and I am quite sure of it now.

Jack. Bunburyist? What on earth do you mean by a Bunburyist?

Algernon. I'll reveal to you the meaning of that incomparable expression as soon as you are kind enough to inform me why you are Ernest in town and Jack in the country.

Jack. Well, produce my cigarette case first.

Algernon. Here it is. (*hands cigarette case*) Now produce your explanation, and pray make it improbable. (*sits on sofa*)

Jack. My dear fellow, there is nothing improbable about my explanation at all. In fact it's perfectly ordinary. Old Mr. Thomas Cardew, who adopted me when I was a little boy, made me in his will guardian to his granddaughter, Miss Cecily Cardew. Cecily, who addresses me as her uncle from motives of respect that you could not possibly appreciate, lives at my place in the country under the charge of her admirable governess, Miss Prism.

Algernon. Where is that place in the country, by the way?

Jack. That is nothing to you, dear boy. You are not going to be invited. . . . I may tell you candidly that the place is not in Shropshire.

Algernon. I suspected that, my dear fellow! I have Bunburyed all over Shropshire on two separate occasions. Now, go on. Why are you Ernest in town and Jack in the country?

Jack. My dear Algy, I don't know whether you will be able to understand my real motives. You are hardly serious enough. When one is placed in the position of guardian, one has to adopt a very high moral tone on all subjects. It's one's duty to do so. And as a high moral tone can hardly be said to conduce[3] very much to either one's health or one's happiness, in order to get up to town I have always pretended to have a younger brother of the name of Ernest, who lives in the Albany, and gets into the most dreadful scrapes. That, my dear Algy, is the whole truth pure and simple.

Algernon. The truth is rarely pure and never simple. Modern life would be very tedious if it were either, and modern literature a complete impossibility!

Jack. That wouldn't be at all a bad thing.

Algernon. Literary criticism is not your forte, my dear fellow. Don't try it. You should leave that to people who haven't been at a University. They do it so well in the daily papers. What you really are is a Bunburyist. I was quite right in saying you were a Bunburyist. You are one of the most advanced Bunburyists I know.

Jack. What on earth do you mean?

Algernon. You have invented a very useful younger brother called Ernest, in order that you may be able to come up to town as often as you like. I have invented an invaluable permanent invalid called Bunbury, in order that I may be able to go down into the country whenever I choose. Bunbury is perfectly invaluable. If it wasn't for Bunbury's extraordinary bad health, for instance, I wouldn't be able to dine with you at Willis's tonight, for I have been really engaged to[4] Aunt Augusta for more than a week.

Jack. I haven't asked you to dine with me anywhere tonight.

Algernon. I know. You are absurdly careless about sending out invitations. It is very foolish of you. Nothing annoys people so much as not receiving invitations.

Jack. You had much better dine with your Aunt Augusta.

Algernon. I haven't the smallest intention of doing anything of the kind. To begin with, I dined there on Monday, and once a week is quite enough to dine with one's own relations. In the second place, whenever I do dine there I am always treated as a member of the family, and sent down with either no woman at all, or two.[5] In the third place, I know perfectly well whom she will place me next to, tonight. She will place me next to Mary Farquhar, who always flirts with her own husband across the dinner-table. That is not very pleasant. Indeed, it is not even decent . . . and that sort of thing is enormously on the increase. The amount of women in London who flirt with their own husbands is perfectly scandalous. It looks so bad. It is simply washing one's clean linen in public. Besides, now that I know you to be a confirmed Bunburyist I naturally want to talk to you about Bunburying. I want to tell you the rules.

Jack. I'm not a Bunburyist at all. If Gwendolen accepts me, I am going to kill my brother, indeed I think I'll kill him in any case. Cecily is a little too much interested in him. It is rather a bore. So I am going to get rid of Ernest. And I strongly advise you to do the same with Mr. . . . with your invalid friend who has the absurd name.

Algernon. Nothing will induce me to part with Bunbury, and if you ever get married, which

3. **conduce:** contribute.

4. **engaged to:** scheduled to dine with.

5. **sent down . . . or two:** Dinner-party guests were usually matched in couples. In the situations Algernon describes, he has had to assume a family member's duty of partnering two unaccompanied women, or he has not been matched with any partner.

seems to me extremely problematic, you will be very glad to know Bunbury. A man who marries without knowing Bunbury has a very tedious time of it.

Jack. That is nonsense. If I marry a charming girl like Gwendolen, and she is the only girl I ever saw in my life that I would marry, I certainly won't want to know Bunbury.

Algernon. Then your wife will. You don't seem to realize, that in married life three is company and two is none.

Jack (*sententiously*).[6] That, my dear young friend, is the theory that the corrupt French Drama has been propounding[7] for the last fifty years.

Algernon. Yes; and that the happy English home has proved in half the time.

Jack. For heaven's sake, don't try to be cynical. It's perfectly easy to be cynical.

Algernon. My dear fellow, it isn't easy to be anything nowadays. There's such a lot of beastly competition about. (*The sound of an electric bell is heard.*) Ah! that must be Aunt Augusta. Only relatives, or creditors, ever ring in that Wagnerian[8] manner. Now, if I get her out of the way for ten minutes, so that you can have an opportunity for proposing to Gwendolen, may I dine with you tonight at Willis's?

Jack. I suppose so, if you want to.

Algernon. Yes, but you must be serious about it. I hate people who are not serious about meals. It is so shallow of them.

(*Enter* Lane.)

Lane. Lady Bracknell and Miss Fairfax.

(Algernon *goes forward to meet them. Enter* Lady Bracknell *and* Gwendolen.)

Lady Bracknell. Good afternoon, dear Algernon, I hope you are behaving very well.

Algernon. I'm feeling very well, Aunt Augusta.

Lady Bracknell. That's not quite the same thing. In fact the two things rarely go together. (*sees* Jack *and bows to him with icy coldness*)

Algernon (*to* Gwendolen). Dear me, you are smart!

Gwendolen. I am always smart! Am I not, Mr. Worthing?

Jack. You're quite perfect, Miss Fairfax.

Gwendolen. Oh! I hope I am not that. It would leave no room for developments, and I intend to develop in many directions. (Gwendolen *and* Jack *sit down together in the corner.*)

Lady Bracknell. I'm sorry if we are a little late, Algernon, but I was obliged to call on dear Lady Harbury. I hadn't been there since her poor husband's death. I never saw a woman so altered; she looks quite twenty years younger. And now I'll have a cup of tea, and one of those nice cucumber sandwiches you promised me.

Algernon. Certainly, Aunt Augusta. (*goes over to tea-table*)

Lady Bracknell. Won't you come and sit here, Gwendolen?

Gwendolen. Thanks, mamma, I'm quite comfortable where I am.

Algernon (*picking up empty plate in horror*). Good heavens! Lane! Why are there no cucumber sandwiches? I ordered them specially.

Lane (*gravely*). There were no cucumbers in the market this morning, sir. I went down twice.

Algernon. No cucumbers!

Lane. No, sir. Not even for ready money.

Algernon. That will do, Lane, thank you.

Lane. Thank you, sir. (*goes out*)

Algernon. I am greatly distressed, Aunt Augusta, about there being no cucumbers, not even for ready money.

---

6. **sententiously** (sĕn-tĕn′shəs-lē): in a pompously moralizing way.

7. **propounding:** putting forward.

8. **Wagnerian** (väg-nîr′ē-ən): here, loud and pompous. Richard Wagner (1813–1883) was a German romantic composer of operas featuring grand, mythical themes.

Lady Bracknell. It really makes no matter, Algernon. I had some crumpets[9] with Lady Harbury, who seems to me to be living entirely for pleasure now.

Algernon. I hear her hair has turned quite gold from grief.

Lady Bracknell. It certainly has changed its color. From what cause I, of course, cannot say. (Algernon *crosses and hands tea.*) Thank you. I've quite a treat for you tonight, Algernon. I am going to send you down with Mary Farquhar. She is such a nice woman, and so attentive to her husband. It's delightful to watch them.

Algernon. I am afraid, Aunt Augusta, I shall have to give up the pleasure of dining with you tonight after all.

Lady Bracknell (*frowning*). I hope not, Algernon. It would put my table completely out. Your uncle would have to dine upstairs. Fortunately he is accustomed to that.

Algernon. It is a great bore, and, I need hardly say, a terrible disappointment to me, but the fact is I have just had a telegram to say that my poor friend Bunbury is very ill again. (*exchanges glances with* Jack) They seem to think I should be with him.

Lady Bracknell. It is very strange. This Mr. Bunbury seems to suffer from curiously bad health.

Algernon. Yes; poor Bunbury is a dreadful invalid.

Lady Bracknell. Well, I must say, Algernon, that I think it is high time that Mr. Bunbury made up his mind whether he was going to live or to die. This shilly-shallying[10] with the question is absurd. Nor do I in any way approve of the modern sympathy with invalids. I consider it morbid.[11] Illness of any kind is hardly a thing to be encouraged in others. Health is the primary duty of life. I am always telling that to your poor uncle, but he never seems to take much notice . . . as far as any improvement in his ailment goes. I should be much obliged if you would ask Mr. Bunbury, from me, to be kind enough not to have a relapse on Saturday, for I rely on you to arrange my music for me. It is my last reception, and one wants something that will encourage conversation, particularly at the end of the season[12] when everyone has practically said whatever they had to say, which, in most cases, was probably not much.

Algernon. I'll speak to Bunbury, Aunt Augusta, if he is still conscious, and I think I can promise you he'll be all right by Saturday. Of course the music is a great difficulty. You see, if one plays good music, people don't listen, and if one plays bad music, people don't talk. But I'll run over the program I've drawn out, if you will kindly come into the next room for a moment.

Lady Bracknell. Thank you, Algernon. It is very thoughtful of you. (*rising and following* Algernon) I'm sure the program will be delightful, after a few expurgations.[13] French songs I cannot possibly allow. People always seem to think that they are improper, and either look shocked, which is vulgar, or laugh, which is worse. But German sounds a thoroughly respectable language, and indeed, I believe is so. Gwendolen, you will accompany me.

Gwendolen. Certainly, mamma.

(Lady Bracknell *and* Algernon *go into the music-room,* Gwendolen *remains behind.*)

Jack. Charming day it has been, Miss Fairfax.

Gwendolen. Pray don't talk to me about the weather, Mr. Worthing. Whenever people talk to me about the weather, I always feel quite certain that they mean something else. And that makes me so nervous.

Jack. I do mean something else.

---

9. **crumpets:** small biscuits, served with tea.
10. **shilly-shallying:** procrastination or indecision.
11. **morbid:** psychologically unwholesome.
12. **the season:** in high society, the months during which people give dinner parties, receptions, and so on.
13. **expurgations:** deletions of incorrect, vulgar, or otherwise objectionable material.

Gwendolen. I thought so. In fact, I am never wrong.

Jack. And I would like to be allowed to take advantage of Lady Bracknell's temporary absence . . .

Gwendolen. I would certainly advise you to do so. Mamma has a way of coming back suddenly into a room that I have often had to speak to her about.

Jack (*nervously*). Miss Fairfax, ever since I met you I have admired you more than any girl . . . I have ever met since . . . I met you.

Gwendolen. Yes, I am quite well aware of the fact. And I often wish that in public, at any rate, you had been more demonstrative. For me you have always had an irresistible fascination. Even before I met you I was far from indifferent to you. (Jack *looks at her in amazement.*) We live, as I hope you know, Mr. Worthing, in an age of ideals. The fact is constantly mentioned in the more expensive monthly magazines, and has reached the provincial pulpits,[14] I am told; and my ideal has always been to love some one of the name of Ernest. There is something in that name that inspires absolute confidence. The moment Algernon first mentioned to me that he had a friend called Ernest, I knew I was destined to love you.

Jack. You really love me, Gwendolen?

Gwendolen. Passionately!

Jack. Darling! You don't know how happy you've made me.

Gwendolen. My own Ernest!

Jack. But you don't really mean to say that you couldn't love me if my name wasn't Ernest?

Gwendolen. But your name is Ernest.

Jack. Yes, I know it is. But supposing it was something else? Do you mean to say you couldn't love me then?

Gwendolen (*glibly*).[15] Ah! that is clearly a metaphysical speculation,[16] and like most metaphysical speculations has very little reference at all to the actual facts of real life, as we know them.

Jack. Personally, darling, to speak quite candidly, I don't much care about the name of Ernest. . . . I don't think the name suits me at all.

Gwendolen. It suits you perfectly. It is a divine name. It has music of its own. It produces vibrations.

Jack. Well, really, Gwendolen, I must say that I think there are lots of other much nicer names. I think Jack, for instance, a charming name.

Gwendolen. Jack? . . . No, there is very little music in the name Jack, if any at all, indeed. It does not thrill. It produces absolutely no vibrations. . . . I have known several Jacks, and they all, without exception, were more than usually plain. Besides, Jack is a notorious domesticity[17] for John! And I pity any woman who is married to a man called John. She would probably never be allowed to know the entrancing pleasure of a single moment's solitude. The only really safe name is Ernest.

Jack. Gwendolen, I must get christened at once—I mean we must get married at once. There is no time to be lost.

Gwendolen. Married, Mr. Worthing?

Jack (*astounded*). Well . . . surely. You know that I love you, and you led me to believe, Miss Fairfax, that you were not absolutely indifferent to me.

Gwendolen. I adore you. But you haven't proposed to me yet. Nothing has been said at all about marriage. The subject has not even been touched on.

Jack. Well . . . may I propose to you now?

Gwendolen. I think it would be an admirable opportunity. And to spare you any possible

---

14. **provincial pulpits:** sermons of country ministers.
15. **glibly:** in a smooth manner that suggests insincerity or superficiality.
16. **metaphysical speculation:** a philosophical theory.
17. **domesticity:** nickname used by relatives and close friends.

disappointment, Mr. Worthing, I think it only fair to tell you quite frankly beforehand that I am fully determined to accept you.

Jack. Gwendolen!

Gwendolen. Yes, Mr. Worthing, what have you got to say to me?

Jack. You know what I have got to say to you.

Gwendolen. Yes, but you don't say it.

Jack. Gwendolen, will you marry me? (*goes on his knees*)

Gwendolen. Of course I will, darling. How long you have been about it! I am afraid you have had very little experience in how to propose.

Jack. My own one, I have never loved any one in the world but you.

Gwendolen. Yes, but men often propose for practice. I know my brother Gerald does. All my girlfriends tell me so. What wonderfully blue eyes you have, Ernest! They are quite, quite, blue. I hope you will always look at me just like that, especially when there are other people present.

(*Enter* Lady Bracknell.)

Lady Bracknell. Mr. Worthing! Rise, sir, from this semi-recumbent[18] posture. It is most indecorous.

Gwendolen. Mamma! (*He tries to rise; she restrains him.*) I must beg you to retire. This is no place for you. Besides, Mr. Worthing has not quite finished yet.

Lady Bracknell. Finished what, may I ask?

Gwendolen. I am engaged to Mr. Worthing, mamma. (*They rise together.*)

Lady Bracknell. Pardon me, you are not engaged to any one. When you do become engaged to some one, I, or your father, should his health permit him, will inform you of the fact. An engagement should come on a young girl as a surprise, pleasant or unpleasant, as the case may be. It is hardly a matter that she could be allowed to arrange for herself. . . . And now I have a few questions to put to you, Mr. Worthing. While I am making these inquiries, you, Gwendolen, will wait for me below in the carriage.

Gwendolen (*reproachfully*). Mamma!

Lady Bracknell. In the carriage, Gwendolen! (Gwendolen *goes to the door. She and* Jack *blow kisses to each other behind* Lady Bracknell's *back.* Lady Bracknell *looks vaguely about as if she could not understand what the noise was. Finally turns round.*) Gwendolen, the carriage!

Gwendolen. Yes, mamma. (*goes out, looking back at* Jack)

Lady Bracknell (*sitting down*). You can take a seat, Mr. Worthing. (*looks in her pocket for notebook and pencil*)

Jack. Thank you, Lady Bracknell, I prefer standing.

Lady Bracknell (*pencil and notebook in hand*). I feel bound to tell you that you are not down on my list of eligible young men, although I have

18. **semi-recumbent:** half lying down. (Lady Bracknell is referring to Jack's kneeling at Gwendolen's feet.)

the same list as the dear Duchess of Bolton has. We work together, in fact. However, I am quite ready to enter your name, should your answers be what a really affectionate mother requires. Do you smoke?

Jack. Well, yes, I must admit I smoke.

Lady Bracknell. I am glad to hear it. A man should always have an occupation of some kind. There are far too many idle men in London as it is. How old are you?

Jack. Twenty-nine.

Lady Bracknell. A very good age to be married at. I have always been of opinion that a man who desires to get married should know either everything or nothing. Which do you know?

Jack (*after some hesitation*). I know nothing, Lady Bracknell.

Lady Bracknell. I am pleased to hear it. I do not approve of anything that tampers with natural ignorance. Ignorance is like a delicate exotic fruit; touch it and the bloom is gone. The whole theory of modern education is radically unsound. Fortunately in England, at any rate, education produces no effect whatsoever. If it did, it would prove a serious danger to the upper classes, and probably lead to acts of violence in Grosvenor[19] Square. What is your income?

Jack. Between seven and eight thousand a year.

Lady Bracknell (*makes a note in her book*). In land, or in investments?

Jack. In investments, chiefly.

Lady Bracknell. That is satisfactory. What between the duties expected of one during one's lifetime, and the duties exacted from one after one's death, land has ceased to be either a profit or a pleasure. It gives one position, and prevents one from keeping it up. That's all that can be said about land.

Jack. I have a country house with some land, of course, attached to it, about fifteen hundred acres, I believe; but I don't depend on that for my real income. In fact, as far as I can make out, the poachers[20] are the only people who make anything out of it.

Lady Bracknell. A country house! How many bedrooms? Well, that point can be cleared up afterwards. You have a town house, I hope? A girl with a simple, unspoiled nature, like Gwendolen, could hardly be expected to reside in the country.

Jack. Well, I own a house in Belgrave Square, but it is let by the year to Lady Bloxham. Of course, I can get it back whenever I like, at six months' notice.

Lady Bracknell. Lady Bloxham? I don't know her.

Jack. Oh, she goes about very little. She is a lady considerably advanced in years.

Lady Bracknell. Ah, nowadays that is no guarantee of respectability of character. What number in Belgrave Square?

Jack. 149.

Lady Bracknell (*shaking her head*). The unfashionable side. I thought there was something. However, that could easily be altered.

Jack. Do you mean the fashion, or the side?

Lady Bracknell (*sternly*). Both, if necessary, I presume. What are your politics?

Jack. Well, I am afraid I really have none. I am a Liberal Unionist.

Lady Bracknell. Oh, they count as Tories.[21] They dine with us. Or come in the evening, at any rate. Now to minor matters. Are your parents living?

Jack. I have lost both my parents.

Lady Bracknell. To lose one parent, Mr. Worthing, may be regarded as a misfortune; to lose both looks like carelessness. Who was your father? He was evidently a man of some wealth. Was he born in what the Radical papers call

---

19. **Grosvenor** (grōv′nər).

20. **poachers:** people who hunt illegally on others' land.

21. **Liberal Unionist . . . Tories:** references to two British political parties.

the purple of commerce,[22] or did he rise from the ranks of the aristocracy?

Jack. I am afraid I really don't know. The fact is, Lady Bracknell, I said I had lost my parents. It would be nearer the truth to say that my parents seem to have lost me. . . . I don't actually know who I am by birth. I was . . . well, I was found.

Lady Bracknell. Found!

Jack. The late Mr. Thomas Cardew, an old gentleman of a very charitable and kindly disposition, found me, and gave me the name of Worthing, because he happened to have a first-class ticket for Worthing in his pocket at the time. Worthing is a place in Sussex. It is a seaside resort.

Lady Bracknell. Where did the charitable gentleman who had a first-class ticket for this seaside resort find you?

Jack (*gravely*). In a handbag.

Lady Bracknell. A handbag?

Jack (*very seriously*). Yes, Lady Bracknell. I was in a handbag—a somewhat large, black leather handbag, with handles to it—an ordinary handbag in fact.

Lady Bracknell. In what locality did this Mr. James, or Thomas, Cardew come across this ordinary handbag?

Jack. In the cloakroom at Victoria Station. It was given to him in mistake for his own.

Lady Bracknell. The cloakroom at Victoria Station?

Jack. Yes. The Brighton line.

Lady Bracknell. The line is immaterial. Mr. Worthing, I confess I feel somewhat bewildered by what you have just told me. To be born, or at any rate bred, in a handbag, whether it had handles or not, seems to me to display a contempt for the ordinary decencies of family life that reminds one of the worst excesses of the French Revolution. And I presume you know what that unfortunate movement led to? As for the particular locality in which the handbag was found, a cloakroom at a railway station might serve to conceal a social indiscretion—has probably, indeed, been used for that purpose before now—but it could hardly be regarded as an assured basis for a recognized position in good society.

Jack. May I ask you then what you would advise me to do? I need hardly say I would do anything in the world to ensure Gwendolen's happiness.

Lady Bracknell. I would strongly advise you, Mr. Worthing, to try and acquire some relations as soon as possible, and to make a definite effort to produce at any rate one parent, of either sex, before the season is quite over.

Jack. Well, I don't see how I could possibly manage to do that. I can produce the handbag at any moment. It is in my dressing room at home. I really think that should satisfy you, Lady Bracknell.

Lady Bracknell. Me, sir! What has it to do with me? You can hardly imagine that I and Lord Bracknell would dream of allowing our only daughter—a girl brought up with the utmost care—to marry into a cloakroom, and form an alliance with a parcel? Good morning, Mr. Worthing!

(Lady Bracknell *sweeps out in majestic indignation.*)

Jack. Good morning! (Algernon, *from the other room, strikes up the Wedding March.* Jack *looks perfectly furious, and goes to the door.*) For goodness' sake don't play that ghastly tune, Algy! How idiotic you are!

(*The music stops and* Algernon *enters cheerily.*)

Algernon. Didn't it go off all right, old boy? You don't mean to say Gwendolen refused you? I know it is a way she has. She is always refusing people. I think it is most ill-natured of her.

22. **the purple of commerce:** Purple is often associated with royalty or high rank. To the "Radical papers," the most exalted people are those who have achieved success and power in the business world.

WORDS TO KNOW

indiscretion (ĭn′dĭ-skrĕsh′ən) *n.* a lapse of good judgment in speech or behavior

Jack. Oh, Gwendolen is as right as a trivet.[23] As far as she is concerned, we are engaged. Her mother is perfectly unbearable. Never met such a Gorgon.[24] . . . I don't really know what a Gorgon is like, but I am quite sure that Lady Bracknell is one. In any case, she is a monster, without being a myth, which is rather unfair. . . . I beg your pardon, Algy, I suppose I shouldn't talk about your own aunt in that way before you.

Algernon. My dear boy, I love hearing my relations abused. It is the only thing that makes me put up with them at all. Relations are simply a tedious pack of people, who haven't got the remotest knowledge of how to live, nor the smallest instinct about when to die.

Jack. Oh, that is nonsense!

Algernon. It isn't!

Jack. Well, I won't argue about the matter. You always want to argue about things.

Algernon. That is exactly what things were originally made for.

Jack. Upon my word, if I thought that, I'd shoot myself. . . . (*a pause*) You don't think there is any chance of Gwendolen becoming like her mother in about a hundred and fifty years, do you, Algy?

Algernon. All women become like their mothers. That is their tragedy. No man does. That's his.

Jack. Is that clever?

Algernon. It is perfectly phrased! and quite as true as any observation in civilized life should be.

Jack. I am sick to death of cleverness. Everybody is clever nowadays. You can't go anywhere without meeting clever people. The thing has become an absolute public nuisance. I wish to goodness we had a few fools left.

Algernon. We have.

Jack. I should extremely like to meet them. What do they talk about?

Algernon. The fools? Oh! about the clever people, of course.

Jack. What fools!

Algernon. By the way, did you tell Gwendolen the truth about your being Ernest in town, and Jack in the country?

Jack (*in a very patronizing*[25] *manner*). My dear fellow, the truth isn't quite the sort of thing one tells to a nice, sweet, refined girl. What extraordinary ideas you have about the way to behave to a woman!

Algernon. The only way to behave to a woman is to make love to her, if she is pretty, and to some one else, if she is plain.

Jack. Oh, that is nonsense.

Algernon. What about your brother? What about the profligate Ernest?

Jack. Oh, before the end of the week I shall have got rid of him. I'll say he died in Paris of apoplexy.[26] Lots of people die of apoplexy, quite suddenly, don't they?

Algernon. Yes, but it's hereditary, my dear fellow. It's a sort of thing that runs in families. You had much better say a severe chill.

Jack. You are sure a severe chill isn't hereditary, or anything of that kind?

Algernon. Of course it isn't!

Jack. Very well, then. My poor brother Ernest is carried off suddenly, in Paris, by a severe chill. That gets rid of him.

Algernon. But I thought you said that . . . Miss Cardew was a little too much interested in your poor brother Ernest? Won't she feel his loss a good deal?

---

23. **as right as a trivet** (trĭv′ĭt): perfectly all right; A-OK.
24. **Gorgon:** in Greek mythology, any of three sisters who had snakes for hair and eyes that turned the beholder into stone.
25. **patronizing** (pā′trə-nī′zĭng): condescending.
26. **apoplexy** (ăp′ə-plĕk′sē): a stroke.

WORDS TO KNOW

profligate (prŏf′lĭ-gĭt) *adj.* lacking moral restraint; reckless, shameless, and immoral

Jack. Oh, that is all right. Cecily is not a silly romantic girl, I am glad to say. She has got a capital appetite, goes for long walks, and pays no attention at all to her lessons.

Algernon. I would rather like to see Cecily.

Jack. I will take very good care you never do. She is excessively pretty, and she is only just eighteen.

Algernon. Have you told Gwendolen yet that you have an excessively pretty ward who is only just eighteen?

Jack. Oh! one doesn't blurt these things out to people. Cecily and Gwendolen are perfectly certain to be extremely great friends. I'll bet you anything you like that half an hour after they have met, they will be calling each other sister.

Algernon. Women only do that when they have called each other a lot of other things first. Now, my dear boy, if we want to get a good table at Willis's, we really must go and dress. Do you know it is nearly seven?

Jack (*irritably*). Oh! it always is nearly seven.

Algernon. Well, I'm hungry.

Jack. I never knew you when you weren't. . . .

Algernon. What shall we do after dinner? Go to a theater?

Jack. Oh no! I loathe listening.

Algernon. Well, let us go to the Club?

Jack. Oh, no! I hate talking.

Algernon. Well, we might trot round to the Empire at ten?

Jack. Oh, no! I can't bear looking at things. It is so silly.

Algernon. Well, what shall we do?

Jack. Nothing!

Algernon. It is awfully hard work doing nothing. However, I don't mind hard work where there is no definite object of any kind.

(*Enter* Lane.)

Lane. Miss Fairfax.

(*Enter* Gwendolen. Lane *goes out.*)

Algernon. Gwendolen, upon my word!

Gwendolen. Algy, kindly turn your back. I have something very particular to say to Mr. Worthing.

Algernon. Really, Gwendolen, I don't think I can allow this at all.

Gwendolen. Algy, you always adopt a strictly immoral attitude towards life. You are not quite old enough to do that. (Algernon *retires to the fireplace.*)

Jack. My own darling!

Gwendolen. Ernest, we may never be married. From the expression on mamma's face I fear we never shall. Few parents nowadays pay any regard to what their children say to them. The old-fashioned respect for the young is fast dying out. Whatever influence I ever had over mamma, I lost at the age of three. But although she may prevent us from becoming man and wife, and I may marry some one else, and marry often, nothing that she can possibly do can alter my eternal devotion to you.

Jack. Dear Gwendolen!

Gwendolen. The story of your romantic origin, as related to me by mamma, with unpleasing comments, has naturally stirred the deeper fibers of my nature. Your Christian name has an irresistible fascination. The simplicity of your character makes you exquisitely incomprehensible to me. Your town address at the Albany I have. What is your address in the country?

Jack. The Manor House,[27] Woolton, Hertfordshire.

(Algernon, *who has been carefully listening, smiles to himself, and writes the address on his shirt cuff. Then picks up the Railway Guide.*)

Gwendolen. There is a good postal service, I suppose? It may be necessary to do something desperate. That of course will require serious consideration. I will communicate with you daily.

Jack. My own one!

Gwendolen. How long do you remain in town?

27. **Manor House:** In England, a manor house is the principal residence on a lord's estate.

Jack. Till Monday.

Gwendolen. Good! Algy, you may turn round now.

Algernon. Thanks, I've turned round already.

Gwendolen. You may also ring the bell.

Jack. You will let me see you to your carriage, my own darling?

Gwendolen. Certainly.

Jack (*to* Lane, *who now enters*). I will see Miss Fairfax out.

Lane. Yes, sir. (Jack *and* Gwendolen *go off.*)

(Lane *presents several letters on a salver to* Algernon. *It is to be surmised that they are bills, as* Algernon, *after looking at the envelopes, tears them up.*)

Algernon. A glass of sherry, Lane.

Lane. Yes, sir.

Algernon. Tomorrow, Lane, I'm going Bunburying.

Lane. Yes, sir.

Algernon. I shall probably not be back till Monday. You can put up my dress clothes, my smoking jacket, and all the Bunbury suits . . .

Lane. Yes, sir. (*handing sherry*)

Algernon. I hope tomorrow will be a fine day, Lane.

Lane. It never is, sir.

Algernon. Lane, you're a perfect pessimist.

Lane. I do my best to give satisfaction, sir.

(*Enter* Jack. Lane *goes off.*)

Jack. There's a sensible, intellectual girl! the only girl I ever cared for in my life. (Algernon *is laughing immoderately.*) What on earth are you so amused at?

Algernon. Oh, I'm a little anxious about poor Bunbury, that is all.

Jack. If you don't take care, your friend Bunbury will get you into a serious scrape some day.

Algernon. I love scrapes. They are the only things that are never serious.

Jack. Oh, that's nonsense, Algy. You never talk anything but nonsense.

Algernon. Nobody ever does.

(Jack *looks indignantly at him, and leaves the room.* Algernon *lights a cigarette, reads his shirt cuff, and smiles.*)

Act Drop

Second Act

Scene:

Garden at the Manor House. A flight of grey stone steps leads up to the house. The garden, an old-fashioned one, full of roses. Time of year, July. Basket chairs, and a table covered with books, are set under a large yew-tree. (Miss Prism *discovered seated at the table.* Cecily *is at the back watering flowers.*)

Miss Prism (*calling*). Cecily, Cecily! Surely such a utilitarian occupation as the watering of flowers is rather Moulton's duty than yours? Especially at a moment when intellectual pleasures await you. Your German grammar is on the table. Pray open it at page fifteen. We will repeat yesterday's lesson.

Cecily (*coming over very slowly*). But I don't like German. It isn't at all a becoming language. I know perfectly well that I look quite plain after my German lesson.

Miss Prism. Child, you know how anxious your guardian is that you should improve yourself in every way. He laid particular stress on your

WORDS TO KNOW

utilitarian (yo͞o-tĭl′ĭ-târ′ē-ən) *adj.* stressing usefulness over beauty or truth; practical

German, as he was leaving for town yesterday. Indeed, he always lays stress on your German when he is leaving for town.

Cecily. Dear Uncle Jack is so very serious! Sometimes he is so serious that I think he cannot be quite well.

Miss Prism (*drawing herself up*). Your guardian enjoys the best of health, and his gravity of demeanor is especially to be commended in one so comparatively young as he is. I know no one who has a higher sense of duty and responsibility.

Cecily. I suppose that is why he often looks a little bored when we three are together.

Miss Prism. Cecily! I am surprised at you. Mr. Worthing has many troubles in his life. Idle merriment and triviality would be out of place in his conversation. You must remember his constant anxiety about that unfortunate young man his brother.

Cecily. I wish Uncle Jack would allow that unfortunate young man, his brother, to come down here sometimes. We might have a good influence over him, Miss Prism. I am sure you certainly would. You know German, and geology, and things of that kind influence a man very much. (Cecily *begins to write in her diary.*)

Miss Prism (*shaking her head*). I do not think that even I could produce any effect on a character that according to his own brother's admission is irretrievably weak and vacillating. Indeed I am not sure that I would desire to reclaim him. I am not in favor of this modern mania for turning bad people into good people at a moment's notice. As a man sows so let him reap. You must put away your diary, Cecily. I really don't see why you should keep a diary at all.

Cecily. I keep a diary in order to enter the wonderful secrets of my life. If I didn't write them down, I should probably forget all about them.

Miss Prism. Memory, my dear Cecily, is the diary that we all carry about with us.

Cecily. Yes, but it usually chronicles the things that have never happened, and couldn't possibly have happened. I believe that Memory is responsible for nearly all the three-volume novels that Mudie[28] sends us.

Miss Prism. Do not speak slightingly of the three-volume novel, Cecily. I wrote one myself in earlier days.

Cecily. Did you really, Miss Prism? How wonderfully clever you are! I hope it did not end happily? I don't like novels that end happily. They depress me so much.

Miss Prism. The good ended happily, and the bad unhappily. That is what Fiction means.

Cecily. I suppose so. But it seems very unfair. And was your novel ever published?

Miss Prism. Alas! no. The manuscript unfortunately was abandoned. (Cecily *starts.*) I use the word in the sense of lost or mislaid. To your work, child, these speculations are profitless.

Cecily (*smiling*). But I see dear Dr. Chasuble coming up through the garden.

Miss Prism (*rising and advancing*). Dr. Chasuble! This is indeed a pleasure.

(*Enter* Canon Chasuble.)

Chasuble. And how are we this morning? Miss Prism, you are, I trust, well?

Cecily. Miss Prism has just been complaining of a slight headache. I think it would do her so much good to have a short stroll with you in the park, Dr. Chasuble.

Miss Prism. Cecily, I have not mentioned anything about a headache.

Cecily. No, dear Miss Prism, I know that, but I felt instinctively that you had a headache. Indeed I

28. **Mudie** (mo͞o′dē): Mudie's Lending Library in London.

WORDS TO KNOW

demeanor (dĭ-mē′nər) *n.* the way in which a person behaves

vacillating (văs′ə-lā′tĭng) *adj.* swinging from one course of action or opinion to another; indecisive **vacillate** *v.*

was thinking about that, and not about my German lesson, when the Rector[29] came in.

Chasuble. I hope, Cecily, you are not inattentive.

Cecily. Oh, I am afraid I am.

Chasuble. That is strange. Were I fortunate enough to be Miss Prism's pupil, I would hang upon her lips. (Miss Prism *glares.*) I spoke metaphorically.—My metaphor was drawn from bees. Ahem! Mr. Worthing, I suppose, has not returned from town yet?

Miss Prism. We do not expect him till Monday afternoon.

Chasuble. Ah yes, he usually likes to spend his Sunday in London. He is not one of those whose sole aim is enjoyment, as, by all accounts, that unfortunate young man his brother seems to be. But I must not disturb Egeria[30] and her pupil any longer.

Miss Prism. Egeria? My name is Laetitia,[31] Doctor.

Chasuble (*bowing*). A classical allusion merely, drawn from the Pagan[32] authors. I shall see you both no doubt at Evensong?[33]

Miss Prism. I think, dear Doctor, I will have a stroll with you. I find I have a headache after all, and a walk might do it good.

Chasuble. With pleasure, Miss Prism, with pleasure. We might go as far as the schools and back.

Miss Prism. That would be delightful. Cecily, you will read your Political Economy in my absence. The chapter on the fall of the Rupee[34] you may omit. It is somewhat too sensational. Even these metallic problems have their melodramatic side. (*goes down the garden with* Dr. Chasuble)

Cecily (*picks up books and throws them back on table*). Horrid Political Economy! Horrid Geography! Horrid, horrid German!

(*Enter* Merriman *with a card on a salver.*)

Merriman. Mr. Ernest Worthing has just driven over from the station. He has brought his luggage with him.

Cecily (*takes the card and reads it*). "Mr. Ernest Worthing, B. 4, The Albany, W." Uncle Jack's brother! Did you tell him Mr. Worthing was in town?

Merriman. Yes, Miss. He seemed very much disappointed. I mentioned that you and Miss Prism were in the garden. He said he was anxious to speak to you privately for a moment.

Cecily. Ask Mr. Ernest Worthing to come here. I suppose you had better talk to the housekeeper about a room for him.

Merriman. Yes, Miss.

(Merriman *goes off.*)

Cecily. I have never met any really wicked person before. I feel rather frightened. I am so afraid he will look just like every one else.

(*Enter* Algernon, *very gay and debonair.*)

He does!

Algernon (*raising his hat*). You are my little cousin[35] Cecily, I'm sure.

Cecily. You are under some strange mistake. I am not little. In fact, I believe I am more than usually tall for my age. (Algernon *is rather taken aback.*) But I am your cousin Cecily. You, I see from your card, are Uncle Jack's brother, my cousin Ernest, my wicked cousin Ernest.

Algernon. Oh! I am not really wicked at all, cousin Cecily. You mustn't think that I am wicked.

Cecily. If you are not, then you have certainly been deceiving us all in a very inexcusable manner. I hope you have not been leading a double

---

29. **Rector:** in the Church of England, a priest in charge of a parish church.
30. **Egeria** (ĭ-jîr′ē-ə): in Roman legend, a goddess who acted as adviser to a king; hence, any female adviser.
31. **Laetitia** (lĭ-tĭsh′ə).
32. **Pagan:** non-Christian.
33. **Evensong:** in the Church of England, a daily evening prayer service.
34. **the fall of the Rupee** (ro͞o′pē): the decline in the value of the primary monetary unit of India.
35. **cousin:** here used in the general sense of "relative."

life, pretending to be wicked and being really good all the time. That would be hypocrisy.

Algernon (*looks at her in amazement*). Oh! Of course I have been rather reckless.

Cecily. I am glad to hear it.

Algernon. In fact, now you mention the subject, I have been very bad in my own small way.

Cecily. I don't think you should be so proud of that, though I am sure it must have been very pleasant.

Algernon. It is much pleasanter being here with you.

Cecily. I can't understand how you are here at all. Uncle Jack won't be back till Monday afternoon.

Algernon. That is a great disappointment. I am obliged to go up by the first train on Monday morning. I have a business appointment that I am anxious . . . to miss?

Cecily. Couldn't you miss it anywhere but in London?

Algernon. No: the appointment is in London.

Cecily. Well, I know, of course, how important it is not to keep a business engagement, if one wants to retain any sense of the beauty of life, but still I think you had better wait till Uncle Jack arrives. I know he wants to speak to you about your emigrating.

Algernon. About my what?

Cecily. Your emigrating. He has gone up to buy your outfit.

Algernon. I certainly wouldn't let Jack buy my outfit. He has no taste in neckties at all.

Cecily. I don't think you will require neckties. Uncle Jack is sending you to Australia.

Algernon. Australia! I'd sooner die.

Cecily. Well, he said at dinner on Wednesday night, that you would have to choose between this world, the next world, and Australia.

Algernon. Oh, well! The accounts I have received of Australia and the next world, are not particularly encouraging. This world is good enough for me, cousin Cecily.

Cecily. Yes, but are you good enough for it?

Algernon. I'm afraid I'm not that. That is why I want you to reform me. You might make that your mission, if you don't mind, cousin Cecily.

Cecily. I'm afraid I've no time, this afternoon.

Algernon. Well, would you mind my reforming myself this afternoon?

Cecily. It is rather Quixotic[36] of you. But I think you should try.

Algernon. I will. I feel better already.

Cecily. You are looking a little worse.

Algernon. That is because I am hungry.

Cecily. How thoughtless of me. I should have remembered that when one is going to lead an entirely new life, one requires regular and wholesome meals. Won't you come in?

Algernon. Thank you. Might I have a buttonhole[37] first? I never have any appetite unless I have a buttonhole first.

Cecily. A Maréchal Niel?[38] (*picks up scissors*)

Algernon. No, I'd sooner have a pink rose.

Cecily. Why? (*cuts a flower*)

Algernon. Because you are like a pink rose, cousin Cecily.

Cecily. I don't think it can be right for you to talk to me like that. Miss Prism never says such things to me.

Algernon. Then Miss Prism is a shortsighted old lady. (Cecily *puts the rose in his buttonhole.*) You are the prettiest girl I ever saw.

Cecily. Miss Prism says that all good looks are a snare.

---

36. **Quixotic** (kwĭk-sŏt′ĭk): idealistic but impractical—from the name of Don Quixote (kē-hō′tē), a character in a Spanish novel who was led into absurd adventures in his effort to perform noble deeds and pursue unreachable goals.

37. **buttonhole:** a flower to wear in a jacket buttonhole.

38. **Maréchal Niel** (mä-rā-shäl′ nyĕl′): a variety of yellow climbing rose.

Algernon. They are a snare that every sensible man would like to be caught in.

Cecily. Oh, I don't think I would care to catch a sensible man. I shouldn't know what to talk to him about.

(*They pass into the house.* Miss Prism *and* Dr. Chasuble *return.*)

Miss Prism. You are too much alone, dear Dr. Chasuble. You should get married. A misanthrope I can understand—a womanthrope,[39] never!

Chasuble (*with a scholar's shudder*). Believe me, I do not deserve so neologistic[40] a phrase. The precept as well as the practice of the Primitive Church was distinctly against matrimony.[41]

Miss Prism (*sententiously*). That is obviously the reason why the Primitive Church has not lasted up to the present day. And you do not seem to realize, dear Doctor, that by persistently remaining single, a man converts himself into a permanent public temptation. Men should be more careful; this very celibacy[42] leads weaker vessels astray.

Chasuble. But is a man not equally attractive when married?

Miss Prism. No married man is ever attractive except to his wife.

Chasuble. And often, I've been told, not even to her.

Miss Prism. That depends on the intellectual sympathies of the woman. Maturity can always be depended on. Ripeness can be trusted. Young women are green. (Dr. Chasuble *starts.*) I spoke horticulturally. My metaphor was drawn from fruit. But where is Cecily?

Chasuble. Perhaps she followed us to the schools.

(*Enter* Jack *slowly from the back of the garden. He is dressed in the deepest mourning, with crepe hatband and black gloves.*)

Miss Prism. Mr. Worthing!

Chasuble. Mr. Worthing?

Miss Prism. This is indeed a surprise. We did not look for you till Monday afternoon.

Jack (*shakes* Miss Prism's *hand in a tragic manner*). I have returned sooner than I expected. Dr. Chasuble, I hope you are well?

Chasuble. Dear Mr. Worthing, I trust this garb of woe does not betoken some terrible calamity?

Jack. My brother.

Miss Prism. More shameful debts and extravagance?

Chasuble. Still leading his life of pleasure?

Jack (*shaking his head*). Dead!

Chasuble. Your brother Ernest dead?

Jack. Quite dead.

Miss Prism. What a lesson for him! I trust he will profit by it.

Chasuble. Mr. Worthing, I offer you my sincere condolence. You have at least the consolation of knowing that you were always the most generous and forgiving of brothers.

Jack. Poor Ernest! He had many faults, but it is a sad, sad blow.

Chasuble. Very sad indeed. Were you with him at the end?

Jack. No. He died abroad; in Paris, in fact. I had a telegram last night from the manager of the Grand Hotel.

Chasuble. Was the cause of death mentioned?

Jack. A severe chill, it seems.

Miss Prism. As a man sows, so shall he reap.

Chasuble (*raising his hand*). Charity, dear Miss Prism, charity! None of us are perfect. I myself

---

39. **misanthrope** (mĭs′ən-thrōp′) . . . **womanthrope:** A misanthrope is a person who hates or mistrusts mankind. A person who hates or mistrusts women is called a misogynist (mĭ-sŏj′ə-nĭst). *Womanthrope* is an invented word of Miss Prism's.

40. **neologistic** (nē-ŏl′ə-jĭs′tĭk): relating to a newly created word or expression.

41. **The precept . . . matrimony:** Both the principles and the practice of early Christians discouraged the marriage of priests.

42. **celibacy** (sĕl′ə-bə-sē): the condition of being unmarried.

am peculiarly susceptible to drafts. Will the interment[43] take place here?

Jack. No. He seems to have expressed a desire to be buried in Paris.

Chasuble. In Paris! (*shakes his head*) I fear that hardly points to any very serious state of mind at the last. You would no doubt wish me to make some slight allusion to this tragic domestic affliction next Sunday. (Jack *presses his hand convulsively.*) My sermon on the meaning of the manna in the wilderness[44] can be adapted to almost any occasion, joyful, or, as in the present case, distressing. (*All sigh.*) I have preached it at harvest celebrations, christenings, confirmations, on days of humiliation and festal days. The last time I delivered it was in the Cathedral, as a charity sermon on behalf of the Society for the Prevention of Discontent among the Upper Orders. The Bishop, who was present, was much struck by some of the analogies I drew.

Jack. Ah! that reminds me, you mentioned christenings I think, Dr. Chasuble? I suppose you know how to christen all right? (Dr. Chasuble *looks astounded.*) I mean, of course, you are continually christening, aren't you?

Miss Prism. It is, I regret to say, one of the Rector's most constant duties in this parish. I have often spoken to the poorer classes on the subject. But they don't seem to know what thrift is.

Chasuble. But is there any particular infant in whom you are interested, Mr. Worthing? Your brother was, I believe, unmarried, was he not?

Jack. Oh yes.

Miss Prism (*bitterly*). People who live entirely for pleasure usually are.

Jack. But it is not for any child, dear Doctor. I am very fond of children. No! the fact is, I would like to be christened myself, this afternoon, if you have nothing better to do.

Chasuble. But surely, Mr. Worthing, you have been christened already?

Jack. I don't remember anything about it.

Chasuble. But have you any grave doubts on the subject?

Jack. I certainly intend to have. Of course I don't know if the thing would bother you in any way, or if you think I am a little too old now.

Chasuble. Not at all. The sprinkling, and, indeed, the immersion[45] of adults is a perfectly canonical practice.

Jack. Immersion!

Chasuble. You need have no apprehensions. Sprinkling is all that is necessary, or indeed I think advisable. Our weather is so changeable. At what hour would you wish the ceremony performed?

Jack. Oh, I might trot round about five if that would suit you.

Chasuble. Perfectly, perfectly! In fact I have two similar ceremonies to perform at that time. A case of twins that occurred recently in one of the outlying cottages on your own estate. Poor Jenkins the carter,[46] a most hard-working man.

Jack. Oh! I don't see much fun in being christened along with other babies. It would be childish. Would half-past five do?

Chasuble. Admirably! Admirably! (*takes out watch*) And now, dear Mr. Worthing, I will not intrude any longer into a house of sorrow. I would merely beg you not to be too much bowed down by grief. What seem to us bitter trials are often blessings in disguise.

Miss Prism. This seems to me a blessing of an extremely obvious kind.

---

43. **interment** (ĭn-tûr′mənt): burial.

44. **manna in the wilderness:** in the Old Testament, the food miraculously provided for the Israelites during their flight from Egypt.

45. **sprinkling . . . immersion:** In the Church of England, the christening ceremony includes baptism, which may be performed either by sprinkling water on the head or by submerging the whole body in water.

46. **carter:** one whose job it is to transport goods in a horse-drawn cart.

(*Enter* Cecily *from the house.*)

Cecily. Uncle Jack! Oh, I am pleased to see you back. But what horrid clothes you have got on! Do go and change them.

Miss Prism. Cecily!

Chasuble. My child! my child! (Cecily *goes towards* Jack; *he kisses her brow in a melancholy manner.*)

Cecily. What is the matter, Uncle Jack? Do look happy! You look as if you had toothache, and I have got such a surprise for you. Who do you think is in the dining-room? Your brother!

Jack. Who?

Cecily. Your brother Ernest. He arrived about half an hour ago.

Jack. What nonsense! I haven't got a brother.

Cecily. Oh, don't say that. However badly he may have behaved to you in the past he is still your brother. You couldn't be so heartless as to disown him. I'll tell him to come out. And you will shake hands with him, won't you, Uncle Jack? (*runs back into the house*)

Chasuble. These are very joyful tidings.

Miss Prism. After we had all been resigned to his loss, his sudden return seems to me peculiarly distressing.

Jack. My brother is in the dining-room? I don't know what it all means. I think it is perfectly absurd.

(*Enter* Algernon *and* Cecily *hand in hand. They come slowly up to* Jack.)

Jack. Good Heavens! (*motions* Algernon *away*)

Algernon. Brother John, I have come down from town to tell you that I am very sorry for all the trouble I have given you, and that I intend to lead a better life in the future. (Jack *glares at him and does not take his hand.*)

Cecily. Uncle Jack, you are not going to refuse your own brother's hand?

Jack. Nothing will induce me to take his hand. I think his coming down here disgraceful. He knows perfectly well why.

Cecily. Uncle Jack, do be nice. There is some good in every one. Ernest has just been telling me about his poor invalid friend Mr. Bunbury whom he goes to visit so often. And surely there must be much good in one who is kind to an invalid, and leaves the pleasures of London to sit by a bed of pain.

Jack. Oh! he has been talking about Bunbury, has he?

Cecily. Yes, he has told me all about poor Mr. Bunbury, and his terrible state of health.

Jack. Bunbury! Well, I won't have him talk to you about Bunbury or about anything else. It is enough to drive one perfectly frantic.

Algernon. Of course I admit that the faults were all on my side. But I must say I think that Brother John's coldness to me is peculiarly painful. I expected a more enthusiastic welcome, especially considering it is the first time I have come here.

Cecily. Uncle Jack, if you don't shake hands with Ernest I will never forgive you.

Jack. Never forgive me?

Cecily. Never, never, never!

Jack. Well, this is the last time I shall ever do it. (*shakes hands with* Algernon *and glares*)

Chasuble. It's pleasant, is it not, to see so perfect a reconciliation?[47] I think we might leave the two brothers together.

Miss Prism. Cecily, you will come with us.

Cecily. Certainly, Miss Prism. My little task of reconciliation is over.

Chasuble. You have done a beautiful action today, dear child.

Miss Prism. We must not be premature in our judgments.

Cecily. I feel very happy. (*They all go off except* Jack *and* Algernon.)

---

47. **reconciliation:** the restoring of a close relationship.

Jack. You young scoundrel, Algy, you must get out of this place as soon as possible. I don't allow any Bunburying here.

(*Enter* Merriman.)

Merriman. I have put Mr. Ernest's things in the room next to yours, sir. I suppose that is all right?

Jack. What?

Merriman. Mr. Ernest's luggage, sir. I have unpacked it and put it in the room next to your own.

Jack. His luggage?

Merriman. Yes, sir. Three portmanteaus,[48] a dressing case, two hat boxes, and a large luncheon basket.

Algernon. I am afraid I can't stay more than a week this time.

Jack. Merriman, order the dog cart at once. Mr. Ernest has been suddenly called back to town.

Merriman. Yes, sir. (*goes back into the house*)

Algernon. What a fearful liar you are, Jack. I have not been called back to town at all.

Jack. Yes, you have.

Algernon. I haven't heard any one call me.

Jack. Your duty as a gentleman calls you back.

Algernon. My duty as a gentleman has never interfered with my pleasures in the smallest degree.

Jack. I can quite understand that.

Algernon. Well, Cecily is a darling.

Jack. You are not to talk of Miss Cardew like that. I don't like it.

Algernon. Well, I don't like your clothes. You look perfectly ridiculous in them. Why on earth don't you go up and change? It is perfectly childish to be in deep mourning for a man who is actually staying for a whole week with you in your house as a guest. I call it grotesque.

Jack. You are certainly not staying with me for a whole week as a guest or anything else. You have got to leave . . . by the four-five train.

Algernon. I certainly won't leave you as long as you are in mourning. It would be most unfriendly. If I were in mourning you would stay with me, I suppose. I should think it very unkind if you didn't.

Jack. Well, will you go if I change my clothes?

Algernon. Yes, if you are not too long. I never saw anybody take so long to dress, and with such little result.

Jack. Well, at any rate, that is better than being always overdressed as you are.

Algernon. If I am occasionally a little overdressed, I make up for it by being always immensely overeducated.

Jack. Your vanity is ridiculous, your conduct an outrage, and your presence in my garden utterly absurd. However, you have got to catch the four-five, and I hope you will have a pleasant journey back to town. This Bunburying, as you call it, has not been a great success for you. (*goes into the house*)

Algernon. I think it has been a great success. I'm in love with Cecily, and that is everything.

(*Enter* Cecily *at the back of the garden. She picks up the can and begins to water the flowers.*)

But I must see her before I go, and make arrangements for another Bunbury. Ah, there she is.

Cecily. Oh, I merely came back to water the roses. I thought you were with Uncle Jack.

Algernon. He's gone to order the dog cart for me.

Cecily. Oh, is he going to take you for a nice drive?

Algernon. He's going to send me away.

Cecily. Then have we got to part?

Algernon. I am afraid so. It's a very painful parting.

Cecily. It is always painful to part from people whom one has known for a very brief space of time. The absence of old friends one can endure

48. **portmanteaus** (pôrt-măn′tōz): large leather suitcases.

with equanimity. But even a momentary separation from any one to whom one has just been introduced is almost unbearable.

Algernon. Thank you.

(*Enter* Merriman.)

Merriman. The dog cart is at the door, sir. (Algernon *looks appealingly at* Cecily.)

Cecily. It can wait, Merriman . . . for . . . five minutes.

Merriman. Yes, Miss.

(*Exit* Merriman.)

Algernon. I hope, Cecily, I shall not offend you if I state quite frankly and openly that you seem to me to be in every way the visible personification of absolute perfection.

Cecily. I think your frankness does you great credit, Ernest. If you will allow me, I will copy your remarks into my diary. (*goes over to table and begins writing in diary*)

Algernon. Do you really keep a diary? I'd give anything to look at it. May I?

Cecily. Oh no. (*puts her hand over it*) You see, it is simply a very young girl's record of her own thoughts and impressions, and consequently meant for publication. When it appears in volume form I hope you will order a copy. But pray, Ernest, don't stop. I delight in taking down from dictation. I have reached "absolute perfection." You can go on. I am quite ready for more.

Algernon (*somewhat taken aback*). Ahem! Ahem!

Cecily. Oh, don't cough, Ernest. When one is dictating one should speak fluently and not cough. Besides, I don't know how to spell a cough. (*writes as* Algernon *speaks*)

Algernon (*speaking very rapidly*). Cecily, ever since I first looked upon your wonderful and incomparable beauty, I have dared to love you wildly, passionately, devotedly, hopelessly.

Cecily. I don't think that you should tell me that you love me wildly, passionately, devotedly, hopelessly. Hopelessly doesn't seem to make much sense, does it?

Algernon. Cecily!

(*Enter* Merriman.)

Merriman. The dog cart is waiting, sir.

Algernon. Tell it to come round next week, at the same hour.

Merriman (*looks at* Cecily, *who makes no sign*). Yes, sir.

(Merriman *retires.*)

Cecily. Uncle Jack would be very much annoyed if he knew you were staying on till next week, at the same hour.

Algernon. Oh, I don't care about Jack. I don't care for anybody in the whole world but you. I love you, Cecily. You will marry me, won't you?

Cecily. You silly boy! Of course. Why, we have been engaged for the last three months.

Algernon. For the last three months?

Cecily. Yes, it will be exactly three months on Thursday.

Algernon. But how did we become engaged?

Cecily. Well, ever since dear Uncle Jack first confessed to us that he had a younger brother who was very wicked and bad, you of course have formed the chief topic of conversation between myself and Miss Prism. And of course a man who is much talked about is always very attractive. One feels there must be something in him, after all. I daresay it was foolish of me, but I fell in love with you, Ernest.

Algernon. Darling. And when was the engagement actually settled?

Cecily. On the 14th of February last. Worn out by your entire ignorance of my existence, I determined to end the matter one way or the other, and after a long struggle with myself I accepted you under this dear old tree here. The next day

WORDS TO KNOW

equanimity (ē'kwə-nĭm'ĭ-tē) *n.* the quality of being calm and even-tempered; self-control

I bought this little ring in your name, and this is the little bangle with the true lover's knot I promised you always to wear.

Algernon. Did I give you this? It's very pretty, isn't it?

Cecily. Yes, you've wonderfully good taste, Ernest. It's the excuse I've always given for your leading such a bad life. And this is the box in which I keep all your dear letters. (*kneels at table, opens box, and produces letters tied up with blue ribbon*)

Algernon. My letters! But, my own sweet Cecily, I have never written you any letters.

Cecily. You need hardly remind me of that, Ernest. I remember only too well that I was forced to write your letters for you. I wrote always three times a week, and sometimes oftener.

Algernon. Oh, do let me read them, Cecily?

Cecily. Oh, I couldn't possibly. They would make you far too conceited. (*replaces box*) The three you wrote me after I had broken off the engagement are so beautiful, and so badly spelled, that even now I can hardly read them without crying a little.

Algernon. But was our engagement ever broken off?

Cecily. Of course it was. On the 22nd of last March. You can see the entry if you like. (*shows diary*) "Today I broke off my engagement with Ernest. I feel it is better to do so. The weather still continues charming."

Algernon. But why on earth did you break it off? What had I done? I had done nothing at all. Cecily, I am very much hurt indeed to hear you broke it off. Particularly when the weather was so charming.

Cecily. It would hardly have been a really serious engagement if it hadn't been broken off at least once. But I forgave you before the week was out.

Algernon (*crossing to her, and kneeling*). What a perfect angel you are, Cecily.

Cecily. You dear romantic boy. (*He kisses her, she puts her fingers through his hair.*) I hope your hair curls naturally, does it?

Algernon. Yes, darling, with a little help from others.

Cecily. I am so glad.

Algernon. You'll never break off our engagement again Cecily?

Cecily. I don't think I could break it off now that I have actually met you. Besides, of course, there is the question of your name.

Algernon. Yes, of course. (*nervously*)

Cecily. You must not laugh at me, darling, but it had always been a girlish dream of mine to love some one whose name was Ernest. (Algernon *rises,* Cecily *also.*) There is something in that

name that seems to inspire absolute confidence. I pity any poor married woman whose husband is not called Ernest.

Algernon. But, my dear child, do you mean to say you could not love me if I had some other name?

Cecily. But what name?

Algernon. Oh, any name you like—Algernon—for instance . . .

Cecily. But I don't like the name of Algernon.

Algernon. Well, my own dear, sweet, loving little darling, I really can't see why you should object to the name of Algernon. It is not at all a bad name. In fact, it is rather an aristocratic name. Half of the chaps who get into the Bankruptcy Court are called Algernon. But seriously, Cecily . . . (*moving to her*) . . . if my name was Algy, couldn't you love me?

Cecily (*rising*). I might respect you, Ernest, I might admire your character, but I fear that I should not be able to give you my undivided attention.

Algernon. Ahem! Cecily! (*picking up hat*) Your Rector here is, I suppose, thoroughly experienced in the practice of all the rites and ceremonials of the Church?

Cecily. Oh, yes. Dr. Chasuble is a most learned man. He has never written a single book, so you can imagine how much he knows.

Algernon. I must see him at once on a most important christening—I mean on most important business.

Cecily. Oh!

Algernon. I shan't be away more than half an hour.

Cecily. Considering that we have been engaged since February the 14th, and that I only met you today for the first time, I think it is rather hard that you should leave me for so long a period as half an hour. Couldn't you make it twenty minutes?

Algernon. I'll be back in no time. (*kisses her and rushes down the garden*)

Cecily. What an impetuous boy he is! I like his hair so much. I must enter his proposal in my diary.

(*Enter* Merriman.)

Merriman. A Miss Fairfax has just called to see Mr. Worthing. On very important business, Miss Fairfax states.

Cecily. Isn't Mr. Worthing in his library?

Merriman. Mr. Worthing went over in the direction of the Rectory some time ago.

Cecily. Pray ask the lady to come out here; Mr. Worthing is sure to be back soon. And you can bring tea.

Merriman. Yes, Miss. (*goes out*)

Cecily. Miss Fairfax! I suppose one of the many good elderly women who are associated with Uncle Jack in some of his philanthropic[49] work in London. I don't quite like women who are interested in philanthropic work. I think it is so forward of them.

(*Enter* Merriman.)

Merriman. Miss Fairfax.

(*Enter* Gwendolen.)

(*Exit* Merriman.)

Cecily (*advancing to meet her*). Pray let me introduce myself to you. My name is Cecily Cardew.

Gwendolen. Cecily Cardew? (*moving to her and shaking hands*) What a very sweet name! Something tells me that we are going to be great friends. I like you already more than I can say. My first impressions of people are never wrong.

Cecily. How nice of you to like me so much after we have known each other such a comparatively short time. Pray sit down.

49. **philanthropic** (fĭl′ən-thrŏp′ĭk): charitable.

WORDS TO KNOW

impetuous (ĭm-pĕch′o͞o-əs) *adj.* characterized by sudden and forceful energy or emotion; impulsive

Gwendolen (*still standing up*). I may call you Cecily, may I not?

Cecily. With pleasure!

Gwendolen. And you will always call me Gwendolen won't you?

Cecily. If you wish.

Gwendolen. Then that is all quite settled, is it not?

Cecily. I hope so. (*A pause. They both sit down together.*)

Gwendolen. Perhaps this might be a favorable opportunity for my mentioning who I am. My father is Lord Bracknell. You have never heard of papa, I suppose?

Cecily. I don't think so.

Gwendolen. Outside the family circle, papa, I am glad to say, is entirely unknown. I think that is quite as it should be. The home seems to me to be the proper sphere for the man. And certainly once a man begins to neglect his domestic duties he becomes painfully effeminate,[50] does he not? And I don't like that. It makes men so very attractive. Cecily, mamma, whose views on education are remarkably strict, has brought me up to be extremely shortsighted; it is part of her system; so do you mind my looking at you through my glasses?

Cecily. Oh! not at all, Gwendolen. I am very fond of being looked at.

Gwendolen (*after examining* Cecily *carefully through a lorgnette*[51]). You are here on a short visit, I suppose.

Cecily. Oh no! I live here.

Gwendolen (*severely*). Really? Your mother, no doubt, or some female relative of advanced years, resides here also?

Cecily. Oh no! I have no mother, nor, in fact, any relations.

Gwendolen. Indeed?

Cecily. My dear guardian, with the assistance of Miss Prism, has the arduous task of looking after me.

Gwendolen. Your guardian?

Cecily. Yes, I am Mr. Worthing's ward.

Gwendolen. Oh! It is strange he never mentioned to me that he had a ward. How secretive of him! He grows more interesting hourly. I am not sure, however, that the news inspires me with feelings of unmixed delight. (*rising and going to her*) I am very fond of you, Cecily; I have liked you ever since I met you! But I am bound to state that now that I know that you are Mr. Worthing's ward, I cannot help expressing a wish you were—well, just a little older than you seem to be—and not quite so very alluring in appearance. In fact, if I may speak candidly—

Cecily. Pray do! I think that whenever one has anything unpleasant to say, one should always be quite candid.

Gwendolen. Well, to speak with perfect candor, Cecily, I wish that you were fully forty-two, and more than usually plain for your age. Ernest has a strong upright nature. He is the very soul of truth and honor. Disloyalty would be as impossible to him as deception. But even men of the noblest possible moral character are extremely susceptible to the influence of the physical charms of others. Modern, no less than Ancient History, supplies us with many most painful examples of what I refer to. If it were not so, indeed, History would be quite unreadable.

Cecily. I beg your pardon, Gwendolen, did you say Ernest?

Gwendolen. Yes.

Cecily. Oh, but it is not Mr. Ernest Worthing who is my guardian. It is his brother—his elder brother.

---

50. **effeminate** (ĭ-fĕm′ə-nĭt): feminine; lacking in manliness.

51. **lorgnette** (lôrn-yĕt′): a pair of eyeglasses with a short handle.

WORDS TO KNOW

arduous (är′jo͞o-əs) *adj.* demanding great effort or labor; difficult

Gwendolen (*sitting down again*). Ernest never mentioned to me that he had a brother.

Cecily. I am sorry to say they have not been on good terms for a long time.

Gwendolen. Ah! that accounts for it. And now that I think of it I have never heard any man mention his brother. The subject seems distasteful to most men. Cecily, you have lifted a load from my mind. I was growing almost anxious. It would have been terrible if any cloud had come across a friendship like ours, would it not? Of course you are quite, quite sure that it is not Mr. Ernest Worthing who is your guardian?

Cecily. Quite sure. (*a pause*) In fact, I am going to be his.

Gwendolen (*inquiringly*). I beg your pardon?

Cecily (*rather shy and confidingly*). Dearest Gwendolen, there is no reason why I should make a secret of it to you. Our little country newspaper is sure to chronicle the fact next week. Mr. Ernest Worthing and I are engaged to be married.

Gwendolen (*quite politely, rising*). My darling Cecily, I think there must be some slight error. Mr. Ernest Worthing is engaged to me. The announcement will appear in the *Morning Post* on Saturday at the latest.

Cecily (*very politely, rising*). I am afraid you must be under some misconception. Ernest proposed to me exactly ten minutes ago. (*shows diary*)

Gwendolen (*examines diary through her lorgnette carefully*). It is certainly very curious, for he asked me to be his wife yesterday afternoon at 5:30. If you would care to verify the incident, pray do so. (*produces diary of her own*) I never travel without my diary. One should always have something sensational to read in the train. I am so sorry, dear Cecily, if it is any disappointment to you, but I am afraid I have the prior claim.

Cecily. It would distress me more than I can tell you, dear Gwendolen, if it caused you any mental or physical anguish, but I feel bound to point out that since Ernest proposed to you he clearly has changed his mind.

Gwendolen (*meditatively*). If the poor fellow has been entrapped into any foolish promise I shall consider it my duty to rescue him at once, and with a firm hand.

Cecily (*thoughtfully and sadly*). Whatever unfortunate entanglement my dear boy may have got into, I will never reproach him with it after we are married.

Gwendolen. Do you allude to me, Miss Cardew, as an entanglement? You are presumptuous. On an occasion of this kind it becomes more than a moral duty to speak one's mind. It becomes a pleasure.

Cecily. Do you suggest, Miss Fairfax, that I entrapped Ernest into an engagement? How dare you? This is no time for wearing the shallow mask of manner. When I see a spade I call it a spade.

Gwendolen (*satirically*). I am glad to say that I have never seen a spade. It is obvious that our social spheres have been widely different.

(*Enter* Merriman, *followed by the footman. He carries a salver, tablecloth, and plate stand.* Cecily *is about to retort. The presence of the servants exercises a restraining influence, under which both girls chafe.*)

Merriman. Shall I lay tea here as usual, Miss?

Cecily (*sternly, in a calm voice*). Yes, as usual. (Merriman *begins to clear table and lay cloth. A long pause.* Cecily *and* Gwendolen *glare at each other.*)

Gwendolen. Are there many interesting walks in the vicinity, Miss Cardew?

Cecily. Oh! yes! a great many. From the top of one of the hills quite close one can see five counties.

WORDS TO KNOW

misconception (mĭs'kən-sĕp'shən) *n.* a mistaken idea or notion; misunderstanding

Gwendolen. Five counties! I don't think I should like that; I hate crowds.

Cecily (*sweetly*). I suppose that is why you live in town? (Gwendolen *bites her lip, and beats her foot nervously with her parasol.*)

Gwendolen (*looking round*). Quite a well-kept garden this is, Miss Cardew.

Cecily. So glad you like it, Miss Fairfax.

Gwendolen. I had no idea there were any flowers in the country.

Cecily. Oh, flowers are as common here, Miss Fairfax, as people are in London.

Gwendolen. Personally I cannot understand how anybody manages to exist in the country, if anybody who is anybody does. The country always bores me to death.

Cecily. Ah! This is what the newspapers call agricultural depression, is it not? I believe the aristocracy are suffering very much from it just at present. It is almost an epidemic amongst them, I have been told. May I offer you some tea, Miss Fairfax?

Gwendolen (*with elaborate politeness*). Thank you. (*aside*) Detestable girl. But I require tea!

Cecily (*sweetly*). Sugar?

Gwendolen (*superciliously*). No, thank you. Sugar is not fashionable any more. (Cecily *looks angrily at her, takes up the tongs and puts four lumps of sugar into the cup.*)

Cecily (*severely*). Cake or bread and butter?

Gwendolen (*in a bored manner*). Bread and butter, please. Cake is rarely seen at the best houses nowadays.

Cecily (*cuts a very large slice of cake, and puts it on the tray*). Hand that to Miss Fairfax.

(Merriman *does so, and goes out with footman.* Gwendolen *drinks the tea and makes a grimace. Puts down cup at once, reaches out her hand to the bread and butter, looks at it, and finds it is cake. Rises in indignation.*)

Gwendolen. You have filled my tea with lumps of sugar, and though I asked most distinctly for bread and butter, you have given me cake. I am known for the gentleness of my disposition, and the extraordinary sweetness of my nature, but I warn you, Miss Cardew, you may go too far.

Cecily (*rising*). To save my poor, innocent, trusting boy from the machinations of any other girl there are no lengths to which I would not go.

Gwendolen. From the moment I saw you I distrusted you. I felt that you were false and deceitful. I am never deceived in such matters. My first impressions of people are invariably right.

Cecily. It seems to me, Miss Fairfax, that I am trespassing on your valuable time. No doubt you have many other calls of a similar character to make in the neighborhood.

(*Enter* Jack.)

Gwendolen (*catching sight of him*). Ernest! My own Ernest!

Jack. Gwendolen! Darling! (*offers to kiss her*)

Gwendolen (*drawing back*). A moment! May I ask if you are engaged to be married to this young lady? (*points to* Cecily)

Jack (*laughing*). To dear little Cecily! Of course not! What could have put such an idea into your pretty little head?

Gwendolen. Thank you. You may! (*offers her cheek*)

Cecily (*very sweetly*). I knew there must be some misunderstanding, Miss Fairfax. The gentleman whose arm is at present round your waist is my guardian, Mr. John Worthing.

Gwendolen. I beg your pardon?

Cecily. This is Uncle Jack.

Gwendolen (*receding*). Jack! Oh!

(*Enter* Algernon.)

WORDS TO KNOW

superciliously (sōō'pər-sĭl'ē-əs-lē) *adv.* disdainfully; arrogantly

machination (măk'ə-nā'shən) *n.* a crafty scheme or cunning plot, usually for some evil end

Cecily. Here is Ernest.

Algernon (*goes straight over to* Cecily *without noticing any one else*). My own love! (*offers to kiss her*)

Cecily (*drawing back*). A moment, Ernest! May I ask you—are you engaged to be married to this young lady?

Algernon (*looking round*). To what young lady? Good heavens! Gwendolen!

Cecily. Yes! to good heavens, Gwendolen, I mean to Gwendolen.

Algernon (*laughing*). Of course not! What could have put such an idea into your pretty little head?

Cecily. Thank you. (*presenting her cheek to be kissed*) You may. (Algernon *kisses her.*)

Gwendolen. I felt there was some slight error, Miss Cardew. The gentleman who is now embracing you is my cousin, Mr. Algernon Moncrieff.

Cecily (*breaking away from* Algernon). Algernon Moncrieff! Oh! (*The two girls move towards each other and put their arms round each other's waists as if for protection.*)

Cecily. Are you called Algernon?

Algernon. I cannot deny it.

Cecily. Oh!

Gwendolen. Is your name really John?

Jack (*standing rather proudly*). I could deny it if I liked. I could deny anything if I liked. But my name certainly is John. It has been John for years.

Cecily (*to* Gwendolen). A gross deception has been practiced on both of us.

Gwendolen. My poor wounded Cecily!

Cecily. My sweet wronged Gwendolen!

Gwendolen (*slowly and seriously*). You will call me sister, will you not? (*They embrace.* Jack *and* Algernon *groan and walk up and down.*)

Cecily (*rather brightly*). There is just one question I would like to be allowed to ask my guardian.

Gwendolen. An admirable idea! Mr. Worthing, there is just one question I would like to be permitted to put to you. Where is your brother Ernest? We are both engaged to be married to your brother Ernest, so it is a matter of some importance to us to know where your brother Ernest is at present.

Jack (*slowly and hesitatingly*). Gwendolen—Cecily—it is very painful for me to be forced to speak the truth. It is the first time in my life that I have ever been reduced to such a painful position, and I am really quite inexperienced in doing anything of the kind. However, I will tell you quite frankly that I have no brother Ernest. I have no brother at all. I never had a brother in my life, and I certainly have not the smallest intention of ever having one in the future.

Cecily (*surprised*). No brother at all?

Jack (*cheerily*). None!

Gwendolen (*severely*). Had you never a brother of any kind?

Jack (*pleasantly*). Never. Not even of any kind.

Gwendolen. I am afraid it is quite clear, Cecily, that neither of us is engaged to be married to any one.

Cecily. It is not a very pleasant position for a young girl suddenly to find herself in. Is it?

Gwendolen. Let us go into the house. They will hardly venture to come after us there.

Cecily. No, men are so cowardly, aren't they?

(*They retire into the house with scornful looks.*)

Jack. This ghastly state of things is what you call Bunburying, I suppose?

Algernon. Yes, and a perfectly wonderful Bunbury it is. The most wonderful Bunbury I have ever had in my life.

Jack. Well, you've no right whatsoever to Bunbury here.

Algernon. That is absurd. One has a right to Bunbury anywhere one chooses. Every serious Bunburyist knows that.

Jack. Serious Bunburyist! Good heavens!

Algernon. Well, one must be serious about something, if one wants to have any amusement in life. I happen to be serious about Bunburying. What on earth you are serious about I haven't got the remotest idea. About everything, I should fancy. You have such an absolutely trivial nature.

Jack. Well, the only small satisfaction I have in the whole of this wretched business is that your friend Bunbury is quite exploded. You won't be able to run down to the country quite so often as you used to do, dear Algy. And a very good thing too.

Algernon. Your brother is a little off color, isn't he, dear Jack? You won't be able to disappear to London quite so frequently as your wicked custom was. And not a bad thing either.

Jack. As for your conduct towards Miss Cardew, I must say that your taking in a sweet, simple, innocent girl like that is quite inexcusable. To say nothing of the fact that she is my ward.

Algernon. I can see no possible defense at all for your deceiving a brilliant, clever, thoroughly experienced young lady like Miss Fairfax. To say nothing of the fact that she is my cousin.

Jack. I wanted to be engaged to Gwendolen, that is all. I love her.

Algernon. Well, I simply wanted to be engaged to Cecily. I adore her.

Jack. There is certainly no chance of your marrying Miss Cardew.

Algernon. I don't think there is much likelihood, Jack, of you and Miss Fairfax being united.

Jack. Well, that is no business of yours.

Algernon. If it was my business, I wouldn't talk about it. (*begins to eat muffins*) It is very vulgar to talk about one's business. Only people like stockbrokers do that, and then merely at dinner parties.

Jack. How can you sit there, calmly eating muffins when we are in this horrible trouble, I can't make out. You seem to be perfectly heartless.

Algernon. Well, I can't eat muffins in an agitated manner. The butter would probably get on my cuffs. One should always eat muffins quite calmly. It is the only way to eat them.

Jack. I say it's perfectly heartless your eating muffins at all, under the circumstances.

Algernon. When I am in trouble, eating is the only thing that consoles me. Indeed, when I am in really great trouble, as any one who knows me intimately will tell you, I refuse everything except food and drink. At the present moment I am eating muffins because I am unhappy. Besides, I am particularly fond of muffins. (*rising*)

Jack (*rising*). Well, that is no reason why you should eat them all in that greedy way. (*takes muffins from* Algernon)

Algernon (*offering tea-cake*). I wish you would have tea-cake instead. I don't like tea-cake.

Jack. Good heavens! I suppose a man may eat his own muffins in his own garden.

Algernon. But you have just said it was perfectly heartless to eat muffins.

Jack. I said it was perfectly heartless of you, under the circumstances. That is a very different thing.

Algernon. That may be. But the muffins are the same. (*He seizes the muffin dish from* Jack.)

Jack. Algy, I wish to goodness you would go.

Algernon. You can't possibly ask me to go without having some dinner. It's absurd. I never go without my dinner. No one ever does, except vegetarians and people like that. Besides, I have just made arrangements with Dr. Chasuble to be christened at a quarter to six under the name of Ernest.

Jack. My dear fellow, the sooner you give up that nonsense the better. I made arrangements this morning with Dr. Chasuble to be christened myself at 5:30, and I naturally will take the name of Ernest. Gwendolen would wish it. We can't both be christened Ernest. It's absurd. Besides, I have a perfect right to be christened if I like. There is no evidence at all that I have ever been christened by anybody. I should think it extremely probable I never was, and so does Dr. Chasuble. It is entirely different in your case. You have been christened already.

Algernon. Yes, but I have not been christened for years.

Jack. Yes, but you have been christened. That is the important thing.

Algernon. Quite so. So I know my constitution can stand it. If you are not quite sure about your ever having been christened, I must say I think it rather dangerous your venturing on it now. It might make you very unwell. You can hardly have forgotten that some one very closely connected with you was very nearly carried off this week in Paris by a severe chill.

Jack. Yes, but you said yourself that a severe chill was not hereditary.

Algernon. It usen't to be, I know—but I daresay it is now. Science is always making wonderful improvements in things.

Jack (*picking up the muffin dish*). Oh, that is nonsense; you are always talking nonsense.

Algernon. Jack, you are at the muffins again! I wish you wouldn't. There are only two left. (*takes them*) I told you I was particularly fond of muffins.

Jack. But I hate tea-cake.

Algernon. Why on earth then do you allow tea-cake to be served up for your guests? What ideas you have of hospitality!

Jack. Algernon! I have already told you to go. I don't want you here. Why don't you go!

Algernon. I haven't quite finished my tea yet! and there is still one muffin left. (Jack *groans, and sinks into a chair.* Algernon *still continues eating.*)

Act Drop

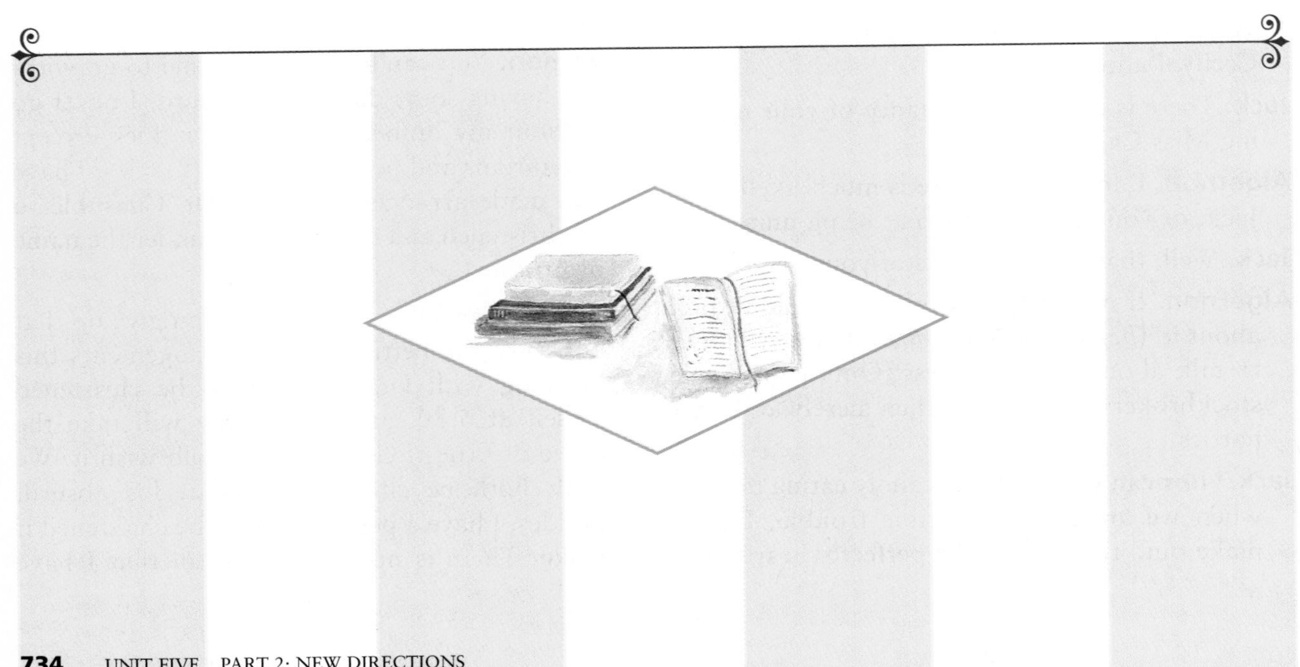

Third Act

Scene:

Morning-room at the Manor House.

(Gwendolen *and* Cecily *are at the window, looking out into the garden.*)

Gwendolen. The fact that they did not follow us at once into the house, as any one else would have done, seems to me to show that they have some sense of shame left.

Cecily. They have been eating muffins. That looks like repentance.

Gwendolen (*after a pause*). They don't seem to notice us at all. Couldn't you cough?

Cecily. But I haven't got a cough.

Gwendolen. They're looking at us. What effrontery!

Cecily. They're approaching. That's very forward of them.

Gwendolen. Let us preserve a dignified silence.

Cecily. Certainly. It's the only thing to do now.

WORDS TO KNOW

effrontery (ĭ-frŭn′tə-rē) *n.* shameless boldness; nerve

(*Enter* Jack *followed by* Algernon. *They whistle some dreadful popular air from a British Opera.*)

Gwendolen. This dignified silence seems to produce an unpleasant effect.

Cecily. A most distasteful one.

Gwendolen. But we will not be the first to speak.

Cecily. Certainly not.

Gwendolen. Mr. Worthing, I have something very particular to ask you. Much depends on your reply.

Cecily. Gwendolen, your common sense is invaluable. Mr. Moncrieff, kindly answer me the following question. Why did you pretend to be my guardian's brother?

Algernon. In order that I might have an opportunity of meeting you.

Cecily (*to* Gwendolen). That certainly seems a satisfactory explanation, does it not?

Gwendolen. Yes, dear, if you can believe him.

Cecily. I don't. But that does not affect the wonderful beauty of his answer.

Gwendolen. True. In matters of grave importance, style, not sincerity, is the vital thing. Mr. Worthing, what explanation can you offer to me for pretending to have a brother? Was it in order that you might have an opportunity of coming up to town to see me as often as possible?

Jack. Can you doubt it, Miss Fairfax?

Gwendolen. I have the gravest doubts upon the subject. But I intend to crush them. This is not the moment for German skepticism.[52] (*moving to* Cecily) Their explanations appear to be quite satisfactory, especially Mr. Worthing's. That seems to me to have the stamp of truth upon it.

Cecily. I am more than content with what Mr. Moncrieff said. His voice alone inspires one with absolute credulity.[53]

Gwendolen. Then you think we should forgive them?

Cecily. Yes. I mean no.

Gwendolen. True! I had forgotten. There are principles at stake that one cannot surrender. Which of us should tell them? The task is not a pleasant one.

Cecily. Could we not both speak at the same time?

Gwendolen. An excellent idea! I nearly always speak at the same time as other people. Will you take the time from me?

Cecily. Certainly. (Gwendolen *beats time with uplifted finger.*)

Gwendolen and **Cecily** (*speaking together*). Your Christian names are still an insuperable barrier. That is all!

Jack and **Algernon** (*speaking together*). Our Christian names! Is that all? But we are going to be christened this afternoon.

Gwendolen (*to* Jack). For my sake you are prepared to do this terrible thing?

Jack. I am.

Cecily (*to* Algernon). To please me you are ready to face this fearful ordeal?

Algernon. I am!

Gwendolen. How absurd to talk of the equality of the sexes! Where questions of self-sacrifice are concerned, men are infinitely beyond us.

Jack. We are. (*clasps hands with* Algernon)

Cecily. They have moments of physical courage of which we women know absolutely nothing.

Gwendolen (*to* Jack). Darling!

Algernon (*to* Cecily). Darling! (*They fall into each other's arms.*)

(*Enter* Merriman. *When he enters he coughs loudly, seeing the situation.*)

Merriman. Ahem! Ahem! Lady Bracknell!

Jack. Good heavens!

---

52. **skepticism:** a philosophy holding that it is impossible to be certain of the truth of any knowledge.

53. **credulity** (krĭ-do͞o′lĭ-tē): willingness to believe.

(*Enter* Lady Bracknell. *The couples separate in alarm.*)

(*Exit* Merriman.)

Lady Bracknell. Gwendolen! What does this mean?

Gwendolen. Merely that I am engaged to be married to Mr. Worthing, mamma.

Lady Bracknell. Come here. Sit down. Sit down immediately. Hesitation of any kind is a sign of mental decay in the young, of physical weakness in the old. (*turns to* Jack) Apprised, sir, of my daughter's sudden flight by her trusty maid, whose confidence I purchased by means of a small coin, I followed her at once by a luggage train. Her unhappy father is, I am glad to say, under the impression that she is attending a more than usually lengthy lecture by the University Extension Scheme on the Influence of a permanent income on Thought. I do not propose to undeceive him. Indeed I have never undeceived him on any question. I would consider it wrong. But of course, you will clearly understand that all communication between yourself and my daughter must cease immediately from this moment. On this point, as indeed on all points, I am firm.

Jack. I am engaged to be married to Gwendolen, Lady Bracknell!

Lady Bracknell. You are nothing of the kind, sir. And now, as regards Algernon! . . . Algernon!

Algernon. Yes, Aunt Augusta.

Lady Bracknell. May I ask if it is in this house that your invalid friend Mr. Bunbury resides?

Algernon (*stammering*). Oh! No! Bunbury doesn't live here. Bunbury is somewhere else at present. In fact, Bunbury is dead.

Lady Bracknell. Dead! When did Mr. Bunbury die? His death must have been extremely sudden.

Algernon (*airily*). Oh! I killed Bunbury this afternoon. I mean poor Bunbury died this afternoon.

Lady Bracknell. What did he die of?

Algernon. Bunbury? Oh, he was quite exploded.

Lady Bracknell. Exploded! Was he the victim of a revolutionary outrage? I was not aware that Mr. Bunbury was interested in social legislation. If so, he is well punished for his morbidity.

Algernon. My dear Aunt Augusta, I mean he was found out! The doctors found out that Bunbury could not live, that is what I mean—so Bunbury died.

Lady Bracknell. He seems to have had great confidence in the opinion of his physicians. I am glad, however, that he made up his mind at the last to some definite course of action, and acted under proper medical advice. And now that we have finally got rid of this Mr. Bunbury, may I ask, Mr. Worthing, who is that young person whose hand my nephew Algernon is now holding in what seems to me a peculiarly unnecessary manner?

Jack. That lady is Miss Cecily Cardew, my ward. (Lady Bracknell *bows coldly to* Cecily.)

Algernon. I am engaged to be married to Cecily, Aunt Augusta.

Lady Bracknell. I beg your pardon?

Cecily. Mr. Moncrieff and I are engaged to be married, Lady Bracknell.

Lady Bracknell (*with a shiver, crossing to the sofa and sitting down*). I do not know whether there is anything peculiarly exciting in the air of this particular part of Hertfordshire, but the number of engagements that go on seems to me considerably above the proper average that statistics have laid down for our guidance. I think some preliminary inquiry on my part would not be out of place. Mr. Worthing, is Miss Cardew at all connected with any of the larger railway stations in London? I merely desire information. Until yesterday I had no idea that there were any families or persons whose origin was a Terminus.[54] (Jack *looks perfectly furious, but restrains himself.*)

Jack (*in a clear, cold voice*). Miss Cardew is the granddaughter of the late Mr. Thomas Cardew of 149 Belgrave Square, S.W.; Gervase Park, Dorking, Surrey; and the Sporran, Fifeshire, N.B.

Lady Bracknell. That sounds not unsatisfactory. Three addresses always inspire confidence, even in tradesmen. But what proof have I of their authenticity?

Jack. I have carefully preserved the Court Guides of the period. They are open to your inspection, Lady Bracknell.

Lady Bracknell (*grimly*). I have known strange errors in that publication.

Jack. Miss Cardew's family solicitors are Messrs.[55] Markby, Markby, and Markby.

Lady Bracknell. Markby, Markby, and Markby? A firm of the very highest position in their profession. Indeed I am told that one of the Mr. Markbys is occasionally to be seen at dinner parties. So far I am satisfied.

Jack (*very irritably*). How extremely kind of you, Lady Bracknell! I have also in my possession, you will be pleased to hear, certificates of Miss Cardew's birth, baptism, whooping cough, registration, vaccination, confirmation, and the measles; both the German and the English variety.

Lady Bracknell. Ah! A life crowded with incident, I see; though perhaps somewhat too exciting for a young girl. I am not myself in favor of premature experiences! (*rises, looks at her watch*) Gwendolen! the time approaches for our depar-

---

54. **Terminus:** a station at the end of a railroad line.

55. **Messrs.** (mĕs′ərz): the plural of *Mr.*

ture. We have not a moment to lose. As a matter of form, Mr. Worthing, I had better ask you if Miss Cardew has any little fortune?

Jack. Oh! about a hundred and thirty thousand pounds in the Funds.[56] That is all. Goodbye, Lady Bracknell. So pleased to have seen you.

Lady Bracknell (*sitting down again*). A moment, Mr. Worthing. A hundred and thirty thousand pounds! And in the Funds! Miss Cardew seems to me a most attractive young lady, now that I look at her. Few girls of the present day have any really solid qualities, any of the qualities that last, and improve with time. We live, I regret to say, in an age of surfaces. (*To* Cecily) Come over here, dear. (Cecily *goes across.*) Pretty child! your dress is sadly simple, and your hair seems almost as Nature might have left it. But we can soon alter all that. A thoroughly experienced French maid produces a really marvelous result in a very brief space of time. I remember recommending one to young Lady Lancing, and after three months her own husband did not know her.

Jack. And after six months nobody knew her.

Lady Bracknell. (*Glares at* Jack *for a few moments. Then bends, with a practiced smile, to* Cecily.) Kindly turn round, sweet child. (Cecily *turns completely round.*) No, the side view is what I want. (Cecily *presents her profile.*) Yes, quite as I expected. There are distinct social possibilities in your profile. The two weak points in our age are its want of principle and its want of profile. The chin a little higher, dear. Style largely depends on the way the chin is worn. They are worn very high, just at present. Algernon!

Algernon. Yes, Aunt Augusta!

Lady Bracknell. There are distinct social possibilities in Miss Cardew's profile.

Algernon. Cecily is the sweetest, dearest, prettiest girl in the whole world. And I don't care twopence about social possibilities.

Lady Bracknell. Never speak disrespectfully of Society, Algernon. Only people who can't get into it do that. (*To* Cecily) Dear child, of course you know that Algernon has nothing but his debts to depend upon. But I do not approve of mercenary marriages. When I married Lord Bracknell I had no fortune of any kind. But I never dreamed for a moment of allowing that to stand in my way. Well, I suppose I must give my consent.

Algernon. Thank you, Aunt Augusta.

Lady Bracknell. Cecily, you may kiss me!

Cecily (*kisses her*). Thank you, Lady Bracknell.

Lady Bracknell. You may also address me as Aunt Augusta for the future.

Cecily. Thank you, Aunt Augusta.

Lady Bracknell. The marriage, I think, had better take place quite soon.

Algernon. Thank you, Aunt Augusta.

Cecily. Thank you, Aunt Augusta.

Lady Bracknell. To speak frankly, I am not in favor of long engagements. They give people the opportunity of finding out each other's character before marriage, which I think is never advisable.

Jack. I beg pardon for interrupting you, Lady Bracknell, but this engagement is quite out of the question. I am Miss Cardew's guardian, and she cannot marry without my consent until she comes of age. That consent I absolutely decline to give.

Lady Bracknell. Upon what grounds may I ask? Algernon is an extremely, I may almost say an ostentatiously, eligible young man. He has nothing, but he looks everything. What more can one desire?

Jack. It pains me very much to have to speak frankly to you, Lady Bracknell, about your nephew, but the fact is that I do not approve at all of his moral character. I suspect him of being

56. **the Funds:** government bonds.

WORDS TO KNOW

mercenary (mûr′sə-nĕr′ē) *adj.* motivated solely by a desire for monetary or material gain

untruthful. (Algernon *and* Cecily *look at him in indignant amazement.*)

Lady Bracknell. Untruthful! My nephew Algernon? Impossible! He is an Oxonian.[57]

Jack. I fear there can be no possible doubt about the matter. This afternoon during my temporary absence in London on an important question of romance, he obtained admission to my house by means of the false pretense of being my brother. Under an assumed name he drank, I've just been informed by my butler, an entire pint bottle of my Perrier-Jouet, Brut,[58] '89; wine I was specially reserving for myself. Continuing his disgraceful deception, he succeeded in the course of the afternoon in alienating the affections of my only ward. He subsequently stayed to tea, and devoured every single muffin. And what makes his conduct all the more heartless is, that he was perfectly well aware from the first that I have no brother, that I never had a brother, and that I don't intend to have a brother, not even of any kind. I distinctly told him so myself yesterday afternoon.

Lady Bracknell. Ahem! Mr. Worthing, after careful consideration I have decided entirely to overlook my nephew's conduct to you.

Jack. That is very generous of you, Lady Bracknell. My own decision, however, is unalterable. I decline to give my consent.

Lady Bracknell (*to* Cecily). Come here, sweet child. (Cecily *goes over.*) How old are you, dear?

Cecily. Well, I am really only eighteen, but I always admit to twenty when I go to evening parties.

Lady Bracknell. You are perfectly right in making some slight alteration. Indeed, no woman should ever be quite accurate about her age. It looks so calculating. . . . (*in a meditative manner*) Eighteen, but admitting to twenty at evening parties. Well, it will not be very long before you are of age and free from the restraints of tutelage.[59] So I don't think your guardian's consent is, after all, a matter of any importance.

Jack. Pray excuse me, Lady Bracknell, for interrupting you again, but it is only fair to tell you that according to the terms of her grandfather's will Miss Cardew does not come legally of age till she is thirty-five.

Lady Bracknell. That does not seem to me to be a grave objection. Thirty-five is a very attractive age. London society is full of women of the very highest birth who have, of their own free choice, remained thirty-five for years. Lady Dumbleton is an instance in point. To my own knowledge she has been thirty-five ever since she arrived at the age of forty, which was many years ago now. I see no reason why our dear Cecily should not be even still more attractive at the age you mention than she is at present. There will be a large accumulation of property.

Cecily. Algy, could you wait for me till I was thirty-five?

Algernon. Of course I could, Cecily. You know I could.

Cecily. Yes, I felt it instinctively, but I couldn't wait all that time. I hate waiting even five minutes for anybody. It always makes me rather cross. I am not punctual myself, I know, but I do like punctuality in others, and waiting, even to be married, is quite out of the question.

Algernon. Then what is to be done, Cecily?

Cecily. I don't know, Mr. Moncrieff.

Lady Bracknell. My dear Mr. Worthing, as Miss Cardew states positively that she cannot wait till she is thirty-five—a remark which I am bound to say seems to me to show a somewhat impatient nature—I would beg of you to reconsider your decision.

Jack. But my dear Lady Bracknell, the matter is entirely in your own hands. The moment you

---

57. **Oxonian** (ŏk-sō′nē-ən): a person who has studied at Oxford University.

58. **Perrier-Jouet, Brut** (pĕ-ryā′zhwĕ′ brüt′): a dry champagne.

59. **tutelage** (to͞ot′l-ĭj): the state of being under the direction of a guardian or tutor.

consent to my marriage with Gwendolen, I will most gladly allow your nephew to form an alliance with my ward.

Lady Bracknell (*rising and drawing herself up*). You must be quite aware that what you propose is out of the question.

Jack. Then a passionate celibacy is all that any of us can look forward to.

Lady Bracknell. That is the destiny I propose for Gwendolen. Algernon, of course, can choose for himself. (*pulls out her watch*) Come, dear, (Gwendolen *rises*) we have already missed five, if not six, trains. To miss any more might expose us to comment on the platform.

(*Enter* Dr. Chasuble)

Chasuble. Everything is quite ready for the christenings.

Lady Bracknell. The christenings, sir! Is not that somewhat premature?

Chasuble (*looking rather puzzled, and pointing to* Jack *and* Algernon). Both these gentlemen have expressed a desire for immediate baptism.

Lady Bracknell. At their age! The idea is grotesque and irreligious. Algernon, I forbid you to be baptized. I will not hear of such excesses. Lord Bracknell would be highly displeased if he learned that that was the way in which you wasted your time and money.

Chasuble. Am I to understand then that there are to be no christenings at all this afternoon?

Jack. I don't think that, as things are now, it would be of much practical value to either of us, Dr. Chasuble.

Chasuble. I am grieved to hear such sentiments from you, Mr. Worthing. They savor of the heretical views of the Anabaptists,[60] views that I have completely refuted[61] in four of my unpublished sermons. However, as your present mood seems to be one peculiarly secular, I will return to the church at once. Indeed, I have just been informed by the pew-opener that for the last hour and a half Miss Prism has been waiting for me in the vestry.[62]

Lady Bracknell (*starting*). Miss Prism! Did I hear you mention a Miss Prism?

Chasuble. Yes, Lady Bracknell. I am on my way to join her.

Lady Bracknell. Pray allow me to detain you for a moment. This matter may prove to be one of vital importance to Lord Bracknell and myself. Is this Miss Prism a female of repellent aspect, remotely connected with education?

Chasuble (*somewhat indignantly*). She is the most cultivated of ladies, and the very picture of respectability.

Lady Bracknell. It is obviously the same person. May I ask what position she holds in your household?

Chasuble (*severely*). I am a celibate, madam.

Jack (*interposing*). Miss Prism, Lady Bracknell, has been for the last three years Miss Cardew's esteemed governess and valued companion.

Lady Bracknell. In spite of what I hear of her, I must see her at once. Let her be sent for.

Chasuble (*looking off*). She approaches; she is nigh.

(*Enter* Miss Prism *hurriedly.*)

Miss Prism. I was told you expected me in the vestry, dear Canon. I have been waiting for you there for an hour and three-quarters. (*Catches sight of* Lady Bracknell, *who has fixed her with a stony glare.* Miss Prism *grows pale and quails. She looks anxiously round as if desirous to escape.*)

Lady Bracknell (*in a severe, judicial voice*). Prism! (Miss Prism *bows her head in shame.*) Come here, Prism! (Miss Prism *approaches in a humble manner.*) Prism! Where is that baby? (*General*

---

60. **the heretical** (hə-rĕt′ĭ-kəl) **views of the Anabaptists:** the views, contrary to accepted church beliefs, of a 16th-century Protestant group. (Dr. Chasuble seems to think that the Anabaptists rejected adult baptism; in fact, they believed adult baptism to be the only valid kind.)

61. **refuted:** proved to be false.

62. **vestry:** the room in a church where clerical robes and implements are stored.

consternation. The Canon *starts back in horror.* Algernon *and* Jack *pretend to be anxious to shield* Cecily *and* Gwendolen *from hearing the details of a terrible public scandal.*) Twenty-eight years ago, Prism, you left Lord Bracknell's house, Number 104, Upper Grosvenor Street, in charge of a perambulator[63] that contained a baby of the male sex. You never returned. A few weeks later, through the elaborate investigations of the Metropolitan police, the perambulator was discovered at midnight, standing by itself in a remote corner of Bayswater. It contained the manuscript of a three-volume novel of more than usually revolting sentimentality. (Miss Prism *starts in involuntary indignation.*) But the baby was not there! (*Every one looks at* Miss Prism.) Prism! Where is that baby? (*a pause*)

Miss Prism. Lady Bracknell, I admit with shame that I do not know. I only wish I did. The plain facts of the case are these. On the morning of the day you mention, a day that is for ever branded on my memory, I prepared as usual to take the baby out in its perambulator. I had also with me a somewhat old, but capacious[64] handbag in which I had intended to place the manuscript of a work of fiction that I had written during my few unoccupied hours. In a moment of mental abstraction, for which I never can forgive myself, I deposited the manuscript in the basinette, and placed the baby in the handbag.

Jack (*who has been listening attentively*). But where did you deposit the handbag?

Miss Prism. Do not ask me, Mr. Worthing.

Jack. Miss Prism, this is a matter of no small importance to me. I insist on knowing where you deposited the handbag that contained that infant.

Miss Prism. I left it in the cloakroom of one of the larger railway stations in London.

Jack. What railway station?

Miss Prism (*quite crushed*). Victoria. The Brighton line. (*sinks into a chair*)

Jack. I must retire to my room for a moment. Gwendolen, wait here for me.

Gwendolen. If you are not too long, I will wait here for you all my life.

(*Exit* Jack *in great excitement.*)

Chasuble. What do you think this means, Lady Bracknell?

Lady Bracknell. I dare not even suspect, Dr. Chasuble. I need hardly tell you that in families of high position strange coincidences are not supposed to occur. They are hardly considered the thing.

(*Noises are heard overhead as if some one was throwing trunks about. Every one looks up.*)

Cecily. Uncle Jack seems strangely agitated.

Chasuble. Your guardian has a very emotional nature.

Lady Bracknell. This noise is extremely unpleasant. It sounds as if he was having an argument. I dislike arguments of any kind. They are always vulgar, and often convincing.

Chasuble (*looking up*). It has stopped now. (*The noise is redoubled.*)

Lady Bracknell. I wish he would arrive at some conclusion.

Gwendolen. This suspense is terrible. I hope it will last.

(*Enter* Jack *with a handbag of black leather in his hand.*)

Jack (*rushing over to* Miss Prism). Is this the handbag, Miss Prism? Examine it carefully before you speak. The happiness of more than one life depends on your answer.

Miss Prism (*calmly*). It seems to be mine. Yes, here is the injury it received through the upsetting of a Gower Street omnibus in younger and happier days. Here is the stain on the lining caused by the explosion of a temperance beverage,[65] an incident that occurred at Leamington.

---

63. **perambulator:** a baby carriage.
64. **capacious:** large and roomy.
65. **temperance beverage:** a nonalcoholic drink for people who reject the use of intoxicating liquors.

And here, on the lock, are my initials. I had forgotten that in an extravagant mood I had had them placed there. The bag is undoubtedly mine. I am delighted to have it so unexpectedly restored to me. It has been a great inconvenience being without it all these years.

Jack (*in a pathetic voice*). Miss Prism, more is restored to you than this handbag. I was the baby you placed in it.

Miss Prism (*amazed*). You?

Jack (*embracing her*). Yes . . . mother!

Miss Prism (*recoiling in indignant astonishment*). Mr. Worthing! I am unmarried!

Jack. Unmarried! I do not deny that is a serious blow. But after all, who has the right to cast a stone against one who has suffered? Cannot repentance wipe out an act of folly? Why should there be one law for men, and another for women? Mother, I forgive you. (*tries to embrace her again*)

Miss Prism (*still more indignant*). Mr. Worthing, there is some error. (*Pointing to* Lady Bracknell) There is the lady who can tell you who you really are.

Jack (*after a pause*). Lady Bracknell, I hate to seem inquisitive, but would you kindly inform me who I am?

Lady Bracknell. I am afraid that the news I have to give you will not altogether please you. You are the son of my poor sister, Mrs. Moncrieff, and consequently Algernon's elder brother.

Jack. Algy's elder brother! Then I have a brother after all. I knew I had a brother! I always said I had a brother! Cecily,—how could you have ever doubted that I had a brother? (*seizes hold of* Algernon) Dr. Chasuble, my unfortunate brother. Miss Prism, my unfortunate brother. Gwendolen, my unfortunate brother. Algy, you young scoundrel, you will have to treat me with more respect in the future. You have never behaved to me like a brother in all your life.

Algernon. Well, not till today, old boy, I admit. I did my best, however, though I was out of practice. (*shakes hands*)

Gwendolen (*to* Jack). My own! But what own are you? What is your Christian name, now that you have become some one else?

Jack. Good heavens! . . . I had quite forgotten that point. Your decision on the subject of my name is irrevocable, I suppose?

Gwendolen. I never change, except in my affections.

Cecily. What a noble nature you have, Gwendolen!

Jack. Then the question had better be cleared up at once. Aunt Augusta, a moment. At the time when Miss Prism left me in the handbag, had I been christened already?

Lady Bracknell. Every luxury that money could buy, including christening, had been lavished on you by your fond and doting parents.

Jack. Then I was christened! That is settled. Now, what name was I given? Let me know the worst.

Lady Bracknell. Being the eldest son you were naturally christened after your father.

Jack (*irritably*). Yes, but what was my father's Christian name?

Lady Bracknell (*meditatively*). I cannot at the present moment recall what the General's Christian name was. But I have no doubt he had one. He was eccentric, I admit. But only in later years. And that was the result of the Indian climate, and marriage, and indigestion, and other things of that kind.

Jack. Algy! Can't you recollect what our father's Christian name was?

Algernon. My dear boy, we were never even on speaking terms. He died before I was a year old.

Jack. His name would appear in the Army Lists of the period, I suppose, Aunt Augusta?

WORDS TO KNOW

irrevocable (ĭ-rĕv′ə-kə-bəl) *adj.* impossible to take back or undo

Lady Bracknell. The General was essentially a man of peace, except in his domestic life. But I have no doubt his name would appear in any military directory.

Jack. The Army Lists of the last forty years are here. These delightful records should have been my constant study. (*rushes to bookcase and tears the books out*) M. Generals . . . Mallam, Maxbohm, Magley, what ghastly names they have—Markby, Migsby, Mobbs, Moncrieff! Lieutenant 1840, Captain, Lieutenant-Colonel, Colonel, General 1869, Christian names, Ernest John. (*puts book very quietly down and speaks quite calmly*) I always told you, Gwendolen, my name was Ernest, didn't I? Well, it is Ernest after all. I mean it naturally is Ernest.

Lady Bracknell. Yes, I remember now that the General was called Ernest. I knew I had some particular reason for disliking the name.

Gwendolen. Ernest! My own Ernest! I felt from the first that you could have no other name!

Jack. Gwendolen, it is a terrible thing for a man to find out suddenly that all his life he has been speaking nothing but the truth. Can you forgive me?

Gwendolen. I can. For I feel that you are sure to change.

Jack. My own one!

Chasuble (*to* Miss Prism). Laetitia! (*embraces her*)

Miss Prism (*enthusiastically*). Frederick! At last!

Algernon. Cecily! (*embraces her*) At last!

Jack. Gwendolen! (*embraces her*) At last!

Lady Bracknell. My nephew, you seem to be displaying signs of triviality.

Jack. On the contrary, Aunt Augusta, I've now realized for the first time in my life the vital Importance of Being Earnest.

Tableau

Curtain

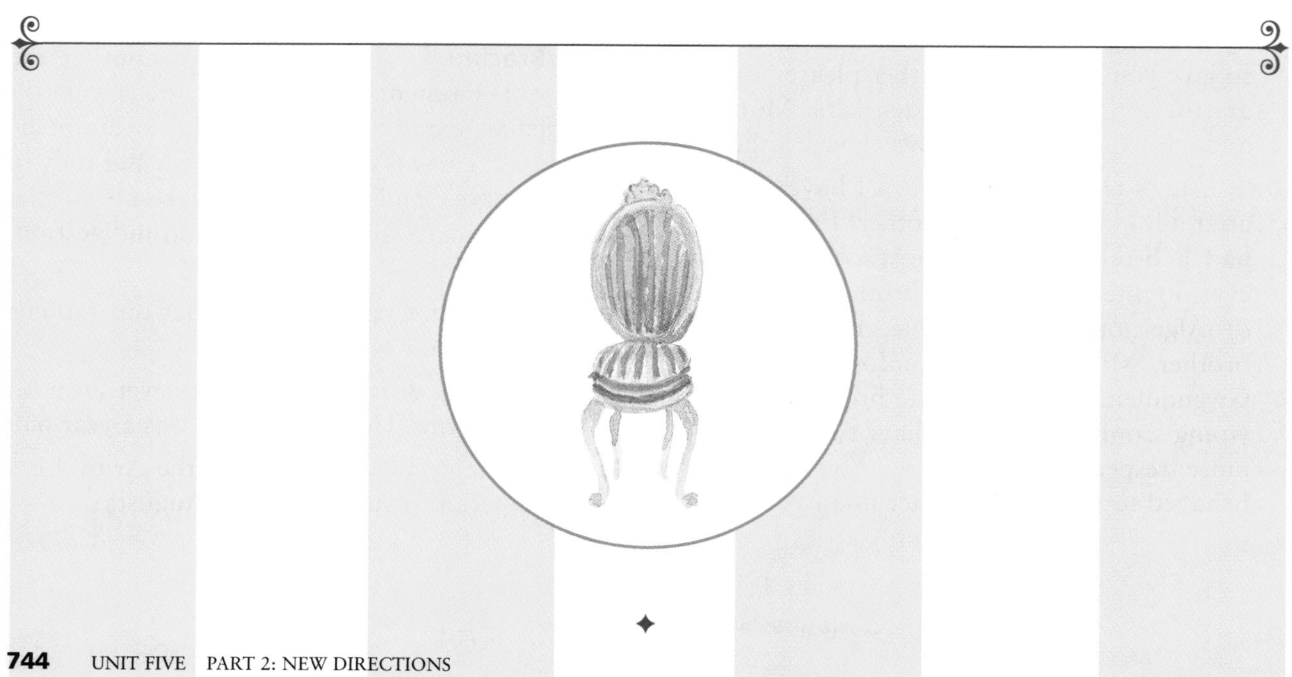

RESPONDING OPTIONS

FROM PERSONAL RESPONSE *TO* CRITICAL ANALYSIS

REFLECT 1. Did you find this play funny? Why or why not? Jot down your reasons in your notebook, then share them with classmates.

RETHINK 2. After your reading of the play, what is your view of Victorian society?

Consider
- the aspects of life that seem most important to each character
- the attitudes toward courtship and marriage expressed by various characters
- the portrayal of Dr. Chasuble

3. Which character do you think is the most clever? Give reasons to support your opinion.

4. Why do you suppose Wilde used the word *earnest* instead of the name Ernest in the title of this play?

5. Recall that Wilde originally gave this play a subtitle: "A Trivial Comedy for Serious People." What do you think he meant by this description of the play?

RELATE 6. In your opinion, could this play serve as a commentary on contemporary society, or does its satire apply only to the late Victorian era? Give reasons for your answer.

ANOTHER PATHWAY

Cooperative Learning

With a group of classmates, choose two or three comic vignettes—brief segments of the play—to act out. Assign parts so that everyone in the group has an opportunity to perform, and decide as a group how each part should be played. Read through each vignette you choose at least once as a group, and then perform them for the rest of the class.

LITERARY CONCEPTS

The Importance of Being Earnest is often described as a **farce,** a type of exaggerated comedy that features an absurd plot, ridiculous situations, and humorous dialogue. The main purpose of a farce is to keep an audience laughing. The characters are usually stereotypes, or simplified examples of different traits or qualities. They may seem reasonable at the start but soon become far-fetched and laughable. Comic devices typically used in farces include mistaken identity, deception, wordplay—such as puns and double meanings—and exaggeration. Find at least one example of each of these devices in *The Importance of Being Earnest,* and explain how it adds to the comic effect of the play.

QUICKWRITES

1. Write a **character profile** that would help a director cast one of the parts in the play. In your profile, mention what you consider to be the character's significant traits or qualities, as well as his or her age and general appearance.
2. Write and design a **program** for a production of *The Importance of Being Earnest.* Include lists of the acts, the cast of characters, and the names of the actors playing the roles. You might also include biographies of your actors and even advertising.
3. As a drama critic, write a **review** of this play. Tell what you like or don't like about it, and give an evaluation of its plot, comic devices, and overall effectiveness.

PORTFOLIO *Save your writing. You may want to use it later as a springboard to a piece for your portfolio.*

ALTERNATIVE ACTIVITIES

1. Use a diagram like the one shown here to create a **stage plan** for one act of the play. On the diagram, map out the location of scenery, furniture, and other stage props, and indicate the position and movement of each character who will be on the stage.

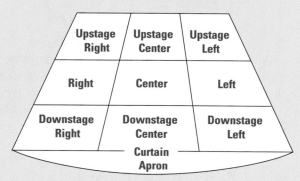

2. Using information provided in the stage directions and elsewhere in the play, work with a partner to create a **model** of the set for one act.
3. Research clothing styles of the Victorian era. Then create **costume designs** appropriate to the occupations and social positions of three characters in the play.
4. Create a **poster** advertising a local performance of *The Importance of Being Earnest.*

CRITIC'S CORNER

The English poet W. H. Auden admired Wilde's writing style in *The Importance of Being Earnest,* describing the play as a "verbal opera" in which "the plot is nothing but a succession of opportunities" for dialogue. What do you think Auden meant by this observation? Explain your answer.

LITERARY LINKS

Compare the views of Victorian society expressed in *The Importance of Being Earnest* with those expressed in Elizabeth Gaskell's "Christmas Storms and Sunshine" (page 606). What similarities can you find? What are some differences?

THE WRITER'S STYLE

Throughout this play, Wilde enhances the comic effect of the dialogue by including amusing **epigrams,** or pointed observations about life. Wilde's epigrams are often witty and unconventional. For example, in the first act, Algernon says, "All women become like their mothers. That is their tragedy. No man does. That's his." Find at least two other witty epigrams and explain how each adds to the comic effect of the play.

ACROSS THE CURRICULUM

Drama/History Investigate the history of comedy in the English theater. What are some of the most popular comedies ever performed in London? Which roles have been especially appealing to English actors and audiences? What famous actors have played these roles?

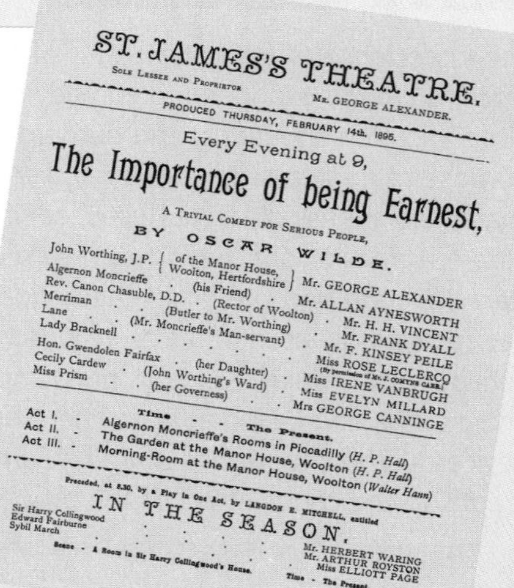

ST. JAMES'S THEATRE.
SOLE LESSEE AND PROPRIETOR MR. GEORGE ALEXANDER.
PRODUCED THURSDAY, FEBRUARY 14th. 1895.
Every Evening at 9,
The Importance of being Earnest,
A TRIVIAL COMEDY FOR SERIOUS PEOPLE,
BY OSCAR WILDE.

John Worthing, J.P. (of the Manor House, Woolton, Hertfordshire) . . . Mr. GEORGE ALEXANDER
Algernon Moncrieffe . (his Friend) . . . Mr. ALLAN AYNESWORTH
Rev. Canon Chasuble, D.D. . (Rector of Woolton) . . . Mr. H. H. VINCENT
Merriman . . (Butler to Mr. Worthing) . . . Mr. FRANK DYALL
Lane . . (Mr. Moncrieffe's Man-servant) . . . Mr. F. KINSEY PEILE
Lady Bracknell . . . . Miss ROSE LECLERCQ (By permission of Mr. J. COMYNS CARR.)
Hon. Gwendolen Fairfax . (her Daughter) . . . Miss IRENE VANBRUGH
Cecily Cardew . (John Worthing's Ward) . . . Miss EVELYN MILLARD
Miss Prism . . (her Governess) . . . Mrs GEORGE CANNINGE

Time - - The Present.
Act I. - Algernon Moncrieffe's Rooms in Piccadilly (*H. P. Hall*)
Act II. - The Garden at the Manor House, Woolton (*H. P. Hall*)
Act III. - Morning-Room at the Manor House, Woolton (*Walter Hann*)

Preceded, at 8.30, by a Play in One Act, by LANGDON E. MITCHELL, entitled
IN THE SEASON.
Sir Harry Collingwood . . . Mr. HERBERT WARING
Edward Fairburne . . . Mr. ARTHUR ROYSTON
Sybil March . . . Miss ELLIOTT PAGE
Scene - A Room in Sir Harry Collingwood's House. Time - The Present.

WORDS TO KNOW

EXERCISE A For each group of words below, write the letter of the word that is an antonym of the boldfaced word.

1. **indiscretion:** (a) clarity, (b) wit, (c) prudence
2. **mercenary:** (a) sparse, (b) permanent, (c) charitable
3. **vacillating:** (a) sensitive, (b) steady, (c) indifferent
4. **impetuous:** (a) careful, (b) cruel, (c) polite
5. **equanimity:** (a) panic, (b) prejudice, (c) superiority
6. **arduous:** (a) clear, (b) easy, (c) modern
7. **superciliously:** (a) correctly, (b) deeply, (c) humbly
8. **profligate:** (a) moral, (b) wealthy, (c) poor

EXERCISE B Write the vocabulary word, not used in Exercise A, that best completes each sentence.

1. Oscar Wilde believed in art for art's sake and disagreed strongly with those who felt that art must have a _____ purpose.
2. It is clear that social comedy, complete with wonderfully witty dialogue, was his _____.
3. In *The Importance of Being Earnest,* there is no scheming so sinister or evil that it could be called a _____.
4. In some of Wilde's other plays, the characters' actions cannot be undone, for they are _____.
5. In *Lady Windermere's Fan,* a wife becomes suspicious of her husband's _____ with another woman.
6. When he invites the lady to a party in their home, the wife is shocked and infuriated by what she believes to be an act of horrifying _____.
7. The wife's outrage is based on a _____ about who the "other woman" is, an error that nearly destroys her marriage and her good name.

OSCAR WILDE

1854–1900

Oscar Fingal O'Flahertie Wills Wilde was born in Dublin, Ireland, and attended schools in both Ireland and England, receiving a scholarship to Oxford University. After graduating with honors, Wilde remained in England, where he proved to be one of the most colorful and unforgettable figures in English literature. He was known for his witty and often outrageous conversation and for his flamboyant lifestyle. His attire was colorful and, like his conversation, often outrageous. Instead of the conservative dress typical of Victorian society, Wilde wore velvet jackets and knee breeches, silk shirts, and black silk stockings. He was flippant and unmindful of authority, frequently annoying or offending his superiors.

While a student at Oxford, Wilde became fascinated with aestheticism, a philosophy of life that advocated "art for art's sake" and the pursuit of art and beauty in preference to all other principles of life. He lived his life accordingly, frowning upon those aspects of society that he considered ugly, such as all sports and anything industrial. His outspoken adherence to aestheticism occasionally made him the object of ridicule in London periodicals.

For most of his life, Wilde sought notoriety, but the scandal that occurred at the pinnacle of his career provided a kind of notoriety that he had never anticipated. Shortly after the first performance of *The Importance of Being Earnest,* Wilde was arrested and imprisoned for behavior that Victorian society considered immoral. His name was removed from theater handbills, and the public rejected his plays. After serving a two-year prison term, Wilde went to France, where he lived under an assumed name until his death three years later at age 46. Ironically, like the imaginary Ernest Worthing in *The Importance of Being Earnest,* Wilde died in a Paris hotel. Eventually, however, his plays regained their popularity, and they continue to be performed today.

OTHER WORKS *Lady Windermere's Fan, A Woman of No Importance, An Ideal Husband*

LASERLINKS
• *ART GALLERY*

WRITING FROM EXPERIENCE

WRITING TO PERSUADE

In her essay "A Warning Against Passion," Charlotte Brontë argued from one point of view—hers. Most controversial topics, however, have more than one valid point of view. That's why you'll find people with strong feelings and arguments on each side of the issue. To make your own judgment, you must look fairly at both sides of a two-sided issue.

GUIDED ASSIGNMENT

Write a Two-Sided Argument Write a persuasive essay in which you present both sides of a controversial issue. Present the arguments on each side as fairly and as fully as you can, even if you yourself favor one particular view.

1 Find an Issue

Start by finding an issue that really interests you—one that has two distinct sides to it. You may already have some ideas of your own. Here are some additional sources of ideas. Make a list of the issues that interest you.

- Tune in to daily news broadcasts for controversial issues.
- Scan recent newspapers and magazines.
- Brainstorm with a group of peers.
- Interview people involved in a controversy.
- Think about current issues covered in the literature you've read recently.
- Consider the items on these two pages.

2 Evaluate Your Topics

Ask yourself the following questions about each issue that interests you.

- Does this issue have two clear sides?
- Are the two sides equally valid? Can I find strong support for each side?
- Where do I stand on the issue? Can I treat both sides fairly?
- Am I interested enough in this issue to spend more time on it?

Environmental Magazine Article

In recent decisions, courts have granted Indians of the Pacific Northwest "an environmental right" to the preservation of fish habitats. These decisions have important implications.

Salmon hatch in small upland streams and migrate through bigger rivers into the ocean. After a few years, they return to where they were hatched. The salmon's existence can be affected by anything that interferes with this migratory pattern. This means that logging, mining, dams—anything that affects the waters the salmon depend on—can be considered a danger to the fish and, therefore, to the Indians' environmental rights.

3 Write from Both Sides

Pick the topic you'd most like to write about. Using what you already know, write a paragraph presenting the arguments for one side of the issue. Then write a second paragraph presenting the other side of the issue. Try to present arguments for each side without bias.

Article on Health Care

What Price Life?

They're writing about it in books, newspapers, and magazines; talking about it in hospitals and at medical conventions; arguing about it in private homes, public meetings, and the halls of Congress. The rising cost of medical care is a hot topic.

When Frenchman Julius Herisson developed a device to measure blood pressure in 1835, physicians sneered. "This is one of the most ridiculous baubles ever foisted on the profession," said one.

No one sneers at medical technology anymore. In little more than a generation, applied science has transformed medicine beyond recognition, lengthening lives and alleviating previously painful diseases. Yet health care also has become an insidious and ever-escalating cost to the economy.

The uncomfortable fact is this: Medicine is now capable of more than this economy—any foreseeable economy—can afford. Such new medical technologies as organ transplants balloon into enormous expenditures as patients everywhere begin insisting on the right to treatment. Where life itself is concerned, should ability to pay be the sole criterion? This is a moral issue, but it is difficult to avoid considering the economic aspects.

Richard Greene,
from "What Price Life?" *Forbes*

Grandma had to sell her home to pay medical bills. Is that fair? I should look into this issue.

Federal Budget, 1994
(estimated, in millions of dollars)

Pie Chart

Education gets only a small fraction of this budget. Can this be justified?

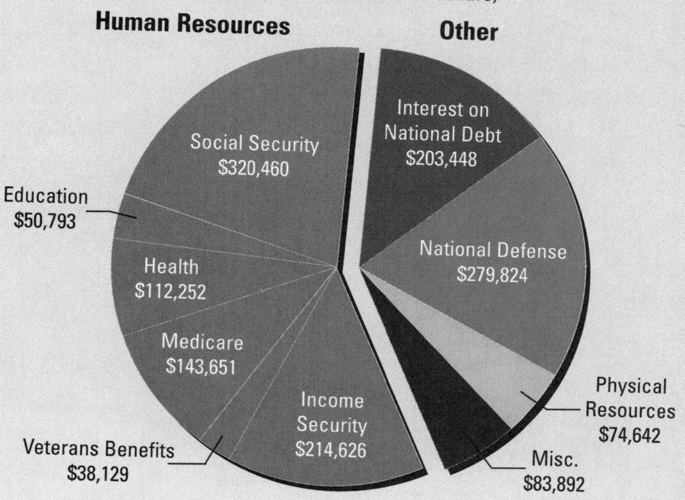

Source: *Statistical Abstract of the United States: 1994*

How do you feel about the ways your government spends money? List three issues you can derive from reading this graph.

PREWRITING

Examining the Issue

First Steps Once you've chosen your topic, take time to think about the issue, plan your approach, and familiarize yourself with the arguments on both sides. Keep in mind that your purpose will be to present both sides of the controversy without bias, even if you have strong feelings of your own on one side of the controversy.

1 Clarify the Issues

To fairly present a controversial topic, you'll need to understand both sides of the issue involved. Before you begin planning your essay, try the following.

Summarize Each Side What is the main issue? What are the different opinions people have about this issue? (Your topic may have more than two sides.) Try to summarize each side's position in a few sentences.

Organize the Issues How can the main issue be broken down into smaller sub-issues? What is each side's position on each sub-issue? You can use a chart like the one on this page to organize these sub-issues.

Examine Points of View How do the people on each side of the issue view those on the other side? For example, do they disagree but respect each other? Would they be willing to compromise?

2 Talk About It

To help you clarify the issue, try discussing it with a group of your peers. Another possibility is to ask one or two classmates on each side of the issue to hold an informal debate on the topic. As you listen, take notes on and evaluate their ideas, their positions, and their arguments. List any questions that arise so that you can later look for the answers.

Student's Notes

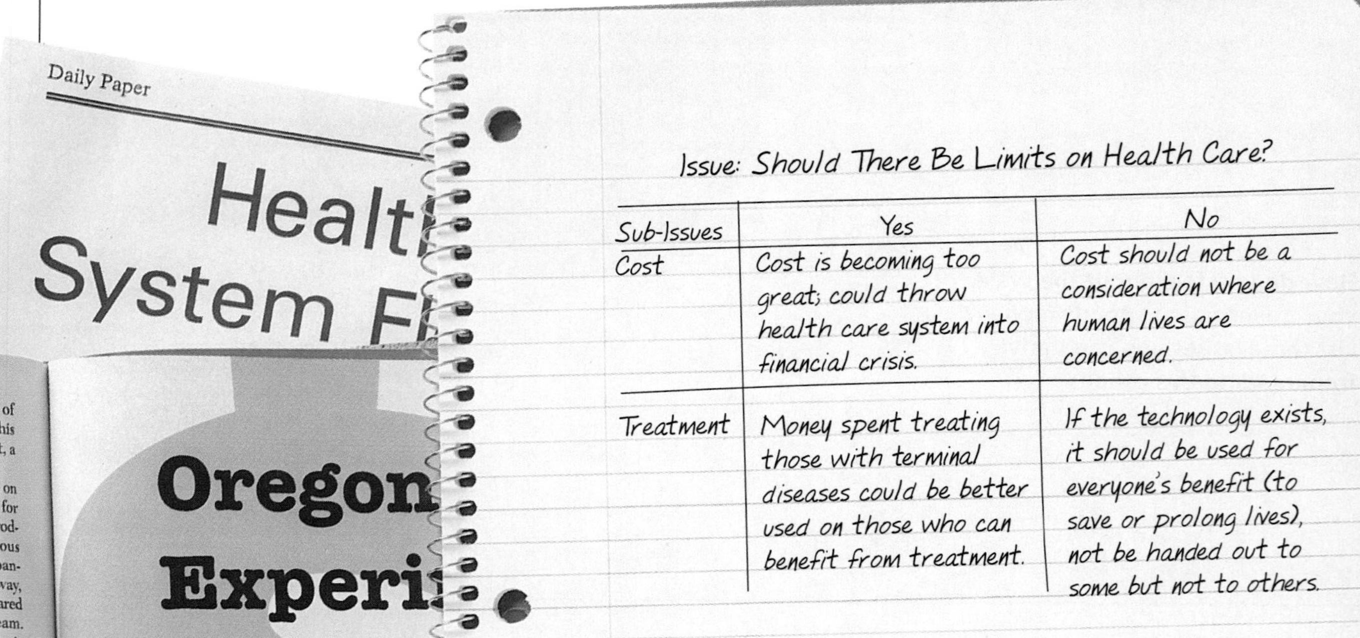

Issue: Should There Be Limits on Health Care?

Sub-Issues	Yes	No
Cost	Cost is becoming too great; could throw health care system into financial crisis.	Cost should not be a consideration where human lives are concerned.
Treatment	Money spent treating those with terminal diseases could be better used on those who can benefit from treatment.	If the technology exists, it should be used for everyone's benefit (to save or prolong lives), not be handed out to some but not to others.

❸ Research Your Topic

After you have clarified the issue, explored the arguments, and listed questions about the topic, start your research. You can use the following, as well as library sources and the Internet.

Read the News Editorials and news articles are good sources for opinions, as are letters to the editor. Choose newspapers that are likely to show opposing views on the topic.

Take a Survey or Poll Find out what others think by polling neighbors or students in your school.

Conduct Interviews Interview people from organizations or agencies involved with the issue. Try to find representatives on each side of the issue.

Seek Referrals Ask those you talk to if they can suggest additional people or organizations you could contact.

❹ Analyze the Arguments

Look for the ideas or attitudes behind the opinions expressed in the arguments. What values influence the opinions? For example, suppose the issue is federal spending on education. One side says the government doesn't spend enough; the other side says it spends too much. It may be possible that the two sides really differ over whether the federal government should be involved with education at all.

Your analysis of underlying assumptions can help you determine whether the differences between sides will allow for any compromise. Parties who disagree about whether the federal government should be involved with education are less likely to compromise on how much the federal government should spend on it.

SkillBuilder

CRITICAL THINKING

Evaluating Arguments
As you examine the arguments presented on both sides of an issue, ask yourself questions such as the following.

- Is the person making this argument an expert on the topic?
- What are the logical consequences of each argument?
- Is this argument biased or objective? On what assumptions is it based?
- Is this statement a fact that can be confirmed in another source, or is it only an opinion? Are the facts accurate and up-to-date?

APPLYING WHAT YOU'VE LEARNED
What's wrong with each of these statements?

1. A woman president? Women are much too emotional to lead a country.
2. It's just stupid to spend millions of dollars looking for neutrinos, whatever they are.

THINK & PLAN

Reflecting on Your Ideas

1. What is the issue involved and the arguments used on each side?
2. Which arguments are based on facts and which are based on opinions or emotional responses?
3. What are the underlying assumptions of the arguments?

Presenting the Issue

Drafting Decisions As you start your first draft, don't worry about creating a masterpiece right away. Don't worry if your rough draft looks pretty rough. Just start getting your ideas down. The student model below begins by stating the main issue and summarizing the arguments on each side.

Student's Rough Draft

This is an important issue. How can I reach a really wide audience?

Should There Be Limits on Health Care?

People are becoming concerned over the cost of health care, which is continuing to rise steeply. New technologies are helping to save the lives of people once considered unsavable, but these advances are very expensive.

Dull beginning. Could I find an example of some kind to start with?

Growing medical costs and high health insurance premiums and the possibility of Medicare and Medicaid going broke—all of these have led to controversy over whether limits should be put on health care.

I should include some actual price tags. Find cost of transplants, dialysis, etc.

Those who favor limits say that they are a necessity. Without them, the entire health care system could collapse. Those who oppose limits say that everyone should be entitled to the best possible care no matter what it costs.

Get at their assumptions. Is health care an economic issue or a moral one? Isn't it both?

The pro-limits side says that money spent to keep people with terminal diseases alive might be better spent elsewhere. Those against limits say this is a "let them die" argument. They ask, Who has the right to decide who will be denied treatment?

I need to flesh out these arguments.

1 Start Your Draft

Your essay may employ a number of techniques, including those used in writing an analysis. (See page 567.) The following are some strategies you may find useful.

Explanation and Definition Much of your essay may be devoted to explaining the various arguments you have found and defining the terms you have used.

Comparison and Contrast Often your analysis will compare and contrast the ideas and assumptions of people involved in the controversy.

Narration Use some narrative details to enliven your analysis of the controversy. Often, an example can make a point more effectively than any other kind of support.

Quotations and Documentation Use quotations from people involved in the controversy to help your readers understand their points of view. Be sure you give the sources of quotations and other information.

❷ Analyze Your Draft

The following questions can help you analyze your draft.

- Have I clearly stated both sides of the argument?
- Have I treated both sides fairly?
- Have I identified and examined the underlying assumptions of the opposing parties?
- Have I considered what format to use for my final draft?

❸ Rework and Share

Your essay should include a clear statement of what the issue is, the arguments on each side of the issue, and evidence to support each side. Also keep in mind the following points.

Organize Your Draft You can show the evidence on each side of the controversy in one of two ways.

- Present all the evidence on one side of the issue, and then all the evidence on the other side.
- Divide the arguments into smaller points and contrast the two sides point by point.

Consider Using Visuals Visuals can help clarify the contrast between the two sides of a controversy. Consider presenting information in the form of charts, tables, graphs, time lines, or maps. See the SkillBuilder at the right for more on visual aids.

Draw a Conclusion Your essay should contain a conclusion. The following are four ways in which you can conclude your two-sided argument.

- Tell why you favor one side over the other.
- Recommend a compromise solution.
- Decide that the two positions are so rigid they can't be reconciled.
- Restate the positions and leave it up to the reader to decide.

PEER RESPONSE

Have a friend or classmate read your essay, and ask him or her these questions.

- How would you restate what the controversy is about?
- How would you state the arguments of each side?
- Was my analysis fair to both sides? Why or why not?

SkillBuilder

WRITER'S CRAFT

Elaborating with Visuals

Writing often can be more effective if supplemented by visuals.

- Charts can show how something works or how something is organized.
- Tables organize information into columns and rows.
- Graphs make statistical information easier to grasp by showing relationships or changes over time.

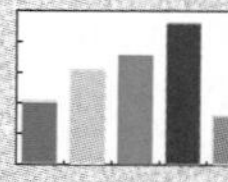

Bar graphs compare amounts.

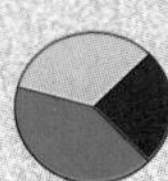

Pie charts show proportions of a whole.

Line graphs show changes in data over time.

- Time lines and maps help readers understand relationships of time and place.

APPLYING WHAT YOU'VE LEARNED

Describe one visual aid you could effectively use with your topic.

RETHINK & EVALUATE

Preparing to Revise

1. How can you improve your presentation of both sides?
2. How can you make sure you have treated both sides fairly?
3. How can you make your conclusion more effective?

Finishing Up

Your Revision Before you begin revising, put your draft aside for a while. Then come back to it and read it fresh. Does it accomplish all that you meant it to? You can also check your work against the Standards for Evaluation on the next page. Be sure that your revision takes into consideration the format you have chosen.

1 Revise and Edit

Ask yourself these questions as you think about your revision.

- Have I provided enough background information?
- How could I more clearly contrast the arguments of the two sides?
- Have I considered all of the underlying assumptions?
- What part of my essay could be considered biased?
- In what way could I improve my conclusion?

The example below was distributed as a pamphlet. Its student author wanted to bring this important issue to the attention of as many people as possible.

Student's Final Draft

New medical technologies save lives, but they also have contributed to rising health care costs. The nation now spends $415 million a year just for heart and liver transplants. Hospitals pass these costs on to patients, who must either pay huge bills or hope that their health insurance will cover the cost. Health insurance rates rise to cover the increased expense to insurance companies.

These new medical marvels and other factors (such as malpractice suits and longer life spans, leading to more medical problems among the aged) increase health care costs. The total cost to the nation rose from $74.4 billion in 1970 to $675 billion in 1990, nearly a tenfold increase in 20 years, and the costs could reach $1.6 trillion by the year 2000. How long will it

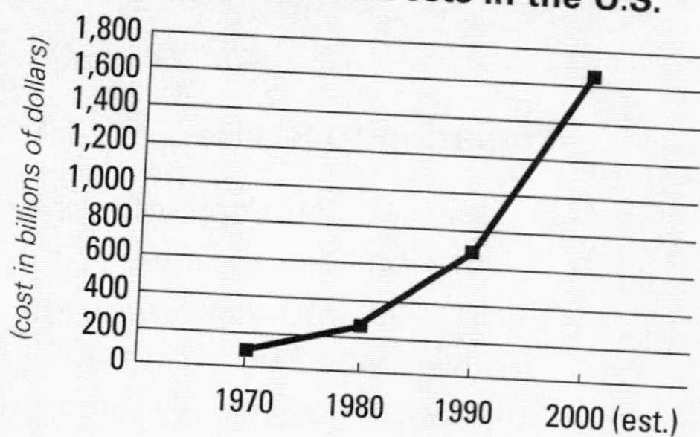

2

be before only the rich can afford health care? That question has led to a controversy over whether limits should be placed on health care.

A chief argument of those who want limits placed on health care concerns its cost. High costs, they say, will soon bring the health-care system into a state of economic crisis, possibly causing a breakdown of the entire system.

Those who argue against limits on health care point out that people pay for their health insurance, including Medicare. They have a right to expect that if they become ill they will receive whatever treatment they need.

Advocates of limits point out that many terminally ill patients require expensive treatment that will do nothing more than prolong lives of discomfort or pain, draining hospital resources that could be better spent on those whose medical problems are less serious.

The patient's condition should not be a factor, opponents of limits say. If a person needs and wants medical treatment, no one—not an insurance company or a hospital or doctor, and certainly not the government—has the right to deny it to them. If the medical technology is available to keep a person—even a terminally ill person—alive, it should be used.

3

card 8

Arguments for—4

card 7

Arguments for—3

Medical insurance costs are soaring.
Some people can no longer afford insurance.

card 6

Arguments for—2

Money spent on hopeless causes (expensive treatment for someone who is expected to die anyway) could be better spent on

- patients who have a better chance of recovery
- health care for the poor
- research on diseases that may be curable
- lowering health care costs for all by eliminating high costs to insurance companies

Note Cards for Speech

2 Share Your Work

A brochure and a speech about the topic are two ways of sharing your work. Here are some additional formats.

- Prepare an opening statement for a panel discussion.
- Write a letter to an editor or to the parties involved in the issue.
- Submit an article to your school newspaper or a magazine that publishes student writing.
- Write a script for a video documentary on the topic.

Standards for Evaluation

A two-sided argument

- provides enough background information to make the issue understandable
- clearly states the two sides of an issue
- presents the arguments of both sides without bias
- tries to uncover the assumptions and biases that underlie the arguments of the opposing sides
- includes a conclusion that summarizes the controversy or states the writer's conclusion about the issue

SkillBuilder

Using Quotations
Your essay may include both direct and indirect quotations.

Direct quotation *He said, "This was not an easy issue to resolve."*
Indirect quotation *He said that this was not an easy issue to resolve.*

GRAMMAR HANDBOOK

For more information about quotations, see page 1292 of the Grammar Handbook.

Editing Checklist Use the following questions as you edit.

- Have you correctly punctuated direct and indirect quotations?
- Have you avoided errors in agreement between subjects and verbs? between pronouns and their referents?
- Do you notice any groups of short, choppy sentences that could be combined?

REFLECT & ASSESS

Evaluate the Experience

1. In what way did your analysis of the arguments improve your understanding of the issue?
2. How did your opinion on the issue change as you learned more about it?

PORTFOLIO Put your answers to the questions above in your portfolio with your essay.

Reflect & Assess

UNIT FIVE: THE VICTORIANS

How has reading the selections in this unit helped you understand the Victorian era? Have you discovered any links between your life and the lives of people you have read about? Choose one or more of the options in each section to help you explore these questions.

REFLECTING ON THE UNIT

OPTION 1 Considering Relationships In this unit you have read about many kinds of personal relationships. Which of these relationships did you find the most inspiring? the most frightening? the most saddening? Which of the relationships seemed like ones that you might encounter today? Discuss your opinions with a classmate.

OPTION 2 Reflecting on Life's Ironies In several of the selections in this unit, you encountered speakers and narrators who reflect on life and its ironies. In a paragraph, compare two selections that you found ironic, exploring the speakers' or narrators' attitudes and circumstances. Then reflect on some of the ironies you have experienced in your own life.

OPTION 3 Looking at Character Think about the quotation from George Eliot at the beginning of this unit: "Our deeds determine us, as much as we determine our deeds." With a partner, choose a character or speaker from each part of the unit and brainstorm some ways in which each has been "determined" by his or her deeds. Then, for the class, role-play a conversation in which the two individuals discuss the quotation.

REFLECT & ASSESS *Self-Assessment: To explore how your understanding of the Victorian era has developed over the course of this unit, make a before-and-after chart. In it, show how your ideas about the lives and relationships of some Victorians have changed as a result of reading the selections.*

REVIEWING LITERARY CONCEPTS

OPTION 1 Understanding an Author's Purpose You have learned that an author's purpose may be to entertain, to inform, to express opinions, or to persuade. In a chart like the one shown, group this unit's selections according to their authors' purposes. Do any seem to fall under more than one heading? Are there any headings under which no selection fits? Compare your groupings with a partner's, and discuss any differences between the two.

To Entertain	To Inform	To Express Opinions	To Persuade

OPTION 2 **Analyzing Setting** In both fiction and poetry, setting often plays an important role—though the settings of poems are frequently implied rather than stated directly. From each part of this unit, choose three selections in which settings are either obvious or implied. List their titles, and describe, next to each, as much as you know about that work's setting. Then rank the selections according to how important you think setting is in them, with 1 representing the selection in which setting plays the most crucial role. Discuss your rankings with the rest of the class.

REFLECT & ASSESS *Self-Assessment: In addition to* setting *and* author's purpose, *the following literary terms were discussed in Unit Five. Copy this list in your notebook. Next to each term, write* W *(for "well"),* S *(for "somewhat"), or* N *(for "not at all") to indicate how well you think you understand it. Review the terms you are not sure about in the Handbook of Literary Terms (page 1192).*

elegy
dramatic monologue
third-person point of view
omniscient point of view
folk tale
controlling image
extended metaphor
sprung rhythm
satire
rhythm
rhyme
title
farce

PORTFOLIO BUILDING

- **QuickWrites** Several of the QuickWrites options in this unit asked you to present your responses to the messages, or themes, of selections. Choose two of your pieces in which you think you explored your reactions to themes most thoroughly. Then write a cover note describing why you found these pieces particularly insightful, and add the note, along with the pieces, to your portfolio.
- **Writing About Literature** Earlier in this unit, you evaluated a writer's ideas and presentation of those ideas. Reread your essay now. If you could give the writer advice on how to present his or her ideas more effectively, what would you say? If you wish, add your notes to your portfolio.
- **Writing from Experience** Reread the essay in which you presented both sides of a controversial issue. Think about how your attitude toward the subject changed as you researched it. How do you account for your change in attitude? Write several sentences about the evidence that influenced you the most.
- **Personal Choice** Think back over the various activities and writing assignments that you completed for this unit, as well as any work that you have done on your own. Is there any work that you would do differently now, in light of what you have learned since doing it? Write a brief paragraph explaining the changes you would make, attach it to your writing or activity record, and add both to your portfolio.

REFLECT & ASSESS *Self-Assessment: Compare what you have chosen for your portfolio during your work on Unit Five with what was already in your portfolio. Do you see any progress in your work? In what areas? Jot down your thoughts in your notebook.*

SETTING GOALS

You have read short stories, poems, nonfiction, and even a full-length play in this unit. At this point, which genre of literature appeals to you the most, and why? What other works belonging to that genre would you like to read this year? Explore these questions in a paragraph or two.

1901–1950

1 9 0 1 - 1 9 5 0

Emerging Modernism

I feel suddenly attached not to the past but to the **future.**

Virginia Woolf
novelist, critic, and essayist

Abstraction on Spectrum (Organization, 5) (about 1914–1917), Stanton MacDonald-Wright. Oil on canvas, 30 ⅛″ × 24 3⁄16″, purchased with funds from the Coffin Fine Arts Trust, Nathan Emory Coffin Collection of the Des Moines (Iowa) Art Center (1962.21).

TIME LINE

Emerging Modernism

1901–1950

1901

Queen Victoria dies and is succeeded by her son Edward VII

1903

Emmeline Pankhurst founds Women's Social and Political Union, dedicated to obtaining women's suffrage in Britain

1907

Britain, France, and Russia form alliance known as Triple Entente

1910

Edward VII dies and is succeeded by his son George V

1912

More than 1,500 drown when S.S. *Titanic* sinks in Atlantic

1913

First production of George Bernard Shaw's *Pygmalion;* D. H. Lawrence's *Sons and Lovers* published

1914

Assassination of Archduke Francis Ferdinand in Sarajevo leads to outbreak of World War I; Britain enters war after Germany invades Belgium

1916

Easter Rebellion fails to achieve Irish independence

1918

World War I ends with signing of armistice on November 11; British women over 30 are granted right to vote

1919

Treaty of Versailles signed; Britain joins League of Nations; Lady Astor becomes first female member of Parliament

1921

Irish Free State established; Northern Ireland remains in union with Great Britain

1922

James Joyce's *Ulysses* published in Paris; T. S. Eliot's *The Waste Land* published; regular radio broadcasts begin in Britain

Period *Pieces*

1923
William Butler Yeats receives Nobel Prize in literature

1927
Virginia Woolf's *To the Lighthouse* published

1929
Worldwide depression begins, during which British unemployment reaches 3 million

1933
Adolf Hitler comes to power in Germany; first German concentration camp built at Dachau

1936
George V dies; when his son Edward VIII abdicates, Edward's younger brother becomes king as George VI

1937
Pablo Picasso's revolutionary painting *Guernica,* expressing horrors of modern warfare, displayed at Paris Exposition

1939
World War II begins with German invasion of Poland

1940
Winston Churchill becomes prime minister; France falls to German forces; Battle of Britain begins

1945
World War II ends

1947
Britain grants independence to India and Pakistan

1949
Britain joins North Atlantic Treaty Organization (NATO); Irish Free State becomes independent Republic of Ireland

1949
George Orwell's *1984* published

California Clipper, mid-1930s

Telephone, 1920s–1930s

Clock in style known as Art Deco, c. 1935

INTRODUCTION

Emerging Modernism
1901–1950

From the accession of Edward VII in 1901 until the outbreak of World War I, Britain remained the dominant political, economic, and military power in the world. The world, however, was rapidly changing. Recent advances, including electric power and the automobile, were completely transforming everyday life. Through strikes and the emergence of the Labor party, British workers were obtaining economic and political power. Women were growing increasingly vocal in public demonstrations, demanding the right to vote. In Ireland, as well as India and other British colonies, nationalist movements were gaining momentum. At the same time, colonial and commercial rivalries were driving European powers into competing alliances, such as the Triple Entente of Britain, France, and Russia, formed in 1907. These rivalries would escalate into World War I, shattering the Victorian way of life forever.

Far left: George V, Victoria, Edward VII, and Edward VIII. *Above:* Women demanding the right to vote.

World War I

Known at the time as the Great War, World War I was precipitated by the assassination of Archduke Francis Ferdinand, heir to the throne of Austria-Hungary, by a Serbian nationalist in Sarajevo on June 28, 1914. Austria's demands for satisfaction from Serbia were impossibly harsh, and when Serbia was unable to meet them, Austria declared war on Serbia. The Russian czar came to the aid of his fellow Slavs in Serbia, mobilizing troops along the border of Austria's strongest ally, Germany,

Scenes of World War I trench warfare. *Right:* Body armor.

which proceeded to declare war on Russia and France. A German invasion of neutral Belgium prompted Britain, already committed by the Triple Entente, to join the war on the side of France and Russia. After British and French forces halted the Germans' westward advance at the First Battle of the Marne in September 1914, both sides dug in, locked together in bloody trench warfare—a chaos of mud, barbed wire, exploding shells and hand grenades, machine guns, tanks, and poison gas. This stalemate would drag on for four years, with massive propaganda intensifying the bitterness and leaders refusing to admit that the carnage and devastation were in vain.

In 1917 disillusionment with the failures of the war effort led to revolution in Russia. A moderate government was formed to replace the czar, but it was soon overthrown by Lenin's Bolsheviks, who promptly established a Communist state, agreed to a separate peace with Germany, and withdrew from the war. By then, however, the United States had entered it, tipping the balance in favor of Britain and France and forcing Germany to sue for peace. In the subsequent negotiations, French fears and anti-German sentiment resulted in the highly punitive Treaty of Versailles. To help defuse future crises, the treaty established the League of Nations, brainchild of the U.S. president Woodrow Wilson. The moderating U.S. influence was lost, however, when Congress refused to sign the treaty and join the league.

Aftermath of the War

Through the provisions of the Treaty of Versailles, Britain acquired several former German colonies in Africa and became "trustee" of large chunks of the Middle East that had been part of the Turkish (or Ottoman) Empire, a German ally. With France a war-torn shambles, Russia ravaged by internal conflict, and the United States abandoning the international scene, Britain seemed to be the

Language

In the 20th century, the English language has increasingly reflected the fads and fancies of popular culture. The horrors of World War I made the delicacies of Victorian usage seem inappropriate, and by the 1920s a spirit of "anything goes" had made slang and colloquial language far more

acceptable. Modern warfare generated new words—*blimp* and *camouflage* in World War I, for example, and *radar* and *blitz* in World War II—as did new technologies, the terminologies of which sometimes differed from one side of the Atlantic to the other. Thus, what Americans called the phonograph and the radio were known as the gramophone and the wireless by their British counterparts. Later, when Americans watched TV, Britons were watching the telly. Despite these verbal differences, the main effect of the two world wars and the communications revolution was to bring speakers of English even closer together. In Britain, U.S. soldiers, Hollywood films, and recordings of American music all helped to spread American popular culture, including its distinctive vocabulary.

"Never in the field of human conflict was so much owed by so many to so few."

war's greatest victor. However, the nation had lost almost an entire generation of young men—over 750,000 killed and more than twice as many wounded—including a disproportionate number from the upper class, which had traditionally provided military leadership.

The casualties resulting from trench warfare had been so great, in fact, that halfway through the war the British government had been forced to make military service compulsory for the first time. Meanwhile, with so many of the nation's men fighting in France, British women had been forced to take on traditionally male jobs. Their contribution was acknowledged in 1918, when women over 30 were granted the right to vote.

Also acknowledged after the war was the military support supplied by Canada, Australia, New Zealand, and South Africa. By 1931, these former colonies, already largely self-governing, had been granted equal footing with Britain in the British Commonwealth of Nations. Britain moved more slowly with India, however, where nonviolent resistance to British rule, under the direction of the spiritual leader Mohandas K. Gandhi, was making Britain look bad in the eyes of the world. Britain did reach a compromise of sorts with Ireland, however. During the war, Irish republican extremists had courted German support, and on Easter Monday, 1916, they had launched an armed rebellion, seizing the General Post Office in Dublin. Although the rebellion had quickly been crushed, the British government's brutal punishment of its leaders led to widespread sympathy for their cause. In 1921, Britain succeeded in negotiating a partition with a group of Irish delegates, establishing the Irish Free State but allowing northern Ireland, with its Protestant majority loyal to the crown, to remain in the United Kingdom. The Irish Free State later became the Republic of Ireland.

While Britain was facing these problems, political turmoil was rocking nations dissatisfied with the terms of the Treaty of Versailles. Italy fell into the hands of the dictator Benito Mussolini, whose Fascist movement was based on an ideal of military glory. In the Soviet Union—the Communist successor of the Russian

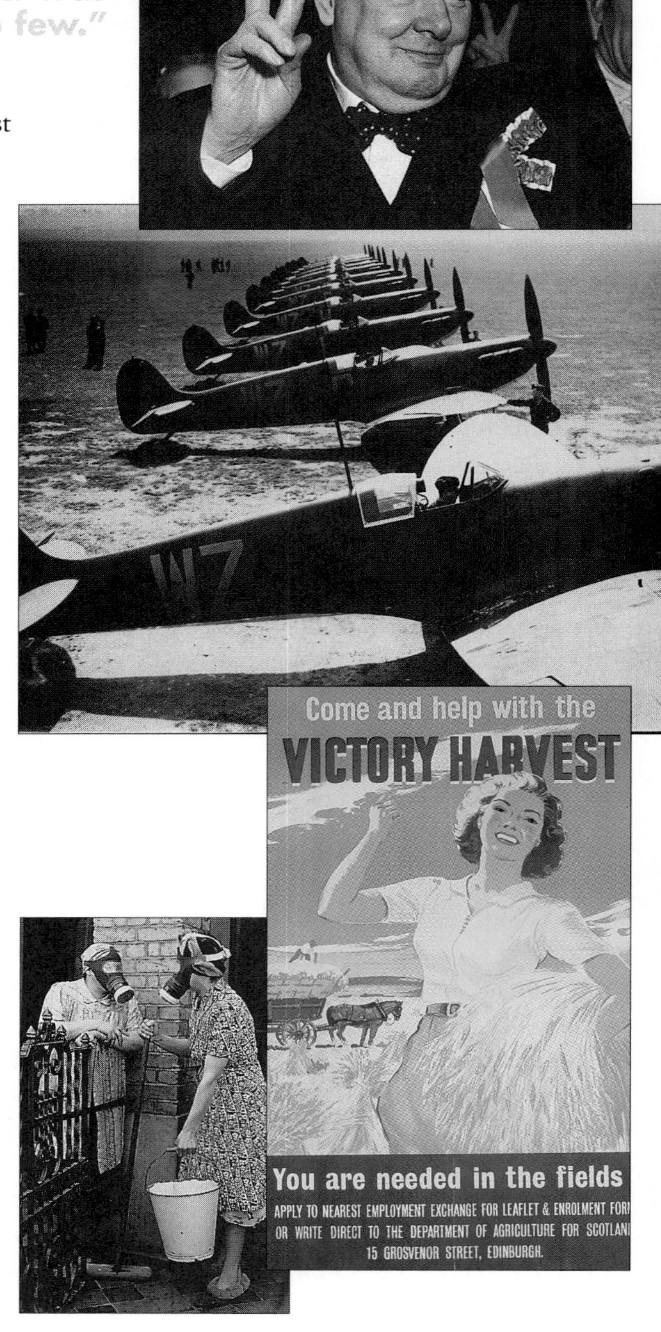

Top to bottom: Winston Churchill giving "victory" sign; World War II Spitfires; war poster asking for volunteers in war effort; London residents with gas masks

empire—another dictator, Joseph Stalin, came to power. The fear and confusion caused by the global economic depression that began in 1929 also favored the rise of dictators. Germany's postwar experiment with democracy ended abruptly in 1933, when its parliament gave dictatorial powers to Adolf Hitler, leader of the Nazi party and advocate of German racial and military supremacy. Soon Hitler was rebuilding the German army (in violation of the Treaty of Versailles) and constructing concentration camps where he secretly planned to exterminate Jews and other "racial undesirables."

In the wake of World War I, the Western democracies had little stomach for further violent confrontations. In 1931, when Japan invaded the Chinese region of Manchuria, China's appeals to the West were largely ignored. Four years later, when Italy invaded Ethiopia, the League of Nations invoked only mild economic sanctions. In the Spanish civil war of 1936, Fascists aided by Italy and Germany defeated the democratic loyalists, whose pleas for formal aid from the Western democracies went unheeded. Two years later, when Hitler forcibly annexed Austria and marched into Czechoslovakia, Britain and France maintained their policy of appeasement. Only when Hitler—after signing a secret pact with Stalin—invaded Poland on September 1, 1939, did Britain and France declare war on Germany. Italy and Japan soon allied themselves with Germany. World War II had begun.

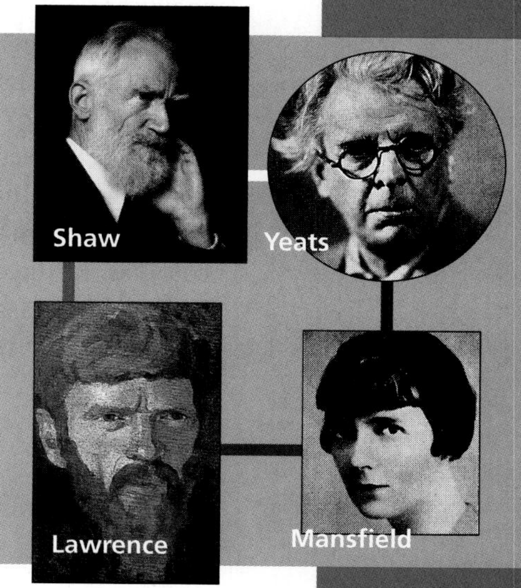

World War II

For a year after the fall of France in June 1940, Britain stood alone. With its entire population mobilized, civilian volunteers acted as plane spotters, firefighters, and rescue workers. All citizens endured severe shortages and rationing. Londoners

Literature

During the first decade of the 20th century—known as the Edwardian era— the major literary movements of Victorian times continued to flourish. The novelists John Galsworthy and Arnold Bennett; the short story writers W. Somerset Maugham, P. G. Wodehouse, and Saki; and the playwright George Bernard Shaw, among others, explored the changes and conflicts in the British class system in a realistic and often witty style. At the same time, a strong romantic spirit marked the work of Rupert Brooke, John Masefield, and other Edwardian poets. Romanticism was also evident in the early poetry of William Butler Yeats, the writings of Lady Gregory, and other works of the Irish Literary Renaissance—a movement propelled by the growing Irish nationalism and a renewed interest in the Celtic myths and legends of Ireland's past.

By 1910, however, Victorian ideas were yielding to the spirit of modernism, the movement that would dominate Western literature in the first half of the 20th century. Modernists stressed innovation as they attempted to create a new kind of literature for a new age. Such modernist poets as T. S. Eliot—and later Yeats—abandoned traditional patterns of stanza and meter for the more natural flow of **free verse.** Influenced by the French symbolists, they discarded the refined sentiment of the 19th century, preferring to convey emotions by means of strong images and unusual symbols. The works of modernist fiction writers —including Joseph Conrad, Katherine Mansfield, E. M. Forster, and D. H. Lawrence—began to reflect the new psychological theories of Sigmund Freud and Carl Jung.

Literature

Psychology also had a major impact on the pioneering fiction of James Joyce and Virginia Woolf. In different ways, each became a master of **stream of consciousness,** a narrative technique that attempts to depict the leaps and associations of the human mind.

The excitement of early modernism, however, crumbled into disillusionment for many of the writers who survived the devastation of World War I. In the aftermath of the war, writers tended to see the world as bleak and fragmentary—a Waste Land like that presented by T. S. Eliot in his most famous poem. The tone of many writers became bitter, expressing the cynicism of what has come to be called the Lost Generation. Others turned away from society altogether, exploring private concerns, personal experience, and the role of the artist.

Auden

Thomas

In the 1930s and 1940s, the growth of fascism and communism and the trauma of World War II prompted many British writers to focus again on social concerns. W. H. Auden and Stephen Spender examined and criticized society in much of their poetry; Aldous Huxley, Graham Greene, and George Orwell did likewise in their fiction. Aspects of modernism were increasingly accepted as they became more familiar, and mere novelty played a less important role in literature than before. Free verse remained popular, but such poets as Auden and Dylan Thomas were equally at home with more traditional forms. In fiction, the use of the stream-of-consciousness technique became more widespread and less obscure.

slept in subways while bombs rained on the city above. During this period, known as the Battle of Britain, a handful of well-trained fighter pilots battered away at the German bombers. Prime Minister Winston Churchill praised these heroes of the Royal Air Force, stating that "never in the field of human conflict was so much owed by so many to so few."

In 1941, Hitler broke his pact with Stalin and invaded the Soviet Union. Later that year Japan bombed Pearl Harbor, and the United States entered the war. With these new allies, Britain was able to persevere until the war ended in 1945. Nearly 50 million people died in World War II, including over 10 million in concentration camps and almost a quarter million British civilians. The war also drained Britain financially.

After the war, devastated by widespread poverty and in desperate need of refashioning their social order, Britons turned to the nation's young liberals, electing a Parliament overwhelmingly dominated by Labor members. Over the next few years, the Labor government transformed Britain into a welfare state, setting up a national health-care system and nationalizing such industries as steel, coal, and railroads. Britain also began slowly to relinquish its colonies. In the climate of the cold war, with the United States assuming a leading role in international affairs, Britain was no longer to be the world's greatest power.

LASERLINKS
• *HISTORICAL LITERARY CONNECTION*

Through his nonviolent resistance to British rule, Mohandas K. Gandhi helped win independence for India in 1947.

PART 1 *Appearance Versus Reality*

In the early 20th century, many people began to challenge the Victorian sense of decorum and class structure. They probed beneath society's mannered surface to explore the disquieting realities of an imperfect and sometimes harsh world. Writers began to pen detailed descriptions of city and social life—some writing stories merely to entertain, others seeking to expose the deceptions and disillusionment of modern life. As you read the selections in this part of Unit Six, consider how honestly today's society confronts reality.

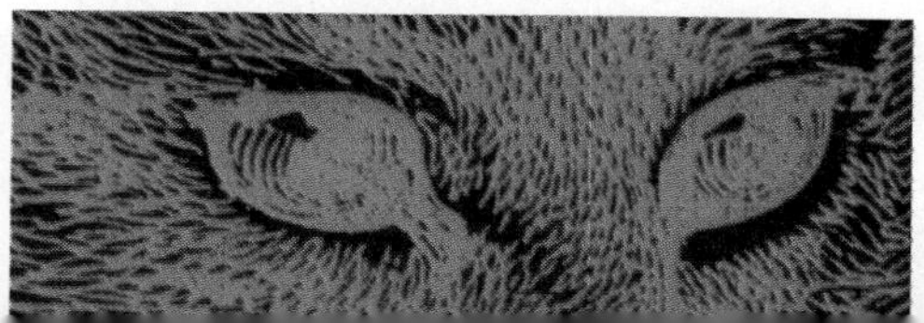

PREVIEWING

FICTION

The Kit-Bag

Algernon Blackwood

PERSONAL CONNECTION

Think about the best ghost story you know. Did you read it in a book, see it in a movie, or listen to someone tell it? How old were you at the time? What was it about the story that frightened you the most? After sharing your story with a classmate, try to decide why people enjoy this kind of story.

LITERARY/CULTURAL CONNECTION

In Britain, the ghost story emerged as a literary genre during the 1820s and steadily grew in popularity, reaching its greatest heights between 1890 and 1940. During this time, many notable British writers—including Rudyard Kipling, Joseph Conrad, and Thomas Hardy—tried their hand at tales of horror. Others, like Algernon Blackwood, devoted their writing efforts almost exclusively to this genre.

"The Kit-Bag," written in the early years of the 20th century, deals with the aftermath of a murder trial in the British courts. In the British legal system, only certain lawyers, known as barristers, are allowed to represent clients in the higher courts. Some of the most senior barristers are selected to serve as King's (or Queen's) Counsels—"K.C.'s" or "Q.C.'s."

WRITING CONNECTION

In your notebook, create a chart similar to the one shown. Use one of three adjectives—*unaffected, nervous,* or *terrified*—to indicate how much fear you feel in each of the circumstances listed. Feel free to add one or more other circumstances that frighten you or that may frighten others. With classmates, discuss the various circumstances and your reactions to them. Then, as you read "The Kit-Bag," compare your personal threshold of fear with that of the main character.

Circumstance	Reaction
dark places	
being alone at night	
the sight of blood	
thunderstorms	
graveyards	

LASERLINKS
• *ART GALLERY*

Algernon Blackwood

The Kit-Bag

When the words "Not Guilty" sounded through the crowded courtroom that dark December afternoon, Arthur Wilbraham, the great criminal K.C., and leader for the triumphant defense, was represented by his junior: but Johnson, his private secretary, carried the verdict across to his chambers like lightning.

"It's what we expected, I think," said the barrister, without emotion; "and, personally, I am glad the case is over." There was no particular sign of pleasure that his defense of John Turk, the murderer, on a plea of insanity, had been successful, for no doubt he felt, as everybody who had watched the case felt, that no man had ever better deserved the gallows.

"I'm glad too," said Johnson. He had sat in the court for ten days watching the face of the man who had carried out with callous detail one of the most brutal and cold-blooded murders of recent years.

The counsel glanced up at his secretary. They were more than employer and employed; for family and other reasons, they were friends. "Ah, I remember; yes," he said with a kind smile, "and you want to get away for Christmas? You're going to skate and ski in

WORDS TO KNOW
callous (kăl′əs) *adj.* unfeeling; heartless

the Alps, aren't you? If I was your age I'd come with you."

Johnson laughed shortly. He was a young man of twenty-six, with a delicate face like a girl's. "I can catch the morning boat now," he said; "but that's not the reason I'm glad the trial is over. I'm glad it's over because I've seen the last of that man's dreadful face. It positively haunted me. That white skin, with the black hair brushed low over the forehead, is a thing I shall never forget, and the description of the way the dismembered body was crammed and packed with lime[1] into that—"

"Don't dwell on it, my dear fellow," interrupted the other, looking at him curiously out of his keen eyes, "don't think about it. Such pictures have a trick of coming back when one least wants them." He paused a moment. "Now go," he added presently, "and enjoy your holiday. I shall want all your energy for my Parliamentary work when you get back. And don't break your neck skiing."

Johnson shook hands and took his leave. At the door he turned suddenly.

"I knew there was something I wanted to ask you," he said. "Would you mind lending me one of your kit-bags? It's too late to get one tonight, and I leave in the morning before the shops are open."

"Of course; I'll send Henry over with it to your rooms. You shall have it the moment I get home."

"I promise to take great care of it," said Johnson gratefully, delighted to think that within thirty hours he would be nearing the brilliant sunshine of the high Alps in winter. The thought of that criminal court was like an evil dream in his mind.

He dined at his club and went on to Bloomsbury, where he occupied the top floor in one of those old, gaunt houses in which the rooms are large and lofty. The floor below his own was vacant and unfurnished, and below that were other lodgers whom he did not know. It was cheerless, and he looked forward heartily to a change. The night was even more cheerless: it was miserable, and few people were about. A cold, sleety rain was driving down the streets before the keenest east wind he had ever felt. It howled dismally among the big, gloomy houses of the great squares, and when he reached his rooms he heard it whistling and shouting over the world of black roofs beyond his windows.

In the hall he met his landlady, shading a candle from the drafts with her thin hand. "This come by a man from Mr. Wilbr'im's, sir."

She pointed to what was evidently the kit-bag, and Johnson thanked her and took it upstairs with him. "I shall be going abroad in the morning for ten days, Mrs. Monks," he said. "I'll leave an address for letters."

"And I hope you'll 'ave a merry Christmas, sir," she said, in a raucous, wheezy voice that suggested spirits, "and better weather than this."

"I hope so too," replied her lodger, shuddering a little as the wind went roaring down the street outside.

When he got upstairs he heard the sleet volleying against the windowpanes. He put his kettle on to make a cup of hot coffee, and then set about putting a few things in order for his absence. "And now I must pack—such as my packing is," he laughed to himself, and set to work at once.

He liked the packing, for it brought the snow mountains so vividly before him, and made him forget the unpleasant scenes of the past ten days. Besides, it was not elaborate in nature. His friend had lent him the very thing—a stout canvas kit-bag, sack-shaped, with holes round the neck for the brass bar and padlock. It was a bit shapeless, true, and not much to look at, but its capacity

1. **the dismembered . . . lime:** the body was cut into pieces and packed with quicklime (calcium oxide), a chemical that inhibits the rotting of flesh.

was unlimited, and there was no need to pack carefully. He shoved in his waterproof coat, his fur cap and gloves, his skates and climbing boots, his sweaters, snow boots, and ear-caps; and then on the top of these he piled his woolen shirts and underwear, his thick socks, puttees,[2] and knickerbockers.[3] The dress suit came next, in case the hotel people dressed for dinner, and then, thinking of the best way to pack his white shirts, he paused a moment to reflect. "That's the worst of these kit-bags," he mused vaguely, standing in the center of the sitting room, where he had come to fetch some string.

A furious gust of wind rattled the windows...

It was after ten o'clock. A furious gust of wind rattled the windows as though to hurry him up, and he thought with pity of the poor Londoners whose Christmas would be spent in such a climate, whilst he was skimming over snowy slopes in bright sunshine, and dancing in the evening with rosy-cheeked girls—Ah! that reminded him; he must put in his dancing pumps and evening socks. He crossed over from his sitting room to the cupboard on the landing where he kept his linen.

And as he did so he heard someone coming softly up the stairs.

He stood still a moment on the landing to listen. It was Mrs. Monks's step, he thought; she must be coming up with the last post. But then the steps ceased suddenly, and he heard no more. They were at least two flights down, and he came to the conclusion they were too heavy to be those of his bibulous[4] landlady. No doubt they belonged to a late lodger who had mistaken his floor. He went into his bedroom and packed his pumps and dress shirts as best he could.

The kit-bag by this time was two-thirds full, and stood upright on its own base like a sack of flour. For the first time he noticed that it was old and dirty, the canvas faded and worn, and that it had obviously been subjected to rather rough treatment. It was not a very nice bag to have sent him—certainly not a new one, or one that his chief valued. He gave the matter a passing thought, and went on with his packing. Once or twice, however, he caught himself wondering who it could have been wandering down below, for Mrs. Monks had not come up with letters, and the floor was empty and unfurnished. From time to time, moreover, he was almost certain he heard a soft tread of someone padding about over the bare boards—cautiously, stealthily, as silently as possible—and, further, that the sounds had been lately coming distinctly nearer.

For the first time in his life he began to feel a little creepy. Then, as though to emphasize this feeling, an odd thing happened: as he left the bedroom, having just packed his recalcitrant white shirts, he noticed that the top of the kit-bag lopped over towards him with an extraordinary resemblance to a human face. The canvas fell into a fold like a nose and forehead, and the brass rings for the padlock just filled the position of the eyes. A shadow—or was it a travel stain? for he could not tell exactly—looked like hair. It gave him rather a turn, for it was so absurdly, so outrageously, like the face of John Turk, the murderer.

He laughed, and went into the front room, where the light was stronger.

"That horrid case has got on my mind," he thought; "I shall be glad of a change of scene and air." In the sitting room, however, he was

2. **puttees:** heavy cloth coverings for the lower legs.
3. **knickerbockers:** short, loose-fitting trousers gathered just below the knee.
4. **bibulous** (bĭb′yə-ləs): fond of alcoholic beverages.

WORDS TO KNOW

stealthily (stĕl′thĭ-lē) *adv.* in a quiet, secretive, or sneaky manner
recalcitrant (rĭ-kăl′sĭ-trənt) *adj.* stubborn; hard to deal with

not pleased to hear again that stealthy tread upon the stairs, and to realize that it was much closer than before, as well as unmistakably real. And this time he got up and went out to see who it could be creeping about on the upper staircase at so late an hour.

But the sound ceased; there was no one visible on the stairs. He went to the floor below, not without trepidation, and turned on the electric light to make sure that no one was hiding in the empty rooms of the unoccupied suite. There was not a stick of furniture large enough to hide a dog. Then he called over the banisters to Mrs. Monks, but there was no answer, and his voice echoed down into the dark vault of the house, and was lost in the roar of the gale that howled outside. Everyone was in bed and asleep—everyone except himself and the owner of this soft and stealthy tread.

"My absurd imagination, I suppose," he thought. "It must have been the wind after all, although—it seemed so *very* real and close, I thought." He went back to his packing. It was by this time getting on towards midnight. He drank his coffee up and lit another pipe—the last before turning in.

It is difficult to say exactly at what point fear begins, when the causes of that fear are not plainly before the eyes. Impressions gather on the surface of the mind, film by film, as ice gathers upon the surface of still water, but often so lightly that they claim no definite recognition from the consciousness. Then a point is reached where the accumulated impressions become a definite emotion, and the mind realizes that something has happened. With something of a start, Johnson suddenly recognized that he felt nervous—oddly nervous; also, that for some time past the causes of this feeling had been gathering slowly in his mind, but that he had only just reached the point where he was forced to acknowledge them.

The Haunted House (1896), Odilon Redon.

WORDS TO KNOW

trepidation (trĕp′ĭ-dā′shən) *n.* fearful uncertainty or worry

It was a singular and curious malaise that had come over him, and he hardly knew what to make of it. He felt as though he were doing something that was strongly objected to by another person, another person, moreover, who had some right to object. It was a most disturbing and disagreeable feeling, not unlike the persistent promptings of conscience; almost, in fact, as if he were doing something he knew to be wrong. Yet, though he searched vigorously and honestly in his mind, he could nowhere lay his finger upon the secret of this growing uneasiness, and it perplexed him. More, it distressed and frightened him.

"Pure nerves, I suppose," he said aloud with a forced laugh. "Mountain air will cure all that! Ah," he added, still speaking to himself, "and that reminds me—my snow glasses."

He was standing by the door of the bedroom during this brief soliloquy,[5] and as he passed quickly towards the sitting-room to fetch them from the cupboard he saw out of the corner of his eye the indistinct outline of a figure standing on the stairs, a few feet from the top. It was someone in a stooping position, with one hand on the banisters, and the face peering up towards the landing. And at the same moment he heard a shuffling footstep. The person who had been creeping about below all this time had at last come up to his own floor. Who in the world could it be? And what in the name of Heaven did he want?

Johnson caught his breath sharply and stood stock still. Then, after a few seconds' hesitation, he found his courage, and turned to investigate. The stairs, he saw to his utter amazement, were empty; there was no one. He felt a series of cold shivers run over him, and something about the muscles of his legs gave a little and grew weak. For the space of several minutes he peered steadily into the shadows that congregated about the top of the staircase where he had seen the figure, and then he walked fast—almost ran, in fact—into the light of the front room; but hardly had he passed inside the doorway when he heard someone come up the stairs behind him with a quick bound and go swiftly into his bedroom. It was a heavy, but at the same time a stealthy footstep—the tread of somebody who did not wish to be seen. And it was at this precise moment that the nervousness he had hitherto experienced leaped the boundary line, and entered the state of fear, almost of acute, unreasoning fear. Before it turned into terror there was a further boundary to cross, and beyond that again lay the region of pure horror. Johnson's position was an unenviable one.

"By Jove! That *was* someone on the stairs, then," he muttered, his flesh crawling all over; "and whoever it was has now gone into my bedroom." His delicate, pale face turned absolutely white, and for some minutes he hardly knew what to think or do. Then he realized intuitively that delay only set a premium upon fear; and he crossed the landing boldly and went straight into the other room, where, a few seconds before, the steps had disappeared.

"Pure nerves, I suppose,"

"Who's there? Is that you, Mrs. Monks?" he called aloud, as he went, and heard the first half of his words echo down the empty stairs, while the second half fell dead against the curtains in a room that apparently held no other human figure than his own.

"Who's there?" he called again, in a voice unnecessarily loud and that only just held firm. "What do you want here?"

The curtains swayed very slightly, and, as he saw it, his heart felt as if it almost missed a beat;

5. **soliloquy** (sə-lĭl'ə-kwē): the utterance of a person who is alone; monologue.

WORDS TO KNOW

singular (sĭng'gyə-lər) *adj.* unique, unusual, or remarkable
malaise (mă-lāz') *n.* a vague feeling of discomfort
intuitively (ĭn-to͞o'ĭ-tĭv-lē) *adv.* without conscious reasoning; instinctively

yet he dashed forward and drew them aside with a rush. A window, streaming with rain, was all that met his gaze. He continued his search, but in vain; the cupboards held nothing but rows of clothes, hanging motionless; and under the bed there was no sign of anyone hiding. He stepped backwards into the middle of the room, and, as he did so, something all but tripped him up. Turning with a sudden spring of alarm he saw—the kit-bag.

"Odd!" he thought. "That's not where I left it!" A few moments before it had surely been on his right, between the bed and the bath; he did not remember having moved it. It was very curious. What in the world was the matter with everything? Were all his senses gone queer? A terrific gust of wind tore at the windows, dashing the sleet against the glass with the force of a small gun-shot, and then fled away howling dismally over the waste of Bloomsbury roofs. A sudden vision of the Channel[6] next day rose in his mind and recalled him sharply to realities.

"There's no one here at any rate; that's quite clear!" he exclaimed aloud. Yet at the time he uttered them he knew perfectly well that his words were not true and that he did not believe them himself. He felt exactly as though someone was hiding close about him, watching all his movements, trying to hinder his packing in some way. "And two of my senses," he added, keeping up the pretense, "have played me the most absurd tricks: the steps I heard and the figure I saw were both entirely imaginary."

He went back to the front room, poked the fire into a blaze, and sat down before it to think. What impressed him more than anything else was the fact that the kit-bag was no longer where he had left it. It had been dragged nearer to the door.

What happened afterwards that night happened, of course, to a man already excited by fear, and was perceived by a mind that had not the full and proper control, therefore, of the senses. Outwardly, Johnson remained calm and master of himself to the end, pretending to the very last that everything he witnessed had a natural explanation, or was merely delusions of his tired nerves. But inwardly, in his very heart, he knew all along that someone had been hiding downstairs in the empty suite when he came in, that this person had watched his opportunity and then stealthily made his way up to the bedroom, and that all he saw and heard afterwards, from the moving of the kit-bag to—well, to the other things this story has to tell—were caused directly by the presence of this invisible person.

And it was here, just when he most desired to keep his mind and thoughts controlled, that the vivid pictures received day after day upon the mental plates exposed in the courtroom of the Old Bailey,[7] came strongly to light and developed themselves in the darkroom of his inner vision. Unpleasant, haunting memories have a way of coming to life again just when the mind least desires them—in the silent watches of the night, on sleepless pillows, during the lonely hours spent by sick and dying beds. And so now, in the same way, Johnson saw nothing but the dreadful face of John Turk, the murderer, lowering[8] at him from every corner of his mental field of vision; the white skin, the evil eyes, and the fringe of black hair low over the forehead. All the pictures of those ten days in court crowded back into his mind unbidden, and very vivid.

"This is all rubbish and nerves," he exclaimed at length, springing with sudden energy from his chair. "I shall finish my packing and go to bed. I'm overwrought, overtired. No doubt, at this

6. **Channel:** the English Channel—a stretch of ocean separating southern England from France. (Crossing the Channel is the first leg of Johnson's planned trip to the Alps.)

7. **Old Bailey:** the headquarters of the Central Criminal Court in London.

8. **lowering** (lou′ər-ĭng): scowling in a dark and threatening way.

WORDS TO KNOW

overwrought (ō′vər-rôt′) *adj.* excessively nervous or excited

rate I shall hear steps and things all night!"

But his face was deadly white all the same. He snatched up his field glasses and walked across to the bedroom, humming a music-hall song as he went—a trifle too loud to be natural; and the instant he crossed the threshold and stood within the room something turned cold about his heart, and he felt that every hair on his head stood up.

The kit-bag lay close in front of him, several feet nearer to the door than he had left it, and just over its crumpled top he saw a head and face slowly sinking down out of sight as though someone were crouching behind it to hide, and at the same moment a sound like a long-drawn sigh was distinctly audible in the still air about him between the gusts of the storm outside.

Johnson had more courage and willpower than the girlish indecision of his face indicated; but at first such a wave of terror came over him that for some seconds he could do nothing but stand and stare. A violent trembling ran down his back and legs, and he was conscious of a foolish, almost a hysterical, impulse to scream aloud. That sigh seemed in his very ear, and the air still quivered with it. It was unmistakably a human sigh.

"Who's there?" he said at length, finding his voice; but though he meant to speak with loud decision, the tones came out instead in a faint whisper, for he had partly lost the control of his tongue and lips.

He stepped forward, so that he could see all round and over the kit-bag. Of course there was nothing there, nothing but the faded carpet and the bulging canvas sides. He put out his hands and threw open the mouth of the sack where it had fallen over, being only three parts full, and then he saw for the first time that round the inside, some six inches from the top, there ran a broad smear of dull crimson. It was an old and faded blood stain. He uttered a scream, and drew back his hands as if they had been burnt. At the same moment the kit-bag gave a faint, but unmistakable, lurch forward towards the door.

Johnson collapsed backwards, searching with his hands for the support of something solid, and the door, being farther behind him than he realized, received his weight just in time to prevent his falling, and shut to with a resounding bang. At the same moment the swinging of his left arm accidentally touched the electric switch, and the light in the room went out.

"Who's there?"

It was an awkward and disagreeable predicament, and if Johnson had not been possessed of real pluck he might have done all manner of foolish things. As it was, however, he pulled himself together, and groped furiously for the little brass knob to turn the light on again. But the rapid closing of the door had set the coats hanging on it a-swinging, and his fingers became entangled in a confusion of sleeves and pockets, so that it was some moments before he found the switch. And in those few moments of bewilderment and terror two things happened that sent him beyond recall over the boundary into the region of genuine horror—he distinctly heard the kit-bag shuffling heavily across the floor in jerks, and close in front of his face sounded once again the sigh of a human being.

In his anguished efforts to find the brass button on the wall he nearly scraped the nails from his fingers, but even then, in those frenzied moments of alarm—so swift and alert are the impressions of a mind keyed up by a vivid emotion—he had time to realize that he dreaded the return of the light, and that it might be better for him to stay hidden in the merciful screen of

WORDS TO KNOW

pluck (plŭk) *n.* courage and daring in the face of difficulties

darkness. It was but the impulse of a moment, however, and before he had time to act upon it he had yielded automatically to the original desire, and the room was flooded again with light.

But the second instinct had been right. It would have been better for him to have stayed in the shelter of the kind darkness. For there, close before him, bending over the half-packed kit-bag, clear as life in the merciless glare of the electric light, stood the figure of John Turk, the murderer. Not three feet from him the man stood, the fringe of black hair marked plainly against the pallor of the forehead, the whole horrible presentment[9] of the scoundrel, as vivid as he had seen him day after day in the Old Bailey, when he stood there in the dock, cynical and callous, under the very shadow of the gallows.

In a flash Johnson realized what it all meant: the dirty and much-used bag; the smear of crimson within the top; the dreadful stretched condition of the bulging sides. He remembered how the victim's body had been stuffed into a canvas bag for burial, the ghastly, dismembered fragments forced with lime into this very bag; and the bag itself produced as evidence—it all came back to him as clear as day. . . .

Very softly and stealthily his hand groped behind him for the handle of the door, but before he could actually turn it the very thing that he most of all dreaded came about, and John Turk lifted his devil's face and looked at him. At the same moment that heavy sigh passed through the air of the room, formulated somehow into words: "It's my bag. And I want it."

Johnson just remembered clawing the door open, and then falling in a heap upon the floor of the landing, as he tried frantically to make his way into the front room.

He remained unconscious for a long time, and it was still dark when he opened his eyes and realized that he was lying, stiff and bruised, on the cold boards. Then the memory of what he had seen rushed back into his mind, and he promptly fainted again. When he woke the second time the wintry dawn was just beginning to peep in at the windows, painting the stairs a cheerless, dismal grey, and he managed to crawl into the front room, and cover himself with an overcoat in the armchair, where at length he fell asleep.

For some minutes Johnson could not find his voice.

A great clamor woke him. He recognized Mrs. Monks's voice, loud and voluble.

"What! You ain't been to bed, sir! Are you ill, or has anything 'appened? And there's an urgent gentleman to see you, though, it ain't seven o'clock yet, and—"

"Who is it?" he stammered. "I'm all right, thanks. Fell asleep in my chair, I suppose."

"Someone from Mr. Wilb'rim's, and he says he ought to see you quick before you go abroad, and I told him—"

"Show him up, please, at once," said Johnson, whose head was whirling, and his mind was still full of dreadful visions.

Mr. Wilbraham's man came in with many apologies, and explained briefly and quickly that an absurd mistake had been made, and that the wrong kit-bag had been sent over the night before.

"Henry somehow got hold of the one that came over from the courtroom, and Mr. Wilbraham only discovered it when he saw his own lying in his room, and asked why it had not gone to you," the man said.

"Oh!" said Johnson stupidly.

"And he must have brought you the one from the murder case instead, sir, I'm afraid," the man continued, without the ghost of an expression on his face. "The one John Turk packed the dead body in. Mr. Wilbraham's awful upset about it,

9. **presentment:** image; appearance.

WORDS TO KNOW

voluble (vŏl'yə-bəl) *adj.* characterized by a rapid flow of words; talkative

sir, and told me to come over first thing this morning with the right one, as you were leaving by the boat."

He pointed to a clean-looking kit-bag on the floor, which he had just brought. "And I was to bring the other one back, sir," he added casually.

For some minutes Johnson could not find his voice. At last he pointed in the direction of his bedroom. "Perhaps you would kindly unpack it for me. Just empty the things out on the floor."

The man disappeared into the other room, and was gone for five minutes. Johnson heard the shifting to and fro of the bag, and the rattle of the skates and boots being unpacked.

"Thank you, sir," the man said, returning with the bag folded over his arm. "And can I do anything more to help you, sir?"

"What is it?" asked Johnson, seeing that he still had something he wished to say.

The man shuffled and looked mysterious. "Beg pardon, sir, but knowing your interest in the Turk case, I thought you'd maybe like to know what's happened—"

"Yes."

"John Turk killed himself last night with poison immediately on getting his release, and he left a note for Mr. Wilbraham saying as he'd be much obliged if they'd have him put away, same as the woman he murdered, in the old kit-bag."

"What time—did he do it?" asked Johnson.

"Ten o'clock last night, sir, the warder[10] says." ❖

10. **warder:** prison guard.

RESPONDING OPTIONS

FROM PERSONAL RESPONSE *TO* CRITICAL ANALYSIS

REFLECT 1. Were you surprised by the ending of the story? Explain your thoughts.

RETHINK 2. In your opinion, was Johnson's mind playing tricks on him, or did he really see John Turk's ghost? Find details in the story to support your view.

3. Do you think Johnson will still go on his holiday? Why or why not?

4. What aspects of this story seem believable to you?

5. How does the mood of this story compare with the mood of the ghost story you recalled for the Personal Connection on page 768?

Consider
- the setting of each story
- the use of the supernatural in each story
- how predictable each story was
- the outcome of each story
- how frightened you were by each story

RELATE 6. Many people complain that there is too much violence in the scary stories, movies, and television shows of today. Is there much explicit violence in this story? Can a story be scary without violence?

ANOTHER PATHWAY

As this story progresses, Johnson is gripped by increasing levels of fear—from feeling "a little creepy" to experiencing "genuine horror." Trace the emotions and physical sensations that Johnson experiences during his ordeal, and use a diagram like the one shown below to arrange them in the order of occurrence. Compare your findings with those of your classmates.

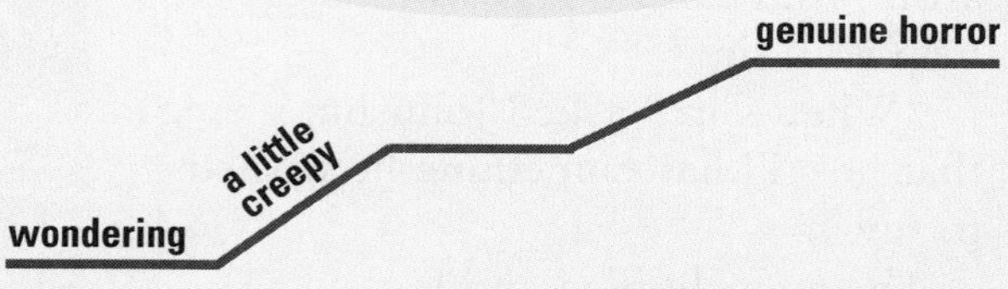

QUICKWRITES

1. Write a **newspaper article** informing the public of John Turk's suicide. Be sure to include a headline.
2. Read another story by Algernon Blackwood and draft an **essay** in which you compare it with "The Kit-Bag."
3. Write a **proposal** for a movie version of "The Kit-Bag." Include information on how you would adapt the story for the screen, what actors you would want for the main roles, and what special effects and music you would use.
4. Write a **supernatural tale** of your own, being sure to include foreshadowing.

PORTFOLIO *Save your writing. You may want to use it later as a spring-board to a piece for your portfolio.*

LITERARY CONCEPTS

A **supernatural tale** is a story that passes beyond the bounds of reality, usually by involving beings, powers, or events that are unexplainable by known forces or laws of nature. In many supernatural tales, **foreshadowing**—hints or clues that point to later events—is used to encourage readers to anticipate the unthinkable. Sometimes readers are left wondering whether a supernatural event has really taken place or is the product of a character's imagination. In an effective supernatural tale, the writer manipulates readers' feelings of curiosity and fear to produce a mounting sense of excitement. In what ways does Blackwood manipulate readers of "The Kit Bag"?

THE WRITER'S STYLE

In "The Kit-Bag," Blackwood introduces an ingredient that is common to many tales of the supernatural—the element of doubt. When describing a seemingly unnatural event, he often creates doubt in readers' minds by suggesting either that the event is not happening or that it has a natural explanation. Look through the story for passages in which the author introduces this element of doubt.

ALTERNATIVE ACTIVITIES

1. Make a papier-mâché or clay **mask** of John Turk's face. Use details from the story to guide you in painting the mask.
2. Tape-record **sound effects** appropriate for a radio broadcast of "The Kit-Bag." Play the sound effects as you read the story aloud in your scariest voice.
3. Create three **illustrations** that might accompany "The Kit-Bag" in an anthology of supernatural tales. Use quotations from the story as your captions.
4. Use resources in your school or public library to research accounts of ghosts by people who believe they have actually seen them. Present your findings to the class in an **oral report,** being sure to indicate whether you think the accounts are convincing.

CRITIC'S CORNER

The American author H. P. Lovecraft, known for his own tales of the supernatural, wrote of Algernon Blackwood's ability to understand the workings of "sensitive minds" and to "evoke . . . a story from a simple . . . psychological description." In what ways might "The Kit-Bag" be considered a psychological description?

ACROSS THE CURRICULUM

Civics ***Cooperative Learning*** Working with a small group of classmates, research the various strategies that might be used by an attorney to defend someone charged with murder. If possible, base your report on actual cases that the members of your group have heard or read about. Present your findings to the class.

WORDS TO KNOW

EXERCISE A For each group of words below, write the letter of the word that is most nearly synonymous with the boldfaced word.

1. **singular:** (a) lonely, (b) exceptional, (c) unimportant
2. **malaise:** (a) evil, (b) overconfidence, (c) uneasiness
3. **recalcitrant:** (a) abusive, (b) unmanageable, (c) critical
4. **stealthily:** (a) slyly, (b) abundantly, (c) dangerously
5. **overwrought:** (a) distressed, (b) clumsy, (c) fancy

EXERCISE B Review the Words to Know at the bottom of the selection pages. Then write the vocabulary word, not used in Exercise A, that is suggested by each set of idioms below.

1. feel in one's bones, have a sixth sense, have a knack for
2. be a windbag, have the gift of gab, shoot the breeze, chew the fat
3. have ice water in one's veins, not give a hoot, be hardhearted
4. scared to death, with one's heart in one's throat, living in fear
5. show gumption, tough it out, have starch in one's spine, take the bull by the horns

ALGERNON BLACKWOOD

1869–1951

Algernon Blackwood lived a life as fascinating as the strange supernatural tales for which he is famous. Born to strict parents in Kent, England, he escaped the confines of family life at the age of 20 by moving to Canada. After managing to lose his entire inheritance within a year, he lived on the fringes of starvation between jobs as a reporter, artist's model, actor, and soap maker. He tried prospecting for gold and spent a brief but comfortable period as private secretary to a millionaire banker before returning to England when he was 30.

Blackwood felt no desire to write and, despite some newspaper work, believed that he had little talent. He was, however, consumed by three passions: he was a voracious reader of books in French, German, and English; he loved nature; and he was fascinated with the idea of psychic powers. At age 36, to amuse himself, Blackwood began to express his thoughts in story form. He had no intention of publishing the stories; but without his knowledge a friend submitted them to a publisher, who issued the first of what was to be more than 30 books written by Blackwood.

OTHER WORKS *The Empty House and Other Ghosts, The Listener and Other Stories, The Lost Valley and Other Stories, Pan's Garden*

PREVIEWING

FICTION

The Infant Prodigy

Thomas Mann

PERSONAL CONNECTION

Have you ever heard about a child who was a prodigy—one, that is, who had an extraordinary talent or ability? If so, what talent or ability did the child possess? What is your reaction to stories of child prodigies? Share your thoughts with classmates.

Portrait of Mozart as a child at the piano (about 1766–1767), unknown artist. Mozart House, Salzburg, Austria, Scala/Art Resource, New York.

LITERARY/BIOGRAPHICAL CONNECTION

Thomas Mann has been called Germany's greatest novelist of the 20th century. He became internationally famous during the early 1900s and was awarded the Nobel Prize in literature in 1929. Like most of the other writers represented in this unit, Mann tended to focus on discrepancies between appearance and reality—how, for example, a person who outwardly appears to fit into society may be inwardly struggling with isolation and loneliness. He also frequently explored the power of illusion to disguise and distort reality.

Many of Mann's writings deal with the role of the individual in society, and especially with the life of the artist—the gifted creator of music, paintings, or literature who, like the prodigy in this story, is in a sense the ultimate individual, since extraordinary talent sets him or her apart. Often Mann depicts artists as outcasts, people who seem to blend into society but who in reality are never comfortable outside the realm of their imagination or creative environment. Although he sympathized with the artist, Mann also recognized the need for the creative genius to resolve the conflicts that make it difficult for him or her to live in the real world.

READING CONNECTION

Recognizing Tone Tone—a writer's attitude toward his or her subject—plays a major role in "The Infant Prodigy." As you read the story, write in your notebook the words and phrases that you think reveal the tone. Try to gather an overall impression of Mann's attitude toward the characters and their actions.

Using Your Reading Log Use your reading log to record your responses to the questions inserted in the selection. Also jot down any other thoughts and feelings that come to you as you read.

THOMAS MANN
The
Infant
Prodigy

The infant prodigy entered. The hall became quiet.

It became quiet and then the audience began to clap, because somewhere at the side a leader of mobs, a born organizer, clapped first. The audience had heard nothing yet, but they applauded; for a mighty publicity organization had heralded the prodigy and people were already hypnotized, whether they knew it or not.

The prodigy came from behind a splendid screen embroidered with Empire garlands and great conventionalized[1] flowers, and climbed nimbly up the steps to the platform, diving into the applause as into a bath; a little chilly and shivering, but yet as though into a friendly element. He advanced to the edge of the platform and smiled as though he were about to be photographed; he made a shy, charming gesture of greeting, like a little girl.

He was dressed entirely in white silk, which the audience found enchanting. The little white jacket was fancifully cut, with a sash underneath it, and even his shoes were made of white silk. But against the white socks his bare little legs stood out quite brown; for he was a Greek boy.

He was called Bibi Saccellaphylaccas.[2] And such indeed was his name. No one knew what Bibi was the pet name for, nobody but the impresario,[3] and he regarded it as a trade secret. Bibi had smooth black hair reaching to his shoulders; it was parted on the side and fastened back from the narrow domed forehead by a little silk bow. His was the most harmless childish countenance in the world, with an unfinished nose and guileless mouth. The area beneath his pitch-black mouselike eyes was already a little tired and visibly lined. He looked as though he were nine years old but was really eight and

1. **conventionalized:** stylized.
2. **Bibi Saccellaphylaccas** (bē′bē sə-kĕl′ə-fĭ-lä′kəs).
3. **impresario** (ĭm′prĭ-sär′ē-ō′): the manager or producer of a concert or performance.

given out for seven. It was hard to tell whether to believe this or not. Probably everybody knew better and still believed it, as happens about so many things. The average man thinks that a little falseness goes with beauty. Where should we get any excitement out of our daily life if we were not willing to pretend a bit? And the average man is quite right, in his average brains!

CLARIFY

What does the narrator think about "the average man"?

The prodigy kept on bowing until the applause died down, then he went up to the grand piano, and the audience cast a last look at its programs. First came a *Marche solennelle*,[4] then a *Rêverie*,[5] and then *Le Hibou et les moineaux*[6]—all by Bibi Saccellaphylaccas. The whole program was by him, they were all his compositions. He could not score[7] them, of course, but he had them all in his extraordinary little head and they possessed real artistic significance, or so it said, seriously and objectively, in the program. The program sounded as though the impresario had wrested these concessions from his critical nature after a hard struggle.

The prodigy sat down upon the revolving stool and felt with his feet for the pedals, which were raised by means of a clever device so that Bibi could reach them. It was Bibi's own piano, he took it everywhere with him. It rested upon wooden trestles and its polish was somewhat marred by the constant transportation—but all that only made things more interesting.

Bibi put his silk-shod feet on the pedals; then he made an artful little face, looked straight ahead of him, and lifted his right hand. It was a brown, childish little hand; but the wrist was strong and unlike a child's, with well-developed bones.

Bibi made his face for the audience because he was aware that he had to entertain them a little. But he had his own private enjoyment in the thing too, an enjoyment which he could never convey to anybody. It was that prickling delight, that secret shudder of bliss, which ran through him every time he sat at an open piano—it would always be with him. And here was the keyboard again, these seven black and white octaves, among which he had so often lost himself in abysmal[8] and thrilling adventures—and yet it always looked as clean and untouched as a newly washed blackboard. This was the realm of music that lay before him. It lay spread out like an inviting ocean, where he might plunge in and blissfully swim, where he might let himself be borne and carried away, where he might go under in night and storm, yet keep the mastery: control, <u>ordain</u>—he held his right hand poised in the air.

A breathless stillness reigned in the room—the tense moment before the first note came. . . . How would it begin? It began so. And Bibi, with his index finger, fetched the first note out of the piano, a quite unexpectedly powerful first note in the middle register, like a trumpet blast. Others followed, an introduction developed—the audience relaxed.

The concert was held in the palatial hall of a fashionable first-class hotel. The walls were covered with mirrors framed in gilded arabesques,[9] between frescoes of the rosy and fleshly school.[10] Ornamental columns supported a ceiling that displayed a whole universe of electric bulbs, in clusters darting a brilliance far brighter than day and filling the whole space

4. ***Marche solennelle*** (märsh′ sô-lä-nĕl′) *French:* "Solemn March."
5. ***Rêverie*** (rĕ-vrē′) *French:* "Daydream."
6. ***Le Hibou et les moineaux*** (lə ĕ-bo͞o′ ā lĕ mwä-nō′) *French:* "The Owl and the Sparrows."
7. **score:** write in musical notation.
8. **abysmal** (ə-bĭz′məl): very deep; profound.
9. **gilded arabesques** (ăr′ə-bĕsks′): elaborate designs covered with gold or gold paint.
10. **frescoes** (frĕs′kōz) . . . **school:** wall paintings featuring nude and seminude figures (probably in imitation of baroque artworks like those of Rubens).

WORDS TO KNOW

ordain (ôr-dān′) *v.* to command or decree

with thin, vibrating golden light. Not a seat was unoccupied, people were standing in the side aisles and at the back. The front seats cost twelve marks; for the impresario believed that anything worth having was worth paying for. And they were occupied by the best society, for it was in the upper classes, of course, that the greatest enthusiasm was felt. There were even some children, with their legs hanging down demurely from their chairs and their shining eyes staring at their gifted little white-clad contemporary.

Down in front on the left side sat the prodigy's mother, an extremely obese woman with a powdered double chin and a feather on her head. Beside her was the impresario, a man of oriental appearance with large gold buttons on his conspicuous cuffs. The princess was in the middle of the front row—a wrinkled, shriveled

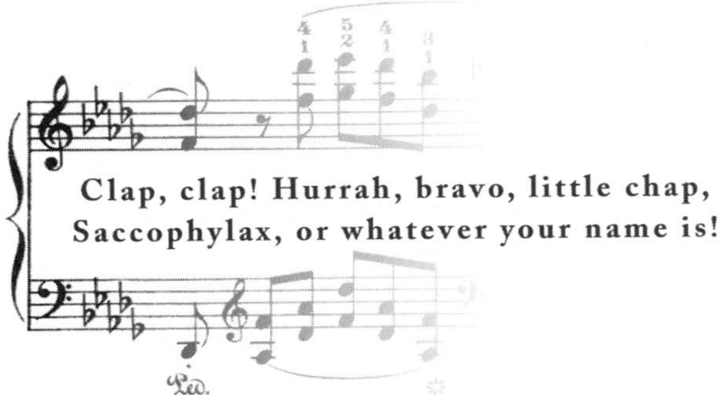
Clap, clap! Hurrah, bravo, little chap,
Saccophylax, or whatever your name is!

little old princess but still a patron of the arts, especially everything full of sensibility. She sat in a deep, velvet-upholstered armchair, and a Persian carpet was spread before her feet. She held her hands folded over her gray striped-silk breast, put her head on one side, and presented a picture of elegant composure as she sat looking up at the performing prodigy. Next to her sat her lady-in-waiting, in a green striped-silk gown. Being only a lady-in-waiting she had to sit up very straight in her chair.

Bibi ended in a grand climax. With what power this wee manikin[11] belabored[12] the keyboard! The audience could scarcely trust its ears. The march theme, an infectious, swinging tune, broke out once more, fully harmonized, bold and showy; with every note Bibi flung himself back from the waist as though he were marching in a triumphal procession. He ended *fortissimo,*[13] bent over, slipped sideways off the stool, and stood with a smile awaiting the applause.

And the applause burst forth, unanimously, enthusiastically; the child made his demure little maidenly curtsy and people in the front seat thought: "Look what slim little hips he has! Clap, clap! Hurrah, bravo, little chap, Saccophylax, or whatever your name is! Wait, let me take off my gloves—what a little devil of a chap he is!"

Bibi had to come out three times from behind the screen before they would stop. Some latecomers entered the hall and moved about looking for seats. Then the concert continued. Bibi's *Rêverie* murmured its numbers, consisting almost entirely of arpeggios,[14] above which a bar of melody rose now and then, weak-winged. Then came *Le Hibou et les moineaux*. This piece was brilliantly successful, it made a strong impression; it was an effective childhood fantasy, remarkably well envisaged.[15] The bass represented the owl, sitting morosely rolling his filmy eyes; while in the treble the impudent, half-frightened sparrows chirped. Bibi received an ovation when he finished, he was called out four times. A hotel page with shiny buttons carried up three great laurel wreaths onto the stage and proffered them from one side while Bibi nodded and expressed his thanks. Even the princess shared in the applause, daintily and noiselessly pressing her palms together.

Ah, the knowing little creature understood how to make people clap! He stopped behind the

---

11. **manikin** (măn′ĭ-kĭn): little man.
12. **belabored:** attacked with blows; pounded.
13. ***fortissimo*** (fôr-tĕ′sē-mō′) *Italian:* most strongly. (As a musical direction, the term means "in a very loud manner.")
14. **arpeggios** (är-pĕj′ē-ōz′): chords in which the notes are played in rapid succession rather than simultaneously.
15. **envisaged** (ĕn-vĭz′ĭjd): imagined.

WORDS TO KNOW

proffer (prŏf′ər) *v.* to offer for acceptance

screen, they had to wait for him; lingered a little on the steps of the platform, admired the long streamers on the wreaths—although actually such things bored him stiff by now. He bowed with the utmost charm, he gave the audience plenty of time to rave itself out, because applause is valuable and must not be cut short. "*Le Hibou* is my drawing card,"[16] he thought—this expression he had learned from the impresario. "Now I will play the fantasy, it is a lot better than *Le Hibou,* of course, especially the C-sharp passage. But you idiots dote on the *Hibou,* though it is the first and the silliest thing I wrote." He continued to bow and smile.

CLARIFY

How does Bibi's behavior differ from his attitude?

Next came a *Méditation*[17] and then an *Étude*[18]—the program was quite comprehensive. The *Méditation* was very like the *Rêverie*—which was nothing against it—and the *Étude* displayed all of Bibi's virtuosity, which naturally fell a little short of his inventiveness. And then the *Fantaisie.*[19] This was his favorite; he varied it a little each time, giving himself free rein and sometimes surprising even himself, on good evenings, by his own inventiveness.

He sat and played, so little, so white and shining, against the great black grand piano, elect and alone, above that confused sea of faces, above the heavy, insensitive mass soul, upon which he was laboring to work with his individual, differentiated soul. His lock of soft black hair with the white silk bow had fallen over his forehead, his trained and bony little wrists pounded away, the muscles stood out visibly on his brown childish cheeks.

Sitting there he sometimes had moments of oblivion and solitude, when the gaze of his strange little mouselike eyes with the big rings beneath them would lose itself and stare through the painted stage into space that was peopled with strange vague life. Then out of the corner of his eye he would give a quick look back into the hall and be once more with his audience.

"Joy and pain, the heights and the depths—that is my *Fantaisie,*" he thought lovingly. "Listen, here is the C-sharp passage." He lingered over the approach, wondering if they would notice anything. But no, of course not, how should they? And he cast his eyes up prettily at the ceiling so that at least they might have something to look at.

All these people sat there in their regular rows, looking at the prodigy and thinking all sorts of things in their regular brains. An old gentleman with a white beard, a seal ring on his finger and a bulbous swelling on his bald spot, a growth if you like, was thinking to himself: "Really, one ought to be ashamed." He had never got any further than "Ah, thou dearest Augustin" on the piano, and here he sat now, a gray old man, looking on while this little hop-o'-my-thumb[20] performed miracles. Yes, yes, it is a gift of God, we must remember that. God grants His gifts, or He withholds them, and there is no shame in being an ordinary man. Like with the Christ Child—Before a child one may kneel without feeling ashamed. Strange that thoughts like these should be so satisfying—he would even say so sweet, if it was not too silly for a tough old man like him to use the word. That was how he felt, anyhow.

"Art . . ." the business man with the parrot nose was thinking. "Yes, it adds something

16. **drawing card:** something that attracts an audience.
17. ***Méditation*** (mā-dē-tä-syôN′) *French:* "Meditation."
18. ***Étude*** (ā-tüd′) *French:* "Study." (In music, the term is used to refer to a short work that is designed to provide practice in some technique but may be performed for its artistic merit.)
19. ***Fantaisie*** (fäN-tĕ-zē′) *French:* "Fantasia" (a loosely structured musical work based on the free play of the composer's imagination).
20. **hop-o'-my-thumb:** a very small person.

WORDS TO KNOW

dote (dōt) *v.* to show excessive love or fondness
virtuosity (vûr′cho͞o-ŏs′ĭ-tē) *n.* the ability, skill, or style shown by a great musician or artist
differentiated (dĭf′ə-rĕn′shē-ā′tĭd) *adj.* different from others; distinctive **differentiate** *v.*
oblivion (ə-blĭv′ē-ən) *n.* a state of total forgetfulness or unawareness

cheerful to life, a little good white silk and a little tumty-ti-ti-tum. Really he does not play so badly. Fully fifty seats, twelve marks apiece, that makes six hundred marks—and everything else besides. Take off the rent of the hall, the lighting and the programs, you must have fully a thousand marks profit.[21] That is worthwhile."

"That was Chopin[22] he was just playing," thought the piano teacher, a lady with a pointed nose; she was of an age when the understanding sharpens as the hopes decay. "But not very original—I will say that afterwards, it sounds well. And his hand position is entirely amateur. One must be able to lay a coin on the back of the hand—I would use a ruler on him."

Then there was a young girl, at that self-conscious and chlorotic[23] time of life when the most ineffable ideas come into the mind. She was thinking to herself: "What is it he is playing? It is expressive of passion, yet he is a child. If he kissed me it would be as though my little brother kissed me—no kiss at all. Is there such a thing as passion all by itself, without any earthly object, a sort of child's play of passion? What nonsense! If I were to say such things aloud they would just be at me with some more cod-liver oil. Such is life."

At the Opera (1879), Mary Stevenson Cassatt. Oil on canvas, 31½" × 25½", courtesy of Museum of Fine Arts, Boston, The Hayden Collection.

An officer was leaning against a column. He looked on at Bibi's success and thought: "Yes, you are something and I am something, each in his own way." So he clapped his heels together and paid to the prodigy the respect which he felt to be due to all the powers that be.

Then there was a critic, an elderly man in a shiny black coat and turned-up trousers splashed with mud. He sat in his free seat and thought: "Look at him, this young beggar of a Bibi. As an individual he has still to develop, but as a type he is already quite complete, the artist *par excellence*.[24] He has in himself all the artist's exaltation and his utter worthlessness, his charlatanry[25] and his sacred fire, his burning contempt and his secret raptures. Of course I can't write all that, it is too good. Of course, I should have been an artist myself if I had not seen through the whole business so clearly."

Then the prodigy stopped playing and a perfect storm arose in the hall. He had to come out again and again from behind his screen. The man with

21. **Fully fifty . . . profit:** The "fifty seats" the businessman refers to are the front seats costing 12 marks each. There must be a considerable number of cheaper seats if his estimate of the profit—a thousand marks—is correct.
22. **Chopin** (shō-păn′): a reference to Frédéric Chopin, a Polish-born composer of the 19th century.
23. **chlorotic** (klə-rŏt′ĭk): characterized by chlorosis, a form of anemia that mainly affects adolescent girls.
24. ***par excellence*** (pär ĕk-sĕ-läɴs′) *French:* supreme; above all.
25. **charlatanry** (shär′lə-tən-rē): fraudulence; trickery.

WORDS TO KNOW

ineffable (ĭn-ĕf′ə-bəl) *adj.* unable to be expressed in words
exaltation (ĕg′zôl-tā′shən) *n.* a feeling of intense joy, pride, or well-being; ecstasy

the shiny buttons carried up more wreaths: four laurel wreaths, a lyre made of violets, a bouquet of roses. He had not arms enough to convey all these tributes, the impresario himself mounted the stage to help him. He hung a laurel wreath round Bibi's neck, he tenderly stroked the black hair—and suddenly as though overcome he bent down and gave the prodigy a kiss, a resounding kiss, square on the mouth. And then the storm became a hurricane. That kiss ran through the room like an electric shock, it went direct to peoples' marrow and made them shiver down their backs. They were carried away by a helpless compulsion of sheer noise. Loud shouts mingled with the hysterical clapping of hands. Some of Bibi's commonplace little friends down there waved their handkerchiefs. But the critic thought: "Of course that kiss had to come—it's a good old gag. Yes, good Lord, if only one did not see through everything quite so clearly—"

EVALUATE

Why do you think the critic views the kiss as "a good old gag"?

And so the concert drew to a close. It began at half past seven and finished at half past eight. The platform was laden with wreaths and two little pots of flowers stood on the lamp stands of the piano. Bibi played as his last number his *Rhapsodie grecque,*[26] which turned into the Greek national hymn at the end. His fellow countrymen in the audience would gladly have sung it with him if the company had not been so august. They made up for it with a powerful noise and hullabaloo, a hot-blooded national demonstration. And the aging critic was thinking: "Yes, the hymn had to come too. They have to exploit every vein—publicity cannot afford to neglect any means to its end. I think I'll criticize that as inartistic. But perhaps I am wrong, perhaps that is the most artistic thing of all. What is the artist? A jack-in-the-box. Criticism is on a higher plane. But I can't say that." And away he went in his muddy trousers.

After being called out nine or ten times the prodigy did not come any more from behind the screen but went to his mother and the impresario down in the hall. The audience stood about among the chairs and applauded and pressed forward to see Bibi close at hand. Some of them wanted to see the princess too. Two dense circles formed, one round the prodigy, the other round the princess, and you could actually not tell which of them was receiving more homage. But the court lady was commanded to go over to Bibi; she smoothed down his silk jacket a bit to make it look suitable for a court function, led him by the arm to the princess, and solemnly indicated to him that he was to kiss the royal hand. "How do you do it, child?" asked the princess. "Does it come into your head of itself when you sit down?" *"Oui, madame,"*[27] answered Bibi. To himself he thought: "Oh, what a stupid old princess!" Then he turned round shyly and uncourtierlike and went back to his family.

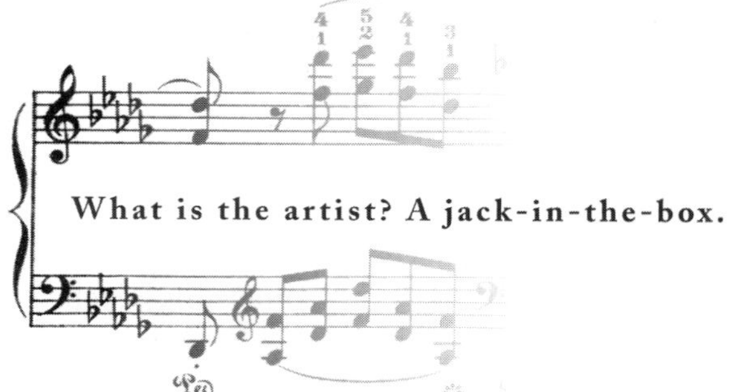
What is the artist? A jack-in-the-box.

Outside in the cloakroom there was a crowd. People held up their numbers and received with open arms furs, shawls, and galoshes. Somewhere among her acquaintances the piano teacher stood making her critique.[28] "He is not very original," she said audibly and looked about her.

26. ***Rhapsodie grecque*** (räp-sô-dē′ grĕk′) *French:* "Greek Rhapsody."
27. ***Oui, madame*** (wē′ mä-däm′) *French:* Yes, madam.
28. **critique** (krĭ-tēk′): a critical review, especially of a work of art or literature.

WORDS TO KNOW

august (ô-gŭst′) *adj.* imposing; exalted; awe-inspiring
exploit (ĭk-sploit′) *v.* to use to the greatest possible advantage

The Charterhouse Matinee, Haymarket Theatre, 1899.

In front of one of the great mirrors an elegant young lady was being arrayed in her evening cloak and fur shoes by her brothers, two lieutenants. She was exquisitely beautiful, with her steel-blue eyes and her clean-cut, well-bred face. A really noble dame. When she was ready she stood waiting for her brothers. "Don't stand so long in front of the glass, Adolf," she said softly to one of them, who could not tear himself away from the sight of his simple, good-looking young features. But Lieutenant Adolf thinks: "What cheek! He would button his overcoat in front of the glass, just the same." Then they went out on the street where the arc lights gleamed cloudily through the white mist. Lieutenant Adolf struck up a little . . . dance on the frozen snow to keep warm, with his hands in his slanting overcoat pockets and his collar turned up.

A girl with untidy hair and swinging arms, accompanied by a gloomy-faced youth, came out just behind them. A child! she thought. A charming child. But in there he was an awe-inspiring . . . and aloud in a toneless voice she said: "We are all infant prodigies, we artists."

"Well, bless my soul!" thought the old gentleman who had never got further than Augustin on the piano, and whose boil was now concealed by a top hat. "What does all that mean? She sounds very oracular."[29] But the gloomy youth understood. He nodded his head slowly.

Then they were silent and the untidy-haired girl gazed after the brothers and sister. She rather despised them, but she looked after them until they had turned the corner. ❖

29. **oracular** (ô-răk′yə-lər): mysterious; enigmatic.

RESPONDING OPTIONS

FROM PERSONAL RESPONSE *TO* CRITICAL ANALYSIS

REFLECT **1.** What is your impression of Bibi? Jot down your thoughts in your notebook, and then share them with classmates.

RETHINK **2.** Do you think Bibi enjoys his status as a prodigy? Why or why not?

3. Do you think most members of the audience appreciate Bibi's talent? Give reasons to support your answer.

4. In your opinion, how does appearance contrast with reality in this story?

Consider

- Bibi's physical appearance
- the irony in some of Bibi's actions
- the thoughts and responses of the audience

5. How would you describe the view of art and artists expressed in the story?

Consider

- Bibi's feelings about his music
- Bibi's reaction to his audience
- the critic's opinion that "they have to exploit every vein"
- the untidy-haired girl's statement "We are all infant prodigies, we artists"

RELATE **6.** At the start of this story, the narrator suggests that "a mighty publicity organization" has influenced the thinking of Bibi's audience. In your opinion, how important is publicity for modern artists and entertainers? Does it influence the way audiences respond? Give examples to support your answers.

ANOTHER PATHWAY

Cooperative Learning

With several classmates, create a list of the descriptive details Mann uses to characterize various members of the audience, including each person's response to the prodigy. Compare your list with those of other groups. Then discuss what Mann might be revealing about human nature through his depiction of the audience.

QUICKWRITES

1. Imagine that you are Bibi's publicity agent. Write a **press release** announcing an upcoming concert in which Bibi will be the featured performer.

2. Pretend that you are the music critic described in the story, and write a **review** of Bibi's concert for a local newspaper.

3. Plan and write a **program** that could be handed out to the audience in this story. Include information about the prodigy and each composition he will perform. You might want to create your program on a computer to give it a professional appearance.

PORTFOLIO *Save your writing. You may want to use it later as a springboard to a piece for your portfolio.*

LITERARY CONCEPTS

In a story told from an **omniscient** (all-knowing) **point of view,** the writer can see into the mind of every character. This narrative style enables the writer to reveal several characters' perspectives, or personal thoughts and feelings, toward the same situation. In most cases, the writer has a specific reason for revealing the thoughts of two or more characters involved in the same incident. What different perspectives does Mann reveal in "The Infant Prodigy"? What reason do you think he had for presenting the thoughts of more than one character?

ALTERNATIVE ACTIVITIES

1. Create a **T-shirt design** that would appeal to fans of Bibi Saccellaphylaccas.
2. With a partner, conduct a **talk-show interview** in which Bibi reveals his feelings about being a child prodigy and about its effect on his life.
3. Design and create a **poster** advertising the concert described in the story.

LITERARY LINKS

Compare Mann's fictional portrayal of the artist in society with Fanny Burney's description of her real-life encounter with Lady Say and Sele in *The Diary and Letters of Madame d'Arblay* (page 440). Do you think the celebrities experience any of the same feelings in these two situations? Explain your response.

THE WRITER'S STYLE

In this story, Mann repeats specific words and phrases to emphasize certain aspects of Bibi's appearance. Look through the story for **repetitions** that emphasize Bibi's small stature and white outfit. Why do you think Mann focuses on these particular aspects of Bibi's appearance?

CRITIC'S CORNER

In an essay on Mann's short stories, the American writer and poet laureate Howard Nemerov stated that in "The Infant Prodigy" Mann depicts "some sinister qualities belonging to the underside of the artist nature." Which of Bibi's qualities do you think Nemerov would consider sinister?

ACROSS THE CURRICULUM

Music Find definitions of the musical terms *etude, fantasia,* and *rhapsody.* Then try to locate recordings of these types of compositions. Play a segment of each composition for the class, and discuss the differences in style.

WORDS TO KNOW

Review the Words to Know at the bottom of the selection pages. Then write the word that best completes each sentence.

1. A young child with amazing talent can often impress the public with his or her _____.
2. The public may _____ on such an "infant prodigy," especially if the child is charming and adorable as well as talented.
3. It is sometimes not the prodigy's skill but only his or her youth that makes him or her seem _____ from older artists.
4. Few prodigies stand the test of time and enter the _____ ranks of the masters of their art, but Wolfgang Amadeus Mozart was one who did.
5. Mozart was able to _____ his flair for melody and harmony, his talent for musical composition, and his great imagination to create an amazing body of work.
6. The emotional range of his works is enormous; a single symphony or opera may move from sadness and misery to _____.
7. His music can convey more than any spoken language; a few notes from a flute, violin, or bassoon can communicate _____ feelings.
8. Many a listener has found that a Mozart sonata can lift the heart and, at least until the music stops, cause all sorrow to sink into _____.
9. It is hard to believe that Mozart traveled from city to city to _____ his talent and his work, only to be continually rejected by those in power in the music world.
10. How much longer might he have lived and created beauty if someone in power had possessed the wisdom to _____ that he be well treated and well paid?

THOMAS MANN

1875–1955

Although Thomas Mann devoted his life to creative pursuits, he did not ignore the important social and political issues of his day, becoming an outspoken commentator on his country's political activities. Mann lived during a critical period in Germany's history and experienced the effects of two world wars. At the start of World War I, his unwavering patriotism made him realize the importance of an artist's commitment to social issues. In his writings of that time, he enthusiastically defended Germany's wartime activities and disagreed vehemently with those who criticized their country's involvement.

In later years Mann's interests in his country's politics did not wane, but in the wake of World War I they took a very different turn. During the 1930s, his outspoken criticism of Nazi policies landed his name on a list of Adolf Hitler's potential enemies. In 1933, while Mann and his wife vacationed in Switzerland, Hitler became chancellor of Germany. Recognizing the danger of returning home, the Manns decided to remain in Zurich and did not see their homeland again for 16 years. During his exile, Mann was stripped of his German citizenship and an honorary doctorate that had been bestowed upon him by the University of Bonn. In 1938, he moved his family from Switzerland to the United States, eventually becoming a U.S. citizen. Throughout most of the war, Mann worked diligently to help other German refugees relocate and find employment. Although he visited Germany after the war, he refused to live there ever again. In 1952, Mann and his family moved back to Switzerland, settling near Zurich, where the author died three years later.

OTHER WORKS "The Way to the Churchyard," *Buddenbrooks, Death in Venice, The Magic Mountain, Doctor Faustus*

PREVIEWING

FICTION

The Truth About George

P. G. Wodehouse

PERSONAL CONNECTION

Think about someone you know who is especially gifted at telling funny stories. What makes that person a good storyteller? What qualities, in your opinion, make a story amusing? Reflect on these questions in your notebook, then share your thoughts with a classmate.

LITERARY/BIOGRAPHICAL CONNECTION

P. G. Wodehouse, who has aptly been described as one of the greatest humorists of the 20th century, is familiar to readers around the world. In a writing career that lasted over 75 years, this English-born author produced more than 90 novels and volumes of short stories, wrote or collaborated on lyrics for over 30 musical comedies, and wrote scripts for more than 20 films.

Wodehouse's popularity is due largely to his unique brand of humor and the gentle, good-natured tone of his works. His primary purpose was not to send a deep or critical message but simply to entertain—to make people laugh. As he remarked once, "I believe there are two ways of writing novels. One is mine, making a sort of musical comedy without music and ignoring real life altogether; the other is going right deep down into life."

Another secret of his success is undoubtedly his creation of some unforgettable recurring characters who have become popular favorites. Perhaps his most famous characters are the comic pair of Bertie Wooster and his valet, Jeeves; but almost as popular is Mr. Mulliner, a genial storyteller who frequents an English fishermen's club called the Anglers' Rest. In "The Truth About George," Mr. Mulliner tells one of his outrageous tales.

READING CONNECTION

Understanding a Frame Story The main events of "The Truth About George" are told in the context of a **frame story,** a story within a story. At the beginning of the work, the narrator, a patron of the Angler's Rest, establishes a frame, or narrative setting, in which the amusing tale about George will be told. The storyteller, who is actually someone other than the narrator, is introduced in this frame. As you read the selection, see if you can figure out why the author encloses the tale in a frame.

The Truth About George

P. G. Wodehouse

Two men were sitting in the bar-parlor of the Anglers' Rest as I entered it; and one of them, I gathered from his low, excited voice and wide gestures, was telling the other a story. I could hear nothing but an occasional "Biggest I ever saw in my life!" and "Fully as large as that!" but in such a place it was not difficult to imagine the rest; and when the second man, catching my eye, winked at me with a sort of humorous misery, I smiled sympathetically back at him.

The action had the effect of establishing a bond between us; and when the storyteller finished his tale and left, he came over to my table as if answering a formal invitation.

"Dreadful liars some men are," he said genially.

"Fishermen," I suggested, "are traditionally careless of the truth."

"He wasn't a fisherman," said my companion. "That was our local doctor. He was telling me about his latest case of dropsy.[1] Besides"—he tapped me earnestly on the knee—"you must not fall into the popular error about fishermen. Tradition has maligned them. I am a fisherman myself, and I have never told a lie in my life."

I could well believe it. He was a short, stout, comfortable man of middle age, and the thing that struck me first about him was the extraordinarily childlike candor of his eyes. They were large and round and honest. I would have bought oil stock from him without a tremor.

The door leading into the white dusty road opened, and a small man with rimless pince-nez[2] and an anxious expression shot in like a rabbit and had consumed a gin and ginger beer almost before we knew he was there. Having thus refreshed himself, he stood looking at us, seemingly ill at ease.

"N-n-n-n-n-n——" he said.

We looked at him inquiringly.

"N-n-n-n-n-n-ice d-d-d-d——"

His nerve appeared to fail him, and he vanished as abruptly as he had come.

"I think he was leading up to telling us that it was a nice day," hazarded my companion.

"It must be very embarrassing," I said, "for a man with such a painful impediment in his speech to open conversation with strangers."

"Probably trying to cure himself. Like my nephew George. Have I ever told you about my nephew George?"

I reminded him that we had only just met, and that this was the first time I had learned that he had a nephew George.

"Young George Mulliner. My name is Mulliner. I will tell you about George's case—in many ways a rather remarkable one."

My nephew George (said Mr. Mulliner) was as nice a young fellow as you would ever wish to meet, but from childhood up he had been cursed with a terrible stammer. If he had had to earn his living, he would undoubtedly have found this affliction a great handicap, but fortunately his father had left him a comfortable income; and George spent a not unhappy life, residing in the village where he had been born and passing his days in the usual country sports and his evenings in doing crossword puzzles. By the time he was thirty he knew more about Eli, the prophet, Ra, the Sun God, and the bird Emu than anybody else in the county except Susan Blake, the vicar's[3] daughter, who had also taken up the solving of crossword puzzles and was the first girl in Worcestershire[4] to find out the meaning of "stearine" and "crepuscular."

It was his association with Miss Blake that first turned George's thoughts to a serious endeavor to cure himself of his stammer. Naturally, with this hobby in common, the young people saw a great deal of one another: for George was always looking in at the vicarage[5] to ask her if she knew a word of seven letters meaning "appertaining to the profession of plumbing," and Susan was just as constant a caller at George's cozy little cottage—being frequently stumped, as girls will be, by words of eight letters signifying "largely used in the manufacture of poppet-valves." The consequence was that one evening,

1. **dropsy:** an abnormal accumulation of fluid in the body—now usually called edema (ĭ-dē′mə).
2. **pince-nez** (păns′nā′): eyeglasses without earpieces, kept in place by being clipped to the bridge of the nose.
3. **vicar's** (vĭk′ərz): A vicar is a kind of parish priest in the Church of England.
4. **Worcestershire** (wo͝os′tə-shîr): a county of England.
5. **vicarage** (vĭk′ər-ĭj): the residence of a vicar.

WORDS TO KNOW

malign (mə-līn′) *v.* to speak evil of; slander

candor (kăn′dər) *n.* frankness; sincerity; openness

just after she had helped him out of a tight place with the word "disestablishmentarianism," the boy suddenly awoke to the truth and realized that she was all the world to him—or, as he put it to himself from force of habit, precious, beloved, darling, much-loved, highly esteemed or valued.

And yet, every time he tried to tell her so, he could get no further than a sibilant gurgle which was no more practical use than a hiccup.

Something obviously had to be done, and George went to London to see a specialist.

"Yes?" said the specialist.

"I-I-I-I-I-I——" said George.

"You were saying—?"

"Woo-woo-woo-woo-woo-woo——"

"Sing it," said the specialist.

"S-s-s-s-s-s-s——?" said George, puzzled.

The specialist explained. He was a kindly man with moth-eaten whiskers and an eye like a meditative cod fish.

"Many people," he said, "who are unable to articulate clearly in ordinary speech find themselves lucid and bell-like when they burst into song."

It seemed a good idea to George. He thought for a moment; then threw his head back, shut his eyes, and let it go in a musical baritone.

"I love a lassie, a bonny, bonny lassie," sang George. "She's as pure as the lily in the dell."

"No doubt," said the specialist, wincing a little.

"She's as sweet as the heather, the bonny purple heather—Susan, my Worcestershire bluebell."

"Ah!" said the specialist. "Sounds a nice girl. Is this she?" he asked, adjusting his glasses and peering at the photograph which George had extracted from the interior of the left side of his under-vest.

George nodded, and drew in breath.

"Yes, sir," he caroled, "that's my baby. No, sir, don't mean maybe. Yes, sir, that's my baby now. And, by the way, by the way, when I meet that preacher I shall say— 'Yes, sir, that's my ——' "

"Quite," said the specialist, hurriedly. He had a sensitive ear. "Quite, quite."

"If you knew Susie like I know Susie," George was beginning, but the other stopped him.

"Quite. Exactly. I shouldn't wonder. And now," said the specialist, "what precisely is the trouble? No," he added, hastily, as George inflated his lungs, "don't sing it. Write the particulars on this piece of paper."

George did so.

"H'm!" said the specialist, examining the screed.[6] "You wish to woo, court, and become betrothed, engaged, affianced to this girl, but you find yourself unable, incapable, incompetent, impotent, and powerless. Every time you attempt it, your vocal cords fail, fall short, are insufficient, wanting, deficient, and go blooey."

George nodded.

"A not unusual case. I have had to deal with this sort of thing before. The effect of love on the vocal cords of even a normally eloquent subject is frequently deleterious. As regards the habitual stammerer, tests have shown that in ninety-seven point five six nine recurring of cases the divine passion reduces him to a condition where he sounds like a soda-water siphon trying to recite 'Gunga Din.' There is only one cure."

"W-w-w-w-w——?" asked George.

"I will tell you. Stammering," proceeded the specialist, putting the tips of his fingers together and eyeing George benevolently, "is mainly mental and is caused by shyness, which is caused by the inferiority complex, which in its turn is caused by suppressed desires or introverted inhibitions or something. The advice I give to all young men who come in here behaving like soda-water siphons is to go out and make a point of speaking to at least three perfect strangers every day. Engage these strangers in conversation, persevering no matter how priceless a chump

6. **screed:** written document.

WORDS TO KNOW

sibilant (sĭb′ə-lənt) *adj.* hissing
lucid (lo͞o′sĭd) *adj.* easily understood
deleterious (dĕl′ĭ-tîr′ē-əs) *adj.* harmful; injurious
benevolently (bə-nĕv′ə-lənt-lē) *adv.* in a way that shows kindness and goodwill

you may feel, and before many weeks are out you will find that the little daily dose has had its effect. Shyness will wear off, and with it the stammer."

And, having requested the young man—in a voice of the clearest timbre,[7] free from all trace of impediment—to hand over a fee of five guineas, the specialist sent George out into the world.

Light, Power & Speed (1910), Charles Sharland. London Transport Museum.

The more George thought about the advice he had been given, the less he liked it. He shivered in the cab that took him to the station to catch the train back to East Wobsley. Like all shy young men, he had never hitherto looked upon himself as shy—preferring to attribute his distaste for the society of his fellows to some subtle rareness of soul. But now that the thing had been put squarely up to him, he was compelled to realize that in all essentials he was a perfect rabbit. The thought of accosting perfect strangers and forcing his conversation upon them sickened him.

But no Mulliner has ever shirked an unpleasant duty. As he reached the platform and strode along it to the train, his teeth were set, his eyes shone with an almost fanatical light of determination, and he intended before his journey was over to conduct three heart-to-heart chats if he had to sing every bar of them.

The compartment into which he had made his way was empty at the moment, but just before the train started a very large, fierce-looking man got in. George would have preferred somebody a little less formidable for his first subject, but he braced himself and bent forward. And, as he did so, the man spoke.

"The wur-wur-wur-wur-weather," he said, "sus-sus-seems to be ter-ter-taking a tur-tur-turn for the ber-ber-better, der-doesn't it?"

George sank back as if he had been hit between the eyes. The train had moved out of the dimness of the station by now, and the sun was shining brightly on the speaker, illuminating his knobbly shoulders, his craggy jaw, and, above all, the shockingly choleric[8] look in his eyes. To reply "Y-y-y-y-y-y-y-yes" to such a man would obviously be madness.

But to abstain from speech did not seem to be much better as a policy. George's silence appeared to arouse this man's worst passions. His face had turned purple and he glared painfully.

"I uk-uk-asked you a sus-sus-civil quk-quk-quk," he said, irascibly. "Are you d-d-d-d-deaf?"

All we Mulliners have been noted for our presence of mind. To open his mouth, point to his tonsils, and utter a strangled gurgle was with George the work of a moment.

7. **timbre** (tăm′bər): the distinctive quality of a sound.

8. **choleric** (kŏl′ə-rĭk): showing anger; bad-tempered.

The tension relaxed. The man's annoyance abated.

"D-d-d-dumb?" he said, commiseratingly. "I beg your p-p-p-p-pup. I t-t-trust I have not caused you p-p-p-p-pup. It m-must be tut-tut-tut-tut-tut not to be able to sus-sus-speak fuf-fuf-fuf-fuf-fluently."

He then buried himself in his paper, and George sank back in his corner, quivering in every limb.

To get to East Wobsley, as you doubtless know, you have to change at Ippleton and take the branch-line. By the time the train reached this junction, George's composure was somewhat restored. He deposited his belongings in a compartment of the East Wobsley train, which was waiting in a glued manner on the other side of the platform, and, finding that it would not start for some ten minutes, decided to pass the time by strolling up and down in the pleasant air.

It was a lovely afternoon. The sun was gilding the platform with its rays, and a gentle breeze blew from the west. A little brook ran tinkling at the side of the road; birds were singing in the hedgerows; and through the trees could be discerned dimly the noble facade of the County Lunatic Asylum. Soothed by his surroundings, George began to feel so refreshed that he regretted that in this wayside station there was no one present whom he could engage in talk.

It was at this moment that the distinguished-looking stranger entered the platform.

The newcomer was a man of imposing physique, simply dressed in pajamas, brown boots, and a mackintosh.[9] In his hand he carried a top hat, and into this he was dipping his fingers, taking them out, and then waving them in a curious manner to right and left. He nodded so affably to George that the latter, though a little surprised at the other's costume, decided to speak. After all, he reflected, clothes do not make the man, and, judging from the other's smile, a warm heart appeared to beat beneath that orange-and-mauve striped pajama jacket.

"N-n-n-n-nice weather," he said.

"Glad you like it," said the stranger. "I ordered it specially."

George was a little puzzled by this remark, but he persevered.

"M-might I ask wur-wur-what you are dud-doing?"

"Doing?"

"With that her-her-her-her-hat?"

"Oh, with this hat? I see what you mean. Just scattering largesse to the multitude," replied the stranger, dipping his fingers once more and waving them with a generous gesture. "Devil of a bore, but it's expected of a man in my position. The fact is," he said, linking his arm in George's and speaking in a confidential undertone, "I'm the Emperor of Abyssinia.[10] That's my palace over there," he said, pointing through the trees. "Don't let it go any further. It's not supposed to be generally known."

It was with a rather sickly smile that George now endeavored to withdraw his arm from that of his companion, but the other would have none of this aloofness. He seemed to be in complete agreement with Shakespeare's dictum that a friend, when found, should be grappled to you with hooks of steel. He held George in a vice-like grip and drew him into a recess of the platform. He looked about him, and seemed satisfied.

"We are alone at last," he said.

This fact had already impressed itself with sickening clearness on the young man. There are few spots in the civilized world more deserted than the platform of a small country station. The sun shone on the smooth asphalt, on the gleaming

9. **mackintosh:** raincoat.

10. **Abyssinia** (ăb′ĭ-sĭn′ē-ə): the African country now known as Ethiopia.

WORDS TO KNOW

commiseratingly (kə-mĭz′ə-rā′tĭng-lē) *adv.* in a way that shows sorrow for another's suffering or trouble
imposing (ĭm-pō′zĭng) *adj.* impressive in size, power, or appearance
affably (ăf′ə-blē) *adv.* in a friendly, pleasant manner
largesse (lär-zhĕs′) *n.* money or gifts given out of generosity

Dorking by Motor-Bus (1920), F. Gregory Brown. London Transport Museum.

rails, and on the machine which, in exchange for a penny placed in the slot marked "Matches," would supply a package of wholesome butter-scotch—but on nothing else.

What George could have done with at the moment was a posse of police armed with stout clubs, and there was not even a dog in sight.

"I've been wanting to talk to you for a long time," said the stranger, genially.

"Huh-huh-have you?" said George.

"Yes. I want your opinion of human sacrifices."

George said he didn't like them.

"Why not?" asked the other, surprised.

George said it was hard to explain. He just didn't.

"Well, I think you're wrong," said the Emperor. "I know there's a school of thought growing up that holds your views, but I disapprove of it. I hate all this modern advanced thought. Human sacrifices have always been good enough for the Emperors of Abyssinia, and they're good enough for me. Kindly step in here, if you please."

He indicated the lamp-and-mop room, at which they had now arrived. It was a dark and sinister apartment, smelling strongly of oil and porters, and was probably the last place on earth in which George would have wished to be closeted with a man of such peculiar views. He shrank back.

"You go in first," he said.

"No larks," said the other, suspiciously.

"L-l-l-l-larks?"

"Yes. No pushing a fellow in and locking the door and squirting water at him through the window. I've had that happen to me before."

"Sus-certainly not."

"Right!" said the Emperor. "You're a gentleman and I'm a gentleman. Both gentlemen. Have you a knife, by the way? We shall need a knife."

"No. No knife."

"Ah, well," said the Emperor, "then we'll have to look about for something else. No doubt we shall manage somehow."

And with the debonair manner which so

became him, he scattered another handful of largesse and walked into the lamp room.

It was not the fact that he had given his word as a gentleman that kept George from locking the door. There is probably no family on earth more nicely scrupulous as regards keeping its promises than the Mulliners, but I am compelled to admit that, had George been able to find the key, he would have locked that door without hesitation. Not being able to find the key, he had to be satisfied with banging it. This done, he leaped back and raced away down the platform. A confused noise within seemed to indicate that the Emperor had become involved with some lamps.

George made the best of the respite. Covering the ground at a high rate of speed, he flung himself into the train and took refuge under the seat.

There he remained, quaking. At one time he thought that his uncongenial acquaintance had got upon his track, for the door of the compartment opened and a cool wind blew in upon him. Then, glancing along the floor, he perceived feminine ankles. The relief was enormous, but even in his relief George, who was the soul of modesty, did not forget his manners. He closed his eyes.

A voice spoke.

"Porter!"

"Yes, ma'am?"

"What was all that disturbance as I came into the station?"

"Patient escaped from the asylum, ma'am."

"Good gracious!"

The voice would undoubtedly have spoken further, but at this moment the train began to move. There came the sound of a body descending upon a cushioned seat, and some little time later the rustling of a paper. The train gathered speed and jolted on.

George had never before traveled under the seat of a railway carriage; and, though he belonged to the younger generation, which is supposed to be so avid of new experiences, he had no desire to do so now. He decided to emerge, and if possible, to emerge with the minimum of ostentation. Little as he knew of women, he was aware that as a sex they are apt to be startled by the sight of men crawling out from under the seats of compartments. He began his maneuvers by poking out his head and surveying the terrain.

All was well. The woman, in her seat across the way, was engrossed in her paper. Moving in a series of noiseless wriggles, George extricated himself from his hiding-place and, with a twist which would have been impossible to a man not in the habit of doing Swedish exercises daily before breakfast, heaved himself into the corner seat. The woman continued reading her paper.

The events of the past quarter of an hour had tended rather to drive from George's mind the mission which he had undertaken on leaving the specialist's office. But now, having leisure for reflection, he realized that, if he meant to complete his first day of the cure, he was allowing himself to run sadly behind schedule. Speak to three strangers, the specialist had told him, and up to the present he had spoken to only one. True, this one had been a pretty considerable stranger, and a less conscientious young man than George Mulliner might have considered himself justified in chalking him up on the scoreboard as one and a half or even two. But George had the dogged, honest Mulliner streak in him, and he refused to quibble.

He nerved himself for action, and cleared his throat.

"Ah-h'rm!" said George.

And, having opened the ball, he smiled a winning smile and waited for his companion to make the next move.

The move which his companion made was in an upwards direction, and measured from six to eight inches. She dropped her paper and regarded George with a pale-eyed horror. One pictures her a little in the position of Robinson Crusoe when he saw the footprint in the sand. She had been

WORDS TO KNOW

avid (ăv'ĭd) *adj.* eager and enthusiastic
extricate (ĕk'strĭ-kāt') *v.* to release; disentangle

convinced that she was completely alone, and lo! out of space a voice had spoken to her. Her face worked, but she made no remark.

George, on his side, was also feeling a little ill at ease. Women always increased his natural shyness. He never knew what to say to them.

Then a happy thought struck him. He had just glanced at his watch and found the hour to be nearly four-thirty. Women, he knew, loved a drop of tea at about this time, and fortunately there was in his suitcase a full thermos flask.

"Pardon me, but I wonder if you would care for a cup of tea?" was what he wanted to say, but, as so often happened with him when in the presence of the opposite sex, he could get no further than a sort of sizzling sound like a cockroach calling to its young.

The woman continued to stare at him. Her eyes were now about the size of regulation standard golf-balls, and her breathing suggested the last stages of asthma. And it was at this point that George, struggling for speech, had one of those inspirations which frequently come to Mulliners. There flashed into his mind what the specialist had told him about singing. Say it with music—that was the thing to do.

He delayed no longer.

"Tea for two and two for tea and me for you and you for me——"

He was shocked to observe his companion turning Nile-green. He decided to make his meaning clearer.

"I have a nice thermos. I have a full thermos. Won't you share my thermos, too? When skies are gray and you feel you are blue, tea sends the sun smiling through. I have a nice thermos. I have a full thermos. May I pour out some for you?"

You will agree with me, I think, that no invitation could have been more happily put, but his companion was not responsive. With one last agonized look at him, she closed her eyes and sank back in her seat. Her lips had now turned a curious gray-blue color, and they were moving feebly. She reminded George, who, like myself, was a keen fisherman, of a newly gaffed[11] salmon.

George sat back in his corner, brooding. Rack his brain as he might, he could think of no topic which could be guaranteed to interest, elevate, and amuse. He looked out of the window with a sigh.

The train was now approaching the dear old familiar East Wobsley country. He began to recognize landmarks. A wave of sentiment poured over George as he thought of Susan, and he reached for the bag of buns which he had bought at the refreshment room at Ippleton. Sentiment always made him hungry.

He took his thermos out of the suitcase, and, unscrewing the top, poured himself out a cup of tea. Then, placing the thermos on the seat, he drank.

He looked across at his companion. Her eyes were still closed, and she uttered little sighing noises. George was half inclined to renew his offer of tea, but the only tune he could remember was "Hard-Hearted Hannah, the Vamp from Savannah," and it was difficult to fit suitable words to it. He ate his bun and gazed out at the familiar scenery.

Now, as you approach East Wobsley, the train, I must mention, has to pass over some points; and so violent is the sudden jerking that strong men have been known to spill their beer. George, forgetting this in his preoccupation, had placed the thermos only a few inches from the edge of the seat. The result was that, as the train reached the points, the flask leaped like a live thing, dived to the floor, and exploded.

Even George was distinctly upset by the sudden sharpness of the report. His bun sprang from his hand and was dashed to fragments. He blinked thrice in rapid succession. His heart tried to jump out of his mouth and loosened a front tooth.

But on the woman opposite, the effect of the untoward occurrence was still more marked. With a single piercing shriek, she rose from her seat straight into the air like a rocketing pheasant;

11. **gaffed:** pulled from the water with a large hook attached to a pole.

and, having clutched the communication cord, fell back again. Impressive as her previous leap had been, she excelled it now by several inches. I do not know what the existing record for the Sitting High-Jump is, but she undoubtedly lowered it; and if George had been a member of the Olympic Games Selection Committee, he would have signed this woman up immediately.

It is a curious thing that, in spite of the railway companies' sporting willingness to let their patrons have a tug at the extremely moderate price of five pounds a go, very few people have ever either pulled a communication cord or seen one pulled. There is, thus, a widespread ignorance as to what precisely happens on such occasions.

The procedure, George tells me, is as follows: First there comes a grinding noise, as the brakes are applied. Then the train stops. And finally, from every point of the compass, a seething mob of interested onlookers begins to appear.

It was about a mile and a half from East Wobsley that the affair had taken place, and as far as the eye could reach, the countryside was totally devoid of humanity. A moment before nothing had been visible but smiling cornfields and broad pasturelands; but now from east, west, north, and south running figures began to appear. We must remember that George at the time was in a somewhat overwrought frame of mind, and his statements should therefore be accepted with caution; but he tells me that out of the middle of a single empty meadow, entirely devoid of cover, no fewer than twenty-seven distinct rustics[12] suddenly appeared, having undoubtedly shot up through the ground.

The rails, which had been completely unoccupied, were now thronged with so dense a crowd of navvies[13] that it seemed to George absurd to pretend that there was any unemployment in England. Every member of the laboring classes throughout the country was so palpably present. Moreover, the train, which at Ippleton had seemed sparsely occupied, was disgorging passengers from every door. It was the sort of mob scene which would have made David W. Griffith[14] scream with delight; and it looked, George says, like Guest Night at the Royal Automobile Club. But, as I say, we must remember that he was overwrought.

It is difficult to say what precisely would have been the correct behavior of your polished man of the world in such a situation. I think myself that a great deal of sang-froid and address[15] would be required even by the most self-possessed in order to pass off such a contretemps.[16] To George, I may say at once, the crisis revealed itself immediately as one which he was totally incapable of handling. The one clear thought that stood out from the welter of his emotions was the reflection that it was advisable to remove himself, and to do so without delay. Drawing a deep breath, he shot swiftly off the mark.

All we Mulliners have been athletes; and George, when at the University, had been noted for his speed of foot. He ran now as he had never run before. His statement, however, that as he sprinted across the first field he distinctly saw a rabbit shoot an envious glance at him as he passed and shrug its shoulders hopelessly, I am inclined to discount. George, as I have said before, was a little overexcited.

Nevertheless, it is not to be questioned that he made good going. And he had need to, for after the first instant of surprise, which had enabled him to secure a lead, the whole mob was pouring across country after him; and dimly, as he ran, he could hear voices in the throng informally

---

12. **rustics:** country people.
13. **navvies:** laborers; workers.
14. **David W. Griffith:** a pioneering American filmmaker, famous for historical epics featuring huge casts.
15. **sang-froid and address:** coolness and composure, as well as skill and tact.
16. **contretemps** (kŏn′trə-täɴ′): a confusing or embarrassing situation.

WORDS TO KNOW

devoid (dĭ-void′) *adj.* empty; completely lacking

discussing the advisability of lynching him. Moreover, the field through which he was running, a moment before a bare expanse of green, was now black with figures, headed by a man with a beard who carried a pitch-fork. George swerved sharply to the right, casting a swift glance over his shoulder at his pursuers. He disliked them all, but especially the man with the pitch-fork.

It is impossible for one who was not an eyewitness to say how long the chase continued and how much ground was covered by the interested parties. I know the East Wobsley country well, and I have checked George's statements; and, if it is true that he traveled east as far as Little-Wigmarsh-in-the-Dell and as far west as Higgleford-cum-Wortlebury-beneath-the-Hill,[17] he must undoubtedly have done a lot of running.

But a point which must not be forgotten is that, to a man not in a condition to observe closely, the village of Higgleford-cum-Wortlebury-beneath-the-Hill might easily not have been Higgleford-cum-Wortlebury-beneath-the-Hill at all, but another hamlet which in many respects closely resembles it. I need scarcely say that I allude to Lesser-Snodsbury-in-the-Vale.

Let us assume, therefore, that George, having touched Little-Wigmarsh-in-the-Dell, shot off at a tangent and reached Lesser-Snodsbury-in-the-Vale. This would be a considerable run. And, as he remembers flitting past Farmer Higgins's pigsty and the Dog and Duck at Pondlebury Parva and splashing through the brook Wipple at the point where it joins the River Wopple, we can safely assume that, wherever else he went, he got plenty of exercise.

But the pleasantest of functions must end, and, just as the setting sun was gilding the spire of the ivy-covered church of St. Barnabas the

17. **Little-Wigmarsh-in-the-Dell . . . Higgleford-cum-Wortlebury-beneath-the-Hill:** Wodehouse often spoofs England's many unusual place names by inventing exaggeratedly silly ones like these.

Resilient, where George as a child had sat so often, enlivening the tedium of the sermon by making faces at the choirboys, a damp and bedraggled figure might have been observed crawling painfully along the High Street of East Wobsley in the direction of the cozy little cottage known to its builder as Chatsworth and to the village tradesmen as "Mulliner's."

It was George, home from the hunting-field.

Slowly George Mulliner made his way to the familiar door, and, passing through it, flung himself into his favorite chair. But a moment later a more imperious need than the desire to rest forced itself upon his attention. Rising stiffly, he tottered to the kitchen and mixed himself a revivifying[18] whisky and soda. Then, refilling his glass, he returned to the sitting room, to find that it was no longer empty. A slim, fair girl, tastefully attired in tailor-made tweeds, was leaning over the desk on which he kept his Dictionary of English Synonyms.

She looked up as he entered, startled.

"Why, Mr. Mulliner!" she exclaimed. "What has been happening? Your clothes are torn, rent, ragged, tattered, and your hair is all disheveled, untrimmed, hanging loose or negligently, at loose ends!"

George smiled a wan smile.

"You are right," he said. "And what is more, I am suffering from extreme fatigue, weariness, lassitude, exhaustion, prostration, and languor."

The girl gazed at him, a divine pity in her soft eyes.

"I'm so sorry," she murmured. "So very sorry, grieved, distressed, afflicted, pained, mortified, dejected, and upset."

George took her hand. Her sweet sympathy had effected the cure for which he had been seeking so long. Coming on top of the violent emotions through which he had been passing all day, it seemed to work on him like some healing spell, charm, or incantation. Suddenly, in a flash, he realized that he was no longer a stammerer. Had he wished at that moment to say "Peter Piper picked a peck of pickled peppers," he could have done it without a second thought.

But he had better things to say than that.

"Miss Blake—Susan—Susie." He took her other hand in his. His voice rang out clear and unimpeded. It seemed to him incredible that he had ever yammered at this girl like an overheated steam-radiator. "It cannot have escaped your notice that I have long entertained towards you sentiments warmer and deeper than those of ordinary friendship. It is love, Susan, that has been animating my bosom. Love, first a tiny seed, has burgeoned in my heart till, blazing into flame, it has swept away on the crest of its wave my diffidence, my doubt, my fears, and my foreboding, and now, like the topmost topaz of some ancient tower, it cries to all the world in a voice of thunder: 'You are mine! My mate! Predestined to me since Time first began!' As the star guides the mariner when, battered by boiling billows, he hies him home to the haven of hope and happiness, so do you gleam upon me along life's rough road and seem to say, 'Have courage, George! I am here!' Susan, I am not an eloquent man—I cannot speak fluently as I could wish—but these simple words which you have just heard come from the heart, from the unspotted heart of an English gentleman. Susan, I love you. Will you be my wife, married woman, matron, spouse, helpmeet, consort, partner, or better half?"

"Oh, George!" said Susan. "Yes, yea, ay, aye! Decidedly, unquestionably, indubitably, incontrovertibly, and past all dispute!"

He folded her in his arms. And, as he did so, there came from the street outside—faintly, as from a distance—the sound of feet and voices. George leaped to the window. Rounding the corner, just by the Cow and Wheelbarrow public

18. **revivifying** (rē-vĭv′ə-fī′ĭng): giving new life, energy, or spirit.

WORDS TO KNOW

tedium (tē′dē-əm) *n.* boredom; dullness
imperious (ĭm-pîr′ē-əs) *adj.* urgent; pressing

house, licensed to sell ales, wines, and spirits, was the man with the pitch-fork, and behind him followed a vast crowd.

"My darling," said George, "for purely personal and private reasons, into which I need not enter, I must now leave you. Will you join me later?"

"I will follow you to the ends of the earth," replied Susan, passionately.

"It will not be necessary," said George. "I am only going down to the coal-cellar. I shall spend the next half-hour or so there. If anybody calls and asks for me, perhaps you would not mind telling them that I am out."

"I will, I will," said Susan. "And, George, by the way. What I really came here for was to ask you if you knew a hyphenated word of nine letters, ending in *k* and signifying an implement employed in the pursuit of agriculture."

"Pitch-fork, sweetheart," said George. "But you may take it from me, as one who knows, that agriculture isn't the only thing it is used in pursuit of."

And since that day (concluded Mr. Mulliner) George, believe me or believe me not, has not had the slightest trace of an impediment in his speech. He is now the chosen orator at all political rallies for miles around; and so offensively self-confident has his manner become that only last Friday he had his eye blacked by a hay-corn-and-feed merchant of the name of Stubbs. It just shows you, doesn't it? ❖

RESPONDING OPTIONS

FROM PERSONAL RESPONSE *TO* CRITICAL ANALYSIS

REFLECT 1. Would you rate this story as slightly amusing, very funny, or hilarious? In your notebook, give reasons for your rating. Then share your opinion with the class.

RETHINK 2. Which part of the story did you find most amusing? Explain your answer.

3. Review the Reading Connection on page 793. Do you think it was a good idea for the author to use the frame-story technique?

   Consider
   - the description of the patrons of the Anglers' Rest
   - the narrator's opinion of Mr. Mulliner, the storyteller
   - the kind of story you might expect from Mr. Mulliner

4. In your opinion, are the situations in the story believable? Give reasons for your answer.

5. How would you describe the tone of the story? Support your answer with details from the text.

RELATE 6. If you were a movie producer, would you consider making a film based on this story? Why or why not?

ANOTHER PATHWAY

Make a time line to chart the main actions or events in this story. Below the time line, explain how and why each event is misinterpreted by characters in the story. Then discuss with a partner how each misunderstanding helps to advance the plot.

QUICKWRITES

1. Create a **wedding invitation** for George and Susan, employing their crossword-puzzle-solving habit of using multiple synonyms to describe things.
2. Write a **police report** in which the woman on the train explains the circumstances that caused her to pull the train's emergency cord.
3. Decide what actors you would choose for a movie based on this story, and then write a **casting call** in which you identify and explain your choice for each role.
4. Write an amusing personal **anecdote** about an incident from your past. Feel free to spice up the story with exaggeration to make it more funny.

PORTFOLIO *Save your writing. You may want to use it later as a springboard to a piece for your portfolio.*

LITERARY CONCEPTS

Humor is the quality possessed by a literary work that entertains by evoking laughter. In "The Truth About George," Wodehouse uses a variety of elements to create humor, including absurd situations and ridiculous characters. He also uses humorous language—including such comic devices as exaggeration, irony, puns, and unexpected or inappropriate remarks. With a partner, choose a passage of the story that you find particularly funny, and discuss what elements contribute to its humor.

ALTERNATIVE ACTIVITIES

1. ***Cooperative Learning*** With a small group of classmates, rehearse and present one scene from the story as a **radio play** in which members of the group read (or sing!) the parts of different characters, including the storyteller.
2. Create a **storyboard,** or sequence of sketches, depicting a scene from the story as you envision that it would be portrayed in a film or on stage.
3. Create a **television commercial** in which the specialist in this story advertises his program for overcoming speech impediments and uses George as an example of the program's stunning success.

LITERARY LINKS

Compare the characters in "The Truth About George" with those in Oscar Wilde's farce *The Importance of Being Earnest* (page 701). In which work do the characters seem more realistic? Give reasons to support your opinion.

THE WRITER'S STYLE

Many other writers have admired the unique style of P. G. Wodehouse. One characteristic of his style is a subtle blending of **formal** and **informal language.** He skillfully mingles unsophisticated descriptions and slang with the eloquent, and occasionally pompous, language used by fashionable English society. Look for examples of this blending of formal and informal language in "The Truth About George." What, in your opinion, might be the purpose of this style?

CRITIC'S CORNER

The British writer V. S. Pritchett wrote: "The strength of Wodehouse lies not in his almost incomprehensibly intricate plots . . . but in his prose style and there, above all, in his command of mind-splitting metaphor. To describe a girl [as Wodehouse once did] as 'the sand in civilization's spinach' enlarges and decorates the imagination." Look through "The Truth About George" for metaphors or similes that you think illustrate Pritchett's point.

ACROSS THE CURRICULUM

Media Watch a videotape of one of the BBC (British Broadcasting Corporation) programs based on Wodehouse novels and stories, and then answer the following questions. Be sure to explain your answers.

- Is the type of humor in the program similar to that in "The Truth About George"?
- Does the program contain both situational and verbal humor?
- Do you think the program effectively captures the Wodehouse tone? Why or why not?

Television portrayal of Bertie Wooster and his valet, Jeeves.

WORDS TO KNOW

EXERCISE A Identify each pair of words as synonyms or antonyms.

1. malign—praise
2. commiseratingly—sympathetically
3. benevolently—cruelly
4. largesse—stinginess
5. lucid—clear
6. tedium—monotony
7. devoid—overflowing
8. candor—frankness
9. affably—disagreeably
10. extricate—imprison

EXERCISE B Review the Words to Know at the bottom of the selection pages. Then write the vocabulary word, not used in Exercise A, that could be used to describe each group of items.

1. smoke, viruses, and oil spills
2. teakettles, snakes, and angry cats
3. extreme hunger, medical emergencies, and important appointments
4. the U.S. Capitol, grizzly bears, and NFL linebackers
5. true sports fans, garage-sale addicts, and dogs at feeding time

P. G. WODEHOUSE

1881–1975

From the time he began contributing stories to his school magazine, Pelham Grenville Wodehouse knew that he wanted to earn his living as a writer; but his father pushed him into the business world, and he worked unhappily in a bank for two years. During this period, however, he managed to find the time to write and publish over 80 stories. Their success enabled him to pursue his dream, and in 1902 he became a full-time humorist for a London newspaper.

After 1909, a good deal of Wodehouse's time was spent living and working in the United States and France. Unfortunately, he and his wife were in France when the country was invaded by Germany in 1940. Being English and therefore an enemy, Wodehouse was captured and imprisoned for almost a year. Afterward, reunited with his wife, he was forced to remain under German surveillance, first in Berlin and then in Paris, until 1944.

During his confinement, Wodehouse had been allowed to make several radio broadcasts from Germany to the United States. Although the Germans may have been using his broadcasts for propaganda, Wodehouse innocently accepted the chance to let the world know his whereabouts and to subtly poke fun at his captors. The English, however, were outraged by his use of the German airwaves, and Wodehouse became the subject of sharp criticism in his homeland. Wodehouse's friends, many of whom were famous authors, came to his defense, and he was eventually forgiven by the English people for what was, after all, an error of judgment. After the war, Wodehouse settled in New York, becoming a U.S. citizen in 1955.

Even during his most dismal wartime experiences, Wodehouse had access to writing materials and remained devoted to his work. His flair for telling a good story never waned. In fact, the celebrated storyteller was perched in front of his typewriter right up until his death at the age of 93. In the words of his biographer Joseph Connolly, "All Wodehouse did, if his achievement may be thought of as in any sense mere, was write a far greater number of consistently funny books than anyone else in the history of literature. And he did it superbly well. And he enjoyed it most utterly."

OTHER WORKS "Mulliner's Buck-U-Uppo," "Jeeves and the Impending Doom," "Ukridge's Accident Syndicate," "The Metropolitan Touch," "Tried in the Furnace"

PREVIEWING

FICTION

The Duchess and the Jeweller

Virginia Woolf

PERSONAL CONNECTION

Have you ever agreed to do something unpleasant in return for a favor? What was the driving force that moved you to accept the bargain? Looking back on the situation, do you think you made the right decision? Explore your thoughts in your notebook.

LITERARY CONNECTION

Virginia Woolf was one of the most celebrated members of the Bloomsbury group, a circle of intellectual writers, painters, and philosophers who met and conversed frequently from about 1907 to 1930. Many in the group lived in the Bloomsbury district of London, and they often met in Woolf's house. Members questioned existing ideas and sought ways of improving not only their literary and artistic expression but society in general. They rejected many 19th-century views about literature, art, politics, and social issues and supported writers and artists who were breaking new ground.

Woolf, who greatly influenced the direction of modern fiction, continually experimented with the form of the novel and excelled at revealing the inner thoughts and feelings of her characters. In her essay "Modern Fiction," she wrote that "everything is the proper stuff of fiction, every feeling, every thought; every quality of brain and spirit is drawn upon; no perception comes amiss." Her brilliantly original fiction has won wide acclaim from prominent literary figures, including the novelist E. M. Forster (also a member of the Bloomsbury group), whose description of Woolf appears on page 816.

Woolf with fellow Bloomsbury writer Lytton Strachey

READING CONNECTION

Understanding Motivation Understanding what impels a character is often the key to understanding an entire story. Sometimes the character's **motivation**—the driving force behind his or her thoughts, feelings, and actions—is obvious; at other times it is difficult to understand and must be inferred from clues buried within the story. As you read Woolf's story, look for clues to the motivations of both the duchess and the jeweller. Record each motivation in a diagram like the one shown here.

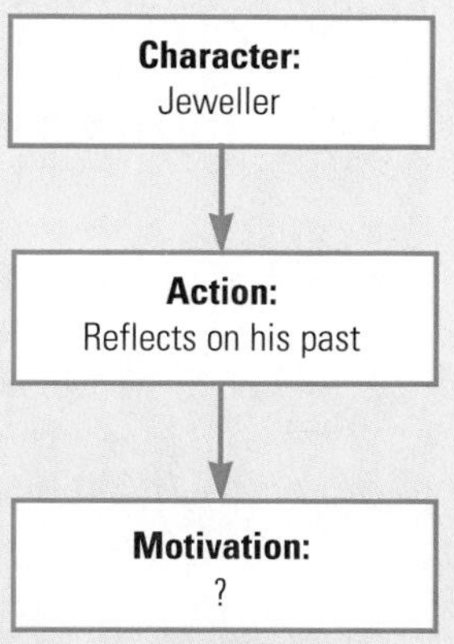

Virginia Woolf

The Duchess and the Jeweller

Oliver Bacon lived at the top of a house overlooking the Green Park. He had a flat; chairs jutted out at the right angles—chairs covered in hide. Sofas filled the bays of the windows—sofas covered in tapestry. The windows, the three long windows, had the proper allowance of discreet net and figured satin.[1] The mahogany sideboard bulged discreetly with the right brandies, whiskeys and liqueurs. And from the middle window he looked down upon the glossy roofs of fashionable cars packed in the narrow straits of Piccadilly.[2] A more central position could not be imagined. And at eight in the morning he would have his breakfast brought in on a tray by a manservant; the manservant would unfold his crimson dressing gown; he would rip his letters open with his long pointed nails and would extract thick white cards of invitation upon which the engraving stood up roughly from duchesses, countesses, viscountesses[3] and Honorable Ladies. Then he would wash; then he would eat his toast; then he would read his paper by the bright burning fire of electric coals.

"Behold Oliver," he would say, addressing himself. "You who began life in a filthy little alley, you who . . ." and he would look down at his legs, so shapely in their perfect trousers; at his boots; at his spats. They were all shapely, shining; cut from the best cloth by the best scissors in Savile Row.[4] But he dismantled himself[5] often and became again a little boy in a dark alley. He had once thought that[6] the height of his ambition—selling stolen dogs to fashionable women in Whitechapel.[7] And once he had been done.[8] "Oh, Oliver," his mother had wailed. "Oh, Oliver! When will you have sense, my son?" . . . Then he had gone behind a counter; had sold cheap watches; then he had taken a wallet to Amsterdam. . . . At that memory he would chuckle—the old Oliver remembering the young. Yes, he had done well with the three diamonds; also there was the commission on the emerald. After that he went into the private room behind the shop in Hatton Garden;[9] the room with the scales, the safe, the thick magnifying glasses. And then . . . and then . . . He chuckled. When he passed through the knots of jewellers in the hot evening who were discussing prices, gold mines, diamonds, reports from South Africa, one of them would lay a finger to the side of his nose and murmur, "Hum–m–m," as he passed. It was no more than a murmur; no more than a nudge on the shoulder, a finger on the nose, a buzz that ran through the cluster of jewellers in Hatton Garden on a hot afternoon—oh, many years ago now! But still Oliver felt it purring down his spine, the nudge, the murmur that meant, "Look at him—young Oliver, the young jeweller—there he goes." Young he was then. And he dressed better and better; and had, first a hansom cab;[10] then a car; and first he went up to the dress circle, then down into the stalls.[11] And he had a villa at Richmond, overlooking the river, with trellises of red roses; and Mademoiselle used to pick one every morning and stick it in his buttonhole.

---

1. **discreet net and figured satin:** curtains made of lace that is not showy and satin with a design woven into it.
2. **Piccadilly** (pĭk′ə-dĭl′ē): one of London's main business streets.
3. **viscountesses** (vī′koun′tĭs-ĭz): noblewomen ranking below duchesses and countesses but above baronesses.
4. **Savile** (săv′ĭl) **Row:** a London street in which many exclusive men's clothing stores are located.
5. **dismantled himself:** took himself apart (that is, mentally removed the outer symbols of success in order to see the person he once was).
6. **that:** The word is used as a pronoun here, referring to the selling of stolen dogs mentioned later in the sentence.
7. **Whitechapel:** a seedy area in eastern London.
8. **done:** British slang meaning "arrested and charged with a crime."
9. **Hatton Garden:** the center of London's jewelry trade.
10. **hansom cab:** a two-wheeled horse-drawn carriage.
11. **dress circle . . . stalls:** In a theater or concert hall, the dress circle is a section of seats—usually in the first balcony—that are expensive but available to all. The stalls are seats near the stage that are usually reserved for royalty or others of very high rank.

"So," said Oliver Bacon, rising and stretching his legs. "So . . ."

And he stood beneath the picture of an old lady on the mantelpiece and raised his hands. "I have kept my word," he said, laying his hands together, palm to palm, as if he were doing homage to her. "I have won my bet." That was so; he was the richest jeweller in England; but his nose, which was long and flexible, like an elephant's trunk, seemed to say by its curious quiver at the nostrils (but it seemed as if the whole nose quivered, not only the nostrils) that he was not satisfied yet; still smelt something under the ground a little further off. Imagine a giant hog in a pasture rich with truffles;[12] after unearthing this truffle and that, still it smells a bigger, a blacker truffle under the ground further off. So Oliver snuffed always in the rich earth of Mayfair[13] another truffle, a blacker, a bigger further off.

For was he not still a sad man, a dissatisfied man, a man who seeks something that is hidden, though he had won his bet?

Now then he straightened the pearl in his tie, cased himself in his smart blue overcoat; took his yellow gloves and his cane; and swayed as he descended the stairs and half snuffed, half sighed through his long sharp nose as he passed out into Piccadilly. For was he not still a sad man, a dissatisfied man, a man who seeks something that is hidden, though he had won his bet?

He swayed slightly as he walked, as the camel at the zoo sways from side to side when it walks along the asphalt paths laden with grocers and their wives eating from paper bags and throwing little bits of silver paper crumpled up on to the path. The camel despises the grocers; the camel is dissatisfied with its lot; the camel sees the blue lake and the fringe of palm trees in front of it. So the great jeweller, the greatest jeweller in the whole world, swung down Piccadilly, perfectly dressed, with his gloves, with his cane; but dissatisfied still, till he reached the dark little shop, that was famous in France, in Germany, in Austria, in Italy, and all over America—the dark little shop in the street off Bond Street.[14]

As usual he strode through the shop without speaking, though the four men, the two old men, Marshall and Spencer, and the two young men, Hammond and Wicks, stood straight behind the counter as he passed and looked at him, envying him. It was only with one finger of the amber-colored glove, waggling, that he acknowledged their presence. And he went in and shut the door of his private room behind him.

Then he unlocked the grating that barred the window. The cries of Bond Street came in; the purr of the distant traffic. The light from reflectors at the back of the shop struck upwards. One tree waved six green leaves, for it was June. But Mademoiselle had married Mr. Pedder of the local brewery—no one stuck roses in his button-hole now.

"So," he half sighed, half snorted, "so . . ."

Then he touched a spring in the wall and slowly the paneling slid open, and behind it were the steel safes, five, no, six of them, all of burnished steel. He twisted a key; unlocked one; then another. Each was lined with a pad of deep crimson velvet; in each lay jewels—bracelets, necklaces, rings, tiaras, ducal coronets;[15] loose stones in glass shells; rubies, emeralds, pearls, diamonds. All safe, shining, cool, yet burning, eternally, with their own compressed light.

"Tears!" said Oliver, looking at the pearls.

"Heart's blood!" he said, looking at the rubies.

"Gunpowder!" he continued, rattling the diamonds so that they flashed and blazed.

"Gunpowder enough to blow up Mayfair—sky high, high, high!" He threw his head back and

---

12. **truffles:** edible fungi that grow underground, considered a rare delicacy. (Hogs are often used to sniff them out.)
13. **Mayfair:** a fashionable residential section of London.
14. **Bond Street:** a main business street passing through the jewelers' district in London.
15. **ducal** (do͞o′kəl) **coronets:** small crowns worn by dukes and duchesses.

A Dinner Table at Night (The Glass of Claret) (1884), John Singer Sargent. Oil on canvas, 20¼" × 26¼", The Fine Arts Museums of San Francisco, gift of the Atholl McBean Foundation (73.12).

made a sound like a horse neighing as he said it.

The telephone buzzed obsequiously in a low muted voice on his table. He shut the safe.

"In ten minutes," he said. "Not before." And he sat down at his desk and looked at the heads of the Roman emperors that were graved[16] on his sleeve links. And again he dismantled himself and became once more the little boy playing marbles in the alley where they sell stolen dogs on Sunday. He became that wily astute little boy, with lips like wet cherries. He dabbled his fingers in ropes of tripe;[17] he dipped them in pans of frying fish; he dodged in and out among the crowds. He was slim, lissome, with eyes like licked stones. And now—now—the hands of the clock ticked on. One, two, three, four . . . The Duchess of Lambourne waited his pleasure; the Duchess of Lambourne, daughter of a hundred Earls. She would wait for ten minutes on a chair at the counter. She would wait his pleasure. She would wait till he was ready to see her. He watched the clock in its shagreen[18] case. The

16. **graved:** engraved.

17. **tripe:** the stomach lining of a cow or calf, used as a food.

18. **shagreen** (shə-grēn′): untanned leather, often dyed green.

WORDS TO KNOW

obsequiously (ŏb-sē′kwē-əs-lē) *adv.* in a subservient or fawning manner

astute (ə-stōōt′) *adj.* clever; shrewd

lissome (lĭs′əm) *adj.* easy and graceful in movement

hand moved on. With each tick the clock handed him—so it seemed—pâté de foie gras;[19] a glass of champagne; another of fine brandy; a cigar costing one guinea. The clock laid them on the table beside him, as the ten minutes passed. Then he heard soft slow footsteps approaching; a rustle in the corridor. The door opened. Mr. Hammond flattened himself against the wall.

"Her Grace!" he announced.

And he waited there, flattened against the wall.

And Oliver, rising, could hear the rustle of the dress of the Duchess as she came down the passage. Then she loomed up, filling the door, filling the room with the aroma, the prestige, the arrogance, the pomp, the pride of all the Dukes and Duchesses swollen in one wave. And as a wave breaks, she broke, as she sat down, spreading and splashing and falling over Oliver Bacon the great jeweller, covering him with sparkling bright colors, green, rose, violet; and odors; and iridescences;[20] and rays shooting from fingers, nodding from plumes, flashing from silk; for she was very large, very fat, tightly girt[21] in pink taffeta, and past her prime. As a parasol with many flounces,[22] as a peacock with many feathers, shuts its flounces, folds its feathers, so she subsided and shut herself as she sank down in the leather armchair.

"Good morning, Mr. Bacon," said the Duchess. And she held out her hand which came through the slit of her white glove. And Oliver bent low as he shook it. And as their hands touched the link was forged between them once more. They were friends, yet enemies; he was master, she was mistress; each cheated the other, each needed the other, each feared the other, each felt this and knew this every time they touched hands thus in the little back room with the white light outside, and the tree with its six leaves, and the sound of the street in the distance and behind them the safes.

"And today, Duchess—what can I do for you today?" said Oliver, very softly.

The Duchess opened; her heart, her private heart, gaped wide. And with a sigh, but no words, she took from her bag a long washleather pouch—it looked like a lean yellow ferret.[23] And from a slit in the ferret's belly she dropped pearls—ten pearls. They rolled from the slit in the ferret's belly—one, two, three, four—like the eggs of some heavenly bird.

"All that's left me, dear Mr. Bacon," she moaned. Five, six, seven—down they rolled, down the slopes of the vast mountainsides that fell between her knees into one narrow valley—the eighth, the ninth, and the tenth. There they lay in the glow of the peach-blossom taffeta. Ten pearls.

"From the Appleby cincture,"[24] she mourned. "The last . . . the last of them all."

Oliver stretched out and took one of the pearls between finger and thumb. It was round, it was lustrous. But real was it, or false? Was she lying again? Did she dare?

She laid her plump padded finger across her lips. "If the Duke knew . . ." she whispered. "Dear Mr. Bacon, a bit of bad luck . . ."

Been gambling again, had she?

"That villain! That sharper!"[25] she hissed.

The man with the chipped cheek bone? A bad 'un. And the Duke was straight as a poker; with side whiskers; would cut her off, shut her up down there if he knew—what I know, thought Oliver, and glanced at the safe.

"Araminta, Daphne, Diana," she moaned. "It's for *them*."

---

19. **pâté de foie gras** (pä-tā′ də fwä grä′): a delicacy made from goose liver.
20. **iridescences** (ĭr′ĭ-dĕs′ən-sĭz): brilliant displays of changing, rainbowlike colors.
21. **girt:** wrapped; encircled.
22. **parasol with many flounces:** umbrella with many ruffles.
23. **ferret:** a small weasel-like mammal.
24. **cincture** (sĭngk′chər): an ornamental belt.
25. **sharper:** a cheating gambler.

WORDS TO KNOW

arrogance (ăr′ə-gəns) *n.* overbearing pride; exaggerated self-importance
forge (fôrj) *v.* to form, shape, or produce

The Ladies Araminta, Daphne, Diana—her daughters. He knew them; adored them. But it was Diana he loved.

"You have all my secrets," she leered. Tears slid; tears fell; tears, like diamonds, collecting powder in the ruts of her cherry-blossom cheeks.

"Old friend," she murmured, "old friend."

"Old friend," he repeated, "old friend," as if he licked the words.

"How much?" he queried.

She covered the pearls with her hand.

"Twenty thousand," she whispered.

But was it real or false, the one he held in his hand? The Appleby cincture—hadn't she sold it already? He would ring for Spencer or Hammond. "Take it and test it," he would say. He stretched to the bell.

"You will come down tomorrow?" she urged, she interrupted. "The Prime Minister—His Royal Highness . . ." She stopped. "And Diana," she added.

Oliver took his hand off the bell.

He looked past her, at the backs of the houses in Bond Street. But he saw, not the houses in Bond Street, but a dimpling river; and trout rising and salmon; and the Prime Minister; and himself too; in white waistcoats; and then, Diana. He looked down at the pearl in his hand. But how could he test it, in the light of the river, in the light of the eyes of Diana? But the eyes of the Duchess were on him.

"Twenty thousand," she moaned. "My honor!"

The honor of the mother of Diana! He drew his checkbook towards him; he took out his pen.

"Twenty," he wrote. Then he stopped writing. The eyes of the old woman in the picture were on him—of the old woman, his mother.

The eyes of the old woman in the picture were on him—of the old woman, his mother.

"Oliver!" she warned him. "Have sense! Don't be a fool!"

"Oliver!" the Duchess entreated—it was "Oliver" now, not "Mr. Bacon." "You'll come for a long weekend?"

Alone in the woods with Diana! Riding alone in the woods with Diana!

"Thousand," he wrote, and signed it.

"Here you are," he said.

And there opened all the flounces of the parasol, all the plumes of the peacock, the radiance of the wave, the swords and spears of Agincourt,[26] as she rose from her chair. And the two old men and the two young men, Spencer and Marshall, Wicks and Hammond, flattened themselves behind the counter envying him as he led her through the shop to the door. And he waggled his yellow glove in their faces, and she held her honor—a check for twenty thousand pounds with his signature—quite firmly in her hands.

"Are they false or are they real?" asked Oliver, shutting his private door. There they were, ten pearls on the blotting paper on the table. He took them to the window. He held them under his lens to the light. . . . This, then, was the truffle he had routed out of the earth! Rotten at the center—rotten at the core!

"Forgive me, oh my mother!" he sighed, raising his hands as if he asked pardon of the old woman in the picture. And again he was a little boy in the alley where they sold dogs on Sunday.

"For," he murmured, laying the palms of his hands together, "it is to be a long weekend." ❖

---

26. **Agincourt** (ăj′ĭn-kôrt′): a French village where, in 1415, Henry V's English forces defeated a much larger French army in what is considered one of England's most glorious victories.

INSIGHT

from Virginia Woolf

E. M. Forster

She liked receiving sensations—sights, sounds, tastes—passing them through her mind, where they encountered theories and memories, and then bringing them out again, through a pen, on to a bit of paper. Now began the higher delights of authorship. For these pen-marks on paper were only the prelude to writing, little more than marks on a wall. They had to be combined, arranged, emphasized here, eliminated there, new relationships had to be generated, new pen-marks born, until out of the interactions; something, one thing, one, arose. This one thing, whether it was a novel or an essay or a short story or a biography or a private paper to be read to her friends, was, if it was successful, itself analogous to a sensation. Although it was so complex and intellectual, although it might be large and heavy with facts, it was akin to the very simple things which had started it off, to the sights, sounds, tastes. It could be best described as we describe them. For it was not about something. It was something.

RESPONDING OPTIONS

FROM PERSONAL RESPONSE *TO* CRITICAL ANALYSIS

REFLECT

1. Is the jeweller someone you would like to know? In your notebook, give reasons for your response.

RETHINK

2. Why do you think the jeweller is dissatisfied with his life?

   Consider
   - what has been the driving force in his life
   - the image of him as a hog searching for truffles
   - the references to Mademoiselle and the red roses
3. Why do you think the jeweller keeps thinking about his mother and his past?
4. How would you describe the relationship between the jeweller and the duchess?

   Consider
   - what motive he might have for making her wait ten minutes
   - his concerns about the pearls
   - what motivates her to mention the prime minister and Diana
5. Would you call the jeweller a winner or a loser in his transactions with the duchess? Give reasons to support your answer.

RELATE

6. In your opinion, what aspects of this story might support E. M. Forster's assertion, in the Insight selection on page 816, that Virginia Woolf "liked receiving sensations—sights, sounds, tastes"?
7. What do you think are some of the main driving forces that motivate successful businesspeople today? Do you think there are pros and cons to achieving great success? Explain your answer.

ANOTHER PATHWAY

Create a chart like the one below to analyze the encounter between the duchess and the jeweller. Begin by identifying the characters' goals and the strategies they use to achieve the goals. Then describe the results of the strategies and decide whether the characters succeed in achieving their goals.

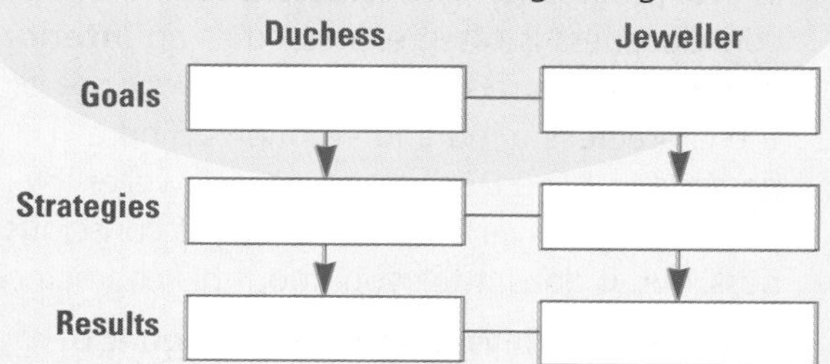

QUICKWRITES

1. Write a new **ending** for this story—one that you think the jeweller's mother would prefer.
2. Imagine that you are a psychologist and that the jeweller has just shared all his thoughts with you. Write a **psychological profile** for your records, in which you describe the forces motivating him and the conflicts in his personality.
3. Compose an imaginary **dialogue** in which the duchess tells her daughter Diana the truth about her encounter with the jeweller and advises Diana how to behave during his impending visit.

PORTFOLIO *Save your writing. You may want to use it later as a spring-board to a piece for your portfolio.*

LITERARY CONCEPTS

The **style** of a literary work is the distinctive way in which it is written—not *what* is said but *how* it is said. It is an expression of the writer's individual way of communicating ideas. Many elements contribute to style, including word choice, tone, figurative language, and point of view. Virginia Woolf used with great skill a style of writing called **stream of consciousness,** a technique of presenting the flow of thoughts and sensations in a character's mind. In this kind of writing, ideas and images occur as loosely connected associations rather than in a logical progression. A character's stream of consciousness is often expressed as an **interior monologue,** a record of the total workings of the character's mind and emotions. Find a passage in "The Duchess and the Jeweller" that records Oliver Bacon's stream of consciousness. What does it tell you about his character?

CONCEPT REVIEW: Figurative Language **Similes** and **metaphors** are types of figurative language in which basically unlike things are compared. Look through the story to find at least three examples of similes and metaphors involving animals. What two things are compared in each figure of speech? How does each influence your understanding of the story?

CRITIC'S CORNER

A student reviewer, Sarah Slezak, commented that she enjoyed the characters in Woolf's story because they "seemed very realistic." Did you have a similar response to the characters, or did you view them differently? Cite details from the story to support your opinion.

ALTERNATIVE ACTIVITIES

1. Draw a **caricature** that depicts the duchess and the jeweller conducting their business deal. Share your work with the class.
2. With a partner, rehearse and perform for the class a **pantomime** of the encounter between the jeweller and the duchess.
3. As the duchess, deliver a stream-of-consciousness **soliloquy** in which you reveal your thoughts and feelings as you wait to see the jeweller.
4. ***Cooperative Learning*** With a small group of classmates, hold a **roundtable discussion** in which you consider whether the jeweller is a greedy person.

ACROSS THE CURRICULUM

History Locate information on the Bloomsbury group, and find the names of three of its members (other than Virginia Woolf, Leonard Woolf, and E. M. Forster). Share your findings with the class, briefly describing the contributions each of the three persons made to society.

Science/Economics Collect information on the production and sale of precious jewels. Research the production process from the finding of the raw stones to the creation of the highest-quality jewels for sale. Include information about the characteristics that make some gems more valuable than others, as well as details about famous jewels of the past and present. Report to the class on your findings.

WORDS TO KNOW

EXERCISE A Use your knowledge of the boldfaced words to answer the following questions.

1. If you **forge** an agreement, are you making it, breaking it, or shaking it?
2. Is an **astute** person one who is conceited, one who is honest, or one who is bright?
3. Is being **lissome** most necessary for a lawyer, for a gymnast, or for a weight lifter?
4. Would someone known for **arrogance** be considered appealing, obnoxious, or wise?
5. Does a person who behaves **obsequiously** give the impression of being proud, of being meek, or of being trustworthy?

EXERCISE B Work with four classmates to develop a short scene involving five characters. The scene can deal with any situation—the important thing is to portray the characters in such a way that, by the end of the scene, each has become associated with one of the five vocabulary words. Do not use the words themselves in the scene; develop the associations through the characters' actions and dialogue.

VIRGINIA WOOLF

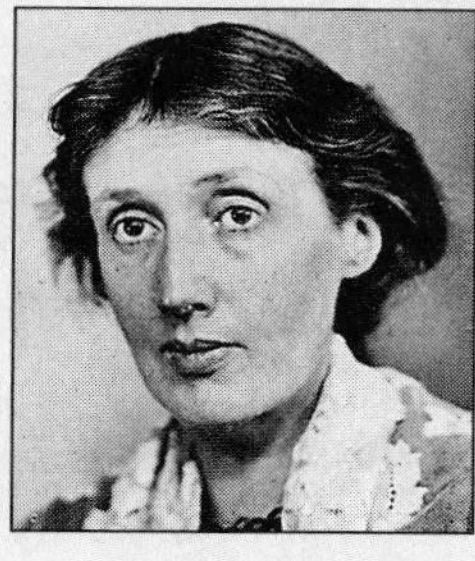

1882–1941

Childhood experiences greatly influenced the path Virginia Woolf would take as an adult. Born Adeline Virginia Stephen and raised in a cultured upper-middle-class family, whose friends included leading artists and thinkers of the late Victorian era, she was writing by the time she was nine. Although her parents encouraged her literary efforts, they adhered to the Victorian custom of sending only their sons to school. While her brothers went off to private schools and to Cambridge University, she remained at home with tutors. Although she would never forget this injustice, she fortunately had free access to her father's vast library and was continually exposed to the brilliant ideas and conversation of the family's intellectual friends. Through these avenues, she managed to gain an education that was rich and varied, though unusual.

As a young woman, Woolf rejected the restrictions of Victorian society and eagerly embraced the free-thinking ideas of her brothers' university friends, who eventually formed the nucleus of the Bloomsbury group. In 1912 she married Leonard Woolf, a member of the group, with whom she founded the Hogarth Press and began to publish her own fiction as well as the poetry of T. S. Eliot and the short stories of Katherine Mansfield. Throughout her life, Woolf was also an articulate feminist. Her long essay *A Room of One's Own* is considered by many to be the first major literary achievement in the movement for female equality in England.

The death of Woolf's mother when Woolf was 13 contributed to the first of many battles with mental illness that the author would face during her lifetime. At the start of World War II, her anxieties about a German invasion of England accelerated the deterioration of her mental health. In 1941, deeply depressed and fearful that she was going insane, Woolf drowned herself in the river Ouse at the age of 59.

OTHER WORKS *A Haunted House and Other Short Stories, To the Lighthouse, A Room of One's Own, Flush*

Milestones in British Literature

Virginia Woolf

The Novels of Virginia Woolf

"Life is not a series of gig-lamps symmetrically arranged; life is a luminous halo, a semi-transparent envelope surrounding us from the beginning of consciousness to the end," wrote Virginia Woolf in her essay "Modern Fiction." Although her vision of life and art seemed clear in her mind, the problem for Woolf was how to re-create this luminous halo in her art. After her early efforts in fiction, she found herself less interested in using the traditional devices of the novel, such as chronological plot structure and conventional point of view, and more in portraying the subtle web of impressions that she believed constituted true reality.

Woolf found her reality in the "world within." Instead of simply writing about surface actions, events, and settings in the orderly fashion that most Victorians had done before her, Woolf became a master of interior monologue and stream of consciousness in order to "record the atoms [of thought] as they fall upon the mind." Believing that one flash of insight could be a more powerful reflection of reality than line after line of literal description, she wove the evocative details and flowing rhythms of lyric poetry into her fiction.

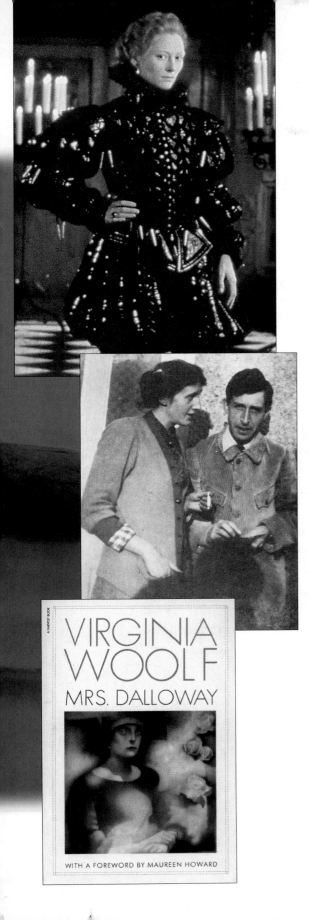

Mrs. Dalloway was the first novel in which Woolf displayed mastery of this distinctive prose style. It depicts a single day in the life of a middle-class Englishwoman preparing to give a party. The novel's reality, however, is composed of the characters' memories and thoughts about life, loved ones, and even strangers—thoughts that create a delicate montage of impressions as they rise to the surface. In similar fashion, *To the Lighthouse* explores the thoughts of a family and their friends on holiday. In the process, one glimpses aspects of daily life that reveal subtle truths about love, death, and art.

In the novel *Orlando,* employing a very different time span, Woolf displays her fascination with male and female identity and with the interplay of past and present. At the opening of the novel, Orlando is a young man in Elizabethan times, but by the work's midpoint, Orlando has become a young woman in the 1920s. *The Waves,* Woolf's most experimental novel, consists almost entirely of interior monologues representing the thoughts of its six major characters from childhood through old age.

In addition to these and other novels, Woolf's literary contributions included numerous reviews and critical essays, as well as the journals that she kept throughout her life. Her most remarkable offerings, however, were undoubtedly her novels, which challenged the existing structures and traditions of literature and inspired future generations of writers to share in her luminous vision of reality.

Top:
The recent film version of the novel Orlando *used lush visuals, music, and voice-overs to convey Orlando's inner life.* Photofest.
Middle:
Leonard and Virginia Woolf.
Left:
Cover of Woolf's novel Mrs. Dalloway

PREVIEWING

POETRY

What I Expected

Stephen Spender

PERSONAL CONNECTION

Recall a time when what you hoped or dreamed for didn't turn out the way you wanted. How did you react to the disappointment? What realities were you forced to face? Jot down your thoughts in your notebook.

BIOGRAPHICAL CONNECTION

When he entered Oxford University in 1928, Stephen Spender had already decided that he wanted to be a famous poet. There, he showed his poems to W. H. Auden, a slightly older student who had already achieved recognition within the school for his poetic genius. Auden approved of Spender's work, and a famous literary alliance was formed. The two poets were key members of a small group of Oxford students—the so-called Auden Generation—who became prominent literary figures during the 1930s. In addition to Auden and Spender, the group included the poets Louis MacNeice and C. Day Lewis and the novelist Christopher Isherwood.

The 1930s were turbulent years in European history—the time of the Great Depression, the Spanish civil war, and the start of World War II. Many English writers, particularly those of the Auden Generation, were appalled by what they saw taking place in the world. Sharing a hatred of war and a disgust for the deplorable living conditions endured by the swelling ranks of England's unemployed, they believed that it was their job to reflect the political and social concerns of the time in their writings. Although Spender did notable work as a critic, editor, translator, and travel writer, it is for his political poetry that he is best known. In "What I Expected," written during the early 1930s, he deals with the realities he faced during that period.

WRITING CONNECTION

In a cluster diagram like the one shown, note some of the unpleasant realities you have had to confront at different times in your life—when moving to a new city or going to a new school, for instance. Then, as you read "What I Expected," notice the realities that the speaker acknowledges.

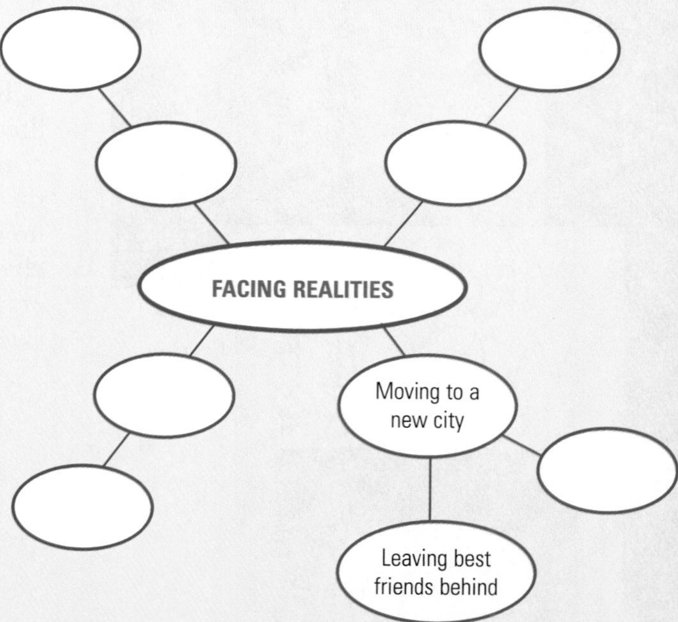

What I Expected

Stephen Spender

What I expected, was
Thunder, fighting,
Long struggles with men
And climbing.
After continual straining
I should grow strong;
Then the rocks would shake
And I rest long.

What I had not foreseen
Was the gradual day
Weakening the will
Leaking the brightness away,
The lack of good to touch,
The fading of body and soul
Smoke before wind,
Corrupt, unsubstantial.

The wearing of Time,
And the watching of cripples pass
With limbs shaped like questions
In their odd twist,
The pulverous grief
Melting the bones with pity,
The sick falling from earth—
These, I could not foresee.

Expecting always
Some brightness to hold in trust
Some final innocence
Exempt from dust,
That, hanging solid,
Would dangle through all
Like the created poem,
Or the faceted crystal.

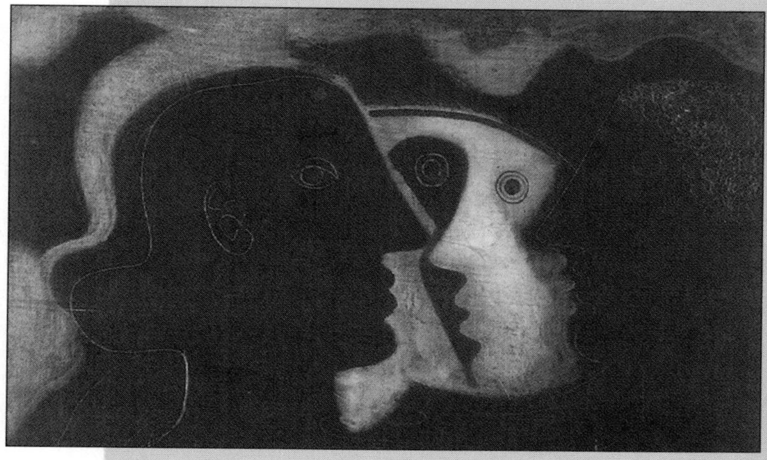

Detail of *1933 (St. Rémy-Provence)* (1933), Ben Nicholson.

21 pulverous: devastating; crushing.

32 faceted: having flat, smooth surfaces.

RESPONDING OPTIONS

FROM PERSONAL RESPONSE TO CRITICAL ANALYSIS

REFLECT **1.** Which images from "What I Expected" remain with you? Jot them down in your notebook.

RETHINK **2.** Summarize what you think the speaker expected to feel at this point in his life. Cite details from the poem to support your ideas.

3. In your own words, tell what you think the speaker "had not foreseen." Compare your thoughts with those of your classmates.

4. In your opinion, what theme or message is expressed in this poem?

Consider

- the speaker's reference to fighting (lines 2–7)
- what the speaker says about "brightness" (lines 12 and 26)
- the image of "smoke before wind" (line 15)
- the reference to "Time" (line 17)

RELATE **5.** Think of the realities that the speaker acknowledges in the poem. Do you think most people come to similar realizations during the course of their lives?

ANOTHER PATHWAY

Examine the imagery in this poem. In a chart like the one shown, distinguish between the images that express the speaker's expectations and those that express the reality the speaker has had to face. Decide what different impressions the two types of images convey. Then share your ideas with the class.

Images That Describe Expectations	Images That Describe Reality
1.	1.
2.	2.

QUICKWRITES

1. Imagine that you are the speaker of "What I Expected." Rewrite each stanza as an individual **diary entry.**
2. Write an **opinion paper** in which you disagree with the speaker's attitude toward life and the passing of time. Be sure to support your opinions with reasons.
3. Refer to the cluster diagram you created for the Writing Connection on page 822. In a **paragraph,** describe one of the events you noted, explaining how your expectations were modified by reality.

***PORTFOLIO** Save your writing. You may want to use it later as a springboard to a piece for your portfolio.*

LITERARY CONCEPTS

Most of Spender's poems are written in **free verse**—verse without regular patterns of rhythm and rhyme. Although free verse lacks conventional meter, it may contain various rhythmic and sound effects—such as recurring syllables or words. Free verse can also contain rhyme, but if so, it is used with great freedom. How would you characterize the overall rhythm of "What I Expected"? How does the rhythm relate to the content of the poem?

ALTERNATIVE ACTIVITIES

1. ***Cooperative Learning*** With a small group of classmates, stage and present a **dramatic reading** of the poem for your class. Select appropriate background music and prepare a simple cloth backdrop or screen to enhance your performance.
2. Create a **montage** that conveys your interpretation of "What I Expected." Include lines from the poem as well as illustrations or photographs. If you have access to a computer, use it to create designs or to set lines of the poem in different sizes and fonts.

LITERARY LINKS

Do you think the speaker of Gerard Manley Hopkins's "Spring and Fall: To a Young Child" (page 679) would agree with the depiction of reality in "What I Expected"? Why or why not?

CRITIC'S CORNER

The critic Geoffrey Thurley considers "What I Expected" to be one of Spender's best poems. He says that Spender conceived the poem "as an act, rather than as a statement" and that for this reason the reader "experiences the poem." Explain what you think Thurley means, and tell how you experience the poem.

ART CONNECTION

In your opinion, how do the visual images in the painting *1933 (St. Rémy-Provence)* on page 823 relate to the verbal images in "What I Expected"? Support your answer.

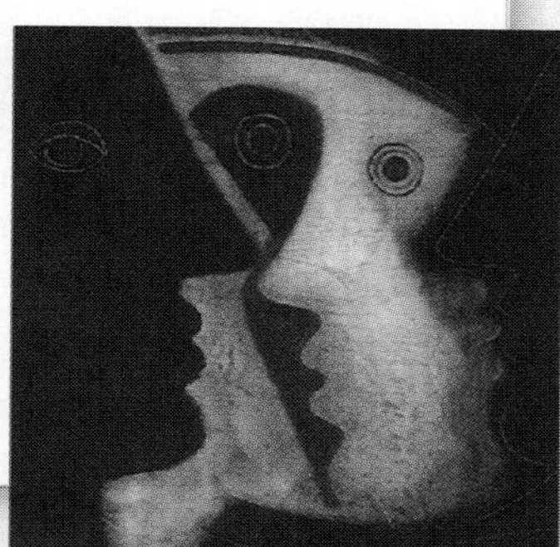

ACROSS THE CURRICULUM

Science Read about the properties of crystals. What significant qualities, shapes, and uses do they have? In the last lines of "What I Expected," the speaker equates a "created poem" with a "faceted crystal." How do you think the properties of a crystal might be like those of a poem?

STEPHEN SPENDER

1909–1995

Throughout his career, Stephen Spender had a reputation for creating humanistic works that struck a balance between bleak pessimism and unfailing optimism. A modest and sometimes shy man, he nevertheless enjoyed a camaraderie with his fellow writers. He eagerly accepted invitations to visit the gatherings of London's numerous literary circles, where he met such distinguished writers as Virginia Woolf and T. S. Eliot, and in later years his reputation for witty conversation made him a popular guest in the homes of the socially prominent both in Britain and in the United States.

Spender's strong interest in humanity was reflected not only in his writing but in his other activities. For approximately 20 years, he acted as a cultural ambassador, lecturing throughout the world on the importance of the artistic and intellectual dimensions of life. From 1970 to 1975, he was a full-time professor of English at University College in London, and he also served as a visiting professor at many universities in the United States and as poetry consultant to the Library of Congress. In 1983 Spender was knighted for his many contributions to literature.

OTHER WORKS "The Vase of Tears," "Two Armies," "Moving Through the Silent Crowd," "Dark and Light," "Fall of a City"

REFLECT & ASSESS

Tobermory

Saki

"Saki" was the pen name of the Scottish writer Hector Hugh Munro. "Tobermory" is one of a series of stories about the adventures of a character named Clovis, in which Munro pokes fun at the follies of British society during the early 1900s. One of Munro's most popular stories, it was praised by the English actor and playwright Noel Coward as a masterpiece of high comedy.

It was a chill, rain-washed afternoon of a late August day, that indefinite season when partridges are still in security or cold storage, and there is nothing to hunt—unless one is bounded on the north by the Bristol Channel, in which case one may lawfully gallop after fat red stags. Lady Blemley's house party was not bounded on the north by the Bristol Channel, hence there was a full gathering of her guests round the tea table on this particular afternoon. And, in spite of the blankness of the season and the triteness of the occasion, there was no trace in the company of that fatigued restlessness which means a dread of the pianola[1] and a subdued hankering for auction bridge.[2] The undisguised open-mouthed attention of the entire party was fixed on the homely negative personality of Mr. Cornelius Appin. Of all her guests, he was the one who had come to Lady Blemley with the vaguest reputation. Someone had said he was "clever," and he had got his invitation in the moderate expectation, on the part of his hostess, that some portion at least of his cleverness would be contributed to the general entertainment. Until tea time that day she had been unable to discover in what direction, if any, his cleverness lay. He was neither a wit nor a croquet champion, a hypnotic force nor a begetter of amateur theatricals. Neither did his exterior suggest the sort of man in whom women are willing to pardon a generous measure of mental deficiency. He had subsided into mere Mr. Appin, and the Cornelius seemed a piece of transparent baptismal bluff. And now he was claiming to have launched on the world a discovery beside which the invention of gunpowder, of the printing press, and of steam locomotion were inconsiderable trifles. Science had made bewildering strides in many directions during recent decades, but this thing seemed to belong to the domain of miracle rather than to scientific achievement.

"And do you really ask us to believe," Sir Wilfrid was saying, "that you have discovered a means for instructing animals in the art of human speech, and that dear old Tobermory has proved your first successful pupil?"

---

1. **pianola** (pē′ə-nō′lə): player piano.
2. **auction bridge:** a card game popular in the early 1900s.

"It is a problem at which I have worked for the last seventeen years," said Mr. Appin, "but only during the last eight or nine months have I been rewarded with glimmerings of success. Of course I have experimented with thousands of animals, but latterly only with cats, those wonderful creatures which have assimilated[3] themselves so marvelously with our civilization while retaining all their highly developed feral[4] instincts. Here and there among cats one comes across an outstanding superior intellect, just as one does among the ruck[5] of human beings, and when I made the acquaintance of Tobermory a week ago I saw at once that I was in contact with a 'Beyond-cat' of extraordinary intelligence. I had gone far along the road to success in recent experiments; with Tobermory, as you call him, I have reached the goal."

Mr. Appin concluded his remarkable statement in a voice which he strove to divest[6] of a triumphant inflection. No one said "Rats," though Clovis's lips moved in a monosyllabic contortion which probably invoked those rodents of disbelief.

"And do you mean to say," asked Miss Resker, after a slight pause, "that you have taught Tobermory to say and understand easy sentences of one syllable?"

"My dear Miss Resker," said the wonder-worker patiently, "one teaches little children and savages and backward adults in that piecemeal fashion; when one has once solved the problem of making a beginning with an animal of highly developed intelligence one has no need for those halting methods. Tobermory can speak our language with perfect correctness."

This time Clovis very distinctly said, "Beyond-rats!" Sir Wilfrid was more polite, but equally skeptical.

"Hadn't we better have the cat in and judge for ourselves?" suggested Lady Blemley.

Sir Wilfrid went in search of the animal, and the company settled themselves down to the languid expectation of witnessing some more or less adroit[7] drawing-room ventriloquism.

In a minute Sir Wilfrid was back in the room, his face white beneath its tan and his eyes dilated with excitement.

"By Gad, it's true!"

His agitation was unmistakably genuine, and his hearers started forward in a thrill of awakened interest.

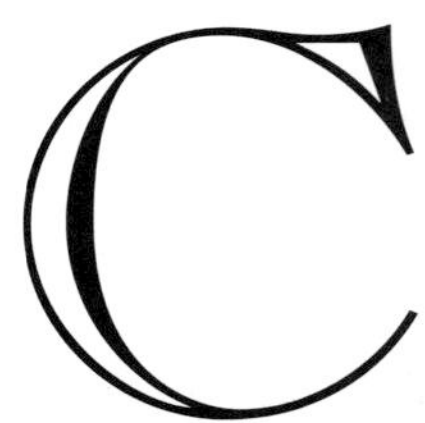ollapsing into an armchair he continued breathlessly: "I found him dozing in the smoking room and called out to him to come for his tea. He blinked at me in his usual way, and I said, 'Come on, Toby; don't keep us waiting'; and, by Gad! he drawled out in a most horribly natural voice that he'd come when he dashed well pleased! I nearly jumped out of my skin!"

Appin had preached to absolutely incredulous hearers; Sir Wilfrid's statement carried instant conviction. A Babel-like[8] chorus of startled exclamation arose, amid which the scientist sat mutely enjoying the first fruit of his stupendous discovery.

In the midst of the clamor Tobermory entered the room and made his way with velvet tread and studied unconcern across to the group seated round the tea table.

A sudden hush of awkwardness and constraint fell on the company. Somehow there seemed an element of embarrassment in addressing on equal terms a domestic cat of acknowledged mental ability.

"Will you have some milk, Tobermory?" asked Lady Blemley in a rather strained voice.

---

3. **assimilated** (ə-sĭm′ə-lā′tĭd): fitted in; adapted.
4. **feral** (fîr′əl): wild; untamed.
5. **ruck:** undistinguished masses.
6. **divest** (dĭ-vĕst′): rid; free.
7. **adroit:** skillful; clever.
8. **Babel-like** (bā′bəl līk′): noisy and confused. (In the biblical story of Babel [Genesis 11], people who tried to build a tower reaching to heaven were punished by God's changing their one language into a multitude of new ones, resulting in violent confusion.)

"I don't mind if I do," was the response, couched in a tone of even indifference. A shiver of suppressed excitement went through the listeners, and Lady Blemley might be excused for pouring out the saucerful of milk rather unsteadily.

"I'm afraid I've spilt a good deal of it," she said apologetically.

"After all, it's not my Axminster,"[9] was Tobermory's rejoinder.[10]

Another silence fell on the group, and then Miss Resker, in her best district-visitor manner, asked if the human language had been difficult to learn. Tobermory looked squarely at her for a moment and then fixed his gaze serenely on the middle distance. It was obvious that boring questions lay outside his scheme of life.

"What do you think of human intelligence?" asked Mavis Pellington lamely.

"Of whose intelligence in particular?" asked Tobermory coldly.

"Oh, well, mine for instance," said Mavis, with a feeble laugh.

"You put me in an embarrassing position," said Tobermory, whose tone and attitude certainly did not suggest a shred of embarrassment. "When your inclusion in this house party was suggested Sir Wilfrid protested that you were the most brainless woman of his acquaintance, and that there was a wide distinction between hospitality and the care of the feeble-minded. Lady Blemley replied that your lack of brainpower was the precise quality which had earned you your invitation, as you were the only person she could think of who might be idiotic enough to buy their old car. You know, the one they call 'The Envy of Sisyphus,'[11] because it goes quite nicely uphill if you push it."

Lady Blemley's protestations would have had greater effect if she had not casually suggested to Mavis only that morning that the car in question would be just the thing for her down at her Devonshire home.

Major Barfield plunged in heavily to effect a diversion.

"How about your carryings-on with the tortoise-shell puss up at the stables, eh?"

The moment he had said it everyone realized the blunder.

"One does not usually discuss these matters in public," said Tobermory frigidly. "From a slight observation of your ways since you've been in this house I should imagine you'd find it inconvenient if I were to shift the conversation on to your own little affairs."

The panic which ensued was not confined to the Major.

"Would you like to go and see if cook has got your dinner ready?" suggested Lady Blemley hurriedly, affecting to ignore the fact that it wanted at least two hours to Tobermory's dinnertime.

"Thanks," said Tobermory, "not quite so soon after my tea. I don't want to die of indigestion."

"Cats have nine lives, you know," said Sir Wilfrid heartily.

"Possibly," answered Tobermory; "but only one liver."

"Adelaide!" said Mrs. Cornett, "do you mean to encourage that cat to go out and gossip about us in the servants' hall?"

The panic had indeed become general. A narrow ornamental balustrade[12] ran in front of most of the bedroom windows at the Towers, and it was recalled with dismay that this had formed a favorite promenade for Tobermory at all hours, whence he could watch the pigeons—and heaven knew what else besides. If he intended to become reminiscent in his present outspoken strain the effect would be something

9. **Axminster:** a fine, expensive carpet.

10. **rejoinder:** reply.

11. **Sisyphus** (sĭs′ə-fəs): in Greek mythology, a cruel king condemned to spend the afterlife forever rolling uphill a huge stone that rolls back down each time he nears the top.

12. **balustrade** (băl′ə-strād′): a railing supported by posts or pillars.

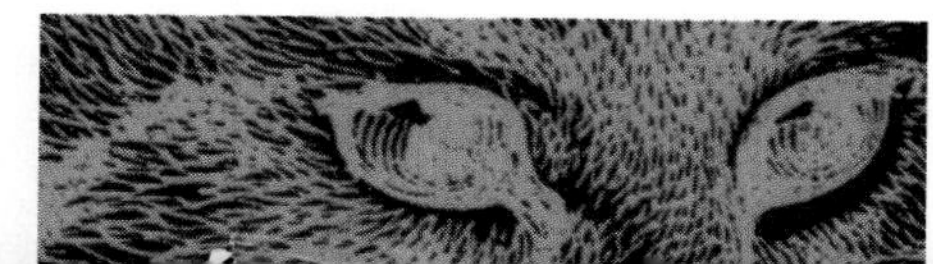

more than disconcerting.[13] Mrs. Cornett, who spent much time at her toilet table, and whose complexion was reputed to be of a nomadic though punctual disposition, looked as ill at ease as the Major. Miss Scrawen, who wrote fiercely sensuous poetry and led a blameless life, merely displayed irritation; if you are methodical and virtuous in private you don't necessarily want everyone to know it. Bertie van Tahn, who was so depraved[14] at seventeen that he had long ago given up trying to be any worse, turned a dull shade of gardenia white, but he did not commit the error of dashing out of the room like Odo Finsberry, a young gentleman who was understood to be reading for the Church[15] and who was possibly disturbed at the thought of scandals he might hear concerning other people. Clovis had the presence of mind to maintain a composed exterior; privately he was calculating how long it would take to procure a box of fancy mice through the agency of the *Exchange and Mart* as a species of hush money.

Even in a delicate situation like the present, Agnes Resker could not endure to remain too long in the background.

"Why did I ever come down here?" she asked dramatically.

Tobermory immediately accepted the opening.

"Judging by what you said to Mrs. Cornett on the croquet lawn yesterday, you were out for food. You described the Blemleys as the dullest people to stay with that you knew, but said they were clever enough to employ a first-rate cook; otherwise they'd find it difficult to get anyone to come down a second time."

"There's not a word of truth in it! I appeal to Mrs. Cornett—" exclaimed the discomfited[16] Agnes.

"Mrs. Cornett repeated your remark afterwards to Bertie van Tahn," continued Tobermory, "and said, 'That woman is a regular Hunger Marcher; she'd go anywhere for four square meals a day,' and Bertie van Tahn said—"

At this point the chronicle mercifully ceased. Tobermory had caught a glimpse of the big yellow Tom from the Rectory working his way through the shrubbery towards the stable wing. In a flash he had vanished through the open French window.

With the disappearance of his too brilliant pupil Cornelius Appin found himself beset by a hurricane of bitter upbraiding, anxious inquiry, and frightened entreaty. The responsibility for the situation lay with him, and he must prevent matters from becoming worse. Could Tobermory impart his dangerous gift to other cats? was the first question he had to answer. It was possible, he replied, that he might have initiated his intimate friend the stable puss into his new accomplishment, but it was unlikely that his teaching could have taken a wider range as yet.

"Then," said Mrs. Cornett, "Tobermory may be a valuable cat and a great pet; but I'm sure you'll agree, Adelaide, that both he and the stable cat must be done away with without delay."

"You don't suppose I've enjoyed the last quarter of an hour, do you?" said Lady Blemley bitterly. "My husband and I are very fond of Tobermory—at least, we were before this horrible accomplishment was infused into him; but now, of course, the only thing is to have him destroyed as soon as possible."

"We can put some strychnine[17] in the scraps he always gets at dinner time," said Sir Wilfrid, "and I will go and drown the stable cat myself. The coachman will be very sore at losing his pet, but I'll say a very catching form of mange[18] has

13. **disconcerting** (dĭs′kən-sûr′tĭng): upsetting; embarrassing.
14. **depraved:** immoral; corrupt.
15. **reading for the Church:** studying to become a priest in the Church of England.
16. **discomfited** (dĭs-kŭm′fĭ-tĭd): uneasy; embarrassed.
17. **strychnine** (strĭk′nīn′): a highly poisonous drug.
18. **mange** (mānj): a disease of animals that causes a loss of hair.

broken out in both cats and we're afraid of its spreading to the kennels."

"But my great discovery!" expostulated Mr. Appin; "after all my years of research and experiment—"

"You can go and experiment on the shorthorns at the farm, who are under proper control," said Mrs. Cornett, "or the elephants at the Zoological Gardens. They're said to be highly intelligent, and they have this recommendation, that they don't come creeping about our bedrooms and under chairs, and so forth."

An archangel ecstatically proclaiming the Millennium,[19] and then finding that it clashed unpardonably with Henley[20] and would have to be indefinitely postponed, could hardly have felt more crestfallen than Cornelius Appin at the reception of his wonderful achievement. Public opinion, however, was against him—in fact, had the general voice been consulted on the subject it is probable that a strong minority vote would have been in favor of including him in the strychnine diet.

Defective train arrangements and a nervous desire to see matters brought to a finish prevented an immediate dispersal of the party, but dinner that evening was not a social success. Sir Wilfrid had had rather a trying time with the stable cat and subsequently with the coachman. Agnes Resker ostentatiously limited her repast to a morsel of dry toast, which she bit as though it were a personal enemy; while Mavis Pellington maintained a vindictive[21] silence throughout the meal. Lady Blemley kept up a flow of what she

19. **the Millennium:** in Christian theology, a period of 1,000 years during which Christ will reign on earth.

20. **Henley:** the Henley Royal Regatta, an annual series of rowing races in England.

21. **vindictive:** revengeful; spiteful.

Interior in Venice (1898), John Singer Sargent. Royal Academy of Arts, London, Bridgeman/Art Resource, New York.

Lotty and the Lady (1906), George Lambert. Oil on canvas, 102.6 cm × 127.6 cm, National Gallery of Victoria, Melbourne, Australia, Felton Bequest, 1910.

hoped was conversation, but her attention was fixed on the doorway. A plateful of carefully dosed fish scraps was in readiness on the sideboard, but sweets and savory[22] and dessert went their way, and no Tobermory appeared either in the dining room or kitchen.

The sepulchral[23] dinner was cheerful compared with the subsequent vigil in the smoking room. Eating and drinking had at least supplied a distraction and cloak to the prevailing embarrassment. Bridge was out of the question in the general tension of nerves and tempers, and after Odo Finsberry had given a lugubrious rendering of "Mélisande in the Wood" to a frigid audience, music was tacitly avoided. At eleven the servants went to bed, announcing that the small window in the pantry had been left open as usual for Tobermory's private use. The guests read steadily through the current batch of magazines, and fell back gradually on the "Badminton Library" and bound volumes of *Punch*. Lady Blemley made periodic visits to the pantry, returning each time with an expression of listless depression which forestalled questioning.

At two o'clock Clovis broke the dominating silence.

"He won't turn up tonight. He's probably in the local newspaper office at the present moment, dictating the first installment of his reminiscences. Lady What's-her-name's book won't be in it. It will be the event of the day."

Having made this contribution to the general cheerfulness, Clovis went to bed. At long intervals the various members of the house party followed his example.

The servants taking round the early tea made a uniform announcement in reply to a uniform question. Tobermory had not returned.

22. **savory** (sā′və-rē): a highly seasoned or pickled food served at the end of dinner.

23. **sepulchral** (sə-pŭl′krəl): tomblike; gloomy.

Breakfast was, if anything, a more unpleasant function than dinner had been, but before its conclusion the situation was relieved. Tobermory's corpse was brought in from the shrubbery, where a gardener had just discovered it. From the bites on his throat and the yellow fur which coated his claws it was evident that he had fallen in unequal combat with the big Tom from the Rectory.

By midday most of the guests had quitted the Towers, and after lunch Lady Blemley had sufficiently recovered her spirits to write an extremely nasty letter to the Rectory about the loss of her valuable pet.

Tobermory had been Appin's one successful pupil, and he was destined to have no successor. A few weeks later an elephant in the Dresden Zoological Garden, which had shown no previous signs of irritability, broke loose and killed an Englishman who had apparently been teasing it. The victim's name was variously reported in the papers as Oppin and Eppelin, but his front name was faithfully rendered Cornelius.

"If he was trying German irregular verbs on the poor beast," said Clovis, "he deserved all he got." ❖

SAKI

1870–1916

Hector Hugh Munro was born in Burma, where his father was serving with the British military police. Less than two years later, after his mother's death, Munro was sent with his brother and sister to live with a pair of unmarried aunts in Barnstaple, England. These stern women did not understand children and raised the young Munros in isolation from the outside world. Forbidden to play outside, seeing other children only rarely, and frequently punished, Munro and his siblings were nevertheless quite inventive, sometimes reacting to their confinement by staging elaborate practical jokes. Munro never forgot the tyranny of his guardians and later satirized them by depicting aunts in his stories as cold, unfeeling, and sometimes evil.

At the age of 23, Munro went back to Burma to follow in his father's footsteps as a police officer, but recurring bouts of malaria forced him to resign his position. He returned to England, where he spent three years researching and writing his only serious historical work, *The Rise and Fall of the Russian Empire,* which was published in 1900. During this time he also began to write political satire for a London newspaper, using the pen name Saki, taken from a character in Omar Khayyám's *Rubáiyát.* In 1902, he combined his interests in history and journalism by accepting a job as a foreign correspondent, and for the next seven years he traveled throughout Europe and the Balkans. Returning to England in 1908, he settled again in London and bravely began a new career—writing fiction.

At the start of World War I, Munro was resolute in his desire to fight. Although 43 years old and physically frail, he enlisted in the British army. Three years later, he was killed during an attack on the Germans at Beaumont-Hamel, France.

OTHER WORKS "The Open Window," "Laura," "The Story-Teller," "The Schartz-Metterklume Method"

WRITING ABOUT LITERATURE

SETTING THE STANDARDS

Every week, new movies come to theaters and new books appear in bookstores. One way to figure out which of these products is worth your time and money is to read reviews. Another way is to read books or watch movies with a critical eye so you can make better choices about what to pay attention to in the future. In this lesson you will

- study how writers use sentence variety to make their writing more interesting
- evaluate and criticize elements of a Unit Six selection
- set criteria to guide you in real-world decisions

Writer's Style: Sentence Variety Good writers vary the length and structure of their sentences in order to add information and keep the writing interesting.

Read the Literature

Beginning writers often overuse the most common sentence structure—sentences that begin with a subject followed by a verb. What variations on this structure do you see in the excerpts below?

Literature Models

Sentence Openers and Subject-Verb Splits
How does the first sentence begin, or open? In the second sentence what separates the subject from its verb? How does this presentation help build suspense?

Then, after a few seconds' hesitation, he found his courage, and turned to investigate. The stairs, he saw to his utter amazement, were empty; there was no one. He felt a series of cold shivers run over him, and something about the muscles of his legs gave a little and grew weak.

Algernon Blackwood, from "The Kit-Bag"

Sentence Closers
How does each sentence end, or close? How does this affect the rhythm of the passage?

Imagine a giant hog in a pasture rich with truffles; after unearthing this truffle and that, still it smells a bigger, a blacker truffle under the ground further off. So Oliver snuffed always in the rich earth of Mayfair another truffle, a blacker, a bigger further off.

Virginia Woolf, from "The Duchess and the Jeweller"

Connect to Life

Writers may use more than one phrase or clause to open or close a sentence or to divide a subject and a verb. Notice how this nonfiction writer varies her sentences. For what purpose is the additional information used?

Magazine Article

> In most mystery series, particularly those in the domestic tradition, setting plays as central a role as sleuth. In few mysteries is that more true than the two Arkansas series written by Joan Hess. Readers familiar with the small backwoods town of Maggody, where Arly Hanks is sheriff, or the university town of Farberville, where single mother and bookstore owner Claire Malloy solves crimes, won't be surprised to learn that the author is as rooted in place as her heroines are.
>
> Dulcy Brainard, from "Joan Hess," *Publishers Weekly*

Adding Phrases
How does this writer use phrases and clauses to create sentence variety? What effect does this have in each sentence?

Try Your Hand: Sentence Variety

1. **Imitate the Models** Write sentences that imitate the structure of each of the following:
   - the first sentence of the first literature model
   - the last sentence of the second literature model
   - the first sentence of the model above
2. **Revise a QuickWrite** Don't worry about sentence structure when you're freewriting; you can strive for sentence variety when it's time to revise. Rewrite a QuickWrite now, taking care to vary your sentences.
3. **Make It Interesting** Write a short paragraph about a frightening experience you've had. Add words and phrases at the beginning, middle, and end of your sentences to provide information, build suspense, and create variety.

SkillBuilder

WRITER'S CRAFT

Varying Sentence Openers
Using the same kind of sentence opener repeatedly can get as dull as constantly using the same kind of sentence. There are several types of openers, and each one creates a different rhythm, provides a different amount of detail, or gives a different emphasis. Vary the kinds you use.

Adverb: *Suddenly, the door swung open.*

Participle: *Shaken, she turned toward the door.*

Prepositional phrase: *In the dim light, Rebbie could hardly see a thing.*

Participial phrase: *Reaching for her baseball bat, she prepared herself for the worst.*

APPLYING WHAT YOU'VE LEARNED
Use your imagination to create a different kind of opener for each of the following sentences.

1. Lightning struck the tree.
2. The animals howled.
3. I ran for cover.
4. The branch hanging above the barn was torn off.

Criticism

Do you ever get halfway through a movie or book and know already whether you love it or hate it? What causes that reaction? Examining each element of a piece and seeing how it works with the whole can help you understand your reactions and express your opinions. It can also improve your own writing.

GUIDED ASSIGNMENT

Write a Literary Review Write a review of one of the selections in Unit Six, based on criteria you establish. Explain what it is you liked or disliked about the work, and how each element of the story contributed to your conclusion.

1 Prewrite and Explore

Which Unit Six selections did you particularly enjoy? Which didn't appeal to you? Choose a selection that you had a strong opinion about.

READ AND RESPOND

Look through the selection again, paying attention to your reactions. Where did you become interested in the story? When did you lose interest? Notice what you notice—for example, the questions that go through your mind when you're reading and the expectations you have about the plot.

SET CRITERIA FOR A GOOD STORY

What makes a story good? Believable characters, thought-provoking subject matter, and good writing are some of the criteria commonly applied in judging literary works. However, different types of literature demand different criteria. Refer to the SkillBuilder on the opposite page for help in setting criteria to judge your story by.

ANALYZE

Once you've established a list of criteria, examine how the selection meets them. Be specific, and look carefully at each literary element. Do the setting and imagery help build suspense? Do the characters make you care about the plot? Consider making a chart like the one shown below.

Student's Chart

Criteria for a ghost story	How well met in "The Kit-Bag"?	Examples
builds suspense	Very well	Foreshadowing. The creepy setting helps to build suspense: rainy night, old house, no close neighbors.
has a compelling plot	It's fairly compelling.	The main character's conflict with the murderer is set up at the beginning. The climax of this conflict is frightening and powerful.
raises questions	Very well—you're left wondering if it's real or not.	Johnson doubts his own observations, calls them "rubbish and nerves," but the details of the murderer's suicide suggest a ghost.

2 Write a Discovery Draft

In a discovery draft, discuss how well the selection meets your criteria. Support your statements with examples from the text. As you're writing, keep your mind open to new ideas and more appropriate criteria.

I'll need to mention setting when I write my thesis statement.

Student's Discovery Draft

From the first scene the setting is ominous; it is a "dark December afternoon." The house that Johnson lives in is creepy, too, and the writer plays this up through his use of language. Johnson's apartment is described as being "the top floor in one of those old, gaunt houses in which the rooms are large and lofty."

3 Draft and Share

A strong introduction will help you turn your discovery draft into a more polished essay and will determine the organization of your body paragraphs. As you write the introduction to your literary review, keep the following tips in mind.

- Formulate a thesis statement. Remember, a thesis statement states the main idea of a piece of nonfiction.
- Identify the title and author of the selection, and briefly summarize its plot.
- State your opinion of the selection and the criteria that you used to judge it.

When you've completed your introduction, body paragraphs, and conclusion, ask a classmate to give you feedback.

- Why do you or don't you think my criteria for judging this selection are fair?
- What made you understand why I did or didn't feel the criteria were met?
- How do my criteria help you understand my opinion of the selection?

SkillBuilder

Setting Criteria

When you make judgments about what you read, you probably are basing your opinion on a list of what did or didn't work for you as you read the selection. By paying attention to this list, you can develop a set of criteria, or standards, that will make clear what you were looking for in a particular work. The kind of comments you make will vary depending on the kind of literature you're reading. For example, if you're reading a mystery story, you may notice whether or not you can follow the clues. This concern wouldn't even come up in a story dealing with a boy's first hunting trip.

Noting your reactions to a mystery story could lead to the following criteria.

A good mystery story should have

- an intriguing set-up
- an interesting main character
- some tension or suspense
- believable clues
- a logical ending

APPLYING WHAT YOU'VE LEARNED

What expectations did you have about the selection you chose? How did you react as you read the selection? Use these reactions to create a set of criteria for judging the kind of story you selected.

4 Revise and Edit

As you revise, remember that most works have strong points as well as weak points. Don't hesitate to discuss both in your review. When you're finished with your paper, reflect on movies or TV shows that have elements similar to those of the selection you reviewed. Consider collecting a group of final papers into a book of Unit Six critiques.

Student's Final Draft

A Ghost Story That Works

"The Kit-Bag" by Algernon Blackwood proves itself to be a first-rate ghost story by providing a compelling plot, building suspense, and raising questions. Setting, imagery, and character all work together to send shivers up the reader's spine. The story concerns a young legal secretary who returns to his gloomy apartment after seeing a murderer escape charges and who spends the night withstanding a terrifying series of events involving a borrowed bag and the image of the criminal. The secretary finally faints from fright, only to be awakened by a servant who informs him that the bag he had borrowed belonged to the murderer and that the murderer killed himself during the night.

Where does the student state the criteria used to review the selection?

How does the student support statements with details from the selection?

One way Blackwood creates suspense is through foreshadowing. The barrister who appears at the beginning of the story speaks "without emotion." "Don't dwell on it," he tells his employee and looks at him "curiously out of his keen eyes." This distinguished lawyer seems to know more than he shows, and his behavior serves as one of the first foreshadowings that something sinister is about to happen.

Standards for Evaluation

A literary review
- clearly expresses an opinion
- states the criteria for evaluation
- supports opinions with details from the text
- examines how literary elements work to meet the criteria

Grammar in Context

Compound-Complex Sentences A compound-complex sentence consists of two or more independent clauses and one or more subordinate clauses. Subordinate clauses either modify a word in one of the independent clauses or act as a noun in one of the independent clauses. The independent clauses in a compound-complex sentence can be joined in the following ways:

- by a coordinating conjunction (such as *and*, *but*, or *or*) preceded by a comma
- by a conjunctive adverb (such as *however*, *therefore*, or *consequently*) preceded by a semicolon and followed by a comma
- by a semicolon alone

When writing your literary review, consider using compound-complex sentences to create sentence variety and express relationships between ideas. Two or more sentences can be combined into one compound-complex sentence.

> This distinguished lawyer seems to know more than he shows, ~~His~~ , and his behavior serves as one of the first foreshadowings that something sinister is about to happen.

In the example above, the subordinate clause *that something sinister is about to happen* modifies the word *foreshadowings*.

Try Your Hand: Using Compound-Complex Sentences

Combine the following sentences into compound-complex sentences. Remember that one of the original sentences must become a subordinate clause.

1. This story is a page-turner. Setting plays a major role in creating suspense. There are also other elements.
2. We learn about Johnson's personality. He packs. He appears to be a nice, regular guy.
3. Everyone has heard things. Things go bump in the night. We can all relate to Johnson's predicament.

SkillBuilder

GRAMMAR FROM WRITING

Avoiding Phrase and Clause Fragments

A sentence must express a complete thought and contain both a subject and a verb. Although this definition may seem elementary, keep it in mind as you combine and separate sentences to create sentence variety. During revision, phrase and clause fragments can easily be mistaken for sentences.

Fragment: *Up the staircase and onto the landing*

In order to correct fragments, combine them with subjects and verbs to create sentences.

Sentence: *The noise traveled up the staircase and onto the landing.*

APPLYING WHAT YOU'VE LEARNED
Rewrite the following paragraph, correcting the phrase and clause fragments.

Blackwood's descriptions help create an ominous mood. Adjectives used, such as *cheerless, miserable,* and *gloomy.* Details about the weather abound, and we can almost feel and hear the winter wind. "A furious gust of wind." How could Johnson be sure about what he was hearing?

GRAMMAR HANDBOOK

For more help avoiding phrase and clause fragments, see page 1254 in the Grammar Handbook.

SPORTY
$1995
CASH
STATE INSPECTED
SALE
$2495
CASH
STATE INSPECTED

READING
THE WORLD

MAKING DECISIONS

Setting criteria can help you evaluate not only a story or film but also products, performances, and decisions. For example, when you're shopping you may be dazzled by a slick car, a stylish outfit, or the words "no fat" written in bold letters on a shiny box. However, you probably consider many other factors before reaching for your wallet. Consider the situation below.

View Examine the cars in the lot pictured on these pages. What is the first thing you notice? What else do you see?

Interpret What can you tell about these cars just by looking at them? What can you guess about them? Why do you think the red car is the least expensive? If you could buy one of these cars, what would you base your decision on?

Discuss In a group, discuss which car you would buy and compare the criteria each of you would use to make that decision. You may want to refer to the SkillBuilder on using criteria in order to help you think through this issue.

SkillBuilder

 CRITICAL THINKING

Using Criteria to Make Decisions

Just as you ask questions to determine whether or not something was worth reading, you can ask questions to determine whether or not a particular product or option is worth choosing. These questions can help you decide what you're looking for in a particular product. For example, if you're thinking about buying a used car, you might ask the following questions.

- Can I afford to purchase this car?
- Is this car likely to need repairs?
- How much money a month will I have to spend on gas, upkeep, and insurance?

Those questions could lead to the following criteria:

- An inexpensive purchase price
- A body and engine that are in good shape
- Efficient gas mileage

APPLYING WHAT YOU'VE LEARNED
What economic decisions will you soon need to make? Will you have to decide whether or not to accept a particular job? where to continue your education? what kind of computer to start saving for? Develop a set of criteria to help you make each decision.

PART 2

Shocking Realities

The first half of the 20th century was one of the most violent times in human history. The bloodshed and atrocities of two world wars shocked people everywhere and altered the course of British life. Throughout the century, many writers have explored the purposes, experiences, and consequences of war. The selections in this part of Unit Six will challenge you to define your own views and beliefs.

POETRY

An Irish Airman Foresees His Death

William Butler Yeats

The Soldier

Rupert Brooke

Dreamers

Siegfried Sassoon

PERSONAL CONNECTION

What if your country were suddenly engaged in a full-scale war with another country? Would you volunteer for military service? Would your decision depend on what caused the war, where it was fought, or who the enemy was? Share your thoughts.

HISTORICAL CONNECTION

At the start of the 20th century, the British were for the most part optimistic. Few anticipated a major conflict. However, a feverish sense of nationalism—the belief that loyalty to one's nation comes before all other loyalties—had led the British government and the governments of other nations to stockpile weapons and to issue increasingly alarming threats to their rivals. Tension mounted between countries with opposing goals, and the assassination of an Austrian archduke in 1914 ignited a war that quickly pulled in all the major powers of Europe. The war, known at the time as the Great War and later as World War I, was a devastating four-year conflict that spread to the Middle East, Africa, Asia, and the Pacific, although most of the major battles were fought in Europe. The casualty count was enormous—more than 8.5 million soldiers killed and approximately 21 million wounded.

Perhaps because World War I affected a large portion of the British population, it inspired an abundance of literature. The military ranks included not only professional soldiers like those who had fought in previous wars but also civilian volunteers and draftees, most of whom were unprepared for the grim realities of warfare. Many experienced changes in attitude during the course of the war, with the patriotism and enthusiasm of the first two years turning into disillusionment and despair as the war dragged on. Rupert Brooke and Siegfried Sassoon were among those who set off to defend their nation.

READING CONNECTION

Determining Attitudes These three poems present three different perspectives on World War I. In your notebook, create a chart like the one shown, recording words and phrases that you think describe the attitude toward war expressed in each poem.

Poem	Attitude Toward War
"An Irish Airman . . ."	
"The Soldier"	
"Dreamers"	

LASERLINKS
• *HISTORICAL CONNECTION*

Detail of *The Bombing of El-Afuleh Railway Junction,* C. R. Fleming-Williams. Imperial War Museum, London.

William Butler Yeats

An Irish Airman Foresees His Death

I know that I shall meet my fate
Somewhere among the clouds above;
Those that I fight I do not hate,
Those that I guard I do not love;
My country is Kiltartan Cross,
My countrymen Kiltartan's poor,
No likely end could bring them loss
Or leave them happier than before.
Nor law, nor duty bade me fight,
Nor public men, nor cheering crowds.
A lonely impulse of delight
Drove to this tumult in the clouds;
I balanced all, brought all to mind,
The years to come seemed waste of breath,
A waste of breath the years behind
In balance with this life, this death.

4 Those that I guard . . . love: Many of the Irish—even those who fought beside the English against the Germans—resented their English rulers.

5 Kiltartan: a district in the west of Ireland.

FROM PERSONAL RESPONSE *TO* CRITICAL ANALYSIS

REFLECT

1. In your notebook, write words that come to mind when you think about the speaker of this poem.

RETHINK

2. How do you think the speaker feels each time he gets into his plane?

3. What factors may have influenced the speaker's decision to go to war?

The Soldier

Rupert Brooke

Wounded in the Chest: "Just Out of the Trenches near Arras," Sir William Orpen. Imperial War Museum, London.

If I should die, think only this of me,
That there's some corner of a foreign field
That is forever England. There shall be
In that rich earth a richer dust concealed,
A dust whom England bore, shaped, made aware,
Gave, once, her flowers to love, her ways to roam,
A body of England's, breathing English air,
Washed by the rivers, blest by suns of home.

And think, this heart, all evil shed away,
A pulse in the Eternal mind, no less
Gives somewhere back the thoughts by England given,
Her sights and sounds; dreams happy as her day;
And laughter, learnt of friends; and gentleness,
In hearts at peace, under an English heaven.

FROM PERSONAL RESPONSE *TO* CRITICAL ANALYSIS

REFLECT **1.** After reading this poem, what thoughts or questions do you have?

RETHINK **2.** How would you describe the tone of the poem?

3. In your opinion, would the sentiments expressed in this poem console the speaker's loved ones? Explain your view.

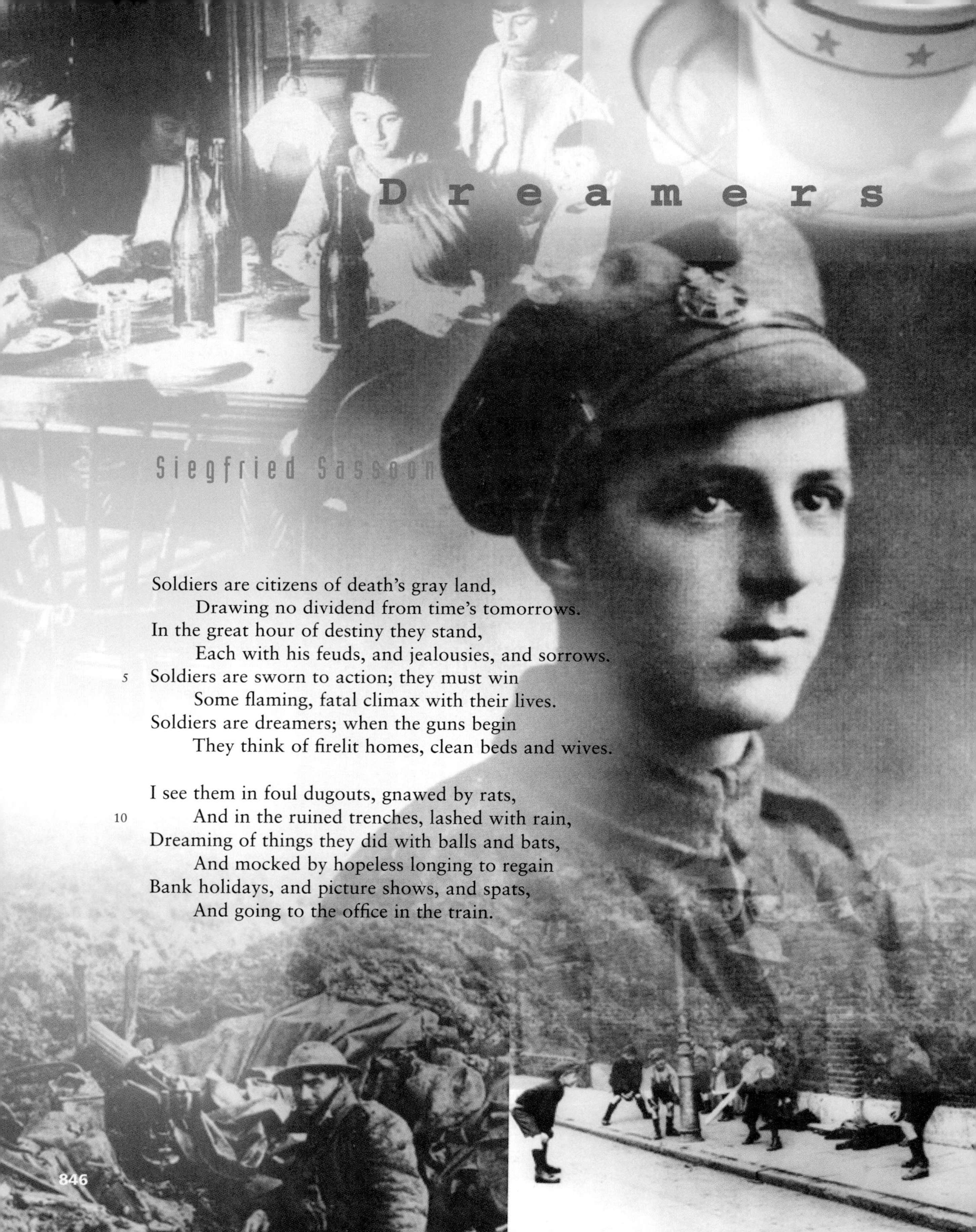

Dreamers

Siegfried Sassoon

Soldiers are citizens of death's gray land,
Drawing no dividend from time's tomorrows.
In the great hour of destiny they stand,
Each with his feuds, and jealousies, and sorrows.
Soldiers are sworn to action; they must win
Some flaming, fatal climax with their lives.
Soldiers are dreamers; when the guns begin
They think of firelit homes, clean beds and wives.

I see them in foul dugouts, gnawed by rats,
And in the ruined trenches, lashed with rain,
Dreaming of things they did with balls and bats,
And mocked by hopeless longing to regain
Bank holidays, and picture shows, and spats,
And going to the office in the train.

RESPONDING OPTIONS

FROM PERSONAL RESPONSE *TO* CRITICAL ANALYSIS

REFLECT 1. In your notebook, describe the images left in your mind after reading "Dreamers." Then share your impressions with the class.

RETHINK 2. How would you describe the speaker's attitude toward war?

3. Do you think the speaker expects that the soldiers' dreams will be fulfilled? Give reasons to support your opinion.

RELATE 4. Compare the speakers of "An Irish Airman Foresees His Death," "The Soldier," and "Dreamers." Review the chart you created for the Reading Connection on page 843, and explain how you think the speakers' attitudes toward war differ.

5. Which poem, "The Soldier" or "Dreamers," was most likely written at the start of the war? Explain your answer.

6. Do you think any of the thoughts expressed in these three poems would be relevant to soldiers fighting in wars today? Give reasons for your opinion.

ANOTHER PATHWAY

Cooperative Learning

With a small group of classmates, discuss the qualities—both strengths and weaknesses—of the speaker of each poem, and decide how those qualities might affect his performance as a soldier. In an informal vote, choose the speaker you think would make the best soldier; then write a rationale for your choice.

LITERARY CONCEPTS

The **speaker** of a poem may be either a distant observer, not directly involved in the situation he or she describes, or a participant in the situation presented in the poem. In either case, the speaker is not necessarily to be identified with the poet. How important are the identities of the speakers of "An Irish Airman Foresees His Death," "The Soldier," and "Dreamers"? How would each poem be different if the speaker were a distant observer?

QUICKWRITES

1. Compose brief **epitaphs** for the speakers of "An Irish Airman Foresees His Death," "The Soldier," and "Dreamers." In each epitaph, include details that convey the unique qualities of the individual who is its subject.

2. If you were sending a "CARE package" to one of the speakers, what might you include in it? Write a **letter** to accompany the package, explaining what you are sending and why you chose those things.

3. If the speakers of these poems chose to express their attitudes toward war on bumper stickers, what sentiments might they express? Write messages for three different **bumper stickers,** one for each speaker.

PORTFOLIO Save your writing. You may want to use it later as a springboard to a piece for your portfolio.

ALTERNATIVE ACTIVITIES

1. With a partner, role-play a **counseling session** in which you offer advice to the speaker of either "An Irish Airman Foresees His Death" or "Dreamers."
2. With a small group of classmates, plan and present a **dramatic choral reading** of the three poems. Use special effects—such as lighting, background music, and costumes—to help convey the moods and messages of the poems.
3. Create a **miniature diorama** depicting the setting presented in one of the three poems.

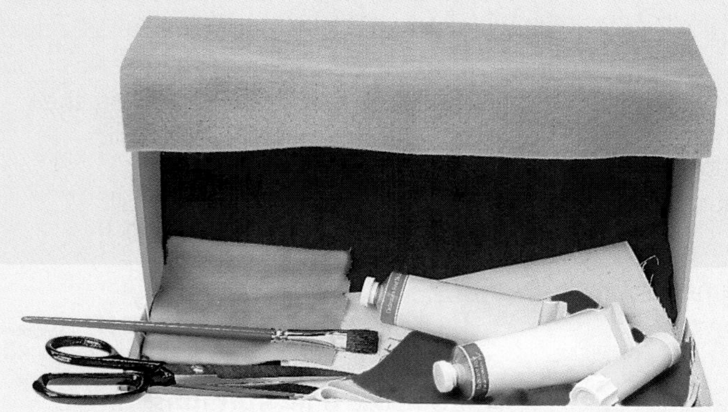

CRITIC'S CORNER

In an essay written in 1919, the British poet Walter de la Mare referred to the "life-giving youthfulness" of Rupert Brooke's poetry. Do you think that "The Soldier" conveys a youthful perspective? Why or why not?

LITERARY LINKS

In your opinion, which speaker in these three war poems would be most likely to share the feelings expressed by the speaker of Thomas Hardy's "The Man He Killed" (page 684)? Give reasons for your choice.

ACROSS THE CURRICULUM

Music Locate printed versions or recordings of songs that were popular during World War I. Read or play a few of the songs for the class. As you listen to the lyrics of each song, try to answer these questions: What message about war does the song convey? How might wartime listeners react to the message?

THE WRITER'S STYLE

All three of these poems contain **repetition** and **parallelism**—the use of similar grammatical structures to express related or equally important ideas. Find examples of repetition or parallelism in the three poems. How do these devices contribute to the overall effect of each poem?

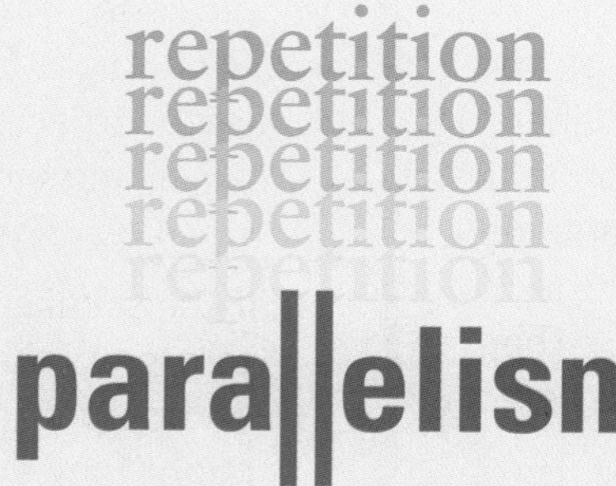

William Butler Yeats

1865–1939

A biography of William Butler Yeats appears on page 927.

Rupert Brooke

1887–1915

Rupert Brooke, an extraordinarily handsome and intelligent young man who excelled at both athletics and academics while attending Cambridge University, was regarded as one of Britain's most promising poets. During his brief life, he mingled with such prominent figures as Virginia Woolf and Winston Churchill. At the outbreak of World War I, he joined the Royal Navy and began training for combat. During this time he wrote *1914,* a series of five war sonnets that included "The Soldier." The young poet saw very little wartime action, however, for he fell victim to blood poisoning on the way to his first major conflict. He died at the age of 27 on a hospital ship in the Aegean Sea and was buried on the Aegean island of Skíros. Upon learning of Brooke's death, Churchill, then first lord of the admiralty, recalled that the poet-soldier was "joyous, fearless, versatile . . . all one could wish England's noblest sons to be."

OTHER WORKS "The Dead," "Peace," "Safety," "The Old Vicarage," "Grantchester"

Siegfried Sassoon

1886–1967

Although Siegfried Sassoon began writing poetry as a child, he was more interested in sports than in scholastic achievement. Born to a prosperous family in Kent, he attended Cambridge University but left without a degree. He joined the army just a few days before England declared war and, while serving as an infantry officer in France, was wounded several times and received the Military Cross for bravery. His experiences in trench warfare affected him profoundly, however, and his early idealism turned to bitter disillusionment as the war progressed. In 1917, having become a pacifist, he wrote his commanding officer a letter protesting the continuation of the war. The letter might have led to a court-martial, but Sassoon was instead briefly hospitalized for shell shock, then sent back to the battlefield, where he was wounded in the head. His wartime experiences were not easily forgotten, and he continued to write about them long after the conflict ended.

OTHER WORKS "Absolution," "To Victory," "To My Brother," "Golgotha," "A Working Party"

PREVIEWING

NONFICTION

from Testament of Youth

Vera Brittain

PERSONAL CONNECTION

Most of us live in a web of relationships. We have ties to our families, to friends, to the communities in which we live, and to society as a whole. We also have a responsibility for our own well-being. How committed are you to your family? your friends? society? yourself? Make a bar graph like the one shown, rating your senses of obligation to the different groups in your life. Then, with your classmates, discuss times when a person might experience conflicting obligations.

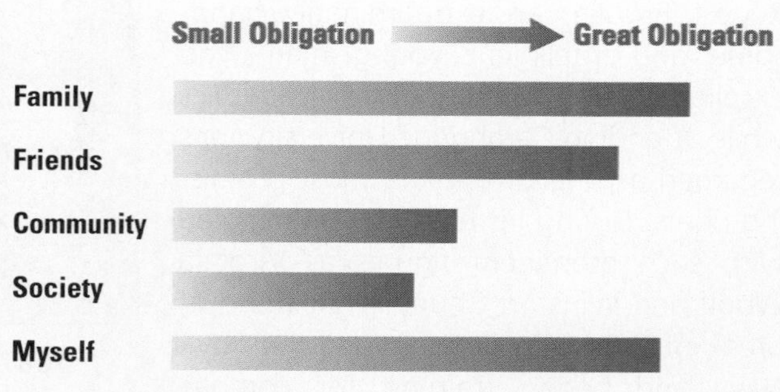

BIOGRAPHICAL CONNECTION

Vera Brittain's autobiographical *Testament of Youth* is a rare account of World War I from the perspective of a young woman. Brittain lived at a time when options for women were limited. Her childhood was sheltered and comfortable, yet she grew up to find few opportunities for personal and professional growth. Although she had a close relationship with her brother, Edward, Brittain was well aware that many choices open to him were denied to her. For example, Brittain's father—like many people of the time—thought that a university education was valuable for a son but wasted on a daughter. Yet Brittain convinced her father to let her attend Somerville College at Oxford University. She entered in 1914, shortly after World War I broke out in Europe.

Although the war seemed somewhat remote to Brittain at first, it soon changed her life. After her fiancé, Roland Leighton, was sent to the front lines, and then as news of war casualties began to come through, Brittain felt a sense of obligation to join the war effort. She interrupted her education to train as an army nurse—nursing being one of the few war-related jobs available to women. In 1915, while caring for wounded soldiers in London, Brittain learned that her fiancé had been killed by enemy fire. In 1916 she requested duty near the front lines, and she was eventually assigned to a field hospital near Étaples (ā-täp′ lə), France. This selection begins during Brittain's time in Étaples.

LASERLINKS
• *BIOGRAPHICAL CONNECTION*

READING CONNECTION

Understanding History Through a Memoir

A **memoir** is a form of autobiographical writing in which a person recalls significant events in his or her life. Most memoirs share the following characteristics:

- They usually are structured as narratives told by the writers themselves, using the first-person point of view.
- Though some names may be changed to protect the privacy of others, they are true accounts of actual events.
- Although basically personal, they may deal with newsworthy events having a significance beyond the confines of the writers' own lives.
- Unlike strictly historical accounts, they often include the writers' feelings and opinions about historical events, giving readers insight into the impact of history on people's lives.

As you read these excerpts from *Testament of Youth,* keep two lists in your notebook. In one, record the historical information that Brittain provides in her memoir; in the other, record Brittain's personal feelings and opinions.

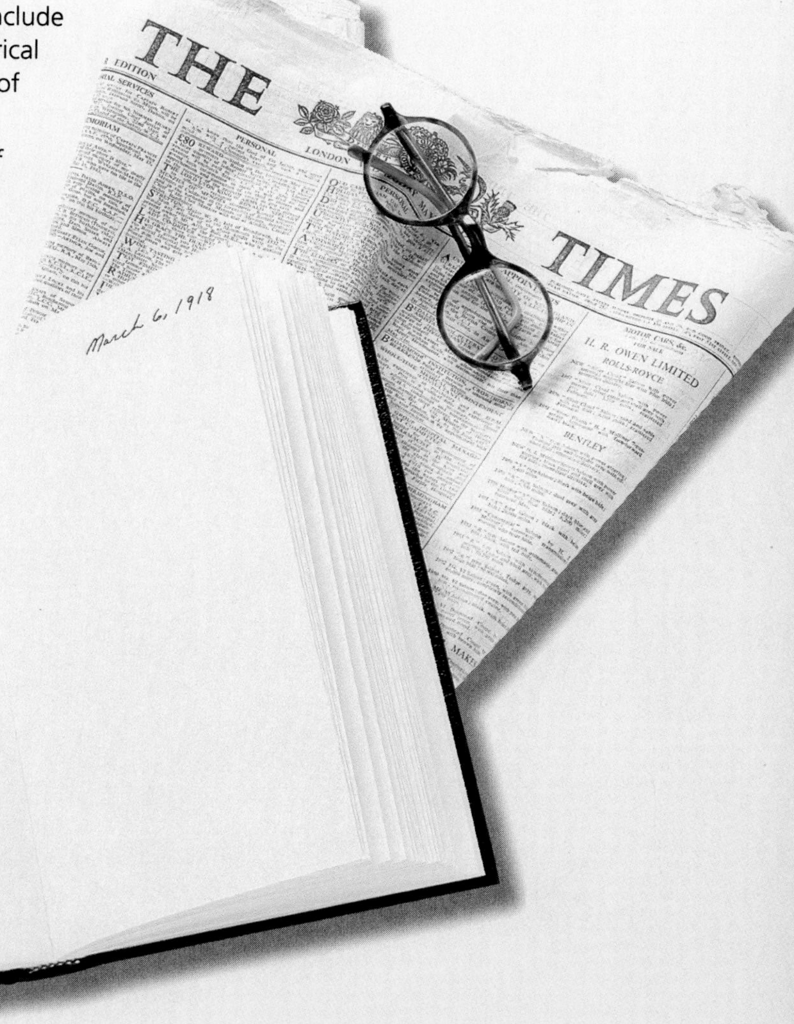

from

TESTAMENT *of* Youth

Vera Brittain

After days of continuous heavy duty and scamped,[1] inadequate meals, our nerves were none too reliable, and I don't suppose I was the only member of the staff whose teeth chattered with sheer terror as we groped our way to our individual huts in response to the order to scatter. Hope Milroy and I, thinking that we might as well be killed together, sat glassy-eyed in her small, pitch-black room. Suddenly, intermittent flashes half blinded us, and we listened frantically in the deafening din for the bugle call which we knew would summon us to join the night staff in the wards if bombs began to fall on the hospital.

1. **scamped:** hurried.

One young Sister,[2] who had previously been shelled at a Casualty Clearing Station, lost her nerve and rushed screaming through the Mess;[3] two others seized her and forcibly put her to bed, holding her down while the raid lasted to prevent her from causing a panic. I knew that I was more frightened than I had ever been in my life, yet all the time a tense, triumphant pride that I was not revealing my fear to the others held me to the semblance of self-control.

When a momentary lull came in the booms and the flashes, Hope, who had also been under fire at a C.C.S., gave way to the sudden bravado of rushing into the open to see whether the raiders had gone; she was still wearing her white cap, and a dozen trembling hands instantly pulled her indoors again, a dozen shakily shrill voices scolded her indiscretion. Gradually, after another brief burst of firing, the camp became quiet, though the lights were not turned on again that night. Next day we were told that most of the bombs had fallen on the village; the bridge over the Canche,[4] it was reported, had been smashed, and the train service had to be suspended while the engineers performed the exciting feat of mending it in twelve hours. . . .

. . . Within the next few weeks a good night's rest proved impossible for most of us. The liability to be called up for late convoys[5] had already induced a habit of light, restless dozing, and the knowledge that the raiders meant business and might return at any moment after sunset did not help us to settle down quietly and confidently during the hours of darkness. Whenever a particularly tiring day had battered our exhausted nerves into indifference, the lights went out as the result of alarming reports from Abbeville or Camiers[6] and revived our apprehensions. Rumor declared that we were all to be issued with steel helmets, and further spasmodic efforts were made to provide us with trenches in case of emergency.

Three weeks of such days and nights, lived without respite or off-duty time under the permanent fear of defeat and flight, reduced the staffs of the Étaples hospitals to the negative conviction that nothing mattered except to end the strain. England, panic-stricken, was frantically raising the military age to fifty and agreeing to the appointment of Foch[7] as Commander-in-Chief, but to us with our blistered feet, our swollen hands, our wakeful, reddened eyes, victory and defeat began—as indeed they were afterwards to prove—to seem very much the same thing. . . .

Just when the Retreat had reduced the strip of coast between the line and the sea to its narrowest dimensions, the summons came that I had subconsciously dreaded ever since my uncomfortable leave.

Early in April a letter arrived from my father to say that my mother had "crocked up" and had been obliged, owing to the inefficiency of the domestic help then available, to go into a nursing home. What exactly was wrong remained unspecified, though phrases referred to "toxic heart" and "complete general breakdown." My father had temporarily closed the flat and moved into a hotel, but he did not, he told me, wish to remain there. "As your mother and I can no longer manage without you," he concluded, "it is now your duty to leave France immediately and return to Kensington."[8]

---

2. **Sister:** nurse.
3. **Mess:** mess hall—the place where people in the armed forces eat meals.
4. **Canche** (känsh): the river on which Étaples is located.
5. **convoys:** groups of vehicles traveling with protective escorts (here, they are bringing wounded soldiers).
6. **reports from Abbeville** (äb-vēl′) **or Camiers** (kä-myā′): In March 1918, the Germans were advancing on these French towns, which lie directly between Étaples and Paris. As the British retreated toward the coast, it was feared that Étaples itself might be captured or cut off.
7. **Foch** (fôsh): Ferdinand Foch, a French general who in March 1918 became commander of all Allied forces on the western front.
8. **Kensington:** a residential section of London.

WORDS TO KNOW
semblance (sĕm′bləns) *n.* an outward appearance
bravado (brə-vä′dō) *n.* a reckless or false show of courage

I read these words with real dismay, for my father's interpretation of my duty was not, I knew only too well, in the least likely to agree with that of the Army, which had always been singularly unmoved by the worries of relatives. What was I to do? I wondered desperately. There was my family, confidently demanding my presence, and here was the offensive, which made every pair of experienced hands worth ten pairs under normal conditions. I remembered how the hastily imported VADs had gone sick at the 1st London[9] during the rush after the Somme;[10] a great push was no time in which to teach a tyro[11] her job. How much of my mother's breakdown was physical and how much psychological—the cumulative result of pessimism at home? It did not then occur to me that my father's sense of emergency was probably heightened by a subconscious determination to get me back to London before the Germans reached the Channel ports,[12] as everyone in England felt certain they would. I only knew that no one in France would believe a domestic difficulty to be so insoluble; if I were dead, or a male, it would have to be settled without me. I should merely be thought to have "wind-up,"[13] to be using my mother's health as an excuse to escape the advancing enemy or the threatening air raids.

Half-frantic with the misery of conflicting obligations, I envied Edward his complete powerlessness to leave the Army whatever happened at home. . . . What exhausts women in wartime is not the strenuous and unfamiliar tasks that fall upon them, nor even the hourly dread of death for husbands or lovers or brothers or sons; it is the incessant conflict between personal and national claims which wears out their energy and breaks their spirit.

That night, dizzy from work and indecision, I sat up in bed listening for an air raid and gazing stupidly at the flickering shadows cast by the candle lantern which was all the illumination that we were now allowed. Through my brain ran perpetually a short sentence which—having become, like the men, liable to sudden lightheaded intervals—I could not immediately identify with anything that I had read.

" 'The strain all along,' " I repeated dully, " 'is very great . . . very great.' " What exactly did those words describe? The enemy within shelling distance—refugee Sisters crowding in with nerves all awry—bright moonlight, and airplanes carrying machine guns—ambulance trains jolting noisily into the siding, all day, all night—gassed men on stretchers, clawing the air—dying men, reeking with mud and foul green-stained bandages, shrieking and writhing in a grotesque travesty of manhood—dead men with fixed, empty eyes and shiny, yellow faces. . . . Yes, perhaps the strain all along *had* been very great. . . .

Then I remembered; the phrase came out of my father's letter, and it described, not the offensive in France, but the troubles at home. The next day I went to the Matron's[14] office and interviewed the successor to the friendly Scottish Matron who had sent me on leave, and whose health had obliged her to leave Étaples and return to the calmer conditions of home service. The new Matron was old and charitable, but she naturally did not welcome my problem with enthusiasm. The application for long leave which I had hoped to put in would have, she said, no chance at all while this push was on; the only possibility was to break my contract, which I might be allowed to do if I made conditions at home sound serious enough.

---

9. **VADs . . . at the 1st London:** Voluntary Aid Detachment nurses at another Étaples hospital.
10. **the Somme** (sŏm): In July 1916, the Allies had launched what turned into a devastating, months-long battle along the Somme River; it resulted in more than a million casualties.
11. **tyro** (tī′rō): beginner.
12. **Channel ports:** seaports on the English Channel.
13. **"wind-up"** (wĭnd′ŭp′): a British slang term meaning "nervousness" or "anxious excitement."
14. **Matron's:** head nurse's.

WORDS TO KNOW

insoluble (ĭn-sŏl′yə-bəl) *adj.* incapable of being solved
incessant (ĭn-sĕs′ənt) *adj.* never ceasing; constant
awry (ə-rī′) *adj.* twisted; faulty; disordered
travesty (trăv′ĭ-stē) *n.* a distorted, bizarre imitation

"I'm giving you this advice against my will," she added. "I'm already short of staff and I can't hope to replace you."

So, with a sinking heart, I asked for leave to break my contract owing to "special circumstances," and returned to my ward feeling a cowardly deserter. Only to Edward could I express the explosive misery caused by my dilemma, and he replied with his usual comprehending sympathy.

"I can well understand how exasperating it must be for you to have to go home now . . . when you have just been in the eddying backwater of the sternest fight this War has known; it is one of those little ironies which life has ready to offer at a most inopportune moment. I suppose that the Armentières[15] push will have affected you more nearly still as it is not so very far away. . . ."

I was glad that my orders did not come through until almost the end of April, when the offensive against the British had slackened, and we knew for certain that we had not yet lost the War.

Early one morning I bade a forlorn farewell to my friends and went down alone in an ambulance to the station. . . . As the train passed through Hardelot,[16] I noticed that the woods on either side of the line were vivid with a golden green latticework of delicate leaves. For a whole month in which off-duty time had been impossible, I had ceased to be aware of the visible world of the French countryside; my eyes had seen nothing but the wards and the dying, the dirt and dried blood, the obscene wounds of mangled men and the lotions and lint with which I had dressed them. Looking, now, at the pregnant buds, the green veil flung over the trees and the spilt cream of primroses in the bright, wet grass, I realized with a pang of astonishment that the spring had come.

I can look back more readily, I think, upon the War's tragedies—which at least had dignity—than upon those miserable weeks that followed my return from France. From a world in which life or death, victory or defeat, national survival or national extinction, had been the sole issues, I returned to a society where no one discussed anything but the price of butter and the incompetence of the latest "temporary."[17]. . .

Keyed up as I had been by the month-long strain of daily rushing to and fro in attendance on the dying, and nightly waiting for the death which hovered darkly in the sky overhead, I found it excruciating to maintain even an appearance of interest and sympathy. Probably I did not succeed, for the triviality of everything drove me to despair. The old feeling of frustration that I had known . . . came back a thousand times intensified; while disasters smashed up the world around me I seemed to be marooned in a kind of death-in-life, with the three years' experience that now made me of some use to the Army all thrown away.

. . . Most bitterly of all I resented the constant dissipation of energy on what appeared to me to be nonessentials. My youth and health had mattered so much when the task was that of dragging wounded men back to life; I believed that the vitality which kept me going had helped others who had lost their own to live, and it seemed rather thrown away when it was all exploded upon persuading the grocer to give us a pot of jam. The agony of the last few weeks in France appeared not to interest London in comparison with the struggle to obtain sugar; the latter was discussed incessantly, but no one wanted even to hear about the former. . . .

I was no better reconciled to staying at home when I read in *The Times* a few weeks after my return that the persistent German raiders had at last succeeded in their intention of smashing up

15. **Armentières** (är-mäɴ-tyĕr′): a town, only 40 miles from Étaples, taken by the Germans in April 1918.

16. **Hardelot** (är-də-lō′).

17. **temporary:** a domestic servant hired for a short time.

WORDS TO KNOW

excruciating (ĭk-skrōō′shē-ā′tĭng) *adj.* intensely painful; agonizing
dissipation (dĭs′ə-pā′shən) *n.* a wasteful expenditure of resources

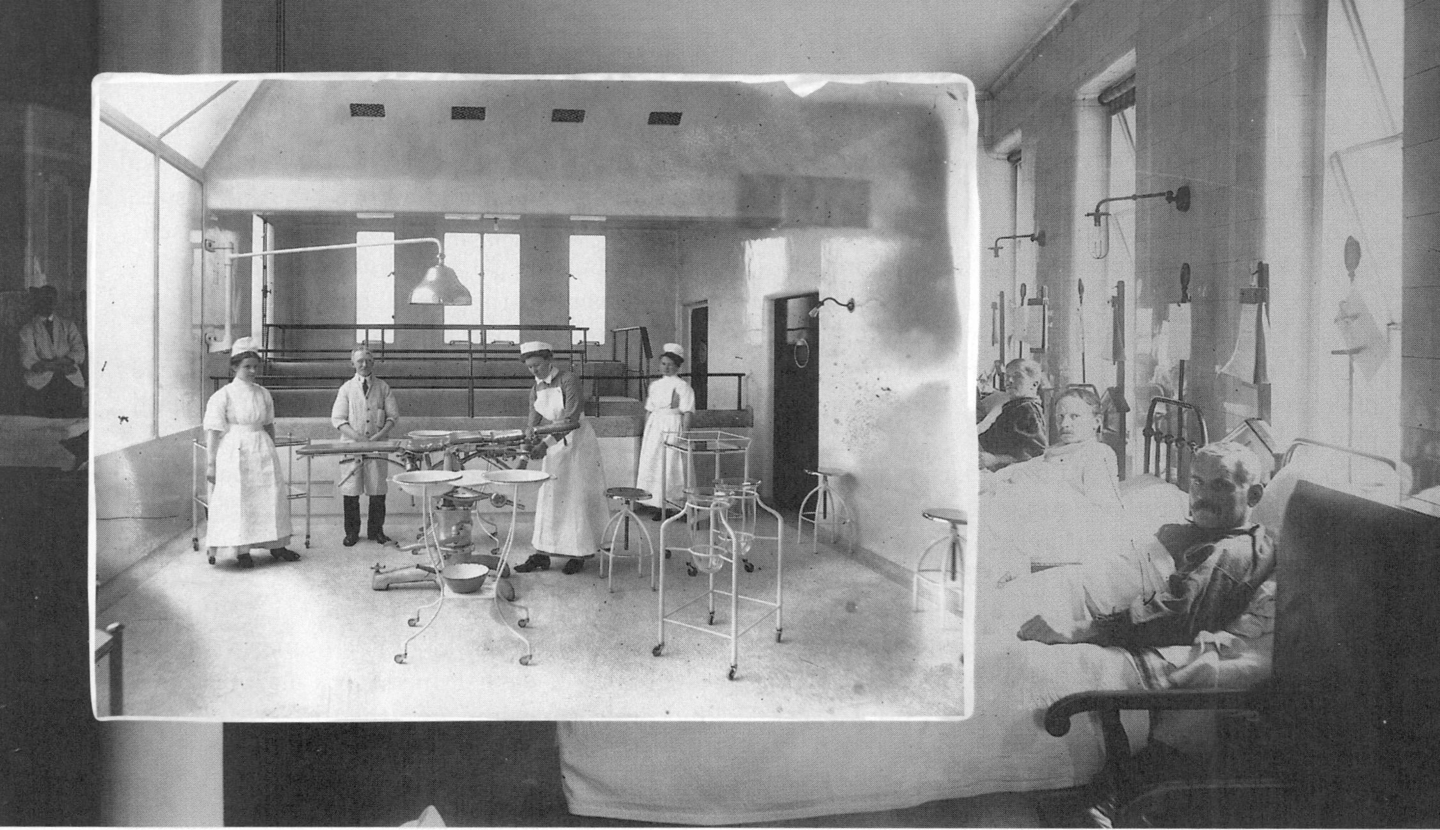

the Étaples hospitals, which, with the aid of the prisoner-patients, had so satisfactorily protected the railway line for three years without further trouble or expense to the military authorities.

It was clear from the guarded *communiqué*[18] that this time the bombs had dropped on the hospitals themselves, causing many casualties and far more damage than the breaking of the bridge over the Canche in the first big raid. Hope Milroy, I was thankful to remember, had been moved to Havre[19] a fortnight earlier, but a few days later a letter from Norah filled in the gaps of the official report. The hospital next door, she told me, had suffered the worst, and several Canadian Sisters had been killed. At 24 General one of the death-dealing bombs had fallen on Ward 17, where I had nursed the pneumonias on night duty; it had shattered the hut, together with several patients, and wounded the VAD in charge, who was in hospital with a fractured skull. The Sisters' quarters were no longer safe after dark, she concluded, and they all had to spend their nights in trenches in the woods.

More than ever, as I finished her letter, I felt myself a deserter, a coward, a traitor to my patients and the other nurses.

How could I have played with the idea—as I had, once or twice lately—of returning to Oxford[20] before the end of the War? What did the waste of an immature intellect matter, when such things could happen to one's friends? My comrades of the push had been frightened, hurt, smashed up—and I was not there with them, skulking[21] safely in England. Why, oh why, had I listened to home demands when my job was out there?

A brief note that came just afterwards from Edward seemed an appropriate—and fear-

18. ***communiqué*** (kô-mü-nē-kā′) *French:* an official communication.
19. **Havre** (hä′vrə): Le Havre, a French seaport used as an Allied troop and supply base.
20. **Oxford:** Oxford University.
21. **skulking:** hiding out.

provoking—comment on the news from Étaples.

"Ma chère," he had written just before midnight on May 12th, *"la vie est brève*[22]—usually too short for me to write adequate letters, and likely to be shorter still."

For some time now, my apprehensions for his safety had been lulled by the long quiescence of the Italian front, which had seemed a haven of peace in contrast to our own raging vortex.[23] Repeatedly, during the German offensive, I had thanked God and the Italians who fled at Caporetto[24] that Edward was out of it, and rejoiced that the worst I had to fear from this particular push was the comparatively trivial danger that threatened myself. But now I felt the familiar stirrings of the old tense fear which had been such a persistent companion throughout the War. . . .

On Sunday morning, June 16th, I opened the *Observer,* which appeared to be chiefly concerned with the new offensive—for the moment at a standstill—in the Noyon-Montdidier[25] sector of the Western Front, and instantly saw at the head of a column the paragraph for which I had looked so long and so fearfully:

ITALIAN FRONT ABLAZE
GUN DUELS FROM MOUNTAIN TO SEA
BAD OPENING OF AN OFFENSIVE

. . . There was nothing to do in the midst of one's family but practice that concealment of fear which the long years of war had instilled, thrusting it inward until one's subconscious became a regular prison house of apprehensions and inhibitions which were later to take their revenge. My mother had arranged to stay with my grandmother at Purley[26] that week in order to get a few days' change from the flat; it was the first time that she had felt well enough since her breakdown to think of going away, and I did not want the news from Italy to make her change her plans. At length, though with instinctive reluctance, she allowed herself to be prevailed upon to go, but a profound depression hung over our parting at Charing Cross.[27]

A day or two later, more details were published of the fighting in Italy, and I learnt that the Sherwood Foresters[28] had been involved in the "show" on the plateau.[29] After that I made no pretense at doing anything but wander restlessly round Kensington or up and down the flat, and, though my father retired glumly to bed every evening at nine o'clock, I gave up writing the semi-fictitious record which I had begun of my life in France. Somehow I couldn't bring myself even to wrap up the *Spectator* and *Saturday Review* that I sent every week to Italy, and they remained in my bedroom, silent yet eloquent witnesses to the dread which my father and I, determinedly conversing on commonplace topics, each refused to put into words.

By the following Saturday we had still heard nothing of Edward. The interval usually allowed for news of casualties after a battle was seldom so long as this, and I began, with an artificial sense of lightness unaccompanied by real conviction, to think that there was perhaps, after all, no news to come. I had just announced to my father, as we sat over tea in the dining room, that I really must do up Edward's papers and take them to the post office before it closed for the weekend, when there came the sudden loud

22. ***Ma chère, . . . la vie est brève*** (mä shĕr′ lä vē′ ā brĕv′) *French:* My dear, . . . life is short.
23. **vortex:** whirl of activity.
24. **Caporetto** (kăp′ə-rĕt′ō): a 1917 battle near the Italian–Austro-Hungarian border that resulted in a major Allied defeat. (Edward was stationed in Italy.)
25. **Noyon-Montdidier** (nwä-yôɴ′ môɴ-dē-dyā′).
26. **Purley:** a town south of London.
27. **Charing Cross:** Charing Cross Station, a railway terminal in central London.
28. **Sherwood Foresters:** the British regiment to which Edward belonged.
29. **"show" on the plateau:** battle on the Asiago Plateau in northeastern Italy.

WORDS TO KNOW

quiescence (kwē-ĕs′əns) *n.* a state of quiet, stillness, or rest; inactivity

clattering at the front-door knocker that always meant a telegram.

For a moment I thought that my legs would not carry me, but they behaved quite normally as I got up and went to the door. I knew what was in the telegram—I had known for a week—but because the persistent hopefulness of the human heart refuses to allow intuitive certainty to persuade the reason of that which it knows, I opened and read it in a tearing anguish of suspense.

"Regret to inform you Captain E. H. Brittain M.C.[30] killed in action Italy June 15th."

"No answer," I told the boy mechanically, and handed the telegram to my father, who had followed me into the hall. As we went back into the dining room I saw, as though I had never seen them before, the bowl of blue delphiniums on the table; their intense color, vivid, ethereal, seemed too radiant for earthly flowers.

Then I remembered that we should have to go down to Purley and tell the news to my mother.

Late that evening, my uncle brought us all back to an empty flat. Edward's death and our sudden departure had offered the maid—at that time the amateur prostitute—an agreeable opportunity for a few hours' freedom of which she had taken immediate advantage. She had not even finished the household handkerchiefs, which I had washed that morning and intended to iron after tea; when I went into the kitchen I found them still hanging, stiff as boards, over the clotheshorse near the fire where I had left them to dry.

Long after the family had gone to bed and the world had grown silent, I crept into the dining room to be alone with Edward's portrait. Carefully closing the door, I turned on the light and looked at the pale, pictured face, so dignified, so steadfast, so tragically mature. He had been through so much—far, far more than those beloved friends who had died at an earlier stage of the interminable War, leaving him alone to mourn their loss. Fate might have allowed him the little, sorry compensation of survival, the chance to make his lovely music[31] in honor of their memory. It seemed indeed the last irony that he should have been killed by the countrymen of Fritz Kreisler, the violinist whom of all others he had most greatly admired.

And suddenly, as I remembered all the dear afternoons and evenings when I had followed him on the piano as he played his violin, the sad, searching eyes of the portrait were more than I could bear, and falling on my knees before it I began to cry "Edward! Oh, Edward!" in dazed repetition, as though my persistent crying and calling would somehow bring him back.

The loss of Brittain's fiancé, brother, and friends in the war, as well as the death and suffering she witnessed in the hospitals, shaped the rest of her life. She became a pacifist and worked tirelessly to oppose war and to urge the resolving of differences through rational and peaceful means. Testament of Youth *was published in 1933, the same year Adolf Hitler became the head of government in Germany. Brittain wrote in the foreword to the book that her object was "to challenge that too easy, too comfortable relapse into forgetfulness which is responsible for history's most grievous repetitions." The following paragraph comes near the end of the book and gives her perspective on war several years after the end of World War I.*

30. **M.C.:** holder of the Military Cross, a medal of honor.

31. **his lovely music:** Edward was an accomplished musician.

WORDS TO KNOW

ethereal (ĭ-thîr′ē-əl) *adj.* delicate; heavenly

. . . In spite of the War, which destroyed so much hope, so much beauty, so much promise, life is still here to be lived; so long as I am in the world, how can I ignore the obligation to be part of it, cope with its problems, suffer claims and interruptions? The surge and swell of its movements, its changes, its tendencies, still mold me and the surviving remnant of my generation whether we wish it or not, and no one now living will ever understand so clearly as ourselves, whose lives have been darkened by the universal breakdown of reason in 1914, how completely the future of civilized humanity depends upon the success of our present halting endeavors to control our political and social passions, and to substitute for our destructive impulses the vitalizing[32] authority of constructive thought. To rescue mankind from that domination by the irrational which leads to war could surely be a more exultant fight than war itself, a fight capable of enlarging the souls of men and women with the same heightened consciousness of living, and uniting them in one dedicated community whose common purpose transcends the individual. Only the purpose itself would be different, for its achievement would mean, not death, but life. ❖

32. **vitalizing:** life-giving; invigorating.

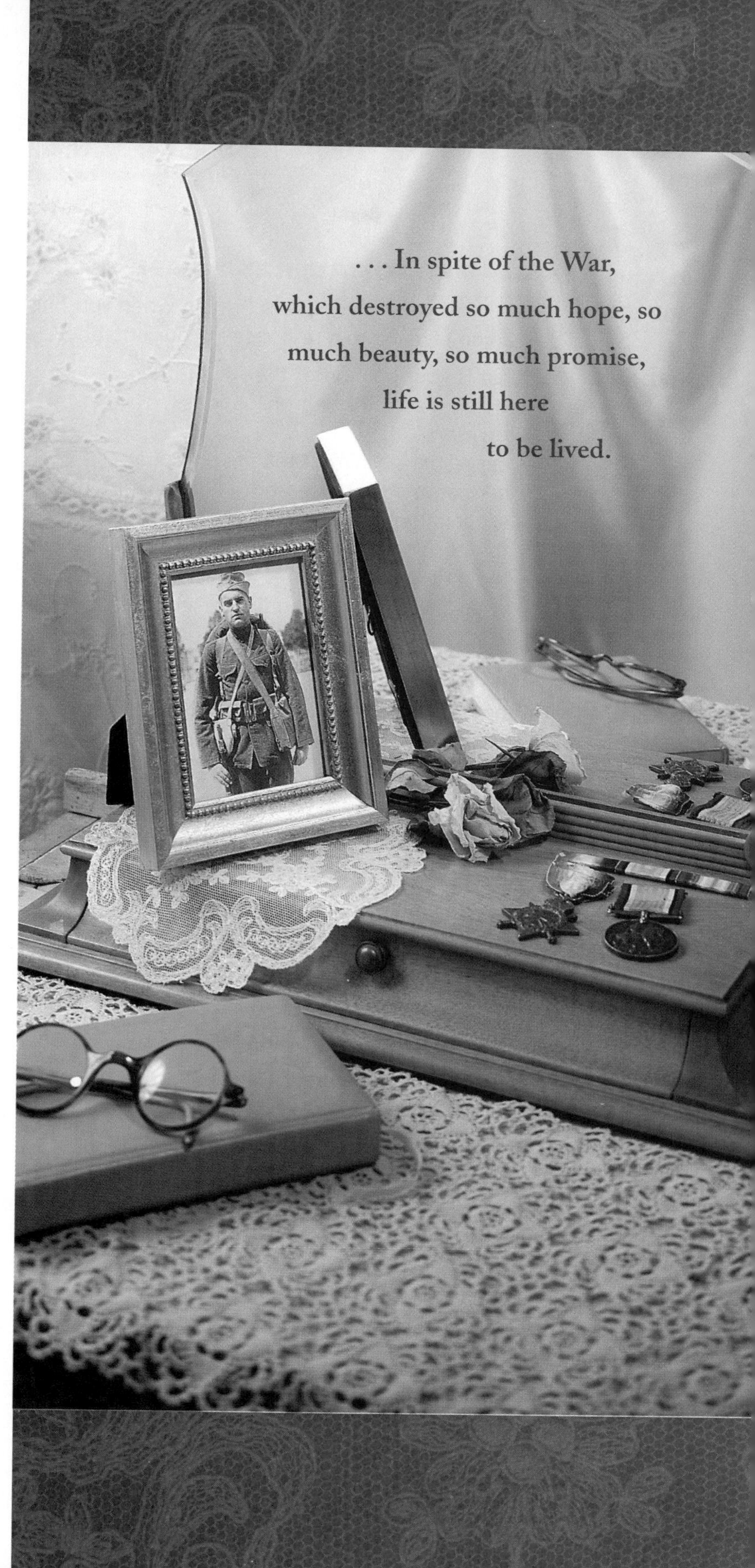
. . . In spite of the War,
which destroyed so much hope, so
much beauty, so much promise,
life is still here
to be lived.

RESPONDING OPTIONS

FROM PERSONAL RESPONSE *TO* CRITICAL ANALYSIS

REFLECT 1. What did you think of Vera Brittain when you finished reading? Freewrite a response in your notebook.

RETHINK 2. What is your opinion of the way Brittain handled her conflicting obligations?
Consider
- her responsibilities at the field hospital
- her parents' situation and expectations
- the position of women in society at the time
- what she most wanted for herself

3. What might have happened if Brittain had not returned to England when she did?

4. What do you think was hardest for Brittain to deal with after she returned to England?

5. If Brittain had been a man, how would her obligations have been different during World War I?

6. Reread the last paragraph of the selection. Do you agree with Brittain's ideas about humanity and war? Explain your opinion.

RELATE 7. Do you think that women today face conflicting obligations similar to those experienced by Brittain? Support your answer with examples.

LITERARY CONCEPTS

A **theme** is an idea or message communicated by a work of literature. It is a perception about life or human nature that the writer chooses to share with the reader. Some themes are stated directly, and some are implied; but every theme is an expression of the significance of the story being told. Certain works of literature contain more than one theme. Get together with a group of classmates to determine the theme or themes of Brittain's memoir. State each theme in a single sentence, and then compare your ideas with those of other groups.

ANOTHER PATHWAY

Cooperative Learning

Conduct a class survey to determine how many people think Brittain's decision to return home at her father's request was the right one. Tabulate the results and discuss why people responded as they did.

QUICKWRITES

1. If Vera Brittain had decided to remain in France, how might she have explained her decision to her father? Imagine that you are Brittain, and write a **letter** to your father, explaining why you are not returning to England as he has requested.
2. After returning to England, Brittain felt herself to be "a deserter, a coward, a traitor to my patients and the other nurses." Make **notes** of what you might say to Brittain in response to her feelings.
3. Create a **poem** that conveys Brittain's thoughts and emotions about the nighttime bombing raids, about the death of her brother, or about war's effects on humanity.

PORTFOLIO Save your writing. You may want to use it later as a spring-board to a piece for your portfolio.

ALTERNATIVE ACTIVITIES

1. Work with a partner to design an eye-catching **book jacket** for Vera Brittain's *Testament of Youth.* Illustrate a scene from the excerpts you have read, and compose a brief advertising message that would appeal to people of Brittain's generation.
2. Work on a design team to help plan and produce a **memorial** honoring the army nurses of World War I. Each team of students should create a painting, sculpture, song, quilt, documentary film or video, poem, or play for the memorial, as well as a written description of the work. Then work with your classmates to present a program featuring all the works.

LITERARY LINKS

Compare and contrast Vera Brittain's reflections on war with those expressed by the speakers of the Yeats, Brooke, and Sassoon poems (pages 843–849). How do you think Brittain would respond to each of the poems?

CRITIC'S CORNER

According to the writer Carolyn Heilbrun, Vera Brittain's memoirs are effective because she "understood the terror of the world she lived through." Find passages in this selection that support Heilbrun's claim, and share them with a partner.

THE WRITER'S STYLE

Testament of Youth differs from most World War I narratives by presenting the facts and emotions of war from a woman's point of view. In addition, the book is autobiographical. Although Brittain at first planned to fictionalize her war experiences in a long novel, the real events and people were still too fresh in her memory to treat them in an imaginative form. How does the selection's being a memoir rather than a fictionalized account affect its impact?

ACROSS THE CURRICULUM

Science Research and report on the development of chemical warfare and the use of poison gas during World War I. What chemical weapons and other technologies used in World War I were new? How did the technological developments affect the nature of war?

History On a large map of the world, mark the battlefronts of World War I. Use encyclopedias or books about the war as resources. Be sure to identify the area of France where Vera Brittain served as a nurse and the area of Italy where her brother, Edward, was killed. Keep the map on display in the classroom.

History Research the specific conditions and events that led to the start of World War I, and report your findings to the class.

HEIR TO AUSTRIA'S THRONE IS SLAIN WITH HIS WIFE BY A BOSNIAN YOUTH TO AVENGE SEIZURE OF HIS COUNTRY

Francis Ferdinand Shot During State Visit to Sarajevo.

TWO ATTACKS IN A DAY

Archduke Saves His Life First Time by Knocking Aside a Bomb Hurled at Auto.

SLAIN IN SECOND ATTEMPT

Lad Dashes at Car as the Royal Couple Return from Town Hall and Kills Both of Them.

LAID TO A SERVIAN PLOT

Heir Warned Not to Go to Bosnia, Where Populace Met Him with Servian Flags.

AGED EMPEROR IS STRICKEN

Shock of Tragedy Prostrates Fran-

Archduke Francis Ferdinand and his Consort the Duchess of Hohenberg

Slain by Assassin's Bullets.

could only certify they were both dead.

The authors of both attacks upon the Archduke are born Bosnians. Gabrinovics is a compositor, and worked for a few weeks in the Government printing works at Belgrade. He returned to Sarajevo a Servian chauvinist, and made no concealment of

by splinters from the bomb. Several persons on the pavement were very seriously hurt by the explosion of the bomb, which was thrown by a young man named Tabrinovitch, (Gabrinovics.) who is a typist from Trebenje, in Herzegovina, and is of Servian nationality. He was arrested some twenty minutes later.

The Archduke and his wife left the

it is feared that it will lead to serious complications with that unruly kingdom, and may have far-reaching results. The future of the empire is a subject of general discussion. It is felt that the Servians have been treated too leniently, and some hard words are being said about the present foreign policy.

All the public buildings are draped in long black streamers and the flags

WORDS TO KNOW

Review the Words to Know at the bottom of the selection pages. Then, on your paper, write the word that is described by each clue below.

1. Recyclers and conservationists oppose this in people's use of nature.
2. A person who wears expensive clothes may be wealthy only in this.
3. It would be foolish to expect to find this in an emergency room or a basketball game.
4. One's clothing might be this after a wrestling match, as might one's emotions after an argument.
5. Dentists use Novocain and other anesthetics to keep their treatments from being this.
6. Most people will quit working on a problem that seems this.
7. This is a harsh misrepresentation of what it copies.
8. Rain during a monsoon, cold at the North Pole, and complaints about taxes can all be said to be this.
9. Certain otherworldly works of art might be called this.
10. This is what a dog demonstrates by barking fiercely at a bigger dog that is safely on the other side of a sturdy fence.

VERA BRITTAIN

1893–1970

Vera Brittain was reared in a comfortable middle-class home in northern England. She grew up, fell in love, and expected to live a rather conventional life—except for attending college, which few women of her time could do—but World War I got in the way of her plans. By the time she entered Oxford University's Somerville College in 1914, the war was already underway in Europe, and in 1915 she decided to postpone her studies to serve in the war like her brother, her fiancé, and her friends. From 1915 to 1919, she worked as a Red Cross nurse in several British army hospitals.

Brittain lost her fiancé, two friends, and her brother in the war. She also lost her youth. "My work and experiences during the war," she wrote, "turned me from an ordinary patriotic young woman into a convinced pacifist." Yet when Brittain finally returned to college after the war, she found herself serving as an unwelcome reminder of the war that her fellow students longed to forget.

Throughout the war years, Brittain had recorded her experiences in a diary. At first, she attempted to fictionalize her experiences, but finding that her efforts rang false, she began writing a personal account of the war in the hope that she could "rescue something that might be of value . . . from the smashing up of my own youth by the war." She also hoped to remind her readers of the great suffering caused by war and to convince them to work for peace. First published in 1933, *Testament of Youth* became an immediate success, with more than 167,000 copies sold in the first year. It was acclaimed as "a moving elegy to a lost generation."

Brittain continued to write memoirs about her experiences; she also continued to break new ground for women by persisting in her career after marrying. Throughout her life, Brittain was active in peace movements, for she firmly believed that "war, which is man-created, can be man-prevented."

OTHER WORKS *Testament of Friendship, Testament of Experience*

PREVIEWING

NONFICTION

from The Speeches, May 19, 1940

Winston Churchill

PERSONAL CONNECTION

Think about the most memorable speech you have ever heard. It may be one delivered by a classmate or a politician, or it may be one in a play or movie you have seen. In your notebook, jot down words and phrases that describe your most vivid memories of the speech. Your description may touch on powerful statements made by the speaker, details of the speaker's tone of voice and body language, emotions you felt during the speech, or the reaction of the audience. Share your experience with some classmates.

HISTORICAL/BIOGRAPHICAL CONNECTION

World War II began in Europe two years before the United States became involved. Between September 1939 and May 1940, Germany—which had already annexed Austria and most of Czechoslovakia—conquered Poland, Denmark, and Norway. Just nine days before Churchill's speech, Hitler's army invaded Holland and Belgium, sweeping through those countries on its way into France. By the morning of May 19, 1940, the British troops that had been fighting in western Europe had been backed up against the ocean, ready to retreat to England.

Winston Churchill, who had just been chosen prime minister, had only three hours to prepare this speech for delivery on a BBC (British Broadcasting Corporation) radio broadcast. Although Churchill had been in politics for years, his wartime speeches made him famous and inspired the British people working on the home front to greater efforts. The spirit and determination of these workers, both male and female, during the darkest moments of the war are reflected in Churchill's speeches.

READING CONNECTION

Evaluating a Speech Winston Churchill made this radio speech to raise the spirits of the British people at a time when the Germans appeared to be winning World War II. Though the speech was meant to be read aloud, it is powerful in print as well. As you read it, note the techniques Churchill uses to influence his audience.

from

The SPEECHES

May 19, 1940

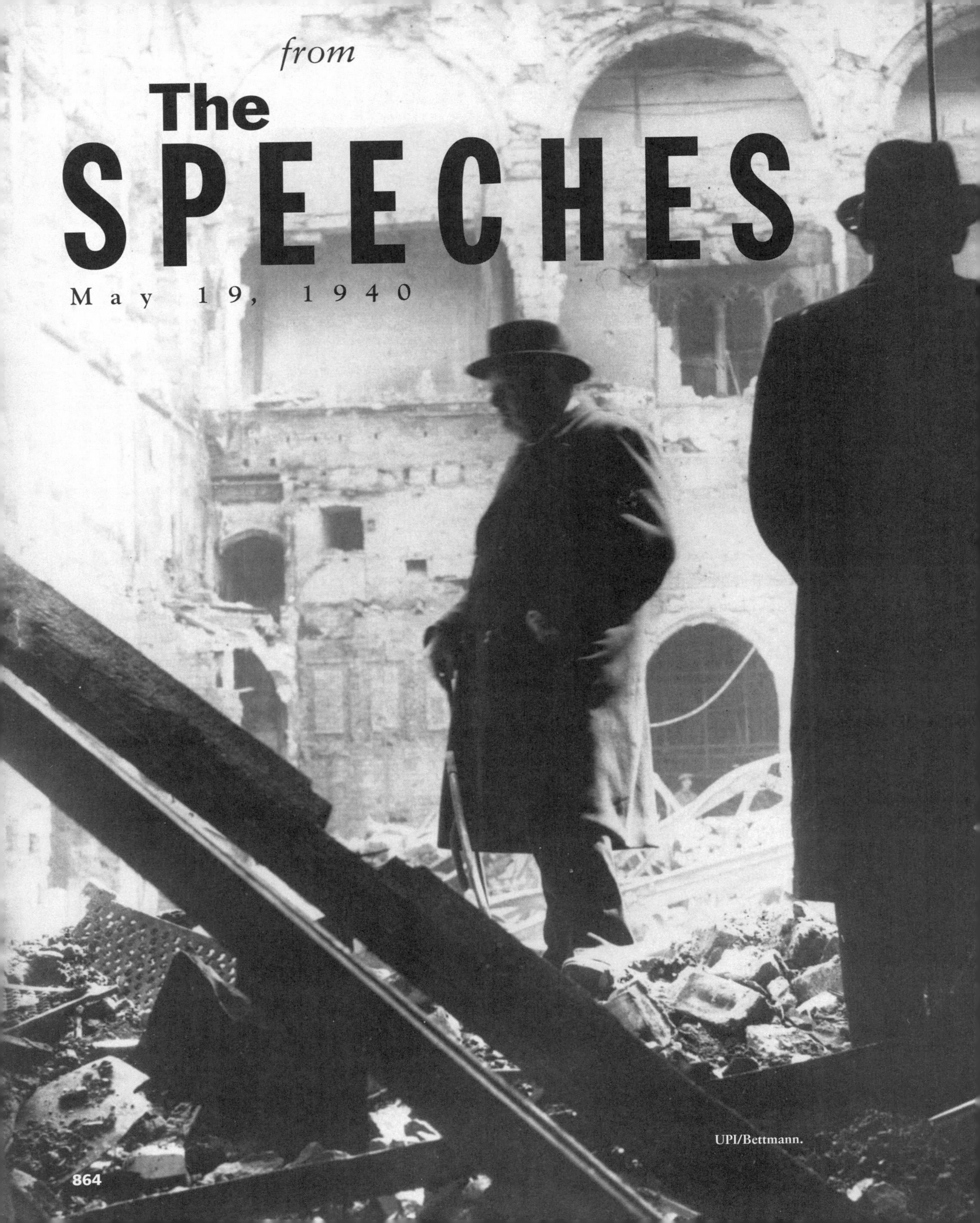

UPI/Bettmann.

Winston Churchill

I speak to you for the first time as Prime Minister in a solemn hour for the life of our country, of our Empire, of our Allies, and, above all, of the cause of Freedom. A tremendous battle is raging in France and Flanders.[1] The Germans, by a remarkable combination of air bombing and heavily armored tanks, have broken through the French defenses north of the Maginot Line, and strong columns of their armored vehicles are ravaging the open country, which for the first day or two was without defenders. They have penetrated deeply and spread alarm and confusion in their track. Behind them there are now appearing infantry in lorries,[2] and behind them, again, the large masses are moving forward. The regroupment of the French armies to make head against, and also to strike at, this intruding wedge has been proceeding for several days, largely assisted by the magnificent efforts of the Royal Air Force.

We must not allow ourselves to be intimidated by the presence of these armored vehicles in unexpected places behind our lines. If they are behind our Front, the French are also at many points fighting actively behind theirs. Both sides are therefore in an extremely dangerous position. And if the French Army, and our own Army, are well handled, as I believe they will be; if the French retain that genius for recovery and counterattack for which they have so long been famous; and if the British Army shows the dogged endurance and solid fighting power of which there have been so many examples in the past—then a sudden transformation of the scene might spring into being.

It would be foolish, however, to disguise the gravity of the hour. It would be still more foolish to lose heart and courage or to suppose that well-trained, well-equipped armies numbering three or four millions of men can be overcome in the space of a few weeks, or even months, by a scoop, or raid of mechanized vehicles, however formidable. We may look with confidence to the stabilization of the Front in France, and to the general engagement of the masses, which will enable the qualities of the French and British soldiers to be matched squarely against those of their adversaries. For myself, I have invincible confidence in the French Army and its leaders. Only a very small part of that splendid army has yet been heavily engaged; and only a very small part of France has yet been invaded. There is good evidence to show that practically the whole of the specialized and mechanized forces of the enemy have been already thrown into the battle; and we know that very heavy losses have been inflicted upon them. No officer or man, no brigade or division, which grapples at close quarters with the enemy, wherever encountered, can fail to make a worthy contribution to the general result. The Armies must cast away the idea of resisting behind concrete lines or natural obstacles, and must realize that mastery can only be regained by furious and unrelenting assault. And this spirit must not only animate the High Command, but must inspire every fighting man.

In the air—often at serious odds—often at odds hitherto thought overwhelming—we have

---

1. **Flanders:** western Belgium.
2. **lorries:** the British term for motor trucks.

WORDS TO KNOW

dogged (dô′gĭd) *adj.* persistent; stubborn
gravity (grăv′ĭ-tē) *n.* seriousness; importance
animate (ăn′ə-māt′) *v.* to encourage; motivate

Our task is not only to win the battle—but to win the War.

been clawing down three or four to one of our enemies; and the relative balance of the British and German Air Forces is now considerably more favorable to us than at the beginning of the battle. In cutting down the German bombers, we are fighting our own battle as well as that of France. My confidence in our ability to fight it out to the finish with the German Air Force has been strengthened by the fierce encounters which have taken place and are taking place. At the same time, our heavy bombers are striking nightly at the taproot of German mechanized power, and have already inflicted serious damage upon the oil refineries on which the Nazi effort to dominate the world directly depends.

We must expect that as soon as stability is reached on the Western Front, the bulk of that hideous apparatus of aggression which gashed Holland into ruin and slavery in a few days, will be turned upon us. I am sure I speak for all when I say we are ready to face it; to endure it; and to retaliate against it—to any extent that the unwritten laws of war permit. There will be many men, and many women, in this island who when the ordeal comes upon them, as come it will, will feel comfort, and even a pride—that they are sharing the perils of our lads at the Front—soldiers, sailors and airmen, God bless

WORDS TO KNOW

retaliate (rĭ-tăl'ē-āt') *v.* to take revenge; pay back in kind

them—and are drawing away from them a part at least of the onslaught they have to bear. Is not this the appointed time for all to make the utmost exertions in their power? If the battle is to be won, we must provide our men with ever-increasing quantities of the weapons and ammunition they need. We must have, and have quickly, more airplanes, more tanks, more shells, more guns. There is imperious[3] need for these vital munitions. They increase our strength against the powerfully armed enemy. They replace the wastage of the obstinate struggle; and the knowledge that wastage will speedily be replaced enables us to draw more readily upon our reserves and throw them in now that everything counts so much.

Our task is not only to win the battle—but to win the War. After this battle in France abates its force, there will come the battle for our island—for all that Britain is, and all that Britain means. That will be the struggle. In that supreme emergency we shall not hesitate to take every step, even the most drastic, to call forth from our people the last ounce and the last inch of effort of which they are capable. The interests of property, the hours of labor, are nothing compared with the struggle for life and honor, for right and freedom, to which we have vowed ourselves.

I have received from the Chiefs of the French Republic, and in particular from its indomitable Prime Minister, M. Reynaud,[4] the most sacred pledges that whatever happens they will fight to the end, be it bitter or be it glorious. Nay, if we fight to the end, it can only be glorious.

Having received His Majesty's commission, I have found an administration of men and women of every party and of almost every point of view. We have differed and quarreled in the past; but now one bond unites us all—to wage war until victory is won, and never to surrender ourselves to servitude and shame, whatever the cost and the agony may be. This is one of the most awe-striking periods in the long history of France and Britain. It is also beyond doubt the most sublime. Side by side, unaided except by their kith and kin[5] in the great Dominions[6] and by the wide Empires which rest beneath their shield—side by side, the British and French peoples have advanced to rescue not only Europe but mankind from the foulest and most soul-destroying tyranny which has ever darkened and stained the pages of history. Behind them—behind us—behind the armies and fleets of Britain and France—gather a group of shattered States and bludgeoned races: the Czechs, the Poles, the Norwegians, the Danes, the Dutch, the Belgians—upon all of whom the long night of barbarism will descend, unbroken even by a star of hope, unless we conquer, as conquer we must; as conquer we shall.

Today is Trinity Sunday.[7] Centuries ago words were written to be a call and a spur to the faithful servants of Truth and Justice: "Arm yourselves, and be ye men of valor, and be in readiness for the conflict; for it is better for us to perish in battle than to look upon the outrage of our nation and our altar. As the Will of God is in Heaven, even so let it be."[8] ❖

---

3. **imperious** (ĭm-pîr′ē-əs): urgent; pressing.
4. **M. Reynaud:** Paul Reynaud, who had long argued, like Churchill, for firmness toward Germany and for a close British-French alliance. (*M.* is an abbreviation of *Monsieur,* "Mister.")
5. **kith and kin:** friends and relatives.
6. **Dominions:** self-governing nations within the British Commonwealth.
7. **Trinity Sunday:** the eighth Sunday after Easter, dedicated to the Trinity (Father, Son, and Holy Spirit).
8. **"Arm yourselves . . . let it be":** a quotation from 1 Maccabees 3:58–60. This book of the Apocrypha (found in only some versions of the Bible) tells of the heroism of the Maccabees, a Jewish family, in preventing the destruction of Judaism by the Syrians during the second century B.C.

WORDS TO KNOW

indomitable (ĭn-dŏm′ĭ-tə-bəl) *adj.* not easily discouraged or defeated; unconquerable

INSIGHT

To My Mother

George Barker

Portrait of Mrs. B. (1937), Edwin Dickinson. The Baltimore (Maryland) Museum of Art, Thomas E. Benesch Memorial Collection (BMA 1974.5).

Most near, most dear, most loved and most far,
Under the window where I often found her
Sitting as huge as Asia, seismic with laughter,
Gin and chicken helpless in her Irish hand,
Irresistible as Rabelais, but most tender for
The lame dogs and hurt birds that surround her,—
She is a procession no one can follow after
But be like a little dog following a brass band.

She will not glance up at the bomber, or condescend
To drop her gin and scuttle to a cellar,
But lean on the mahogany table like a mountain
Whom only faith can move, and so I send
O all my faith, and all my love to tell her
That she will move from mourning into morning.

RESPONDING OPTIONS

FROM PERSONAL RESPONSE *TO* CRITICAL ANALYSIS

REFLECT

1. If you had been living in England at the time of this speech, would Churchill's words have inspired you to help the war effort? Why or why not?

RETHINK

2. If you had been a British citizen listening to Churchill's speech in 1940, what would your reaction have been?
3. In your opinion, which parts of the speech are most effective? Support your answer with details from the speech.
4. How would you describe Churchill's attitudes toward the English, the French, and the Germans? Cite words and phrases that suggest those attitudes.

RELATE

5. Reread the Insight poem "To My Mother" on page 868. How do you think the speaker's mother would react to Churchill's speech?
6. If Churchill were to give his speech today, it would be televised. How might he change it? Do you think the speech would be more or less powerful on television? Why?

Aftermath of London bombing

ANOTHER PATHWAY

Cooperative Learning

Even though speeches usually do not have titles, quotations from speeches are sometimes used in referring to them. This speech has been called "Be Ye Men of Valor." With a group, find another quotation from the speech that could be used as an alternative title. Then vote as a class to select the best title.

QUICKWRITES

1. Churchill ends his speech by quoting a statement that "it is better for us to perish in battle than to look upon the outrage of our nation and our altar." In one or two **paragraphs,** explain this statement and explain why you agree or do not agree with it.
2. In this speech, Churchill provides compelling reasons for going to war. Yet many people around the world remained pacifists throughout World War II. Consider what the pacifist position might be, and write a short **persuasive speech** presenting arguments against fighting in World War II.

PORTFOLIO *Save your writing. You may want to use it later as a springboard to a piece for your portfolio.*

LITERARY CONCEPTS

Persuasion is the technique of convincing an audience to adopt an opinion, perform an action, or both. Churchill's speech is considered one of the greatest persuasive speeches of all time because it stirred the British people to hold out against the German assault on their homeland. The speech is effective largely because it balances intellectual and emotional appeals. Churchill's arguments are logical and clearly stated, but he also uses **loaded language**—words and phrases with strong emotional content—to seek support for his idea of defeating the enemy at all costs. Reread the speech, paying particular attention to Churchill's use of loaded language. In a chart like the one shown, record the examples you find, the information they convey, the ideas they suggest, and the emotions they inspire.

Loaded Word or Phrase	Information Provided	Ideas Suggested	Emotions Inspired

ACROSS THE CURRICULUM

History Using a historical atlas and books about World War II, find out what happened in France, England, and the rest of western Europe during the six months following Churchill's speech. Write a documentary news report explaining your findings, and present it to the class.

Math Look up statistical information about the costs and casualties incurred by Britain, France, Germany, the United States, and Russia in World War II. Present your findings in a chart showing the cost of World War II in money and lives.

WORDS TO KNOW

For each group of words below, write the letter of the word that is an antonym of the boldfaced word.

1. **animate:** (a) stifle, (b) appreciate, (c) liberate
2. **gravity:** (a) height, (b) clearness, (c) insignificance
3. **dogged:** (a) respectable, (b) nonchalant, (c) friendly
4. **retaliate:** (a) praise, (b) forgive, (c) discourage
5. **indomitable:** (a) angry, (b) strong, (c) vulnerable

WINSTON CHURCHILL

1874–1965

The son of a noble English father and an American mother, Winston Churchill received a traditional English secondary education. Because his school record was not particularly distinguished, he did not go on to a university, instead entering the Royal Military College at Sandhurst at the age of 18 and then joining the military. There he found his niche, serving both as a war correspondent and as an officer. He entered politics in 1900, and 40 years later he became a compromise prime minister in a deeply divided government. With his public-speaking ability and talent at working with opposing forces, he was able to unite the British people and lead them to victory over the Germans in World War II. Despite his lifetime involvement in politics, Churchill never stopped writing. He was awarded the Nobel Prize in literature in 1953.

OTHER WORKS *The Gathering Storm; Blood, Sweat, and Tears; Their Finest Hour; History of the English-Speaking Peoples* (4 volumes); *The Second World War* (6 volumes)

LASERLINKS
• *AUTHOR BACKGROUND*

PREVIEWING

NONFICTION

from Letters from Westerbork

Etty Hillesum (hĭl′ə-süm′)

PERSONAL CONNECTION

What do you know about the Holocaust—the Nazis' systematic slaughter of Jews and members of other minority groups during World War II? Where did you get your information? How did you react when you learned about it? Share your knowledge and experiences with your classmates.

HISTORICAL CONNECTION

When Adolf Hitler became chancellor of Germany in 1933, he was determined to make his country a world empire. As leader of the controlling Nazi party, he carried out a policy of military aggression and expansion. When German troops invaded Poland in September 1939, World War II began. In 1940, undaunted by the threat of war, the Germans invaded Denmark, Norway, the Netherlands, Belgium, and France.

In his quest for German supremacy, Hitler was also determined to rid his country of Jews, whom he blamed for every evil in the world. As the war progressed, his goals expanded to include the elimination of all European Jews. Under Hitler's orders, Jews were forced by the thousands into concentration camps, where many were killed in gas chambers or by firing squads. Others died as a result of torture, starvation, and disease. By the end of the war, about 6 million Jews—over two-thirds of the Jewish population of Europe—had perished.

In the Netherlands, more than 100,000 Dutch Jews were sent to Westerbork, a Nazi transit camp near the German border. From there, most were transported by train to Auschwitz (oush′vĭts′) in Poland, one of the largest Nazi death camps. For a few months in 1943, a spirited young woman named Etty Hillesum was confined at Westerbork along with her parents and her brother Mischa. Hillesum, who was 29 years old, worked in the hospital barracks during her imprisonment, providing care and comfort to her fellow Jews. She also kept a diary and wrote letters—possibly more than 100—to friends outside the camp. Hillesum's letters vividly attest to the atrocities that have come to be known as the Holocaust.

WRITING CONNECTION

In your notebook, list words and phrases that might describe the feelings of someone living in a concentration camp during the Holocaust. Then, as you read this selection, compare your ideas with the thoughts and feelings described by Etty Hillesum.

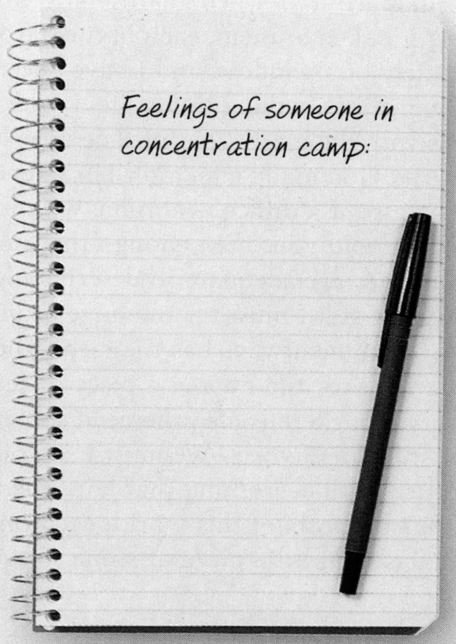

LASERLINKS
• *HISTORICAL CONNECTION*

from Letters from

Westerbork

Etty Hillesum

24 August 1943[1]

There was a moment when I felt in all seriousness that after this night, it would be a sin ever to laugh again. But then I reminded myself that some of those who had gone away had been laughing, even if only a handful of them this time. . . . There will be some who will laugh now and then in Poland too, though not many from this transport,[2] I think.

When I think of the faces of that squad of armed, green-uniformed guards—my God, those faces! I looked at them, each in turn, from behind the safety of a window, and I have never been so frightened of anything in my life. I sank to my knees with the words that preside over human life: And God made man after His likeness. That passage spent a difficult morning with me.

I have told you often enough that no words and images are adequate to describe nights like these. But still I must try to convey something of it to you. One always has the feeling here of being the ears and eyes of a piece of Jewish history, but there is also the need sometimes to be a still, small voice. We must keep one another in touch with everything that happens in the various outposts of this world, each one contributing his own little piece of stone to the great mosaic that will take shape once the war is over.

After a night in the hospital barracks, I took an early-morning walk past the punishment barracks. And prisoners were being moved out. The deportees, mainly men, stood with their packs behind the barbed wire. So many of them looked tough and ready for anything. An old acquaintance—I didn't recognize him straightaway; a shaven head often changes people completely—called out to me with a smile, "If they don't manage to do me in, I'll be back."

But the babies, those tiny piercing screams of the babies, dragged from their cots in the middle of the night . . . I have to put it all down quickly, in a muddle, because if I leave it until later I probably won't be able to go on believing that it really happened. It is like a vision, and drifts further and further away. The babies were easily the worst.

And then there was that paralyzed young girl, who didn't want to take her dinner plate along and found it so hard to die. Or the terrified young boy: he had thought he was safe, that was his mistake, and when he realized he was going to have to go anyway, he panicked and ran off. His fellow Jews had to hunt him down. If they didn't find him, scores of others would be put on the transport in his place. He was caught soon enough, hiding in a tent, but "notwithstanding"

1. This letter was probably written to friends with whom Hillesum had once shared a house in Amsterdam.
2. **this transport:** the most recent group of people sent by train to a concentration camp in Poland.

WORDS TO KNOW **notwithstanding** (nŏt′wĭth-stăn′dĭng) *adv.* in spite of that; nevertheless

. . . "notwithstanding," all those others had to go on transport anyway, as a deterrent, they said. And so, many good friends were dragged away by that boy. Fifty victims for one moment of insanity. Or rather: he didn't drag them away—our commandant did, someone of whom it is sometimes said that he is a gentleman. Even so, will the boy be able to live with himself, once it dawns on him exactly what he's been the cause of? And how will all the other Jews on board the train react to him? That boy is going to have a very hard time. The episode might have been overlooked, perhaps, if there hadn't been so much unnerving activity over our heads that night. The commandant must have been affected by that too. "*Donnerwetter,*[3] some flying tonight!" I heard a guard say as he looked up at the stars.

People still harbor such childish hopes that the transport won't get through. Many of us were able from here to watch the bombardment of a nearby town, probably Emden. So why shouldn't it be possible for the railway line to be hit too, and for the train to be stopped from leaving? It's never been known to happen yet. But people keep hoping it will, with each new transport and with never-flagging hope. . . .

The evening before, I had walked through the camp. People were grouped together between the barracks under a gray, cloudy sky. "Look, that's just how people behave after a disaster, standing about on street corners discussing what's happened," my companion said to me. "But that's what makes it so impossible to understand," I burst out. "This time, it's *before* the disaster!"

Whenever misfortune strikes, people have a natural instinct to lend a helping hand and to save what can be saved. Tonight I shall be helping to dress babies and to calm mothers—and that is all I can hope to do. I could almost curse myself for that. For we all know that we are yielding up our sick and defenseless brothers and sisters to hunger, heat, cold, exposure, and destruction, and yet we dress them and escort them to the bare cattle cars—and if they can't walk, we carry them on stretchers. What is going on, what mysteries are these, in what sort of fatal mechanism have we become enmeshed? The answer cannot simply be that we are all cowards. We're not that bad. We stand before a much deeper question. . . .

In the afternoon I did a round of the hospital barracks one more time, going from bed to bed. Which beds would be empty the next day? The transport lists are never published until the very last moment, but some of us know well in advance that our names will be down. A young girl called me. She was sitting bolt upright in her bed, eyes wide open. This girl has thin wrists and a peaky[4] little face. She is partly paralyzed, and has just been learning to walk again, between two nurses, one step at a time. "Have you heard? I have to go." We look at each other for a long moment. It is as if her face has disappeared; she is all eyes. Then she says in a level, gray little voice, "Such a pity, isn't it? That everything you have learned in life goes for nothing." And, "How hard it is to die." Suddenly the unnatural rigidity of her expression gives way and she sobs, "Oh, and the worst of it all is having to leave Holland!" And, "Oh, why wasn't I allowed to die before . . ." Later, during the night, I saw her again, for the last time.

There was a little woman in the washhouse, a basket of dripping clothes on her arm. She grabbed hold of me; she looked deranged. A flood of words poured over me: "That isn't right, how can that be right? I've got to go and I won't even be able to get my washing dry by tomorrow. And my child is sick, he's feverish, can't you fix

3. ***Donnerwetter*** (dôn′ər-vĕt′ər): a German exclamation of anger or annoyance (literally, "thunder weather").

4. **peaky:** sharp; pinched.

WORDS TO KNOW

enmeshed (ĕn-mĕsht′) *adj.* entangled, involved, or entrapped **enmesh** *v.*
deranged (dĭ-rānjd′) *adj.* mentally disturbed; insane **derange** *v.*

things so that I don't have to go? And I don't have enough things for the child, the rompers they sent me are too small, I need the bigger size, oh, it's enough to drive you mad. And you're not even allowed to take a blanket along, we're going to freeze to death, you didn't think of that, did you? There's a cousin of mine here, he came here the same time I did, but he doesn't have to go, he's got the right papers. Couldn't you help me to get some too? Just say I don't have to go, do you think they'll leave the children with their mothers, that's right, you come back again tonight, you'll help me then, won't you, what do you think, would my cousin's papers . . . ?"

If I were to say that I was in hell that night, what would I really be telling you? I caught myself saying it aloud in the night, aloud to myself and quite soberly, "So that's what hell is like." You really can't tell who is going and who isn't this time. Almost everyone is up, the sick help each other to get dressed. There are some who have no clothes at all, whose luggage has been lost or hasn't arrived yet. Ladies from the "Welfare" walk about doling out clothes, which may fit or not, it doesn't matter so long as you've covered yourself with something. Some old women look a ridiculous sight. Small bottles of milk are being prepared to take along with the babies, whose pitiful screams punctuate all the frantic activity in the barracks. A young mother says to me almost apologetically, "My baby doesn't usually cry; it's almost as if he can tell what's happening." She picks up the child, a lovely baby about eight months old, from a makeshift crib and smiles at it. "If you don't behave yourself, Mummy won't take you along with her!" She tells me about some friends. "When those men in green came to fetch them in Amsterdam, their children cried terribly. Then their father said, 'If you don't behave yourselves, you won't be allowed to go in that green car, this green gentleman won't take you.' And that helped—the children calmed down." She winks at me bravely, a trim, dark little woman with a lively, olive-skinned face. She is dressed in long gray trousers and a green woolen sweater. "I may be smiling," she says, "but I feel pretty awful." The little woman with the wet washing is on the point of hysterics. "Can't you hide my child for me? Go on, please, won't you hide him, he's got a high fever, how can I possibly take him along?" She points to a little bundle of misery with blond curls and a burning, bright-red little face. The child tosses about in his rough wooden cot. The nurse wants the mother to put on an extra woolen sweater, tries to pull it over her dress. She refuses. "I'm not going to take anything along, what use would it be? . . . my child." And she sobs, "They take the sick children away and you never get them back."

Then a woman comes up to her, a stout working-class woman with a kindly snub-nosed face, draws the desperate mother down with her on the edge of one of the iron bunks, and talks to her almost crooningly. "There now, you're just an ordinary Jew, aren't you? So you'll just have to go, won't you . . . ?"

A few beds further along I suddenly catch sight of the ash-gray, freckled face of a colleague. She is squatting beside the bed of a dying woman who has swallowed some poison and who happens to be her mother. . . .

"God Almighty, what are You doing to us?" The words just escape me. Over there is that affectionate little woman from Rotterdam. She is in her ninth month. Two nurses try to get her dressed. She just stands there, her swollen body leaning against her child's cot. Drops of sweat run down her face. She stares into the distance, a distance into which I cannot follow her, and says in a toneless, worn-out voice, "Two months ago I volunteered to go with my husband to Poland. And then I wasn't allowed to, because I always have such difficult pregnancies. And now I do have to go . . . just because someone tried to run away tonight." The wailing of the babies grows louder still, filling every nook and cranny of the

Photograph of camp at Westerbork. U.S. Holocaust Memorial Museum, Washington, D.C.

barracks, now bathed in ghostly light. It is almost too much to bear. A name occurs to me: Herod.[5]

On the stretcher on the way to the train, her labor pains begin, and we are allowed to carry the woman to the hospital instead of to the freight train—which, this night, seems a rare act of humanity. . . .

I pass the bed of the paralyzed girl. The others have helped to dress her. I never saw such great big eyes in such a little face. "I can't take it all in," she whispers to me. A few steps away stands my little hunchbacked Russian woman; I told you about her before. She stands there as if spun in a web of sorrow. The paralyzed girl is a friend of hers. Later she said sadly to me, "She doesn't even have a plate, I wanted to give her mine, but she wouldn't take it. She said, 'I'll be dead in ten days anyway, and then those horrible Germans will get it.' "

She stands there in front of me, a green silk kimono wrapped around her small, misshapen figure. She has the very wise, bright eyes of a child. She looks at me for a long time in silence, searchingly, and then says, "I would like, oh, I really would like, to be able to swim away in my tears." And "I long so desperately for my dear mother." (Her mother died a few months ago from cancer, in the washroom near the WC.[6] At

5. **Herod:** a king of Judea who, according to the New Testament, attempted to kill the infant Jesus by ordering the execution of all male children under the age of two in the region of Bethlehem.

6. **WC:** water closet; toilet.

least she was left alone there for a moment, left to die in peace.) She asks me with her strange accent in the voice of a child that begs for forgiveness, "Surely God will be able to understand my doubts in a world like this, won't He?" Then she turns away from me, in an almost loving gesture of infinite sadness, and throughout the night I see the misshapen, green, silk-clad figure moving between the beds, doing small services for those about to depart. She herself doesn't have to go, not this time, anyway. . . .

Slowly but surely six o'clock in the morning has arrived. The train is due to depart at eleven, and they are starting to load it with people and luggage. Paths to the train have been staked out by men of the *Ordedienst,*[7] the Camp Service Corps. Anyone not involved with the transport has to keep to barracks. I slip into one just across from the siding. "There's always been a splendid view from here," I hear a cynical voice say. The camp has been cut in two halves since yesterday by the train: a depressing series of bare, unpainted freight cars in the front, and a proper coach for the guards at the back. Some of the cars have paper mattresses on the floor. These are for the sick. There is more and more movement now along the asphalt path beside the train.

Men from the "Flying Column"[8] in brown overalls are bringing the luggage up on wheelbarrows. Among them I spot two of the commandant's court jesters: the first is a comedian and a songwriter. Some time ago his name was down, irrevocably, for transport, but for several nights in a row he sang his lungs out for a delighted audience, including the commandant and his retinue. He sang *"Ich kann es nicht verstehen, dass die Rosen blühen"*[9] ("I know not why the roses bloom") and other topical songs. The commandant, a great lover of art, thought it all quite splendid. The singer got his exemption. He was even allocated a house, where he now lives behind red-checked curtains with his peroxide-blonde wife, who spends all her days at a mangle[10] in the boiling-hot laundry. Now here he is, dressed in khaki overalls, pushing a wheelbarrow piled high with the luggage of his fellow Jews. He looks like death warmed over. And over there is another court jester: the commandant's favorite pianist. Legend has it that he is so accomplished that he can play Beethoven's Ninth as a jazz number, which is certainly saying something. . . .

Suddenly there are a lot of green-uniformed men swarming over the asphalt. I can't imagine where they have sprung from. Knapsacks and guns over their shoulders. I study their faces. I try to look at them without prejudice.

I can see a father, ready to depart, blessing his wife and child and being himself blessed in turn by an old rabbi with a snow-white beard and the profile of a fiery prophet. I can see . . . ah, I can't begin to describe it all. . . .

On earlier transports, some of the guards were simple, kindly types with puzzled expressions, who walked about the camp smoking their pipes and speaking in some incomprehensible dialect. One would have found their company not too objectionable on the journey. Now I am transfixed with terror. Oafish, jeering faces, in which one seeks in vain for even the slightest trace of human warmth. At what fronts did they learn their business? In what punishment camps were they

---

7. **Ordedienst** (ôr′də-dēnst′) *German.*
8. **"Flying Column:"** the inmates' joking term for those assigned to transport the luggage belonging to new arrivals. (In the military, a flying column is a strong unit that operates at a distance from the main body of troops.)
9. ***"Ich kann es nicht verstehen, dass die Rosen blühen"*** (ĭkh kän′ ĕs nĭkht′ fĕr-shtā′ən däs′ dē rō′zən blü′ən) *German.*
10. **mangle:** a hand-cranked device for wringing water from clothes.

WORDS TO KNOW

topical (tŏp′ĭ-kəl) *adj.* of current interest
allocate (ăl′ə-kāt′) *v.* to give out; assign
transfix (trăns-fĭks′) *v.* to make motionless, as with fear, amazement, or awe

trained? For after all, this is a punishment, isn't it? A few young women are already sitting in a freight car. They hold their babies on their laps, their legs dangling outside—they are determined to enjoy the fresh air as long as possible. Sick people are carried past on stretchers. I almost find myself laughing; the disparity between the guards and the guarded is too absurd. My companion at the window shudders. Months ago he was brought here from Amersfoort, in bits and pieces. "Oh, yes, that's what those fellows were like," he says. "That's what they looked like."

Etty Hillesum. Collection Jewish Historical Museum, Amsterdam, the Netherlands.

A couple of young children stand with their noses pressed to the windowpane. I listen in to their earnest conversation. "Why do those nasty, horrid men wear green; why don't they wear black? Bad people wear black, don't they?" "Look over there, that man is really sick!" A shock of gray hair above a rumpled blanket on a stretcher. "Look, there's another sick one . . ."

And, pointing at the green uniforms, "Look at them, now they're laughing!" "Look, look, one of them's already drunk!"

More and more people are filling up the spaces in the freight cars. A tall, lonely figure paces the asphalt, a briefcase under his arm. He is the head of the so-called *Antragstelle,*[11] the camp Appeals Department. He strives right up to the last moment to get people out of the commandant's clutches. Horse trading[12] here always continues until the train has actually pulled out. It's even been known for him to manage to free people from the moving train. The man with the briefcase has the brow of a scholar, and tired, very tired shoulders. A bent little old woman, with a black, old-fashioned hat on her gray, wispy hair, bars his way, gesticulating and brandishing a bundle of papers under his nose. He listens to her for a while, then shakes his head and turns away, his shoulders sagging just a little bit more. This time it won't be possible to get many people off the train in the nick of time. The commandant is annoyed. A young Jew has had the effrontery to run away. One can't really call it a serious attempt to escape—he absconded from the hospital in a moment of panic, a thin jacket over his blue pajamas, and in a clumsy, childish way took refuge in a tent, where he was picked up quickly enough after a search of the camp. But if you are a Jew you may not run away, may not allow yourself to be stricken with panic. The commandant is remorseless. As a reprisal, and without warning, scores of others are being sent on the

11. ***Antragstelle*** (än'träKH-shtĕl'ə) *German.*
12. **horse trading:** negotiations characterized by hard, shrewd bargaining.

WORDS TO KNOW
disparity (dĭ-spăr'ĭ-tē) *n.* a lack of equality; difference
abscond (ăb-skŏnd') *v.* to leave quickly and secretly; run away
reprisal (rĭ-prī'zəl) *n.* an act of punishment or retaliation

transport with the boy, including quite a few who had thought they were firmly at anchor here. This system happens to believe in collective punishment. And all those planes overhead couldn't have helped to improve the commandant's mood, though that is a subject on which he prefers to keep his own counsel. . . .

My God, are the doors really being shut now? Yes, they are. Shut on the herded, densely packed mass of people inside. Through small openings at the top we can see heads and hands, hands that will wave to us later when the train leaves. The commandant takes a bicycle and rides once again along the entire length of the train. Then he makes a brief gesture, like royalty in an operetta. A little orderly comes flying up and deferentially relieves him of the bicycle. The train gives a piercing whistle. And 1,020 Jews leave Holland.

This time the quota was really quite small, all considered: a mere thousand Jews, the extra twenty being reserves. For it is always possible—indeed, quite certain this time—that a few will die or be crushed to death on the way. So many sick people and not a single nurse. . . .

The tide of helpers gradually recedes; people go back to their sleeping quarters. So many exhausted, pale, and suffering faces. One more piece of our camp has been amputated. Next week yet another piece will follow. This is what has been happening now for over a year, week in, week out. We are left with just a few thousand. A hundred thousand Dutch members of our race are toiling away under an unknown sky or lie rotting in some unknown soil. We know nothing of their fate. It is only a short while, perhaps, before we find out, each one of us in his own time. For we are all marked down to share that fate, of that I have not a moment's doubt. But I must go now and lie down and sleep for a little while. I am a bit tired and dizzy. Then later I have to go to the laundry to track down the facecloth that got lost. But first I must sleep. As for the future, I am firmly resolved to return to you after my wanderings. In the meantime, my love once again, you dear people.

[postmarked 15 September 1943]

Christine,
Opening the Bible at random I find this: "The Lord is my high tower."[13] I am sitting on my rucksack in the middle of a full freight car. Father, Mother, and Mischa are a few cars away. In the end, the departure came without warning. On sudden special orders from the Hague.[14] We left the camp singing, Father and Mother firmly and calmly, Mischa too. We shall be traveling for three days. Thank you for all your kindness and care. Friends left behind will still be writing to Amsterdam; perhaps you will hear something from them. Or from my last letter from camp.

Good-bye for now from the four of us.
Etty

Translated by Arnold J. Pomerans

13. **"The Lord is my high tower":** a paraphrase of 2 Samuel 22:2–3: "The Lord is my rock, and my fortress, and my deliverer; . . . He is my shield, and the horn of my salvation, my high tower, and my refuge, my saviour; . . . I will call on the Lord . . . so shall I be saved from mine enemies."
14. **the Hague** (hāg): the seat of government of the Netherlands, site of Nazi headquarters during the German occupation of the country.

WORDS TO KNOW

collective (kə-lĕk'tĭv) *adj.* having to do with people considered as a group rather than as individuals

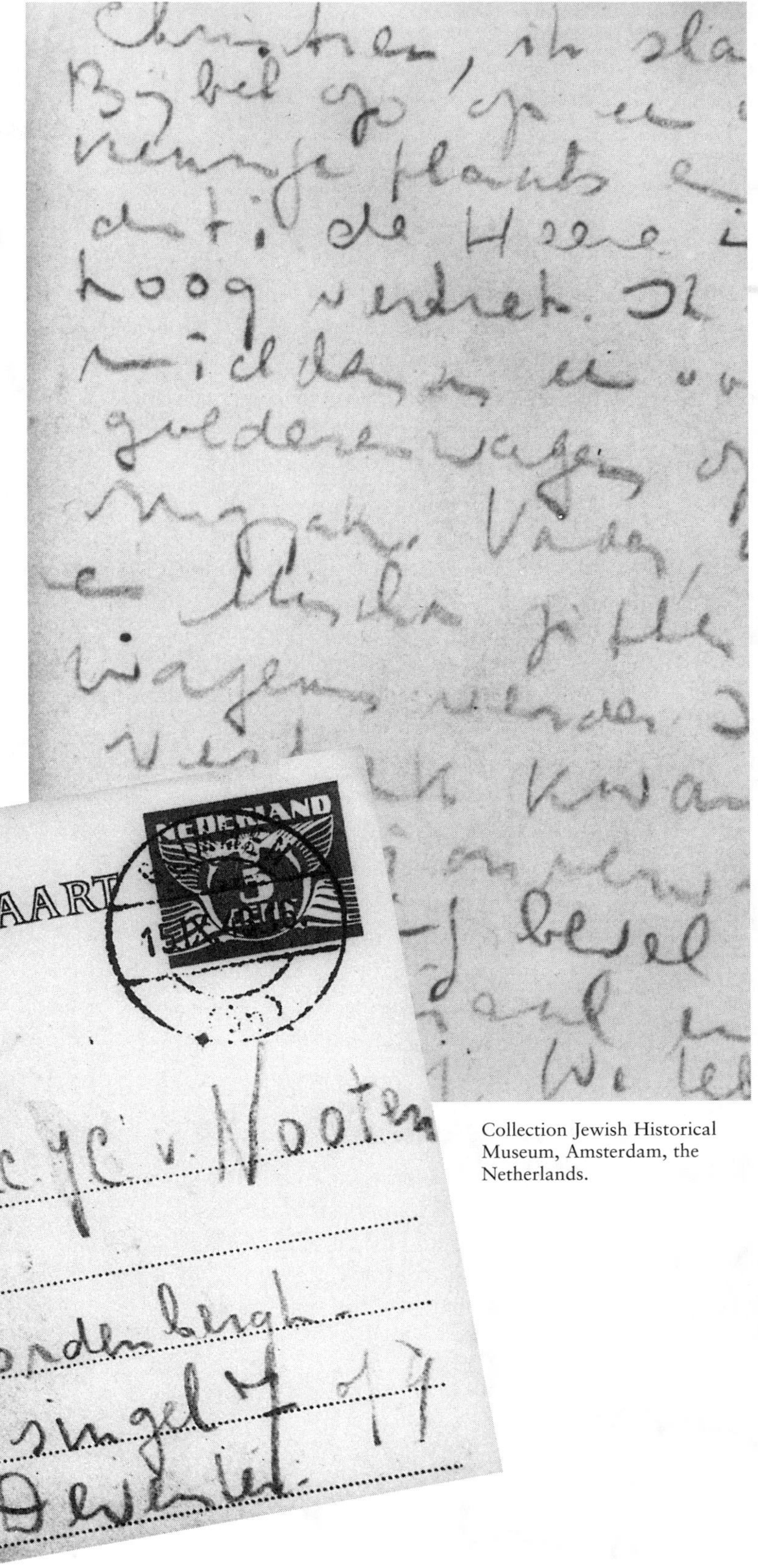

This card, thrown out of the train by Etty on 7 September, was found by farmers outside Westerbork camp and posted by them.

Etty Hillesum died in Auschwitz on 30 November 1943.

Collection Jewish Historical Museum, Amsterdam, the Netherlands.

RESPONDING OPTIONS

FROM PERSONAL RESPONSE *TO* CRITICAL ANALYSIS

REFLECT 1. To which parts of Hillesum's letters did you react most strongly? Describe your reaction in your notebook, and then share your thoughts with classmates.

RETHINK 2. On the basis of these letters, what would you consider the most difficult part of Hillesum's experience at Westerbork? Explain your answer.

3. How would you describe the various feelings Hillesum expresses in her letters?
   Consider
   - her comments about helping the sick so that they can board the train
   - her thoughts about her relationship to God
   - her attitude toward her own fate

4. Why do you think the Jews laughed and sang as they left Westerbork?

5. Do you think Hillesum ever considered the possibility that her letters would become valuable to future generations? Give reasons to support your answer.

RELATE 6. In your opinion, could a tragedy like the Holocaust happen today to members of any race, religion, or culture? Why or why not?

LITERARY LINKS

On the basis of the excerpts from *Letters from Westerbork* and *Testament of Youth* (page 850), how would you compare Etty Hillesum and Vera Brittain? Do you think the two women shared any personal traits or qualities?

ANOTHER PATHWAY

Cooperative Learning

Other than a knowledge of the deplorable conditions in concentration camps, what messages or themes can one glean from Etty Hillesum's writing? Hold a group discussion in which you explore the themes of this selection. Then share your conclusions with the rest of the class.

QUICKWRITES

1. Write a **eulogy** for Etty Hillesum that might be read at a memorial service.
2. Imagine that you are one of Hillesum's close friends. Write her a **letter** in response to her letter of August 24, 1943.
3. Write a **poem** that expresses your reaction to Hillesum's letters.

PORTFOLIO *Save your writing. You may want to use it later as a springboard to a piece for your portfolio.*

LITERARY CONCEPTS

A **source** is a book, document, or person from which a researcher obtains information. A **primary source** is a book, document, or person that provides original, firsthand information about a topic. If a book is the topic, that book itself is the primary source. A primary source for an event or period of history might be a document written at the time. A person can be a primary source for events that he or she has experienced or witnessed. Etty Hillesum's letters are a primary source for information about the Holocaust. What information in the letters could come only from a primary source?

CONCEPT REVIEW: Description Hillesum creates vivid images of the scenes and people at Westerbork by making extensive use of description. How did her descriptions affect you? Find examples of descriptive passages that seem especially vivid to you.

CRITIC'S CORNER

The American critic Terrence Des Pres praised Hillesum's "literary flair" and suggested that her diaries "are written with the interior richness and woven design of a . . . novel." Might the same be said of these letters? Support your opinion with examples from the selection.

ACROSS THE CURRICULUM

History Investigate and prepare an oral report on one of the following topics related to Nazism and the Holocaust: the anti-Jewish policies leading up to the Holocaust, the conditions at Auschwitz, the Jewish resistance to Nazi policies, or the Nuremberg trials.

ALTERNATIVE ACTIVITIES

1. Create a design for a **monument** memorializing victims of the Holocaust.
2. ***Cooperative Learning*** With a small group of classmates, create a large **flow chart** showing the process by which simple prejudices can evolve into the kind of hatred that inspired the Holocaust. Present and explain your chart to the class.
3. Design a **book jacket** for *Letters from Westerbork.* Use the artistic style that you think best conveys the impact of Hillesum's experience in the camp.

WORDS TO KNOW

Review the Words to Know at the bottom of the selection pages. Then write the word that best completes each of the following sentences.

1. A four-year-old is likely to cry "That's not fair!" if someone seems to _____ snacks, toys, or privileges in an unjust manner.
2. There is something basic and human that yearns for justice, that objects to a _____ in the way people are treated.
3. It is no wonder that the first photographs of concentration-camp victims were able to _____ those who saw them, almost paralyzing the viewers with horror.
4. The atrocities committed against these victims might be seen as the acts of _____ individuals.
5. Some world events become "old news" rather quickly, but the Holocaust remains _____ today, many years after the Nazi war crimes occurred.
6. Time has passed, and the world has changed; _____, the memories of those injustices live on.
7. Simon Wiesenthal's memories kept him hunting for Nazi war criminals who had managed to _____ before they could be captured and tried.
8. The goal of the Jewish Documentation Center that he founded is not _____ so much as simple justice.
9. The group's researchers seek to _____ Nazi criminals in a web of convincing evidence against them.
10. The enormity of the _____ evil of the Nazi leaders is beyond comprehension.

ETTY HILLESUM

1914–1943

Much of what is known about Etty (Esther) Hillesum has been gleaned from the diaries she kept between 1941 and 1943. Born in Middelburg, Netherlands, where her father was a teacher, she was an avid reader who, before the war, earned a law degree at the University of Amsterdam, where she also studied psychology, philosophy, and foreign languages. Her brothers, too, appeared to have bright futures. Mischa was one of the most talented pianists in Europe, and Jaap was a doctor.

When the war broke out, Hillesum at first tried to ignore it. She concentrated instead on personal relationships, spiritual matters, and her interest in palm reading. As the Nazi threat became more real, however, she was forced to acknowledge its presence. In the summer of 1942, she began working as a typist for the Jewish Council, an organization established by the Nazis to decide which Jews would report for work assignments and which were needed at home. She found the job disgusting, and although it exempted her from being sent to Westerbork, she requested to be sent there anyway to work in the camp's hospital.

For over a year, Hillesum was allowed to make occasional trips back to Amsterdam. During these visits, her non-Jewish friends frequently offered to help her escape to a safer place, but she refused their assistance, feeling very strongly that it was her duty to share the destiny of her fellow Jews, whatever it might be. In June 1943 her traveling privileges were revoked, and in September she was sent to Auschwitz, where she was put to death in a gas chamber. Another Westerbork inmate later described Hillesum, preparing to board the train on that fateful day, as "talking gaily, smiling, a kind word for everyone she met on the way, full of sparkling humor, perhaps just a touch of sadness, but every inch the Etty you all know so well."

OTHER WORKS *An Interrupted Life: The Diaries of Etty Hillesum, 1941–1943*

NONFICTION

Words and Behavior

Aldous Huxley

PERSONAL CONNECTION

Suppose that you accidentally backed the family car into a tree, causing serious damage to the vehicle. How would you break the news to your parents? Would you describe the damage accurately and completely, or would you try to conceal or gloss over the facts? Share your thoughts with classmates.

BIOGRAPHICAL/HISTORICAL CONNECTION

Throughout his life, the English novelist Aldous Huxley was concerned with social and political issues. His earliest novels satirize the vanity and foolishness of English society, and his later works reflect his skepticism about the direction in which the world was headed. Today, Huxley is best known for his novel *Brave New World,* a satiric portrayal of society. Published in 1932, *Brave New World* was viewed as a warning of how dismal the world could become as a result of technology and political manipulation.

In the late 1930s, Huxley became alarmed at the turmoil that seemed to be leading up to a second world war. During the 20th century, most governments at war, or about to enter into a war, have naturally been concerned about the manner in which their activities are reported to the general public. Often, they have formed special bureaus to control the type and amount of information released to the public. The information that has been released has usually been presented in carefully worded language designed to evoke feelings of patriotism and to diminish antiwar sentiment. A few years before the start of World War II, Huxley wrote the essay "Words and Behavior," in which he reflects upon the nature of wartime communication.

WRITING CONNECTION

Think about words and phrases that people use to gloss over facts or to make references to unpleasant or controversial subjects less offensive. In your notebook, list any words or phrases that come to mind, and note what they actually refer to. Then, as you read this essay, compare the examples in your list with those mentioned by Huxley.

Using Your Reading Log Use your reading log to record your responses to the questions inserted at various places in the selection. Also jot down other thoughts and feelings that come to you as you read.

• *HISTORICAL CONNECTION*

Words and Behavior

ALDOUS HUXLEY

Words form the thread on which we string our experiences. Without them we should live spasmodically and intermittently. Hatred itself is not so strong that animals will not forget it, if distracted, even in the presence of the enemy. Watch a pair of cats, crouching on the brink of a fight. Balefully the eyes glare; from far down in the throat of each come bursts of a strange, strangled noise of defiance; as though animated by a life of their own, the tails twitch and tremble. With aimed intensity of loathing! Another moment and surely there must be an explosion. But no; all of a sudden one of the two creatures turns away, hoists a hind leg in a more than fascist salute[1] and, with the same fixed and focused attention as it had given a moment before to its enemy, begins to make a lingual toilet.[2] Animal love is as much at the mercy of distractions as animal hatred. The dumb creation lives a life made up of discrete[3] and mutually irrelevant episodes. Such as it is, the consistency of human characters is due to the words upon which all human experiences are strung. We are purposeful because we can describe our feelings in rememberable words, can justify and rationalize our desires in terms of some kind of argument. Faced by an enemy we do not allow an itch to distract us from our emotions; the mere word "enemy" is enough to keep us reminded of our hatred, to convince us that we do well to be angry. Similarly the word "love" bridges for us those chasms of momentary indifference and boredom which gape from time to time between even the most ardent lovers. Feeling and desire provide us with our motive power; words give continuity to what we do and to a considerable extent determine our direction. Inappropriate and badly chosen words vitiate thought and lead to wrong or foolish conduct. Most ignorances are vincible,[4] and in the greater number of cases stupidity is what the Buddha pronounced it to be, a sin. For, consciously, or subconsciously, it is with deliberation that we do not know or fail to understand—because incomprehension allows us, with a good conscience, to evade unpleasant obligations and responsibilities, because ignorance is the best excuse for going on doing what one likes, but ought not, to do. Our egotisms are incessantly fighting to preserve themselves, not only from external enemies, but also from the assaults of the other and better self with which they are so uncomfortably associated. Ignorance is egotism's most effective defense against that Dr. Jekyll[5] in us who desires perfection; stupidity, its subtlest stratagem. If, as so often happens, we choose to give continuity to our experience by means of words which falsify the facts, this is because the falsification is somehow to our advantage as egotists.

CLARIFY

According to Huxley, how do people use ignorance as a defense?

Consider, for example, the case of war. War is enormously discreditable to those who order it to be waged and even to those who merely tolerate its existence. Furthermore, to developed sensibilities the facts of war are revolting and horrifying. To falsify these facts, and by so doing to make war seem less evil than it really is, and our own responsibility in tolerating war less heavy, is doubly to our advantage. By suppressing and distorting the truth, we protect our sensibilities and preserve our self-esteem. Now, language is, among other things, a device which men use for suppressing and distorting the truth. Finding the

1. **fascist** (făsh'ĭst) **salute:** a salute, used in Nazi Germany, in which the arm is rigidly extended forward, slightly above the horizontal.
2. **make a lingual toilet:** clean itself with its tongue.
3. **discrete:** separate; distinct.
4. **vincible** (vĭn'sə-bəl): capable of being overcome.
5. **Dr. Jekyll:** in Robert Louis Stevenson's novel *The Strange Case of Dr. Jekyll and Mr. Hyde,* an idealistic medical researcher who is transformed by an experimental drug into the murderously evil Mr. Hyde.

WORDS TO KNOW

balefully (bāl'fə-lē) *adv.* in a menacing way; wickedly
ardent (är'dnt) *adj.* passionate
vitiate (vĭsh'ē-āt') *v.* to destroy the quality of; corrupt; debase

reality of war too unpleasant to contemplate, we create a verbal alternative to that reality, parallel with it, but in quality quite different from it. That which we contemplate thenceforward is not that to which we react emotionally and upon which we pass our moral judgments, is not war as it is in fact, but the fiction of war as it exists in our pleasantly falsifying verbiage. Our stupidity in using inappropriate language turns out, on analysis, to be the most refined cunning.

The most shocking fact about war is that its victims and its instruments are individual human beings, and that these individual human beings are condemned by the monstrous conventions of politics to murder or be murdered in quarrels not their own, to inflict upon the innocent and, innocent themselves of any crime against their enemies, to suffer cruelties of every kind.

The language of strategy and politics is designed, so far as it is possible, to conceal this fact, to make it appear as though wars were not fought by individuals drilled to murder one another in cold blood and without provocation, but either by impersonal and therefore wholly non-moral and impassible forces, or else by personified abstractions.

Here are a few examples of the first kind of falsification. In place of "cavalrymen" or "foot soldiers" military writers like to speak of "sabers" and "rifles." Here is a sentence from a description of the Battle of Marengo:[6] "According to Victor's report, the French retreat was orderly; it is certain, at any rate, that the regiments held together, for the six thousand Austrian sabers found no opportunity to charge home." The battle is between sabers in line and muskets in échelon[7]—a mere clash of ironmongery.[8]

On other occasions there is no question of anything so vulgarly material as ironmongery. The battles are between Platonic ideas,[9] between the abstractions of physics and mathematics. Forces interact; weights are flung into scales; masses are set in motion. Or else it is all a matter of geometry. Lines swing and sweep; are protracted or curved; pivot on a fixed point.

Alternatively the combatants are personal, in the sense that they are personifications. There is "the enemy," in the singular, making "his" plans, striking "his" blows. The attribution of personal characteristics to collectivities,[10] to geographical expressions, to institutions, is a source, as we shall see, of endless confusions in political thought, of innumerable political mistakes and crimes. Personification in politics is an error which we make because it is to our advantage as egotists to be able to feel violently proud of our country and of ourselves as belonging to it, and to believe that all the misfortunes due to our own mistakes are really the work of the Foreigner. It is easier to feel violently toward a person than toward an abstraction; hence our habit of making political personifications. In some cases military personifications are merely special instances of political personifications. A particular collectivity, the army or the warring nation, is given the name and, along with the name, the attributes of a single person, in order that we may be able to love or hate it more intensely than we could do if we thought of it as what it really is: a number of diverse individuals. In other cases personification is used for the purpose of concealing the

---

6. **Battle of Marengo:** a battle fought in 1800, in which French troops led by Napoleon Bonaparte defeated an Austrian army near the town of Marengo in northern Italy.

7. **échelon** (ĕsh′ə-lŏn′): an arrangement of groups of soldiers in a steplike formation.

8. **ironmongery** (ī′ərn-mŭng′gə-rē): hardware.

9. **Platonic ideas:** in the thought of Plato (a Greek philosopher of the fourth century B.C.), immaterial realities that all actual things are copies of.

10. **collectivities:** groups of people.

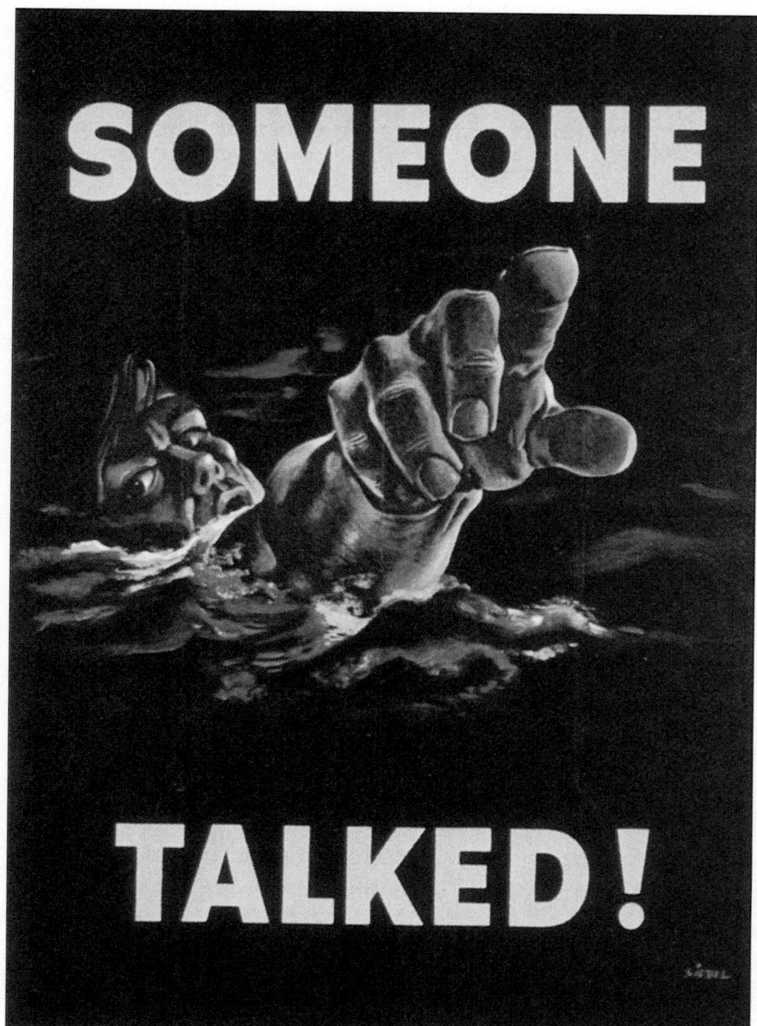

Official Photograph, United States Air Force, courtesy of Sam. R. Quincey.

fundamental absurdity and monstrosity of war. What is absurd and monstrous about war is that men who have no personal quarrel should be trained to murder one another in cold blood. By personifying opposing armies or countries, we are able to think of war as a conflict between individuals. The same result is obtained by writing of war as though it were carried on exclusively by the generals in command and not by the private soldiers in their armies. ("Rennenkampf had pressed back von Schubert.") The implication in both cases is that war is indistinguishable from a bout of fisticuffs[11] in a bar room. Whereas in reality it is profoundly different. A scrap between two individuals is forgivable; mass murder, deliberately organized, is a monstrous iniquity. We still choose to use war as an instrument of policy; and to comprehend the full wickedness and absurdity of war would therefore be inconvenient. For, once we understood, we should have to make some effort to get rid of the abominable thing. Accordingly, when we talk about war, we use a language which conceals or embellishes its reality. Ignoring the facts, so far as we possibly can, we imply that battles are not fought by soldiers, but by things, principles, allegories, personified collectivities, or (at the most human) by opposing commanders, pitched against one another in single combat. For the same reason, when we have to describe the processes and the results of war, we employ a rich variety of euphemisms. Even the most violently patriotic and militaristic are reluctant to call a spade by its own name. To conceal their intentions even from themselves, they make use of picturesque metaphors. We find them, for example, clamoring for war planes numerous and powerful enough to go and "destroy the hornets in their nests"—in other words, to go and throw

11. **fisticuffs** (fĭs′tĭ-kŭfs′): fighting with the fists.

WORDS TO KNOW

iniquity (ĭ-nĭk′wĭ-tē) *n.* immorality; wickedness
embellish (ĕm-bĕl′ĭsh) *v.* to add ornamental or fictitious details to; decorate
euphemism (yo͞o′fə-mĭz′əm) *n.* a mild or vague term used in place of a blunt or offensive one

thermite,[12] high explosives and vesicants[13] upon the inhabitants of neighboring countries before they have time to come and do the same to us. And how reassuring is the language of historians and strategists! They write admiringly of those military geniuses who know "when to strike at the enemy's line" (a single combatant deranges the geometrical constructions of a personification); when to "turn his flank"; when to "execute an enveloping movement." As though they were engineers discussing the strength of materials and the distribution of stresses, they talk of abstract entities called "man power" and "fire power." They sum up the long-drawn sufferings and atrocities of trench warfare in the phrase, "a war of attrition";[14] the massacre and mangling of human beings is assimilated to the grinding of a lens.[15]

CLARIFY

How can words conceal the reality of war?

A dangerously abstract word, which figures in all discussions about war, is "force." Those who believe in organizing collective security by means of military pacts against a possible aggressor are particularly fond of this word. "You cannot," they say, "have international justice unless you are prepared to impose it by force." "Peace-loving countries must unite to use force against aggressive dictatorships." "Democratic institutions must be protected, if need be, by force." And so on.

Now, the word "force," when used in reference to human relations, has no single, definite meaning. There is the "force" used by parents when, without resort to any kind of physical violence, they compel their children to act or refrain from acting in some particular way. There is the "force" used by attendants in an asylum when they try to prevent a maniac from hurting himself or others. There is the "force" used by the police when they control a crowd, and that other "force" which they use in a baton charge.[16] And finally there is the "force" used in war. This, of course, varies with the technological devices at the disposal of the belligerents, with the policies they are pursuing, and with the particular circumstances of the war in question. But in general it may be said that, in war, "force" connotes violence and fraud used to the limit of the combatants' capacity. Variations in quantity, if sufficiently great, produce variations in quality. The "force" that is war, particularly modern war, is very different from the "force" that is police action, and the use of the same abstract word to describe the two dissimilar processes is profoundly misleading. (Still more misleading, of course, is the explicit assimilation of a war, waged by allied League-of-Nations powers against an aggressor, to police action against a criminal. The first is the use of violence and fraud without limit against innocent and guilty alike; the second is the use of strictly limited violence and a minimum of fraud exclusively against the guilty.)

Reality is a succession of concrete and particular situations. When we think about such situations we should use the particular and concrete words which apply to them. If we use abstract words which apply equally well (and equally badly) to other, quite dissimilar situations, it is certain that we shall think incorrectly.

Let us take the sentences quoted above and translate the abstract word "force" into language that will render (however inadequately) the con-

12. **thermite:** a mixture of chemicals that burns very intensely, used in certain kinds of bombs.
13. **vesicants** (vĕs'ĭ-kənts): chemical agents, such as mustard gas, that cause inflammation and blistering of the skin and internal tissues.
14. **attrition:** a gradual process of wearing down.
15. **assimilated . . . lens:** likened to the process by which glass is ground into lenses.
16. **baton charge:** the beating back of a mob by policemen wielding wooden clubs.

crete and particular realities of contemporary warfare.

"You cannot have international justice, unless you are prepared to impose it by force." Translated, this becomes: "You cannot have international justice unless you are prepared, with a view to imposing a just settlement, to drop thermite, high explosives and vesicants upon the inhabitants of foreign cities and to have thermite, high explosives and vesicants dropped in return upon the inhabitants of your cities." At the end of this proceeding, justice is to be imposed by the victorious party—that is, if there is a victorious party. It should be remarked that justice was to have been imposed by the victorious party at the end of the last war. But, unfortunately, after four years of fighting, the temper of the victors was such that they were quite incapable of making a just settlement. The Allies are reaping in Nazi Germany what they sowed at Versailles.[17] The victors of the next war will have undergone intensive bombardments with thermite, high explosives and vesicants. Will their temper be better than that of the Allies in 1918? Will they be in a fitter state to make a just settlement? The answer, quite obviously, is: No. It is psychologically all but impossible that justice should be secured by the methods of contemporary warfare.

He's Watching You (1942), Glenn Grohe. American World War II poster, The Granger Collection, New York.

The next two sentences may be taken together. "Peace-loving countries must unite to use force against aggressive dictatorships. Democratic institutions must be protected, if need be, by force." Let us translate. "Peace-loving countries must unite to throw thermite, high explosives and vesicants on the inhabitants of countries ruled by aggressive dictators. They must do this, and of course abide the consequences, in order to preserve peace and democratic institutions." Two questions immediately propound[18] themselves. First, is it likely that peace can be secured by a process calculated to reduce the orderly life of our complicated societies to chaos? And, second, is it likely that democratic institutions will flourish in a state of chaos? Again, the answers are pretty clearly in the negative.

By using the abstract word "force," instead of terms which at least attempt to describe the realities of war as it is today, the preachers of collective security through military collaboration disguise from themselves and from others, not only the contemporary facts, but also the probable consequences of their favorite policy. The attempt to secure justice, peace and democracy by "force" seems reasonable enough until we realize, first, that this noncommittal word stands, in the circumstances of our age, for activities which can hardly fail to result in social chaos; and second, that the consequences of social chaos are injustice,

17. **The Allies . . . Versailles** (vər-sī′): The peace treaty ending World War I—signed at the Palace of Versailles, near Paris, in 1919—imposed humiliating punishments on Germany, which led to the rise of German nationalism and Nazism in the 1920s and 1930s.

18. **propound:** to put forward for consideration; pose.

chronic warfare and tyranny. The moment we think in concrete and particular terms of the concrete and particular process called "modern war," we see that a policy which worked (or at least didn't result in complete disaster) in the past has no prospect whatever of working in the immediate future. The attempt to secure justice, peace and democracy by means of a "force," which means, at this particular moment of history, thermite, high explosives and vesicants, is about as reasonable as the attempt to put out a fire with a colorless liquid that happens to be, not water, but petrol.

What applies to the "force" that is war applies in large measure to the "force" that is revolution. It seems inherently very unlikely that social justice and social peace can be secured by thermite, high explosives and vesicants. At first, it may be, the parties in a civil war would hesitate to use such instruments on their fellow-countrymen. But there can be little doubt that, if the conflict were prolonged (as it probably would be between the evenly balanced Right and Left of a highly industrialized society), the combatants would end by losing their scruples.

The alternatives confronting us seem to be plain enough. Either we invent and conscientiously employ a new technique for making revolutions and settling international disputes; or else we cling to the old technique and, using "force" (that is to say, thermite, high explosives and vesicants), destroy ourselves. Those who, for whatever motive, disguise the nature of the second alternative under inappropriate language, render the world a grave disservice. They lead us into one of the temptations we find it hardest to resist—the temptation to run away from reality, to pretend that facts are not what they are. Like Shelley (but without Shelley's acute awareness of what he was doing) we are perpetually weaving

A shroud of talk to hide us from the sun
Of this familiar life.

We protect our minds by an elaborate system of abstractions, ambiguities, metaphors and similes from the reality we do not wish to know too clearly; we lie to ourselves, in order that we may still have the excuse of ignorance, the alibi of stupidity and incomprehension, possessing which we can continue with a good conscience to commit and tolerate the most monstrous crimes:

The poor wretch who has learned his only prayers
From curses, who knows scarcely words enough
To ask a blessing from his Heavenly Father,
Becomes a fluent phraseman, absolute
And technical in victories and defeats,
And all our dainty terms for fratricide;[19]
Terms which we trundle smoothly o'er our tongues
Like mere abstractions, empty sounds to which
We join no meaning and attach no form!
As if the soldier died without a wound:
As if the fibers of this godlike frame
Were gored without a pang: as if the wretch
Who fell in battle, doing bloody deeds,
Passed off to Heaven translated and not killed;
As though he had no wife to pine for him,
No God to judge him.

The language we use about war is inappropriate, and its inappropriateness is designed to conceal a reality so odious that we do not wish to know it. The language we use about politics is also inap-

19. **fratricide** (frăt′rĭ-sīd′): the killing of one's brother or sister.

WORDS TO KNOW

inherently (ĭn-hîr′ənt-lē) *adv.* essentially; naturally
odious (ō′dē-əs) *adj.* disgusting; hateful

propriate; but here our mistake has a different purpose. Our principal aim in this case is to arouse and, having aroused, to rationalize and justify such intrinsically[20] agreeable sentiments as pride and hatred, self-esteem and contempt for others. To achieve this end we speak about the facts of politics in words which more or less completely misrepresent them. . . .

The evil passions are further justified by another linguistic error—the error of speaking about certain categories of persons as though they were mere embodied abstractions. Foreigners and those who disagree with us are not thought of as men and women like ourselves and our fellow-countrymen; they are thought of as representatives and, so to say, symbols of a class. In so far as they have any personality at all, it is the personality we mistakenly attribute to their class—a personality that is, by definition, intrinsically evil. We know that the harming or killing of men and women is wrong, and we are reluctant consciously to do what we know to be wrong. But when particular men and women are thought of merely as representatives of a class, which has previously been defined as evil and personified in the shape of a devil, then the reluctance to hurt or murder disappears. Brown, Jones and Robinson are no longer thought of as Brown, Jones and Robinson, but as heretics, gentiles, Yids, niggers, barbarians, Huns, communists, capitalists, fascists, liberals[21]—whichever the case may be. When they have been called such names and assimilated to the accursed class to which the names apply, Brown, Jones and Robinson cease to be conceived as what they really are—human persons—and become for the users of this fatally inappropriate language mere vermin or, worse, demons whom it is right and proper to destroy as thoroughly and as painfully as possible. Wherever persons are present, questions of morality arise. Rulers of nations and leaders of parties find morality embarrassing. That is why they take such pains to depersonalize their opponents. All propaganda directed against an opposing group has but one aim: to substitute diabolical abstractions for concrete persons. The propagandist's purpose is to make one set of people forget that certain other sets of

ugh Darkness to Light
THE ONLY ROAD FOR AN ENGLISHMAN
Through Fighting to Triumph

The Only Road for an Englishman (1914), Gerald Spencer Pryse. Imperial War Museum, London.

20. **intrinsically** (ĭn-trĭn′zĭk-lē): inherently; essentially.

21. **heretics . . . liberals:** terms used to disparage groups of people. (*Yid* is an offensive term for a Jew, and *Huns* was what some British people called the Germans during World War I.)

WORDS TO KNOW **diabolical** (dī′ə-bŏl′ĭ-kəl) *adj.* extremely wicked or cruel; devilish

people are human. By robbing them of their personality, he puts them outside the pale of moral obligation. Mere symbols can have no rights—particularly when that of which they are symbolical is, by definition, evil.

CLARIFY

According to the author, why do rulers "depersonalize their opponents"?

Politics can become moral only on one condition: that its problems shall be spoken of and thought about exclusively in terms of concrete reality; that is to say, of persons. To depersonify human beings and to personify abstractions are complementary errors which lead, by an inexorable logic, to war between nations and to idolatrous worship of the State, with consequent governmental oppression. All current political thought is a mixture, in varying proportions, between thought in terms of concrete realities and thought in terms of depersonified symbols and personified abstractions. In the democratic countries the problems of internal politics are thought about mainly in terms of concrete reality; those of external politics, mainly in terms of abstractions and symbols. In dictatorial countries the proportion of concrete to abstract and symbolic thought is lower than in democratic countries. Dictators talk little of persons, much of personified abstractions, such as the Nation, the State, the Party, and much of depersonified symbols, such as Yids, Bolshies,[22] Capitalists. The stupidity of politicians who talk about a world of persons as though it were not a world of persons is due in the main to self-interest. In a fictitious world of symbols and personified abstractions, rulers find that they can rule more effectively, and the ruled, that they can gratify instincts which the conventions of good manners and the imperatives of morality demand that they should repress. To think correctly is the condition of behaving well. It is also in itself a moral act; those who would think correctly must resist considerable temptations. ❖

Enjoy Your War Work (1941), unknown artist. London Transport Museum.

22. **Bolshies:** Communists (after *Bolshevik,* the name of the Russian Communist faction that came to power in the 1917 revolution).

WORDS TO KNOW **inexorable** (ĭn-ĕk'sər-ə-bəl) *adj.* unyielding; relentless

RESPONDING OPTIONS

FROM PERSONAL RESPONSE *TO* CRITICAL ANALYSIS

REFLECT **1.** What is your overall reaction to Huxley's ideas in this essay? Summarize your thoughts in your notebook.

RETHINK **2.** Adopting the role of Aldous Huxley, explain what you hoped to achieve by writing this essay.

3. What general concerns does Huxley seem to have about the power of words?

Consider

- his statement that "words give continuity to what we do" (page 885)
- the examples of euphemisms and abstractions that he gives
- his opinion that most people have trouble resisting "the temptation to run away from reality" (page 890)

4. If Huxley were asked to describe the worst effect of using euphemisms to gloss over the facts of war, what do you think he would say?

5. Do you think Huxley's arguments are objective and convincing? Explain your answer.

RELATE **6.** If people always spoke as directly as possible and never used euphemisms or abstractions to gloss over facts, what do you think would be the results? Be specific in your answer.

ANOTHER PATHWAY

Look through Huxley's essay for sentences that you think are especially powerful or persuasive. Jot down your choices. Then share them with the whole class and discuss what makes certain sentences in the essay more appealing or persuasive than others.

QUICKWRITES

1. Review the list of euphemistic words and phrases that you made for the Writing Connection on page 883. Choose two or three and write a brief **analysis** of each, in which you explain why you think the euphemism is used and what would be the effect of replacing it with more direct language.

2. Design and write a **job application** in which you use euphemisms to gloss over your faults or to make yourself seem more experienced than you are.

3. Imagine that you are the leader of a country about to go to war. Write a **speech** in which you report your plans to the public in a way that might satisfy Aldous Huxley.

PORTFOLIO *Save your writing. You may want to use it later as a springboard to a piece for your portfolio.*

LITERARY CONCEPTS

One important element of any writer's style is **diction,** or choice of words. Diction includes both vocabulary (individual words) and syntax (the order or arrangement of words). A writer's diction may be described as formal or informal, as technical or ordinary, as abstract or concrete. Most of the diction in Huxley's essay is rather formal, as in the sentence beginning "Most ignorances are vincible . . ." (page 885). Rewrite this sentence in informal language. Then find two other examples of formal diction in the essay and rewrite them as well.

ALTERNATIVE ACTIVITIES

1. Draw a **political cartoon** dealing with one of the euphemisms or examples of inappropriate language mentioned in the essay.
2. With a partner, conduct a **debate** in which the two of you argue for and against the use of euphemisms and abstract language during wartime. Be sure to support your position with sufficient facts and reasons.

LITERARY LINKS

How do you think Huxley might have reacted to Winston Churchill's speech of May 19, 1940 (page 864)? Cite specific passages in your answer.

THE WRITER'S STYLE

In various sections of this essay, Huxley repeats particular words and phrases. Find two examples of such **repetition.** Why do you think Huxley uses this technique? Be specific in your answer.

WORDS TO KNOW

For each phrase in the first column, write the letter of the synonymous phrase in the second column.

1. **odious** poultry
2. **ardent** protection
3. a fiendish romp
4. **vitiate** the efforts
5. destined to **embellish**
6. direct **balefully**
7. sayin' "powder room"
8. **inherently** harmonious
9. an unrelenting power
10. an evil from ancient days

a. spoil the toil
b. naturally matchable
c. an **iniquity** from antiquity
d. born to adorn
e. usin' a **euphemism**
f. sickening chicken
g. intense defense
h. administer sinisterly
i. a **diabolical** frolic
j. an **inexorable** force

ALDOUS HUXLEY

1894–1963

Aldous Huxley was born in Surrey, England, into a family of gifted intellectuals, including scientists, educators, and writers. As a student at Eton College, a prestigious English prep school, he was pursuing studies in science when he contracted keratitis, an eye disease that resulted in near-blindness. Although he had to abandon any hope of a career in science or medicine, he learned Braille in order to continue his education. He studied English literature at Oxford University, where his sight improved, and he was awarded an honors degree in 1916. During the same year, he published his first book, a collection of poetry.

After working briefly as a teacher and as a journalist for a literary magazine, Huxley concentrated on his own writing, moving away from poetry to fiction and essays. The witty skepticism of his first two novels, published in the 1920s, established his reputation as a novelist and also brought him a certain popularity as a rebel. During the 1930s, Huxley's writing focused on political and cultural trends that he felt to be alarming.

Huxley and his wife, Maria, had been traveling extensively since the mid-1920s, and in 1937 they settled in California, where both the climate and new medical treatments improved Huxley's vision. His later work, which reflected his wide range of interests and skills, included film scripts and explorations of mysticism and parapsychology. Huxley endured a painful battle with cancer at the end of his life, but he continued to write, relentless in his attention to the problems facing contemporary society.

OTHER WORKS *Crome Yellow, Point Counter Point, Brave New World Revisited, Island*

PREVIEWING

FICTION

The Demon Lover

Elizabeth Bowen

PERSONAL CONNECTION

Most people are intrigued by unexplained events—mysterious occurrences or strange coincidences that seem outside the limits of ordinary life. Jot down descriptions of any events of this sort that you have read about, heard about, or experienced yourself. Discuss these events with your classmates.

HISTORICAL CONNECTION

During World War II, German aircraft bombed British cities for more than four years. From September 1940 to May 1941, Germany hit London with a series of nightly air attacks—known as the Blitz—designed to force Britain to surrender. Londoners sought safety in subway tunnels and air-raid shelters during the bombings. Those who could afford to do so left the city and moved to the countryside.

Mrs. Drover, the main character in this story, lived with her family in the wealthy Kensington district of London before moving to the country to escape the Blitz. As the story begins, she is returning to her Kensington home to reclaim some valued personal belongings. The story includes a brief flashback to World War I, when Mrs. Drover became engaged to a young soldier.

Children leaving London during war.

READING CONNECTION

Understanding Flashbacks A **flashback** is an account of a conversation, an episode, or an event that happened before the main sequence of events in a story. Most flashbacks share some or all of the following characteristics:

- They interrupt the chronological flow of events to give readers information needed for an understanding of characters' present situations.
- They reveal significant thoughts, experiences, or events in characters' lives.
- They take the form of reminiscences, dream sequences, or descriptions by third-person narrators.
- They contain foreshadowing or other clues to stories' outcomes.

As you read "The Demon Lover," look for evidence of these characteristics in Bowen's use of flashback. In a chart like the one shown, identify important details presented in flashback and the characteristics shown by each. Then note how you think each detail might relate to the unexplained events in the story.

Flashback Detail	Characteristics	Relation to Unexplained Events

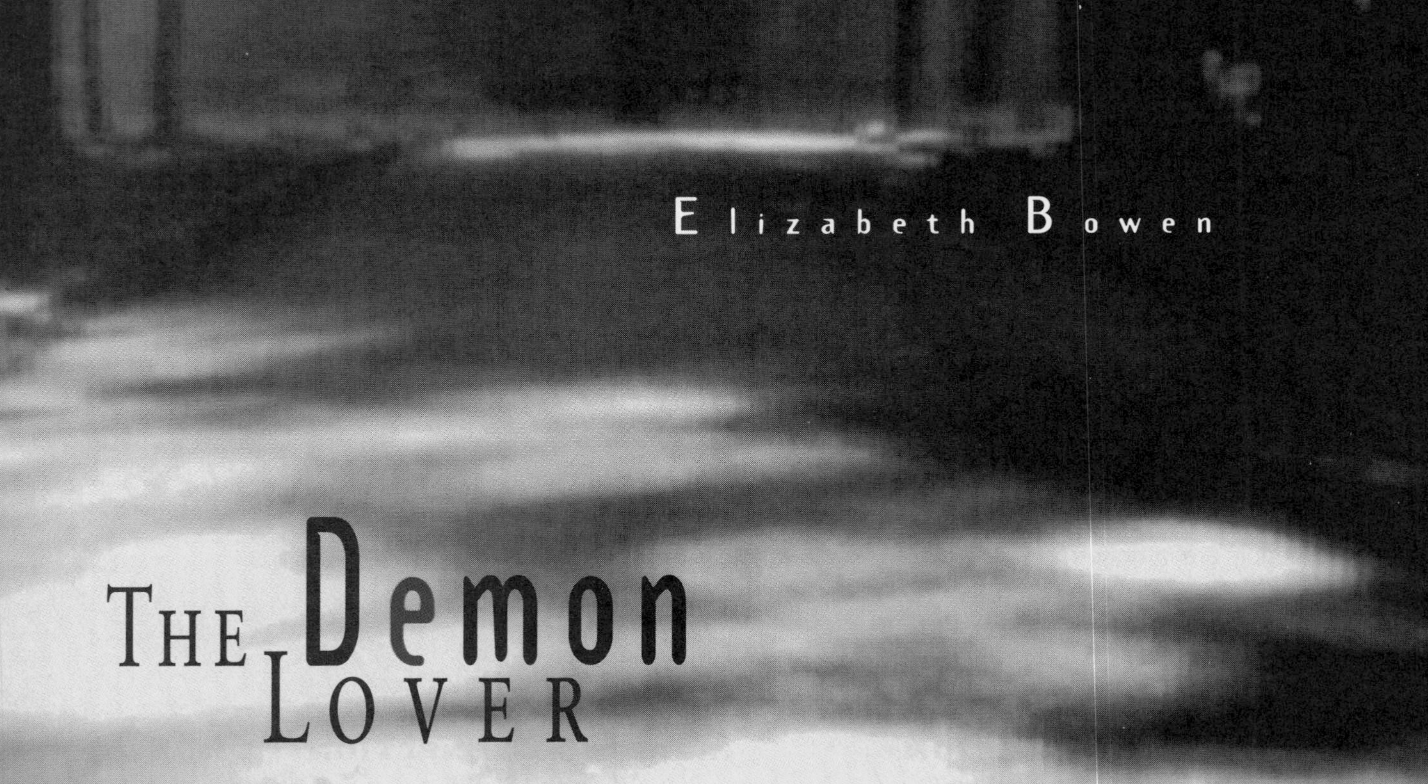

THE Demon LOVER

Elizabeth Bowen

Towards the end of her day in London Mrs. Drover went round to her shut-up house to look for several things she wanted to take away. Some belonged to herself, some to her family, who were by now used to their country life. It was late August; it had been a steamy, showery day: at the moment the trees down the pavement glittered in an escape of humid yellow afternoon sun. Against the next batch of clouds, already piling up ink-dark, broken chimneys and parapets stood out. In her once familiar street, as in any unused channel, an unfamiliar queerness had silted up;[1] a cat wove itself in and out of railings, but no human eye watched Mrs. Drover's return. Shifting some parcels under her arm, she slowly forced round her latchkey in an unwilling lock, then gave the door, which had warped, a push with her knee. Dead air came out to meet her as she went in.

The staircase window having been boarded up, no light came down into the hall. But one door, she could just see, stood ajar, so she went quickly through into the room and unshuttered the big window in there. Now the prosaic woman, looking about her, was more perplexed than she knew by everything that she saw, by traces of her long former habit of life—the yellow smoke stain up the white marble mantelpiece, the ring left by a vase on the top of the escritoire;[2] the bruise in the wallpaper where, on the door being thrown open widely, the china handle had always hit the wall. The piano, having gone away to be stored, had left what looked like claw marks on its part of the parquet.[3] Though not much dust had seeped in, each object wore a film of another kind; and, the only

1. **silted up:** piled up, like sediment deposited in a river channel.
2. **escritoire** (ĕs′krĭ-twär′): a writing desk or table.
3. **parquet** (pär-kā′): a wood floor made of small blocks laid in a geometric pattern.

WORDS TO KNOW **prosaic** (prō-zā′ĭk) *adj.* commonplace; ordinary; dull

ventilation being the chimney, the whole drawing room smelled of the cold hearth. Mrs. Drover put down her parcels on the escritoire and left the room to proceed upstairs; the things she wanted were in a bedroom chest.

She had been anxious to see how the house was—the part-time caretaker she shared with some neighbors was away this week on his holiday, known to be not yet back. At the best of times he did not look in often, and she was never sure that she trusted him. There were some cracks in the structure, left by the last bombing, on which she was anxious to keep an eye. Not that one could do anything—

A shaft of refracted daylight now lay across the hall. She stopped dead and stared at the hall table—on this lay a letter addressed to her.

She thought first—then the caretaker *must* be back. All the same, who, seeing the house shuttered, would have dropped a letter in at the box? It was not a circular, it was not a bill. And the post office redirected, to the address in the country, everything for her that came through the post. The caretaker (even if he *were* back) did not know she was due in London today—her call here had been planned to be a surprise—so his negligence in the manner of this letter, leaving it to wait in the dusk and the dust, annoyed her. Annoyed, she picked up the letter, which bore no stamp. But it cannot be important, or they would know . . . She took the letter rapidly upstairs with her, without a stop to look at the writing till she reached what had been her bedroom, where she let in light. The room looked over the garden and other gardens: the sun had gone in; as the clouds sharpened and lowered, the trees and rank lawns seemed already to smoke with dark. Her reluctance to look again at the letter came from the fact that she felt intruded upon—and by someone contemptuous of her ways. However, in the tenseness preceding the fall of rain she read it: it was a few lines.

Dear Kathleen: You will not have forgotten that today is our anniversary, and the day we said. The years have gone by at once slowly and fast. In view of the fact that nothing has changed, I shall rely upon you to keep your promise. I was sorry to see you leave London, but was satisfied that you would be back in time. You may expect me, therefore, at the hour arranged. Until then . . . K.

Mrs. Drover looked for the date: it was today's. She dropped the letter onto the bedsprings, then picked it up to see the writing again—her lips, beneath the remains of lipstick, beginning to go white. She felt so much the change in her own face that she went to the mirror, polished a clear patch in it and looked at once urgently and stealthily in. She was confronted by a woman of forty-four, with eyes starting out under a hat brim that had been rather carelessly pulled down. She had not put on any more powder since she left the shop where she ate her solitary tea. The pearls her husband had given her on their marriage hung loose round her now rather thinner throat, slipping in the V of the pink wool jumper her sister knitted last autumn as they sat round the fire. Mrs. Drover's most normal expression was one of controlled worry, but of assent. Since the birth of the third of her little boys, attended by a quite serious illness, she had had an intermittent muscular flicker to the left of her mouth, but in spite of this she could always sustain a manner that was at once energetic and calm.

Turning from her own face as precipitately as she had gone to meet it, she went to the chest where the things were, unlocked it, threw up the lid and knelt to search. But as rain began to come crashing down she could not keep from looking over her shoulder at the stripped bed on which the letter lay. Behind the blanket of rain the clock of the church that still stood struck six—with rapidly heightening apprehension she counted each of the slow strokes. "The hour

WORDS TO KNOW

assent (ə-sĕnt′) *n.* agreement; acceptance
precipitately (prĭ-sĭp′ĭ-tĭt-lē) *adv.* hurriedly; suddenly

arranged . . . My God," she said, "*what* hour? How should I . . . ? After twenty-five years . . ."

The young girl talking to the soldier in the garden had not ever completely seen his face. It was dark; they were saying goodbye under a tree. Now and then—for it felt, from not seeing him at this intense moment, as though she had never seen him at all—she verified his presence for these few moments longer by putting out a hand, which he each time pressed, without very much kindness, and painfully, onto one of the breast buttons of his uniform. That cut of the button on the palm of her hand was, principally, what she was to carry away. This was so near the end of a leave from France that she could only wish him already gone. It was August 1916. Being not kissed, being drawn away from and looked at, intimidated Kathleen till she imagined spectral[4] glitters in the place of his eyes. Turning away and looking back up the lawn she saw, through branches of trees, the drawing-room window alight: she caught a breath for the moment when she could go running back there into the safe arms of her mother and sister, and cry: "What shall I do, what shall I do? He has gone."

Hearing her catch her breath, her fiancé said, without feeling: "Cold?"

"You're going away such a long way."

"Not so far as you think."

"I don't understand?"

"You don't have to," he said. "You will. You know what we said."

"But that was—suppose you—I mean, suppose."

"I shall be with you," he said, "sooner or later. You won't forget that. You need do nothing but wait."

Only a little more than a minute later she was free to run up the silent lawn. Looking in through the window at her mother and sister, who did not for the moment perceive her, she already felt that unnatural promise drive down between her and the rest of all humankind. No other way of having given herself could have made her feel so apart, lost and foresworn.[5] She could not have plighted a more sinister troth.[6]

Kathleen behaved well when, some months later, her fiancé was reported missing, presumed killed. Her family not only supported her but were able to praise her courage without stint[7] because they could not regret, as a husband for her, the man they knew almost nothing about. They hoped she would, in a year or two, console herself—and had it been only a question of consolation things might have gone much straighter ahead. But her trouble, behind just a little grief, was a complete dislocation from everything. She did not reject other lovers, for these failed to appear: for years she failed to attract men—and with the approach of her thirties she became natural enough to share her family's anxiousness on this score. She began to put herself out, to wonder; and at thirty-two she was very greatly relieved to find herself being courted by William Drover. She married him, and the two of them settled down in this quiet, arboreal[8] part of Kensington:[9] in this house the years piled up, her children were born and they all lived till they were driven out by the bombs of the next war. Her movements as Mrs. Drover were circumscribed,[10] and she dismissed any idea that they were still watched.

As things were—dead or living the letter-writer sent her only a threat. Unable, for some minutes, to go on kneeling with her back exposed to the empty room, Mrs. Drover rose from the chest to sit on an upright chair whose back was firmly against the wall. The desuetude[11] of her former bedroom, her married London home's whole air

---

4. **spectral:** ghostly; phantomlike.
5. **foresworn:** guilty of perjury.
6. **plighted . . . troth:** made a more ominous promise of marriage.
7. **stint:** limitation or restriction.
8. **arboreal** (är-bôr′ē-əl): tree-filled.
9. **Kensington:** a residential section of London.
10. **circumscribed:** restricted; confined.
11. **desuetude** (dĕs′wĭ-to͞od′): disuse.

of being a cracked cup from which memory, with its reassuring power, had either evaporated or leaked away, made a crisis—and at just this crisis the letter-writer had, knowledgeably, struck. The hollowness of the house this evening canceled years on years of voices, habits and steps. Through the shut windows she only heard rain fall on the roofs around. To rally herself, she said she was in a mood—and for two or three seconds shutting her eyes, told herself that she had imagined the letter. But she opened them—there it lay on the bed.

On the supernatural side of the letter's entrance she was not permitting her mind to dwell. Who, in London, knew she meant to call at the house today? Evidently, however, this had been known. The caretaker, *had* he come back, had had no cause to expect her: he would have taken the letter in his pocket, to forward it, at his own time, through the post. There was no other sign that the caretaker had been in—but, if not? Letters dropped in at doors of deserted houses do not fly or walk to tables in halls. They do not sit on the dust of empty tables with the air of certainty that they will be found. There is needed some human hand—but nobody but the caretaker had a key. Under circumstances she did not care to consider, a house can be entered without a key. It was possible that she was not alone now. She might be being waited for, downstairs. Waited for—until when? Until "the hour arranged." At least that was not six o'clock: six has struck.

She rose from the chair and went over and locked the door.

Interior with Seated Woman (1908), Vilhelm Hammershøi. Oil on canvas, 76 cm × 66 cm, Aarhus (Denmark) Kunstmuseum.

The thing was, to get out. To fly? No, not that: she had to catch her train. As a woman whose utter dependability was the keystone of her family life she was not willing to return to the country, to her husband, her little boys and her sister, without the objects she had come up to fetch. Resuming work at the chest she set about making up a number of parcels in a rapid, fumbling-decisive way. These, with her shopping parcels, would be too much to carry; these meant a taxi—at the thought of the taxi her heart went up and her normal breathing resumed. I will ring up the taxi now; the taxi cannot come too soon: I shall hear the taxi out there running its engine, till I walk calmly down to it through the hall. I'll ring up—But no: the telephone is cut off . . . She tugged at a knot she had tied wrong.

The idea of flight . . . He was never kind to me, not really. I don't remember him kind at all. Mother said he never considered me. He was set on me, that was what it was—not love. Not love, not meaning a person well. What did he do, to make me promise like that? I can't remember—But she found that she could.

She remembered with such dreadful acuteness that the twenty-five years since then dissolved like smoke and she instinctively looked for the weal[12] left by the button on the palm of her hand. She remembered not only all that he said and did but the complete suspension of *her* existence during that August week. I was not myself—they all told me so at the time. She remembered—but with one white burning blank as where acid has dropped on a photograph: *under no conditions* could she remember his face.

So, wherever he may be waiting, I shall not know him. You have no time to run from a face you do not expect.

The thing was to get to the taxi before any clock struck what could be the hour. She would slip down the street and round the side of the square to where the square gave on the main road. She would return in the taxi, safe, to her own door, and bring the solid driver into the house with her to pick up the parcels from room to room. The idea of the taxi driver made her decisive, bold: she unlocked her door, went to the top of the staircase and listened down.

She heard nothing—but while she was hearing nothing the *passé*[13] air of the staircase was disturbed by a draft that traveled up to her face. It emanated from the basement: down there a door or window was being opened by someone who chose this moment to leave the house.

The rain had stopped; the pavements steamily shone as Mrs. Drover let herself out by inches from her own front door into the empty street. The unoccupied houses opposite continued to meet her look with their damaged stare. Making towards the thoroughfare and the taxi, she tried not to keep looking behind. Indeed, the silence was so intense—one of those creeks of London silence exaggerated this summer by the damage of war—that no tread could have gained on hers unheard. Where her street debouched[14] on the square where people went on living, she grew conscious of, and checked, her unnatural pace. Across the open end of the square two buses impassively passed each other: women, a

12. **weal:** a mark or ridge raised on the skin.

13. ***passé*** (pä-sā′) *French:* old; stale; past its prime.

14. **debouched** (dĭ-boucht′): emerged.

WORDS TO KNOW

emanate (ĕm′ə-nāt′) *v.* to come forth; flow out

impassively (ĭm-păs′ĭv-lē) *adv.* without feeling or emotion

perambulator,[15] cyclists, a man wheeling a barrow signalized, once again, the ordinary flow of life. At the square's most populous corner should be—and was—the short taxi rank. This evening, only one taxi—but this, although it presented its blank rump, appeared already to be alertly waiting for her. Indeed, without looking round the driver started his engine as she panted up from behind and put her hand on the door. As she did so, the clock struck seven. The taxi faced the main road: to make the trip back to her house it would have to turn—she had settled back on the seat and the taxi *had* turned before she, surprised by its knowing movement, recollected that she had not "said where." She leaned forward to scratch at the glass panel that divided the driver's head from her own.

The driver braked to what was almost a stop, turned round and slid the glass panel back: the jolt of this flung Mrs. Drover forward till her face was almost into the glass. Through the aperture[16] driver and passenger, not six inches between them, remained for an eternity eye to eye. Mrs. Drover's mouth hung open for some seconds before she could issue her first scream. After that she continued to scream freely and to beat with her gloved hands on the glass all round as the taxi, accelerating without mercy, made off with her into the hinterland of deserted streets. ❖

15. **perambulator:** baby carriage.

16. **aperture** (ăp′ər-chər): opening.

At the square's most populous corner
should be—and was—
the short taxi rank.

RESPONDING OPTIONS

FROM PERSONAL RESPONSE *TO* CRITICAL ANALYSIS

REFLECT 1. What do you think of Mrs. Drover? In your notebook briefly describe your reaction to her and her experience.

RETHINK 2. What conclusions can you draw about Mrs. Drover's former fiancé?

Consider
- his words and actions during their 1916 farewell meeting
- her reactions to him during their farewell
- her current memories of him

3. How would you describe Mrs. Drover's emotions during the course of the story?

Consider
- her attitude at the beginning of the story
- her reactions to the letter and other unexplained events
- what she decides to do

4. How would you describe the tone of the story's narrator?

5. Do you think there is a rational explanation for the events in this story? Explain your answer.

RELATE 6. Mrs. Drover's life is dramatically affected by two wars. People in many parts of the world today are suffering through wars, some of them prolonged. What do you think it might be like to experience such events as a teenager or a young adult?

ANOTHER PATHWAY

Make three lists—one of details about this story's setting, one of details about Mrs. Drover's personality and behavior, and one of details about the soldier. Then decide how you think each kind of detail contributes to the total effect of the story.

QUICKWRITES

1. The story ends with Mrs. Drover screaming and pounding her fists on the windows of a speeding taxi. What do you think happens next? Write a new **scene** to add to the end of the story.
2. Using evidence from the story, write a **missing-person report** about Mrs. Drover. Describe her physical appearance and her actions and state of mind before her disappearance. Provide clues to her whereabouts and offer a reward for her return.
3. In a **paragraph,** explain what you think Bowen's purpose for writing this story might have been. Support your ideas with evidence from the story.

PORTFOLIO *Save your writing. You may want to use it later as a springboard to a piece for your portfolio.*

LITERARY CONCEPTS

A **surprise ending** is an unexpected twist at the end of a story's plot. The surprise may be a sudden turn in the action or a revelation that provides a different perspective on the entire story. The last paragraph of "The Demon Lover" reveals an unexpected turn in the action. Identify the twist in the plot, and explain what contributes to making it a surprise. Are there, in retrospect, any details that might have prepared you for the ending?

ALTERNATIVE ACTIVITIES

1. ***Cooperative Learning*** Work with classmates to select appropriate music, create sound effects, and develop lighting for a **dramatic reading** of the story. Assign a team of directors, and cast different people to read the soldier's letter, the thoughts of Mrs. Drover, and the narration. Then rehearse the reading and perform it, complete with effects. If possible, videotape the performance for later review.
2. Suppose that a movie version of this story has been made. Draw or paint a **poster,** depicting the taxi scene, to advertise the movie. Include actors' names as well as quotations from reviews.
3. Imagine that you are the editor in chief of a sensational tabloid newspaper. Choose several classmates to act as reporters and editors, and hold a **staff meeting** to discuss how you want to cover the disappearance of Mrs. Drover.

LITERARY LINKS

Compare and contrast the mystery of Mrs. Drover's fate with the mystery that unfolds in "The Kit-Bag" (page 768). Both stories describe frightening events that seem to defy rational explanation. Which of the two mysteries is more easily explained? Which do you find more frightening?

THE WRITER'S STYLE

Bowen creates **suspense** and builds atmosphere in "The Demon Lover" by choosing words carefully. Such phrases as "no human eye" (page 896), "spectral glitters" (page 898), and "damaged stare" (page 900) contribute to a mood of tension and foreboding. Look for other examples of words and phrases that have similar effects. How important do you think word choice is in making the action and conclusion of this story convincing?

CRITIC'S CORNER

Critics have noted Bowen's sensitivity and precision in conveying setting, mood, and character—in particular, the relationships between characters and the places where they live. In your opinion, how important is this story's setting—wartime London, the time of day, the empty house—to its plot? Be specific in your answer.

ART CONNECTION

The painting *Interior with Seated Woman,* reproduced on page 899, shows a woman with her back to the viewer and a series of rooms opening before her. What is mysterious about the scene depicted in the painting? What might lie beyond the partially opened door in the adjoining room?

ACROSS THE CURRICULUM

History Research what life in London was like during World War II. In addition to descriptions in history books and encyclopedias, try to find firsthand accounts in biographies. Prepare a report that includes copies of photos of wartime London, as well as quotations from people who experienced the Blitz.

WORDS TO KNOW

EXERCISE A Answer the following questions.

1. Would you be most likely to signal **assent** by nodding your head up and down, yawning and stretching, or holding your nose?
2. Would a person who is reacting **impassively** be laughing, gasping, or shrugging?
3. What **emanates** from a bouquet of roses—fragrance, thorns, or roots?
4. Would a **prosaic** lifestyle tend to be full of excitement, routine, or danger?
5. If you needed to act **precipitately,** would you be cautious, quick, or sneaky?

EXERCISE B Work with four classmates to describe a fictional school or social event, using the five vocabulary words. One student should begin the description and keep going until he or she has used one of the words; then another student should continue the description, using a second vocabulary word; and so on until all the words have been used.

Elizabeth Bowen

1899–1973

Born in Dublin, Ireland, of Anglo-Irish parents, Elizabeth Bowen spent her early childhood at Bowen's Court, an estate that had been in the family since the 17th century. Although her early childhood was happy, her later childhood years were difficult. When she was seven, her father suffered a nervous breakdown, and she was sent to England with her mother and a governess. Six years later, her mother died after a three-year battle with cancer. Bowen then attended a boarding school for a few years, increasingly feeling herself part of neither England nor Ireland. During the last year of World War I, she returned to Dublin and nursed soldiers suffering from shell shock.

In 1918 Bowen returned to London, where she began writing stories. She later wrote of that time, "From the moment that my pen touched paper, I thought of nothing but writing, and since then I have thought of practically nothing else. . . . [W]hen I have nothing to write, I feel only half alive." In 1923, she married Alan C. Cameron, an educator, and published her first collection of stories, *Encounters.* Her first novel, *The Hotel,* appeared in 1927, when she also inherited Bowen's Court, becoming the first woman owner of the estate, although she did not move there until 1952.

Bowen had a prolific career, publishing more than 20 novels and volumes of short stories. Her fiction, which deals primarily with the upper middle class, is beautifully crafted, with finely drawn characters and detailed, evocative descriptions of setting. Many of her best works are set in wartime London, a setting she presents with realism and force.

Bowen's career was diversified as well as distinguished. She was a reviewer for the *Tatler* in 1941 and worked for the Ministry of Information during the early years of World War II. In addition to short stories and novels, she published *Bowen's Court* (a history of her family) and nonfiction works dealing with her life and writing. She is considered a major 20th-century British writer.

OTHER WORKS *The Death of the Heart, The Heat of the Day, Collected Stories*

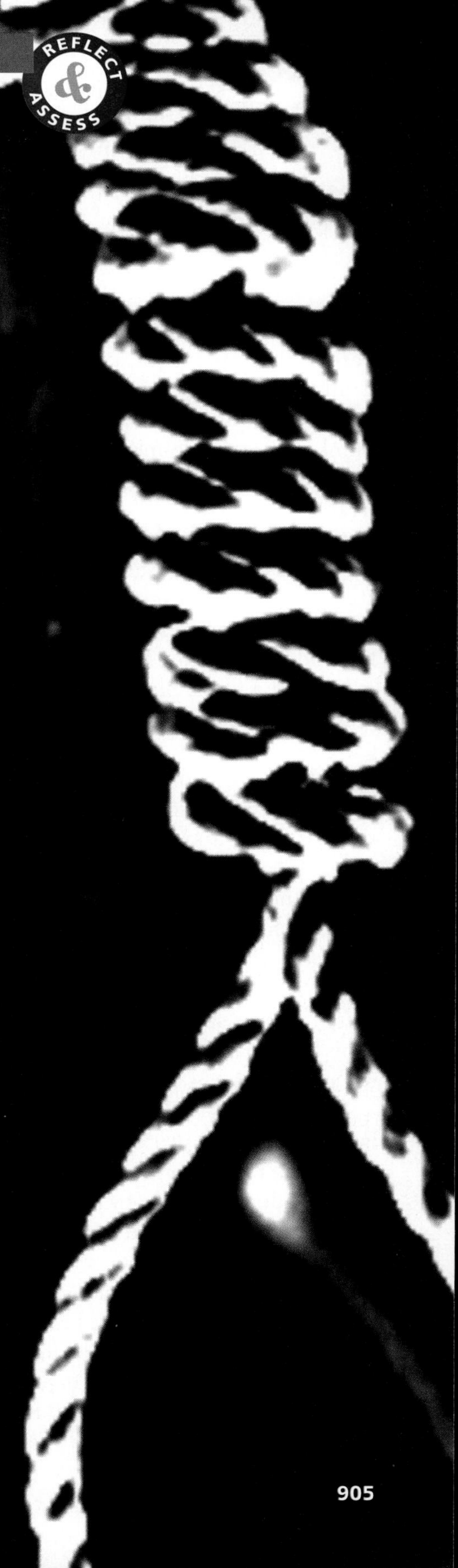

A Hanging

George Orwell

Although best known for the political novels 1984 *and* Animal Farm, *George Orwell was also one of the great essayists of the 20th century. Like his novels, many of his essays contain social and political commentary. "A Hanging" is Orwell's eyewitness account of an event that occurred during the 1920s in Burma, where he was employed as an assistant superintendent with the Indian Imperial Police.*

IT was in Burma, a sodden morning of the rains. A sickly light, like yellow tinfoil, was slanting over the high walls into the jail yard. We were waiting outside the condemned cells, a row of sheds fronted with double bars, like small animal cages. Each cell measured about ten feet by ten and was quite bare within except for a plank bed and a pot of drinking water. In some of them brown silent men were squatting at the inner bars, with their blankets draped round them. These were the condemned men, due to be hanged within the next week or two.

One prisoner had been brought out of his cell. He was a Hindu, a puny wisp of a man, with a shaven head and vague liquid eyes. He had a thick, sprouting moustache, absurdly too big for his body, rather like the moustache of a comic man on the films. Six tall Indian warders[1] were guarding him and getting him ready for the gallows. Two of them stood by with rifles and fixed bayonets, while the others handcuffed him, passed a chain through his handcuffs and fixed it to their belts, and lashed his arms tight to his sides. They crowded very close about him, with their hands always on him in a careful, caressing grip, as though all the while feeling him to make sure he was there. It was like men handling a fish which is still alive and may jump back into the water. But he stood quite unresisting, yielding his arms limply to the ropes, as though he hardly noticed what was happening.

Eight o'clock struck and a bugle call, desolately thin in the wet air, floated from the distant barracks. The superintendent of the jail, who was standing apart from the rest of us, moodily prodding the gravel with his stick, raised his head at the sound. He was an army doctor, with a grey toothbrush moustache and a gruff voice. "For God's sake hurry up, Francis," he said irritably. "The man ought to have been dead by this time. Aren't you ready yet?"

Francis, the head jailer, a fat Dravidian[2] in a white drill suit and gold spectacles, waved his black hand. "Yes sir, yes sir," he bubbled. "All iss satisfactorily prepared. The hangman iss waiting. We shall proceed."

"Well, quick march, then. The prisoners can't get their breakfast till this job's over."

We set out for the gallows. Two warders marched on either side of the prisoner, with their rifles at the slope; two others marched close against him, gripping him by arm and shoulder, as though at once pushing and supporting him. The rest of us, magistrates and the like, followed behind. Suddenly, when we had gone ten yards, the procession stopped short without any order or warning. A dreadful thing had happened—a dog, come goodness knows whence, had appeared in the yard. It came bounding among us with a loud volley of barks, and leapt round us wagging its whole body, wild with glee at finding so many human beings together. It was a large, wooly dog, half Airedale, half pariah.[3] For a moment it pranced round us, and then, before anyone could stop it, it had made a dash for the prisoner, and jumping up tried to lick his face. Everyone stood aghast, too taken aback even to grab at the dog.

"Who let that bloody brute in here?" said the superintendent angrily. "Catch it, someone!"

A warder, detached from the escort, charged clumsily after the dog, but it danced and gamboled[4] just out of his reach, taking everything as part of the game. A young Eurasian jailer picked up a handful of gravel and tried to stone the dog away, but it dodged the stones and came after us again. Its yaps echoed from the jail walls. The prisoner, in the grasp of the two warders, looked on incuriously, as though this was another

---

1. **warders:** prison guards.
2. **Dravidian** (drə-vĭd′ē-ən): a member of a dark-skinned people of southern India.
3. **pariah:** a wild or domesticated mongrel dog.
4. **gamboled** (găm′bəld): jumped about playfully.

formality of the hanging. It was several minutes before someone managed to catch the dog. Then we put my handkerchief through its collar and moved off once more, with the dog still straining and whimpering.

It was about forty yards to the gallows. I watched the bare brown back of the prisoner marching in front of me. He walked clumsily with his bound arms, but quite steadily, with that bobbing gait of the Indian who never straightens his knees. At each step his muscles slid neatly into place, the lock of hair on his scalp danced up and down, his feet printed themselves on the wet gravel. And once, in spite of the men who gripped him by each shoulder, he stepped slightly aside to avoid a puddle on the path.

It is curious, but till that moment I had never realized what it means to destroy a healthy, conscious man. When I saw the prisoner step aside to avoid the puddle, I saw the mystery, the unspeakable wrongness, of cutting a life short when it is in full tide. This man was not dying, he was alive just as we were alive. All the organs of his body were working—bowels digesting food, skin renewing itself, nails growing, tissues forming—all toiling away in solemn foolery. His nails would still be growing when he stood on the drop, when he was falling through the air with a tenth of a second to live. His eyes saw the yellow gravel and the grey walls, and his brain still remembered, foresaw, reasoned—reasoned even about puddles. He and we were a party of men walking together, seeing, hearing, feeling, understanding the same world; and in two minutes, with a sudden snap, one of us would be gone—one mind less, one world less.

The gallows stood in a small yard, separate from the main grounds of the prison, and overgrown with tall prickly weeds. It was a brick erection like three sides of a shed, with planking on top, and above that two beams and a crossbar with the rope dangling. The hangman, a grey-haired convict in the white uniform of the prison, was waiting beside his machine. He greeted us with a servile[5] crouch as we entered. At a word from Francis the two warders, gripping the prisoner more closely than ever, half led, half pushed him to the gallows and helped him clumsily up the ladder. Then the hangman climbed up and fixed the rope round the prisoner's neck.

We stood waiting, five yards away. The warders had formed in a rough circle round the gallows. And then, when the noose was fixed, the prisoner began crying out to his god. It was a high, reiterated cry of "Ram! Ram! Ram! Ram!"[6] not urgent and fearful like a prayer or a cry for help, but steady, rhythmical, almost like the tolling of a bell. The dog answered the sound with a whine. The hangman, still standing on the gallows, produced a small cotton bag like a flour bag and drew it down over the prisoner's face. But the sound, muffled by the cloth, still persisted, over and over again: "Ram! Ram! Ram! Ram! Ram!"

The hangman climbed down and stood ready, holding the lever. Minutes seemed to pass. The steady, muffled crying from the prisoner went on and on, "Ram! Ram! Ram!" never faltering for an instant. The superintendent, his head on his chest, was slowly poking the ground with his stick; perhaps he was counting the cries, allowing the prisoner a fixed number—fifty, perhaps, or a hundred. Everyone had changed color. The Indians had gone grey like bad coffee, and one or two of the bayonets were wavering. We looked at the lashed, hooded man on the drop, and listened to his cries—each cry another second of life; the same thought was in all our minds: oh, kill him quickly, get it over, stop that abominable noise!

Suddenly the superintendent made up his

---

5. **servile:** slavelike; cringing.

6. **Ram** (räm): a form of *Rama,* the name of an incarnation of Vishnu, one of the three main Hindu gods.

mind. Throwing up his head he made a swift motion with his stick. "Chalo!"[7] he shouted almost fiercely.

There was a clanking noise, and then dead silence. The prisoner had vanished, and the rope was twisting on itself. I let go of the dog, and it galloped immediately to the back of the gallows; but when it got there it stopped short, barked, and then retreated into a corner of the yard, where it stood among the weeds, looking timorously out at us. We went round the gallows to inspect the prisoner's body. He was dangling with his toes pointed straight downwards, very slowly revolving, as dead as a stone.

The superintendent reached out with his stick and poked the bare body; it oscillated, slightly. "*He's* all right," said the superintendent. He backed out from under the gallows, and blew out a deep breath. The moody look had gone out of his face quite suddenly. He glanced at his wristwatch. "Eight minutes past eight. Well, that's all for this morning, thank God."

7. **Chalo!** (chä'lō) *Hindi:* Go!

George Orwell at the police training school at Mandalay, Burma, in 1922. Photo courtesy of Roger Beadon. Orwell is circled.

The warders unfixed bayonets and marched away. The dog, sobered and conscious of having misbehaved itself, slipped after them. We walked out of the gallows yard, past the condemned cells with their waiting prisoners, into the big central yard of the prison. The convicts, under the command of warders armed with lathis,[8] were already receiving their breakfast. They squatted in long rows, each man holding a tin pannikin,[9] while two warders with buckets marched round ladling out rice; it seemed quite a homely, jolly scene, after the hanging. An enormous relief had come upon us now that the job was done. One felt an impulse to sing, to break into a run, to snigger. All at once everyone began chattering gaily.

Eurasian boy walking beside me nodded towards the way we had come, with a knowing smile: "Do you know, sir, our friend (he meant the dead man), when he heard his appeal had been dismissed, he pissed on the floor of his cell. From fright.—Kindly take one of my cigarettes, sir. Do you not admire my new silver case, sir? From the boxwallah,[10] two rupees eight annas.[11] Classy European style."

Several people laughed—at what, nobody seemed certain.

Francis was walking by the superintendent, talking garrulously:[12] "Well, sir, all hass passed off with the utmost satisfactoriness. It wass all finished—flick! like that. It iss not always so—oah, no! I have known cases where the doctor wass obliged to go beneath the gallows and pull the prisoner's legs to ensure decease. Most disagreeable!"

"Wriggling about, eh? That's bad," said the superintendent.

"Ach, sir, it iss worse when they become refractory![13] One man, I recall, clung to the bars of hiss cage when we went to take him out. You will scarcely credit, sir, that it took six warders to dislodge him, three pulling at each leg. We reasoned with him. 'My dear fellow,' we said, 'think of all the pain and trouble you are causing to us!' But no, he would not listen! Ach, he wass very troublesome!"

I found that I was laughing quite loudly. Everyone was laughing. Even the superintendent

---

8. **lathis** (lä′tēz): heavy bamboo sticks bound with iron, used as weapons by the police in India.
9. **pannikin:** a small pan or shallow cup.
10. **boxwallah:** in India, a peddler.
11. **rupees** (ro͞o-pēz′) . . . **annas** (ä′nəz): Indian units of money. (Annas, which are no longer used, were coins worth 1/16 of a rupee.)
12. **garrulously** (găr′ə-ləs-lē): in a wordy, long-winded manner.
13. **refractory:** hard to manage; stubborn.

grinned in a tolerant way. "You'd better all come out and have a drink," he said quite genially. "I've got a bottle of whisky in the car. We could do with it."

We went through the big double gates of the prison, into the road. "Pulling at his legs!" exclaimed a Burmese magistrate suddenly, and burst into a loud chuckling. We all began laughing again. At that moment Francis's anecdote seemed extraordinarily funny. We all had a drink together, native and European alike, quite amicably.[14] The dead man was a hundred yards away. ❖

14. **amicably:** in a friendly manner.

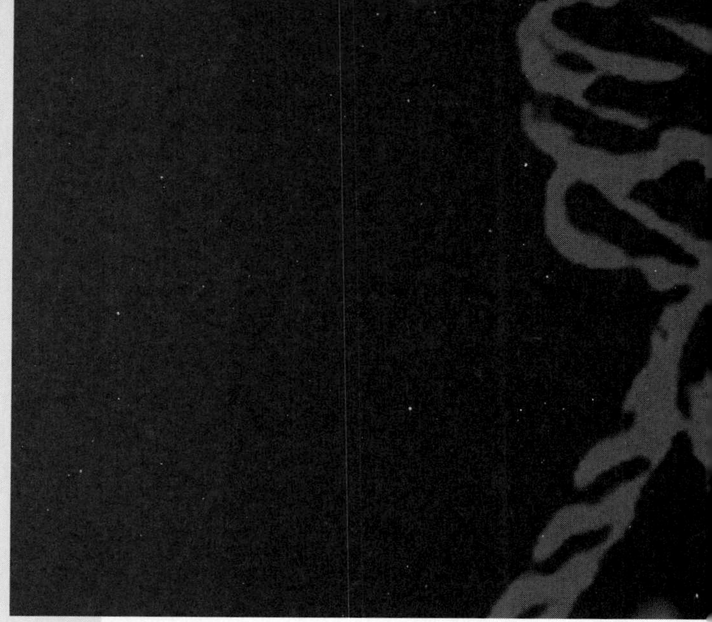

George Orwell

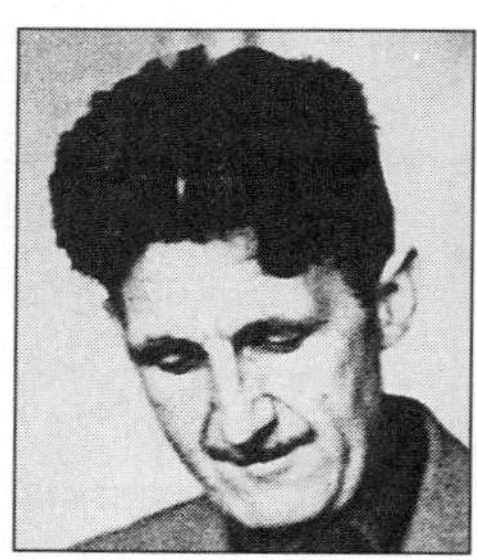

1903–1950

"George Orwell" was the pen name of Eric Arthur Blair, who was born in India, where his father was serving in the Indian civil service. After his family returned to England, he attended excellent schools and proved to be an extremely bright student. When offered a college scholarship, however, he turned it down, deciding instead to follow in his father's footsteps. In 1922 he joined the Indian Imperial Police and left for Burma, which was at that time under British rule.

When Orwell discovered how much the Burmese disliked British rule, he became disenchanted with Britain's imperialist policies, eventually quitting his job. Having developed deep sympathies for the poor and downtrodden, he decided to live their life. At the age of 25, he gave up the trappings of a middle-class existence and adopted the life of the impoverished, dressing in rags and living in the poorest sections of London and Paris. Working as a dishwasher and a day laborer, he tramped through the countryside with the homeless. Out of these varied experiences came his first book, *Down and Out in Paris and London,* published in 1933.

Throughout his short life, Orwell continued to sympathize with the underdog and to speak out against social and political injustice. During the Spanish civil war, he enlisted with the anti-Fascist forces and was wounded in the fighting. Near the end of World War II, he completed the first of his famous novels—*Animal Farm,* in which he warned prophetically of the dangers of dictatorships. In 1949 he published *1984,* focusing on the appalling possibilities of life in a totalitarian state. Orwell completed *1984* while battling tuberculosis, from which he died at the peak of his career.

OTHER WORKS "Shooting an Elephant," "How the Poor Die"

PART 3 *New Images of Reality*

The profound changes of the first half of the 20th century gave rise to a sharpened anxiety and sense of irony. Many writers began to experiment with new and highly personal forms to express these feelings. In this part of Unit Six, you will encounter writers who examine relationships and search for meaning in modern life. As you read, consider whether their new images of reality express any ideas similar to your own.

PREVIEWING

DRAMA

The Rising of the Moon

Lady Isabella Augusta Gregory

PERSONAL CONNECTION

This play focuses on a moral dilemma—a man must choose between two opposing sides, each of which seems to be right. Think of a time when you had to make a hard choice between two sides of an issue. In your notebook, describe your experience and tell how you made your decision. Then compare your experience with those of your classmates.

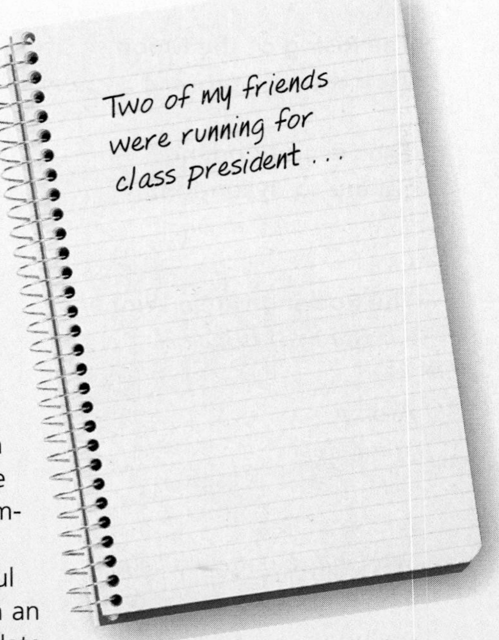

Two of my friends
were running for
class president . . .

HISTORICAL CONNECTION

When *The Rising of the Moon* was first performed in 1907, the Irish were struggling to gain independence from Great Britain, and individual citizens found themselves in the position of having to take sides. Some patriots worked for gradual change through peaceful means; others were willing to use violence to obtain an immediate separation from Great Britain. Set in the late 1800s, this play is about the search for an Irish rebel who has plotted to overthrow the British.

Two popular revolutionary songs are important in the play. The song "The Rising of the Moon" celebrates a famous Irish rebellion in 1798. It describes a gathering of rebels at moonrise, armed and ready to fight, and ends with thanks to God that there are still men "who would follow in their footsteps at the rising of the moon." In the other song, "Granuaile" (grän'o͞o-āl'), Ireland is portrayed as a maiden who has been brutalized by the "ruffian band" of the English. At one time, when the English outlawed even the speaking of the name of Ireland, *Granuaile* was one of the many metaphorical names that Irish patriots applied to their homeland.

READING CONNECTION

Appreciating Dialect In Ireland, the dialects of spoken English vary from county to county. This play reflects the dialect of County Galway in western Ireland. Longer vowel sounds and differences in grammar, sentence structure, and idiom—such as the use of *me* for *my*—give a musical quality to the language. As you read this play about a man who takes sides in the Irish-English conflict, choose some passages to recite aloud so that you can better appreciate the language.

THE RISING OF THE MOON

Lady Isabella Augusta Gregory

CAST OF CHARACTERS

Sergeant
Policeman X
Policeman B
A Ragged Man

Scene: *Side of a quay*[1] *in a seaport town. Some posts and chains. A large barrel. Enter three policemen. Moonlight.*

Sergeant, *who is older than the others, crosses the stage to right and looks down steps. The others put down a pastepot and unroll a bundle of placards.*[2]

1. **quay** (kē): a landing place for boats; wharf.
2. **placards** (plăk′ärdz′): posters.

Policeman B. I think this would be a good place to put up a notice. (*He points to barrel.*)

Policeman X. Better ask him. (*calls to* Sergeant) Will this be a good place for a placard? (*no answer*)

Policeman B. Will we put up a notice here on the barrel? (*no answer*)

Sergeant. There's a flight of steps here that leads to the water. This is a place that should be minded well. If he got down here, his friends might have a boat to meet him; they might send it in here from outside.

Policeman B. Would the barrel be a good place to put a notice up?

Sergeant. It might; you can put it there. (*They paste the notice up.*)

Sergeant (*reading it*). Dark hair—dark eyes, smooth face, height five feet five—there's not much to take hold of in that—It's a pity I had no chance of seeing him before he broke out of jail. They say he's a wonder, that it's he makes all the plans for the whole organization. There isn't another man in Ireland would have broken jail the way he did. He must have some friends among the jailers.

Policeman B. A hundred pounds is little enough for the Government to offer for him. You may be sure any man in the force that takes him will get promotion.

Sergeant. I'll mind this place myself. I wouldn't wonder at all if he came this way. He might come slipping along there (*points to side of quay*), and his friends might be waiting for him there (*points down steps*), and once he got away it's little chance we'd have of finding him; it's maybe under a load of kelp[3] he'd be in a fishing boat, and not one to help a married man that wants it to the reward.

Policeman X. And if we get him itself, nothing but abuse on our heads for it from the people, and maybe from our own relations.

Sergeant. Well, we have to do our duty in the force. Haven't we the whole country depending on us to keep law and order? It's those that are down would be up and those that are up would be down, if it wasn't for us. Well, hurry on, you have plenty of other places to placard yet, and come back here then to me. You can take the lantern. Don't be too long now. It's very lonesome here with nothing but the moon.

Policeman B. It's a pity we can't stop with you. The Government should have brought more police into the town, with *him* in jail, and at assize[4] time too. Well, good luck to your watch. (*They go out.*)

Sergeant (*walks up and down once or twice and looks at placard*). A hundred pounds and promotion sure. There must be a great deal of spending in a hundred pounds. It's a pity some honest man not to be the better of that. (*A ragged man appears at left and tries to slip past.* Sergeant *suddenly turns.*)

Sergeant. Where are you going?

Man. I'm a poor ballad singer, your honor. I thought to sell some of these (*holds out bundle of ballads*) to the sailors. (*He goes on.*)

Sergeant. Stop! Didn't I tell you to stop? You can't go on there.

Man. Oh, very well. It's a hard thing to be poor. All the world's against the poor!

Sergeant. Who are you?

Man. You'd be as wise as myself if I told you, but I don't mind. I'm one Jimmy Walsh, a ballad singer.

Sergeant. Jimmy Walsh? I don't know that name.

Man. Ah, sure, they know it well enough in Ennis. Were you ever in Ennis, Sergeant?

Sergeant. What brought you here?

Man. Sure, it's to the assizes I came, thinking I might make a few shillings here or there. It's in

3. **kelp:** a seaweed used to keep fish fresh until they get to market.

4. **assize** (ə-sīz′): in Britain, a court session held periodically in a county.

the one train with the judges I came.

Sergeant. Well, if you came so far, you may as well go farther, for you'll walk out of this.

Man. I will, I will; I'll just go on where I was going. (*goes toward steps*)

Sergeant. Come back from those steps; no one has leave to pass down them tonight.

Man. I'll just sit on the top of the steps till I see will some sailor buy a ballad off me that would give me my supper. They do be late going back to the ship. It's often I saw them in Cork carried down the quay in a handcart.

Sergeant. Move on, I tell you. I won't have anyone lingering about the quay tonight.

Man. Well, I'll go. It's the poor have the hard life! Maybe yourself might like one, Sergeant. Here's a good sheet now. (*turns one over*) "Content and a pipe"—that's not much. "The Peeler[5] and the Goat"—you wouldn't like that. "Johnny Hart"—that's a lovely song.

Sergeant. Move on.

Man. Ah, wait till you hear it. (*sings*)

There was a rich farmer's daughter lived near the town of Ross;
She courted a Highland soldier, his name was Johnny Hart;
Says the mother to her daughter, "I'll go distracted mad
If you marry that Highland soldier[6] dressed up in Highland plaid."

Sergeant. Stop that noise. (Man *wraps up his ballads and shuffles toward the steps.*)

Sergeant. Where are you going?

Man. Sure you told me to be going, and I am going.

Sergeant. Don't be a fool. I didn't tell you to go that way; I told you to go back to the town.

Man. Back to the town, is it?

Sergeant (*taking him by the shoulder and shoving him before him*). Here, I'll show you the way. Be off with you. What are you stopping for?

Man (*who has been keeping his eye on the notice, points to it*). I think I know what you're waiting for, Sergeant.

Sergeant. What's that to you?

Man. And I know well the man you're waiting for—I know him well—I'll be going. (*He shuffles on.*)

Sergeant. You know him? Come back here. What sort is he?

Man. Come back is it, Sergeant? Do you want to have me killed?

Sergeant. Why do you say that?

Man. Never mind. I'm going. I wouldn't be in your shoes if the reward was ten times as much. (*goes on offstage to left*) Not if it was ten times as much.

Sergeant (*rushing after him*). Come back here, come back. (*drags him back*) What sort is he? Where did you see him?

Man. I saw him in my own place, in the County Clare. I tell you you wouldn't like to be looking at him. You'd be afraid to be in the one place with him. There isn't a weapon he doesn't know the use of, and as to strength, his muscles are as hard as that board. (*slaps barrel*)

Sergeant. Is he as bad as that?

Man. He is then.

Sergeant. Do you tell me so?

Man. There was a poor man in our place, a sergeant from Ballyvaughan.[7]—It was with a lump of stone he did it.

Sergeant. I never heard of that.

Man. And you wouldn't, Sergeant. It's not everything that happens gets into the papers. And

5. **Peeler:** policeman (from the name of the British politician Robert Peel, who established the Irish constabulary in the early 1800s).

6. **If you marry that Highland soldier:** Scottish soldiers were hated by the Irish because of Scotland's close ties to England.

7. **Ballyvaughan** (băl′ē-vôn′).

there was a policeman in plain clothes, too . . . It is in Limerick he was. . . . It was after the time of the attack on the police barrack at Kilmallock. . . . Moonlight . . . just like this . . . waterside. . . . Nothing was known for certain.

Sergeant. Do you say so? It's a terrible county to belong to.

Man. That's so, indeed! You might be standing there, looking out that way, thinking you saw him coming up this side of the quay (*points*), and he might be coming up this other side (*points*), and he'd be on you before you knew where you were.

Sergeant. It's a whole troop of police they ought to put here to stop a man like that.

Man. But if you'd like me to stop with you, I could be looking down this side. I could be sitting up here on this barrel.

Sergeant. And you know him well, too?

Man. I'd know him a mile off, Sergeant.

Sergeant. But you wouldn't want to share the reward?

Man. Is it a poor man like me, that has to be going the roads and singing in fairs, to have the name on him that he took a reward? But you don't want me. I'll be safer in the town.

Sergeant. Well, you can stop.

Man (*getting up on barrel*). All right, Sergeant. I wonder, now, you're not tired out, Sergeant, walking up and down the way you are.

Sergeant. If I'm tired I'm used to it.

Man. You might have hard work before you tonight yet. Take it easy while you can. There's plenty of room up here on the barrel, and you see farther when you're higher up.

Sergeant. Maybe so. (*Gets up beside him on barrel, facing right. They sit back to back, looking different ways.*) You made me feel a bit queer with the way you talked.

Man. Give me a match, Sergeant (*He gives it and* Man *lights pipe.*); take a draw yourself? It'll quiet you. Wait now till I give you a light, but you needn't turn round. Don't take your eye off the quay for the life of you.

Sergeant. Never fear, I won't. (*Lights pipe. They both smoke.*) Indeed it's a hard thing to be in the force, out at night and no thanks for it, for all the danger we're in. And it's little we get but abuse from the people, and no choice but to obey our orders, and never asked when a man is sent into danger, if you are a married man with a family.

Man (*sings*).

As through the hills I walked to view the hills
and shamrock plain,
I stood awhile where nature smiles to view the
rocks and streams,
On a matron fair I fixed my eyes beneath a
fertile vale,
As she sang her song it was on the wrong of
poor old Granuaile.

Sergeant. Stop that; that's no song to be singing in these times.[8]

Man. Ah, Sergeant, I was only singing to keep my heart up. It sinks when I think of him. To think of us two sitting here, and he creeping up the quay, maybe, to get to us.

Sergeant. Are you keeping a good lookout?

Man. I am; and for no reward too. Amn't I the foolish man? But when I saw a man in trouble, I never could help trying to get him out of it. What's that? Did something hit me? (*rubs his heart*)

Sergeant (*patting him on the shoulder*). You will get your reward in heaven.

Man. I know that. I know that, Sergeant, but life is precious.

Sergeant. Well, you can sing if it gives you more courage.

---

8. **that's no song . . . these times:** "Granuaile" is an anti-British revolutionary anthem.

Man (*sings*).

Her head was bare, her hands and feet with iron bands were bound,
Her pensive[9] *strain and plaintive*[10] *wail mingles with the evening gale,*
And the song she sang with mournful air, I am old Granuaile.
Her lips so sweet that monarchs kissed . . .

Sergeant. That's not it. . . . "Her gown she wore was stained with gore." . . . That's it—you missed that.

Man. You're right, Sergeant, so it is; I missed it. (*repeats line*) But to think of a man like you knowing a song like that.[11]

Sergeant. There's many a thing a man might know and might not have any wish for.

Man. Now, I daresay, Sergeant, in your youth, you used to be sitting up on a wall, the way you are sitting up on this barrel now, and the other lads beside you, and you singing "Granuaile"? . . .

Sergeant. I did then.

Man. And the "Shan Bhean Bhocht"?[12] . . .

Sergeant. I did then.

Man. And the "Green on the Cape"?

Sergeant. That was one of them.

Man. And maybe the man you are watching for tonight used to be sitting on the wall, when he was young, and singing those same songs. . . . It's a queer world.

Sergeant. Whisht! . . . I think I see something coming. . . . It's only a dog.

Man. And isn't it a queer world? . . . Maybe it's one of the boys you used to be singing with that time you will be arresting today or tomorrow, and sending into the dock.[13]

Sergeant. That's true indeed.

Man. And maybe one night, after you had been singing, if the other boys had told you some plan they had, some plan to free the country, you might have joined with them . . . and maybe it is you might be in trouble now.

Sergeant. Well, who knows but I might? I had a great spirit in those days.

Man. It's a queer world, Sergeant, and it's little any mother knows when she sees her child creeping on the floor what might happen to it before it has gone through its life, or who will be who in the end.

Sergeant. That's a queer thought now, and a true thought. Wait now till I think it out. . . . If it wasn't for the sense I have, and for my wife and family, and for me joining the force the time I did, it might be myself now would be after breaking jail and hiding in the dark, and it might be him that's hiding in the dark and that got out of jail would be sitting up where I am on this barrel. . . . And it might be myself would be creeping up trying to make my escape from himself, and it might be himself would be keeping the law, and myself would be breaking it, and myself would be trying maybe to put a bullet in his head, or to take up a lump of a stone the way you said he did . . . no, that myself did. . . . Oh! (*gasps; after a pause*) What's that? (*grasps* Man's *arm*)

Man (*jumps off barrel and listens, looking out over water*). It's nothing, Sergeant.

Sergeant. I thought it might be a boat. I had a notion there might be friends of his coming about the quays with a boat.

Man. Sergeant, I am thinking it was with the people you were, and not with the law you were, when you were a young man.

---

9. **pensive:** thoughtful in a serious or sad way.
10. **plaintive:** mournful; melancholy.
11. **to think of . . . song like that:** Since the sergeant is a police officer, paid to uphold British laws, the man is surprised that he is familiar with an anti-British song.
12. **"Shan Bhean Bhocht"** (shăn′ văn′ vôKHt′): a revolutionary song from the 1798 rebellion. Its title (meaning "the poor old woman"), like that of "Granuaile," is a reference to Ireland.
13. **dock:** the place where the accused person stands in a criminal court.

Captain Ned Bishop with Officers on the Bridge of the SS Eagle (1969), David Blackwood. Original etching.

Sergeant. Well, if I was foolish then, that time's gone.

Man. Maybe, Sergeant, it comes into your head sometimes, in spite of your belt and your tunic, that it might have been as well for you to have followed Granuaile.

Sergeant. It's no business of yours what I think.

Man. Maybe, Sergeant, you'll be on the side of the country yet.

Sergeant (*gets off barrel*). Don't talk to me like that. I have my duties and I know them. (*looks round*) That was a boat; I hear the oars. (*goes to the steps and looks down*)

Man (*sings*).

Oh then tell me, Shawn O'Farrell,
Where the gathering is to be.
In the old spot by the river
Right well known to you and me!

Sergeant. Stop that! Stop that, I tell you!

Man (*sings louder*).

One word more, for signal token,
Whistle up the marching tune,
With your pike upon your shoulder,
At the Rising of the Moon.

Sergeant. If you don't stop that, I'll arrest you. (*A whistle from below answers, repeating the air.*)

Sergeant. That's a signal. (*stands between him and steps*) You must not pass this way. . . . Step farther back. . . . Who are you? You are no ballad singer.

Man. You needn't ask who I am; that placard will tell you. (*points to placard*)

Sergeant. You are the man I am looking for.

Man (*takes off hat and wig.* Sergeant *seizes them*). I am. There's a hundred pounds on my head. There is a friend of mine below in a boat. He knows a safe place to bring me to.

Sergeant (*looking still at hat and wig*). It's a pity!

It's a pity. You deceived me. You deceived me well.

Man. I am a friend of Granuaile. There is a hundred pounds on my head.

Sergeant. It's a pity, it's a pity!

Man. Will you let me pass, or must I make you let me?

Sergeant. I am in the force. I will not let you pass.

Man. I thought to do it with my tongue. (*puts hand in breast*) What is that?

(*Voice of* Policeman X *outside*) Here, this is where we left him.

Sergeant. It's my comrades coming.

Man. You won't betray me . . . the friend of Granuaile. (*slips behind barrel*)

(*Voice of* Policeman B) That was the last of the placards.

Policeman X (*as they come in*). If he makes his escape it won't be unknown he'll make it. (Sergeant *puts hat and wig behind his back.*)

Policeman B. Did anyone come this way?

Sergeant (*after a pause*). No one.

Policeman B. No one at all?

Sergeant. No one at all.

Policeman B. We had no orders to go back to the station; we can stop along with you.

Sergeant. I don't want you. There is nothing for you to do here.

Policeman B. You bade us to come back here and keep watch with you.

Sergeant. I'd sooner be alone. Would any man come this way and you making all that talk? It is better the place to be quiet.

Policeman B. Well, we'll leave you the lantern anyhow. (*hands it to him*)

Sergeant. I don't want it. Bring it with you.

Policeman B. You might want it. There are clouds coming up and you have the darkness of the night before you yet. I'll leave it over here on the barrel. (*goes to barrel*)

Sergeant. Bring it with you I tell you. No more talk.

Policeman B. Well, I thought it might be a comfort to you. I often think when I have it in my hand and can be flashing it about into every dark corner (*doing so*) that it's the same as being beside the fire at home, and the bits of bogwood blazing up now and again. (*flashes it about, now on the barrel, now on* Sergeant)

Sergeant (*furious*). Be off the two of you, yourselves and your lantern! (*They go out.* Man *comes from behind barrel. He and* Sergeant *stand looking at one another.*)

Sergeant. What are you waiting for?

Man. For my hat, of course, and my wig. You wouldn't wish me to get my death of cold? (Sergeant *gives them.*)

Man (*going toward steps*). Well, good night, comrade, and thank you. You did me a good turn tonight, and I'm obliged to you. Maybe I'll be able to do as much for you when the small rise up and the big fall down . . . when we all change places at the Rising (*waves his hand and disappears*) of the Moon.

Sergeant (*turning his back to audience and reading placard*). A hundred pounds reward! A hundred pounds! (*turns toward audience*) I wonder, now, am I as great a fool as I think I am?

RESPONDING OPTIONS

FROM PERSONAL RESPONSE *TO* CRITICAL ANALYSIS

REFLECT 1. In your notebook, jot down words and phrases that describe your reaction to this play.

RETHINK 2. Do you think the sergeant does the right thing by allowing the man to escape?

Consider

- Policeman X's statement that "the people" might give them "nothing but abuse" if they catch the man
- what the reward might do for the sergeant's family
- the sergeant's duty to enforce the law
- the sergeant's background

3. Think about the different strategies the man uses to persuade the sergeant to let him go. Which do you think works best?

Consider

- the man's stories about the dangerousness of the escapee
- the songs he sings
- how he compares the sergeant to himself

4. Which of the two main characters do you admire more? Give reasons for your answer.

5. What would you say was Lady Gregory's purpose in writing this play?

RELATE 6. The sergeant obviously breaks the law by letting the man escape. What are your feelings about breaking the law for the sake of a cause? Explain your opinion.

ANOTHER PATHWAY

Create a chart, like the one shown, to analyze the sergeant's conflicting loyalties. In the first column, list the reasons he has for turning the man in; in the second, list the reasons he has for letting the man escape. Use the third column to record your opinions about the validity of the reasons.

Reasons for Turning In the Man	Reasons for Letting the Man Escape	My Opinions

LITERARY CONCEPTS

Suspense is created when a writer purposely leaves readers uncertain or apprehensive about what will happen. Writers rely on suspense to entertain their audiences and to hold the audiences' interest. Lady Gregory uses suspense-building techniques by having the sergeant refer to the sounds he thinks he hears in the dark. With a partner, look through the play for other statements and events that add to the suspense.

QUICKWRITES

1. Write a **dramatic scene** in which the sergeant tells his wife about his encounter with the man. Try to convey his concern for his family as well as for the revolutionary cause.
2. What might the future hold for the two main characters? Will the sergeant's life go on as usual? Will the man stay out of trouble with the law? Write an **outline** of a short story that explains what happens to each man in the weeks following their encounter.
3. Write an original **ballad** that tells the story of the sergeant and the rebel.

PORTFOLIO *Save your writing. You may want to use it later as a springboard to a piece for your portfolio.*

ALTERNATIVE ACTIVITIES

1. ***Cooperative Learning*** Role-play with a small group of classmates to improvise a new **ending** for the play, in which Policeman B discovers the revolutionary's disguise and hiding place. As you perform your improvisation for the class, try to imitate the Irish dialect that you practiced for the Reading Connection on page 912.
2. *The Rising of the Moon* opened in 1907 at the now-famous Abbey Theatre in Dublin. Create an **advertising poster** for the play. Draw an appropriate picture and write an attention-getting caption.

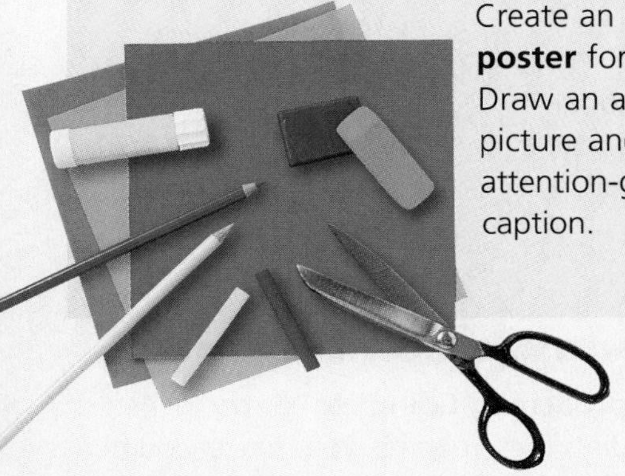

ACROSS THE CURRICULUM

History Although much of Ireland gained independence in 1922, organizations such as Sinn Fein and the Irish Republican Army have continued to fight for the independence of Northern Ireland, which is still part of the United Kingdom. Scan current newspapers and magazines to learn about the recent activities of these groups and the current status of English-Irish negotiations. Share your findings with the class.

Music Research traditional Irish ballads to find out more about their characteristics. Present your findings to your classmates, along with a few recordings of Irish ballads. Some of the more popular singers of such ballads are the Clancy Brothers, Michael O'Donnaill, and a group called De Dannaan.

LADY ISABELLA AUGUSTA GREGORY

1852–1932

The pastoral life of a titled young Irish gentlewoman seems far removed from Isabella Gregory's eventual achievements as a dramatist, Irish partisan, and "godmother" of Dublin's Abbey Theatre. Lady Gregory did not take an active interest in literature until after the death of her husband in 1892. When her son told her that he wanted to learn to speak with the people who lived on their estate, she began to study Gaelic (gā'lĭk), the language of the Celtic people of Ireland, and became fascinated with Gaelic myths, legends, and folk tales.

Her interest in Irish traditions led her to a close friendship with William Butler Yeats, Ireland's foremost poet. The two became leading figures in the Irish Literary Revival, which sought to preserve and renew the country's cultural traditions. It was her son, Major Robert Gregory, whom Yeats commemorated in his poem "An Irish Airman Foresees His Death" (page 844).

Together, Lady Gregory and Yeats helped found the Abbey Theatre expressly for the purpose of staging works such as *The Rising of the Moon.* The theater provided a forum for works celebrating the speech, history, and spirit of the Irish people—topics considered revolutionary in the Ireland of the time.

After writing her first play at the age of 52, Lady Gregory went on to write or translate 40 more plays. She also published three collections of Irish oral histories and legends, based on what she called her "imperfect, stumbling" knowledge of Gaelic. These efforts to bring Irish tales and legends to English-speaking readers met with high critical acclaim when they were published and are still highly regarded today.

OTHER WORKS *Spreading the News, The Workhouse Ward*

PREVIEWING

POETRY

The Second Coming
Sailing to Byzantium

William Butler Yeats

PERSONAL CONNECTION

Most people have concerns and questions about the future—both their own and the world's. What are your main hopes and fears for the future? Do your friends and relatives have similar hopes and fears? Jot down some of your thoughts, and share them with your classmates.

LITERARY/BIOGRAPHICAL CONNECTION

William Butler Yeats, considered by many the greatest poet of the 20th century, was a visionary who developed his own set of beliefs to answer his questions about life and help him interpret the uncertainties of the future. Among these beliefs was the view that history occurs in 2,000-year cycles and that as each era comes to an end, another era—its opposite—is ushered in by a momentous occurrence. In "The Second Coming"—written in January 1919, after the upheavals of World War I and the Russian Revolution of 1917—Yeats employed this view of history to explain what he and many others saw as a breakdown of society at the beginning of the 20th century.

In the 1920s, Yeats became fascinated with the history and art of medieval Byzantium. This interest is reflected in his 1926 poem "Sailing to Byzantium," one of his most celebrated and closely studied poems. He later commented, "Byzantium was the center of European civilization and the source of its spiritual philosophy, so I symbolize the search for spiritual life by a journey to that city."

READING CONNECTION

Approaching Complex Poetry When reading these poems, you may encounter some unfamiliar ideas and images. If a poem seems obscure, try reading it several times. On your first reading, refer to the explanations in the notes and think about the poem's subject. The next time you read the poem, jot down in your notebook any images that stand out in your mind. On subsequent readings, write down any lines that you think are especially difficult.

William Butler Yeats

THE SECOND COMING

Turning and turning in the widening gyre
The falcon cannot hear the falconer;
Things fall apart; the center cannot hold;
Mere anarchy is loosed upon the world,
The blood-dimmed tide is loosed, and everywhere
The ceremony of innocence is drowned;
The best lack all conviction, while the worst
Are full of passionate intensity.

Surely some revelation is at hand;
Surely the Second Coming is at hand.
The Second Coming! Hardly are those words out
When a vast image out of *Spiritus Mundi*
Troubles my sight: somewhere in sands of the desert
A shape with lion body and the head of a man,
A gaze blank and pitiless as the sun,
Is moving its slow thighs, while all about it
Reel shadows of the indignant desert birds.
The darkness drops again; but now I know
That twenty centuries of stony sleep
Were vexed to nightmare by a rocking cradle,
And what rough beast, its hour come round at last,
Slouches towards Bethlehem to be born?

1 gyre (jīr): spiral. (Yeats, however, pronounced this word with a hard *g* [gīr].)

2 falcon: a hawklike bird of prey; **falconer:** a person who uses trained falcons to hunt small game.

6 ceremony of innocence: the rituals (such as the rites of baptism and marriage) that give order to life.

10 Second Coming: Christ's return to earth, predicted in the New Testament as an event preceded by a time of terror and chaos.

12 *Spiritus Mundi* (spîr'ĭ-to͝os mo͝on'dē) *Latin:* Spirit of the World. Yeats used this term to refer to the collective unconscious, a supposed source of images and memories that all human beings share.

14 This image suggests the Great Sphinx in Egypt, built more than 40 centuries ago.

20 rocking cradle: a reference to the birth of Christ.

FROM PERSONAL RESPONSE *TO* CRITICAL ANALYSIS

REFLECT 1. After your reading of this poem, what image from it remains most vivid in your mind? Describe the image in your notebook.

RETHINK 2. What concerns does the poem's speaker seem to be expressing?

3. How would you describe the speaker's view of the future?

Consider
- the speaker's apparent attitude toward the Second Coming
- the speaker's feelings about the "rough beast"
- the effect of the rocking cradle

William Butler Yeats

SAILING TO BYZANTIUM

That is no country for old men. The young
In one another's arms, birds in the trees
—Those dying generations—at their song,
The salmon-falls, the mackerel-crowded seas,
Fish, flesh, or fowl, commend all summer long
Whatever is begotten, born, and dies.
Caught in that sensual music all neglect
Monuments of unaging intellect.

An aged man is but a paltry thing,
A tattered coat upon a stick, unless
Soul clap its hands and sing, and louder sing
For every tatter in its mortal dress,
Nor is there singing school but studying
Monuments of its own magnificence;
And therefore I have sailed the seas and come
To the holy city of Byzantium.

4 salmon-falls: the rapids in rivers that salmon swim up to spawn.

13 but: except for.

14 its: the soul's.

16 Byzantium (bĭ-zăn′shē-əm): a city of southeastern Europe (now Istanbul, Turkey) that was a center of European civilization, especially art and religion, in the Middle Ages.

Saint Mark arriving in Venice (about A.D. 800–1000). Byzantine mosaic from San Marco, Venice, Italy, Scala/Art Resource, New York.

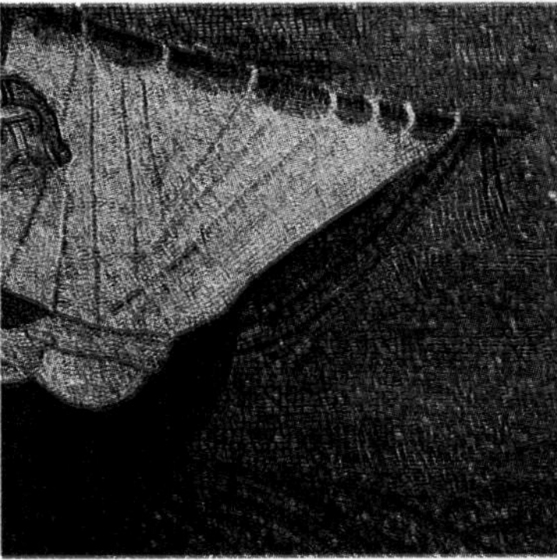

III

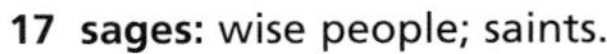

O sages standing in God's holy fire
As in the gold mosaic of a wall,
Come from the holy fire, perne in a gyre,
And be the singing-masters of my soul.
Consume my heart away; sick with desire
And fastened to a dying animal
It knows not what it is; and gather me
Into the artifice of eternity.

IV

Once out of nature I shall never take
My bodily form from any natural thing,
But such a form as Grecian goldsmiths make
Of hammered gold and gold enameling
To keep a drowsy Emperor awake;
Or set upon a golden bough to sing
To lords and ladies of Byzantium
Of what is past, or passing, or to come.

17 sages: wise people; saints.

18 gold mosaic of a wall: artwork in an ancient church.

19 perne (pûrn) **in a gyre:** whirl in a spiral.

23 it: the speaker's heart.

24 artifice: skilled craftsmanship.

29 Emperor: the ninth-century Byzantine emperor Theophilus, said to have possessed a golden sculpture of a tree with mechanical singing birds on its branches.

RESPONDING OPTIONS

FROM PERSONAL RESPONSE *TO* CRITICAL ANALYSIS

REFLECT

1. What impressions of growing old do you have after reading "Sailing to Byzantium"? Share your thoughts with classmates.

RETHINK

2. What conflict does the speaker seem to be facing at the start of the poem?
3. Why do you think the speaker decides to go to Byzantium?
   Consider
   - what the speaker might mean by "monuments of unaging intellect"
   - the possible meanings of *singing*
   - the references to sages, holy fire, and gold mosaic
4. What do you think the speaker expects from the future?

RELATE

5. Compare and contrast the ways in which the speakers of "The Second Coming" and "Sailing to Byzantium" view the future. Do they share any attitudes or expectations? Explain your answer.
6. Some people see uncertainty and change as a challenge; others, as a threat. What kinds of uncertainties and changes do you think people will face in the 21st century? Do you think these two poems offer any perspectives that might be useful in today's world?

ANOTHER PATHWAY

With a partner, read through each poem, making a list of the visual images that you think are essential to the poem's meaning. Decide what feelings or ideas each image conveys and how it contributes to the meaning of the whole poem. Then discuss your list and thoughts with the whole class.

LITERARY CONCEPTS

Symbols—persons, places, objects, or actions that stand for things beyond themselves—are a central element in Yeats's poetry. One of his most important symbols is the spiral, or gyre, which he uses to express his view of history and his belief that life repeats itself even as it moves forward. In a chart like the one below, list other possibly symbolic details in the two poems, noting what each symbol might represent.

"The Second Coming"		"Sailing to Byzantium"	
Symbol	**What It Represents**	**Symbol**	**What It Represents**
gyre	repetition in life		

QUICKWRITES

1. Compose **subtitles** for the four stanzas of "Sailing to Byzantium." Try to make each subtitle reflect your interpretation of the stanza it applies to.
2. Write a **symbolic description** of a major event or change in the world or in your life. Use an original symbol that you think captures the intensity or significance of the event.

PORTFOLIO *Save your writing. You may want to use it later as a springboard to a piece for your portfolio.*

ALTERNATIVE ACTIVITIES

1. Work with a partner to prepare a reading-and-dance **presentation** of one of these poems. As one of you reads the poem, the other should use gesture and movement to interpret the images and the development of ideas in the poem.
2. Draw a **design** for a sculpture that conveys your interpretation of part or all of either poem.

ACROSS THE CURRICULUM

Art Research the art of medieval Byzantium. What was the style of Byzantine art like? What materials were used? Look in art-history books for photographs of Byzantine art, and share some of the best examples with the class.

LITERARY LINKS

Do you think the speaker of "Sailing to Byzantium" would agree with the views about the realities of old age expressed by the speaker of Stephen Spender's "What I Expected" (page 822)? Give reasons to support your answer.

THE WRITER'S STYLE

Yeats once wrote, "I tried to make the language of poetry coincide with that of passionate, normal speech." Find examples of normal, or everyday, language in these two poems. Keeping in mind the importance of both word choice and rhythm, comment on how successful you think Yeats was in his attempt to reflect "passionate, normal speech."

WILLIAM BUTLER YEATS

Born in Dublin of Protestant parents, William Butler Yeats was educated in large part by his father, a portrait painter. After a brief period at an art school, Yeats decided to write instead of paint. He published his first poems in 1885, and from that time until the end of his life, he was constantly writing—producing drama and criticism as well as poetry.

1865–1939

Yeats was passionately committed to Ireland—its people, culture, and political destiny. At the age of 24, he met and fell in love with the actress Maud Gonne, a fiery Irish patriot. Although Gonne refused to marry him, she inspired some of his finest lyrics and deepened his commitment to Irish nationalism. In 1896, he met Lady Gregory, an Irish aristocrat; together they worked to create a national drama for Ireland, founding Dublin's Abbey Theatre in 1904. Their work was vital to the 20th-century revival of Irish literature.

Throughout his life, Yeats had an intense interest in mysticism and the supernatural—an interest that received a fresh impetus after his marriage in 1917, when he discovered that his wife could apparently convey "spirit messages" by means of automatic writing. Yeats used the metaphors and symbols he found in these messages to pursue new directions in his poetry and to create his mythological system. Many of his best works were produced in the following decade.

In 1923 Yeats received the Nobel Prize in literature. He died in France in January 1939, but after World War II his remains were reburied in Ireland, as he had wished.

OTHER WORKS "No Second Troy," "A Prayer for My Daughter," "Byzantium," "Under Ben Bulben"

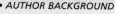

LASERLINKS
- *AUTHOR BACKGROUND*
- *ART GALLERY*

PREVIEWING

FICTION

The Rocking-Horse Winner

D. H. Lawrence

PERSONAL CONNECTION

What do you think of when you hear the word *luck?* Are good luck and bad luck always what they appear to be? With a group of classmates, discuss your thoughts about luck, sharing any notable examples of good luck or bad luck you can think of.

CULTURAL CONNECTION

In England, where this story is set, horseracing dates back more than 800 years. Two of the five great annual horseraces in England are the St. Leger Stakes and the Derby. Other notable English races mentioned in this story are the Grand National, the Ascot Gold Cup, and the Lincolnshire.

Large sums of money are bet on horseraces. The amount a bettor can win depends on the odds. The odds on each horse are expressed as a ratio—3 to 1, for example—and are determined by what proportion of the total amount bet on the race is bet on that horse. The more money bet on a horse, the lower the odds and the lower the payoff. For example, the odds on a "favorite" (a horse that many people have bet on) might be 2 to 1; if that horse wins, each person who has bet on the horse receives 2 dollars for every dollar bet. The odds on a "long shot" (a horse that few people have bet on) might be 20 to 1; if that horse wins, each person who has bet on the horse wins 20 dollars for every dollar bet.

Bettors can wager on horses to win, to place, or to show. A holder of a win ticket collects only if the horse finishes first. A holder of a place ticket collects if the horse comes in first or second, and a holder of a show ticket collects if the horse comes in first, second, or third; but holders of place and show bets on a winning horse receive smaller payoffs than holders of win tickets.

WRITING CONNECTION

In your opinion, how important are love, money, and luck in achieving happiness? In your notebook, rank these things in order of their importance to you. Jot down reasons for your ranking. Then, as you read this story, determine the importance of each in the lives of the various characters.

There must be more money! There must be more money!
There must be more money!

The Rocking-Horse WINNER

D. H. Lawrence

There was a woman who was beautiful, who started with all the advantages, yet she had no luck. She married for love, and the love turned to dust. She had bonny[1] children, yet she felt they had been thrust upon her, and she could not love them. They looked at her coldly, as if they were finding fault with her. And hurriedly she felt she must cover up some fault in herself. Yet what it was that she must cover up she never knew. Nevertheless, when her children were present, she always felt the center of her heart go hard. This troubled her, and in her manner she was all the more gentle and anxious for her children, as if she loved them very much. Only she herself knew that at the center of her heart was a hard little place that could not feel love, no, not for anybody. Everybody else said of her: "She is such a good mother. She adores her children." Only she herself, and her children themselves, knew it was not so. They read it in each other's eyes.

1. **bonny:** pretty.

There were a boy and two little girls. They lived in a pleasant house, with a garden, and they had discreet servants, and felt themselves superior to anyone in the neighborhood.

Although they lived in style, they felt always an anxiety in the house. There was never enough money. The mother had a small income, and the father had a small income, but not nearly enough for the social position which they had to keep up. The father went into town to some office. But though he had good prospects, these prospects never materialized. There was always the grinding sense of the shortage of money, though the style was always kept up.

At last the mother said: "I will see if *I* can't make something." But she did not know where to begin. She racked[2] her brains, and tried this thing and the other, but could not find anything successful. The failure made deep lines come into her face. Her children were growing up, they would have to go to school. There must be more money, there must be more money. The father, who was always very handsome and expensive in his tastes, seemed as if he never *would* be able to do anything worth doing. And the mother, who had a great belief in herself, did not succeed any better, and her tastes were just as expensive.

And so the house came to be haunted by the unspoken phrase: *There must be more money! There must be more money!* The children could hear it all the time, though nobody said it aloud. They heard it at Christmas, when the expensive and splendid toys filled the nursery. Behind the shining modern rocking-horse, behind the smart doll's house, a voice would start whispering: "There *must* be more money! There *must* be more money!" And the children would stop playing, to listen for a moment. They would look into each other's eyes, to see if they had all heard. And each one saw in the eyes of the other two that they too had heard. "There *must* be more money! There *must* be more money!"

It came whispering from the springs of the still-swaying rocking-horse, and even the horse, bending his wooden, champing head, heard it. The big doll, sitting so pink and smirking in her new pram,[3] could hear it quite plainly, and seemed to be smirking all the more self-consciously because of it. The foolish puppy, too, that took the place of the teddy bear, he was looking so extraordinarily foolish for no other reason but that he heard the secret whisper all over the house: "There *must* be more money!"

Yet nobody ever said it aloud. The whisper was everywhere, and therefore no one spoke it. Just as no one ever says: "We are breathing!" in spite of the fact that breath is coming and going all the time.

"Mother," said the boy Paul one day, "why don't we keep a car of our own? Why do we always use uncle's, or else a taxi?"

"Because we're the poor members of the family," said the mother.

"But why *are* we, mother?"

"Well—I suppose," she said slowly and bitterly, "it's because your father has no luck."

The boy was silent for some time.

"Is luck money, mother?" he asked, rather timidly.

"No, Paul. Not quite. It's what causes you to have money."

"Oh!" said Paul vaguely. "I thought when Uncle Oscar said *filthy lucker,* it meant money."

"*Filthy lucre*[4] does mean money," said the mother. "But it's lucre, not luck."

"Oh!" said the boy. "Then what *is* luck, mother?"

"It's what causes you to have money. If you're lucky you have money. That's why it's better to

---

2. **racked:** strained; tortured.
3. **pram:** baby carriage (a shortened form of *perambulator*).
4. **filthy lucre** (lo͞o′kər): money, especially that obtained through fraud or greed (an expression from the King James Bible [Titus 1:11] that has passed into familiar usage).

be born lucky than rich. If you're rich, you may lose your money. But if you're lucky, you will always get more money."

"Oh! Will you? And is father not lucky?"

"Very unlucky, I should say," she said bitterly.

The boy watched her with unsure eyes.

"Why?" he asked.

"I don't know. Nobody ever knows why one person is lucky and another unlucky."

"Don't they? Nobody at all? Does *nobody* know?"

"Perhaps God. But He never tells."

"He ought to, then. And aren't you lucky either, mother?"

"I can't be, if I married an unlucky husband."

"But by yourself, aren't you?"

"I used to think I was, before I married. Now I think I am very unlucky indeed."

"Why?"

"Well—never mind! Perhaps I'm not really," she said.

The child looked at her to see if she meant it. But he saw, by the lines of her mouth, that she was only trying to hide something from him.

"Well, anyhow," he said stoutly,[5] "I'm a lucky person."

"Why?" said his mother, with a sudden laugh.

He stared at her. He didn't even know why he had said it.

"God told me," he asserted, brazening it out.

"I hope He did, dear!" she said, again with a laugh, but rather bitter.

"He did, mother!"

"Excellent!" said the mother, using one of her husband's exclamations.

The boy saw she did not believe him; or rather, that she paid no attention to his assertion. This angered him somewhere, and made him want to compel her attention.

He went off by himself, vaguely, in a childish way, seeking for the clue to "luck." Absorbed, taking no heed of other people, he went about with a sort of stealth, seeking inwardly for luck. He wanted luck, he wanted it, he wanted it. When the two girls were playing dolls in the nursery, he would sit on his big rocking-horse, charging madly into space, with a frenzy that made the little girls peer at him uneasily. Wildly the horse careered, the waving dark hair of the boy tossed, his eyes had a strange glare in them. The little girls dared not speak to him.

When he had ridden to the end of his mad little journey, he climbed down and stood in front of his rocking-horse, staring fixedly into its lowered face. Its red mouth was slightly open, its big eye was wide and glassy-bright.

"Now!" he would silently command the snorting steed. "Now, take me to where there is luck! Now take me!"

And he would slash the horse on the neck with the little whip he had asked Uncle Oscar for. He *knew* the horse could take him to where there was luck, if only he forced it. So he would mount again and start on his furious ride, hoping at last to get there. He knew he could get there.

"You'll break your horse, Paul!" said the nurse.

"He's always riding like that! I wish he'd leave off!" said his elder sister Joan.

But he only glared down on them in silence. Nurse gave him up. She could make nothing of him. Anyhow, he was growing beyond her.

One day his mother and his Uncle Oscar came in when he was on one of his furious rides. He did not speak to them.

"Hallo, you young jockey! Riding a winner?" said his uncle.

"Aren't you growing too big for a rocking-horse? You're not a very little boy any longer, you know," said his mother.

But Paul only gave a blue glare from his big, rather close-set eyes. He would speak to nobody

5. **stoutly:** bravely; firmly.

WORDS TO KNOW

career (kə-rîr′) *v.* to move at full speed; rush

when he was in full tilt.[6] His mother watched him with an anxious expression on her face.

At last he suddenly stopped forcing his horse into the mechanical gallop and slid down.

"Well, I got there!" he announced fiercely, his blue eyes still flaring, and his sturdy long legs straddling apart.

"Where did you get to?" asked his mother.

"Where I wanted to go," he flared back at her.

"That's right, son!" said Uncle Oscar. "Don't you stop till you get there. What's the horse's name?"

"He doesn't have a name," said the boy.

"Gets on without all right?" asked the uncle.

"Well, he has different names. He was called Sansovino last week."

"Sansovino, eh? Won the Ascot. How did you know this name?"

"He always talks about horse races with Bassett," said Joan.

The uncle was delighted to find that his small nephew was posted with all the racing news. Bassett, the young gardener, who had been wounded in the left foot in the war and had got his present job through Oscar Cresswell, whose batman[7] he had been, was a perfect blade of the "turf."[8] He lived in the racing events, and the small boy lived with him.

Oscar Cresswell got it all from Bassett.

"Master Paul comes and asks me, so I can't do more than tell him, sir," said Bassett, his face terribly serious, as if he were speaking of religious matters.

"And does he ever put anything on a horse he fancies?"

"Well—I don't want to give him away—he's a young sport,[9] a fine sport, sir. Would you mind asking him himself? He sort of takes a pleasure in it, and perhaps he'd feel I was giving him away, sir, if you don't mind."

Bassett was serious as a church.

The uncle went back to his nephew and took him off for a ride in the car.

"Say, Paul, old man, do you ever put anything on a horse?" the uncle asked.

The boy watched the handsome man closely.

"Why, do you think I oughtn't to?" he parried.

6. **in full tilt:** moving at full speed.

7. **batman:** in Britain, a soldier who acts as an officer's servant.

8. **blade of the "turf":** one who is very knowledgeable about horseracing.

9. **sport:** good fellow.

WORDS TO KNOW

parry (păr'ē) *v.* to respond by turning aside or evading (a question or argument)

The Races at Longchamp (1866), Édouard Manet. Oil on canvas, 43.9 cm × 84.5 cm, The Art Institute of Chicago, Mr. and Mrs. Potter Palmer Collection (1922.424).

"Not a bit of it! I thought perhaps you might give me a tip for the Lincoln."

The car sped on into the country, going down to Uncle Oscar's place in Hampshire.

"Honor bright?"[10] said the nephew.

"Honor bright, son!" said the uncle.

"Well, then, Daffodil."

"Daffodil! I doubt it, sonny. What about Mirza?"

"I only know the winner," said the boy. "That's Daffodil."

"Daffodil, eh?"

There was a pause. Daffodil was an obscure horse comparatively.

"Uncle!"

"Yes, son?"

"You won't let it go any further, will you? I promised Bassett."

"Bassett be damned, old man! What's he got to do with it?"

10. **honor bright:** an expression meaning "on your (or my) honor."

WORDS TO KNOW **obscure** (ŏb-skyŏŏr′) *adj.* not well-known; undistinguished

"We're partners. We've been partners from the first. Uncle, he lent me my first five shillings,[11] which I lost. I promised him, honor bright, it was only between me and him; only you gave me that ten-shilling note I started winning with, so I thought you were lucky. You won't let it go any further, will you?"

The boy gazed at his uncle from those big, hot, blue eyes, set rather close together. The uncle stirred and laughed uneasily.

"Right you are, son! I'll keep your tip private. Daffodil, eh? How much are you putting on him?"

"All except twenty pounds,"[12] said the boy. "I keep that in reserve."

The uncle thought it a good joke.

"You keep twenty pounds in reserve, do you, you young romancer? What are you betting, then?"

"I'm betting three hundred," said the boy gravely. "But it's between you and me, Uncle Oscar! Honor bright?"

The uncle burst into a roar of laughter.

"It's between you and me all right, you young Nat Gould,"[13] he said, laughing. "But where's your three hundred?"

"Bassett keeps it for me. We're partners."

"You are, are you! And what is Bassett putting on Daffodil?"

"He won't go quite as high as I do, I expect. Perhaps he'll go a hundred and fifty."

"What, pennies?" laughed the uncle.

"Pounds," said the child, with a surprised look at his uncle. "Bassett keeps a bigger reserve than I do."

Between wonder and amusement Uncle Oscar was silent. He pursued the matter no further, but he determined to take his nephew with him to the Lincoln races.

"Now, son," he said, "I'm putting twenty on Mirza, and I'll put five on for you on any horse you fancy. What's your pick?"

"Daffodil, uncle."

"No, not the fiver on Daffodil!"

"I should if it was my own fiver," said the child.

"Good! Good! Right you are! A fiver for me and a fiver for you on Daffodil."

The child had never been to a race-meeting before, and his eyes were blue fire. He pursed his mouth tight and watched. A Frenchman just in front had put his money on Lancelot. Wild with excitement, he flayed his arms up and down, yelling *"Lancelot! Lancelot!"* in his French accent.

Daffodil came in first, Lancelot second, Mirza third. The child, flushed and with eyes blazing, was curiously serene. His uncle brought him four five-pound notes, four to one.

"What am I to do with these?" he cried, waving them before the boy's eyes.

"I suppose we'll talk to Bassett," said the boy. "I expect I have fifteen hundred now; and twenty in reserve; and this twenty."

His uncle studied him for some moments.

"Look here, son!" he said. "You're not serious about Bassett and that fifteen hundred, are you?"

"Yes, I am. But it's between you and me, uncle. Honor bright?"

"Honor bright all right, son! But I must talk to Bassett."

"If you'd like to be a partner, uncle, with Bassett and me, we could all be partners. Only, you'd have to promise, honor bright, uncle, not to let it go beyond us three. Bassett and I are lucky, and you must be lucky, because it was your ten shillings I started winning with. . . ."

Uncle Oscar took both Bassett and Paul into Richmond Park for an afternoon, and there they talked.

---

11. **shillings:** coins formerly used in Britain. (There were 20 shillings in a pound.)
12. **twenty pounds:** the equivalent of about $1,000 in today's dollars. (In the mid-1920s, a pound was worth about $5, and the purchasing power of a dollar was about 10 times what it is now.)
13. **Nat Gould:** a well-known British horseracing authority and writer.

"It's like this, you see, sir," Bassett said. "Master Paul would get me talking about racing events, spinning yarns, you know, sir. And he was always keen on knowing if I'd made or if I'd lost. It's about a year since, now, that I put five shillings on Blush of Dawn for him: and we lost. Then the luck turned, with that ten shillings he had from you: that we put on Singhalese. And since that time, it's been pretty steady, all things considering. What do you say, Master Paul?"

"We're all right when we're sure," said Paul. "It's when we're not quite sure that we go down."

"Oh, but we're careful then," said Bassett.

"But when are you *sure?*" smiled Uncle Oscar.

"It's Master Paul, sir," said Bassett in a secret, religious voice. "It's as if he had it from heaven. Like Daffodil, now, for the Lincoln. That was as sure as eggs."[14]

"Did you put anything on Daffodil?" asked Oscar Cresswell.

"Yes, sir. I made my bit."

"And my nephew?"

Bassett was obstinately silent, looking at Paul.

"I made twelve hundred, didn't I, Bassett? I told uncle I was putting three hundred on Daffodil."

"That's right," said Bassett, nodding.

"But where's the money?" asked the uncle.

"I keep it safe locked up, sir. Master Paul he can have it any minute he likes to ask for it."

"What, fifteen hundred pounds?"

"And twenty! And *forty,* that is, with the twenty he made on the course."

"It's amazing!" said the uncle.

"If Master Paul offers you to be partners, sir, I would, if I were you: if you'll excuse me," said Bassett.

Oscar Cresswell thought about it.

"I'll see the money," he said.

They drove home again, and, sure enough, Bassett came round to the garden-house with fifteen hundred pounds in notes. The twenty pounds reserve was left with Joe Glee, in the Turf Commission deposit.[15]

"You see, it's all right, uncle, when I'm *sure!* Then we go strong, for all we're worth. Don't we, Bassett?"

"We do that, Master Paul."

"And when are you sure?" said the uncle, laughing.

"Oh, well, sometimes I'm *absolutely* sure, like about Daffodil," said the boy; "and sometimes I have an idea; and sometimes I haven't even an idea, have I, Bassett? Then we're careful, because we mostly go down."

"You do, do you! And when you're sure, like about Daffodil, what makes you sure, sonny?"

"Oh, well, I don't know," said the boy uneasily. "I'm sure, you know, uncle; that's all."

"It's as if he had it from heaven, sir," Bassett reiterated.

"I should say so!" said the uncle.

But he became a partner. And when the Leger was coming on Paul was "sure" about Lively Spark, which was a quite inconsiderable horse. The boy insisted on putting a thousand on the horse, Bassett went for five hundred, and Oscar Cresswell two hundred. Lively Spark came in first, and the betting had been ten to one against him. Paul had made ten thousand.

"You see," he said, "I was absolutely sure of him."

Even Oscar Cresswell had cleared two thousand.

"Look here, son," he said, "this sort of thing makes me nervous."

"It needn't, uncle! Perhaps I shan't be sure again for a long time."

14. **as sure as eggs:** absolutely certain (a shortened form of the expression "as sure as eggs is eggs").

15. **Turf Commission deposit:** a bank where bettors keep money for future bets.

WORDS TO KNOW

inconsiderable (ĭn'kən-sĭd'ər-ə-bəl) *adj.* not worth consideration; insignificant

"But what are you going to do with your money?" asked the uncle.

"Of course," said the boy, "I started it for mother. She said she had no luck, because father is unlucky, so I thought if I was lucky, it might stop whispering."

"What might stop whispering?"

"Our house. I *hate* our house for whispering."

"What does it whisper?"

"Why—why"—the boy fidgeted—"why, I don't know. But it's always short of money, you know, uncle."

"I know it, son, I know it."

"You know people send mother writs,[16] don't you, uncle?"

"I'm afraid I do," said the uncle.

"And then the house whispers, like people laughing at you behind your back. It's awful, that is! I thought if I was lucky—"

"You might stop it," added the uncle.

The boy watched him with big blue eyes, that had an uncanny cold fire in them, and he said never a word.

"Well, then!" said the uncle. "What are we doing?"

"I shouldn't like mother to know I was lucky," said the boy.

"Why not, son?"

"She'd stop me."

"I don't think she would."

"Oh!"—and the boy writhed in an odd way—"I *don't* want her to know, uncle."

"All right, son! We'll manage it without her knowing."

They managed it very easily. Paul, at the other's suggestion, handed over five thousand pounds to his uncle, who deposited it with the family lawyer, who was then to inform Paul's mother that a relative had put five thousand pounds into his hands, which sum was to be paid out a thousand pounds at a time, on the mother's birthday, for the next five years.

"So she'll have a birthday present of a thousand pounds for five successive years," said Uncle Oscar. "I hope it won't make it all the harder for her later."

Paul's mother had her birthday in November. The house had been "whispering" worse than ever lately, and, even in spite of his luck, Paul could not bear up against it. He was very anxious to see the effect of the birthday letter, telling his mother about the thousand pounds.

When there were no visitors, Paul now took his meals with his parents, as he was beyond the nursery control. His mother went into town nearly every day. She had discovered that she had an odd knack of sketching furs and dress materials, so she worked secretly in the studio of a friend who was the chief "artist" for the leading drapers.[17] She drew the figures of ladies in furs and ladies in silk and sequins for the newspaper advertisements. This young woman artist earned several thousand pounds a year, but Paul's mother only made several hundreds, and she was again dissatisfied. She so wanted to be first in something, and she did not succeed, even in making sketches for drapery advertisements.

She was down to breakfast on the morning of her birthday. Paul watched her face as she read her letters. He knew the lawyer's letter. As his mother read it, her face hardened and became more expressionless. Then a cold, determined look came on her mouth. She hid the letter under the pile of others, and said not a word about it.

"Didn't you have anything nice in the post for your birthday, mother?" said Paul.

"Quite moderately nice," she said, her voice cold and absent.

She went away to town without saying more.

But in the afternoon Uncle Oscar appeared. He said Paul's mother had had a long interview

16. **writs:** legal documents (in this case, demands for the payment of debts).

17. **drapers:** in Britain, dealers in cloth and dry goods.

with the lawyer, asking if the whole five thousand could not be advanced at once, as she was in debt.

"What do you think, uncle?" said the boy.

"I leave it to you, son."

"Oh, let her have it, then! We can get some more with the other," said the boy.

"A bird in the hand is worth two in the bush, laddie!" said Uncle Oscar.

"But I'm sure to *know* for the Grand National; or the Lincolnshire; or else the Derby. I'm sure to know for *one* of them," said Paul.

So Uncle Oscar signed the agreement, and Paul's mother touched[18] the whole five thousand. Then something very curious happened. The voices in the house suddenly went mad, like a chorus of frogs on a spring evening. There were certain new furnishings, and Paul had a tutor. He was *really* going to Eton, his father's school, in the following autumn. There were flowers in the winter, and a blossoming of the luxury Paul's mother had been used to. And yet the voices in the house, behind the sprays of mimosa and almond-blossom, and from under the piles of iridescent[19] cushions, simply trilled and screamed in a sort of ecstasy: "There *must* be more money! Oh-h-h; there *must* be more money. Oh, now, now-w! Now-w-w—there *must* be more money!—more than ever! More than ever!"

It frightened Paul terribly. He studied away at his Latin and Greek with his tutor. But his intense hours were spent with Bassett. The Grand National had gone by: he had not "known," and had lost a hundred pounds. Summer was at hand. He was in agony for the Lincoln. But even for the Lincoln he didn't "know," and he lost fifty pounds. He became wild-eyed and strange, as if something were going to explode in him.

"Let it alone, son! Don't you bother about it!" urged Uncle Oscar. But it was as if the boy couldn't really hear what his uncle was saying.

"I've got to know for the Derby! I've got to know for the Derby!" the child reiterated, his big blue eyes blazing with a sort of madness.

His mother noticed how overwrought he was.

"You'd better go to the seaside. Wouldn't you like to go now to the seaside, instead of waiting?

18. **touched:** took.

19. **iridescent** (ĭr′ĭ-dĕs′ənt): shining with a rainbowlike display of colors.

Spotted rocking horse, late 1800s. Wood with polychrome, 29″ × 53″, courtesy of Ricco Moresca Gallery.

I think you'd better," she said, looking down at him anxiously, her heart curiously heavy because of him.

But the child lifted his uncanny blue eyes.

"I couldn't possibly go before the Derby, mother!" he said. "I couldn't possibly!"

"Why not?" she said, her voice becoming heavy when she was opposed. "Why not? You can still go from the seaside to see the Derby with your Uncle Oscar, if that's what you wish. No need for you to wait here. Besides, I think you care too much about these races. It's a bad sign. My family has been a gambling family, and you won't know till you grow up how much damage it has done. But it has done damage. I shall have to send Bassett away, and ask Uncle Oscar not to talk racing to you, unless you promise to be reasonable about it: go away to the seaside and forget it. You're all nerves!"

"I'll do what you like, mother, so long as you don't send me away till after the Derby," the boy said.

"Send you away from where? Just from this house?"

"Yes," he said, gazing at her.

"Why, you curious child, what makes you care about this house so much, suddenly? I never knew you loved it."

He gazed at her without speaking. He had a secret within a secret, something he had not divulged, even to Bassett or to his Uncle Oscar.

But his mother, after standing undecided and a little bit sullen for some moments, said:

"Very well, then! Don't go to the seaside till after the Derby, if you don't wish it. But promise me you won't let your nerves go to pieces. Promise you won't think so much about horse-racing and *events,* as you call them!"

"Oh no," said the boy casually. "I won't think much about them, mother. You needn't worry. I wouldn't worry, mother, if I were you."

"If you were me and I were you," said his mother, "I wonder what we *should* do!"

"But you know you needn't worry, mother, don't you?" the boy repeated.

"I should be awfully glad to know it," she said wearily.

"Oh, well, you *can,* you know. I mean, you *ought* to know you needn't worry," he insisted.

"Ought I? Then I'll see about it," she said.

Paul's secret of secrets was his wooden horse, that which had no name. Since he was emancipated from a nurse and a nursery-governess, he had had his rocking-horse removed to his own bedroom at the top of the house.

"Surely you're too big for a rocking-horse!" his mother had remonstrated.

"Well, you see, mother, till I can have a *real* horse, I like to have *some* sort of animal about," had been his quaint answer.

"Do you feel he keeps you company?" she laughed.

"Oh yes! He's very good, he always keeps me company, when I'm there," said Paul.

So the horse, rather shabby, stood in an arrested prance in the boy's bedroom.

The Derby was drawing near, and the boy grew more and more tense. He hardly heard what was spoken to him, he was very frail, and his eyes were really uncanny. His mother had sudden strange seizures of uneasiness about him. Sometimes, for half an hour, she would feel a sudden anxiety about him that was almost anguish. She wanted to rush to him at once, and know he was safe.

Two nights before the Derby, she was at a big party in town, when one of her rushes of anxiety about her boy, her first-born, gripped her heart till she could hardly speak. She fought with the feeling, might and main,[20] for she believed in common sense. But it was too strong. She had to

20. **might and main:** with all her strength.

WORDS TO KNOW

remonstrate (rĭ-mŏn′strāt′) *v.* to protest or object

leave the dance and go downstairs to telephone to the country. The children's nursery-governess was terribly surprised and startled at being rung up in the night.

"Are the children all right, Miss Wilmot?"

"Oh yes, they are quite all right."

"Master Paul? Is he all right?"

"He went to bed as right as a trivet.[21] Shall I run up and look at him?"

"No," said Paul's mother reluctantly. "No! Don't trouble. It's all right. Don't sit up. We shall be home fairly soon." She did not want her son's privacy intruded upon.

"Very good," said the governess.

It was about one o'clock when Paul's mother and father drove up to their house. All was still. Paul's mother went to her room and slipped off her white fur cloak. She had told her maid not to wait up for her. She heard her husband downstairs, mixing a whisky and soda.

And then, because of the strange anxiety at her heart, she stole upstairs to her son's room. Noiselessly she went along the upper corridor. Was there a faint noise? What was it?

She stood, with arrested muscles, outside his door, listening. There was a strange, heavy, and yet not loud noise. Her heart stood still. It was a soundless noise, yet rushing and powerful. Something huge, in violent, hushed motion. What was it? What in God's name was it? She ought to know. She felt that she knew the noise. She knew what it was.

Yet she could not place it. She couldn't say what it was. And on and on it went, like a madness.

Softly, frozen with anxiety and fear, she turned the door handle.

The room was dark. Yet in the space near the window, she heard and saw something plunging to and fro. She gazed in fear and amazement.

Then suddenly she switched on the light, and saw her son, in his green pajamas, madly surging on the rocking-horse. The blaze of light suddenly lit him up, as he urged the wooden horse, and lit her up, as she stood, blonde, in her dress of pale green and crystal, in the doorway.

"Paul!" she cried. "Whatever are you doing?"

"It's Malabar!" he screamed in a powerful, strange voice. "It's Malabar!"

His eyes blazed at her for one strange and senseless second, as he ceased urging his wooden horse. Then he fell with a crash to the ground, and she, all her tormented motherhood flooding upon her, rushed to gather him up.

But he was unconscious, and unconscious he remained, with some brain-fever. He talked and tossed, and his mother sat stonily by his side.

"Malabar! It's Malabar! Bassett, Bassett, I *know!* It's Malabar!"

So the child cried, trying to get up and urge the rocking-horse that gave him his inspiration.

"What does he mean by Malabar?" asked the heart-frozen mother.

"I don't know," said the father stonily.

"What does he mean by Malabar?" she asked her brother Oscar.

"It's one of the horses running for the Derby," was the answer.

And, in spite of himself, Oscar Cresswell spoke to Bassett, and himself put a thousand on Malabar: at fourteen to one.

The third day of the illness was critical: they were waiting for a change. The boy, with his rather long, curly hair, was tossing ceaselessly on the pillow. He neither slept nor regained consciousness, and his eyes were like blue stones. His mother sat, feeling her heart had gone, turned actually into a stone.

In the evening, Oscar Cresswell did not come, but Bassett sent a message, saying could he come up for one moment, just one moment? Paul's mother was very angry at the intrusion, but on second thoughts she agreed. The boy was the same. Perhaps Bassett might bring him to consciousness.

21. **as right as a trivet:** in perfect condition.

The gardener, a shortish fellow with a little brown mustache and sharp little brown eyes, tiptoed into the room, touched his imaginary cap to Paul's mother, and stole to the bedside, staring with glittering, smallish eyes at the tossing, dying child.

"Master Paul!" he whispered. "Master Paul! Malabar came in first all right, a clean win. I did as you told me. You've made over seventy thousand pounds, you have; you've got over eighty thousand.[22] Malabar came in all right, Master Paul."

"Malabar! Malabar! Did I say Malabar, mother? Did I say Malabar? Do you think I'm lucky, mother? I knew Malabar, didn't I? Over eighty thousand pounds! I call that lucky, don't you, mother? Over eighty thousand pounds! I knew, didn't I know I knew? Malabar came in all right. If I ride my horse till I'm sure, then I tell you, Bassett, you can go as high as you like. Did you go for all you were worth, Bassett?"

"I went a thousand on it, Master Paul."

"I never told you, mother, that if I can ride my horse, and *get there,* then I'm absolutely sure—oh, absolutely! Mother, did I ever tell you? I *am* lucky!"

"No, you never did," said his mother.

But the boy died in the night.

And even as he lay dead, his mother heard her brother's voice saying to her: "My God, Hester, you're eighty-odd thousand to the good, and a poor devil of a son to the bad. But, poor devil, poor devil, he's best gone out of a life where he rides his rocking-horse to find a winner." ❖

22. **eighty thousand:** the equivalent of about $4 million in today's dollars.

RESPONDING OPTIONS

FROM PERSONAL RESPONSE *TO* CRITICAL ANALYSIS

REFLECT 1. What scene or image in the story did you find most memorable? Describe it in your notebook.

RETHINK 2. Why do you think Paul becomes obsessed with racing?

Consider
- his mother's attitude toward money
- the "voices" in the house
- what happens when he rides the rocking horse

3. How would you describe the relationship between Paul and his mother?

Consider
- his mother's view of herself and her family
- what she says about luck
- what Paul wants to do for his mother

4. Why do you think the voices get louder after Paul's mother receives the 5,000 pounds?

5. Think back to your discussion of luck for the Personal Connection on page 928. Has reading this story changed your view of luck? Explain your answer.

RELATE 6. In the United States, popular culture is full of suggestions that people can achieve happiness by acquiring as many possessions as possible. What is your opinion of this approach to life? What other lifestyles do you think are possible?

ANOTHER PATHWAY

Cooperative Learning

Working with a small group of classmates, list all the characters in the story, and record each character's experiences with luck. Then decide whether luck is a negative, a positive, or a neutral force in each character's life. Present your conclusions to the rest of the class.

LITERARY CONCEPTS

Foreshadowing consists of hints or clues that suggest what events will occur later in a narrative. The use of foreshadowing creates suspense while preparing readers for what is to come. In "The Rocking-Horse Winner," for example, the strange, mad frenzy with which Paul rides his rocking horse early in the story foreshadows the tragedy of his final ride. List other examples of foreshadowing in the story, noting how each prepares readers for the ending.

CONCEPT REVIEW: Title The title of a literary work usually reveals something about its subject or theme. What do you think Lawrence might have been trying to convey with the title "The Rocking-Horse Winner"?

QUICKWRITES

1. Pretend that you are Paul's mother and write a **letter** to an advice columnist, describing Paul's strange behavior and asking for advice. Then write the columnist's response.
2. Write a new **ending** for this story, in which Paul does not predict the winner of the Derby and does not die.
3. As a police detective, write a **report** of your investigation into Paul's unusual death. Include statements from witnesses and a list of evidence gathered at the scene, as well as your own conclusions about the death.

***PORTFOLIO** Save your writing. You may want to use it later as a springboard to a piece for your portfolio.*

ALTERNATIVE ACTIVITIES

1. ***Cooperative Learning*** Work with a small group of classmates to rewrite a scene from this story in the form of a **radio dramatization.** Remember that a radio dramatization relies heavily upon dialogue, and be sure to include sound effects, such as the "whispering" of the house. You might also include descriptive passages for a narrator to read between your scene and other scenes. Collaborate with other groups to tape-record a performance of the entire story.
2. Tell Paul's story as it might be told by Bassett, the gardener, in an **interview** with a TV news reporter. Explain what you think Paul was trying to do and what kind of person he was.
3. Think about the emotions you had as you read this story. Create an **abstract painting** that expresses one or more of your feelings. Use colors that convey the intensity of your emotions.

THE WRITER'S STYLE

Lawrence uses **irony** to explore the meaning of luck for Paul, his mother, his uncle, and the gardener. For example, Paul's mother's statement "If you're lucky you have money" (page 930) is ironic when read in the light of the story's ending. List other examples of irony, explaining how each contributes to Lawrence's exploration of luck.

LITERARY LINKS

Like "The Demon Lover" (page 895), "The Rocking-Horse Winner" contains unusual, mysterious events and a surprise ending. Which of the two stories seems more believable to you? Explain your answer.

CRITIC'S CORNER

Critics have observed that much of Lawrence's fiction expresses a dissatisfaction with the values and limited viewpoint of conventional middle-class people. What evidence for this attitude can you find in "The Rocking-Horse Winner"? Be specific in your response.

ACROSS THE CURRICULUM

Sports Research the career of a professional jockey. Find out what physical characteristics, skills, and education a jockey must have. List the outstanding achievements of one or two well-known jockeys, and investigate the entrance of women into the profession. Report your findings to the class.

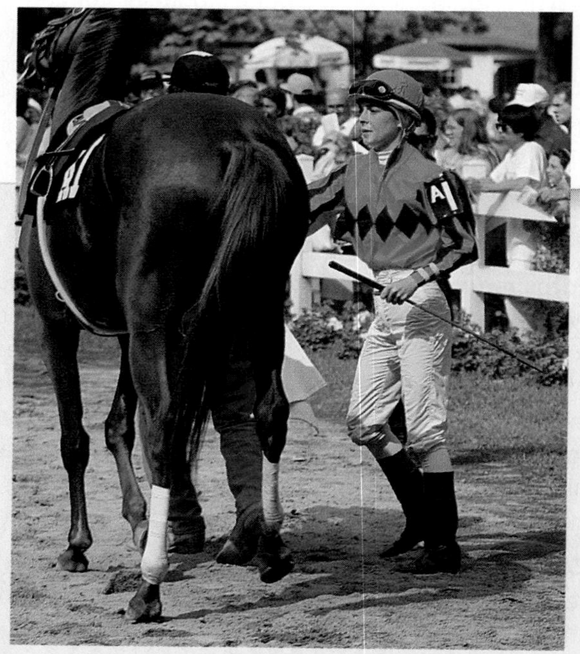

WORDS TO KNOW

EXERCISE A For each pair of words, indicate whether the words are synonyms or antonyms.

1. **remonstrate**—agree
2. **career**—speed
3. **parry**—avoid
4. **obscure**—illustrious
5. **inconsiderable**—outstanding

EXERCISE B Review the Words to Know at the bottom of the selection pages. In groups of five, take turns pantomiming the meaning of each word. Then, in your group, choose the person who you think did the best job of conveying the meaning of his or her word. Challenge members of other groups to guess which word is being pantomimed as the person repeats the performance.

D. H. Lawrence

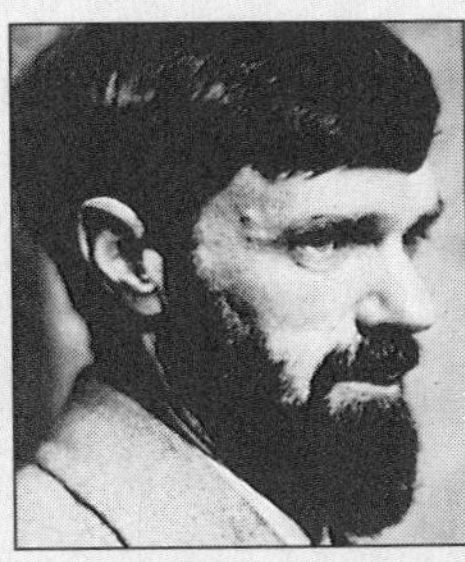

1885–1930

One of five children, David Herbert Lawrence was born in a coal-mining village in the central English county of Nottinghamshire. His early semiautobiographical novel *Sons and Lovers* (1913) is set in this region and reflects the conflict between his mother, who had been a teacher and poet, and his father, an uneducated miner. Lawrence was often ill as a child, and his mother, determined to keep him out of the mines, encouraged him in school, where he remained until he was 15, when financial problems forced him to take a job as a clerk and then as an elementary school teacher. After earning a teaching certificate at the University of Nottingham, he taught school in London for four years. He had already begun writing poetry and fiction, and his first novel, *The White Peacock,* was published when he was 26.

Although Lawrence was recognized as brilliant and imaginative, the passionate, sensual nature of his work made him one of the most controversial writers of the early 20th century. He not only broke literary conventions but also fought against the restrictive social, political, and moral conventions of his day. Many of his novels, short stories, and books of poetry were destroyed or had their publication delayed because censors objected to his treatment of relationships between men and women.

Despite censorship, chronic poverty, and advancing tuberculosis, Lawrence wrote a remarkable number of stories, poems, and novels. He and his wife, Frieda, lived all over the world, trying to discover a better way to relate, live, and grow with other people. Later in his life, Lawrence wrote that "the magnificent here and now of life in the flesh is ours, and ours alone, and ours only for a time. We ought to dance with rapture that we should be alive." Today, Lawrence is studied and admired for the fresh perspective and style he brought to literature and living.

OTHER WORKS "Tickets, Please," "Odor of Chrysanthemums"

PREVIEWING

FICTION

Araby

James Joyce

PERSONAL CONNECTION

Try to recall a time in your childhood or adolescence when you came to a sudden realization about yourself or someone close to you. Perhaps you discovered that you had a new ability or hidden talent, or maybe you suddenly understood why a friend was treating you a certain way. Share the insight with your classmates, explaining the impact it had on you.

LITERARY/BIOGRAPHICAL CONNECTION

The Irish writer James Joyce is best known for his novel *Ulysses,* published in 1922. (See pages 954–955). In writing it and his other works, Joyce called upon his own remembrances of Dublin at the turn of the century. His father's financial problems forced the Joyce family to move frequently, each time to a poorer and shabbier section of the city, and Joyce thus became acquainted with many facets of Dublin society. As a young man, Joyce was critical of the "paralysis," or immobility, of the Irish people, and he left the country to live abroad. Nevertheless, his mind was preoccupied with the people of Dublin, and the life of the city became the focal point of all his fiction.

"Araby" is one of a series of short stories that Joyce began writing in 1904 and that were eventually published in the collection *Dubliners.* Joyce explained that the collection's stories are grouped to present four aspects of Dublin life: childhood, adolescence, maturity, and public life. The events in each story lead up to what Joyce called an epiphany—an ordinary moment or situation in which an important truth about a character's life is suddenly revealed.

James Joyce, 1904

READING CONNECTION

Understanding Point of View "Araby" is told from the **first-person point of view**—that is, the narrator is a participant (in this case, as a young boy) in the events he recounts. Readers see everything through the narrator's eyes, and it is his comments and descriptions that convey the intensity of his situation. As you read the story, be aware of what Joyce's use of the first-person point of view helps to reveal about the narrator.

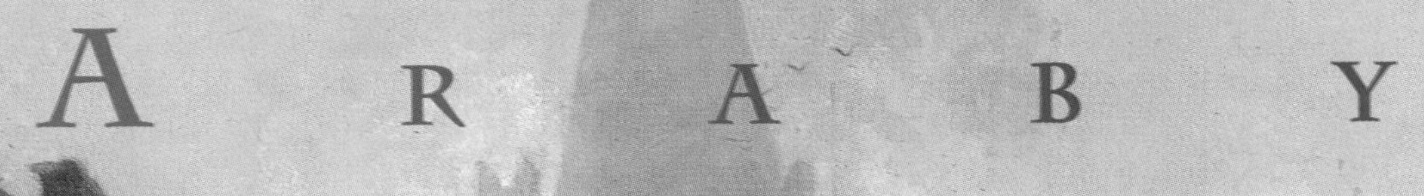

ARABY

JAMES JOYCE

North Richmond Street, being blind, was a quiet street except at the hour when the Christian Brothers' School set the boys free. An uninhabited house of two stories stood at the blind end, detached from its neighbors in a square ground.

• • •

The other houses of the street, conscious of decent lives within them, gazed at one another with brown imperturbable faces.

The former tenant of our house, a priest, had died in the back drawing-room. Air, musty from having been long enclosed, hung in all the rooms, and the waste room behind the kitchen was littered with old useless papers. Among these I found a few paper-covered books, the pages of which were curled and damp: *The Abbot,* by Walter Scott, *The Devout Communicant* and *The Memoirs of Vidocq.*[1] I liked the last best because its leaves were yellow. The wild garden behind the house contained a central apple-tree and a few straggling bushes under one of which I found the late tenant's rusty bicycle-pump. He had been a very charitable priest; in his will he had left all his money to institutions and the furniture of his house to his sister.

When she came out on the doorstep my heart leaped.

When the short days of winter came dusk fell before we had well eaten our dinners. When we met in the street the houses had grown somber. The space of sky above us was the color of ever-changing violet and towards it the lamps of the street lifted their feeble lanterns. The cold air stung us and we played till our bodies glowed. Our shouts echoed in the silent street. The career of our play brought us through the dark muddy lanes behind the houses where we ran the gantlet[2] of the rough tribes from the cottages, to the back doors of the dark dripping gardens where odors arose from the ashpits, to the dark odorous stables where a coachman smoothed and combed the horse or shook music from the buckled harness. When we returned to the street light from the kitchen windows had filled the areas. If my uncle was seen turning the corner we hid in the shadow until we had seen him safely housed. Or if Mangan's sister came out on the doorstep to call her brother in to his tea we watched her from our shadow peer up and down the street. We waited to see whether she would remain or go in and, if she remained, we left our shadow and walked up to Mangan's steps resignedly. She was waiting for us, her figure defined by the light from the half-opened door. Her brother always teased her before he obeyed and I stood by the railings looking at her. Her dress swung as she moved her body and the soft rope of her hair tossed from side to side.

Every morning I lay on the floor in the front parlor watching her door. The blind was pulled down to within an inch of the sash so that I could not be seen. When she came out on the doorstep my heart leaped. I ran to the hall, seized my books and followed her. I kept her brown figure always in my eye and, when we came near the point at which our ways diverged, I quickened my pace and passed her. This happened morning after morning. I had never spoken to her, except for a few casual words, and yet her name was like a summons to all my foolish blood.

Her image accompanied me even in places the most hostile to romance. On Saturday evenings when my aunt went marketing I had to go to carry some of the parcels. We walked through the flaring streets, jostled by drunken men and bargaining women, amid the curses of laborers, the shrill litanies of shopboys who stood on guard by the barrels of pigs' cheeks, the nasal chanting of street-singers, who sang a *come-all-*

1. ***The Abbot . . . Vidocq*** (vē-dôk′): three widely varying 19th-century works—the first a historical novel, the second a book of religious instruction, and the third an autobiography of a French police detective.
2. **ran the gantlet:** passed through an area of hostility or attack. (A gantlet [or gauntlet] is a punishment in which a person is made to run between two rows of people who strike him with clubs.)

WORDS TO KNOW

imperturbable (ĭm′pər-tûr′bə-bəl) *adj.* not easily disturbed; calm
litany (lĭt′n-ē) *n.* a repetitive chant or recital

you about O'Donovan Rossa, or a ballad about the troubles in our native land. These noises converged in a single sensation of life for me: I imagined that I bore my chalice safely through a throng of foes. Her name sprang to my lips at moments in strange prayers and praises which I myself did not understand. My eyes were often full of tears (I could not tell why) and at times a flood from my heart seemed to pour itself out into my bosom. I thought little of the future. I did not know whether I would ever speak to her or not or, if I spoke to her, how I could tell her of my confused adoration. But my body was like a harp and her words and gestures were like fingers running upon the wires.

One evening I went into the back drawing-room in which the priest had died. It was a dark rainy evening and there was no sound in the house. Through one of the broken panes I heard the rain impinge[3] upon the earth, the fine incessant needles of water playing in the sodden beds. Some distant lamp or lighted window gleamed below me. I was thankful that I could see so little. All my senses seemed to desire to veil themselves and, feeling that I was about to slip from them, I pressed the palms of my hands together until they trembled, murmuring: *O love! O love!* many times.

At last she spoke to me. When she addressed the first words to me I was so confused that I did not know what to answer. She asked me was I going to *Araby*. I forgot whether I answered yes or no. It would be a splendid bazaar, she said; she would love to go.

—And why can't you? I asked.

While she spoke she turned a silver bracelet round and round her wrist. She could not go, she said, because there would be a retreat that week in her convent. Her brother and two other boys were fighting for their caps and I was alone at the railings. She held one of the spikes, bowing her head towards me. The light from the lamp opposite our door caught the white curve of her neck, lit up her hair that rested there and, falling, lit up the hand upon the railing. It fell over one side of her dress and caught the white border of a petticoat, just visible as she stood at ease.

—It's well for you, she said.

—If I go, I said, I will bring you something.

What innumerable follies laid waste my waking and sleeping thoughts after that evening! I wished to annihilate the tedious intervening days. I chafed against the work of school. At night in my bedroom and by day in the classroom her image came between me and the page I strove to read. The syllables of the word *Araby* were called to me through the silence in which my soul luxuriated, and cast an Eastern enchantment over me. I asked for leave to go to the bazaar on Saturday night. My aunt was surprised and hoped it was not some Freemason[4] affair. I answered few questions in class. I watched my master's face pass from amiability to sternness; he hoped I was not beginning to idle. I could not call my wandering thoughts together. I had hardly any patience with the serious work of life which, now that it stood between me and my desire, seemed to me child's play, ugly monotonous child's play.

On Saturday morning I reminded my uncle that I wished to go to the bazaar in the evening. He was fussing at the hallstand,

3. **impinge** (ĭm-pĭnj'): hit; strike.

4. **Freemason:** having to do with the Free and Accepted Masons, a worldwide charitable and social organization. (Freemasonry has often been opposed by Roman Catholics and other religious groups, in part because of its secret rituals and signs.)

WORDS TO KNOW **luxuriate** (lŭg-zhŏŏr'ē-āt') *v.* to take great delight

looking for the hat-brush, and answered me curtly:

—Yes, boy, I know.

As he was in the hall I could not go into the front parlor and lie at the window. I left the house in bad humor and walked slowly towards the school. The air was pitilessly raw and already my heart misgave[5] me.

When I came home to dinner my uncle had not yet been home. Still it was early. I sat staring at the clock for some time and, when its ticking began to irritate me, I left the room. I mounted the staircase and gained the upper part of the house. The high cold empty gloomy rooms liberated me and I went from room to room singing. From the front window I saw my companions playing below in the street. Their cries reached me weakened and indistinct and, leaning my forehead against the cool glass, I looked over at the dark house where she lived. I may have stood there for an hour, seeing nothing but the brown-clad figure cast by my imagination, touched discreetly by the lamp-light at the curved neck, at the hand upon the railings and at the border below the dress.

When I came downstairs again I found Mrs. Mercer sitting at the fire. She was an old garrulous woman, a pawnbroker's widow, who collected used stamps for some pious purpose. I had to endure the gossip of the tea table. The meal was prolonged beyond an hour and still my uncle did not come. Mrs. Mercer stood up to go: she was sorry she couldn't wait any longer, but it was after eight o'clock and she did not like to be out late, as the night air was bad for her. When she had gone I began to walk up and down the room, clenching my fists. My aunt said:

—I'm afraid you may put off your bazaar for this night of Our Lord.

At nine o'clock I heard my uncle's latchkey in the hall-door. I heard him talking to himself and heard the hall-stand rocking when it had received the weight of his overcoat. I could interpret these signs. When he was midway through his dinner I asked him to give me the money to go to the bazaar. He had forgotten.

—The people are in bed and after their first sleep now, he said.

I did not smile. My aunt said to him energetically:

—Can't you give him the money and let him go? You've kept him late enough as it is.

My uncle said he was very sorry he had forgotten. He said he believed in the old saying: *All work and no play makes Jack a dull boy.* He asked me where I was going and, when I had told him a second time he asked me did I know *The Arab's Farewell to His Steed.* When I left the kitchen he was about to recite the opening lines of the piece to my aunt.

I held a florin[6] tightly in my hand as I strode down Buckingham Street towards the station. The sight of the streets thronged with buyers and glaring with gas[7] recalled to me the purpose of my journey. I took my seat in a third-class carriage of a deserted train. After an intolerable delay the train moved out of the station slowly. It crept onward among ruinous houses and over the twinkling river. At Westland Row Station a crowd of people pressed

5. **misgave:** caused to feel doubt or anxiety.

6. **florin:** a former British coin worth 2 shillings (24 pence).

7. **gas:** gaslight.

WORDS TO KNOW

garrulous (găr'ə-ləs) *adj.* rambling in speech; tiresomely talkative

to the carriage doors; but the porters moved them back, saying that it was a special train for the bazaar. I remained alone in the bare carriage. In a few minutes the train drew up beside an improvised wooden platform. I passed out on to the road and saw by the lighted dial of a clock that it was ten minutes to ten. In front of me was a large building which displayed the magical name.

I allowed the two pennies to fall against the sixpence in my pocket.

I could not find any sixpenny entrance and, fearing that the bazaar would be closed, I passed in quickly through a turnstile, handing a shilling to a weary-looking man. I found myself in a big hall girdled at half its height by a gallery. Nearly all the stalls were closed and the greater part of the hall was in darkness. I recognized a silence like that which pervades a church after a service. I walked into the center of the bazaar timidly. A few people were gathered about the stalls which were still open. Before a curtain, over which the words *Café Chantant*[8] were written in colored lamps, two men were counting money on a salver.[9] I listened to the fall of the coins.

Remembering with difficulty why I had come I went over to one of the stalls and examined porcelain vases and flowered tea-sets. At the door of the stall a young lady was talking and laughing with two young gentlemen. I remarked their English accents and listened vaguely to their conversation.

—O, I never said such a thing!

—O, but you did!

—O, but I didn't!

—Didn't she say that?

—Yes. I heard her.

—O, there's a . . . fib!

Observing me the young lady came over and asked me did I wish to buy anything. The tone of her voice was not encouraging; she seemed to have spoken to me out of a sense of duty. I looked humbly at the great jars that stood like eastern guards at either side of the dark entrance to the stall and murmured:

—No, thank you.

The young lady changed the position of one of the vases and went back to the two young men. They began to talk of the same subject. Once or twice the young lady glanced at me over her shoulder.

I lingered before her stall, though I knew my stay was useless, to make my interest in her wares seem the more real. Then I turned away slowly and walked down the middle of the bazaar. I allowed the two pennies to fall against the sixpence in my pocket. I heard a voice call from one end of the gallery that the light was out. The upper part of the hall was now completely dark.

Gazing up into the darkness I saw myself as a creature driven and derided by vanity; and my eyes burned with anguish and anger. ❖

8. ***Café Chantant*** (kä-fā′ shäɴ-täɴ′): a café providing musical entertainment.

9. **salver:** serving tray.

St. Patrick's Close, Dublin (1887), Walter Frederick Osborne. Oil on canvas, 27 ¼″ × 20″, National Gallery of Ireland, Dublin.

WORDS TO KNOW **pervade** (pər-vād′) *v.* to spread throughout; completely fill

RESPONDING OPTIONS

FROM PERSONAL RESPONSE *TO* CRITICAL ANALYSIS

REFLECT 1. Were you surprised by the way this story ended? In your notebook, briefly explain your reactions. Then share them with the class.

RETHINK 2. How would you describe the relationship between the narrator and Mangan's sister?

3. What might be the cause of the narrator's "anguish and anger" at the end of the story?

Consider
- his expectations and excitement about going to the bazaar
- his experiences at the bazaar
- his reference to himself as "a creature driven . . . by vanity"

4. What epiphany, or sudden awareness, does the narrator seem to experience?

RELATE 5. Do you think the narrator's actions and feelings are typical? Why or why not?

ANOTHER PATHWAY

Cooperative Learning

With a small group of classmates, identify and describe the feelings experienced by the narrator during the various events he recalls in the story. After recording your findings in a chart like the one shown, discuss them with the rest of the class.

Narrator's Situation	Narrator's Feelings
before talking to Mangan's sister	longing, amazement
during conversation with Mangan's sister	
at school	

LITERARY CONCEPTS

Realism in fiction is a truthful representation of actual life. In a realistic work, ordinary, everyday events are presented in clear, direct prose. Detailed characterization, focusing on characters' thoughts and values, is also an important element of realism. Look back through "Araby," listing at least four descriptive sentences that you find particularly realistic in their depiction of actual life. Share and discuss your list with the class.

CONCEPT REVIEW: Setting The importance of setting—the time and place in which a story's action occurs—varies from story to story. It may play a major role in what happens, contributing to the story's mood, tone, or theme, or it may be only incidental. Think about the different settings described in "Araby," and discuss what they add to the story.

QUICKWRITES

1. Write a short **sequel** to "Araby," using the first-person point of view to present the next encounter between the narrator and Mangan's sister.
2. Write a **journal entry** that the narrator might compose after arriving home from the bazaar.
3. Write a **biographical sketch** of the narrator as a child, based on the information given about him and his family in the story. Feel free to add missing pieces of information.

PORTFOLIO *Save your writing. You may want to use it later as a springboard to a piece for your portfolio.*

ALTERNATIVE ACTIVITIES

1. Practice and perform a **pantomime** of the narrator's actions on the day and evening of the bazaar.
2. Design an **advertisement** for Araby that reflects the narrator's anticipation of what the bazaar will be like.
3. Look through books to find **photographs** illustrating your impression of the early-20th-century city life portrayed in "Araby." Display them in the classroom.

LITERARY LINKS

Compare and contrast the portrayals of adults in "Araby" and D. H. Lawrence's "The Rocking-Horse Winner."

ART CONNECTION

Look again at the photograph of the boy on page 949. Does his appearance match your mental image of the narrator of this story? Discuss your impressions with a partner.

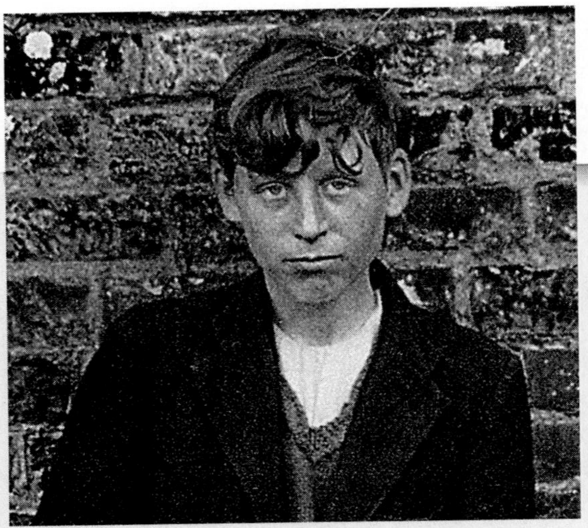

THE WRITER'S STYLE

The **images** that Joyce uses add a rich layer of intensity and interest to his stories. Sometimes a single image will recur several times in a story. Choose your favorite images in "Araby." Explain why you selected them and what impact you think they have on the story.

CRITIC'S CORNER

According to the American poet and critic Ezra Pound (a contemporary of Joyce's), one of Joyce's merits is that "he carefully avoids telling you a lot that you don't want to know." Similarly, Eva Tanner, a student reviewer, praised "Araby" for its "simplicity" and thoughtful use of detail. Do you agree that Joyce is frugal in his use of detail? Use evidence from this story to support your opinion.

ACROSS THE CURRICULUM

History Find out more about Dublin life in the early 1900s. Write a brief report describing the class structure, schooling, clothing, housing, occupations, and transportation of the city's residents.

WORDS TO KNOW

Review the Words to Know at the bottom of the selection pages. Then write the word that is best described by each clue.

1. Joy, light, or a fragrance can do this to a group or a place.
2. A person who is this is someone you don't want to have a conversation with when you're in a hurry.
3. You might do this in a hot bath on a cold day or in a cool lake on a hot day.
4. It can require great patience not to interrupt this, because you're tempted to say, "So you've said . . . and said and said!"
5. A person who is this might gaze serenely from the stands while the rest of the fans are leaping to their feet to cheer a home run.

JAMES JOYCE

1882–1941

James Joyce overcame many handicaps to become one of the greatest novelists of the 20th century. Born into a large Dublin family, he began feeling the effects of poverty as a young child. His father was extremely irresponsible and drank heavily, and during Joyce's childhood the family sank further and further into debt. The children grew accustomed to bill collectors, frequent moves, and the loss of family possessions. At one point, Joyce was forced to leave a grammar school when his parents could no longer afford the tuition. After two years of trying to educate himself at home, he finally had his tuition fees waived so that he might finish his formal education.

In 1902, Joyce graduated from University College in Dublin, where he first began to write seriously. Writing, however, was not the only interest that Joyce pursued—he had a fine voice and as a young man considered a singing career—but even after he focused his attention more exclusively on writing, he knew that it was an uncertain profession and that he would probably need another source of income. He began the study of medicine but quickly abandoned it because he had neither the tuition nor the proper educational background. During his lifetime, he tried his hand at various other jobs and enterprises, including teaching, banking, and the movie-theater business.

In June 1904, Joyce met Nora Barnacle, a young girl from Galway, and a few months later the couple moved to Austria-Hungary. Over the next few years, they lived in several European cities—including Trieste, Paris, and Zurich—but never returned to Ireland. Throughout much of his adult life, Joyce faced financial disaster but managed to continue writing with assistance from friends. He also faced serious problems with his vision, undergoing eye surgery 25 times between 1917 and 1930. While working on his last novel, *Finnegans Wake,* he was occasionally forced to write in crayon on large sheets of paper in order to see his own work.

OTHER WORKS "An Encounter," "The Sisters," "Eveline," "Counterparts"

MILESTONES IN BRITISH LITERATURE

James Joyce

ULYSSES

Above:
Images of Dublin, early 20th century

Is it possible to write an epic set in the modern world? Where could one find characters of suitably heroic dimensions? The Irish writer James Joyce faced these questions after leaving his homeland, which he believed to be too narrow in its cultural and religious views, to live in self-imposed exile in Trieste, Zurich, and Paris. From 1914 to 1921, impoverished and struggling to support his family, he produced his masterwork, *Ulysses,* probably the most influential novel of the 20th century.

On one level the plot of *Ulysses* reflects the events recounted in Homer's *Odyssey*—the return of the Greek hero Odysseus (in Latin, Ulysses) to his faithful wife, Penelope, and his son,

Telemachus, after ten years of wandering throughout the Mediterranean after the Trojan War. In typical Joycean fashion, however, the Greek epic is turned on its ear. The hero of *Ulysses* is Leopold Bloom, a middle-aged advertising salesman who lives in Dublin with his unfaithful wife, Molly. He wanders about the city on a single day—June 16, 1904—beginning and ending his journey at his home in Eccles Street. During the course of his wanderings, he encounters Stephen Dedalus, a 22-year-old poet who was the protagonist of Joyce's first novel, *A Portrait of the Artist as a Young Man*. As their lives intersect, the two men form a bond, and in a way Stephen becomes a son to Bloom—a Telemachus to Bloom's Odysseus.

What elevates the story to truly epic proportions is Joyce's presentation of the amazing inner life of his characters through interior monologues. Their thoughts, including the most intimate ones, come rushing by in a stream of consciousness. In the following passage, for example, Bloom, having just attended the funeral of Patrick Dignam, is in a pub, deciding what to have for lunch. Notice how, in the space of a few lines, his thoughts range from sensory experience to a biblical pun to an advertising slogan to Dignam's corpse to a flight of fancy:

> Sardines on the shelves. Almost taste them by looking. Sandwich? Ham and his descendants musterred and bred there. Potted meats. What is home without Plumtree's potted meat? Incomplete. What a stupid ad! Under the obituary notices they stuck it. All up a plumtree. Dignam's potted meat. Cannibals would with lemon and rice. . . .

In addition to the Homeric parallels, allusions to Shakespeare and Dante abound, along with references to the Roman Catholic Church, music, psychology, philosophy, pulp fiction, and a multitude of other topics. Every imaginable aspect of a day in the life of a 20th-century Odysseus, Penelope, and Telemachus is captured in exacting detail, as if their thoughts were our very own.

It is ironic that Joyce, a man who spent his lifetime wandering about Europe, searching for a home, should have spent so much time writing about the very homeland he rejected. Once, when asked if he had plans to return to Ireland at some point, Joyce replied, "Have I ever left?"

Below:
Ulysses and the Sirens *(third century A.D.), unknown artist. Musée National du Bardo, Le Bardo, Tunisia, Giraudon/Art Resource, New York.*

PREVIEWING

FICTION

A Cup of Tea

Katherine Mansfield

PERSONAL CONNECTION

Although class distinctions based on wealth are not as pronounced in the United States as they once were, they do still exist. In your notebook, make three lists, noting what seem to you to be (1) typically upper-class, (2) typically middle-class, and (3) typically lower-class places, events, and institutions. Discuss your lists with classmates.

CULTURAL CONNECTION

In the early 1900s, when "A Cup of Tea" was written, class distinctions were quite evident in Britain. The best schools and neighborhoods were typically reserved for the rich, who also tended to shop in separate stores on exclusive streets and to avoid contact with people of lower classes whenever possible. An upper-class wife never worked, either inside or outside the home—instead spending her days shopping, visiting, and entertaining. It was considered improper for her to associate with people of lower classes unless they were serving her in some way. In "A Cup of Tea," Mansfield portrays a character named Rosemary who belongs to this pampered upper class.

WRITING CONNECTION

In your notebook, make a copy of the diagram shown. After reading the two definitions of the word *patronize* in the first box, illustrate each definition with an example of your own in the second box. Then, as you read this story about an upper-class wife's encounter with a poor woman, look for an action of Rosemary's that illustrates each definition. Record your findings in the third box.

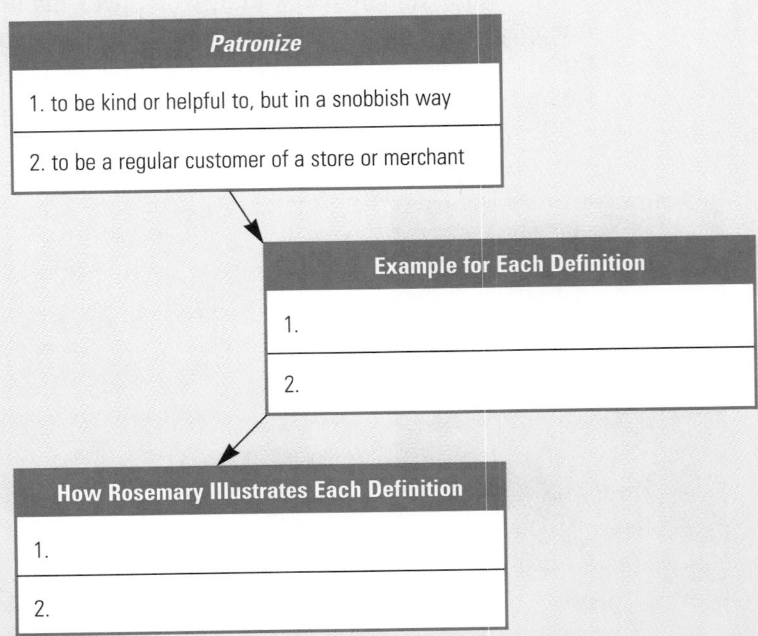

Patronize
1. to be kind or helpful to, but in a snobbish way
2. to be a regular customer of a store or merchant
Example for Each Definition
1.
2.
How Rosemary Illustrates Each Definition
1.
2.

A Cup of Tea

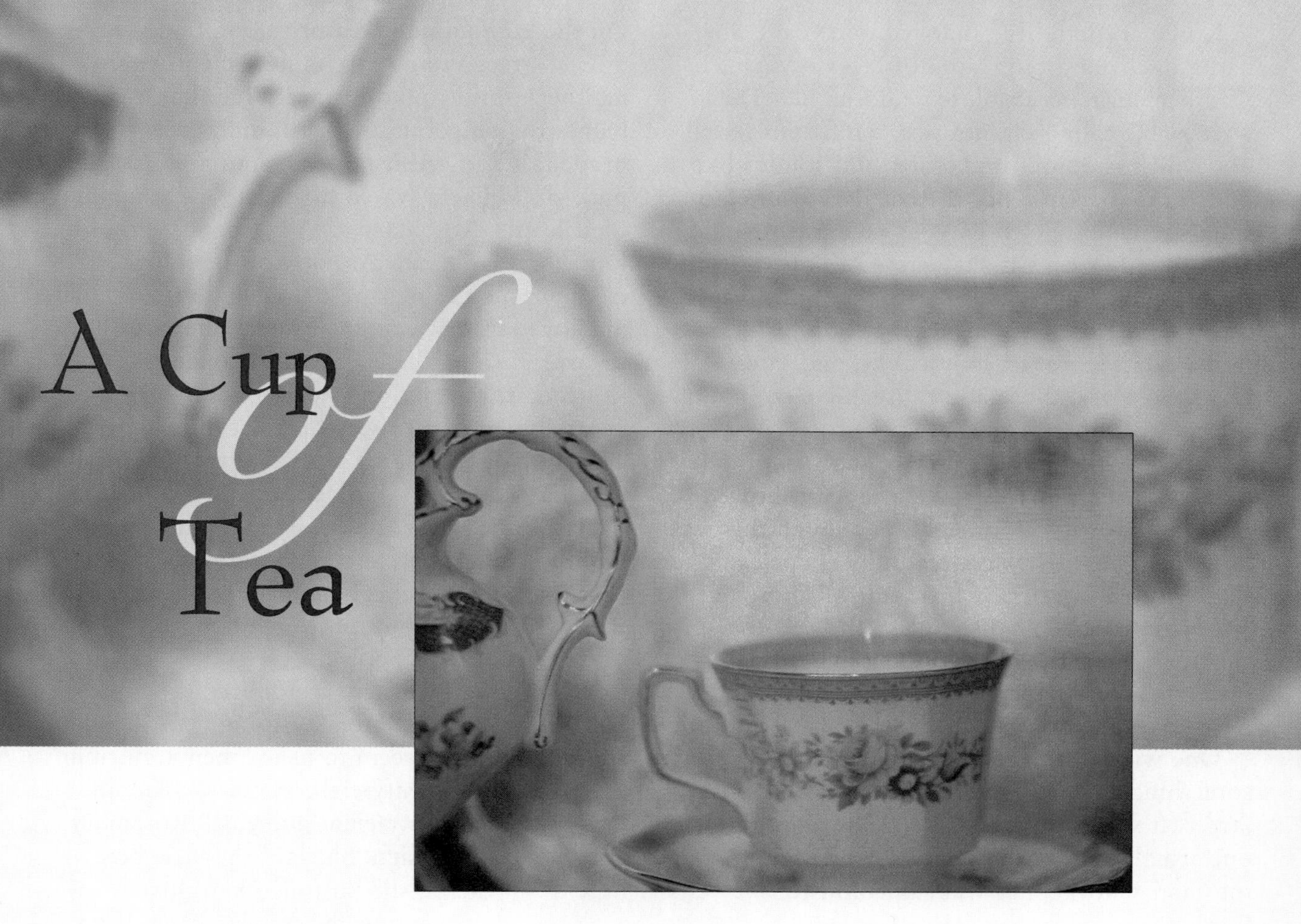

Katherine Mansfield

Rosemary Fell was not exactly beautiful. No, you couldn't have called her beautiful. Pretty? Well, if you took her to pieces . . . But why be so cruel as to take anyone to pieces? She was young, brilliant, extremely modern, exquisitely well dressed, amazingly well read in the newest of the new books, and her parties were the most delicious mixture of the really important people and . . . artists—quaint creatures, discoveries of hers, some of them too terrifying for words, but others quite presentable and amusing.

Rosemary had been married two years. She had a duck[1] of a boy. No, not Peter—Michael. And her husband absolutely adored her. They were rich, really rich, not just comfortably well off, which is odious and stuffy and sounds like one's grandparents. But if Rosemary wanted to shop she would go to Paris as you and I would go to Bond Street.[2] If she wanted to buy flowers, the car pulled up at that perfect shop in Regent Street, and Rosemary inside the shop just gazed in her dazzled, rather exotic way, and said: "I want those and those and those. Give me four bunches of those. And that jar of roses. Yes, I'll have all the roses in the jar. No, no lilac. I hate lilac. It's got no shape." The attendant bowed and put the lilac out of sight, as though this was only too true; lilac was dreadfully shapeless. "Give me those stumpy little tulips. Those red and white ones." And she was followed to the car by a thin shopgirl staggering under an immense white paper armful that looked like a baby in long clothes. . . .

One winter afternoon she had been buying something in a little antique shop in Curzon Street. It was a shop she liked. For one thing, one usually had it to oneself. And then the man who kept it was ridiculously fond of serving her. He beamed whenever she came in. He clasped his hands; he was so gratified he could scarcely speak. Flattery, of course. All the same, there was something . . .

"You see, madam," he would explain in his low respectful tones, "I love my things. I would rather not part with them than sell them to someone who does not appreciate them, who has not that fine feeling which is so rare. . . ." And, breathing deeply, he unrolled a tiny square of blue velvet and pressed it on the glass counter with his pale fingertips.

Today it was a little box. He had been keeping it for her. He had shown it to nobody as yet. An exquisite little enamel box with a glaze so fine it looked as though it had been baked in cream. On the lid a minute creature stood under a flowery tree, and a more minute creature still had her arms around his neck. Her hat, really no bigger than a geranium petal, hung from a branch; it had green ribbons. And there was a pink cloud like a watchful cherub[3] floating above their heads. Rosemary took her hands out of her long gloves. She always took off her gloves to examine such things. Yes, she liked it very much. She loved it; it was a great duck. She must have it. And, turning the creamy box, opening and shutting it, she couldn't help noticing how charming her hands were against the blue velvet. The shopman, in some dim cavern of his mind, may have dared to think so too. For he took a pencil, leaned over the counter, and his pale bloodless fingers crept timidly towards those rosy, flashing ones, as he murmured gently: "If I may venture to point out to madam, the flowers on the little lady's bodice."[4]

"Charming!" Rosemary admired the flowers. But what was the price? For a moment the shopman did not seem to hear. Then a murmur reached her. "Twenty-eight guineas,[5] madam."

"Twenty-eight guineas." Rosemary gave no sign. She laid the little box down; she buttoned her gloves again. Twenty-eight guineas. Even if one is rich . . . She looked vague. She stared at a plump teakettle like a plump hen above the shopman's head, and her voice was dreamy as she answered: "Well, keep it for me—will you? I'll . . ."

But the shopman had already bowed as though keeping it for her was all any human being could ask. He would be willing, of course, to keep it for her forever.

---

1. **duck:** in British usage, a darling person or thing.
2. **Bond Street:** one of London's main business streets.
3. **cherub:** an angel depicted as a chubby child with wings.
4. **bodice** (bŏd′ĭs): the upper part of a dress.
5. **guineas** (gĭn′ēz): units of British money (equal to 21 shillings each), used mainly for pricing luxury items.

The discreet door shut with a click. She was outside on the step, gazing at the winter afternoon. Rain was falling, and with the rain it seemed the dark came too, spinning down like ashes. There was a cold bitter taste in the air, and the new-lighted lamps looked sad. Sad were the lights in the houses opposite. Dimly they burned as if regretting something. And people hurried by, hidden under their hateful umbrellas. Rosemary felt a strange pang.[6] She pressed her muff to her breast; she wished she had the little box, too, to cling to. Of course, the car was there. She'd only to cross the pavement. But still she waited. There are moments, horrible moments in life, when one emerges from shelter and looks out, and it's awful. One oughtn't to give way to them. One ought to go home and have an extra-special tea. But at the very instant of thinking that, a young girl, thin, dark, shadowy—where had she come from?—was standing at Rosemary's elbow and a voice like a sigh, almost like a sob, breathed: "Madam, may I speak to you a moment?"

"Speak to me?" Rosemary turned. She saw a little battered creature with enormous eyes, someone quite young, no older than herself, who clutched at her coat-collar with reddened hands, and shivered as though she had just come out of the water.

"M-madam," stammered the voice. "Would you let me have the price of a cup of tea?"

"A cup of tea?" There was something simple, sincere in that voice; it wasn't in the least the voice of a beggar. "Then have you no money at all?" asked Rosemary.

"None, madam," came the answer.

"How extraordinary!" Rosemary peered through the dusk, and the girl gazed back at her. How more than extraordinary! And suddenly it seemed to Rosemary such an adventure. It was like something out of a novel by Dostoyevsky,[7] this meeting in the dusk. Supposing she took the girl home? Supposing she did do one of those things she was always reading about or seeing on the stage, what would happen? It would be thrilling. And she heard herself saying afterwards to the amazement of her friends: "I simply took her home with me," as she stepped forward and said to that dim person beside her: "Come home to tea with me."

The Mirror (1890), Dennis Miller Bunker. Oil on canvas, 50⅜″ × 40⅜″, Terra Foundation for the Arts, Daniel J. Terra Collection (43.1980). Photo Copyright © 1995 courtesy of Terra Museum of American Art, Chicago.

The girl drew back startled. She even stopped shivering for a moment. Rosemary put out a hand and touched her arm. "I mean it," she said, smiling. And she felt how simple and kind her smile was. "Why won't you? Do. Come home with me now in my car and have tea."

"You—you don't mean it, madam," said the girl, and there was pain in her voice.

---

6. **pang:** a sudden sharp pain or feeling.
7. **Dostoyevsky** (dŏs′tə-yĕf′skē): Feodor Dostoyevsky, a 19th-century Russian writer of novels and short stories. He wrote a number of works dealing with the lives of the poor and the underprivileged.

The First Cloud (1887), Sir William Quiller Orchardson. Tate Gallery, London/Art Resource, New York.

"But I do," cried Rosemary. "I want you to. To please me. Come along."

The girl put her fingers to her lips and her eyes devoured Rosemary. "You're—you're not taking me to the police station?" she stammered.

"The police station!" Rosemary laughed out. "Why should I be so cruel? No, I only want to make you warm and to hear—anything you care to tell me."

Hungry people are easily led. The footman held the door of the car open, and a moment later they were skimming through the dusk.

"There!" said Rosemary. She had a feeling of triumph as she slipped her hand through the velvet strap. She could have said, "Now I've got you," as she gazed at the little captive she had netted. But of course she meant it kindly. Oh, more than kindly. She was going to prove to this girl that—wonderful things did happen in life, that—fairy godmothers were real, that—rich people had hearts, and that women *were* sisters. She turned impulsively, saying: "Don't be frightened. After all, why shouldn't you come back with me? We're both women. If I'm the more fortunate, you ought to expect . . ."

But happily at that moment, for she didn't know how the sentence was going to end, the car stopped. The bell was rung, the door opened, and with a charming, protecting, almost embracing movement, Rosemary drew the other into the hall. Warmth, softness, light, a sweet scent, all those things so familiar to her she never even thought about them, she watched that other receive. It was fascinating. She was like the little rich girl in her nursery with all the cupboards to open, all the boxes to unpack.

"Come, come upstairs," said Rosemary, longing to begin to be generous. "Come up to my room." And, besides, she wanted to spare this poor little thing from being stared at by the servants; she decided as they mounted the stairs she would not even ring for Jeanne, but take off her things by herself. The great thing was to be natural!

And "There!" cried Rosemary again, as they reached her beautiful big bedroom with the curtains drawn, the fire leaping on her wonderful lacquer furniture, her gold cushions and the primrose and blue rugs.

The girl stood just inside the door; she seemed dazed. But Rosemary didn't mind that.

"Come and sit down," she cried, dragging her big chair up to the fire, "in this comfy chair. Come and get warm. You look so dreadfully cold."

"I daren't, madam," said the girl, and she edged backwards.

"Oh, please,"—Rosemary ran forward—"you mustn't be frightened, you mustn't, really. Sit down, and when I've taken off my things we shall go into the next room and have tea and be cozy. Why are you afraid?" And gently she half pushed the thin figure into its deep cradle.

But there was no answer. The girl stayed just as she had been put, with her hands by her sides and her mouth slightly open. To be quite sincere, she looked rather stupid. But Rosemary wouldn't acknowledge it. She leaned over her, saying: "Won't you take off your hat? Your pretty hair is all wet. And one is so much more comfortable without a hat, isn't one?"

There was a whisper that sounded like "Very good, madam," and the crushed hat was taken off.

"Let me help you off with your coat, too," said Rosemary.

The girl stood up. But she held on to the chair with one hand and let Rosemary pull. It was quite an effort. The other scarcely helped her at all. She seemed to stagger like a child, and the thought came and went through Rosemary's mind, that if people wanted helping they must respond a little, just a little, otherwise it became very difficult indeed. And what was she to do with the coat now? She left it on the floor, and the hat too. She was just going to take a cigarette off the mantelpiece when the girl said quickly, but so lightly and strangely: "I'm very sorry, madam, but I'm going to faint. I shall go off, madam, if I don't have something."

"Good heavens, how thoughtless I am!" Rosemary rushed to the bell.

"Tea! Tea at once! And some brandy immediately!"

The maid was gone again, but the girl almost cried out. "No, I don't want no brandy. I never drink brandy. It's a cup of tea I want, madam." And she burst into tears.

It was a terrible and fascinating moment. Rosemary knelt beside her chair.

"Don't cry, poor little thing," she said. "Don't cry." And she gave the other her lace handkerchief. She really was touched beyond words. She put her arm round those thin, birdlike shoulders.

Now at last the other forgot to be shy, forgot everything except that they were both women, and gasped out: "I can't go on no longer like this. I can't bear it. I shall do away with myself. I can't bear no more."

"You shan't have to. I'll look after you. Don't cry anymore. Don't you see what a good thing it was that you met me? We'll have tea and you'll tell me everything. And I shall arrange something. I promise. *Do* stop crying. It's so exhausting. Please!"

The other did stop just in time for Rosemary to get up before the tea came. She had the table placed between them. She plied the poor little creature with everything, all the sandwiches, all the bread and butter, and every time her cup was empty she filled it with tea, cream and sugar. People always said sugar was so nourishing. As for herself she didn't eat; she smoked and looked away tactfully so that the other should not be shy.

And really the effect of that slight meal was marvelous. When the tea table was carried away a new being, a light, frail creature with tangled hair, dark lips, deep, lighted eyes, lay back in the big chair in a kind of sweet languor,[8] looking at the blaze. Rosemary lit a fresh cigarette; it was time to begin.

"And when did you have your last meal?" she asked softly.

But at that moment the door-handle turned.

"Rosemary, may I come in?" It was Philip.

"Of course."

He came in. "Oh, I'm so sorry," he said, and stopped and stared.

"It's quite all right," said Rosemary smiling. "This is my friend, Miss—"

"Smith, madam," said the languid figure, who was strangely still and unafraid.

"Smith," said Rosemary. "We are going to have a little talk."

"Oh, yes," said Philip. "Quite," and his eye caught sight of the coat and hat on the floor. He came over to the fire and turned his back to it. "It's a beastly afternoon," he said curiously, still looking at that listless figure, looking at its hands and boots, and then at Rosemary again.

"Yes, isn't it?" said Rosemary enthusiastically. "Vile."[9]

Philip smiled his charming smile. "As a matter of fact," said he, "I wanted you to come into the library for a moment. Would you? Will Miss Smith excuse us?"

The big eyes were raised to him, but Rosemary answered for her. "Of course she will." And they went out of the room together.

"I say," said Philip, when they were alone. "Explain. Who is she? What does it all mean?"

Rosemary, laughing, leaned against the door and said: "I picked her up in Curzon Street. Really. She's a real pick-up. She asked me for the price of a cup of tea, and I brought her home with me."

"But what on earth are you going to do with her?" cried Philip.

"Be nice to her," said Rosemary quickly. "Be frightfully nice to her. Look after her. I don't know how. We haven't talked yet. But show her—treat her—make her feel—"

"My darling girl," said Philip, "you're quite mad, you know. It simply can't be done."

"I knew you'd say that," retorted Rosemary. "Why not? I want to. Isn't that a reason? And besides, one's always reading about these things. I decided—"

"But," said Philip slowly, and he cut the end of a cigar, "she's so astonishingly pretty."

"Pretty?" Rosemary was so surprised that she blushed. "Do you think so? I—I hadn't thought about it."

"Good Lord!" Philip struck a match. "She's absolutely lovely. Look again, my child. I was bowled over when I came into your room just now. However . . . I think you're making a ghastly mistake. Sorry, darling, if I'm crude and all that. But let me know if Miss Smith is going to dine with us in time for me to look up *The Milliner's Gazette*."[10]

"You absurd creature!" said Rosemary, and she went out of the library, but not back to her bedroom. She went to her writing-room and sat down at her desk. Pretty! Absolutely lovely! Bowled over! Her heart beat like a heavy bell. Pretty! Lovely! She drew her checkbook towards her. But no, checks would be no use, of course. She opened a drawer and took out five pound notes, looked at them, put two back, and holding the three squeezed in her hand, she went back to her bedroom.

---

8. **languor** (lăng′gər): a dreamy, lazy mood.
9. **vile:** unpleasant; highly disagreeable.
10. ***The Milliner's Gazette:*** an imaginary newsletter for working-class women. (A milliner is a maker of women's hats.)

Half an hour later Philip was still in the library, when Rosemary came in.

"I only wanted to tell you," said she, and she leaned against the door again and looked at him with her dazzled exotic gaze, "Miss Smith won't dine with us tonight."

Philip put down the paper. "Oh, what's happened? Previous engagement?"

Rosemary came over and sat down on his knee. "She insisted on going," said she, "so I gave the poor little thing a present of money. I couldn't keep her against her will, could I?" she added softly.

Rosemary had just done her hair, darkened her eyes a little, and put on her pearls. She put up her hands and touched Philip's cheeks.

"Do you like me?" said she, and her tone, sweet, husky, troubled him.

"I like you awfully," he said, and he held her tighter. "Kiss me."

There was a pause.

Then Rosemary said dreamily, "I saw a fascinating little box today. It cost twenty-eight guineas. May I have it?"

Philip jumped her on his knee. "You may, little wasteful one," said he.

But that was not really what Rosemary wanted to say.

"Philip," she whispered, and she pressed his head against her bosom, "am I *pretty?*" ❖

RESPONDING OPTIONS

FROM PERSONAL RESPONSE *TO* CRITICAL ANALYSIS

REFLECT 1. In your notebook, describe your reaction to Rosemary's question at the end of the story. Share your writing with a classmate.

RETHINK 2. Why do you think Rosemary invites Miss Smith to her home?

Consider
- Rosemary's mood when she meets Miss Smith
- her thoughts when Miss Smith asks her for money
- the reasons she gives to Miss Smith and to Philip

3. Why do you think Miss Smith doesn't stay for dinner? Support your answer with evidence from the story.

4. What is your opinion of Rosemary, Philip, and the upper-class lifestyle presented in this story?

Consider
- Rosemary's appearance
- her shopping habits
- her conversations with Philip

RELATE 5. In real life, some people help others out of a true sense of charity, whereas others have strictly self-serving motives for lending a helping hand. With a group of classmates, discuss which type of assistance is, in your opinion, more prevalent.

LITERARY CONCEPTS

Tone is the expression of a writer's attitude toward his or her subject. Throughout "A Cup of Tea," Mansfield suggests her view of Rosemary through her choice of words and through details of Rosemary's appearance, actions, and thoughts. What, for example, might Rosemary's response to Miss Smith's tears—"*Do* stop crying. It's so exhausting. Please!"—imply about her character? After looking through the story to find details that reveal Mansfield's attitude, try to formulate a description of the story's overall tone.

ANOTHER PATHWAY

With a partner, develop a scene in which you, as Miss Smith, tell a friend about your unusual encounter with a rich woman. Be sure to discuss the actions or experiences that made the strongest impression on you, the differences between yourself and Rosemary, and the separate worlds you inhabit in London.

QUICKWRITES

1. Write down your idea of the **conversation** that Rosemary and Miss Smith have just before Miss Smith leaves. Remember the social class of each character in the dialogue.

2. The story ends before Philip answers Rosemary's final question. Write the **answer** you think he would give. Try to match Mansfield's writing style and Philip's manner of speech.

3. Write a **diary entry** in which Rosemary describes her day. Include details Rosemary would be likely to dwell on, and exclude those she would rather forget.

PORTFOLIO Save your writing. You may want to use it later as a spring-board to a piece for your portfolio.

ALTERNATIVE ACTIVITIES

1. ***Cooperative Learning*** With a small group of classmates, brainstorm ideas for a contemporary version of the **scene** in which Rosemary meets Miss Smith. Look back at your ideas for the Personal Connection on page 956 to help you decide on a setting. Then choose two students to play the characters and have them perform the scene for the class.
2. Imagine that having decided to make Miss Smith her protégée, Rosemary wants to throw a party to introduce the woman to her rich friends. Design an **invitation** she might send, including a description of Miss Smith and of the evening's entertainment.
3. Create a **drawing** of the enamel box described in the story.

THE WRITER'S STYLE

You may have noticed that Katherine Mansfield uses dashes (—) and ellipses (. . .) frequently in "A Cup of Tea." In your opinion, what stylistic purpose do they serve in the story? Cite at least three uses of each that illustrate your point.

CRITIC'S CORNER

John Middleton Murry, the critic who became Katherine Mansfield's husband, praised her work for its purity, recalling the judgment of a printer who remarked after reading a manuscript of hers, "But these kids are *real!"* Do the characters in "A Cup of Tea" seem real to you? Support your answer with evidence from the story.

ACROSS THE CURRICULUM

Social Studies Research and report on the British class system today. Is it as rigid as it was at the time of this story? If not, how has it changed?

KATHERINE MANSFIELD

1888–1923

Although she lived to be only 34 years old, Katherine Mansfield was a master of the short story who developed a distinctive prose style characterized by mood and suggestion rather than dramatic action. Born Kathleen Mansfield Beauchamp in Wellington, New Zealand, she published her first story when she was 9. In 1903 she was sent to college in London, where she played the cello and edited the college literary magazine. On her return to New Zealand, she was so unhappy that her father sent her back to London, where her interest quickly shifted from music to literature. She married in 1909 but left her husband after a few days and began reviewing and writing short stories.

In 1911, Mansfield met the English critic John Middleton Murry, and they began a creative but stormy relationship. In 1919, after she obtained a divorce from her first husband, she and Murry were married. The couple stayed some weeks with Frieda and D. H. Lawrence, and Lawrence loosely based the main characters in his novel *Women in Love* on the four of them.

Mansfield suffered from ill health and traveled often in search of a favorable climate. She spent her last years as an invalid, fighting a losing battle with tuberculosis, but at the same time she was at the height of her powers as a writer. Despite the shortness of her writing career, she is considered a major contributor to the form and style of the modern short story.

OTHER WORKS *Bliss and Other Stories, Something Childish and Other Stories, The Garden Party and Other Stories*

MILESTONES IN BRITISH LITERATURE

Graham Greene

The Novels of

Graham Greene

A stranger arrives in Vienna, or Vietnam, or Cuba—a scene of conflict and intrigue. He intends to live quietly, but trouble soon finds him. Torn between conscience and friendship, duty and love, evidence and faith, the stranger must betray one or the other. Which will he choose?

Situations such as this fascinated Graham Greene, who used them as frameworks for many of his novels. First and foremost, Greene saw himself as an entertainer, even characterizing some of his books as "entertainments" rather than novels. A number of his works, including *Our Man in Havana* and *Brighton Rock,* have been made into films; one, *The Third Man,* was actually conceived as a film before it was published as a novel. Greene's style is itself basically cinematic, sometimes displaying a wide view from a distance, sometimes zooming in for a close-up of details. It is a style that has had a tremendous influence on other writers, especially writers of the spy novel—brimming with suspense, danger, and international intrigue—a form of which Greene was a master.

The settings of Greene's novels tend to be the world's trouble spots, including such far-flung places as Africa, Mexico, London, South America, and Haiti. Most of these exotic locales are places Greene knew well. *The Ministry of Fear* grew out of his wartime service in West Africa, and *The Heart of the Matter* evolved from his experiences in Freetown, Sierra Leone. Similarly, a visit to Vienna resulted in *The Third Man,* and trips to Vietnam, Cuba, and South America provided material for *The Quiet American, Our Man in Havana,* and *The Honorary Consul.*

Like his settings, the themes of Greene's novels spring from personal experience. The web of conflicting loyalties in which his characters are caught resembles his own boyhood sense of dual loyalty—to his headmaster father on the one hand and to his school chums on the other. His concern with moral dilemmas reflects his personal interest in spiritual growth as well as his conversion to Roman Catholicism. His political themes reflect his lifelong involvement in world affairs and his experience as a spy.

Recognizing these various influences, critics have labeled Graham Greene a Catholic novelist, a political novelist, and a spy novelist. He is all of these, of course, and more. Despite their varied themes and settings, Greene's novels essentially center on complex, unpredictable people. Like real people, they refuse to be classified or pigeonholed. Instead, they live as best they know how in a world that is in turmoil.

Far top left:
The giant Ferris wheel in Vienna used in filming The Third Man. *Photofest.*
Top right:
Freetown, Sierra Leone, one of the many places Greene lived in and wrote about.
Middle right:
Joseph Cotton and Orson Welles in The Third Man. *Photofest.*
Bottom right:
Greene in Havana.

PREVIEWING

POETRY

Preludes

T. S. Eliot

PERSONAL CONNECTION

People in the late 20th century frequently speak of being alienated from one another. Many people don't know their neighbors, for example, and commuters spend hours with strangers in trains and buses. Think about other examples of this kind of alienation that you have either observed or experienced. In your notebook, create a chart like the one shown to explore some of the causes and consequences of alienation. Discuss your completed chart with a group of classmates.

Examples of Alienation	Causes of Alienation	Immediate Consequences	Long-Term Effects

LITERARY/BIOGRAPHICAL CONNECTION

T. S. Eliot, more than any other writer, defined the contours of modern poetry. Not satisfied with traditional structures and language, Eliot strove to use rhythms, images, forms, and words that expressed the fragmentation and alienation of Western society in the early 20th century. His most radical break with traditional poetry was his avoidance of explicit transitions and connections in his poems. He made extensive use of both irony and symbolism, relying on the juxtaposition of images to create meaning. His poems suggest rather than explain.

Eliot's first volume of poems, *Prufrock and Other Observations,* was published in 1917. Its revolutionary impact has been compared to that of *Lyrical Ballads,* the volume published in 1798 by William Wordsworth and Samuel Taylor Coleridge. Just as *Lyrical Ballads* heralded the age of romanticism, making a break with neoclassicism, *Prufrock and Other Observations* heralded the era of modern poetry, making a sharp break with the poetic conventions of the prewar years. In 1922, Eliot published *The Waste Land,* perhaps the key poem of the period and certainly one of the major poems of the 20th century. In this extremely complex work, a variety of rhythms, images, allusions, ideas, and styles are combined to evoke the isolation, disillusionment, and despair of the time.

The sections of the poem "Preludes" were written over a period of several years, and the completed work was published in *Prufrock and Other Observations.* In music, the term *prelude* refers either to a short piece based on a single motif or to a piece that serves as an introduction to another work.

READING CONNECTION

Approaching Modern Poetry

READING STRATEGIES

The changes in technique and subject matter that appeared in much poetry of the early 20th century were part of a revolution that was taking place in all the arts—painting, music, sculpture, architecture—at that time. As artists began to look at themselves and the world in radically different ways, they created new forms and approaches. The two paintings below—one from the 19th century and one from the early 20th century—illustrate some of the shifts and innovations that occurred. Comparing the styles of the two works can help you to gain insights into some of the developments in 20th-century poetry.

- realistic-looking figure
- appealing subject and setting
- colors and shapes used in recognizable ways
- an orderly world

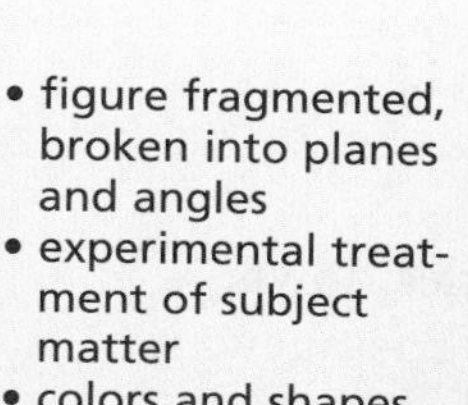

- figure fragmented, broken into planes and angles
- experimental treatment of subject matter
- colors and shapes used in unexpected ways
- inner tensions

If you compare poems by Victorian poets with poems by T. S. Eliot and other early-20th-century poets, you will notice differences that are similar to those between the two paintings. The earlier poems tend to be written in formal language, with regular patterns of rhyme and rhythm, idealistic or dignified subjects, readily understandable images, and clearly developed ideas and themes. In contrast, many 20th-century poems have the following characteristics:

- everyday language
- free-verse forms
- subjects that are ordinary, and sometimes unpleasant
- unusual and complex images and allusions
- patterns of imagery that imply meaning rather than state it

As you read "Preludes," pay attention to the length and arrangement of the lines on the page. Read each section of the poem aloud to hear its sounds, lingering over words or images that engage your attention. Identify the parts that seem clear to you and the parts that are puzzling. Consider possible interpretations—note what you think are the main directions, images, and themes and how they work together. Don't expect to understand the poem immediately, but do expect to discover new insights each time you reread it.

Above left: Alphonsine Fournaise at La Grenouillère (1879), Auguste Renoir. Musée d'Orsay, Paris, Giraudon/Art Resource, New York.
Above right: Portrait of Wilhelm Uhde (1910), Pablo Picasso. Collection Penrose, London, Giraudon/Art Resource, New York. Copyright © 1996 Estate of Pablo Picasso/Artists Rights Society (ARS), New York.

PRELUDES

T. S. ELIOT

I

The winter evening settles down
With smell of steaks in passageways.
Six o'clock.
The burnt-out ends of smoky days.
And now a gusty shower wraps
The grimy scraps
Of withered leaves about your feet
And newspapers from vacant lots;
The showers beat
On broken blinds and chimney-pots,
And at the corner of the street
A lonely cab-horse steams and stamps.
And then the lighting of the lamps.

II

The morning comes to consciousness
Of faint stale smells of beer
From the sawdust-trampled street
With all its muddy feet that press
To early coffee-stands.
With the other masquerades
That time resumes,
One thinks of all the hands
That are raising dingy shades
In a thousand furnished rooms.

GUIDE FOR READING

2 steaks: In the early 20th century, steaks (usually cheap cuts from low-grade beef) were primarily a food of the working class.

7 As you read, note how pronouns are used and how they affect the point of view.

10 What picture do you have of the place being described?

14 Why do you think morning is personified?

18 early coffee-stands: stands of venders who cater to early-morning pedestrians.

23 furnished rooms: one-room apartments with furniture included, usually cheap and rundown.

III

You tossed a blanket from the bed,
You lay upon your back, and waited;
You dozed, and watched the night revealing
The thousand sordid images
Of which your soul was constituted;
They flickered against the ceiling.
And when all the world came back
And the light crept up between the shutters
And you heard the sparrows in the gutters,
You had such a vision of the street
As the street hardly understands;
Sitting along the bed's edge, where
You curled the papers from your hair,
Or clasped the yellow soles of feet
In the palms of both soiled hands.

27 sordid: wretched; dirty; morally degraded.

33–38 Lines 35–36 suggest that the person being addressed is a woman. What kind of vision do you think she had?

IV

His soul stretched tight across the skies
That fade behind a city block,
Or trampled by insistent feet
At four and five and six o'clock;
And short square fingers stuffing pipes,
And evening newspapers, and eyes
Assured of certain certainties,
The conscience of a blackened street
Impatient to assume the world.

I am moved by fancies that are curled
Around these images, and cling:
The notion of some infinitely gentle
Infinitely suffering thing.

Wipe your hand across your mouth, and laugh;
The worlds revolve like ancient women
Gathering fuel in vacant lots.

39 his: the street's. Think about why the street is personified.

42 A reference to afternoon and early evening.

48–49 What metaphor is used here?

50–51 Note the rhythm of these lines.

53–54 What aspect of the women's activity is focused on in this simile?

RESPONDING OPTIONS

FROM PERSONAL RESPONSE *TO* CRITICAL ANALYSIS

REFLECT 1. In your notebook, jot down any questions that this poem raised in your mind.

RETHINK 2. How would you describe the setting of the poem?

3. What impression do you have of the people mentioned in the poem?

4. What thoughts about life does the poem suggest to you?

   Consider
   - the sense of alienation suggested by such words as *lonely* and *sordid*
   - what the speaker means by "the other masquerades / That time resumes" (lines 19–20)
   - the types of activities described
   - the speaker's "notion of some infinitely gentle / Infinitely suffering thing" (lines 50–51)

5. What do you think is the speaker's attitude toward the scenes and people he presents? Be specific in your answer.

RELATE 6. Think back to your responses for the Personal Connection on page 968. Do you find any evidence of the causes and consequences of alienation in "Preludes"? Explain your answer.

ANOTHER PATHWAY

Cooperative Learning

With the class divided into four groups, one for each section of the poem, work with your group to rewrite your section as stage directions for a scene in a play. Try to include as many details from the poem as possible. When you are finished, share your work with the whole class.

LITERARY CONCEPTS

Synecdoche (sĭ-nĕk'də-kē) is a figure of speech in which the name of a part is used to refer to a whole—for example, the use of *wheels* to mean "automobile." In "Preludes," Eliot sometimes uses words for body parts to refer to people, as in line 17, where "muddy feet" refers to early-morning crowds of people going to work. Find at least two examples of this kind of synecdoche in the fourth section of the poem. How do Eliot's references to people in terms of their body parts contribute to the tone and theme of the poem? Cite evidence from the poem to support your answer.

CONCEPT REVIEW: Mood The imagery in a poem usually contributes to its mood—that is, the feeling or atmosphere that the writer creates for the reader. How would you describe the mood of "Preludes"? Find specific words or images that you think help to convey the mood.

QUICKWRITES

1. Outline a **short story** based on one scene in the poem. Create your own characters and plot.
2. Compose a **list** of images that convey your idea of the sights, sounds, and smells of a typical winter morning or evening.
3. Imagine that you are one of the people mentioned in the poem. Write a **diary entry** describing a single day in your life.

PORTFOLIO *Save your writing. You may want to use it later as a springboard to a piece for your portfolio.*

ALTERNATIVE ACTIVITIES

1. Create a **collage** of pictures that illustrate various images in the poem.
2. Find two or three contemporary **songs** that contain imagery similar to that in "Preludes." Share the lyrics of the songs with the class, comparing the thoughts about life expressed in each song with those expressed in the poem.
3. With three classmates, practice and perform a **dramatic reading** of "Preludes." Each person should read a section of the poem in a style appropriate to its mood and subject matter.

THE WRITER'S STYLE

In "Preludes," Eliot uses precise and evocative **images** to express ideas, emotions, and attitudes. Choose five images that you think are particularly forceful. Explain how they contribute to the development of the poem's theme.

LITERARY LINKS

Contrast the images in "Preludes" with those in William Wordsworth's "Composed upon Westminster Bridge, September 3, 1802" (page 504). What does your analysis suggest about the differences between modern and romantic poetry?

ACROSS THE CURRICULUM

Sociology Search magazines and newspapers for articles that describe living conditions in poor sections of large cities. What struggles do people living in these areas deal with in their daily lives? What obstacles do they face in trying to improve their situation?

CRITIC'S CORNER

The English poet Stephen Spender once pointed out that T. S. Eliot "deliberately . . . cultivated impersonality in his poetry"—that is, he attempted to keep the poet out of the poems. Do you think Eliot succeeded in achieving such impersonality in "Preludes"? Why or why not?

T. S. ELIOT

1888–1965

Thomas Stearns Eliot was born in St. Louis, Missouri, and studied at Harvard, the Sorbonne in Paris, and Oxford University in England. Unable to return to the United States during World War I, he settled in London, becoming a British citizen 13 years later. His early work, including "Preludes" and "The Love Song of J. Alfred Prufrock," reflects his reading of French symbolist poets, his study of philosophy, and his involvement in the avant-garde London literary circles of the time. To support himself and his wife, he worked successively as a teacher, a bank clerk, and an editor at a London publishing firm. Meanwhile, he poured his energies into writing both prose and poetry. In 1921, exhausted from overwork, Eliot went to Switzerland to recuperate. While there, he completed most of *The Waste Land.* Its expression of the spiritual infirmities of the age reverberated throughout the literary world, and the poem stands as one of the definitive statements of the human condition.

Eliot joined the Church of England in 1927, and religious themes and symbols came to pervade his later poetry, as well as the plays he began writing in the 1930s. He was also a prominent critic, whose interpretations and observations as a working poet made him an authoritative voice in the literary world. The numerous honors he received included the Nobel Prize, England's Order of Merit, and 23 honorary doctorates.

OTHER WORKS "The Hollow Men," "Journey of the Magi"

POETRY

Musée des Beaux Arts
The Unknown Citizen

W. H. Auden

PERSONAL CONNECTION

How do the teenagers you know respond to the world's major problems, such as war, famine, and natural disasters? In your opinion, are teenagers apathetic and indifferent, or are they genuinely concerned about what is happening in the world? Share your thoughts with classmates.

LITERARY/BIOGRAPHICAL CONNECTION

Generally regarded as one of the foremost modern English poets, W. H. Auden produced a large and complex body of work. At times obscure, his poetry defies easy description or categorization, for it is at times religious, at times lyrical, and frequently satirical. His interest in the problems of modern society and the psychological aspects of human existence is revealed throughout his writing.

Auden, who wanted the style of his poetry to reflect his concern for the common person, strove to write simply and avoid the finery of "grand poetry." He believed that his role as a poet was to present ordinary aspects of human existence in a way that readers could understand and relate to their own lives.

The two poems you are about to read reveal Auden's knack for simplicity of style and biting satire. "Musée des Beaux Arts" was inspired by a trip to Brussels, where Auden viewed the paintings in the Royal Museum of Fine Arts, including several by the 16th-century Flemish artist Pieter Brueghel (broi′gəl) the Elder. In "The Unknown Citizen," Auden explores the quality of life in the 20th century.

WRITING CONNECTION

In your notebook, create a bar graph like the one shown, indicating the extents to which you think other people are concerned about your personal well-being. In addition to groups with whom you are directly involved—family members, friends, teachers, coaches, employers, doctors—include some with whom you are involved more indirectly, such as government leaders. Then, as you read these poems, notice the messages expressed by their speakers.

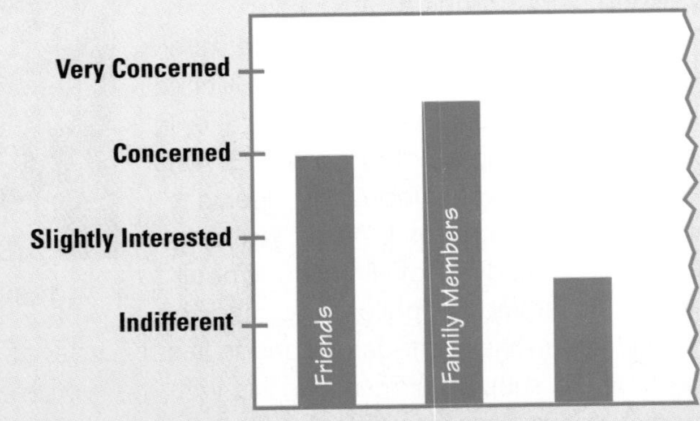

Landscape with the Fall of Icarus (about 1560), Pieter Brueghel the Elder. Musée Royaux des Beaux Arts de Belgique, Brussels, Belgium/Superstock.

Musée des Beaux Arts

W. H. AUDEN

About suffering they were never wrong,
The Old Masters: how well they understood
Its human position; how it takes place
While someone else is eating or opening a window or just
walking dully along;
How, when the aged are reverently, passionately waiting
For the miraculous birth, there always must be

2 Old Masters: great European artists of the 16th–18th centuries.

Children who did not specially want it to happen, skating
On a pond at the edge of the wood:
They never forgot
That even the dreadful martyrdom must run its course
Anyhow in a corner, some untidy spot
Where the dogs go on with their doggy life and the
torturer's horse
Scratches its innocent behind on a tree.

In Breughel's *Icarus,* for instance: how everything turns
away
Quite leisurely from the disaster; the ploughman may
Have heard the splash, the forsaken cry,
But for him it was not an important failure; the sun shone
As it had to on the white legs disappearing into the green
Water; and the expensive delicate ship that must have seen
Something amazing, a boy falling out of the sky,
Had somewhere to get to and sailed calmly on.

14 Breughel's *Icarus* (ĭk′ər-əs): the painting *Landscape with the Fall of Icarus* by Pieter Brueghel (also spelled *Bruegel* and *Breughel*). In Greek mythology, Icarus and his father, Daedalus (dĕd′l-əs), escape imprisonment by flying away on wings crafted of wax and feathers. When Icarus flies too near the sun, the wax melts and he falls into the sea and drowns.

FROM PERSONAL RESPONSE *TO* CRITICAL ANALYSIS

REFLECT

1. In your notebook, jot down words or phrases that describe your reaction to this poem.

RETHINK

2. Do you agree with the speaker's ideas about suffering and indifference? Give reasons for your answer.

3. How would you describe the tone of this poem?

Golconde [Golconda] (1953), René Magritte. Oil on canvas, 31½″ × 39½″, The Menil Collection, Houston. Photo by Hickey-Robertson.

The Unknown Citizen

(To JS/07/M/378
This Marble Monument
Is Erected by the State)

W. H. AUDEN

He was found by the Bureau of Statistics to be
One against whom there was no official complaint,
And all the reports on his conduct agree
That, in the modern sense of an old-fashioned word, he was a saint,
For in everything he did he served the Greater Community.
Except for the War till the day he retired
He worked in a factory and never got fired,
But satisfied his employers, Fudge Motors Inc.
Yet he wasn't a scab or odd in his views,

9 scab: a worker who refuses to support a union strike and crosses a picket line.

For his Union reports that he paid his dues,
(Our report on his Union shows it was sound)
And our Social Psychology workers found
That he was popular with his mates and liked a drink.
The Press are convinced that he bought a paper every day
And that his reactions to advertisements were normal in
every way.
Policies taken out in his name prove that he was fully insured,
And his Health-card shows he was once in hospital but left it cured.
Both Producers Research and High-Grade Living declare
He was fully sensible to the advantages of the Installment Plan
And had everything necessary to the Modern Man,
A phonograph, a radio, a car and a frigidaire.
Our researchers into Public Opinion are content
That he held the proper opinions for the time of year;
When there was peace, he was for peace; when there was
war, he went.
He was married and added five children to the population,
Which our Eugenist says was the right number for a parent
of his generation,
And our teachers report that he never interfered with their
education.
Was he free? Was he happy? The question is absurd:
Had anything been wrong, we should certainly have heard.

21 frigidaire: refrigerator.

26 Eugenist (yo͞o′jə-nĭst): a scientist who tries to improve the human race by controlling hereditary factors.

La grande guerre [The great war] (1964), René Magritte. Private collection, Giraudon/Art Resource, New York. Copyright © 1996 Herscovici/Artists Rights Society (ARS), New York.

RESPONDING OPTIONS

FROM PERSONAL RESPONSE *TO* CRITICAL ANALYSIS

REFLECT 1. What is your opinion of the person memorialized in "The Unknown Citizen"? Share your thoughts with your classmates.

RETHINK 2. How would you describe the tone of the poem?

Consider
- the dedication in parentheses at the beginning of the poem
- the types of accomplishments cited by the speaker
- the speaker's conclusions

3. Do you think the unknown citizen was free and happy? Explain why or why not.

RELATE 4. After reading "Musée des Beaux Arts" and "The Unknown Citizen," how would you describe Auden's view of the average person?

5. Refer to the graph you created for the Writing Connection on page 974. Compare any indifference you noted with the types of indifference portrayed in the two poems. Do you think indifference is an inevitable fact of life?

ANOTHER PATHWAY

Cooperative Learning

Working with a small group of classmates, list some ideas expressed in these poems that readers in the 1930s may have seen as reflections of new social and political realities. Then discuss which of the ideas might be relevant in today's society. Share your conclusions with the class.

LITERARY CONCEPTS

In a literary work, **situational irony** is a contrast between what readers expect and what actually happens. **Verbal irony** is a character's or writer's saying one thing and meaning another. Give your interpretation of Auden's use of situational irony in "Musée des Beaux Arts," citing lines from the poem to support your ideas. Then explain how you think he uses verbal irony in "The Unknown Citizen." With your classmates, speculate on how the two poems might be different if they contained no irony.

LITERARY LINKS

Compare the themes of Auden's poems with the theme of Stephen Spender's "What I Expected" (page 822). What conclusions can you draw about the literary group to which both poets belonged?

QUICKWRITES

1. Write a **newspaper editorial** in which you urge average citizens to cast aside the kinds of indifference portrayed in these two poems.
2. What do you suppose the unknown citizen was really like? Write a **eulogy** to convey your impression of him.
3. Draft a short **essay** in which you compare Auden's depiction of the unknown citizen with your impression of workers in today's society.

PORTFOLIO *Save your writing. You may want to use it later as a springboard to a piece for your portfolio.*

ALTERNATIVE ACTIVITIES

1. With a partner, role-play an **interview** in which a police officer asks either the plowman or the captain of the ship in Brueghel's *Landscape with the Fall of Icarus* for more details about the boy's accident.
2. Create two **census forms** for the Bureau of Statistics—one that seeks only the kind of information presented in "The Unknown Citizen" and one that might elicit a more in-depth picture of people.

CRITIC'S CORNER

The literary critic Richard Hoggart has remarked on the conversational style of Auden's poems, saying that reading them is like "listening to the poet thinking aloud." Do you agree with Hoggart? Cite examples from both poems to support your answer.

ART CONNECTION

Look at the reproduction of Brueghel's painting *Landscape with the Fall of Icarus* on page 975. Why do you think Auden chose this particular painting as the focus of "Musée des Beaux Arts"?

W.H. AUDEN

1907–1973

Wystan Hugh Auden was born in York, England, the son of a doctor. His earliest interest was science, and as a boy he planned to become a mining engineer. From his mother, who loved music, he derived a lifelong interest in many kinds of music, particularly opera. At the age of 15, however, he discovered his talent for writing poetry; thereafter, he knew that writing would be his career.

While a student at Oxford University, Auden exerted a significant influence on a group of young writers who would become the literary leaders of the 1930s. Later known as the Auden Generation, this group included Stephen Spender, who in 1928 printed Auden's first published book of poems on a hand-operated press. Auden's poetic genius was also encouraged by the celebrated poet T. S. Eliot, then an editor at the publishing firm of Faber and Faber.

Although a prolific poet, Auden assumed various other roles during his lifetime, including those of teacher, playwright, documentary-film maker, critic, and editor. In 1939 he moved to New York City, becoming a U.S. citizen in 1946. He spent most of his literary career in the United States, where he regularly taught and lectured at colleges and universities, including Yale, Swarthmore, Penn State, and the University of Michigan.

Even after becoming a renowned literary figure who mingled with the rich and famous, Auden chose to live the life of an eccentric, residing in messy, rundown apartments; dressing in shabby attire; and frequently appearing in public wearing jeans and bedroom slippers. Although disordered in his daily life, he maintained a strict sense of order in his poetry.

Auden never had a family of his own, but he appreciated home life and liked to be surrounded by good friends and their families. Extremely clever and witty, he hosted parties that were attended by guests from all walks of life. In 1972, a year before his death, his college at Oxford offered him a rent-free residence, and he returned to England to live his remaining days in security and comfort on the Oxford campus.

OTHER WORKS "On This Island," "Their Lonely Betters," "In Praise of Limestone"

• *ART GALLERY*

PREVIEWING

POETRY

Do Not Go Gentle into That Good Night
In My Craft or Sullen Art

Dylan Thomas

PERSONAL CONNECTION

If you were a poet, what topics would you be inspired to write about? What personal events would motivate you to take pen in hand? Explore these questions in your notebook. As you read these two poems by Dylan Thomas, compare your own ideas about topics for poems with the topics that he treats.

LITERARY CONNECTION

The poetry of Dylan Thomas has provoked strong and widely divergent reactions. The style of his poems, which are unique and difficult to classify but also quite lyrical and moving, seemed bold, unconventional, and unfamiliar to readers in the 1930s and 1940s and aroused responses ranging from adoration to contempt.

In the late 1940s and early 1950s, while critics argued over the merit of his writing, adoring fans flocked to hear the poet read his works. Not all of them fully understood his poetry, but they loved to listen to it—to hear its sounds. In explaining why he began writing, Thomas once said, "I wanted to write poetry in the beginning because I had fallen in love with words. . . . What the words stood for, symbolized, or meant, was of very secondary importance. What mattered was the *sound* of them." Like the 19th-century poet Gerard Manley Hopkins, Thomas frequently experimented with language, playing with sound devices, coining new words, and creating fresh images.

Thomas wrote about the things closest to his heart, calling his poetry "the record of my individual struggle from darkness towards some measure of light." He was motivated not by social and political issues but by his own experiences, writing about topics such as childhood, holidays, nature, and death. The intensely personal nature of his writing is revealed in both of the poems that you are about to read. In "Do Not Go Gentle into That Good Night," Thomas reacts to his father's deteriorating health; in "In My Craft or Sullen Art," he explores his fundamental motivation for writing.

READING CONNECTION

Visualizing Setting in Poetry Although neither of these poems is what would normally be considered a narrative poem, each poem's topic implies a setting. As you read them, look for words and phrases that help you visualize a time and place for each speaker.

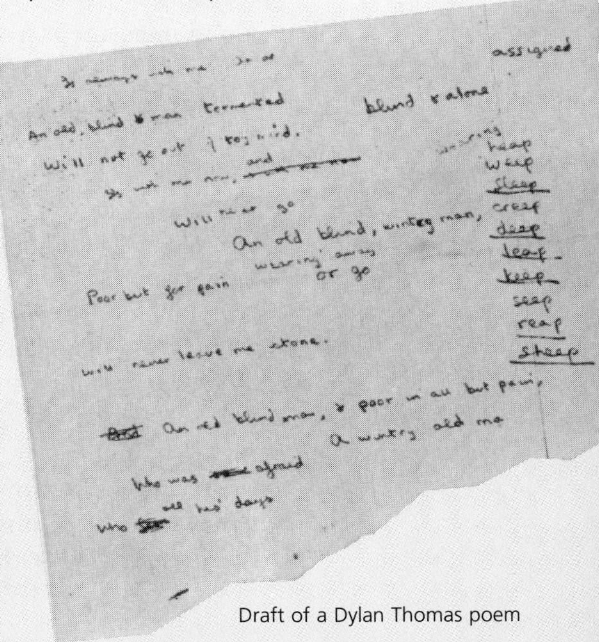

Draft of a Dylan Thomas poem

Do Not Go Gentle into That Good Night

Dylan Thomas

Do not go gentle into that good night,
Old age should burn and rave at close of day;
Rage, rage against the dying of the light.

Though wise men at their end know dark is right,
Because their words had forked no lightning they
Do not go gentle into that good night.

Good men, the last wave by, crying how bright
Their frail deeds might have danced in a green bay,
Rage, rage against the dying of the light.

Wild men who caught and sang the sun in flight,
And learn, too late, they grieved it on its way,
Do not go gentle into that good night.

Grave men, near death, who see with blinding sight
Blind eyes could blaze like meteors and be gay,
Rage, rage against the dying of the light.

And you, my father, there on the sad height,
Curse, bless, me now with your fierce tears, I pray.
Do not go gentle into that good night.
Rage, rage against the dying of the light.

Portrait of Father III (1972), Leon Kossoff. Oil on board, 60″ × 48″, private collection.

FROM PERSONAL RESPONSE *TO* CRITICAL ANALYSIS

REFLECT 1. In your notebook, jot down two or three phrases that convey your reaction to this poem.

RETHINK 2. How would you describe the speaker's attitude toward death? Give evidence from the poem to support your answer.

3. What can you infer about the relationship between the speaker and his father?

In My Craft or Sullen Art

Dylan Thomas

In my craft or sullen art
Exercised in the still night
When only the moon rages
And the lovers lie abed
With all their griefs in their arms,
I labor by singing light
Not for ambition or bread
Or the strut and trade of charms
On the ivory stages
But for the common wages
Of their most secret heart.

Not for the proud man apart
From the raging moon I write
On these spindrift pages
Nor for the towering dead
With their nightingales and psalms
But for the lovers, their arms
Round the griefs of the ages,
Who pay no praise or wages
Nor heed my craft or art.

14 spindrift: spray blown up from the sea by the wind.

Les amoureux aux fleurs [Lovers with flowers] (1927), Marc Chagall. Israel Museum (IDAM), Jerusalem, Israel, Giraudon/Art Resource, New York. Copyright © 1996 Artists Rights Society (ARS), New York/ADAGP, Paris.

RESPONDING OPTIONS

FROM PERSONAL RESPONSE *TO* CRITICAL ANALYSIS

REFLECT 1. What images linger in your mind after your reading of "In My Craft or Sullen Art"? Sketch them in your notebook.

RETHINK 2. How would you describe the speaker?
Consider
- why he refers to writing as his "sullen art"
- his use of the words *labor* (line 6) and *wages* (line 10)
- his fascination with lovers
- what he might mean by "the towering dead / With their nightingales and psalms" (lines 15–16)

3. Review your responses to the Personal Connection on page 981. How does the topic of this poem compare with your own notions of topics that might inspire a poet?

RELATE 4. The verb *rage* appears in both "Do Not Go Gentle into That Good Night" and "In My Craft or Sullen Art." Why do you think Thomas chose to include this word in both poems?

5. Think back to the Reading Connection on page 981. How would you describe the settings of the two poems?

ANOTHER PATHWAY

Reread the poems, writing down any words, phrases, or sentences that you think are used in unusual or ambiguous ways—for example, "spindrift pages" in line 14 of "In My Craft or Sullen Art." Then think up an interpretation of each word, phrase, or sentence, based on its use in the poem. Share your interpretations with the class.

LITERARY CONCEPTS

Thomas's love of the sound of words is reflected in the sound devices used in these two poems. Examples of both **consonance,** a repetition of consonant sounds within and at the ends of words, and **assonance,** a repetition of vowel sounds in words, can be found in each poem. Both assonance and consonance are used to emphasize particular words, to create moods, and to add a musical quality to poems. Find examples of consonance and assonance in both poems, and explain their effectiveness.

QUICKWRITES

1. Write a **letter** to Dylan Thomas, explaining your opinion of the view of death expressed in "Do Not Go Gentle into That Good Night."
2. Write a **speech** that the speaker of "In My Craft or Sullen Art" might deliver to a class of aspiring poets.

PORTFOLIO *Save your writing. You may want to use it later as a springboard to a piece for your portfolio.*

ALTERNATIVE ACTIVITIES

Locate a **recording** of Dylan Thomas reading his poetry—including, if possible, the two poems you have read in this lesson. After playing the recording for the class, discuss the effect of hearing the works in the poet's own voice.

THE WRITER'S STYLE

"Do Not Go Gentle into That Good Night" is an example of an intricate verse form called the **villanelle.** Although the rules of the form are quite rigid, several modern poets have used it to produce highly personal works. Examine the patterns of rhyme and repetition in Thomas's poem and write a definition of the term *villanelle* based on your observations. Then look up the word in a dictionary and compare the dictionary's definition with your own.

CRITIC'S CORNER

According to the American poet and critic Karl Shapiro, Thomas's poems are characterized by "a fatal pessimism . . . offset by a few bursts of joy and exuberance." Do you detect pessimism, joy, or exuberance in these poems—or perhaps all three? Give examples to support your answer.

LITERARY LINKS

Do you think the speaker of A. E. Housman's "To an Athlete Dying Young" (page 692) shares the attitude toward life expressed by the speaker of "Do Not Go Gentle into That Good Night"? Why or why not?

DYLAN THOMAS

1914–1953

Dylan Thomas was considered by many the most original English poet since Yeats and Eliot. He was born in Swansea in southwestern Wales, and his writing is rooted in the countryside and culture of his homeland. Although he did not learn to speak the Welsh language, he captured its cadences and word sequences in both his poetry and prose.

Thomas attended Swansea Grammar School, where his father taught English and where Thomas performed poorly in every subject but literature. At the age of 16, he quit school and went to work as a newspaper reporter. Already, he had become a prolific poet. By the time he was 20, his first book of poems had been published.

In the late 1930s, Thomas moved to London to look for more lucrative writing assignments and began writing fewer poems and more short stories, radio scripts, and screenplays. Unfortunately, Thomas had no business sense and was always in dire financial straits. He fell behind on his taxes and had to borrow money to support his wife and family. In 1949, Thomas and his family moved back to Wales. The following year, in an attempt to improve his finances, he booked his first series of poetry readings in the United States.

A gifted performer, Thomas captivated audiences with dramatic readings of his own works as well as those of earlier poets. To his many fans in America and Great Britain, he personified the typical image of the bohemian poet—reckless and romantic. Sadly, he was also self-destructive. Thomas had a serious drinking problem, and at the age of 39, in the midst of his fourth American tour, he died in a hotel room from complications of alcoholism. He nevertheless left a legacy of innovative, lyrical work that helped set a new standard for modern poetry.

OTHER WORKS "And Death Shall Have No Dominion," "Fern Hill," "Poem in October," *Portrait of the Artist as a Young Dog, Under Milk Wood, A Child's Christmas in Wales*

PREVIEWING

POETRY

Writing/Escritura

Octavio Paz

PERSONAL CONNECTION

Think about what the word *creativity* means to you. In a word web like the one shown, jot down the characteristics that you associate with the concept of creativity. Then share your ideas with your classmates.

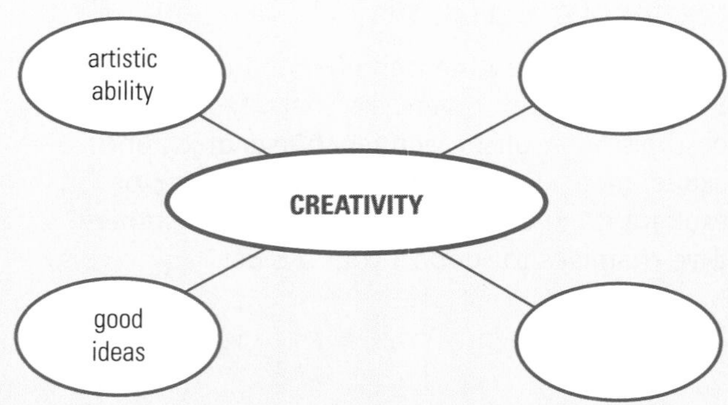

CULTURAL/LITERARY CONNECTION

Although the history of English poetry extends back many centuries, poetry did not become a popular literary genre in the Spanish-speaking countries of Latin America until the late 19th century and did not flourish until after World War I. In 1933, when a 19-year-old Mexican writer named Octavio Paz published his first volume of poetry, he began a literary career that has spanned more than 60 years. Paz has achieved widespread recognition for both his poetry and his prose, including the 1990 Nobel Prize in literature. In exploring themes that reflect the universal human condition, his writing presents images of reality that appeal to people in all countries.

In his writing, as Dylan Thomas did in "In My Craft or Sullen Art," Paz has explored the creative process—what it means to be a poet and what steps lead to a finished work. According to Paz, the meaning of a poem depends entirely on the way a reader interprets the work; thus, the reader's response is a part of the creative process.

WRITING CONNECTION

What is your impression of the way a poem is created? In your notebook, list what you think are the steps of the creative process—the series of thoughts and decisions that lead to a completed poem. Then, as you read this poem, notice what the speaker says about the creative process.

Octavio Paz as a young man

Writing

Octavio Paz

When over the paper the pen goes writing
in any solitary hour,
who drives the pen?
To whom is he writing, he who writes for me,
this shore made of lips, made of dream,
a hill of stillness, abyss,
shoulder on which to forget the world forever?

Someone in me is writing, moves my hand,
hears a word, hesitates,
halted between green mountain and blue sea.
With icy fervor
contemplates what I write.
All is burned in this fire of justice.
But this judge is nevertheless the victim
and in condemning me condemns himself:
He writes to anyone, he calls nobody,
to his own self he writes, and in himself forgets,
and is redeemed, becoming again me.

Translated by Muriel Rukeyser

11 fervor: heat; intensity of feeling.

Escritura

Octavio Paz

Cuando sobre el papel la pluma escribe,
a cualquier hora solitaria,
¿quién la guía?
¿A quién escribe el que escribe por mí,
orilla hecha de labios y de sueño,
quieta colina, golfo,
hombro para olvidar al mundo para siempre?

Alguien escribe en mí, mueve mi mano,
escoge una palabra, se detiene,
duda entre el mar azul y el monte verde.
Con un ardor helado
contempla lo que escribo.
Todo lo quema, fuego justiciero.
Pero este juez también es víctima
y al condenarme, se condena:
no escribe a nadie, a nadie llama,
a sí mismo se escribe, en sí se olvida,
y se rescata, y vuelve a ser yo mismo.

RESPONDING OPTIONS

FROM PERSONAL RESPONSE *TO* CRITICAL ANALYSIS

REFLECT **1.** In your notebook, write down a few words or phrases that describe your response to this poem.

RETHINK **2.** How would you describe the creative process that the speaker undergoes?

Consider
- his reference to "he who writes for me" (line 4)
- the description in lines 5–8
- the "icy fervor" with which the writer contemplates what he has written (line 11)
- the meaning of "becoming again me" (line 18)

3. What would you say is the speaker's attitude toward this process?

4. Do you think that other poets share Paz's vision of the creative process?

RELATE **5.** Over the centuries, many poets have chosen to write about writing. Why do you think this is so?

ANOTHER PATHWAY

Rewrite each stanza of the poem in prose, using words of your own. Then compare your paraphrase with those of your classmates. Discuss whether some of the words and lines might be interpreted in different ways by readers with different responses to the poem.

LITERARY LINKS

Compare the ideas of the speakers of "Writing" and Dylan Thomas's "In My Craft or Sullen Art." Do you think their motives for writing poetry are similar? Use evidence from the poems to support your answer.

CRITIC'S CORNER

The critic John M. Fein has suggested that Octavio Paz's poetry might seem "unconcluded" to a reader who does not realize that Paz "invites him to feel his own version of the poem." Explain what you think Fein means and why you agree or disagree with him.

QUICKWRITES

1. Write a **definition** of the word *creativity* from the perspective of this poem's speaker.
2. Write an **interior monologue** to represent the thoughts of the poem's "he" during the creative process.

PORTFOLIO *Save your writing. You may want to use it later as a springboard to a piece for your portfolio.*

ALTERNATIVE ACTIVITIES

1. Create a **design** for a postage stamp commemorating the art of writing.
2. ***Cooperative Learning*** With a group of classmates, look for books, essays, and interviews in which well-known writers explore the creative process. Then create a **booklet** called "Writers on Writing," in which you include inspirational quotations from those works. You may want to use a computer to design the booklet and its cover, selecting appropriate borders and styles of type.

THE WRITER'S STYLE

The integration of opposites is an important component of Paz's literary style. In "Writing," he frequently juxtaposes contrasting images, such as fire and ice. He also uses **paradox**—statements that seem contradictory but nevertheless express truths. Look for examples of contrast and contradiction in the poem, and discuss their effects with your classmates.

OCTAVIO PAZ

1914–

Octavio Paz was born on the outskirts of Mexico City during the Mexican Revolution. The war left his family in financial ruin, and Paz remembers that as a child he lived in a large house that was gradually crumbling to the ground. In spite of these circumstances, he had a fairly pleasant childhood, spending many hours in his grandfather's extensive library. After attending the National Autonomous University of Mexico, he traveled extensively in Spain, France, and the United States, becoming immersed in the literature, history, art, and philosophy of other nations. His experiences are reflected in his writing, which embraces a diversity of topics, including politics, Eastern philosophy, psychology, art, and anthropology. Despite his interest in travel and other cultures, however, Paz never forgot his heritage: his first book of prose, *The Labyrinth of Solitude,* was an exploration of Mexican culture and thought. Published in 1950, it was well received and brought the author international recognition.

Paz has also worked as an ambassador, editor, and teacher. In 1946, he joined the Mexican diplomatic corps and served for 22 years in such countries as France, Switzerland, Japan, and India. He has founded and been editor of several literary magazines and, since resigning from his diplomatic post in 1968, has taught at various universities, including the Universities of Texas and California, Harvard, and Cambridge.

OTHER WORKS "Two Bodies," "Wind and Water and Stone," "Fable," "The Spoken Word," "Nightfall"

WRITING FROM EXPERIENCE

Writing a Report

Have you ever become so interested in or excited about some topic, problem, or issue that you just couldn't let it go? People who feel this way often research a topic further to understand it better. They may even end up writing about it to allow others to share their excitement.

Write a Research Paper Write a research paper in which you investigate the background or history of a topic of current interest in order to understand it better or draw a conclusion about it.

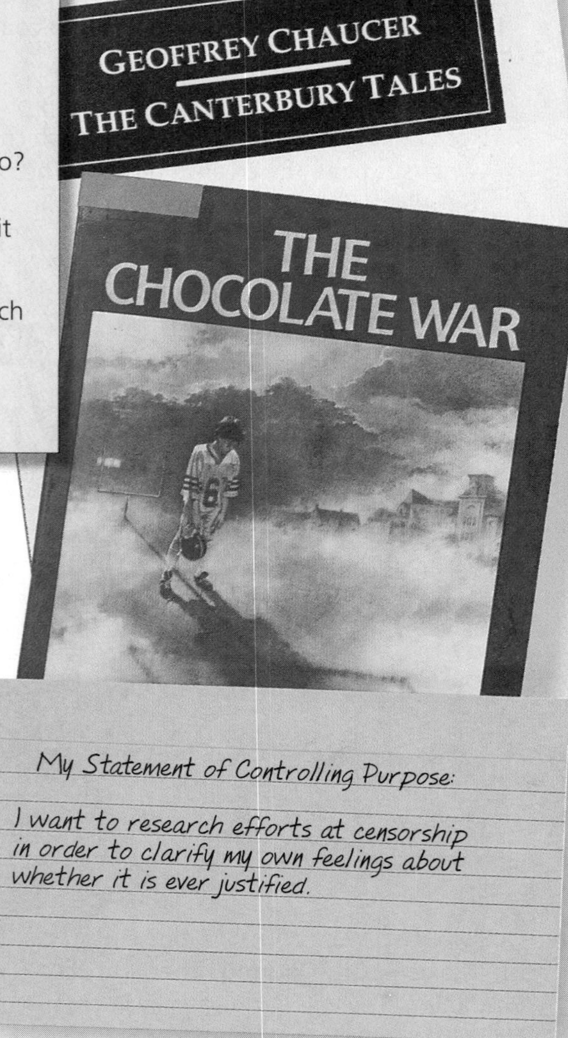

GEOFFREY CHAUCER
THE CANTERBURY TALES
THE CHOCOLATE WAR
My Statement of Controlling Purpose:
I want to research efforts at censorship in order to clarify my own feelings about whether it is ever justified.

Books

1 Gather Ideas

Look for a report topic you'd like to research further to help you understand a problem or answer a question. The following are some suggestions for exploring ideas.

- Examine the items on these pages. Think also about other controversial issues or disputes that are currently in the news. How might research help you understand the issues?
- Brainstorm with a group of friends about topics suitable for a report.
- Think about issues raised by the literature you've read recently.

2 Choose and Narrow Your Topic

Look over your list of possible topics and evaluate them.

- Pick the topic that appeals to you most and freewrite about it for a few minutes—what you know about it and what you'd like to find out.
- To make sure your topic isn't too broad, do a little preliminary research in a general source (such as an encyclopedia). Then narrow down the topic to one you can handle in a report.

3 Define Your Goal

Before you begin your research, you need to know exactly what you want to accomplish. Look at the freewriting you did earlier. Do your comments lead you to a goal?

Write a statement of controlling purpose This statement will guide your research and later will help you develop a thesis statement.

Excerpt from Report

Films Under Attack

The number of attempts to censor the showing of films in public school classrooms rose sharply this year, with a substantial number of incidents involving blanket bans on the showing of films altogether or, more commonly, on the showing of films that have a specific rating. Of particular interest is the number of times that a showing of *Schindler's List*, Steven Spielberg's moving, Academy Award-winning film about the Holocaust, sparked controversy.

People for the American Way,
from *Attacks on the Freedom to Learn*

I wonder what reasons people gave for wanting to keep others from seeing this movie.

Magazine Article

Both sides seem to make some sense. I'm not sure which viewpoint I agree with.

The battle over rock lyrics is not being fought only on the floors of state legislatures. In Alabama, a record-store owner was arrested for selling a rap cassette to an undercover policeman, and convicted of selling obscene materials. In Georgia, five nationally known artists were arrested last year for "suggestive" performances. And the city of Memphis, Tennessee, has banned minors from attending potentially "harmful" rock concerts.

It is the collective impact of all this that concerns civil libertarians and many rock fans. "This is just another one of those attempts to legislate morality," says Barry Lynn of the American Civil Liberties Union (ACLU). "You cannot force individuals or record dealers to speak in ways the government wants them to speak."

The supporters of labeling laws strongly disagree. "All we're doing is labeling the contents of a package or a performance just like we do with cornflakes and cigarettes, just like we rate movies," says Pennsylvania State Representative Ron Gamble.

Steven Manning,
from "X-Rated Rock and Roll," *Scholastic Update*

Is a warning to parents just a label that gives information or is it a subtle form of censorship?

PARENTAL ADVISORY EXPLICIT LYRICS

Compact Disc

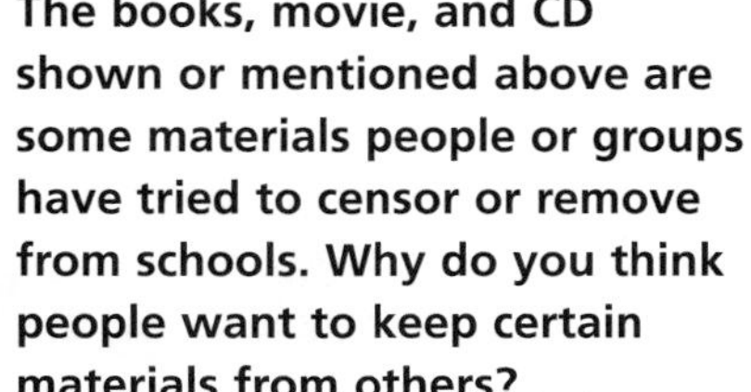

The books, movie, and CD shown or mentioned above are some materials people or groups have tried to censor or remove from schools. Why do you think people want to keep certain materials from others?

Getting the Information

Source Search Even if you know a great deal about your topic, you'll need to do research to find more information, to get other people's points of view, and to make sure the information you use is accurate.

1 Start Your Research

The purpose of research is to find information in reliable sources. The materials you find will be either primary or secondary sources. **Primary sources** are firsthand accounts, such as diaries, journals, letters, and original documents. **Secondary sources** provide secondhand information. Encyclopedia articles, most books, newspaper stories, and magazine articles are examples of secondary sources.

2 Evaluate Your Sources

Use these guidelines to evaluate your sources.

Is the author biased? An author may have a particular point of view. Be certain to explore a variety of viewpoints.

Is the source up-to-date? A 1980 article on personal computers, for example, would have only historical value now.

Is the source reliable? Sources such as supermarket tabloids are not reliable sources of information.

For what audience is the source intended? Books written for younger readers often oversimplify material; those written for experts may be too complex.

3 Create Source Cards

Use index cards, like the examples at the right, to keep track of the sources you decide to use. Study the format of each type of source card. You'll need these cards if you want to find a source again and when you credit your sources in your report.

Source Cards for Encyclopedia and Book

(1)

Anastaplo, George. "Censorship." Encyclopaedia Britannica: Macropaedia. 15th ed. 1992

School Library

(2)

Burress, Lee. Battle of the Books: Literary Censorship in the Public Schools, 1950–1985. Metuchen: Scarecrow, 1989.

Public Library Z658U5 B87

Source Card for Article in Periodical

(3)

Gray, Timothy. "Ratings Still Rankle after All These Years." Variety 10–16 Jan. 1994: 1+.

Public Library

4 Take Notes

Keep your purpose in mind as you research. Take notes on the useful information you find, using a separate index card for each piece of information. For each card, write the number of the source. Study the format of the sample note cards below. Your notes can take these basic forms.

Paraphrase Restate a passage in your own words. Use a paraphrase when you want to be especially detailed.

Quotation Copy the original words exactly, including all the punctuation. Use quotation marks at the beginning and end of the quoted words. Use this form when you think you may want to use an author's exact words in your report.

General Knowledge General knowledge is something that is widely known. Facts that can be found in many different sources and that you think your readers will not question need not be referenced to a specific source.

For more information on source cards and note taking, see page 1241 of the Writing Handbook.

Note Cards

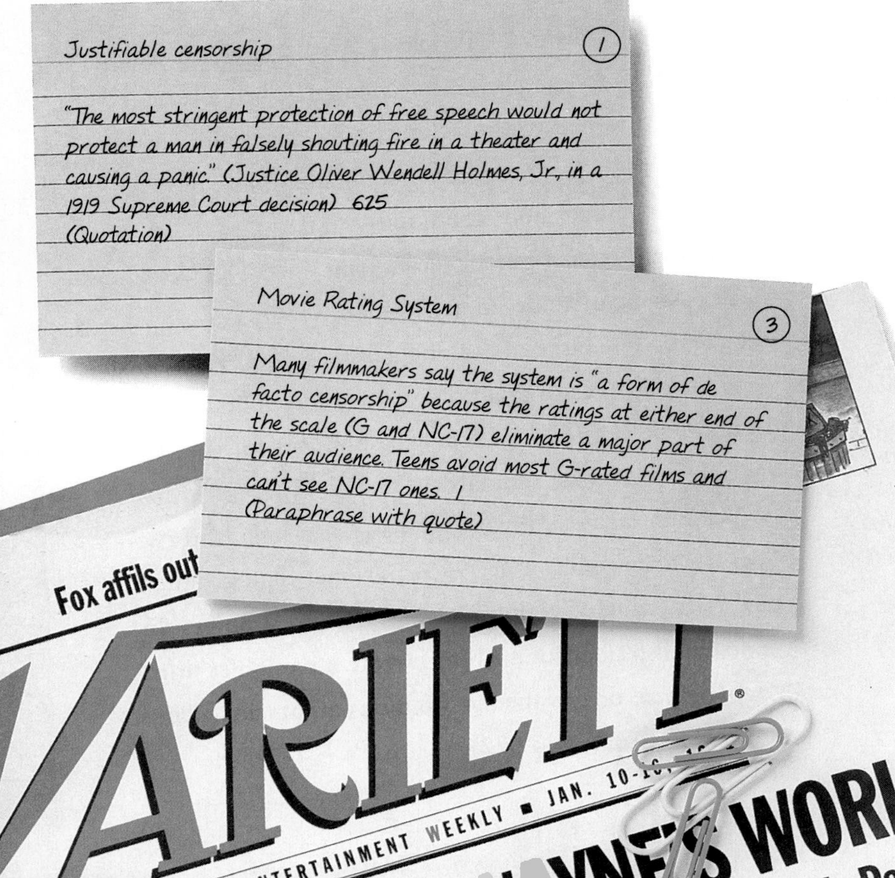

Justifiable censorship
1
"The most stringent protection of free speech would not protect a man in falsely shouting fire in a theater and causing a panic." (Justice Oliver Wendell Holmes, Jr., in a 1919 Supreme Court decision) 625
(Quotation)
Movie Rating System
3
Many filmmakers say the system is "a form of de facto censorship" because the ratings at either end of the scale (G and NC-17) eliminate a major part of their audience. Teens avoid most G-rated films and can't see NC-17 ones. 1
(Paraphrase with quote)
Fox affils out
VARIETY
ENTERTAINMENT WEEKLY • JAN. 10-

SkillBuilder

RESEARCH SKILLS

Outlining

An outline will help you organize your material. You can use the main ideas on your note cards to create a topic outline. In this kind of outline, words, phrases, or clauses are used for entries.

Start by organizing your note cards into separate piles of related information. Then try to sum up what information each pile contains. Next, think about the order in which you could best present the information in these separate piles of note cards. Use that order to prepare a topic outline using the following format. (See also the example on the next page.)

I. Major section
  A. Main idea
  B. Main idea
II. Major section

APPLYING WHAT YOU'VE LEARNED
Make an outline to organize the information for your report.

THINK & PLAN

Reflecting on Your Research

1. If you need to find additional information, what sources will you use?
2. Which of the authorities you used as sources were biased? How could you tell?
3. How did your statement of controlling purpose help guide your research?

DRAFTING

Writing Your Report

From Beginning to End Your report, like many other essays, will begin with an introduction that states your thesis and end with a conclusion that restates this thesis and summarizes your main points. The largest part of your report, the body, should be organized to suit your topic.

1 Write a Thesis Statement

After completing your research, write a statement that expresses the main idea you will develop in your report. For an example, see the thesis statement at the top of the student outline at the left.

Student's Outline and Rough Draft

Censorship: Is It Ever Justified?

Thesis Statement: Censorship efforts are sometimes necessary, sometimes unreasonable or unjust, and sometimes difficult to categorize one way or the other.

I. Introduction
  A. Censorship today
  B. Historical background
II. Military censorship
  A. In wartime
  B. In peacetime
  C. Of the Pentagon Papers
III. Political censorship
  A. Authoritarian governments
  B. Watergate
IV. Moral or ethical censorship
  A. Conservative efforts
  B. Liberal efforts
V. Conclusion
  A. Clear-cut cases
  B. Gray cases

I should include more on censorship today. This ancient-history material may not be needed.

All these numbers don't make for a particularly gripping opening. Try a different approach.

According to People for the American Way, there were 229 attempts at censorship of school materials in the 1990–1991 school year, 347 in 1992–1993, and 338 in 1994–1995 (Fields 1; McGowan 15; People 5). The level of censorship remains high today. The kinds of materials being censored are varied. The targets today include books, magazines, newspapers, television programs, movies, popular-music recordings, and even paintings and other kinds of art.

Censorship has been around a long time. The word goes back to ancient Rome. In the Roman Republic a censor was the person in charge of "taking a census of all Roman citizens for purposes of taxation, voting, and military service." In time, the censor also became responsible for Roman manners and moral standards (O'Neill 13).

The fight against censorship also has a long history. Socrates drank poison in 399 B.C. rather than give up his teachings, which Greek authorities tried to suppress. In 1644 English poet John Milton wrote a pamphlet titled *Areopagitica*, one of the most famous arguments against censorship (Anastaplo 622).

❷ Write Your Draft

Use your outline and note cards to write a rough draft of your report.

Work with Your Research Use evidence from your research (facts, quotes, statistics, examples) to support your ideas. Don't just repeat information—analyze, synthesize, and (if it's part of your writing goal) evaluate it. If you find as you write that you don't have enough information on some aspect of the topic, do additional research to find it.

Identify Sources Credit your sources carefully and avoid plagiarism (using someone else's words or ideas without giving credit). If you use a source's exact words, use quotation marks around them. The SkillBuilder on this page has more information about citing sources.

❸ Evaluate Your Draft

Ask yourself these questions as you evaluate your rough draft:

- Is my thesis statement clearly written? Have I adequately supported my thesis?
- Where do I need to add more information?
- What unnecessary information can be deleted?
- How can I organize my material more effectively?
- Have I used direct quotations effectively? Would any of them be more effective if I paraphrased them?
- Are all of my facts accurate?
- Have I correctly documented my sources?

❹ Rework and Share

Rework your draft, using what you learned in your evaluation. Then share your draft with a classmate.

After a peer reader has read your report, ask these questions:
- How could I make my report more interesting?
- Can you restate the main idea of my report?
- Which parts seem confusing or unclear?
- What should I add more information about? What information could I leave out?

SkillBuilder

WRITER'S CRAFT

Citing Sources

A research report should let readers know where each piece of information came from. Add a reference in parentheses after each quotation or paraphrase of material from a source. Give the name of the source's author (or the title if no author is given) and the page number. A reader can use the list of sources you will provide at the end of your report to get the full information about the source.

Example:
Except for animated films, the G rating is considered "the kiss of death" to a movie producer because teens won't go to see what they believe to be a "kiddie" movie (Gray 44).

WRITING HANDBOOK

For more information on citing sources, see page 1242 of the Writing Handbook.

RETHINK & EVALUATE

Preparing to Revise

1. Does the body of your report support your thesis statement? If not, what should you change—your thesis statement or your evidence?
2. Is your report about the right length to cover the topic, or is it longer than necessary or not long enough?

Coming Back to It

Final Touches After putting your draft aside for a day or so, go back and give it a critical appraisal. What improvements do you think are needed? Does it need to be reorganized? Does anything need to be expanded or cut? Check it against the Standards for Evaluation on the next page as you work on your final draft.

Student's Final Research Paper

Watanabe 1

Lisa Watanabe
Ms. Jackson
English
26 April 1997

Censorship: When Can It Be Justified?

Some computer on-line services refuse to allow their users access to Internet areas they consider "objectionable" (Ness 25). In California a parent objects to the singing of "Dixie" in a middle school's music program (People 61). The ratings code of the Motion Picture Association of America continues to be criticized as "a form of de facto censorship" (Gray 1). A supplementary textbook on human sexuality is accused of being "a how-to book" and is removed from use in a Georgia high school's health education classes (People 84). In incidents all over the country, books by authors such as Mark Twain, John Steinbeck, William Faulkner, Alice Walker, Maya Angelou, and Toni Morrison are attacked as somehow harmful to young readers (People 9–11).

People opposed to censorship in any form view these developments with alarm. Many others see them as justified. Both sides base their arguments on legal or moral principles. Which side, if any, is right? A brief survey of some censorship cases of the past will show that some censorship efforts are justified, even necessary, while others are a violation of people's rights.

1 Revise and Edit

Ask yourself these questions as you work on your revision:

- How can my introduction keep people interested in reading the full report?
- Do I need to add information from additional sources? If so, from what sources?
- Do I have all the data I need to identify my sources?
- Does the evidence that I've included back up my conclusion?

2 List Your Sources

Use your source cards to make a Works Cited list at the end of your report. Include all the sources used for the report. The model on page 999 shows the style one student used to create her Works Cited list. For help creating a Works Cited list, see page 1243 of the Writing Handbook.

Watanabe 8

Works Cited

Anastaplo, George. "Censorship." Encyclopaedia Britannica: Macropaedia. 15th ed. 1992

Burress, Lee. Battle of the Books: Literary Censorship in the Public Schools, 1950–1985. Metuchen: Scarecrow, 1989.

Downs, Robert B., and Ralph E. McCoy, eds. The First Freedom Today. Chicago: ALA, 1984.

Gray, Timothy. "Ratings Still Rankle after All These Years." Variety 10–16 Jan. 1994: 1+.

McClenaghan, William A. Magruder's American Government. Rev. ed. Needham: Prentice, 1990.

Ness, Erik. "Big Brother at Cyberspace: Will Your Freedom and Privacy Be Roadkill on the Information Superhighway?" The Progressive Dec. 1994: 22–27.

O'Neill, Terry, ed. Censorship: Opposing Viewpoints. St. Paul: Greenhaven, 1985.

Patterson, James T. America in the Twentieth Century: A History. Orlando: Harcourt, 1989.

People for the American Way. Attacks on the Freedom to Learn: 1994–1995 Report. Washington: People for Amer. Way, 1995.

Standards for Evaluation

A research report

- is logically organized, with an attention-getting introduction, a body, and an effective conclusion
- includes a thesis statement
- uses evidence from a variety of sources to develop and support its thesis
- credits the sources used for information, direct quotations, and paraphrases
- includes a list of works cited, giving full publication information for all the works used as sources

SkillBuilder

GRAMMAR FROM WRITING

Punctuating Quotations

You quote a source that reads, "I believe that censorship by any government agency is wrong." In your report, the quotation reads,

> *Some people believe that "censorship by any government agency is wrong," as Ms. Jones insists in her essay.*

Notice that to punctuate *your* sentence correctly, you had to change the period that came after the word *wrong* to a comma.

GRAMMAR HANDBOOK

To learn more about punctuating quotations, see page 1292 of the Grammar Handbook.

Editing Checklist Use these tips as you edit your draft:

- Did you credit all sources?
- Have you used a good balance of sentence types and lengths?

REFLECT & ASSESS

Evaluate the Experience

1. What did you learn about gathering information as you worked on your report?
2. How did your ideas about your topic change as you investigated and wrote your report?

PORTFOLIO Put your answers to the questions above in your portfolio with your report.

REFLECT & ASSESS

UNIT SIX: EMERGING MODERNISM

What important issues of the first half of the 20th century can you identify from your reading of the selections in this unit? In what ways do you think your life has been influenced by the ideas and views of reality expressed in the unit? To explore these questions, choose one or more options in each of the following sections.

REFLECTING ON THE UNIT

OPTION 1 Comparing Perspectives In these works from the first half of the 20th century, the writers approach various aspects of reality—war, love, motivation, truth—from different perspectives. Pick two selections from the unit, in which writers offer differing interpretations of some topic or experience. In a chart, identify the topic or experience, list the important points each writer makes, and summarize the opinion of each. Then comment on which perspective matches your own most closely.

OPTION 2 Tracking Sudden Changes In many selections in this unit, circumstances take unexpected turns, or actions have unforeseen consequences. With a small group of classmates, choose four or five selections in which such shifts occur. How do the speakers or characters react to the new developments? What effect do they have on the speakers' or characters' understanding of the world and other people? Discuss whether you think such sudden changes can lead to important insights into reality.

OPTION 3 Evaluating Public and Private Realities Some of the writers represented in this unit address public issues, and some deal with private concerns. Work with a partner to identify the main focus of each selection as public or private. Then look for relationships between the public and the private: How do the larger issues of public life affect people's private lives? How do people's personal experiences and viewpoints affect their interpretation of public events? Summarize your conclusions and present them to the class.

REFLECT & ASSESS *Self-Assessment: To examine what you have discovered about the ways in which writers perceived and interpreted reality in the first half of the 20th century, identify a view of reality that you found evidence of in each of the three parts of the unit. Then briefly record your thoughts about how the three views of reality relate to one another and what attitudes toward life they convey.*

REVIEWING LITERARY CONCEPTS

OPTION 1 Appreciating Suspense Many of the selections in this unit contain a great deal of suspense. Identify the two selections that you found the most suspenseful, and make a cluster diagram to identify the elements of suspense at work in each. In each diagram, underline the element that you think contributes most to the tension felt by readers.

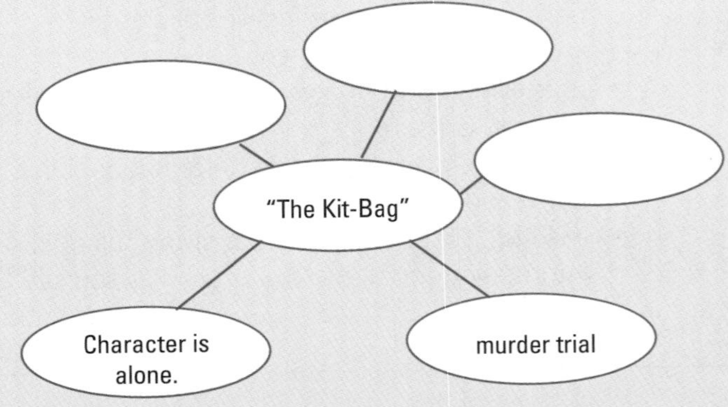

OPTION 2 **Analyzing Style** Writers convey their ideas and attitudes in part through details of style. From this unit, choose two selections that you think have particularly interesting or forceful styles. List the main characteristics of each style, and then make notes about how the styles work to express the writers' thoughts and feelings.

REFLECT & ASSESS *Self-Assessment: Some of the literary terms presented in this unit relate to only one genre, or type of writing, but many relate to two or more. In your notebook, copy the following list of terms, and use the letters* F *(for "fiction"),* P *(for "poetry"),* N *(for "nonfiction"), and* D *(for "drama") to identify the genres each term relates to. Exchange lists with a partner and discuss any terms you categorized differently.*

supernatural tale	*diction*
omniscient point of view	*surprise ending*
humor	*suspense*
style	*symbol*
stream of consciousness	*foreshadowing*
interior monologue	*realism*
free verse	*tone*
speaker	*synecdoche*
theme	*situational irony*
persuasion	*verbal irony*
loaded language	*consonance*
primary source	*assonance*

PORTFOLIO BUILDING

- **QuickWrites** Some of the QuickWrites in this unit asked you to look at the world from an unusual viewpoint—in order to write an epitaph or a bumper sticker, for example. Choose the piece that you think is your most interesting and successful attempt at seeing life from a different angle. Write a brief note explaining your choice, and include it with the piece in your portfolio.
- **Writing About Literature** Earlier, you wrote a literary review of a selection in this unit. Reread your review now, paying special attention to the criteria you developed. Which criteria influenced your evaluation the most? On the basis of those criteria alone, would you recommend the selection to someone else? Write your comments and attach them to your review if you choose.
- **Writing from Experience** By now you have finished your research paper. Reflect on the process you used in writing the paper. Which part of the process was most successful for you? Which part was the most difficult? In a brief note, describe how you might change your process when doing another research project.
- **Personal Choice** Look back at the writing, activities, and projects you have worked on for this unit—either for assignments or on your own. Which one do you think taught you the most about yourself and your world? Write a note explaining your choice, and include it in your portfolio.

REFLECT & ASSESS *Self-Assessment: By now you have put together a substantial collection of pieces in your portfolio. Look through them and decide if there are any that you think you would like to replace. Which ones do you think are the most outstanding examples of your work?*

SETTING GOALS

As you reviewed your writing and projects for this unit, you undoubtedly noted some significant events and viewpoints that influenced the literature of the first half of the 20th century. Jot down some questions and ideas that you would like to explore as you read works from the later part of the century in Unit Seven.

UNIT SEVEN

CONTEMPORARY VOICES

1950–PRESENT

IT WAS A BRIGHT COLD DAY IN APRIL, AND THE CLOCKS WERE STRIKING THIRTEEN.

George Orwell
novelist, essayist, and critic

Invasion (1987–1988), Carel Weight. Oil on canvas, 48″ × 60″, The Saatchi Collection, London.

PRESENT

TIME LINE

Contemporary Voices

1950–PRESENT

1950

Beginning of Korean War, in which British troops join United Nations force led by United States

1952

George VI dies and is succeeded by his daughter, Elizabeth II; Britain becomes atomic power; Samuel Beckett's play *Waiting for Godot* published

1954

William Golding's *Lord of the Flies* published

1956

British troops sent to Egypt in Suez crisis

1957

Soviet Union launches *Sputnik 1,* beginning space age

1961

Muriel Spark's *The Prime of Miss Jean Brodie* published

1962

Anthony Burgess's *A Clockwork Orange* published

1964

Beatles enjoy huge international popularity, heralding "British invasion" of American rock music; U.S. begins air attacks on North Vietnam

1967

Christiaan Barnard performs the world's first successful heart transplant in South Africa

1968

C. Day Lewis becomes poet laureate

1969

Violence erupts in Northern Ireland following attempt to grant civil rights to Catholic minority

1970

Equal Pay Act ensures that British women's wages will be equal to those of men performing same jobs

1973

Worldwide energy crisis spurs efforts to begin North Sea oil production; Britain and Ireland join Common Market

1977
Elizabeth II celebrates her Silver Jubilee

1979
Margaret Thatcher becomes Britain's first female prime minister

1981
Racial tensions and unemployment lead to riots in Brixton area of London; Charles, Prince of Wales and heir to British throne, marries Lady Diana Spencer

1982
Britain defeats Argentina in Falklands War

1984
Ted Hughes becomes poet laureate

1991
Britain joins with United States and other nations in Persian Gulf War

1993
Britain and other Common Market countries form European Union (EU)

1994
Black leader Nelson Mandela is elected president of South Africa in nation's first one-person, one-vote election

1995
Seamus Heaney wins Nobel Prize in literature

Period *Pieces*

The Concorde, a supersonic passenger plane

1950s television

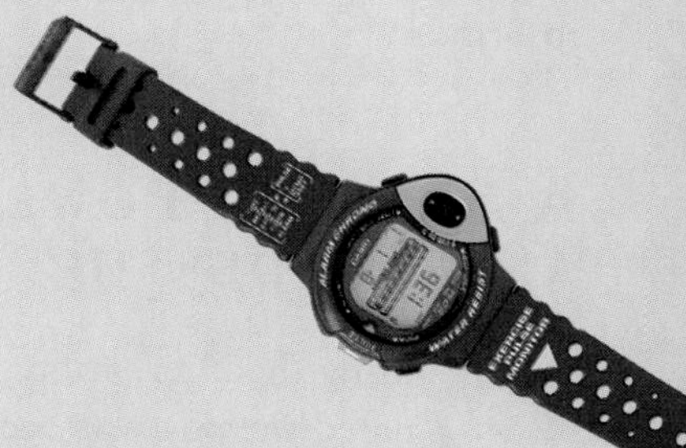

Contemporary-styled watch

INTRODUCTION

Contemporary Voices

1950–PRESENT

In 1953, a year after succeeding her father, George VI, as Britain's monarch, Elizabeth II was crowned in a glorious ceremony in Westminster Abbey. To many, the coronation symbolized a return of hope after the enormous loss and suffering of World War II, yet even though the ceremony recalled Britain's long tradition of greatness, there was no question that Britain was a greatly altered nation. The political power of the working class had been firmly established, and the influence of the upper class substantially diminished. The economic instability caused by Britain's huge war debt, which affected all classes, had prompted a series of nationwide strikes and other crises. The Labor government's social welfare programs and nationalization of industries, begun just after the war to address the dire economic situation, had continued even when the Conservatives returned to power in the 1950s. The dismantling of the empire was also continuing, with Britain—in response to both economic and nationalistic pressures—relinquishing control of most of its colonies in Asia, Africa, and the West Indies. At the same time, immigration from the former colonies was transforming what had formerly been a homogeneous population, creating racial and ethnic tensions on a scale never before known in Britain.

Top: Queen Elizabeth II at her coronation ceremony, 1953. *Center:* Newly built row houses in postwar England. *Above left* and *above:* Increasing religious and ethnic diversity is shown in two London photographs, one of a Hindu temple and the other of spectators watching a cricket match between a team of West Indians and a police team. *Right:* The Beatles, 1966.

A Shift in Power and Leadership

During the international political struggle that dominated the postwar decades—the so-called cold war between Western democracies and Communist nations—the United States became the chief champion of the West. Britain, though it became an atomic power and an important member of both the United Nations and the North Atlantic Treaty Organization (NATO), generally followed the lead of its powerful American ally. One exception was the Suez crisis of the mid-1950s, in which Britain joined with France in an unsuccessful military effort to reverse the Egyptian government's nationalization of the Suez Canal. Although the United States criticized the policy, the differences were soon smoothed over, and Britain retained its position as one of the United States' closest allies.

The new international supremacy of the United States extended beyond the political arena. As the world's most powerful nation and richest market, the United States became the center of Western technological development, particularly in the decades preceding the full recovery of the Japanese and German economies. Britain made valuable contributions in such areas as DNA research and fiber optics but clearly had lost the preeminent position in science and technology that it had once enjoyed. During the "brain drain" of the early 1960s, many of Britain's top scientists and engineers emigrated to the United States, lured by greater opportunities and financial resources. Similarly, the worldwide dominance of U.S. popular culture attracted much of Britain's entertainment talent to American shores.

Britain's greatest international success in the sphere of popular culture came in the 1960s, with the "British invasion" of the American rock-music scene. Led by the Beatles and the Rolling Stones, British rock groups not only dominated international pop

Language

Since the 1960s, the women's movement has left its mark on the English language, promoting existing alternatives and new coinages as replacements for terms perceived as sexist. For example, the title *Ms.* was introduced, and efforts were made to secure acceptance of such gender-neutral terms as *humanity* and *firefighter* in place of *mankind* and *fireman.* Technology, however, has proved the greatest source of vocabulary expansion. From space exploration have come a host of new or rejuvenated terms, including *liftoff, astronaut,* and *A-OK;* the spread of computer technology has given us such terms as *software, floppy disk,* and *user-friendly.*

At the same time, satellite broadcasting, computer modems, FAX machines, and other advances in communications have helped turn the world into a "global village" in which English—spread originally by British and more recently by American influence—has become a universal language. If a Greek does business with someone in Japan, or a Norwegian diplomat negotiates with an Israeli, they are likely to communicate in English, a second language common to both. In such former British colonies as India and Malaysia, English bridges the gaps between dozens of native languages and dialects.

Literature

British writers have responded in several ways to the changes of the contemporary era. During the 1950s, a group of young poets called the Movement—including Ted Hughes, Thom Gunn, Elizabeth Jennings, and Philip Larkin—achieved recognition by rejecting complex styles and producing clear, rational, understated poetry on subjects drawn from everyday

music but also launched a teenage craze for long hair and for things British—British TV shows, British slang, and the "mod" fashions of London's Carnaby Street, for example.

Although prominence in the pop-culture scene had its economic rewards, the weaknesses of the British economy required far more extensive remedies. One was provided by the discovery in 1969 of oil beneath the North Sea off the Scottish coast; in the next 12 years, Britain would be transformed from an oil-importing nation to one self-sufficient in energy. Another solution to the nation's economic problems, according to some Britons—particularly members of the Conservative party—lay in joining the European Community (EC), or Common Market, which several Western European nations had established in 1957. Opponents of this view, mainly in the Labor party, felt that EC membership would weaken trade ties within the British Commonwealth, entangle Britain in continental politics, and threaten the nation's sovereignty and agricultural interests. Since the Labor party held sway for most of the 1960s, British efforts to join the Common Market were not vigorously pursued during those years. Soon after the Conservative party returned to power in 1970, however, Britain's application for membership was accepted.

Above: Twiggy, an internationally famous model of the 1960s, poses in front of a life-size poster of herself. *Right:* Margaret Thatcher, Great Britain's first woman prime minister. *Below:* A 1940s bronze sculpture, *Family Group,* by Henry Moore, one of Britain's most renowned sculptors

The Thatcher Era

In 1975, following defeats in two general elections the year before, the Conservative party elected a new leader who four years later would become Britain's first woman prime minister. The daughter of a small-town grocer, Margaret Thatcher had risen in the ranks of Britain's new "meritocracy," in which success was attained not through birth or wealth but through hard work and talent. Her 11 years as prime minister (1979–1990), known as the Thatcher Era, left their mark on both Britain and the rest of the world. A pragmatist in the fight against communism, Thatcher was the first Western leader to recognize and promote the changes that were occurring in the Soviet Union, and she encouraged President Ronald Reagan to do the same. Under her leadership, Britain successfully waged the Falklands War of 1982 and joined the victorious U.S.-led coalition in the Persian Gulf War of 1991. Meanwhile, on the domestic front, Thatcher was leading her country in a new economic direction. Insisting that Britain become a "wealth-producing" rather than merely a "wealth-redistributing" nation, she

began privatizing the previously nationalized industries and instituting other changes to make British industry more competitive.

A significant problem faced by Thatcher and her successor, John Major, was the ongoing conflict in Northern Ireland. A decade before Thatcher took office, Northern Ireland's Roman Catholic minority had begun a civil-rights movement, calling for an end to discrimination against Catholics there. When clashes broke out between Catholics and Protestants, the British government sent in troops that the Catholics perceived as favoring the Protestants. Before long, Irish Republican Army (IRA) extremists had gained prominence over the civil-rights moderates among the Catholics, and Protestant extremists had formed militant groups of their own, including the Ulster Defense League (UDL). For over two decades, violence between these factions rocked Northern Ireland and spilled over, in the form of bombings and other terrorist attacks, into other parts of the United Kingdom. A peace effort led by two Northern Irish women, Mairead Corrigan and Betty Williams, earned them the Nobel Peace Prize but failed to end the violence. Finally, in 1994, both the IRA and the UDL agreed to a cease-fire, and British and Irish officials began peace negotiations that seemed more promising than past efforts.

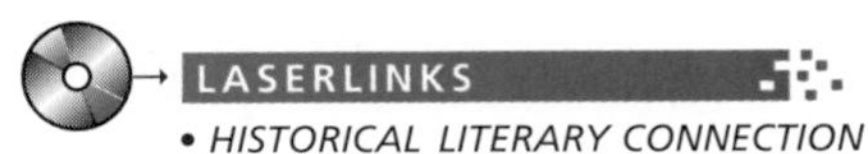

• *HISTORICAL LITERARY CONNECTION*

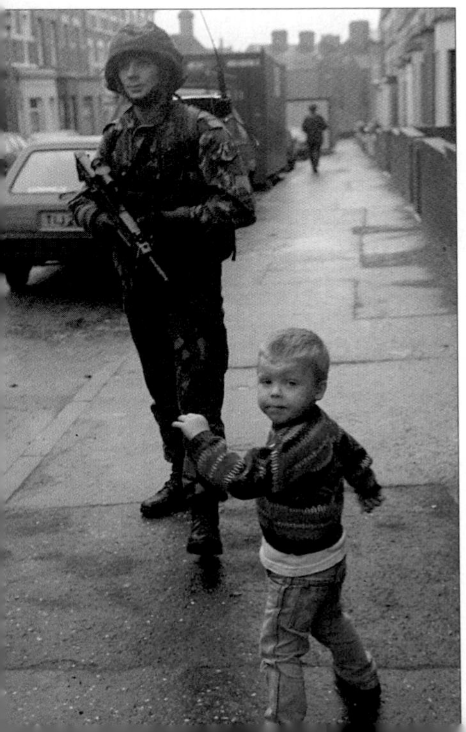

Street scene in Northern Ireland, 1991

LITERATURE

experience. Even more simple in style was the work of Stevie Smith, who—like Dylan Thomas before her—helped popularize the oral reading of poetry for modern audiences.

The 1950s also gave birth to the fiction of the so-called Angry Young Men and to the "kitchen sink" school of drama. Works like John Osborne's play *Look Back in Anger* (1956) and Alan Sillitoe's story collection *The Loneliness of the Long Distance Runner* (1959) expressed the contempt for authority and middle-class values felt by British working-class and student radicals. The social radicalism of these works was matched by the stylistic radicalism of the plays of Samuel Beckett and others associated with the "theater of the absurd," who abandoned realism, plot, and characterization in order to focus on the isolation and absurdity of contemporary life—themes that have also reverberated in the plays of Harold Pinter. Meanwhile, some contemporary dramatists have drawn on British tradition: in *A Man for All Seasons* (1960), for example, Robert Bolt dramatized the life of the Renaissance hero Thomas More, and in *Rosenkrantz and Guildenstern Are Dead* (1967), Tom Stoppard retold Shakespeare's *Hamlet* from the viewpoint of two minor characters.

Another significant contemporary trend is the increasingly favorable reception given to regional and commonwealth writers, broadening the concept of "English" literature. Seamus Heaney (Northern Ireland), Muriel Spark (Scotland), Nadine Gordimer (South Africa), Chinua Achebe (Nigeria), Margaret Atwood (Canada), Judith Wright (Australia), and Derek Walcott (St. Lucia and Trinidad) are just a few of the talented writers who have enriched English letters with their unique perceptions of human experience.

PART 1 *Moments of Insight*

In the second half of the 20th century, technological development has threatened to depersonalize society. In contrast, contemporary writers have frequently concentrated on the individual. Through a single character's experiences and insights, a writer may explore the nature of love, motivation, and mortality. As you will discover in this part of Unit Seven, flashes of insight can occur at any place and time: in a museum, at dawn, during a celebration. As you read the selections, try to recall where you were during a recent moment of insight.

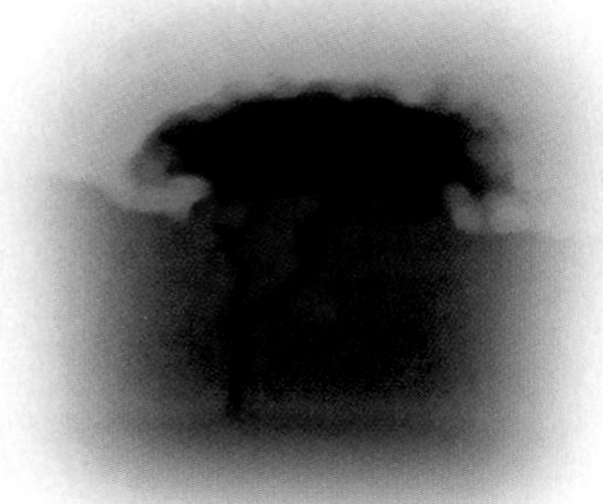

FICTION

At the Pitt-Rivers

Penelope Lively

PERSONAL CONNECTION

Recall a time when you became completely engrossed in the conversation or activities of strangers you observed in a park, restaurant, or other public place. What attracted your attention to these people? Did you begin to speculate about their lives or situations? Share your thoughts with classmates.

CULTURAL/LITERARY CONNECTION

"At the Pitt-Rivers" takes place in 20th-century Oxford, a city northwest of London. More specifically, it takes place in the Pitt-Rivers, an actual museum located on the campus of Oxford University. The Pitt-Rivers Museum was established in 1883 when a collection of early weapons, tools, pottery, and other artifacts was donated to the university by an English soldier and archaeologist, Lieutenant-General Pitt-Rivers. He believed that by sharing his treasures with the public, he could give ordinary people a better understanding of their ancestors. The Pitt-Rivers Museum is well-known for its exhibits in anthropology (the study of the origin and development of human beings) and archaeology (the excavation and study of items belonging to ancient cultures). It also contains an extensive collection of musical instruments from around the world.

Penelope Lively, the award-winning author of "At the Pitt-Rivers," has a personal link to the setting of her story, being a graduate of Oxford University, with a degree in modern history. In many of her stories, Lively reveals her preoccupation with history, especially its ability to change one's perspective on life. She frequently relates experiences in which a child matures greatly as a result of a new awareness about history or humanity. In the following story, a teenage boy gains insights into life by observing the relationship of two adults.

READING CONNECTION

Recognizing Idioms and Slang The language in Lively's story is quite informal. She uses an abundance of **idioms** (phrases or expressions unique to a particular language that mean something different from their literal, word-for-word translation) and **slang** (highly informal speech that is outside conventional or standard usage). Many of the idioms and slang expressions she employs are uniquely British; it is through context that you will be able to decipher them. As you read this story about a teenage boy's observations, jot down, in a chart like the one shown, any idioms or slang that you encounter. Also note what you infer each expression to mean.

Idiom or Slang	What Expression Means
having a snooze	sleeping

LASERLINKS
• CULTURAL CONNECTION

At the Pitt-Rivers

Penelope Lively

They've got this museum in Oxford,[1] called the Pitt-Rivers; I spend a lot of time there. It's a weird place, really weird, stuff from all over the world crammed into glass cases like some kind of mad junk-shop—native things from New Guinea and Mexico and Sumatra and wherever you like to think of. Spears and stone axes and masks and a thousand different kinds of fish-hook. And bead jewelry and peculiar musical instruments. And a great totem from Canada. You can learn a lot there about what people get up to: it makes you think. Mostly it's pretty depressing—umpteen different nasty ways of killing each other.

I didn't start going there to learn anything; just because it was a nice quiet place to mooch around and be on my own, Saturdays, or after school. It got to be a kind of habit. There aren't often people there—the odd art student, a few kids gawping at the shrunken heads, one or two serious-looking blokes[2] wandering around. The porter's[3] usually reading the *Sun* or having a snooze; there's not a lot of custom.[4] The Natural History Museum is a bigger draw; you have to go through that to get into the Pitt-Rivers. You'll always get an audience for a dinosaur and a few nasty-looking jellyfish in formalin.[5] Actually I'm partial to the Natural History Museum myself; that makes you think, too. All those fossils, and then in the end you and me. I had a go at reading *The Origin of Species* last term, not that I got very far. There's a room upstairs in the museum where Darwin's friend—Huxley[6]—had this great argument with that bishop and the rest of them. It says so on the door. I like that, it seems kind of respectful. Putting up a plaque to an argument, instead of just JOE SOAP WAS BORN HERE or whatever. It should be done more often.

It was in the Natural History Museum—underneath the central whale—that I first saw her, and since my mind was on natural selection I thought she wasn't all that good an example of it. I remember thinking that it was funny it doesn't seem to operate with girls, so you got them getting prettier and prettier, because good-looking girls have a better deal than bad-looking ones, you've only got to observe a bit to see that. I always notice girls, to see if they're pretty or not, and she wasn't. She wasn't specially ugly; just very ordinary—you wouldn't look at her twice. She was sitting on a bench, watching the entrance.

All the girls I know—at school or round where I live—are either attractive or they're not. If they're attractive they have lots of blokes after them and if they're not they don't. It's as simple as that. If they're attractive just looking at them makes you think of all sorts of things, imagine what it would be like and so forth, and if they're not then it doesn't really occur to you, except in so far as it occurs to you a good deal of the time,

---

1. **Oxford:** a city in England that is the site of Oxford University, the world's oldest English-speaking university.
2. **blokes:** British slang meaning "fellows," "guys."
3. **porter:** a British term for a doorman.
4. **custom:** the customers or patrons of a business or store. (The narrator is saying that there are usually not many visitors in the museum.)
5. **formalin** (fôr′mə-lĭn): a solution of formaldehyde in water, used as a preservative.
6. **Huxley:** One of the main supporters of Darwin's theory of evolution was Thomas Henry Huxley (1825–1895), a British biologist.

actually. This girl was definitely not attractive. In the first place she was in fact quite old, not far off thirty, I should think, and in the second she hadn't got a nice figure; her legs were kind of dumpy and she didn't have pretty hair or anything like that. I gave her a look, just automatically, to check, and then didn't bother with her.

. . . she had the most beautiful expression I've ever seen in my life. She glowed; that's the only way I can put it.

Until I came alongside, where I could see her face clearly, and then I looked again. And again. She still wasn't pretty, but she had the most beautiful expression I've ever seen in my life. She glowed; that's the only way I can put it. She sat there with her hands in her lap, watching the door, and radiating away so that in a peculiar fashion it made you feel good just to look at her, a bit like you were joining in how she felt. Stupid, I daresay, but that's how it was.

And I thought to myself: oh ho . . . I mean, I've seen films and I've read books and I know a bit about things.

As a matter of fact I've been in love myself twice. The first time was with a girl in my class at school and I suppose it was a bit of a trial run, really, I mean I'm not altogether sure how much I was feeling it but it seemed quite important when it was going on. The second time was last year, when I was fifteen. She came to stay with her married sister who lives round the corner from us and though it's months and months ago now I still feel quite faint and weak when I go past the house.

Oh ho, I thought. I felt kindly—sort of benign—and a bit curious to see what the bloke would be like. I thought he couldn't be much because of her not being pretty. I mean, in films you can always tell who's going to fall for who because they'll be the two good-lookers and while I'm not saying real life's like that there is a way people match each other, isn't there, you've only got to look round at married people. Let me hasten to say that I'm not all that good-looking myself, only about B+. Not too bad, but not all that marvelous, either.

But he didn't show up and I wanted to get on into the Pitt-Rivers, so I left her there, waiting. What I haven't said is that one of the things I go to the Pitt-Rivers for is to write poetry. I write quite a lot of poetry. I could do it at home—I often do—and it's not that I'm coy or anything, my parents know about it and they're quite interested, but I just like the idea of having a special place to go to. It's quiet there, and a bit odd like I've said, and nobody takes any notice of me.

Sometimes I feel I'm getting somewhere with this poetry, and other times it looks to me pretty awful. I showed a few poems to our English master[7] and he was very helpful: he said what was good and pointed out where I'd used words badly, or not worked out what I was thinking very well, so that was quite encouraging. He's a nice bloke. I like his lessons. He's very good at explaining poetry. I mean, I think poetry's amazingly difficult: sometimes you read a thing again and again and you just can't see what the hell the person's getting at. He reads all sorts of poetry to us, our English master, and you really get the hang of it after a bit—hard stuff like Hopkins and *The Hound of Heaven*,[8] and Donne. He read us some of those Donne poems about love the other day which are all very explicit and I must say first time round I hadn't quite got the point—"License my roving hands . . ." and so forth—but he wasn't embarrassed or anything, our English master, and when you realize that it's not geography he's talking about, the poet, then as a matter of fact I think that

7. **English master:** English teacher.
8. ***The Hound of Heaven:*** a poem by the English poet Francis Thompson (1859–1907).

WORDS TO KNOW
benign (bĭ-nīn′) *adj.* gentle; mild
explicit (ĭk-splĭs′ĭt) *adj.* clear and fully expressed

poem's lovely. I got a bit fed up with the way some of my mates were sniggering about it, being all-knowing; truth to tell I doubt if they know any more than I do, it's all just show. And that's a beautiful poem: I mean, if anything makes it clear that there's nothing wrong about sex, that poem does, they ought to make it compulsory reading for some people.

Anyway, I went on into the Pitt-Rivers and I was up on the first floor, in a favorite corner of mine among the arrow-heads, when I saw her again, and I must say I got quite a shock. Because the man with her was an old bloke: he was older than my father, fiftyish and more, he must have been at least twenty years older than her. So I reckoned I must have made a mistake. Not that at all.

They were talking, though I couldn't hear what they were saying because they were on the far side of the gallery. They stopped in front of a case and I could see their faces quite clearly. They stood there looking at each other, not talking any more, and I realized I hadn't made a mistake after all. Absolutely not. They didn't touch each other, they just stood and looked; it seemed like ages. I don't imagine they knew I was there.

And that time I was shocked. Really shocked. I don't mind telling you, I thought it was disgusting. He was an ordinary-looking person—he might have been a schoolmaster or something, he wore those kind of clothes, old trousers and sweater, and he had greyish hair, a bit long. And there was she, and as I've said she wasn't pretty, not at all, but she had this marvelous look about her, and she was years and years younger.

It was because of him, I realized, that she had that look.

I didn't like it at all. I got up, from where I was sitting, with quite a clatter to make sure they heard me and I went stumping off out of the museum. I wasn't going to write any more poetry that day, I could see. I went off home and truth to tell I didn't really think much more about them, that man and the girl, mainly because of being rather disgusted, like I said.

A couple of weeks later they were there again. They were on the ground floor, at the back, by the rush matting[9] and ceremonial gear for with-it tribesmen, leaning up against a glass case that they weren't looking into, and talking. At least he was talking, quiet and serious, and she was listening, and nodding from time to time. I was busy with some thinking I wanted to do, and I tried not to take any notice of them; I mean, they were neither here nor there as far as I was concerned, none of my business, though I still thought it was a bit creepy. I couldn't see *why*, frankly. You fancy people your own age, and that's all there is to it, is what I thought. What I'd always thought.

So I ignored them, except that I couldn't quite. I kept sneaking a look, every now and then, and the more I did the more I felt kind of friendly towards them; I liked them. Which was a bit weird considering they didn't know I even existed—they certainly weren't interested in *me*—so it was a pretty one-sided kind of relationship. I thought he seemed like a nice bloke, whatever you thought about him and her and all that. It was something about the way he smiled, and the way he told her things (not that I ever heard a word they said, I wasn't eavesdropping, not ever, let's be quite clear about that) that made her look interested and say things back and so on. I thought it was obvious they liked talking to each other, quite apart from anything else. I thought that was nice.

I only took out that girl I mentioned—the one who came to stay with her sister—once, and

9. **rush matting:** mats made from the stems of stiff marsh plants called rushes.

WORDS TO KNOW

compulsory (kəm-pŭl′sə-rē) *adj.* required; mandatory

Portrait of Scott (1968), Robert Vickrey. Collection of Remson Scott Vickrey.

I found myself imagining what it must be like being able to feel that you've made someone look like that.

as a matter of fact we couldn't find much to talk about. I was still in love with her—no doubt about that—but it was a bit sticky, I don't mind admitting. In fact I was quite glad when it was time to take her back to her sister's. In many ways the best part was just thinking about her.

Every time I looked at the girl—the Pitt-Rivers one, that is—I found myself imagining what it must be like being able to feel that you've made someone look like that. Radiant, like she was. Which is what that bloke must have been able to feel. I found myself putting myself in his place, as it were, and wondering. I've done a lot of wondering about things like that—everybody does, I suppose—but mostly it's been more kind of basic. Now, I began to think I didn't really know anything. Looking at those two—watching them, if you like—was a bit like seeing something go on behind a thick glass window, so it was half removed from you. You could see but not hear, hear but not touch, or whatever. I could see, but I didn't know.

I suppose you could say I was envious, in a funny kind of way. I don't mean jealous in that I fancied the girl, or anything like that. As I've said already, she wasn't pretty, or even attractive. And I wasn't envious like you might be envious of someone for being happier than you are, because I'm not specially unhappy, as it happens. I think I was envious of them for being what they were—as though one fossil creature might be envious of a more evolved kind of fossil creature, which of course is a stupid idea.

When I was in the Pitt-Rivers again I looked for them, quite deliberately, but they weren't there. I was disappointed, though I pretended to myself it really didn't matter. I wondered about why they went there in the first place; I mean, people have to meet each other somewhere but why *there?* It doesn't exactly spring to mind as a romantic spot. I supposed there were reasons they didn't want to meet somewhere obvious and public: maybe he was married, I thought, or maybe she was, even. I wondered if that was the only place they met, or did they have others. Once walking through the botanical gardens, I found myself looking for them in the big glasshouses there.

I know the inside of the Pitt-Rivers pretty well by now. Considering it's not anthropology or ethnology[10] or whatever I went there for in the first place, it's quite surprising what a lot I could tell you about the things people believe and do. Primitive people, that is—what the Pitt-Rivers calls primitive people. And I think it's all very sad, actually: sad because it's like children, not understanding how things work and getting it all wrong, and carving each other up because of it a lot of the time. It does actually make you feel things get better—wars and bombs and everything notwithstanding. Nobody wants to go on being a child all their lives.

I was thinking about this—looking at a case full of particularly loony stuff to do with witchcraft—when I saw them again. At least I saw her first, standing by the totem with her hands in her coat pockets, and I didn't have to look at the door to know he'd arrived: her face told you that. He came up to her and gave her a kind of hug—arm round her shoulders and then quickly off again—and they wandered away up the stairs, heads together, talking.

I didn't follow them; it had been nice to see them again, and know they were there, and that was it. I was busy on a poem I'd been writing and unpicking and rewriting for some time. It was a poem about an old man sitting on a bench in a park and getting into conversation with a boy—someone around my age—and they swap opinions and observations (it's all dialogue, this poem, like a long conversation) and it's not till the end you realize they're the same person. It sounds

10. **ethnology** (ĕth-nŏl′ə-jē): the branch of anthropology that involves the study and comparison of human cultures.

either corny, or pretentious, I know; and what I could never decide was whether to have it as though the old man's looking back, or the boy's kind of projecting forward—imagining himself, as it were. So I went on fiddling about with this, and didn't really think much about the man and the girl, until I saw it was latish and there was no one else in the museum except me and some feet on the wooden floor of the gallery overhead, walking round and round, round and round. Two pairs of feet. They'd been doing that for ages, I realized; I'd been hearing them without registering.

I saw them go past—just their heads, above the glass cases—and something wasn't right. They weren't talking. She had her arm through his, and she was looking straight in front of her, and when I saw her face I had a nasty kind of twinge in my stomach. Because she was miserable. Once, she looked at him, and they both managed a bleak sort of smile. And then they walked on, round the gallery again, and next time past they still weren't talking, just holding on to each other like that, like people who're ill, or very old. And then the attendant rang the bell, and I heard them come down the stairs, and they came past me and went out into the Natural History Museum.

I don't know what had happened. I never will.

I went after them. I saw them stop—under the central whale, just where I first saw her—and then they did say something to each other. I couldn't see her face; she had her back to me. He went off then, on his own, out through the main entrance, quickly, and she sat down on a bench. For a moment or two she just sat staring at that wretched whale, and then she felt in her bag and got out a comb and did her hair, as though that might help. And then she dropped the comb and didn't seem to have noticed, even, because she just sat; she didn't bother to pick it up or anything. I could see her face then, and I hope I don't ever see anyone look so unhappy again. I truly hope that.

I don't know what had happened. I never will. Somehow, I don't think they were ever going to see each other again, but why . . . well, that's their concern, just like the rest of it was, except that in this peculiar way I'd come to feel it was mine too. I didn't think there was anything disgusting about them any more, or creepy—I hadn't for a long time. I suppose you could say I'd learned something else in the Pitt-Rivers, by accident. I never did go on with that poem. I tore it up, as far as it had got; I wasn't so sure any more about that conversation, that there could even be one, or not like I'd been imagining, anyway. ❖

WORDS TO KNOW

pretentious (prĭ-tĕn′shəs) *adj.* marked by an artificial display intended to impress others

bleak (blēk) *adj.* gloomy; hopeless

RESPONDING OPTIONS

FROM PERSONAL RESPONSE TO CRITICAL ANALYSIS

REFLECT

1. Did you like the narrator in this story? Jot down your opinions in your notebook.

RETHINK

2. Why do you think the narrator becomes so interested in the woman at the museum?
3. How would you explain the narrator's reaction to the couple the first time he observes them?
4. The narrator says that he "learned something else in the Pitt-Rivers, by accident." What do you think he learned?
5. Why do you think the narrator tears up his poem at the end of the story?
6. Look back at the expressions you noted for the Reading Connection on page 1011. Why do you think the author used idioms and slang in this story?

RELATE

7. Consider the narrator's thoughts, feelings, and interests. In your estimation, is he a believable teenager? In other words, does he seem like a real person, like someone you might know? Why or why not?

ANOTHER PATHWAY

For each of the three times the boy encounters the couple, briefly describe, in a chart like the one shown, what the boy tells us about the couple and what he reveals about himself. Then discuss with your classmates whether your opinion of the couple or of the boy changed as you read the story.

	The Couple	The Boy
1st Visit		
2nd Visit		
3rd Visit		

LITERARY CONCEPTS

In many stories, the **setting,** or time and place of the action, is critical to a complete understanding of the plot, characters, and theme. In other stories, the setting plays a more subtle role, perhaps supporting or enhancing the theme. Consider both the atmosphere and the function of the Pitt-Rivers Museum. Why do you think Lively chose it as the setting for this story?

QUICKWRITES

1. As the narrator of this story, write a **poem** expressing your feelings about the couple.
2. Write a **character sketch** of the narrator, based on what he reveals about himself and on your own judgment of his attitudes.
3. Unravel the mystery of the couple at the Pitt-Rivers Museum. Write a **summary** of a short story that focuses on their relationship.

***PORTFOLIO** Save your writing. You may want to use it later as a spring-board to a piece for your portfolio.*

ALTERNATIVE ACTIVITIES

1. With a partner, rehearse and present a **dramatization** of a conversation the narrator might have had with the woman in the story.
2. Plan and shoot a **silent movie** that depicts a variety of relationships and conversations between couples of all ages. Stage your film with friends or family members role-playing the different couples. Share your work with the class.

CRITIC'S CORNER

Critic John Mellors said of Lively: "She is particularly good at showing how one generation looks at, or ignores, the activities and preoccupations of another." Describe how this comment applies to "At the Pitt-Rivers." Use evidence from the story to support your opinion.

ACROSS THE CURRICULUM

History Research the origins of a famous museum or a museum in your community. Find out why the museum was founded, who funded it, and what its early collections consisted of. Share your information with the class in an oral report.

WORDS TO KNOW

For each phrase in the first column, write the letter of the synonymous phrase from the second column.

1. **pretentious** nonsense	a. mandatory story
2. **explicit** counsel	b. **benign** design
3. harmless scheme	c. phony baloney
4. dreary pinnacle	d. precise advice
5. **compulsory** bedtime ritual	e. **bleak** peak

PENELOPE LIVELY

1933–

In a memoir of her childhood called *Oleander, Jacaranda,* Penelope Lively describes what it was like growing up in Egypt—a culture that included mosquito netting, water buffalo, pyramids, and annual visits from the snake charmer. Although her parents were English, Lively was born in Egypt, which at that time was a protectorate of the British government. Her father had moved from England as a young man to accept a position with the National Bank of Egypt. Lively's world was vastly different from that of her English contemporaries, but it was a world she would desperately miss when forced to leave Cairo at the age of 12.

While living in Egypt, Lively was educated at home by her governess, who used a program designed for teaching English children living in foreign countries. In 1945, after the divorce of her parents, she was sent to England and enrolled in a boarding school. For a long time, Lively was an unhappy exile, living in an unfamiliar country and attending a school where success was equated with athletic and social skills rather than intellectual ability. It was a family friend who eventually sparked Lively's interest in history, an interest she later pursued at Oxford University.

Lively has earned considerable recognition as a versatile author. She has successfully woven her historical knowledge into numerous books for younger readers, including *The Ghost of Thomas Kempe* and *A Stitch in Time.* In the late 1970s, after writing juvenile literature for about ten years, the author turned her energies to adult fiction, writing both novels and short stories.

OTHER WORKS "Customers," "Miss Carlton and the Pop Concert," "A World of Her Own," "Yellow Trains," "Black Dogs"

LASERLINKS
• *ART GALLERY*

PREVIEWING

FICTION

Significant Moments in the Life of My Mother

Margaret Atwood

PERSONAL CONNECTION

Do your parents or other adults you know ever share memories of the years when they were growing up? If so, what kinds of stories do they tell? How do you generally react to their stories? Share your experiences with classmates.

HISTORICAL/BIOGRAPHICAL CONNECTION

Canada was long a British colony and is still a member of the Commonwealth of Nations. Although the reigning British monarch is the official head of state, Canada is self-governing. British influence is seen in the structure of Canada's government, which is modeled on Britain's, but Canada has developed its own heritage and is a blend of distinctly different cultures, of which English is only one.

Canadian literature did not begin to flourish until the 1960s, when a sense of nationalism spurred efforts to promote Canadian culture. One of the most effective promoters of Canadian literature, and one of its most talented contributors, is Margaret Atwood.

"Significant Moments in the Life of My Mother" appears in Atwood's second collection of short stories, *Bluebeard's Egg.* A statement on the copyright page of that volume declares that the characters in the stories are fictional and that "any resemblance to actual persons or happenings is coincidental." Nevertheless, the writer has acknowledged that some of the stories contain "portraits" of her parents, and Atwood may have based some of the events described in "Significant Moments in the Life of My Mother" on actual memories her mother shared with her. In the story, the narrator relates events that took place from around the 1920s, when Atwood's own parents were growing up in the Canadian province of Nova Scotia, to the 1940s and 1950s, when the writer herself progressed through childhood and adolescence in Ontario and Quebec.

LASERLINKS

• *GEOGRAPHICAL CONNECTION*

WRITING CONNECTION

Imagine yourself 20 years from now, recalling your own youth and sharing your memories with a young child. What stories would you most likely tell? In your notebook, write a brief account of one childhood memory that you might share.

Significant Moments in the Life of My Mother

Margaret Atwood

When my mother was very small, someone gave her a basket of baby chicks for Easter. They all died.

"I didn't know you weren't supposed to pick them up," says my mother. "Poor little things. I laid them out in a row on a board, with their little legs sticking out straight as pokers, and wept over them. I'd loved them to death."

Possibly this story is meant by my mother to illustrate her own stupidity, and also her sentimentality. We are to understand she wouldn't do such a thing now.

Possibly it's a commentary on the nature of love; though, knowing my mother, this is unlikely.

My mother's father was a country doctor. In the days before cars he drove a team of horses and a buggy around his territory, and in the days before snow ploughs he drove a team and a sleigh, through blizzards and rainstorms and in the middle of the night, to arrive at houses lit with oil lamps where water would be boiling on the wood range and flannel sheets warming on the plate rack, to deliver babies who would subsequently be named after him. His office was in the house, and as a child my mother would witness people arriving at the office door, which was reached through the front porch, clutching parts of themselves—thumbs, fingers, toes, ears, noses—which had accidentally been cut off, pressing these severed parts to the raw stumps of their bodies as if they could be stuck there like dough, in the mostly vain hope that my grandfather would be able to sew them back on, heal the gashes made in them by axes, saws, knives, and fate.

My mother and her younger sister would loiter near the closed office door until shooed away. From behind it would come groans, muffled screams, cries for help. For my mother, hospitals have never been glamorous places, and illness offers no respite or holiday. "Never get sick," she says, and means it. She hardly ever does.

Once, though, she almost died. It was when her appendix burst. My grandfather had to do the operation. He said later that he shouldn't have been the person to do it: his hands were shaking too much. This is one of the few admissions of weakness on his part that my mother has ever reported. Mostly he is portrayed as severe and in charge of things. "We all respected him, though," she says. "He was widely respected." (This is a word which has slipped a little in the scale since my mother's youth. It used to outrank *love.*)

It was someone else who told me the story of my grandfather's muskrat farm: how he and one of my mother's uncles fenced in the swamp at the back of their property and invested my mother's maiden aunt's savings in muskrats. The idea was that these muskrats would multiply and eventually be made into muskrat coats, but an adjoining apple farmer washed his spraying equipment upstream, and the muskrats were all killed by the poison, as dead as doornails. This was during the Depression, and it was no joke.

When they were young—this can cover almost anything these days, but I put it at seven or eight—my mother and her sister had a tree house, where they spent some of their time playing dolls' tea parties and so forth. One day they found a box of sweet little bottles outside my grandfather's dispensary.[1] The bottles were being thrown out, and my mother (who has always hated waste) appropriated them for use in their dolls' house. The bottles were full of yellow liquid, which they left in because it looked so pretty. It turned out that these were urine samples.

"We got Hail Columbia[2] for that," says my mother. "But what did we know?"

My mother's family lived in a large white house near an apple orchard, in Nova Scotia.[3] There was a barn and a carriage-house; in the kitchen there was a pantry. My mother can remember the days before commercial bakeries, when flour came in barrels and all the bread was made at home. She can remember the first radio broadcast she ever heard, which was a singing commercial about socks.

---

1. **dispensary:** a place from which medicines and medical care are given out.
2. **Hail Columbia:** old slang for a punishment or a sharp scolding.
3. **Nova Scotia** (nō′və skō′shə): a province in southeastern Canada.

WORDS TO KNOW

appropriate (ə-prō′prē-āt′) *v.* to take possession of or make use of, often without permission

In this house there were many rooms. Although I have been there, although I have seen the house with my own eyes, I still don't know how many. Parts of it were closed off, or so it seemed; there were back staircases. Passages led elsewhere. Five children lived in it, two parents, a hired man and a hired girl, whose names and faces kept changing. The structure of the house was hierarchical,[4] with my grandfather at the top, but its secret life—the life of pie crusts, clean sheets, the box of rags in the linen closet, the loaves in the oven—was female. The house, and all the objects in it, crackled with static electricity; undertows washed through it, the air was heavy with things that were known but not spoken. Like a hollow log, a drum, a church, it amplified, so that conversations whispered in it sixty years ago can be half-heard even today.

The air was heavy with things that were known but not spoken.

In this house you had to stay at the table until you had eaten everything on your plate. "'Think of the starving Armenians,' mother used to say," says my mother. "I didn't see how eating my bread crusts was going to help them out one jot."

It was in this house that I first saw a stalk of oats in a vase, each oat wrapped in the precious silver paper which had been carefully saved from a chocolate box. I thought it was the most wonderful thing I had ever seen, and began saving silver paper myself. But I never got around to wrapping the oats, and in any case I didn't know how. Like many other art forms of vanished civilizations, the techniques for this one have been lost and cannot quite be duplicated.

"We had oranges at Christmas," says my mother. "They came all the way from Florida; they were very expensive. That was the big treat: to find an orange in the toe of your stocking. It's funny to remember how good they tasted, now."

When she was sixteen, my mother had hair so long she could sit on it. Women were bobbing[5] their hair by then; it was getting to be the twenties. My mother's hair was giving her headaches, she says, but my grandfather, who was very strict, forbade her to cut it. She waited until one Saturday when she knew he had an appointment with the dentist.

"In those days there was no freezing," says my mother. "The drill was worked with a foot pedal, and it went *grind, grind, grind.* The dentist himself had brown teeth: he chewed tobacco, and he would spit the tobacco juice into a spittoon while he was working on your teeth."

Here my mother, who is a good mimic, imitates the sounds of the drill and the tobacco juice: *"Rrrrr! Rrrrr! Rrrrr! Phtt! Rrrrr! Rrrrr! Rrrrr! Phtt!* It was always sheer agony. It was a heaven-sent salvation when gas came in."

My mother went into the dentist's office, where my grandfather was sitting in the chair, white with pain. She asked him if she could have her hair cut. He said she could do anything in tarnation as long as she would get out of there and stop pestering him.

"So I went out straight away and had it all chopped off," says my mother jauntily. "He was furious afterwards, but what could he do? He'd given his word."

My own hair reposes in a cardboard box in a steamer trunk in my mother's cellar, where I picture it becoming duller and more brittle with each passing year, and possibly moth-eaten; by now it will look like the faded wreaths of hair in

4. **hierarchical:** (hī′ə-rär′kĭ-kəl): ranked according to status or authority.

5. **bobbing:** cutting short.

WORDS TO KNOW

jauntily (jôn′tə-lē) *adv.* in a lighthearted, cheerful, and self-confident manner

repose (rĭ-pōz′) *v.* to rest or lie

Victorian funeral jewelry. Or it may have developed a dry mildew; inside its tissue-paper wrappings it glows faintly, in the darkness of the trunk. I suspect my mother has forgotten it's in there. It was cut off, much to my relief, when I was twelve and my sister was born. Before that it was in long curls: "Otherwise," says my mother, "it would have been just one big snarl." My mother combed it by winding it around her index finger every morning, but when she was in the hospital my father couldn't cope. "He couldn't get it around his stubby fingers," says my mother. My father looks down at his fingers. They are indeed broad compared with my mother's long elegant ones, which she calls boney. He smiles a pussy-cat smile.

So it was that my hair was sheared off. I sat in the chair in my first beauty parlor and watched it falling, like handfuls of cobwebs, down over my shoulders. From within it my head began to emerge, smaller, denser, my face more angular. I aged five years in fifteen minutes. I knew I could go home now and try out lipstick.

"Your father was upset about it," says my mother, with an air of collusion. She doesn't say this when my father is present. We smile, over the odd reactions of men to hair.

I used to think that my mother, in her earlier days, led a life of sustained hilarity and hair-raising adventure. (That was before I realized that she never put in the long stretches of uneventful time that must have made up much of her life: the stories were just the punctuation.) Horses ran away with her, men offered to, she was continually falling out of trees or off the ridgepoles of barns, or nearly being swept out to sea in rip-tides; or, in a more minor vein, suffering acute embarrassment in trying circumstances.

Churches were especially dangerous. "There was a guest preacher one Sunday," she says. "Of course we had to go to church every Sunday. There he was, in full career,[6] preaching hellfire and damnation"—she pounds an invisible pulpit—"and his full set of false teeth shot out of his mouth—*phoop!*—just like that. Well, he didn't miss a stride. He stuck his hand up and caught them and popped them back into his mouth, and he kept right on, condemning us all to eternal torment. The pew was shaking! The tears were rolling down our faces, and the worst of it was, we were in the front pew, he was looking right at us. But of course we couldn't laugh out loud: father would have given us Hail Columbia."

Other people's parlors were booby-trapped for her; so were any and all formal social occasions. Zippers sprang apart on her clothes in strategic places, hats were unreliable. The shortage of real elastic during the war demanded constant alertness: underpants then had buttons, and were more taboo and therefore more significant than they are now. "There you would be," she says, "right on the street, and before you knew it they'd be down around your galoshes. The way to do was to step out of them with one foot, then kick them up with your other foot and whip them into your purse. I got quite good at it."

This particular story is told only to a few, but other stories are for general consumption. When she tells them, my mother's face turns to rubber. She takes all the parts, adds the sound effects, waves her hands around in the air. Her eyes gleam, sometimes a little wickedly, for although my mother is sweet and old and a lady, she avoids being a sweet old lady. When people are in danger of mistaking her for one, she flings in something from left field; she refuses to be taken for granted.

But my mother cannot be duped into telling stories when she doesn't want to. If you prompt her, she becomes self-conscious and clams up. Or she will laugh and go out into the kitchen, and shortly after that you will hear the whir of the Mixmaster.[7] Long ago I gave up attempting to make her do tricks at parties. In gatherings of

6. **in full career:** going full speed.

7. **Mixmaster:** the brand name of an electric mixer.

WORDS TO KNOW

collusion (kə-lo͞o'zhən) *n.* a secret agreement for a deceitful purpose
dupe (do͞op) *v.* to deceive; trick

unknown people, she merely listens intently, her head tilted a little, smiling a smile of glazed politeness. The secret is to wait and see what she will say afterwards.

At the age of seventeen my mother went to the Normal School in Truro. This name—"Normal School"—once held a certain magic for me. I thought it had something to do with learning to be normal, which possibly it did, because really it was where you used to go to learn how to be a schoolteacher. Subsequently my mother taught in a one-room school house not far from her home. She rode her horse to and from the school house every day, and saved up the money she earned and sent herself to university with it. My grandfather wouldn't send her: he said she was too frivolous-minded. She liked ice-skating and dancing too much for his taste.

At Normal School my mother boarded with a family that contained several sons in more or less the same age group as the girl boarders. They all ate around a huge dining-room table (which I pictured as being of dark wood, with heavy carved legs, but covered always with a white linen tablecloth), with the mother and father presiding, one at each end. I saw them both as large and pink and beaming.

"The boys were great jokers," says my mother. "They were always up to something." This was desirable in boys: to be great jokers, to be always up to something. My mother adds a key sentence: "We had a lot of fun."

Having fun has always been high on my mother's agenda. She has as much fun as possible, but what she means by this phrase cannot be understood without making an adjustment, an allowance for the great gulf across which this phrase must travel before it reaches us. It comes from another world, which, like the stars that originally sent out the light we see hesitating in the sky above us these nights, may be or is already gone. It is possible to reconstruct the facts of this world—the furniture, the clothing, the ornaments on the mantelpiece, the jugs and basins and even the chamber pots in the bedrooms, but not the emotions, not with the same exactness. So much that is now known and felt must be excluded.

This was a world in which guileless flirtation was possible, because there were many things that were simply not done by nice girls, and more girls were nice then. To fall from niceness was to fall not only from grace: sexual acts, by girls at any rate, had financial consequences. Life was more joyful and innocent then, and at the same time permeated with guilt and terror, or at least the occasions for them, on the most daily level. It was like the Japanese haiku: a limited form, rigid in its perimeters, within which an astonishing freedom was possible.

There are photographs of my mother at this time, taken with three or four other girls, linked arm in arm or with their arms thrown jestingly around each other's necks. Behind them, beyond the sea or the hills or whatever is in the background, is a world already hurtling towards ruin, unknown to them: the theory of relativity has been discovered, acid is accumulating at the roots of trees, the bull-frogs are doomed. But they smile with something that from this distance you could almost call gallantry, their right legs thrust forward in parody of a chorus line.

One of the great amusements for the girl boarders and the sons of the family was amateur theater. Young people—they were called "young people"—frequently performed in plays which were put on in the church basement. My mother was a regular actor. (I have a stack of the scripts somewhere about the house, yellowing little booklets with my mother's parts checked in pencil. They are all comedies, and all impenetrable.) "There was no television then," says my mother. "You made your own fun."

For one of these plays a cat was required, and my mother and one of the sons borrowed the family cat. They put it into a canvas bag and

WORDS TO KNOW

permeated (pûr'mē-ā-tĭd) *adj.* penetrated throughout; filled **permeate** *v.*

Hilda, Unity and Dolls,

Sir Stanley Spencer (1891–1959). Leeds (England) Museums and Galleries, City Art Gallery.

drove to the rehearsal (there were cars by then), with my mother holding the cat on her lap. The cat, which must have been frightened, wet itself copiously, through the canvas bag and all over my mother's skirt. At the same time it made the most astonishingly bad smell.

"I was ready to sink through the floorboards," says my mother. "But what could I do? All I could do was sit there. In those days things like that"—she means cat pee, or pee of any sort—"were not mentioned." She means in mixed company.

I think of my mother driven through the night, skirts dripping, overcome with shame, the young man beside her staring straight ahead, pretending not to notice anything. They both feel that this act of unmentionable urination has been done, not by the cat, but by my mother. And so they continue, in a straight line that takes them over the Atlantic and past the curvature of the earth, out through the moon's orbit and into the dark reaches beyond.

Meanwhile, back on earth, my mother says: "I had to throw the skirt out. It was a good skirt, too, but nothing could get rid of the smell."

"**I** only heard your father swear once," says my mother. My mother herself never swears. When she comes to a place in a story in which swearing is called for, she says "dad-ratted" or "blankety-blank."

"It was when he mashed his thumb, when he was sinking the well, for the pump." This story, I know, takes place before I was born, up north, where there is nothing underneath the trees and their sheddings but sand and bedrock. The well was for a hand pump, which in turn was for the first of the many cabins and houses my parents built together. But since I witnessed later wells being sunk and later hand pumps being installed, I know how it's done. There's a pipe with a point at one end. You pound it into the ground with a sledge hammer, and as it goes down you screw other lengths of pipe onto it, until you hit drinkable water. To keep from ruining the thread on the top end, you hold a block of wood between the sledge hammer and the pipe. Better, you get someone else to hold it for you. This is how my father mashed his thumb: he was doing both the holding and the hammering himself.

"It swelled up like a radish," says my mother. "He had to make a hole in the nail, with his toad-sticker,[8] to ease the pressure. The blood spurted out like pips from a lemon. Later on the whole nail turned purple and black and dropped off. Luckily he grew another one. They say you only get two chances. When he did it though, he turned the air blue[9] for yards around. I didn't even know he knew those words. I don't know where he picked them up." She speaks as if these words are a minor contagious disease, like chicken pox.

Here my father looks modestly down at his plate. For him, there are two worlds: one containing ladies, in which you do not use certain expressions, and another one—consisting of logging camps and other haunts of his youth, and of gatherings of acceptable sorts of men—in which you do. To let the men's world slip over verbally into the ladies' would reveal you as a mannerless boor, but to carry the ladies' world over into the men's brands you a prig and maybe even a pansy. This is the word for it. All of this is well understood between them.

This story illustrates several things: that my father is no pansy, for one; and that my mother behaved properly by being suitably shocked. But my mother's eyes shine with delight while she tells this story. Secretly, she thinks it funny that my father got caught out, even if only once. The thumbnail that fell off is, in any significant way, long forgotten.

There are some stories which my mother does not tell when there are men present: never at

8. **toad-sticker:** pocketknife.
9. **turned the air blue:** filled the air with the sound of swearing.

WORDS TO KNOW

copiously (kō′pē-əs-lē) *adv.* abundantly; plentifully

dinner, never at parties. She tells them to women only, usually in the kitchen, when they or we are helping with the dishes or shelling peas, or taking the tops and tails off the string beans, or husking corn. She tells them in a lowered voice, without moving her hands around in the air, and they contain no sound effects. These are stories of romantic betrayals, unwanted pregnancies, illnesses of various horrible kinds, marital infidelities, mental breakdowns, tragic suicides, unpleasant lingering deaths. They are not rich in detail or embroidered with incident: they are stark and factual. The women, their own hands moving among the dirty dishes or the husks of vegetables, nod solemnly.

Some of these stories, it is understood, are not to be passed on to my father, because they would upset him. It is well known that women can deal with this sort of thing better than men can. Men are not to be told anything they might find too painful; the secret depths of human nature, the sordid physicalities,[10] might overwhelm or damage them. For instance, men often faint at the sight of their own blood, to which they are not accustomed. For this reason you should never stand behind one in the line at the Red Cross donor clinic. Men, for some mysterious reason, find life more difficult than women do. (My mother believes this, despite the female bodies, trapped, diseased, disappearing, or abandoned, that litter her stories.) Men must be allowed to play in the sandbox of their choice, as happily as they can, without disturbance; otherwise they get cranky and won't eat their dinners. There are all kinds of things that men are simply not equipped to understand, so why expect it of them? Not everyone shares this belief about men; nevertheless, it has its uses.

"She dug up the shrubs from around the house," says my mother. This story is about a shattered marriage: serious business. My mother's eyes widen. The other women lean forward. "All she left him were the shower curtains." There is a collective sigh, an expelling of breath. My father enters the kitchen, wondering when the tea will be ready, and the women close ranks, turning to him their deceptive blankly smiling faces. Soon afterwards, my mother emerges from the kitchen, carrying the tea pot, and sets it down on the table in its ritual place.

"**I** remember the time we almost died," says my mother. Many of her stories begin this way. When she is in a certain mood, we are to understand that our lives have been preserved only by a series of amazing coincidences and strokes of luck; otherwise the entire family, individually or collectively, would be dead as doornails. These stories, in addition to producing adrenaline, serve to reinforce our sense of gratitude. There is the time we almost went over a waterfall, in a canoe, in a fog; the time we almost got caught in a forest fire; the time my father almost got squashed, before my mother's very eyes, by a ridgepole he was lifting into place; the time my brother almost got struck by a bolt of lightning, which went by him so close it knocked him down. "You could hear it sizzle," says my mother.

This is the story of the hay wagon. "Your father was driving," says my mother, "at the speed he usually goes." We read between the lines: *too fast.* "You kids were in the back." I can remember this day, so I can remember how old I was, how old my brother was. We were old enough to think it was funny to annoy my father by singing popular songs of a type he disliked, such as "Mockingbird Hill"; or perhaps we were imitating bagpipe music by holding our noses and

10. **sordid physicalities:** the basic physical needs and workings of the human body.

humming, while hitting our Adam's apples with the edges of our hands. When we became too irritating my father would say, "Pipe down." We weren't old enough to know that his irritation could be real: we thought it was part of the game.

"We were going down a steep hill," my mother continues, "when a hay wagon pulled out right across the road, at the bottom. Your father put on the brakes, but nothing happened. The brakes were gone! I thought our last moment had come." Luckily the hay wagon continued across the road, and we shot past it, missing it by at least a foot. "My heart was in my mouth," says my mother.

I didn't know until afterwards what had really happened. I was in the back seat, making bagpipe music, oblivious. The scenery was the same as it always was on car trips: my parents' heads, seen from behind, sticking up above the front seat. My father had his hat on, the one he wore to keep things from falling off the trees into his hair. My mother's hand was placed lightly on the back of his neck.

"**Y**ou had such an acute sense of smell when you were younger," says my mother.

Now we are on more dangerous ground: my mother's childhood is one thing, my own quite another. This is the moment at which I start rattling the silverware, or ask for another cup of tea. "You used to march into houses that were strange to you, and you would say in a loud voice, 'What's that funny smell?'" If there are guests present, they shift a little away from me, conscious of their own emanations, trying not to look at my nose.

"I used to be so embarrassed," says my mother absent-mindedly. Then she shifts gears. "You were such an easy child. You used to get up at six in the morning and play by yourself in the play room, singing away. . . ." There is a pause. A distant voice, mine, high and silvery, drifts over the space between us. "You used to talk a blue streak. Chatter, chatter, chatter, from morning to night." My mother sighs imperceptibly, as if wondering why I have become so silent, and gets up to poke the fire.

Hoping to change the subject, I ask whether or not the crocuses have come up yet, but she is not to be diverted. "I never had to spank you," she says. "A harsh word, and you would be completely reduced." She looks at me sideways; she isn't sure what I have turned into, or how. "There were just one or two times. Once, when I had to go out and I left your father in charge." (This may be the real point of the story: the inability of men to second-guess small children.) "I came back along the street, and there were you and your brother, throwing mud balls at an old man out of the upstairs window."

We both know whose idea this was. For my mother, the proper construction to be put on this event is that my brother was a hell-raiser and I was his shadow, "easily influenced," as my mother puts it. "You were just putty in his hands."

"Of course, I had to punish both of you equally," she says. Of course. I smile a forgiving smile. The real truth is that I was sneakier than my brother, and got caught less often. No front-line charges into enemy machine-gun nests for me, if they could be at all avoided. My own solitary acts of wickedness were devious and well concealed; it was only in partnership with my brother that I would throw caution to the winds.

"He could wind you around his little finger," says my mother. "Your father made each of you a toy box, and the rule was—" (my mother is good at the devising of rules) "—the rule was that neither of you could take the toys out of the other one's toy box without permission. Otherwise he would have got all your toys away from you. But he got them anyway, mind you. He used to talk you into playing house, and he would pretend to be the baby. Then he would pretend to cry, and when you asked what he wanted, he'd demand whatever it was out of

WORDS TO KNOW

imperceptibly (ĭm′pər-sĕp′tə-blē) *adv.* subtly or slightly; in a barely noticeable way

your toy box that he wanted to play with at the moment. You always gave it to him."

I don't remember this, though I do remember staging World War Two on the living-room floor, with armies of stuffed bears and rabbits; but surely some primal patterns were laid down. Have these early toy-box experiences—and "toy box" itself, as a concept, reeks with implications —have they made me suspicious of men who wish to be mothered, yet susceptible to them at the same time? Have I been conditioned to believe that if I am not solicitous, if I am not forthcoming, if I am not a never-ending cornucopia[11] of entertaining delights, they will take their collections of milk-bottle tops and their mangy one-eared teddy bears and go away into the woods by themselves to play snipers? Probably. What my mother thinks was merely cute may have been lethal.

But this is not her only story about my suckiness and gullibility. She follows up with the *coup de grâce,*[12] the tale of the bunny-rabbit cookies.

"It was in Ottawa. I was invited to a government tea," says my mother, and this fact alone should signal an element of horror: my mother hated official functions, to which however she was obliged to go because she was the wife of a civil servant. "I had to drag you kids along; we couldn't afford a lot of babysitters in those days." The hostess had made a whole plateful of decorated cookies for whatever children might be present, and my mother proceeds to describe these: wonderful cookies shaped like bunny rabbits, with faces and clothes of colored icing, little skirts for the little girl bunny rabbits, little pants for the little boy bunny rabbits.

"You chose one," says my mother. "You went off to a corner with it, by yourself. Mrs. X noticed you and went over. 'Aren't you going to eat your cookie?' she said. 'Oh, no,' you said. 'I'll just sit here and talk to it.' And there you sat, as happy as a clam. But someone had made the mistake of leaving the plate near your brother. When they looked again, there wasn't a single cookie left. He'd eaten every one. He was very sick that night, I can tell you."

Some of my mother's stories defy analysis. What is the moral of this one? That I was a simp is clear enough, but on the other hand it was my brother who got the stomach ache. Is it better to eat your food, in a straightforward materialistic way, and as much of it as possible, or go off into the corner and talk to it? This used to be a favorite of my mother's before I was married, when I would bring what my father referred to as "swains"[13] home for dinner. Along with the dessert, out would come the bunny-rabbit cookie story, and I would cringe and twiddle my spoon while my mother forged blithely on with it. What were the swains supposed to make of it? Were my kindliness and essential femininity being trotted out for their inspection? Were they being told in a roundabout way that I was harmless, that they could expect to be talked to by me, but not devoured? Or was she, in some way, warning them off? Because there is something faintly crazed about my behavior, some tinge of the kind of person who might be expected to leap up suddenly from the dinner table and shout, "Don't eat that! It's alive!"

There is, however, a difference between symbolism and anecdote. Listening to my mother, I sometimes remember this.

"**I**n my next incarnation," my mother said once, "I'm going to be an archaeologist and go around digging things up." We were sitting on the bed that had once been my brother's, then mine, then my sister's; we were sorting out things from one of the trunks, deciding what could now be given away or

---

11. **cornucopia** (kôr′nə-kō′pē-ə): abundant, overflowing supply.

12. ***coup de grâce*** (ko͞o′ də gräs′) *French:* a deathblow that ends a victim's suffering; a finishing stroke or decisive event.

13. **swains:** boyfriends.

WORDS TO KNOW **solicitous** (sə-lĭs′ĭ-təs) *adj.* expressing or showing care or concern

thrown out. My mother believes that what you save from the past is mostly a matter of choice.

At that time something wasn't right in the family; someone wasn't happy. My mother was angry: her good cheer was not paying off.

This statement of hers startled me. It was the first time I'd ever heard my mother say that she might have wanted to be something other than what she was. I must have been thirty-five at the time, but it was still shocking and slightly offensive to me to learn that my mother might not have been totally contented fulfilling the role in which fate had cast her: that of being my mother. What thumb-suckers we all are, I thought, when it comes to mothers.

Shortly after this I became a mother myself, and this moment altered for me.

While she was combing my next-to-impossible hair, winding it around her long index finger, yanking out the snarls, my mother used to read me stories. Most of them are still in the house somewhere, but one has vanished. It may have been a library book. It was about a little girl who was so poor she had only one potato left for her supper, and while she was roasting it the potato got up and ran away. There was the usual chase, but I can't remember the ending: a significant lapse.

"That story was one of your favorites," says my mother. She is probably still under the impression that I identified with the little girl, with her hunger and her sense of loss; whereas in reality I identified with the potato.

Early influences are important. It took that one a while to come out; probably until after I went to university and started wearing black stockings and pulling my hair back into a bun, and having pretensions.[14] Gloom set in. Our next-door neighbor, who was interested in wardrobes, tackled my mother: "'If she would only *do* something about herself,'" my mother quotes, "'She could be *quite attractive.*'"

"You always kept yourself busy," my mother says charitably, referring to this time. "You always had something cooking. Some project or other."

It is part of my mother's mythology that I am as cheerful and productive as she is, though she admits that these qualities may be occasionally and temporarily concealed. I wasn't allowed much angst[15] around the house. I had to indulge it in the cellar, where my mother wouldn't come upon me brooding and suggest I should go out for a walk, to improve my circulation. This was her answer to any sign, however slight, of creeping despondency. There wasn't a lot that a brisk sprint through dead leaves, howling winds, or sleet couldn't cure.

It was, I knew, the *zeitgeist*[16] that was afflicting me, and against it such simple remedies were powerless. Like smog I wafted through her days, dankness spreading out from around me. I read modern poetry and histories of Nazi atrocities, and took to drinking coffee. Off in the distance, my mother vacuumed around my feet while I sat in chairs, studying, with car rugs tucked around me, for suddenly I was always cold.

My mother has few stories to tell about these times. What I remember from them is the odd look I would sometimes catch in her eyes. It struck me, for the first time in my life, that my mother might be afraid of me. I could not even reassure her, because I was only dimly aware of the nature of her distress, but there must have been something going on in me that was beyond her: at any time I might open my mouth and out would come a language she had never heard before. I had become a visitant from outer space, a time-traveler come back from the future, bearing news of a great disaster. ❖

14. **pretensions:** behavior or appearances meant to impress other people.

15. **angst:** a feeling of anxiety or apprehension, often accompanied by depression.

16. ***zeitgeist*** (tsīt'gīst'): the spirit of the time; the outlook characteristic of a period or generation. The word is German in origin, from *zeit,* meaning "time," and *geist,* meaning "spirit."

WORDS TO KNOW

despondency (dĭ-spŏn'dən-sē) *n.* a state of extreme discouragement due to a loss of confidence, courage, or hope

RESPONDING OPTIONS

FROM PERSONAL RESPONSE *TO* CRITICAL ANALYSIS

REFLECT 1. Which of the stories told by the narrator's mother was your favorite? In your notebook, briefly describe it and tell why you liked it.

RETHINK 2. What is your opinion of the narrator? Give evidence from the selection to support your answer.

3. How would you describe the male-female relationships presented in this selection?

Consider
- the hair-cutting stories
- the various roles of fathers and husbands in the stories
- the attitudes toward men expressed by the narrator and her mother

4. Why do you think the narrator calls the stories of her own childhood "dangerous ground"?

RELATE 5. Would you like to have someone like the narrator's mother in your family? Why or why not?

ANOTHER PATHWAY

Cooperative Learning

Working in small groups, discuss how the mother's personality is revealed through her stories. In a chart like the one shown, note the stories she tells and the qualities that you think she displays in each story. Compare your findings with those of other classmates.

The Narrator's Mother

Story		Qualities
Baby chicks	→	sensitive, curious
	→	
	→	

LITERARY CONCEPTS

The **narrator** of a literary work is the person or voice that tells the story. The narrator can be a character in the story or a voice outside the action. In this selection, the narrator is not only the recorder and judge of her mother's tales but an active participant in some of those tales.

Atwood intertwines fact and fiction in this story and bases her characters—to some degree—on actual people, a technique that is fairly common in contemporary fiction. In this type of story, the writer often creates a fictional narrator, who may or may not reflect the personality and views of the writer. Do you think of the narrator in this selection as the writer, or do you give her a different identity? Give reasons for your answer.

QUICKWRITES

1. Write out an **interview** in which the narrator's mother answers questions about the changes in lifestyle that have occurred since she was a young girl.
2. Using details from the selection, write a **historical sketch** that describes life during the early 20th century, when the narrator's mother was growing up in Nova Scotia.
3. Draft a short **essay** in which you compare and contrast the story you wrote for the Writing Connection on page 1021 with one of the stories told by the narrator's mother.

PORTFOLIO *Save your writing. You may want to use it later as a spring-board to a piece for your portfolio.*

ALTERNATIVE ACTIVITIES

1. Using at least two of the mother's stories, try the art of **storytelling.** Retell the stories in your own words, and attempt to capture the interest of your listeners by varying the tone of your voice and by incorporating appropriate facial expressions and gestures into your performance. Be sure to rehearse your routine several times before performing in front of the class.
2. Create a **cartoon strip** to illustrate one of the stories told by the mother or the narrator. Share your work with your classmates.
3. With a group of classmates, plan and perform a **dramatic skit** based on one of the stories in the selection. You might want to use props or costumes to make your presentation more realistic.

CRITIC'S CORNER

In commenting on Atwood's writing, critic Linda Sandler has said: "Margaret Atwood is all things to all people. If you want, she's a nationalist . . . a feminist . . . or a psychologist or a comedian." Look for evidence in the selection that might support some or all of the roles Sandler assigns to the author.

LITERARY LINKS

Compare the mother in this selection with the mother portrayed in George Barker's poem "To My Mother" (page 868). What similarities or differences do you find between the two women? Explain your answer.

THE WRITER'S STYLE

Atwood uses extensive **imagery** in her writing. Look through the selection and find examples of imagery that you think are particularly vivid. What is their sensory appeal? What effect does each example have on you as a reader?

ACROSS THE CURRICULUM

Psychology Investigate the typical transitions that occur in the relationship between a parent and a child as the child progresses from infancy to adulthood. How do the roles of both the parent and the child change? How do their attitudes change? Present your findings in an oral report to the class.

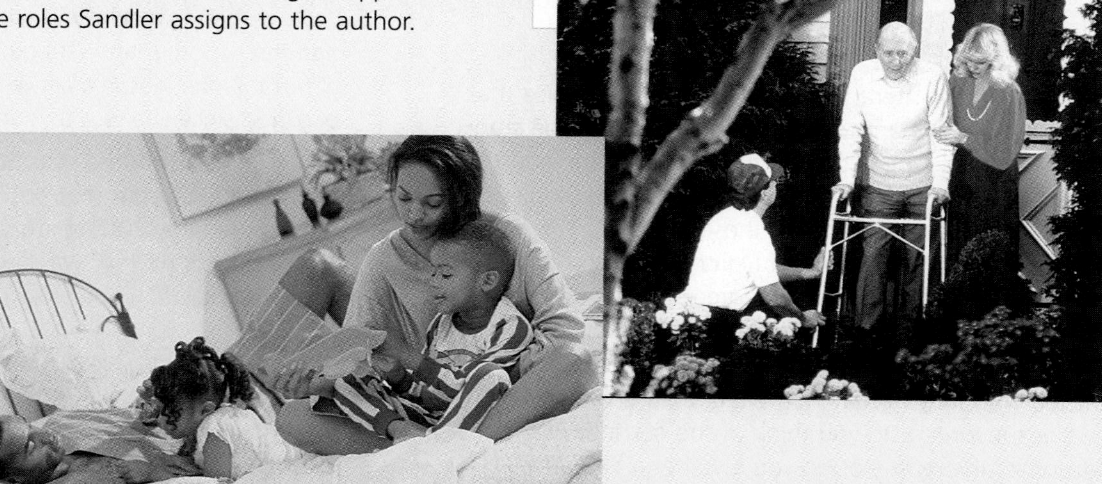

WORDS TO KNOW

EXERCISE A Identify each pair of words by writing *Synonyms* or *Antonyms.*

1. solicitous—indifferent
2. permeated—saturated
3. jauntily—gravely
4. copiously—insufficiently
5. dupe—mislead
6. repose—work
7. collusion—conspiracy
8. despondency—despair
9. imperceptibly—obviously
10. appropriate—donate

EXERCISE B With a partner, take turns acting out the meanings of the following words: *jauntily, repose, collusion, dupe, imperceptibly, solicitous,* and *despondency.* After your partner guesses your word, try to guess your partner's word.

MARGARET ATWOOD

1939–

During much of her childhood, Margaret Atwood and her family spent six or seven months of every year living in the Canadian bush, the sparsely populated areas of northern Quebec and Ontario. These trips were an important part of her father's job as an entomologist, a scientist who collects and studies insects. For Atwood, the trips provided vast knowledge of the natural world, knowledge that would appear in her writing many years later.

Atwood began writing poems at age 5, and by age 16, she knew that writing was her sole ambition. She has credited her parents for their supportive role in her early pursuits. Although they did not urge her to become a writer, they did expect her to put her intelligence and creative talent to good use. Atwood grew up in a highly educated family of readers and storytellers who believed that girls as well as boys should acquire all the education they could. In this respect, her parents were unlike many of their contemporaries during the 1950s, when society generally pushed young women toward marriage and often discouraged them from other pursuits.

In 1961, Atwood graduated with honors in English from the University of Toronto, where she had displayed her creativity not only in writing but in drama and art. That same year, her first collection of poetry was published. She received a master of arts degree in English from Radcliffe College at Harvard University in 1962 and later began working toward a doctorate at Harvard. She has taught English literature and creative writing at universities in Canada, Australia, and the United States.

By the 1970s, Atwood's writing had gained worldwide attention, and by 1982 her work had been published in 14 different languages. She is especially popular in her native Canada, where she has gained the status usually accorded only to movie stars and musicians. Atwood was honored for her first book of poems and has been receiving awards for both her poetry and her prose ever since. She has twice been the recipient of the Governor General's Award, Canada's most prestigious literary honor.

OTHER WORKS "Hurricane Hazel," "In Search of the Rattlesnake Plantain," "Unearthing Suite"

LASERLINKS
- *AUTHOR BACKGROUND*
- *ART GALLERY*

PREVIEWING

FICTION

A Sunrise on the Veld

Doris Lessing

PERSONAL CONNECTION

Think about how easy or hard it is for you to change your ideas and viewpoints. How do you respond when an experience leads you to new insights? Do you enjoy being challenged to see the world in a new way or to think about your life from a different perspective? Jot down some of your thoughts in your notebook.

BIOGRAPHICAL CONNECTION

Doris Lessing grew up on a farm in the African country of Southern Rhodesia (rō-dē'zhə), today known as Zimbabwe (zĭm-bäb'wē). The farm was situated on the edge of the veld (fĕlt), a vast grassy land having only a few bushes and almost no trees, but a land that teemed with wildlife in the years of Lessing's childhood. She spent her youth exploring her surroundings and later claimed that her real education came not from school but from observing nature on the veld. In her nonfiction work *African Laughter,* she wrote about what the veld was like for her and her brother:

> Lying in our blankets under the trees on the sandveld of Marandellas, or in the house on the farm in Banket, the shrilling, clamoring, exulting of the birds as the sun appeared was so loud the ears seemed to curl up and complain before . . . we leaped up into the early morning, to become part of all that tumult and activity.

Not surprisingly, the same veld that taught Lessing so much about nature and life became the setting for many of her stories, including "A Sunrise on the Veld."

READING CONNECTION

Interpreting a Title The title of a short story can give the reader help in understanding the characters, plot, and themes. Sometimes the significance of a title changes as the story develops. As you read "A Sunrise on the Veld," jot down any insights you have about the relationship of the title to the main character, plot, and themes in the story.

LASERLINKS
• *ZOOLOGICAL CONNECTION*

A Sunrise on the Veld

DORIS LESSING

Every night that winter he said aloud into the dark of the pillow: Half-past four! Half-past four! till he felt his brain had gripped the words and held them fast. Then he fell asleep at once, as if a shutter had fallen; and lay with his face turned to the clock so that he could see it first thing when he woke.

It was half-past four to the minute, every morning. Triumphantly pressing down the alarm-knob of the clock, which the dark half of his mind had outwitted, remaining vigilant all night and counting the hours as he lay relaxed in sleep, he huddled down for a last warm moment under the clothes, playing with the idea of lying abed for this once only. But he played with it for the fun of knowing that it was a weakness he could defeat without effort; just as he set the alarm each night for the delight of the moment when he woke and stretched his limbs, feeling the muscles tighten, and thought: Even my brain—even that! I can control every part of myself.

Luxury of warm rested body, with the arms and legs and fingers waiting like soldiers for a word of command! Joy of knowing that the precious hours were given to sleep voluntarily!—for he had once stayed awake three nights running, to prove that he could, and then worked all day, refusing even to

WORDS TO KNOW

vigilant (vĭj′ə-lənt) *adj.* ever watchful and alert

admit that he was tired; and now sleep seemed to him a servant to be commanded and refused.

The boy stretched his frame full-length, touching the wall at his head with his hands, and the bedfoot with his toes; then he sprung out, like a fish leaping from water. And it was cold, cold.

He always dressed rapidly, so as to try and conserve his night-warmth till the sun rose two hours later; but by the time he had on his clothes his hands were numbed and he could scarcely hold his shoes. These he could not put on for fear of waking his parents, who never came to know how early he rose.

As soon as he stepped over the lintel,[1] the flesh of his soles contracted on the chilled earth, and his legs began to ache with cold. It was night: the stars were glittering, the trees standing black and still. He looked for signs of day, for the greying of the edge of a stone, or a lightening in the sky where the sun would rise, but there was nothing yet. Alert as an animal he crept past the dangerous window, standing poised with his hand on the sill for one proudly fastidious moment, looking in at the stuffy blackness of the room where his parents lay.

Feeling for the grass-edge of the path with his toes, he reached inside another window further along the wall, where his gun had been set in readiness the night before. The steel was icy, and numbed fingers slipped along it, so that he had to hold it in the crook of his arm for safety. Then he tiptoed to the room where the dogs slept, and was fearful that they might have been tempted to go before him; but they were waiting, their haunches crouched in reluctance at the cold, but ears and swinging tails greeting the gun ecstatically. His warning undertone kept them secret and silent till the house was a hundred yards back: then they bolted off into the bush, yelping excitedly. The boy imagined his parents turning in their beds and muttering: Those dogs again! before they were dragged back in sleep; and he smiled scornfully. He always looked back over his shoulder at the house before he passed a wall of trees that shut it from sight. It looked so low and small, crouching there under a tall and brilliant sky. Then he turned his back on it, and on the frowsting[2] sleepers, and forgot them.

THE AIR SMELLED OF MORNING AND THE STARS WERE DIMMING.

He would have to hurry. Before the light grew strong he must be four miles away; and already a tint of green stood in the hollow of a leaf, and the air smelled of morning and the stars were dimming.

He slung the shoes over his shoulder, veld *skoen*[3] that were crinkled and hard with the dews of a hundred mornings. They would be necessary when the ground became too hot to bear. Now he felt the chilled dust push up between his toes, and he let the muscles of his feet spread and settle into the shapes of the earth; and he thought: I could walk a hundred miles on feet like these! I could walk all day, and never tire!

He was walking swiftly through the dark tunnel of foliage that in day-time was a road. The dogs were invisibly ranging the lower travelways of the bush, and he heard them panting. Sometimes he felt a cold muzzle on his leg before they were off again, scouting for a trail to follow. They were not trained, but free-running companions of the hunt, who often tired of the long stalk before the final shots, and went off on their own pleasure. Soon he could see them, small and wild-looking in a wild

1. **lintel:** used here to mean "threshold" (the wood or stone sill at the bottom of a doorway).

2. **frowsting** (frou′stĭng): a British term for lounging about.

3. ***skoen*** (sko͞on) *Afrikaans*: shoes.

WORDS TO KNOW **fastidious** (fă-stĭd′ē-əs) *adj.* displaying meticulous attention to detail

strange light, now that the bush stood trembling on the verge of color, waiting for the sun to paint earth and grass afresh.

The grass stood to his shoulders; and the trees were showering a faint silvery rain. He was soaked; his whole body was clenched in a steady shiver.

Once he bent to the road that was newly scored with animal trails, and regretfully straightened, reminding himself that the pleasure of tracking must wait till another day.

He began to run along the edge of a field, noting jerkily how it was filmed over with fresh spiderweb, so that the long reaches of great black clods seemed netted in glistening grey. He was using the steady lope he had learned by watching the natives, the run that is a dropping of the weight of the body from one foot to the next in a slow balancing movement that never tires, nor shortens the breath; and he felt the blood pulsing down his legs and along his arms, and the exultation and pride of body mounted in him till he was shutting his teeth hard against a violent desire to shout his triumph.

Soon he had left the cultivated part of the farm. Behind him the bush was low and black. In front was a long vlei,[4] acres of long pale grass that sent back a hollowing gleam of light to a satiny sky. Near him thick swathes of grass were bent with the weight of water, and diamond drops sparkled on each frond.

The first bird woke at his feet and at once a flock of them sprang into the air calling shrilly that day had come; and suddenly, behind him, the bush woke into song, and he could hear the guinea fowl[5] calling far ahead of him. That meant they would now be sailing down from their trees into thick grass, and it was for them he had come: he was too late. But he did not mind. He forgot he had come to shoot. He set his legs wide, and balanced from foot to foot, and swung his gun up and down in both hands horizontally, in a kind of improvised exercise, and let his head sink back till it was pillowed in his neck muscles, and watched how above him small rosy clouds floated in a lake of gold.

Suddenly it all rose in him: it was unbearable. He leapt up into the air, shouting and yelling wild, unrecognizable noises. Then he began to run, not carefully, as he had before, but madly, like a wild thing. He was clean crazy, yelling mad with the joy of living and a superfluity of youth. He rushed down the vlei under a tumult of crimson and gold, while all the birds of the world sang about him. He ran in great leaping strides, and shouted as he ran, feeling his body rise into the crisp rushing air and fall back surely on to sure feet; and thought briefly, not believing that such a thing could happen to him, that he could break his ankle any moment, in this thick tangled grass. He cleared bushes like a duiker,[6] leapt over rocks; and finally came to a dead stop at a place where the ground fell abruptly away below him to the river. It had been a two-mile-long dash through waist-high growth, and he was breathing hoarsely and could no longer sing. But he poised on a rock and looked down at stretches of water that gleamed through stooping trees, and thought suddenly, I am fifteen! Fifteen! The words came new to him; so that he kept repeating them wonderingly, with swelling excitement; and he felt the years of his life with his hands, as if he were counting marbles, each one hard and separate and compact, each one a wonderful shining thing. That was what he was: fifteen years of this rich soil, and this slow-moving water, and air that smelt like a challenge whether it was warm and sultry at noon, or as brisk as cold water, like it was now.

There was nothing he couldn't do, nothing! A vision came to him, as he stood there, like when a child hears the word "eternity" and tries to understand it, and time takes possession of the mind. He felt his life ahead of him as a great and wonderful thing, something that was his; and he

4. **vlei** (flā): low, swampy land.

5. **guinea fowl:** pheasantlike birds that have dark gray bodies flecked with white.

6. **duiker** (dī′kər): small African antelope.

WORDS TO KNOW **superfluity** (so͞o′pər-flo͞o′ĭ-tē) *n.* excess; overabundance; oversupply

Horned Forms (1944), Graham Sutherland. Tate Gallery, London/Art Resource, New York.

said aloud, with the blood rising to his head: all the great men of the world have been as I am now, and there is nothing I can't become, nothing I can't do; there is no country in the world I cannot make part of myself, if I choose. I contain the world. I can make of it what I want. If I choose, I can change everything that is going to happen: it depends on me, and what I decide now.

The urgency, and the truth and the courage of what his voice was saying exulted him so that he began to sing again, at the top of his voice, and the sound went echoing down the river gorge. He stopped for the echo, and sang again: stopped and shouted. That was what he was!—he sang, if he chose; and the world had to answer him.

And for minutes he stood there, shouting and singing and waiting for the lovely eddying[7] sound of the echo; so that his own new strong thoughts came back and washed round his head, as if someone were answering him and encouraging him; till the gorge was full of soft voices clashing back and forth from rock to rock over the river. And then it seemed as if there was a new voice. He listened, puzzled, for it was not his own. Soon he was leaning forward, all his nerves alert, quite still: somewhere close to him there was a noise that was no joyful bird, nor tinkle of falling water, nor ponderous[8] movement of cattle.

There it was again. In the deep morning hush that held his future and his past, was a sound of pain, and repeated over and over: it was a kind of shortened scream, as if someone, something, had no breath to scream. He came to himself, looked about him, and called for the dogs. They did not appear: they had gone off on their own business, and he was alone. Now he was clean sober, all the madness gone. His heart beating fast, because of that frightened screaming, he stepped carefully off the rock and went towards a belt of trees. He was moving cautiously, for not so long ago he had seen a leopard in just this spot.

At the edge of the trees he stopped and peered, holding his gun ready; he advanced, looking steadily about him, his eyes narrowed. Then, all at once, in the middle of a step, he faltered, and his face was puzzled. He shook his head impatiently, as if he doubted his own sight.

There, between two trees, against a background of gaunt black rocks, was a figure from a dream, a strange beast that was horned and drunken-legged, but like something he had never even imagined. It seemed to be ragged. It looked like a small buck

7. **eddying** (ĕd′ē-ĭng): moving contrary to the main current; circling.

8. **ponderous:** clumsy because of heaviness and size.

that had black ragged tufts of fur standing up irregularly all over it, with patches of raw flesh beneath . . . but the patches of rawness were disappearing under moving black and came again elsewhere; and all the time the creature screamed, in small gasping screams, and leaped drunkenly from side to side, as if it were blind.

Then the boy understood: it *was* a buck. He ran closer, and again stood still, stopped by a new fear. Around him the grass was whispering and alive. He looked wildly about, and then down. The ground was black with ants, great energetic ants that took no notice of him, but hurried and scurried towards the fighting shape, like glistening black water flowing through the grass.

And, as he drew in his breath and pity and terror seized him, the beast fell and the screaming stopped. Now he could hear nothing but one bird singing, and the sound of the rustling, whispering ants.

He peered over at the writhing blackness that jerked convulsively with the jerking nerves. It grew quieter. There were small twitches from the mass that still looked vaguely like the shape of a small animal.

It came into his mind that he should shoot it and end its pain; and he raised the gun. Then he lowered it again. The buck could no longer feel; its fighting was a mechanical protest of the nerves. But it was not that which made him put down the gun. It was a swelling feeling of rage and misery and protest that expressed itself in the thought: if I had not come it would have died like this: so why should I interfere? All over the bush things like this happen; they happen all the time; this is how life goes on, by living things dying in anguish. He gripped the gun between his knees and felt in his own limbs the myriad swarming pain of the twitching animal that could no longer feel, and set his teeth, and said over and over again under his breath: I can't stop it. I can't stop it. There is nothing I can do.

He was glad that the buck was unconscious and had gone past suffering so that he did not have to make a decision to kill it even when he was feeling with his whole body: this is what happens, this is how things work.

It was right—that was what he was feeling. *It was right and nothing could alter it.*

The knowledge of fatality, of what has to be, had gripped him and for the first time in his life; and he was left unable to make any movement of brain or body, except to say: "Yes, yes. That is what living is." It had entered his flesh and his bones and grown in to the furthest corners of his brain and would never leave him. And at that moment he could not have performed the smallest action of mercy, knowing as he did, having lived on it all his life, the vast unalterable, cruel veld, where at any moment one might stumble over a skull or crush the skeleton of some small creature.

Suffering, sick, and angry, but also grimly satisfied with his new stoicism,[9] he stood there leaning on his rifle, and watched the seething black mound grow smaller. At his feet, now, were ants trickling back with pink fragments in their mouths, and there was a fresh acid smell in his nostrils. He sternly controlled the uselessly convulsing muscles of his empty stomach, and reminded himself: the ants must eat too! At the same time he found that the tears were streaming down his face, and his clothes were soaked with the sweat of that other creature's pain.

The shape had grown small. Now it looked like nothing recognizable. He did not know how long it was before he saw the blackness thin, and bits of white showed through, shining in the sun—yes, there was the sun, just up, glowing over the rocks. Why, the whole thing could not have taken longer than a few minutes.

He began to swear, as if the shortness of the time was in itself unbearable, using the words he had heard his father say. He strode forward, crushing ants with each step, and brushing them

9. **stoicism** (stō'ĭ-sĭz'əm): calm acceptance of events as inevitable. This viewpoint is identified with ancient Greek Stoic philosophy.

WORDS TO KNOW

myriad (mĭr'ē-əd) *adj.* made up of many different elements or parts

off his clothes, till he stood above the skeleton, which lay sprawled under a small bush. It was clean-picked. It might have been lying there years, save that on the white bone were pink fragments of gristle. About the bones ants were ebbing away, their pincers full of meat.

The boy looked at them, big black ugly insects. A few were standing and gazing up at him with small glittering eyes.

"Go away!" he said to the ants, very coldly. "I am not for you—not just yet, at any rate. Go away." And he fancied that the ants turned and went away.

He bent over the bones and touched the sockets in the skull; that was where the eyes were, he thought incredulously, remembering the liquid dark eyes of a buck. And then he bent the slim foreleg bone, swinging it horizontally in his palm.

That morning, perhaps an hour ago, this small creature had been stepping proud and free through the bush, feeling the chill on its hide even as he himself had done, exhilarated by it. Proudly stepping the earth, tossing its horns, frisking a pretty white tail, it had sniffed the cold morning air. Walking like kings and conquerors it had moved through this free-held bush, where each blade of grass grew for it alone, and where the river ran pure sparkling water for its slaking.[10]

And then—what had happened? Such a swift surefooted thing could surely not be trapped by a swarm of ants?

The boy bent curiously to the skeleton. Then he saw that the back leg that lay uppermost and strained out in the tension of death, was snapped midway in the thigh, so that broken bones jutted over each other uselessly. So that was it! Limping into the ant-masses it could not escape, once it had sensed the danger. Yes, but how had the leg been broken? Had it fallen, perhaps? Impossible, a buck was too light and graceful. Had some jealous rival horned it?

What could possibly have happened? Perhaps some Africans had thrown stones at it, as they do, trying to kill it for meat, and had broken its leg. Yes, that must be it.

Even as he imagined the crowd of running, shouting natives, and the flying stones, and the leaping buck, another picture came into his mind. He saw himself, on any one of these bright ringing mornings, drunk with excitement, taking a snap shot at some half-seen buck. He saw himself with the gun lowered, wondering whether he had missed or not; and thinking at last that it was late, and he wanted his breakfast, and it was not worth while to track miles after an animal that would very likely get away from him in any case.

For a moment he would not face it. He was a small boy again, kicking sulkily at the skeleton, hanging his head, refusing to accept the responsibility.

Then he straightened up, and looked down at the bones with an odd expression of dismay, all the anger gone out of him. His mind went quite empty: all around him he could see trickles of ants disappearing into the grass. The whispering noise was faint and dry, like the rustling of a cast snakeskin.

At last he picked up his gun and walked homewards. He was telling himself half defiantly that he wanted his breakfast. He was telling himself that it was getting very hot, much too hot to be out roaming the bush.

Really, he was tired. He walked heavily, not looking where he put his feet. When he came within sight of his home he stopped, knitting his brows. There was something he had to think out. The death of that small animal was a thing that concerned him, and he was by no means finished with it. It lay at the back of his mind uncomfortably.

Soon, the very next morning, he would get clear of everybody and go to the bush and think about it. ❖

10. **slaking:** quenching of thirst.

WORDS TO KNOW

incredulously (ĭn-krĕj′ə-ləs-lē) *adv.* in a manner showing disbelief

RESPONDING OPTIONS

FROM PERSONAL RESPONSE *TO* CRITICAL ANALYSIS

REFLECT

1. What was your reaction to the events of this story? Jot down your reactions in your notebook, and share them with your classmates.

RETHINK

2. Why do you think it is so important to the boy to go out on the veld each morning?
   Consider
   - his attitude toward his abilities and powers
   - his attitude toward his parents
   - the scene on the veld at sunrise
3. Why do you think the buck's death upsets the boy so much?
4. Do you think the boy's experience with the buck will change him? Cite evidence from the story to support your answer.
5. Review any notes you created for the Reading Connection on page 1036. What do you think is the significance of the title "A Sunrise on the Veld" ?

RELATE

6. Would you have reacted to the buck's death in the same way as the boy in the story? Explain your answer.
7. For what different reasons do people around the world hunt wild animals? Do you think hunting is an acceptable activity? Why or why not?

ANOTHER PATHWAY

Identify the climax of the story, and record it on a diagram like the one shown. On the left side, list the boy's thoughts and actions leading up to the climax, and on the right side, list his thoughts and actions following it. Below the diagram, write any changes you see in his view of the world.

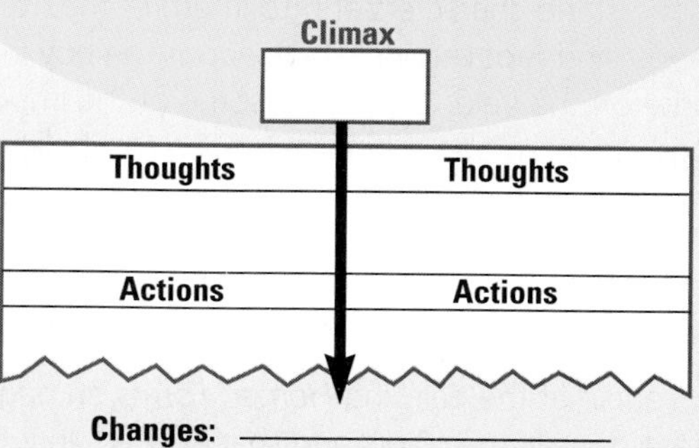

LITERARY CONCEPTS

In addition to using **imagery** that relates to the five senses—sight, hearing, taste, touch, and smell—Lessing employs kinesthetic imagery. **Kinesthetic imagery** re-creates the tension felt through muscles, tendons, or joints in the body. An example of kinesthetic imagery in "A Sunrise on the Veld" is the description of the boy's feet at the beginning of the sixth paragraph: "the flesh of his soles contracted on the chilled earth." With a partner, find other examples of kinesthetic imagery in the story. Discuss why you think Lessing uses this kind of imagery. Be specific in your answer.

QUICKWRITES

1. Imagine that you are the boy in this story. Write a **diary entry** describing your thoughts and feelings after witnessing the buck's death.
2. With a partner, take a walk in a nature preserve. Keep a **log** of things you see, hear, smell, or feel and of your reaction to each. You may want to continue keeping your log over a period of time, recording experiences with nature in other settings, such as your own yard or parks.

PORTFOLIO *Save your writing. You may want to use it later as a springboard to a piece for your portfolio.*

ALTERNATIVE ACTIVITIES

1. The boy in the story experiences both the beauty and the cruelty of nature on the veld. Make a **collage** of pictures that illustrates these two opposing views of life on the veld.
2. Using voice, musical instruments, sound effects, and brief passages from recordings, create a **soundtrack** expressing your impression of the veld. Record your sound landscape on tape and present it to the class.

CRITIC'S CORNER

Critics have noted that Lessing has a remarkable ability to understand characters and to interpret their thoughts, feelings, and motivations. Think about the boy in "A Sunrise on the Veld." What are some of the important things you learn about him that make him believable and worth your attention?

ART CONNECTION

Look again at the painting *Horned Forms* on page 1040. Note especially the colors and shapes used. In what ways does the painting convey the mood and themes of the story?

THE WRITER'S STYLE

One of the ways in which Lessing develops the character of the boy in the story is by directly recording his thoughts. For example, early in the story, she describes the boy thinking to himself, "Even my brain—even that! I can control every part of myself." Find as many other examples of the boy's actual thoughts as you can. How does this technique contribute to the development of the character of the boy?

LITERARY LINKS

In both "At the Pitt-Rivers" by Penelope Lively and "A Sunrise on the Veld," the main character is a teenage boy. Compare the attitudes of the two boys. How do they view themselves, others, and the world? Do their views change from the beginning to the end of the stories? Explain your answer.

ACROSS THE CURRICULUM

History/Geography Locate two political maps of Africa, one from about 1955 and one from the present. List all the countries that were once colonies and are now independent nations; include their former and current names. What European countries held colonies in Africa? Approximately how much of the continent was colonized? Summarize your information for the class.

Science With a small group, research the importance of balance within an ecosystem. Explain what an ecosystem is, how the balance of nature is maintained, and what can happen if the balance is upset. Present your findings to the rest of the class.

WORDS TO KNOW

Write the vocabulary word that is suggested by each set of idioms below.

1. over and above; too much of a good thing; the icing on the cake; money to burn
2. countless as the sands of the sea; more than you can count; a thousand and one; everything but the kitchen sink
3. be a fussbudget; cross all *t*'s and dot all *i*'s; be persnickety
4. be on the lookout; stay on one's toes; keep one ear to the ground; look alive
5. have to pinch oneself; that'll be the day; take with a grain of salt

DORIS LESSING

1919–

Doris Lessing was born in Persia (now Iran), but when she was 5, her British parents moved to Southern Rhodesia, where her father bought a farm. Lessing was not interested in socializing with other British settlers—a part of life that was important to her mother—and she disliked school intensely, much preferring to wander the lonely veld. Rebelling against her parents' wishes, Lessing left school at the age of 14 and worked for several years as a nursemaid, a typist, and a telephone operator in Salisbury, Southern Rhodesia. During these years, she read a great deal, especially the works of 19th-century novelists, and began to write fiction. When she was in her mid-20s, she quit her job in a lawyer's office to write what turned out to be her first major novel. Lessing was married and divorced twice, and in 1949 she moved to Great Britain with her youngest child, Peter. The publication of her novel *The Grass Is Singing* in the following year marked the beginning of her professional career.

Lessing has been a prolific writer—publishing more than 30 works in several genres—and is considered by many to be one of the most important novelists of the 20th century. Her early fiction was based on her own life and on her intimate knowledge of the culture and people of Southern Rhodesia, especially the problems between blacks and whites. Because of her outspoken criticism of racism and her radical political sympathies, Lessing was banned for many years from her homeland and from South Africa.

Lessing's fiction has become increasingly more complex and ambitious, ranging from novels of social realism to science fiction. Her most widely read and controversial work is *The Golden Notebook,* a novel exploring women's concerns and experiences that is written in the form of conventional narrative interwoven with a writer's notebooks. Lessing feels that contemporary society is in the midst of monumental change and crisis and that the writer must speak with integrity, imagination, and a clear sense of moral responsibility. Her work continues to evolve as she develops new formats and addresses the dilemmas of the late 20th century.

OTHER WORKS "The Old Chief Mshlanga," "No Witchcraft for Sale," "Through the Tunnel," "Homage for Isaac Babel," "A Mild Attack of Locusts," *Under My Skin* (autobiography)

LASERLINKS
• *SCIENCE CONNECTION*

PREVIEWING

POETRY

Digging

Seamus Heaney (shā′məs hā′nē)

The Horses

Ted Hughes

PERSONAL CONNECTION

Think about the kinds of experiences that have made lasting impressions on you. Did those experiences involve ordinary events or extraordinary moments? In your notebook, jot down some of your lasting impressions and your thoughts about them.

BIOGRAPHICAL/LITERARY CONNECTION

The Irish poet Seamus Heaney grew up on a farm in Northern Ireland. Although much of Heaney's work is concerned with the political unrest in his native land, there is also a concern with the poet as a craftsman who interacts with the force and mystery of language. Heaney's poems are characterized by themes and images taken from the natural world and rural life. His early poems, in particular, reflect the land and experiences of his childhood. His work shows the influence of both William Wordsworth and Gerard Manley Hopkins. "Digging" was the opening poem in his first book, *Death of a Naturalist,* published in 1966. In describing the poem, Heaney once said, "This was the first place where I felt I had done more than make an arrangement of words: I felt that I had let down a shaft into real life."

As a young man, Heaney was inspired by the writing of a slightly older contemporary, the English poet Ted Hughes. Many of Hughes's poems describe wild natural settings. He frequently focuses on the savage, predatory aspects of animals and sometimes uses animals to probe the instinctual, nonrational side of human life. Hughes's fascination with nature began during his youth, when he loved to hunt. Gradually, his passion shifted from literal hunting to searching for the essential qualities and energies of animals and writing about his discoveries in poetry. "The Horses," one of Hughes's earliest poems, appeared in his first book, *The Hawk in the Rain,* published in 1957.

READING CONNECTION

Identifying a Writer's Focus One way to explore the meaning of a poem is to determine the focus of the poem. In your notebook, create for each poem a cluster diagram like the one shown. As you read each poem, first identify the main impression of a past experience that the speaker focuses on. Then find the details that contribute to creating this lasting impression. Jot down the details you think are the most important in each poem.

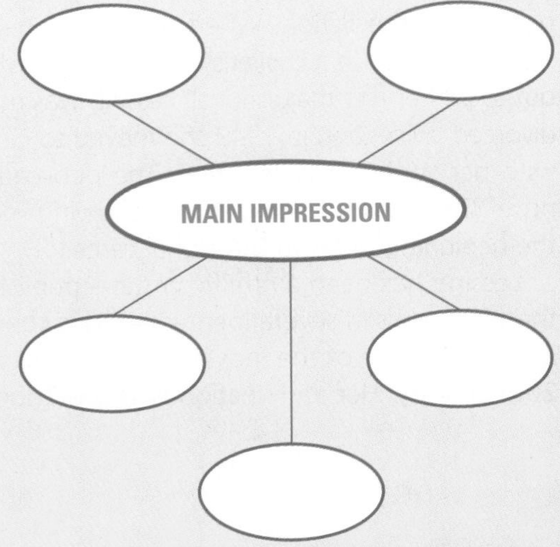

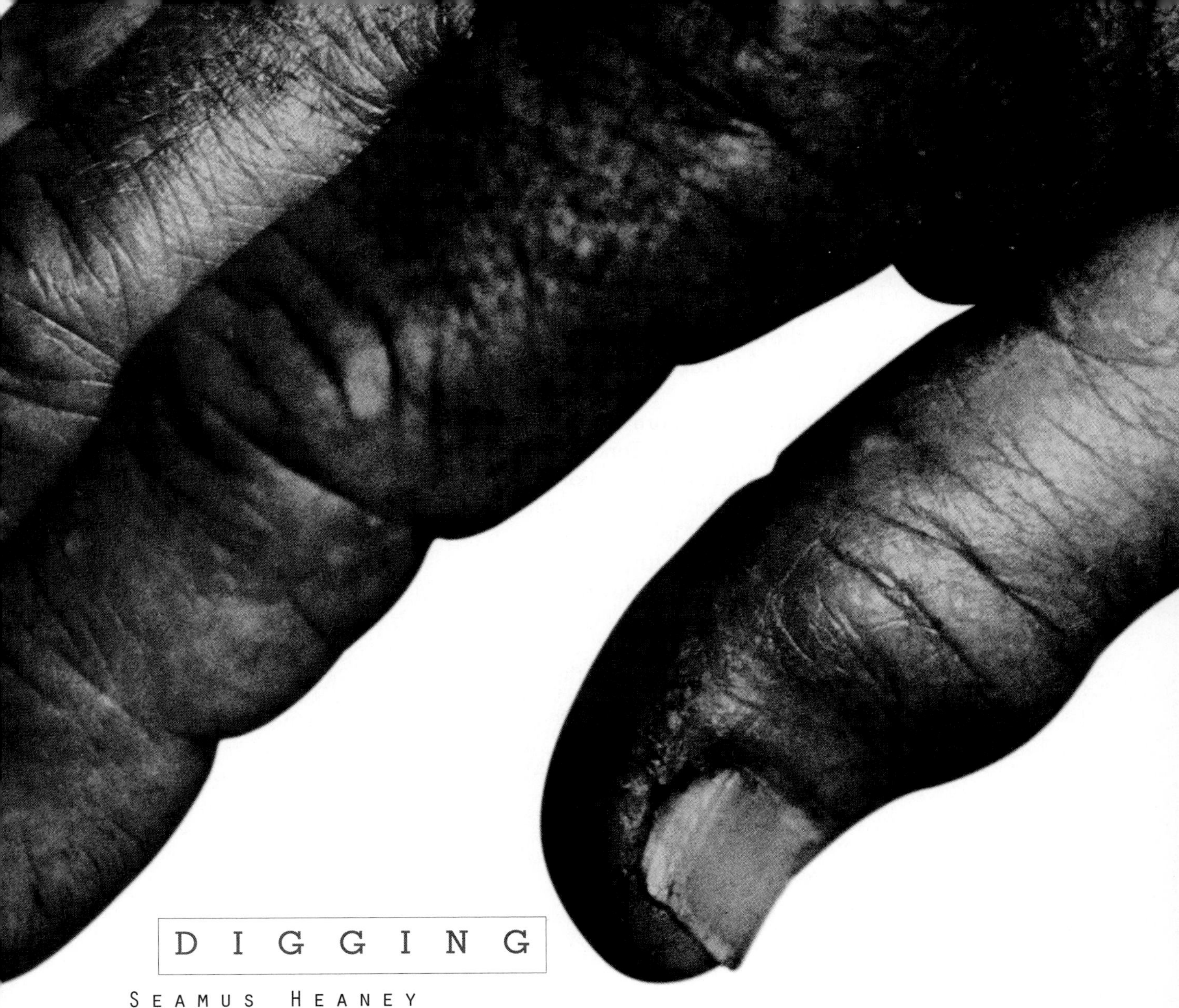

DIGGING

SEAMUS HEANEY

Between my finger and my thumb
The squat pen rests; snug as a gun.

Under my window, a clean rasping sound
When the spade sinks into gravelly ground:
My father, digging. I look down

Till his straining rump among the flowerbeds
Bends low, comes up twenty years away
Stooping in rhythm through potato drills
Where he was digging.

8 drills: furrows for planting seeds.

The coarse boot nestled on the lug, the shaft
Against the inside knee was levered firmly.
He rooted out tall tops, buried the bright edge deep
To scatter new potatoes that we picked
Loving their cool hardness in our hands.

By God, the old man could handle a spade.
Just like his old man.

My grandfather cut more turf in a day
Than any other man on Toner's bog.
Once I carried him milk in a bottle
Corked sloppily with paper. He straightened up
To drink it, then fell to right away
Nicking and slicing neatly, heaving sods
Over his shoulder, going down and down
For the good turf. Digging.

The cold smell of potato mold, the squelch and slap
Of soggy peat, the curt cuts of an edge
Through living roots awaken in my head.
But I've no spade to follow men like them.

Between my finger and my thumb
The squat pen rests.
I'll dig with it.

10 lug: a widening at the top of a shovel blade to support the foot.

17–18 Turf, or peat—partially decayed vegetable matter found in wet areas called bogs—was cut in blocks, called sods, and used as fuel in Ireland.

FROM PERSONAL RESPONSE *TO* CRITICAL ANALYSIS

REFLECT **1.** In your notebook, jot down words and phrases that reveal your reactions to the speaker. Then share your opinions with classmates.

RETHINK **2.** How would you describe the relationship between the speaker and his father and grandfather? Be specific in your answer.

3. How important are the lasting impressions of the past to the speaker's understanding of his future?

Consider

- how his father "buried the bright edge deep" (line 12)
- his grandfather "heaving sods" (line 22) and "going down and down" (line 23)
- what kind of digging the speaker plans to do

The Horses

Ted Hughes

I climbed through woods in the hour-before-dawn dark.
Evil air, a frost-making stillness,

Not a leaf, not a bird—
A world cast in frost. I came out above the wood

Where my breath left tortuous statues in the iron light.
But the valleys were draining the darkness

Till the moorline—blackening dregs of the brightening gray—
Halved the sky ahead. And I saw the horses:

Huge in the dense gray—ten together—
Megalith-still. They breathed, making no move,

With draped manes and tilted hind-hooves,
Making no sound.

I passed: not one snorted or jerked its head.
Gray silent fragments

Of a gray silent world.

5 tortuous: winding or twisting.

7 moorline: the horizon at the edge of a moor, a large area of high, open land; **dregs:** small amounts left over.

10 megalith: a very large stone of the sort used in various prehistoric formations, such as Stonehenge in England.

I listened in emptiness on the moor-ridge.
The curlew's tear turned its edge on the silence.

Slowly detail leafed from the darkness. Then the sun
Orange, red, red, erupted

Silently, and splitting to its core tore and flung cloud,
Shook the gulf open, showed blue,

And the big planets hanging.
I turned,

Stumbling in the fever of a dream, down toward
The dark woods, from the kindling tops,

And came to the horses.
There, still they stood,
But now steaming and glistening under the flow of light,

Their draped stone manes, their tilted hind-hooves
Stirring under a thaw while all around them

The frost showed its fires. But still they made no sound.
Not one snorted or stamped,

Their hung heads patient as the horizons,
High over valleys, in the red leveling rays—

In din of the crowded streets, going among the years, the faces,
May I still meet my memory in so lonely a place

Between the streams and the red clouds, hearing curlews,
Hearing the horizons endure.

17 curlew: a large, brownish, long-legged shore bird with a long, slender, downward-curving bill.

RESPONDING OPTIONS

FROM PERSONAL RESPONSE *TO* CRITICAL ANALYSIS

REFLECT 1. In your notebook, try to sketch the one image from "The Horses" that you remember most clearly.

RETHINK 2. How would you describe the mood of this poem? Cite details from the poem to support your answer.

3. Why do you think the horses made such an impression on the speaker?
   Consider
   - the phrase "a world cast in frost"
   - his references to darkness and silence
   - his descriptions of the horses after sunrise

4. How would you describe the relationship between the speaker and the horses?

RELATE 5. Compare the speakers' experiences as described in "Digging" and "The Horses." Which experience had the stronger effect on you as a reader?

6. As noted on page 1046, Heaney admires the poetry of Hughes. What aspects of Hughes's poetry do you think might appeal to Heaney?

ANOTHER PATHWAY

Read through each poem and look for images that appeal to one or more of the five senses—sight, hearing, smell, taste, touch. Then list the images from each poem in five columns corresponding to the five senses. Decide how each group of images helps convey the lasting impressions of the speaker.

LITERARY CONCEPTS

The **connotation** of a word refers to the attitudes and feelings associated with the word. The connotation may be positive or negative. For example, *thrifty* has positive associations, but *stingy* has negative ones. From each poem, choose two words that have strong connotations for you. What associations do you have with each word? Discuss how those associations affect your interpretation of each poem.

CONCEPT REVIEW: Sound Devices Both Heaney and Hughes experiment with sound devices such as the **repetition** of words and phrases, **alliteration** (the repetition of consonant sounds at the beginning of words), **consonance** (the repetition of consonant sounds within words), and **assonance** (the repetition of vowel sounds within words). Look for at least one example of each technique in each of the poems. Explain how each example provides focus or reinforces meaning.

QUICKWRITES

1. In "Digging" the speaker implies that, figuratively, he'll use his writing to "dig," just as his father and grandfather dug with a spade. Develop as many comparisons as you can think of that equate writing with other actions. Then, with other students, combine your comparisons in a **booklet** titled "Writing Is Like . . ."

2. In a **descriptive paragraph,** try to capture the images of an experience that made a lasting impression on you.

PORTFOLIO Save your writing. You may want to use it later as a springboard to a piece for your portfolio.

ALTERNATIVE ACTIVITIES

Create a **series of drawings** to illustrate three or more scenes from either "Digging" or "The Horses."

LITERARY LINKS

Both Dylan Thomas in "Do Not Go Gentle into That Good Night" (page 982) and Seamus Heaney in "Digging" write about their fathers. What kinds of feelings and attitudes toward the father does each poet express? Compare the impression of the father that each poet leaves with the reader.

THE WRITER'S STYLE

Writers occasionally use an image that describes one sensation in terms of another. This technique is called **synesthesia.** For example, writers may describe colors in terms of temperatures (hot pink), smells in terms of sounds (blaring scent), or sounds in terms of colors (white noise). Find one example of synesthesia in "Digging" and one in "The Horses." What different sensations are combined in each example?

SEAMUS HEANEY

1939–

Seamus Heaney was the oldest of nine children. He went to Queen's University in Belfast on a scholarship and, while there, became interested in poets who wrote about their local surroundings. The work of these poets affirmed for Heaney the validity of his own background, and after graduating in 1961, he began to write poetry regularly. His first book was published when he was 27.

Heaney took a teaching position at Queen's University and later lectured at other universities in Ireland and at universities in England and the United States. In 1969, violent conflicts erupted in Northern Ireland between the Irish Protestant allies of England and the Irish Republican Army. Shortly thereafter, Heaney, a Catholic, left Queen's and eventually settled near Dublin.

Today, Heaney divides his time between Dublin and Harvard University, where he has taught since 1982. Although Heaney is not comfortable being viewed as a political poet, he has dealt with the tensions and devastation of the Irish struggles with deep feeling and power. Many consider him to be the most important Irish poet since W. B. Yeats. Heaney won the Nobel Prize in literature in 1995.

OTHER WORKS "Blackberry-Picking," "Follower," "Personal Helicon," "A Drink of Water"

TED HUGHES

1930–

Ted Hughes grew up in Yorkshire, England, and began writing poetry when he was 15. After serving in the Royal Air Force, he went to Cambridge University, where he first studied English and then anthropology and archaeology. In 1956 he met and married the American poet Sylvia Plath, and for two years they lived in the United States, where Hughes taught at the University of Massachusetts. Hughes's first book of poetry, *The Hawk in the Rain,* was published in 1957 to critical acclaim.

Hughes and Plath returned to England in late 1959, and his second book, *Lupercal,* was published the next year, establishing his reputation as an important new poet. In 1962 Hughes and Plath separated, and in 1963 Plath committed suicide; for nearly three years, Hughes wrote no poetry at all. When he began writing again, however, he was prolific, producing numerous works for adults and children that included poetry, drama, short stories, and criticism. Hughes has received many awards for his literary achievements and in 1984 was named England's poet laureate.

OTHER WORKS "Thistles," "Hawk Roosting," "The Thought-Fox," "Wind," "A March Calf"

PREVIEWING

POETRY

In Music

Czeslaw Milosz (chĕ′släv mē′wŏsh′)

PERSONAL CONNECTION

Are there any sounds, smells, tastes, or sights that you associate with a certain time or activity, or with an incident from your past? If so, what do you think triggers these associations? Share your experiences with your classmates.

LITERARY CONNECTION

Like Seamus Heaney and many other contemporary poets, Czeslaw Milosz frequently examines the past and its associations as he searches for insights into life's experiences. Sometimes called the greatest poet in Poland, he has not lived in that country since 1951, the year he defected to the West. Even after moving to the United States in 1960, Milosz continued writing in his native language, but in the 1970s he began translating his own poetry into English with the help of some of his graduate students. When his *Selected Poems* was published in 1973, his readership and his international reputation grew rapidly. In 1980 he was awarded the Nobel Prize in literature.

READING CONNECTION

Looking for Transitions in Thought Writers occasionally make transitions in the direction of their thinking. They may shift from one setting to another, from one perspective to another, or from the conscious world to the subconscious world. These transitions are often quick and subtle, particularly in poetry, where ideas are usually expressed briefly and compactly. As you read "In Music," look for the transition that occurs between the first and second stanzas. Then, in your notebook, jot down your response to the transition.

In Music

Czeslaw Milosz

Wailing of a flute, a little drum.
A small wedding cortege accompanies a couple
Going past clay houses on the street of a village.
In the dress of the bride much white satin.
How many pennies put away to sew it, once in a lifetime.
The dress of the groom black, festively stiff.
The flute tells something to the hills, parched, the color of deer.
Hens scratch in dry mounds of manure.

I have not seen it, I summoned it listening to music.
The instruments play for themselves, in their own eternity.
Lips glow, agile fingers work, so short a time.
Soon afterwards the pageant sinks into the earth.
But the sound endures, autonomous, triumphant,
For ever visited by, each time returning,
The warm touch of cheeks, interiors of houses,
And particular human lives
Of which the chronicles make no mention.

Translated by the poet
and Robert Hass

2 cortege (kôr-tĕzh'): a ceremonial procession, as at a funeral or wedding.

Wedding Procession. Elek Györy. Hungarian National Gallery, Budapest.

RESPONDING OPTIONS

FROM PERSONAL RESPONSE *TO* CRITICAL ANALYSIS

REFLECT **1.** In your notebook, jot down your thoughts after reading this poem.

RETHINK **2.** Summarize what you think has happened in the poem.

3. What aspects of life seem to concern the speaker?

Consider
- the scene he describes in the first stanza
- the kinds of details he notices
- what he means by "particular human lives / Of which the chronicles make no mention" (lines 16–17)

RELATE **4.** What different effects can music have on its listeners? Base your response on your own experience or observations.

ANOTHER PATHWAY

Decide how you would create a short story based on the experience described in the poem. Consider what point of view you would use and what information you would reveal in the opening paragraphs. Jot down some ideas, and then outline the framework of your story. Share your ideas with the class.

LITERARY CONCEPTS

To clarify ideas or to elicit an emotional response from the reader, writers sometimes use **contrast,** a technique in which one element is put in opposition with another. These opposing elements might be contrasting structures—such as sentences of varying lengths or stanzas of different configurations—or they might be contrasting ideas or images. Look for examples of contrast in the selection. What effect do these contrasts have on your response to the poem?

LITERARY LINKS

Compare "In Music" with Thomas Gray's "Elegy Written in a Country Churchyard" (page 433). Can you find any similarities in the framework of the two poems or in the thoughts expressed about humanity? Cite lines from the poems to help you explain your answer.

QUICKWRITES

1. Write a **character sketch** of the speaker based on the thoughts and observations he expresses in the poem. Explain what type of person you would expect him to be.
2. In a **letter** to a friend, explain how a certain song or type of music has affected you and what thoughts or images it suggests.

PORTFOLIO Save your writing. You may want to use it later as a spring-board to a piece for your portfolio.

ALTERNATIVE ACTIVITIES

1. With a group of classmates, play an **association game** in which everyone responds independently to various pictures of people, places, or objects. As each picture is shown to your group, write down whatever associations come to your mind. Then compare and discuss your responses with those of other group members.
2. Plan and present for your class a **dramatic reading** of the poem, accompanied by flute and drum music. Students who play in your school band or orchestra could provide live music, or you could play an appropriate tape recording.

ACROSS THE CURRICULUM

Music Find and play recordings of the following three musical compositions: Tchaikovsky's *1812 Overture,* Rimsky-Korsakov's *The Flight of the Bumblebee,* and Chopin's *Funeral March.* As you listen to each recording, jot down words or phrases that describe your associations—for example, any scenes, activities, or moods that come to your mind. Compare your responses with those of your classmates. Discuss how each composition might have been written to provoke a specific response.

CZESLAW MILOSZ

1911–

Czeslaw Milosz was born in Lithuania, a country that once existed as a Polish-Lithuanian confederation. Long before Milosz's birth, the confederation collapsed and was taken over by Russia. As a result, the poet, during his early years, was exposed to the language and customs of three different cultures.

Milosz attended the Stefan Batory University in Wilno (now called Vilnius), where he studied law and published his first book of poems at the age of 21. At the university, he also became involved with a group of poets called the Catastrophists, who predicted the outbreak of World War II. After the war erupted, Milosz moved to Nazi-occupied Warsaw, where he helped the Polish Resistance movement by contributing anti-Nazi writings and by promoting the cultural activities of the Polish underground. In order to have access to books, he worked as a janitor in a university library that had been closed to the general public.

When the war ended, Poland's new Communist government rewarded Milosz with a job in the foreign service. He was assigned as a cultural ambassador first to the United States and then to France. Milosz became disillusioned with Poland's totalitarian government, however, and in 1951 he asked the French government for political asylum. That same year he began writing his prose work *The Captive Mind,* an explanation of his reasons for defecting and of the effects of communism on creativity.

In 1960, Milosz moved to the United States to accept a teaching position at the University of California in Berkeley. Ten years later, he became an American citizen. His poetry and political writings reflect his diverse life experiences, and his recent poetry also probes aspects of American culture.

OTHER WORKS "Song on Porcelain," "Rivers," "Incantation," "Earth," "Should, Should Not"

LASERLINKS
• *AUTHOR BACKGROUND*

We'll Never Conquer Space

Arthur C. Clarke

Arthur C. Clarke is probably best known for his science fiction. His most famous achievement, in collaboration with film director Stanley Kubrick, is the 1968 science fiction film *2001: A Space Odyssey*, which was based on his 1951 short story "The Sentinel" and which he subsequently developed into a novel. Clarke is also a knowledgeable and respected author of numerous scientific essays. Even in his fiction, Clarke bases his ideas on sound scientific data; he has contributed greatly to making science fiction an intellectually respectable genre. In many instances, his futuristic speculations have been closely paralleled in real life.

In the following nonfiction essay, written before the first manned space flights, Clarke expresses his thoughts on the limitations of space exploration. →

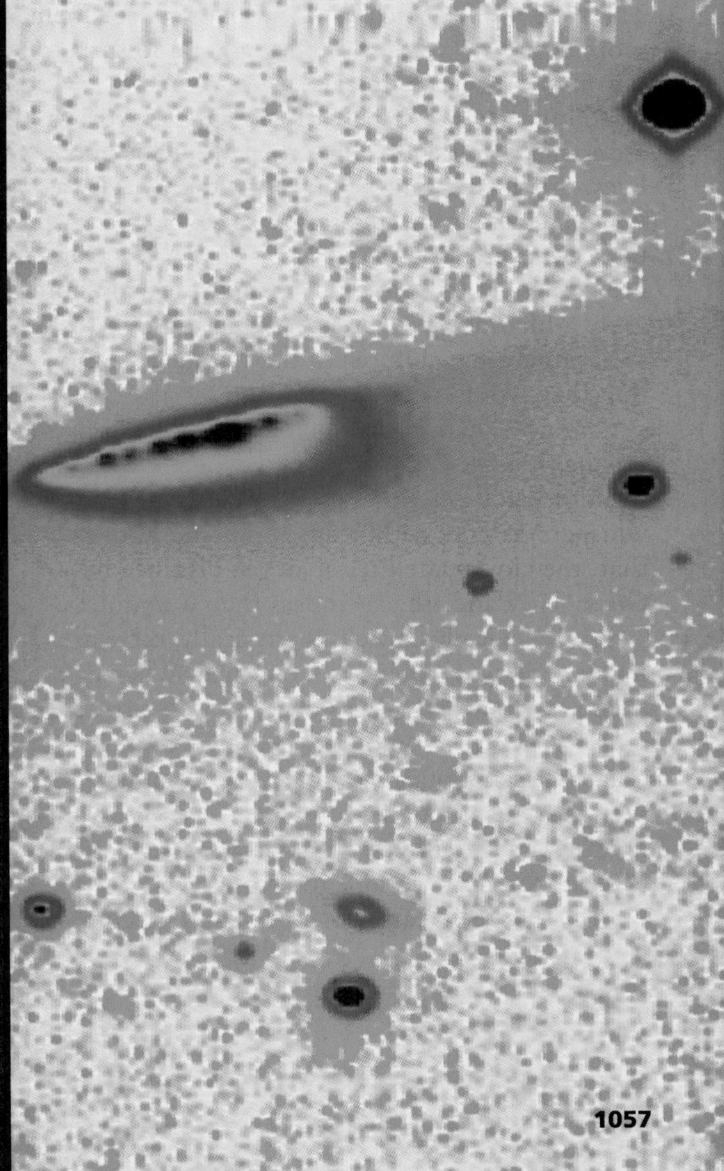

Man will never conquer space. Such a statement may sound ludicrous, now that our rockets are already 100 million miles beyond the moon and the first human travelers are preparing to leave the atmosphere. Yet it expresses a truth which our forefathers knew, one we have forgotten—and our descendants must learn again, in heartbreak and loneliness.

Our age is in many ways unique, full of events and phenomena which never occurred before and can never happen again. They distort our thinking, making us believe that what is true now will be true forever, though perhaps on a larger scale. Because we have annihilated distance on this planet, we imagine that we can do it once again. The facts are far otherwise, and we will see them more clearly if we forget the present and turn our minds towards the past.

To our ancestors, the vastness of the earth was a dominant fact controlling their thoughts and lives. In all earlier ages than ours, the world was wide indeed, and no man could ever see more than a tiny fraction of its immensity. A few hundred miles—a thousand at the most—was infinity. Only a lifetime ago, parents waved farewell to their emigrating children in the virtual certainty that they would never meet again.

And now, within one incredible generation, all this has changed. Over the seas where Odysseus wandered for a decade, the Rome-Beirut Comet[1] whispers its way within the hour. And above that, the closer satellites span the distance between Troy and Ithaca[2] in less than a minute.

Psychologically as well as physically, there are no longer any remote places on earth. When a friend leaves for what was once a far country, even if he has no intention of returning, we cannot feel that same sense of irrevocable separation that saddened our forefathers. We know that he is only hours away by jet liner, and that we have merely to reach for the telephone to hear his voice.

In a very few years, when the satellite communication network[3] is established, we will be able to see friends on the far side of the earth as easily as we talk to them on the other side of the town. Then the world will shrink no more, for it will have become a dimensionless point.

FOREVER TOO LARGE

But the new stage that is opening up for the human drama will never shrink as the old one has done. We have abolished space here on the little earth; we can never abolish the space that yawns between the stars. Once again we are face to face with immensity and must accept its grandeur and terror, its inspiring possibilities and its dreadful restraints. From a world that has become too small, we are moving out into one that will be forever too large, whose frontiers will recede from us always more swiftly than we can reach out towards them.

Consider first the fairly modest solar, or planetary, distances which we are now preparing to assault. The very first Lunik[4] made a substantial impression upon them, traveling more than 200

1. **Over the seas . . . Rome-Beirut Comet:** The distance between Rome in the west and Beirut in the east—the general area of the Mediterranean around which Odysseus wandered, as described by Homer in *The Odyssey*—can be covered in less than an hour by a modern airplane such as the *Comet.*
2. **Troy and Ithaca:** ancient locales in *The Odyssey,* about 500 miles apart.
3. **satellite communication network:** It was Arthur C. Clarke who first proposed the idea of using satellites for communication. Since *Telstar,* the first commercial communications satellite, was placed in earth orbit in 1962 to relay television signals between the United States and Europe, an entire satellite communications network has evolved. Today, satellites assist in the transmission of radio, telegraph, telephone, and television signals.
4. **Lunik:** *Luna I,* an unmanned space probe launched by the former Soviet Union on January 2, 1959. It missed the moon and went into orbit around the sun. *Luna I* was, for a while, called *Lunik* by the American press, possibly in imitation of the name *Sputnik.*

million miles from the earth—six times the distance to Mars. When we have harnessed nuclear energy for spaceflight, the solar system will contract until it is little larger than the earth today. The remotest of the planets will be perhaps no more than a week's travel from the earth, while Mars and Venus will be only a few hours away.

This achievement, which will be witnessed within a century, might appear to make even the solar system a comfortable, homely place, with such giant planets as Saturn and Jupiter playing much the same role in our thoughts as do Africa or Asia today. (Their qualitative differences of climate, atmosphere and gravity, fundamental though they are, do not concern us at the moment.) To some extent this may be true, yet as soon as we pass beyond the orbit of the moon, a mere quarter-million miles away, we will meet the first of the barriers that will separate the earth from her scattered children.

The marvelous telephone and television network that will soon enmesh the whole world, making all men neighbors, cannot be extended into space. It will never be possible to converse with anyone on another planet.

Do not misunderstand this statement. Even with today's radio equipment, the problem of sending speech to the other planets is almost trivial. But the messages will take minutes—sometimes hours—on their journey, because radio and light waves travel at the same limited speed of 186,000 miles a second.

Twenty years from now you will be able to listen to a friend on Mars, but the words you hear will have left his mouth at least three minutes earlier, and your reply will take a corresponding time to reach him. In such circumstances, an exchange of verbal messages is possible—but not a conversation.

Even in the case of the nearby moon, the 2½ second time-lag will be annoying. At distances of more than a million miles, it will be intolerable.

"Time Barrier"

To a culture which has come to take instantaneous communication for granted, as part of the very structure of civilized life, this "time barrier" may have a profound psychological impact. It will be a perpetual reminder of universal laws and limitations against which not all our technology can ever prevail. For it seems as certain as anything can be that no signal—still less any material object—can ever travel faster than light.

The velocity of light is the ultimate speed limit, being part of the very structure of space and time. Within the narrow confines of the solar system, it will not handicap us too severely, once we have accepted the delays in communication which it involves. At the worst, these will amount to 20 hours—the time it takes a radio signal to span the orbit of Pluto, the outermost planet.

Between the three inner worlds the earth, Mars, and Venus, it will never be more than 20 minutes—not enough to interfere seriously with commerce or administration, but more than sufficient to shatter those personal links of sound or vision that can give us a sense of direct contact with friends on earth, wherever they may be.

It is when we move out beyond the confines of the solar system that we come face to face with an altogether new order of cosmic reality. Even today, many otherwise educated men—like those savages who can count to three but lump together all numbers beyond four—cannot grasp the profound distinction between solar and stellar space. The first is the space enclosing our neighboring worlds, the planets; the second is that which embraces those distant suns, the stars, and it is literally millions of times greater.

There is no such abrupt change of scale in terrestrial[5] affairs. To obtain a mental picture of

5. **terrestrial:** of or representing Earth.

the distance to the nearest star, as compared with the distance to the nearest planet, you must imagine a world in which the closest object to you is only five feet away—and then there is nothing else to see until you have traveled a thousand miles.

Many conservative scientists, appalled by these cosmic gulfs, have denied that they can ever be crossed. Some people never learn; those who 60 years ago scoffed at the possibility of flight, and ten (even five!) years ago laughed at the idea of travel to the planets, are now quite sure that the stars will always be beyond our reach. And again they are wrong, for they have failed to grasp the great lesson of our age—that if something is possible in theory, and no fundamental scientific laws oppose its realization, then sooner or later it will be achieved.

One day, it may be in this century, or it may be a thousand years from now, we shall discover a really efficient means of propelling our space vehicles. Every technical device is always developed to its limit (unless it is superseded by something better) and the ultimate speed for spaceships is the velocity of light. They will never reach that goal, but they will get very close to it. And then the nearest star will be less than five years' voyaging from the earth.

Our exploring ships will spread outwards from their home over an ever-expanding sphere of space. It is a sphere which will grow at almost—but never quite—the speed of light. Five years to the triple system of Alpha Centauri, 10 to the strangely-matched doublet Sirius A and B, 11 to the tantalizing enigma of 61 Cygni,[6] the first star suspected to possess a planet. These journeys are long, but they are not impossible. Man has always accepted whatever price was necessary for his explorations and discoveries, *and the price of Space is Time.*

Even voyages which may last for centuries or millennia will one day be attempted. Suspended animation has already been achieved in the laboratory, and may be the key to interstellar travel. Self-contained cosmic arks which will be tiny traveling worlds in their own right may be another solution, for they would make possible journeys of unlimited extent, lasting generation after generation.

The famous Time Dilation effect predicted by the Theory of Relativity, whereby time appears to pass more slowly for a traveler moving at

6. **Alpha Centauri . . . Cygni:** Alpha Centauri is a multiple-star system. It includes Proxima Centauri, which, at 4.3 light-years from Earth, is the closest star other than the sun. Sirius (also called the Dog Star) is the brightest star in the night skies. It is a binary, or double, star consisting of Sirius A and Sirius B. The binary star 61 Cygni is in the constellation Cygnus.

almost the speed of light, may be yet a third. And there are others.

Looking far into the future, therefore, we must picture a slow (little more than half a billion miles an hour!) expansion of human activities outwards from the solar system, among the suns scattered across the region of the galaxy in which we now find ourselves. These suns are on the average five light-years apart; in other words, we can never get from one to the next in less than five years.

To bring home what this means, let us use a down-to-earth analogy. Imagine a vast ocean, sprinkled with islands—some desert, others perhaps inhabited. On one of these islands an energetic race has just discovered the art of building ships. It is preparing to explore the ocean, but must face the fact that the very nearest island is five years' voyaging away, and that no possible improvement in the technique of ship-building will ever reduce this time.

In these circumstances (which are those in which we will soon find ourselves) what could the islanders achieve? After a few centuries, they might have established colonies on many of the nearby islands and have briefly explored many others. The daughter colonies might themselves have sent out further pioneers, and so a kind of chain reaction would spread the original culture over a steadily expanding area of the ocean.

But now consider the effects of the inevitable, unavoidable time-lag. There could be only the most tenuous contact between the home island and its offspring. Returning messengers could report what had happened on the nearest colony—five years ago. They could never bring information more up to date than that, and dispatches from the more distant parts of the ocean would be from still further in the past—perhaps centuries behind the times. There would never be news from the other islands, but only history.

INDEPENDENT "COLONIES"

All the star-borne colonies of the future will be independent, whether they wish it or not. Their liberty will be inviolably protected by Time as well as Space. They must go their own way and achieve their own destiny, with no help or hindrance from Mother Earth.

At this point, we will move the discussion on to a new level and deal with an obvious objection. Can we be sure that the velocity of light is indeed a limiting factor? So many "impassible" barriers have been shattered in the past; perhaps this one may go the way of all the others.

We will not argue the point, or give the reasons why scientists believe that light can never be outraced by any form of radiation or any material object. Instead, let us assume the contrary and see just where it gets us. We will even take the most optimistic possible case and imagine that the speed of transportation may eventually become infinite.

Picture a time when, by the development of techniques as far beyond our present engineering as a transistor is beyond a stone axe, we can reach anywhere we please instantaneously, with no more effort than by dialing a number. This would indeed cut the universe down to size and reduce its physical immensity to nothingness. What would be left?

Everything that really matters. For the universe has two aspects—its scale, and its overwhelming, mind-numbing complexity. Having abolished the first, we are now face-to-face with the second.

What we must now try to visualize is not size, but quantity. Most people today are familiar with the simple notation which scientists use to describe large numbers; it consists merely of counting zeroes, so that a hundred becomes 10^2, a million, 10^6, a billion, 10^9 and so on. This useful trick enables us to work with quantities of any magnitude, and even defense budget totals look modest when expressed as $\$5.76 \cdot 10^9$ instead of \$5,760,000,000.

The number of other suns in our own galaxy (that is, the whirlpool of stars and cosmic dust of which our sun is an out-of-town member, lying in one of the remoter spiral arms) is estimated at about 10^{11}—or written in full, 100,000,000,000. Our present telescopes can observe something like 10^9 other galaxies, and they show no sign of thinning out even at the extreme limit of vision.

There are probably at least as many galaxies in the whole of creation as there are stars in our own galaxy, but let us confine ourselves to those we can see. They must contain a total of about 10^{11} times 10^9 stars, or 10^{20} stars altogether. 1 followed by 20 other digits is, of course, a number beyond all understanding.

Before such numbers, even spirits brave enough to face the challenge of the light-years must quail.[7] The detailed examination of all the grains of sand on all the beaches of the world is a far smaller task than the exploration of the universe.

And so we return to our opening statement. Space can be mapped and crossed and occupied without definable limit; but it can never be conquered. When our race has reached its ultimate achievements, and the stars themselves are scattered no more widely than the seed of Adam, even then we shall still be like ants crawling on the face of the earth. The ants have covered the world but have they conquered it—for what do their countless colonies know of it, or of each other?

So it will be with us as we spread outwards from Mother Earth, loosening the bonds of kinship and understanding, hearing faint and belated rumors at second—or third—or thousandth—hand of an ever-dwindling fraction of the entire human race.

Though Earth will try to keep in touch with her children, in the end all the efforts of her archivists and historians will be defeated by time and distance, and the sheer bulk of material. For the number of distinct societies or nations, when our race is twice its present age, may be far greater than the total number of all the men who have ever lived up to the present time.

We have left the realm of human comprehension in our vain effort to grasp the scale of the universe; so it must always be, sooner rather than later.

When you are next outdoors on a summer night, turn your head towards the zenith. Almost vertically above you will be shining the brightest

7. **quail:** draw back in fear; lose courage.

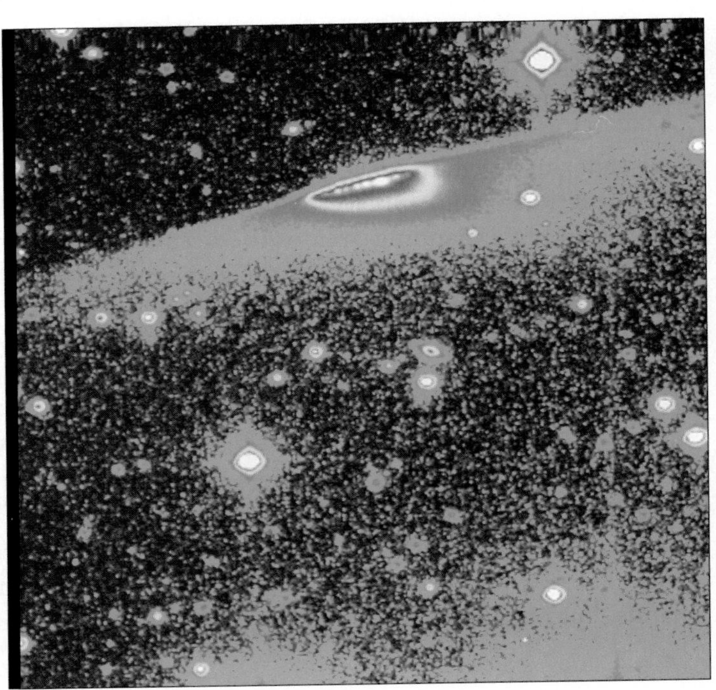

star of the northern skies—Vega of the Lyre,[8] 26 years away at the speed of light, near enough the point-of-no-return for us short-lived creatures. Past this blue-white beacon, 50 times as brilliant as our sun, we may send our minds and bodies, but never our hearts.

For no man will ever turn homewards from beyond Vega, to greet again those he knew and loved on the earth. ❖

8. **Vega of the Lyre:** a very bright star in the constellation Lyra, so named because its shape suggests a lyre, or harp.

Arthur C. Clarke

1917–

Born in Somerset, England, Arthur C. Clarke showed an intense interest in science even as a child. While still a young boy, he created a map of the moon, using a telescope he had constructed on his own. Clarke's talent was further manifested at the age of 13, when he began writing science fiction stories for his school magazine. Unable to afford a college education after high school, Clarke went to work as a government auditor. In 1941 he was drafted into the Royal Air Force, eventually serving as an instructor and technician on the first attempts at ground-controlled approach radar. During this time, Clarke wrote an article for a magazine called *Wireless World* in which he predicted in detail the use of satellites for communication, a feat that was accomplished 20 years later.

After World War II, Clarke studied at King's College in London, graduating with honors in physics and mathematics. He then went to work as an assistant editor of a journal called *Science Abstracts,* a job that enabled him to stay abreast of the latest scientific discoveries. At this time, he also began a prolific career as a science fiction writer, publishing both novels and short stories. In the 1950s, Clarke's scientific curiosity turned to underwater exploration and photography, and he became involved in explorations of the coast of Sri Lanka and the Great Barrier Reef of Australia.

In the 1980s, Clarke published two sequels to the story depicted in the film *2001: A Space Odyssey.* The first sequel, a novel titled *2010: Odyssey Two,* was also made into a film. This was followed in 1987 by the novel *2061: Odyssey Three.*

OTHER WORKS "The Star," "History Lesson," "The Call of the Stars," "The Songs of Distant Earth"

WRITING ABOUT LITERATURE

Put It in Context

Just as a story is a combination of people, places, events, and times, so is every experience in your life. The key to understanding an experience, then—whether it is fictional or as real as this morning's news—is to analyze the elements within it. In this lesson you will

- examine how writers use setting to tell part of a story
- use comparison to analyze the effect of literary elements in two selections from Unit Seven
- study the effect of setting in your own life

Writer's Style: Using Setting Good writers know that a setting is more than a description of where and when a story takes place. They may use setting to create a mood, shape the plot, or help define a character.

Read the Literature

Setting doesn't play a vital part in every story, but when it does, it often is being used to reinforce another key element.

Literature Models

Setting Defines a Character
This description of setting is from the opening paragraph of "At the Pitt-Rivers." What does it tell you about the narrator?

They've got this museum in Oxford, called the Pitt-Rivers; I spend a lot of time there. It's a weird place, really weird, stuff from all over the world crammed into glass cases like some kind of mad junk-shop—native things from New Guinea and Mexico and Sumatra and wherever you like to think of. Spears and stone axes and masks and a thousand different kinds of fish-hook. And bead jewelry and peculiar musical instruments. And a great totem from Canada. You can learn a lot there about what people get up to: it makes you think.

Penelope Lively, from "At the Pitt-Rivers"

Setting Creates a Mood
What mood does this setting evoke in you? What words help create this mood?

Soon he had left the cultivated part of the farm. Behind him the bush was low and black. In front was a long vlei, acres of long pale grass that sent back a hollowing gleam of light to a satiny sky. Near him thick swathes of grass were bent with the weight of water, and diamond drops sparkled on each frond.

Doris Lessing, from "A Sunrise on the Veld"

Connect to Life

Real-life surroundings can also provide information and affect mood. Notice how this nonfiction writer uses setting to communicate something about the person she's interviewing.

Magazine Article

As she sits behind a large granite-block desk in her office, Oprah is more serious and pensive than she has been in earlier interviews. Yet somehow you can't help expecting a touch of whimsy to flow from her at any minute, especially considering the surroundings. The decor of Oprah's office is a little, well, jarring. Huge modern paintings with splashes of green, yellow, blue and pink adorn bright-blue walls. A large black-and-white zebra rug lies on the floor. The furniture is black—an overstuffed sofa and two lacquer chairs with lion's-head arms. It looks like a psychedelic episode of *Wild Kingdom.*

Mary-Ann Bendel, from "TV's Superwomen," *Ladies' Home Journal*

Setting Provides Elaboration
How does this writer use setting to elaborate on her statement about Oprah's personality?

Try Your Hand: Creating Setting

1. **Provide Details** The meaning a setting communicates often depends on the details used to describe it. Picture a place that has special meaning for you, and write down the details that communicate your feelings.
2. **Set the Mood** Depending on how they're described, similar settings can create different moods. Choose a setting and describe it twice, creating different moods.
3. **Describe a Character** Write a short paragraph in which you use setting to introduce a character. For example, you may describe your character's bedroom.

SkillBuilder

GRAMMAR FROM WRITING

Using Compound Prepositions

A preposition is a word used to show the relationship between a noun or pronoun and another word in a sentence. The relationships most often expressed are location, direction, and association.

Compound prepositions are formed by combining two or more words. The following sentences contain examples of compound prepositions.

Location: *Margaret Atwood was sitting* **next to** *her brother, "making bagpipe music."*

Direction: *Atwood's mother said that as a girl she often fell* **out of** *trees.*

Association: *Margaret did not like having to put* **up with** *her mother's embarrassing stories.*

A compound preposition, like any other preposition, must be followed by an object. The object can be a noun, a pronoun, or a clause. In the second sentence above, *trees* is the object of the preposition.

APPLYING WHAT YOU'VE LEARNED
In order to create vivid settings, you will need to use prepositions. Write a paragraph describing your classroom or cafeteria. Then circle the prepositions and underline the objects of the prepositions. Use at least one compound preposition.

WRITING ABOUT LITERATURE

Analysis

How can you assess the effect literary elements such as setting have on a story as a whole? Sometimes comparing one piece of literature with another can help you understand the impact of the elements each consists of. Examining the differences and similarities between two stories can also reveal how each communicates its meaning.

GUIDED ASSIGNMENT

Write a Comparative Analysis Analyze two Unit Seven stories. Compare the effects the two stories' literary elements have on the whole works.

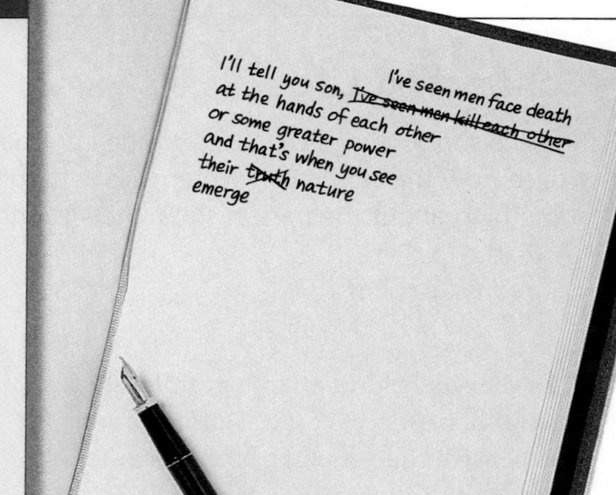

I'll tell you son, I've seen men face death
at the hands of each other
or some greater power
and that's when you see
their nature
emerge

1 Prewrite and Explore

Choose two stories to compare. Consider works that have either noticeable similarities or glaring differences.

BUILD AN INTERPRETATION

Before considering the individual elements of a story, be sure you understand the work as a whole. As you read and reflect on the selections, form interpretations of them. Develop your interpretations by discussing them with someone else or by making lists of evidence that supports your conclusions.

EXAMINE THE ELEMENTS

Once you've formed interpretations, identify the specific elements of each selection. Consider listing these elements in charts like the ones at the right. Then begin analyzing the stories. Asking questions like the following may help get you started.

- Do any events in the plot repeat or contrast with other events?
- What meanings are suggested by each character's actions, thoughts, and way of talking?
- How does the setting affect actual and psychological events? What mood does it set?
- How does the point of view affect the story?
- Does the story address any universal theme?

Student's Chart

A Sunrise on the Veld

At the Pitt-Rivers

Plot	A boy watches the progress of a couple's relationship.
Character	16-year-old boy
Setting	An anthropological museum—displays show many artifacts of human cruelty.
Point of view	First person—we are inside the narrator's head.
Theme	Life is unpredictable; the more you learn the less you know!

2 Write a Discovery Draft

After you've analyzed each of the two stories individually, you can compare them in a discovery draft. There are several ways that you can explore their similarities and differences. You may want to compare

- the effects different literary elements have on the communication of similar themes
- the ways the elements work to create meaning
- the effects of a particular element in the two stories

Student's Discovery Draft

In both "A Sunrise on the Veld" and "At the Pitt-Rivers" a teenage boy discovers cruelty. The setting of each story helps the boys discover this. But "Veld" is set in nature and "Pitt-Rivers" is set in a museum. The cruelty in "Veld" happens in the animal kingdom. The boy says, "There is nothing I can do." The boy in the Pitt-Rivers museum is looking at human events and artifacts. I can imagine him saying about humans beings, "We all do it."

The different points of view seem important to what I'm saying here. How can I bring that up?

3 Draft and Share

When you're ready to write a more structured draft, you'll have to decide how you want to organize your analysis. After starting with an introduction that includes your interpretation of both stories, you may want to discuss each selection separately, saving the comparison for the end. Or you may want to devote each paragraph to a different literary element and compare the stories throughout. When you're finished with your draft, ask a classmate to give you feedback.

PEER RESPONSE

- How did the paper's organization help you or confuse you?
- What aspects of the comparison helped you understand the selections better? What aspects seem unnecessary?
- What important similarities or differences did I ignore?

SkillBuilder

WRITER'S CRAFT

Using Transitional Words

Transitional words indicate relationships between ideas. These words can be used to connect sentences or paragraphs. You can use them to help achieve coherence in your comparative analysis.

The bleakness of the setting drew attention to her isolation. ***Therefore,*** *I wasn't surprised to learn that she was a solitary woman.*

The following chart lists the kinds of relationships transitional words can show and gives examples of transitional words in each category.

Time or sequence	*then, before, eventually*
Logical relationships	*therefore, because, since*
Similarity	*as, similarly*
Degree	*better, greatest*
Contrast	*however, still*

APPLYING WHAT YOU'VE LEARNED

Look through your discovery draft. Which relationships are unclear? When you write your analysis, use transitional words to make the links between ideas clear.

WRITING HANDBOOK

For more information on transitions, see page 1223 of the Writing Handbook.

4 Revise and Edit

As you revise, make sure that your comparison of the two works is complete. For example, if you discuss a particular element in one selection, you should discuss it in the other. When you're finished, consider reading the essay of someone who compared a selection you chose with one you did not. Reflect on the different aspects of the selection highlighted by this other comparison.

Student's Final Draft

Coming of Age

"A Sunrise on the Veld" by Doris Lessing and "At the Pitt-Rivers" by Penelope Lively tell coming-of-age stories in different ways and with different effects. In each story, a teenage boy's view of life is complicated by bearing witness to another's pain. Setting, character, and point of view affect the portrayal of both boys' turning points. However, because of the way these elements are used in each selection, a reader may come away from the two similar endings with very different feelings about each boy's revelation and about life in general.

What do you think the student hopes to demonstrate by comparing these two stories?

The setting of both "A Sunrise on the Veld" and "At the Pitt-Rivers" is central to the meaning of the story. "A Sunrise on the Veld" is set in the African bush, a sparsely populated wilderness with extremes in temperature and a variety of wildlife. The main character takes this setting as a personal challenge. He gets so much joy from meeting that challenge that when running alone through the grassland, "He leapt up into the air, shouting and yelling."

How does this analysis appear to be organized?

Standards for Evaluation

A comparative analysis
- identifies two selections and provides an interpretation of them both
- compares the literary elements of one selection with those of another
- is organized in a way that makes the comparison clear

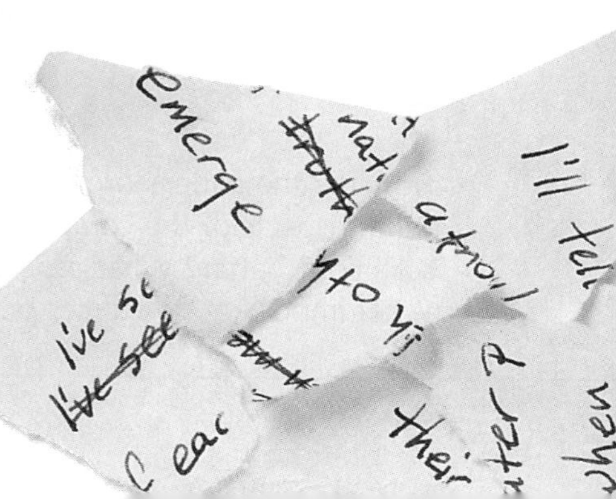

Grammar in Context

Adverb Clauses When you're comparing elements from two selections, you'll need to address the questions *where, when, how, why, to what extent,* and *under what circumstances.* Adverb clauses answer these questions. An adverb clause is a subordinate clause that modifies a verb, an adjective, another adverb, or a verbal. In the first sentence below, the adverb clause modifies a verb; in the second, it modifies an infinitive.

> *The narrator of Lively's short story* ***visited*** *the Pitt-Rivers* ***when he wanted to be alone.***

> *The boy in Lessing's story learned* ***to awaken*** *early* ***so that he could hunt alone.***

Most adverb clauses begin with a subordinating conjunction that relates the clause to the word it modifies and establishes a specific relationship between them. In the first sentence above, the subordinating conjunction *when* indicates a time relationship. In the second sentence, the conjunction *so that* shows purpose. Subordinating conjunctions may also show cause, comparison, condition, manner, or place. For examples of other subordinating conjunctions, refer to the SkillBuilder on page 375.

When an adverb clause begins a sentence, it should be followed by a comma.

> As the reader comes to know the young poet sitting in the museum, it becomes easier to identify with him.

Try Your Hand: Using Adverb Clauses

Rewrite the following sentences, adding adverb clauses that answer the questions in parentheses.

- The main character in "A Sunrise on the Veld" resolved to rise early the next morning. (*Why did he rise early?*)
- The narrator of "At the Pitt-Rivers" rips up his poem. (*When did he rip up his poem?*)
- The boy ran across the veld. (*How did he run?*)

SkillBuilder

Using Elliptical Clauses
If there is no possibility that readers will misunderstand the meaning of an adverb clause, a writer may choose to omit one or more words from the clause. A clause from which a word or words have been omitted is called an **elliptical clause.**

When dressing on cold mornings, the boy would move as rapidly as he could.

The words *he was* have been omitted: *When* ***he was*** *dressing on cold mornings . . .*

Doris Lessing's character seems more self-aware than most 15-year-old boys.

The final verb *do* was omitted:

. . . than most 15-year-old boys **do.**

APPLYING WHAT YOU'VE LEARNED
Rewrite these adverb clauses as elliptical clauses.

1. When Lessing is writing about the boy, she appears to enter into the mind of her 15-year-old character.
2. Penelope Lively's short story appeals to me more than Doris Lessing's story does.
3. While he watched the couple, the narrator found himself wondering about human relationships.

Ohio

FLORIDA

FORT WORTH STOCK YARDS
Fort Worth, Texas

R E A D I N G
THE WORLD

SEEING THE BIG PICTURE

When you compared two literary selections, you probably noticed how a change in a single element could alter the effect of similar selections. Have you ever realized how a change in some aspect of your own life might affect the way you think, act, and feel? Have you considered how such changes might affect other people and events?

View Look at the postcards on these pages. What are the first things you notice about the places pictured on each one? Write the name of each place and then jot down your observations.

Interpret What would your reaction be if you were asked to spend a week in each of the places pictured? How might each location affect your mood and actions for that week? Record your responses, as well as your reasons for them.

Discuss Compare your reactions to each place with those of some classmates. How did each person feel about each place? Why did he or she feel that way? Notice the differences and the similarities between your responses.

SkillBuilder

CRITICAL THINKING

Considering All Factors

How often have you heard an excuse that places blame on the circumstances of an event rather than on the person involved? Different factors—elements or circumstances—connected to a situation may indeed have an impact on its outcome. For example, think again about visiting each of the places on these pages. Would you be equally comfortable in each place?

Whenever you evaluate a situation, consider all the factors that come into play. For example, here are some of the factors that might affect the success of a presidential campaign:

- the funds available
- the behavior of the opponent
- the revelation of personal history

To determine whether a particular factor is important, compare the situation at hand with the situation that might have occurred had that factor been different. Would the outcome change significantly?

APPLYING WHAT YOU'VE LEARNED
Write down at least three factors that might affect your reaction to the following situations.

- A friend picks you up half an hour late.
- You are turned down for a job.

PART 2 # *Culture and Conflict*

England has had complex relationships with other countries—especially the other parts of the United Kingdom and the countries that were once British colonies, some of which still belong to the British Commonwealth. Political conflicts have ravaged Northern Ireland, and citizens of former colonies find themselves caught in transition within their own countries and faced with the tensions of culture clash when they immigrate to England. Some of the writers represented in this part of Unit Seven describe struggles for peace and justice in their homelands, whereas others detail the prejudice many immigrants experience in England. As you read the selections, think about how you would react in similar situations.

PREVIEWING

FICTION

The Distant Past

William Trevor

PERSONAL CONNECTION

Do you know someone who seems to live in the past—who likes to think and talk about events that happened long ago? What do you think might make such a person dwell on past experiences? Share your thoughts with classmates.

HISTORICAL/BIOGRAPHICAL CONNECTION

Conflicts between the English and the Irish extend back to the 12th century, when England first succeeded in gaining control of part of Ireland. Later, when the English tried to establish Protestantism as the sole religion in the predominantly Roman Catholic land, they naturally met with resistance and considerable anti-English sentiment. In the late 1800s, Irish Catholics began demanding self-rule, but the mostly Protestant settlements in northern Ireland opposed the plan, fearing control by an all-Catholic parliament.

In 1920, Britain divided Ireland into two countries with some powers of self-government. Northern Ireland, with its Protestant majority, readily accepted the decision. The Catholics in the rest of Ireland, however, wanted complete independence. In 1921, after a series of bloody revolts, southern Ireland agreed to become a self-governing dominion called the Irish Free State. By 1949, the nation had severed all ties with Great Britain, becoming the totally independent Republic of Ireland. Meanwhile, dissension between Protestants and Catholics living in Northern Ireland continued, and in the late 1960s the Irish Republican Army (IRA), an outlawed group of Catholic militants, began a series of terrorist attacks aimed at removing the British from that country as well.

The author William Trevor was born in 1928 to a Protestant family living in the Irish Free State. Although he attended Catholic schools, Trevor felt no prejudice during his early childhood. He does remember, however, that the few Protestants of the town formed a close alliance, ignoring all class distinctions within the group for the sake of unity. He also recalls the persistent loyalty of certain Protestants to England. According to Trevor, "keeping faith with the irretrievable past . . . was often the hallmark of the dispossessed." Many of Trevor's stories are set in Ireland, and his characters are often forced to confront the realities of a long history of violence and hatred.

LASERLINKS
- *HISTORICAL CONNECTION*
- *GEOGRAPHICAL CONNECTION*

READING CONNECTION

Literature as Social Commentary

The selections in this part of Unit Seven are representative of the type of literature that imparts social commentary. Throughout the history of English literature, many writers have used fiction, poetry, and nonfiction to convey their insights into social and political issues. The novelist Charles Dickens, for example, addressed the darker side of England's industrial development in the 19th century, and the poet Siegfried Sassoon graphically depicted the horrors of World War I. Since World War II, social commentary has become prevalent not only in the literature of Great Britain but in the works of writers around the world.

Typically, writers who include social commentary in their works hope to do more than merely entertain their readers. Although their individual reasons for addressing political or social problems may vary, most undoubtedly feel that they have a responsibility to enlighten their audience, to make readers aware of important facts. Sometimes a writer's motives may be very personal, based on direct experience with an unpleasant situation; in other instances, the writer may simply be presenting thoughts or observations on a problem that has bothered his or her conscience. Clearly, most such writers hope that their writing will change the way people think or act. The Chilean author Isabel Allende has stated that she considers this type of writing "an act of hope."

Writers of fiction differ in the way they introduce social commentary into their works. In some stories, for example, a profound political or social issue may dominate the entire plot and become the central theme around which all other actions revolve. In other stories, the social commentary is less direct, and the political or social issue is merely a backdrop for another situation. Typically, writers cast their characters as ordinary individuals caught up in the context of larger world issues. The reader then observes how the larger issues affect the motives, behaviors, and destinies of real people. Often the best examples of social commentary in fiction are those in which writers present the truth about situations without injecting their personal beliefs, thus allowing readers to form their own opinions.

"The Distant Past" belongs with the best examples of social commentary in literature. Trevor, as the author and critic V. S. Pritchett has noted, "truthfully allows life to present itself without preaching." In your reading of the story, try to focus on the author's message about the effects of the conflicts in Ireland on individual lives and upon Irish society as a whole. Make a chart like the one shown, noting incidents that you think are significant and explaining how they affect the characters and society depicted in the story.

Significant Incidents	Effects
Father leaves children only a dozen acres.	Children become bitter about Catholic woman and new regime.

Jonathan Swift

Charles Dickens

George Orwell

Nadine Gordimer

The Distant Past

WILLIAM TREVOR

In the town and beyond it they were regarded as harmlessly peculiar. Odd, people said, and in time this reference took on a burnish[1] of affection.

They had always been thin, silent with one another, and similar in appearance: a brother and sister who shared a family face. It was a bony countenance, with pale blue eyes and a sharp, well-shaped nose and high cheek-bones. Their father had had it too, but unlike them their father had been an irresponsible and careless man, with red flecks in his cheeks that they didn't have at all. The Middletons of Carraveagh the family had once been known as, but now the brother and sister were just the Middletons, for Carraveagh didn't count any more, except to them.

1. **burnish:** a smooth, polished finish.

They owned four Herefords,[2] a number of hens, and the house itself, three miles outside the town. It was a large house, built in the reign of George II,[3] a monument that reflected in its glory and later decay the fortunes of a family. As the brother and sister aged, its roof increasingly ceased to afford protection, rust ate at its gutters, grass thrived in two thick channels all along its avenue. Their father had mortgaged his inherited estate, so local rumor claimed, in order to keep a Catholic Dublin woman in brandy and jewels. When he died, in 1924, his two children discovered that they possessed only a dozen acres. It was locally said also that this adversity hardened their will and that because of it they came to love the remains of Carraveagh more than they could ever have loved a husband or a wife. They blamed for their ill-fortune the Catholic Dublin woman whom they'd never met and they blamed as well the new national regime, contriving in their eccentric way to relate the two. In the days of the Union Jack[4] such women would have known their place: wasn't it all part and parcel?

Twice a week, on Fridays and Sundays, the Middletons journeyed into the town, first of all in a trap[5] and later in a Ford Anglia car. In the shops and elsewhere they made, quite gently, no secret of their continuing loyalty to the past. They attended on Sundays St. Patrick's Protestant Church, a place that matched their mood, for prayers were still said there for the King whose sovereignty[6] their country had denied. The revolutionary regime would not last, they quietly informed the Reverend Packham: what sense was there in green-painted pillar-boxes and a language that nobody understood?[7]

On Fridays, when they took seven or eight dozen eggs to the town, they dressed in pressed tweeds and were accompanied over the years by a series of red setters, the breed there had always been at Carraveagh. They sold the eggs in Keogh's grocery and then had a drink with Mrs. Keogh in the part of her shop that was devoted to the consumption of refreshment. Mr. Middleton had whisky and his sister Tio Pepe.[8] They enjoyed the occasion, for they liked Mrs. Keogh and were liked by her in return. Afterwards they shopped, chatting to the shopkeepers about whatever news there was, and then they went to Healy's Hotel for a few more drinks before driving home.

Drink was their pleasure and it was through it that they built up, in spite of their loyalty to the past, such convivial relationships with the people of the town. Fat Driscoll, who kept the butcher's shop, used even to joke about the past when he stood with them in Healy's Hotel or stood behind his own counter cutting their slender chops or thinly slicing their liver. "Will you ever forget it, Mr. Middleton? I'd ha' run like a rabbit if you'd lifted a finger at me." Fat Driscoll would laugh then, rocking back on his heels with a glass of stout in his hand or banging their meat on to his weighing-scales. Mr. Middleton would smile. "There was alarm in your eyes, Mr. Driscoll," Miss Middleton would murmur, smiling also at the memory of the distant occasion.

Fat Driscoll, with a farmer called Maguire and another called Breen, had stood in the hall of Carraveagh, each of them in charge of a shotgun. The Middletons, children then, had been locked with their mother and father and an aunt

2. **Herefords** (hûr'fərdz): cattle of a breed raised for beef.
3. **George II:** king of Great Britain, 1727–1760.
4. **Union Jack:** the flag of Great Britain.
5. **trap:** a light two-wheeled carriage.
6. **sovereignty:** royal authority.
7. **green-painted . . . understood:** mailboxes painted Irish green (instead of red British mailboxes) and Gaelic—also known as Irish—the traditional language of Ireland's Celtic inhabitants and one of the official languages of the Republic of Ireland.
8. **Tio Pepe:** a brand of Spanish sherry.

WORDS TO KNOW
adversity (ăd-vûr'sĭ-tē) *n.* hardship; misfortune
regime (rā-zhēm') *n.* a government in power
convivial (kən-vĭv'ē-əl) *adj.* characterized by friendly companionship; sociable

into an upstairs room. Nothing else had happened: the expected British soldiers had not, after all, arrived and the men in the hall had eventually relaxed their vigil. "A massacre they wanted," the Middletons' father said after they'd gone. "Damn bloody ruffians."

The Second World War took place. Two Germans, a man and his wife called Winkelmann who ran a glove factory in the town, were suspected by the Middletons of being spies for the Third Reich.[9] People laughed, for they knew the Winkelmanns well and could lend no credence to the Middletons' latest fantasy: typical of them, they explained to the Winkelmanns, who had been worried. Soon after the War the Reverend Packham died and was replaced by the Reverend Bradshaw, a younger man who laughed also and regarded the Middletons as an anachronism. They protested when prayers were no longer said for the Royal Family in St. Patrick's, but the Reverend Bradshaw considered that their protests were as absurd as the prayers themselves had been. Why pray for the monarchy of a neighboring island when their own island had its chosen President now? The Middletons didn't reply to that argument. In the Reverend Bradshaw's presence they rose to their feet when the BBC[10] played "God Save the King," and on the day of the coronation of Queen Elizabeth II[11] they drove into the town with a small Union Jack propped up in the back window of their Ford Anglia. "Bedad, you're a holy terror, Mr. Middleton!" Fat Driscoll laughingly exclaimed, noticing the flag as he lifted a tray of pork-steaks from his display shelf. The Middletons smiled. It was a great day for the Commonwealth of Nations, they replied, a remark which further amused Fat Driscoll and which he later repeated in Phelan's public house. "Her Britannic Majesty," guffawed[12] his friend Mr. Breen.

A Self-Portrait (about 1965), William Leech. National Gallery of Ireland, Dublin.

Situated in a valley that was noted for its beauty and with convenient access to rich rivers and bogs over which game-birds flew, the town benefited from post-war tourism. Healy's Hotel changed its title and became, overnight, the New Ormonde. Shopkeepers had their shop-fronts painted and Mr. Healy organized an annual Salmon Festival. Even Canon[13] Kelly, who had

9. **Third Reich** (rīk): Nazi-controlled Germany.
10. **BBC:** British Broadcasting Corporation.
11. **the day . . . Queen Elizabeth II:** June 2, 1953—more than four years after Ireland withdrew from the British Commonwealth of Nations, severing all official ties with England.
12. **guffawed:** laughed loudly.
13. **Canon:** the title of certain Roman Catholic priests.

WORDS TO KNOW

anachronism (ə-năk′rə-nĭz′əm) *n.* something out of keeping with a specified time; especially, something proper to a former age but not to the present

Au Cinquième [On the fifth floor]: *A Portrait of the Artist's Wife* (about 1940), William Leech. Oil on canvas, 74 cm × 60 cm, National Gallery of Ireland, Dublin.

at first commented severely on the habits of the tourists, and in particular on the summertime dress of the women, was in the end obliged to confess that the morals of his flock remained unaffected. "God and good sense," he proclaimed, meaning God and his own teaching. In time he even derived pride from the fact that people with other values came briefly to the town and that the values esteemed by his parishioners were in no way diminished.

The town's grocers now stocked foreign cheeses, brie and camembert and Port Salut, and wines were available to go with them. The plush Cocktail Room of the New Ormonde set a standard: the wife of a solicitor, a Mrs. O'Brien, began to give six o'clock parties once or twice a year, obliging her husband to mix gin and Martini in glass jugs and herself handing round a selection of nuts and small Japanese crackers. Canon Kelly looked in as a rule and satisfied himself that all was above board. He rejected, though, the mixture in the jugs, retaining his taste for a glass of John Jameson.[14]

From the windows of their convent the Loretto nuns[15] observed the long, sleek cars with G.B. plates; English and American accents drifted on the breeze to them. Mothers cleaned up their children and sent them to the Golf Club to seek employment as caddies. Sweet shops sold holiday mementoes. The brown, soda and currant breads of Murphy-Flood's bakery were declared to be delicious. Mr. Healy doubled the number of local girls who served as waitresses in his dining-room, and in the winter of 1961 he had the builders in again, working on an extension for which the Munster and Leinster Bank had lent him twenty-two thousand pounds.

But as the town increased its prosperity Carraveagh continued its decline. The Middletons were in their middle-sixties now and were reconciled to a life that became more uncomfortable with every passing year. Together they roved the vast lofts of their house, placing old paint tins and flowerpot saucers beneath the drips from the roof. At night they sat over their thin chops in a dining-room that had once been gracious and which in a way was gracious still, except for the faded appearance of furniture that was dry from lack of polish and of a wallpaper that time had rendered colorless. In the hall their father gazed down at them, framed in ebony and gilt, in the uniform of the Irish Guards. He had conversed with Queen Victoria, and even in their middle-sixties they could still hear him saying that God and Empire and Queen formed a trinity

14. **John Jameson:** a brand of Irish whiskey.
15. **Loretto nuns:** members of a Roman Catholic religious order founded near Dublin in 1822.

unique in any worthy soldier's heart. In the hall hung the family crest, and on ancient Irish linen the Cross of St. George.[16]

The dog that accompanied the Middletons now was called Turloch, an animal whose death they dreaded for they felt they couldn't manage the antics of another pup. Turloch, being thirteen, moved slowly and was blind and a little deaf. He was a reminder to them of their own advancing years and of the effort it had become to tend the Herefords and collect the weekly eggs. More and more they looked forward to Fridays, to the warm companionship of Mrs. Keogh and Mr. Healy's chatter in the hotel. They stayed longer now with Mrs. Keogh and in the hotel, and idled longer in the shops, and drove home more slowly. Dimly, but with no less loyalty, they still recalled the distant past and were listened to without ill-feeling when they spoke of it and of Carraveagh as it had been, and of the Queen whose company their careless father had known.

The visitors who came to the town heard about the Middletons and were impressed. It was a pleasant wonder, more than one of them remarked, that old wounds could heal so completely, that the Middletons continued in their loyalty to the past and that, in spite of it, they were respected in the town. When Miss Middleton had been ill with a form of pneumonia in 1958 Canon Kelly had driven out to Carraveagh twice a week with pullets and young ducks that his housekeeper had dressed. "An upright couple," was the Canon's public opinion of the Middletons, and he had been known to add that eccentric views would hurt you less than malice. "We can disagree without guns in this town," Mr. Healy pronounced in his Cocktail Room, and his visitors usually replied that as far as they could see that was the result of living in a Christian country. That the Middletons bought their meat from a man who had once locked them into an upstairs room and had then waited to shoot soldiers in their hall was a fact that amazed the seasonal visitors. You lived and learned, they remarked to Mr. Healy.

The Middletons, privately, often considered that they led a strange life. Alone in their two beds at night they now and again wondered why they hadn't just sold Carraveagh forty-eight years ago when their father had died: why had the tie been so strong and why had they in perversity encouraged it? They didn't fully know, nor did they attempt to discuss the matter in any way. Instinctively they had remained at Carraveagh, instinctively feeling that it would have been cowardly to go. Yet often it seemed to them now to be no more than a game they played, this worship of the distant past. And at other times it seemed as real and as important as the remaining acres of land, and the house itself.

"Isn't that shocking?" Mr. Healy said one day in 1967. "Did you hear about that, Mr. Middleton, blowing up them post offices in Belfast?"[17]

Mr. Healy, red-faced and short-haired, spoke casually in his Cocktail Room, making midday conversation. He had commented in much the same way at breakfast-time, looking up from the *Irish Independent*. Everyone in the town had said it too: that the blowing up of sub–post offices in Belfast was a shocking matter.

"A bad business," Fat Driscoll remarked, wrapping the Middletons' meat. "We don't want that old stuff all over again."

"We didn't want it in the first place," Miss Middleton reminded him. He laughed, and she laughed, and so did her brother. Yes, it was a game, she thought: how could any of it be as real or as important as the afflictions and problems of the old butcher himself, his rheumatism and

16. **Cross of St. George:** horizontal and vertical red bars crossing on a white background—an ancient flag of England.

17. **blowing up . . . in Belfast:** In Northern Ireland, Belfast (the capital) and the town of Londonderry were sites of terrorist attacks by members of the IRA.

WORDS TO KNOW

perversity (pər-vûr'sĭ-tē) *n.* a stubborn determination to act in an inappropriate or unexpected way

his reluctance to retire? Did her brother, she wondered, privately think so too?

"Come on, old Turloch," he said, stroking the flank of the red setter with the point of his shoe, and she reflected that you could never tell what he was thinking. Certainly it wasn't the kind of thing you wanted to talk about.

"I've put him in a bit of mince," Fat Driscoll said, which was something he often did these days, pretending the mince would otherwise be thrown away. There'd been a red setter about the place that night when he waited in the hall for the soldiers: Breen and Maguire had pushed it down into a cellar, frightened of it.

"There's a heart of gold in you, Mr. Driscoll," Miss Middleton murmured, nodding and smiling at him. He was the same age as she was, sixty-six: he should have shut up shop years ago. He would have, he'd once told them, if there'd been a son to leave the business to. As it was, he'd have to sell it and when it came to the point he found it hard to make the necessary arrangements. "Like us and Carraveagh," she'd said, even though on the face of it it didn't seem the same at all.

Every evening they sat in the big old kitchen, hearing the news. It was only in Belfast and Derry,[18] the wireless[19] said; outside Belfast and Derry you wouldn't know anything was happening at all. On Fridays they listened to the talk in Mrs. Keogh's bar and in the hotel. "Well, thank God it has nothing to do with the South," Mr. Healy said often, usually repeating the statement.

The first British soldiers landed in the North of Ireland, and soon people didn't so often say that outside Belfast and Derry you wouldn't know anything was happening. There were incidents in Fermanagh and Armagh, in Border villages and towns. One Prime Minister resigned and then another one. The troops were unpopular, the newspapers said; internment[20] became part of the machinery of government. In the town, in St. Patrick's Protestant Church and in the Church of the Holy Assumption, prayers for peace were offered, but no peace came.

"We're hit, Mr. Middleton," Mr. Healy said one Friday morning. "If there's a dozen visitors this summer it'll be God's own stroke of luck for us."

"Luck?"

"Sure, who wants to come to a country with all that malarkey[21] in it?"

"But it's only in the North."

"Tell that to your tourists, Mr. Middleton."

The town's prosperity ebbed. The Border was more than sixty miles away, but over that distance had spread some wisps of the fog of war. As anger rose in the town at the loss of fortune so there rose also the kind of talk there had been in the distant past. There was talk of atrocities and counter-atrocities, and of guns and gelignite[22] and the rights of people. There was bitterness suddenly in Mrs. Keogh's bar because of the lack of trade, and in the empty hotel there was bitterness also.

On Fridays, only sometimes at first, there was a silence when the Middletons appeared. It was as though, going back nearly twenty years, people remembered the Union Jack in the window of their car and saw it now in a different light. It wasn't something to laugh at any more, nor were certain words that the Middletons had gently spoken, nor were they

---

18. **Derry:** another name for Londonderry.
19. **wireless:** radio.
20. **internment:** confinement or imprisonment, especially in wartime.
21. **malarkey:** foolishness.
22. **gelignite** (jĕl′ĭg-nīt′): a powerful explosive.

themselves just an old, peculiar couple. Slowly the change crept about, all around them in the town, until Fat Driscoll didn't wish it to be remembered that he had ever given them mince for their dog. He had stood with a gun in the enemy's house, waiting for soldiers so that soldiers might be killed: it was better that people should remember that.

One day Canon Kelly looked the other way when he saw the Middletons' car coming and they noticed this movement of his head, although he hadn't wished them to. And on another day Mrs. O'Brien, who had always been keen to talk to them in the hotel, didn't reply when they addressed her.

The Middletons naturally didn't discuss these rebuffs but they each of them privately knew that there was no conversation they could have at this time with the people of the town. The stand they had taken and kept to for so many years no longer seemed ridiculous in the town. Had they driven with a Union Jack now they would, astoundingly, have been shot.

"It will never cease." He spoke disconsolately one night, standing by the dresser where the wireless was.

She washed the dishes they'd eaten from, and the cutlery. "Not in our time," she said.

"It is worse than before."

"Yes, it is worse than before."

They took from the walls of the hall the portrait of their father in the uniform of the Irish Guards because it seemed wrong to them that at this time it should hang there. They took down also the crest of their family and the Cross of St. George, and from a vase on the drawing-room mantelpiece they removed the small Union Jack that had been there since the Coronation of Queen Elizabeth II. They did not remove these articles in fear but in mourning for the *modus vivendi*[23] that had existed for so long between them and the people of the town. They had given their custom[24] to a butcher who had planned to shoot down soldiers in their hall and he, in turn, had given them mince for their dog. For fifty years they had experienced, after suspicion had seeped away, a tolerance that never again in the years that were left to them would they know.

One November night their dog died and he said to her after he had buried it that they must not be depressed by all that was happening. They would die themselves and the house would become a ruin because there was no one to inherit it, and the distant past would be set to rest. But she disagreed: the *modus vivendi* had been easy for them, she pointed out, because they hadn't really minded the dwindling of their fortunes while the town prospered. It had given them a life, and a kind of dignity: you could take a pride out of living in peace.

He did not say anything and then, because of the emotion that both of them felt over the death of their dog, he said in a rushing way that they could no longer at their age hope to make a living out of the remains of Carraveagh. They must sell the hens and the four Herefords. As he spoke, he watched her nodding, agreeing with the sense of it. Now and again, he thought, he would drive slowly into the town, to buy groceries and meat with the money they had saved, and to face the silence that would sourly thicken as their own two deaths came closer and death increased in another part of their island. She felt him thinking that and she knew that he was right. Because of the distant past they would die friendless. It was worse than being murdered in their beds. ❖

---

23. ***modus vivendi*** (mō′dəs vĭ-vĕn′dē) *Latin:* way of life.

24. **custom:** business; trade.

RESPONDING OPTIONS

FROM PERSONAL RESPONSE *TO* CRITICAL ANALYSIS

REFLECT 1. What parts of the story did you find most thought-provoking? Describe your reactions in your notebook before sharing them with a partner.

RETHINK 2. How would you describe the relationship between the Middletons and the people of the town?

Consider
- how the townspeople felt about the Middletons' parents
- the Middletons' behavior
- the changing feelings of all involved
- the political loyalties of all involved

3. In your opinion, what is the true cause of the conflict between the Middletons and the townspeople?

4. Do you think the townspeople are justified in their behavior? Why or why not?

5. How would you describe the Middletons' feelings about the past, and how do these feelings change at the end of the story?

RELATE 6. Does the person you thought about for the Personal Connection on page 1073 share any qualities with the Middletons? How is he or she different from them?

7. Do you think that a situation similar to the one depicted in "The Distant Past" could occur in your own community?

ANOTHER PATHWAY

Cooperative Learning

With a partner, create a time line on which you indicate how you think the attitudes of the Middletons and the townspeople change as time passes and important events occur in their lives. Discuss with your classmates the reasons for each of the changes in attitude.

LITERARY CONCEPTS

Consider the examples of **conflict**—the struggle between opposing forces—presented in this story. In your opinion, are most of the conflicts **external** (occurring between a character and an outside force, such as another character or society in general), or are most **internal** (occurring within a character)? Explain your answer, citing specific details from the story.

QUICKWRITES

1. As Miss Middleton, express your feelings about life in two different **diary entries,** the first written before World War II and the second written in the late 1960s, after the violence has erupted.
2. As one of the townspeople, write a **letter to the editor** of your local newspaper, expressing your views about the terrorism in Northern Ireland and its effect on your town.
3. In a **paragraph,** describe your reaction to the last sentence of the story: "It was worse than being murdered in their beds."

PORTFOLIO *Save your writing. You may want to use it later as a springboard to a piece for your portfolio.*

ALTERNATIVE ACTIVITIES

1. With a partner, role-play two different **conversations** between Fat Driscoll and Mrs. Keogh, one during the 1950s and one in the late 1960s, after the British soldiers land in Northern Ireland. Discuss the Middletons as well as current events.
2. Create two **political cartoons** that reflect the contrasting political sentiments of the Middletons and the townspeople. Display your work in the classroom.

ACROSS THE CURRICULUM

Geography Display a map of Ireland in your classroom. Use information from "The Distant Past" to identify the sites of the terrorist activities mentioned in the story, as well as possible locations of the town where the story is set.

LITERARY LINKS

Compare the characters in "The Distant Past" with those in Lady Gregory's *The Rising of the Moon* (page 912). What conflicts do they share? Are those conflicts resolved in either selection?

WORDS TO KNOW

Review the Words to Know at the bottom of the selection pages. Then write the word suggested by each of the following descriptions.

1. An example of this might be a Neanderthal man in modern Berlin or a helicopter hovering over King Arthur and his Round Table.
2. More exasperating than mere misbehavior and harder to deal with than simple stubbornness, this is a trait found in real brats and people we call ornery.
3. This may or may not change when there's a national election, but it does change when there's a successful revolution.
4. This word describes the guests we are happiest to entertain and most likely to invite again.
5. If you retire to a bed of thorns after having a hard row to hoe, your life has a good deal of this in it.

WILLIAM TREVOR

1928–

William Trevor was born William Trevor Cox in County Cork, Ireland. During his childhood, his family relocated often, moving from town to town throughout southern Ireland as his father pursued a career in banking. As a result, Trevor's education was somewhat irregular; he went to 13 different grammar schools and, at times, no school at all. Later, he attended St. Columba's College and Trinity College in Dublin. Immediately after receiving a degree from Trinity, he accepted a position as a history teacher in Northern Ireland. In 1952, he moved to England, where he taught art and began a career as a sculptor.

As a youth, Trevor never entertained thoughts of a writing career. In fact, he always assumed that he would someday enter the business world, perhaps working in a store or a bank. He did not publish his first novel until 1958, and not until he was in his mid-30s did he abandon art in order to write full-time. The numerous novels, plays, and short stories he has published since then have been commended for their restrained style, subtle humor, and compassionate characterization. Although his writing often deals with the people, culture, and history of his native Ireland, he has continued to reside and work in England.

OTHER WORKS "Mrs. Silly," "Autumn Sunshine," "The Tennis Court," *Mrs. Acland's Ghosts*

PREVIEWING

FICTION

Civil Peace

Chinua Achebe (chĭn′wä ä-chā′bā)

PERSONAL CONNECTION

Think about articles or books you have read that describe the aftermath of war. What is life typically like for ordinary civilians after a war has been fought on their land? Share your knowledge with classmates.

HISTORICAL/CULTURAL CONNECTION

Chinua Achebe often writes about the conflicts and transitions in his native Nigeria, a former British colony on the western coast of Africa. After more than 100 years of British influence, Nigeria finally gained its independence in 1960. Although English is the country's official language, over 250 ethnic groups, each with its own language and customs, live there. The three largest of these are the Hausa, the Yoruba, and the Ibo.

Throughout the 1960s, various ethnic groups struggled, often violently, for control of Nigeria's government. The principal opponents were the Ibo and the Hausa. In 1967, the Ibo in the eastern part of the country seceded from Nigeria and formed their own republic, called Biafra. A period of civil war followed, lasting until 1970 and causing massive hardship and devastation —especially in Biafra, which suffered from a lack of supplies. It is estimated that over 1.5 million Biafrans starved to death before their leaders surrendered. Chinua Achebe was a tireless spokesperson for the Biafran cause, but in the war's aftermath he just as diligently joined in the long process of unifying and rebuilding the country.

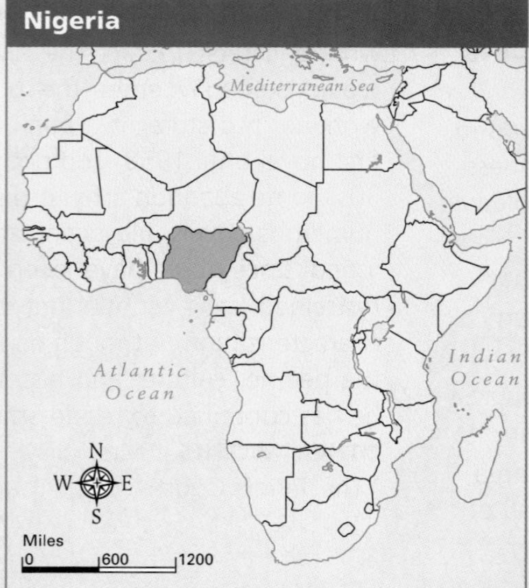

READING CONNECTION

Reading Dialect In "Civil Peace," Achebe shows how one man deals with his return to his home in the aftermath of the Biafran war. Some of the characters in the story speak a **dialect,** or local version, of English that may seem almost a foreign language to you. Here are some examples of the dialect terms in "Civil Peace," along with their meanings:

na ("is" or "it is")	*commot* ("leave")
wetin ("what")	*soja* ("soldiers")
am ("it")	*katakata* ("trouble")

If you have difficulty understanding any of the dialect as you read this story, try reading it aloud. Jot down in your notebook any phrases or sentences that you still find confusing.

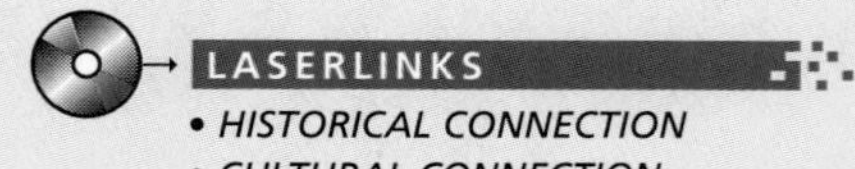

- *HISTORICAL CONNECTION*
- *CULTURAL CONNECTION*

CIVIL PEACE

Chinua Achebe

Jonathan Iwegbu counted himself extraordinarily lucky. "Happy survival!" meant so much more to him than just a current fashion of greeting old friends in the first hazy days of peace. It went deep to his heart. He had come out of the war with five inestimable blessings—his head, his wife Maria's head and the heads of three out of their four children. As a bonus he also had his old bicycle—a miracle too but naturally not to be compared to the safety of five human heads.

The bicycle had a little history of its own. One day at the height of the war it was commandeered "for urgent military action." Hard as its loss would have been to him he would still have let it go without a thought had he not had some doubts about the genuineness of the officer. It wasn't his disreputable rags, nor the toes peeping out of one blue and one brown canvas shoes, nor yet the two stars of his rank done obviously in a hurry in biro,[1] that troubled Jonathan; many good and heroic soldiers looked the same or worse. It was rather a certain lack of grip and firmness in his manner. So Jonathan, suspecting he might be amenable to influence, rummaged in his raffia[2] bag and produced the two pounds with which he had been going to buy firewood which his wife, Maria, retailed to camp officials for extra stock-fish and corn meal, and got his bicycle back. That night he buried it in the little clearing in the bush where the dead of the camp, including his own youngest son, were buried. When he dug it up again a year later after the surrender all it needed was a little palm-oil greasing. "Nothing puzzles God," he said in wonder.

He put it to immediate use as a taxi and accumulated a small pile of Biafran money ferrying camp officials and their families across the four-mile stretch to the nearest tarred road. His standard charge per trip was six pounds and those who had the money were only glad to be rid of some of it in this way. At the end of a fortnight he had made a small fortune of one hundred and fifteen pounds.

Then he made the journey to Enugu[3] and found another miracle waiting for him. It was unbelievable. He rubbed his eyes and looked again and it was still standing there before him. But, needless to say, even that monumental blessing must be accounted also totally inferior to the five heads in the family. This newest miracle was his little house in Ogui Overside. Indeed nothing puzzles God! Only two houses away a huge concrete edifice some wealthy contractor had put up just before the war was a mountain of rubble. And here was Jonathan's little zinc house[4] of no regrets built with mud blocks quite intact! Of course the doors and windows were missing and five sheets off the roof. But what was that? And anyhow he had returned to Enugu early enough to pick up bits of old zinc and wood and soggy sheets of card-board lying around the neighborhood before thousands more came out of their forest holes looking for the same things. He got a destitute carpenter with one old hammer, a blunt plane and a few bent and rusty nails in his tool bag to turn this assortment of wood, paper and metal into door and window shutters for five Nigerian shillings or fifty Biafran pounds. He paid the

1. **biro** (bîr′ō) a British term for a ballpoint pen. (The officer's insignia, that is, had been drawn in ink.)
2. **raffia:** a palm fiber used for weaving such items as mats, baskets, and hats.
3. **Enugu** (ā-nōō′gōō): a city in southeastern Nigeria.
4. **zinc house:** a house roofed with sheets of galvanized metal.

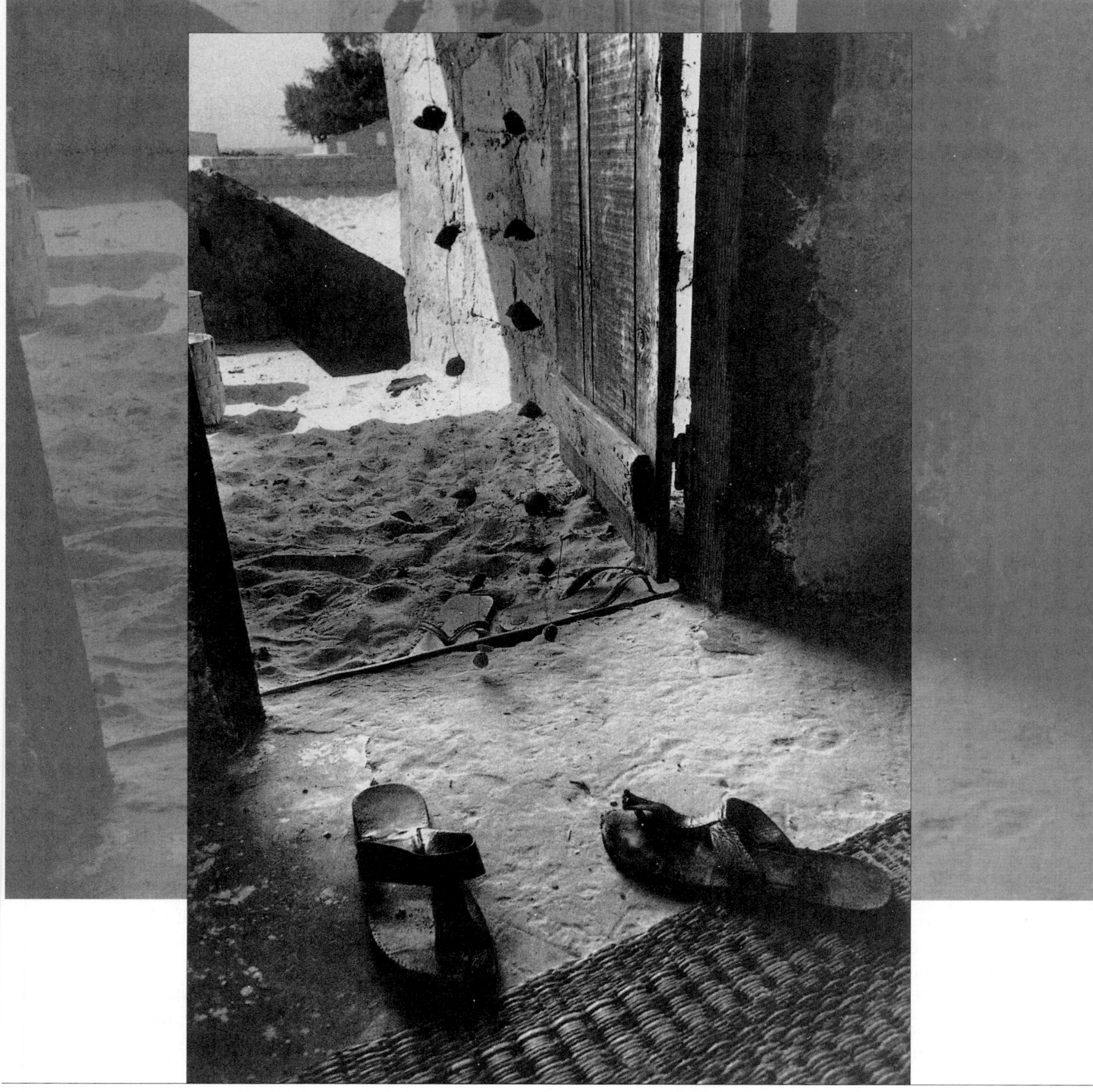

pounds, and moved in with his overjoyed family carrying five heads on their shoulders.

His children picked mangoes near the military cemetery and sold them to soldiers' wives for a few pennies—real pennies this time—and his wife started making breakfast akara[5] balls for neighbors in a hurry to start life again. With his family earnings he took his bicycle to the villages around

5. **akara** (ä-kä′rä) **balls:** bean cakes.

and bought fresh palm-wine which he mixed generously in his rooms with the water which had recently started running again in the public tap down the road, and opened up a bar for soldiers and other lucky people with good money.

At first he went daily, then every other day and finally once a week, to the offices of the Coal Corporation where he used to be a miner, to find out what was what. The only thing he did find out in the end was that that little house of his was even a greater blessing than he had thought. Some of his fellow examiners who had nowhere to return at the end of the day's waiting just slept outside the doors of the offices and cooked what meal they could scrounge together in Bournvita tins. As the weeks lengthened and still nobody could say what was what Jonathan discontinued his weekly visits altogether and faced his palm-wine bar.

But nothing puzzles God. Came the day of the windfall when after five days of endless scuffles in queues[6] and counter-queues in the sun outside the Treasury he had twenty pounds counted into his palms as ex-gratia[7] award for the rebel money he had turned in. It was like Christmas for him and for many others like him when the payments began. They called it (since few could manage its proper official name) *egg-rasher*.

As soon as the pound notes were placed in his palm Jonathan simply closed it tight over them and buried fist and money inside his trouser pocket. He had to be extra careful because he had seen a man a couple of days earlier collapse into near-madness in an instant before that oceanic crowd because no sooner had he got his twenty pounds than some heartless ruffian picked it off him. Though it was not right that a man in such an extremity of agony should be blamed yet many in the queues that day were able to remark quietly on the victim's carelessness, especially after he pulled out the innards of his pocket and revealed a hole in it big enough to pass a thief's head. But of course he had insisted that the money had been in the other pocket, pulling it out too to show its comparative wholeness. So one had to be careful.

Jonathan soon transferred the money to his left hand and pocket so as to leave his right free for shaking hands should the need arise, though by fixing his gaze at such an elevation as to miss all approaching human faces he made sure that the need did not arise, until he got home.

He was normally a heavy sleeper but that night he heard all the neighborhood noises die down one after another. Even the night watchman who knocked the hour on some metal somewhere in the distance had fallen silent after knocking one o'clock. That must have been the last thought in Jonathan's mind before he was finally carried away himself. He couldn't have been gone for long, though, when he was violently awakened again.

"Who is knocking?" whispered his wife lying beside him on the floor.

Who is knocking?

"I don't know," he whispered back breathlessly.

The second time the knocking came it was so loud and imperious that the rickety old door could have fallen down.

"Who is knocking?" he asked then, his voice parched and trembling.

"Na tief-man and him people," came the cool reply. "Make you hopen de door." This was followed by the heaviest knocking of all.

Maria was the first to raise the alarm, then he followed and all their children.

"Police-o! Thieves-o! Neighbors-o! Police-o! We are lost! We are dead! Neighbors, are you asleep? Wake up! Police-o!"

This went on for a long time and then stopped suddenly. Perhaps they had scared the thief away. There was total silence. But only for a short while.

"You done finish?" asked the voice outside. "Make we help you small. Oya, everybody!"

"Police-o! Tief-man-o! Neighbors-o! we done loss-o! Police-o! . . ."

---

6. **queues** (kyo͞oz): lines of waiting people.

7. **ex-gratia** (ĕks′grā′shə): given as a favor rather than as a legal obligation.

There were at least five other voices besides the leader's.

Jonathan and his family were now completely paralyzed by terror. Maria and the children sobbed inaudibly like lost souls. Jonathan groaned continuously.

The silence that followed the thieves' alarm vibrated horribly. Jonathan all but begged their leader to speak again and be done with it.

"My frien," said he at long last, "we don try our best for call dem but I tink say dem all done sleep-o. . . . So wetin we go do now? Sometaim you wan call soja? Or you wan make we call dem for you? Soja better pass police. No be so?"

"Na so!" replied his men. Jonathan thought he heard even more voices now than before and groaned heavily. His legs were sagging under him and his throat felt like sand-paper.

"My frien, why you no de talk again. I de ask you say you wan make we call soja?"

"No."

"Awrighto. Now make we talk business. We no be bad tief. We no like for make trouble. Trouble done finish. War done finish and all the katakata wey de for inside.[8] No Civil War again. This time na Civil Peace. No be so?"

"Na so!" answered the horrible chorus.

"What do you want from me? I am a poor man. Everything I had went with this war. Why do you come to me? You know people who have money. We . . ."

"Awright! We know say you no get plenty money. But we sef no get even anini.[9] So derefore make you open dis window and give us one hundred pound and we go commot. Orderwise we de come for inside now to show you guitar-boy like dis . . ."

A volley of automatic fire rang through the sky. Maria and the children began to weep aloud again.

"Ah, missisi de cry again. No need for dat. We done talk say we na good tief. We just take our small money and go nwayorly. No molest. Abi we de molest?"

"At all!" sang the chorus.

"My friends," began Jonathan hoarsely. "I hear what you say and I thank you. If I had one hundred pounds . . ."

"Lookia my frien, no be play we come play for your house. If we make mistake and step for inside you no go like am-o. So derefore . . ."

"To God who made me; if you come inside and find one hundred pounds, take it and shoot me and shoot my wife and children. I swear to God. The only money I have in this life is this twenty-pounds *egg-rasher* they gave me today . . ."

"OK. Time de go. Make you open dis window and bring the twenty pound. We go manage am like dat."

There were now loud murmurs of dissent among the chorus: "Na lie de man de lie; e get plenty money. . . . Make we go inside and search properly well. . . . Wetin be twenty pound? . . ."

"Shurrup!" rang the leader's voice like a lone shot in the sky and silenced the murmuring at once. "Are you dere? Bring the money quick!"

"I am coming," said Jonathan fumbling in the darkness with the key of the small wooden box he kept by his side on the mat.

At the first sign of light as neighbors and others assembled to commiserate with him he was already strapping his five-gallon demijohn[10] to his bicycle carrier and his wife, sweating in the open fire, was turning over akara balls in a wide clay bowl of boiling oil. In the corner his eldest son was rinsing out dregs of yesterday's palm wine from old beer bottles.

"I count it as nothing," he told his sympathizers, his eyes on the rope he was tying. "What is *egg-rasher?* Did I depend on it last week? Or is it greater than other things that went with the war? I say, let *egg-rasher* perish in the flames! Let it go where everything else has gone. Nothing puzzles God." ❖

---

8. **wey de for inside:** Nigerian dialect for "that went with it."

9. **anini** (ä-nē′nē): a small coin worth less than a penny.

10. **demijohn** (dĕm′ē-jŏn′): a large bottle with a narrow neck, usually encased in wicker.

RESPONDING OPTIONS

FROM PERSONAL RESPONSE *TO* CRITICAL ANALYSIS

REFLECT 1. How did you react to the events in this story? Describe your reactions in your notebook.

RETHINK 2. How would you describe Jonathan's approach to life?

Consider

- the value he places on "the safety of five human heads"
- his ways of earning money
- his reaction to the thieves
- what he means when he says "Nothing puzzles God"

3. What ironies did you find in this story?

4. What ideas about the aftermath of war do you think the story conveys?

RELATE 5. Do you think Jonathan's attitude in the wake of the war's destruction and tragedy is common among the survivors of wars? Give reasons for your opinion.

ANOTHER PATHWAY

Jonathan considers himself "extraordinarily lucky." Make a chart like the one shown here, recording what *you* consider to be his losses and his blessings. Then decide whether you agree with his assessment of his lot in life. Share your opinion and reasons with the rest of the class.

Jonathan's Luck	
Losses	**Blessings**

LITERARY CONCEPTS

A **dialect** is a form of English, or another language, that is spoken in one place by a certain group of people. It reflects the pronunciations, vocabulary, and grammatical rules that are typical of a region. In "Civil Peace," Chinua Achebe actually uses two dialects of English, the Nigerian dialect of the thieves and the near-standard dialect of Jonathan and his family. Why do you think Achebe chose to include both dialects?

LITERARY LINKS

Compare Jonathan in "Civil Peace" with Miss Middleton in "The Distant Past" (page 1073). What similarities and differences can you find in their attitudes toward life? Which character is more prepared to cope with hardship?

QUICKWRITES

1. Write a **job recommendation** for Jonathan, telling a prospective employer what you consider to be his strengths and weaknesses.

2. With a group of classmates, plan and write the **front page** of a newspaper for the residents of Jonathan's town. Include a report of the robbery and other articles based on newsworthy details in the story. If a desktop-publishing program is available to you, use it to design your page. Make copies of your work to share with classmates.

PORTFOLIO *Save your writing. You may want to use it later as a spring-board to a piece for your portfolio.*

ALTERNATIVE ACTIVITIES

1. With a small group of classmates, practice and perform an **oral reading** of the robbery scene. Use appropriate tones of voice to convey the characters' emotions, and try to reproduce the thieves' dialect.
2. Imagine that "Civil Peace" is to be published as a small book. Design a **book jacket** that might entice people to read the story. Display your work in the classroom.
3. Using pictures or real objects, put together a **package** of items that you might send Jonathan and his family to help them adjust to life after the war.

CRITIC'S CORNER

The student reviewer Carrie Mitchell indicated that the suspense in "Civil Peace" kept her attention and that she "couldn't read fast enough" to discover the outcome of Jonathan's encounter with the thieves. Did you experience a similar feeling during your reading? Explain your answer.

CHINUA ACHEBE

1930–

A son of Ibo missionaries in eastern Nigeria, Chinua Achebe was raised a Christian and attended British-run schools, studying first in the Ibo language and later in English. A gifted student, Achebe became one of the few 14-year-olds chosen to attend Government College, one of the best high schools in Nigeria. At the age of 18, he left high school with a scholarship to study medicine at the University of Ibadan in western Nigeria. Achebe quickly changed his course of study, however, and it was in English literature that he received his degree in 1953.

After teaching for a year, Achebe went to work for the Nigerian Broadcasting Corporation in Lagos, where he eventually became the director of external broadcasting. In 1966, amidst the often violent strife between the Ibo and other ethnic groups, Achebe felt that he and his family were no longer safe in Lagos. He quit his job and returned to eastern Nigeria, where he became an outspoken advocate of—and fundraiser for—the Biafran cause. He also started a publishing company with the poet Christopher Okigbo, who was later killed in the war.

In addition to short stories, Achebe has written novels, essays, poems, and children's books. His first novel, *Things Fall Apart* (1958), focuses on the effects of European colonialism in Nigeria. Many of his other works focus on problems associated with Nigeria's emergence as a modern nation. Throughout his literary career, Achebe has taught and lectured at universities in both Nigeria and the United States.

OTHER WORKS "Marriage Is a Private Affair," "Vengeful Creditor," "The Sacrificial Egg," "Dead Men's Path"

PREVIEWING

POETRY

Telephone Conversation

Wole Soyinka (wō′lĕ shô-yĭng′kə)

from Midsummer

Derek Walcott

PERSONAL CONNECTION

Recall a time when you read about or witnessed an obvious display of prejudice against someone because of his or her race, gender, nationality, or religion. What was your reaction? Do you think any form of prejudice exists in your school or community? Share your thoughts with classmates.

CULTURAL/BIOGRAPHICAL CONNECTION

A native of Nigeria, on the west coast of Africa, Wole Soyinka was awarded the 1986 Nobel Prize in literature, becoming the first African to receive that honor. In 1992, Derek Walcott—born on St. Lucia, a small island in the West Indies—became the first native Caribbean author to receive the Nobel literature prize. For many years, the now-independent countries of Nigeria and St. Lucia were British colonies, and both Soyinka's and Walcott's works draw upon the often antagonistic African and English cultures that have played such a significant role in their lives.

Both authors include social commentary—on racial prejudice and other issues—in their writing, undoubtedly in an attempt to enlighten their readers and encourage change. According to Soyinka, writers must become "a part of that machinery that will actually shape events." He often speaks out against political corruption and violations of human rights and is frequently at odds with government leaders in his own country. Walcott, while appreciating the literary traditions of England, often voices opposition to the neglect of West Indian culture by the islands' British colonizers and by present-day tourists. Acknowledging his own diverse cultural background, Walcott from time to time contemplates his own identity and role as a poet. In his Nobel Prize acceptance speech, he stated that "the process of poetry is one of excavation and of self-discovery."

WRITING CONNECTION

In your notebook, create a word web like the one below, recording words or images that you associate with the word *prejudice*. Then, as you read these two poems, add any other images that come to mind.

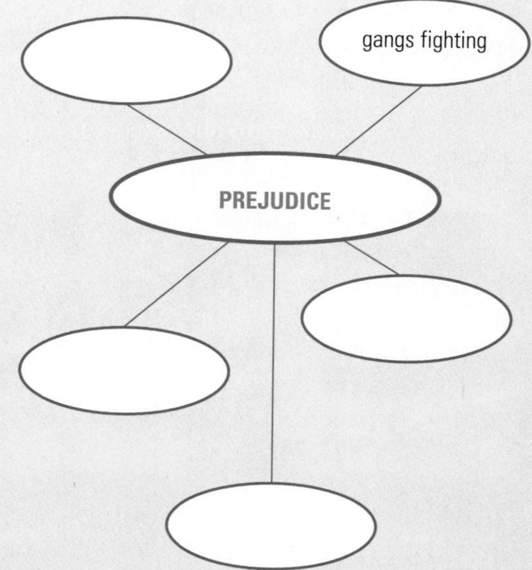

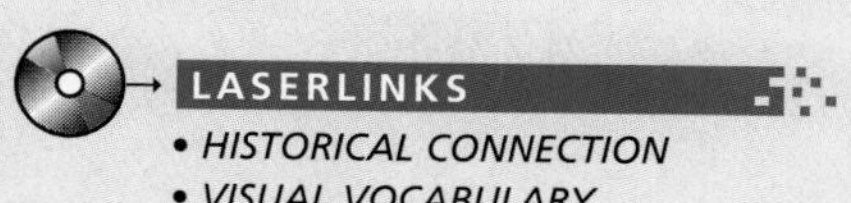

- *HISTORICAL CONNECTION*
- *VISUAL VOCABULARY*

TELEPHONE CONVERSATION

WOLE SOYINKA

The price seemed reasonable, location
Indifferent. The landlady swore she lived
Off premises. Nothing remained
But self-confession. "Madam," I warned,
"I hate a wasted journey—I am African."
Silence. Silenced transmission of
Pressurized good-breeding. Voice, when it came,
Lipstick-coated, long gold-rolled
Cigarette-holder pipped. Caught I was, foully.

"HOW DARK?" . . . I had not misheard . . . "ARE YOU LIGHT
"OR VERY DARK?" Button B. Button A. Stench
Of rancid breath of public hide-and-speak.
Red booth. Red pillar-box. Red double-tiered
Omnibus squelching tar. It *was* real! Shamed
By ill-mannered silence, surrender
Pushed dumbfoundment to beg simplification.
Considerate she was, varying the emphasis—

12 rancid (răn′sĭd): smelling of decay; rotten.

13 pillar-box: a pillar-shaped mailbox.

Second Bus (1962), Allen Jones. Oil on canvas, collection of Granada Television, Manchester, England, reproduced by courtesy of the artist.

"ARE YOU DARK? OR VERY LIGHT?" Revelation came.
"You mean—like plain or milk chocolate?"
Her assent was clinical, crushing in its light
Impersonality. Rapidly, wave-length adjusted,
I chose, "West African sepia"—and as an afterthought,
"Down in my passport." Silence for spectroscopic
Flight of fancy, till truthfulness clanged her accent
Hard on the mouthpiece "WHAT'S THAT?", conceding,
"DON'T KNOW WHAT THAT IS." "Like brunette."

"THAT'S DARK, ISN'T IT?" "Not altogether.
"Facially, I am brunette, but madam, you should see
"The rest of me. Palm of my hand, soles of my feet
"Are a peroxide blonde. Friction, caused—
"Foolishly, madam—by sitting down, has turned
"My bottom raven black.—One moment madam!"—sensing
Her receiver rearing on the thunder clap
About my ears—"Madam," I pleaded, "wouldn't you rather
"See for yourself?"

22 sepia (sē′pē-ə): a dark yellow brown or olive brown.

23 spectroscopic: here, pertaining to the analysis of colors. (A spectroscope is an instrument that separates light into its various wavelengths—colors—for scientific study.)

FROM PERSONAL RESPONSE *TO* CRITICAL ANALYSIS

REFLECT

1. What is your impression of the landlady? Describe your thoughts in your notebook and then share them with classmates.

RETHINK

2. How and why does the speaker's attitude change as the poem progresses? Cite evidence to support your answer.
3. How would you describe the tone of this poem?

The Sniper (1987), R. B. Kitaj. Oil on canvas, 120″ × 36″. The Saatchi Collection, London.

from **Midsummer**

Derek Walcott

With the stampeding hiss and scurry of green lemmings,
midsummer's leaves race to extinction like the roar
of a Brixton riot tunneled by water hoses;
they seethe toward autumn's fire—it is in their nature,
being men as well as leaves, to die for the sun.
The leaf stems tug at their chains, the branches bending
like Boer cattle under Tory whips that drag every wagon
nearer to apartheid. And, for me, that closes
the child's fairy tale of an antic England—fairy rings,
thatched cottages fenced with dog roses,
a green gale lifting the hair of Warwickshire.
I was there to add some color to the British theater.
"But the blacks can't do Shakespeare, they have no experience."
This was true. Their thick skulls bled with rancor
when the riot police and the skinheads exchanged quips
you could trace to the Sonnets, or the Moor's eclipse.
Praise had bled my lines white of any more anger,
and snow had inducted me into white fellowships,
while Calibans howled down the barred streets of an empire
that began with Caedmon's raceless dew, and is ending
in the alleys of Brixton, burning like Turner's ships.

1 lemmings: small rodents whose migrations in northern Europe sometimes end in mass drownings.

3 Brixton: an area in London.

7 Boer (bōr): belonging to South Africans of Dutch ancestry.

8 apartheid (ə-pärt'hīt'): the official policy of racial segregation formerly practiced in South Africa.

11 Warwickshire (wär'ĭk-shîr'): the English county where Shakespeare was born.

14 rancor (răng'kər): bitter resentment; ill will.

15 skinheads: young British working-class hoodlums—typically having hair cut very short—who are known for their use of violence against members of minority groups.

16 Sonnets: Shakespeare's 154 sonnets; **Moor's eclipse:** a reference to the downfall of the black hero of Shakespeare's *Othello*.

19 Calibans: beastlike human beings (from the name of a grotesque slave in Shakespeare's *The Tempest).*

20 Caedmon (kăd'mən): a seventh-century Anglo-Saxon poet.

21 Turner's ships: burning ships in paintings by the 19th-century British artist J. M. W. Turner.

RESPONDING OPTIONS

FROM PERSONAL RESPONSE *TO* CRITICAL ANALYSIS

REFLECT 1. What image in the excerpt from *Midsummer* made the greatest impression on you? Jot down your thoughts in your notebook.

RETHINK 2. With what specific social issues does the speaker of this poem seem to be most concerned?

Consider
- his comparison of leaves to human beings
- his references to historical events and works of art
- the quotation about blacks in the theater

3. What message about the English, or about European culture in general, do you think the speaker is trying to convey?

4. How does the speaker appear to feel about his own role in society? Cite evidence from the poem to support your answer.

RELATE 5. Do you think that similar kinds of racial prejudice are revealed in "Telephone Conversation" and the excerpt from *Midsummer?* Explain your answer.

6. Do you think there will ever be a time when the majority of the world's people accept cultural and racial differences? Why or why not?

ANOTHER PATHWAY

In a chart like the one shown, summarize what each poem suggests to you about its speaker's character and feelings and about the society in which the speaker lives. Then discuss whether the two speakers have any qualities in common.

Observations		
	"Telephone Conversation"	*from* Midsummer
Speaker		
Society		

LITERARY CONCEPTS

In these poems, both Soyinka and Walcott make use of **satire,** a literary technique that combines criticism with wit or humor for the purpose of improving society. The attitudes of satirists range from mildly or playfully critical to bitter or scornful. Who or what is being satirized in "Telephone Conversation"? in the excerpt from *Midsummer?* How would you describe the attitude underlying the satire in each poem?

QUICKWRITES

1. In an **opinion paper,** tell whether you think the speaker of "Telephone Conversation" handles the landlady's questions appropriately. Give reasons for your opinion.
2. With a partner, create an **advice column,** writing letters in which the speakers of these poems seek help in dealing with the issues presented in the poems, then responding to each letter.
3. Write a guest **editorial** for your school paper, expressing your concerns about a specific violation of human rights that you have either read about or witnessed.

PORTFOLIO *Save your writing. You may want to use it later as a springboard to a piece for your portfolio.*

ALTERNATIVE ACTIVITIES

1. Create a design for a **T-shirt** that promotes what one or both of the speakers might consider an ideal society. Display your work in the classroom.
2. ***Cooperative Learning*** With a group of classmates, prepare a **mock trial** in which the speaker of "Telephone Conversation" accuses the landlady of discrimination. With different members of the group taking on the roles of prosecutor, defense attorney, plaintiff, defendant, and judge, prepare questions and arguments for both sides of the case. Then conduct your trial while the rest of the class acts as the jury.
3. Create a **scrapbook** of photographs, political cartoons, news articles, and other items that you think reflect the social issues dealt with in these poems.

CRITIC'S CORNER

The critic Sven Birkerts has written that in Walcott's *Midsummer* "sharply etched descriptions give way to dark surges." What do you think he meant by this statement? Support your answer with examples from the excerpt presented here.

LITERARY LINKS

Do you think either of these poems share any messages about humanity with W. H. Auden's "The Unknown Citizen" (page 977)? Explain your opinion.

THE WRITER'S STYLE

Derek Walcott is an accomplished painter as well as a writer, and his talent as a poet is often described in terms of his artistic sense. What evidence of this artistic sense, or "artist's eye," can you find in the excerpt from *Midsummer?*

ACROSS THE CURRICULUM

History Investigate the history of civil rights legislation in the United States since 1950. What civil rights laws have been enacted? What events led to their enactment? How have the laws affected racial prejudice?

Wole Soyinka

1934–

Though his travels extend far beyond Nigeria, Wole Soyinka's main interest is in promoting his native Yoruba culture. Like his Nigerian contemporary Chinua Achebe, Soyinka attended high school at Government College and then entered the University of Ibadan. Later, he studied at the University of Leeds in England, graduating with honors in English. His early jobs included work as a bricklayer and a nightclub bouncer, but a job as play reader for London's Royal Court Theatre proved more suitable to his temperament. In 1960, he returned to Nigeria and launched his own theater company, called The 1960 Masks.

Soyinka is probably best known as a playwright. His first major play, *A Dance of the Forests,* was commissioned as a salute to Nigeria's independence in 1960. Since then, his works have been presented in cities throughout the world. In addition, he has produced, directed, and acted in plays and films—both in English and in his native Yoruba language—has organized theater groups at various schools in Nigeria, and has lectured at universities in Britain and the United States.

Like Achebe, Soyinka was actively involved in the Nigerian civil war of the late 1960s. Accused of helping the Biafrans secede, he was arrested by the Nigerian government and imprisoned for over two years. His confinement did not stifle his writing voice, however; in 1969, while he was still incarcerated, his volume *Poems from Prison* was published.

OTHER WORKS "After the Deluge," "Your Logic Frightens Me, Mandela," "Massacre, October 66," "Civilian and Soldier"

Derek Walcott

1930–

Derek Walcott's interest in the arts was inspired by his parents. His mother was a teacher on St. Lucia and acted in a local theater group, and his father, who died when Walcott was just a baby, was an aspiring painter and poet. Walcott once said, "I have felt from my boyhood that I had one function and that was somehow to articulate, not my own experience, but what I saw around me." While hoping to preserve his own culture through his writing, the witty and outgoing writer also relishes cultural diversity. His closest friends include two other Nobel Prize winners featured in this book—the Irish poet Seamus Heaney and the Polish poet, essayist, and novelist Czeslaw Milosz.

Walcott's literary talent developed early. He recalls that as a child he rejected sports for reading, writing, and playing with puppets. At the age of 18, he borrowed $200 from his mother to publish his first book of poems and then sold copies on the street to pay back the loan. At the age of 20, he and his twin brother organized a theater group in St. Lucia and staged a play that Walcott had written. While still a student at the University of the West Indies in Jamaica, he published several works, among them a play.

After studying drama in New York for a year, Walcott moved to Trinidad, where he recruited and trained the first professional West Indian acting troupe. Since 1970, he has taught at various schools in the United States—including Yale, Columbia, and Boston University—in recent years dividing his time between homes in Boston, Trinidad, and St. Lucia.

OTHER WORKS "A Far Cry from Africa," "A Sea Change," "The Liberator," "Port of Spain," "Hurucan"

PREVIEWING

FICTION

Six Feet of the Country

Nadine Gordimer

PERSONAL CONNECTION

Have you ever encountered a situation in which a person claimed to understand and respect another race or culture but really showed little understanding or respect? Discuss your experiences and insights with your classmates.

HISTORICAL CONNECTION

Nadine Gordimer writes about the people of her South African homeland and reveals how the system of apartheid has affected their lives. The term *apartheid*—which means "separateness" in Afrikaans, the language of the Dutch settlers of South Africa—refers to an official system of racial separation enforced by the South African government from 1948 to 1991. During the first 20 years of that period, laws were enacted that segregated education and housing, restricted the movement and voting rights of nonwhites, and gave the government far-reaching police powers to ensure compliance with apartheid. In 1961, South Africa withdrew from the United Nations after other member nations severely criticized its racial policies.

In the 1970s and 1980s, the government of South Africa, responding to years of national and international protest, began to repeal some apartheid laws and to open public facilities and transportation systems to all races. Many apartheid regulations remained, however, as did segregation of schools and neighborhoods. Finally, in 1991, the government granted full rights to nonwhites, repealing the last of the discriminatory laws that had formed the basis of apartheid. Although apartheid has now been officially dismantled, its economic and social effects are likely to linger for some time.

From the first days of apartheid, many white South Africans opposed the system for its inhumanity and lack of respect for people of other cultures. A few, like Nadine Gordimer, openly expressed their disapproval of the system. In "Six Feet of the Country," first published in the 1950s, she examines the experiences and attitudes of a British couple—a businessman and a former actress—who have moved to the South African countryside.

WRITING CONNECTION

On the basis of the title "Six Feet of the Country" and the information provided in the Historical Connection, what do you think this story will be about? Jot down your ideas in your notebook. As you read, compare your predictions with what actually happens in the story.

Using Your Reading Log Use your reading log to record your responses to the questions inserted in this selection. Also jot down other thoughts and feelings that come to you as you read.

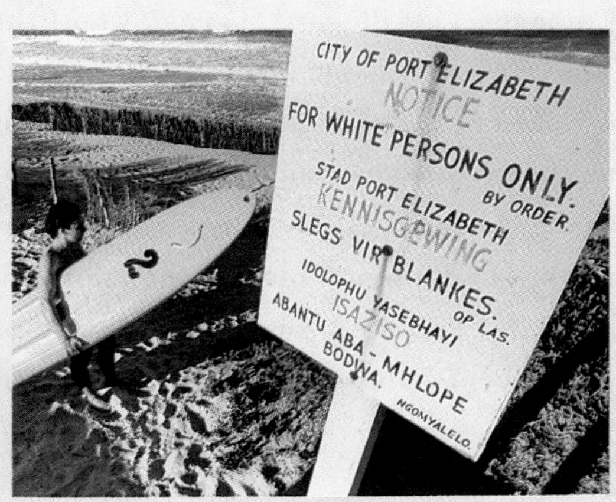

• CULTURAL/HISTORICAL CONNECTION

Six Feet of the Country

Nadine Gordimer

My wife and I are not real farmers—not even Lerice, really. We bought our place, ten miles out of Johannesburg on one of the main roads, to change something in ourselves, I suppose; you seem to rattle about so much within a marriage like ours. You long to hear nothing but a deep, satisfying silence when you sound a marriage. The farm hasn't managed that for us, of course, but it has done other things, unexpected, illogical. Lerice, who I thought would retire there in Chekhovian sadness for a month or two, and then leave the place to the servants while she tried yet again to get a part she wanted and become the actress she would like to be, has sunk into the business of running the farm with all the serious intensity with which she once imbued the shadows in a playwright's mind. I should have given it up long ago if it had not been for her. Her hands, once small and plain and well-kept—she was not the sort of actress who wears red paint and diamond rings—are hard as a dog's pads.

WORDS TO KNOW

imbue (ĭm-byo͞o') *v.* to fill with a quality; saturate

I, of course, am there only in the evenings and at week-ends. I am a partner in a luxury-travel agency, which is flourishing—needs to be, as I tell Lerice, in order to carry on the farm. Still, though I know we can't afford it, and though the sweetish smell of the fowls Lerice breeds sickens me, so that I avoid going past their runs, the farm is beautiful in a way I had almost forgotten—especially on a Sunday morning when I get up and go out into the paddock and see not the palm trees and fish pond and imitation-stone bird-bath of the suburbs but white ducks on the dam, the lucerne[1] field brilliant as window-dresser's grass, and the little, stocky, mean-eyed bull, lustful but bored, having his face tenderly licked by one of his ladies. Lerice comes out with her hair uncombed, in her hand a stick dripping with cattle-dip. She will stand and look dreamily for a moment, the way she would pretend to look sometimes in those plays. "They'll mate tomorrow," she will say. "This is their second day. Look how she loves him, my little Napoleon." So that when people come out to see us on Sunday afternoon, I am likely to hear myself saying, as I pour out the drinks, "When I drive back home from the city every day, past those rows of suburban houses, I wonder how the devil we ever did stand it. . . . Would you care to look around?" And there I am, taking some pretty girl and her young husband stumbling down to our river-bank, the girl catching her stockings on the mealie-stooks[2] and stepping over cow-turds humming with jewel-green flies while she says, ". . . the *tensions* of the damned city. And you're near enough to get into town to a show, too! I think it's wonderful. Why, you've got it both ways!"

And for a moment I accept the triumph as if I *had* managed it—the impossibility that I've been trying for all my life—just as if the truth was that you could get it "both ways," instead of finding yourself with not even one way or the other but a third, one you had not provided for at all.

But even in our saner moments, when I find Lerice's earthy enthusiasms just as irritating as I once found her histrionical[3] ones, and she finds what she calls my "jealousy" of her capacity for enthusiasm as big a proof of my inadequacy for her as a mate as ever it was, we do believe that we have at least honestly escaped those tensions peculiar to the city about which our visitors speak. When Johannesburg people speak of "tension" they don't mean hurrying people in crowded streets, the struggle for money, or the general competitive character of city life. They mean the guns under the white men's pillows and the burglar bars on the white men's windows. They mean those strange moments on city pavements when a black man won't stand aside for a white man.

Out in the country, even ten miles out, life is better than that. In the country, there is a lingering remnant of the pretransitional stage; our relationship with the blacks is almost feudal.[4] Wrong, I suppose, obsolete, but more comfortable all round. We have no burglar bars, no gun. Lerice's farm-boys have their wives and their piccanins[5] living with them on the land. They brew their sour beer without the fear of police raids. In fact, we've always rather prided ourselves that the poor devils have nothing much to fear, being with us; Lerice even keeps an eye on their children, with all the competence of a woman who has never had a child of her own, and she certainly doctors

---

1. **lucerne** (lo͞o-sûrn′): a British term for alfalfa.
2. **mealie-stooks:** a South African term for cornstalks.
3. **histrionical:** theatrical; dramatic.
4. **feudal** (fyo͞od′l): characteristic of feudalism—the medieval European economic, political, and social system in which the serfs who worked the land were protected by, and owed allegiance to, their overlords.
5. **piccanins** (pĭk′ə-nĭnz′): in South Africa, a term (usually considered derogatory) for native African children.

them all—children and adults—like babies whenever they happen to be sick.

It was because of this that we were not particularly startled one night last winter when the boy Albert came knocking at our window long after we had gone to bed. I wasn't in our bed but sleeping in the little dressing-room-cum-linen room next door, because Lerice had annoyed me, and I didn't want to find myself softening toward her simply because of the sweet smell of the talcum powder on her flesh after her bath. She came and woke me up. "Albert says one of the boys is very sick," she said. "I think you'd better go down and see. He wouldn't get us up at this hour for nothing."

"What time is it?"

"What does it matter?" Lerice is maddeningly logical.

I got up awkwardly as she watched me—how is it I always feel a fool when I have deserted her bed? After all, I know from the way she never looks at me when she talks to me at breakfast the next day that she is hurt and humiliated at my not wanting her—and I went out, clumsy with sleep.

"Which of the boys is it?" I asked Albert as we followed the dance of my torch.

"He's too sick. Very sick, *Baas,*"[6] he said.

"But who? Franz?" I remembered Franz had had a bad cough for the past week.

Albert did not answer; he had given me the path, and was walking along beside me in the tall dead grass. When the light of the torch caught his face, I saw that he looked acutely embarrassed. "What's this all about?" I said.

He lowered his head under the glance of the light. "It's not me, *Baas.* I don't know. Petrus he send me."

Irritated, I hurried him along to the huts. And there, on Petrus's iron bedstead, with its brick stilts, was a young man, dead. On his forehead there was still a light, cold sweat; his body was warm. The boys stood around as they do in the kitchen when it is discovered that someone has broken a dish—uncooperative, silent. Somebody's wife hung about in the shadows, her hands wrung together under her apron.

EVALUATE

What does the narrator reveal about himself as he shares his observations of the others?

I had not seen a dead man since the war. This was very different. I felt like the others—extraneous, useless.

"What was the matter?" I asked.

The woman patted at her chest and shook her head to indicate the painful impossibility of breathing.

He must have died of pneumonia.

I turned to Petrus. "Who was this boy? What was he doing here?" The light of a candle on the floor showed that Petrus was weeping. He followed me out the door.

When we were outside, in the dark, I waited for him to speak. But he didn't. "Now come on, Petrus, you must tell me who this boy was. Was he a friend of yours?"

"He's my brother, *Baas.* He come from Rhodesia to look for work."

The story startled Lerice and me a little. The young boy had walked down from Rhodesia to look for work in Johannesburg, had caught a chill from sleeping out along the way, and had lain ill in his brother Petrus's hut since his arrival three days before. Our boys had been

6. ***baas*** (bäs) *Afrikaans:* master; boss (formerly used as a term of address by black South Africans when speaking to a white man).

WORDS TO KNOW

extraneous (ĭk-strā′nē-əs) *adj.* not relevant; inessential

frightened to ask us for help for him because we had not been intended ever to know of his presence. Rhodesian natives are barred from entering the Union[7] unless they have a permit; the young man was an illegal immigrant. No doubt our boys had managed the whole thing successfully several times before; a number of relatives must have walked the seven or eight hundred miles from poverty to the paradise of zoot suits,[8] police raids, and black slum townships that is their *Egoli,*[9] City of Gold—the Bantu name for Johannesburg. It was merely a matter of getting such a man to lie low on our farm until a job could be found with someone who would be glad to take the risk of prosecution for employing an illegal immigrant in exchange for the services of someone as yet untainted by the city.

Well, this was one who would never get up again.

"You would think they would have felt they could tell *us,*" said Lerice next morning. "Once the man was ill. You would have thought at least—" When she is getting intense over something, she has a way of standing in the middle of a room as people do when they are shortly to leave on a journey, looking searchingly about her at the most familiar objects as if she had never seen them before. I had noticed that in Petrus's presence in the kitchen, earlier, she had the air of being almost offended with him, almost hurt.

In any case, I really haven't the time or inclination any more to go into everything in our life that I know Lerice, from those alarmed and pressing eyes of hers, would like us to go into. She is the kind of woman who doesn't mind if she looks plain, or odd; I don't suppose she would even care if she knew how strange she looks when her whole face is out of proportion with urgent uncertainty. I said, "Now, I'm the one who'll have to do all the dirty work, I suppose."

She was still staring at me, trying me out with those eyes—wasting her time, if she only knew.

"I'll have to notify the health authorities," I said calmly. "They can't just cart him off and bury him. After all, we don't really know what he died of."

She simply stood there, as if she had given up—simply ceased to see me at all.

I don't know when I've been so irritated. "It might have been something contagious," I said. "God knows?" There was no answer.

I am not enamored of holding conversations with myself. I went out to shout to one of the boys to open the garage and get the car ready for my morning drive to town.

As I had expected, it turned out to be quite a business. I had to notify the police as well as the health authorities, and answer a lot of tedious questions: How was it I was ignorant of the boy's presence? If I did not supervise my native quarters, how did I know that that sort of thing didn't go on all the time? Et cetera, et cetera. And when I flared up and told them that so long as my natives did their work, I didn't think it my right or concern to poke my nose into their private lives, I got from the coarse, dull-witted police sergeant one of those looks that come not from any thinking process going on in the brain but from that faculty common to all who are possessed by the master-race theory—a look of insanely inane certainty. He grinned at me with a mixture of scorn and delight at my stupidity.

Then I had to explain to Petrus why the health authorities had to take away the body

7. **Union:** Union of South Africa—the South African state preceding the formation of the Republic of South Africa in 1961.

8. **zoot suits:** flashy men's suits with broad padded shoulders and baggy trousers.

9. ***Egoli*** (ā-gō′lē).

WORDS TO KNOW	
	untainted (ŭn-tān′tĭd) *adj.* not contaminated; unspoiled
	enamor (ĭ-năm′ər) *v.* to inspire with love; fascinate
	inane (ĭn-ān′) *adj.* foolish; senseless

for a post-mortem[10]—and, in fact, what a post-mortem was. When I telephoned the health department some days later to find out the result, I was told the cause of death was, as we had thought, pneumonia, and that the body had been suitably disposed of. I went out to where Petrus was mixing a mash for the fowls and told him that it was all right, there would be no trouble; his brother had died from that pain in his chest. Petrus put down the paraffin tin and said, "When can we go to fetch him, *Baas?*"

"To fetch him?"

"Will the *Baas* please ask them when we must come?"

I went back inside and called Lerice, all over the house. She came down the stairs from the spare bedrooms, and I said, "*Now* what am I going to do? When I told Petrus, he just asked calmly when they could go and fetch the body. They think they're going to bury him themselves."

"Well, go back and tell him," said Lerice. "You must tell him. Why didn't you tell him then?"

When I found Petrus again, he looked up politely. "Look, Petrus," I said. "You can't go to fetch your brother. They've done it already—they've *buried* him, you understand?"

"Where?" he said, slowly, dully, as if he thought that perhaps he was getting this wrong.

"You see, he was a stranger. They knew he wasn't from here, and they didn't know he had some of his people here, so they thought they must bury him." It was difficult to make a pauper's grave sound like a privilege.

"Please, *Baas,* the *Baas* must ask them?" But he did not mean that he wanted to know the burial-place. He simply ignored the incomprehensible machinery I told him had set to work on his dead brother; he wanted the brother back.

"But Petrus," I said, "how can I? Your brother is buried already. I can't ask them now."

"Oh *Baas!*" he said. He stood with his bran-smeared hands uncurled at his sides, one corner of his mouth twitching.

"Good God, Petrus, they won't listen to me! They can't, anyway. I'm sorry, but I can't do it. You understand?"

He just kept on looking at me, out of his knowledge that white men have everything, can do anything; if they don't, it is because they won't.

And then, at dinner Lerice started. "You could at least phone," she said.

"*Christ,* what d'you think I am? Am I supposed to bring the dead back to life?"

But I could not exaggerate my way out of this ridiculous responsibility that had been thrust on me. "Phone them up," she went on. "And at least you'll be able to tell him you've done it and they've explained that it's impossible."

She disappeared somewhere into the kitchen quarters after coffee. A little later she came back to tell me, "The old father's coming down from Rhodesia to be at the funeral. He's got a permit and he's already on his way."

Unfortunately, it was not impossible to get the body back. The authorities said that it was somewhat irregular, but that since the hygiene conditions had been fulfilled, they could not refuse permission for exhumation.[11] I found out that, with the undertaker's charges, it would cost twenty pounds. Ah, I thought, that settles it. On five pounds a month, Petrus won't have twenty pounds—and just as well, since it couldn't do the dead any good. Certainly I should not offer it to him myself. Twenty pounds—or anything else within reason, for that matter—I would have spent without grudging it on doctors or medicines that might have helped the boy when he was alive. Once he was dead, I had no intention of encouraging Petrus to throw away, on a gesture, more than he spent to clothe his whole family in a year.

When I told him, in the kitchen that night, he said, "Twenty pounds?"

---

10. **post-mortem:** an examination of a corpse to determine the cause of death.

11. **exhumation** (ĕg′zyo͞o-mā′shən): the removal of a corpse from a grave.

I said, "Yes, that's right, twenty pounds."

For a moment, I had the feeling, from the look on his face, that he was calculating. But when he spoke again I thought I must have imagined it. "We must pay twenty pounds!" he said in the far-away voice in which a person speaks of something so unattainable that it does not bear thinking about.

"All right, Petrus," I said in dismissal, and went back to the living-room.

The next morning before I went to town, Petrus asked to see me. "Please *Baas,*" he said, awkwardly handing me a bundle of notes. They're so seldom on the giving rather than the receiving side, poor devils, that they don't really know how to hand money to a white man. There it was, the twenty pounds, in ones and halves, some creased and folded until they were soft as dirty rags, others smooth and fairly new—Franz's money, I suppose, and Albert's, and Dora the cook's, and Jacob the gardener's, and God knows who else's besides, from all the farms and small holdings round about. I took it in irritation more than in astonishment, really—irritation at the waste, the uselessness of this sacrifice by people so poor. Just like the poor everywhere, I thought, who stint themselves the decencies of life in order to insure themselves the decencies of death. So incomprehensible to people like Lerice and me, who regard life as something to be spent extravagantly and, if we think about death at all, regard it as the final bankruptcy.

CLARIFY

Why is the narrator so surprised by the farm hands' efforts?

The servants don't work on Saturday afternoon anyway, so it was a good day for the funeral. Petrus and his father had borrowed our donkey-cart to fetch the coffin from the city, where, Petrus told Lerice on their return, everything was "nice"—the coffin waiting for them, already sealed up to save them from what must have been a rather unpleasant sight after two weeks' interment. (It had taken all that time for the authorities and the undertaker to make

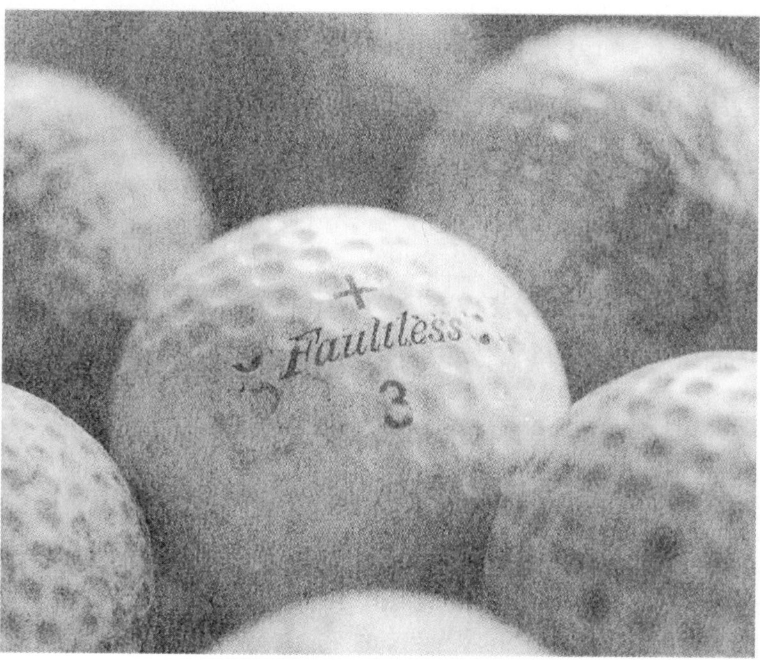

the final arrangements for moving the body.) All morning, the coffin lay in Petrus's hut, awaiting the trip to the little old burial-ground, just outside the eastern boundary of our farm, that was a relic of the days when this was a real farming district rather than a fashionable rural estate. It was pure chance that I happened to be down there near the fence when the procession came past; once again Lerice had forgotten her promise to me and had made the house uninhabitable on a Saturday afternoon. I had come home and been infuriated to find her in a pair of filthy old slacks and with her hair uncombed since the night before, having all the varnish scraped off the living-room floor, if you

WORDS TO KNOW

stint (stĭnt) *v.* to limit to a small amount; give sparingly

please. So I had taken my No. 8 iron and gone off to practice my approach shots. In my annoyance I had forgotten about the funeral, and was reminded only when I saw the procession coming up the path along the outside of the fence toward me; from where I was standing, you can see the graves quite clearly, and that day the sun glinted on bits of broken pottery, a lopsided homemade cross, and jam-jars brown with rain-water and dead flowers.

Funeral Procession (1940), Ellis Wilson. Armistad Research Center, Tulane University, New Orleans, Louisiana.

I felt a little awkward, and did not know whether to go on hitting my golf ball or stop at least until the whole gathering was decently past. The donkey-cart creaks and screeches with every revolution of the wheels and it came along in a slow, halting fashion somehow peculiarly suited to the two donkeys who drew it, their little potbellies rubbed and rough, their heads sunk between the shafts, and their ears flattened back with an air submissive and downcast; peculiarly suited, too, to the group of men and women who came along slowly behind. The patient ass. Watching, I thought, you can see now why the creature became a Biblical symbol. Then the procession drew level with me and stopped, so I had to put down my club. The coffin was taken down off the cart—it was a shiny, yellow-varnished wood, like cheap furniture—and the donkeys twitched their ears against the flies. Petrus, Franz, Albert and the old father from Rhodesia hoisted it on their shoulders and the procession moved on, on foot. It was really a very awkward moment. I stood there rather foolishly at the fence, quite still, and slowly they filed past, not looking up, the four men bent beneath the shiny wooden box, and the straggling troop of mourners. All of them were servants or neighbors' servants whom I knew as casual, easygoing gossipers about our lands or kitchen. I heard the old man's breathing.

QUESTION

Why does the narrator feel awkward as the funeral passes?

I had just bent to pick up my club again when there was a sort of jar in the flowing solemnity of their processional mood; I felt it at once, like a wave of heat along the air, or one of those sudden currents of cold catching at your legs in a placid stream. The old man's voice was muttering

WORDS TO KNOW

submissive (səb-mĭs'ĭv) *adj.* yielding to the control of another

something, and they bumped into one another, some pressing to go on, others hissing at them to be still. I could see that they were embarrassed, but they could not ignore the voice; it was much the way that the mumblings of a prophet, though not clear at first, arrest the mind. The corner of the coffin the old man carried was sagging at an angle; he seemed to be trying to get out from under the weight of it. Now Petrus expostulated with him.

The little boy who had been left to watch the donkeys dropped the reins and ran to see. I don't know why—unless it was for the same reason people crowd round someone who has fainted in a cinema—but I parted the wires of the fence and went through, after him.

Petrus lifted his eyes to me—to anybody—with distress and horror. The old man from Rhodesia had let go of the coffin entirely, and the three others, unable to support it on their own, had laid it on the ground, in the pathway. Already there was a film of dust lightly wavering up its shiny sides. I did not understand what the old man was saying; I hesitated to interfere. But now the whole seething group turned on my silence. The old man himself came over to me, with his hands outspread and shaking, and spoke directly to me, saying something that I could tell from the tone, without understanding the words, was shocking and extraordinary.

"What is it, Petrus? What's wrong?" I appealed.

Petrus threw up his hands, bowed his head in a series of hysterical shakes, then thrust his face up at me suddenly.

"He says, 'My son was not so heavy.'"

Silence. I could hear the old man breathing; he kept his mouth a little open as old people do.

"My son was young and thin," he said, at last, in English.

Again silence. Then babble broke out. The old man thundered against everybody; his teeth were yellowed and few, and he had one of those fine, grizzled, sweeping moustaches that one doesn't often see nowadays, which must have been grown in emulation of early Empire builders.[12] It seemed to frame all his utterances with a special validity, perhaps merely because it was the symbol of the traditional wisdom of age—an idea so fearfully rooted that it carries still something awesome beyond reason. He shocked them; they thought he was mad, but they had to listen to him. With his own hands he began to prise the lid off the coffin and three of the men came forward to help him. Then he sat down on the ground; very old, very weak, and unable to speak, he merely lifted a trembling hand toward what was there. He abdicated, he handed it over to them; he was no good any more.

They crowded round to look (and so did I), and now they forgot the nature of this surprise and the occasion of grief to which it belonged, and for a few minutes were carried up in the astonishment of the surprise itself. They gasped and flared noisily with excitement. I even noticed the little boy who had held the donkeys jumping up and down, almost weeping with rage because the backs of the grown-ups crowded him out of his view.

In the coffin was someone no one had ever seen before: a heavily built, rather light-skinned native with a neatly stitched scar on his forehead—perhaps from a blow in a brawl that had also dealt him some other, slower-working injury which had killed him.

I wrangled with the authorities for a week over that body. I had the feeling that they were shocked, in a laconic fashion, by their own mistake, but that in the confusion of their anonymous dead they were helpless to put it right. They said to me, "We are trying to find out," and "We are still making enquiries." It was as if at any moment they might conduct me into their mortuary and say, "There! Lift up the sheets; look for him—your poultry boy's brother. There are so many black faces—surely one will do?"

12. **Empire builders:** British colonizers.

WORDS TO KNOW
expostulate (ĭk-spŏs′chə-lāt′) *v.* to reason earnestly in an effort to correct or dissuade
laconic (lə-kŏn′ĭk) *adj.* making use of few words

And every evening when I got home Petrus was waiting in the kitchen. "Well, they're trying. They're still looking. The *Baas* is seeing to it for you, Petrus," I would tell him. "God, half the time I should be in the office I'm driving around the back end of town chasing after this affair," I added aside, to Lerice, one night.

She and Petrus both kept their eyes turned on me as I spoke, and, oddly, for those moments they looked exactly alike, though it sounds impossible: my wife, with her high, white forehead and her attenuated Englishwoman's body, and the poultry boy, with his horny bare feet below khaki trousers tied at the knee with string and the peculiar rankness of his nervous sweat coming from his skin.

QUESTION

Why do Lerice and Petrus look alike to the narrator at this point?

"What makes you so indignant, so determined about this now?" said Lerice suddenly.

I stared at her. "It's a matter of principle. Why should they get away with a swindle? It's time these officials had a jolt from someone who'll bother to take the trouble."

She said, "Oh." And as Petrus slowly opened the kitchen door to leave, sensing that the talk had gone beyond him, she turned away too.

I continued to pass on assurances to Petrus every evening, but although what I said was the same, and the voice in which I said it was the same, every evening it sounded weaker. At last, it became clear that we would never get Petrus's brother back, because nobody really knew where he was. Somewhere in a graveyard as uniform as a housing scheme, somewhere under a number that didn't belong to him, or in the medical school, perhaps, laboriously reduced to layers of muscles and strings of nerves? Goodness knows. He had no identity in this world anyway.

It was only then, and in a voice of shame, that Petrus asked me to try and get the money back.

"From the way he asks, you'd think he was robbing his dead brother," I said to Lerice later. But as I've said, Lerice had got so intense about this business that she couldn't even appreciate a little ironic smile.

I tried to get the money; Lerice tried. We both telephoned and wrote and argued, but nothing came of it. It appeared that the main expense had been the undertaker, and, after all, he had done his job. So the whole thing was a complete waste, even more of a waste for the poor devils than I had thought it would be.

The old man from Rhodesia was about Lerice's father's size, so she gave him one of her father's old suits and he went back home rather better off, for the winter, than he had come. ❖

WORDS TO KNOW

attenuated (ə-tĕn′yo͞o-ā′tĭd) *adj.* slender; thin **attenuate** *v.*

RESPONDING OPTIONS

FROM PERSONAL RESPONSE TO CRITICAL ANALYSIS

REFLECT

1. How did you react to the ending of this story? Share your impressions with your classmates.

RETHINK

2. What do you think of the narrator's comment, in the last sentence of the story, that the old man "went back home rather better off . . . than he had come"?
3. Could the narrator have done anything differently in dealing with the mix-up of the corpses?
4. How would you describe the relationship between the narrator and Lerice?
   Consider
   - how he describes their marriage
   - each character's values and interests
   - the effect of this incident on their relationship
5. What do you consider the most powerful conflict in this story? Give reasons for your opinion.
6. How did the predictions you made for the Writing Connection on page 1099 compare with the actual events of the story?

RELATE

7. The characters in "Six Feet of the Country" find that dealing with government officials can be horribly frustrating. Could anything this frustrating happen in your own community?

ANOTHER PATHWAY

Cooperative Learning

With a small group of classmates, discuss and record the ideas, impulses, and circumstances that seem to motivate the narrator, Lerice, Petrus, Petrus's father, and the health authorities. After comparing your group's findings with those of other groups, compile a class chart like the one shown.

Character or Group	Motivations
narrator	obeying the rules, avoiding controversy
Lerice	

LITERARY CONCEPTS

As you know, the term ***point of view*** refers to the narrative method used in a literary work. "Six Feet of the Country" is told from the first-person point of view of a narrator who is also the story's main character. All we know about him, his wife, Petrus, Petrus's father, and the story's events is based on his observations and thoughts, which may be colored or distorted by his personal perspective. With a partner, go back through the story to identify passages that have a strong effect on you. Then rewrite one of those passages, telling the events from a third-person point of view. Discuss the two versions and speculate about Gordimer's reasons for using the first-person point of view.

QUICKWRITES

1. Nadine Gordimer has been praised for her ability to convey the importance of respecting other cultures. Write a **review** of "Six Feet of the Country," in which you explain how the story demonstrates this idea.
2. Compose a **memo** to a history teacher, recommending that Gordimer's story be required reading for a unit on South Africa.

PORTFOLIO *Save your writing. You may want to use it later as a springboard to a piece for your portfolio.*

ALTERNATIVE ACTIVITIES

1. Create a design for a **monument** to Petrus's brother, symbolizing the plight of his family and others like them.
2. With a classmate, improvise a **dialogue** in which the narrator and Lerice, after the old man's departure, talk over the events of the story. Try to convey the nature of their marital relationship, as well as the reactions of each to the events.

THE WRITER'S STYLE

Dashes are frequently used as punctuation in "Six Feet of the Country." Locate instances of their use throughout the story, and think about what other punctuation might be substituted in each case. Explain why the dashes might be more effective than the alternative forms of punctuation.

LITERARY LINKS

Both "Telephone Conversation" and "Six Feet of the Country" explore interactions between people of different races. Which selection do you find more bitter in tone? Explain your answer.

CRITIC'S CORNER

Critics praise the way Gordimer concisely and graphically conveys meaning by using figurative language, such as similes (comparisons expressed through the use of *like* or *as*). On page 1100, for example, Gordimer writes, "Her hands . . . are hard as a dog's pads." Find other similes in the story, and tell how they affect your impressions of the characters and events.

ACROSS THE CURRICULUM

History As a result of the April 1994 election in South Africa, in which blacks were permitted to vote for the first time, Nelson Mandela became the leader of the nation. Use the *Readers' Guide to Periodical Literature* to locate recent articles on Mandela and events in South Africa. Summarize the articles and share the information with the class.

Geography Using a reliable atlas as a resource, draw a map of South Africa, outlining its four provinces and highlighting the one in which this story is set. Be sure to indicate the main cities and physical features of each province.

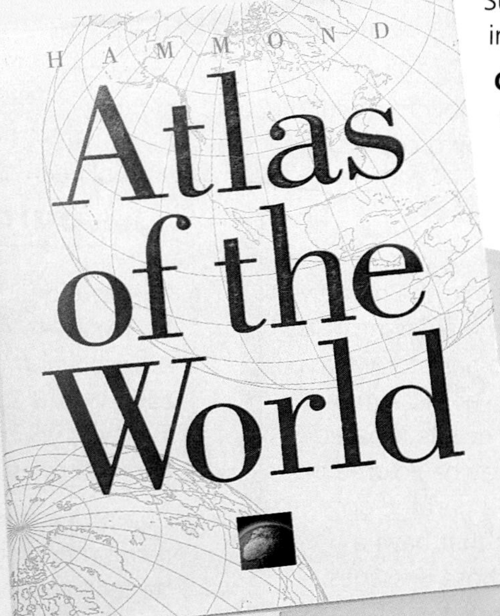

WORDS TO KNOW

EXERCISE A For each phrase in the first column, write the letter of the synonymous phrase in the second column.

1. **laconic** account
2. idiotic chorus
3. manageable sibling
4. infatuated faltering
5. pure pigment
6. **stint** the stallion
7. **expostulate** on the way
8. permeate with sadness
9. **attenuated** agent
10. variety of unnecessary things

a. dispute en route
b. **untainted** paint
c. short report
d. **inane** refrain
e. delicate delegate
f. **enamored** stammering
g. **submissive** sister
h. **imbue** with the blues
i. **extraneous** miscellany
j. underfeed the steed

EXERCISE B Work with a partner to come up with an appropriate phrase—such as "**extraneous** details" or "**inane** chatter"—for each vocabulary word. Then challenge another pair of students to compete with each other to guess one of the phrases, allowing them to suggest letters one by one (as in the game hangman or the TV show *Wheel of Fortune*). When one has guessed the phrase, compete with your partner to guess a phrase that they have written.

NADINE GORDIMER

1923–

Nadine Gordimer is known for her beautifully crafted novels and short stories dealing with themes of exile, alienation, and life's missed opportunities. Born into a white middle-class family in the Transvaal province of South Africa, she spent much of her childhood in solitude, which she relieved by visiting her local library. She began to write while still a child, publishing her first short story at the age of 15.

At first Gordimer concentrated on writing short stories, but as her subject matter grew increasingly complex, she turned to the novel. Almost from the beginning, critics noted her precise ear for spoken language, her sensitivity to the rhythm of the spoken word, her keen sense of social satire, and the strong moral purpose of her work. Since much of her writing is set in South Africa, her characters have inevitably been shaped by the political situation there; yet even as she has used her talents and influence to oppose apartheid, she has refused to let her writing become propaganda. Instead, she has said, she strives simply to portray the society in which she lives: "I thrust my hand as deep as it will go, deep into the life around me, and I write about what comes up."

In 1974 Gordimer won the Booker Prize for her novel *The Conservationist,* and in 1991 she received the Nobel Prize in literature. She has been called "one of the most gifted practitioners of the short story anywhere in English."

OTHER WORKS *Burger's Daughter, July's People, Jump and Other Stories*

PREVIEWING

NONFICTION

from Writing as an Act of Hope

Isabel Allende

PERSONAL CONNECTION

With a group of classmates, create a list of 15 writers whose work you have read in this book, including poets, essayists, playwrights, and short story writers. In a discussion, decide what you think each writer's main reason for writing was. How many of the reasons you've identified have something to do with social commentary? Share your findings with other classmates.

LITERARY/CULTURAL CONNECTION

Like South African literature, the literature of Latin America—where political unrest and economic hardship have been facts of life during much of the past century—is characterized by a good deal of social commentary. Since the 19th century, many Latin American writers, even those living in exile elsewhere, have had a strong reason for writing—to speak out about the social and political problems of their homelands. Until recently, however, the handling of such issues was the exclusive domain of male writers. In the region's male-dominated culture, female writers were discouraged from engaging in political or intellectual commentary, even in fiction. It was the Chilean author Isabel Allende who, in the 1980s, became the first Latin American female to produce a widely read novel that focuses on the effects of social and political turmoil.

Allende's writing is inspired principally by her Chilean roots and her family's experiences. For example, her popular first novel, *The House of the Spirits,* is a family saga based on the history of her own family and is set in a Latin American country that many readers assume to be Chile. In all of her novels, she skillfully interweaves realism and fantasy—so much so that she herself claims to find it difficult to distinguish reality from the inventions of her mind in her writing.

WRITING CONNECTION

In your notebook, list all the different kinds of writing—such as essays, letters, notes, receipts, poetry, and diary entries—that you do on a regular basis at school, at home, and (if you have a job) at work. Next to each item, briefly identify your reasons for engaging in that type of writing. Then, as you read the following excerpt from "Writing as an Act of Hope," decide whether you share any of Allende's motivations for writing.

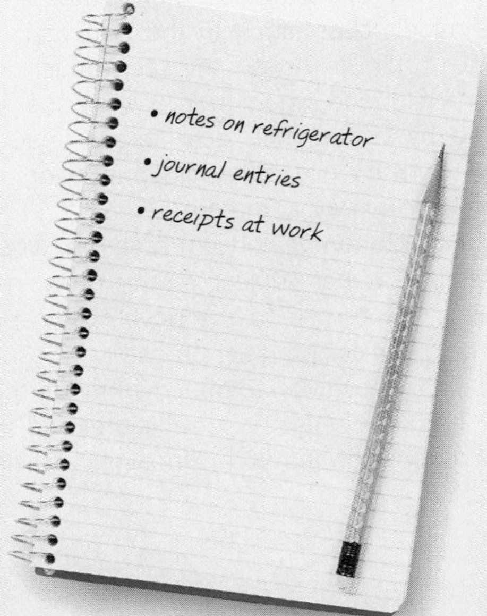

• notes on refrigerator
• journal entries
• receipts at work

LASERLINKS
• CULTURAL CONNECTION

FROM

Writing as an Act of Hope

ISABEL ALLENDE

IN EVERY INTERVIEW DURING THE LAST FEW YEARS I ENCOUNTERED TWO QUESTIONS THAT FORCED ME TO DEFINE MYSELF AS A WRITER AND AS A HUMAN BEING: WHY DO I WRITE? AND WHO DO I WRITE FOR? TONIGHT I WILL TRY TO ANSWER THOSE QUESTIONS.

IN 1981, IN CARACAS, I PUT A SHEET OF PAPER IN MY TYPEWRITER AND WROTE THE FIRST SENTENCE OF *THE HOUSE OF THE SPIRITS:* "BARABBAS CAME TO US BY SEA." AT THAT MOMENT I DIDN'T KNOW WHY I WAS DOING IT, OR FOR WHOM.

In fact, I assumed that no one would ever read it except my mother, who reads everything I write. I was not even conscious that I was writing a novel. I thought I was writing a letter—a spiritual letter to my grandfather, a formidable old patriarch,[1] whom I loved dearly. He had reached almost one hundred years of age and decided that he was too tired to go on living, so he sat in his armchair and refused to drink or eat, calling for Death, who was kind enough to take him very soon.

I wanted to bid him farewell, but I couldn't go back to Chile, and I knew that calling him on the telephone was useless, so I began this letter. I wanted to tell him that he could go in peace because all his memories were with me. I had forgotten nothing. I had all his anecdotes, all the characters of the family, and to prove it I began writing the story of Rose, the fiancée my grandfather had had, who is called Rose the Beautiful in the book. She really existed; she's not a copy from García Márquez,[2] as some people have said.

For a year I wrote every night with no hesitation or plan. Words came out like a violent torrent. I had thousands of untold words stuck in my chest, threatening to choke me. The long silence of exile was turning me to stone; I needed to open a valve and let the river of secret words find a way out. At the end of that year there were five hundred pages on my table; it didn't look like a letter anymore. On the other hand, my grandfather had died long before, so the spiritual message had already reached him. So I thought, "Well, maybe in this way I can tell some other people about him, and about my country, and about my family and myself." So I just organized it a little bit, tied the manuscript with a pink ribbon for luck, and took it to some publishers.

The spirit of my grandmother was protecting the book from the very beginning, so it was refused everywhere in Venezuela. Nobody wanted it—it was too long; I was a woman; nobody knew me. So I sent it by mail to Spain, and the book was published there. It had reviews, and it was translated and distributed in other countries.

In the process of writing the anecdotes of the past, and recalling the emotions and pains of my fate, and telling part of the history of my country, I found that life became more comprehensible and the world more tolerable. I felt that my roots had been recovered and that during that patient exercise of daily writing I had also recovered my own soul. I felt at that time that writing was unavoidable—that I couldn't keep away from it. Writing is such a pleasure; it is always a private orgy, creating and recreating the world according to my own laws, fulfilling in those pages all my dreams and exorcising some of my demons.

but

BUT that is a rather simple explanation. There are other reasons for writing.

Six years and three books have passed since *The House of the Spirits*. Many things have changed for me in that time. I can no longer pretend to be naïve, or elude questions, or find refuge in irony. Now I am constantly confronted

1. **patriarch** (pā′trē-ärk′): a respected old man, especially one who is head of a family, clan, or tribe.
2. **García Márquez** (gär-sē′ə mär′kĕs): Gabriel García Márquez (1928–), a Colombian novelist and short story writer.

WORDS TO KNOW **exorcising** (ĕk′sôr-sī′zĭng) *adj.* driving out (an evil spirit) by prayer, ceremony, or command **exorcise** *v.*

Sin título [Untitled] (1985), Rocío Maldonado. Acrylic with collaged elements on canvas with painted frame, 69″ × 85″ × 6″, courtesy of Gallery OMR, Mexico City.

by my readers, and they can be very tough. It's not enough to write in a state of trance, overwhelmed by the desire to tell a story. One has to be responsible for each word, each idea. Be very careful: the written word cannot be erased. . . .

Maybe the most important reason for writing is to prevent the erosion of time, so that memories will not be blown away by the wind. Write to register history, and name each thing. Write what should not be forgotten. But then, why write novels? Probably because I come from Latin America, a land of crazy, illuminated people, of geological and political cataclysms—a land so large and profound, so beautiful and frightening, that only novels can describe its fascinating complexity.

A novel is like a window, open to an infinite landscape. In a novel we can put all the interrogations, we can register the most extravagant, evil, obscene, incredible or magnificent facts—which, in Latin America, are not hyperbole, because that is the dimension of our reality. In a novel we can give an illusory order to chaos. We can find the key to the labyrinth of history. We can make excursions into the past, to try to understand the present and dream the future. In a novel we can use everything: testimony, chronicle, essay, fantasy, legend, poetry and other devices that might help us to decode the mysteries of our world and discover our true identity.

For a writer who nourishes himself or herself on images and passions, to be born in a fabulous continent is a privilege. In Latin America we don't have to stretch our imaginations. Critics in Europe and the United States often stare in disbelief at Latin American books, asking how the authors dare to invent those incredible lies of young women who fly to heaven wrapped in linen sheets; of black emperors who build fortresses with cement and the blood of emasculated bulls; of outlaws who die of hunger in the Amazon with bags full of emeralds on their backs; of ancient tyrants who order their mothers to be flogged naked in front of the troops and modern tyrants who order children to be tortured in front of their parents; of hurricanes and earthquakes that turn the world upside down; of revolutions made with machetes, bullets, poems and kisses; of hallucinating landscapes where reason is lost.

It is very hard to explain to critics that these things are not a product of our pathological imaginations. They are written in our history; we can find them every day in our newspapers. We hear them in the streets; we suffer them frequently in our own lives. It is impossible to speak of Latin America without mentioning violence. We inhabit a land of terrible contrasts and we have to survive in times of great violence.

Contrast and violence, two excellent ingredients for literature, although for us, citizens of that reality, life is always suspended from a very fragile thread.

The first, the most naked and visible form of violence is the extreme poverty of the majority, in contrast with the extreme wealth of the very few. In my continent two opposite realities coexist. One is a legal face, more or less comprehensible and with a certain pretension to dignity and civilization. The other is a dark and tragic face, which we do not like to show but which is always threatening us. There is an apparent

WORDS TO KNOW

cataclysm (kăt′ə-klĭz′əm) *n.* a violent change or sudden upheaval
hyperbole (hī-pûr′bə-lē) *n.* an exaggeration used for emphasis or effect
illusory (ĭ-lo͞o′sə-rē) *adj.* unreal; deceptive
pathological (păth′ə-lŏj′ĭ-kəl) *adj.* diseased; unhealthy
pretension (prĭ-tĕn′shən) *n.* a claim or aspiration

world and a real world—nice neighborhoods where blond children play on their bicycles and servants walk elegant dogs, and other neighborhoods, of slums and garbage, where dark children play naked with hungry mutts. There are offices of marble and steel where young executives discuss the stock market, and forgotten villages where people still live and die as they did in the Middle Ages. There is a world of fiction created by the official discourse, and another world of blood and pain and love, where we have struggled for centuries.

In Latin America we all survive on the borderline of those two realities. Our fragile democracies exist as long as they don't interfere with imperialist interests. Most of our republics are dependent on submissiveness. Our institutions and laws are inefficient. Our armed forces often act as mercenaries[3] for a privileged social group that pays tribute to transnational enterprises. We are living in the worst economic, political and social crisis since the conquest of America by the Spaniards. There are hardly two or three leaders in the whole continent. Social inequality is greater every day, and to avoid an outburst of public rancor, repression also rises day by day. Crime, drugs, misery and ignorance are present in every Latin American country, and the military is an immediate threat to society and civil governments. We try to keep straight faces while our feet are stuck in a swamp of violence, exploitation, corruption, the terror of the state and the terrorism of those who take arms against the status quo.

BUT Latin America is also a land of hope and friendship and love. Writers navigate in these agitated waters. They don't live in ivory towers; they cannot remove themselves from this brutal reality. In such circumstances there is no time and no wish for narcissistic literature. Very few of our writers contemplate their navel in self-centered monologue. The majority want desperately to communicate.

I feel that writing is an act of hope, a sort of communion with our fellow men. The writer of good will carries a lamp to illuminate the dark corners. Only that, nothing more—a tiny beam of light to show some hidden aspect of reality, to help decipher and understand it and thus to initiate, if possible, a change in the conscience of some readers. This kind of writer is not seduced by the mermaid's voice of celebrity or tempted by exclusive literary circles. He has both feet planted firmly on the ground and walks hand in hand with the people in the streets. He knows that the lamp is very small and the shadows are immense. This makes him humble. ❖

3. **mercenaries** (mûr′sə-nĕr′ēz): soldiers who will do anything for money.

WORDS TO KNOW

imperialist (ĭm-pîr′ē-ə-lĭst′) *adj.* pertaining to a government's domination of the economic or political affairs of a weaker nation

rancor (răng′kər) *n.* bitter resentment; ill will

repression (rĭ-prĕsh′ən) *n.* the act of subduing or keeping down by force

narcissistic (när′sĭ-sĭs′tĭk) *adj.* characterized by excessive self-love or self-involvement

RESPONDING OPTIONS

FROM PERSONAL RESPONSE *TO* CRITICAL ANALYSIS

REFLECT **1.** In your notebook, describe your response to this excerpt from "Writing as an Act of Hope."

RETHINK **2.** On the basis of this essay, how would you describe Allende?

Consider
- her reasons for writing
- her relationship with her family
- her feelings of responsibility to her readers

3. What qualities do you think Allende most admires in other writers? Cite evidence to support your answer.

4. Do you think Allende feels that it is important for a writer to be able to answer the questions "Why do I write?" and "Whom do I write for?" Give reasons to support your answer.

5. Does reading this essay make you want to read Allende's fiction? Why or why not?

RELATE **6.** Review the list that you and other classmates created for the Personal Connection on page 1112, and add to it the names of at least three writers whose works you have read in this unit. Generally speaking, in which type of writing included in this book—short stories, poems, or essays—have the writers most frequently tried to, in Allende's words, "illuminate the dark corners"?

ANOTHER PATHWAY

With a partner, role-play an interview in which a TV talk-show host asks Allende the questions "Why do you write?" and "Whom do you write for?" Allende's responses should be based on ideas expressed in this essay. The host can also ask other questions dealing with the writer's role in society.

LITERARY CONCEPTS

An essay—whether intended to inform, to persuade, or to entertain—serves to express the opinions of its writer. In an **informative essay,** the writer's purpose is to reveal information on a subject about which he or she is particularly knowledgeable or concerned. In a **persuasive essay,** the writer's intent is to persuade readers to adopt a particular opinion or to perform a certain action. Both kinds of essays usually contain facts, reasons, and examples that support the writers' opinions. Would you describe Allende's essay as informative or as persuasive? Back up your opinion with reasons.

QUICKWRITES

1. In a **paragraph,** identify your favorite passage in this selection, giving reasons for your choice.
2. Write a **letter** to Isabel Allende, in which you express your thoughts or questions about ideas she presents in her essay.
3. For your school newspaper, write an **article** that addresses a present-day social or political issue and that could be described as "writing as an act of hope."

PORTFOLIO *Save your writing. You may want to use it later as a springboard to a piece for your portfolio.*

ALTERNATIVE ACTIVITIES

1. Deliver a **speech** in which you nominate Allende for an award on the basis of her ideas about writing.
2. Create a **collage** of pictures to illustrate some of the contrasts that, according to Allende's essay, exist in Latin America.
3. "Writing as an Act of Hope" originated as a lecture that Allende gave at the New York Public Library—part of a series of lectures by writers on particular aspects of the craft of writing. Allende was one of a group of writers who were asked why they wrote political novels. Design a **poster** advertising Allende's speech, being sure to include all pertinent information and to make the poster interesting and eye-catching.

CRITIC'S CORNER

The author Amy Tan has said that her friend Isabel Allende writes "with great passion." Review this excerpt from "Writing as an Act of Hope" to identify passages that seem to show great passion. Be prepared to explain why you think those passages are especially passionate. Do you think Allende would consider it important for a writer to be passionate about his or her writing? Discuss your opinions with your classmates.

LITERARY LINKS

Do you think Isabel Allende and Octavio Paz (page 988) have any of the same feelings about the process of writing? Support your opinion with specific evidence from her essay and his poem.

THE WRITER'S STYLE

Allende includes an abundance of **imagery** in both her fiction and her nonfiction—as in the sentence "I had thousands of untold words stuck in my chest, threatening to choke me" in the fourth paragraph of this selection. Find other examples of imagery in the essay. Which do you think are the most vivid or powerful? How do they affect your reaction to Allende and her writing?

ACROSS THE CURRICULUM

History ***Cooperative Learning*** Work with a group of classmates to prepare an oral report on Chile, Allende's native country. Individual group members can investigate different aspects of Chile's culture and history—for example, its geography, its early history, the military coup of 1973, and the current political and social conditions in the country. Where appropriate, use slides, pictures, maps, charts, and graphs in presenting your report to the class.

WORDS TO KNOW

EXERCISE A Review the Words to Know at the bottom of the selection pages. Then write the word that best completes each sentence.

1. "The pen is mightier than the sword" is not a _____; it is quite true.
2. Thomas Paine's widely read pamphlet *Common Sense* spoke so harshly against British _____ of the American colonists that it helped to inspire the American Revolution.
3. The novel *Uncle Tom's Cabin,* written by an abolitionist, created so much antislavery _____ that it is considered one of the causes of the Civil War.
4. Not every change that a book or article may help to bring about is a _____; some are more gradual and subtle alterations of people's perceptions of reality.
5. Rudyard Kipling's writings, which made the British presence in India look both appealing and righteous, were influential in perpetuating Great Britain's _____ attitude toward its colonies.

EXERCISE B Write the letter of the word that is a synonym of each boldfaced word.

1. **exorcise:** (a) maneuver, (b) expel, (c) glorify
2. **pretension:** (a) claim, (b) ability, (c) decision
3. **illusory:** (a) imaginary, (b) evasive, (c) flexible
4. **pathological:** (a) skillful, (b) lasting, (c) sick
5. **narcissistic:** (a) numb, (b) addictive, (c) self-centered

ISABEL ALLENDE

1942–

Isabel Allende traveled extensively as a child. Born in Peru, she moved to Chile with her mother after her parents' divorce. Although she lost contact with her father, she remained close to his family—especially to her uncle, a prominent politician. After her mother remarried, the family moved again, first to Bolivia, then to Europe and the Middle East, and finally, when Allende was 15, back to Chile. Allende's mother nurtured her creativity by encouraging her to record all her thoughts in a notebook and to draw anything she wanted on a bedroom wall.

A rebellious teenager, Allende quit school early, married, and eventually found a job as a journalist, writing and reporting for television and magazines. By the time she was 30, she felt settled and expected to spend the rest of her life in Chile, but a military coup in 1973 changed her plans dramatically. The Chilean government was overthrown, and Allende's uncle, who was then president, was assassinated. In spite of the widespread violence in Chile, she remained there for a time, secretly helping those who opposed the new regime. After her own life was threatened, however, she fled to Venezuela, where she lived in exile for 13 years before coming to the United States. She currently resides near San Francisco.

Allende was in her late 30s before she started writing fiction. After gaining worldwide attention with her first novel, *The House of the Spirits,* she has continued to write in Spanish, but her work has been translated into 27 languages, including English. In 1994, she published an autobiography, entitled *Paula* in memory of a daughter who had died a year earlier.

OTHER WORKS *Of Love and Shadows, Eva Luna, The Stories of Eva Luna*

PART 3 # *Ironic Perspectives*

Contemporary society has witnessed revolutionary advances. In many people, however, the increasingly fast pace of life and the global scale of events have produced a growing sense of isolation, alienation, and anxiety. Writers have responded by taking an ironic look at the contradictions and absurdities of modern life. In this part of Unit Seven, you will read a plotless play and poems that question life's meaning. You will also encounter characters who grapple with unexpected—and even horrifying—events. As you read the selections, try to identify the ironies they present.

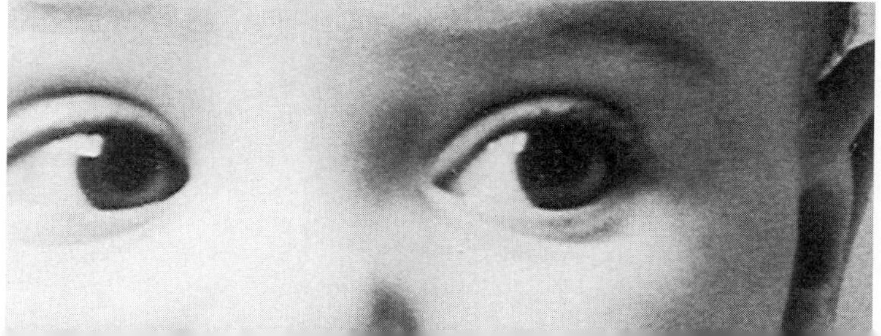

PREVIEWING

DRAMA

That's All

Harold Pinter

PERSONAL CONNECTION

What kinds of conversations do people engage in most of the time? Do you think people typically talk about important issues, or do most conversations consist of small talk about everyday routines and events? Jot down your responses to these questions in your notebook, and discuss them with your classmates.

LITERARY CONNECTION

Harold Pinter began writing plays in the late 1950s, when various new styles were emerging in British drama. Some critics saw similarities between Pinter's style of writing and that of the "kitchen sink" school of realists, with its focus on the language and lifestyle of the working class. Others likened his plays to those of the "theater of the absurd," in which disjointed, seemingly meaningless dialogue was used to convey the absurdity of many of life's circumstances.

Pinter, however, has never belonged to a single school. Instead, he has drawn from various dramatic styles to create his own distinctive approach—a style sometimes referred to as Pinteresque. Typically, a Pinter play involves just one setting, only two or three characters, and a minimal amount of action. The dialogue tends to be very simple—sometimes even ordinary and conversational—but it usually conveys a level of meaning beyond the literal meanings of the words that are spoken. According to Pinter, "The speech we hear is an indication of that which we don't hear."

That's All, written in 1959, is one of Pinter's early works. It is a short dramatic sketch intended to be performed either as one segment of a variety show or as a short radio skit.

READING CONNECTION

Reading Unconventional Works The play you are about to read is unconventional both in subject matter and in the conversational style of the dialogue. As you read it, try to abandon your expectations of dramatic works so that you can experience Pinter's unique brand of humor.

THAT'S ALL

Harold Pinter

Mrs. A. I always put the kettle on about that time.

Mrs. B. Yes. (*pause*)

Mrs. A. Then she comes round.

Mrs. B. Yes. (*pause*)

Mrs. A. Only on Thursdays.

Mrs. B. Yes. (*pause*)

Mrs. A. On Wednesdays I used to put it on. When she used to come round. Then she changed it to Thursdays.

Mrs. B. Oh yes.

Mrs. A. After she moved. When she used to live round the corner, then she always came in on Wednesdays, but then when she moved she used to come down to the butcher's on Thursdays. She couldn't find a butcher up there.

May Shield (1974), Nancy Hellebrand. Copyright © 1974 Nancy Hellebrand.

Mrs. B. No.

Mrs. A. Anyway, she decided she'd stick to her own butcher. Well, I thought, if she can't find a butcher, that's the best thing.

Mrs. B. Yes. (*pause*)

Mrs. A. So she started to come down on Thursdays. I didn't know she was coming down on Thursdays until one day I met her in the butcher.

Mrs. B. Oh yes.

Mrs. A. It wasn't my day for the butcher, I don't go to the butcher on Thursdays.

Mrs. B. No, I know. (*pause*)

Mrs. A. I go on Friday.

Mrs. B. Yes. (*pause*)

Mrs. A. That's where I see you.

Mrs. B. Yes. (*pause*)

Mrs. A. You're always in there on Fridays.

Mrs. B. Oh yes. (*pause*)

Mrs. A. But I happened to go in for a bit of meat, it turned out to be a Thursday. I wasn't going in for my usual weekly on Friday. I just slipped in, the day before.

Mrs. B. Yes.

Mrs. A. That was the first time I found out she couldn't find a butcher up there, so she decided to come back here, once a week, to her own butcher.

Mrs. B. Yes.

Mrs. A. She came on Thursday so she'd be able to get meat for the weekend. Lasted her till Monday, then from Monday to Thursday they'd have fish. She can always buy cold meat, if they want a change.

Mrs. B. Oh yes. (*pause*)

Mrs. A. So I told her to come in when she came down after she'd been to the butcher's and I'd put a kettle on. So she did. (*pause*)

Mrs. B. Yes. (*pause*)

Mrs. A. It was funny because she always used to come in Wednesdays. (*pause*) Still, it made a break. (*long pause*)

Mrs. B. She doesn't come in no more, does she? (*pause*)

Mrs. A. She comes in. She doesn't come in so much, but she comes in. (*pause*)

Mrs. B. I thought she didn't come in. (*pause*)

Mrs. A. She comes in. (*pause*) She just doesn't come in so much. That's all.

RESPONDING OPTIONS

FROM PERSONAL RESPONSE *TO* CRITICAL ANALYSIS

REFLECT 1. What word best describes your impression of this play? Record it in your notebook and compare it with the words suggested by your classmates.

RETHINK 2. How does *That's All* differ from other dramas or skits you have encountered? Cite details in your answer.

3. What do you think was Pinter's purpose in writing this play?
   Consider
   - the subject matter of the characters' conversation
   - the way the characters interact

4. Why do you think Pinter chose to use Mrs. A's last remark, "That's all," as the title of his play?

RELATE 5. Review your responses to the Personal Connection on page 1122. Do you think the conversation in this play is typical of small talk between friends? Why or why not?

ANOTHER PATHWAY

Cooperative Learning

Work with a small group of classmates to give several dramatic readings of the play, taking turns in the roles of Mrs. A and Mrs. B and experimenting with inflections, facial expressions, and ways of observing the pauses. With the rest of the class, discuss how different ways of reading the play can affect its meaning.

QUICKWRITES

1. Compose dialogue and stage directions for a second **scene** in the encounter between Mrs. A and Mrs. B. Then, with a partner, perform your scene for your classmates.
2. Write a **review** of *That's All*, stating your overall opinion of the play and pointing out its strengths and weaknesses.
3. Imagine that you are going to direct a production of this play. Write a **casting call** in which you specify the ages, physical traits, and other qualities of the actresses you want to portray Mrs. A and Mrs. B.

PORTFOLIO *Save your writing. You may want to use it later as a springboard to a piece for your portfolio.*

LITERARY CONCEPTS

In drama, **dialogue** is the main means of characterization and the main vehicle for conveying events and themes. One characteristic of Pinter's dialogue is repetition; another is the use of pauses, always indicated by stage directions. Analyze the dialogue in *That's All.* What effect do you think Pinter creates by having his characters repeat certain words and phrases? What effects does he achieve with pauses?

ALTERNATIVE ACTIVITIES

1. Create a three-dimensional model of the **set design** you would use for a production of *That's All.*
2. Prepare a **cover design** for a program to be handed out at a performance of the play.
3. Draw **costume sketches** of the clothing you think would be most appropriate for the actresses playing Mrs. A and Mrs. B.

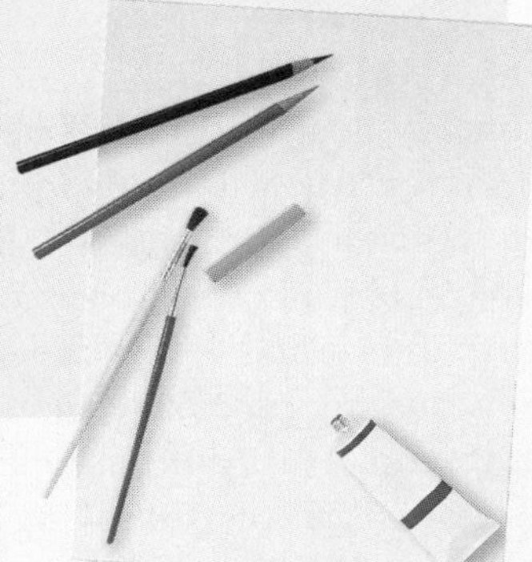

CRITIC'S CORNER

The critic Alrene Sykes has written that Pinter tends to establish a "lack of communication between his characters" at the beginning of each of his plays. Do you see any evidence of this in *That's All?* Support your answer.

LITERARY LINKS

Compare *That's All* with Oscar Wilde's *The Importance of Being Earnest* (page 701). What similarities and differences can you find in the ways Pinter and Wilde use dialogue to create humor?

HAROLD PINTER

1930–

Harold Pinter was born and educated in a working-class neighborhood of London's East End. Though he was a child during World War II, he vividly recalls the German bombing raids that took him away from his parents for a year, when he was evacuated to the country along with other London children. A son of Jewish parents, he also recalls the anti-Jewish sentiment that was widespread in some sectors of British society during and after the war. On many occasions, he found himself involved in fistfights as a result of attacks by unruly neighborhood thugs.

As a teenager, Pinter acted in plays and wrote poetry for a school magazine, but he also showed his proficiency in sports. He played soccer, broke a school record in sprinting, and received an award for his accomplishments in cricket, a sport that he continued to play into adulthood. At the age of 18, he received a grant to study at London's Royal Academy of Dramatic Art, but he left the school after only a few months. Later, he studied acting with more success at the Central School of Speech and Drama, and he spent his early and middle 20s acting in various productions and repertory theaters throughout England.

During his years as an actor, Pinter continued to write, but all his early works were poetry and fiction. In 1957, he composed his first play—a one-act drama called *The Room,* which he wrote in four days. In explaining how he started writing plays, Pinter has stated, "I went into a room one day and saw a couple of people in it. . . . I started off with this picture of the two people and let them carry on from there. . . . It was quite a natural movement." Pinter has since written scripts for television and movies as well as for the theater and has won numerous literary prizes, including a Tony Award.

OTHER WORKS *Last to Go, Trouble in the Works, The Black and White, The Birthday Party, The Dumb Waiter, The Caretaker*

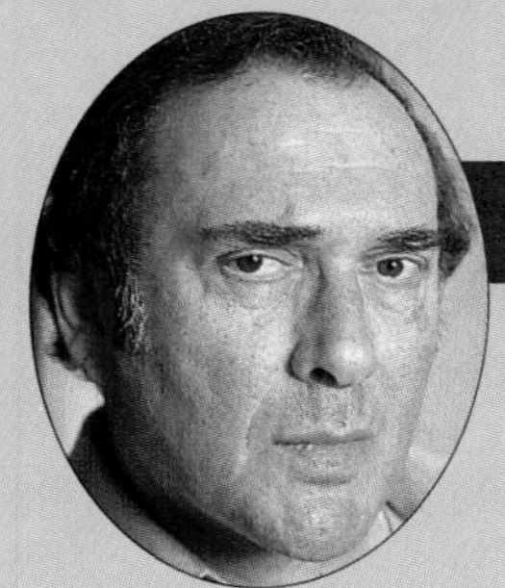

MILESTONES IN BRITISH LITERATURE

Harold Pinter

THE LONGER PLAYS OF HAROLD PINTER

When is comedy dead serious? When it's comedy in a play by Harold Pinter. All of Pinter's longer plays open on an ordinary note, even lightheartedly. Realistic but rather eccentric characters inhabit unremarkable rooms. They converse or banter about everyday subjects—breakfast, family life, a missing pair of scissors. These conversations often seem to consist of dull and clichéd—albeit humorous—small talk, as in the following exchange between Mick and Davies in *The Caretaker:*

> **Davies.** I was saying, he's . . . he's a bit of a funny bloke, your brother.
>
> (Mick *stares at him.*)
>
> **Mick.** Funny? Why?
>
> **Davies.** Well . . . he's funny. . . .
>
> **Mick.** What's funny about him?
>
> (*pause*)
>
> **Davies.** Not liking work.
>
> **Mick.** What's funny about that?
>
> **Davies.** Nothing.
>
> (*pause*)
>
> **Mick.** I don't call it funny.
>
> **Davies.** Nor me.

As more and more information is revealed, one begins to notice some odd twists and turns, such as the shifting alliances revealed in the conversation above. Characters lie or contradict themselves; their memories are faulty; sometimes they can't recall their own past. Their pauses can amputate their thoughts, cut off communication with others, and fail to cover up extreme emotions and dangerous intentions. Buried conflicts loom, but no one will admit their existence. Pinter carefully weaves language and silence into a subtle web of fear and menace.

Pinter's characters engage in seemingly harmless, everyday activities, such as maintaining a household, welcoming a returned relative, or attending a gathering of friends. In a Pinter play, however, the surface reality is completely unreliable; ordinary activities can take on another layer of meaning. As the action intensifies, hidden rivalries and hostilities, lurking danger, or devastating isolation may be revealed. In *The Birthday Party,* for example, breakfast comes to stand for mental and emotional nourishment. At the beginning of the play, breakfast is plentiful, but by the end, two intruders have eaten all the breakfast before the main characters can get any. The intruders also have complete control over the main characters' household.

To achieve the tense and startling atmosphere of his plays, Pinter draws on the techniques of such absurdist playwrights as Eugène Ionesco and Samuel Beckett; yet his plays, unlike theirs, open on a realistic note. They rest, as John Osborne's plays do, on a foundation of violence, but they don't celebrate the "angry young man," as Osborne's do. Instead, Pinter allows his plays to be haunting explorations of the hopes, fears, memories, and dreams that give shape to each moment of life.

Above left:
Donald Pleasence and Alan Bates in The Guest, *the film version of Harold Pinter's* The Caretaker.
Above:
Dirk Bogarde and James Fox in the movie The Servant, *screenplay by Pinter.*
Below left:
The National Theatre's production of No Man's Land *at the Old Vic, with Ralph Richardson and John Gielgud.*

PREVIEWING

FICTION

The First Year of My Life

Muriel Spark

PERSONAL CONNECTION

What kind of baby were you, according to your parents and other relatives? Were you happy? cranky? Did you seem interested in the world around you or indifferent to it? In your notebook, briefly describe yourself at that point in your life. Then, as you read this story, compare yourself with the rather astonishing baby being depicted.

HISTORICAL CONNECTION

The story you are about to read is set in 1918, the final year of World War I. By that time, the bloodshed and devastation of the Great War, as it was then called, had reached levels never seen in any previous conflict. The use of advanced weaponry and poison gas in the brutal stalemate of trench warfare had resulted in heavy casualties, and many families across Europe suffered the loss of loved ones. The war also left deep political and economic scars on almost every European country—scars that eventually led to the eruption of World War II only two decades later.

In her account of her life as an infant, the narrator of this story provides an unusual perspective on the final year of World War I. Although the premise of the story is pure fantasy, the narrator makes allusions to many individuals who actually lived during the time, including figures famous in history and the arts.

READING CONNECTION

Appreciating Satire As you may recall, **satire** is a literary technique in which criticism is mixed with humor in order to expose the faults of society. The tone of a satirical work may be gently witty, mildly abrasive, or even bitterly critical. As you read "The First Year of My Life," look for specific instances of satire and decide what effects are created by the narrator's unusual perspective. Note passages in which you think the satire is particularly effective.

Using Your Reading Log Use your reading log to record your responses to the questions inserted in the story. Also jot down other thoughts and feelings that come to you as you read.

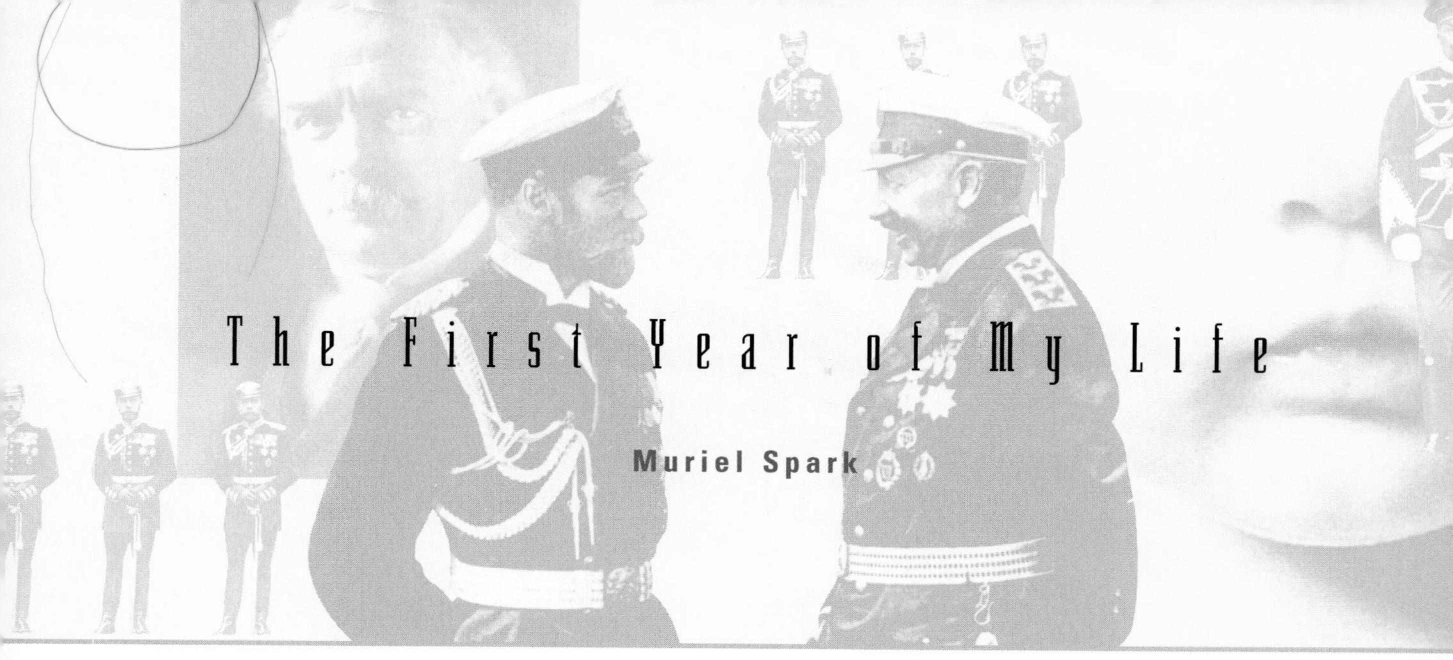

The First Year of My Life

Muriel Spark

I was born on the first day of the second month of the last year of the First World War, a Friday. Testimony abounds that during the first year of my life I never smiled. I was known as the baby whom nothing and no one could make smile. Everyone who knew me then has told me so. They tried very hard, singing and bouncing me up and down, jumping around, pulling faces. Many times I was told this later by my family and their friends; but, anyway, I knew it at the time.

You will shortly be hearing of that new school of psychology, or maybe you have heard of it already, which after long and far-adventuring research and experiment has established that all of the young of the human species are born omniscient. Babies, in their waking hours, know everything that is going on everywhere in the world; they can tune in to any conversation they choose, switch on to any scene. We have all experienced this power. It is only after the first year that it was brainwashed out of us; for it is demanded of us by our immediate environment that we grow to be of use to it in a practical way. Gradually, our know-all brain-cells are blacked out, although traces remain in some individuals in the form of E.S.P., and in the adults of some primitive tribes.

It is not a new theory. Poets and philosophers, as usual, have been there first. But scientific proof is now ready and to hand. Perhaps the final touches are being put to the new manifesto[1] in some cell[2] at Harvard University. Any day now it will be given to the world, and the world will be convinced.

PREDICT

What will this information about a "new school of psychology" have to do with the events in the story?

Let me therefore get my word in first, because

1. **manifesto:** a declaration of principles.
2. **cell:** a small group forming a unit of a larger organization.

WORDS TO KNOW

omniscient (ŏm-nĭsh′ənt) *adj.* having complete knowledge; all-knowing

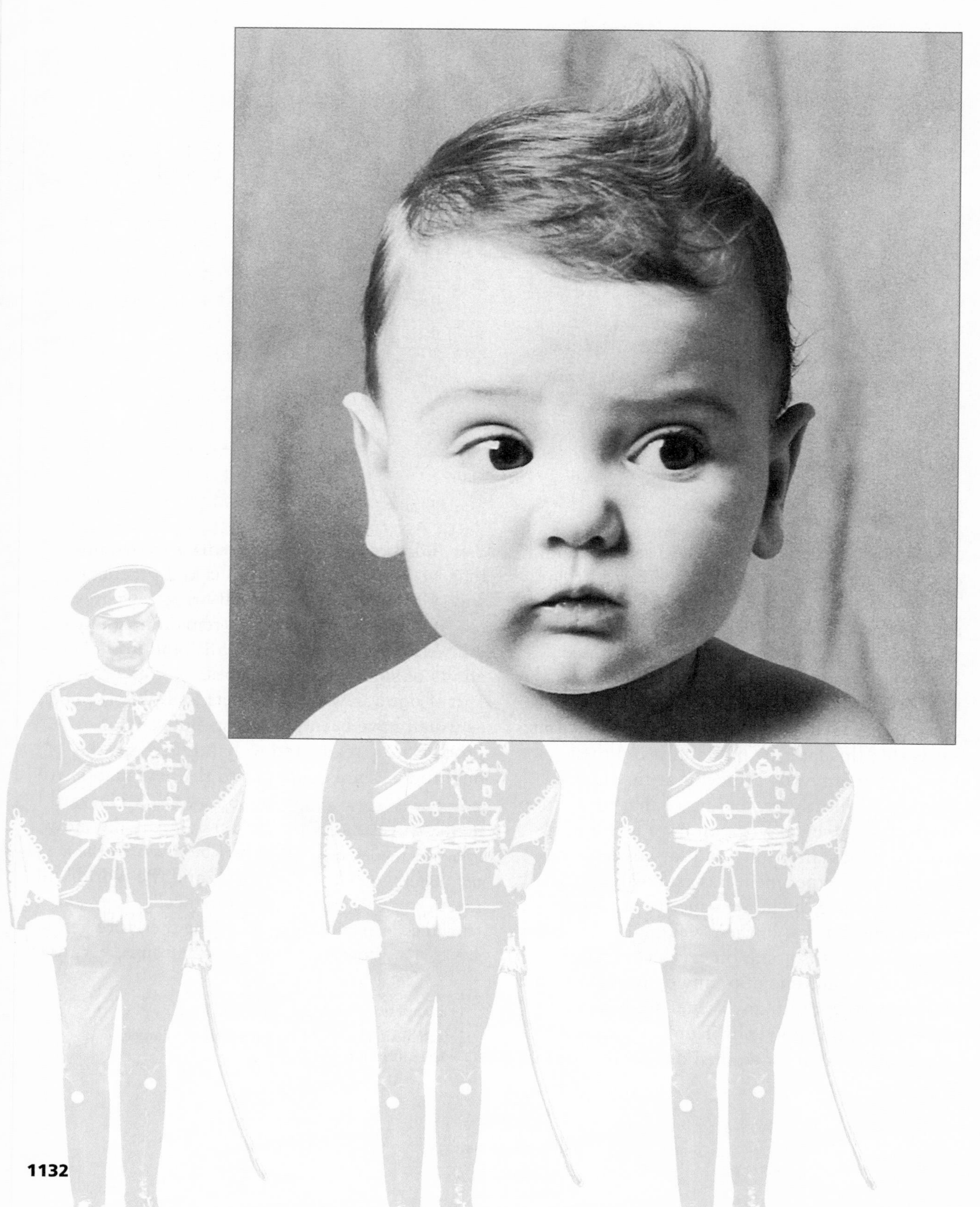

I feel pretty sure, now, about the authenticity of my remembrance of things past. My autobiography, as I very well perceived at the time, started in the very worst year that the world had ever seen so far. Apart from being born bedridden and toothless, unable to raise myself on the pillow or utter anything but farmyard squawks or police-siren wails, my bladder and my bowels totally out of control, I was further depressed by the curious behavior of the two-legged mammals around me. There were those black-dressed people, females of the species to which I appeared to belong, saying they had lost their sons. I slept a great deal. Let them go and find their sons. It was like the special pin for my nappies[3] which my mother or some other hoverer dedicated to my care was always losing. These careless women in black lost their husbands and their brothers. Then they came to visit my mother and clucked and crowed over my cradle. I was not amused.

CLARIFY

Why are the women dressed in black?

"Babies never really smile till they're three months old," said my mother. "They're not *supposed* to smile till they're three months old."

My brother, aged six, marched up and down with a toy rifle over his shoulder:

The grand old Duke of York
He had ten thousand men;
He marched them up to the top of the hill
And he marched them down again.

And when they were up, they were up.
And when they were down, they were down.
And when they were neither down nor up
They were neither up nor down.

"Just listen to him!"

"Look at him with his rifle!"

I was about ten days old when Russia stopped fighting. I tuned in to the Czar,[4] a prisoner, with the rest of his family, since evidently the country had put him off his throne and there had been a revolution not long before I was born. Everyone was talking about it. I tuned in to the Czar. "Nothing would ever induce me to sign the treaty of Brest-Litovsk,"[5] he said to his wife. Anyway, nobody had asked him to.

CLARIFY

How does the narrator know what the czar said? Reread the beginning of the story if you need further clarification.

At this point I was sleeping twenty hours a day to get my strength up. And from what I discerned in the other four hours of the day I knew I was going to need it. The Western Front[6] on my frequency was sheer blood, mud, dismembered bodies, blistering crashes, hectic flashes of light in the night skies, explosions, total terror. Since it was plain I had been born into a bad moment in the history of the world, the future bothered me, unable as I was to raise my head from the pillow and as yet only twenty inches long. "I truly wish I were a fox or a bird," D. H. Lawrence was writing to somebody. Dreary old creeping Jesus. I fell asleep.

Red sheets of flame shot across the sky. It was 21st March, the fiftieth day of my life, and the German Spring Offensive[7] had started before my morning feed. Infinite slaughter. I scowled at the

3. **nappies:** the British term for diapers.
4. **Czar:** Nicholas II, the last czar of Russia, who was forced from power in the Russian Revolution of 1917.
5. **treaty of Brest-Litovsk:** the treaty—signed on March 3, 1918—by which the new Communist government of Russia made peace with Germany, withdrawing from World War I eight months before its end.
6. **Western Front:** a 450-mile-long battlefront across Belgium and northeastern France, along which the Allies and Germany were locked in bloody trench warfare from 1914 to 1918.
7. **German Spring Offensive:** In late March 1918, after its peace treaty with Russia ended the fighting on the eastern front, Germany began a major push to win the war on the western front.

WORDS TO KNOW

authenticity (ô'thĕn-tĭs'ĭ-tē) *n.* genuineness
discern (dĭ-sûrn') *v.* to observe; perceive

scene, and made an effort to kick out. But the attempt was feeble. Furious, and impatient for some strength, I wailed for my feed. After which I stopped wailing but continued to scowl.

The grand old Duke of York
He had ten thousand men . . .

They rocked the cradle. I never heard a sillier song. Over in Berlin and Vienna the people were starving, freezing, striking, rioting and yelling in the streets. In London everyone was bustling to work and muttering that it was time the whole damn business was over.

The big people around me bared their teeth; that meant a smile, it meant they were pleased or amused. They spoke of ration cards[8] for meat and sugar and butter.

"Where will it all end?"

I went to sleep. I woke and tuned in to Bernard Shaw[9] who was telling someone to shut up. I switched over to Joseph Conrad[10] who, strangely enough, was saying precisely the same thing. I still didn't think it worth a smile, although it was expected of me any day now. I got on to Turkey. Women draped in black huddled and chattered in their harems; yak-yak-yak. This was boring, so I came back to home base.

In and out came and went the women in British black. My mother's brother, dressed in his uniform, came coughing. He had been poison-gassed in the trenches. *"Tout le monde à la bataille!"*[11] declaimed Marshal Foch[12] the old swine. He was now Commander-in-Chief of the Allied Forces. My uncle coughed from deep within his lungs, never to recover but destined to return to the Front. His brass buttons gleamed in the firelight. I weighed twelve pounds by now; I stretched and kicked for exercise, seeing that I had a lifetime before me, coping with this crowd. I took six feeds a day and kept most of them down by the time the *Vindictive* was sunk in Ostend harbor,[13] on which day I kicked with special vigor in my bath.

In France the conscripted[14] soldiers leapfrogged over the dead on the advance and littered the fields with limbs and hands, or drowned in the mud. The strongest men on all fronts were dead before I was born. Now the sentries used bodies for barricades and the fighting men were unhealthy from the start. I checked my toes and fingers, knowing I was going to need them. *The Playboy of the Western World*[15] was playing at the Court Theatre in London, but occasionally I beamed over to the House of Commons[16] which made me drop off gently to sleep. Generally, I preferred the Western Front where one got the true state of affairs. It was essential to know the worst, blood and explosions and all, for one had to be prepared, as the boy scouts said. Virginia Woolf yawned and reached for her diary. Really, I preferred the Western Front.

---

8. **ration cards:** cards entitling the bearers to limited amounts of certain foods and other goods that were in short supply during the war.
9. **Bernard Shaw:** George Bernard Shaw, an Irish-born British playwright and social critic.
10. **Joseph Conrad:** a Polish-born British novelist.
11. ***Tout le monde à la bataille!*** (to͞o′ lə môɴd′ ä lä bä-tī′) *French:* The whole world into the battle!
12. **Marshal Foch** (fôsh): Ferdinand Foch, a French general who in March 1918 became commander of all Allied forces on the western front.
13. ***Vindictive* . . . Ostend harbor:** In May 1918, a crew of Allied volunteers sunk the ship *Vindictive* to block the entrance of the harbor of Ostend, Belgium, which the Germans had been using as a submarine base.
14. **conscripted:** drafted into military service.
15. ***The Playboy of the Western World:*** a controversial drama by the Irish playwright John Millington Synge.
16. **House of Commons:** the lower house of the British parliament.

In the fifth month of my life I could raise my head from my pillow and hold it up. I could grasp the objects that were held out to me. Some of these things rattled and squawked. I gnawed on them to get my teeth started. "She hasn't smiled yet?" said the dreary old aunties. My mother, on the defensive, said I was probably one of those late smilers. On my wavelength Pablo Picasso[17] was getting married and early in that month of July the Silver Wedding of King George V and Queen Mary was celebrated in joyous pomp at St. Paul's Cathedral. They drove through the streets of London with their children. Twenty-five years of domestic happiness. A lot of fuss and ceremonial handing over of swords went on at the Guildhall where the King and Queen received a check for £53,000 to dispose of for charity as they thought fit. *Tout le monde à la bataille!* Income tax in England had reached six shillings in the pound. Everyone was talking about the Silver Wedding; yak-yak-yak, and ten days later the Czar and his family, now in Siberia, were invited to descend to a little room in the basement. Crack, crack, went the guns; screams and blood all over the place, and that was the end of the Romanoffs.[18] I flexed my muscles. "A fine healthy baby," said the doctor; which gave me much satisfaction.

Tout le monde à la bataille! That included my gassed uncle. My health had improved to the point where I was able to crawl in my playpen. Bertrand Russell[19] was still cheerily in prison for writing something seditious about pacifism. Tuning in as usual to the Front Lines it looked as if the Germans were winning all the battles yet losing the war. And so it was. The upper-income people were upset about the income tax at six shillings to the pound. But all women over thirty got the vote. "It seems a long time to wait," said one of my drab old aunts, aged twenty-two. The speeches in the House of Commons always sent me to sleep which was why I missed, at the actual time, a certain oration by Mr. Asquith[20] following the armistice on 11th November.[21] Mr. Asquith was a greatly esteemed former prime minister later to be an Earl, and had been ousted by Mr. Lloyd George.[22] I clearly heard Asquith, in private, refer to Lloyd George as "that damned Welsh goat."

The armistice was signed and I was awake for that. I pulled myself on to my feet with the aid of the bars of my cot. My teeth were coming through very nicely in my opinion, and well worth all the trouble I was put to in bringing them forth. I weighed twenty pounds. On all the world's fighting fronts the men killed in action or dead of wounds numbered 8,538,315 and the warriors wounded and maimed were 21,219,452. With these figures in mind I sat up in my high chair and banged my spoon on the table. One of my mother's black-draped friends recited:

I have a rendezvous with Death
At some disputed barricade,
When spring comes back with rustling shade
And apple blossoms fill the air—
I have a rendezvous with Death.[23]

Most of the poets, they said, had been killed. The poetry made them dab their eyes with clean white handkerchiefs.

17. **Pablo Picasso:** a Spanish painter and sculptor.
18. **Romanoffs:** the ruling family of Russia from 1613 to 1917.
19. **Bertrand Russell:** a British philosopher, mathematician, and writer.
20. **Mr. Asquith:** Herbert Henry Asquith, prime minister of Britain from 1908 to 1916.
21. **armistice on 11th November:** the agreement that marked the end of fighting in World War I.
22. **Lloyd George:** David Lloyd George, prime minister of Britain from 1916 to 1922.
23. ***I . . . Death:*** the beginning of "I Have a Rendezvous with Death" by the American poet Alan Seeger, who was killed in action during World War I. (Another quotation from the poem appears three paragraphs farther on.)

WORDS TO KNOW

seditious (sĭ-dĭsh'əs) *adj.* stirring up discontent or rebellion

Next February on my first birthday, there was a birthday-cake with one candle. Lots of children and their elders. The war had been over two months and twenty-one days. "Why doesn't she smile?" My brother was to blow out the candle. The elders were talking about the war and the political situation. Lloyd George and Asquith, Asquith and Lloyd George. I remembered recently having switched on to Mr. Asquith at a private party where he had been drinking a lot. He was playing cards and when he came to cut the cards he tried to cut a large box of matches by mistake. On another occasion I had seen him putting his arm around a lady's shoulder in a Daimler[24] motor car, and generally behaving towards her in a very friendly fashion. Strangely enough she said, "If you don't stop this nonsense immediately I'll order the chauffeur to stop and I'll get out." Mr. Asquith replied, "And pray, what reason will you give?" Well anyway it was my feeding time.

The guests arrived for my birthday. It was so sad, said one of the black widows, so sad about Wilfred Owen who was killed so late in the war, and she quoted from a poem of his:

What passing-bells for these who die as cattle?
Only the monstrous anger of the guns.[25]

The children were squealing and toddling around. One was sick and another wet the floor and stood with his legs apart gaping at the puddle. All was mopped up. I banged my spoon on the table of my high chair.

But I've a rendezvous with Death
At midnight in some flaming town;
When spring trips north again this year,
And I to my pledged word am true,
I shall not fail that rendezvous.

More parents and children arrived. One stout man who was warming his behind at the fire, said, "I always think those words of Asquith's after the armistice were so apt . . ."

They brought the cake close to my high chair for me to see, with the candle shining and flickering above the pink icing. "A pity she never smiles."

"She'll smile in time," my mother said, obviously upset.

"What Asquith told the House of Commons just after the war," said that stout gentleman with his backside to the fire, "—so apt, what Asquith said. He said that the war has cleansed and purged the world, by God! I recall his actual words: 'All things have become new. In this great cleansing and purging it has been the privilege of our country to play her part . . .' "

That did it. I broke into a decided smile and everyone noticed it, convinced that it was provoked by the fact that my brother had blown out the candle on the cake. "She smiled!" my mother exclaimed. And everyone was clucking away about how I was smiling. For good measure I crowed like a demented raven. "My baby's smiling!" said my mother.

"It was the candle on her cake," they said.

The cake be damned. Since that time I have grown to smile quite naturally, like any other healthy and house-trained person, but when I really mean a smile, deeply felt from the core, then to all intents and purposes it comes in response to the words uttered in the House of Commons after the First World War by the distinguished, the immaculately dressed and the late Mr. Asquith. ❖

24. **Daimler** (dīm′lər): a German automobile-manufacturing company.

25. ***What . . . guns:*** the beginning of Owen's "Anthem for Doomed Youth."

WORDS TO KNOW **demented** (dĭ-mĕn′tĭd) *adj.* insane

RESPONDING OPTIONS

FROM PERSONAL RESPONSE *TO* CRITICAL ANALYSIS

REFLECT **1.** In your notebook, jot down your reaction to the story. Then share your thoughts with your classmates.

RETHINK **2.** Why do you think Muriel Spark chose to tell the story from the unusual perspective of a baby?

3. Why do you think the narrator finally smiles after hearing Asquith's postwar remarks?

4. Review the definition of *satire* given in the Reading Connection on page 1130. What words would you use to describe the tone of the satire in this story? Cite examples to support your answer.

RELATE **5.** If an author chose to tell a similar story from the perspective of a baby living today, what people and events might the baby "tune in to"?

ANOTHER PATHWAY

In a chart like the one shown, list the individuals and groups that are satirized in this story, and explain what fault the narrator finds with each one. Share your observations with the class, discussing how and why the narrator calls attention to each fault.

Individual or Group Satirized	Reason for Criticism
Narrator's family	

QUICKWRITES

1. As the narrator of this story, write a **letter** to Mr. Asquith, giving your opinion of his comments to the House of Commons.
2. Compose the **lyrics** for a song in which you lament some of the conditions or faults referred to in the story.
3. Draft a **review** in which you recommend that history teachers use this story in a unit on World War I.

PORTFOLIO *Save your writing. You may want to use it later as a springboard to a piece for your portfolio.*

LITERARY CONCEPTS

Many stories are told from a **first-person point of view,** by narrators who participate in the stories' action. Another common narrative point of view is the **third-person omniscient** (all-knowing) **point of view,** in which the narrator is outside the story's action but can see into the minds of more than one character. It is unusual, however, for these two narrative techniques to be merged in a first-person omniscient point of view like that used in "The First Year of My Life."

With a partner, look through the story and choose a passage that you find particularly amusing. Rewrite the passage, telling the events from either a third-person or a first-person limited point of view. What changes do you notice in the tone of the passage?

CRITIC'S CORNER

The critic Michiko Kakutani has remarked that Spark presents a "distinctly dark view of human nature" in her stories. What do you think of this comment?

ACROSS THE CURRICULUM

History *Cooperative Learning*
With a group of classmates, research the views on war that were held by the writers and politicians mentioned in this story. Then conduct a forum in which the members of your group role-play these individuals and summarize their views for the class.

WORDS TO KNOW

EXERCISE A Answer the following questions.

1. If you called someone **demented,** would you mean that the person was insulting, powerful, or crazy?
2. If you were **omniscient,** would someone find it difficult to see you, to soothe you, or to fool you?
3. What cannot be successful without the involvement of **seditious** people—a contest, a mutiny, or a charity fundraiser?
4. If you questioned the **authenticity** of something, would you be doubting its truth, its safety, or its legality?
5. What do soldiers sometimes use to make it difficult for the enemy to **discern** them—radar, helmets, or camouflage?

EXERCISE B Work with four classmates to develop a short skit involving five characters—a skit that will lead the audience to associate each character with one of the five vocabulary words. Do *not* use the words themselves; develop the associations only by means of the characters' actions and dialogue.

MURIEL SPARK

1918–

Born in Edinburgh, Scotland, Muriel Spark attended James Gillespie's Girls' School in that city, where her literary efforts were encouraged and she was considered the school's "poet and dreamer." In 1937, at the age of 19, she moved to Central Africa, marrying there shortly afterward. Although her African venture provided her with excellent material for some of the stories she would later publish, her marriage was not successful; after a divorce, she returned to Great Britain in 1944. In order to have a closer view of the realities of World War II, which was then raging, she decided to live in London rather than Edinburgh. There she worked for the Intelligence Service's anti-Nazi propaganda department until the war's end.

Spark remained in London for more than a decade after the war, writing poetry, short stories, and biographies and working as an editor. In 1957, she published the first of her many novels, *The Comforters.* A few of her best-known works, including *The Prime of Miss Jean Brodie,* have been made into movies.

Many of the characters in Spark's stories are based on real people who have touched her life. In her autobiography, *Curriculum Vitae,* she states, "I can't remember a time when I was not a person-watcher, a behaviorist." Of her very early years, she remarks, "People were far more important to me than toys or nature."

OTHER WORKS "The Twins," "The Ormolu Clock," "Miss Pinkerton's Apocalypse," "You Should Have Seen the Mess," "The Playhouse Called Remarkable"

LASERLINKS
• *HISTORICAL CONNECTION*

PREVIEWING

FICTION

The Happy Man

Naguib Mahfouz

PERSONAL CONNECTION

Imagine that you awoke one morning to find that a magical change had occurred within you. Suddenly, you felt so incredibly happy that all worries and troubles had lost their power to affect you. How do you think you would react to such happiness? Do you think it could last? Discuss your reactions with your classmates.

CULTURAL/BIOGRAPHICAL CONNECTION

The contemporary Egyptian writer Naguib Mahfouz lives in Cairo, the capital of Egypt. Located on the Nile River and having a population of about 6 million (the greatest of all African cities), Cairo, like many large cities, is home to a wide variety of people, businesses, political views, and problems. It is a city of contrasts—encompassing great wealth and extreme poverty, ancient and modern ways of life, and Eastern and Western cultural influences. It has been the scene of political struggles as well.

Many of Mahfouz's works deal with the problems and concerns of modern Egypt's residents, especially the members of the middle class. Although Mahfouz focused on philosophy in his university studies, he had a long and productive career as a government official, in which he obtained firsthand knowledge of bureaucratic life and the questions, conflicts, and absurdities of the people involved in it. "The Happy Man" is from *God's World,* a collection of stories in which Mahfouz explores the dilemmas of human existence and the search for a meaningful life.

Café in Cairo

READING CONNECTION

Identifying Irony The term ***irony*** refers to a contrast between what is expected and what actually happens. Sometimes irony in stories involves actions or circumstances, and sometimes it involves ways in which words are used. As you read "The Happy Man," look for details and statements that might be considered ironic. Keep a list of examples in your notebook, noting the effects of the irony on your understanding of the story.

THE HAPPY MAN

NAGUIB MAHFOUZ

HE woke up in the morning and discovered that he was happy. "What's this?" he asked himself. He could not think of any word which described his state of mind more accurately and precisely than "happy." This was distinctly peculiar when compared with the state he was usually in when he woke up. He would be half-asleep from staying so late at the newspaper office. He would face life with a sense of strain and contemplation. Then he would get up, whetting his determination to face up to all inconveniences and withstand all difficulties.

Today he felt happy, full of happiness as a matter of fact. There was no arguing about it. The symptoms were quite clear and their vigor and obviousness were such as to impose themselves on his senses and mind all at once. Yes, indeed; he was happy. If this was not happiness, then what was? He felt that his limbs were well proportioned and functioning perfectly. They were working in superb harmony with each other and with the world around him. Inside him, he felt a boundless power, an imperishable energy, an ability to achieve anything with confidence, precision, and obvious success. His heart was overflowing with love for people, animals and things, and with an all-engulfing sense of optimism and joy. It was as if he were no longer troubled or bothered by fear, anxiety, sickness, death, argument, or the question of earning a living. Even more important than that, and something he could not analyze, it was a feeling which penetrated to every cell of his body and soul, it played a tune full of delight, pleasure, serenity and peace, and hummed in its incredible melodies the whispering sound of the world which is denied to the unhappy.

He felt drunk with ecstasy and savored it slowly with a feeling of surprise. He asked himself where it had come from and how; the past provided no explanation and the future could not justify it. Where did it come from, then, and how? How long would it last? Would it stay with him till breakfast? Would it give him enough time to get to the newspaper office? Just a minute though, he thought . . . it won't last because it can't. If it did, man would be turned into an angel or something even higher. So he told himself that he should devote his attention to savoring it, living with it, and storing up its nectar before it became a mere memory with no way of proving it or even being sure that it had ever existed.

He ate his breakfast with a relish, and this time nothing distracted his attention while he was eating. He gave "Uncle" Bashir who was waiting on him such a beaming smile that the poor man felt rather alarmed and taken aback. Usually he would only look in his direction to give orders or ask questions; although, on most occasions, he treated him fairly well.

"Tell me, 'Uncle' Bashir," he asked the servant, "am I a happy man?"

The poor man was startled. He realized why his servant was confused; for the first time ever he was talking to him as a colleague or friend. He encouraged his servant to forget about his worries and asked him with unusual insistence to answer his question.

"Through God's grace and favor, you are happy," the servant replied.

"You mean, I should be happy. Anyone with my job, living in my house, and enjoying my health, should be happy. That's what you want to say. But do you think I'm really happy?"

WORDS TO KNOW

savor (sā′vər) *v.* to appreciate; enjoy; relish

Hombre radiante de alegria [Man glowing with happiness] (1968), Rufino Tamayo. Reproduction authorized by The Olga and Rufino Tamayo Foundation, A.C.

The servant replied, "You work too hard, Sir," after yet more insistence, "it's more than any man can stand. . . ."

He hesitated, but his master gestured to him to continue with what he had to say.

"You get angry a lot," he said, "and have fierce arguments with your neighbors. . . ."

He interrupted him by laughing loudly. "What about you," he asked, "don't you have any worries?"

"Of course, no man can be free of worry."

"You mean that complete happiness is an impossible quest?"

"That applies to life in general. . . ."

How could he have dreamed up this incredible happiness? He or any other human being? It was a strange, unique happiness, as though it were a private secret he had been given. In the meeting hall of the newspaper building, he spotted his main rival in this world sitting down thumbing through a magazine. The man heard his footsteps, but did not look up from the magazine. He had undoubtedly noticed him in some way and was therefore pretending to ignore him so as to keep his own peace of mind. At some circulation meetings, they would argue so violently with each other that sparks began to fly and they would exchange bitter words. One stage more, and they would come to blows. A week ago, his rival had won in the union elections and he had lost. He had felt pierced by a sharp, poisoned arrow, and the world had darkened before his eyes. Now here he was approaching his rival's seat; the sight of him sitting there did not make him excited, nor did the memories of their dispute spoil his composure. He approached him with a pure and carefree heart, feeling drunk with his incredible happiness; his face showed an expression full of tolerance and forgiveness. It was as though he were approaching some other man towards whom he had never had any feelings of enmity, or perhaps he might be renewing a friendship again. "Good morning!" he said without feeling any compunction.

The man looked up in amazement. He was silent for a few moments until he recovered, and then returned the greeting curtly. It was as though he did not believe his eyes and ears.

He sat down alongside the man. "Marvelous weather today . . . ," he said.

"Okay . . . ," the other replied guardedly.

"Weather to fill your heart with happiness."

His rival looked at him closely and cautiously. "I'm glad that you're so happy . . . ," he muttered.

"Inconceivably happy . . . ," he replied with a laugh.

"I hope," the man continued in a rather hesitant tone of voice, "that I shan't spoil your happiness at the meeting of the administrative council. . . ."

"Not at all. My views are well known, but I don't mind if the members adopt your point of view. That won't spoil my happiness!"

"You've changed a great deal overnight," the man said with a smile.

"The fact is that I'm happy, inconceivably happy."

WORDS TO KNOW

enmity (ĕn'mĭ-tē) *n.* bitter hatred; hostility

compunction (kəm-pŭngk'shən) *n.* uneasiness caused by a feeling of guilt

The man examined his face carefully. "I bet your dear son has changed his mind about staying in Canada?" he asked.

"Never, never, my friend," he replied, laughing loudly. "He is still sticking to his decision. . . ."

"But that was the principal reason for your being so sad. . . ."

"Quite true. I've often begged him to come back out of pity for me in my loneliness and to serve his country. But he told me that he's going to open an engineering office with a Canadian partner; in fact, he's invited me to join him in it. Let him live where he'll be happy. I'm quite happy here—as you can see, inconceivably happy. . . ."

The man still looked a little doubtful. "Quite extraordinarily brave!" he said.

"I don't know what it is, but I'm happy in the full meaning of the word."

Yes indeed, this was full happiness; full, firm, weighty, and vital. As deep as absolute power, widespread as the wind, fierce as fire, bewitching as scent, transcending nature. It could not possibly last.

The other man warmed to his display of affection. "The truth is," he said, "that I always picture you as someone with a fierce and violent temperament which causes him a good deal of trouble and leads him to trouble other people."

"Really?"

"You don't know how to make a truce, you've no concept of intermediate solutions. You work with your nerves, with the marrow in your bones. You fight bitterly as though any problem is a matter of life and death!"

"Yes, that's true."

He accepted the criticism without any difficulty and with an open heart. His wave expanded into a boundless ocean of happiness. He struggled to control an innocent, happy laugh which the other man interpreted in a way far removed from its pure motives.

"So then," he asked, "you think it's necessary to be able to take a balanced view of events, do you?"

"Of course. I remember, by way of example, the argument we had the day before yesterday about racism. We both had the same views on the subject; it's something worth being zealous about, even to the point of anger. But what kind of anger? An intellectual anger, abstract to a certain extent; not the type which shatters your nerves, ruins your digestion, and gives you palpitations. Not so?"

"That's obvious; I quite understand. . . ." He struggled to control a second laugh and succeeded. His heart refused to renounce one drop of its joy. Racism, Vietnam, Palestine, . . . no problem could assail that fortress of happiness which was encircling his heart. When he remembered a problem, his heart guffawed. He was happy. It was a tyrannical happiness, despising all misery and laughing at any hardship; it wanted to laugh, dance, sing, and distribute its spirit of laughter, dancing and singing among the various problems of the world.

HE COULD NOT BEAR TO STAY IN HIS office at the newspaper; he felt no desire to work at all. He hated the very idea of thinking about his daily business, and completely failed to bring his mind down from its stronghold in the kingdom of happiness. How could he possibly write about a trolley bus falling into the Nile when he was so intoxicated by this frightening happiness? Yes, it really was frightening. How could it be anything else, when there was no reason for it at all, when it was so strong that it made him exhausted and paralyzed his will; apart from the fact that it had been with him for half a day without letting up in the slightest degree?

He left the pages of paper blank and started walking backwards and forwards across the room, laughing and cracking his fingers. . . .

WORDS TO KNOW

palpitation (păl'pĭ-tā'shən) *n.* a rapid fluttering of the heartbeat, often caused by stress or nervousness

He felt slightly worried; it did not penetrate deep enough to spoil his happiness, but paused on the surface of his mind like an abstract idea. It occurred to him that he might recall the tragedies of his life so that he could test their effect on his happiness. Perhaps they would be able to bring back some idea of balance or security, at least until his happiness began to flag a little. For example, he remembered his wife's death in all its various aspects and details. What had happened? The event appeared to him as a series of movements without any meaning or effect, as though it had happened to some other woman, the wife of another man, in some distant historical age. In fact, it had a contagious effect which prompted a smile, and then even provoked laughter. He could not stop himself laughing, and there he was guffawing, ha . . . ha . . . ha!

The same thing happened when he remembered the first letter his son had sent him saying that he wanted to emigrate to Canada. The sound of his guffaws as he paraded the bloody tragedies of the world before him would have attracted the attention of the newspaper workers and passersby in the street, had it not been for the thickness of the walls. He could do nothing to dislodge his happiness. Memories of unhappy times hit him like waves being thrown onto a sandy beach under the golden rays of the sun.

He excused himself from attending the administrative council and left the newspaper office without writing a word. After lunch, he lay down on his bed as usual but could not sleep. In fact, sleep seemed an impossibility to him. Nothing gave him any indication that it was coming, even slowly. He was in a place alight and gleaming, resounding with sleeplessness and joy. He had to calm down and relax, to quieten his senses and limbs, but how could he do it? He gave up trying to sleep, and got up. He began to hum as he was walking around his house. If this keeps up, he told himself, I won't be able to sleep, just as I can't work or feel sad. It was almost time for him to go to the club, but he did not feel like meeting any friends. What was the point of exchanging views on public affairs and private worries? What would they think if they found him laughing at every major problem? What would they say? How would they picture things? How would they explain it? No, he did not need anyone, nor did he want to spend the evening talking. He should be by himself, and go for a long walk to get rid of some of his excess vitality and think about his situation. What had happened to him? How was it that this incredible happiness had overwhelmed him? How long would he have to carry it on his shoulders? Would it keep depriving him of work, friends, sleep and peace of mind? Should he resign himself to it? Should he abandon himself to the flood to play with him as the whim took it? Or should he look for a way out for himself through thought, action, or advice?

When he was called into the examination room in the clinic of his friend, the specialist in internal medicine, he felt a little alarmed. The doctor looked at him with a smile. "You don't look like someone who's complaining about being ill," he said.

"I haven't come to see you because I'm ill," he told the doctor in a hesitant tone of voice, "but because I'm happy!"

The doctor looked piercingly at him with a questioning air.

"Yes," he repeated to underline what he had said, "because I'm happy!"

There was a period of silence. On one side, there was anxiety, and on the other, questioning and amazement.

"It's an incredible feeling which can't be defined in any other way, but it's very serious. . . ."

The doctor laughed. "I wish your illness was contagious," he said, prodding him jokingly.

"Don't treat it as a joke. It's very serious, as I told you. I'll describe it to you. . . ."

He told him all about his happiness from the time he had woken up in the morning till he had felt compelled to visit him.

"Haven't you been taking drugs, alcohol, or

Great Pyramid at Giza with Broken Head from Thebes (1963), David Hockney. Oil, 72″ × 72″. Copyright © David Hockney.

tranquilizers?"

"Absolutely nothing like that."

"Have you had some success in an important sphere of your life; work . . . love . . . money?"

"Nothing like that either. I've twice as much to worry about as I have to make me feel glad. . . ."

"Perhaps if you were patient for a while. . . ."

"I've been patient all day. I'm afraid I'll be spending the night wandering around. . . ."

The doctor gave him a precise, careful, and comprehensive examination and then shrugged his shoulders in despair. "You're a picture of health," he said.

"And so?"

"I could advise you to take a sleeping pill, but it would be better if you consulted a nerve specialist. . . ."

The examination was repeated in the nerve specialist's clinic with the selfsame precision, care, and comprehensiveness. "Your nerves are sound," the doctor told him, "they're in enviable condition!"

"Haven't you got a plausible explanation for my condition?" he asked hopefully.

"Consult a gland specialist!" the doctor replied, shaking his head.

The examination was conducted for a third time in the gland specialist's clinic with the same precision, care, and comprehensiveness. "I congratulate you!" the doctor told him. "Your glands are in good condition."

He laughed. He apologized for laughing, laughing as he did so. Laughter was his way of expressing his alarm and despair.

HE LEFT THE CLINIC WITH THE FEELING that he was alone; alone in the hands of his tyrannical happiness with no helper, no guide and no friend. Suddenly, he remembered the doctor's sign he sometimes saw from the window of his office in the newspaper building. It was true that he had no confidence in psychiatrists even though he had read about the significance of psychoanalysis. Apart from that, he knew that their tentacles were very long and they kept their patients tied in a sort of long association. He laughed as he remembered the method of cure through free association and the problems which it eventually uncovers. He was laughing as his feet carried him towards the psychiatrist's clinic, and imagined the doctor listening to his incredible complaints about feeling happy, when he was used to hearing people complain about hysteria,[1] schizophrenia,[2] anxiety, and so on.

"The truth is, Doctor, that I've come to see you because I'm happy!"

He looked at the doctor to see what effect his statement had had on him, but noticed that he was keeping his composure. He felt ridiculous. "I'm inconceivably happy . . . ," he said in a tone of confidence.

He began to tell the doctor his story, but the latter stopped him with a gesture of his hand. "An overwhelming, incredible, debilitating happiness?" he asked quietly.

He stared at him in amazement and was on the point of saying something, but the doctor spoke first. "A happiness which has made you stop working," he asked, "abandon your friends, and detest going to sleep . . . ?"

"You're a miracle!" he shouted.

"Every time you get involved in some misfortune," the psychiatrist continued quietly, "you dissolve into laughter . . . ?"

"Sir . . . are you familiar with the invisible?"

"No!" he said with a smile, "nothing like that. But I get a similar case in my clinic at least once a week!"

"Is it an epidemic?" he asked.

"I didn't say that, and I wouldn't claim that it's been possible to analyze one case into its primary elements as yet."

"But is it a disease?"

"All the cases are still under treatment."

"But are you satisfied without any doubt that they aren't natural cases . . . ?"

"That's a necessary assumption for the job; there's only . . ."

"Have you noticed any of them to be deranged in . . . ," he asked anxiously, pointing to his head.

"Absolutely not," the doctor replied convincingly. "I assure you that they're all intelligent in every sense of the word. . . ."

The doctor thought for a moment. "We should have two sessions a week, I think?" he said.

"Very well. . . ." he replied in resignation.

"There's no sense in getting alarmed or feeling sad. . . ."

Alarmed, sad? He smiled, and his smile kept on getting broader. A laugh slipped out, and before long, he was dissolving into laughter. He was determined to control himself, but his resistance collapsed completely. He started guffawing loudly. . . . ❖

---

1. **hysteria:** a neurotic condition characterized by emotional excitability and the presence of physical disorders without organic causes.
2. **schizophrenia** (skĭt′sə-frē′nē-ə): a severe mental disorder characterized by a distorted perception of reality.

WORDS TO KNOW

debilitating (dĭ-bĭl′ĭ-tā′tĭng) *adj.* producing weakness or loss of energy
debilitate *v.*

RESPONDING OPTIONS

FROM PERSONAL RESPONSE *TO* CRITICAL ANALYSIS

REFLECT 1. How did you react to the end of this story? Record your reaction in your notebook.

RETHINK 2. What effect does happiness seem to have on the main character's thoughts and actions?

Consider
- what his servant and his main rival say about how he used to be
- changes in his attitudes
- changes in his behavior

3. Why do you think the man seeks medical treatment for his happiness?

4. Do you think the kind of happiness the man experiences is desirable? Explain your answer.

5. What message about life do you think Mahfouz tries to convey in this story?

Consider
- the use of irony in the story
- what happens at the end of the story

RELATE 6. Like the main character in this story, many people have good health, comfortable surroundings, and a secure job but are not happy or content. What do you think prevents people in good circumstances from being happy?

ANOTHER PATHWAY

Cooperative Learning

With a small group of classmates, discuss what you think happiness means and what a person needs to be happy. Then compare and contrast your group's ideas with what happiness means to the main character in the story. Summarize your results in the form of a list of similarities and differences.

LITERARY CONCEPTS

Fantasy is literature in which the constraints of reality are intentionally disregarded. In many cases, it serves as a vehicle for explorations of the nature of reality and the hidden desires and capabilities of human beings. Some works of fantasy are set in fabulous dream worlds; in others, unbelievable elements are introduced into a mostly realistic world. The narration may leave readers unsure of the story's outcome or even what exactly is happening throughout the story. What elements of this story do you think could be considered fantastic? How do the fantastic elements relate to the story's realistic elements?

QUICKWRITES

1. Write a **definition** of happiness as it is depicted in this story. Then, in a few sentences, explain whether you think the definition is applicable to real life.

2. Write a **letter** in which the happy man explains to the psychiatrist why he does or does not want to be "cured" of his happiness.

PORTFOLIO *Save your writing. You may want to use it later as a springboard to a piece for your portfolio.*

LITERARY LINKS

In both "A Sunrise on the Veld" (page 1036) and "The Happy Man," the main characters experience exuberant happiness. Compare their experiences, their reactions to the experiences, and the ways the experiences affect their lives.

ALTERNATIVE ACTIVITIES

1. Sometimes the writer of a story or poem includes an epigraph at the beginning of the work—a quotation that sheds some light on the work's theme. Using books such as *Bartlett's Familiar Quotations,* find a quotation that could serve as an **epigraph** for "The Happy Man."
2. With a partner, improvise a **dialogue** between the happy man and his boss, who has discovered the happy man leaving the office without having done any work.

CRITIC'S CORNER

Critics have pointed out that much of Mahfouz's work—with its portrayals of injustice, uncertainty, and despair in modern Egypt—expresses a tragic view of life. Do you see any evidence of such a view in "The Happy Man"? Explain your answer.

WORDS TO KNOW

Write the letter of the word pair that expresses a relationship most like that of the capitalized pair.

1. ENMITY : FOE :: (a) cat : dog, (b) thunder : lightning, (c) rain : umbrella, (d) goodwill : friend
2. COMPUNCTION : APOLOGY :: (a) race : contest, (b) embarrassment : blush, (c) pride : shame, (d) dancer : gracefulness
3. STARVATION : DEBILITATING :: (a) speech : shouting, (b) hunter : hunting, (c) exercise : strengthening, (d) oxygen : breathing
4. PALPITATION : HEARTBEAT :: (a) cramp : muscle, (b) drawl : speech, (c) desperation: emotion, (d) panting : respiration
5. SAVOR : DISLIKE :: (a) accelerate : decelerate, (b) hope : encourage, (c) thirst : hunger, (d) care : protect

ART CONNECTION

Look carefully at the painting *Great Pyramid at Giza with Broken Head from Thebes* (page 1145). What message do you think is conveyed by the combination of realistic and fantastic elements in the painting?

NAGUIB MAHFOUZ

1911–

Naguib Mahfouz was born in Cairo, the youngest child in a large, lower-middle-class family. He attended state-supported schools, where, because of the abilities he displayed, he was one of the few students chosen to pursue university studies. He began writing in his teens, and his first novel was published when he was 28. Most of his stories and novels portray the tensions and contradictions of life in modern urban Egypt, revealing, through a mixture of realism, allegory, and symbolism, the struggles and moral crises faced by people at all levels of society. His most famous work is the so-called Cairo Trilogy—three novels chronicling the lives of three generations of a Cairo family—in which he depicts the turbulent development of modern Egypt from the end of World War I into the mid-1950s.

Mahfouz has published more than 50 works and is considered one of the foremost writers of fiction in the Arab world. He was, however, largely unknown outside Egypt until 1988, when he won the Nobel Prize in literature. Since then, many of his works have been translated into English to critical acclaim.

OTHER WORKS *Midaq Alley, The Thief and the Dogs, Miramar*

LASERLINKS
• *AUTHOR BACKGROUND*

PREVIEWING

FICTION

Paintbox Place

Ruth Rendell

PERSONAL CONNECTION

Get together with a group of classmates and brainstorm a list of associations you have with the form of fiction known as the detective story. In addition to descriptive words and phrases, your list may include names of famous fictional detectives and titles of stories written about them.

LITERARY CONNECTION

Sir Arthur Conan Doyle set the standard for the detective-story genre in 1887, when he introduced the fictional sleuth Sherlock Holmes. By the early 1900s, the formula for a successful detective mystery included a murder, a long list of suspects, assorted clues, and the use of scientific techniques to track and expose the murderer. A traditional detective story typically focuses on the resolution of a crime either by an astute police detective or by an amateur detective who puts the professional sleuths to shame.

In more recent decades, however, the detective story has undergone some changes. Instead of focusing on crimes and the techniques used to solve them, contemporary writers frequently focus on the personalities and motives of the characters, emphasizing the psychology of criminals and detectives. Ruth Rendell, the author of "Paintbox Place" and currently one of England's most popular writers of detective stories, believes that modern research in psychology and sociology has changed the way detective stories are written.

Although many British writers of detective stories are women, most successful fictional detectives are still male. Of the few female sleuths that have been created, the most memorable—such as Agatha Christie's Miss Jane Marple—are elderly women who try their hand at amateur investigation.

READING CONNECTION

Understanding Characters As you read the detective story "Paintbox Place," make your own judgments about the traits and inner qualities of each character, based on his or her behavior in the story. Make a chart, like the one shown, in your notebook to record your thoughts. Be ready to modify your chart as the story progresses and your judgments change.

Character	Behavior	Trait or Quality Inferred

PAINTBOX PLACE

RUTH RENDELL

Elderly ladies as detectives are not unknown in fiction. Avice Julian could think of two or three, the creations of celebrated authors, and no doubt there were more. It would seem that the quiet routine of an old woman's life, her penchant for gossip and knitting and her curiosity, born of boredom, provide a suitable climate for the consideration of motive and the assessment of clues. In fiction, that is. Would it, Mrs. Julian sometimes wondered, also be true in reality?

WORDS TO KNOW

penchant (pĕn′chənt) *n.* a strong taste or liking

She took a personal interest. She was eighty-four years old, thin, sharp-witted, arthritic, cantankerous and intolerant. Most of her time she spent sitting in an upright chair in the bay window of her drawing room in her very large house, observing what her neighbors got up to. From the elderly ladies of mystery fiction, though, she differed in one important respect. They were spinsters, she was a widow. In fact, she had been twice married and twice widowed. Could that, she asked herself after reading a particularly apposite[1] detective novel, be of significance? Could it affect the deductive powers and it be her spinsterhood which made Miss Marple, say, a detective of genius? Perhaps. Anthropologists say (Mrs. Julian was an erudite person) that in ancient societies maidenhood was revered as having awesome and unique powers. It might be that this was true and that prolonged virginity, though in many respects disagreeable, only serves to enhance them. Possibly, one day, she would have an opportunity to put to the test the Aged Female Sleuth Theory. She saw enough from her window, sitting there knitting herself a twinset[2] in dark blue two-ply. Mostly she eyed the block of houses opposite, on the other side of broad, tree-lined Abelard Avenue.

POSSIBLY, ONE DAY, SHE WOULD HAVE AN OPPORTUNITY TO PUT TO THE TEST THE AGED FEMALE SLEUTH THEORY.

There were six of them, all joined together, all exactly the same. They all had three stories, plate-glass windows, a bit of concrete to put the car on, a flowerbed, an outside cupboard to put parcels in and an outside cupboard to put the rubbish sack in. Mrs. Julian thought that unhygienic. She had an old-fashioned dustbin,[3] though she had to keep a black plastic bag inside it if she wanted Northway Borough Council to collect her rubbish.

The houses had been built on the site of an old mansion. There had been several such in Abelard Avenue, as well as big houses like Mrs. Julian's which were not quite mansions. Most of these had been pulled down and those which remained converted into flats. They would do that to hers when she was gone, thought Mrs. Julian, those nephews and nieces and great nephews and great nieces of hers would do that. She had watched the houses opposite being built. About ten years ago it had been. She called them the paintbox houses because there was something about them that reminded her of a child's drawing and because each had its front door painted a different color, yellow, red, blue, lime, orange and chocolate.

"It's called Paragon Place," said Mrs. Upton, her cleaner and general help, when the building was completed.

"What a ridiculous name! Paintbox Place would be far more suitable."

Mrs. Upton ignored this as she ignored all of Avice Julian's remarks which she regarded as "showing off," affected or just plain senile. "They do say," she said, "that the next thing'll be they'll start building on that bit of waste ground next door."

"Waste ground?" said Mrs. Julian distantly. "Can you possibly mean the wood?"

"Waste ground" had certainly been a

1. **apposite** (ăp'ə-zĭt): appropriate; relevant.
2. **twinset:** matching pullover and cardigan sweaters.
3. **dustbin:** trash can.

WORDS TO KNOW
erudite (ĕr'yə-dīt') *adj.* knowledgeable; learned
enhance (ĕn-hăns') *v.* to make greater; increase
paragon (păr'ə-gŏn') *n.* a model of perfection or excellence

misnomer, though "wood" was an exaggeration. It was a couple of rustic acres, more or less covered with trees of which part of one side bordered Mrs. Julian's garden, part the Great North Road, and which had its narrow frontage on Abelard Avenue. People used the path through it as a short cut from the station. At Mrs. Upton's unwelcome forebodings, Avice Julian had got up and gone to the right-hand side of the bay window which overlooked the "wood" and thought how disagreeable it would be to have another Paintbox Place on her back doorstep. In these days when society seemed to have gone mad, when the cost of living was frightening, when there were endless strikes and she was asked to pay 98 per cent income tax on the interest on some of her investments, it was quite possible, anything could happen.

However, no houses were built next door to Mrs. Julian. It appeared that the "wood," though hardly National Trust or an Area of Outstanding Natural Beauty, was nevertheless scheduled as "not for residential development." For her lifetime, it seemed, she would look out on birch trees and green turf and small hawthorn bushes—when she was not, that is, looking out on the inhabitants of Paintbox Place, on Mr. and Mrs. Arnold and Mr. Laindon and the Nicholsons, all young people, none of them much over forty. Their activities were of absorbing interest to Mrs. Julian as she knitted away in dark blue two-ply, and a source too of disapproval and sometimes outright condemnation.

After Christmas, in the depths of the winter, when Mrs. Julian was in the kitchen watching Mrs. Upton peeling potatoes for lunch, Mrs. Upton said: "You're lucky I'm private, have you thought of that?"

This was beyond Mrs. Julian's understanding. "I beg your pardon?"

"I mean it's lucky for you I'm not one of those council home helps. They're all coming out on strike, the lot of them coming out. They're NUPE, see? Don't you read your paper?"

Mrs. Julian certainly did read her paper, the *Daily Telegraph,* which was delivered to her door each morning. She read it from cover to cover after she had had her breakfast, and she was well aware that the National Union of Public Employees was making rumbling noises and threatening to bring its members out over a pay increase. It was typical, in her view, of the age in which she found herself living. Someone or other was always on strike. But she had very little idea of how to identify the Public Employee and had hoped the threatened action would not affect her. To Mrs. Upton she said as much.

"Not affect you?" said Mrs. Upton, furiously scalping brussels sprouts. She seemed to find Mrs. Julian's innocence uproariously funny. "Well, there'll be no gritters[4] on the roads for a start and maybe you've noticed it's snowing again. Gritters are NUPE. They'll have to close the schools so there'll be kids all over the streets. School caretakers are NUPE. No ambulances if you fall on the ice and break your leg, no hospital porters, and what's more, no dustmen. We won't none of us get our rubbish collected on account of dustmen are NUPE. So how about that for not affecting you?"

Mrs. Julian's dustbin, kept just inside the front gate on a concrete slab and concealed from view by a laurel bush and a cotoneaster, was not emptied that week. On the following Monday she looked out of the right-hand side of the bay window and saw under the birch trees, on the frosty ground, a dozen or so black plastic sacks, apparently filled with rubbish, their tops secured with wire fasteners. There was no end to the propensities of some people for making disgusting litter,

4. **gritters:** workers who spread sand and salt on icy roads.

WORDS TO KNOW **misnomer** (mĭs-nō′mər) *n.* a name that is unsuitable or inaccurate

Detail of *Hillside in Wales* (1962), Laurence Stephen Lowry. Tate Gallery, London/Art Resource, New York.

thought Mrs. Julian, give them half a chance. She would telephone Northway Council, she would telephone the police. But first she would put on her squirrel coat and take her stick and go out and have a good look.

The snow had melted, the pavement was wet. A car had pulled up and a young woman in jeans and a pair of those silly boots that came up to the thighs like in a pantomime was taking two more black plastic sacks out of the back of it. Mrs. Julian was on the point of telling her in no uncertain terms to remove her rubbish at once, when she caught sight of a notice stuck up under the trees. The notice was of plywood with printing on it in red chalk: *Northway Council Refuse Tip.*[5] *Bags This Way.*

Mrs. Julian went back into her house. She told Mrs. Upton about the refuse tip and Mrs. Upton said she already knew but hadn't told Mrs. Julian because it would only upset her.

"You don't know what the world's coming to, do you?" said Mrs. Upton, opening a tin of peaches for lunch.

"I most certainly do know," said Mrs. Julian. "Anarchy. Anarchy is what it is coming to."

Throughout the week the refuse on the tip mounted. Fortunately, the weather was very cold; as yet there was no smell. In Paintbox Place black plastic sacks of rubbish began to appear outside the cupboard doors, on the steps beside the colored front doors, overflowing into the narrow flowerbeds. Mrs. Upton came five days a week but

5. **refuse** (rĕf'yo͞os) **tip:** garbage dump.

WORDS TO KNOW

anarchy (ăn'ər-kē) *n.* disorder and confusion; lawlessness

not on Saturdays or Sundays. When the doorbell rang at ten on Saturday morning Mrs. Julian answered it herself and there outside was Mr. Arnold from the house with the red front door, behind him on the gravel drive a wheelbarrow containing five black plastic sacks of rubbish.

He was a good-looking, cheerful, polite man was Mr. Arnold. Forty-two or three, she supposed. Sometimes she fancied she had seen a melancholy look in his eyes. No wonder, she could well understand if he was melancholic. He said good morning, and he was on his way to the tip with his rubbish and Mr. Laindon's and could he take hers too?

"That's very kind and thoughtful of you, Mr. Arnold," said Mrs. Julian. "You'll find my bag inside the dustbin at the gate. I do appreciate it."

"No trouble," said Mr. Arnold. "I'll make a point of collecting your bag, shall I, while the strike lasts?"

Mrs. Julian thought. A plan was forming in her mind. "That won't be necessary, Mr. Arnold. I shall be disposing of my waste by other means. Composting,[6] burning," she said, "beating tins flat, that kind of thing. Now if everyone were to do the same . . ."

"Ah, life's too short for that, Mrs. Julian," said Mr. Arnold and he smiled and went off with his wheelbarrow before she could say what was on the tip of her tongue, that it was shorter for her than for most people.

She watched him take her sack out of the dustbin and trundle his barrow up the slope and along the path between the wet black mounds. Poor man. Many an evening, when Mr. Arnold was working late, she had seen the chocolate front door open and young Mr. Laindon, divorced, they said, just before he came there, emerge and tap at the red front door and be admitted. Once she had seen Mrs. Arnold and Mr. Laindon coming back from the station together, taking the short cut through the "wood." They had been enjoying each other's company and laughing, though it had been cold and quite late, all of ten at night. And here was Mr. Arnold performing kindly little services for Mr. Laindon, all innocent of how he was deceived. Or perhaps he was not quite innocent, not ignorant and that accounted for his sad eyes. Perhaps he was like Othello who doted yet doubted, suspected yet strongly loved.[7] It was all very disagreeable, thought Avice Julian, employing one of her favorite words.

She went back into the kitchen and examined the boiler, a small coke-burning furnace disused since 1963 when the late Alexander Julian had installed central heating. The chimney, she was sure, was swept, the boiler could be used again. Tins could be hammered flat and stacked temporarily in the garden shed. And—why not?—she would start a compost heap. No one should be without a compost heap at the best of times, any alternative was most wasteful.

Her neighbors might contribute to the squalor; she would not. Presently she wrapped herself up in her late husband's Burberry and made her way down to the end of the garden. On the "wood" side, in the far corner, that would be the place. Up against the fence, thought Mrs. Julian. She found a bundle of stout sticks in the shed—Alexander had once grown runner beans up them—and selecting four of these, managed to drive them into the soft earth, one at each of the angles of a roughly conceived square. Next, a strip of chicken wire went round the posts to form an enclosure. She would get Mrs. Upton to buy her some garotta next time she went shopping. Avice Julian knew all about making compost heaps, she and her first husband had

6. **composting:** allowing vegetable refuse and other organic matter to decompose into a mixture that can be used to fertilize and condition soil.

7. **Othello . . . strongly loved:** In Shakespeare's play *Othello,* the title character murders his beloved wife in a jealous rage after being falsely persuaded that she has been unfaithful.

WORDS TO KNOW **squalor** (skwŏl′ər) *n.* a dismal state of filthiness

been experts during the war.

In the afternoon, refreshed by a nap, she emptied the vegetable cupboard and found some strange potatoes growing stems and leaves and some carrots covered in blue fur. Mrs. Upton was not a hygienic housekeeper. The potatoes and carrots formed the foundation of the new compost heap. Mrs. Julian pulled up a handful of weeds and scattered them on the top.

"I shall have my work cut out, I can see that," said Mrs. Upton on Monday morning. She laughed unpleasantly. "I'm sure I don't know when the cleaning'll get done if I'm traipsing up and down the garden path all day long."

Between them they got the boiler alight and fed it Saturday's *Daily Telegraph* and Sunday's *Observer.* Mrs. Upton hammered out a can that had contained baked beans and banged her thumb. She made a tremendous fuss about it which Mrs. Julian tried to ignore. Mrs. Julian went back to her window, cast on for the second sleeve of the dark blue two-ply jumper,[8] and watched women coming in cars with their rubbish sacks for the tip. Some of them hardly bothered to set foot on the pavement but opened the boots of their cars and hurled the sacks from where they stood. With extreme distaste, Mrs. Julian watched one of these sacks strike the trunk of a tree and burst open, scattering tins and glass and peelings and leavings and dregs and grounds in all directions.

During the last week of January, Mrs. Julian always made her marmalade. She saw no reason to discontinue this custom because she was eighty-four. Grumbling and moaning about her back and varicose veins, Mrs. Upton went out to buy preserving sugar and Seville oranges. Mrs. Julian peeled potatoes and prepared a cabbage for lunch, carrying the peelings and the outer leaves down the garden to the compost heap herself. Most of the orange peel would go on there in due course. Mrs. Julian's marmalade was the clear jelly kind with only strands of rind in it, pared hair-thin.

They made the first batch in the afternoon. Mr. Arnold called on the following morning with his barrow. "Your private refuse operative, Mrs. Julian, at your service."

"Ah, but I've done what I told you I should do," she said and insisted on his coming down the garden with her to see the compost heap.

"You eat a lot of oranges," said Mr. Arnold.

Then she told him about the marmalade and Mr. Arnold said he had never tasted home-made marmalade, he didn't know people made it any more. This shocked Mrs. Julian and rather confirmed her opinion of Mrs. Arnold. She gave him a jar of marmalade and he was profuse in his thanks.

She was glad to get indoors again. The meteorological people had been right when they said there was another cold spell coming. Mrs. Julian knitted and looked out of the window and saw Mrs. Arnold brought back from somewhere or other by Mr. Laindon in his car. By lunchtime it had begun to snow. The heavy, grey, louring sky looked full of snow.

This did not deter Mrs. Julian's great-niece from dropping in unexpectedly with her boyfriend. They said frankly that they had come to look at the rubbish tip which was said to be the biggest in London apart from the one which filled the whole of Leicester Square. They stood in the window staring at it and giggling each time anyone arrived with fresh offerings.

"It's surrealistic!" shrieked the great-niece as a sack, weighted down with snow, rolled slowly out of the branches of a tree where it had been suspended for some days. "It's fantastic! I could stand here all day just watching it."

Mrs. Julian was very glad that she did not but

8. **jumper:** in Britain, a pullover sweater.

WORDS TO KNOW

traipse (trāps) *v.* to walk or tramp about
profuse (prə-fyōōs') *adj.* extremely generous; lavish; abundant

departed after about an hour (with a jar of marmalade) to something called the Screen on the Hill which turned out to be a cinema in Hampstead. After they had gone it snowed harder than ever. There was a heavy frost that night and the next.

"You don't want to set foot outside," said Mrs. Upton on Monday morning. "The pavements are like glass." And she went off into a long tale about her son Stewart who was a police constable finding an old lady who had slipped over and was lying helpless on the ice.

Mrs. Julian nodded impatiently. "I have no intention whatsoever of going outside. And you must be very careful when you go down that path to the compost heap."

They made a second batch of marmalade. The boiler refused to light so Mrs. Julian said to leave it but try it again tomorrow, for there was quite an accumulation of newspapers to be burnt. Mrs. Julian sat in the window, sewing together the sections of the dark blue two-ply jumper and watching the people coming through the snow to the refuse tip. Capped with snow, the mounds on the tip resembled a mountain range. In the Arctic perhaps, thought Mrs. Julian fancifully, or on some planet where the temperature was always sub-zero.

All the week it snowed and froze and snowed and melted and froze again. Mrs. Julian stayed indoors. Her nephew, the one who wrote science fiction, phoned to ask if she was all right, and her other nephew, the one who was a commercial photographer, came round to sweep her drive clear of snow. By the time he arrived Mr. Laindon had already done it, but Mrs. Julian gave him a jar of marmalade just the same. She had resisted giving one to Mr. Laindon because of the way he carried on with Mrs. Arnold.

It started thawing on Saturday. Mrs. Julian sat in the window, casting on for the left front of her cardigan and watching the snow and ice drip away and flow down the gutters. She left the curtains undrawn, as she often did, when it got dark.

At about eight Mrs. Arnold came out of the red front door and Mr. Laindon came out of the chocolate front door and they stood chatting and laughing together until Mr. Arnold came out. Mr. Arnold unlocked the doors of his car and said something to Mr. Laindon. How Mrs. Julian wished she could have heard what it was! Mr. Laindon only shook his head. She saw Mrs. Arnold get quickly into the car and shut the door. Very cowardly, not wanting to get involved, thought Mrs. Julian. Mr. Arnold was arguing now with Mr. Laindon, trying to persuade him to something, apparently. Perhaps to leave Mrs. Arnold alone. But all Mr. Laindon did was give a silly sort of laugh and retreat into the house with the chocolate door. The Arnolds went off, Mr. Arnold driving quite recklessly fast in this sort of weather, as if he were fearfully late for wherever they were going or, more likely, in a great rage.

THE ARNOLDS WENT OFF, MR. ARNOLD DRIVING QUITE RECKLESSLY FAST IN THIS SORT OF WEATHER, AS IF HE WERE FEARFULLY LATE FOR WHEREVER THEY WERE GOING OR, MORE LIKELY, IN A GREAT RAGE.

Mrs. Julian saw nothing of Mr. Laindon on the following day, the Sunday, but in the afternoon she saw Mrs. Arnold go out on her own. She crossed the road from Paintbox Place and took the path, still mercifully clear of rubbish sacks, through the "wood" towards the station. Off to a secret assignation,[9] Mrs. Julian supposed. The weather was drier and less cold but she felt no inclination to go out. She sat in the window, doing the ribbing part of the left front of her cardigan and noting that the rubbish sacks were mounting again in Paintbox Place. For

9. **assignation** (ăs′ĭg-nā′shən): a meeting between lovers.

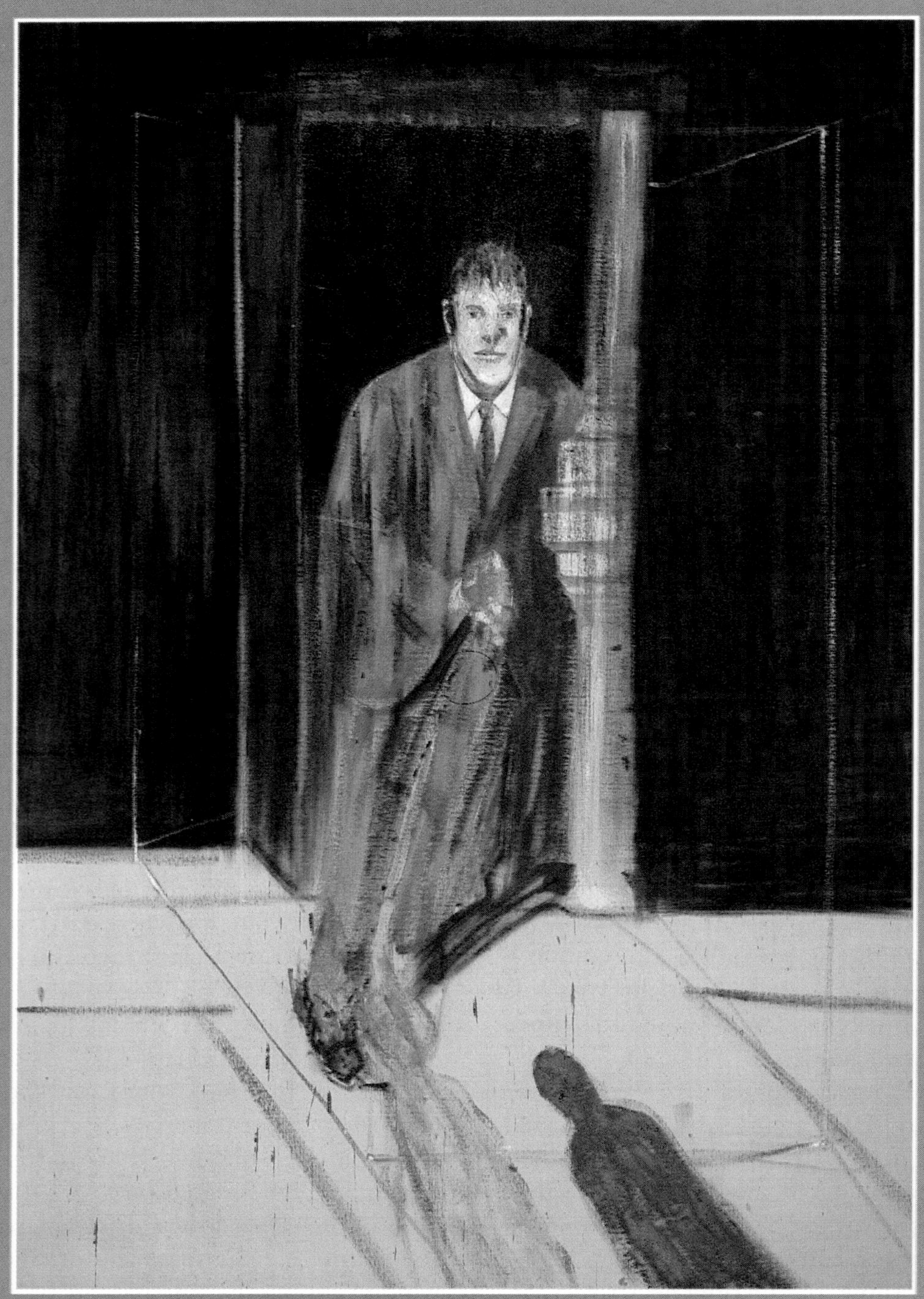

Portrait of Lucien Freud (1951), Francis Bacon. Oil on canvas. The Whitworth Art Gallery, University of Manchester, England (0.1980.3).

some reason, laziness perhaps, Mr. Arnold had failed to clear them away on Saturday morning. Mrs. Julian had a nap and a cup of tea and read the *Observer*.

It pleased her that Mrs. Upton had burnt up all the old newspapers. At any rate, there were none to be seen. But what had she done with the empty tins? Mrs. Julian looked everywhere for the hammered-out, empty tins. She looked in the kitchen cupboards and the cupboards under the stairs and even in the dining room and the morning room. You never knew with people like Mrs. Upton. Perhaps she had put them in the shed, perhaps she had actually done what her employer suggested and put them in the shed.

Mrs. Julian went back to the living room, back to her window, and got there just in time to see Mr. Arnold letting himself into his house. Time tended to pass slowly for her at weekends and she was surprised to find it was as late as nine o'clock. It had begun to rain. She could see the slanting rain shining gold in the light from the lamps in Paintbox Place.

She sat in the window and picked up her knitting. After a little while the red front door opened and Mr. Arnold came out. He had changed out of his wet clothes, changed grey trousers for dark brown, blue jacket for sweater and anorak.[10] He took hold of the nearest rubbish sack and dragged it just inside the door. Within a minute or two he had come out again, carrying the sack, which he loaded onto the barrow he fetched from the parking area.

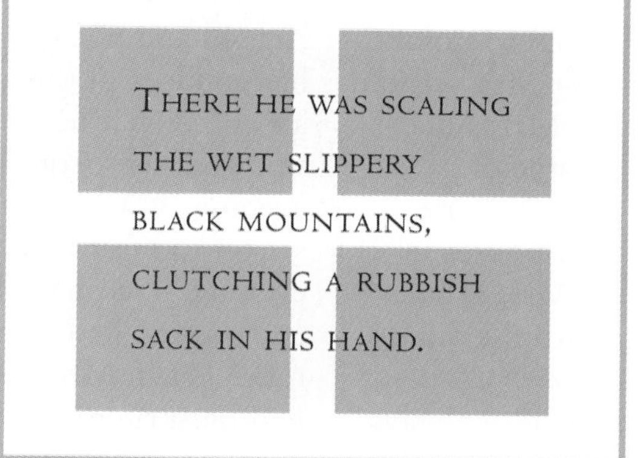
THERE HE WAS SCALING
THE WET SLIPPERY
BLACK MOUNTAINS,
CLUTCHING A RUBBISH
SACK IN HIS HAND.

It was at this point that Mrs. Julian's telephone rang. The phone was at the other end of the room. Her caller was the elder of her nephews, the commercial photographer, wanting to know if he might borrow pieces from her Second Empire[11] bedroom furniture for some set or background. They had all enjoyed the marmalade, it was nearly gone. Mrs. Julian said he should have another jar of marmalade next year but he certainly could not borrow her furniture. She didn't want pictures of her wardrobe and dressing table all over those vulgar magazines, thank you very much. When she returned to her point of vantage at the window Mr. Arnold had disappeared.

Disappeared, that is, from the forecourt of Paintbox Place. Mrs. Julian crossed to the right-hand side of the bay to draw the curtains and shut out the rain, and there he was scaling the wet slippery black mountains, clutching a rubbish sack in his hand. The sack looked none too secure, for its side had been punctured by the neck of a bottle and its top was fastened not with a wire fastener but wound round and round with blue string. Finally, he dropped it at the side of one of the high mounds round the birch tree. Mrs. Julian drew the curtains.

Mrs. Upton arrived punctually in the morning, agog with her news. It was a blessing she had such a strong constitution, Mrs. Julian thought. Many a woman of her advanced years would have been made ill—or worse—by hearing a thing like that.

"How can you possibly know?" she said. "There's nothing in this morning's paper."

Stewart, of course. Stewart, the policeman.

"She was coming home from the station," said Mrs. Upton, "through that bit of waste ground."

---

10. **anorak** (ăn′ə-răk′): a hooded jacket; parka.

11. **Second Empire:** a style of furniture popular in France in the mid-19th century. (The term *Second Empire* refers to the period, from 1852 to 1870, when the emperor Napoleon III ruled France.)

She cocked a thumb in the direction of the "wood." "Asking for trouble, wasn't she? Nasty dark lonely place. This chap, whoever he was, he clouted her over the head with what they call a blunt instrument. That was about half-past eight, though they never found her till ten. Stewart says there was blood all over, turned him up proper it did, and him used to it."

"What a shocking thing," said Mrs. Julian. "What a dreadful thing. Poor Mrs. Arnold."

"Murdered for the cash in her handbag, though there wasn't all that much. No one's safe these days."

When such an event takes place it is almost impossible for some hours to deflect one's thoughts onto any other subject. Her knitting lying in her lap, Mrs. Julian sat in the window, contemplating the paintbox houses. A vehicle that was certainly a police car, though it had no blue lamp, arrived in the course of the morning and two policemen in plain clothes were admitted to the house with the red front door. Presumably by Mr. Arnold who was not, however, visible to Mrs. Julian.

What must it be like to lose, in so violent a manner, one's marriage partner? Even so unsatisfactory a marriage partner as poor Mrs. Arnold had been. Did Mr. Laindon know? Mrs. Julian wondered. She found herself incapable of imagining what his feelings must be. No one came out of or went into any of the houses in Paintbox Place and at one o'clock Mrs. Julian had to leave her window and go into the dining room for lunch.

"Of course you know what the police always say, don't you?" said Mrs. Upton, sticking a rather underdone lamb chop down in front of her. "The husband's always the first to be suspected. Shows marriage up in a shocking light, don't you reckon?"

Mrs. Julian made no reply but merely lifted her shoulders. Both her husbands had been devoted to her and she told herself that she had no personal experience of the kind of uncivilized relationship Mrs. Upton was talking about. But could she say the same for Mrs. Arnold? Had she not, in fact, for weeks, for months, now been deploring the state of the Arnolds' marriage and even awaiting some fearful climax?

It was at this point, or soon after when she was back in her window, that Avice Julian began to see herself as a possible Miss Marple or Miss Silver,[12] though she had not recently been reading the works of either of those ladies' creators. Rather it was that she saw the sound common-sense which lay behind the notion of elderly women as detectives. Who else has the leisure to be so observant? Who else had behind them a lifetime of knowledge of human nature? Who else has suffered sufficient disillusionment to be able to face so squarely such unpalatable facts?

Beyond a doubt, the facts Mrs. Julian was facing were unpalatable. Nevertheless, she marshaled them. Mrs. Arnold had been an unfaithful wife. She had been conducting some sort of love affair with Mr. Laindon. That Mr. Arnold had not known of it was evident from her conduct of this extra-marital adventure in his absence. That he was beginning to be aware of it was apparent from his behavior of Saturday evening. What more probable than that he had set off to meet his wife at the station on Sunday evening, had quarreled with her about this very matter, and had struck her down in a jealous rage? When Mrs. Julian had seen him first he had been running home from the scene of the crime, clutching to him under his jacket the weapon for which Mrs. Upton said the police were now searching.

The morning had been dull and damp but after lunch it had dried up and a weak, watery sun came out. Mrs. Julian put on her squirrel

12. **Miss Silver:** the fictional spinster detective Maud Silver—a retired governess—created by the author Patricia Wentworth.

coat and went out into the garden, the first time she had been out for nine days.

The compost heap had not increased much in size. Perhaps the weight of snow had flattened it down or, more likely, Mrs. Upton had failed in her duty. Displeased, Mrs. Julian went back into the front garden and down to the gate where she lifted the lid of her dustbin, confident of what she would find inside. But, no, she had done Mrs. Upton an injustice. The dustbin was empty and quite clean. She stood by the fence and viewed the tip.

What an eyesore it was! A considerable amount of leakage, due to careless packing and fastening, had taken place, and the wet, fetid, black hillocks were strewn all over with torn and soggy paper, cartons and packages, while in the valleys between clustered, like some evil growth, a conglomeration of decaying fruit and vegetable parings, mildewed bread, tea leaves, coffee grounds and broken glass. In one hollow there was movement. Maggots or the twitching nose of a rat? Mrs. Julian shuddered and looked hastily away. She raised her eyes to take in the continued presence under the birch tree of the sack Mr. Arnold had deposited there on the previous evening, the sack that was punctured by the neck of a bottle and bound with blue string.

She returned to the house. Was she justified in keeping this knowledge of hers to herself? There was by then no doubt in her mind as to what Mr. Arnold had done. After killing his wife he had run home, changed his bloodstained clothes for clean ones and, fetching in the rubbish sack from outside, inserted into it the garments he had just removed and the blunt instrument, so-called, he had used. An iron bar perhaps or a length of metal piping he had picked up in the "wood." In so doing he had mislaid the wire fastener and could find no other, so he had been obliged to fasten the sack with the nearest thing to hand, a piece of string. Then across the road with it as he had been on several previous occasions, this time to deposit there a sack containing evidence that would incriminate him if found on his property. But what could be more anonymous than a black plastic sack on a council refuse tip? There it would be only one among a thousand and, he must have supposed, impossible to identify.

Mrs. Julian disliked the idea of harming her kind and thoughtful neighbor. But justice must be done. If she was in possession of knowledge the police could not otherwise acquire, it was plainly her duty to reveal it. And the more she thought of it the more convinced she was that there was the correct solution to the crime against Mrs. Arnold. Would not Miss Seaton[13] have thought so? Would not Miss Marple, having found parallels between Mr. Arnold's behavior and that of some St. Mary Mead[14] husband, having considered and weighed the awful significance of the quarrel on Saturday night and the extraordinary circumstance of taking rubbish to a tip at nine-thirty on a wet Sunday evening, would she not have laid the whole matter before the CID?[15]

She hesitated for only a few minutes before fetching the telephone directory and looking up the number. By three o'clock in the afternoon she was making a call to her local police station.

The detective sergeant and constable who came to see Mrs. Julian half an hour later showed no surprise at being supplied with information by such as she. Perhaps they too read the works of the inventors of elderly lady sleuths. They treated Mrs. Julian with great courtesy and after she had told them what she suspected they suggested she accompany them to the vicinity of the tip and point out the incriminating sack.

However, it was quite possible for her to do this from the right-hand side of the bay window.

13. **Miss Seaton:** the fictional spinster detective Emily D. Seaton—a retired art teacher—created by the author Heron Carvic.

14. **St. Mary Mead:** the small English village where Miss Marple lives.

15. **CID:** the Criminal Investigation Department of the London police force.

The detectives nodded and wrote things in notebooks and thanked her and went away, and after a little while a van arrived and a policeman in uniform got out and removed the sack. Mrs. Julian sat in the window, working away at the lacy pattern on the front of her dark blue cardigan and watching for the arrest of Mr. Arnold. She watched with trepidation and fear for him and a reluctant sympathy. There were policemen about the area all day, tramping around among the rubbish sacks, investigating gardens and ringing doorbells, but none of them went to arrest Mr. Arnold.

Nothing happened at all apart from Mr. Laindon calling at eight in the evening. He seemed very upset and his face looked white and drawn. He had come, he said, to ask Mrs. Julian if she would care to contribute to the cost of a wreath for Mrs. Arnold or would she be sending flowers personally?

"I should prefer to see to my own little floral tribute," said Mrs. Julian rather frostily.

"Just as you like, of course. I'm really going round asking people to give myself something to do. I feel absolutely bowled over by this business. They were wonderful to me, the Arnolds, you know. You couldn't have better friends. I was feeling pretty grim when I first came here—my divorce and all that—and the Arnolds, well, they looked after me like a brother, never let me be on my own, even insisted I go out with them. And now a terrible thing like this has to happen and to a wonderful person like that . . ."

Mrs. Julian had no wish to listen to this sort of thing. No doubt, there were some gullible enough to believe it. She went to bed wondering if the arrest would take place during the night, discreetly, so that the neighbors should not witness it.

The paintbox houses looked just the same in the morning. But of course they would. The arrest of Mr. Arnold would hardly affect their appearance. The phone rang at 9:30 and Mrs. Upton took the call. She came into the morning room where Mrs. Julian was finishing her breakfast.

"The police want to come round and see you again. I said I'd ask. I said you mightn't be up to it, not being so young as you used to be."

"Neither are you or they," said Mrs. Julian and then she spoke to the police herself and told them to come whenever it suited them.

During the next half hour some not disagreeable fantasies went round in Mrs. Julian's head. Such is often the outcome of identifying with characters in fiction. She imagined herself congratulated on her acumen and even, on a future occasion when some other baffling crime had taken place, consulted by policemen of high rank. Mrs. Upton had served her well on the whole, as well as could be expected in these trying times. Perhaps one day, when it came to the question of Stewart's promotion, a word from her in the right place . . .

"I HOPE YOU WON'T FIND IT TOO DISTASTEFUL . . . TO CAST YOUR EYES OVER SOME OF THE CONTENTS OF THIS BAG."

The doorbell rang. It was the same detective sergeant and detective constable. Mrs. Julian was a little disappointed, she thought she rated an inspector now. They greeted her with jovial smiles and invited her into her own kitchen where they said they had something to show her. Between them they were lugging a large canvas bag.

The sergeant asked Mrs. Upton if she could find them a sheet of newspaper, and before Mrs. Julian could say that they had burnt all the newspapers, Saturday's *Daily Telegraph* was produced from where it had been secreted. Then,

WORDS TO KNOW

acumen (ə-kyōō′mən) *n.* keen insight

to Mrs. Julian's amazement, he pulled out of the canvas bag the black plastic rubbish sack, punctured on one side and secured at the top with blue string, which she had seen Mr. Arnold deposit on the tip on Sunday evening.

"I hope you won't find it too distasteful, madam," he said, "just to cast your eyes over some of the contents of this bag."

Mrs. Julian was astounded that he should ask such a thing of someone of her age. But she indicated with a faint nod and wave of her hand that she would comply, while inwardly she braced herself for the sight of some hideous bludgeon,[16] perhaps encrusted with blood and hair, and for the emergence from the depths of the sack of a bloodstained jacket and pair of trousers. She would not faint or cry out, she was determined on that, whatever she might see.

It was the constable who untied the string and spread open the neck of the sack. With care, the sergeant began to remove its contents and to drop them on the newspaper Mrs. Upton had laid on the floor. He dropped them, in so far as he could, in small separate heaps: a quantity of orange peel, a few lengths of dark blue two-ply knitting wool, innumerable Earl Grey tea bags, potato peelings, cabbage leaves, a lamb chop bone, the sherry bottle whose neck had pierced the side of the sack, and seven copies of the *Daily Telegraph* with one of the *Observer,* all with "Julian, 1 Abelard Avenue" scrawled above the masthead . . .

Mrs. Julian surveyed her kitchen floor. She looked at the sergeant and the constable and at the yard or so of dark blue two-ply knitting wool which he still held in his hand and which he had unwound from the neck of the sack.

"I fail to understand," she said.

"I'm afraid this sack would appear to contain waste from your own household, Mrs. Julian," said the sergeant. "In other words to have been yours and been disposed of from your premises."

Mrs. Julian sat down. She sat down rather heavily on one of the bentwood chairs and fixed her eyes on the opposite wall and felt a strange tingling hot sensation in her face that she hadn't experienced for some sixty years. She was blushing.

"I see," she said.

The constable began stuffing the garbage back into the sack. Mrs. Upton watched him, giggling.

"If you haven't consumed all our stock of sherry, Mrs. Upton," said Mrs. Julian, "perhaps we might offer these two gentlemen a glass."

The policemen, though on duty—which Mrs. Julian had formerly supposed put the consumption of alcohol out of the question—took two glasses apiece. They were not at a loss for words and chatted away with Mrs. Upton, possibly on the subject of the past and future exploits of Stewart. Mrs. Julian scarcely listened and said nothing. She understood perfectly what had happened, Mr. Arnold changing his clothes because they were wet, deciding to empty his rubbish that night because he had forgotten or failed to do so on the Saturday morning, gathering up his own and very likely Mr. Laindon's too. At that point she had left the window to go to the telephone. In the few minutes during which she had been talking to her nephew, Mr. Arnold had passed her gate with his barrow, lifted the lid of her dustbin and, finding a full sack within, taken it with him. It was this sack, her own, that she had seen him disposing of on the tip when she had next looked out.

No wonder the boiler had hardly ever been alight, no wonder the compost heap had scarcely grown. Once the snow and frost began and she knew her employer meant to remain indoors, Mrs. Upton had abandoned the hygiene regimen and reverted to sack and dustbin. And this was what it had led to.

The two policemen left, obligingly discarding the sack on to the tip as they passed it. Mrs. Upton looked at Mrs. Julian and Mrs. Julian looked at Mrs. Upton and Mrs. Upton said very brightly: "Well, I wonder what all that was about then?"

Mrs. Julian longed and longed for the old days when she would have given her notice on the spot, but that was impossible now. Where would

16. **bludgeon:** a short, heavy club.

she find a replacement? So all she said was, knowing it to be incomprehensible: "A faux pas,[17] Mrs. Upton, that's what it was," and walked slowly off and into the living room where she picked up her knitting from the chair by the window and carried it into the furthest corner of the room.

As a detective she was a failure. Yet, ironically, it was directly due to her efforts that Mrs. Arnold's murderer was brought to justice. Mrs. Julian could not long keep away from her window and when she returned to it the next day it was to see the council men dismantling the tip and removing the sacks to some distant disposal unit or incinerator. As her newspaper had told her, the strike was over. But the hunt for the murder weapon was not. There was more room to maneuver and investigate now the rubbish was gone. By nightfall the weapon had been found and twenty-four hours later the young out-of-work mechanic who had struck Mrs. Arnold down for the contents of her handbag had been arrested and charged.

They traced him through the spanner[18] with which he had killed her and which, passing Mrs. Julian's garden fence, he had thrust into the depths of her compost heap. ❖

---

17. **faux pas** (fō pä'): a social blunder; mistake.
18. **spanner:** the British term for a wrench.

INSIGHT

It Is Not Bred in Me

Molly Holden

It is not bred in me to overlook
the close at hand, the particular.
I turn my head to gaze at every meadow,
to stare through every gate that's left ajar;

am always ravished by a width of view
but see the harebell at the bottom edge,
notice the thorn that gives the panorama
scale,
brown roots, white garlic, beneath the tallest
hedge.

It's just as well these are my inclinations,
to cry: Stop here—or here, that I may stare,
now that I have no choice but to travel slowly
or watch the seasons stroll from dark to fair.

For now I'm set in soul as well as tissue
and doubly urgent longing fills my days
to put down surely what is my obsession
—the small cold characters of plants, each
phase

of sunlight on the grass, color of thickets,
the shapes of leaves, the self-sufficiency of
birds
—urgent because so relevant, their life's as
strong
as ours and will outlast me and my words.

RESPONDING OPTIONS

FROM PERSONAL RESPONSE *TO* CRITICAL ANALYSIS

REFLECT **1.** Were you surprised by the way this story ended? Share your thoughts with classmates.

RETHINK **2.** Review the Reading Connection on page 1149. What qualities does Mrs. Julian have that, in your opinion, would help her to be a good detective, and which of her qualities might make her a bad detective? Explain your responses.

3. Why do you think the setting is described in such detail?

4. Think about the relationship between Mrs. Julian and Mrs. Upton. What purpose do you think the character Mrs. Upton serves?

5. How would you describe the tone of the story?

RELATE **6.** Reread the Insight poem "It Is Not Bred in Me" on page 1164. What characteristics does the poem's speaker share with Mrs. Julian?

7. How common do you think it is for people to be very curious about the activities and whereabouts of their neighbors? Cite examples as part of your answer.

ANOTHER PATHWAY

In a chart like the one shown, briefly identify the incorrect assumptions Mrs. Julian makes, as well as the actual facts of each circumstance. Then discuss with your classmates whether, in your opinion, Mrs. Julian deserves her embarrassment and whether you think she will try to be less judgmental in the future.

What Mrs. Julian Assumes	versus	The Facts
______	→	______
______	→	______
______	→	______

LITERARY LINKS

Compare Mrs. Julian with the narrator of Penelope Lively's "At the Pitt-Rivers" (page 1011). What do they have in common? How do they differ in their reactions to the people they observe?

QUICKWRITES

1. Imagine that you are Mrs. Upton, and write a **character sketch** of Avice Julian.
2. Design and complete a **police report** that details the events surrounding Mrs. Arnold's murder. You may want to use a computer to give your report a professional appearance.
3. What if something other than Mrs. Julian's trash were found in the plastic bag? Consider some possibilities, and then write an alternative **ending** for "Paintbox Place."

PORTFOLIO *Save your writing. You may want to use it later as a springboard to a piece for your portfolio.*

LITERARY CONCEPTS

Characterization consists of all the ways in which writers form readers' impressions of characters. An author may use several methods of characterization, but often one method is especially effective in revealing traits or qualities important to the plot of a particular story. Consider how Rendell uses each of the following methods to characterize Mrs. Julian: (1) physical description, (2) presentation of the character's speech, thoughts, feelings, and actions, (3) presentation of the speech, thoughts, feelings, and actions of other characters, and (4) direct comments by the narrator. Which of these methods do you think is most effective in establishing Mrs. Julian's role in the story? Give reasons to support your opinion.

CONCEPT REVIEW: Foreshadowing Think about the use of foreshadowing in this story. What hints or clues pointing to later events does the author provide? Did you recognize the clues while you were reading the story? Share your observations with your classmates.

CRITIC'S CORNER

The critic Douglas Johnson has noted that Rendell is "meticulous in describing the details of everyday life," with an "emphasis on the real and ordinary." Find examples in the story to support this evaluation of Rendell's style. Why do you think she devotes so much attention to everyday details?

ALTERNATIVE ACTIVITIES

1. ***Cooperative Learning*** With a small group of classmates, create a **map** of the neighborhood in which "Paintbox Place" is set. Include all streets, houses, paths, and landmarks identified in the story, and indicate the exact locations of all major occurrences. Display your map in the classroom.
2. Draw a **caricature** satirizing Mrs. Julian's image of herself at the beginning of the story.
3. ***Cooperative Learning*** Imagine that you have been given the task of creating a **dramatization** of this story for a radio series titled *Murder Mystery.* With a small group of classmates, choose a scene that you find especially interesting and practice performing it, with some members of the group playing the characters and others providing sound effects. Record your performance and play the recording for the class.

ACROSS THE CURRICULUM

Science Identify the methods employed by Mrs. Julian to handle her trash. How would today's environmentalists react to each of those methods? What are the merits and drawbacks of each method?

WORDS TO KNOW

Review the Words to Know at the bottom of the selection pages. Then write the word that best completes each sentence.

1. People who have a _____ for reading mystery novels have probably already encountered Miss Jane Marple, one of Agatha Christie's best-known characters.
2. Try to imagine a mild, sweet old lady and you will visualize someone much like Jane Marple—a _____ of this type if ever there was one.
3. She is perhaps not as _____ as the intellectual and scholarly Sherlock Holmes, but she is by no means ignorant.
4. The crimes she becomes involved with are usually domestic ones rather than ones involving mob action or episodes of sweeping _____.
5. She lives in St. Mary Mead—the name of which is somewhat of a _____, since a mead is a meadow and St. Mary Mead is a village.
6. The village is _____ in examples of human faults and weaknesses, and Miss Marple notices how these defects influence the residents' behavior.
7. She is wise enough to know that human nature is human nature, whether people live in the splendor of huge country estates or in the _____ of miserable huts.
8. Her shrewdness about people's motivations, and her ability to apply specific knowledge to new situations, exemplify her surprising _____.
9. Her mildness and advanced age _____ her ability to solve crimes, because victims trust her and criminals tend to disregard her.
10. If you haven't met this charming detective yet, you may want to _____ down to the local library and check out one of the many novels that feature her.

RUTH RENDELL

1930–

The first novel Ruth Rendell ever submitted to a publisher was a comedy, which was returned to her with a letter suggesting that she make some major changes in it. Not wanting to rewrite the comedy, Rendell instead submitted another novel she had written, a detective story called *From Doon with Death.* Its publication in 1964 launched her career as a mystery writer.

Rendell, who currently lives in Polstead, England, was born in London and educated in Essex. Both of her parents were teachers, and she recalls that her father read to her frequently when she was a child. For several years after graduating from high school, she worked as a newspaper writer, reporter, and editor. Since the publication of her first novel, she has received numerous awards for her literary achievements. Two of her award-winning novels were published in the 1980s under the pen name Barbara Vine because, according to Rendell, their style seemed different from that of the typical "Ruth Rendell novel."

Many of Rendell's most popular works feature the crime-solving abilities of Chief Inspector Reginald Wexford, who solves murders through his keen attention to the psychology of the suspects. He also reflects his creator's own voracious reading habits and broad literary background as he quotes frequently from all types of literature. Rendell herself generally reads about five books a week.

OTHER WORKS "Front Seat," "The Venus Fly Trap," "Fen Hall," "May and June," "Divided We Stand"

MILESTONES IN BRITISH LITERATURE

John le Carré

The Novels of *John le Carré*

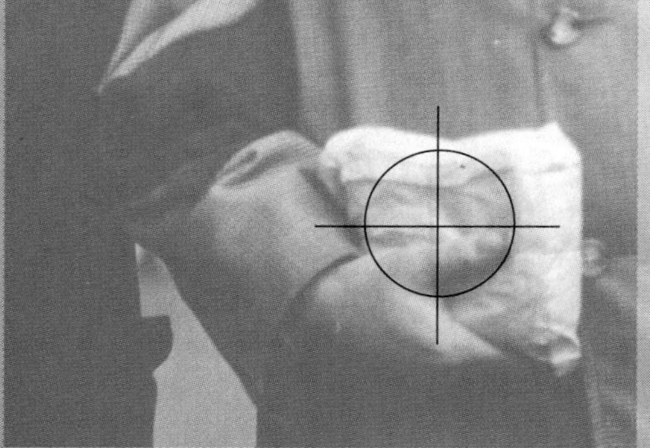

John le Carré's aging master spy George Smiley is no James Bond. Bond—Ian Fleming's Agent 007—is elegant, tall, and suave; Smiley is rumpled, squat, and plain. Bond manipulates technological wonders; Smiley avoids using even the telephone. Whereas Bond goes on thrilling foreign adventures, Smiley spends his time wading through oceans of paperwork. Unlike the jet-set playboy Bond, faithful Smiley goes home to an unfaithful wife.

However exciting Bond and his adventures may be, they are inventions of pure fantasy. It is George Smiley who is modeled in the likeness of a real British spy—on the type of fellow le Carré, whose real name is David Cornwell, encountered when he himself worked as an agent in the British Secret Service. In fact, part of le Carré's purpose in writing his novels about Smiley and other secret agents has been to rip the veil of false glamour from the world of espionage.

George Smiley made his first appearance in *Call for the Dead*—le Carré's first novel, published in 1961. He played a minor role in *The Spy Who Came In from the Cold,* then returned as the main character of *Tinker, Tailor, Soldier, Spy; The Honourable Schoolboy;* and *Smiley's People.* In these and his other novels, a number of which have been made into motion pictures, le Carré depicts the spy's world as an underground realm of lies, betrayal, and treachery. It is a world in which there is "no victory and no virtue," explains le Carré. A spy who "gets his man" most likely has to compromise his principles in the process, and one who manages to retain his ethical values is likely to get killed.

In order to perform their assigned roles, le Carré's spies routinely undermine the principles that uphold their governments. According to le Carré, "We are in the process of doing things in defense of our society which may very well produce a society which is not worth defending." For that reason, the suspense in a le Carré novel is two-sided: readers wonder whether the hero will survive, but they also wonder whether he *should* survive.

Critics and writers alike have hailed le Carré as a brilliant craftsman of the spy novel, praising his ability to tell a thrilling adventure story with real moral and ethical dimensions. Graham Greene called *The Spy Who Came In from the Cold* "the best spy novel I have ever read." However, le Carré's ability to detect and record conflicts between the values people claim to have and those they actually live by makes him more than just a spy novelist. He is a chronicler of the era that evolved in the aftermath of World War II, an era of fear and duplicity—the era of the cold war.

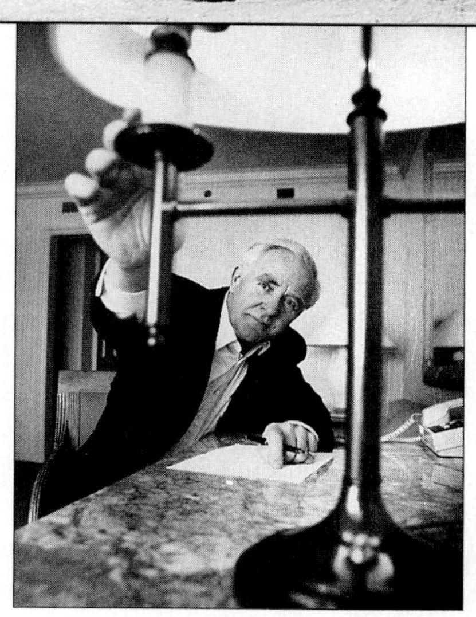

Top:
Alec Guinness as George Smiley in the film version of Smiley's People.
Middle:
Diane Keaton starred in the movie adaptation of The Little Drummer Girl.
Bottom:
John le Carré at work in his study.
Opposite page:
Claire Bloom and Richard Burton in the film version of The Spy Who Came In from the Cold.

PREVIEWING

POETRY

The Frog Prince
Not Waving but Drowning

Stevie Smith

PERSONAL CONNECTION

Get together with a partner and examine the image on this page. What do you see? Look at it longer. Do you see something different? This type of image is sometimes referred to as an optical illusion; what you see on the surface at first glance becomes something different as you look longer. Literature, too, can have this effect, as you will see in the poems you are about to read.

BIOGRAPHICAL/LITERARY CONNECTION

During her early years as a writer, Florence Margaret Smith—better known as Stevie Smith—read widely in older works of literature, avoiding the poetic works of her contemporaries for fear that their influence would keep her from developing her own style. She did indeed achieve a distinctive style, and critics have therefore found her work hard to compare with that of other poets. At first glance, her poems appear simple both in subject matter and in their use of conventional rhyme, but closer scrutiny often reveals deep insights in her supposedly "light" verse.

Although Smith did not consider herself a visual artist, she illustrated many of her poems with drawings—she called them doodles—that she thought helped readers to understand the poetry. The drawing that appears on page 1175 is the one Smith chose to print with "The Frog Prince."

READING CONNECTION

Understanding Connotations The development of meaning in poems often depends on the connotations of the poems' words. A **connotation** is an emotional response evoked by a word—as distinguished from the word's **denotation,** or dictionary definition. Words may have different connotations even though their denotations are quite similar—consider, for example, the different connotations of *food* and *cuisine.* As you read the following poems, notice how you react to certain words, and consider whether your reactions to those words change as you continue reading.

THE Frog Prince

STEVIE SMITH

I am a frog,
I live under a spell,
I live at the bottom
Of a green well.

And here I must wait
Until a maiden places me
On her royal pillow,
And kisses me,
In her father's palace.

The story is familiar,
Everybody knows it well,
But do other enchanted people feel as nervous
As I do? The stories do not tell,

Ask if they will be happier
When the changes come,
As already they are fairly happy
In a frog's doom?

I have been a frog now
For a hundred years
And in all this time
I have not shed many tears,

I am happy, I like the life,
Can swim for many a mile
(When I have hopped to the river)
And am for ever agile.

And the quietness,
Yes, I like to be quiet
I am habituated
To a quiet life,

But always when I think these thoughts
As I sit in my well
Another thought comes to me and says:
It is part of the spell

To be happy
To work up contentment
To make much of being a frog
To fear disenchantment

Says, It will be *heavenly*
To be set free,
Cries, *Heavenly* the girl who disenchants
And the royal times, *heavenly,*
And I think it will be.

Come, then, royal girl and royal times,
Come quickly,
I can be happy until you come
But I cannot be heavenly,
Only disenchanted people
Can be heavenly.

FROM PERSONAL RESPONSE *TO* CRITICAL ANALYSIS

REFLECT **1.** Did you enjoy this poem? Why or why not? Briefly describe your opinion in your notebook.

RETHINK **2.** Why do you think the frog prince is nervous?

Consider
- what his life is like now
- what changes he anticipates

3. What do you think the underlying message of this poem is?

Not Waving but Drowning

Stevie Smith

Nobody heard him, the dead man,
But still he lay moaning:
I was much further out than you thought
And not waving but drowning.

Poor chap, he always loved larking
And now he's dead
It must have been too cold for him his heart gave way,
They said.

Oh, no no no, it was too cold always
(Still the dead one lay moaning)
I was much too far out all my life
And not waving but drowning.

RESPONDING OPTIONS

FROM PERSONAL RESPONSE *TO* CRITICAL ANALYSIS

REFLECT 1. What emotions did "Not Waving but Drowning" evoke in you? In your notebook, describe those feelings.

RETHINK 2. What different voices, or speakers, do you hear in the poem?

3. Although the poem has more than one speaker, it has a single overall tone. How would you describe the tone?
   Consider
   - the attitude of the first speaker
   - the fact that a dead man speaks
   - what the dead man says
   - the fact that the dead man is heard by no one

4. What do you think the speaker means in the last stanza?

5. Consider the title of this part of the unit—"Ironic Perspectives." How do you think that title applies to this poem? Explain your answer by citing specific details from the poem.

RELATE 6. What similarities and differences between "The Frog Prince" and "Not Waving but Drowning" do you notice?

7. A critic has remarked that Smith's voice is "very much that of what she once called the 'age of unrest' through which she lived." Do you think her poetry also speaks to your generation? Explain your opinion.

ANOTHER PATHWAY

Draw a step diagram, like the one shown, for each of the poems. Starting with the lowest step in each diagram, show how the poem's ideas progress from simple to complex. Identify specific lines where the level of meaning shifts, and summarize the ideas conveyed in each level.

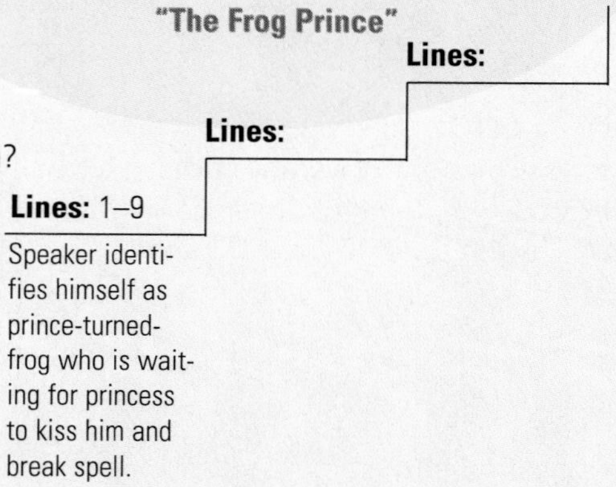

"The Frog Prince"

Lines:

Lines:

Lines: 1–9

Speaker identifies himself as prince-turned-frog who is waiting for princess to kiss him and break spell.

LITERARY CONCEPTS

In both "The Frog Prince" and "Not Waving but Drowning," Smith relies on **wordplay**—a clever use of the multiple meanings of words—to convey her messages. For example, in "The Frog Prince" she plays with different meanings of *disenchantment* and *heavenly.* How does such wordplay contribute to the meaning of "The Frog Prince"? What examples of wordplay can you find in "Not Waving but Drowning"?

QUICKWRITES

1. Following the style of "The Frog Prince," write your own **poem** based on a famous fairy tale or nursery rhyme. Try to give the original story a humorous twist while at the same time conveying an insight about life.

2. As the man in "Not Waving but Drowning," write a **diary entry** in which you explain why you've felt "much too far out" all your life and been "not waving but drowning."

***PORTFOLIO** Save your writing. You may want to use it later as a springboard to a piece for your portfolio.*

ALTERNATIVE ACTIVITIES

1. Create a **collage** of photographs or illustrations that reflect the contrasting viewpoints expressed in "Not Waving but Drowning."
2. ***Cooperative Learning*** With a partner, create a series of **drawings** depicting the frog prince as he sits in his well. Be sure to convey his various thoughts about his impending "disenchantment." Add your drawings to a class display, and discuss any similarities and differences between them and Stevie Smith's frog "doodle" shown to the left.

THE WRITER'S STYLE

One distinguishing characteristic of Smith's style is a simple, straightforward **diction,** or choice of words. How do you think her reliance on simple words affects the tone of these two poems?

CRITIC'S CORNER

Muriel Spark once wrote that Smith's "style is comic and her vision melancholy but dry-eyed." Do you think Smith displays both a comic style and a melancholy vision in "The Frog Prince" and "Not Waving but Drowning"? Support your opinion with details from the two poems.

LITERARY LINKS

Compare and contrast the speaker of "The Frog Prince" with the main character in Naguib Mahfouz's "The Happy Man" (page 1139). What similarities or differences can you find in their responses to happiness? in their thoughts about the future?

STEVIE SMITH

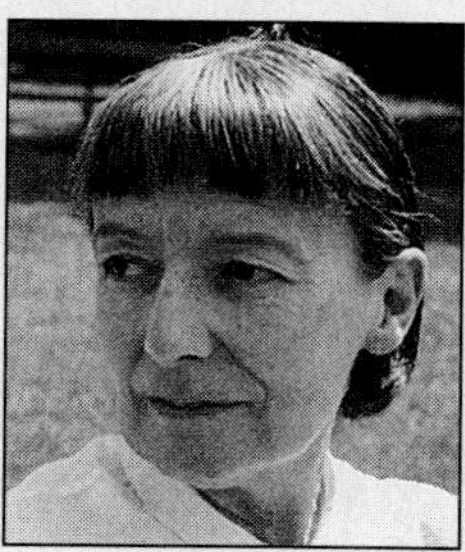

1902–1971

Florence Margaret Smith acquired her nickname in the early 1930s, while horseback riding. Alluding to a well-known jockey named Steve Donaghue, some boys jokingly called her Steve; her friends picked up the name, changing it to "Stevie." Smith loved the nickname and continued to use it the rest of her life.

For most of her life, Smith lived in a house in Palmers Green, a northern suburb of London, having moved there at the age of three with her mother, her sister, and a favorite aunt (whom she affectionately called the Lion Aunt) shortly after her father deserted the family. After her mother died and her sister left home, Smith and her best friend, the Lion Aunt, continued to live together until the older woman died at the age of 96.

In grammar school and high school, Smith was an average student. Instead of going on to college, she entered a secretarial school and then worked for the next 30 years as secretary to a magazine publisher. She found the job boring, but it did afford her ample free time to write stories and poems. Her first published work was a novel she wrote on the yellow paper used in her office, to which she gave the title *Novel on Yellow Paper*.

Although she first gained recognition as a novelist, Smith is known primarily for her achievements as a poet. She was awarded the Cholmondeley Poetry Award in 1966, and in 1969 Queen Elizabeth II personally presented Smith with the Queen's Gold Medal for Poetry. She undoubtedly would have received many more honors for her unique work, but she died in 1971, at the height of her popularity. A few years later, her life and literary achievements became the subject of a stage play and a movie, both entitled *Stevie*.

OTHER WORKS "There Is an Old Man," "Tender Only to One," "The New Age," "Pretty," "Is It Wise?"

WRITING FROM EXPERIENCE

PERSUASIVE WRITING

Several selections in Unit Seven, "Contemporary Voices," deal with important issues of recent times. Many individuals have identified similar problems or needs in their community, proposed solutions, and used persuasion to get help in attacking the problems. What current problem interests you? In the following pages you'll learn how you can bring about a needed change.

GUIDED ASSIGNMENT

Write a Proposal Write a proposal that identifies an issue calling for action in your school or community. Suggest a way to solve the problem or meet the need you identify.

1 Explore the Issues

Read the items on these pages. What problems do they suggest? Situations like these have caused many people to stop reading and take action. Where could you make a difference?

Use the following ideas to find some issues that interest you.

- List some conditions or situations that upset or concern you.
- Brainstorm about current issues.
- Interview classmates, teachers, or parents.
- Clip articles from newspapers and newsmagazines and listen to TV and radio news.

Magazine Article

Give Me Shelter

Yetta Adams lay down to sleep at a bus shelter in the nation's capital, Washington, D.C. As the temperature plummeted into the low 30s, Adams, a 43-year-old homeless woman, covered herself with an old, tattered blanket and placed a crumpled paper bag under her head.

The next morning, Yetta Adams was found dead—across the street from the headquarters of the very government agency that is supposed to help America's homeless: the Department of Housing and Urban Development (HUD).

A decade ago, when the sight of people sleeping in the streets still shocked Americans, such an incident might have caused a national uproar. Today, with homelessness common nearly everywhere, Adams's death attracted only a brief spurt of media attention. Then it was forgotten.

Ken Silverstein,
from *Scholastic Update*

The Toughest Jump

From High School to Work World, No Easy Leap

Earl Jones and Nancy Rus look at job hunting differently, but they both find the ordeal frustrating.

Jones graduated from Cardozo High School with Bs and Cs. Because his attempts to find a sales job have failed, he works for $5.50 an hour in a fast-food restaurant.

"My main problem is experience," said Jones, 20. "But most of the people hiring don't give me a chance. They're not willing to give you training. You never get any experience that way."

Rus doesn't know Jones, but she's met youths in his situation. They interview at her company, but only a handful are hired.

"The problem with high schools is that they're very inconsistent in terms of the qualities of the graduates," said Rus, vice president and director of organizational development at Motorola Inc., an electronic equipment manufacturer based in Schaumburg, Ill.

"If they're interested in working in manufacturing and growing with a company like Motorola," Rus said, "it would be to their benefit to have computer abilities as well as basic electronic skills, not just the reading and math. But high schools don't have tracks for electronic occupations. We just don't see that."

Alex Pham,
from *The Washington Post*

How can we get more help with the technical training we'll need to find work?

I wonder if it'll be this hard for seniors at Amherst High to find jobs after graduation.

Education Article

Jefferson High School students work together to convert an empty lot at Park and Davis into a community garden.

Newspaper Photo

There's an empty lot in my neighborhood that could be cleaned up and made into a garden.

2 Explore Possible Solutions

Which problem or need intrigues you the most? Choose one you would like to propose a solution for.

Freewrite Try freewriting about your problem or need. Tell how you propose to solve or meet it. Describe what—and whose—support you would need.

Collaborate Get together with a partner. Discuss your ideas for a proposal and take turns evaluating ideas and offering suggestions. Take notes about your discussion.

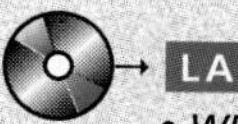

LASERLINKS
• *WRITING SPRINGBOARD*

WRITING COACH

PREWRITING

Investigate Issues

Planning Pointers A proposal is a formal document or speech that identifies a need and offers a specific plan to meet that need. The tips on these pages will help you make sure that your proposal suggests something that can be done and is likely to be accepted by others.

1 Understand the Issue

Make sure that you are completely familiar with the problem or situation your proposal involves. Do the necessary research. Consider the following sources for additional information:

- Published interviews with experts
- Information from books or articles
- Information you can request by letter
- Personal research through observation, interviews, and polls or surveys

You might also want to find out what other people feel about your issue, or even how other communities have resolved similar issues.

2 Think Through Your Proposal

Think about the nature of the problem or issue you've chosen and develop a workable proposal. Answer questions like the following.

- How do you propose to solve the problem? How will your suggested solution help the situation?
- What steps are involved? How would you tackle each one? In what order will you propose to complete these steps?
- What resources must you ask for in order to implement your proposal? What will you need in terms of assistance, time, money, and materials? How will you allocate any money given to put your plan into action?
- How will you put your solution into practice?

3 Consider Your Audience

A proposal expresses your concerns about an issue and calls for action. An effective proposal also is addressed to the person or group who can actually do something about the problem. The chart below will help you decide to whom you will present your proposal.

Send a proposal about	to
laws	government officials
community issues	local government
neighborhood concerns	family, neighbors
school issues	school officials, faculty

4 Identify and Address Weaknesses

Consider getting together with a few other students to evaluate your proposal. Ask questions such as the following.

- Will my proposal really work? What difficulties can you foresee? How can I overcome them?
- What are the arguments against my proposal? How can I counter them?
- What concerns will my audience have? What will I need to do to make my plan acceptable to my audience?

To guide your research process, make a list of your audience's possible objections. Then consider how you could overcome each one.

Can you think of any other questions you might add to a survey like the one below?

Student's Survey Questions

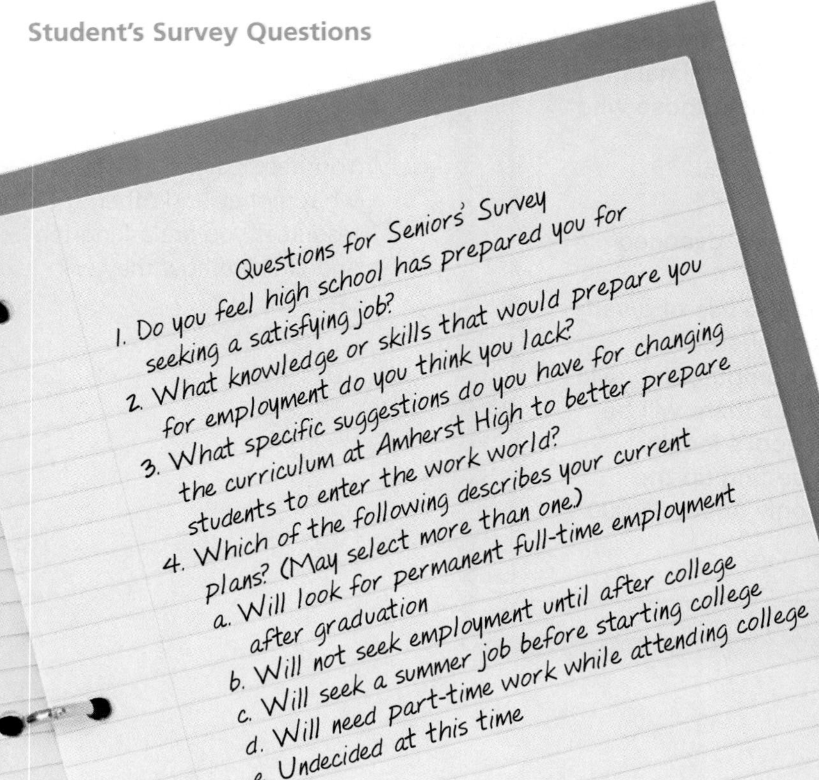
Questions for Seniors' Survey

1. Do you feel high school has prepared you for seeking a satisfying job?
2. What knowledge or skills that would prepare you for employment do you think you lack?
3. What specific suggestions do you have for changing the curriculum at Amherst High to better prepare students to enter the work world?
4. Which of the following describes your current plans? (May select more than one.)
   a. Will look for permanent full-time employment after graduation
   b. Will not seek employment until after college
   c. Will seek a summer job before starting college
   d. Will need part-time work while attending college
   e. Undecided at this time

SkillBuilder

SPEAKING & LISTENING

Conducting Surveys

Here are some hints for conducting an effective survey.

- Plan ahead. Know what you want to find out and whom you will need to survey.
- Write questions that require brief answers. This will enable you to pull together information from many respondents quickly and efficiently.
- Avoid questions that show any bias toward your subject. You want to get at the truth rather than influence respondents.
- If possible, prepare a form that you can use to check off or enter responses on.
- Study the sample survey questions at the left for additional ideas.

APPLYING WHAT YOU'VE LEARNED

List the questions you want to ask your survey subjects about your issue or proposal. Let a friend look at your list and suggest additional questions you could ask.

THINK & PLAN

Reflecting on Your Plan

1. How can you make this issue important to your audience?
2. Do you need to acquire more information before you can begin drafting your proposal?
3. What information will be most effective in your proposal?

DRAFTING

Draft Your Proposal

Your Solution to the Problem It's one thing to envision a solution to a problem. It's quite another to take the next step—convincing other people that your solution will work. With a persuasive proposal directed to the right people, you can help bring about a necessary change.

Student's Rough Draft

Proposal for Computer Course

My Rough Draft

This proposal requests a new computer course that will give Amherst students an opportunity to increase their computer skills and give students who do not plan to attend college an edge in the job market.

Statement of Need:
Many Amherst students lack the computer skills they need to find a good job. The computer lab provides only minimal training in computer use. Much more is needed to help those who will soon be seeking work.

Plan:

1. Amherst High School will offer a course in advanced computer training.
2. The course will also include training in the use of a variety of software and other computer peripherals.
3. Ms. Ferguson, who currently runs the computer lab, will take on the teaching of this course. Thus there will be no need to increase the size of the school's faculty.
4. Very little expense will be involved in setting up the course. Ms. Ferguson estimates that only about $5,000 of new equipment will be needed.

1 Start Your Draft

Write a rough draft of your proposal. Use your earlier freewriting, any ideas you got when you collaborated with a partner during the exploration stage, and the information you acquired through research, surveys, or interviews. As a guide, you can use the standard outline shown below. Look at the student example on the Writing Coach at the left for further ideas about starting a draft.

Standard Outline for a Proposal

I. Preview. Summarize your proposal.
II. Statement of need. Support with examples, testimony, and data, as appropriate.
III. Plan of action. Identify steps to be taken and describe the benefits of the plan and how they will outweigh any disadvantages.
IV. Your request. Tell exactly what money and other resources you are asking for, and indicate how they will be used.

2 Evaluate Your Draft

The following questions can help you evaluate your draft.

- Am I sure that what I propose to do really can be done?
- Have I identified the resources I will need to implement my proposal? Have I told how these resources will be used?
- Have I included information about the people who will help execute my proposal if it is approved?
- Have I demonstrated how any obstacles to my plan can be overcome?

3 Rework Your Draft and Share

Consider how you can use the following techniques as you rework your proposal.

Tone The tone of a proposal is usually formal. It should show your audience how strongly you feel about the project you propose and inspire confidence in your ability. Remember also to be respectful of your audience—the person or persons you want to agree to your proposal. Use words that will help you achieve the right tone.

Persuasion Use persuasive techniques to convince your audience that a need exists and that what you propose can meet that need. Include sufficient evidence—facts, examples, statistical data, expert testimony—to support your proposal. (See the SkillBuilder on this page for more information about using facts and statistics.) Be sure you have refuted all of the possible objections to your plan.

PEER RESPONSE

After sharing your draft with peer readers, ask these questions:

- How can I make my proposal more convincing? What other persuasive arguments can you think of that I could use?
- What problems can you think of that might make my plan difficult to implement?
- What additional advantages and disadvantages of my plan can you think of?
- What else might I ask for to support my plan?
- Who might oppose my plan? Why would they oppose it? Can you think of ways I could overcome their opposition?

SkillBuilder

WRITER'S CRAFT

Using Facts and Statistics
Facts and statistics can help you elaborate on the details you include in your proposal. Facts are statements that can be proved. Statistics are facts in numerical form. The following is a statistic.

The official unemployment rate among 16- to 19-year-olds is 21 percent.

The kinds of facts and statistics you use will depend on your purpose for writing and on your audience. Except for surveys or polls, try to verify each fact by using more than one source.

WRITING HANDBOOK

For more information about using facts and statistics, see page 1225 of the Writing Handbook.

APPLYING WHAT YOU'VE LEARNED
As you look through your draft, put a check mark beside each detail that needs to be elaborated on with facts or statistics. Where can you find the information?

RETHINK & EVALUATE

Preparing to Revise

1. What do you like best about your proposal?
2. How will you use your peer reviewer's comments?
3. How can you make your proposal more convincing?

Revise Your Proposal

Absolute Accuracy Accuracy is particularly important for a proposal that will be read by people whose support you are seeking. Revise and proofread your proposal carefully. Don't let any minor errors prejudice your readers against the project for which you're trying to gain support.

1 Reevaluate Your Proposal

As you review your draft, think about how you and your peer reviewers responded to it. Use the following suggestions, as well as the Standards for Evaluation and the Editing Checklist on the next page, as you revise.

- Use headings to show the main parts of your proposal.
- Be sure your proposal defines what needs to be done and how it can be accomplished.
- See that your plan is detailed enough but not overly so.
- Look for ways to improve the tone of your proposal.
- Be sure to refute all possible objections to it.

Student's Final Draft

A Proposal for an Advanced Computer Course
Presented to the Principal and Faculty of Amherst High School
by Sherry Albert

This proposal requests the establishment of an advanced course that will give Amherst students an opportunity to increase their computer skills and give students who do not plan to attend college an edge in the job market.

The Need

Good jobs are scarce today. Many high school graduates are unable to find work anywhere but in low-paying fast-food restaurants, supermarkets, or other businesses that promise little hope for advancement or job satisfaction. Many of the good positions require at least some familiarity with computers, and some employers will consider only applicants with considerable computer skills. At the very least, an applicant who can demonstrate computer competence may have an edge over his or her competition for a job.

Amherst's computer lab offers an opportunity for every student to learn to use a computer and to have access to one for up to two periods a week. However, the school gives no training beyond that introduction and what little time Ms. Ferguson can spare for students who want to further increase their skills.

How has the student's expansion of the section on the need for additional computer training increased the proposal's effectiveness?

What other methods of presenting your proposal can you think of? What are the advantages and disadvantages of each method?

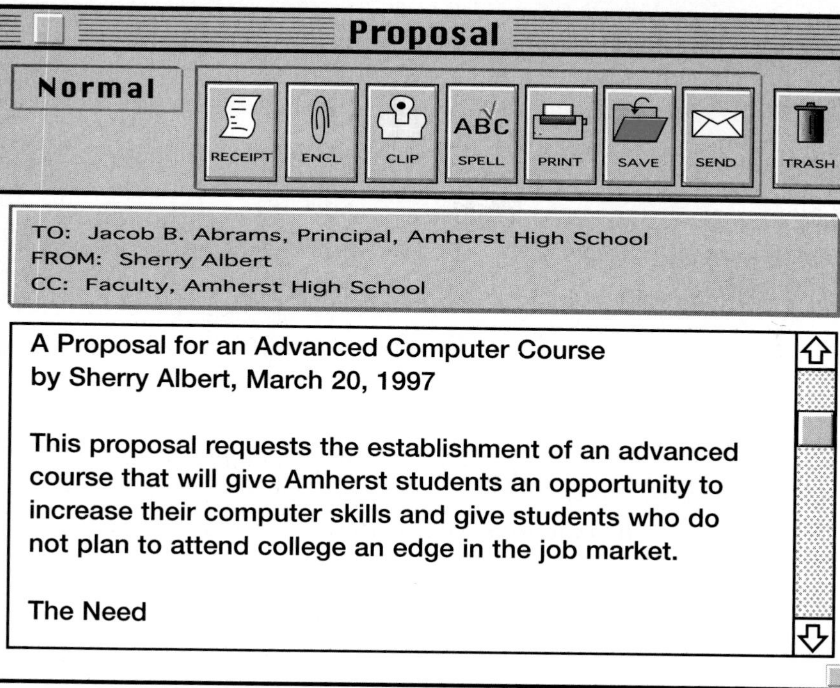
Proposal
Normal
RECEIPT
ENCL
CLIP
SPELL
PRINT
SAVE
SEND
TRASH
TO: Jacob B. Abrams, Principal, Amherst High School
FROM: Sherry Albert
CC: Faculty, Amherst High School
A Proposal for an Advanced Computer Course
by Sherry Albert, March 20, 1997
This proposal requests the establishment of an advanced course that will give Amherst students an opportunity to increase their computer skills and give students who do not plan to attend college an edge in the job market.
The Need

2 Share Your Work

Here are some ways you can share your completed proposal.

- Send your proposal—in writing or, as demonstrated above, by e-mail—to a person or agency that can support it.
- Present it orally in class, at a school assembly, or to a community group concerned with the issue you discuss.
- Submit it to your school or community newspaper.

Standards for Evaluation

An effective proposal
- clearly defines a problem or need, using such evidence as statistics, examples, and testimony
- presents a clear plan for solving the problem or meeting the need, with enough details to demonstrate that the plan is workable
- demonstrates that the writer understands how to implement the plan and knows what resources will be involved
- persuasively shows how the advantages of the plan outweigh any disadvantages
- addresses and refutes possible objections to the plan
- makes clear how any requested funds will be spent and how requested resources will be used

SkillBuilder

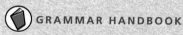

GRAMMAR FROM WRITING

Organizing with Adverbs and Adverb Phrases
Effective adverbs and adverb phrases can help you clearly identify your points and priorities.

- Words like *first* and *later* clarify the order of events in a plan.
- Words like *most importantly* show what your priorities are.
- Words like *urgently* and *immediately* show degree of need.

GRAMMAR HANDBOOK

For more information on adverbs and adverb phrases, see page 1272 of the Grammar Handbook.

Editing Checklist Use the following tips as you edit and proofread your final draft.

- Have you carefully checked your punctuation?
- Have you capitalized and correctly spelled all proper nouns?
- Have you used adverbs and adverb phrases effectively?

REFLECT & ASSESS

Evaluate the Experience

1. How did your proposal change in the course of your work on it?
2. What influences led to the changes you made?

PORTFOLIO Put a summary of this writing experience in your portfolio along with your proposal.

REFLECT & ASSESS

UNIT SEVEN: CONTEMPORARY VOICES

The selections in this unit depict contemporary conflicts, characters, and speakers who gain insights into life by observing the world. How did you respond to the perspectives presented? Which of the selections caused you to think more about particular problems or to change your own attitudes? Choose one or more of the options in each of the following sections to help you answer these questions and further analyze your reactions as a reader.

REFLECTING ON THE UNIT

OPTION 1 **Examining Insights** Draw a horizontal line in the middle of a sheet of paper. Then consider the individuals you encountered in Part 1 of this unit. In the top half of the sheet, list those who you think benefit from the insights they gain; in the bottom half, list those whose insights may have negative effects. If you think that certain individuals' insights have both positive and negative results, list those individuals directly on the horizontal line. Discuss your conclusions with a small group of classmates.

OPTION 2 **Comparing and Contrasting** The selections in Part 2 of this unit focus on social and political issues, revealing how individuals are affected by conflict. Select two of these individuals that you find most memorable. With a partner, role-play a conversation in which the two reflect on their experiences with conflict. You may also want to have them comment on each other's words and actions, as depicted in the selections.

OPTION 3 **Applying a Quotation** Think about the quotation from George Orwell that introduces this unit: "It was a bright cold day in April, and the clocks were striking thirteen." Which selection in Part 3 of the unit do you think best reflects the tone and mood of Orwell's sentence? Write a paragraph explaining your opinion.

REFLECT & ASSESS *Self-Assessment: Recall the thoughts and impressions that the selections in this unit conveyed to you. Then, working with a small group of classmates, create a cluster diagram for each part of the unit—"Moments of Insight," "Culture and Conflict," and "Ironic Perspectives." In each diagram, record the messages, ideas, and insights you and your group members received from the selections.*

REVIEWING LITERARY CONCEPTS

OPTION 1 **Looking at Style** A writer's style is an expression of his or her individuality. Although writers may have similar styles, there are usually certain characteristics that distinguish each writer's work from the work of others. With a small group of classmates, review the selections in this unit, selecting from each a passage that you think exemplifies the writer's style. Then quiz other groups by reading each a passage and asking them to identify the writer and the selection. Allow groups to glance over the Table of Contents if they need help recalling the names of the writers and selections.

OPTION 2 **Appreciating Poetry** In poetry, literary techniques are used to provide focus and to reinforce meaning for readers. Select two poems from this unit that you found particularly meaningful. In each, identify some devices the poet uses to focus the poem or to help convey its message. List them in a graphic like the one shown here.

"Digging"	"Not Waving but Drowning"
alliteration	irony

REFLECT & ASSESS *Self-Assessment: From the literary concepts featured in this unit, select the five that had the greatest impact on you as a reader. Define the concepts, give examples of how they were used, and explain how they influenced your appreciation and understanding of the selections.*

PORTFOLIO BUILDING

- **QuickWrites** Some of the QuickWrites assignments in this unit asked you to reflect on experiences and people's reactions to them—either your own or those of characters or speakers in the selections. Look over your responses and select one or two pieces that you think give the best accounts of experiences and reactions. Write a short note explaining why you think those pieces are successful. Add the pieces and the note to your portfolio.
- **Writing About Literature** Earlier in this unit, you wrote an essay in which you compared two selections. Reread your essay now. Which selection would you recommend more strongly to someone else? In a brief note, use information you gathered for your analysis to persuade someone else to read that selection.
- **Writing from Experience** Reread the proposal you wrote earlier in this unit. Then draft a letter to someone who you think could help you implement your proposal. In the letter, explain why you chose that person and how he or she could help. If you like, attach the letter to your proposal.
- **Personal Choice** In this unit you have had many opportunities to explore human-rights and civil-rights issues in other cultures. Look back through your records and evaluations of all activities you completed in this unit, including work that you did on your own. Which project or piece of writing do you feel best expresses an insight into or understanding of a conflict in another culture? Write a paragraph explaining why you are satisfied with your work. Add the paragraph to your portfolio.

REFLECT & ASSESS *Self-Assessment: At this stage, the contents of your writing portfolio should represent the work of an entire year. Review the pieces in your portfolio and choose three of your best works—one done in the fall, one in the winter, and one in the spring. Write a note explaining what these works reveal about your progress and abilities as a writer.*

SETTING GOALS

Reflect on all the goals that you set for yourself during the course of the year. Which goals did you reach? Which goals seem nearly within your reach? Which goals seem as far away as ever? Write an evaluation of your progress this year, and identify three goals for the future.

Student Resource Bank

Words to Know: Access Guide

Q

R

S

T

U

V

W

Z

Pronunciation Key

Symbol	Examples	Symbol	Examples	Symbol	Examples
ă	at, gas	m	man, seem	v	van, save
ā	ape, day	n	night, mitten	w	web, twice
ä	father, barn	ng	sing, anger	y	yard, lawyer
âr	fair, dare	ŏ	odd, not	z	zoo, reason
b	bell, table	ō	open, road, grow	zh	treasure, garage
ch	chin, lunch	ô	awful, bought, horse	ə	awake, even, pencil, pilot, focus
d	dig, bored	oi	coin, boy	ər	perform, letter
ĕ	egg, ten	o͝o	look, full		
ē	evil, see, meal	o͞o	root, glue, through		
f	fall, laugh, phrase	ou	out, cow		**Sounds in Foreign Words**
g	gold, big	p	pig, cap	KH	*German* ich, auch; *Scottish* loch
h	hit, inhale	r	rose, star	N	*French* entre, bon, fin
hw	white, everywhere	s	sit, face	œ	*French* feu, cœur; *German* schön
ĭ	inch, fit	sh	she, mash	ü	*French* utile, rue; *German* grün
ī	idle, my, tried	t	tap, hopped		
îr	dear, here	th	thing, with		
j	jar, gem, badge	*th*	then, other		
k	keep, cat, luck	ŭ	up, nut		
l	load, rattle	ûr	fur, earn, bird, worm		

Stress Marks

′ This mark indicates that the preceding syllable receives the primary stress. For example, in the word *language,* the first syllable is stressed: lăng′gwĭj.

′ This mark is used only in words in which more than one syllable is stressed. It indicates that the preceding syllable is stressed, but somewhat more weakly than the syllable receiving the primary stress. In the word *literature,* for example, the first syllable receives the primary stress, and the last syllable receives a weaker stress: lĭt′ər-ə-cho͝or′.

LITERARY HANDBOOK

Handbook of Literary Terms

Alliteration Alliteration is the repetition of consonant sounds at the beginning of words, as in the phrase "wild winds of winter." Writers use alliteration to emphasize certain words, to heighten mood, to establish a musical effect, to unify a passage, and to help create meaning. Often alliteration is reinforced by repeating the same consonant sound within and at the end of other words. Look for examples of alliteration in the following lines from Samuel Taylor Coleridge's "Kubla Khan":

In Xanadu did Kubla Khan
A stately pleasure dome decree:
Where Alph, the sacred river, ran
Through caverns measureless to man
Down to a sunless sea.

See also **Assonance; Consonance.**

Allusion An allusion is a reference to a historical or fictional person, place, or event with which the reader is assumed to be familiar. Understanding the allusions in a work can give the reader a better understanding of it. For example, in Thomas Gray's "Elegy Written in a Country Churchyard," the speaker alludes to Milton, the famous English poet, and Cromwell, the leader of the Puritan revolt in the 17th century. These allusions to two of the most well-known figures in English life emphasize the poet's ideas about what the lives of the obscure people buried in the churchyard might have been like had they had different opportunities. In the excerpt from Derek Walcott's poem *Midsummer,* allusions contribute to the satiric tone of the poem.

Analogy An analogy is a point-by-point comparison between two dissimilar things in order to clarify the less familiar of the two. In "We'll Never Conquer Space," Arthur C. Clarke compares the colonizing of distant planets and galaxies to the colonizing of distant islands in a vast ocean by island dwellers with primitive ships.

Anglo-Saxon Poetry Anglo-Saxon poetry, which was written between the 7th and 12th centuries, is characterized by a strong rhythm, or cadence, that makes it easily chanted or sung. It was originally recited by **scops,** poet-singers who traveled from place to place. Lines of Anglo-Saxon poetry are unified through alliteration and through use of the same number of accented syllables in each line. Typically, a line is divided by a **caesura,** or pause, into two parts, with each part having two accented syllables. Usually, one or both of the accented syllables in the first part alliterate with an accented syllable in the second part. This passage from *Beowulf* illustrates some of these characteristics:

He took what he wanted, // all the treasures
That pleased his eye, // heavy plates
And golden cups // and the glorious banner,
Loaded his arms // with all they could hold.

Another characteristic of Anglo-Saxon poetry is the use of **kennings,** metaphorical compound words or phrases substituted for simple nouns. Examples include "whale's way" for the sea, "shepherd of evil" for Grendel, and "folk-king" for Beowulf.

Antagonist The antagonist of a novel, short story, drama, or narrative poem is the character or force against which the main character, or **protagonist,** is pitted. The antagonist may be another character, some aspect of society or nature, or an internal force within the protagonist. In *Sir Gawain and the Green Knight,* the antagonist is the Green Knight, who challenges Sir Gawain. In Doris Lessing's "A Sunrise on the Veld," the antagonist is the natural world, which confronts the boy with his limits.

See also **Conflict; Protagonist.**

Antithesis Antithesis is a figure of speech in which sharply contrasting words, phrases, clauses, or sentences are juxtaposed to emphasize a point. In true antithesis, both the ideas and the grammatical structures are balanced. An example is the second line of the following couplet from Alexander Pope's *An Essay on Criticism:*

> Regard not then if wit be old or new,
> But blame the false, and value still the true.

Aphorism An aphorism is a brief statement that expresses a general observation about life in a witty, pointed way. Unlike proverbs, which may stem from oral folk tradition, aphorisms originate with specific authors. "A blighted spring makes a barren year," from Samuel Johnson's essay "On Spring," is an example of an aphorism.

Apostrophe Apostrophe is a figure of speech in which an object, an abstract quality, or an absent or imaginary person is addressed directly, as if present and able to understand. Writers use apostrophe to express powerful emotions. Lines 10 to 63 of the excerpt from Lord Byron's *Childe Harold's Pilgrimage* are an apostrophe to the ocean:

> Roll on, thou deep and dark blue Ocean, roll!
> Ten thousand fleets sweep over thee in vain;
> Man marks the earth with ruin, his control
> Stops with the shore; upon the watery plain
> The wrecks are all thy deed, nor doth remain
> A shadow of man's ravage, save his own,
> When, for a moment, like a drop of rain,
> He sinks into thy depths with bubbling groan,
> Without a grave, unknell'd, uncoffin'd, and
> unknown. . . .

Argumentation Argumentation is speech or writing intended to convince an audience that a proposal should be adopted or rejected. Most argumentation begins with a statement of an idea or opinion, which is then supported with logical evidence. Another technique of argumentation is the anticipation and rebuttal of opposing views. An example of argumentation is the excerpt from *A Vindication of the Rights of Woman,* in which Mary Wollstonecraft argues for the rights of women and argues against views that would subjugate women.

Aside In drama, an aside is a remark spoken in an undertone by a character, either to the audience or to another character. A traditional dramatic convention, the aside is heard by the audience but supposedly not by the other characters on stage. Asides can be used to express characters' feelings, opinions, and reactions, so they function as a method of characterization. Note the following aside from Oscar Wilde's *The Importance of Being Earnest*:

> **Gwendolen** (*with elaborate politeness*). Thank you.
> (*aside*) Detestable girl. But I require tea!

See also **Drama.**

Assonance Assonance is the repetition of a vowel sound in two or more stressed syllables that do not end with the same consonant. Poets use assonance to emphasize certain words, to impart a musical quality, to create a mood, or to unify a passage. An example of assonance is the repetition of the long *e* sound in the following lines from a sonnet by John Keats. Note that the repeated sounds are not always spelled the same.

> When I have fears that I may cease to be
> Before my pen has glean'd my teeming brain

See also **Alliteration; Consonance; Rhyme.**

Author's Purpose An author's purpose may be to entertain, to inform, to express opinions, or to persuade. Although a writer can fulfill more than one of these purposes in a work, one is usually the most important. The purposes of the excerpt from the Venerable Bede's *A History of the English Church and People* are to inform and to persuade. The purpose of P. G. Wodehouse's humorous story "The Truth About George" is to entertain.

Autobiography An autobiography is a writer's account of his or her own life. Autobiographies often convey profound insights as writers recount past events from the perspective of greater understanding and distance. A formal autobiography involves a sustained, lengthy narrative of a person's history, but other autobiographical narratives may be less formal and briefer. Under the general category of autobiography fall such writings as diaries, journals, memoirs, and letters. Both formal and informal autobiographies provide revealing insights into the writer's character, attitudes, and motivations, as well as some understanding of the society in which the writer lived. *The Book of Margery Kempe* is an autobiography.

See also **Diary; Memoir.**

Ballad A ballad is a narrative poem that was originally intended to be sung. Traditional **folk ballads,** written by unknown authors and handed down orally, usually depict ordinary people in the midst of tragic events and adventures of love and bravery. They tend to begin abruptly, focus on a single incident, use dialogue and repetition, and suggest more than they actually state. They often contain supernatural elements.

Typically, a ballad consists of four-line stanzas, or quatrains, with the second and fourth lines of each stanza rhyming. Each stanza has a strong rhythmic pattern, usually with four stressed syllables in the first and third lines and three stressed syllables in the second and fourth lines. The rhyme scheme is usually *abcb* or *aabb.* "Barbara Allan" and "Sir Patrick Spens" are examples of ballads. The following stanza is from "Barbara Allan":

O slowly, slowly rase she up, *a*
To the place where he was lyin', *b*
And when she drew the curtain by: *c*
"Young man, I think you're dyin'." *b*

See also **Narrative Poem; Quatrain.**

Biography A biography is an account of a person's life written by another person. In a good biography, the presentation of the subject's life is comprehensive, unified, and accurate. The skilled biographer synthesizes information from sources such as letters, journals, interviews, and documents and strives for a balanced portrayal through detailed anecdotes, reconstructed dialogue, description, quotations, and interpretive passages. An outstanding example of a biography is James Boswell's *The Life of Samuel Johnson.*

Although full-length biographies cover the life history of a person from birth to death, less extensive writings also may be considered biographical. These include the anecdote, which relates a revealing incident in a person's life, and the character sketch, a brief descriptive essay that highlights certain qualities of the subject.

Blank Verse Blank verse is unrhymed poetry written in iambic pentameter. Because iambic pentameter resembles the natural rhythm of spoken English, it has been considered the most suitable meter for dramatic verse in English. Shakespeare's plays are written largely in blank verse. Blank verse has also been used frequently for long poems. An example is William Wordsworth's poem "Lines Composed a Few Miles Above Tintern Abbey":

And now, with gleams of half-extinguished thought
With many recognitions dim and faint,
And somewhat of a sad perplexity,
The picture of the mind revives again;

See also **Iambic Pentameter; Meter.**

Caesura *See* **Anglo-Saxon Poetry.**

Character Characters are the people who participate in the action of a work. The most important characters are the **main characters.** Less prominent characters are known as **minor characters.** In Katherine Mansfield's "A Cup of Tea," Rosemary and the girl are main characters, and the shopman is a minor character.

Whereas some characters are two-dimensional, with only one or two dominant traits, a fully developed character possesses many traits, mirroring the psychological complexity of a real person. In longer works of fiction, main characters often undergo change as the plot unfolds. Such characters are called **dynamic characters,** as opposed to **static characters,** who remain the same. In D. H. Lawrence's story "The Rocking-Horse Winner," Paul is a dynamic character, because he becomes increasingly absorbed by his obsession to get money for his mother. Uncle Oscar is a static character, who primarily observes and responds to Paul's actions.

See also **Characterization.**

Characterization *Characterization* refers to the techniques that writers use to develop characters. There are four basic methods of characterization:

1. A writer may describe the physical appearance of a character. In William Trevor's "The Distant Past," the narrator describes the Middletons: "They had always been thin, silent with one another, and similar in appearance: a brother and sister who shared a family face. It was a bony countenance, with pale blue eyes and a sharp, well-shaped nose and high cheekbones."

2. A character's nature may be revealed through his or her own speech, thoughts, feelings, or actions. In Trevor's story, the reader learns about the kind of life the Middletons lead: "Together they roved the vast lofts of their house, placing old paint tins and flowerpot saucers beneath the drips from the roof. At night they sat over their thin chops in a dining-room that had once been gracious . . ."
3. The speech, thoughts, feelings, and actions of other characters can be used to develop a character. The attitudes of the townspeople to the Middletons help the reader understand the old couple better: "'An upright couple,' was the Canon's public opinion of the Middletons, and he had been known to add that eccentric views would hurt you less than malice."
4. The narrator can make direct comments about the character's nature. The narrator in Trevor's story comments, "The Middletons were in their middle-sixties now and were reconciled to a life that became more uncomfortable with every passing year."

See also **Character.**

Climax *See* **Plot.**

Comedy A comedy is a dramatic work that is light and often humorous in tone, usually ending happily with a peaceful resolution of the main conflict. A comedy differs from a farce by having a more believable plot, more realistic characters, and less boisterous behavior. Shakespeare's *A Midsummer Night's Dream* is a comedy.

See also **Drama; Farce.**

Conflict A conflict is a struggle between opposing forces that moves a plot forward. The conflict provides the interest or suspense in a short story, drama, novel, narrative poem, or nonfiction narrative. Conflict may be **external,** with a character being pitted against some outside force—another person, a physical obstacle, nature, or society. Conflict may also be **internal,** occurring within a character. In Elizabeth Gaskell's "Christmas Storms and Sunshine," Mrs. Hodgson is in a running conflict with Mrs. Jenkins. The sergeant in Lady Gregory's *The Rising of the Moon* faces an external conflict with the escaped prisoner and an internal conflict involving his double loyalties.

See also **Plot.**

Connotation *Connotation* refers to the attitudes and feelings associated with a word, in contrast to **denotation,** which is the literal or dictionary meaning of a word. The connotation of a word may be positive or negative. For example, *enthusiastic* has positive associations, but *rowdy* has negative ones. Connotations of words can have an important influence on style and meaning and are particularly important in poetry. In W. B. Yeats's poem "Sailing to Byzantium," the connotations of the words *paltry* and *tattered* in the lines "An aged man is but a paltry thing, / A tattered coat upon a stick, . . ." help to create the image of a thin, ragged scarecrow.

Consonance Consonance is the repetition of consonant sounds within and at the ends of words, as in "lonely afternoon." Consonance is unlike rhyme in that the vowels preceding or following the repeated consonant sounds differ. Sometimes the repeated sounds have different spellings, as in *hours* and *squeeze.* Consonance is often used together with alliteration, assonance, and rhyme to create a musical quality, to emphasize certain words, or to unify a poem. The repetition of the *l* sound in the following lines from W. H. Auden's "Musée des Beaux Arts" reinforces the meaning of *leisurely* and helps create a slow pace:

> In Breughel's *Icarus,* for instance: how everything
> turns away
> Quite leisurely from the disaster; the ploughman may
> Have heard the splash, the forsaken cry,
> But for him it was not an important failure; . . .

See also **Assonance.**

Contrast Contrast is a stylistic device in which one element is put into opposition with another. The opposing elements might be contrasting structures, such as sentences of varying lengths or stanzas of different configurations. They could also be contrasting ideas or images juxtaposed within phrases, sentences, paragraphs, stanzas, or sections of a longer work of literature. Writers use contrast to clarify or emphasize ideas and to elicit emotional responses from the reader. Part of the force of Siegfried Sassoon's poem "Dreamers" lies in the contrast between images of war, such as "death's gray land," and images of ordinary life, such as "firelit homes."

Controlling Image *See* **Imagery.**

Couplet A couplet is a rhymed pair of lines. A simple couplet may be written in any rhythmic pattern. The following couplet from Andrew Marvell's "To His Coy Mistress" is written in iambic tetrameter (lines of four iambs):

> Hăd wé bŭt wórld ĕnóugh, ănd tíme,
> Thĭs cóynĕss, ládў, wére nŏ críme.

A **heroic couplet** consists of two rhyming lines written in iambic pentameter. The term *heroic* comes from the fact that English poems having heroic themes and elevated style have often been written in iambic pentameter. Alexander Pope's masterful use of the heroic couplet made it a popular verse form during the neoclassical period. The following lines from *An Essay on Criticism* are one of many possible examples from his work:

> Ăvóid ĕxtrémes; ănd shŭn thĕ fáult ŏf súch,
> Whŏ stíll ăre pléased tŏo líttlĕ ór tŏo múch.

Denotation *See* **Connotation.**

Denouement *See* **Plot.**

Description Description is writing that helps a reader to picture scenes, events, and characters. It helps the reader understand exactly what someone or something is like. To create description, writers often use sensory images—words and phrases that enable the reader to see, hear, smell, taste, or feel the subject described—and figurative language. Effective description also relies on precise nouns, verbs, adjectives, and adverbs, as well as carefully selected details. The following passage from James Joyce's "Araby" contains clear details and images:

> Air, musty from having been long enclosed, hung in all the rooms, and the waste room behind the kitchen was littered with old useless papers. Among these I found a few paper-covered books, the pages of which were curled and damp. . . . The wild garden behind the house contained a central apple-tree and a few straggling bushes under one of which I found the late tenant's rusty bicycle-pump.

Dialect Dialect is a particular variety of language spoken in one place by a distinct group of people. A dialect reflects the colloquialisms, grammatical constructions, distinctive vocabulary, and pronunciations that are typical of a region. At times writers use dialect to establish or emphasize settings, as well as to develop characters. The runaway in Lady Gregory's play *The Rising of the Moon* speaks in a broad Irish dialect, which underscores his links to Irish nationalism.

Dialogue Written conversation between two or more people, in either fiction or nonfiction, is called dialogue. Writers use dialogue to bring characters to life and to give readers insights into the characters' qualities, personality traits, and reactions to other people. Realistic, well-paced dialogue also advances the plot of a narrative.

Dialogue in drama is critical to an understanding of the playwright's story or message. How the dialogue is read or performed will determine to a great extent the reactions of the reader or audience to the play. Dramatists use **stage directions** to indicate how they intend the dialogue to be interpreted by the actors. In the first act of Oscar Wilde's play *The Importance of Being Earnest,* the words *languidly* and *stiffly* are stage directions used to indicate how the character Algernon is supposed to speak at two different times. In Harold Pinter's play *That's All,* the frequent pauses and breaks in conversation are indicated by stage directions.

Although dialogue is most common in novels, short stories, and dramas, it is also used in other forms of prose as well as in poetry. Fanny Burney's account of the party in the excerpt from *The Diary and Letters of Madame d'Arblay* makes effective use of dialogue.

See also **Characterization; Drama.**

Diary A diary is a writer's personal day-to-day account of his or her experiences and impressions. Most diaries are private and not intended to be shared. Some, however, have been published because they are well written and provide useful perspectives on historical events or on the everyday life of particular eras. The excerpt from *The Diary of Samuel Pepys* is an example of a well-written diary of great historical interest.

See also **Autobiography.**

Diction Diction is a writer's choice of words, a significant component of style. Diction encompasses both vocabulary (individual words) and syntax (the order or arrangement of words). Diction can be described with terms such as *formal* or *informal, technical* or *common, abstract* or *concrete.* Much of the diction in Aldous Huxley's essay "Words and Behavior" is formal, which is appropriate to the seriousness of his subject. In W. H. Auden's "The Unknown Citizen," the blandness of the diction—for example, the words *employers, advertisements, advantages,* and *population*—helps establish the detached, ironic tone of the poem.

See also **Connotation; Style.**

Drama Drama is literature that develops plot and character through dialogue and action; in other words, drama is literature in play form. Dramas are meant to be performed by actors who appear on a stage, before radio microphones, or in front of television or movie cameras.

Unlike other forms of literature, such as fiction and poetry, a drama requires the collaboration of many people in order to come to life. In an important sense, a drama in printed form is an incomplete work of art. It is a skeleton that must be fleshed out by a director, actors, set designers, and others who interpret the work and stage a performance. When the members of an audience become caught up in a drama and forget to a degree the artificiality of the play, the process is called the "suspension of disbelief."

Most plays are divided into acts, with each act having an emotional peak, or climax, of its own. The acts sometimes are divided into scenes; each scene is limited to a single time and place. Shakespeare's plays have five acts; Wilde's *The Importance of Being Earnest* has three. Contemporary plays usually have two or three acts, although some, such as Lady Gregory's *The Rising of the Moon* and Harold Pinter's *That's All,* have only one.

All plays have **stage directions,** instructions included in the script to help performers and directors put on the play or to help readers visualize the action. Stage directions can describe setting, lighting, sound effects, the movement of actors, or the way in which dialogue is spoken.

See also **Aside; Dialogue; Plot; Soliloquy.**

Dramatic Irony *See* **Irony.**

Dramatic Monologue A dramatic monologue is a lyric poem in which a speaker addresses a silent or absent listener in a moment of high intensity or deep emotion, as if engaged in private conversation. The speaker proceeds without interruption or argument, and the effect on the reader is that of hearing just one side of a conversation. This technique allows the poet to focus on the feelings, personality, and motivations of the speaker—in a sense, taking the reader inside the speaker's mind. Robert Browning's poems "Porphyria's Lover" and "My Last Duchess" are both dramatic monologues.

Elegy An elegy is an extended meditative poem in which the speaker reflects upon death—often in tribute to a person who has died recently—or on an equally serious subject. Most elegies are written in formal, dignified language and are serious in tone. Alfred, Lord Tennyson's *In Memoriam,* written in memory of his friend Arthur Henry Hallam, is a famous elegy.

Elizabethan (Shakespearean) Sonnet *See* **Sonnet.**

End Rhyme *See* **Rhyme.**

English (Shakespearean) Sonnet *See* **Sonnet.**

Epic An epic is a long narrative poem on a serious subject, presented in an elevated or formal style. It traces the adventures of a great hero. Most epics share some or all of the following characteristics:

1. The hero is a figure of high social status and often of great historical or legendary importance.
2. The actions of the hero often determine the fate of a nation or group of people.
3. The hero performs exceedingly courageous, sometimes even superhuman, deeds that reflect the ideas and values of the era.
4. The plot is complicated by supernatural beings and events.
5. The setting is large in scale, involving more than one nation and often a long and dangerous journey through foreign lands.
6. Long formal speeches are often given by the main character.

7. The poem treats universal ideas, such as good and evil, life and death.

Beowulf and the *Iliad* are both epics.

Epic Simile *See* **Simile.**

Epigram The epigram is a literary form that originated in ancient Greece. It developed from simple inscriptions on monuments into a literary genre—short poems or sayings characterized by conciseness, balance, clarity, and wit. A classic epigram is written in two parts, the first establishing the occasion or setting the tone and the second stating the main point. A few lines taken from a longer poem can also be an epigram. Epigrams are used for many purposes, including the expression of friendship, grief, criticism, praise, and philosophy. Many passages in Pope's *An Essay on Criticism* constitute epigrams, as in the following example:

> Good nature and good sense must ever join;
> To err is human, to forgive, divine.

Epitaph An epitaph is an inscription on a tomb or monument to honor the memory of a deceased person. The term *epitaph* is also used to describe any verse commemorating someone who has died. Although a few humorous epitaphs have been composed, most are serious in tone. Ben Jonson's "On My First Son" is sometimes called an epitaph.

Epithet An epithet is a brief phrase that points out traits associated with a particular person or thing. Homer's *Iliad* contains many examples of epithets, such as the references to Achilles as "the great runner" (line 34) and to Hector as "killer of men" (line 328).

Essay An essay is a brief work of nonfiction that offers an opinion on a subject. The purpose of an essay may be to express ideas and feelings, to analyze, to inform, to entertain, or to persuade. In a **persuasive essay,** a writer attempts to convince readers to adopt a particular opinion or to perform a certain action. Most persuasive essays present a series of facts, reasons, or examples in support of an opinion or proposal. Sir Francis Bacon's "Of Studies" and "Of Marriage and Single Life" are good examples of the persuasive essay.

Essays can be formal or informal. A **formal essay** examines a topic in a thorough, serious, and highly organized manner. An **informal essay** presents an opinion on a subject, but not in a completely serious or formal tone. Characteristics of this type of essay include humor, a personal or confidential approach, a loose and sometimes rambling style, and often a surprising or unconventional topic. Daniel Defoe's essay "An Academy for Women" is a formal essay, meant to analyze and persuade. Joseph Addison's essays from *The Spectator* are informal, meant to express observations, ideas, and feelings and to entertain with gentle humor and wit.

Exaggeration *See* **Hyperbole.**

Exposition *See* **Plot.**

Extended Metaphor Like any metaphor, an extended metaphor is a comparison between two essentially unlike things that nevertheless have something in common. It does not contain the word *like* or *as.* In an extended metaphor, two things are compared at length and in various ways—perhaps throughout a stanza, a paragraph, or even an entire work. The likening of God to a shepherd in Psalm 23 is an example of an extended metaphor.

See also **Figurative Language; Metaphor; Simile.**

External Conflict *See* **Conflict.**

Fable A fable is a brief tale, in either prose or verse, told to illustrate a moral or teach a lesson. Often, the moral of a fable appears in a distinct and memorable statement near the tale's beginning or end. Jean de La Fontaine's "The Acorn and the Pumpkin" and "The Value of Knowledge" are both fables.

Falling Action *See* **Plot.**

Fantasy *Fantasy* is a term applied to works of fiction that display a disregard for the restraints of reality. The aim of a fantasy may be purely to delight or may be to make a serious comment. Some fantasies include extreme or grotesque characters. Others portray realistic characters in a realistic world who only marginally overstep the bounds of reality. In Muriel Spark's "The First Year of My Life," the presentation of events from the perspective of an infant is an element of fantasy.

Farce A farce is a type of exaggerated comedy that features an absurd plot, ridiculous situations, and humorous dialogue. The main purpose of a farce is to keep an audience laughing. The characters are usually stereotypes, or simplified examples of different traits or qualities. They may seem reasonable at the start but soon become far-fetched. Comic devices typically used in farces include mistaken identity, deception, wordplay—such as puns and double meanings—and exaggeration. Many of the characteristics and comic devices of farce are present in Oscar Wilde's play *The Importance of Being Earnest* and in P. G. Wodehouse's story "The Truth About George."

See also **Stereotype.**

Fiction *Fiction* refers to imaginative works of prose, primarily the novel and the short story. Although fiction sometimes draws on actual events and real people, it springs mainly from the imagination of the writer. The purpose of fiction is to entertain, but it also enlightens by providing a deeper understanding of the human condition. The basic elements of fiction are plot, character, setting, and theme.

See also **Character; Fable; Fantasy; Novel; Plot; Setting; Short Story; Theme.**

Figurative Language Language that communicates meanings beyond the literal meanings of the words is called figurative language. A figurative expression is not literally true, but rather creates an impression in the reader's mind. Writers use figurative language to create effects, to emphasize ideas, and to evoke emotions. Figurative language is used in both prose and poetry, as well as in oral expression. Special types of figurative language, called figures of speech, include simile, metaphor, personification, hyperbole, and apostrophe. In his poem "Preludes," T. S. Eliot uses each of these kinds of figurative language: (1) simile—"The worlds revolve like ancient women / Gathering fuel in vacant lots"; (2) metaphor—"The burnt-out ends of smoky days"; (3) personification—"The morning comes to consciousness"; (4) hyperbole—"The thousand sordid images"; (5) apostrophe—the third section, beginning "You tossed a blanket from the bed."

See also **Apostrophe; Hyperbole; Metaphor; Personification; Simile.**

First-Person Point of View *See* **Point of View.**

Flashback A flashback is an account of a conversation, an episode, or an event that happened before the beginning of a story. By revealing significant thoughts, experiences, or events in a character's life, a flashback can help readers understand a character's present situation. Flashbacks may take the form of reminiscences, dream sequences, or descriptions by third-person narrators; they usually interrupt the chronological flow of a story. Flashbacks may contain foreshadowing or other clues to the outcome of a story. The use of flashback in Virginia Woolf's "The Duchess and the Jeweller" helps to reveal the conflicting emotions and motivations of the jeweller. The use of flashback in William Trevor's "The Distant Past" provides important background for understanding the relationship of the Middletons to the townspeople.

Foil A foil is a character who provides a striking contrast to another character. By using a foil, a writer can call attention to certain traits possessed by a main character or simply enhance a character by contrast. In Ruth Rendell's "Paintbox Place," the down-to-earth and practical Mrs. Upton is a foil to the proud and self-centered Mrs. Julian.

Folk Ballad *See* **Ballad.**

Folk Tale A folk tale is a story that is handed down, usually by word of mouth, from generation to generation. Folk tales reflect the unique characteristics of the regions they come from, showing how the inhabitants live and what their values are. Many involve supernatural events, and most suggest morals. Often, things happen in threes in folk tales. Leo Tolstoy's "What Men Live By" is a version of a Russian folk tale.

Foreshadowing Foreshadowing is a writer's use of hints or clues that suggest what events will occur later in a narrative. The use of foreshadowing creates suspense while preparing readers for what is to come. In "The Rocking-Horse Winner," the strange mad frenzy with which Paul rides his rocking horse early in the story foreshadows the tragedy of his final ride.

Form When applied to poetry, the term *form* refers to all the principles of arrangement in a poem—

the ways in which the words and images are organized and patterned to produce a pleasing whole, including the length and placement of lines and the grouping of lines into stanzas. Elements of form—such as the sound devices of rhythm, rhyme, alliteration, consonance, and assonance—work together with elements such as figurative language and imagery to shape a poem, convey meaning, and create a total experience for the reader. The term *form* can also refer to a type of poetry, such as the sonnet or the dramatic monologue. William Wordsworth's "The World Is Too Much with Us," "It Is a Beauteous Evening," and "I Wandered Lonely As a Cloud" all provide good examples of the poet's artful use of form.

See also **Structure.**

Frame Story A frame story exists when a story is told within a narrative setting or frame—hence creating a story within a story. An example is P. G. Wodehouse's "The Truth About George." At the beginning of the work, the narrator establishes a frame in which the tale will be told. The storyteller, who is actually someone other than the narrator, is introduced in this frame. Geoffrey Chaucer's "The Pardoner's Tale" and Giovanni Boccaccio's "Federigo's Falcon" also contain frame stories.

Free Verse Free verse is verse that does not contain regular patterns of rhythm and rhyme. The lines in free verse often flow more naturally than do rhymed, metrical lines and thus achieve a rhythm more like that of everyday speech. Although free verse lacks conventional meter, it may contain various rhythmic and sound effects, such as repetitions of syllables or words. Free verse can also contain rhyme, although the rhyme will not follow predictable patterns. Much 20th-century poetry, such as Stephen Spender's "What I Expected" and T. S. Eliot's "Preludes," is written in free verse.

Haiku Haiku is a form of Japanese poetry that embodies three qualities greatly valued in Japanese art: precision, economy, and delicacy. Nature is a particularly important source of inspiration for Japanese haiku poets, and details from nature are often the subject of their poems. The rules of haiku are strict—in only 17 syllables, arranged in 3 lines of 5, 7, and 5 syllables, the poet must create a clear picture that will evoke a strong emotional response in the reader. The poems of Matsuo Bashō and Kobayashi Issa are examples of haiku.

Hero A hero, or **protagonist,** is a central character in a work of fiction, drama, or epic poetry. A traditional hero possesses good qualities that enable him or her to triumph over an antagonist who is bad or evil in some way.

The term ***tragic hero,*** first used by the Greek philosopher Aristotle, refers to a central character in a drama who is dignified or noble. According to Aristotle, a tragic hero possesses a defect, or tragic flaw, that brings about or contributes to his or her downfall. This flaw may be poor judgment, pride, weakness, or an excess of an admirable quality. The tragic hero, Aristotle noted, recognizes his or her flaw and its consequences, but only after it is too late to change the course of events. The characters Macbeth and Hamlet in Shakespeare's tragedies are tragic heroes.

A **cultural hero** is a hero who represents the values of his or her culture. Such a hero ranks somewhere between ordinary human beings and the gods. The role of a cultural hero is to provide a noble image that will inspire and guide the actions of mortals. Beowulf is a cultural hero.

In more recent literature, heroes do not necessarily command the attention and admiration of an entire culture. They tend to be individuals whose actions and decisions reflect personal courage. The conflicts they face are not on an epic scale but instead involve moral dilemmas presented in the course of living. Such heroes are often in a struggle with established authority because their actions challenge accepted beliefs. The sergeant in Lady Gregory's play *The Rising of the Moon* might be viewed as such a hero.

See also **Epic; Protagonist; Tragedy.**

Heroic Couplet *See* **Couplet.**

Historical Writing Historical writing is the systematic telling, often in narrative form, of the past of a nation or group of people. Historical writing generally has the following characteristics: (1) it is concerned with real events; (2) it uses chronological order; and (3) it is usually an objective retelling of facts rather than a personal interpretation. The Venerable Bede's *A History of the English Church and People* is an example of historical writing.

Humor In literature there are three basic types of humor, all of which may involve exaggeration or irony. **Humor of situation** is derived from the plot of a work. It usually involves exaggerated events or situational irony, which occurs when something happens that is different from what was expected. **Humor of character** is often based on exaggerated personalities or on characters who fail to recognize their own flaws, a form of dramatic irony. **Humor of language** may include sarcasm, exaggeration, puns, or verbal irony, which occurs when what is said is not what is meant. In "The Truth About George," P. G. Wodehouse uses all three kinds of humor, including absurd situations, ridiculous characters, and unexpected or inappropriate remarks.

Hyperbole Hyperbole is a figure of speech in which the truth is exaggerated for humorous effect or for emphasis. In Edmund Spenser's "Sonnet 75," the speaker uses hyperbole in the last four lines to express his love:

> My verse your virtues rare shall eternize,
> And in the heavens write your glorious name,
> Where whenas death shall all the world subdue,
> Our love shall live, and later life renew.

See also **Figurative Language.**

Iambic Pentameter Iambic pentameter is a metrical line of five feet, or units, each of which is made up of two syllables, the first unstressed and the second stressed. Iambic pentameter is the most common form of meter used in English poetry; it is the meter used in blank verse, the heroic couplet, and the sonnet. The following line from Milton's sonnet "How Soon Hath Time" is an example of iambic pentameter:

> How soon hath Time, the subtle thief of youth

Iambic pentameter is also the meter Milton used in his epic *Paradise Lost.*

See also **Blank Verse; Couplet; Meter; Sonnet.**

Imagery The term *imagery* refers to words and phrases that create vivid sensory experiences for the reader. The majority of images are visual, but imagery may also appeal to the senses of smell, hearing, taste, and touch. In addition, images may re-create sensations of heat (thermal), movement (kinetic), and bodily tension (kinesthetic). Effective writers of both prose and poetry frequently use imagery that appeals to more than one sense simultaneously. For example, in John Keats's ode "To Autumn," the image "Thy hair soft-lifted by the winnowing wind," appeals to two senses—sight and touch.

When an image describes one sensation in terms of another, the technique is called **synesthesia.** For example, the phrase "cold smell of potato mold" from Seamus Heaney's poem "Digging" is an image appealing to smell described in terms of touch (temperature).

A poet may use a controlling image to convey thoughts or feelings. A **controlling image** is a single image or comparison that extends throughout a literary work and shapes its meaning. A controlling image sometimes is an **extended metaphor.** The image of the Greek vase in Keats's "Ode on a Grecian Urn" and the image of digging in Heaney's poem "Digging" are controlling images.

See also **Kinesthetic Imagery.**

Informal Essay *See* **Essay.**

Interior Monologue *See* **Stream of Consciousness.**

Internal Conflict *See* **Conflict.**

Internal Rhyme *See* **Rhyme.**

Irony Irony is a contrast between expectation and reality. This incongruity often has the effect of surprising the reader or viewer. The techniques of irony include hyperbole, understatement, and sarcasm. Irony is often subtle and easily overlooked or misinterpreted.

There are three main types of irony. **Situational irony** occurs when a character or the reader expects one thing to happen but something else actually happens. In Thomas Hardy's poem "Ah, Are You Digging on My Grave?" the speaker questions who is digging on her grave and why. The responses to her questions and the final revelation shock the speaker and create a shattering irony in the poem.

Verbal irony occurs when a writer or character says one thing but means another. An example of verbal irony is the title of Jonathan Swift's essay "A Modest Proposal." The reader soon discovers that the narrator's proposal is outrageous rather than modest and unassuming.

Dramatic irony occurs when the reader or viewer knows something that a character does not know. In Muriel Spark's story "The First Year of My Life," the characters in the final scene think that the baby smiles because her brother blows out the candle on her birthday cake. The reader knows, however, that she smiles in response to hearing someone quote a prominent politician.

Italian (Petrarchan) Sonnet *See* **Sonnet.**

Kenning *See* **Anglo-Saxon Poetry.**

Kinesthetic Imagery Kinesthetic imagery re-creates the tension felt through muscles, tendons, or joints in the body. An example of kinesthetic imagery is the following description from Doris Lessing's "A Sunrise on the Veld": "the flesh of his soles contracted on the chilled earth."

See also **Imagery.**

Lyric A lyric is a short poem in which a single speaker expresses personal thoughts and feelings. Most poems other than dramatic and narrative poems are lyrics. In ancient Greece, lyrics were meant to be sung—the word *lyric* comes from the word *lyre,* the name of a musical instrument that was used to accompany songs. Modern lyrics are not usually intended for singing, but they are characterized by strong, melodic rhythms. Lyrics can be in a variety of forms and cover many subjects, from love and death to everyday experiences. They are marked by imagination and create for the reader a strong, unified impression. "The Wife's Lament," Shakespeare's sonnets, Keats's odes, and Eliot's "Preludes" are all lyrics. Sir Thomas Wyatt's "My Lute, Awake!" is an example of a lyric that was written to be set to music.

See also **Poetry.**

Major Character *See* **Character.**

Memoir A memoir is a form of autobiographical writing in which a person recalls significant events in his or her life. Most memoirs share the following characteristics: (1) they usually are structured as narratives told by the writers themselves, using the first-person point of view; (2) though some names may be changed to protect privacy, memoirs are true accounts of actual events; (3) although basically personal, memoirs may deal with newsworthy events having a significance beyond the confines of the writers' lives; (4) unlike strictly historical accounts, memoirs often include the writers' feelings and opinions about historical events, giving the reader insight into the impact of history on people's lives. Vera Brittain's *Testament of Youth* is a memoir from the period of World War I.

See also **Autobiography.**

Metaphor A metaphor is a figure of speech that makes a comparison between two things that are basically unlike but have something in common. Unlike a simile, a metaphor does not contain the word *like* or *as.* In Andrew Marvell's poem "To His Coy Mistress," the phrase "Time's wingéd chariot" is a metaphor in which the swift passage of time is compared to a speeding chariot:

> But at my back I always hear
> Time's wingéd chariot hurrying near

See also **Extended Metaphor; Figurative Language; Simile.**

Metaphysical Poetry Metaphysical poetry is a style of poetry written by a group of 17th-century poets, of whom John Donne was the first. The metaphysical poets rejected the conventions of Elizabethan love poetry, with its musical quality and themes of courtly love. Instead, they approached subjects such as religion, death, and even love by analyzing them logically and philosophically. The metaphysical poets were intellectuals who, like the ideal Renaissance man, were well-read in a broad spectrum of subjects. The characteristics of metaphysical poetry include more than just an intellectual approach to subject matter, however. Instead of the lyrical style of most Elizabethan poetry, metaphysical poets used a more colloquial, or conversational, style. In spite of the simplicity of the words, the ideas may seem obscure or confusing at first, because metaphysical poets loved to play with language. Donne's writing is filled with surprising twists: unexpected images and comparisons, as well as the use of **paradox,** seemingly contradictory statements that in fact reveal some element of truth. Donne's poem "A Valediction: Forbidding Mourning" contains many characteristics of metaphysical poetry.

See also **Paradox.**

Meter Meter is the repetition of a regular rhythmic unit in poetry. The meter of a poem emphasizes the musical quality of the language. Each unit of meter is known as a **foot,** consisting of one stressed syllable and one or two unstressed syllables. In representations of meter, a stressed syllable is often indicated by the symbol ´, an unstressed syllable by the symbol ˘. The four basic types of metrical feet are the **iamb,** an unstressed syllable followed by a stressed syllable (˘ ´); the **trochee,** a stressed syllable followed by an unstressed syllable (´ ˘); the **anapest,** two unstressed syllables followed by a stressed syllable (˘ ˘ ´); and the **dactyl,** a stressed syllable followed by two unstressed syllables (´ ˘ ˘).

Two words are used to identify the meter of a line of poetry. The first word describes the predominant type of metrical foot in the line. The second word describes the number of feet in the line: dimeter (two feet), trimeter (three feet), tetrameter (four feet), pentameter (five feet), hexameter (six feet), and so forth. The meter that Alfred, Lord Tennyson, used in his poem *In Memoriam* is iambic tetrameter:

I hold it true, whate'er befall;
I feel it, when I sorrow most;
'Tis better to have loved and lost
Than never to have loved at all.

Poets use variations within a regular metrical pattern—adding an extra syllable or reversing the stressed and unstressed syllables in a foot—to create the effects they want and to reinforce meaning. In his poem "Still to Be Neat," Ben Jonson also uses iambic tetrameter, but he frequently changes iambs to trochees to achieve emphasis and to create interesting rhythmic effects:

Still to be neat, still to be dressed,
As you were going to a feast;
Still to be powdered, still perfumed;
Lady, it is to be presumed,
Though art's hid causes are not found,
All is not sweet, all is not sound.

See also **Free Verse; Iambic Pentameter; Rhythm.**

Minor Character *See* **Character.**

Miracle Play *See* **Mystery Play.**

Monologue *See* **Dramatic Monologue; Soliloquy.**

Mood Mood is the feeling, or atmosphere, that a writer creates for the reader. The use of connotation, details, dialogue, imagery, figurative language, foreshadowing, setting, and rhythm can help set the mood. The mood of Rudyard Kipling's "The Miracle of Purun Bhagat" is one of peace and reflection, created in part by the descriptions of the main character and his relationships with other people, the land, and the animals.

See also **Tone.**

Morality Play *See* **Mystery Play.**

Motif A motif is a recurring word, phrase, image, object, idea, or action in a work of literature. Motifs function as unifying devices and often relate directly to one or more major themes. Motifs in "The Prologue" to *The Canterbury Tales,* for example, include images of earthly love along with images of spiritual devotion.

Mystery Play A mystery play is a drama, written in the Middle Ages, that portrays a biblical story. Mystery plays were first performed in churches but were later staged outdoors. Closely related to mystery plays were **miracle plays,** which dramatized saints' lives, and **morality plays,** which dramatized moral conflicts through allegory; the characters in morality plays were allegorical figures, such as Vice, Mercy, Death, and Good Deeds. These types of plays became increasingly elaborate and popular, and some were performed well into the Renaissance period.

Narration *See* **Narrative; Narrator; Point of View.**

Narrative A narrative is any type of writing that is primarily concerned with relating an event or a series of events. A narrative can be imaginary, like a short story or a novel, or it can be factual, like a newspaper account or a work of history. *Memoirs of Madame Vigée-Lebrun* and Algernon Blackwood's story "The Kit-Bag" are both narratives.

Narrative Poem A narrative poem tells a story. Like a short story or a novel, a narrative poem has the following elements: characters, setting, plot, and point of view, all of which combine to develop a theme. Epics, such as *Beowulf* and the *Iliad,* are narrative poems, as are ballads.

Narrator The narrator of a literary work is the person or voice that tells the story. The narrator can be a character in the story or a voice outside the action. In Margaret Atwood's story "Significant Moments in the Life of My Mother," the narrator is sometimes a participant in the incidents she recounts. The narrator of Saki's story "Tobermory" is, on the other hand, observant but detached.

Naturalism An extreme form of realism, naturalism in fiction involves the depiction of life objectively and precisely, without idealizing. Like the realist, the naturalist accurately portrays the world. However, the naturalist creates characters who are victims of environmental forces and internal drives beyond their comprehension and control. Naturalistic fiction conveys the belief that everything that exists is part of the scheme of nature, explainable entirely by natural and physical causes. Doris Lessing's "A Sunrise on the Veld," which depicts a boy who encounters death and brutality in nature, has naturalistic aspects.

See also **Realism.**

Neoclassicism *Neoclassicism* refers to the attitudes toward life and art that dominated English literature during the Restoration and the 18th century. Neoclassicists respected order, reason, and rules and viewed humans as limited and imperfect. To them, the intellect was more important than emotions, and society was more important than the individual. Imitating classical literature, neoclassical writers developed a style that was characterized by strict form, logic, symmetry, grace, good taste, restraint, clarity, and conciseness. Their works were meant not only to delight readers but also to instruct them in moral virtues and correct social behavior. Among the literary forms that flourished during the neoclassical period were the essay, the literary letter, and the epigram. The heroic couplet was the dominant verse form, and satire and parody prevailed in both prose and poetry. For examples, see the selections by Alexander Pope, Jonathan Swift, and Samuel Johnson.

See also **Romanticism.**

Nonfiction Nonfiction is prose writing that is about real people, places, and events. Unlike fiction, nonfiction is largely concerned with factual information, although the writer selects and interprets the information according to his or her purpose and viewpoint. Although the subject matter of nonfiction is not imaginative, the writer's style may be individualistic and innovative. Types of nonfiction include autobiographies, biographies, letters, essays, diaries, journals, memoirs, and speeches. Examples include *The Paston Letters* and Winston Churchill's speeches.

See also **Autobiography; Biography; Diary; Essay; Memoir.**

Novel A novel is an extended work of fiction. Like a short story, a novel is essentially the product of a writer's imagination. The most obvious difference between a novel and a short story is length. Because the novel is considerably longer, a novelist can develop a wider range of characters and a more complex plot.

Octave *See* **Sonnet.**

Ode An ode is an exalted, complex lyric that develops a serious and dignified theme. Odes appeal to both the imagination and the intellect, and many commemorate events or praise people or elements of nature. Examples of odes that celebrate an element of nature are Percy Bysshe Shelley's "Ode to the West Wind" and "To a Skylark."

Off Rhyme *See* **Rhyme.**

Omniscient Point of View *See* **Point of View.**

Onomatopoeia Onomatopoeia is the use of words whose sounds echo their meanings, such as *buzz, whisper, gargle,* and *murmur.* Onomatopoeia as a literary technique goes beyond the use of simple echoic words, however. Skilled writers, especially poets, choose words whose sounds in combination suggest meaning. In "Pied Beauty," Gerard Manley Hopkins uses onomatopoeia to help convey the images and meanings he wants to express:

> Whatever is fi<u>ck</u>le, fre<u>ck</u>led (who knows how?)
> With swift, <u>slow</u>; sweet, sour; <u>adazzle</u>, <u>dim</u>

Oxymoron *See* **Paradox.**

Parable A parable is a brief story that is meant to teach a lesson or illustrate a moral truth. A parable is more than a simple story, however. Each detail of the parable corresponds to some aspect of the problem or moral dilemma to which it is directed. The story of the prodigal son in the Bible is a classic parable.

Paradox A paradox is a statement that seems to contradict itself but, in fact, reveals some element of truth. Paradox is found frequently in the poetry of the 16th and 17th centuries. The first line of the following couplet from Elizabeth I's poem "On Monsieur's Departure" contains two examples of paradox:

> I am and not, I freeze and yet am burned,
> Since from myself another self I turned.

A special kind of concise paradox is the **oxymoron,** which brings together two contradictory terms. Examples are "cruel kindness" and "brave fear."

See also **Metaphysical Poetry.**

Parallelism Parallelism is the use of similar grammatical constructions to express ideas that are related or equal in importance. The parallel elements may be words, phrases, sentences, or paragraphs. In the first paragraph of the excerpt from *The Crisis,* Thomas Paine uses the parallel phrases "the harder the conflict, the more glorious the triumph" and "what we obtain too cheap, we esteem too lightly."

See also **Repetition.**

Parody A parody imitates or mocks another work or type of literature. Like caricature in art, parody in literature mimics a subject or a style. The purpose of a parody may be to ridicule through broad humor. On the other hand, a parody may broaden understanding of or add insight to the original work. Some parodies are even written in tribute to a work of literature. Shakespeare's "Sonnet 130" is in part a parody of love poetry of other Renaissance poets. The sonnet mocks some of the characteristics of the traditional beautiful woman praised in the earlier poems.

Pastoral A pastoral is a poem presenting shepherds in rural settings, usually in an idealized manner. The language and form of pastorals are artificial. The supposedly simple, rustic characters tend to use formal, courtly speech, and the meters and rhyme schemes are characteristic of formal poetry. Renaissance poets were drawn to the pastoral as a means of conveying their own emotions and ideas, particularly about love. Christopher Marlowe's "The Passionate Shepherd to His Love" is a pastoral.

Personification Personification is a figure of speech in which human qualities are attributed to an object, animal, or idea. Writers use personification to communicate feelings and images in a concise, concrete way. In line 117 of Thomas Gray's "Elegy Written in a Country Churchyard," for example, the earth is personified: *"Here rests his head upon the lap of Earth."* In Shakespeare's "Sonnet 116," time is personified:

> Love's not Time's fool, though rosy lips and cheeks
> Within his bending sickle's compass come,

See also **Figurative Language; Metaphor; Simile.**

Persuasion Persuasion is a technique used by speakers and writers to convince an audience to adopt a particular opinion, perform an action, or both. Effective persuasion appeals to both the intellect and the emotions. The most common form of persuasion is the oration, or speech, as in Winston's Churchill's speech of May 19, 1940.

See also **Essay.**

Persuasive Essay *See* **Essay; Persuasion.**

Persuasive Speech *See* **Persuasion.**

Petrarchan (Italian) Sonnet *See* **Sonnet.**

Plot Plot is the sequence of actions and events in a narrative. Usually, the events of a plot progress because of a **conflict,** or struggle between opposing forces. Most plots include the following stages:

1. The **exposition** lays the groundwork for the plot and provides the reader with essential background information. Characters are introduced, the setting is described, and the major conflict is identified. Although the exposition generally appears at the opening of a work, it may also occur later in the narrative.

2. In the **rising action,** complications usually arise, causing difficulties for the main characters and making the conflict more difficult to resolve. As the characters struggle to find solutions to the conflict, suspense builds.
3. The **climax** is the turning point of the action, the moment when interest and intensity reach their peak. The climax of a work usually involves an important event, decision, or discovery that affects the final outcome.
4. The **falling action** consists of the events that occur after the climax. Often, the conflict is resolved, and the intensity of the action subsides. Sometimes this phase of the plot is called the **resolution** or the **denouement** (dā'no͞o-mäɴ'). *Denouement* is from a French word that means "untying"—in this stage the tangles of the plot are untied and mysteries are solved.

See also **Conflict.**

Poetry Poetry is an arrangement of lines on the page in which form and content fuse to suggest meanings beyond the literal meanings of the words. Like other forms of literature, poetry attempts to re-create emotions and experiences. Poetry, however, is usually more compressed and suggestive than prose. Because poetry frequently does not include the kind of explanation common in the short story or the novel, it tends to leave more to the reader's imagination.

Many poems are divided into stanzas. The stanzas of a poem may contain the same number of lines, or they may vary in length. Some poems have definite patterns of meter and rhyme. Others, especially poems of the 20th century, rely more on the sounds of words and less on fixed rhythms and rhyme schemes. Characteristic of poetry is the use of imagery, language that appeals to the senses. Poetry is also rich in connotative words and figurative language.

See also **Figurative Language; Form; Free Verse; Imagery; Meter; Repetition; Rhyme; Rhythm; Stanza.**

Point of View *Point of view* refers to the method of narrating a short story, novel, narrative poem, or work of nonfiction. The three most common points of view are first-person, third-person omniscient, and third-person limited. The point of view that a writer employs determines to a great degree the reader's view of the action and the characters; manipulation of point of view creates many striking effects in fiction.

In **first-person point of view,** the narrator is a character in the work, narrating the action as he or she perceives and understands it. First-person narration imparts an immediacy to the narrative and usually leads to involvement with the narrating character. Two short stories using first-person narration are "Araby" by James Joyce and "At the Pitt-Rivers" by Penelope Lively. Almost all autobiographies have first-person narration.

In **third-person point of view,** events and characters are described by a narrator outside the action. In **third-person omniscient point of view,** the narrator is omniscient, or all-knowing, and can see into the mind of more than one character. The use of a third-person omniscient narrator gives the writer great flexibility and provides the reader with access to all the characters' motivations and responses and to events that may be occurring simultaneously. In D. H. Lawrence's "The Rocking-Horse Winner," the use of a third-person omniscient narrator allows for psychological complexity and depth that would not be possible with a first-person narrator.

When a writer uses **third-person limited point of view,** the narrator tells the story from the perspective of only one of the characters. The reader learns only what that character thinks, feels, observes, and experiences. Algernon Blackwood's "The Kit-Bag" is told from a third-person limited point of view. Blackwood's use of this point of view helps to create suspense and intensity in the story.

See also **Narrator.**

Primary Source A primary source is a book, document, or person that provides original, firsthand information about a topic. Primary sources for an event or period of history might include letters, wills, diaries, tape recordings, and government records. A person can be a primary source for events that he or she has experienced or witnessed. Etty Hillesum's letters are a primary source for information about the Holocaust.

Prop The word *prop,* an abbreviation of *property,* refers to any physical object that is used in a stage production. In Oscar Wilde's *The Importance of Being Earnest,* the props include a cigarette case and a black leather handbag.

See also **Drama.**

Prose Generally, *prose* refers to all forms of written or spoken expression that are organized and that lack regular rhythmic patterns. Prose is characterized by logical order, continuity of thought, and individual style. Prose style varies from one writer to another, depending on such elements as word choice, sentence length and structure, use of figurative language, and tone. Examples of the variety of prose styles can be seen in John Donne's religious meditations from the 17th century, Samuel Johnson's essays from the 18th century, Elizabeth Gaskell's fiction from the 19th century, and Katherine Mansfield's fiction from the 20th century.

See also **Poetry.**

Protagonist The central character in a story, novel, or play is called the protagonist. The protagonist is always involved in the main conflict of the plot and often changes during the course of the work. The force or person who opposes the protagonist is the antagonist. In Boccaccio's story "Federigo's Falcon," the protagonist is Federigo, who considers himself opposed by Fortune. In 20th-century fiction and drama, the conflict may be subtle, and the protagonist is not always opposed by an antagonist. In Penelope Lively's story "At the Pitt-Rivers," for example, the main character changes in his perceptions as the story develops, but he is not opposed by another character or by an outside force.

See also **Antagonist; Hero.**

Quatrain A quatrain is a four-line stanza, or unit, of poetry. The most common stanza in English poetry, the quatrain can display a variety of meters and rhyme schemes. The following quatrain from Robert Herrick's "To the Virgins, to Make Much of Time," follows a typical *abab* rhyme scheme:

Gather ye rosebuds while ye may, *a*
  Old time is still a-flying; *b*
And this same flower that smiles today *a*
  Tomorrow will be dying. *b*

See also **Ballad; Form; Sonnet; Stanza.**

Realism As a general term, *realism* refers to any effort to offer an accurate and detailed portrayal of actual life. In this sense, realism has been a significant element in almost every school of writing in human history. Thus, critics praise Geoffrey Chaucer's realistic descriptions of people from all social classes and analyze Shakespeare's realistic portrayals of character.

Realism also refers to a literary method developed in the 19th century. The 19th-century realists based their writing on careful observations of ordinary life, often focusing on the middle or lower classes. They attempted to present life objectively and honestly, without the sentimentality or idealism that had characterized earlier literature, particularly fiction. Typically, the realists developed settings in great detail in an effort to re-create specific times and places for the reader. Modern realists focus on characterization and avoid contrived plot structures. Elements of realism can be found in the novels of Jane Austen and Charles Dickens, but it is not fully developed until the fiction of George Eliot. James Joyce's story "Araby" and Ruth Rendell's "Paintbox Place" are examples of 20th-century realistic fiction.

See also **Naturalism.**

Repetition Repetition is a technique in which a sound, word, phrase, or line is repeated for emphasis or unity. The use of repetition often helps to reinforce meaning and to create an appealing rhythm. *Repetition* is a general term that includes specific devices associated with both prose and poetry, such as alliteration and parallelism. Examples of effective repetition can be found in William Blake's "The Lamb" and "The Tyger" and in Elizabeth Barrett Browning's "Sonnet 43."

See also **Alliteration; Assonance; Consonance; Parallelism; Rhyme; Rhyme Scheme.**

Resolution *See* **Plot.**

Rhyme Words rhyme when the sounds of their accented vowels and all succeeding sounds are identical, as in *amuse* and *confuse.* For **true rhyme,** the consonants that precede the vowels must be different. Rhyme that occurs at the end of lines of poetry is called **end rhyme,** as in

Thomas Hardy's rhyming of *face* and *place* in "The Man He Killed." End rhymes that are not exact but approximate are called **off rhyme,** or **slant rhyme,** as in the words *come* and *doom* in Stevie Smith's "The Frog Prince." Rhyme that occurs within a single line, as in A. E. Housman's "When I Was One-and-Twenty" is called **internal rhyme:**

Give crowns and pounds and guineas

Rhyme Scheme A rhyme scheme is the pattern of end rhyme in a poem. A rhyme scheme is charted by assigning a letter of the alphabet, beginning with *a,* to each line. Lines that rhyme are given the same letter—in Sir Thomas Wyatt's "My Lute, Awake!" for example, the rhyme scheme of each stanza is *aabab:*

Vengeance shall fall on thy disdain *a*
That makest but game on earnest pain. *a*
Think not alone under the sun *b*
Unquit to cause thy lovers plain, *a*
Although my lute and I have done. *b*

See also **Ballad; Rhyme; Sonnet; Spenserian Stanza; Villanelle.**

Rhythm Rhythm is a pattern of stressed and unstressed syllables in a line of poetry. Poets use rhythm to bring out the musical quality of language, to emphasize ideas, to create mood, to unify a work, and to heighten emotional response. Devices such as alliteration, rhyme, assonance, consonance, and parallelism often contribute to creating rhythm. The slow rhythms of the following lines from Ted Hughes's "The Horses" help to convey the mysterious mood of the poem:

I listened in emptiness on the moor-ridge.
The curlew's tear turned its edge on the silence.

See also **Anglo-Saxon Poetry; Ballad; Meter; Spenserian Stanza; Sprung Rhythm.**

Rising Action *See* **Plot.**

Romance The romance has been a popular narrative form since the Middle Ages. Generally, the term *romance* refers to any imaginative adventure concerned with noble heroes, gallant love, a chivalric code of honor, daring deeds, and supernatural events. Romances usually have faraway settings, depict events unlike those of ordinary life, and idealize their heroes as well as the eras in which the heroes lived. Medieval romances are often lighthearted in tone, usually consist of a number of episodes, and often involve one or more characters in a quest. Thomas Malory's *Le Morte d'Arthur* is an example of a medieval romance. Its stories of kings, knights, and ladies relate many adventures, tales of love, superhuman feats, and quests for honor and virtue.

Romanticism *Romanticism* refers to a literary movement that flourished in Britain and Europe throughout much of the 19th century. Romantic writers looked to nature for their inspiration, idealized the distant past, and celebrated the individual. In reaction against neoclassicism, their treatment of subjects was emotional rather than rational, imaginative rather than analytical. The romantic period in English literature is generally viewed as beginning with the publication of *Lyrical Ballads,* poems by William Wordsworth and Samuel Taylor Coleridge.

See also **Neoclassicism.**

Satire Satire is a literary technique in which ideas, customs, behaviors, or institutions are ridiculed for the purpose of improving society. Satire may be gently witty, mildly abrasive, or bitterly critical, and it often uses exaggeration to force readers to see something in a more critical light. Often, a satirist will distance himself or herself from a subject by creating a fictional speaker—usually a calm, and often a naive, observer—who can address the topic without revealing the true emotions of the writer. Whether the object of a satiric work is an individual person or a group of people, the force of the satire will almost always cast light on foibles and failings that are universal to human experience.

There are two main types of satire, named for the Roman satirists Horace and Juvenal; they differ chiefly in tone. Horatian satire is playfully amusing and seeks to correct vice or foolishness with gentle laughter and sympathetic understanding. Joseph Addison's essays are examples of Horatian satire. Juvenalian satire provokes a darker kind of laughter. It is biting and criticizes corruption or incompetence with scorn and outrage. Jonathan Swift's essay "A Modest Proposal" is an example of Juvenalian satire.

See also **Irony.**

Scripture Scripture is literature that is considered sacred—that is, it is used in religious rituals of worship, initiation, celebration, and mourning. Such literature is usually preserved in what are considered holy books. The hymns, chants, prayers, myths, and other forms passed down through generations and combined as a body of scripture express the core beliefs of a group of people. The excerpts from the King James Bible are examples of scripture gathered from the Jewish and Christian traditions.

Sestet *See* **Sonnet.**

Setting *Setting* is usually defined as "the time and place of the action of a short story, novel, play, narrative poem, or nonfiction narrative." In addition to time and place, however, setting may include the social and moral environment that form the background for a narrative. Setting is one of the main elements in fiction and often plays an important role in what happens and why. Sometimes it serves as a source of conflict, as in Doris Lessing's story "A Sunrise on the Veld."

See also **Fiction.**

Shakespearean (English) Sonnet *See* **Sonnet.**

Short Story A short story is a work of fiction that can be read in one sitting. Generally, a short story develops one major conflict. The basic elements of a short story are setting, character, plot, and theme.

A short story must be unified; all the elements must work together to produce a total effect. This unity of effect is reinforced through an appropriate title and through the use of symbolism, irony, and other literary devices.

See also **Fiction.**

Simile A simile is a figure of speech that compares two things that are basically unlike yet have something in common. Unlike a metaphor, which implies or suggests a comparison, a simile states it by means of the word *like* or *as.* Both poets and prose writers use similes to intensify emotional response, stimulate vibrant images, provide imaginative delight, and concentrate the expression of ideas. In her story "The Duchess and the Jeweller," Virginia Woolf uses similes to describe the duchess as she sits down:

> As a parasol with many flounces, as a peacock with many feathers, shuts its flounces, folds its feathers, so she subsided and shut herself as she sank down in the leather armchair.

An **epic simile** is a long comparison that often continues for a number of lines. It does not always contain the word *like* or *as.* Here is an example of an epic simile from Homer's *Iliad:*

> Conspicuous as the evening star that comes,
> amid the first in heaven, at fall of night,
> and stands most lovely in the west, so shone
> in sunlight the fine-pointed spear
> Achilles poised in his right hand. . . .

See also **Figurative Language; Metaphor.**

Situational Irony *See* **Irony.**

Slant Rhyme *See* **Rhyme.**

Soliloquy A soliloquy is a speech in a dramatic work in which a character speaks his or her thoughts aloud. Usually the character is on the stage alone, not speaking to other characters and perhaps not even consciously addressing the audience. (If there are other characters on stage, they are ignored temporarily.) The purpose of a soliloquy is to reveal a character's inner thoughts, feelings, and plans to the audience. In *The Rising of the Moon,* the speech the sergeant makes just after the two policemen leave and just before the ragged man appears on stage is an example of a brief soliloquy.

Sonnet A sonnet is a lyric poem of 14 lines, commonly written in iambic pentameter. For centuries the sonnet has been a popular form, because it is long enough to permit development of a complex idea yet short and structured enough to challenge any poet's skills. Sonnets written in English usually follow one of two forms.

The **Petrarchan,** or **Italian, sonnet,** introduced into English by Sir Thomas Wyatt, is named after Petrarch, the 14th-century Italian poet. This type of sonnet consists of two parts, called the **octave** (the first eight lines) and the **sestet** (the last six lines). The usual rhyme scheme for the octave is *abbaabba.* The rhyme scheme for the **sestet** may be *cdecde, cdccdc,* or a similar variation. The octave generally presents a problem or raises a question, and the sestet resolves or comments on the problem. John Milton's sonnets are written in the Petrarchan form.

The **Shakespearean,** or **English, sonnet** is sometimes called the **Elizabethan sonnet.** It consists of three quatrains, or four-line units, and a final couplet. The typical rhyme scheme is *ababcdcdefefgg.* In the English sonnet, the rhymed couplet at the end of the sonnet provides a final commentary on the subject developed in the three quatrains. Shakespeare's sonnets are the finest examples of this type of sonnet.

A variation of the Shakespearean sonnet is the **Spenserian sonnet,** which has the same structure but uses the interlocking rhyme scheme *ababbcbccdcdee.* Spenser's "Sonnet 30" is an example.

Some poets have written a series of related sonnets that have the same subject. These are called **sonnet sequences,** or **sonnet cycles.** Toward the end of the 16th century, writing sonnet sequences became fashionable, with a common subject being love for a beautiful but unattainable woman. Francesco Petrarch, Edmund Spenser, and Elizabeth Barrett Browning wrote sonnet sequences.

See also **Iambic Pentameter; Lyric; Meter; Quatrain.**

Sound Devices *See* **Alliteration; Assonance; Consonance; Meter; Onomatopoeia; Repetition; Rhyme; Rhyme Scheme; Rhythm.**

Speaker The speaker in a poem is the voice that "talks" to the reader, like the narrator in fiction. The speaker is sometimes a distant observer and at other times intimately involved with the experiences and ideas being expressed in the poem. The speaker and poet are not necessarily identical. Often a poet creates a speaker with a distinct identity in order to achieve a particular effect. The speaker of W. H. Auden's poem "Musée des Beaux Arts" is detached and aloof, as though merely recording observations. The speaker in W. B. Yeats's "Sailing to Byzantium," on the other hand, is passionately involved in the ideas and feelings he is expressing.

Spenserian Stanza The Spenserian stanza (named for Edmund Spenser, who invented it for his romance *The Faerie Queene*) consists of nine iambic lines rhyming in the pattern *ababbcbcc.* Each of the first eight lines contains five feet, and the ninth contains six. The rhyming pattern helps to create unity, and the six-foot line, called an **alexandrine,** slows down the stanza and so gives dignity and allows for reflection on the ideas in the stanza. The following example of the Spenserian stanza comes from Byron's *Childe Harold's Pilgrimage:*

There is a pleasure in the pathless woods, *a*
There is a rapture on the lonely shore, *b*
There is society where none intrudes, *a*
By the deep Sea, and music in its roar: *b*
I love not Man the less, but Nature more, *b*
From these our interviews, in which I steal *c*
From all I may be or have been before, *b*
To mingle with the Universe, and feel *c*
What I can ne'er express, yet can not all conceal. *c*

See also **Stanza.**

Sprung Rhythm In order to approximate the rhythms of natural speech in poetry, the poet Gerard Manley Hopkins developed what he called sprung rhythm. The lines of a poem written in sprung rhythm have fixed numbers of stressed syllables but varying numbers of unstressed syllables. A line may contain several consecutive stressed syllables, or a stressed syllable may be followed by one, two, or even three unstressed syllables. The following lines from "Pied Beauty" are written in sprung rhythm:

Landscape plotted and pieced—fold, fallow, and plough;
And all trades, their gear and tackle and trim.

Stage Directions *See* **Drama.**

Stanza A stanza is a group of lines that form a unit in a poem. The stanza is roughly comparable to the paragraph in prose. In traditional poems, the stanzas usually have the same number of lines and often have the same rhyme scheme and meter. In the 20th century, poets have experimented more freely with stanza form, sometimes writing poems that have no stanza breaks at all. The quatrains in Richard Lovelace's "To Lucasta, Going to the Wars," are a traditional stanza form. The two stanzas of W. B. Yeats's "The Second Coming," one 8 lines long and the other 14 lines long, are an example of an unconventional stanza form.

See also **Quatrain; Spenserian Stanza; Villanelle.**

Stereotype In literature, simplified or stock characters who conform to a fixed pattern or are defined by a single trait are called stereotypes. Such characters do not usually demonstrate the complexities of real people. Familiar stereotypes in popular literature include the absent-minded professor, the busybody, and the merciless villain. The figure of the rejected lover in many ballads is an example of a stereotype.

Stream of Consciousness *Stream of consciousness* refers to a style of fiction that takes as its subject the flow of thoughts, responses, and sensations of one or more characters. A stream-of-consciousness narrative is not structured as a coherent, logical presentation of ideas. Rather, the connections between ideas are associative, with one idea suggesting another.

A character's stream of consciousness is often expressed as an **interior monologue,** a record of the total workings of the character's mind and emotions. An interior monologue may reveal the inner experience of the character on many levels of consciousness, often represented through a sequence of images and impressions. Virginia Woolf and James Joyce make extensive use of stream of consciousness in their fiction.

See also **Characterization; Point of View; Style.**

Structure Structure is the way in which the parts of a work of literature are put together. Paragraphs are a basic unit in prose, as are chapters in novels, acts and scenes in plays, and stanzas and lines in poems. A prose selection can be structured by idea or incident, like most essays, short stories, narrative poems, and one-act plays. Structure in poetry involves the arrangement of words and lines to produce a desired effect; a poem's structure takes into account the sounds in the poem as well as the ideas.

The structure of a poem, short story, novel, play, or work of nonfiction usually emphasizes certain important aspects of content. For example, the division of T. S. Eliot's poem "Preludes" into sections enables him to shift between different times of day and between the interior of a room and the street outside. Structure is also a means through which a writer adds layers of psychological complexity to characters. Katherine Mansfield's story "A Cup of Tea" begins and ends with questions about whether Rosemary is pretty. This framework suggests the element in Rosemary's character—her vanity—that proves to be the crux of the story.

See also **Form.**

Style Style is the particular way in which a piece of literature is written. Style is not what is said but how it is said. It is the writer's uniquely individual way of communicating ideas. Many elements contribute to style, including word choice, sentence length, tone, figurative language, use of dialogue, and point of view. A literary style may be described in a variety of ways, such as *formal, conversational, journalistic, wordy, ornate, poetic,* or *dynamic.* The interior monologue and detailed, evocative imagery in Virginia Woolf's "The Duchess and the Jeweller" are important elements of the style of the story.

Supernatural Tale A supernatural tale is a story that goes beyond the bounds of reality, usually by involving beings, powers, or events that are unexplainable by known forces or laws of nature. In many supernatural tales, **foreshadowing**—hints or clues that point to later events—is used to encourage readers to anticipate the unthinkable. Sometimes readers are left wondering whether a supernatural event has really taken place or is the product of a character's imagination. In an effective supernatural tale, the writer manipulates readers' feelings of curiosity and fear to produce a mounting sense of excitement. Both Algernon Blackwood's "The Kit-Bag" and Elizabeth Bowen's "The Demon Lover" are supernatural tales.

Supernatural Elements *See* **Supernatural Tale.**

Surprise Ending A surprise ending is an unexpected twist in the plot at the end of a story. The surprise may be a sudden turn in the action or a revelation that gives a different perspective to the entire story. The final paragraph of "The Demon Lover," which sets off a new direction in the plot instead of bringing it to its expected conclusion, is an example of a surprise ending.

See also **Plot.**

Suspense Suspense is the tension or excitement readers feel as they are drawn into a story and become increasingly eager to learn the outcome of the plot. Suspense is created when a writer purposely leaves readers uncertain or apprehensive about what will happen. Lady Gregory uses suspense-building techniques when she describes the sounds the sergeant hears in the dark.

Symbol A symbol is a person, place, object, or activity that stands for something beyond itself. Certain symbols are commonly used in literature, such as a journey to represent life or night to represent death. Other symbols, however, acquire their meanings within the contexts of the works in which they occur. In Boccaccio's story "Federigo's Falcon," the falcon comes to symbolize the passionate and consuming love of Federigo for Monna Giovanna. Sometimes a literary symbol has more than one possible meaning. For example, the rose in Blake's poem "The Sick Rose" might symbolize goodness, innocence, or all of humanity.

Synecdoche Synecdoche is a figure of speech in which the name of a part is used to refer to a whole—for example, the use of *wheels* to mean "automobile." T. S. Eliot uses synecdoche in his poem "Preludes" when he uses words for body parts to refer to people, as in line 17, where "muddy feet" refers to early-morning crowds of people going to work.

Synesthesia *See* **Imagery.**

Theme A theme is a central idea or message in a work of literature. Theme should not be confused with subject, or what the work is about. Rather, theme is a perception about life or human nature shared with the reader. Sometimes the theme is directly stated within a work; at other times it is implied, and the reader must infer the theme. There may be more than one theme in a work.

One way to discover the theme of a literary work is to think about what happens to the central characters. The importance of those events, stated in terms that apply to all human beings, is the theme. In poetry, imagery and figurative language also help convey theme. In Chaucer's "The Pardoner's Tale," what happens to the three young men illustrates the theme "The love of money is the root of all evil."

Third-Person Point of View *See* **Point of View.**

Title The title of a literary work introduces readers to the piece and usually reveals something about its subject or theme. Although works are occasionally untitled or, in the case of some poems, merely identified by their first line, most literary works have been deliberately and carefully named. Some titles are straightforward, stating exactly what the reader can expect to discover in the work. Others suggest possibilities, perhaps hinting at the subject and forcing the reader to search for interpretations. "1996," the title of a poem by Rabindranath Tagore, gives the reader a direct clue about the subject of the poem, as does "Writing," the title of a poem by Octavio Paz. On the other hand, "Dover Beach," the title of a poem by Matthew Arnold, is open to interpretation, and the reader has to work through the significance of the title in relation to the poem.

Tone Tone is an expression of a writer's attitude toward a subject. Unlike mood, which is intended to shape the reader's emotional response, tone reflects the feelings of the writer. The writer's choice of words and details helps establish the tone, which might be serious, humorous, sarcastic, playful, ironic, bitter, or objective. To identify the tone of a work, you might find it helpful to read the work aloud. The emotions you convey in reading should give you clues to the tone of the work. The tone of Jonathan Swift's "A Modest Proposal" is searingly ironic; the tone of Arthur C. Clarke's essay "We'll Never Conquer Space" is logical and ironic. In "The Prologue" from *The Canterbury Tales,* Chaucer's restrained, detached tone accounts for much of the work's humor.

See also **Mood.**

Tragedy A tragedy is a dramatic work that presents the downfall of a dignified character who is involved in historically or socially significant events. The main character, or **tragic hero,** has a **tragic flaw,** a quality that leads to his or her destruction. The events in a tragic plot are set in motion by a decision that is often an error in judgment caused by the tragic flaw. Succeeding events are linked in a cause-and-effect relationship and lead inevitably to a disastrous conclusion, usually death. A tragic hero evokes both pity and fear in readers or viewers: pity because readers or viewers feel sorry for the character, and fear because they realize that the problems and struggles faced by the character are perhaps a necessary part of human life. At the end of a tragedy, a reader or viewer generally feels a sense of waste, because humans who were in some way superior have been destroyed. Shakespeare's plays *Macbeth, Hamlet, Othello,* and *King Lear* are famous examples of tragedies.

Tragic Flaw *See* **Hero; Tragedy.**

Tragic Hero *See* **Hero; Tragedy.**

Understatement Understatement is a technique of creating emphasis by saying less than is actually or literally true. Understatement is the opposite of hyperbole, or exaggeration. One of the primary devices of irony, understatement can be used to develop a humorous effect, to create biting satire, or to achieve a restrained tone. Understatement is an important element in the dramas of Harold Pinter, as in his one-act play *That's All.*

Verbal Irony *See* **Irony.**

Villanelle The villanelle is an intricately patterned French verse form, planned to give the impression of simplicity. A villanelle has 19 lines, composed of 5 tercets, or 3-line stanzas, followed by a quatrain. The first line is repeated as a refrain at the end of the second and fourth stanzas. The last line of the first stanza is repeated at the end of the third and fifth stanzas. Both lines reappear as the final two lines of the poem. The rhyme scheme of a villanelle is *aba* for each tercet and then *abaa* for the quatrain. Dylan Thomas's "Do Not Go Gentle into That Good Night" is an example of a villanelle.

See also **Quatrain; Stanza.**

Wordplay Wordplay is the intentional use of more than one meaning of a word to express ambiguities, multiple interpretations, and irony. In the excerpt from Derek Walcott's poem *Mid-summer,* he achieves some of his irony through the use of wordplay—for example, through his use of the words *color* and *white.*

WRITING HANDBOOK

1 The Writing Process

The writing process consists of four stages: prewriting, drafting, revising and editing, and publishing and reflecting. As the graphic to the right shows, these stages are not steps that you must complete in a set order. Rather, you may return to any one at any time in your writing process, using feedback from your readers along the way.

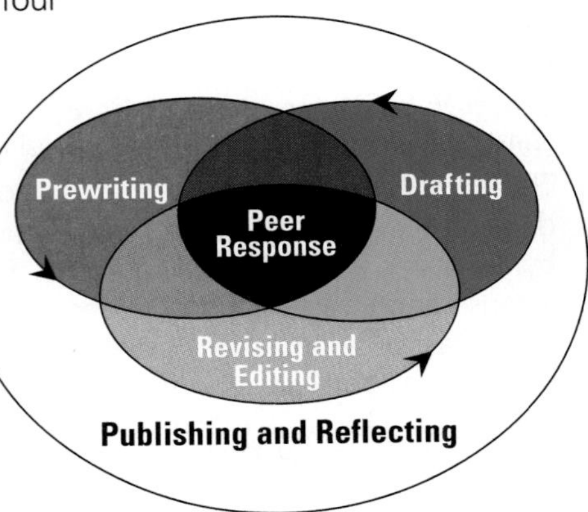

1.1 Prewriting

In the prewriting stage, you explore your ideas and discover what you want to write about.

Finding Ideas for Writing

Ideas for writing can come from just about anywhere: experiences, memories, conversations, dreams, or imaginings. Try one or more of the following techniques to help you find a writing topic.

Personal Techniques
Practice imaging, or trying to remember mainly sensory details about a subject—its look, sound, feel, taste, and smell.
Complete a knowledge inventory to discover what you already know about a subject.
Browse through magazines, newspapers, and on-line bulletin boards for ideas.
Start a clip file of articles that you want to save for future reference. Be sure to label each clip with source information.

Sharing Techniques
With a group, brainstorm a topic by trying to come up with as many ideas as you can without stopping to critique or examine them.
Interview someone who knows a great deal about your topic.

Writing Techniques

After freewriting on a topic, try looping, or choosing your best idea for more freewriting. Repeat the loop at least once.

Make a list to help you organize ideas, examine them, or identify areas for further research.

Graphic Techniques

Create a pro-and-con chart to compare the positive and negative aspects of an idea or a course of action.

Use a cluster map or tree diagram to explore subordinate ideas that relate to your general topic or central idea.

Determining Your Purpose

At some time during your writing process, you need to consider your purpose, or general reason, for writing. For example, your purpose may be one of the following: to express yourself, to entertain, to explain, to describe, to analyze, or to persuade. To clarify your purpose, ask yourself questions like these:

- Why did I choose to write about my topic?
- What aspects of the topic mean the most to me?
- What do I want others to think or feel after they read my writing?

Identifying Your Audience

Knowing who will read your writing can help you clarify your purpose, focus your topic, and choose the details and tone that will best communicate your ideas. As you think about your readers, ask yourself questions like these:

- What does my audience already know about my topic?
- What will they be most interested in?
- What language is most appropriate for this audience?

1.2 Drafting

In the drafting stage, you put your ideas on paper and allow them to develop and change as you write.

There's no right or wrong way to draft. Sometimes you might be adventuresome and dive right into your writing. At other times, you might draft slowly, planning carefully beforehand. You can combine aspects of these approaches to suit yourself and your writing projects.

LINK TO LITERATURE

One purpose for writing is to clarify a subject. For example, the Nigerian writer Chinua Achebe, author of "Civil Peace," page 1084, wrote to correct the errors and misunderstandings about Africans in European literature and to show the value of African cultures.

LINK TO LITERATURE

Sometimes the creative process is accelerated out of necessity. Harold Pinter, author of *That's All*, page 1122, wrote his first play, *The Room,* in just four afternoons while he was working as an actor. Spending mornings in rehearsal and evenings in performance, he wrote the play for a group of college drama students.

Discovery drafting is a good approach when you've gathered some information on your topic or have a rough idea for writing but are not quite sure how you feel about your subject or what exactly you want to say. You just plunge into your draft and let your ideas lead you where they will. After finishing a discovery draft, you may decide to start another draft, do more prewriting, or revise your first draft.

Planned drafting may work better for research reports, critical reviews, and other kinds of formal writing. Try thinking through a writing plan or making an outline before you begin drafting. Then, as you write, you can develop your ideas and fill in the details.

1.3 Using Peer Response

The suggestions and comments your peers or classmates make about your writing are called peer response.

Talking with peers about your writing can help you discover what you want to say or how well you have communicated your ideas. You can ask a peer reader for help at any point in the writing process. For example, your peers can help you develop a topic, narrow your focus, discover confusing passages, or organize your writing.

Questions for Your Peer Readers

You can help your peer readers provide you with the most useful kinds of feedback by following these guidelines:

- Tell readers where you are in the writing process. Are you still trying out ideas, or have you completed a draft?
- Ask questions that will help you get specific information about your writing. Open-ended questions that require more than yes-or-no answers are more likely to give you information you can use as you revise.
- Give your readers plenty of time to respond thoughtfully to your writing.
- Encourage your readers to be honest when they respond to your work. It's OK if you don't agree with them—you always get to decide which changes to make.

The chart on the following page explains different peer-response techniques you might use when you're ready to share your work with others.

Technique	When to Use It	Questions to Ask
Sharing	Use this when you are just exploring ideas or when you want to celebrate the completion of a piece of writing.	Will you please read or listen to my writing without criticizing or making suggestions afterward?
Summarizing	Use this when you want to know if your main idea or goals are clear.	What do you think I'm saying? What's my main idea or message?
Replying	Use this strategy when you want to make your writing richer by adding new ideas.	What are your ideas about my topic? What do you think about what I have said in my piece?
Responding to Specific Features	Use this when you want a quick overview of the strengths and weaknesses of your writing.	Are the ideas supported with enough examples? Did I persuade you? Is the organization clear enough for you to follow the ideas?
Telling	Use this to find out which parts of your writing are affecting readers the way you want and which parts are confusing.	What did you think or feel as you read my words? Would you show me which passage you were reading when you had that response?

Tips for Being a Peer Reader

Follow these guidelines when you respond to someone else's work:

- Respect the writer's feelings.
- Make sure you understand what kind of feedback the writer is looking for, and then respond accordingly.
- Use "I" statements, such as "I like . . . ," "I think . . . ," or "It would help me if . . ." Remember that your impressions and opinions may not be the same as someone else's.

WRITING TIP

Writers are better able to absorb criticism of their work if they first receive positive feedback. When you act as a peer reader, try to start your review by telling something you like about the piece.

1.4 Revising and Editing

In the revising and editing stage, you improve your draft, choose the words that best express your ideas, and proofread for mistakes in spelling, grammar, usage, and punctuation.

The changes you make in your writing during this stage usually fall into three categories: revising for content, revising for structure, and editing to correct mistakes in mechanics. Use the questions and suggestions that follow to help you assess problems in your draft and determine what kinds of changes would improve it.

WRITING TIP

Be sure to consider the needs of your audience as you answer the questions under Revising for Content. For example, before you can determine whether any of your material is unnecessary or irrelevant, you need to identify what your audience already knows.

WRITING TIP

For help identifying and correcting problems that are listed in the Proofreading Checklist, see the Grammar Handbook, pages 1254–1299.

Revising for Content

- Does my writing have a main idea or central focus? Is my thesis clear?
- Have I incorporated adequate detail? Where might I include a telling detail, revealing statistic, or vivid example?
- Is any material unnecessary, irrelevant, or confusing?

Revising for Structure

- Is my writing unified? Do all ideas and supporting details pertain to my main idea or advance my thesis?
- Is my writing clear and coherent? Is the flow of sentences and paragraphs smooth and logical?
- Do I need to add transitional words, phrases, or sentences to make the relationships among ideas clearer?
- Are my sentences well constructed? What sentences might I combine to improve the grace and rhythm of my writing?

Editing to Correct Mistakes in Mechanics

When you are satisfied with your draft, proofread and edit it, correcting any mistakes you might have made in spelling, grammar, usage, and punctuation. You may want to proofread your writing several times, looking for different types of mistakes each time. The following checklist may help you proofread your work.

Proofreading Checklist	
Sentence Structure and Agreement	Are there any run-on sentences or sentence fragments? Do all verbs agree with their subjects? Do all pronouns agree with their antecedents? Are verb tenses correct and consistent?
Forms of Words	Do adverbs and adjectives modify the appropriate words? Are all forms of *be* and other irregular verbs used correctly? Are pronouns used correctly? Are comparative and superlative forms of adjectives correct?
Capitalization, Punctuation, and Spelling	Is any punctuation mark missing or not needed? Are all words spelled correctly? Are all proper nouns and all proper adjectives capitalized?

If you have a printout of your draft or a handwritten copy, mark changes on it by using the proofreading symbols shown in the chart on the next page. The Grammar Handbook, starting on page 1254, includes models for using these symbols.

Proofreading Symbols			
∧	Add letters or words.	/	Make a capital letter lowercase.
⊙	Add a period.	¶	Begin a new paragraph.
≡	Capitalize a letter.	— or ℘	Delete letters or words.
⊂⊃	Close up space.	∽	Switch the positions of letters or words.
∧	Add a comma.		

1.5 Publishing and Reflecting

After you've completed a writing project, consider sharing it with a wider audience—even when you've produced it for a class assignment. Reflecting on your writing process is another good way to bring closure to a writing project.

Creative Publishing Ideas

Following are some ideas for publishing and sharing your writing.

- Post your writing on an electronic bulletin board or send it to others via e-mail.
- Create a multimedia presentation and share it with classmates.
- Publish your writing in a school newspaper or literary magazine.
- Present your work orally in a report, a speech, a reading, or a dramatic performance.
- Submit your writing to a local newspaper or a magazine that publishes student writing.
- Form a writing exchange group with other students.

Reflecting on Your Writing

Think about your writing process and consider whether you'd like to add your writing to your portfolio. You might attach to your work a note in which you answer questions like these:

- What did I learn about myself and my subject through this writing project?
- Which parts of the writing process did I most and least enjoy?
- As I wrote, what was my biggest problem? How did I solve it?
- What did I learn that I can use the next time I write?

WRITING TIP

You might work with other students to publish an anthology of class writing. Then exchange your anthology with another class or another school. Reading the work of other student writers will help you get ideas for new writing projects and for ways to improve your work.

Building Blocks of Good Writing

2.1 Introductions

A good introduction catches your reader's interest and often presents the main idea of your writing. To introduce your writing effectively, try one of the following methods.

Make a Surprising Statement

Beginning with a startling or an interesting fact can capture your reader's curiosity about the subject, as in the example below.

> Since it was first published in 1883, Robert Louis Stevenson's *Treasure Island* has never been out of print, and it has been translated into languages as diverse as Welsh, Zulu, and Ukrainian. This unusual success attests to the universal appeal of Stevenson's storytelling skills.

LINK TO LITERATURE

A vivid description is a good way to introduce readers to the characters or setting of a narrative. In the excerpt from *Testament of Youth*, page 850, Vera Brittain uses striking imagery to capture the sensations of being under fire at an Allied war hospital during World War I.

Provide a Description

A vivid description sets a mood and brings a scene to life for your reader. Here, details about visitors at Ellis Island set the tone for an essay about immigration to the United States.

> The visitors to the museum at Ellis Island wander almost reverently through rooms filled with photos and memorabilia. The walls seem to reverberate with countless stories—many long since forgotten—of immigrants who passed through this island.

Pose a Question

Beginning with a question can make your reader want to read on to find out the answer. The following introduction asks a significant question about the careers of two women writers.

> George Eliot and George Sand were both successful writers in the 19th century; both were also women. At this time in history, why was it important for them to use male pen names?

Relate an Anecdote

Beginning with a brief anecdote, or story, can hook readers and help you make a point in a dramatic way. The anecdote below introduces an essay about gangsters in the 1920s.

> The man, in an immaculate suit with broad lapels, narrowed his eyes against the sun as he stepped from the shadowy doorway. Pulling his hat down, he tossed a dime to the dazed, grubby boy standing before him. "Go get me a coupla Cokes, willya?—and step on it, kid!" So it was that my grandfather met Al Capone.

WRITING TIP

In order to write the best introduction for your paper, you may want to try more than one of the methods and then decide which is the most effective for your purpose and audience.

Address the Reader Directly

Speaking directly to readers in your introduction establishes a friendly, informal tone and involves them in your topic.

> If you are concerned about the appearance of our community, you should learn how you can participate in the Adopt-a-Street program that begins this April.

Begin with a Thesis Statement

A thesis statement expressing a paper's main idea may be woven into both the beginning and the end of nonfiction writing. The following is a thesis statement that introduces a literary analysis.

> In "Words and Behavior," Aldous Huxley argues that language must be used carefully. He shows that its misuse can establish and perpetuate great evil.

2.2 Paragraphs

A paragraph is made up of sentences that work together to develop an idea or accomplish a purpose. Whether or not it contains a topic sentence stating the main idea, a good paragraph must have both unity and coherence.

Unity

A paragraph has unity when all the sentences support and develop one stated or implied idea. Use the following techniques to create unity in your paragraphs.

Write a Topic Sentence A topic sentence states the main idea of the paragraph; all the other sentences in the paragraph provide supporting details. A topic sentence is often the first sentence in a paragraph. However, it may also appear later in the paragraph or at the end, to summarize or reinforce the main idea, as shown in the model below.

> Magnesium is a mineral found in food sources such as beans, nuts, meats, and dairy products. This mineral is necessary for the breakdown of nutrients in cells and is important to the stimulation of muscles and nerves. A healthy body effectively conserves magnesium. Insufficient amounts of the mineral, however, are related to various health problems, including kidney disease and excesses of acids in the body. *Dietary magnesium, therefore, is clearly vital to human health.*

Relate All Sentences to an Implied Main Idea A paragraph can be unified without a topic sentence as long as every sentence supports the implied, or unstated, main idea. In the example below, all the sentences work together to create a unified impression of an impending storm.

> All morning the wind had gently rustled the branches of trees and tossed back curtains from open windows. By early afternoon, however, it had picked up a force that tore green leaves from the trees and pushed thick and menacing clouds across the sky.

WRITING TIP

The same techniques that create unity in paragraphs can be used to create unity in an entire paper. Be sure that all of your paragraphs support the thesis statement or the implied main idea of your paper. If a paragraph includes information irrelevant to the main idea, you should delete it or revise it to establish a clear connection.

Coherence

A paragraph is coherent when all its sentences are related to one another and flow logically from one to the next. The following techniques will help you achieve coherence in paragraphs.

- Present your ideas in the most logical order.
- Use pronouns, synonyms, and repeated words to connect ideas.
- Use transitional devices to show the relationships among ideas.

In the example below, the italicized words show how the writer used some of these techniques to create a unified paragraph.

> Most people know that the gravitational pull of the moon causes tides in the oceans. Are you aware, *though*, that the moon exerts the *same pull* on the solid part of the earth? *Unlike* ocean tides, *however,* earth tides are deformations of as much as a foot in the earth's surface. The extent to which *its* surface bulges is greatest during full moon and new moon, *because* the gravitational pull of the moon combines with *that* of the sun.

WRITING TIP

You can use the techniques at the left to create coherence in an entire paper. Be sure that paragraphs flow logically from one to the next.

2.3 Transitions

Transitions are words and phrases that show the connections between details, such as relationships in time and space, order of importance, causes and effects, and similarities or differences.

Time or Sequence

Some transitions help to clarify the sequence of events over time. When you are telling a story or describing a process, you can connect ideas with such transitional words as *first, second, always, then, next, later, soon, before, finally, after, earlier, afterward,* and *tomorrow.*

> *Before* a blood donation can be used, it must be processed carefully. *First*, a sample is tested for infectious diseases and identified by blood type. *Next*, preservatives are added. *Finally*, a blood cell separator breaks up the blood into its parts, such as red blood cells, platelets, and plasma.

LINK TO LITERATURE

In the excerpt from *Letters from Westerbork*, page 871, notice how Etty Hillesum uses transitions to manage time. She uses them to distinguish between her thoughts, events in the recent past (which she presents in flashback), and ongoing experience (which she shows in present tense).

Spatial Relationships

Transitional words and phrases such as *in front, behind, next to, along, nearest, lowest, above, below, underneath, on the left,* and *in the middle* can help readers visualize a scene.

> A theater-in-the-round stage is constructed *in the middle of* the theater space, with the audience sitting *around* the entire stage. To create a more intimate setting, the seats *nearest* the stage are often only a few feet away.

Degree

Transitions such as *mainly, strongest, weakest, first, second, most important, least important, worst,* and *best* may be used to rank ideas or to show degree of importance.

> Cory made several New Year's resolutions. *Most important,* he decided to cut back on watching TV.

WRITING TIP

Both *but* and *however* may be used to join two independent clauses. When *but* is used as a coordinating conjunction, it is preceded by a comma. When *however* is used as a conjunctive adverb, it is preceded by a semicolon and followed by a comma, as shown in the example at the right.

Compare and Contrast

Words and phrases such as *similarly, likewise, also, like, as, neither . . . nor,* and *either . . . or* show similarity between details. *However, by contrast, yet, but, unlike, instead, whereas,* and *while* show difference. Note the use of both types of transitions in the model below.

> *Like* running and bicycling, swimming helps you maintain aerobic fitness; *however,* swimming has the added benefit of exercising muscles throughout your body.

Cause and Effect

When you are writing about a cause-and-effect relationship, use transitional words and phrases such as *since, because, thus, therefore, so, due to, for this reason,* and *as a result* to help clarify that relationship and to make your writing coherent.

> *Because* the temperature dropped to 28 degrees after it rained for five hours, car door locks froze.

2.4 Elaboration

Elaboration is the process of developing a writing idea by providing specific supporting details that are appropriate for the purpose and form of your writing.

Facts and Statistics

A fact is a statement that can be verified, while a statistic is a fact stated in numbers. As in the model below, the facts and statistics you use should strongly support the statements you make.

> Although lotteries have been a controversial method of generating revenue, the proceeds have benefited many state-funded programs. In fact, 53 percent of the 9 billion dollars of lottery proceeds in the United States in 1993 funded education programs.

WRITING TIP

Facts and statistics can be used to explain more than one idea, depending on how you interpret the information for the reader. Be certain that you clearly and logically establish how the facts you have chosen support your writing.

Sensory Details

Details that show how something looks, sounds, tastes, smells, or feels can enliven a description. Which senses does the writer appeal to in the following paragraph?

> Gina wasn't sure she enjoyed her first hayride. As the wagon bumped along the furrows of the empty field, she clumsily bounced between Marty and Deanna. She tried to imagine she was having fun as she shivered under the scratchy wool blankets that smelled of straw and dust.

Incidents

One way to illustrate a point is to relate an incident or tell a story, as shown in the example on the following page.

LINK TO LITERATURE

In the selection from *The Crisis,* Number 1, page 400, Thomas Paine uses the incident with the tavern owner to reinforce his idea that Americans had no choice but to fight the British if they didn't want to leave the task for future generations.

> Reforms often do not happen until a significant tragedy brings a problem to public attention. The deaths of 146 women workers in a fire at New York City's Triangle Shirtwaist factory in 1911 led to tougher protective labor laws in New York State and national awareness of unsafe management practices.

Examples

An example can help make an abstract or a complex idea concrete or can provide evidence to clarify a point for readers.

> There was a time when many of the foods eaten around the world today were found only in North, Central, and South America. For example, tomatoes, potatoes, beans, and corn all originated in the Americas.

Quotations

Choose quotations that clearly support your points and be sure that you copy each quotation word for word. Remember always to credit the source.

> Technological advances in the design of tennis rackets have changed the nature of the sport, but many players lament the passing of the wood racket. In his article "The Feel of Wood," Marshall Fisher states that after he switched to an aluminum racket in college competition, he concluded that the unavoidable "march of technology had degraded tennis."

2.5 Description

A good description contains carefully chosen details that create a unified impression for the reader.

Description is an important part of most writing genres—essays, stories, biography, and poetry, for example. Effective description can help readers to recognize the significance of an issue, to visualize a scene, or to understand a character.

Use a Variety of Details

If you include plenty of sensory details, readers can better imagine the scene you are describing. In the example below, the sensory details describe a character wading in a stream.

> The water wove through the smooth stones, pulling grains of wet sand from beneath Keiko's toes as if it were unraveling fabric. The swirling around her ankles relaxed her, but the water's coldness reminded her that winter wasn't altogether gone.

Show, Don't Tell

Simply telling your readers about an event or an idea in a general way does not give them a clear impression. Showing your readers the specific details, however, helps them develop a better sense of your subject. The following example tells how the writer's family felt.

> Our grandmother surprised us when she arrived for Thanksgiving dinner.

In the paragraph below, descriptive details are used to show the family's delight at the arrival of their grandmother.

> First, we heard a motor; next came the exuberant slam of a car door and the clicking, tottery sound of a woman in high heels running up our curved walk. It was so late on Thanksgiving Day that we couldn't imagine who this person might be. We smiled at one another when we heard the familiar voice: "You haven't started eating without me, have you?"

Use Figurative Language

Figurative language is descriptive writing that evokes associations beyond the literal meaning of the words. The following types of figurative language can make your descriptions clear and fresh.

LINK TO LITERATURE

Look at the descriptions of Mangan's sister in "Araby," on pages 946 and 947. Notice how James Joyce uses visual details to show the intensity of the narrator's focus on the girl. First, the girl stands silhouetted in a doorway at evening; later, lamplight pours over her in a narrow band.

WRITING TIP

To avoid unclear descriptions, be careful not to mix metaphors or use two or more comparisons that create a confusing image: *Shrouding the entire city, the storm howled through the night.*

WRITING TIP

You can clarify your descriptive writing by choosing precise words. For example, replace general nouns (*tree*) with more specific nouns (*blue spruce*).

- A **simile** is a figure of speech comparing two essentially unlike things, signaling the comparison with a word such as *like* or *as.*
- A **metaphor** is a figure of speech describing something by speaking of it as if it were something else, with no word such as *like* or *as* used to signal the comparison.

In the example below, the writer uses a simile to exaggerated effect.

> By the end of my research project, my room was so thoroughly choked with note cards, papers, and books that cleaning up was like an archaeological excavation.

Organize Your Details

Organize descriptions carefully to create a clear image for your readers. Descriptive details may be organized chronologically, spatially, by order of importance, or by order of impression.

> Rising up in the desert of Nevada like an image from ancient history, Las Vegas's Luxor Hotel replicates the Great Pyramid and Sphinx of Egypt. Inside the structure, however, you can witness everything from choreographed chariot races to simulated race-car driving.

2.6 Conclusions

A conclusion should leave readers with a strong final impression. Try any of these approaches for concluding your writing.

Restate Your Thesis

A good way to conclude an essay is by restating your thesis, or main idea, in different words. The conclusion below restates the thesis introduced in an example on page 1221.

> Aldous Huxley's "Words and Behavior" clearly warns of the danger of misusing language to manipulate and control. Unless we begin using concrete words and plain language to describe our experience, he maintains, we may ultimately destroy our civilization.

Ask a Question

Try asking a question that sums up what you have said and gives readers something new to think about. The question below concludes an appeal against continued funding for space exploration.

> Given all the evidence to the contrary, can you imagine that continued investment in the space program will truly provide a greater good for future generations than an equivalent investment in the basic needs of those living now?

Make a Recommendation

When you are persuading your audience to take a position on an issue, you can conclude by recommending a specific course of action.

> Voting is a vital way to influence your world. Make voter registration a part of your birthday plans.

Make a Prediction

Readers are concerned about matters that may affect them and therefore are moved by a conclusion that predicts the future.

> Reading the works of Chinua Achebe will change your understanding of the history and culture of African nations—a story that for years was told mostly by European writers.

Summarize Your Information

Summarizing reinforces the writer's main ideas, leaving a strong, lasting impression. The model below concludes with a statement that summarizes a review of a book.

> James Gurney's book *Dinotopia* appeals to adult readers, as well as to children, with its imaginative adventures, its realistic and fascinating drawings of dinosaurs, and its timeless theme of cooperation in a diverse community.

LINK TO LITERATURE

In the excerpt from *Testament of Youth*, on page 850, Vera Brittain concludes her discussion of events during World War I with predictions about the outcome of a different kind of war—a fight against the irrational thoughts that divide people.

3

Narrative Writing

Writing Standards

Good narrative writing

- includes descriptive details and dialogue to develop the characters, setting, and plot
- has a clear beginning, middle, and end
- has a logical organization with clues and transitions to help the reader understand the order of events
- maintains a consistent tone and point of view
- uses language that is appropriate for the audience
- demonstrates the significance of events or ideas

Narrative writing tells a story. If you write a story from your imagination, it is called a fictional narrative. A true story about actual events is called a nonfictional narrative.

Key Techniques of Narrative Writing

Clearly Organize the Events

Choose the important events and explain them in an order that is easy to understand. In a fictional narrative, this series of events is the story's plot.

Example

- the morning after my grandfather's funeral, I go to the cemetery
- the wilted funeral wreaths make me feel angry
- I want to find a place to remember my grandfather
- at the beach, I sit on the piece of driftwood near where my grandfather and I used to walk

Describe the Setting

The setting is the time and place of a narrative. In the example below, the details set the scene for the action of the narrative.

Example

The morning after the funeral, my grandfather's grave is covered with flowers and wreaths that are just starting to wilt from the cold.

Depict Characters Vividly

Use vivid details to show your readers what your characters look like, what they say, and what they think.

Example

I know lots of people come to the cemetery to mourn their loved ones, but I feel angry and frustrated. The gray stones and the wilted funeral wreaths don't make me feel closer to my grandfather.

Organizing Narrative Writing

One way to organize a piece of narrative writing is to arrange the events in chronological order, as shown in Option 1 below.

Option 1: Focus on Events	Example
• Introduce characters and setting.	The morning after my grandfather's funeral, I wake up early and walk to the cemetery.
• Show event 1.	I sit by his grave, surrounded by flowers and wreaths, and feel angry.
• Show event 2.	Frustrated and sad, I want to find some place where I can remember my grandfather and all the good times we had together.
• End, perhaps showing the significance of the events.	On the beach, I sit on the huge piece of driftwood where my grandfather and I used to sit. The cool lake wind and the noise of the waves bring back my favorite memories of him.

When the telling of a fictional narrative focuses on a central conflict, the story's plot may follow the model shown in Option 2. It is also possible in narrative writing to arrange the order of events by starting *in medias res,* or in the middle of things (Option 3).

Option 2

Focus on Conflict

- Describe the main characters and setting.
- Present the conflict.
- Relate the events that make the conflict complex and cause the characters to change.
- Present the resolution, or outcome of the conflict.

Option 3

Flashback

- Begin with the conflict.
- Present the events leading up to the conflict.
- Present the resolution, or outcome of the conflict.

Remember: You can use setting to reinforce the mood of your narrative as well as to reveal aspects of your characters.

WRITING TIP

Introductions Try to hook your readers' interest by opening your story with an interesting image that you can develop throughout the story.

WRITING TIP

Dialogue Dialogue is an effective way of depicting characters in a narrative. As you write dialogue, choose words that express your characters' personalities and show how they feel about one another.

Explanatory Writing

LINK TO LITERATURE

Explanatory writing provides many opportunities to explore issues presented by and in literature. The examples on the following pages use explanatory writing techniques to examine the historical and cultural context of Sir Thomas Malory's *Le Morte d'Arthur*, page 155.

Explanatory writing informs and explains. For example, you can use it to evaluate the effects of a new law, to compare two movie reviews, or to analyze a piece of literature.

Types of Explanatory Writing

Compare and Contrast

Compare-and-contrast writing explores the similarities and differences between two or more subjects.

Example
King Arthur and Sir Launcelot share similar qualities that lead to their friendship, but they also share weaknesses that ensure their deaths.

Cause and Effect

Cause-and-effect writing explains why something happened, why certain conditions exist, or what resulted from an action or a condition.

Example
King Arthur dies in battle with Sir Modred because he adheres too closely to the honor of knighthood and believes too much in the knights of his court.

Analysis

Analysis explains how something works, how it is defined, or what its parts are.

Example
Legends, such as the story of King Arthur, change over time as they are retold and take on new interpretations.

Problem-Solution

Problem-solution writing states a problem, analyzes the problem, and then proposes a solution to it.

Example
Arthur has to choose between honor and friendship—two values that are equally desirable until they conflict. Similarly, a teenager may have to choose between protecting a friendship and doing what is right.

4.1 Compare and Contrast

Compare-and-contrast writing explores the similarities and differences between two or more subjects.

Organizing Compare-and-Contrast Writing

Compare-and-contrast writing can be organized in different ways. The examples below demonstrate feature-by-feature organization and subject-by-subject organization.

Option 1

Feature by Feature

- **Feature 1** — Although King Arthur and Sir Launcelot become enemies, they still share similar noble qualities.
  - Subject A — King Arthur is reluctant to fight Launcelot because he still admires him as a great knight.
  - Subject B — Launcelot is reluctant to fight King Arthur because he still respects him as his liege.
- **Feature 2** — Both characters possess weaknesses that cause their own and each other's destruction.
  - Subject A
  - Subject B

Option 2

Subject by Subject

- **Subject A** — Despite King Arthur's noble qualities, his weaknesses ensure his destruction.
  - Feature 1 — King Arthur is reluctant to fight Launcelot because he still admires him as a great knight.
  - Feature 2 — King Arthur too often trusts the judgment of his knights rather than his own intuition.
- **Subject B** — Sir Launcelot's weaknesses similarly ensure his destruction.
  - Feature 1 — Launcelot is reluctant to fight King Arthur because he still respects him as his liege.
  - Feature 2 — His respect for his liege does not prevent him from giving in to his love for Arthur's wife.

Writing Standards

Good compare-and-contrast writing

- clearly identifies the subjects that are being compared and contrasted
- includes specific, relevant details
- follows a clear plan of organization dealing with the same features of both subjects under discussion
- uses language and details appropriate to the audience
- uses transitional words and phrases to clarify similarities and differences

WRITING TIP

Remember your purpose for comparing the items you are writing about and support your purpose with expressive language and specific details.

Writing Standards

Good cause-and-effect writing

- clearly states the cause-and-effect relationship being examined
- shows clear connections between causes and effects
- presents causes and effects in a logical order and uses transitions effectively
- uses facts, examples, and other details to illustrate each cause and effect
- uses language and details appropriate to the audience

WRITING TIP

You cannot assume that a cause-and-effect relationship exists simply because one event follows another. Be sure your facts indicate that the effect could not have happened without the cause.

4.2 Cause and Effect

Cause-and-effect writing explains why something happened, why certain conditions exist, or what resulted from an action or a condition.

Organizing Cause-and-Effect Writing

Your organization will depend on your topic and purpose for writing. If you want to explain the causes of an event such as the closing of a factory, you might first state the effect and then examine its causes (Option 1). If your focus is on explaining the effects of an event, such as the passage of a law, you might first state the cause and then explain the effects (Option 2). Sometimes you'll want to describe a chain of cause-and-effect relationships (Option 3) to explore a topic such as the disappearance of tropical rain forests or the development of home computers.

Option 1

Effect to Cause	Example
Effect	King Arthur dies because of his adherence to the honor of knighthood and belief in his knights.
• Cause 1	Because he believes in the honor of knighthood, he entrusts his kingdom to his son Sir Modred, who proves to be a vengeful and selfish knight.
• Cause 2	Because he adheres to the code of knighthood, he honorably defends a fellow knight at the expense of his friendship with Sir Launcelot.
• Cause 3	For the sake of defending the honor of knighthood, King Arthur fights Sir Modred to the death.

Option 2

Cause to Effect
Cause
• Effect 1
• Effect 2
• Effect 3

Option 3

Cause-and-Effect Chain
Cause
↓
effect (cause)
↓
effect (cause)
↓
effect (cause)

4.3 Problem-Solution

Problem-solution writing clearly states a problem, analyzes the problem, and proposes a solution to the problem.

Organizing Problem-Solution Writing

Your organization will depend on the goal of your problem-solution piece, your intended audience, and the specific problem you choose to address. The organizational methods outlined below are effective for different kinds of problem-solution writing.

Option 1

Simple Problem-Solution	Example
Description of problem and why it needs to be solved	Arthur chooses between honor and friendship—values that are equally desirable until they conflict. Some teenagers face a similar choice—wondering whether to report a friend who is cheating in school, but not wanting to wreck a friendship.
Recommended solution	They should encourage the friend to be honest to the teacher about the cheating.
Explanation of solution	They would then be both honorable people and good friends by encouraging action.
Conclusion	The friend may be angry, but they will feel that they have done what is right.

Option 2

Deciding Between Solutions	Example
Description of problem	Some teenagers have to choose between reporting a friend who is cheating in class and keeping it a secret.
Solution A	They can go to the teacher and explain that a friend is cheating.
• Pros	Then they would stop feeling guilty for protecting someone who is cheating.
• Cons	But they might damage or even end the friendship by doing so.
Solution B	They could tell the friend that they are concerned about the cheating and encourage the friend to be honest with the teacher.
• Pros	
• Cons	
Recommendation	

Writing Standards

Good problem-solution writing

- identifies the problem and helps the reader understand the issues involved
- analyzes the causes and effects of the problem
- has quotations, facts, and statistics integrated into the text
- explores potential solutions to the problem and recommends the best one(s)
- uses language, tone, and details appropriate to the audience

WRITING TIP

Ask a classmate to read and respond to your problem-solution writing. Here are some questions for your peer reader to respond to: Is my language clear? Is the writing organized in a way that is easy to follow? Do the proposed solutions seem logical?

Writing Standards

A good analysis

- hooks the readers' attention with a strong introduction
- clearly states the subject and its individual parts
- uses a specific organizing structure to provide a logical flow of information
- shows connections among facts and ideas through subordinate clauses and transitional words and phrases
- uses language and details appropriate for the audience

WRITING TIP

Introductions You may want to begin your analysis with a vivid description or an interesting detail of the subject to capture readers' attention. For example, an exciting excerpt from the narrative could open the process analysis at the right.

4.4 Analysis

In an analysis you try to help your readers understand a subject by explaining how it works, how it is defined, or what its parts are.

The details you include will depend upon the kind of analysis you're writing.

- A **process analysis** should provide background information—such as definitions of terms and a list of needed equipment—and then explain each important step or stage in the process. For example, you might explain the steps of programming a VCR.
- A **definition** should include the most important characteristics of the subject. To define a quality, such as honesty, you might include the characteristic of telling the truth.
- A **parts analysis** should describe each of the parts, groups, or types that make up the subject. For example, you might analyze the human brain by looking at its parts, analyze a new law by looking at how different groups are affected by it, or analyze jazz music by describing the different styles of jazz.

Organizing Your Analysis

Organize your details in a logical order appropriate for the kind of analysis you're writing. A process analysis is usually organized chronologically, with steps or stages in the order they occur.

Option 1: Process Analysis	Example
Introduce topic	The legends of King Arthur changed over time as they were retold and reinterpreted.
Background information	The early legends of King Arthur are believed to be based on a British ruler of the early 500s.
Explain steps	
• Step 1	Around 1469 Thomas Malory finished compiling *Le Morte d'Arthur* from various French and English versions of the story.
• Step 2	Between 1842 and 1885 Lord Tennyson published *Idylls of the King*, which implies comparisons between Arthur and Prince Albert of Britain.
• Step 3	In 1960 Alan Lerner and Frederick Loewe transformed the legend into the musical *Camelot*.

You can organize the details in a definition or parts analysis in order of importance or impression.

Option 2

Definition

- **Introduce term** — In *Le Morte d'Arthur,* the characters' motivation for action depends on preserving their honor.
- **General definition** — In the story of King Arthur, honor is defined among the knights as a code of integrity, dignity, and pride.
- **Explain qualities**
  - Quality 1 — King Arthur demonstrates his integrity by fighting his enemy even when he has been warned of certain death.
  - Quality 2 — Sir Launcelot demonstrates his dignity by attempting to make peace and avoid battling King Arthur's family members.
  - Quality 3 — Sir Gawain's pride leads him into his fatal battle with Sir Launcelot.

WRITING TIP

Conclusions An effective way to conclude an analysis is to return to your thesis and restate it in different words.

The following parts analysis explores three elements of a medieval knight's code of chivalry.

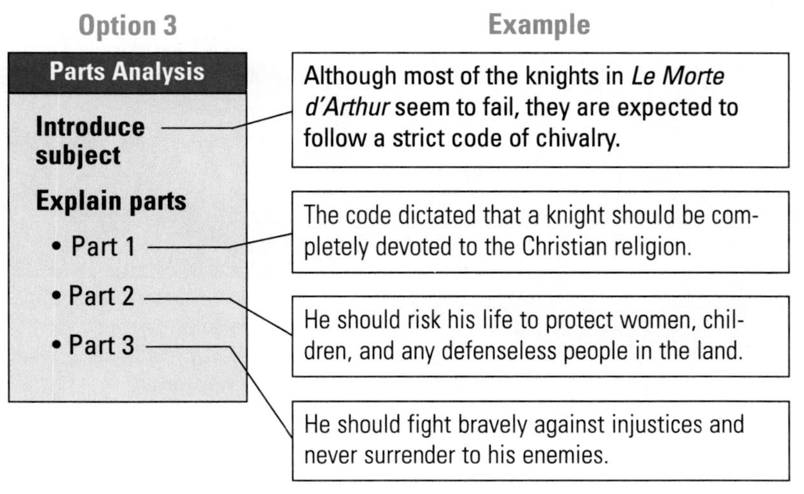

Option 3
Example
Parts Analysis
Introduce subject
Although most of the knights in Le Morte d'Arthur seem to fail, they are expected to follow a strict code of chivalry.
Explain parts
• Part 1
The code dictated that a knight should be completely devoted to the Christian religion.
• Part 2
He should risk his life to protect women, children, and any defenseless people in the land.
• Part 3
He should fight bravely against injustices and never surrender to his enemies.

Persuasive Writing

Writing Standards

Good persuasive writing

- clearly states the issue and the writer's position
- gives opinions and supports them with facts or reasons
- has a reasonable and respectful tone
- takes into account and answers opposing views
- uses sound logic and effective language
- concludes by summing up reasons or calling for action

Persuasive writing allows you to use the power of language to inform and influence others.

Key Techniques of Persuasive Writing

State Your Opinion

Taking a stand on an issue and clearly stating your opinion are essential to every piece of persuasive writing you do.

Example
It is important that we continue to spend money on space exploration and colonization.

Know Your Audience

Knowing who will read your writing will help you decide what information you need to share and what tone you should use to communicate your message. In the example below, the writer has chosen an informal tone appropriate for a report to be presented to fellow students.

Example
One day we may even find an answer to problems such as overpopulation by exploring ways for people to live in space.

Support Your Opinion

Using reasons, examples, facts, statistics, and anecdotes to support your opinion will show your audience why you feel the way you do.

Example
There will always be people who argue that something cannot be done. However, as Arthur C. Clarke points out in his essay, people used to scoff at the possibility of flight.

Organizing Persuasive Writing

In a two-sided persuasive essay you want to show the weaknesses of other opinions as you explain the strengths of your own. The example below demonstrates one method of organizing your persuasive essay to convince your audience.

Option 1

Why Another Opinion Is Weaker	Example
Other opinion	Many people believe that we cannot justify the enormous costs of space exploration.
• reasons	They argue that the money should be spent on solving social problems, such as hunger and homelessness.
Your opinion	While we must not neglect social problems here on the earth, we should also continue our exploration of space.
• reasons supporting your opinion and pointing out the weaknesses of the other side	One day this exploration might even provide solutions to social problems on our overpopulated planet.

Two more options for persuasive writing are shown below. Option 2 includes opposing viewpoints, and Option 3 organizes information to support your opinion.

Option 2

Why Your Opinion Is Stronger

Your opinion
- your reasons

Other opinion
- evidence refuting reasons for other opinion and showing strengths of your opinion

Option 3

Reasons for Your Opinion

Your opinion
- Reason 1
- Reason 2
- Reason 3

Remember: When writing an effective two-sided persuasive essay, you should present both arguments as fairly and fully as possible, even if you favor one particular view.

LINK TO LITERATURE

Statements from Arthur C. Clarke's essay "We'll Never Conquer Space" are used to support the opinions presented in the persuasive essay outlined here.

WRITING TIP

Introductions Capture your readers' attention in the introduction to your piece. Try opening with a quote, a statistic, or an anecdote that shows the importance of your topic.

6

Research Report Writing

A research report explores a topic in depth, incorporating information from a variety of sources.

Writing Standards

Good research report writing

- clearly states the purpose of the report in a thesis statement
- uses evidence and details from a variety of sources to support the thesis
- contains only accurate and relevant information
- documents sources correctly
- develops the topic logically and includes appropriate transitions
- includes a properly formatted Works Cited list

Key Techniques of Research Report Writing

Clarify Your Thesis

A thesis statement is one or two sentences clearly stating the main idea that you will develop in your report. A thesis may also indicate the organizational pattern you will follow and reflect your tone and point of view.

Example

In *Oliver Twist,* instead of drawing clear lines between the dark underworld of London and the light of the more civilized world, Charles Dickens blurs the distinction, making good and evil in society difficult to define.

Document Your Sources

You need to document, or credit, the sources where you find your evidence. In the example below, the writer uses and documents a quotation from the novel.

Example

In *Oliver Twist,* Dickens shows the intertwining of good and evil in the world. The narrator states, "Men who look on nature . . . and cry that all is dark and gloomy, are in the right; but the sombre colours are reflections from their own jaundiced eyes and hearts. The real hues . . . need a clearer vision" (Pool 256–257).

Support Your Ideas

You should support your ideas with relevant evidence—facts, anecdotes, and statistics—from reliable sources. In the example below, the writer includes a fact about the conditions of workhouses during Dickens's time.

Example

Oliver is condemned to a workhouse. The living conditions in workhouses were deliberately worse than in prisons in order to discourage the poor from depending on the publicly funded institutions (Pool 245).

Evaluating Sources

To help you determine whether your sources are reliable and contain useful and accurate information, use the following checklist.

Checklist for Evaluating Your Sources	
Authoritative	Someone who has written several books or articles on your subject or whose work has been published in a well-respected newspaper or journal may be considered an authority.
Up-to-date	Check the publication date to see whether the source reflects the most current research on your subject.
Respected	In general, tabloid newspapers and popular-interest magazines are not reliable sources. If you have questions about whether you are using a respected source, ask your librarian.

WRITING TIP

For additional help, see the research report about censorship on page 998 or McDougal Littell's *Writing Research Papers*.

Making Source Cards

For each source you find, record the bibliographic information on a separate index card. You will need this information to give credit to the sources you use in your paper. The samples at the right show how to make source cards for journal and magazine articles, on-line articles, and books. You will use the source number on each card to identify the notes you take during your research.

Journal Article

On-Line Article

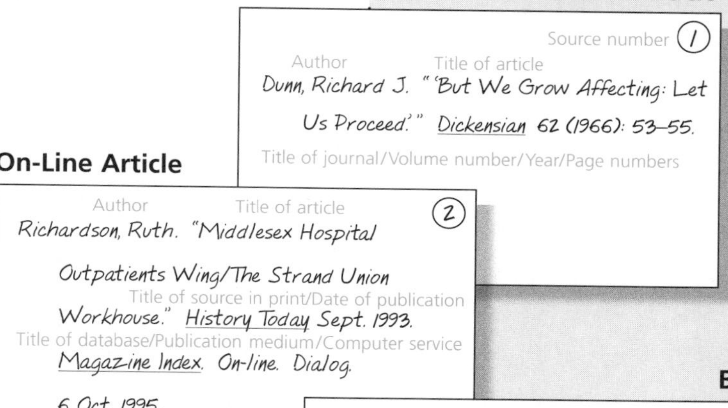

Source number 1
Author
Title of article
Dunn, Richard J. "'But We Grow Affecting: Let Us Proceed.'" Dickensian 62 (1966): 53–55.
Title of journal/Volume number/Year/Page numbers
Author
Title of article
2
Richardson, Ruth. "Middlesex Hospital Outpatients Wing/The Strand Union Workhouse." History Today Sept. 1993.
Title of source in print/Date of publication
Title of database/Publication medium/Computer service
Magazine Index. On-line. Dialog.
6 Oct. 1995.
Date of access

Book

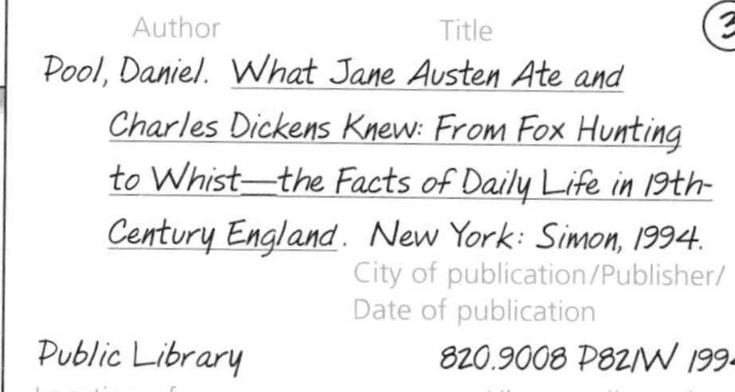

Author
Title
3
Pool, Daniel. What Jane Austen Ate and Charles Dickens Knew: From Fox Hunting to Whist—the Facts of Daily Life in 19th-Century England. New York: Simon, 1994.
City of publication/Publisher/
Date of publication
Public Library
Location of source
820.9008 P82W 1994
Library call number

Taking Notes

As you read your sources, record on note cards information that is relevant to the purpose of your research. You will probably use all three of the following note-taking methods.

- **Paraphrase,** or restate in your own words, the main ideas and supporting details in a passage.
- **Summarize,** or rephrase in fewer words the original material, trying to capture the key ideas.
- **Quote,** or copy word for word the original text, if you think the author's own words best clarify a particular point. Use quotation marks to signal the beginning and the end of the quotation.

Paraphrase

Main idea
Conditions for Orphans Source number (3)

Orphans were often apprenticed without their consent. The judges who approved the apprenticeships could bind children to service from the age of 8 until they were 21. 241–42
Page numbers

(Paraphrase) Type of note

Organizing Your Research Report

Making an outline can help guide the drafting process. Begin by reading over your note cards and sorting them into groups. The main-idea headings may help you find connections among the notes. Then arrange the groups of related note cards so that the ideas flow logically from one group to the next.

Note the format for a topic outline shown below. Remember that in a topic outline, items of the same degree of importance should be parallel in form. For instance, if A is a noun, then B and C should also be nouns. Subtopics need not be parallel with main topics.

The Two Worlds of Oliver Twist

Introduction—Dickens blurs the distinction between good and evil

I. The underworld of London

A. The criminal characters

1. Sikes and Monks

2. Fagin

B. The good characters

II. The civilized world of London

Documenting Your Sources

When you quote, paraphrase, or summarize information from one of your sources, you need to credit that source, using parenthetical documentation.

Guidelines for Parenthetical Documentation	
Work by One Author	Put the author's last name and the page reference in parentheses: **(Pool 191)**. If you mention the author's name in the sentence, put only the page reference in parentheses: **(191)**.
Work by Two or Three Authors	Put the authors' last names and the page reference in parentheses: **(Mitchell and Deane 42)**.
Work by More Than Three Authors	Give the first author's last name followed by *et al.* and the page reference: **(Bentley et al. 122)**.
Work with No Author Given	Give the title or a shortened version and (if appropriate) the page reference: **("Hurried Trials" 742)**.
One of Two or More Works by Same Author	Give the author's last name, the title or a shortened version, and the page reference: **(Dunn, "But We Grow" 54)**.

WRITING TIP

Plagiarism Presenting someone else's writing or ideas as your own is plagiarism. To avoid plagiarism, you need to credit sources as noted at the right. However, if a piece of information is common knowledge—information available in several sources—you do not need to credit a source. For an example of parenthetical documentation, see the report on page 998.

Following MLA Manuscript Guidelines

The final copy of your report should follow the Modern Language Association guidelines for manuscript preparation.

- The heading in the upper left-hand corner of the first page should include your name, your teacher's name, the course name, and the date, each on a separate line.
- Below the heading, center the title on the page.
- Number all the pages consecutively in the upper right-hand corner, one-half inch from the top. Also, include your last name before the page number.
- Double-space the entire paper.
- Except for the margins above the page numbers, leave one-inch margins on all sides of every page.

The Works Cited page at the end of your report is an alphabetized list of the sources you have used and documented. In each entry all lines after the first are indented an additional one-half inch.

WRITING TIP

When your report includes a quotation that is longer than four lines, set it off from the rest of the text by indenting the entire quotation one inch from the left margin. In this case, you should not use quotation marks.

Watanabe 15

Works Cited

Bayley, John. "Oliver Twist: 'Things as They Really Are.'" Dickens and the Twentieth Century. Ed. John Gross and Gabriel Pearson. London: Routledge, 1962. 49–64.

Bentley, Nicholas, et al. The Dickens Index. Oxford: Oxford UP, 1988.

Collins, Philip, ed. Sikes and Nancy: A Facsimile. London: Dickens, 1982.

Dickens, Charles. Oliver Twist. New York: Bantam, 1981.

Dunn, Richard J. "'But We Grow Affecting: Let Us Proceed.'" Dickensian 62 (1966): 53–55.

– – –. Oliver Twist: Whole Heart and Soul. New York: Twayne, 1993.

Mitchell, B. R., and Phyllis Deane. Abstract of British Historical Statistics. Cambridge: Cambridge UP, 1962.

Models for Works Cited Entries

- Selection from a book of collected essays; note that publishers' names are shortened.
- Book with more than three authors
- Book with editor but no single author
- Book with one author
- Article in scholarly journal
- Work with same author as previous entry
- Work with two authors

Getting Information Electronically

Electronic resources provide you with a convenient and efficient way to gather information.

1.1 On-line Resources

When you use your computer to communicate with another computer or with another person using a computer, you are working "on-line." On-line resources include commercial information services and information available on the Internet.

Commercial Information Services

You can subscribe to various services that offer information such as the following:

- up-to-date news, weather, and sports reports
- access to encyclopedias, magazines, newspapers, dictionaries, almanacs, and databases (collections of information)
- electronic mail (e-mail) to and from other users
- forums, or ongoing electronic conversations among users interested in a particular topic

Internet

The Internet is a vast network of computers. News services, libraries, universities, researchers, organizations, and government agencies use the Internet to communicate and to distribute information. The Internet includes two key features:

- **World Wide Web,** which provides you with information on particular subjects and links you to related topics and resources (such as the linked Web pages shown at the left)
- **Electronic mail** (e-mail), which allows you to communicate with other e-mail users worldwide

1.2 CD-ROM

A CD-ROM (compact disc–read-only memory) stores data, which may include text, sound, photographs, and video.

Almost any kind of information can be found on CD-ROMs, which you can use at the library or purchase, including

- encyclopedias, almanacs, and indexes
- other reference books on a variety of subjects
- news reports from newspapers, magazines, television, or radio
- museum art collections
- back issues of magazines
- literature collections

WHAT YOU'LL NEED

- To access on-line resources, you need a computer with a modem linked to a telephone line. Your school computer lab or resource center may be linked to the Internet or to a commercial information service.
- To use CD-ROMs, you need a computer system with a CD-ROM player.

1.3 Library Computer Services

Many libraries offer computerized catalogs and a variety of other electronic resources.

Computerized Catalogs

You may search for a book in a library by typing the title, author, subject, or key words into a computer terminal. If you enter the title of a book, the screen will display the bibliographic information and the current availability of the book. When a particular work is not available, you may be able to search the catalogs of other libraries.

Other Electronic Resources

In addition to computerized catalogs, many libraries offer electronic versions of books or other reference materials. They may also have a variety of indexes on CD-ROM, which allow you to search for magazine or newspaper articles on any topic you choose. When you have found an article on the topic you want, the screen will display the kind of information shown at the right.

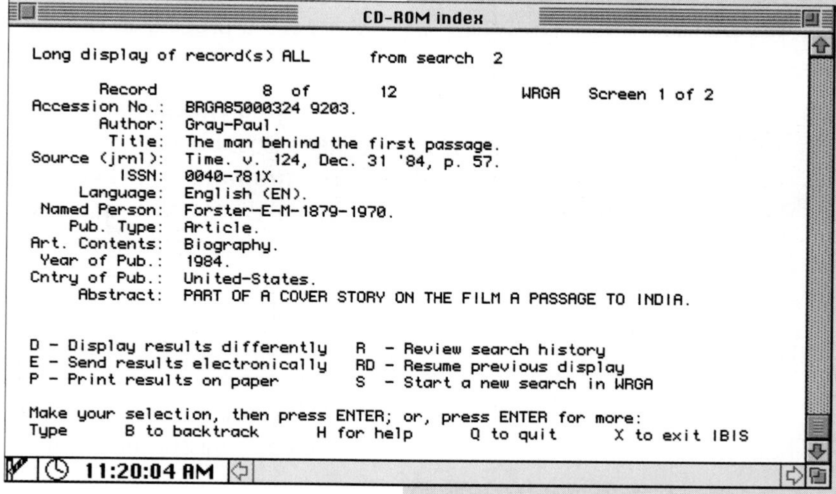

2 Word Processing

WHAT YOU'LL NEED

- Computer
- Word-processing program
- Printer

Word-processing programs allow you to draft, revise, edit, and format your writing and to produce neat, professional-looking papers. They also allow you to share your writing with others.

2.1 Revising and Editing

Improving the quality of your writing becomes easier when you use a word-processing program to revise and edit.

Revising a Document

Most word-processing programs allow you to make the following kinds of changes:

- adding or deleting words
- moving text from one location in your document to another
- undoing a change you have made in the text
- saving a document with a new name, so that you can keep the old draft for reference
- copying text from one document and adding it to another

Editing a Document

Many word-processing programs have the following features to help you catch errors and polish your writing:

- The **spell checker** automatically finds misspelled words and suggests possible corrections.
- The **grammar checker** spots possible grammatical errors and suggests ways you might correct them.
- The **thesaurus** suggests synonyms for a word you want to replace.
- The **dictionary** will give you the definitions of words so that you can be sure you have used words correctly.
- The **search-and-replace** feature searches your whole document and corrects every occurrence of something you want to change, such as a misspelled name.

WRITING TIP

Spell checkers and grammar checkers offer suggestions for corrections, but you must carefully assess these suggestions before picking the right one. Making such an assessment involves looking at the suggested change in the context of your writing.

2.2 Formatting Your Work

Format is the layout and appearance of your writing on the page. You may choose your formatting options before or after you write.

Formatting Type

You may want to make changes in the typeface, type size, and type style of the words in your document. For each of these, your word-processing program will most likely have several options to choose from. These options allow you to

- change the typeface to create a different look for the words in your document
- change the type size of the entire document or of just the headings of sections in the paper
- change the type style when necessary—for example, to italicize or underline the titles of books and magazines

Typeface	Size	Style
Geneva Times **Chicago** `Courier`	7-point Times 10-point Times 12-point Times 14-point Times	*Italic* **Bold** Underline

Formatting Pages

Not only can you change the way individual words look; you can also change the way they are arranged on the page. Some of the formatting decisions you make will depend on how you plan to use a printout of a draft or on the guidelines of an assignment.

- Set the line spacing, or the amount of space between lines of text. Double-spacing is commonly used for final drafts.

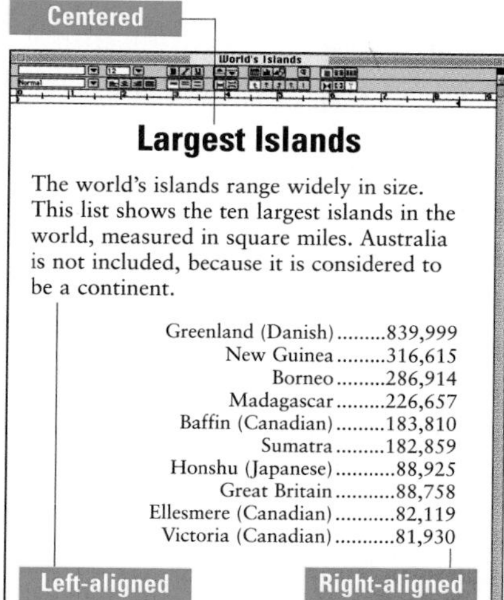

Centered
World's Islands
Largest Islands
The world's islands range widely in size. This list shows the ten largest islands in the world, measured in square miles. Australia is not included, because it is considered to be a continent.
Greenland (Danish).........839,999
New Guinea.........316,615
Borneo.........286,914
Madagascar.........226,657
Baffin (Canadian).........183,810
Sumatra.........182,859
Honshu (Japanese)...........88,925
Great Britain...........88,758
Ellesmere (Canadian)...........82,119
Victoria (Canadian)...........81,930
Left-aligned
Right-aligned

- Set the margins, or the amount of white space around the edges of your text. A one-inch margin on all sides is commonly used for final drafts.
- Create a header for the top of the page or a footer for the bottom if you want to include such information as your name, the date, or the page number on every page.
- Determine the alignment of your text. The screen at the left shows some options.

WRITING TIP

Keep your format simple. Your goal is to create not only an attractive document but also one that is easy to read. Your readers will have difficulty if you change typefaces or type sizes frequently.

TECHNOLOGY TIP

Some word-processing programs and other software packages provide preset templates, or patterns, for writing outlines, memos, letters, newsletters, and invitations. If you use one of these templates, you will not need to adjust the formatting.

2.3 Working Collaboratively

Computers allow you to share your writing electronically. Send a copy of your work to someone via e-mail or put it in someone's drop box if your computer is linked to other computers on a network. Then use the feedback of your peers to help you improve the quality of your writing.

TECHNOLOGY TIP

Some word-processing programs, such as the Writing Coach software referred to in this book, allow you to leave notes for your peer readers in the side column or in a separate text box. If you wish, leave those areas blank so your readers can write comments or questions.

Peer Editing on a Computer

The writer and the reader can both benefit from the convenience of peer editing "on screen," or at the computer.

- Be sure to save your current draft and then make a copy of it for each of your peer readers.
- You might have each peer reader use a different typeface or type style for making comments, as shown in the example below.
- Ask each of your readers to include his or her initials in the file name.

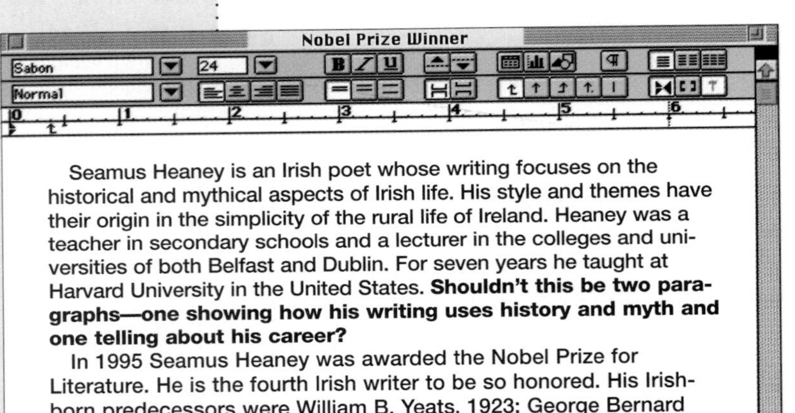

- If your computer allows you to open more than one file at a time, open each reviewer's file and refer to the files as you revise your draft.

Peer Editing on a Printout

Some peer readers prefer to respond to a draft on paper rather than on the computer.

- Double-space or triple-space your document so that your peer editor can make suggestions between the lines.
- Leave extra-wide margins to give your readers room to note their reactions and questions as they read.
- Print out your draft and photocopy it if you want to share it with more than one reader.

Using Visuals

3

Tables, graphs, diagrams, and pictures often communicate information more effectively than words alone do. Many computer programs allow you to create visuals to use with your written text.

3.1 When to Use Visuals

Use visuals in your work to illustrate complex concepts and processes or to make a page look more interesting.

Although you should not expect a visual to do all the work of written text, combining words and pictures or graphics can increase readers' understanding and enjoyment of your writing. Many computer programs allow you to create graphs, tables, time lines, diagrams, and flow charts and insert them into your documents. An art program allows you to create border designs for a title page or to draw an unusual character or setting for narrative or descriptive writing. You may also be able to add clip art, or premade pictures, to your documents. Clip art can be used to illustrate an idea or concept in your writing or to make your writing more appealing for young readers.

WHAT YOU'LL NEED

- A graphics program to create visuals
- Access to clip-art files on a CD-ROM, a diskette, or an on-line service

3.2 Kinds of Visuals

The visuals you choose will depend on the types of information you want to present to your readers.

TECHNOLOGY TIP

A spreadsheet program provides you with a preset table for your statistics and performs any necessary calculations.

Tables

Tables allow you to arrange facts or numbers into rows and columns so that your readers can compare information more easily. In many word-processing programs, you can create a table by choosing the number of vertical columns and horizontal rows you need and then entering information in each box, as the illustration shows.

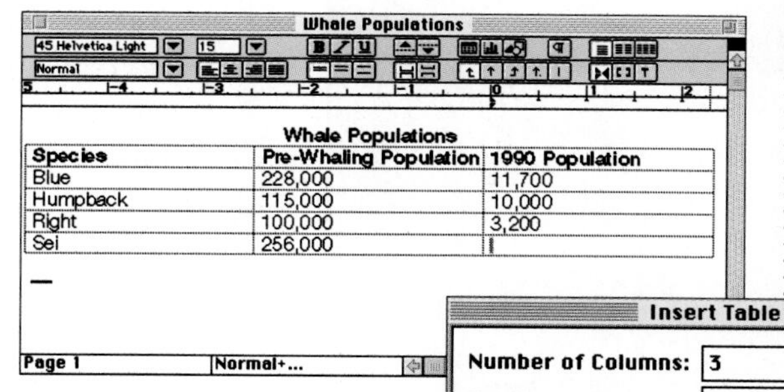

Whale Populations

Whale Populations

Species	Pre-Whaling Population	1990 Population
Blue	228,000	11,700
Humpback	115,000	10,000
Right	100,000	3,200
Sei	256,000	

WRITING TIP

Be sure that you have effectively integrated your written text and visuals. The body of your text should refer to the information in your visuals and explain the relevance of the information. Also, captions, headings, and labels in your visuals should clearly identify each component.

Graphs and Charts

You can sometimes use a graph or chart to help communicate complex information in a clear visual image. For example, you could use a line graph to show how a trend changes over time, a bar graph to compare statistics from different years, or a pie chart like the one at the right to compare percentages. You might want to explore ways of displaying data in more than one visual format before deciding which will work best for you.

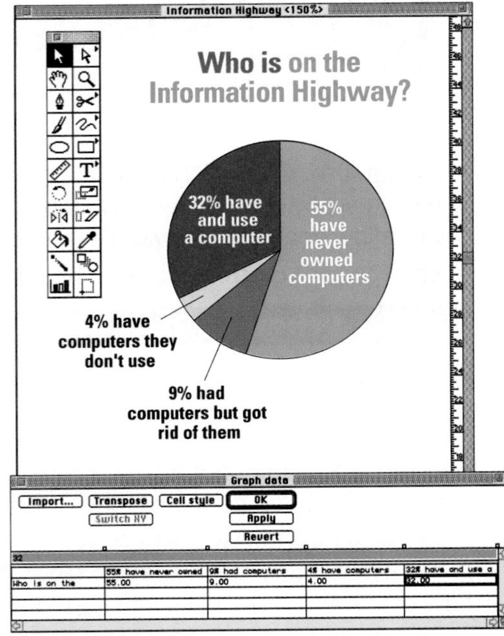

Source: Times Mirror Center for the People and the Press

Other Visuals

Art and design programs allow you to create visuals for your writing. Many programs include the following features:

- drawing tools that allow you to draw, color, and shade pictures
- clip art that you can copy or change with drawing tools
- page borders that you can use to decorate title pages, invitations, or brochures
- text options that allow you to combine words with your illustrations, as in the screen at the left
- tools for making geometric shapes in flow charts, time lines, and diagrams that show a process or sequence of events

Open House <150%>

Only a Dog

"It's only a dog," someone said.
Childhood playmate,
Bed warmer (though Mom said no),
Tennis shoe terminator,
Untiring jokester,
Cohort in mischief,
Unwaveringly loyal friend,
Brother I never had.

Paint Style

Creating a Multimedia Presentation

4

A multimedia presentation is a combination of text, sound, and visuals such as photographs, videos, and animation. Your audience reads, hears, and sees your presentation at a computer, following different "paths" you create to lead the user through the information you have gathered.

4.1 Features of Multimedia Programs

To start planning your multimedia presentation, you need to know what options are available to you. You can combine sound, photos, videos, and animation to enhance any text you write about your topic.

WHAT YOU'LL NEED

- Individual programs to create and edit the text, graphics, sound, and videos you will use
- A multimedia authoring program that allows you to combine these elements and create links between the screens

Sound

Including sound in your presentation can help your audience understand information in your written text. For example, the user may be able to listen and learn from

- the pronunciation of an unfamiliar or foreign word
- a speech
- a recorded news interview
- a musical selection
- a dramatic reading of a work of literature

Photos and Videos

Photographs and live-action videos can make your subject come alive for the user. Here are some examples:

- videotaped news coverage of a historical event
- videos of music, dance, or theater performances
- charts and diagrams
- photos of an artist's work
- photos or video of a geographical setting that is important to the written text

TECHNOLOGY TIP

You can download photos, sound, and video from Internet sources onto your computer. This process allows you to add to your multimedia presentation elements that would usually require complex editing equipment.

Animation

Many graphics programs allow you to add animation, or movement, to the visuals in your presentation. Animated figures add to the user's enjoyment and understanding of what you present. You can use animation to illustrate

- what happens in a story
- the steps in a process
- changes in a chart, graph, or diagram
- how your user can explore information in your presentation

4.2 Planning Your Presentation

To create a multimedia presentation, first choose your topic and decide what you want to include. Then plan how you want your user to move through your presentation.

Imagine that you are creating a multimedia presentation based on the changing faces of heroes through the ages. You'll start with Beowulf and end with a modern hero, such as James Bond or Batman. You might want to include the following items:

- text defining *hero* and discussing heroic qualities
- taped reading from *Beowulf*
- taped reading from Malory's Arthurian tales
- chart comparing heroic qualities of Arthur and a modern superhero
- video interview with a scholar on the mythic origins of modern heroes
- video from Batman or Bond film
- photo of real-life modern hero

TECHNOLOGY TIP

You can now find CD-ROMs with videos of things like wildlife, weather, street scenes, and events, and other CD-ROMs with recordings of famous speeches, musical selections, and dramatic readings.

You can choose one of the following ways to organize your presentation:

- step by step, with only one path, or order, in which the user can see and hear the information
- a branching path that allows users to make some choices about what they will see and hear, and in what order

A flow chart can help you figure out the paths a user can take through your presentation. Each box in the flow chart on the following page represents something about heroes for the user to read, see, or hear. The arrows on the flow chart show the possible paths the user can follow.

Whenever arrows lead to more than one box, the user can choose which item to see or hear first.

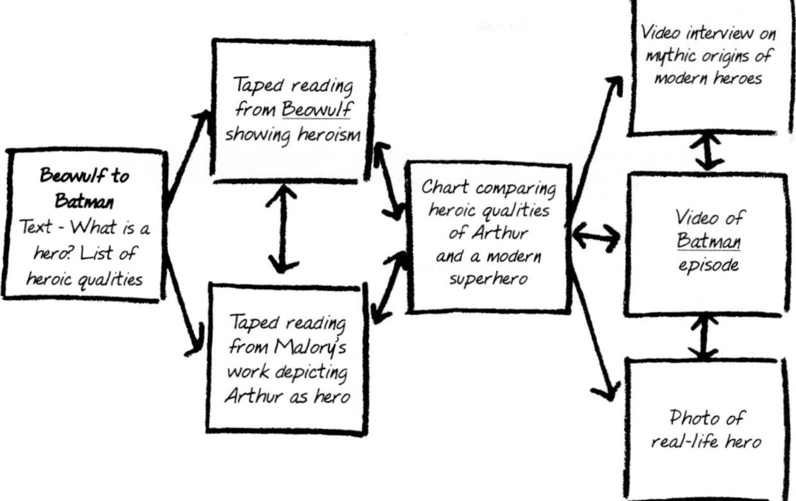

WRITING TIP

You usually need permission from the person or organization that owns the copyright on material that you want to copy. You do not need permission, however, if you are not making money from your presentation, you use it only for educational purposes, and you use only a small percentage of the original material.

4.3 Guiding Your User

Your user will need directions to follow the path you have planned for your multimedia presentation.

Most multimedia authoring programs allow you to create screens that include text or audio directions that guide the user from one part of your presentation to the next. In the example below, the user can choose between several paths, and directions on the screen explain how to make the choice.

If you need help creating your multimedia presentation, ask your school's technology adviser. You may also be able to get help from your classmates or your software manual.

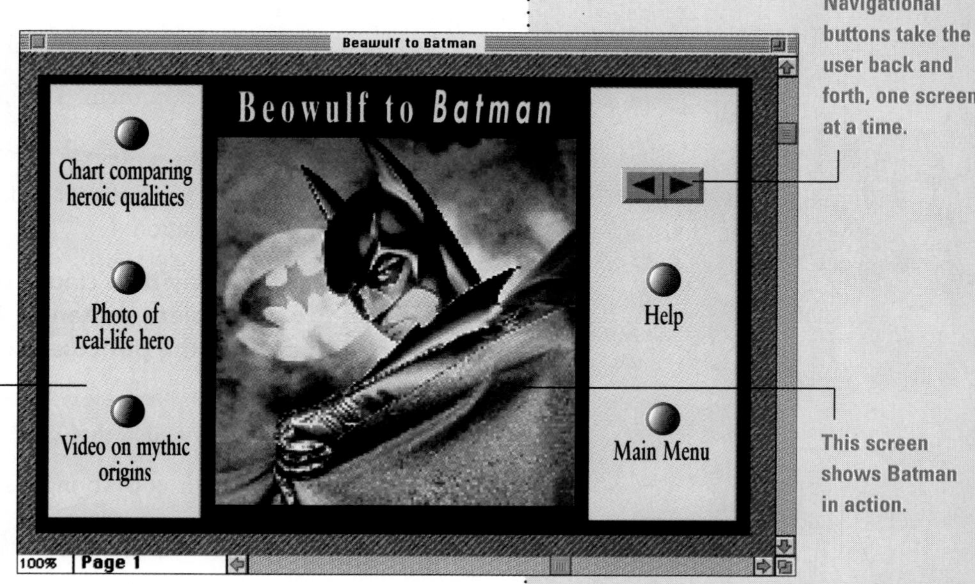

Navigational buttons take the user back and forth, one screen at a time.

The user clicks on a button to select any of these options.

This screen shows Batman in action.

Writing Complete Sentences

1.1 Sentence Fragments

A sentence fragment is a group of words that does not express a complete thought. A sentence fragment may be missing a subject, a predicate, or both.

Completing an Incomplete Thought

You can correct a sentence fragment by adding the missing subject, predicate, or both to complete the thought.

In "An Academy for Women" the author argues for women's education. He presents the standard positive and negative stereotypes of women. He deplores the waste of women's gifts.

When a fragment is a subordinate clause, you can join the fragment to an existing sentence and change the punctuation, or you can rewrite the clause so that it can stand alone.

Because God gives women intellectual gifts, he must expect women to develop them. This is Defoe's position.

Correcting Punctuation

A sentence fragment may be a clause or a phrase that can be connected to a complete sentence. To correct it, you may simply need to change the punctuation.

In the 18th century, the idea that men differed from women mostly because of their education was a radical one.

APPLY WHAT YOU'VE LEARNED

Rewrite this paragraph, correcting the sentence fragments.

[1]As a religious dissenter Daniel Defoe. [2]Ineligible to attend an English university. [3]Received a far broader education from a fine academy, however. [4]His simple and clear writing style. [5]Is probably greatly indebted to the Bible and the works of John Bunyan, in which he was well read. [6]Defoe's freethinking in the religious sphere. [7]Extended to political and social issues as well. [8]For example, his pamphlets. [9]Frequently addressed liberal causes. [10]Defoe's poem *The True-Born Englishman.* [11]Used his wit to address the matter of prejudice against King William III. [12]The cause of women's rights. [13]Also claimed his attention. [14]Because he was married for 47 years and had 8 children. [15]Most people assume that Defoe's marriage was a happy one. [16]Although he never wrote about it specifically.

1.2 Run-On Sentences

A run-on sentence consists of two or more sentences incorrectly written as one. It is unclear where one idea ends and the next begins.

REVISING TIP

To correct run-on sentences, read them to yourself, noticing where you naturally pause between ideas. The pause usually indicates where you should place end punctuation.

Forming Separate Sentences

One way to correct a run-on sentence is to form two separate sentences. Use a period or other end punctuation after the first complete thought, and capitalize the first letter of the next sentence.

> In *A Vindication of the Rights of Woman* the author blames both men and women for women's lot men ask only that women be beautiful women cater to that wish.

A writer may mistakenly use a comma instead of a period to separate two complete thoughts. To correct this kind of mistake, called a comma splice, change the comma to a period and capitalize the first letter of the second sentence.

> Like Daniel Defoe before her, Mary Wollstonecraft decries the inadequacy of women's education, women's intelligence has been judged inadequate, so it has not been cultivated.

Joining Sentences

If the ideas expressed in a run-on sentence are closely related, you may wish to join them to form a compound sentence. One way to do this is to use a comma and a coordinating conjunction to join the main clauses.

> Wollstonecraft regarded herself first as a human being and then as a woman ^(and) most women today would support that position enthusiastically.

Use a semicolon alone, or with a conjunctive adverb, to join main clauses having closely related ideas.

Some commonly used conjunctive adverbs are *however, therefore, nevertheless,* and *besides*.

> The women's movement owes much to the suffragists, who favored granting the vote to women ^(however,) it owes just as much to writers such as Defoe and Wollstonecraft.

APPLY WHAT YOU'VE LEARNED

Rewrite this paragraph, correcting the run-on sentences.

1 Mary Wollstonecraft lived from 1759 to 1797 she considered herself a freethinker. 2 Wollstonecraft taught in her own school and as a governess, she wrote reviews and translations for a publisher of radical materials. 3 In 1787 Wollstonecraft published *Thoughts on the Education of Daughters*, a year later her novel *Mary* was published, followed by *A Vindication of the Rights of Men*. 4 *A Vindication of the Rights of Woman* followed closely afterward it is clear that the author was at the forefront of action on progressive social issues of the day. 5 It is interesting to trace the family connections of the writers of the romantic period, Wollstonecraft married William Godwin, a philosopher and writer. 6 Their daughter, Mary, best known as the author of *Frankenstein*, married the poet Percy Bysshe Shelley, Mary Shelley's stepsister bore a daughter to Lord Byron.

Making Subjects and Verbs Agree

2

2.1 Simple and Compound Subjects

A verb must agree in number with its subject. The word *number* refers to whether a word is singular or plural. When a word refers to one thing, it is singular. When it refers to more than one thing, it is plural.

Agreement with Simple Subjects

Use a singular verb with a singular subject.

When the subject is a singular noun, you use the singular form of the verb. The present-tense third-person singular form of a regular verb usually ends in *-s* or *-es*.

> In "Federigo's Falcon" Giovanni Boccaccio tell a story of true love.

Use a plural verb with a plural subject.

> Federigo's actions qualifies as noble because he does them for the woman he loves.

Agreement with Compound Subjects

Use a plural verb with a compound subject whose parts are joined by *and,* regardless of the number of each part.

> Monna Giovanna and her son asks a real sacrifice of him.

REVISING TIP

To find the subject of a sentence, first find the verb. Then ask *whom* or *what* the verb refers to. Say the subject and the verb together to see whether they agree.

When the parts of a compound subject are joined by *or* or *nor,* make the verb agree in number with the part that is closer to it.

> Neither the mother and her son nor the impoverished man realize^s how much is at stake.

APPLY WHAT YOU'VE LEARNED

Correct verb errors in this paragraph.

[1]Giovanni Boccaccio's "Federigo's Falcon" appear in his *Decameron.* [2]Like other stories in the collection, this tale convey both poignancy and irony. [3]Unrequited love and sacrifice also serves as the theme of his *Fiammetta*. [4]Many scholars believes that Boccaccio had a real "Fiammetta" in his life. [5]One would hope not, because Fiammetta's sweetheart treat her shabbily. [6]The whole book deal with her obsessive love. [7]This beautiful married woman experiences great anguish when the young man abandon her. [8]Her originally remarkable beauty and vivacity diminishes as the months go on. [9]Her appetite and her interest in society fails. [10]Fiammetta revive when she hear news of her lover and sink again when the rumors proves unfounded. [11]So concerned is Fiammetta's husband about her health that he even give her his blessing when she searches for his rival. [12]His love and concern strikes readers as being just as obsessive as Fiammetta's love for someone else.

2.2 Pronoun Subjects

When a pronoun is used as a subject, the verb must agree with it in number.

Agreement with Personal Pronouns

When the subject is a singular personal pronoun, use a singular verb. When the subject is plural, use a plural verb.

Singular pronouns are *I, you, he, she,* and *it.* Plural pronouns are *we, you,* and *they.* Although *I* and *you* are singular, the verb forms they take are almost always identical to the plural forms.

> The *Rubáiyát* of Omar Khayyám is chiefly known to the Western world in its translation by Edward FitzGerald. It contain^s lines that are among the most quoted in poetry.

When *he, she,* or *it* is the part of a compound subject that is closer to the verb and the parts are joined by *or* or *nor,* use a singular verb. When a pronoun is part of a compound subject containing *and,* use a plural verb.

> Khayyám dreams of this—"A Jug of Wine, a Loaf of Bread—and Thou." I can't decide whether the ancient Greek poets or he conjure^s up lovelier images.

Agreement with Indefinite Pronouns

When the subject is a singular indefinite pronoun, use the singular form of the verb.

The following are singular indefinite pronouns: *another, either, nobody, anybody, everybody, no one, anyone, everyone, someone, one, anything, everything, each,* and *neither*.

> Hardly anybody know^s for certain how close FitzGerald's translation comes to the original Persian. Everybody ~~are~~ ^is impressed with the flow of the language, however.

When the subject is a plural indefinite pronoun, use the plural form of the verb.

The following are plural indefinite pronouns: *both, few, many,* and *several*.

> Sadly, many know~~s~~ of no other works by FitzGerald. For example, few ~~has~~ ^have heard of his translations of Attar's *Conference of the Birds* and Jami's *Salámán and Absál.*

REVISING TIP

In many sentences an indefinite pronoun is followed by a prepositional phrase that can help you determine whether the subject is singular or plural. Remember, however, that the object of the preposition is not the subject of the sentence.

The indefinite pronouns *some, all, any, none,* and *most* can be either singular or plural. When the pronoun refers to one thing or part, use a singular verb. When the pronoun refers to more than one thing, use a plural verb.

> None denies the beauty of FitzGerald's poetry. Of course, the meter and rhyme are the poet's own. Most of us appreciates the poem's style, perhaps because much of it ~~are~~ is traditional in form.

APPLY WHAT YOU'VE LEARNED

In each sentence write the correct form of the verb.

[1]Some of the great works of Persian literature (has, have) been translated more than once. [2]Sir Richard Burton's version of *The Arabian Nights* seems to be the most famous one; it (dwarf, dwarfs) most others. [3]However, many (prefer, prefers) John Payne's version as more literal. [4]Burton and he (approach, approaches) the text differently. [5]Payne's translation and Burton's were begun at different times, but both of the versions (was, were) being worked on at the same time. [6]The two men corresponded, so each (was, were) aware of the other's progress; in fact, scholars know that Payne shared his work with Burton. [7]Side-by-side comparisons suggest that Burton plagiarized Payne's work; some of the passages (is, are) identical. [8]Nonetheless, Payne graciously dedicated his first edition to Burton, who was a respected colleague; in this tribute he (reveal, reveals) his humility. [9]Neither Payne's heirs nor he (has, have) ever brought suit against Burton.

2.3 Common Agreement Problems

Several other situations can cause problems in subject-verb agreement.

Interrupting Words and Phrases

REVISING TIP

To find the subject, look carefully at words that come before the verb. Remember that the subject may not be the noun or pronoun closest to the verb.

Be sure the verb agrees with its subject when words or phrases come between them.

The subject of a verb is never found in a prepositional phrase or an appositive, which may follow the subject and come before the verb. Other phrases can also separate the subject and the verb.

This translation of the *Ramayana*, one of two classic Indian epics, tell the story in prose. Other versions, like the original Sanskrit version, appears in verse.

When phrases—such as those beginning with *including, as well as, along with, such as,* and *in addition to*—separate subjects and verbs, be sure that the verbs agree with the subjects.

The hero, Rama—as well as his wife, Sita, and his brother Lakshmana—are incarnations of Vishnu, the Preserver. The demon Ravana, along with his minions, capture Sita and seek to destroy the brothers.

Inverted Sentences

When the simple subject comes after the verb, be sure the verb agrees with the subject in number.

A sentence in which the subject follows the verb is called an inverted sentence. Questions are usually in inverted form, as are sentences beginning with *Here is/are* and *There is/are.* (*What is hope? Here are the books I read.*)

How does Rama, Lakshmana, and Sita combat the power of evil? There is forces of nature that rally to help, such as the monkey Hanuman—according to Hindu mythology, yet another incarnation of the supreme god.

REVISING TIP

The forms of *do, be,* and *have* can be main verbs or helping verbs. They can also be part of contractions with *not* (*doesn't/don't, isn't/aren't, hasn't/haven't*). In every case, the verb should agree in number with its subject.

REVISING TIP

To check subject-verb agreement in inverted sentences, place the subject before the verb. For example, change *Here is Rama* to *Rama is here.*

Singular Nouns with Plural Forms

Be sure to use a singular verb when the subject is a noun that is singular in meaning but appears to be plural.

Words such as *means* and *news* appear to be plural because they end in *-s*. However, these words are singular in meaning. Words ending in *-ics* that refer to sciences or branches of study (*mathematics, apologetics, civics*) are also singular.

> The means to Ravana's destruction ~~are~~ is the Brahmasthra, a weapon designed by the creator Brahma.

Collective Nouns

Use a singular verb when the subject is a collective noun—such as *set, congregation,* or *audience*—that refers to a group acting as a unit. Use a plural verb when the collective noun refers to members of the group acting individually.

> Some have likened the *Ramayana* to the *Odyssey* and the *Mahabharata* to the *Iliad*. The first pair deals with long journeys away from home and back. The second pair features extended battles.

Nouns of Time, Weight, Measure, Number

Use a singular verb with a subject that identifies a period of time, a weight, a measure, or a number.

> In the *Ramayana* 14 years ~~are~~ is the period of Rama's wandering in exile. Odysseus' 20 years of absence ~~are~~ is even longer.

Titles

Use a singular verb when the subject is the title of a work of art, literature, or music, even though the title may contain plural words.

> "Celestial Arms and Chariot," a story taken from the *Panchatantra,* intrigue students of literature as well.

Predicate Nominatives

Use a verb that agrees with the subject, not with the predicate nominative, when the subject is different in number from the predicate nominative.

> Classic works is a major contribution to the field of literature, a means of learning more about past cultures.

REVISING TIP

The fact that a title is set off by quotation marks, italics, or underscoring helps to remind you that it is singular and takes a singular verb.

APPLY WHAT YOU'VE LEARNED

Write the correct form of each verb.

1 The epics of Greece, India, Germany, and Scandinavia (is, are) national heroic myths. 2 They, as well as other writing, (form, forms) an impressive body of ancient literature. 3 The tale of Rama, his brother, and his wife (has, have) been represented artistically in India throughout the ages. 4 Happy (is, are) the villagers when a *harikata* storyteller arrives. 5 Sometimes a series of movies based on the epics (draw, draws) large crowds. 6 Everyone knows the stories, yet there (is, are) always people eager to see a new version. 7 (Was Were) Peter Brook's production of the *Mahabharata* as acclaimed in India as abroad? 8 No, an Indian audience (prefer, prefers) more conventional presentations. 9 A hundred similar performances—including plays, movies, dances, and musical presentations—(do, does) not decrease the pleasure of an audience. 10 A classic comic book series (delight, delights) Indian children here and in India. 11 "Lord Krishna and the Milkmaids" always (appeal, appeals) to children.

3 Using Nouns and Pronouns

3.1 Plural and Possessive Nouns

Nouns refer to people, places, things, and ideas. A noun is plural when it refers to more than one person, place, thing, or idea. A possessive noun shows who or what owns something.

REVISING TIP

The dictionary usually lists the plural form of a noun if it is formed irregularly or if it might be formed in more than one way. For example, the plural of *medium* can be *media* or *mediums.* Dictionary listings are especially helpful for nouns that end in *o, f,* and *fe.*

Plural Nouns

Follow these guidelines to form noun plurals.

- For most nouns, add *-s* (*song—songs, book—books*).
- For nouns ending in *s, sh, ch, x,* or *z,* add *-es* (*watch—watches, wish—wishes*).
- For nouns ending in a consonant and *y,* change the *y* to *i* and add *-es* (*story—stories, folly—follies*).
- For most nouns that end in a consonant and *o,* add *-es* (*hero—heroes, potato—potatoes*).
- For many nouns that end in *f* or *fe,* change the *f* to *v* and add *-s* or *-es* (*life—lives, leaf—leaves*).

Some nouns have the same spelling in both singular and plural forms: *sheep, elk, lox*. Some noun plurals have irregular forms that don't follow any rule: *mice, teeth*.

> In "A Valediction: Forbidding Mourning" John Donne says that death separates bodys but cannot divide peoples joined together by love.

Possessive Nouns

Follow these guidelines to form possessive nouns.

- Add an apostrophe and *-s* to form the possessive of a singular noun or a plural noun that does not end in *-s* (*nephew—nephew's, children—children's*).
- Add only an apostrophe to plural nouns that end in *-s* (*pupils—pupils', teachers—teachers'*).

In "Holy Sonnet 10" Donne addresses death as a person. Death's power is not so great as other's power, he says, because death "dies" when people's lives begin again.

APPLY WHAT YOU'VE LEARNED

Correct the errors in plurals and possessives.

[1]The lifes of those 17th-century writers known as metaphysical poets are interesting. [2]John Donne is not included in this classification just because most of his poemes are religious. [3]He is also included because his work's express feelings more than they record event's. [4]Donne crafted beautiful love poem's, but few of these are accessible today. [5]After Donnes' religious conversion, he took Anglican holy order's. [6]It was then that he attempted to destroy all of his secular writinges. [7]Such action may seem extreme, but not when one considers that he felt that some of his poetrys content was obscene. [8]Fortunately for us, Donnes efforts were thwarted. [9]So many piece's were already in circulation that he could not entirely succeed. [10]The mans follys pursued him despite all of his efforts. [11]Judging from the remarkable sonnet's that remain, however, we can only mourn the poetry that did not survive.

3.2 Pronoun Forms

There are first-person, second-person, and third-person personal pronouns. A personal pronoun has three cases, or forms: the subject form, the object form, and the possessive form.

Subject Pronouns

Use the subject form of a pronoun when it is the subject of a sentence or the subject of a clause. *I, you, he, she, it, we,* and *they* are subject pronouns.

Problems usually arise when a noun and a pronoun—or two pronouns—are used in a compound subject or compound object. To see whether you are using the correct form, read the sentence with just one pronoun.

In William Blake's "The Lamb" the speaker says that a little lamb and ~~him~~ he are like the Christ child.

LINK TO LITERATURE

In "A Valediction: Forbidding Mourning" on page 267, notice how John Donne uses pronouns to avoid repetition of nouns and to prevent confusion.

To check the form of a predicate pronoun, see whether the sentence still makes sense when the subject and the predicate pronoun are reversed. (*It was they. They were it.*)

Use the subject form of a pronoun when it is a predicate pronoun following a linking verb.

You often hear the object form used for a predicate pronoun in casual conversation (*It is him*). However, the subject form is preferred in more formal writing.

> According to one interpretation, in "The Little Boy Lost" and "The Little Boy Found" Blake says that it is ~~him~~ he and ~~us~~ we who need rescuing, much as a wandering child does.

Object Pronouns

Use the object form of a pronoun when it is the object of a verb or verbal or the object of a preposition. *Me, you, him, her, it, us,* and *them* are object pronouns.

> In "The Tyger" the speaker ponders a glory of nature. The tiger may inspire fear in you and ~~I~~ me, but such a magnificent creature causes ~~he~~ him and us to marvel as well.

Possessive Pronouns

Never use an apostrophe in a possessive pronoun. *My, mine, your, yours, his, her, hers, its, our, ours, their,* and *theirs* are possessive pronouns.

> In "The Fly" Blake reflects on the life of a fly. It's life and the poet's—or mine and your's, for that matter—are similar in many respects.

APPLY WHAT YOU'VE LEARNED

Write the following sentences, correcting pronoun errors.

[1]William Blake was one of the early romantic poets; others and him found their inspiration in nature. [2]To other writers and he it was important to be creative in more than one field, so Blake was also a printer, engraver, and artist. [3]In fact, his' artwork for a time attracted as much of a following as his' poetry. [4]The scientist and theologian Emanuel Swedenborg greatly influenced others of his time and he. [5]It was him, Swedenborg, whose mystical writings spoke of visions of spirits and angels, which also appear in Blake's prose, poetry, and art. [6]Them may be what made those who could not understand Blake's work consider him insane. [7]Those same works now strike you and I as profound.

3.3 Pronoun Antecedents

An antecedent is the noun or pronoun to which a personal pronoun refers. The antecedent usually precedes the pronoun.

Pronoun and Antecedent Agreement

A pronoun must agree with its antecedent in number, person, and gender.

Use a singular pronoun to refer to a singular antecedent; use a plural pronoun to refer to a plural antecedent.

Do not allow interrupters to determine the number of the personal pronoun.

> In "Pied Beauty" stripes, shadows, and contrasts help the poet to appreciate nature. Without ~~it~~ them, nature's beauty would not be so apparent.

If the antecedent is a noun that could refer to either a male or a female, use *he or she* (*him or her, his or her*), or reword the sentence to avoid the singular pronoun.

> The reader shares Gerard Manley Hopkins's joy when ~~they~~ he or she realizes the many wonders ~~they~~ he or she takes for granted.

LINK TO LITERATURE

Clearly, Gerard Manley Hopkins's pronouns all agree with their antecedents in "Spring and Fall" on page 679. Notice especially that—because the poem is written to someone, as a letter might be—many of the pronouns are *you* and *your.*

REVISING TIP

You could also revise the second example in either of these ways:

Readers share Gerard Manley Hopkins's joy when they realize the many wonders ***they*** *take for granted.*

or

We readers share Gerard Manley Hopkins's joy when ***we*** *realize the many wonders we take for granted.*

To avoid vague pronoun reference, do not use *this* or *that* alone to start a clause. Instead, include a word stating the thing or idea to which *this* or *that* refers—*this idea, that philosophy, this perception.*

REVISING TIP

Be careful with the indefinite use of *you* and *they*.

~~They~~ People say that ~~you~~ one ought to make use of each day to see and appreciate the beauty all around ~~you.~~

Be sure that the antecedent of a pronoun is clear.

In most cases do not use a pronoun to refer to an entire idea or clause. Your writing will be much clearer if you specify the exact idea.

> In "Spring and Fall" a child is saddened by the sight of bare trees. ~~This~~ Her sorrow comes from her unconscious awareness that her life has seasons too.

Unclear Antecedents

Make sure that each pronoun has a clear reference.

Clarify unidentified references.

The words *it, they, this, which,* and *that* can create problems because they may appear without antecedents.

> ~~It says in~~ Hopkins's poem says that life passes all too soon.

Clarify ambiguous referents.

Ambiguous means "having two or more possible meanings." A pronoun reference is ambiguous if the pronoun may refer to more than one antecedent.

> The leaves in the poem are as transient as our years. We cannot keep ~~them.~~ either. ~~They~~ Both are here and then gone.

Compound Antecedents Joined by *Or* or *Nor*

When two or more singular antecedents are joined by *or* or *nor,* use a singular pronoun. When two or more plural antecedents are joined by *or* or *nor,* use a plural pronoun.

> Neither spring nor fall represents all that life offers.

When one singular and one plural antecedent are joined by *or* or *nor,* use the nearer antecedent to determine whether the pronoun should be singular or plural.

> Either Hopkins's poems or his prose arouses an apprecia-tion of nature through the details ~~they~~ it present^s.

Indefinite Pronouns as Antecedents

When a singular indefinite pronoun is the antecedent, use *he or she* (*him or her, his or her*), or rewrite the sentence.

> Not everyone has pondered ~~their~~ his or her life as Hopkins did.

APPLY WHAT YOU'VE LEARNED

Correct the pronouns to clarify antecedents.

1 Both John Donne and Gerard Manley Hopkins were spiritual men; each wrote profound religious poetry in their own unique style. **2** Although they approached his subject differently, neither resorted to the trite or hackneyed. **3** This is evident in both "God's Grandeur" and "Pied Beauty." **4** The poems speak of seeing God's hand in nature, but it says that power springs from within. **5** Conversely, in the poem "Thou Art Indeed Just, Lord" it asks "Why do sinners' ways prosper?" **6** Everyone, religious or not, asks similar questions sometimes, but they do not ask so eloquently. **7** A poet tries to speak convincingly to their audience. **8** Hopkins's poems and prose achieve this by evoking a strong response.

3.4 Pronoun Usage

The form that a pronoun takes is always determined by its function within its own clause or sentence.

Who and *Whom*

Use *who* or *whoever* as the subject of a clause or a sentence.

> Dylan Thomas is the poet who~~m~~ employs an unusual poetic form in "Do Not Go Gentle into That Good Night."

REVISING TIP

In the example at left, *who* is the subject of the clause *who employs an unusual poetic form in "Do Not Go Gentle into That Good Night."*

REVISING TIP

Sometimes changing the order of the words in a sentence enables one to see an error easily. This technique is helpful in replacing *who* with *whom* in the example at right: (*To*) *whom*—object of the preposition *to*

Use *whom* as the direct or indirect object of a verb or verbal and as the object of a preposition.

People often use *who* for *whom* when speaking informally. However, in written English the pronouns should be used correctly.

> Who^m could you speak to about your feelings?

In trying to determine the correct pronoun form, ignore interrupters that come between the subject and the verb.

In the example that follows, *who* should replace *whom* because the pronoun is the subject of the clause *who would enjoy writing such a poem.*

> ~~Whom~~ Who do you feel would enjoy writing such a poem?

Pronouns in Contractions

Do not confuse the contractions *it's, they're, who's,* and *you're* with possessive pronouns that sound the same—*its, their, whose,* and *your*.

> In Thomas's poem "In My Craft or Sullen Art" it's the rhymes in the first four lines that we see repeated. ~~Their~~ They're also the rhymes in the first four lines of the second stanza.

Pronouns with Nouns

Determine the correct pronoun form in phrases such as *we students* and *us pupils* by imagining what the sentence would look like if the pronoun appeared without the noun that follows it.

> ~~Us~~ We children can all admire Thomas's tribute to his father in "Do Not Go Gentle into That Good Night."

Pronouns in Comparisons

Be sure to use the correct form of a pronoun in a comparison.

Than or *as* often begins an elliptical clause, one in which some words have been left out. To decide which form of the pronoun to use, fill in the missing words.

> In "In My Craft or Sullen Art" Thomas proves that few work harder at poetry than ~~him~~ he (does).

Shifts in Person

Be sure that a pronoun agrees with its antecedent in person.

One, everyone, and *everybody* should be referred to by third-person pronouns.

> Everyone must ultimately write for ~~yourself~~ himself or herself. One should not let others exert pressure on ~~you~~ him or her.

APPLY WHAT YOU'VE LEARNED

Correct the errors in pronoun usage.

1 Us students can relate to Thomas's wish to please himself first. 2 Sometimes its hard to satisfy teachers or friends when your writing. 3 Thomas, whom chose unusual, creative forms for his poems, rarely repeated a form. 4 Who's poems have rhyme schemes as unusual as his? 5 To who would it occur to rhyme the first seven lines with the last seven? 6 It also surprises we students to find the last four lines of the first and second stanzas rhyming. 7 One is startled by a Christmas poem shaped like a star or a pine tree; they must admit that it's shape is appropriate, though. 8 Some scholars who we know consider Thomas's odd forms mere tricks. 9 Whom of other poets you have studied had more fun writing poems than him? 10 The only one who I can think of might be E. E. Cummings, whom threw out the rules of capitalization and punctuation.

Using Modifiers Effectively

4.1 Adjective or Adverb?

REVISING TIP

Always determine first which word is being modified. Note that in the example at right, *complains* is the verb being modified, so it takes an adverb, *mournfully*. *Ocean* is a noun, so its modifier must be an adjective, *merciless*.

Use an adjective to modify a noun or a pronoun. Use an adverb to modify a verb, an adjective, or another adverb.

> The speaker of "The Seafarer" complains so mournful ly of the mercilessly ocean's caprices that readers wonder why he doesn't stay on dry land.

Use an adjective after a linking verb to describe the subject.

In addition to forms of the verb *be*, the following are linking verbs: *become, seem, appear, look, sound, feel, taste, grow,* and *smell*.

> The speaker's explanation seems inadequately. Basically, he says he feels restlessly when he's on land.

APPLY WHAT YOU'VE LEARNED

Select the correct modifier from each pair in parentheses.

1. The Exeter Book, the source of the excerpt from "The Seafarer," holds a (considerable, considerably) number of works from the Anglo-Saxon period.
2. Around A.D. 975 monks (painstaking, painstakingly) copied the works, probably from an older manuscript.
3. (Frequent, Frequently) scholars debate whether "The Seafarer" was written by two different poets.
4. Researchers (careful, carefully) examine the (unique, uniquely) structure of a work before making such a claim.
5. As "The Seafarer" shows, sea travel (certain, certainly) did exist back then.
6. The sailor, who moans so (loud, loudly) about his work, (probable, probably) received a handsome reward for his troubles.
7. He may have been (safer, more safely) at sea.
8. On land he could have been forced to go to war: the call to arms seems to have been (frequent, frequently) in those days.

4.2 Comparisons and Negatives

Comparative and Superlative Modifiers

Use the comparative form of an adjective or adverb to compare two things or actions. Use the superlative form to compare more than two things or actions.

Form the comparative by adding *-er* to short modifiers or by using the word *more* with longer modifiers. Form the superlative by adding *-est* or by adding the word *most.*

> The women who speak in Margaret Cavendish's "Female Orations" raise one of the ~~importantest~~ *most important* questions of Cavendish's time: why don't people take women ~~seriouser~~ *more seriously*? They also wonder what the ~~most~~ high*est* and ~~most~~ best achievements of women could be.

Illogical Comparisons

Avoid comparisons that don't make sense because of missing words or illogical constructions.

> Many men considered Cavendish's views more scandalous than any *other* woman's.

REVISING TIP

Without the added word, the comparison in the example at left states that Cavendish's views are more scandalous than her own views, since Cavendish herself is a woman.

Double Negatives

To avoid double negatives in comparisons, use only one negative word in a clause.

Besides *not* and *no*, the following are negative words: *never, nobody, none, no one, nothing, nowhere, hardly,* and *scarcely*.

> Cavendish strongly implies that the limitations placed on women ~~aren't~~ are hardly reasonable.

APPLY WHAT YOU'VE LEARNED

Rewrite these sentences, correcting mistakes in modifiers.

1. The author of "Female Orations" enjoyed more greater privilege than almost any other Englishwoman of her time.
2. The demands of farm life, including the raising of children, absorbed the time of most women more than any task.
3. In Cavendish's time, universities and schools didn't hardly admit women.
4. Most 17th-century women couldn't neither read nor write.
5. Even some women in the most high ranks of the aristocracy were poorly educated.
6. Many feel that women of the 17th century had the most hardest lives.
7. It is hard to tell whether a farmer's wife or an aristocratic lady had the most interesting life.
8. Back then, some farmers were being forced off the land by rich people who thought it was more importanter to care for sheep than people.
9. Landless people didn't have nowhere to go except the cities, where few people found work.
10. Such women couldn't hardly question their lot—but Cavendish could.

REVISING TIP

Misplaced modifiers cause confusion. In the example at right, the object (*the worst in the humans*) is separated from its verb (*brings*) by a prepositional phrase (*around him*). It sounds as if the cat is surrounding himself with something.

4.3 Misplaced or Dangling Modifiers

A misplaced modifier is separated from the word it modifies. It may appear to modify the wrong word and can confuse the reader. A dangling modifier seems unrelated to any word in the sentence. Misplaced and dangling modifiers are usually phrases or clauses.

Misplaced Modifier

Place a modifier near the word it modifies.

In "Tobermory" a cat speaks the truth and brings out around him the worst in the humans.

Dangling Modifier

Be sure a modifier describes a particular word in the sentence.

If he had escaped and lived ~~Escaping and living~~ elsewhere, what would he have ~~be~~ said of his experience?

APPLY WHAT YOU'VE LEARNED

Correct the misplaced and dangling modifiers in this paragraph.

1 Having the ability to speak, Saki's short story "Tobermory" is about a specially trained cat. 2 Various attempts have been made to teach human speech to animals in recent years. 3 Convinced that gorillas possess enough intelligence to understand speech, one of the most successful of these experiments has been carried out with them. 4 With American Sign Language, the gorilla Koko has learned to respond to questions and directions. 5 Being the focus of the world's longest ongoing ape-language study, signs were used by Koko to tell Dr. Patterson she wanted a kitten. 6 The 230-pound gorilla amazingly has been very gentle with the tiny pet given her by Dr. Patterson.

4.4 Special Problems with Modifiers

The following terms are frequently misused in spoken English. Be careful to use them correctly in written English.

Bad and *Badly*

Always use *bad* as an adjective, whether before a noun or after a linking verb. *Badly* should generally be used to modify an action verb.

Churchill's speech of May 19, 1940, details how bad[ly] the Germans were threatening England.

REVISING TIP

Avoid the use of *here* with *this* and *these*; also, do not use *there* with *that* and *those*.

That ~~there~~ invasion of France by Germany was only one of the harrowing events of the 1940s.

This, That, These, Those, and *Them*

Whether used as adjectives or pronouns, *this* and *these* refer to people and things that are nearby, and *that* and *those* refer to people and things that are farther away.

Them is a pronoun; it never modifies a noun.

He distinguishes between ~~these~~ those powerful Germans across the Channel and ~~those~~ these magnificent Allied forces closer to home.

Few, Fewer, Fewest and *Little, Less, Least*

***Few, fewer,* and *fewest* refer to numbers of things that can be counted. *Little, less,* and *least* refer to amounts or quantities.**

> Churchill knows that he has to give the ~~fewest~~ least credibility possible to the idea of failure. The more the Allies could believe in their own strength, the ~~less~~ fewer lives would be lost.

Misplacement of *Only*

For clarity, *only* should be positioned before the word or words it modifies.

The misplacement of *only* can alter, and sometimes confuse, the meaning of a sentence. Notice in the example below the difference in meaning when *only* is moved.

> The British leader emphasizes that because so many nations had fallen to the Germans, a few only remained to save the world from extraordinary tyranny.

APPLY WHAT YOU'VE LEARNED

Rewrite these sentences, correcting the errors in modifiers.

1. In his May 19, 1940, speech Churchill stated that the nation needed a "furious and unrelenting assault" on the enemy very bad.
2. Unfortunately, the Allies soon lost France to these Germans.
3. Great Britain remained only to challenge the German forces.
4. In early August of 1940, the Germans tackled what they thought would be the fewest of their worries.
5. They began air strikes to wound Britain bad before beginning a naval invasion.
6. With few help, however, Britain's Royal Air Force defeated the German Luftwaffe over a period of 11 months.
7. The Battle of Britain showed the precision of British radar and the technological superiority of them British aircraft.

Using Verbs Correctly

5

5.1 Verb Tenses and Forms

Verb tense shows the time of an action or a condition. Writers sometimes cause confusion when they use different verb tenses in describing actions that occur at the same time.

Consistent Use of Tenses

When two or more actions occur at the same time or in sequence, use the same verb tense to describe the actions.

"Christmas Storms and Sunshine" is a story about two families who shared a house but complain about each other.

A shift in tense is necessary when two events occur at different times or out of sequence. The tenses of the verbs should clearly indicate that one action precedes the other.

In the past, Mrs. Hodgson and Mrs. Jenkins seldom spoke to each other, but they ~~quarreled~~ quarrels openly as the story develops.

Tense	Verb Form
Present	help/helps
Past	helped
Future	will/shall help
Present perfect	has/have helped
Past perfect	had helped
Future perfect	will/shall have helped

REVISING TIP

In telling a story, be careful not to shift tenses so often that the reader finds the sequence of events unclear.

LINK TO LITERATURE

Notice how Elizabeth Gaskell throughout "Christmas Storms and Sunshine," on page 606, is consistent in her use of the past and perfect tenses. She shifts to the present tense only in the quotations.

REVISING TIP

The past tense and past participle of regular verbs have the same spelling. Both forms end in *-d* or *-ed.* However, you usually double a final consonant before adding *-ed* when a short vowel sound precedes the consonant *(slip—slipped, knit—knitted, rot—rotted, pat—patted, stub—stubbed).*

Past Tense and Past Participle

The simple past form of a verb can always stand alone. When used as verbs, the past participles of the following irregular verbs should always be accompanied by helping verbs.

Present Tense	Past Tense	Past Participle
am/is/are	was/were	(have, had) been
begin	began	(have, had) begun
break	broke	(have, had) broken
choose	chose	(have, had) chosen
come	came	(have, had) come
do	did	(have, had) done
drink	drank	(have, had) drunk
eat	ate	(have, had) eaten
fly	flew	(have, had) flown
freeze	froze	(have, had) frozen
give	gave	(have, had) given
go	went	(have, had) gone
speak	spoke	(have, had) spoken
wear	worn	(have, had) worn

Mary Hodgson ~~taken~~ took some sausages to the Jenkinses after Mrs. Jenkins had ~~ran~~ run downstairs with a mustard plaster for the baby.

APPLY WHAT YOU'VE LEARNED

Write the correct form of the verb in parentheses.

1 In "Christmas Storms and Sunshine" Elizabeth Gaskell used the same kind of setting that Charles Dickens (did, does). 2 Gaskell and Dickens were contemporaries, and Gaskell (benefits, benefited) from her association with Dickens. 3 Many of her novels (are, were) published at his invitation. 4 Gaskell (spoke, spoken) with sympathy about the sick infant in the story, because she herself (loses, lost) a child in infancy. 5 Her writing (helps, helped) her overcome her sorrow at the death of her child. 6 Mrs. Gaskell (wrote, written) a number of full-length novels, including *Cranford.* 7 She also (wrote, written) a biography of Charlotte Brontë, which (is, was) not well received because it contained some libelous statements. 8 Mrs. Gaskell (includes, included) among her friends such literary personages as Ruskin, Carlyle, and Norton, and such humanitarians as Florence Nightingale.

5.2 Commonly Confused Verbs

The following verb pairs are often confused.

Affect and *Effect*

Affect **means "to influence."** ***Effect*** **means "to cause."**

> In "Sunrise on the Veld" Doris Lessing describes how the sight of an injured animal ~~effects~~ affects a young boy.

Lie and *Lay*, *Sit* and *Set*

Lie **means "to rest in a flat position" or "to be in a certain place";** ***lay*** **means "to put or place."** ***Sit*** **means "to be in a seated position";** ***set*** **means "to put or place."**

> The boy ~~lays~~ lies in bed for only a short time before he ~~sits~~ sets his feet on the cold floor.

Rise and *Raise*

Rise **means "to move upward."** ***Raise*** **means "to move something upward."**

> The boy has trained himself to ~~raise~~ rise even before the alarm sounds.

Learn and *Teach*

Learn **means "to gain knowledge or skill."** ***Teach*** **means "to help someone learn."**

> Living on the edge of the veld, the boy has ~~learned~~ taught himself about the wildlife that shares the area.

REVISING TIP

If you're uncertain about which verb to use, check to see whether the verb has an object. The verbs *lie* and *sit* never have objects—and they both refer to position. The verbs *lay* and *set* both have objects—and they have the same meaning.

REVISING TIP

When no movement is implied, *bring* may be used to mean "to produce a result." (*War brings hardships to many.*)

Bring and *Take*

***Bring* is used with reference to movement toward a place. *Take* refers to movement away from a place.**

The boy ~~brings~~ takes his shoes with him rather than risk awakening his parents.

Here are the principal parts of these troublesome verb pairs.

Present Tense	Past Tense	Past Participle
affect	affected	(have, had) affected
effect	effected	(have, had) effected
lie	lay	(have, had) lain
lay	laid	(have, had) laid
sit	sat	(have, had) sat
set	set	(have, had) set
rise	rose	(have, had) risen
raise	raised	(have, had) raised
learn	learned	(have, had) learned
teach	taught	(have, had) taught
bring	brought	(have, had) brought
take	took	(have, had) taken

APPLY WHAT YOU'VE LEARNED

Choose the correct verb from each pair in parentheses.

1 In lightly forested parts of southern Africa, the impala (rises, raises) its graceful head. *2* Another area, known as the Highveld, (lies, lays) in the high-plateau country. *3* Most of it (lays, lies) between 4,000 and 6,000 feet above sea level. *4* Over the centuries, erosion has (affected, effected) the terrain there. *5* Wind and water carry away the soil and (sit, set) it elsewhere. *6* It is difficult to (learn, teach) oneself about the characteristics of the Middleveld, because it is geologically complex. *7* The summer months (bring, take) much rainfall to the veld, usually in the form of high-energy thunderstorms.

Correcting Capitalization

6

6.1 Proper Nouns and Adjectives

A common noun is the name of a class of persons, places, things, or ideas. A proper noun is the name of a particular person, place, thing, or idea. A proper adjective is an adjective formed from a proper noun. Capitalize all proper nouns and proper adjectives.

Names and Titles

Capitalize people's names and initials that stand for such names.

In muriel spark's "The First Year of My Life" a baby is psychically aware of world events. She can "tune in" to d. h. lawrence and joseph conrad in their daily lives.

Capitalize a title used before a name or an abbreviation of such a title. In general, do not capitalize a title that follows a name or stands alone.

She can see and hear czar nicholas II, marshal ferdinand foch, and the Prime Minister who had been ousted.

Capitalize a title indicating a family relationship when it is used before or as someone's name (*Uncle Al, Granny*) but not when it is used simply to identify a person (*Jill's uncle*).

The baby thinks her Aunts are much too proud of her Brother's exploits with his toy gun, considering that so many of them have lost their Sons in the war.

LINK TO LITERATURE

Notice how Muriel Spark refers to specific places, people, and things in "The First Year of My Life" on page 1130. The precise names help you visualize scenes. More-general words would probably make the story less plausible and vivid.

REVISING TIP

Prefixes and suffixes such as *ex-* and *-elect* are not capitalized when used with a title. (*President-**elect** Olsen calmed the financial markets with a word.*)

REVISING TIP

Do not capitalize pronouns that refer to a deity. (*Kuan-yin protects all who seek her protection.*)

REVISING TIP

Do not capitalize minor words in a proper noun that is made up of several words. (*Write to the Illinois Department of Tourism.*)

Languages, Nationalities, Religious Terms

Capitalize names of languages and nationalities, as well as religious names and terms. Do not capitalize the words *god* and *goddess* when they refer to mythological deities.

Capitalize names of languages and nationalities, such as *Hindi, Sanskrit, Afrikaans, Korean, German,* and *Nigerian*. Capitalize religious names and terms, such as *God, Buddha, Bible,* and *Koran*.

> The baby sees that the germans and the french are locked in battle along the western front; meanwhile, turkish women sit around gossiping in their harems.

School Subjects

Capitalize the name of a specific school course (*Biology I, World History*). Do not capitalize a general reference to a school subject (*mathematics, history, music*).

> Perhaps the baby can already tell that, in this dreary world she's entered, she'll have to go to school and endure everything from Mathematics to earth science III.

Organizations, Institutions

Capitalize the important words in the official names of organizations and institutions (*Congress, Duke University*).

Do not capitalize words that name kinds of organizations or institutions (*school, church, university*) or words that refer to specific organizations when they are not used as part of the official names (*at the university*).

> The author supposes that the omniscience of newborns is even now being proved by someone at harvard university.

Geographical Names, Events, Time Periods

Capitalize geographical names, as well as the names of events, historical periods and documents, holidays, months, and days, but not the names of seasons.

Names	Examples
Continents	North America, Europe, Asia
Bodies of water	Suez Canal, Hudson River, Indian Ocean
Political units	China, Ottoman Empire, New Jersey
Areas of a country	Midwest, New England
Public areas	Central Park, Trafalgar Square
Roads and structures	Wall Street, Taj Mahal
Events	Boer War, Congress of Berlin
Documents	Treaty of Sèvres, Entente Cordiale
Periods of history	Middle Ages, Restoration
Holidays	Easter, Veterans Day
Months and days	November, Monday
Seasons	spring, winter
Directions	east, northwest

The baby is born near the end of world war I on a friday. She is aware of the signing of the treaty of brest-litovsk, in which russia made peace with the central powers in march 1918.

REVISING TIP

Do not capitalize a reference that does not consist of the full name of a place, an event, or a period. (*The Russian Revolution complicated World War I, but the revolution did not significantly alter the war's outcome.*)

APPLY WHAT YOU'VE LEARNED

Correct any capitalization errors.

1"The First Year of My Life" looks at the close of world war I: important events followed. *2*Great britain entered a short time of prosperity until 1920. *3*A number of british inventions had sparked the industrial revolution. *4*By the 1920s, however, japan had taken over textiles. *5*The treaty of versailles of june 1919 had wounded germany; neither the germans nor the russians could afford british products. *6*By january 1924 a new political party had emerged in Britain: the labor party flourished, but it failed in november in the house of commons. *7*Consequently, the conservative party, led by stanley baldwin, came to power and remained there until 1929 and the great depression. *8*Troubles in ireland continued in the 1920s, with the sinn fein group engaging in guerrilla attacks against british administrators. *9*Eventually, the british created the irish free state, in which most people were roman catholics. *10*Northern ireland had mostly protestant citizens.

6.2 Titles of Created Works

The titles of published material follow certain capitalization rules.

Books, Plays, Magazines, Newspapers, Films

Capitalize the first word, the last word, and all other important words in the title of a book, play, periodical, newspaper, or film. Underline or italicize the title to set it off.

Do not capitalize articles, coordinating conjunctions, and prepositions of fewer than five letters unless they appear at the beginning or the end of the title.

> Stevie Smith's poem "The Frog Prince" has several levels of meaning. She wrote eight books of poetry, one of which is entitled a good time was had by all.

Poems, Stories, Articles

Capitalize the first word, the last word, and all other important words in the title of a poem, a short story, or an article. Enclose the title in quotation marks.

> Multiple levels of meaning characterize another poem of hers, entitled "not waving but drowning."

APPLY WHAT YOU'VE LEARNED

Rewrite the sentences, correcting the punctuation and capitalization of titles.

1. Stevie Smith's poem the frog prince is only a small part of her writing.
2. She published three novels: novel on yellow paper, over the frontier, and the holiday.
3. One of her best-known poems was originally published in a newspaper called the observer.
4. Four years after her death, most of her poetry was gathered into a volume entitled the collected poems of stevie smith.
5. Ten years after she died, her other writings—which include literary reviews, short stories, and essays—were put together into a volume entitled me again: uncollected writings of stevie smith.

Correcting Punctuation

7

7.1 Punctuating Compound Sentences

Punctuation helps organize sentences that have more than one clause.

Commas in Compound Sentences

Use a comma before the conjunction that joins the clauses of a compound sentence.

Do not use a comma before the conjunction that joins the parts of a compound subject or compound predicate.

> In the excerpt from *Memoirs of Madame Vigée-Lebrun,* Vigée-Lebrun admires, and raves about the French royal family and she cannot understand the reasons behind the revolution.

Semicolons in Compound Sentences

Use a semicolon between the clauses of a compound sentence when no conjunction is used. Use a semicolon before a conjunctive adverb that joins the clauses of a compound sentence.

Conjunctive adverbs include *therefore, however, consequently, nevertheless,* and *besides*. You should place a comma after a conjunctive adverb in a compound sentence.

> Some 20th-century art historians find Vigée-Lebrun's work sentimental and irrelevant consequently, they prefer that of Jacques-Louis David.

REVISING TIP

Even when clauses are connected by a coordinating conjunction, you may use a semicolon between them if one or both clauses contain a subordinate clause or a series punctuated with commas. (*Madame Vigée-Lebrun survived the French Revolution; and after she fled from France, she painted portraits of princesses, noblewomen, and even Lord Byron.*)

APPLY WHAT YOU'VE LEARNED

Rewrite this paragraph, correcting problems with commas and semicolons.

[1] *Memoirs of Madame Vigée-Lebrun* shows the effects of the French Revolution on people connected with the court many of them were killed during the Reign of Terror. [2] Vigée-Lebrun left her husband behind in France as she escaped however, she was able to take her daughter with her. [3] She endured the tumult of 1789 consequently she adapted well to life away from France. [4] Vigée-Lebrun became a painter in a predictable way her father drew pastel portraits and he began her training very early. [5] Her minimal impact on art history stems from the teachers with whom she worked, such as Greuze they later were condemned for their sentimentality. [6] Even her early work is warm and graceful and it's no surprise that she later painted an English princess and noblewomen, as well as the poet Lord Byron and the writer Madame de Staël. [7] This adventurous painter lived to be 87 years old but she seems to have stopped painting when she was in her mid-50s.

7.2 Setting Off Elements in a Sentence

Most elements that are not essential to a sentence are set off with commas or other punctuation marks to highlight the main idea of the sentence. A nonessential element merely adds information to an already complete sentence. An essential element is necessary to convey the accurate meaning of the sentence; without it, the meaning is unclear.

Commas

You should often use a comma to separate an introductory word or phrase from the rest of the sentence.

An introductory prepositional phrase usually need not be set off with a comma. However, you should use a comma after two or more prepositional phrases or a phrase that includes a verb or a verbal.

> With its combination of rare grace and humor^ *The Importance of Being Earnest* perennially amuses readers and audiences. Still^ one wonders just how the humor works.

In a complex sentence, set off an introductory subordinate clause with a comma.

> When a character makes an uproarious comment, the words operate first on the level of literal meaning and then on one or two additional levels.

Use commas to set off a word or group of words that interrupts the flow of a sentence. When a subordinate clause interrupts or follows the main clause, set off the subordinate clause only if it is not essential.

> It's as if Wilde, indulging in boundless energy, is playing musical chairs with his characters and his audience.

The words shown in the chart below are commonly used to begin subordinate clauses. Such words often signal the need for one or more commas.

Words Often Used to Introduce Subordinate Clauses				
Subordinating Conjunctions	after although as as if as long as as much as as though	because before even even if if in order that provided	since so that than though till unless until	whatever when whenever where wherever while
Relative Pronouns	which	who	whom	whose

REVISING TIP

Try saying the sentence without the interrupter; if the basic meaning doesn't change, you should use punctuation (commas, dashes, or parentheses) to set off the interrupter.

Parentheses

Use parentheses to set off material that is only incidentally connected to the main idea of a sentence.

I look forward to reading the rest of Wilde's work he wrote other plays, poetry, and a novel so that I can learn about this interesting man.

Dashes

Use dashes to set off a word, or a group of words, that abruptly interrupts the flow of a sentence.

His humor not surprisingly makes me stop and think.

Colons

Use a colon between two sentences when the second explains or summarizes the first.

One is left in doubt who's laughing at whom?

Use a colon to introduce a list of items or a long quotation.

Never use a colon after a preposition or after a verb when the items listed are essential to the clause.

The answer may include the following the playwright laughs at his world, the characters at themselves, the characters at their world, and the characters at each other.

A colon often follows a word or phrase such as *these* or *the following items*. (*The parade started in the following order: police cars, fire engines, marching bands, and children's groups.*)

For Clarity

Use commas to prevent misreading or misunderstanding.

At the very least careful readers will find many treasures.

REVISING TIP

Sometimes when a comma is missing, parts of a sentence can be grouped in more than one way by a reader. A comma separates the parts so that they can be read in only one way.

APPLY WHAT YOU'VE LEARNED

Rewrite these sentences. Add commas, parentheses, dashes, and colons where necessary.

1 *The Importance of Being Earnest* a society comedy has earned great acclaim. 2 Besides that play Wilde wrote three other society comedies *Lady Windermere's Fan, A Woman of No Importance*, and *An Ideal Husband*. 3 Wilde has a way quite clever in fact of raising many questions in very little space. 4 Consider the statement of one of the young women "I never travel without my diary. One should always have something sensational to read in the train." 5 She's implying a great deal at the very least, that fiction perhaps creeps into her account of her own life. 6 Does she write then to entertain? 7 When a Wilde character says something that is quite matter-of-fact and literal readers almost have to stop and scratch their heads. 8 They wonder and necessarily so whether they've missed something.

7.3 Elements in a Series

Use commas to separate three or more elements in a series and to separate multiple adjectives preceding a noun.

Subjects, Verbs, Objects, and Other Elements

Use a comma after every item except the last in a series of three or more items.

The three or more items can be nouns, verbs, adjectives, adverbs, phrases, clauses, or other parts of a sentence.

In "On Spring" Johnson introduces the reader to a new way of looking at life to new habits of thought and to a sure method for living well.

REVISING TIP

Note in the example that a comma followed by a conjunction precedes the last element in the series. That comma is always used.

Two or More Adjectives

In many cases when more than one adjective precedes a noun, use a comma after each adjective except the last one.

If you can't reverse the order of the adjectives without changing the meaning or if you can't use the word *and* between them, do not separate them with a comma.

> Johnson's walks convinced him that spring is a verdant, pleasant, joyous season.

APPLY WHAT YOU'VE LEARNED

Rewrite these sentences, correcting the comma errors.

1. In his essay "On Spring" Samuel Johnson gives advice on living fully deeply and richly.
2. He wrote the essay when he was 41 when it was springtime and when he felt he had wisdom to pass on to others.
3. Just like anyone else, Johnson appreciates the blooms the breezes and the singing birds of springtime.
4. In his essay, however, he moves far away from simple description of the beauty joy and energy of the season.
5. Instead, he presents a complex wide-ranging analysis of what one can and should do in the spring.

7.4 Dates, Addresses, and Letters

Punctuation in addresses, dates, and letters makes information easy to understand.

Dates

Use a comma after the day and the year to set off a date from the rest of the sentence.

> *The Life of Samuel Johnson* exists because Boswell met Johnson on May 16, 1763, at a bookshop in Covent Garden.

REVISING TIP

In dates that include only the month and the year, do not use a comma after the month. (*James Boswell met Samuel Johnson for the first time in May 1763 at a London bookshop.*)

Addresses

In an address with more than one part, use a comma after each part to set it off from the rest of the sentence.

> The house at 17 Gough Square, London, is now the Johnson Museum; it is where he compiled his famous dictionary.

REVISING TIP

In an address that includes the ZIP code, do not use a comma between the state abbreviation and the ZIP code.

Parts of a Letter

Use a comma after the greeting and after the closing of a letter.

An abridged letter from Johnson to his dear friend Mrs. Hester Thrale might read as follows.

> My dear Mrs. Thrale,
>
> Surely all is well with you, Henry, and your children. . . .
>
> The use of traveling is to regulate imagination by reality, and instead of thinking how things may be, to see them as they are. . . .
>
> Yours,
>
> S. Johnson

APPLY WHAT YOU'VE LEARNED

Rewrite the following items, correcting the comma errors.

1 *The Life of Samuel Johnson* was a project of Boswell's from the time of his meeting with Johnson in May, 1763 until the book's publication in 1791. 2 As Boswell traveled in the mid-1760s, he might have written notes such as this:

Esteemed M. Voltaire

M. Rousseau suggested that I write to you. I am eager to meet you and to thank you for your wondrous *Candide.* Might I see you Thursday?

Yours

James Boswell

3 In 1728 Johnson entered Pembroke College Oxford. 4 In 1765 Johnson was granted the degree of LL.D. by Trinity College Dublin Ireland. 5 Johnson's writings touched on diverse subjects: he defended the right of Catholics in Quebec Canada to practice their religion. 6 Johnson died in London on December 13 1784. 7 At the time he was living at 8 Bolt Court London.

7.5 Quotations

Quotation marks tell readers who said what. Incorrectly placed or missing quotation marks lead to misunderstanding.

Direct Quotation from a Source

Use quotation marks at the beginning and the end of a direct quotation from source material and to set off the title of a short work. Do not use quotation marks to set off an indirect quotation.

> The Truth About George uncovers a surprisingly demanding cure for stuttering. George himself would have said that "he was completely transformed."

Introducing a Quotation

Introduce a short direct quotation with a comma. Use a colon for a long quotation. Capitalize the first word in a direct quotation but not in an indirect one.

> P. G. Wodehouse wrote about two men chatting at the Anglers' Rest. One of them remarks "biggest I ever saw in my life!" and shows how exaggeration takes on a life of its own.

REVISING TIP

If quoted words form part of your own sentence rather than a sentence of their own, begin the quotation with a lowercase letter. (*The poet Adrienne Rich speaks of "visionary anger cleansing my sight."*)

End Punctuation

Place periods inside quotation marks. Place question marks and exclamation points inside quotation marks if they belong to the quotation; place them outside if they do not belong to the quotation. Place semicolons outside quotation marks.

> George asked, "Will you be my wife"?
>
> "Oh, George"! said Susan.

REVISING TIP

Use a colon to introduce a long quotation. (*Anne Frank said: "Whoever is happy will make others happy too. He who has courage and faith will never perish in misery!"*)

Use a comma to end a quotation that is a complete sentence followed by explanatory words.

"Dreadful liars some men are" the storyteller said genially.

Divided Quotations

Capitalize the first word of the second part of a direct quotation if it begins a new sentence.

"He wasn't a fisherman" said his companion. "that was our local doctor."

Do not capitalize the first word of the second part of a divided quotation if it does not begin a new sentence.

"Fishermen" he suggested "Are traditionally careless of the truth."

REVISING TIP

Should the first word of the second part of a divided quotation be capitalized? Imagine the quotation without the explanatory words. If a capital letter would not be used, then do not use one in the divided quotation.

APPLY WHAT YOU'VE LEARNED

Rewrite the sentences, inserting quotation marks and correcting punctuation errors.

1In The Truth About George poor George gets in trouble during a train ride across England in the years before World War II. ***2***Steve asked, "what were passenger trains like in those days"? ***3***Angie replied "that one could infer a great deal from reading Wodehouse's story closely." ***4***"In any event" she said "You know that Great Britain was the cradle of railroad technology. ***5***Many of the leading inventors worked in the British Isles in the early 19th century. ***6***"Right enough" Steve responded. "however, you seem to have forgotten the Jesuit missionary in Peking who in 1681 invented what may well have been the first self-propelled steam vehicle." ***7***"Oh, him"! sniffed Angie "some missionary"! ***8***Steve said Well, perhaps he was a Renaissance man a century after the fact. ***9***Angie swirled her coffee dregs in her cup, muttering "that the engineers and inventors Trevithick, Blenkinsop, Hedley, Stephenson, and Hackworth collectively made George's ride possible."

8 Grammar Glossary

This glossary contains various terms you need to understand when you use the Grammar Handbook. Used as a reference source, this glossary will help you explore grammar concepts and the ways they relate to one another.

Abbreviation An abbreviation is a shortened form of a word or word group; it is often made up of initials. (B.C., A.M., *Maj.*)

Active voice. *See* **Voice.**

Adjective An adjective modifies, or describes, a noun or pronoun. (*happy* camper, she is *small*)

A ***predicate adjective*** follows a linking verb and describes the subject. (The day seemed *long*.)

A ***proper adjective*** is formed from a proper noun. (*Jewish* temple, *Alaskan* husky)

The ***comparative*** form of an adjective compares two things. (*more alert, thicker*)

The ***superlative*** form of an adjective compares more than two things. (*most abundant, weakest*)

What Adjectives Tell	Examples
How many	*some* writers *much* joy
What kind	*grand* plans *wider* streets
Which one(s)	*these* flowers *that* star

Adjective phrase. *See* **Phrase.**

Adverb An adverb modifies a verb, an adjective, or another adverb. (Clare sang *loudly*.)

The ***comparative*** form of an adverb compares two actions. (*more generously, faster*)

The ***superlative*** form of an adverb compares more than two actions. (*most sharply, closest*)

What Adverbs Tell	Examples
How	climb *carefully* chuckle *merrily*
When	arrived *late* left *early*
Where	climbed *up* moved *away*
To what extent	*extremely* upset *hardly* visible

Adverb, conjunctive. *See* **Conjunctive adverb.**

Adverb phrase. *See* **Phrase.**

Agreement Sentence parts that correspond with one another are said to be in agreement.

In ***pronoun-antecedent agreement,*** a pronoun and the word it refers to are the same in number, gender, and person. (*Bill* mailed *his* application. The *students* ate *their* lunches.)

In ***subject-verb agreement,*** the subject and verb in a sentence are the same in number. (*A child cries* for help. *They cry* aloud.)

Ambiguous reference An ambiguous reference occurs when a pronoun may refer to more than one word. (Bud asked his brother if *he* had any mail.)

Antecedent An antecedent is the noun or pronoun to which a pronoun refers. (If *Adam* forgets *his* raincoat, *he* will be late for school. *She* learned *her* lesson.)

Appositive An appositive is a noun or phrase that explains one or more words in a sentence. (Cary Grant, *an Englishman,* spent most of his adult life in America.)

An ***essential appositive*** is needed to make the sense of a sentence complete. (A comic strip inspired the musical *Annie*.)

A ***nonessential appositive*** is one that adds information to a sentence but is not necessary to its sense. (O. Henry, *a short-story writer,* spent time in prison.)

Article Articles are the special adjectives *a, an,* and *the*. (*the* day, *a* fly)

The ***definite article*** (the word *the*) is one that refers to a particular thing. (*the* cabin)

An ***indefinite article*** is used with a noun that is not unique but refers to one of many of its kind. (*a* dish, *an* otter)

Auxiliary verb. *See* **Verb.**

Clause A clause is a group of words that contains a verb and its subject. (*they slept*)

An ***adjective clause*** is a subordinate clause that modifies a noun or pronoun. (Hugh bought the sweater *that he had admired.*)

An ***adverb clause*** is a subordinate clause used to modify a verb, an adjective, or an adverb. (Ring the bell *when it is time for class to begin.*)

A ***noun clause*** is a subordinate clause that is used as a noun. (*Whatever you say* interests me.)

An ***elliptical clause*** is a clause from which a word or words have been omitted. (We are not as lucky *as they.*)

A ***main (independent) clause*** can stand by itself as a sentence. (*the flashlight flickered*)

A ***subordinate (dependent) clause*** does not express a complete thought and cannot stand by itself. (*while the nation watched*)

Clause	Example
Main (independent)	The hurricane struck
Subordinate (dependent)	while we were preparing to leave.

Collective noun. *See* **Noun.**

Comma splice A comma splice is an error caused when two sentences are separated with a comma instead of a correct end mark. (*The band played a medley of show tunes, everyone enjoyed the show.*)

Common noun. *See* **Noun.**

Comparative. *See* **Adjective; Adverb.**

Complement A complement is a word or group of words that completes the meaning of a verb. (The kitten finished the *milk.*) *See also* **Direct object; Indirect object.**

An ***objective complement*** is a word or a group of words that follows a direct object and renames or describes that object. (The parents of the rescued child declared Gus a *hero.*)

A ***subject complement*** follows a linking verb and renames or describes the subject. (The coach seemed *anxious.*) *See also* **Noun (predicate noun); Adjective, (predicate adjective).**

Complete predicate The complete predicate of a sentence consists of the main verb plus any words that modify or complete the verb's meaning. (The student *produces work of high caliber.*)

Complete subject The complete subject of a sentence consists of the simple subject plus any words that modify or describe the simple subject. (*Students of history* believe that wars can be avoided.)

Sentence Part	Example
Complete subject	The man in the ten-gallon hat
Complete predicate	wore a pair of silver spurs.

Compound sentence part A sentence element that consists of two or more subjects, verbs, objects, or other parts is compound. (*Lou* and *Jay* helped. Laura *makes* and *models* scarves. Jill sings *opera* and *popular music.*)

Conjunction A conjunction is a word that links other words or groups of words.

A ***coordinating conjunction*** connects related words, groups of words, or sentences. (*and, but, or*)

A ***correlative conjunction*** is one of a pair of conjunctions that work together to connect sentence parts. (*either . . . or, neither . . . nor, not only . . . but also, whether . . . or, both . . . and*)

A ***subordinating conjunction*** introduces a subordinate clause. (*after, although, as, as if, as long as, as though, because, before, if, in order that, since, so that, than, though, till, unless, until, whatever, when, where, while*)

Conjunctive adverb A conjunctive adverb joins the clauses of a compound sentence. (*however, therefore, yet*)

Contraction A contraction is formed by joining two words and substituting an apostrophe for a letter or letters left out of one of the words. (*didn't, we've*)

Coordinating conjunction. *See* **Conjunction.**

Correlative conjunction. *See* **Conjunction.**

Dangling modifier A dangling modifier is one that does not clearly modify any word in the sentence. (*Dashing for the train,* the barriers got in the way.)

Demonstrative pronoun. *See* **Pronoun.**

Dependent clause. *See* **Clause.**

Direct object A direct object receives the action of a verb. Direct objects follow transitive verbs. (Jude planned the *party.*)

Direct quotation. *See* **Quotation.**

Divided quotation. *See* **Quotation.**

Double negative A double negative is the incorrect use of two negative words when only one is needed. (*Nobody didn't* care.)

End mark An end mark is one of several punctuation marks that can end a sentence. See the punctuation chart on page 1298.

Fragment. *See* **Sentence fragment.**

Future tense. *See* **Verb tense.**

Gender The gender of a personal pronoun indicates whether the person or thing referred to is male, female, or neuter. (My cousin plays the tuba; *he* often performs in school concerts.)

Gerund A gerund is a verbal that ends in *-ing* and functions as a noun. (*Making* pottery takes patience.)

Helping verb. *See* **Verb (auxiliary verb).**

Illogical comparison An illogical comparison is a comparison that does not make sense because words are missing or illogical. (My computer is *newer than Kay*.)

Indefinite pronoun. *See* **Pronoun.**

Indefinite reference Indefinite reference occurs when a pronoun is used without a clear antecedent. (My aunt hugged me in front of my friends, and *it* was embarrassing.)

Independent clause. *See* **Clause.**

Indirect object An indirect object tells to whom or for whom (sometimes to what or for what) something is done. (Arthur wrote *Kerry* a letter.)

Indirect question An indirect question tells what someone asked without using the person's exact words. (*My friend asked me if I could go with her to the dentist.*)

Indirect quotation. *See* **Quotation.**

Infinitive An infinitive is a verbal beginning with *to* that functions as a noun, an adjective, or an adverb. (He wanted *to go* to the play.)

Intensive pronoun. *See* **Pronoun.**

Interjection An interjection is a word or phrase used to express strong feeling. (*Wow! Good grief!*)

Interrogative pronoun. *See* **Pronoun.**

Intransitive verb. *See* **Verb.**

Inverted sentence An inverted sentence is one in which the subject comes after the verb. (*How was the movie? Here come the clowns.*)

Irregular verb. *See* **Verb.**

Linking verb. *See* **Verb.**

Main clause. *See* **Clause.**

Main verb. *See* **Verb.**

Modifier A modifier makes another word more precise. Modifiers most often are adjectives or adverbs; they may also be phrases, verbals, or clauses that function as adjectives or adverbs. (*small* box, smiled *broadly,* house *by the sea,* dog *barking loudly*)

An ***essential modifier*** is one that is necessary to the meaning of a sentence. (Everybody *who has a free pass* should enter now. None *of the passengers* got on the train.)

A ***nonessential modifier*** is one that merely adds more information to a sentence that is clear without the addition. (We will use the new dishes, *which are stored in the closet.*)

Noun A noun names a person, a place, a thing, or an idea. (*auditor, shelf, book, goodness*)

An ***abstract noun*** names an idea, a quality, or a feeling. (*joy*)

A ***collective noun*** names a group of things. (*bevy*)

A ***common noun*** is a general name of a person, a place, a thing, or an idea. (*valet, hill, bread, amazement*)

A ***compound noun*** contains two or more words. (*hometown, pay-as-you-go, screen test*)

A ***noun of direct address*** is the name of a person being directly spoken to. (*Lee,* do you have the package? No, *Suki,* your letter did not arrive.)

A ***possessive noun*** shows who or what owns or is associated with something. (*Lil's* ring, a *day's* pay)

A ***predicate noun*** follows a linking verb and renames the subject. (Karen is a *writer.*)

A ***proper noun*** names a particular person, place, or thing. (*John Smith, Ohio, Sears Tower, Congress*)

Number A word is **singular** in number if it refers to just one person, place, thing, idea, or action, and **plural** in number if it refers to more than one person, place, thing, idea, or action. (The words *he, waiter,* and *is* are singular. The words *they, waiters,* and *are* are plural.)

Object of a preposition The object of a preposition is the noun or pronoun that follows a preposition. (The athletes cycled along the *route*. Jane baked a cake for *her*.)

Object of a verb The object of a verb receives the action of the verb. (Sid told *stories*.)

Participle A participle is often used as part of a verb phrase. (had *written*) It can also be used as a verbal that functions as an adjective. (the *leaping* deer, the medicine *taken* for a fever)

The ***present participle*** is formed by adding *-ing* to the present tense of a verb. (*Walking* rapidly, we reached the general store.)

The ***past participle*** of a regular verb is formed by adding *-d* or *-ed* to the present tense. The past participles of irregular verbs do not follow this pattern. (*Startled,* they ran from the house. *Spun* glass is delicate. A *broken* cup lay there.)

Passive voice. *See* **Voice.**

Past tense. *See* **Verb tense.**

Perfect tenses. *See* **Verb tense.**

Person Person is a means of classifying pronouns.

A ***first-person*** pronoun refers to the person speaking. (*We* came.)

A ***second-person*** pronoun refers to the person spoken to. (*You* ask.)

A ***third-person*** pronoun refers to some other person(s) or thing(s) being spoken of. (*They* played.)

Personal pronoun. *See* **Pronoun.**

Phrase A phrase is a group of related words that does not contain a verb and its subject. (*noticing everything, under a chair*)

An ***adjective phrase*** modifies a noun or a pronoun. (The label *on the bottle* has faded.)

An ***adverb phrase*** modifies a verb, an adjective, or an adverb. (Come *to the fair.*)

An ***appositive phrase*** explains one or more words in a sentence. (Mary, *a champion gymnast,* won gold medals at the Olympics.)

A ***gerund phrase*** consists of a gerund and its modifiers and complements. (*Fixing the leak* will take only a few minutes.)

An ***infinitive phrase*** consists of an infinitive, its modifiers, and its complements. (*To prepare for a test,* study in a quiet place.)

A ***participial phrase*** consists of a participle and its modifiers and complements. (*Straggling to the finish line,* the last runners arrived.)

A ***prepositional phrase*** consists of a preposition, its object, and the object's modifiers. (The Saint Bernard does rescue work *in the Swiss Alps.*)

A ***verb phrase*** consists of a main verb and one or more helping verbs. (*might have ordered*)

Possessive A noun or pronoun that is possessive shows ownership or relationship. (*Dan's* story, *my* doctor)

Possessive noun. *See* **Noun.**

Possessive pronoun. *See* **Pronoun.**

Predicate The predicate of a sentence tells what the subject is or does. (The van *runs well even in winter.* The job *seems too complicated.*) *See also* **Complete predicate; Simple predicate.**

Predicate adjective. *See* **Adjective.**

Predicate nominative A predicate nominative is a noun or pronoun that follows a linking verb and renames or explains the subject. (Joan is a computer *operator.* The winner of the prize was *he.*)

Predicate pronoun. *See* **Pronoun.**

Preposition A preposition is a word that relates its object to another part of the sentence or to the sentence as a whole. (Alfredo leaped *onto* the stage.)

Prepositional phrase. *See* **Phrase.**

Present tense. *See* **Verb tense.**

Pronoun A pronoun replaces a noun or another pronoun. Some pronouns allow a writer or speaker to avoid repeating a proper noun. Other pronouns let a writer refer to an unknown or unidentified person or thing.

A ***demonstrative pronoun*** singles out one or more persons or things. (*This* is the letter.)

An ***indefinite pronoun*** refers to an unidentified person or thing. (*Everyone* stayed home. Will you hire *anybody?*)

An ***intensive pronoun*** emphasizes a noun or pronoun. (The teacher *himself* sold tickets.)

An ***interrogative pronoun*** asks a question. (*What* happened to you?)

A ***personal pronoun*** shows a distinction of person. (*I* came. *You* see. *He* knows.)

A ***possessive pronoun*** shows ownership. (*My* spaghetti is always good. Are *your* parents coming to the play?)

A ***predicate pronoun*** follows a linking verb and renames the subject. (The owners of the store were *they.*)

A ***reflexive pronoun*** reflects an action back on the subject of the sentence. (Joe helped *himself.*)

A ***relative pronoun*** relates a subordinate clause to the word it modifies. (The draperies, *which* had been made by hand, were ruined in the fire.)

Pronoun-antecedent agreement. *See* **Agreement.**

Pronoun forms

The ***subject form*** of a pronoun is used when the pronoun is the subject of a sentence or follows a linking verb as a predicate pronoun. (*She* fell. The star was *she*.)

The ***object form*** of a pronoun is used when the pronoun is the direct or indirect object of a verb or verbal or the object of a preposition. (We sent *him* the bill. We ordered food for *them*.)

Proper adjective. *See* **Adjective.**

Proper noun. *See* **Noun.**

Punctuation Punctuation clarifies the structure of sentences. See the punctuation chart below.

Quotation A quotation consists of words from another speaker or writer.

A ***direct quotation*** is the exact words of a speaker or writer. (Martin said, *"The homecoming game has been postponed."*)

A ***divided quotation*** is a quotation separated by words that identify the speaker. (*"The homecoming game,"* said Martin, *"has been postponed."*)

An ***indirect quotation*** reports what a person said without giving the exact words. (*Martin said that the homecoming game had been postponed.*)

Reflexive pronoun. *See* **Pronoun.**

Regular verb. *See* **Verb.**

Relative pronoun. *See* **Pronoun.**

Run-on sentence A run-on sentence consists of two or more sentences written incorrectly as one. (*The sunset was beautiful its brilliant colors lasted only a short time.*)

Sentence A sentence expresses a complete thought. The chart at the top of the next page shows the four kinds of sentences.

A ***complex sentence*** contains one main clause and one or more subordinate clauses. (*Open the windows before you go to bed. If she falls, I'll help her up.*)

A ***compound sentence*** is made up of two or more independent clauses joined by a conjunction, a colon, or a semicolon. (*The ship finally docked, and the passengers quickly left.*)

A ***simple sentence*** consists of only one main clause. (*My friend volunteers at a nursing home.*)

Punctuation	Uses	Examples	
Apostrophe (')	Shows possession	Lou's garage	Alva's script
	Indicates a contraction	I'll help you.	The baby's tired.
Colon (:)	Introduces a list or quotation	three colors: red, green, and yellow	
	Divides some compound sentences	This was the problem: we had to find our own way home.	
Comma (,)	Separates ideas	The glass broke, and the juice spilled all over.	
	Separates modifiers	The lively, talented cheerleaders energized the team.	
	Separates items in series	We visited London, Rome, and Paris.	
Exclamation point (!)	Ends an exclamatory sentence	Have a wonderful time!	
Hyphen (-)	Joins parts of some compound words	daughter-in-law, great-grandson	
Period (.)	Ends a declarative sentence	Swallows return to Capistrano in spring.	
	Indicates most abbreviations	min. qt. Blvd. Gen. Jan.	
Question mark (?)	Ends an interrogative sentence	Where are you going?	
Semicolon (;)	Divides some compound sentences	Marie is an expert dancer; she teaches a class in tap.	
	Separates items in series that contain commas	Jerry visited Syracuse, New York; Athens, Georgia; and Tampa, Florida.	

Kind of Sentence	Example
Declarative (statement)	Our team won.
Exclamatory (strong feeling)	I had a great time!
Imperative (request, command)	Take the next exit.
Interrogative (question)	Who owns the car?

Sentence fragment A sentence fragment is a group of words that is only part of a sentence. (*When he arrived. Merrily yodeling.*)

Simple predicate A simple predicate is the verb in the predicate. (John *collects* foreign stamps.)

Simple subject A simple subject is the key noun or pronoun in the subject. (The new *house* is empty.)

Split infinitive A split infinitive occurs when a modifier is placed between the word *to* and the verb in an infinitive. (*to quickly speak*)

Subject The subject is the part of a sentence that tells whom or what the sentence is about. (*Lou* swam.) *See* **Complete subject; Simple subject.**

Subject-verb agreement. *See* **Agreement.**

Subordinate clause. *See* **Clause.**

Superlative. *See* **Adjective; Adverb.**

Transitive verb. *See* **Verb.**

Unidentified reference An unidentified reference usually occurs when the word *it, they, this, which,* or *that* is used. (In California *they* have good weather most of the time.)

Verb A verb expresses an action, a condition, or a state of being.

An ***action verb*** tells what the subject does, has done, or will do. The action may be physical or mental. (Susan *trains* guide dogs.)

An ***auxiliary verb*** is added to a main verb to express tense, add emphasis, or otherwise affect the meaning of the verb. Together the auxiliary and main verb make up a verb phrase. (*will* intend, *could have* gone)

A ***linking verb*** expresses a state of being or connects the subject with a word or words that describe the subject. (The ice *feels* cold.) Linking verbs include *appear, be* (*am, are, is, was, were, been, being*), *become, feel, grow, look, remain, seem, smell, sound,* and *taste.*

A ***main verb*** expresses action or state of being; it appears with one or more auxiliary verbs. (will be *staying*)

The ***progressive form*** of a verb shows continuing action. (She *is knitting.*)

The past tense and past participle of a ***regular verb*** are formed by adding *-d* or *-ed*. (*open, opened*) An ***irregular verb*** does not follow this pattern. (*throw, threw, thrown; shrink, shrank, shrunk*)

The action of a ***transitive verb*** is directed toward someone or something, called the object of a verb. (Leo *washed* the windows.) An ***intransitive verb*** has no object. (The leaves *scattered.*)

Verb phrase. *See* **Phrase.**

Verb tense Verb tense shows the time of an action or the time of a state of being.

The ***present tense*** places an action or condition in the present. (Jan *takes* piano lessons.)

The ***past tense*** places an action or condition in the past. (We *came* to the party.)

The ***future tense*** places an action or condition in the future. (You *will understand.*)

The ***present perfect tense*** describes an action in an indefinite past time or an action that began in the past and continues in the present. (*has called, have known*)

The ***past perfect tense*** describes one action that happened before another action in the past. (*had scattered, had mentioned*)

The ***future perfect tense*** describes an event that will be finished before another future action begins. (*will have taught, shall have appeared*)

Verbal A verbal is formed from a verb and acts as another part of speech, such as a noun, an adjective, or an adverb.

Verbal	Example
Gerund (used as a noun)	Lamont enjoys *swimming.*
Infinitive (used as an adjective, an adverb, or a noun)	Everyone wants *to help.*
Participle (used as an adjective)	The leaves *covering the drive* made it slippery.

Voice The voice of a verb depends on whether the subject performs or receives the action of the verb.

In the ***active voice*** the subject of the sentence performs the verb's action. (We *knew* the answer.)

In the ***passive voice*** the subject of the sentence receives the action of the verb. (The team *has been eliminated.*)

Index of Fine Art

Index of Skills

Literary Terms

Reading and Critical Thinking Skills

Grammar, Usage, and Mechanics

Writing Skills, Modes, and Formats

Vocabulary Skills

Research and Study Skills

Speaking, Listening, and Viewing

Index of Titles and Authors

Page numbers that appear in italics refer to biographical information.

T

U

V

W

Y

Acknowledgments *(continued)*

Oxford University Press: "The Seafarer," from *An Anthology of Old English Poetry,* translated by Charles W. Kennedy. Copyright © 1960 by Oxford University Press, Inc.; renewed 1988 by Elizabeth D. Kennedy. Reprinted by permission of the publisher.

Rosanna White Norton: "The Wife's Lament," from *The Women Poets in English,* edited by Ann Stanford. Reprinted by permission of Rosanna White Norton, trustee.

Penguin Books Ltd: Excerpts from *A History of the English Church and People* by Bede, translated by Leo Sherley-Price, revised translation by R. E. Latham (Penguin Classics 1955, revised edition 1968); Copyright © 1955, 1968 by Leo Sherley-Price. Excerpts from "The Prologue," "The Pardoner's Prologue," and "The Pardoner's Tale," from *The Canterbury Tales* by Geoffrey Chaucer, translated by Nevill Coghill. (Penguin Classics 1951, fourth revised edition 1977). Copyright © 1951, 1958, 1960, 1975, 1977 by Nevill Coghill.
Excerpts from Chapter 1 from *The Book of Margery Kempe,* translated by B. A. Windeatt (Penguin Classics, 1985); Copyright © 1985 B. A. Windeatt. Reproduced by permission of Penguin Books Ltd.

The Folio Society: Excerpts from *The Pastons: A Family in the Wars of the Roses,* edited by Richard Barber (The Folio Society 1981; Boydell Press [Woodbridge, U.K., and Rochester, NY] 1993). Reprinted by permission of The Folio Society.

University of Chicago Press: Excerpts from *Sir Gawain and the Green Knight,* translated by John Gardner. Copyright © 1965 by The University of Chicago. Reprinted by permission of The University of Chicago Press.

Northwestern University Press: From the preface by William Caxton from *Le Morte d'Arthur,* parts seven and eight by Sir Thomas Malory, edited by D. S. Brewer. Copyright © 1968 by D. S. Brewer. Reprinted by permission.

Viking Penguin: "The Siege of Lanka" and "Rama and Ravana in Battle" from *The Ramayana,* translated by R. K. Narayan. Copyright © 1972 by R. K. Narayan. Used by permission of Viking Penguin, a division of Penguin Books USA Inc.

The New York Times: "How Muggsy Bogues Overcame Such Long Odds" by Ira Berkow, from *The New York Times,* February 26, 1995; Copyright © 1995 by The New York Times Company. Reprinted by permission.

Unit Two

University of Alabama Press: Sonnet 169 and Sonnet 292 from *Petrarch: Selected Poems,* English translation by Anthony Mortimer, Copyright © 1977 by The University of Alabama Press. Used by permission of The University of Alabama Press.

Rondor Music Publishing: "Love over Gold" by Mark Knopfler, from the Dire Straits album *Love over Gold;* Copyright © 1982 Chariscourt Limited (PRS). Almo Music Corporation (ASCAP) administers in the United States and Canada. All rights reserved. International Copyright © secured. Used by permission of Rondor Music Publishing, a division of Almo Music Corporation.

Unit Three

University of California Press: Excerpts from *Diary of Samuel Pepys,* edited by Robert Latham and William Matthews. Copyright © 1972–1986 by The Master, Fellows and Scholars of Magdalen College, Cambridge, Robert Latham, and the Executors of William Matthews. Reprinted by permission of the University of California Press, Berkeley, California.

University of Illinois Press: "The Acorn and the Pumpkin" and "The Value of Knowledge" from *The Fables of La Fontaine,* translated by Norman R. Shapiro. Copyright © 1985, 1988 by Norman R. Shapiro. Used with the permission of the author and of the University of Illinois Press.

Unit Four

Harcourt Brace & Company: "The Lotus-Blossom Cowers," from *Heinrich Heine: Paradox and Poet, The Poems* by Louis Untermeyer, copyright 1937 by Harcourt Brace & Company and renewed 1965 by Louis Untermeyer, reprinted by permission of the publisher.

Lucien Stryk: Selected haiku from *Penguin Book of Zen Poetry,* edited and translated by Lucien Stryk and Takashi Ikemoto. London: Penguin Books Ltd., 1977. Reprinted by permission of the author.

Time Inc.: First two paragraphs in "A New Divide Between Haves and Have-Nots," from *Time* Magazine, Spring 1995; Copyright © 1995 Time Inc. Reprinted by permission.

Unit Five

Henry Holt and Company, Inc., and The Society of Authors: "To an Athlete Dying Young" and "When I Was One-and-Twenty," from *The Collected Poems of A. E. Housman* by A. E. Housman. Copyright 1939, 1940 by Henry Holt & Co., Inc. Copyright © 1967 by Robert E. Symons. Reprinted by permission of Henry Holt and Company, Inc., and The Society of Authors as the literary representative of the Estates of A. E. Housman.

Unit Six

A. P. Watt Ltd.: "The Kit-Bag" by Algernon Blackwood. Reprinted by permission of A. P. Watt Ltd. on behalf of Sheila Reeves.

"The Truth About George," from *The World of Mr. Mulliner* by P. G. Wodehouse. Reprinted by permission of A. P. Watt Ltd. on behalf of The Trustees of the Wodehouse Estate.

Alfred A. Knopf, Inc.: "The Infant Prodigy," from *Stories of Three Decades* by Thomas Mann, edited by H. T. Lowe-Porter. Copyright 1936 by Alfred A. Knopf, Inc.

"A Cup of Tea," from *The Short Stories of Katherine Mansfield* by Katherine Mansfield. Copyright 1923 by Alfred A. Knopf, Inc., and renewed 1951 by John Middleton Murry.

Reprinted by permission of the publisher, Alfred A. Knopf, Inc.

Harcourt Brace & Company and The Hogarth Press: "The Duchess and the Jeweller," from *A Haunted House and Other Short Stories* by Virginia Woolf;

Copyright 1944 and renewed 1972 by Harcourt Brace & Company, reprinted by permission of the publisher and the Hogarth Press.

Cambridge University Press: Excerpt from *Virginia Woolf* by E. M. Forster. Reprinted with the permission of Cambridge University Press.

Random House, Inc., and Faber and Faber Ltd.: "What I Expected," from *Selected Poems* by Stephen Spender. Copyright © 1934 and renewed 1962 by Stephen Spender. Reprinted by permission of Random House, Inc., and Faber and Faber Ltd.

Penguin USA and G. T. Sassoon: "Dreamers," from *Collected Poems of Siegfried Sassoon* by Siegfried Sassoon. Copyright 1918, 1920 by E. P. Dutton. Copyright 1936, 1946, 1947, 1948 by Siegfried Sassoon. Used by permission of Viking Penguin, a division of Penguin Books USA Inc., and George Sassoon.

Paul Berry, Literary Executor, and Virago Press, London: Excerpts from *Testament of Youth* by Vera Brittain are included with the permission of Paul Berry, literary executor for Vera Brittain, and The Virago Press, London.

Curtis Brown Ltd.: "Be Ye Men of Valour," from *Blood, Toil, Tears and Sweat* by Winston Churchill. Reproduced with permission of Curtis Brown Ltd., London, on behalf of the Estate of Sir Winston S. Churchill. Copyright © the Estate of Sir Winston S. Churchill.

"The Demon Lover," from *The Collected Stories of Elizabeth Bowen* by Elizabeth Bowen. Copyright © 1941 by Elizabeth Bowen.

Reproduced by permission of Curtis Brown, London.

Faber and Faber Limited: "To My Mother" from *Collected Poems* by George Barker. Copyright © 1987 by George Barker. Reprinted by permission of Faber and Faber Ltd.

Pantheon Books: Excerpts from *Letters from Westerbork* by Etty Hillesum, translated by Arnold J. Pomerans. Translation copyright © 1986 by Random House, Inc. Reprinted by permission of Pantheon Books, a division of Random House, Inc.

Reece Halsey Agency: Excerpt from "Words and Behavior," from *Collected Essays* by Aldous Huxley. Reprinted by permission of Dorris Halsey, as agent for the Aldous Huxley Literary Estate.

Harcourt Brace & Company: "A Hanging," from *Shooting an Elephant and Other Essays* by George Orwell, copyright 1950 by Sonia Brownell Orwell and renewed 1978 by Sonia Pitt-Rivers. Reprinted by permission of Harcourt Brace & Company, the Estate of the late Sonia Brownell Orwell, and Martin Secker & Warburg Ltd.

Simon & Schuster, Inc.: "Sailing to Byzantium" by William Butler Yeats, Copyright 1928 by Macmillan Publishing Company, renewed 1956 by Georgie Yeats, and "The Second Coming" by William Butler Yeats, Copyright 1924 by Macmillan Publishing Company, renewed 1952 by Bertha Georgie Yeats, from *The Poems of W. B. Yeats: A New Edition,* edited by Richard J. Finneran. Reprinted with the permission of Simon & Schuster, Inc.

Viking Penguin and Laurence Pollinger Ltd.: "The Rocking-Horse Winner" by D. H. Lawrence; Copyright 1933 by the Estate of D. H. Lawrence, renewed © 1961 by Angelo Ravagli and C. M. Weekley, Executors of the Estate of Frieda Lawrence Ravagli. From *Complete Short Stories of D. H. Lawrence* by D. H. Lawrence. Used by permission of Viking Penguin, a division of Penguin Books USA Inc., and Laurence Pollinger Ltd.

Harcourt Brace & Company and Faber and Faber Limited: "Preludes" from *Collected Poems 1909–1962* by T. S. Eliot, copyright 1936 by Harcourt Brace & Company, copyright © 1963, 1964 by T. S. Eliot, reprinted by permission of the publisher and Faber and Faber Limited.

Random House, Inc.: "Musée des Beaux Arts" and "The Unknown Citizen," from *W. H. Auden: Collected Poems* by W. H. Auden, edited by Edward Mendelson. Copyright © 1940 and renewed 1968 by W. H. Auden. Reprinted by permission of Random House, Inc.

New Directions Publishing Corporation and David Higham Associates: "Do Not Go Gentle into That Good Night" and "In My Craft or Sullen Art," from *Poems of Dylan Thomas* by Dylan Thomas. Copyright 1946 by New Directions Publishing Corporation, Copyright 1952 by Dylan Thomas. Reprinted by permission of New Directions Publishing Corporation and David Higham Associates.

Indiana University Press and Fondo de Cultura Económica: "Writing/Escritura" from *Selected Poems of Octavio Paz,* edited and translated by Muriel Rukeyser. Copyright © 1963 by Octavio Paz and Muriel Rukeyser. Reprinted by permission of Indiana University Press and Fondo de Cultura Económica, Mexico.

Unit Seven

Grove/Atlantic, Inc., and Murray Pollinger: "At the Pitt-Rivers," from *Pack of Cards and Other Stories* by Penelope Lively. Copyright © 1986 by Penelope Lively. Used by permission of Grove/Atlantic, Inc., and Murray Pollinger, Literary Agent.

Houghton Mifflin Company and McClelland & Stewart: "Significant Moments in the Life of My Mother," from *Bluebeard's Egg* by Margaret Atwood. Copyright © 1983, 1986 by O. W. Toad, Ltd. First American edition 1986. Reprinted by permission of Houghton Mifflin Company and McClelland & Stewart Inc. All rights reserved.

Simon & Schuster and Jonathan Clowes Ltd.: "A Sunrise on the Veld," from *African Stories* by Doris Lessing. Copyright © 1965 by Doris Lessing; Copyright renewed © 1993 by Doris Lessing. Reprinted by permission of Simon & Schuster, Inc., and of Jonathan Clowes Limited, London, on behalf of Doris Lessing.

Farrar, Straus & Giroux, Inc., and Faber and Faber Ltd.: "Digging," from *Poems 1965–1975* by Seamus Heaney. Copyright © 1980 by Seamus Heaney. Used by arrangement with Farrar, Straus & Giroux, Inc., and Faber and Faber Ltd. All rights reserved.

Faber and Faber Ltd.: "The Horses," from *The Hawk in the Rain* by Ted Hughes. Reprinted by permission of Faber and Faber Ltd.

The Ecco Press: "In Music" from *Provinces* by Czeslaw Milosz. Copyright © 1991 by Czeslaw Milosz Royalties Inc. First printed by The Ecco Press in 1991. Reprinted by permission of The Ecco Press.

Scovil Chichak Galen Literary Agency: "We'll Never Conquer Space" by Arthur C. Clarke. Reprinted by permission of the author and the author's agents, Scovil Chichak Galen Literary Agency, Inc., New York.

Viking Penguin: "The Distant Past," from *Angels at the Ritz and Other Stories* by William Trevor. Copyright © 1975 by William Trevor. Used by permission of Viking Penguin, a division of Penguin Books USA Inc.

Doubleday and Harold Ober Associates: "Civil Peace," from *Girls at War and Other Stories* by Chinua Achebe. Copyright © 1972, 1973 by Chinua Achebe. Used by permission of Doubleday, a division of Bantam Doubleday Dell Publishing Group, Inc., and Harold Ober Associates Incorporated.

Wole Soyinka: "Telephone Conversation" by Wole Soyinka, first published in *Reflections: Nigerian Prose and Verse,* edited by Frances Ademola. Copyright © Wole Soyinka. Reprinted by permission of Wole Soyinka.

Farrar, Straus & Giroux, Inc.: "XXIII" from *Midsummer* by Derek Walcott. Copyright © 1984 by Derek Walcott. Used by arrangement with Farrar, Straus & Giroux, Inc. All rights reserved.

Russell & Volkening, Inc.: "Six Feet of the Country" from *Six Feet of the Country and Other Stories* by Nadine Gordimer. Copyright © 1956 by Nadine Gordimer, Copyright © renewed 1984 by Nadine Gordimer. Reprinted by permission of Russell & Volkening as agents for the author.

Agencia Literaria Carmen Balcells, S.A.: Excerpts from "Writing as an Act of Hope" by Isabel Allende in *Paths of Resistance,* edited by William Zinsser. Copyright © 1989 by Isabel Allende. Reprinted by permission of the author's agent.

Grove/Atlantic, Inc., and Faber and Faber Ltd.: "That's All" from *Revue Sketches* by Harold Pinter. Copyright © 1966 by H. Pinter Ltd. Used by permission of Grove/Atlantic, Inc., and Faber and Faber Ltd.

Georges Borchardt, Inc.: "The First Year of My Life," from *The Stories of Muriel Spark* by Muriel Spark. Copyright © 1985 by Copyright Administration Limited. Reprinted by permission of Georges Borchardt, Inc.

Bibliotheca Islamica: "The Happy Man" from *God's World* by Naguib Mahfouz, translated from the Arabic by Akef Abadir and Roger Allen. Reprinted by permission of the publisher, Bibliotheca Islamica, Inc.

Pantheon Books and Kingsmarkham Enterprises Ltd.: "Paintbox Place" from *Collected Stories* by Ruth Rendell. Copyright © 1987 by Kingsmarkham Enterprises Ltd. Reprinted by permission of Pantheon Books, a division of Random House, Inc., and Kingsmarkham Enterprises Ltd.

Alan Holden: "It Is Not Bred in Me," from *Air and Chill Earth* by Molly Holden. Copyright © by Alan Holden. By permission of Alan Holden.

New Directions Publishing Corp.: "The Frog Prince" and "Not Waving but Drowning" from *Collected Poems* by Stevie Smith. Copyright © 1972 by New Directions Publishing Corp. Reprinted by permission of New Directions Publishing Corp.

Scholastic, Inc.: Excerpt from "Give Me Shelter" by Ken Silverstein, from *Scholastic Update,* March 11, 1994. By permission of Scholastic, Inc.

The editors have made every effort to trace the ownership of all copyrighted material found in this book and to make full acknowledgment for its use. Omissions brought to our attention will be corrected in a subsequent edition.

Art Credits

Author Photographs and Portraits

61 The Bettmann Archive. **108, 117, 216** *bottom left,* **227** *bottom left,* **266** *bottom,* **288** *bottom* The Granger Collection, New York. **216** *bottom right,* **221, 227** *bottom right,* **288** *top* North Wind Picture Archives. **239** *bottom,* **275** *bottom,* **280** *bottom,* **299** *bottom* Culver Pictures. **305** *bottom,* **337, 343, 349, 355** *bottom,* **367** *left,* **367** *right,* **385, 399** The Granger Collection, New York. **404** *bottom* National Gallery of Art, Washington, D.C. **412, 424, 431** *bottom,* **439** *bottom,* **446, 458** The Granger Collection, New York. **461** Mary Evans Picture Library. **490** *bottom,* **510, 515, 780** Culver Pictures. **495** *left, Portrait of Bashō,* Suzuki Manrei. New Orleans (Louisiana) Museum of Art, anonymous donor; *right* Heibonsha Ltd., Tokyo. **516** *top, Jane Austen* (about 1810), Cassandra Austen. Pencil and watercolor. The Granger Collection, New York. **534** *bottom,* **545** *bottom,* **559** *bottom,* **596** The Granger Collection, New York. **549, 792** German Information Center, New York. **587** Stock Montage. **603** *left* Courtesy of Armstrong Browning Library, Baylor University, Waco, Texas; *right* The Granger Collection, New York. **619, 636, 654, 676, 682** *bottom,* **689, 695** The Granger Collection, New York. **700, 921** The Bettmann Archive. **747, 825** *bottom,* **833, 849, 894, 943, 965, 973, 987** The Granger Collection, New York. **953** UPI/Bettmann. **808, 862, 927, 980** *bottom* Hulton Deutsch Collection Ltd. **819** Archive Photos. **870** Woodfin Camp. **904** Elliott Erwitt/Camera Press/Globe Photos. **910, 991, 1045, 1098** *left,* **1127, 1148** *bottom* Globe Photos. **1020** Jane Brown/Camera Press/Globe Photos. **1052** *left* Billet Potter/Camera Press/Globe Photos; *right* Fay Godwin/Camera Press/Globe Photos. **1035, 1098** *right* Copyright © Layle Silbert. **1056, 1138** AP/Wide World. **1063** Jay Kay Klein. **1083** Jane Brown/Camera Press/Globe Photos. **1090** The Schomburg Center for Research in Black Culture, The New York Public Library, Astor, Lenox and Tilden Foundations. **1111** Reuters/Bettmann. **1120** R. Drinkwater/Camera Press/Globe Photos. **1167** Copyright © Sally Soames. **1175** *bottom* Hulton Deutsch Collection Ltd.

Commissioned Art and Photography

xxxii–1, 2 *top,* **4–5, 25, 43** *left, center, right,* **68, 78–82, 88–89, 98, 153** *top,* **190–191, 192** *top,* **194–195, 229, 231, 233, 247, 250, 310–317, 324** *top,* **336, 370–374, 439** *top,* **463** *center,* **464–465, 469, 488, 518–523, 563** *bottom,* **564–567, 599, 639–651** *top,* **682** *top,* **683** *left, right,* **691, 782–783, 834–839, 848, 851, 859, 880, 905, 906, 909** *top,* **910** *top,* **940** *right,* **942** *left,* **958, 961, 963, 992–993, 1007** *background,* **1012, 1064–1066, 1068–1069, 1090, 1110, 1150–1151, 1176–1178, 1182** Sharon Hoogstraten.

2 *bottom,* **84–85, 192–193, 244, 248–249, 376–377, 462** *top,* **463, 464–465, 520** *bottom,* **521** *center,* **562, 563** *top,* **567–568, 662–667, 748–754, 836** *top,* **994–999** Allan Landau.

26–27, 30–31 Stephen Johnson.

35, 36–37, 140, 145, 146 *left,* **148, 492–493, 555** *background,* **556, 708, 714, 717, 720, 725, 726, 727** *bottom,* **727** *top left,* **731, 734, 744, 758** *background* Rebecca McClellan.

89–97, 99–105, 140–141, 145–148 *calligraphy* Sharon D. Siegel.
141, 146, 148–149, 151 Lorraine Silvestri.
704, 707, 712, 718, 727 *top right,* **735, 737** Nina Berkson.
Maps: **14, 16** *background* John Sandford.

Time Lines

12–13 *Hadrian's Wall* Nawrocki Stock Photo, Inc.; *helmet* The Granger Collection, New York; *Battle of Crécy* Bibliothèque National, Paris, and Giraudon/Art Resource, New York; *Prioress* Ellesmere manuscript of *The Canterbury Tales* (about 1410), The Huntington Library, San Marino, California; *candlestick* Photo Copyright © British Museum; *sandals* Museum of London; *sundial* (two images), R. Krubner/H. Armstrong Roberts.

202–203 *Henry VIII* (1518), unknown artist. The Granger Collection, New York; *map of Utopia* The Granger Collection, New York; *Queen Elizabeth* (about 1588), attributed to George Cower. The Granger Collection, New York; *bible* The King James Bible, first edition, 1611, The Granger Collection, New York; *microscope* (about 1675) used by Robert Hooke, Science & Society Picture Library, London; *household items* two basting spoons, an Elizabeth I Apostle spoon (1561), and a William III spoon (late 17th century), Christie's Images, London; *timepiece* (two images), Ashburnham watch (mid-17th century), Courtesy of the Bickersteth Family, Ashburnham, England.

320–321 *King Charles II Landing at Dover* (about 1660–1685), Hess. The Bettmann Archive; *James II* (1684), Sir Godfrey Kneller, Courtesy of the National Portrait Gallery, London; *Anne, England's Last Stuart Monarch* (about 1694), unknown artist. Courtesy of the National Portrait Gallery, London; *coin* British coin commemorating the capture of Quebec, Copyright © Hulton Deutsch Collection Ltd.; *washstand* 18th-century washstand, Cooper-Bridgeman Library; *bed* Carved day bed (1695), private collection, Bridgeman/Art Resource, New York; *watch* (two images), 18th-century painted watch, Copyright © British Museum.

474–475 *William Wordsworth* (1818), Benjamin Robert Haydon. Courtesy of the National Portrait Gallery, London; *Mary Shelley* (1841), Richard Rothwell. The Granger Collection, New York; *Liverpool and Manchester Railway: Stephenson's Bridge near Ranhill* (about 1830), unknown artist. Museum of British Transport, London, Bridgeman/Art Resource; *night lamp* (about 1820), Victoria and Albert Museum/Art Resource; *iron* (early 19th century), from *Everyday Life Through the Ages,* Copyright © 1992 Reader's Digest; *clock* (two images), Twelve-month equation clock (1830), Charles Edward Viner. Collection of L. A. Mayer Memorial Institute for Islamic Art, Jerusalem, Israel.

574–575 *University of London in the 1860s* Copyright © Hulton Deutsch Collection Ltd.; *Prince Albert* (1867), F. X. Winterhalter. Oil on canvas, The Granger Collection, New York; *Treasure Island illustration, Israel Hands* (1911), N. C. Wyeth. Oil on canvas, 47¼″ × 38½″, New Britain (Connecticut) Museum of American Art, Harriet Russell Stanley Fund, Photo by Michael Agee; *mangle* (19th century), Copyright © Marshall Cavendish; *Benz Viktoria* (1895), Photo by Peter Roberts; *Big Ben* (two images), Copyright © Geoffrey C. Garner/Superstock.

760–761 *Emmeline Pankhurst* (1918), UPI/Bettmann; *Titanic* Underwood Collection/The Bettmann Archive, New York; *Guernica* (1937), Pablo Picasso.

Copyright © ARS, New York, Museo del Prado, Madrid, Spain, and Giraudon/Art Resource, New York; *1984* by George Orwell, Copyright © 1949 by Harcourt Brace Jovanovich. Used by permission of Harcourt Brace & Company; *California Clipper* Pan American Airways, H. Armstrong Roberts; *woman on telephone* H. Armstrong Roberts; *Art Deco clock* (two images), General Electric clock (about 1935), from *Pastime* by Philip Collins. Copyright © 1993, published by Chronicle Books. **1004–1005** *Samuel Beckett* Copyright © Beppe Arvidsson/Camera Press, London/Globe Photos; *Sputnik 1* Copyright © Robert Phillips/*Life* Magazine/Time, Inc.; *barrister* Copyright © 1995 Stuart Franklin/Magnum Photos; *Ted Hughes* Copyright © Michael Blackman/Camera Press, London/Globe Photos; *Nelson Mandela* Copyright © 1994 John Harrington/Black Star; *1950s television, Concorde supersonic airplane* H. Armstrong Roberts; *watch* (two images), Casio Pulse Monitor Watch by Casio, Inc.

Miscellaneous Art Credits

xi Pilgrims leaving Canterbury (about 1400), English illuminated manuscript. The Granger Collection, New York. **xii** Detail of Arthur from the Nine Heroes Tapestries (about 1385), probably Nicolas Bataille. The Metropolitan Museum of Art, New York, The Cloisters Collection, Munsey Fund, 1932 (32.130.3a). **xvi** *Portrait of a Young Woman, Called Mademoiselle Charlotte du Val d'Ognes* (about 1800), unknown French artist. Oil on canvas, 63½″ × 50⅝″, The Metropolitan Museum of Art, bequest of Isaac D. Fletcher, 1917. Mr. and Mrs. Isaac D. Fletcher Collection (17.120.204). Copyright © The Metropolitan Museum of Art. **xxi** *Am Meer* [By the sea] (1875), Anselm Feuerbach. Kunstmuseum Düsseldorf im Ehrenhof, Germany. **xxiii** National Archives. **xxv** NASA. **xxvi** Detail of *Au cinquième* [On the fifth floor]: *A Portrait of the Artist's Wife* (about 1940), William Leech. Oil on canvas, 74 cm × 60 cm, National Gallery of Ireland, Dublin. **2** *bottom* The Bettmann Archive. **3** *top* Copyright © 1995 Dilip Mehta/Contact Press Images; *bottom* Copyright © Paul Harris/Tony Stone Images. **14** *top left* Scabbard boss from Sutton Hoo ship burial (seventh century), The Granger Collection, New York; *bottom left* Gundestrup cauldron (about 100 B.C.), Celtic. Detail from inner plate depicting the god Teutates accepting human sacrifice from warriors. Embossed silver, gilded, probably from Gaul. National Museum, Copenhagen, Denmark. Erich Lessing/Art Resource, New York. **15** *top left* M. Berman/H. Armstrong Roberts; *bottom right* Silver groat of King Henry VI of England. Ancient Art and Architecture Collection, London, England. **16** *bottom* The beginning of the Gospel of St. Luke. Lindisfarne Gospels (about A.D. 698) Cott. Nero D. IV. f. 139. British Library, London. Bridgeman/Art Resource, New York; *top* Portrait of St. John, with the tools of a scribe, folio 291v from the Book of Kells. Trinity College Library, by permission of the Board of Trinity College, Dublin. **17** *top* Knudsens-Giraudon/Art Resource, New York; *bottom* Alfred the Great in majesty: detail of jewel worked in cloisonné enamel, late 800s. The Granger Collection, New York. **18** *left* By permission of The British Library, London; *right* John Bethell Photography. **19** MS. Douce 383, f. 16. The Bodleian Library, University of Oxford, Great Britain. **20** *top center* Suit of armor for George IV of Puchheim (about 1515). Kunsthistorisches Museum, Vienna, Austria. Erich

Lessing/Art Resource, New York; *top right, bottom left, bottom right* Bibliothèque Nationale, Paris; *center right* The Magna Carta of Liberties, 1215. Department of the Environment, London. Bridgeman/Art Resource, New York. **21** The Bettmann Archive, New York. **22** *top* Edimedia, Paris; *bottom* Illustration from the Mary Evans Picture Library, London. **29** Knudsens-Giraudon/Art Resource, New York. **31** The Granger Collection, New York. **37** Courtesy of the Royal Ontario Museum, Toronto, Canada. **38, 39** The Granger Collection, New York. **40** Giraudon/Art Resource, New York. **45** Ancient Art and Architecture Collection, London. **51** Copyright © George Hunter/H. Armstrong Roberts. **55** Scala/Art Resource, New York. **63** *bottom right* Detail of the Whale from the Ashmole Bestiary (about 1210). MS. Ashmole 1511, f. 86v, The Bodleian Library, University of Oxford, Great Britain; *top, center left* Copyright © Mapfile/WestLight. **66** The Pierpont Morgan Library/Art Resource, New York. **69** *top* Reproduced by kind permission of *The Times,* London. Copyright. **70** *left* Copyright © Erich Lessing/Art Resource, New York. **71** Trinity College MS. R.17.1 f. 283v. The Master and Fellows of Trinity College, Cambridge, Great Britain. **78, 80, 82** Artifacts courtesy of David Blanding and John Nance. **84–85** Copyright © 1994 Peter Menzel/ Material World. **98** Nawrocki Stock Photo. **103** Detail of the Pardoner. From the Ellesmere manuscript of Chaucer's *Canterbury Tales,* EL 26.C.9 f. 138r, The Huntington Library, San Marino, California. **107** The month of May, from the Playfair Hours. Victoria and Albert Museum, Playfair Hours/ET Archive. **115** Copyright © Julie Habel/West Light. **116** Miniature from Codex Manesse (about 1300), unknown artist. Universitätsbibliothek Heidelberg. Photo by Lossen Foto. **118** Book of Hours, July: Shearing Sheep, Simon Benninck. British Library. Bridgeman/Art Resource, New York. **120** *foreground* Detail of women defending a castle with bow and crossbow (about 1326–1327). Manuscript illumination from *De nobilitatibus, sapientiis, et prudentiis regum* by Walter de Milemete (MS. CH. CH. 92 f. 4r). By permission of the Governing Body of Christ Church, Oxford, Great Britain; *background* With permission of the Trustees of the British Library. **120** *right,* **121, 122, 123** *top left,* **124, 126** *right,* **127** The Governing Body of Christ Church, Oxford, Great Britain. **125** Letter from Richard Calle to Margery Paston, Add. 34889, ff. 78v-79:c, by permission of The British Library. **126** *background* With permission of the Trustees of the British Library. **129** *bottom* The Granger Collection, New York. **130** Canadian Museum of Civilization (#S92-2107). **132** Illustration by Gordon Grant. **152** By permission of The British Library, London. **153** *bottom* Armor (16th century), anonymous, attributed to Chevalier Bayard. Musée de l'Armée, Paris, Giraudon/Art Resource, New York. **170** National Museum of India, New Delhi, India. **171, 172, 174, 176, 178, 179, 181** Photograph from *Angkor* by Michael Freedman and Roger Warner, edited and designed by David Larkin. Photographs copyright © 1990 by Michael Freedman. Reprinted by permission of Houghton Mifflin Company. All rights reserved. **182** *top right* Illustration from *Romance of Alexander* (about 1340), Flemish. The Granger Collection, New York; *top left* By permission of the Folger Shakespeare Library, Washington, D.C. **183** *bottom* By permission of The British Library, London. **185, 186** Woman tending fire and reading. From the Bruges illuminated manuscript, Royal 15.D.1 f.18, by permission of The British Library. **190** *top* UPI/Bettmann; *bottom* Copyright © John Barr/Gamma Liaison. **191** Copyright © 1993 William R. Sallaz/Duomo. **192** The Major League Baseball trademarks and copyrights used with permission from Major League Baseball Properties, Inc. **193** *top* The Major League Baseball trademarks and copyrights used with permission from Major League Baseball

Properties, Inc.; *bottom* Courtesy of Chicago Convention and Tourism Bureau. **197** Courtesy of Image Club Graphics, Inc. **204** *top, Portrait of Henry VIII* (about 1510), Hans Holbein the Younger. Galleria Nazionale d'Arte Antica, Rome, Scala/Art Resource, New York; *bottom, Self-Portrait,* number 15741, Leonardo da Vinci. Biblioteca Reale, Turin, Italy. Scala/Art Resource. **205** *top* Derrick E. Witty/The National Trust Photographic Library, London; *center* Henry VIII's armor (1520). The Board of Trustees of the Royal Armouries; *bottom* The Granger Collection, New York. **206** *top, Edward VI as a Child* (about 1538), Hans Holbein the Younger. Oil on panel, 22⅜″ × 17⅜″, National Gallery of Art, Washington, D.C. Andrew W. Mellon Collection. Photo by Richard Carafelli; *center, Queen Mary I of England* (1544), Master John. The Granger Collection, New York; *bottom* Gold medal of Queen Elizabeth I commemorating defeat of the Spanish Armada in 1588. The Granger Collection, New York. **207** *The Mariners' Mirrour,* map of the English Channel. By permission of the Folger Shakespeare Library, Washington, D.C. **208** *top, Portrait of James I,* Copyright © The Royal Collection, Her Majesty Queen Elizabeth II; *bottom, Charles I on Horseback* (about 1637), Anthony Van Dyck. Canvas, 367 × 292.1 cm, National Gallery, London. **209** *left, Sailing of the Pilgrims from Plymouth, England* (1941), Charles Shimmin. Woolaroc Museum, Bartlesville, Oklahoma; *right* The Granger Collection, New York. **211** *The Huguenot* (1893), Sir John Everett Millais. Christie's, London, Bridgeman/Art Resource, New York. **214** Queen Elizabeth I of England as a princess (about 1542–1547), unknown artist. The Granger Collection, New York. **216** *top* The Granger Collection, New York. **219** Copyright © Dave Bjorn/Tony Stone Worldwide. **224, 225** Details of *The Hireling Shepherd* (1851), William Holman Hunt. Manchester City Art Gallery/A.K.G., Berlin/Superstock. **235** Portrait of Laura, unknown artist. Manuscript Plut. 41, 1. Biblioteca Laurenziana, Florence, Italy. **239** *top* Wolfgang Hille/Leo de Wys. **240** © T. Dietrich/H. Armstrong Roberts. **241** *top* © B. Dobos/H. Armstrong Roberts; *bottom right* © T. Dietrich/H. Armstrong Roberts. **242** *top* The Granger Collection, New York; *bottom* Detail of Globe Theatre, *Visscher's View of London.* By permission of the Folger Shakespeare Library, Washington, D.C. **243** *left* Photofest; *right, Are you sure that we are awake?,* Arthur Rackham. By permission of the Folger Shakespeare Library, Washington, D.C. **246–247** Copyright © Rob Atkins/The Image Bank. **250** *Self-Portrait in Red Jacket,* Mary Mabbutt. Courtesy of Graham Paton Gallery, London. Reproduced from *The Self Portrait—A Modern View* by S. Kelly and E. Lucie Smith, by kind permission of Sarema Press (Publishers) Limited, London. **256** *frame,* **259** Details of *The Return of the Prodigal Son* (1667–1668), Rembrandt van Rijn. The Hermitage Museum, St. Petersburg/Bridgeman Art Library, London/Superstock. **260** Copyright © Chicago Tribune Company. All rights reserved. Used with permission. **263** *center* © Shoji Yoshida/The Image Bank. **266** *top right,* **267, 268** The Granger Collection, New York. **272** *center* The Kremlin Saviour's Tower, Moscow, Russia. © Dave and Les Jacobs/The Stock Broker; *top left background* Camerique/H. Armstrong Roberts; *top right background* H. Abernathy/H. Armstrong Roberts; *bottom left background* Leo de Wys Inc./Casimir; *bottom right background* Leo de Wys Inc./J. Messerschmidt. **277** *background* © Arnulf Husmo/Tony Stone Worldwide. **282–283** *background, The Genus Rosa,* Ellen Willmott. Royal Horticultural Society, Lindley Library. **284** Detail of *The Genus*

Rosa, Ellen Willmott. Royal Horticultural Society, Lindley Library. **285** *background* Erich Lessing/Art Resource, New York. **287** *top right* Detail of *The Proposal* (1872), Adolphe-William Bouguereau. Oil on canvas, 64⅜″ × 44″, The Metropolitan Museum of Art, New York, gift of Mrs. Elliot L. Kamen in memory of her father, Bernard R. Armour, 1960 (60. 122). Copyright © 1994 The Metropolitan Museum of Art. **289** Copyright © Andrew Unangst/The Image Bank. **290–291** *top* Copyright © Suzanne and Nick Geary/Tony Stone Worldwide. **293** Courtesy of the Trustees of the British Museum. **294** The Granger Collection, New York. **295** *background* © 1989 Barry Seidman/The Stock Market. **300** *top* The Granger Collection, New York; *center, The Expulsion from Paradise,* Masaccio. Brancacci Chapel, S. Maria del Carmine, Florence, Italy. Scala/Art Resource, New York. **301** *top, Satan in his Original Glory: "Thou Wast Perfect Till Iniquity Was Found in Thee"* (about 1805), William Blake. Presented by the executors of W. Graham Robertson through the National Art Collections Fund, 1949, Tate Gallery, London/Art Resource, New York; *right, Paradise Lost,* Manuscript of Book I (about 1665). Purchased by Pierpont Morgan, 1904. The Pierpont Morgan Library, New York. (MA 307). **307** Detail of *Adam Tempted by Eve* (1517), Hans Holbein the Younger. Öffentliche Kunstsammlung Basel, Switzerland (313). Photo by Martin Bühler. **309** *album cover* Courtesy Warner Bros. Records, Inc. **310** *top* Copyright © Lee White/WestLight. **314** *center* Copyright © Tim Davis/Tony Stone Images. **322** *top left* Perspective view of the Garden and Chateau de Versailles, France, Pierre Patel. Giraudon/Art Resource, New York; *center* Museum of London; *top right, Charles II,* John M. Wright. The Royal Collection, Copyright © Her Majesty Queen Elizabeth II; *bottom right* Copyright © R. Korh/H. Armstrong Roberts. **323** *top, William III* (1677), unknown artist, after Sir Peter Lely. The Granger Collection, New York; *bottom, Queen Mary II, Wife of William III,* William Wissing. National Portrait Gallery, Edinburgh, Great Britain. Bridgeman/Art Resource. **324** *top, King George I of England* (1716), Sir Godfrey Kneller. Oil on canvas. The Granger Collection, New York; *bottom, George III, Queen Charlotte and Their Six Eldest Children,* Johann Zoffany. The Royal Collection, Copyright © Her Majesty Queen Elizabeth II. **325** *The Boston Massacre, March 5, 1770,* Paul Revere, after a drawing by Henry Pelham. The Granger Collection, New York. **326** *top, Sir Isaac Newton* (about 1726), John Vanderbank. The Granger Collection, New York; *center, The Ladies Waldegrave,* Sir Joshua Reynolds. National Gallery of Scotland; *bottom, Mr. Healey's Sheep,* W. H. Davis. ET Archive/Lincoln Museum and Art Galleries, Great Britain. **338** Copyright © 1993 Richard Laird/FPG International. **343** *top* Detail of *The Sense of Touch* (about 1615–1616), Jusepe de Ribera. Oil on canvas, 45⅝″ × 34¾″, The Norton Simon Foundation, Pasadena, California. **344** *The Crow and the Fox,* Grandville, for *The Fables of La Fontaine.* **345** *background* J. Nettis/H. Armstrong Roberts. **350** Copyright © Chicago Tribune Company. All rights reserved. Used with permission. **355** *center left* The Granger Collection, New York. **368** *top, Daniel Defoe* (1706), unknown artist, after Michiel van der Gucht. Colored engraving, The Granger Collection, New York; *bottom, Rio de Janeiro Bay* (1864), Martin Johnson Heade. Canvas, 17⅞″ × 35⅞″, National Gallery of Art, Washington, D.C., Gift of the Avalon Foundation. **369** *top right* Illustration from *A Field Guide to Eastern Birds.* Copyright © 1980 by Roger Tory Peterson. Reprinted by permission of Houghton Mifflin Company. All rights reserved. **379** Detail of *Woman Reading,* Jerome Janssens. Alte Pinakothek, Munich,

Germany/SEF/Art Resource, New York. **385** *top* Detail of *Portrait of a Young Woman, Called Mademoiselle Charlotte du Val d'Ognes* (about 1800), unknown artist. Oil on canvas, 63½″ × 50⅝″, The Metropolitan Museum of Art, Bequest of Isaac D. Fletcher, 1917. Mr. and Mrs. Isaac D. Fletcher Collection (17.120.204). Copyright © 1981 The Metropolitan Museum of Art. **386** *top, Jonathan Swift,* Charles Jervas. Oil on canvas. The Granger Collection, New York. **388** Copyright © Frank Spooner/Gamma Liaison. **392, 396** Details of *Industry and Idleness: The Idle 'Prentice Executed at Tyburn* (1747), William Hogarth. The Granger Collection, New York. **404** *top* Republican party campaign button from the 1952 presidential election. The Granger Collection, New York. **406–409** Copyright © Hulton Deutsch Collection Ltd. **413** Detail of *Johnson's Ghost Berating Boswell,* unknown artist. Copyright © British Museum. **415** *Solanum macrocarpum,* G. van Spaëndonck, courtesy of the Natural History Museum, London. **424** *top* From *The Thurber Carnival,* published by HarperCollins. Copyright © 1945 James Thurber. Copyright © 1973 Rosemary A. Thurber. **425** *signature* The Granger Collection, New York. **431** *top* Copyright © Obremski Studios/The Image Bank. **432** *Der Träumer* [The dreamer] (about 1835), Caspar David Friedrich. State Hermitage Museum, St. Petersburg, Russia. **433–437** Photo by Allan I. Ludwig. **440** Copyright © David W. Hamilton/The Image Bank. **441–444** *background* Copyright © Phil Brodatz. Reproduction and publication rights reserved. **444** Detail of *The Porten Family,* Gawen Hamilton. Museum of Fine Arts, Springfield, Massachusetts, James Philip Gray Collection. **448** *foreground* Copyright © Editions d'Art Lys, Versailles, France; *background* Department of Rare Books and Special Collections, University of Rochester Library. **451, 452, 453, 455** Copyright © Editions d'Art Lys, Versailles, France. **457** Detail of *Marie Antoinette and Her Children,* Élisabeth Vigée-Lebrun. Chateau de Versailles, France, Giraudon/Art Resource, New York. **478** *bottom* The Granger Collection, New York. **480** *top* Courtesy, Barnaby's Picture Library; *bottom* Manchester Heroes, September 1819. ET Archive. **481** *The Circulating Library,* Isaac Cruikshank (1764–1811). Pen, ink, watercolor and wash on wove paper, 6⅞″ × $8\frac{7}{16}$″, Yale Center for British Art, Paul Mellon Collection (B1975.4.867). **484–485** *background* Copyright © Linda Dufurrena/Grant Heilman Photography, Inc. **486** *background* Tiger in Africa, Mark Newman/Adventure Photo & Film. **490** *top right, above* Detail of title page for *Songs of Innocence* (1789), William Blake. The Granger Collection, New York; *top right, below,* Detail of title page for *Songs of Experience* (1794), William Blake. The Granger Collection, New York. **491** Copyright © Wendy Chan/The Image Bank. **517** *bottom* From *The Repository of Arts, Literature, Commerce, Manufacture, Fashions and Politics,* published by R. Ackerman, London (1809–1828). **524–525** CLB Publishing. **526** Detail of *Cloud Study* (about 1821), John Constable, R.A. Oil on canvas, Victoria and Albert Museum, London/Art Resource, New York. **529** *background* D. Petku/H. Armstrong Roberts. **534** *top* Detail of *Snow Storm: Steam-Boat off a Harbour's Mouth* (1842), Joseph Mallord William Turner. Clore Collection, Tate Gallery, London/Art Resource, New York. **536** *top center* Abu Simbel, Egypt, R. Benson/H. Armstrong Roberts; *left* Calendar of Elephantine, with Egyptian hieroglyphs. Musée du Louvre, Paris, Giraudon/Art Resource, New York; *background* The original manuscript of Shelley's "Ozymandias." The Bodleian Library, University of Oxford,

Great Britain (MS. Shelley e. 4, f. 85r). **546** Copyright © 1980 Hersel E. Abernathy/H. Armstrong Roberts. **547** *background* Copyright © William Thompson/Tony Stone Images. **550** *top* The Granger Collection, New York; *background* Copyright © Superstock. **553** *background* Copyright © Jerry Schad/Science Source/Photo Researchers; *signature* The Granger Collection, New York. **555, 557, 560** *signatures* The Granger Collection, New York. **563** *bottom* Cover of *Frankenstein, or The Modern Prometheus* by Mary Wollstonecraft Shelley, illustration by Everett Henry. Published by The Heritage Press, New York, Copyright © 1934. **568** *bottom* Illustration Copyright © 1995 SoftKey International Inc. **572** *background* Detail of *The Stone Pickers* (1887), Sir George Clausen. Oil on canvas, 42″ × 31″, Tyne and Wear Museums, Newcastle upon Tyne, England. **576** *background* Floral patterns. Victoria and Albert Museum, London/Art Resource, New York; *top, Queen Victoria* (1840), Aaron Edwin Penley. By courtesy of the National Portrait Gallery, London; *bottom, Great Exhibition, 1851: Waiting for the Queen at Coalbrookdale Gates,* Joseph Nash. Lithograph, Guildhall Library, London, Bridgeman/Art Resource, New York. **577** From *The Illustrated London News,* xiii, 1848. **578** *top left* Detail of *Benjamin Disraeli,* Sir John Everett Millais. The Granger Collection, New York; *top right, William E. Gladstone* (1879), Sir John Everett Millais. Oil on canvas, The Granger Collection; *center above, Sketch of a Ward at the Hospital at Scutari,* Joseph-Austin Benwell. Greater London Council, London, Bridgeman/Art Resource, New York; *center below, Florence Nightingale,* Sir William Blake Richmond (1842–1921). Claydon House, Great Britain, Bridgeman/Art Resource, New York. **580** *top* Copyright © Hulton Deutsch Collection Ltd.; *bottom foreground* By permission of the Syndics of Cambridge (England) University Library; *bottom background, Charles Darwin* (1884), John Collier. Oil on canvas, The Granger Collection, New York. **581** *bottom left* Copyright © Hulton Deutsch Collection Ltd. **582, 598** Copyright © G. Heck/Panoramic Images, Chicago 1995. **588** *top, Portrait of Charles Dickens* (1859), William Powell Frith. Victoria and Albert Museum, London, Bridgeman/Art Resource, New York; *bottom* Sam Weller's first appearance in Dickens's *The Pickwick Papers.* Illustration by Phiz. **589** *top* Photofest; *center* The Mansell Collection; *bottom* Copyright © Hulton Deutsch Collection Ltd. **597** The Granger Collection, New York. **604** *top left* Detail of *Charlotte Brontë* (1850), G. Richmond. Chalk drawing, The Granger Collection, New York; *top right, Emily Brontë* (about 1833), Patrick Branwell Brontë. Oil on canvas, The Granger Collection, New York; *bottom left* Copyright © Simon Warner; *bottom right* Copyright © The Brontë Society. **605** *top, The First Meeting of Jane Eyre and Mr. Rochester,* Thomas Davidson. Copyright © The Brontë Society; *bottom, Merlin Hawk,* Emily Brontë. Watercolor. Copyright © The Brontë Society. **608, 611, 615** Illustrations by John Leach. **618** Detail of *Newgate* (late 1800s), Frank Holl. Royal Holloway and Bedford Collection, New College, Egham, Surrey, England, Bridgeman/Art Resource, New York. **620** *top left* The Granger Collection, New York. **621** *center* Photofest; *bottom* From the Castle Howard Archives, by kind permission of the Honourable Simon Howard and Mr. Jonathan Ouvry. **623** *background,* **633** Roloff Beny/National Archives of Canada/1986-009. **635** *bottom* Copyright © 1994 Stephen Wilkes/The Image Bank. **637** Itar-Tass/Sovfoto. **638** Copyright © Greg Heck/Montresor. **653** Detail of *Nightfall at Hradčany* (1909–1913), Jakub Schikaneder. Oil on canvas, 33.7″ × 41.9″, National Gallery, Prague, Czech

Republic. **663** Copyright © 1995 Time Inc. Reprinted by permission. **668–669** Copyright © Donna Binder/Impact Visuals. **672** Copyright © Masao Ota/Photonica. **677** Copyright © Dag Sundberg/The Image Bank, all rights reserved. **678** *top left, center* Copyright © Ross Hamilton/Tony Stone Images; *background* Copyright © E. Cooper/H. Armstrong Roberts. **680** Copyright © Shinichi Eguchi/Photonica. **684** Copyright © Hulton Deutsch Collection Ltd. **686–687** Copyright © H. Abernathy/H. Armstrong Roberts. **690** Copyright © Ron Oulds/Robert Harding Picture Library. **693** The Bettmann Archive. **698** UPI/Bettmann. **746** The Granger Collection, New York. **748** Copyright © Rick Ergenbright/Tony Stone Images. **762** *left, bottom right* Copyright © Hulton Deutsch Collection Ltd; *top right* The Bettmann Archive; *center right, background* Imperial War Museum, London. **763** *left* Imperial War Museum, London; *right* Copyright © Hulton Deutsch Collection Ltd. **764** *top, center, bottom left* Copyright © Hulton Deutsch Collection Ltd.; *bottom right* Imperial War Museum, London. **765** *top left* Photo of George Bernard Shaw, January 1925. Copyright © Hulton Deutsch Collection Ltd.; *top right* William Butler Yeats, The Granger Collection, New York; *bottom left, David Herbert Lawrence* (1920), Jan Juta. By courtesy of the National Portrait Gallery, London; *bottom right* Katherine Mansfield. The Granger Collection, New York. **766** *top left* Wystan Hugh Auden. Copyright © Hulton Deutsch Collection Ltd.; *top right, Portrait of Dylan Thomas,* Augustus John. National Museum of Wales, Cardiff, Great Britain/Bridgeman/Art Resource, New York; *bottom right* Gandhi (1946), Margaret Bourke-White. *Life* magazine. Copyright © Time Inc. **768** Copyright © The Hulton Deutsch Collection Ltd. **769** Copyright © R. Kord/H. Armstrong Roberts. **777, 793** Copyright © H. Armstrong Roberts. **778** Photofest. **794** *When in Doubt* (1913), John Hassall. London Transport Museum; *background* Copyright © *The Times,* London, reproduced by permission. **803** *Please Pass Down the Car* (1944), Cyril Kenneth Bird. London Transport Museum. **805** *The Lure of the Underground* (1927), Alfred Leete. London Transport Museum. **807** Photofest. **809** Copyright © Mrs. Vinogradoff. **810** Copyright © 1994 Rita Maas/The Image Bank. **816** *left* Copyright © Gisèle Freund; *center* Virginia Woolf, 1902. The Bettmann Archive; *right* Copyright © Mrs. Vinogradoff. **818** Copyright © 1994 Andy Caulfield/The Image Bank. **820** *top left* Virginia Woolf. Photo by Man Ray. Copyright © 1996 Artists Rights Society (ARS), New York/ADAGP/Man Ray Trust, Paris; *background* Superstock. **821** *center* Leonard Woolf and Virginia Woolf at Asheham House. By permission of Mrs. Angelica Garnett; *bottom* Cover of *Mrs. Dalloway* by Virginia Woolf. A Harvest Book, Copyright © 1990 Harcourt Brace & Company. By permission of Harcourt Brace and Company. **825** *top* Detail of *1933 (St. Remy-Provence)* (1933), Ben Nicholson. Copyright © 1995 Mrs. Angela Verren-Taunt/Licensed by VAGA, New York/DACS, London. **840–841** Copyright © C. Ferris. **842** Collection Jewish Historical Museum, Amsterdam. **846** *top left* Roger-Viollet, Paris; *top right* Copyright © Robert Tardio/Graphistock; *center* Courtesy Martin Middlebrook, author of *The First Day on the Somme; bottom left* Troops of the Canadian Fourth Division, 1917. Imperial War Museum, London; *bottom right* English boys playing cricket, UPI/Bettmann. **850** *La France Croisée* (1914), Romaine Brooks. National Gallery of American Art, Washington, D.C./Art Resource, New York. **852** National Archives. **856** Copyright © Hulton Deutsch

Collection Ltd. **861** *bottom right* The Bettmann Archive. **866–867** *background,* **869** UPI/Bettmann. **872, 879** *background* Collection Jewish Historical Museum, Amsterdam, the Netherlands. **881** UPI/Bettmann. **884** Official photograph, United States Air Force, courtesy of Sam R. Quincey. **895** Copyright © Hulton Deutsch Collection Ltd. **896** Copyright © 1994 Alain Choisnet/The Image Bank. **899** *top* Courtesy Martin Middlebrook, author of *The First Day on the Somme.* **900** Copyright © 1992 Color Box/FPG International Corp. **901** Copyright © 1994 Masaru Suzuki/Photonica. **903** Detail of *Interior with Seated Woman* (1908), Vilhelm Hammershøi. Oil on canvas, 76 cm × 66 cm, Aarhus (Denmark) Kunstmuseum. **913** H. Armstrong Roberts. **923** Copyright © M. Thonig/H. Armstrong Roberts. **928** Copyright © Hulton Deutsch Collection Ltd. **940** *left* Copyright © William S. Nawrocki, all rights reserved. **942** *right* Copyright © 1991 Frank Whitney/The Image Bank. **944** Courtesy, Beinecke Rare Book and Manuscript Library, Yale University. **945–946, 947** Details of *St. Patrick's Close, Dublin* (1887), Walter Frederick Osborne. Oil on canvas, 27¼″ × 20″, National Gallery of Ireland, Dublin. **948, 949** Copyright © Evelyn Hofer, courtesy of The Witkin Gallery, Inc., New York. **952** *top* Copyright © Obremski Studios/The Image Bank; *bottom* Copyright © Evelyn Hofer, courtesy of The Witkin Gallery, Inc., New York. **954** *top left, Portrait of James Joyce* (1935), Sean O'Sullivan. Red chalk and charcoal with white highlights on gray paper, 21⁷⁄₁₆″ × 15″. National Gallery of Ireland, Dublin; *center left* O'Connell Bridge and Sackville Street, Dublin. National Library of Ireland; *center* The Slide File; *center right* Trinity College Library, Dublin. **955** *left* From the collections of the Library of Congress. **957** Copyright © 1994 Photonica. **966** *top left* Graham Greene. The Bettmann Archive, New York. **966–967** *background,* **967** *top* Photo of Freetown, Sierra Leone, by Islay Lyons. **967** *bottom* Graham Greene in Cuba. Peter Stackpole, *Life* magazine. Copyright © Time, Inc. **976, 980** *top* Details of *Landscape with the Fall of Icarus*, Pieter Brueghel the Elder (about 1560). Musée Royaux des Beaux Arts de Belgique, Brussels, Belgium/Superstock. **981** Copyright © 1965 by the Trustees for the Estate of Dylan Thomas, and printed with the permission of New Directions Publishing Corporation, New York. **988** Octavio Paz. The Granger Collection, New York. **992** Jacket cover for *The Chocolate War* by Robert Cormier. Copyright © 1974 by Robert Cormier. Used by permission of Dell Books, a division of Bantam Doubleday Dell Publishing Group, Inc. **994–995** *bottom* Reprinted with permission from Variety®. **1006** *top* Copyright © R. B. Goodman/National Geographic Society Image Collection; *center left* Alistair Berg FSP/Gamma Liaison; *center right, bottom* Copyright © Hulton Deutsch Collection Ltd. **1007** Copyright © Hulton Deutsch Collection Ltd. **1008** *top* Copyright © Hulton Deutsch Collection Ltd; *center* Copyright © Peter Jordan/Gamma Liaison; *bottom, Family Group* (1945–1949), Henry Moore. Bronze (cast 1950), 59¼″ × 46½″ × 29⅞″, The Museum of Modern Art, New York, A. Conger Goodyear Fund. Photo Copyright © 1996 The Museum of Modern Art, New York. **1009** Copyright © 1991 Peter Stone/Black Star. **1021** Copyright © Jon Riley/Tony Stone Images. **1022, 1026, 1028, 1032** Copyright © Ludovic Moulin/Photonica. **1024, 1029, 1030** Copyright © Kathleen Creighton/Graphistock. **1034** *left* Copyright © David Hanover/Tony Stone Images; *right* Copyright © 1990 Mason Morfit/FPG International. **1036** Copyright © Paul Stover/Tony Stone Images. **1044** Detail of *Horned Forms* (1944), Graham Sutherland. Tate Gallery, London/Art Resource, New York. **1047** Copyright © Michael

La Monica/Graphistock. **1049, 1050** Copyright © Tim Davis/Tony Stone Images. **1053** Copyright © Superstock. **1057, 1058, 1062** Image by J. V. Scotti, University of Arizona. **1060** *left* Image by J. V. Scotti, University of Arizona; *right* NASA. **1070** *top* Photo by James Blank, courtesy of Nu-Vista Prints; *center* Copyright © J. Schwabel/Southern Stock Photo Agency. **1070–1071** *background* Map Copyright © 1995 Rand McNally, R.L. 95-S-294. **1071** Copyright © Chuck O'Rear/WestLight. **1072** Detail of *Sin título* [Untitled] (1985), Rocío Maldonado. Acrylic with collaged elements on canvas with painted frame, 69″ × 85″ × 6″, courtesy of Gallery OMR, Mexico City. **1073** Copyright © Eric Bouvet/Gamma Liaison. **1074** *left, Jonathan Swift* (about 1710), Charles Jervas. Oil on canvas, The Granger Collection, New York; *second from left, second from right* The Granger Collection, New York; *right* UPI/Bettmann. **1075** Copyright © 1991 Steve McCurry/Magnum Photos, Inc. **1080** Portal at Clonfert. Department of Art History, Trinity College, Dublin. **1086** *background* Copyright © Chester Higgins, Jr. **1097** Copyright © Bruce Davidson/ Magnum Photos. **1099** Copyright © 1986 David Turnley/Black Star. **1100, 1102, 1106** *background,* **1108** Copyright © Joshua Sheldon/Photonica. **1105** Copyright © 1995 Mel Curtis/Photonica. **1119** *bottom* Copyright © Gail Shumway/FPG International. **1121, 1132** *foreground* Copyright © A. Kachaturian/Photonica. **1122** Copyright © Hulton Deutsch Collection Ltd. **1123, 1124** *background* Copyright © J. Hohmann/H. Armstrong Roberts. **1125** Copyright © H. Armstrong Roberts. **1128** *top left* Copyright © Jill Furmanovsky/Camera Press London/Globe Photos. **1129** Photofest. **1130** Copyright © Hulton Deutsch Collection Ltd. **1131** *center foreground, center background, left background, right foreground* The Bettmann Archive; *right background* Copyright © A. Kachaturian/Photonica. **1132** *background,* **1133,1134, 1136** The Bettmann Archive. **1139** Copyright © 1981 Inge Morath/Magnum Photos Inc. **1148** *top* Detail of *Great Pyramid at Giza with Broken Head from Thebes* (1963), David Hockney. Oil, 72″ × 72″. Copyright © David Hockney. **1168** *background* Photofest; *top left* AP/Wide World Photos. **1169** *top, center* Photofest; *bottom* AP/Wide World Photos. **1170** Copyright © 1995 M. C. Escher/Cordon Art—Baarn, Holland. All rights reserved. **1171, 1172** *bottom* Copyright © 1971 John Dommers/Photo Researchers, Inc. **1173** *eyes* Copyright © Elma Garcia/Photonica; *water* Copyright © Howard Schatz/Graphistock. **1175** *top* Reproduced by permission of New Directions Publishing Corp., agents for the estate of Stevie Smith. **1176** Copyright © 1989 P. J. Griffiths/Magnum Photos Inc. **1177** Copyright © Richard B. Levine. **1230** Copyright © 1992 Mark E. Gibson. **1232** Photofest. **1238** Copyright © Jinsei Choh/The Image Bank. **1240** The Bettmann Archive. **1244** The Academy of Natural Sciences. Netscape, Netscape Navigator and the Netscape Communications Corporation Logo are trademarks of Netscape Communications Corporation. **1247–1249** Screen shots reprinted with permission from Microsoft Corporation. **1250** Used with express permission. Adobe and Adobe Illustrator are trademarks of Adobe Systems Incorporated. **1251** Illustration from the 1923 edition of *Story of King Arthur & His Knights,* The Granger Collection, New York. **1253** Copyright © 1995 DC Comics/Warner Brothers, courtesy of Photofest.

Teacher Review Panels *(continued)*

Sharon Johnston, Learning Resource Specialist, Evans High School, Orange County School District

Eileen Jones, English Department Chairperson, Spanish River High School, Palm Beach County School District

Jan McClure, Winter Park High School, Orange County School District

Wanza Murray, English Department Chairperson (retired), Vero Beach Senior High School, Indian River City School District

Shirley Nichols, Language Arts Curriculum Specialist Supervisor, Marion County School District

Debbie Nostro, Ocoee Middle School, Orange County School District

Barbara Quinaz, Assistant Principal, Horace Mann Middle School, Dade County School District

OHIO

Joseph Bako, English Department Chairperson, Carl Shuler Middle School, Cleveland City School District

Deb Delisle, Language Arts Department Chairperson, Ballard Brady Middle School, Orange School District

Ellen Geisler, English/Language Arts Department Chairperson, Mentor Senior High School, Mentor School District

Dr. Mary Gove, English Department Chairperson, Shaw High School, East Cleveland School District

Loraine Hammack, Executive Teacher of the English Department, Beachwood High School, Beachwood City School District

Sue Nelson, Shaw High School, East Cleveland School District

Mary Jane Reed, English Department Chairperson, Solon High School, Solon City School District

Nancy Strauch, English Department Chairperson, Nordonia High School, Nordonia Hills City School Dictrict

Ruth Vukovich, Hubbard High School, Hubbard Exempted Village School District

TEXAS

Anita Arnold, English Department Chairperson, Thomas Jefferson High School, San Antonio Independent School District

Gilbert Barraza, J. M. Hanks High School, Ysleta School District

Sandi Capps, Dwight D. Eisenhower High School, Alding Independent School District

Judy Chapman, English Department Chairperson, Lawrence D. Bell High School, Hurst-Euless-Bedford School District

Pat Fox, Grapevine High School, Grapevine-Colley School District

LaVerne Johnson, McAllen Memorial High School, McAllen Independent School District

Donna Matsumura, W. H. Adamson High School, Dallas Independent School District

Ruby Mayes, Waltrip High School, Houston Independent School District

Mary McFarland, Amarillo High School, Amarillo Independent School District

Adrienne Thrasher, A. N. McCallum High School, Austin Independent School District

CALIFORNIA

Steve Bass, 8th Grade Team Leader, Meadowbrook Middle School, Ponway Unified School District

Cynthia Brickey, 8th Grade Academic Block Teacher, Kastner Intermediate School, Clovis Unified School District

Karen Buxton, English Department Chairperson, Winston Churchill Middle School, San Juan School District

Bonnie Garrett, Davis Middle School, Compton School District

Sally Jackson, Madrona Middle School, Torrance Unified School District

Sharon Kerson, Los Angeles Center for Enriched Studies, Los Angeles Unified School District

Gail Kidd, Center Middle School, Azusa School District

Corey Lay, ESL Department Chairperson, Chester Nimitz Middle School, Los Angeles Unified School District

Myra LeBendig, Forshay Learning Center, Los Angeles Unified School District

Dan Manske, Elmhurst Middle School, Oakland Unified School District

Joe Olague, Language Arts Department Chairperson, Alder Middle School, Fontana School District

Pat Salo, 6th Grade Village Leader, Hidden Valley Middle School, Escondido Elementary School District

Manuscript Reviewers *(continued)*

Beverly Ann Barge, Wasilla High School, Wasilla, Alaska

Sharon Batson, Master Teacher, Westbury High School, Houston, Texas

Louann Bohman, Wilbur Cross High School, New Haven, Connecticut

Rose Mary Bolden, J. F. Kimball High School, Dallas, Texas

Angela Boyd, Andrews High School, Andrews, Texas

Judith H. Briant, Armwood High School, Seffner, Florida

Hugh Delle Broadway, McCullough High School, The Woodlands, Texas

Stephan P. Clarke, Spencerport High School, Spencerport, New York

Dr. Shawn Eric DeNight, Miami Edison Senior High School, Miami, Florida

JoAnna R. Exacoustas, La Serna High School, Whittier, California

Linda Ferguson, English Department Head, Tyee High School, Seattle, Washington

Ellen Geisler, Mentor Senior High School, Mentor, Ohio

Ricardo Godoy, English Department Chairman, Moody High School, Corpus Christi, Texas

Robert Henderson, West Muskingum High School, Zanesville, Ohio

Martha Watt Hosenfeld, English Department Chairperson, Churchville-Chili High School, Churchville, New York

Janice M. Johnson, Assistant Principal, Union High School, Grand Rapids, Michigan

Eileen S. Jones, English Department Chair, Spanish River Community High School, Boca Raton, Florida

Paula S. L'Homme, West Orange High School, Winter Garden, Florida

Bonnie J. Mansell, Downey Adult School, Downey, California

Ruth McClain, Paint Valley High School, Bainbridge, Ohio

Rebecca Miller, Taft High School, San Antonio, Texas

Deborah Lynn Moeller, Western High School, Fort Lauderdale, Florida

Bobbi Darrell Montgomery, Batavia High School, Batavia, Ohio

Wanza Murray, Vero Beach High School, Vero Beach, Florida

Marjorie M. Nolan, Language Arts Department Head, William M. Raines Sr. High School, Jacksonville, Florida

Julia Pferdehirt, freelance writer, former Special Education teacher, Middleton, Wisconsin

Pauline Sahakian, English Department Chairperson, San Marcos High School, San Marcos, Texas

Jacqueline Y. Schmidt, Department Chairperson and Coordinator of English, San Marcos High School, San Marcos, Texas

Milinda Schwab, Judson High School, Converse, Texas

John Sferro, Butler High School, Vandalia, Ohio

Faye S. Spangler, Versailles High School, Versailles, Ohio

Rita Stecich, Evergreen Park Community High School, Evergreen Park, Illinois

GayleAnn Turnage, Abiline High School, Abiline, Texas

Ruth Vukovich, Hubbard High School, Hubbard, Ohio

Charlotte Washington, Westwood Middle School, Grand Rapids, Michigan

Tom Watson, Westbridge Academy, Grand Rapids, Michigan